MAKING CONTACT

Readings from
Home and Abroad

MAKING CONTACT

*Readings from
Home and Abroad*

CAROL J. VERBURG

BEDFORD BOOKS ♋ BOSTON

For Bedford Books

President and Publisher: Charles H. Christensen
General Manager and Associate Publisher: Joan E. Feinberg
Managing Editor: Elizabeth M. Schaaf
Developmental Editor: Michelle McSweeney
Editorial Assistant: Joanne Diaz
Production Editor: Sherri Frank
Copyeditor: Joyce Churchill
Text Design: Anna George
Cover Design: Night & Day Design
Cover Art: Diana Ong, *People Power* (detail)/Superstock, Inc.
Map Design: Richard D. Pusey

Library of Congress Catalog Card Number: 96–86782

Manufactured in the United States of America.

1 0 9 8 7 6
f e d c b a

For information, write: Bedford Books, 75 Arlington Street, Boston, MA 02116
(617–426–7440)

ISBN: 0–312–13350–2

Acknowledgments

David Abram, "Making Magic," from *Parabola* 7, No. 3 (Fall 1982). Copyright © 1982 by David Abram. Reprinted by permission of the author.

PREFACE
FOR INSTRUCTORS

What a difference a decade makes! Ten years ago Bedford Books and I launched *Ourselves Among Others* — the first global reader for college composition courses. Back then it was a challenge just to find English translations of outstanding writing from other parts of the world, much less convince doubtful instructors that cross-cultural essays and stories were accessible to students. Those teachers who did believe that such greats as Gabriel García Márquez, Simone de Beauvoir, and Chinua Achebe belonged in the composition classroom still faced the uphill battle of persuading their classes and their departments.

The results have been gratifying beyond our expectations. Teachers wrote to us of students reading more selections than assigned, engaging in lively class discussions, and keeping the book long after the course had ended. Meanwhile, those exotic names in the table of contents grew more and more familiar. Some of them made the best-seller lists; some made the news. Some won Nobel Prizes. Some saw their books turned into movies. Some were imprisoned in their homelands; some were freed. Nearly all of them kept on writing.

We've come a long way from asking if we ought to be reading non-U.S. authors in composition courses; in fact, the very question now seems bizarre. As instructors know, more and more of today's students have networks of family and community that stretch thousands of miles. Even students whose backgrounds are firmly established in this country can benefit from reading about the many cultures that have contributed to both global and national communities. Indeed, go back far enough in time and all of us in the United States have roots elsewhere that have shaped who we are.

While our nation's demographic makeup has been shifting, technological advances have been changing the way we view the world. Students have only to push a few buttons to make contact with their virtual neighbors in other countries. They can delve into thousands of libraries and databases without leaving their chairs. Information about our global village comes fast and cheap; the challenge is reacting to it. Which events are important? Which speakers are trustworthy? How can we judge their motives, their biases, and the accuracy of their reports? What critical and rhetorical skills of our own will help us first to interpret what we read and then to respond appropriately as citizens and neighbors?

v

These questions led us to rework *Ourselves Among Others* to meet the demands of our changing world. We asked users of that book's first three editions to suggest ways that our new volume could help prepare students for the next millennium. Overwhelmingly, instructors asked us to provide a close-up look at a few specific non-U.S. cultures. Although keeping the global perspective is essential, they advised, the book should offer more than a survey of foreign writing. Particularly valuable would be enough information and contrasting viewpoints from selected cultures for students to draw their own conclusions as they read and write. At the same time, students reminded us of the growing wealth of diversity in our own country. Noting that the mainstream is, after all, part of that diversity, they requested more selections from the United States. With a solid base of familiar writers and viewpoints, students suggested they could better appreciate the unfamiliar ones.

The result is the book in your hands. *Making Contact: Readings from Home and Abroad* comprises seventy-two essays and stories representing every continent but Antarctica. Introducing each of the book's six thematic parts are a dozen or so short epigraphs on the theme from diverse cultures both inside and outside the United States. Each part then presents four U.S. selections (Mirrors), four global selections (Windows), and four selections from a particular nation or region (Spotlights): Mexico, Japan, Russia, the Islamic Middle East, Nigeria, and China. For instance, Part Three, "Turning Points," starts with brief observations on life's pivotal experiences by Gail Sheehy, Michael Dorris, Gloria Anzaldúa, Günter Grass, and others. Readers then travel in "Mirrors: The United States" to a coming-of-age with Maya Angelou in Arkansas; an epiphany with Annie Dillard in Washington state; a tragedy with Andre Dubus aboard an aircraft carrier; and a family cataclysm with Richard Ford in Montana. The exploration of turning points expands in "Windows: The World" to Sophronia Liu's Taiwan, Liliana Heker's Argentina, Amitav Ghosh's India, and Nadine Gordimer's South Africa. "Spotlight: Russia" concludes with background on Russia's historic and cultural turning points, followed by reminiscences and critical observations from Vladimir Nabokov, Joseph Brodsky, Galina Dutkina, and Natasha Singer.

The book's six themes are ones that students have found particularly intriguing and teachers have found particularly effective. *Making Contact* begins with the conundrum of "Identifying Ourselves" and progresses outward to "Families," "Turning Points," "Opposite Sexes," "Myth, Ritual, and Magic," and "Institutions and Individuals." Each Mirrors, Windows, and Spotlight section opens with a photograph illustrating some aspect of what follows. To introduce each essay or story, biographical and geographical headnotes supply information about the author's background. In addition, each Spotlight includes an extended headnote on the featured culture.

Questions after each selection help students to think critically about what they have read: "Explorations" probe the author's ideas and rhetorical strategies; "Connections" link one piece with others; "Elaborations" suggest essay topics for students' responses to their reading. "Investigations" at the end of each Spotlight encourage the reader to examine more closely what makes a particular culture idiosyncratic and what makes it universal. Maps of the Spotlight countries locate the events in the selections and headnotes; a world map at the back of the book shows all the countries treated in the book. A comprehensive instructor's manual (bound with the book in an instructor's edition) provides further background on authors and cultures, guidance for student discussions, a rhetorical table of contents and list of writing assignments, and information on multimedia resources, including film, video, and audiocassettes, as well as Internet sites and addresses.

The book's greatest asset, of course, is the writing it comprises. The essays, excerpts, and stories included here blend literary excellence with compelling content. More than a dozen Nobel laureates are represented, along with a wide variety of writers known and unknown, and the many countries included show the diversity of cultural contexts from which good writing emerges. Unlike traditional literary explorations of "foreign lands," *Making Contact* emphasizes insider accounts. We hear about life in Africa's Kalahari desert or a traveling Bedouin camp from the women and men who live there. Within the United States, too, people write about what they know: Leslie Marmon Silko involves us in Native American traditions, and Cornel West reflects on our nation's legacy of racial tension.

Acknowledgments

A book this large and complex is built on many people's contributions. I'm grateful to all those who answered questionnaires and reviewed plans to help shape *Making Contact*: Helen Aron, Union County College; Jan Aslanian, Kalamazoo Valley Community College; Patrick Baliani, University of Arizona; Kelly Belanger, Youngstown State University; Abby Bogemolny, De Anza College; Bege Bowers, Youngstown State University; Susanna Defever, St. Clair County Community College; Simone DeVito, Southern Illinois University of Carbondale; Sheila S. Eswara, Maryville University; Katerie Gladdys,

Southern Illinois University; Lawrence Gorman, East-West University; David Hawkes, Lehigh University; Amy Hudock, Marshall University; Angela Ingram, Southwest Texas State University; R. Janie Isackson, DePaul University; Mary Jellema, Hope College; Delores Johnson, Marshall University; Mary Kennedy, Suffolk University; Damarys Lacayo-Salas, Jersey City State College; Bill Lalicker, West Chester University; Rhoda Maxwell, University of Wisconsin; Mary Moore, Marshall University; Robert Pendleton, Solano Community College; Margaret Racin, West Virginia University; Timothy G. Roufs, University of Minnesota — Duluth; Kim Schmitt, Southern Illinois University — Carbondale; Larry Silverman, Seattle Central Community College; William C. Simonitis, Union County College; and Anna B. Young, Trenton State College.

Essential contributions to *Making Contact* also came from the staff at Bedford Books. Publisher Chuck Christensen, associate publisher Joan Feinberg, and executive editor Karen Henry supplied advice and support throughout. Day by day and page by page, editor Michelle McSweeney was invaluable for her perspicacity, patience, and good humor. Editorial assistant Joanne Diaz played the roles of detective and journalist, among others; associate development editor John E. Sullivan III supervised the creation of the instructor's manual. Nancy Hurrelbrinck's gifts as a teacher and writer will be appreciated by everyone who uses the instructor's manual she created. Noël Yount did her usual thorough job of researching headnotes for the book; Fred Courtright was an uncommonly helpful and persistent permissions editor. Finally, I'm fortunate to have had the easygoing but scrupulous Sherri Frank shepherding the book through production. Every author should be lucky enough to work with a team like this!

Thanks most of all to the worldwide writers represented in *Making Contact*, many of whom make their creative contributions under harsher conditions than most of us in the United States can imagine.

CONTENTS

PART FOUR: OPPOSITE SEXES   389

INTRODUCTION FOR STUDENTS

Cross-Cultural Reading and Critical Thinking

What will you gain from using this book?

If you make the effort to read these selections carefully and critically, you will come away with two useful assets: knowledge of a variety of people and situations you are likely to encounter in and out of college and the ability to communicate effectively.

Both these accomplishments hinge on critical thinking. That is, as a reader, you play an active role: You evaluate what you read, and you respond to it. You do not take someone else's printed words at face value; rather, you examine the assumptions and biases behind those statements, the evidence on which assertions are based, the process by which conclusions are drawn, and the rhetorical and stylistic techniques used to make a case.

Making Contact: Readings from Home and Abroad has several features designed to encourage critical thinking. First, as the subtitle suggests, its essays, stories, and excerpts come from a great range of people and places. The book is organized in six parts, each centered on a theme that has intrigued writers and readers for millennia. From the highly personal topic "Identifying Ourselves," we move outward to "Families" and "Turning Points," then to "Opposite Sexes," "Myth, Ritual, and Magic," and finally "Institutions and Individuals." Each part opens with brief comments on the theme by writers from around the world. Next come four selections representing diverse subcultures in the United States, then four selections from other countries, and finally four selections from a single non-U.S. country or region.

Some of the writers you will have read before, some you may have heard about, and some are probably unfamiliar. Although all of them live on the same planet in the same century, the contrast in their ethnic, religious, political, and personal orientations is striking — a reminder that their points of view also are bound to differ. Some of their beliefs will conflict with yours. By examining your reaction to what you read, and by writing your own response, you can identify the components (both visible and hidden) of opposing arguments. You may discover that your position is even stronger than you thought; or you may change your mind about a position you always took for granted.

To help sharpen your critical thinking skills, questions following each section of the book encourage you to probe and evaluate what you have read. "Explorations" after the opening epigraphs and after each main selection ask you to scrutinize the writer's arguments, biases, supporting evidence, stylistic techniques, and other tools and tactics. "Connections" relate one selection to others with similar or contrasting elements. For example, how does the Canadian writer Margaret Atwood's concept of "American" compare with British expatriate Richard Rayner's and African-American Ishmael Reed's? How do their concepts compare with those of the Peruvian novelist Mario Vargas Llosa or the Colombian Gabriel García Márquez? Looking at the ways different people interpret the same word can sharpen your appreciation of its meaning not only to them but to you. "Elaborations" take your response to your reading a step further by suggesting topics you can write about. Finally, after the "Spotlight" section that concludes each part are "Investigations" questions to help you synthesize what you have read about the featured country or region. All of these questions ask you not only for information, but also to think critically about the way you arrive at an answer. How do you know? On what evidence do you base your conclusions?

The prospect of pushing your mind in this way may seem daunting at first — like learning a new language or navigating in a strange city. The rewards are worth the work. Once you master the foreign vocabulary and constructions for Spanish or Japanese, you can converse with a whole new assortment of people. Once you know your way around the Paris Métro or the streets of Hong Kong, you can find restaurants, museums, shops, and parks. Critical thinking, too, is a mental challenge that takes effort at the beginning but opens up a world of new experiences and insights once you develop the habit.

PART ONE

IDENTIFYING OURSELVES

Richard Rayner • Ishmael Reed • Julio Cortázar • Anita Desai
Roger Rosenblatt • Mario Vargas Llosa • Shelby Steele
Adrienne Rich • Molly Ivins • Jill Ker Conway • Alma Guillermoprieto

MIRRORS: The United States

Walker Percy: *A Short Quiz*
James Baldwin: *The New Lost Generation*
Amy Tan: *Two Kinds*
Susan Orlean: *Quinceañera*

WINDOWS: The World

Salman Rushdie: *The Broken Mirror*
  (INDIA/GREAT BRITAIN)
Margaret Atwood: *A View from Canada*
  (CANADA)
Germaine Greer: *One Man's Mutilation Is
  Another Man's Beautification*
  (AUSTRALIA/GREAT BRITAIN)
Paul Harrison: *The Westernization of the
  World*

SPOTLIGHT: Mexico

Octavio Paz: *The Art of the Fiesta*
Elena Garro: *The Day We Were Dogs*
Carlos Fuentes: *The Two Americas*
Richard Rodriguez: *Mexico's Children*

My wife, from Finland, has a green card; I'm English, in the process of applying for one myself; our son was born an American. When we moved into our house in Venice, California, one of our neighbors, an elderly white woman with whom we're now very friendly, said, "No Americans live on our block anymore."

Maybe she had the jitters about new neighbors, or maybe there was something else at play. I knew that her father had been born in Germany and had journeyed to Detroit, where she was born. I wanted to say that logically, therefore, our son is every bit as American as she is. But in any debate about nationality, I know, logic fades fast.

My own father once traced our family tree back to 1066, when one Baron de Rainier sailed from Normandy to help conquer England. Since then, give or take the occasional Irish excursion, my progenitors were all born within a hundred or so miles of one another in the north of England. So, when I came to America and found that nearly everyone was from somewhere else if they stepped back a generation or two, I found myself thrilled and oddly at ease. It explained America's drive, its generosity and up-for-anything energy. As Melville wrote, "We are not a nation, so much as a world."

– RICHARD RAYNER
"What Immigration Crisis?"
New York Times Magazine, 1996

▼ ▼ ▼

[A] blurring of cultural styles occurs in everyday life in the United States to a greater extent than anyone can imagine. The result is what . . . Yale professor Robert Thompson referred to as a "cultural bouillabaisse." Yet members of the nation's present educational and cultural elect still cling to the notion that the United States belongs to some vaguely defined entity they refer to as "Western civilization," by which they mean, presumably, a civilization created by people of Europe, as if Europe can even be viewed in monolithic terms. Is Beethoven's Ninth Symphony, which includes Turkish marches, a part of Western civilization? Or the late-nineteenth– and twentieth-century French paintings, whose creators were influenced by Japanese art? And what of the cubists, through whom the influence of African art changed modern painting? Or the surrealists, who were so impressed with the art of the Pacific Northwest Indians that, in their map of North America, Alaska dwarfs the lower forty-eight states in size?

– ISHMAEL REED
"What's American about America?"
Utne Reader, 1989

▼ ▼ ▼

In Latin America, during the last fifteen years the predominant subject, the predominant ambiance for our writers, has been anger, fear, and frustration; the feeling of belonging to countries that are being betrayed by their own governments and exploited by foreign governments. These authors are even sometimes rejected by their own people who don't always have a clear consciousness of what they are or of what they ought to be. The Colombian, Venezuelan, or Argentinean contemporary writers lack the kind of sound historical base which the American writer has. They are floating in a universe in which they have very little to cling to. . .

. . . The great advantage of starting from nothingness, or almost nothingness, is analogous to that of the creators of cosmogonies; it allows one to create according to the dictates of one's own desires. We Latin American writers who have achieved this consciousness of floating in the void have realized that everything is permitted in literature. This has given us an extraordinary freedom for good and for bad. There have been many failures because, after all, a tradition is rather important. To be able to lean on a solid base, as French literature does, permits one to progress, within certain limits, knowing what to do and what not to do. We don't know what to do and what not to do. But if we are honest we can do everything.

– JULIO CORTÁZAR
Antaeus, 1988

▼ ▼ ▼

I was born in India, I grew up in India, went to school there, but when one says "India" no Indian really knows what you mean. It's just the opening to a hundred questions. Which region? Which part of India? Which state? Which language? Which religion? What particular background? Because India is a country made up of so many fragments, much smaller than the United States, but each little fragment has a culture which is so distinctly its own — its own language, its own script, its own literature. Which one do I claim as mine? All and none. My parents settled down in a part of India which was home to neither of them. My father came from Bengal, originally from quite a small village in what was then East Bengal, now Bangladesh, probably went to the local village school, belonged to a generation that went to such little local village schools but came out able to quote long passages from Milton's *Paradise Lost* or from Browning with which he used to like to regale us. My mother's home, on the other hand, was in Germany. She left Germany in the late twenties. The Germany she knew was soon after totally destroyed. She never returned to it, and both of them made their home in north India, in Delhi, where I grew up.

It was a home with three languages. Obviously German had to be the very first one because that was the language of infancy, the one my mother spoke to us. With all our neighbors and friends we spoke Hindi, that was the language in Delhi. My parents believed very much in sending us to the local school. I went to the nearest one, the one I could bicycle to, and that happened to be a mission school, run by British missionaries. And so it was a matter of pure chance that the first language I was taught to read and write was English and by that accident it became my literary language. And of course I loved the literature that was given me in the English language, but I very soon became aware that the language did much more than that. It opened up world literature to me in translation. I couldn't have read the Russian literature I did, the French literature I did, the Japanese literature that I did read and love, if it hadn't been for the English language.

– ANITA DESAI
"The Other Voice"
Transition, 1994

▼ ▼ ▼

Enriqué is a 41-year-old fifth-grade math teacher from the Dominican Republic who came here only a few years ago. An "economic refugee," as he calls himself, he packed up with his wife and three young sons, headed for New York, and wound up in Sunset Park.

I ask him if the students here are better or worse than in the Dominican Republic.

"There's a big difference," he replies. "The kids here don't care. In Santo Domingo you have to be dedicated to come to school. I teach math, and nobody cares. It scares me — for the students, and for my own kids, too. My boys are dedicated now, but in a few years, who knows?"

He is especially concerned about bilingualism, which is pushed not by immigrants but by local politicians seeking to build non-English-speaking constituencies. "I want [my boys] to learn English. But here, in this area, they want them to learn Spanish. It's funny, really. I, who know so little English, want my sons to learn English. And others, who speak English perfectly, want to keep them learning in Spanish. What's the point of learning in Spanish?" He tenses up. "This is America."

– ROGER ROSENBLATT
Utne Reader, 1994

▼ ▼ ▼

Immense opportunities brought by the civilization that discovered and conquered America have been beneficial only to a minority, some-

4

times a very small one; whereas the great majority managed to have only the negative share of the conquest — that is, contributing in their serfdom and sacrifice, in their misery and neglect, to the prosperity and refinement of the Westernized elites. One of our worst defects, our best fictions, is to believe that our miseries have been imposed on us from abroad, that others, for example, the conquistadores, have always been responsible for our problems. There are countries in Latin America — Mexico is the best example — in which the Spaniards are even now severely indicted for what they did to the Indians. Did they really do it? We did it; we are the conquistadores.

They were our parents and grandparents who came to our shores and gave us the names we have and the language we speak. They also gave us the habit of passing to the devil the responsibility for any evil we do. Instead of making amends for what they did, by improving and correcting our relations with our indigenous compatriots, mixing with them and amalgamating ourselves to form a new culture that would have been a kind of synthesis of the best of both, we, the Westernized Latin Americans, have persevered in the worst habits of our forebears, behaving toward the Indians during the nineteenth and twentieth centuries as the Spaniards behaved toward the Aztecs and the Incas, and sometimes even worse. We must remember that in countries like Chile and Argentina, it was during the republic (in the nineteenth century), not during the colony, that the native cultures were systematically exterminated. In the Amazon jungle, and in the mountains of Guatemala, the exterminating continues.

— MARIO VARGAS LLOSA
"Questions of Conquest"
Harper's Magazine, 1990

▼ ▼ ▼

I think the racial struggle in America has always been primarily a struggle for innocence. White racism from the beginning has been a claim of white innocence and therefore of white entitlement to subjugate blacks. And in the sixties, as went innocence so went power. Blacks used the innocence that grew out of their long subjugation to seize more power, while whites lost some of their innocence and so lost a degree of power over blacks. Both races instinctively understand that to lose innocence is to lose power (in relation to each other). To be innocent someone else must be guilty, a natural law that leads the races to forge their innocence on each other's backs. The inferiority of the black always makes the white man superior; the evil might of whites makes blacks good. This pattern means that both races have a hidden invest-

5

ment in racism and racial disharmony despite their good intentions to the contrary. Power defines their relations, and power requires innocence, which, in turn, requires racism and racial division. . . .

Historically, blacks have handled white society's presumption of innocence in two ways: They have bargained with it, granting white society its innocence in exchange for entry into the mainstream, or they have challenged it, holding that innocence hostage until their demand for entry (or other concessions) was met. A bargainer says, *I already believe you are innocent (good, fair-minded) and have faith that you will prove it.* A challenger says, *If you are innocent, then prove it.* Bargainers *give* in hope of receiving; challengers *withhold* until they receive. Of course, there is risk in both approaches, but in each case the black is negotiating his own self-interest against the presumed racial innocence of the larger society.

– SHELBY STEELE
"I'm Black, You're White, Who's Innocent?
Race and Power in an Era of Blame"
The Content of Our Character, 1988

▼ ▼ ▼

My mother is a gentile. In Jewish law I cannot count myself a Jew. If it is true that "we think back through our mothers if we are women" (Virginia Woolf) — and I myself have affirmed this — then even according to lesbian theory, I cannot (or need not?) count myself a Jew. . . . It would be easy to push away and deny the gentile in me — that white southern woman, that social Christian. At different times in my life I have wanted to push away one or the other burden of inheritance, to say merely *I am a woman; I am a lesbian.* If I call myself a Jewish lesbian, do I thereby try to shed some of my southern gentile white woman's culpability? If I call myself only through my mother, is it because I pass more easily through a world where being a lesbian often seems like outsiderhood enough?

– ADRIENNE RICH
"Split at the Root: An Essay on Jewish Identity"
*Blood, Bread, and Poetry:
Selected Prose, 1979–1985*, 1986

▼ ▼ ▼

Of all the odd misperceptions current about homosexuality, perhaps the oddest is that it is a choice, that people choose to be homosexual. That strikes me as so patently silly. Did any of us who are straight choose to be heterosexual? When? Did we wake up one morning when

6

we were fifteen and say, "Gosh, I think I'll be a heterosexual?" For heaven's sakes, how can anyone believe that people choose to be a homosexual? "I think it would be a lot of fun to be called *queer* and *sissy* for the rest of my life, so I think I'll be gay."

– MOLLY IVINS
"'Twas a Fine Spring Day to Air
Out Attitudes"
Nothin' But Good Times Ahead, 1993

▼ ▼ ▼

The red earth, the blazing sun, and the broken hearts of [its] settlers were the recurring subjects of great Australian painting. It had never occurred to me before to wonder why we didn't celebrate the plenty and lyrical beauty of the fertile slopes beyond the mountains. . . . I knew that somehow it had to do with our relationship to nature, and with the way in which the first settlers' encounter with this environment had formed the inner landscape of the mind, the unspoken, unanalyzed relationship to the order of creation which governs our psyches at the deepest level. Australians saw that relationship as cruel and harsh . . . I wished there were a clear way to understand the process by which a people's dominant myths and mental imagery took shape. Now that I had seen England and Europe, these myths seemed more important to me than any study of the politics of Federation, or of the precise details of nineteenth-century land policy.

– JILL KER CONWAY
The Road from Coorain, 1989

▼ ▼ ▼

Mexicans know that a party has been outstandingly successful if at the end of it there are at least a couple of clusters of longtime or first-time acquaintances leaning on each other against a wall, sobbing helplessly. The activities one normally associates with a party — flirting and conversation, and even the kind of dancing that leads to an amnesiac dawn in a strange bed — are considered here mere preludes to or distractions from the ultimate goal, which is weeping and the free, luxurious expression of pain. . . .

Now that Mexico is carpeted with Kentucky Fried Chicken, Denny's, and McDonald's outlets, and Coca-Cola is the national drink; now that even low-paid office workers are indentured to their credit cards and auto loans; now that the government of [former] President Carlos Salinas de Gortari has approved a North American Free Trade Agreement, which promises to make Mexico commercially one with its neighbors to the north, there is little scope for magnificent sorrow in the average citizen's life. In the smog-darkened center of Mexico City, or in its monstrous, ticky-tacky suburban spokes, the average citizen on an average day is more concerned with beating the traffic, making the mortgage payment, punching the clock. Progress has hit Mexico in the form of devastation, some of it ecological, much of it aesthetic. Life is rushed, the water may be poisoned, and the new industrial tortillas taste terrible. Favorite ornaments for the home include porcelain dogs and plastic roses, and for the two-thirds of the population which is confined to the cities recreation usually takes the form of a couple of hours with the latest imported sitcom or the local *telenovelas*. Hardly anyone knows anymore what it is to live on a ranch or to die of passion, and yet, when it comes to the defining moments of *mexicanidad*, *ranchera* music, with its odes to love, idyllic landscapes, and death for the sake of honor, continues to reign supreme.

It is a hybrid music. Sung most often to the accompaniment of a mariachi ensemble, *rancheras* generate tension by setting the classic formality of the trumpets and violins against the howling quality of the vocals. The lyrics of many of the best-known songs — "Cielito Lindo," say — include verses that were inherited in colonial days from Spain. Many of the rhetorical flourishes — "lips like rose petals," "eyes like stars" — are Spanish also. But when *rancheras* turn, as they do obsessively, to the topics of death and destruction, alcohol and defeat, and the singer holds up his dying heart for all to see, or calls for the stones in the field to shout at him, he is bleeding from a wound that is uniquely Mexican.

> – ALMA GUILLERMOPRIETO
> "Serenading the Future"
> *The New Yorker*, 1992

EXPLORATIONS

1. Richard Rayner comments on different concepts of "American" (p. 2). Most of the observations you have just read come from Americans of some kind — or more than one kind. Which of them are North Americans? Which are Central Americans? South Americans? Latin Americans?

2. What criteria besides nationality do these writers use to identify themselves? Which of their criteria do you use most often to identify yourself?

3. How do you think Richard Rayner's elderly neighbor (p. 2) would define an American? How do you think Ishmael Reed (p. 2) would define an American? How would you define an American?

4. Compare Mario Vargas Llosa's comments on the problems of Latin America (p. 5) with Shelby Steele's comments on racial problems in the United States (p. 5). What are the similarities in these two analyses? What are some important differences?

MIRRORS:
THE UNITED STATES

Identifying Ourselves: *A boy with a telescope is lost in the cosmos.*

WALKER PERCY

A Short Quiz

Walker Percy was born in Birmingham, Alabama, in 1916. He spent most of his life, and set most of his books, in the South — particularly Louisiana, where he and his bride settled after World War II. Percy's life was as eventful as any Southern novel. His father committed suicide when Walker was thirteen years old; three years later, his mother died in a car accident. In between, Walker was informally adopted by his father's cousin, William Alexander (Will) Percy in Mississippi, for whom he later named a recurring fictional character. Percy graduated from the University of North Carolina at Chapel Hill and received his medical degree from Columbia University. During his internship at Bellevue Hospital, however, Will Percy died of a stroke, and Walker Percy developed tuberculosis. He spent the next three years in a sanitarium, reading intensely, exploring existentialism and other literary and philosophical angles on the cosmos. A year after his marriage, Percy converted to Roman Catholicism, which became a central force in his life and work. He and his wife moved first to New Orleans and then to the nearby small town of Covington. His first novel, *The Moviegoer* (1961), won the National Book Award. Five more novels followed: *The Last Gentleman* (1966), *Love in the Ruins* (1971), *Lancelot* (1977), *The Second Coming* (1980), and *The Thanatos Syndrome* (1987). Percy also published widely in both literary and philosophical journals. "A Short Quiz" comes from *Lost in the Cosmos: The Last Self-Help Book* (1983). Percy died in Covington from cancer in 1990.

Imagine that you are reading a book about the Cosmos. You find it so interesting that you go out and buy a telescope. One fine clear moonless night you set up your telescope and focus on the brightest star in the sky. It is a planet, not a star, with a reddish spot and several moons. Excited, you look up the planets in your book about the Cosmos. You read a description of the planets. You read a sentence about a large yellowish planet with a red spot and several moons. You recognize both the description and the picture. Clearly, you have been looking at Jupiter.

You have no difficulty at all in saying that it is Jupiter, not Mars or Saturn, even though the object you are looking at is something you have never seen before and is hundreds of millions of miles distant.

Now imagine that you are reading the newspaper. You come to the astrology column. You may or may not believe in astrology, but to judge from the popularity of astrology these days, you will probably read your horoscope. According to a recent poll, more Americans set store in astrology than in science or God.

You are an Aries. You open your newspaper to the astrology column and read an analysis of the Aries personality. It says among other things:

> You have the knack of creating an atmosphere of thought and movement, unhampered by petty jealousies. But you have the tendency to scatter your talents to the four winds.

Hm, you say, quite true. I'm like that.

Suddenly you realize you've made a mistake. You've read the Gemini column. So you go back to Aries: 5

> Nothing hurts you more than to be unjustly mistreated or suspected. But you have a way about you, a gift for seeing things through despite all obstacles and distractions. You also have a desperate need to be liked. So you have been wounded more often than you will admit.

Hm, you say, quite true. I'm like that.

The first question is: Why is it that both descriptions seem to fit you — or, for that matter, why do you seem to recognize yourself in the self-analysis of all twelve astrological signs? Or, to put it another way, why is it that you can recognize and identify the planets Jupiter and Venus so readily after reading a bit and taking one look, yet have so much trouble identifying yourself from twelve descriptions when, presumably, you know yourself much better than you know Jupiter and Venus?

(2) Can you explain why it is that there are, at last count, sixteen schools of psychotherapy with sixteen theories of the personality and its disorders and that patients treated in one school seem to do as well or as badly as patients treated in any other — while there is only one generally accepted theory of the cause and cure of pneumococcal pneumonia and only one generally accepted theory of the orbits of the planets and the gravitational attraction of our galaxy and the galaxy M31 in Andromeda? (Hint: If you answer that the human psyche is more complicated than the pneumococcus and the human white-cell response or the galaxies or Einstein's general theory of relativity, keep in mind that the burden of proof is on you. Or if you answer that the study of the human psyche is in its infancy, remember then this infancy has lasted

2,500 years and, unlike physics, we don't seem to know much more about the psyche than Plato did.)

(3) How do you explain these odd little everyday phenomena with which everyone is familiar:

You have seen yourself a thousand times in the mirror, face to face. No sight is more familiar. Yet why is it that the first time you see yourself in a clothier's triple mirror — from the side, so to speak — it comes as a shock? Or the first time you saw yourself in a home movie: were you embarrassed? What about the first time you heard your recorded voice — did you recognize it? Clearly, you should, since you've been hearing it all your life.

Why is it that, when you are shown a group photograph in which you   10
are present, you always (and probably covertly) seek yourself out? To see what you look like? Don't you know what you look like?

Has this ever happened to you? You are walking along a street of stores. There are other people walking. You catch a glimpse in a store window of a reflection of a person. For a second or so you do not recognize the person. He, she, seems a total stranger. Then you realize it is your own reflection. Then in a kind of transformation, the reflection does in fact become your familiar self.

One of the peculiar ironies of being a human self in the Cosmos: A stranger approaching you in the street will in a second's glance see you whole, size you up, place you in a way in which you cannot and never will, even though you have spent a lifetime with yourself, live in the Century of the Self, and therefore ought to know yourself best of all.

The question is: Why is it that in your entire lifetime you will never be able to size yourself up as you can size up somebody else — or size up Saturn — in a ten-second look?

Why is it that the look of another person looking at you is different from everything else in the Cosmos? That is to say, looking at lions or tigers or Saturn or the Ring Nebula or at an owl or at another person from the side is one thing, but finding yourself looking into the eyes of another person looking at you is something else. And why is it that one can look at a lion or a planet or at someone's finger as long as one pleases, but looking into the eyes of another person is, if prolonged past a second, a perilous affair?

(4) The following experiment was performed on a group of ten sub-   15
jects. See how you would answer the questions.

Think of five acquaintances, not close friends, not lovers, not family members.

Describe each by three adjectives (in the experiment, a "personality characteristic chart" was provided on which one could score an acquaintance on a scale of "good" and "bad" qualities, e.g., more or less trustworthy, attractive, boring, intelligent, selfish, flighty, outgoing, introspective, and so on). Thus, you might describe an acquaintance named Gary McPherson as fairly good company, moderately trustworthy, funny but a little malicious, and so on. Or Linda Ellison: fairly good-looking (a 7 or $7\frac{1}{2}$), more intelligent than she lets on, a good listener. And so on.

Note that most if not all of your adjectives could be placed on a finite scale, say from a plus ten to a minus ten.

Now, having described five acquaintances, do the following. Read these two sentences carefully:

(a) You are extraordinarily generous, ecstatically loving of the right person, supremely knowledgeable about what is wrong with the country, about people, capable of moments of insight unsurpassed by any scientist or artist or writer in the country. You possess an infinite potentiality.

(b) You are of all people in the world probably the most selfish, hateful, envious (e.g., you take pleasure in reading death notices in the newspaper and in hearing of an acquaintance's heart attack), the most treacherous, the most frightened, and above all the phoniest.

Now answer this question as honestly as you can: Which of these two sentences more nearly describes you? CHECK *(a)*, *(b)*, (neither), (both).

If you checked both — 60 percent of respondents did — how can   20
that be?

(5) Do you understand sexuality?

That is to say, are you happy with either of the two standard versions of sexuality:

One, the biological — that the sex drive is one among several needs and drives evolved through natural selection as a means of sustaining the life of the organism and ensuring the survival of the species. Thus, sexual desire is one item on a list which includes other such items as hunger, thirst, needs of shelter, nest-building, migration, and so on.

The other, the religious-humanistic — sex is an expression, perhaps the ultimate expression, of love and communication between a man and a woman, and is best exemplified in marriage, raising children, the sharing of a life, family, home, and fireside.

Or do you see sexuality as a unique trait of the present-day self   25
(which is the only self we know), occupying an absolutely central locus
in the consciousness particularly as it relates to other sexual beings, of
an order and magnitude of power incommensurate with other "drives"
and also specified by the very structure of the present-day self as its very
core and as its prime avenue of intercourse with others?

If the sexual drive is but one of several biological needs, why are we
living in the most eroticized society in history? Why don't TV, films,
billboards, magazines feature culinary delights, e.g., huge chocolate
cakes, hams, roasts, strawberries, instead of women's bodies?

Or are you more confused about sexuality than any other phenomenon in the Cosmos?

Do you know why it is that men and women exhibit sexual behavior
undreamed of among the other several million species, with every conceivable sexual relation between persons, or with only one person, or
between a male and female, or between two male persons, or two female persons, or two males and one female, or two females and one
male; relationships moreover which can implicate every orifice and ap-
pendage of the human body and which bear no relation to the reproduction and survival of the species?

Is the following statement true or false:

Pornography is not an aberration of a few sexually frustrated middle-   30
aged men in gray raincoats; it is rather a salient and prime property of
modern consciousness, of three hundred years of technology and the
industrial revolution, and is symptomatic of a radical disorder in the relation of the self to other selves which generally manifests itself in the
abstracted state of one self (male) and the degradation of another self
(female) to an abstract object of satisfaction.

(6) Consider the following short descriptions of different kinds of
consciousness of self. Which of the selves, if any, do you identify with?

(a) *The cosmological self.* The self is either unconscious of itself or
only conscious of itself insofar as it is identified with a cosmological
myth or classificatory system, e.g., totemism. Ask a Bororo tribesman:
Who are you? He may reply: I am parakeet. (Ask an L.S.U. fan at a football game: Who are you? He may reply: I am a tiger.)

(b) *The Brahmin-Buddhist self.* Who are you? What is your self? My
self in this life is impaled on the wheel of non-being, obscured by the
veil of unreality. But it can realize itself by penetrating the veil of *maya*

and plumbing the depths of self until it achieves *nirvana*, nothingness, or the *Brahman*, God. The *atman* (self) is the *Brahman* (God).

(*c*) *The Christian self (and, to a degree, the Judaic and Islamic self).* The self sees itself as a creature, created by God, estranged from God by an aboriginal catastrophe, and now reconciled with him. Before the reconciliation, the self is, as Paul told the Ephesians, a stranger to every covenant, with no promise to hope for, with the world about you and no God. But now the self becomes a son of God, a member of a family of selves, and is conscious of itself as a creature of God embarked upon a pilgrimage in this life and destined for happiness and reunion with God in a later life.

(*d*) *The role-taking self.* One sociological view of the self is that the self achieves its identity by taking roles and modeling its own role from the roles of others, e.g., one's mother, father, housewife, breadwinner, macho-boy-man, feminine-doll-girl, etc. — and also, as George Mead said, upon how one perceives others' perceptions of oneself.

(*e*) *The standard American-Jeffersonian high-school-commencement Republican-and-Democratic-platform self.* The self is an individual entity created by God and endowed with certain inalienable rights and the freedom to pursue happiness and fulfill its potential. It achieves itself through work, participation in society, family, the marketplace, the political process, cultural activities, sports, the sciences, and the arts. It follows that in a free and affluent society the self should succeed more often than not in fulfilling itself. Happiness can be pursued and to a degree caught.

(*f*) *The diverted self.* In a free and affluent society, the self is free to divert itself endlessly from itself. It works in order to enjoy the diversions that the fruit of one's labor can purchase. The pursuit of happiness becomes the pursuit of diversion, and in this society the possibilities of diversion are endless and as readily available as eight hours of television a day: TV, sports, travel, drugs, games, newspapers, magazines, Vegas.

(*g*) *The lost self.* With the passing of the cosmological myths and the fading of Christianity as a guarantor of the identity of the self, the self becomes dislocated, Jefferson or no Jefferson, is both cut loose and imprisoned by its own freedom, yet imprisoned by a curious and paradoxical bondage like a Chinese handcuff, so that the very attempts to free itself, e.g., by ever more refined techniques for the pursuit of happiness, only tighten the bondage and distance the self ever farther from the very world it wishes to inhabit as its homeland. The rational Jeffersonian pursuit of happiness embarked upon in the American Revolution translates into the flaky euphoria of the late twentieth century. Every advance in an objective understanding of the Cosmos and in its technological control further distances the self from the Cosmos precisely in the degree of the advance — so that in the end the self becomes a space-bound ghost which roams the very Cosmos it understands perfectly.

(h) The scientific and artistic self. Or that self which is so totally absorbed in the pursuit of art or science as to be selfless. The modern caricature is the "absentminded professor" or the demonic possessed artist, which is to say that as a self he is "absent" from the usual concerns of the self about itself in the world. E.g., Karl von Frisch and his bees, Schubert in a beer hall writing lieder on the tablecloth, Picasso in a restaurant modeling animals from bread.

(i) The illusory self. Or the conviction that one's sense of oneself is a   40
psychological or cultural illusion and that with the advance of science, e.g., behaviorism, Lévi-Strauss's structuralism, the self will disappear.

(j) The autonomous self. The self sees itself as a sovereign and individual consciousness, liberated by education from the traditional bonds of religion, by democracy from the strictures of class, by technology from the drudgery of poverty, and by self-knowledge from the tyranny of the unconscious — and therefore free to pursue its own destiny without God.

(k) The totalitarian self. The self sees itself as a creature of the state, fascist or communist, and understands its need to be specified by the needs of the state.

(CHECK ONE)

EXPLORATIONS

1. How do you think Walker Percy would define the self? How would you summarize Percy's thesis in "A Short Quiz"? (Refer to the title of the book this essay comes from for one clue.)

2. In what ways does Percy's choice of a quiz format suit his material? Specifically, what advantages does he gain by asking questions rather than making statements? By using the second-person singular ("you") rather than some other pronoun?

3. Reread Question 6 in "A Short Quiz." Which of the selves (6 *a* through *k*) do you identify with, and why?

CONNECTIONS

1. How do you think the "cultural bouillabaisse" described by Ishmael Reed (p. 2) has affected Americans' sense of self? Which of the questions in "A Short Quiz" might not make sense to someone from a culture with only one race, religion, and philosophy?

2. Which of Percy's concepts of self (6 *a* through *k*) are reflected in Adrienne Rich's comments on page 6? What explanation does Percy suggest for Rich's desire to "push away one or the other burden of inheritance"?

3. In items 6 (*e*) and 6 (*f*), Percy alludes to "a free and affluent society." Which writers of the epigraphs on pages 2–8 do you think would agree with that phrase as a description of the United States? Which writers do you think would not agree, and why not?

ELABORATIONS

1. Which of the selves described in Question 6 (*a* through *k*) do you see around you most often? Write an essay applying Percy's definitions to contemporary U.S. culture. Support your position with examples.

2. Choose one of Percy's six items in "A Short Quiz" and answer the subquestions in it. Write an essay replying to the item's central question, incorporating and expanding on Percy's discussion and your answers.

JAMES BALDWIN

The New Lost Generation

As the following essay describes, James Baldwin decided in his twenties to leave the United States for France. Born in New York City's Harlem in 1924, he grew up in a family of ten step- and half-siblings. Not until his late teens did he learn that his father, a rigid disciplinarian who worked in a bottling plant and preached in a local church, was really his stepfather. His mother worked as a maid, often leaving James to babysit. At Frederick Douglass Junior High School, one of his teachers was the poet Countee Cullen, who introduced him to other writers of the Harlem Renaissance and encouraged his obvious talent. Baldwin graduated from a Bronx high school in 1942, having concealed from his literary-minded friends (most of them white, many of them Jewish) that he also preached at the Fire Side Pentecostal Assembly. After his stepfather's funeral, which coincided with a massive riot in Harlem, Baldwin moved downtown to Greenwich Village. There he met Richard Wright, who helped the younger author to win one of many literary prizes that would support his writing. Baldwin published his first novel, the autobiographical *Go Tell It on the Mountain*, in 1953; the essay collection *Notes of a Native Son* followed two years later. A self-described transatlantic commuter, Baldwin continued to produce influential novels, essays, and plays (including *Blues for Mr. Charlie*, 1964) until his death from cancer in 1987.

This is an extremely difficult record to assess. Perhaps it begins for me in 1946, when my best friend took his life. He was an incandescent Negro boy of twenty-four, whose future, it had seemed to all of us, would unfailingly be glorious. He and I were Socialists, as were most of our friends, and we dreamed of this utopia, and worked toward it. We may have evinced more conviction than intelligence or skill, and more youthful arrogance than either, but we, nevertheless, had carried petitions about together, fought landlords together, worked as laborers together, been fired together, and starved together.

But for some time before his death, troubles graver than these had laid hold of my friend. Not only did the world stubbornly refuse his vision; it despised him for his vision, and scourged him for his color. Of course, it despised and scourged me, too, but I was different from my friend in that it took me nearly no time to despise the world right back and decide that I would accomplish, in time, with patience and cunning and by becoming indestructible, what I might not, in the moment, achieve by force or persuasion. My friend did not despise anyone. He really thought that people were good, and that one had only to point out to them the right path in order to have them, at once, come flocking to it in loudly rejoicing droves.

Before his death, we had quarreled very bitterly over this. I had lost my faith in politics, in right paths; if there *were* a right path, one might be sure (I informed him with great venom) that whoever was on it was simply asking to be stoned to death — by all the world's good people. I didn't give a damn, besides, *what* happened to the miserable, the unspeakably petty world. There was probably not a handful of decent people in it. My friend looked very saddened by these original reflections. He said that it seemed to him that I had taken the road which ended in fascism, tyranny, and blood.

So, I told him, have you. One fine day, you'll realize that people don't *want* to be better. So you'll have to make them better. And how do you think you'll go about it?

He said nothing to this. He was sitting opposite me, in a booth, in a   5
Greenwich Village diner.

What about love? he asked me.

His question threw me off guard, and frightened me. With the indescribable authority of twenty-two, I snarled: Love! You'd better forget about that, my friend. That train has *gone*.

The moment I said this, I regretted it, for I remembered that he *was* in love: with a young white girl, also a Socialist, whose family was threatening to have him put in prison. And the week before, a handful of sailors had come across them in the subway and beaten him very badly.

He looked at me and I wanted to unsay what I had said, to say something else. But I could not think of anything which would not sound, simply, like unmanly consolation, which would not sound as though I were humoring him.

You're a poet, he said, and you don't believe in love.   10

And he put his head down on the table and began to cry.

We had come through some grueling things together, and I had never seen him cry. In fact, he went into and came out of battles laughing. We were in a hostile, public place. New York was fearfully hostile in those days, as it still is. He was my best friend, and for the first time in our lives I could do nothing for him; and it had been my ill-considered rage which had hurt him. I wanted to take it back, but I did not know how. I *would* have known how if I had been being insincere. But, though I know now that I was wrong, I did not know it then. I had meant what I had said, and my unexamined life would not allow me to speak otherwise. I really did not, then, as far as I knew, believe that love existed, except as useless pain; and the time was far from me when I would begin to see the contradiction implicit in the fact that I was bending all my forces, or imagined I was, to protect myself against it.

He wept; I sat there; no one, for a wonder, bothered us. By and by we paid, and walked out into the streets. This was the last time, but one, that I ever saw him; it was the very last time that we really spoke. A very short time after this, his body was found in the Hudson River. He had jumped from the George Washington Bridge.

Why do I begin my sketch of Americans abroad with this memory? I suppose that there must be many reasons. I certainly cannot hope to tell or, for that matter, to face them all. One reason, of course, is that I thought for a very long time that I had hastened him to his death. *You're a poet, and you don't believe in love.* But, leaving aside now this hideous and useless speculation, it is from the time of my friend's death that I resolved to leave America. There were two reasons for this. One was that I was absolutely certain, from the moment I learned of his death, that I, too, if I stayed here, would come to a similar end. I felt then, and, to tell the truth, I feel now, that he would not have died in such a way and certainly not so soon, if he had not been black. (Legally speaking. Physically, he was almost, but not quite, light enough to pass.) And this meant that he was the grimmest, until then, of a series of losses for which I most bitterly blamed the American republic. From the time of his death, I began to be afraid of enduring any more. I was afraid that hatred, and the desire for revenge, would reach unmanageable proportions in me, and that my end, even if I should not physically die, would be infinitely more horrible than my friend's suicide.

He was not the only casualty of those days. There were others, white, 15 friends of mine, who, at just about the time his indescribably colored body was recovered from the river, were returning from the world's most hideous war. Some were boys with whom I had been to high school. One boy, Jewish, sat with me all night in my apartment on Orchard Street, telling me about the camps he had seen in Germany and the Germans he had blasted off the face of the earth. I will never forget his face. I had once known it very well — shortly before, when we had been children. It was not a child's face now. He had *seen* what people would do to him — because he was a Jew he knew what he had done to Germans; and not only could nothing be undone, it might very well be that this was all that the world could ever be, over and over again, forever. All political hopes and systems, then, seemed morally bankrupt: for, if Buchenwald was wrong, what, then, *really* made Hiroshima right? He shook his head, an old Jew already, an old man. If all visions of human nature are to be distrusted, and all hopes, what about love?

The people I knew found the most extraordinary ways of dealing with this question, but it was a real question. Girls who had been virgins when they married their husbands — and there were some, I knew them — sometimes had to have abortions before their husbands returned from overseas. The marriages almost never survived the returning pressures, and, very often, the mental equilibrium of the partners — or ex-partners — was lost, never to be regained. Men who had had homosexual adventures in CO camps, or in the service, could not accept what had happened to them, could not forget it, dared not discover if they desired to repeat it, and lapsed into a paralysis from which neither men nor women could rouse them. It was a time of the most terrifying personal anarchy. If one gave a party, it was virtually certain that someone, quite possibly oneself, would have a crying jag or have to be restrained from murder or suicide. It was a time of experimentation, with sex, with marijuana, and minor infringements of the law, such as "boosting" from the A & P and stealing electricity from Con Edison. I knew some people who had a stolen refrigerator for which they had no room and no use, and which they could not sell; it was finally shipped, I believe, of all places, to Cuba. But, finally, it seems to me that life was beginning to tell us who we are, and what life was — news no one has ever wanted to hear: and we fought back by clinging to our vision of ourselves as innocent, of love perhaps imperfect but reciprocal and enduring. And we did not know that the price of this was experience. We had been raised to believe in formulas.

In retrospect, the discovery of the orgasm — or, rather, of the orgone box — seems the least mad of the formulas that came to mind. It seemed to me — though I was, perhaps, already too bitterly inoculated against groups or panaceas — that people turned from the idea of the world being made better through politics to the idea of the world being made better through psychic and sexual health like sinners coming down the aisle at a revival meeting. And I doubted that their conversion was any more to be trusted than that. The converts, indeed, moved in a certain euphoric aura of well-being, which could not last. They had not become more generous, but less, not more open, but more closed. They ceased, totally, to listen and could only proselytize; nor did their private lives become discernibly less tangled. There are no formulas for the improvement of the private, or any other life — certainly not the formula of more and better orgasms. (Who decides?) The people I had been raised among had orgasms all the time, and still chopped each other up with razors on Saturday nights.

By this wild process, then, of failure, elimination and rejection, I, certainly, and most of the people whom I knew got to Europe, and, roughly speaking, "settled there." Many of us have returned, but not all: It is important to remember that many expatriates vanish into the lives of their adopted country, to be flushed out only, and not always then, by grave international emergency. This applies especially, of course, to women, who, given the pressures of raising a family, rarely have time to be homesick, or guilty about "escaping" the problems of American life. Their first loyalties, thank heaven, are to the men they married and the children they must raise. But I know American couples, too, who have made their homes in Europe quite happily, and who have no intention of returning to this country. It is worth observing, too, that these people are nearly always marked by a lack of spite or uneasiness concerning this country which quite fails to characterize what I tend to think of as the "displaced" or "visible" expatriate. That is, remarkable as this may sound, it is not necessary to hate this country in order to have a good time somewhere else. In fact, the people who hate this country never manage, except physically, to leave it, and have a wretched life wherever they go.

And, of course, many of us have become, in effect, commuters; which is a less improbable state now than it was a decade ago. Many have neither returned nor stayed, but can be found in Village bars, talking about Europe, or in European bars, talking about America.

Apart from GIs who remained in Europe, thoughtfully using up all the cheap studios, and nearly all, as it turned out, of the available goodwill, we, who have been described (not very usefully) as the "new" expatriates, began arriving in Paris around '45, '46, '47, and '48. The character of the influx began to change very radically after that, if only because the newcomers had had the foresight to arm themselves with jobs: American government jobs, which also meant that they had housing allowances and didn't care how much rent they paid. Neither, of course, did the French landlords, with the result that rents rose astronomically and we who had considered ourselves forever installed in the Latin Quarter found ourselves living all over Paris. But this, at least for some of us, turned out to be very healthy and valuable. We were in Paris, after all, because we had presumably put down all formulas and all safety in favor of the chilling unpredictability of experience.

Voyagers discover that the world can never be larger than the person that is in the world; but it is impossible to foresee this, it is impossible to be warned. It is only when time has begun spilling through his fingers like water or sand — carrying away with it, forever, dreams, possibilities, challenges, and hopes — that the young man realizes that he will not be young forever. If he wishes to paint a picture, raise a family, write a book, design a building, start a war — well, he does not have forever in which to do it. He has only a certain amount of time, and half of that time is probably gone already. As long as his aspirations are in the realm of the dream, he is safe; when he must bring them back into the world, he is in danger.

Precisely for this reason, Paris was a devastating shock. It was easily recognizable as Paris from across the ocean: that was what the letters on the map spelled out. This was not the same thing as finding oneself in a large, inconvenient, indifferent city. Paris, from across the ocean, looked like a refuge from the American madness; now it was a city four thousand miles from home. It contained — in those days — no dough-nuts, no milk shakes, no Coca-Cola, no dry martinis; nothing resem-bling, for people on our economic level, an American toilet; as for toilet paper, it was yesterday's newspaper. The concierge of the hotel did not appear to find your presence in France a reason for rejoicing; rather, she found your presence, and in particular your ability to pay the rent, a matter for the profoundest suspicion. The policemen, with their re-volvers, clubs, and (as it turned out) weighted capes, appeared to be convinced of your legality only after the most vindictive scrutiny of your passport; and it became clear very soon that they were not kidding about the three-month period during which every foreigner had to buy a new visa or leave the country. Not a few astounded Americans, unable to call their embassy, spent the night in jail, and steady offenders were escorted to the border. After the first street riot, or its aftermath, one wit-nessed in Paris, one took a new attitude toward the Paris paving stones, and toward the café tables and chairs, and toward the Parisians, indeed, who showed no signs, at such moments, of being among the earth's most cerebral or civilized people. Paris hotels had never heard of cen-tral heating or hot baths or showers or clean towels and sheets or ham and eggs; their attitude toward electricity was demonic — once one had seen what they thought of as wiring one wondered why the city had not, long ago, vanished in flame; and it soon became clear that Paris hospi-tals had never heard of Pasteur. Once, in short, one found oneself di-vested of all the things that one had fled from, one wondered how people, meaning, above all, oneself, could possibly do without them.

And yet one did, of course, and in the beginning, and sporadically, thereafter, found these privations a subject for mirth. One soon ceased expecting to be warm in one's hotel room, and read and worked in the cafés. The French, at least insofar as student hotels are concerned, do not appear to understand the idea of a social visit. They expect one's callers to be vastly more intimate, if not utilitarian, than that, and much prefer that they register and spend the night. This aspect of Parisian life would seem vastly to simplify matters, but this, alas, is not the case. It merely makes it all but impossible to invite anyone to your hotel room. Americans do not cease to be Puritans when they have crossed the ocean; French girls, on the other hand, contrary to legend, tend, preponderantly, to be the marrying kind; thus, it was not long before we brave voyagers rather felt that we had been turned loose in a fair in which there was not a damn thing we could buy, and still less that we could sell.

And I think that when we began to be frightened in Paris, to feel baffled and betrayed, it was because we had failed, after all, somehow, and once again, to make the longed-for, magical human contact. It was on this connection with another human being that we had felt that our lives and our work depended. It had failed at home. We had thought we knew why. Everyone at home was too dry and too frightened, mercilessly pinned beneath the thumb of the Puritan God. Yet, here we were, surrounded by quite beautiful and sensual people, who did not, however, appear to find us beautiful or sensual. They said so. By the time we had been abroad two years, each of us, in one way or another, had received this message. It was one of the things that was meant when we were referred to as children. We had been perfectly willing to refer to all the other Americans as children — in the beginning; we had not known what it meant; we had not known that we were included.

By 1950 some of us had already left Paris for more promising ports of 25 call. Tangiers for some, or Italy, or Spain; Sweden or Denmark or Germany for others. Some girls had got married and vanished; some had got married and vanished and reappeared — minus their husbands. Some people got jobs with the ECA and began a slow retreat back into the cocoon from which they had never quite succeeded in emerging. Some of us were going to pieces — spectacularly, as in my own case, quietly, in others. One boy, for example, had embarked on the career which I believe still engages him, that of laboriously writing extremely literary plays in English, translating them — laboriously — into French and Spanish, reading the trilingual results to a coterie of friends who were, even then, beginning to diminish, and then locking them in his trunk. Magazines were popping up like toadstools and vanishing like fog. Painters and poets of thin talent and no industry began to feel abused by the lack of attention their efforts elicited from the French, and made outrageously obvious — and successful — bids for the attention of visiting literary figures from the States, of whose industry, in any case, there could be no doubt. And a certain real malice now began to make itself felt in our attitudes toward the French, as well as a certain defensiveness concerning whatever it was we had come to Paris to do and clearly were not doing. We were edgy with each other, too. Going, going, going, gone — were the days when we walked through Les Halles, singing, loving every inch of France, and loving each other; gone were the jam sessions in Pigalle, and our stories about the whores there; gone were the nights spent smoking hashish in Arab cafés; gone were the mornings which found us telling dirty stories, true stories, sad and earnest stories, in gray, workingmen's cafés. It was all gone. We were secretive with each other. I no longer talked about my novel. We no longer talked about our love affairs, for either they had failed, were failing, or were serious. Above all, they were private — how can love be talked about? It is probably the most awful of all the revelations this little life affords. We no longer walked about, as a friend of mine once put it, in a not dissimilar context, in "friendly groups of five thousand." We were splitting up, and each of us was going for himself. Or, if not precisely for himself, his own way; some of us took to the needle, some returned to the family business, some made loveless marriages, some ceased fleeing and turned to face the demons that had been on the trail so long. The luckiest among us were these last, for they managed to go to pieces and then put themselves back together with whatever was left. This may take away one's dreams, but it delivers one to oneself. Without this coming together, the longed-for love is never possible, for the confused personality can neither give nor take.

In my case, I think my exile saved my life, for it inexorably confirmed something which Americans appear to have great difficulty accepting. Which is, simply, this: A man is not a man until he is able and willing to accept his own vision of the world, no matter how radically this vision departs from that of others. (When I say "vision," I do not mean "dream.") There are long moments when this country resembles nothing so much as the grimmest of popularity contests. The best thing that happened to the "new" expatriates was their liberation, finally, from any need to be smothered by what is really nothing more (though it may be something less) than mother love. It need scarcely, I hope, be said that I have no interest in hurling gratuitous insults at American mothers; they are certainly helpless, if not entirely blameless; and my point has nothing to do with them. My point is involved with the great emphasis placed on public approval here, and the resulting and quite insane system of penalties and rewards. It puts a premium on mediocrity and has all but slaughtered any concept of excellence. This corruption begins in the private life and unfailingly flowers in the public life. Europeans refer to Americans as children in the same way that American Negroes refer to them as children, and for the same reason: They mean that Americans have so little experience — experience referring not to *what* happens, but to *who* — that they have no key to the experience of others. Our current relations with the world forcibly suggest that there is more than a little truth to this. What Europe still gives an American — or gave us — is the sanction, if one can accept it, to become oneself. No artist can survive without this acceptance. But rare indeed is the American artist who achieved this without first becoming a wanderer, and then, upon his return to his own country, the loneliest and most blackly distrusted of men.

EXPLORATIONS

1. In the opening section (paras. 1–13) of "The New Lost Generation," what information does James Baldwin give us about himself? Of the half-dozen identifying categories in which he places himself, which ones are most central to his essay?

2. What aspects of the United States made Baldwin leave it? What did he hope to find in Europe? In what ways did the life of an expatriate match his expectations, and in what ways did it surprise him?

3. At what points does Baldwin use the pronouns "you" and "one" in writing about his own experience? What are the effects of this choice?

CONNECTIONS

1. What comments about U.S. expatriates in "The New Lost Generation" correspond to elements in Walker Percy's definition of "the lost self" (p. 15)? How do you think Percy would explain Baldwin's emigration to Paris?

2. How does Baldwin's vision of America differ from Richard Rayner's (p. 2)? What factors (besides individual idiosyncrasy) may account for the contrast?

3. Compare Baldwin's description of himself and his friend in paragraph 2 with Shelby Steele's description of bargainers and challengers (p. 5). How do they match up?

ELABORATIONS

1. What was "the lost generation"? Why was it so called? What is the meaning of Baldwin's title "The New Lost Generation"? Write an essay defining the term as it was originally used and comparing the meaning Baldwin gives to it.

2. "Voyagers discover that the world can never be larger than the person that is in the world" (para. 21). What does Baldwin mean by this? Do you agree with him? Write an essay explaining and exploring his statement.

AMY TAN

Two Kinds

Amy Tan's parents emigrated from China to Oakland, California, shortly before she was born in 1952. Her Chinese name, An-mei, means "blessing from America." Amy Tan graduated from San Jose State University. She became a language-development consultant and later a business writer. "Two Kinds" comes from her book *The Joy Luck Club* (1989), which began as three short stories and grew into a novel told in the voices of four Chinese women and their California-born daughters. Tan followed up *The Joy Luck Club* (which has been translated into seventeen languages) with two more novels, *The Kitchen God's Wife* (1991) and *The Hundred Secret Senses* (1995), as well as two children's books, *The Moon Lady* (1992) and *The Chinese Siamese Cat* (1994). Tan and her husband live in San Francisco.

For background on China, see p. 730.

My mother believed you could be anything you wanted to be in America. You could open a restaurant. You could work for the government and get good retirement. You could buy a house with almost no money down. You could become rich. You could become instantly famous.

"Of course you can be prodigy, too," my mother told me when I was nine. "You can be best anything. What does Auntie Lindo know? Her daughter, she is only best tricky."

America was where all my mother's hopes lay. She had come here in 1949 after losing everything in China: her mother and father, her family home, her first husband, and two daughters, twin baby girls. But she never looked back with regret. There were so many ways for things to get better.

We didn't immediately pick the right kind of prodigy. At first my mother thought I could be a Chinese Shirley Temple. We'd watch Shirley's old movies on TV as though they were training films. My mother would poke my arm and say, "*Ni kan*" — You watch. And I would see Shirley tapping her feet, or singing a sailor song, or pursing her lips into a very round O while saying, "Oh my goodness."

28

"*Ni kan*," said my mother as Shirley's eyes flooded with tears. "You   5
already know how. Don't need talent for crying!"

Soon after my mother got this idea about Shirley Temple, she took
me to a beauty training school in the Mission district and put me in the
hands of a student who could barely hold the scissors without shaking.
Instead of getting big fat curls, I emerged with an uneven mass of
crinkly black fuzz. My mother dragged me off to the bathroom and
tried to wet down my hair.

"You look like Negro Chinese," she lamented, as if I had done this
on purpose.

The instructor of the beauty training school had to lop off these
soggy clumps to make my hair even again. "Peter Pan is very popular
these days," the instructor assured my mother. I now had hair the
length of a boy's, with straight-across bangs that hung at a slant two
inches above my eyebrows. I liked the haircut and it made me actually
look forward to my future fame.

In fact, in the beginning, I was just as excited as my mother, maybe
even more so. I pictured this prodigy part of me as many different images, trying each one on for size. I was a dainty ballerina girl standing by
the curtains, waiting to hear the right music that would send me floating on my tiptoes. I was like the Christ child lifted out of the straw
manger, crying with holy indignity. I was Cinderella stepping from her
pumpkin carriage with sparkly cartoon music filling the air.

In all of my imaginings, I was filled with a sense that I would soon   10
become *perfect*. My mother and father would adore me. I would be beyond reproach. I would never feel the need to sulk for anything.

But sometimes the prodigy in me became impatient. "If you don't
hurry up and get me out of here, I'm disappearing for good," it warned.
"And then you'll always be nothing."

Every night after dinner, my mother and I would sit at the Formica
kitchen table. She would present new tests, taking her examples from
stories of amazing children she had read in *Ripley's Believe It or Not*, or
Good Housekeeping, Reader's Digest, and a dozen other magazines she
kept in a pile in our bathroom. My mother got these magazines from
people whose houses she cleaned. And since she cleaned many houses
each week, we had a great assortment. She would look through them
all, searching for stories about remarkable children.

The first night she brought out a story about a three-year-old boy who
knew the capitals of all the states and even most of the European countries. A teacher was quoted as saying the little boy could also pronounce
the names of the foreign cities correctly.

"What's the capital of Finland?" my mother asked me, looking at the magazine story.

All I knew was the capital of California, because Sacramento was the name of the street we lived on in Chinatown. "Nairobi!" I guessed, saying the most foreign word I could think of. She checked to see if that was possibly one way to pronounce "Helsinki" before showing me the answer.

The tests got harder — multiplying numbers in my head, finding the queen of hearts in a deck of cards, trying to stand on my head without using my hands, predicting the daily temperatures in Los Angeles, New York, and London.

One night I had to look at a page from the Bible for three minutes and then report everything I could remember. "Now Jehoshaphat had riches and honor in abundance and . . . that's all I remember, Ma," I said.

And after seeing my mother's disappointed face once again, something inside of me began to die. I hated the tests, the raised hopes and failed expectations. Before going to bed that night, I looked in the mirror above the bathroom sink and when I saw only my face staring back — and that it would always be this ordinary face — I began to cry. Such a sad, ugly girl! I made high-pitched noises like a crazed animal, trying to scratch out the face in the mirror.

And then I saw what seemed to be the prodigy side of me — because I had never seen that face before. I looked at my reflection, blinking so I could see more clearly. The girl staring back at me was angry, powerful. This girl and I were the same. I had new thoughts, willful thoughts, or rather thoughts filled with lots of won'ts. I won't let her change me, I promised myself. I won't be what I'm not.

So now on nights when my mother presented her tests, I performed listlessly, my head propped on one arm. I pretended to be bored. And I was. I got so bored I started counting the bellows of the foghorns out on the bay while my mother drilled me in other areas. The sound was comforting and reminded me of the cow jumping over the moon. And the next day, I played a game with myself, seeing if my mother would give up on me before eight bellows. After a while I usually counted only one, maybe two bellows at most. At last she was beginning to give up hope.

Two or three months had gone by without any mention of my being a prodigy again. And then one day my mother was watching *The Ed Sullivan Show* on TV. The TV was old and the sound kept shorting out.

Every time my mother got halfway up from the sofa to adjust the set, the sound would go back on and Ed would be talking. As soon as she sat down, Ed would go silent again. She got up, the TV broke into loud piano music. She sat down. Silence. Up and down, back and forth, quiet and loud. It was like a stiff embraceless dance between her and the TV set. Finally she stood by the set with her hand on the sound dial.

She seemed entranced by the music, a little frenzied piano piece with this mesmerizing quality, sort of quick passages and then teasing lilting ones before it returned to the quick playful parts.

"*Ni kan*," my mother said, calling me over with hurried hand gestures. "Look here."

I could see why my mother was fascinated by the music. It was being pounded out by a little Chinese girl, about nine years old, with a Peter Pan haircut. The girl had the sauciness of a Shirley Temple. She was proudly modest like a proper Chinese child. And she also did this fancy sweep of a curtsy, so that the fluffy skirt of her white dress cascaded slowly to the floor like the petals of a large carnation.

In spite of these warning signs, I wasn't worried. Our family had no   25
piano and we couldn't afford to buy one, let alone reams of sheet music and piano lessons. So I could be generous in my comments when my mother bad-mouthed the little girl on TV.

"Play note right, but doesn't sound good! No singing sound," complained my mother.

"What are you picking on her for?" I said carelessly. "She's pretty good. Maybe she's not the best, but she's trying hard." I knew almost immediately I would be sorry I said that.

"Just like you," she said. "Not the best. Because you not trying." She gave a little huff as she let go of the sound dial and sat down on the sofa.

The little Chinese girl sat down also to play an encore of "Anitra's Dance" by Grieg. I remember the song, because later on I had to learn how to play it.

Three days after watching *The Ed Sullivan Show*, my mother told me   30
what my schedule would be for piano lessons and piano practice. She had talked to Mr. Chong, who lived on the first floor of our apartment building. Mr. Chong was a retired piano teacher and my mother had traded housecleaning services for weekly lessons and a piano for me to practice on every day, two hours a day, from four until six.

When my mother told me this, I felt as though I had been sent to hell. I whined and then kicked my foot a little when I couldn't stand it anymore.

"Why don't you like me the way I am? I'm *not* a genius! I can't play the piano. And even if I could, I wouldn't go on TV if you paid me a million dollars!" I cried.

My mother slapped me. "Who ask you be genius?" she shouted. "Only ask you be your best. For you sake. You think I want you be genius? Hnnh! What for! Who ask you!"

"So ungrateful," I heard her mutter in Chinese. "If she had as much talent as she has temper, she would be famous now."

Mr. Chong, whom I secretly nicknamed Old Chong, was very   35
strange, always tapping his fingers to the silent music of an invisible orchestra. He looked ancient in my eyes. He had lost most of the hair on top of his head and he wore thick glasses and had eyes that always looked tired and sleepy. But he must have been younger than I thought, since he lived with his mother and was not yet married.

I met Old Lady Chong once and that was enough. She had this peculiar smell like a baby that had done something in its pants. And her fingers felt like a dead person's, like an old peach I once found in the back of the refrigerator; the skin just slid off the meat when I picked it up.

I soon found out why Old Chong had retired from teaching piano. He was deaf. "Like Beethoven!" he shouted to me. "We're both listening only in our head!" And he would start to conduct his frantic silent sonatas.

Our lessons went like this. He would open the book and point to different things, explaining their purpose: "Key! Treble! Bass! No sharps or flats! So this is C major! Listen now and play after me!"

And then he would play the C scale a few times, a simple chord, and then, as if inspired by an old, unreachable itch, he gradually added more notes and running trills and a pounding bass until the music was really something quite grand.

I would play after him, the simple scale, the simple chord, and then I   40
just played some nonsense that sounded like a cat running up and down on top of garbage cans. Old Chong smiled and applauded and then said, "Very good! But now you must learn to keep time!"

So that's how I discovered that Old Chong's eyes were too slow to keep up with the wrong notes I was playing. He went through the motions in half-time. To help me keep rhythm, he stood behind me, pushing down on my right shoulder for every beat. He balanced pennies on top of my wrists so I would keep them still as I slowly played scales and arpeggios. He had me curve my hand around an apple and keep that shape when playing chords. He marched stiffly to show me how to make each finger dance up and down, staccato like an obedient little soldier.

He taught me all these things, and that was how I also learned I could be lazy and get away with mistakes, lots of mistakes. If I hit the wrong notes because I hadn't practiced enough, I never corrected myself. I just kept playing in rhythm. And Old Chong kept conducting his own private reverie.

So maybe I never really gave myself a fair chance. I did pick up the basics pretty quickly, and I might have become a good pianist at that young age. But I was so determined not to try, not to be anybody different that I learned to play only the most ear-splitting preludes, the most discordant hymns.

Over the next year, I practiced like this, dutifully in my own way. And then one day I heard my mother and her friend Lindo Jong both talking in a loud bragging tone of voice so others could hear. It was after church, and I was leaning against the brick wall wearing a dress with stiff white petticoats. Auntie Lindo's daughter, Waverly, who was about my age, was standing farther down the wall about five feet away. We had grown up together and shared all the closeness of two sisters squabbling over crayons and dolls. In other words, for the most part, we hated each other. I thought she was snotty. Waverly Jong had gained a certain amount of fame as "Chinatown's Littlest Chinese Chess Champion."

"She bring home too many trophy," lamented Auntie Lindo that 45 Sunday. "All day she play chess. All day I have no time do nothing but dust off her winnings." She threw a scolding look at Waverly, who pretended not to see her.

"You lucky you don't have this problem," said Auntie Lindo with a sigh to my mother.

And my mother squared her shoulders and bragged: "Our problem worser than yours. If we ask Jing-mei wash dish, she hear nothing but music. It's like you can't stop this natural talent."

And right then, I was determined to put a stop to her foolish pride.

A few weeks later, Old Chong and my mother conspired to have me play in a talent show which would be held in the church hall. By then, my parents had saved up enough to buy me a secondhand piano, a black Wurlitzer spinet with a scarred bench. It was the showpiece of our living room.

For the talent show, I was to play a piece called "Pleading Child" 50 from Schumann's *Scenes from Childhood*. It was a simple, moody piece that sounded more difficult than it was. I was supposed to memorize the whole thing, playing the repeat parts twice to make the piece sound longer. But I dawdled over it, playing a few bars and then cheating, looking up to see what notes followed, I never really listened to what I was playing. I daydreamed about being somewhere else, about being someone else.

The part I liked to practice best was the fancy curtsy: right foot out, touch the rose on the carpet with a pointed foot, sweep to the side, left leg bends, look up and smile.

My parents invited all the couples from the Joy Luck Club to witness my debut. Auntie Lindo and Uncle Tin were there. Waverly and her two older brothers had also come. The first two rows were filled with children both younger and older than I was. The littlest ones got to go first. They recited simple nursery rhymes, squawked out tunes on miniature violins, twirled Hula Hoops, pranced in pink ballet tutus, and when they bowed or curtsied, the audience would sigh in unison, "Awww," and then clap enthusiastically.

When my turn came, I was very confident. I remember my childish excitement. It was as if I knew, without a doubt, that the prodigy side of me really did exist. I had no fear whatsoever, no nervousness. I remember thinking to myself, This is it! This is it! I looked out over the audience, at my mother's blank face, my father's yawn, Auntie Lindo's stiff-lipped smile, Waverly's sulky expression. I had on a white dress layered with sheets of lace, and a pink bow in my Peter Pan haircut. As I sat down I envisioned people jumping to their feet and Ed Sullivan rushing up to introduce me to everyone on TV.

And I started to play. It was so beautiful. I was so caught up in how lovely I looked that at first I didn't worry how I would sound. So it was a surprise to me when I hit the first wrong note and I realized something didn't sound quite right. And then I hit another and another followed that. A chill started at the top of my head and began to trickle down. Yet I couldn't stop playing, as though my hands were bewitched. I kept thinking my fingers would adjust themselves back, like a train switching to the right track. I played this strange jumble through two repeats, the sour notes staying with me all the way to the end.

When I stood up, I discovered my legs were shaking. Maybe I had just been nervous and the audience, like Old Chong, had seen me go through the right motions and had not heard anything wrong at all. I swept my right foot out, went down on my knee, looked up and smiled. The room was quiet, except for Old Chong, who was beaming and shouting, "Bravo! Bravo! Well done!" But then I saw my mother's face, her stricken face. The audience clapped weakly, and as I walked back to my chair, with my whole face quivering as I tried not to cry, I heard a little boy whisper loudly to his mother, "That was awful," and the mother whispered back, "Well, she certainly tried."

And now I realized how many people were in the audience, the whole world it seemed. I was aware of eyes burning into my back. I felt the shame of my mother and father as they sat stiffly throughout the rest of the show.

We could have escaped during intermission. Pride and some strange sense of honor must have anchored my parents to their chairs. And so we watched it all: the eighteen-year-old boy with a fake mustache who did a magic show and juggled flaming hoops while riding a unicycle. The breasted girl with white makeup who sang from *Madama Butterfly* and got honorable mention. And the eleven-year-old boy who won first prize playing a tricky violin song that sounded like a busy bee.

After the show, the Hsus, the Jongs, and the St. Clairs from the Joy Luck Club came up to my mother and father.

"Lots of talented kids," Auntie Lindo said vaguely, smiling broadly.

"That was somethin' else," said my father, and I wondered if he was 60 referring to me in a humorous way, or whether he even remembered what I had done.

Waverly looked at me and shrugged her shoulders. "You aren't a genius like me," she said matter-of-factly. And if I hadn't felt so bad, I would have pulled her braids and punched her stomach.

But my mother's expression was what devastated me: a quiet, blank look that said she had lost everything. I felt the same way, and it seemed as if everybody were now coming up, like gawkers at the scene of an accident, to see what parts were actually missing. When we got on the bus to go home, my father was humming the busy-bee tune and my mother was silent. I kept thinking she wanted to wait until we got home before shouting at me. But when my father unlocked the door to our apartment, my mother walked in and then went to the back, into the bedroom. No accusations. No blame. And in a way, I felt disappointed. I had been waiting for her to start shouting, so I could shout back and cry and blame her for all my misery.

I assumed my talent-show fiasco meant I never had to play the piano again. But two days later, after school, my mother came out of the kitchen and saw me watching TV.

"Four clock," she reminded me as if it were any other day. I was stunned, as though she were asking me to go through the talent-show torture again. I wedged myself more tightly in front of the TV.

"Turn off TV," she called from the kitchen five minutes later.   65

I didn't budge. And then I decided. I didn't have to do what my mother said anymore. I wasn't her slave. This wasn't China. I had listened to her before and look what happened. She was the stupid one.

She came out from the kitchen and stood in the arched entryway of the living room. "Four clock," she said once again, louder.

"I'm not going to play anymore," I said nonchalantly. "Why should I? I'm not a genius."

She walked over and stood in front of the TV. I saw her chest was heaving up and down in an angry way.

"No!" I said, and I now felt stronger, as if my true self had finally   70
emerged. So this was what had been inside me all along.

"No! I won't!" I screamed.

She yanked me by the arm, pulled me off the floor, snapped off the TV. She was frighteningly strong, half pulling, half carrying me toward the piano as I kicked the throw rugs under my feet. She lifted me up and onto the hard bench. I was sobbing by now, looking at her bitterly. Her chest was heaving even more and her mouth was open, smiling crazily as if she were pleased I was crying.

"You want me to be someone that I'm not!" I sobbed. "I'll never be the kind of daughter you want me to be!"

"Only two kinds of daughters," she shouted in Chinese. "Those who are obedient and those who follow their own mind! Only one kind of daughter can live in this house. Obedient daughter!"

"Then I wish I wasn't your daughter. I wish you weren't my mother,"   75
I shouted. As I said these things I got scared. I felt like worms and toads and slimy things were crawling out of my chest, but it also felt good, as if this awful side of me had surfaced, at last.

"Too late change this," said my mother shrilly.

And I could sense her anger rising to its breaking point. I wanted to see it spill over. And that's when I remembered the babies she had lost in China, the ones we never talked about. "Then I wish I'd never been born!" I shouted. "I wish I were dead! Like them."

It was as if I had said the magic words. Alakazam! — and her face went blank, her mouth closed, her arms went slack, and she backed out of the room, stunned, as if she were blowing away like a small brown leaf, thin, brittle, lifeless.

It was not the only disappointment my mother felt in me. In the years that followed, I failed her so many times, each time asserting my own will, my right to fall short of expectations. I didn't get straight As. I didn't become class president. I didn't get into Stanford. I dropped out of college.

For unlike my mother, I did not believe I could be anything I 80 wanted to be. I could only be me.

And for all those years, we never talked about the disaster at the recital or my terrible accusations afterward at the piano bench. All that remained unchecked, like a betrayal that was now unspeakable. So I never found a way to ask her why she had hoped for something so large that failure was inevitable.

And even worse, I never asked her what frightened me the most: Why had she given up hope?

For after our struggle at the piano, she never mentioned my playing again. The lessons stopped. The lid to the piano was closed, shutting out the dust, my misery, and her dreams.

So she surprised me. A few years ago, she offered to give me the piano, for my thirtieth birthday. I had not played in all those years. I saw the offer as a sign of forgiveness, a tremendous burden removed.

"Are you sure?" I asked shyly. "I mean, won't you and Dad miss it?" 85

"No, this your piano," she said firmly. "Always your piano. You only one can play."

"Well, I probably can't play anymore," I said. "It's been years."

"You pick up fast," said my mother, as if she knew this was certain. "You have natural talent. You could been genius if you want to."

"No I couldn't."

"You just not trying," said my mother. And she was neither angry nor 90 sad. She said it as if to announce a fact that could never be disproved. "Take it," she said.

But I didn't at first. It was enough that she had offered it to me. And after that, every time I saw it in my parents' living room, standing in front of the bay windows, it made me feel proud, as if it were a shiny trophy I had won back.

Last week I sent a tuner over to my parents' apartment and had the piano reconditioned, for purely sentimental reasons. My mother had died a few months before and I had been getting things in order for my father, a little bit at a time. I put the jewelry in special silk pouches. The sweaters she had knitted in yellow, pink, bright orange — all the colors I hated — I put those in moth-proof boxes. I found some old Chinese silk dresses, the kind with little slits up the sides. I rubbed the old silk against my skin, then wrapped them in tissue and decided to take them home with me.

After I had the piano tuned, I opened the lid and touched the keys. It sounded even richer than I remembered. Really, it was a very good piano. Inside the bench were the same exercise notes with handwritten scales, the same secondhand music books with their covers held together with yellow tape.

I opened up the Schumann book to the dark little piece I had played at the recital. It was on the left-hand side of the page, "Pleading Child." It looked more difficult than I remembered. I played a few bars, surprised at how easily the notes came back to me.

And for the first time, or so it seemed, I noticed the piece on the   95 right-hand side. It was called "Perfectly Contented." I tried to play this one as well. It had a lighter melody but the same flowing rhythm and turned out to be quite easy. "Pleading Child" was shorter but slower; "Perfectly Contented" was longer but faster. And after I played them both a few times, I realized they were two halves of the same song.

EXPLORATIONS

1. How many different meanings for the story's title can you find in "Two Kinds"?
2. What is the primary goal of the narrator's mother in "Two Kinds"? Which of her statements and actions show how important it is to her? What clues in the story's first three paragraphs suggest why she has fixed on this goal?
3. What is the primary goal of the narrator at the beginning of "Two Kinds"? Why has she fixed on this goal? How does her goal change as the story progresses, and why?

CONNECTIONS

1. James Baldwin writes, "A man is not a man until he is able and willing to accept his own vision of the world, no matter how radically this vision departs from that of others" (p. 25). What does he mean? What comments by Tan's narrator Jing-mei express a similar view?
2. Which of Walker Percy's definitions of self (pp. 14–16) do you think Tan's narrator would most identify with, and why? Which of these definitions would the narrator's mother prefer that she identify with?
3. Enriqué, an immigrant to New York from the Dominican Republic, says "My boys are dedicated now, but in a few years, who knows?" (p. 4). After reading "Two Kinds," what reasons can you give why Enriqué's sons may lose their dedication?

ELABORATIONS

1. In "African Literature: What Tradition?" (p. 562), Es'kia Mphahlele comments about parents: "They worry a great deal about the way in which we break loose at one point and ignore some elements of tradition." How is this true of the characters in "Two Kinds"? Reread Amy Tan's story. Then write a cause-and-effect essay about the problems faced by families consisting of traditional parents and nontraditional children.

2. "Two Kinds" begins, "My mother believed you could be anything you wanted to be in America." In the last paragraph of "The New Lost Generation" (p. 25), James Baldwin writes, "There are long moments when this country resembles nothing so much as the grimmest of popularity contests." He refers to "the great emphasis placed on public approval here, and the resulting and quite insane system of penalties and rewards." Baldwin was an American who emigrated to France; Amy Tan is an American whose parents immigrated from China. Write an essay comparing and contrasting their assessments of life in the United States.

SUSAN ORLEAN

Quinceañera

Susan Orlean was born on Halloween in 1955 in Cleveland, Ohio. After graduating from the University of Michigan she became a writer for *Willamette Week* in Portland, Oregon, then for the *Boston Phoenix*, and then for the *Boston Globe*. Her first book was a collection of essays from the *Globe* entitled *Red Sox and Bluefish: Meditations on What Makes New England New England* (1987). Orlean now lives in New York, where she has been a contributing editor for *Rolling Stone* and *Vogue*; in 1992 she became a staff writer for *The New Yorker*. "Quinceañera" comes from her book *Saturday Night* (1990).

Azteca Plaza, the biggest formal wear shopping center in the world, is on a skinny strip of sandy, cactus-studded Arizona real estate, a few miles east of downtown Phoenix, in a neighborhood that does not yet illustrate the vitality of the Sunbelt economy. . . . Azteca Plaza has the corner on the greater metropolitan Phoenix prom-dress trade. It also does a brisk business in the fancy ball gowns Hispanic girls wear at their *quinceañeras,* the ceremony that takes place when they are fifteen years old — *quinceaños* — to celebrate their passage into womanhood, commitment to Catholicism, and debut into society. In the last decade, the number of Hispanics in Phoenix has grown by 125 percent. The *quinceañera* business at Azteca Plaza has enjoyed a corresponding upswing.

Azteca Plaza is just a few blocks away from Immaculate Heart Church, a boxy stucco-colored structure that serves as a central parish for the Hispanic community in the Phoenix diocese. Immaculate Heart was built in 1928, fourteen years after it was revealed that the priests at the main basilica in Phoenix, St. Mary's, had been obliging their Mexican parishioners to hold their masses and weddings and *quinceañeras* in the basement rather than on the main floor of the church. It used to be common for certain churches to serve an ethnic group rather than a geographical area — in most American cities, there would be French, Hispanic, Polish, Irish, and German Catholic churches. The practice is rare these days, and Immaculate Heart is one of the few such ethnic parishes left in the entire country. Someone in Phoenix, recounting for me the history of Hispanic mistreatment at St. Mary's, credited the continued existence of a national parish in Phoenix to the dry Arizona desert air, which, he claimed, had preserved the unpleasant memory of bargain-basement weddings at the basilica in many Hispanics' minds. Hispanics in Phoenix now regularly attend the churches in their immediate neighborhoods, but for sentimental and historical reasons they continue to think of Immaculate Heart as the mother ship. Not coincidentally, Immaculate Heart was for years the site of most of Phoenix's many *quinceañeras* — that is, the site of the mass when the girl is blessed and is asked to affirm her dedication to the Church. The party in which she is introduced to society and celebrates her birthday is held after the mass at a hotel or hall. For a while, there were so many *quinceañeras* at Immaculate Heart that they outnumbered weddings. For that matter, there were so many *quinceañera* masses and parties that they were a standard Saturday-night social occasion in town.

In early summer I was invited to a large *quinceañera* in Phoenix at which sixteen girls were to be presented. The event was being sponsored by the girls' parents and the Vesta Club, a social organization of Hispanic college graduates. In the Southwest, constituents of this subset are sometimes known as "chubbies" — Chicano urban professionals. Chubbies give Azteca Plaza a lot of business. The girls' fathers and the sixteen young men who were going to be escorts at the *quinceañera* had rented their tuxedos from Azteca Plaza and would be picking them up on Saturday morning. The girls, of course, had gotten their gowns months before.

The traditional Mexican *quinceañera* gown is white or pink, floor length but trainless, snug on top and wide at the bottom, with a skirt shaped like a wedding bell. But like most traditions that migrate a few hundred miles from their point of origin and make it through a couple of generations in this country, *quinceañeras* have yielded somewhat to interpretation, and the gowns that the Vesta Club girls were going to wear demonstrated the effects of Americanization on taste as well as a certain American-style expansiveness in price. All of the gowns were white and full-length but otherwise they were freestyle — an array of high necks, fluted necklines, sweetheart necklines, leg-o'-mutton sleeves, cap sleeves, cascade collars, gathered bodices, beaded bodices, bustles, and sequins; one had a train and one had a flouncy peplum and a skirt that was narrow from the hip to the floor. Further Americanization has taken place with regards to scheduling. In Mexico, *quinceañeras* traditionally take place on the day the girl actually turns fifteen. In the United States, *quinceañeras* — like many important ceremonies in American life — take place on Saturday nights.

When I first mentioned to a woman I know in Phoenix that I wanted   5
to attend a *quinceañera,* that I thought they seemed like interesting cer-

emonies and great displays of community feeling and a good example
of how ethnic tradition fits into American Saturday nights, she clucked
sympathetically and said she was very sentimental about her own
quinceañera but had become convinced that they were now going the
way of many other ethnic ceremonies in this country — changed beyond recognition, marketed like theme parks, at the very least irrelevant
to assimilated youngsters who would rather spend Saturday nights at
keg parties than reenacting an old-world ceremony. An inevitable pattern transforms such things: Immigrants gather in their leisure time so
that they can bolster one another and share their imported traditions,
their children tolerate the gatherings occasionally because they have a
likeable familiar ring, and then the children of *those* children deplore
them because they seem corny and pointless, and finally there is a lot of
discussion about how sad it is that the community doesn't get together
anymore.

That is partly what has become of *quinceañeras* in Phoenix, but the
real problem, ironically, is that they have been too popular for their
own good. A few years ago, the bishop of Phoenix, a slight, freckle-faced
man from Indiana named Thomas O'Brien, started hearing complaints
from some priests about *quinceañeras*. According to the bishop, the
chief complaint was that *quinceañera* masses were beginning to dominate church schedules. This would surprise no one with an eye on the
city's demographics: Three-quarters of the Hispanics in Phoenix are
under thirty-five years old and a significant number of them are girls —
all potential subjects of a *quinceañera* mass and party. The priests complained that some girls came to their *quinceañera* mass without the
faintest idea of its religious significance, never came to church otherwise, demanded a mass even if they were pregnant or using drugs or in
some other way drifting outside the categories usually in good stead
with the religious community, and badgered their families — some
chubbies, but many not — into giving them opulent postmass parties.
Some *quinceañera* parties in Phoenix were running into the high four
figures and beyond. Many families could hardly afford this. In response
to these concerns, Father Antonio Sotelo, the bishop's vicar for Hispanic affairs, surveyed the diocese's priests and then wrote a guidebook
for *quinceañeras* similar to ones circulated recently in a few other American parishes with large Hispanic populations, advising that girls take
five classes on Bible study, Hispanic history, *quinceañera* history, and
modern morals, and go on a church-sponsored retreat with their parents
before the event. He also recommended that *quinceañeras* be held for
groups of girls rather than for individuals, in order to offset the queen-

for-a-day quality that many of them had taken on, and so that the cost could be spread around.

One morning before the Vesta Club *quinceañera*, I stopped by Father Sotelo's office at Immaculate Heart. Besides being vicar for Hispanic affairs, Father Sotelo is the pastor of Immaculate Heart. His small office in the back of the church is decorated with pictures of his parishioners and dominated by a whale of a desk. Father Sotelo is short and wiry and has rumpled graying hair, an impish face, and a melodious voice. His manner of address is direct. He is known for holding and broadcasting the opinion that anyone who wears shorts and a T-shirt to church should be escorted out the door, and that the men in his congregation who walk with a sloppy, swinging, barrio-tough gait look like gorillas. Father Sotelo grew up in San Diego. His heritage is Mexican and American Indian. He says that he considered the *quinceañera* issue a simple matter of facing reality, and he doesn't mind that the requirements have discouraged many girls from having *quinceañeras*. "We knew perfectly well that most girls were only thinking about the party," he said. "It was a big dream for them. Everyone wants a fancy *quinceañera* party. Unlike an American debutante ball, *quinceañeras* are not limited to the upper class. Any girl can celebrate it. But there are spoiled brats in every class. Many of these girls were demanding that their parents spend thousands of dollars on them whether they could afford it or not. People at the lower end of the economic scale cling to tradition most fervently, so they were most determined to have a traditional *quinceañera*, and their daughters would have the most expensive dresses and parties. And when these girls would walk down the aisle with their parents at the mass, you could tell that quite often the girls and their parents couldn't stand one another. It was an empty ceremony. For what they were getting out of the church part of the *quinceañera*, they could have gone out and done the whole thing in the desert and had someone sprinkle magic pollen on their heads."

After the guidelines were circulated around the diocese, a few churches, including Immaculate Heart, set up the *quinceañera* classes and retreats. But to the enormous displeasure of parishioners who enjoyed spending Saturday nights at their friends' daughters' *quinceañeras*, and who imagined that on some Saturday night in the future their own daughters would be feted at a mass and nice reception of their own, many priests in Phoenix announced that they agreed with Father Sotelo but they lacked the time and facilities to run classes and retreats. Therefore, they declared, they would no longer perform *quinceañera* masses at all.

The one priest who took exception was Frank Peacock, the pastor of a poor church in a scruffy South Phoenix neighborhood. Father Peacock made it known that he thought the guidelines were too strict, and that they inhibited the exercise of a tradition that rightfully belonged to the people, and that as far as he was concerned, anyone in any condition or situation who wanted a *quinceañera* could come to him. "We get calls here all the time from people asking very meekly for Father Peacock's number," Father Sotelo said to me, looking exasperated. "They're not fooling anyone. I know exactly what they want."

A few weeks before I got to Phoenix, a small yucca plant on the cor-   10
ner of Twelfth and Van Buren, about a half mile down the street from Immaculate Heart, sprouted a stem that then shriveled up into an unusual shape and was subsequently noticed by a passerby who thought it bore a striking resemblance to Our Lady of Guadeloupe. The yucca stem was never certified as a genuine miracle by church hierarchy, but for several weeks, until someone shot at it with a small-caliber handgun and then two artists took it upon themselves to cut it down with a chainsaw as the climax of a performance piece, it attracted large crowds of people who came to marvel at it and pray.

Our Lady of Guadeloupe, the vision who appeared to the Mexican-Indian Juan Diego on December 9, 1531, and who was so awe-inspiring a sight that she more or less nailed down the entire country of Mexico for the Catholic Church, has appeared in other places as unlikely as the corner of Twelfth and Van Buren. For instance, Our Lady of Guadeloupe also happens to be spray-painted on the trunk of at least one souped-up low-rider car in Phoenix, which I noticed bouncing down the street one afternoon when I was in town. Father Peacock had seen this same car and says he finds it remarkable. The day before the Vesta Club Ball, he and I had gotten together so he could show me videotapes of some of the outlaw *quinceañera* masses he had presided over at Our Lady of Fatima. Before we started the tapes, I said that Father Sotelo had pointed out that people were perfectly entitled to have *quinceañeras* that cost ten thousand dollars and celebrated fifteen-year-olds with heavy marijuana habits, but that the Church shouldn't necessarily endorse them or hold celebration masses for them. "People have a right to enjoy things that the Church doesn't endorse," Father Peacock said. "We don't endorse low-riders, do we?" He interrupted himself. "Actually, I endorse low-riders. I love them. Have you ever seen one? Oh, they can be gorgeous, really beautiful. Did you ever see the one painted with Our Lady of Guadeloupe?" . . .

Some of the people who come to Father Peacock for a *quinceañera* are poor, or are recent immigrants who are still attached to the traditional Mexican style of the ceremony and resist what they could well consider pointless time-consuming requirements or irritating Americanizations. Quite often, Father Peacock is approached by affluent Hispanics as well, who tell him they want their daughters to have their own celebrations, not *quinceañeras* with a group of other girls, and that they want to go all out with the six-tiered *quinceañera* cake and the rhinestone crown and the catered sit-down dinner for three hundred and the mariachi band and the lavish gifts from the godparents and the fifteen boy escorts and fifteen girl attendants in matching outfits who traditionally accompany the *quinceañera* girl. Father Peacock says he has given *quinceañera* masses for daughters of state senators as well as for girls whose parents are illiterate. Most of the time, he begins his address at the mass by asking for forgiveness for his failures and then says, "You have asked us to take care of a fifteenth-birthday celebration and we say no — this is one of our failures." Sometimes the people at the altar look bored or are wearing dark sunglasses and conspicuous amounts of jewelry and can't even remember the words to the Lord's Prayer when Father Peacock recites it. "That is one of my motivations," he says. "This might be the only chance I have to get that sort of person into church and try to reach them." Some of the families have experienced child abuse, sexual abuse, divorce, separation, or a combination of all four, and Father Peacock says he loves seeing such families together at the occasional happy affair like a *quinceañera*. Some of them take out loans to pay for their daughters' gowns. Father Peacock usually urges the poorer families to hold their parties at South Mountain Park, a city facility with a hall that can be used for free, but he says he can understand if they prefer a fancier place. On this point, he always says something in the homily like, "Through self-sacrifice we get our pleasure," and has said many times that he would rather that people go into hock for a traditional, ethnic, religious occasion — no matter how marginally religious it might turn out to be — than for something like a car or a boat. "A *quinceañera* costs a lot of money," he says. "But it's worth a lot of money. Anyway, I don't try to change people. I like to meet them in their own way." . . .

"Father Peacock will do anything," a young woman named Alice Coronado-Hernandez, this year's chairman of the Vesta Club *Quinceañera* Ball, said to me one afternoon. "Everyone knows that about Father Peacock, so everyone calls him." At the time, I was having lunch at a bad Mexican restaurant in a good part of Phoenix with Alice, her mother, Caroline, and Mary Jo Franco-French, a physician who helped found the Vesta *quinceañera* fifteen years ago. When she was organizing that first *quinceañera*, Mary Jo had just finished medical school and was pregnant with her daughter Laura. This year, Laura was going to be one of the girls up on the stage.

The Vesta Club is not going to be calling on Father Peacock anytime soon. "We're really happy with doing our *quinceañera* the way Father Sotelo has suggested," Caroline said. "We felt the classes and the retreat were really good for the girls. We saw what was going on with the *quinceañeras* — we saw the problem out there. Even if we could afford it, we knew it wasn't good to continue the old way."

Alice said, "It was crazy what people were spending. When I was that   15 age, the girls were really competitive about their *quinceañeras* and about how nice they would be." Caroline nodded. "My *quinceañera* was at the first Vesta Club Ball," Alice went on. "That year, I must have been invited to *quinceañeras* for friends of mine just about every weekend, so it was a pretty regular Saturday-night activity for me. But even then I could see how some people got very extravagant about it."

"They were hocking their souls for the fancy private *quinceañera*," Caroline added. "The diocese could see that it was becoming detrimental to the economy of their parishioners."

The three of them spent some time talking about last-minute details of the Vesta *quinceañera*. After a mass at Immaculate Heart, there was going to be dinner for the four hundred and fifty guests at Camelback Inn, an elegant resort north of the city, and a short ceremony in which each girl would be presented by her father. Then the girls and their escorts would perform a *quinceañera* waltz — a complicated dance to the "Blue Danube" which the kids had practiced once a week for the last three months. "The waltz is such a beautiful tradition," Mary Jo said. "It's what we have that makes the event really special. That, and having them learn about their Hispanic heritage. The kids have worked so hard at that waltz. They've really practiced, and they've really gotten good at it."

"They *have* gotten good at it, haven't they?" Caroline said, nodding. "It's hard to believe that some of them had never danced a step before they started to learn."

The Fifteenth Annual Vesta Club *Quinceañera* Mass began at five o'clock with a procession of the sixteen girls up the center aisle of Immaculate Heart. I sat on the left side of the church, a row behind Mary Jo Franco-French and her husband, Alfred, an eye surgeon of Gallic ex-

traction who has a large practice in Phoenix. Beside me were four
cousins of Mary Jo's who had flown in from Juarez, Mexico, for the
event. The day had been dry-roasting hot, and at five, the long, dusty
southwestern dusk was just beginning and the light was hitting the city
at a flat angle and giving everything a yellowy glow. The *quinceañera*
girls in their white dresses had been standing on the sidewalk outside
the church when I walked in, and each time a car drove down the street
in front of the church, the updraft would blow their big skirts around.
Immaculate Heart is a bulky, unadorned building with dark wooden
pews, a vaulted ceiling, some stained glass, a wide altar with simple
lines, and a pail hanging just outside the side door into which parishioners are advised to deposit their chewing gum. After I sat down, I noticed Father Sotelo and Bishop O'Brien seated together at the altar.
The Vesta Club *quinceañera* is the only one in Phoenix at which the
bishop celebrates the mass. He told me that it is the only one he attends
because he liked the seriousness with which the club approached the
spiritual content of the ceremony, and also because no one else having
a *quinceañera* had ever invited him.

After a few minutes, the organist hit a chord and the procession   20
began. The Vesta Club girls walked in, trailing satin and netting. The
gowns were a spectacle: Each one was bright white, with different structural embellishments and complicated effects. I noticed the girl wearing the dress with the little train and the one with the narrow skirt.
"Wow," whispered Carmen Gonzalez, one of Mary Jo Franco-French's
cousins, who had celebrated her own *quinceañera* a few years ago at a
country club in Juarez. "Pretty nice dresses. These girls look so *grown-
up.*"

"The third one down is my niece Maria," the woman behind us said.
"Fifteen already, but I still think of her as a baby. I think her mother's
praying that Maria keeps her figure so she can wear the dress again
when she gets married."

The procession took several minutes. Then the girls sat down in two
rows of chairs at the altar, and the bishop made his greetings and began
the mass. After a few prayers, he announced that it was time for the parents to bless their daughters individually. He turned and nodded at the
dark-haired girl at the end of the row. She stood up cautiously, walked
to the center of the apse and down the three steps, turned around and
knelt down, partially disappearing in the folds of her dress. Her parents
stood up in their pew and walked over to her, leaned down and made
the sign of the cross on her forehead, kissed her, whispered something
in her ear, and then returned to their seats. The girl rose up and walked
back to the altar. Someone in a pew behind me sobbed lightly and then

blew loudly into a handkerchief. A faulty key in the church organ stuck and started to squeal. The next girl stood up, smoothed her huge skirt, stepped down, knelt, was blessed by her parents, and returned to her seat. Laura Josefina Franco-French, a tall and elegant-looking fifteen-year-old with long dark hair and a serene expression, came forward and was blessed by Alfred and Mary Jo. Then the girl who was wearing the tight skirt stood up. We all sat forward. She walked in tiny steps across the apse, eased herself down the stairs, turned around, and then, with the agility of a high school cheerleader at the season's big game, she folded her legs beneath her and knelt without straining a seam.

There were still some golfers on the greens at Camelback Inn when the Vesta Club partygoers arrived. The ballroom wasn't ready for us to be seated, so everyone milled around the pool having drinks and talking. I wondered if the golfers were curious about what we were doing — four hundred well-dressed people, mostly adult, and sixteen girls in formal white gowns. It might have looked like a wedding, except there were too many young women in white, and it might have looked like a prom, except no one has parents at her prom. It felt mostly like a community reunion. "It's a big group, but it's a small world," said a woman in a beaded lilac gown standing beside me at the bar.

"Relatives or friends?" I asked.

"Both," she said. "About half of these people were at my daughter's *quinceañera* last year." I must have looked surprised, because she started to laugh and then said, "Some of these families even knew each other in Mexico. You could say that we're just keeping the chain or circle or what have you, intact. I had my *quinceañera* longer ago than I'm happy to say. It's an old-fashioned event but I love it." She took her drink and joined a group of people nearby who were talking about an expensive shopping center just opening in Scottsdale. One of the men in the group kept sweeping his hands out and saying "Boom!" and the woman beside him would then slap his shoulder playfully and say "For godsakes, come on, Adolfo!" Alfred Franco-French III, who was escorting his sister Laura, walked past the bar and muttered that he hoped he would remember the waltz when it came time to waltz. The patio got noisier and noisier. No one was speaking Spanish. One of the girls' fathers started a conversation with me by saying, "There are plenty of bums in the world out there, sad to say," but then he got distracted by someone he hadn't seen in a while and walked away. I had driven out to Camelback with one of Laura Franco-French's school friends, and after a few minutes we ran into each other. She said she was impressed with the *quinceañera* so far. She talked about how there was usually never

25

anything to do on Saturday nights in Phoenix, and then she talked about how favorably Laura's involvement in a formal event, in particular one that required the purchase of a really nice fancy dress, was regarded by other students at their largely non-Hispanic private school. It happened that this girl was not Hispanic and had never been to a *quinceañera* before and had also never before considered what advantages ethnicity might include. She looked across the pool where the debutantes were standing in a cluster and said, "I never thought about it one way or another. But now that I'm at one of these *quinceañeras*, I'm thinking that being Hispanic might be really cool." I walked to the far side of the pool, where I had a long view of all the people at the party, in their fresh tuxes and filmy formals; with their good haircuts and the handsome, relaxed posture common to people whose businesses are doing well and to whom life has been generous; who were standing around the glimmery pool and against the dark, lumpy outline of Camelback Mountain, holding up light-colored drinks in little crystal glasses so that they happened to catch the last bit of daylight. It was a pretty gorgeous sight.

Finally, Alice Coronado-Hernandez and Caroline Coronado sent word that the ballroom was ready. The doors of the Saguaro Room were propped open. The patio emptied as the crowd moved inside. At one end of the ballroom, a mariachi band was ready to play. Around the dance floor were fifty tables set with bunchy flower arrangements and good china. I had been seated with Alice Coronado-Hernandez and her family. At the tables, each place was set with a program printed on stiff, creamy paper; it listed the Vesta Club officers, last year's *quinceañera* debs and escorts, and this year's debs and escorts, and had formal portraits of each of the girls. This was similar in style to the program for the St. Luke's Hospital Visitors' Society Cotillion — Phoenix's premier society event — at which the girls being presented are far more likely to have names like Bickerstaff and Collins than Esparza and Alvarez. I had seen the 1988 St. Luke's program when I had dinner one night with the Franco-Frenches. Laura had been studying the program so energetically that some of the pages were fingerprinted and the binding was broken. In the time since Mexicans in Phoenix were forced to hold their masses in the basement of St. Mary's, a certain amount of social amalgamation has come to pass: Laura Franco-French, half-Mexican in heritage and at least that much in consciousness, will also be presented at St. Luke's in a few years. Similarly, there was a Whitman and a Thornton among the debutantes at the Vesta Ball. . . .

"When do they announce debutante of the year?" Alice's stepdaughter asked her. Alice drummed her fingers on the table and said, "Later."

Just then, the master of ceremonies coughed into the microphone and the room got quiet. The girls lined up around the edge of the dance floor with their fathers. The mothers were stationed near them in chairs, so that they would be readily available for the father-mother waltz, which comes after the father-daughter waltz and after the special *quinceañera* waltz — a complex piece of choreography, in which the girls spin around their escorts and then weave through their arms, form little circles and then big circles and finally waltz in time around the dance floor. After all these waltzes, the mariachi band was going to play — although I had heard that for the sake of the teenagers, who appreciated their heritage but who were, after all, American kids with tastes of their own, the Mexican music was going to be alternated throughout the evening with current selections of rock 'n' roll.

The announcer cleared his throat again and said, "*Buenos noches, damas y caballeros.*" He had a sonorous, rumbling voice that thundered through the ballroom. "*Buenos noches.* We present to you this year's Vesta Club debutantes."

EXPLORATIONS

1. How does the name of the store with which Susan Orlean opens "Quinceañera" illustrate the dual identity of the culture she is writing about?

2. What purposes was a *quinceañera* originally created to serve (para. 1)? What are the current purposes of a *quinceañera* from the point of view of the Roman Catholic Church? The girl involved? Her parents? What do you think are the main reasons for the ceremony's changes in function since its origin in Mexico?

3. What sources of information does Orlean cite in this essay? What kinds of sources would you expect her to cite that she does not? How does that choice affect "Quinceañera"?

CONNECTIONS

1. Like Amy Tan's "Two Kinds" (p. 28), Susan Orlean's "Quinceañera" depicts American families with roots outside the United States. What factors does Tan mention that foster a sense of community among the Chinese Americans in "Two Kinds"? What factors does Orlean mention that foster a sense of community among the Hispanic-Americans in "Quinceañera"?

2. Both "Quinceañera" and "Two Kinds" feature a public performance that functions as a rite of passage. What does the performance mean to the parents in each selection? How is its meaning similar and different for the children who take part in it?

3. In "A Short Quiz" (p. 10), Walker Percy comments on how much easier it is to size up another person than oneself. Which of Percy's definitions of self (pp. 14–16) do you think Orlean would apply to the subjects of "Quinceañera"? What information in her essay suggests which definitions the subjects would apply to themselves?

ELABORATIONS

1. Orlean observes that all the Vesta Club's *quinceañera* girls wear white gowns. Who benefits from this custom, and why? What are the disadvantages of such uniformity, and how do the girls deal with them? What other situations can you think of in which strict unofficial dress codes play an important role? Write an essay about such a situation, describing the clothes involved and analyzing the ways they enable the wearers to identify themselves and each other.

2. Major social occasions such as proms and weddings often are exciting to look forward to, beautiful or comical to look back on, and miserable to experience. (See, for instance, the talent show in Amy Tan's "Two Kinds.") Has this ever happened to you? Write an essay recalling an event that was supposed to be glorious (for you or a friend or family member) but in fact was either painful or ridiculous.

WINDOWS:
THE WORLD

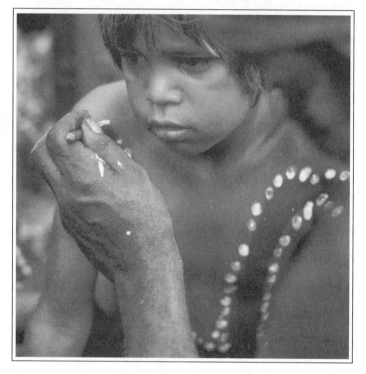

Identifying Ourselves: *An Australian aborigine decorates a child.*

SALMAN RUSHDIE

The Broken Mirror

Ahmed Salman Rushdie was born to a wealthy Muslim family in Bombay, India, in 1947. That same year his homeland won independence from Britain, which partitioned the country into mostly Hindu India and mostly Islamic Pakistan. Rushdie was sent to a British-style private school in Bombay and then to Rugby, an exclusive school in England. He went on to Cambridge University under protest after his family moved to Pakistan, "the unmentionable country across the border" (para. 2). Rushdie published his first novel in 1975; his second, *Midnight's Children*, won the prestigious Booker Prize. The book that made him famous, however, was *The Satanic Verses* (1988). Immediately banned in India, the novel caused a worldwide uproar for allegedly blaspheming Islam. On February 14, 1989, Iran's religious leader, the Ayatollah Khomeini, issued a *fatwa*, or death warrant, and offered a $1 million reward to any Muslim who would assassinate Rushdie. The writer went into hiding in England and has stayed hidden since, although recently he has begun making cautious, usually unannounced public appearances. Rushdie and his wife divorced; in 1990 he declared himself a Muslim, but Khomeini refused to withdraw the *fatwa* and Rushdie recanted. In 1991 the novel's Italian translator was knifed and its Japanese translator was murdered. Despite pressure from the West and from writers and readers around the world, Iran has upheld the *fatwa*, and Khomeini's successor raised the reward to between $2 and $3 million. Rushdie continues to write; recent books include *East, West* (1994) and *The Moor's Last Sigh* (1995). "The Broken Mirror," written before the *fatwa* was issued, comes from *Imaginary Homelands* (1991).

For more information on India, see page 330. For information on Great Britain, see page 705.

An old photograph in a cheap frame hangs on a wall of the room where I work. It's a picture dating from 1946 of a house into which, at the time of its taking, I had not yet been born. The house is rather peculiar — a three-storied gabled affair with tiled roofs and round towers in two corners, each wearing a pointy tiled hat. "The past is a foreign country," goes the famous opening sentence of L. P. Hartley's novel *The Go-Between*, "they do things differently there." But the photograph tells me to invert this idea; it reminds me that it's my present that is foreign, and that the past is home, albeit a lost home in a lost city in the mists of lost time.

A few years ago I revisited Bombay, which is my lost city, after an absence of something like half my life. Shortly after arriving, acting on an impulse, I opened the telephone directory and looked for my father's name. And, amazingly, there it was; his name, our old address, the unchanged telephone number, as if we had never gone away to the unmentionable country across the border. It was an eerie discovery. I felt as if I were being claimed, or informed that the facts of my faraway life were illusions, and that this continuity was the reality. Then I went to visit the house in the photograph and stood outside it, neither daring nor wishing to announce myself to its new owners. (I didn't want to see how they'd ruined the interior.) I was overwhelmed. The photograph had naturally been taken in black and white; and my memory, feeding on such images as this, had begun to see my childhood in the same way, monochromatically. The colors of my history had seeped out of my mind's eye; now my other two eyes were assaulted by colors, by the vividness of the red tiles, the yellow-edged green of cactus-leaves, the brilliance of bougainvillaea creeper. It is probably not too romantic to say that that was when my novel *Midnight's Children* was really born; when I realized how much I wanted to restore the past to myself, not in the faded grays of old family-album snapshots, but whole, in Cinema-Scope and glorious Technicolor.

Bombay is a city built by foreigners upon reclaimed land; I, who had been away so long that I almost qualified for the title, was gripped by the conviction that I, too, had a city and a history to reclaim.

It may be that writers in my position, exiles or emigrants or expatriates, are haunted by some sense of loss, some urge to reclaim, to look back, even at the risk of being mutated into pillars of salt.[1] But if we do look back, we must also do so in the knowledge — which gives rise to profound uncertainties — that our physical alienation from India almost inevitably means that we will not be capable of reclaiming precisely the thing that was lost; that we will, in short, create fictions, not actual cities or villages, but invisible ones, imaginary homelands, Indias of the mind.

Writing my book in North London, looking out through my window   5
onto a city scene totally unlike the ones I was imagining onto paper, I was constantly plagued by this problem, until I felt obliged to face it in

---

[1]Rushdie refers to the biblical story of Lot, whose wife was turned into a pillar of salt when she disobeyed God's order not to look back as the couple fled their homeland. — ED.

the text, to make clear that (in spite of my original and I suppose some-what Proustian ambition to unlock the gates of lost time so that the past reappeared as it actually had been, unaffected by the distortions of memory) what I was actually doing was a novel of memory and about memory, so that my India was just that: "my" India, a version and no more than one version of all the hundreds of millions of possible versions. I tried to make it as imaginatively true as I could, but imaginative truth is simultaneously honorable and suspect, and I knew that my India may only have been one to which I (who am no longer what I was, and who by quitting Bombay never became what perhaps I was meant to be) was, let us say, willing to admit I belonged.

This is why I made my narrator, Saleem, suspect in his narration; his mistakes are the mistakes of a fallible memory compounded by quirks of character and of circumstance, and his vision is fragmentary. It may be that when the Indian writer who writes from outside India tries to re-flect that world, he is obliged to deal in broken mirrors, some of whose fragments have been irretrievably lost.

But there is a paradox here. The broken mirror may actually be as valuable as the one which is supposedly unflawed. Let me again try and explain this from my own experience. Before beginning *Midnight's Children*, I spent many months trying simply to recall as much of the Bombay of the 1950s and 1960s as I could; and not only Bombay — Kashmir, too, and Delhi and Aligarh, which, in my book, I've moved to Agra to heighten a certain joke about the Taj Mahal. I was genuinely amazed by how much came back to me. I found myself remembering what clothes people had worn on certain days, and school scenes, and whole passages of Bombay dialogue verbatim, or so it seemed; I even re-membered advertisements, film posters, the neon Jeep sign on Marine Drive, toothpaste ads for Binaca and for Kolynos, and a footbridge over the local railway line which bore, on one side, the legend "Esso puts a tiger in your tank" and, on the other, the curiously contradictory admo-nition: "Drive like Hell and you will get there." Old songs came back to me from nowhere. . . .

I knew that I had tapped a rich seam; but the point I want to make is that of course I'm not gifted with total recall, and it was precisely the partial nature of these memories, their fragmentation, that made them so evocative for me. The shards of memory acquired greater status, greater resonance, because they were *remains*; fragmentation made triv-ial things seem like symbols, and the mundane acquired numinous qualities. There is an obvious parallel here with archaeology. The bro-ken pots of antiquity, from which the past can sometimes, but always provisionally, be reconstructed, are exciting to discover, even if they are pieces of the most quotidian objects.

It may be argued that the past is a country from which we have all emigrated, that its loss is part of our common humanity. Which seems to me self-evidently true; but I suggest that the writer who is out-of-country and even out-of-language may experience this loss in an intensified form. It is made more concrete for him by the physical fact of discontinuity, of his present being in a different place from his past, of his being "elsewhere." This may enable him to speak properly and concretely on a subject of universal significance and appeal.

But let me go further. The broken glass is not merely a mirror of   10
nostalgia. It is also, I believe, a useful tool with which to work in the present.

John Fowles begins *Daniel Martin* with the words: "Whole sight: or all the rest is desolation." But human beings do not perceive things whole; we are not gods but wounded creatures, cracked lenses, capable only of fractured perceptions. Partial beings, in all the senses of that phrase. Meaning is a shaky edifice we build out of scraps, dogmas, childhood injuries, newspaper articles, chance remarks, old films, small victories, people hated, people loved; perhaps it is because our sense of what is the case is constructed from such inadequate materials that we defend it so fiercely, even to the death. The Fowles position seems to me a way of succumbing to the guru-illusion. Writers are no longer sages, dispensing the wisdom of the centuries. And those of us who have been forced by cultural displacement to accept the provisional nature of all truths, all certainties, have perhaps had modernism forced upon us. We can't lay claim to Olympus, and are thus released to describe our world in the way in which all of us, whether writers or not, perceive it from day to day. . . .

The Indian writer, looking back at India, does so through guilt-tinted spectacles. (I am of course, once more, talking about myself.) I am speaking now of those of us who emigrated . . . and I suspect that there are times when the move seems wrong to us all, when we seem, to ourselves, post-lapsarian[2] men and women. We are Hindus who have crossed the black water; we are Muslims who eat pork. And as a result — as my use of the Christian notion of the Fall indicates — we are now partly of the West. Our identity is at once plural and partial. Sometimes we feel that we straddle two cultures; at other times, that we fall between two stools. But however ambiguous and shifting this ground

---

[2]After the Fall; that is, after Adam and Eve's expulsion from Paradise. — ED.

may be, it is not an infertile territory for a writer to occupy. If literature is in part the business of finding new angles at which to enter reality, then once again our distance, our long geographical perspective, may provide us with such angles.

EXPLORATIONS

1. What does the mirror represent in Salman Rushdie's essay? What does the broken mirror represent?
2. "We are now partly of the West" (para. 12), says Rushdie of writers who have emigrated from India. What references in "The Broken Mirror" show that this statement is true of him?
3. What does Rushdie seem to value most about the Western part of his identity? What does he seem to value most about the Indian part?

CONNECTIONS

1. Salman Rushdie describes the experience of a writer who emigrated from India to England. Compare this with James Baldwin's experience abroad in "The New Lost Generation" (p. 18). What perceptions and conclusions do both writers share? What are some important differences in their viewpoints?
2. What observations in "The Broken Mirror" echo comments by Walker Percy in "A Short Quiz" (p. 10)? Do Rushdie and Percy give the same explanation for the ambiguity of the self? If so, what is that explanation? If not, how do their explanations differ?
3. Anita Desai (p. 4) and Salman Rushdie both are Indian emigrants writing in English. What ideas do the two share? Do you think Desai would agree with Rushdie's statement, "The Indian writer, looking back at India, does so through guilt-tinted spectacles" (para. 12)? Why or why not?

ELABORATIONS

1. "Our identity is at once plural and partial," writes Rushdie (para. 12). "Sometimes we feel that we straddle two cultures; at other times, that we fall between two stools." How do these comments apply to your perception of your own identity? Write an essay examining ways in which your sense of yourself seems fragmented or changeable. (You may want to draw on ideas from Percy's "A Short Quiz.")

2. Reread Rushdie's essay, particularly paragraph 7. Then think back to a by-gone place and time in your own life, and write a description of everything you remember about it: clothes, conversations, signs, songs, and whatever else you can recall. What do you notice is missing? What do you suspect is distorted?

MARGARET ATWOOD

A View from Canada

Margaret Atwood is one of Canada's most distinguished novelists, poets, and critics. Born in Ottawa, Ontario, in 1939, she began writing as a small child; by age six she had started a novel about an ant. Her father was a forest entomologist, so Atwood had plenty of exposure to both insects and solitude in the Canadian wilderness. Having discovered that writing was "suddenly the only thing I wanted to do," she studied at Victoria College and the University of Toronto in Canada and got her master's degree from Radcliffe College at Harvard University. Atwood has taught at colleges and universities in Canada and the United States and has received more than a dozen literary awards and fellowships. Since her earliest poems and her first novel, *The Edible Woman* (1969), Atwood has published more than twenty-five volumes of poetry, nonfiction, and fiction, as well as occasional plays and children's books. Her virtuosity with language ranges from wildly passionate (*Surfacing*, 1972) to coldly controlled (*Life Before Man*, 1979). Her ironic futuristic novel *The Handmaid's Tale* (1986) was made into a motion picture. Atwood currently lives in Toronto with the novelist Graeme Gibson and their daughter. "A View from Canada" comes from a speech given at Harvard University in 1981 and reprinted in *Second Words* (1982).

Canada, the world's second-largest country (after Russia), extends from the Atlantic to the Pacific Ocean and from the North Pole to the U.S. border. The French explorer Jacques Cartier claimed it for France in 1534. Settlers followed, starting in Acadia (now Nova Scotia) and moving into Quebec. As the English colonies to the south became more established, conflicts arose over hunting, trapping, and fishing rights. In the early 1700s the English took over Newfoundland, Hudson Bay, and Acadia. Many of the evicted French speakers migrated south to Louisiana, where "Acadians" became slurred to "Cajuns." Various British colonies united in 1867 as the Dominion of Canada, which stayed subject to British rule until 1982. Although today Canada's head of government is an elected prime minister, its head of state is still the British monarch. Ottawa, the nation's capital, lies in a narrow section of Ontario between New York State and Quebec, a province where French remains the predominant language. Tension continues between Canadians of English and French heritage, with Quebec periodically threatening to secede. A 1990 vote to give Quebec the protection of distinct constitutional status failed to win national approval; in 1995, Quebec voters narrowly defeated a referendum to create a separate state.

I spent a large part of my childhood in northern Quebec, surrounded by many trees and few people. My attitude toward Americans was formed by this environment. Alas, the Americans we encountered were usually pictures of ineptitude. We once met two of them dragging a heaving metal boat, plus the motor, across a portage from one lake to another because they did not want to paddle. Typically American, we thought, as they ricocheted off yet another tree. Americans hooked other people when they tried to cast, got lost in the woods, and didn't burn their garbage. Of course, many Canadians behaved this way too; but somehow not *as* many. And there were some Americans, friends of my father, who could shoot a rapids without splintering their canoe and who could chop down a tree without taking off a foot in the process. But these were not classed as Americans, not *real* Americans. They were from Upper Michigan State or Maine or places like that, and were classed, I blush to admit, not as Americans but as honorary Canadians. I recognize that particular cross-filing system, that particular way of approving of people you as a rule don't approve of, every time a man tells me I think like a man; a sentence I've always felt had an invisible comma after the word *think*. I've since recognized that it's no compliment to be told you are not who you are, but as children we generalized, cheerfully and shamelessly. The truth, from our limited experience, was clear: Americans were wimps who had a lot of money but did not know what they were doing.

That was the rural part of my experience. The urban part was somewhat different. In the city I went to school, and in the early years at any rate the schools I went to were still bastions of the British Empire. In school we learned the Kings of England and how to draw the Union Jack and sing "Rule Britannia," and poems with refrains like, "Little Indian, Sioux or Cree, Don't you wish that you were me?" Our imaginations were still haunted by the war, a war that we pictured as having been fought between us, that is, the British, and the Germans. There wasn't much room in our minds for the Americans and the Japanese. Winston Churchill was a familiar figure to us; Franklin D. Roosevelt was not.

In public school we did not learn much about Americans, or Canadians either, for that matter. Canadian history was the explorers and was mostly brown and green, for all those trees. British history was kings and queens, and much more exciting, since you could use the silver and gold colored pencils for it.

That era of Canadian colonialism was rapidly disappearing, however. One explanation for the reason it practically vanished during the postwar decade — 1946 to 1957, say, the year I graduated from high school — is an economic one. The Canadians, so the theory goes, overextended themselves so severely through the war effort that they created a capital vacuum in Canada. Nature and entrepreneurs hate a vacuum, so money flowed up from the United States to fill it, and when Canadians woke up in the sixties and started to take stock, they discovered they'd sold their birthright for a mess. This revelation was an even greater shock for me; not only was my country owned, but it was owned by the kind of people who carried tin boats across portages and didn't burn their garbage. One doubted their competence.

Looking back on this decade, I can see that the changeover from 5
British cultural colony to American cultural colony was symbolized by what happened after school as opposed to in it. I know it's hard to believe in view of my youthful appearance, but when I was a child there was no television. There were, however, comic books, and these were monolithically American. We didn't much notice, except when we got to the ads at the back, where Popsicle Pete reigned supreme. Popsicle Pete would give you the earth in exchange for a few sticky wrappers, but his promises always had a little asterisk attached: "Offer good only in the United States." International world cynics may be forgiven for thinking that the same little asterisk is present invisibly in the Constitution and the Declaration of Independence and the Bill of Rights, not to mention the public statements of prominent Americans on such subjects as democracy, human dignity and freedom, and civil liberties. Maybe it all goes back to Popsicle Pete. We may all be in this together, but some of us are asterisked.

Such thoughts did not trouble our heads a great deal. When you were finished with Donald Duck and Mickey Mouse (and Walt Disney was, by the way, a closet Canadian), you could always go on to Superman (whose creator was also one of ours). After that it would be time for Sunday night radio, with Jack Benny and Our Miss Brooks. We knew they talked funny, but we didn't mind. Then of course there were movies, none of which were Canadian, but we didn't mind that either. Everyone knew that was what the world was like. Nobody knew there had once been a Canadian film industry.

After that I went to high school, where people listened to American pop music after school instead of reading comic books. During school hours we studied, among other things, history and literature. Literature was still the British tradition: Shakespeare, Eliot, Austen, Thomas Hardy, Keats and Wordsworth and Shelley and Byron; not experiences anyone should miss, but it did tend to give the impression that all literature was written by dead Englishmen, and — this is important — by dead Englishwomen. By this time I wanted to be a writer, and you can see it would be a dilemma: Being female was no hindrance, but how could one be a writer and somehow manage to avoid having to become British and dead? . . .

In history it was much the same story. We started with ancient Egypt and worked our way through Greece, Rome, and medieval Europe, then the Renaissance and the birth of the modern era, the invention of the steam engine, the American revolution, the French revolution, the Civil War, and other stirring events, every single one of which had taken place outside Canada.

Finally, in the very last year, by which time many future citizens had dropped out anyway, we got a blue book called *Canada in the World Today*. It was about who grew the wheat, how happy the French were, how well the parliamentary system worked for everybody, and how nice it was that the Indians had given us all their land in exchange for the amenities of civilization. The country we lived in was presented to us in our schools as colorless, dull, and without much historical conflict to speak of, except for a few massacres, and nobody did *that* any more. Even the British war of conquest was a dud, since both of the generals died. It was like a hockey game in which both teams lost.

As for Canada in the World Today, its role, we were assured, was an   10
important one. It was the upper northwest corner of a triangle consist-ing of Canada, the United States, and Britain, and its position was not one to be sneezed at: Canada, having somehow become an expert at compromise, was the mediator. It was not to be parochial and inward-looking any more but was to be international in outlook. Although in retrospect the role of mediator may shrink somewhat — one cannot quite dispel the image of Canada trotting back and forth across the At-lantic with sealed envelopes, like a glorified errand boy — there's a little truth to be squeezed from this lemon. Canadians, oddly enough, *are* more international in outlook than Americans are; not through any virtue on their part but because they've had to be. If you're a Canadian traveling in the United States, one of the first things you notice is the relative absence of international news coverage. In Canada, one of the most popular news programs ever devised has two radio commentators phoning up just about anyone they can get on the line, anywhere in the world. Canadians live in a small house, which may be why they have their noses so firmly pressed to the windows, looking out.

I remember *Canada in the World Today* with modified loathing — "Canada comes of age," it trumpeted, not bothering to mention that what happened to you when you came of age was that you got pimples or a job or both — and still not a year passes without some politician an-nouncing that Canada has finally grown up. Still, the title is significant. Canada sees itself as part of the world; a small sinking *Titanic* squashed between two icebergs, perhaps, but still inevitably a part. The States, on the other hand, has always had a little trouble with games like chess. Situational strategy is difficult if all you can see is your own borders, and beyond that some wispy brownish fuzz that is barely worth considering. The Canadian experience was a circumference with no center, the American one a center which was mistaken for the whole thing.

A few years ago I was in India and had occasion to visit both the Canadian and American enclaves in New Delhi. The Canadian there lived in a house decorated with Indian things and served us a meal of Indian food and told us all about India. One reason for going into the foreign service, in Canada anyway, is to get out of Canada, and Canadians are good at fitting in, partly because they can't afford to do otherwise. They could not afford, for instance, to have the kind of walled compound the Americans had. We were let in to do some shopping at the supermarket there, and once the gate had closed you were in Syracuse, New York. Hot dogs, hamburgers, cokes, and rock music surrounded you. Americans enter the outside world the way they landed on the moon, with their own oxygen tanks of American air strapped to their backs and their protective spacesuits firmly in place. If they can't stay in America they take it with them. Not for them the fish-in-the-water techniques of the modern urban guerrilla. Those draft dodgers of the sixties who made it as far as Canada nearly died of culture shock: They thought it was going to be like home.

It's not their fault, though. It's merely that they've been oddly educated. Canadians and Americans may look alike, but the contents of their heads are quite different. Americans experience themselves, individually, as small toads in the biggest and most powerful puddle in the world. Their sense of power comes from identifying with the puddle. Canadians as individuals may have more power within the puddle, since there are fewer toads in it; it's the puddle that's seen as powerless. One of our politicians recently gave a speech entitled, "In the Footsteps of the Giant." The United States of course was the giant and Canada was in its footsteps, though some joker wondered whether Canada was in the footstep just before or just after the foot had descended. One of Canada's problems is that it's always comparing itself to the wrong thing. If you stand beside a giant, of course you tend to feel a little stunted. When we stand beside Australia, say, or the ex-British West Indies, we feel more normal. I had lunch recently with two publishers from Poland. "Do Canadians realize," they said, "that they live in one of the most peaceful, happy, and prosperous countries on earth?" "No," I said. . . .

Americans and Canadians are not the same; they are the products of two very different histories, two very different situations. Put simply, south of you you have Mexico and south of us we have you.

But we *are* all in this together, not just as citizens of our respective
nation states but more importantly as inhabitants of this quickly shrink-
ing and increasingly threatened earth. There are boundaries and borders, spiritual as well as physical, and good fences make good neighbors. But there are values beyond national ones. Nobody owns the air;
we all breathe it.

EXPLORATIONS

1. How does Margaret Atwood summarize her childhood concept of "typically
American" (para. 1)? How would you summarize her present concept of
"typically American"? What qualities does Atwood seem to consider typically Canadian?
2. What aspects of "A View from Canada" show that it was written as a speech,
to be heard rather than read by its audience? What can you tell about Atwood's intended audience?
3. Find at least three places where Atwood uses humor in "A View from
Canada." In each case, what purpose(s) does her humor serve?

CONNECTIONS

1. Reread the last paragraph of Salman Rushdie's "The Broken Mirror"
(p. 56). Both India and Canada are former British colonies. What comments by Atwood suggest that she shares Rushdie's mixed feelings about
straddling two cultures?
2. In what ways does Anita Desai's description of growing up in India (p. 4) resemble Margaret Atwood's description of growing up in Canada?
3. Do you think Richard Rayner (p. 2) and Ishmael Reed (p. 2) would agree
with Atwood's assessment of Americans? Why or why not?

ELABORATIONS

1. Go through Atwood's essay and note the main points she makes about
Canadians and about Americans. Rewrite "A View from Canada" as a
shorter, more direct comparison-contrast essay.
2. Did you ever encounter tourists with canoes? The Union Jack? Popsicle
Pete? Make a list of observations and events in Atwood's personal history
that provoked her to think about being Canadian. Then make a similar list
based on your personal history. Use your list as the starting point for an essay
about what it means to you to be an American.

GERMAINE GREER

One Man's Mutilation Is Another Man's Beautification

Germaine Greer was born in Melbourne, Australia, in 1939. She won scholarships first to a convent there and then to Melbourne University, from which she graduated at age twenty. After receiving a First Class Honours master's degree from Sydney University, she taught in a girls' high school and later at the university. Greer went to England in 1964 as a Commonwealth Scholar and received her Ph.D. on Shakespeare from Cambridge University. While working on her thesis she lived in Calabria in southeastern Italy, where she was impressed by the satisfaction and prestige the local women found in a matriarchal role. (Those women feature in her 1985 book *Sex and Destiny*; her feminist interpretation *Shakespeare* appeared in 1986.) Greer went on to teach at Warwick University, simultaneously working in television and journalism, and to write her first book, *The Female Eunuch* (1971). This manifesto of the feminist movement made her a celebrity and spokeswoman, in which capacity she has continued to travel, lecture, research, and write. Her most recent book is *Slip-shod Sibyls* (1995). Greer is currently a Fellow of Newnham College at Cambridge University.

Australia, with an area of almost 3 million square miles, is the world's smallest continent and sixth largest country. It lies south of Indonesia (and Vietnam), across the Indian Ocean from southern Africa, and across the Pacific from South America. The native Aborigines may have migrated there from Southeast Asia as long as 40,000 years ago. By 1770, when Captain James Cook claimed Australia for Britain, the Aborigines numbered around 300,000. The British settled their new domain with shiploads of transported convicts. Gold and copper were discovered, and sheep ranches were established, spurring economic growth but displacing the Aborigines. Australia became a commonwealth in 1901 and gained full independence in 1975. Since World War II its ties with Britain have weakened in favor of the United States.

Humans are the only animals which can consciously and deliberately change their appearance according to their own whims. Most animals groom themselves, but humans are tempted to manipulate their appearance in ways much more radical that those open to other animals, not simply because they are able to use tools upon themselves, but also because of some peculiarities in the way in which humans are made. The human body is a curiously ambiguous structure, partaking of almost contradictory attributes. For example, humans are neither furry nor hairless, but variously naked, slightly hairy, and very hirsute. All these variations may be found on the body of a single individual at the same time. Humans are then confronted with a series of managerial problems: among the ways in which they express their cultural identities are the contrasting ways in which they handle these problems.

The Australian Aborigines used to conserve hair; not only did they not eliminate whatever hair was growing on their bodies, they collected extra human hair to work into a thick girdle for men to wear about their hips. We would look askance at anyone who could not bear to discard fallen hair, now that hair shirts are out of fashion, but sophisticated Western people often wear the hair of others as a postiche or toupee. Where the scalp-hunter once sought to augment his physical or psychic power by acquiring the hair of others, the literate people of the twentieth century feel that they will acquire youth and beauty through bought hair. They will even pay to have hair stitched into their scalps in a very costly and laborious development of the ancient practice of needle-working living flesh.

Some people identify themselves partly by their refusal to cut hair, as do the Sikhs, who twist the long silky hair of their beards together with what grows on their heads, tie the whole lot up in a chignon, and cover it with a turban. Others insist on the removal of any hair, wherever it is, and they too may choose a turban, this time to hide a bald head. Western conventions of hair management often appeal to younger or recalcitrant members of societies with strict rules for hair management because they find them more convenient; in fact, they are very subtle and difficult, requiring minute calculations of the degree of shagginess which is appropriate to age, and economic and social status. The rejection of traditional modes of hair management has less to do with convenience and common sense than with the desire to break out of the confinement of the group. A shaven Sikh might object that he is as much Sikh as ever; he may claim that his elimination of his identifying marks was simply to pour out the bath water while retaining the baby, but in fact he has summarily loosened his ties with his religious group in order to be accepted into another group. If he keeps his steel bracelet, which will be recognized by other Sikhs, it is because he does not wish to lose all the advantages connected with belonging to that group. When a Sikh takes his employer to court for refusing to allow him to wear his turban at work, it is not a mere formality. He is making a serious bid to limit his employer's power over his life.

The impact of technological culture can be measured by the degree of acceptance of Western conventions of body management throughout the world. Fashion, because it is beyond logic, is deeply revealing. Women all over the world have adopted, often in addition to their traditional accoutrements, four Western conventions: high-heeled shoes, lipstick, nail varnish, and the brassiere. The success of all of these fashions, which are not even remotely connected with comfort or common sense, is an indication of the worldwide acceptance of the Western notion that the principal duties of women are sexual attraction and vicarious leisure. The women who have accepted these fashions will justify their decision by saying that all four are more attractive than the alternatives. All that they are really saying is that they themselves were more attracted to alien styles than they were to the styles adopted by their mothers and grandmothers. To give the full answer would be to expose the tensions which are destroying traditional lifestyles all over the world. There is a slight traffic in the opposite direction. Distinguished lady professors of economics may reject high heels, lipstick, nail varnish, and brassiere, and adopt the dress of a Punjabi peasant laborer; Iranian girls may resume the chador. In each case the motive for the change is clearly political; what is not so often realized is that it is equally political when it happens the other way around.

Because what we do with our bodies is so revealing we try to insist that it has no meaning at all. A man whose hair is cut regularly and at great expense, who shaves his face in a careful pattern, will say that he is not concerned with his appearance, while a man with a beard will maintain that he simply cannot be bothered shaving, but the truth is that both have selected an image which they feel best expresses their characters and chosen social roles. The man with a beard probably shaves some part of his face and neck quite regularly, and definitely trims the beard itself. He may frequently be seen grooming it with his hands, patting and stroking it into his preferred shape. Between the shaggy bearded man and the smooth clean-shaven man there lies a vast range of tonsorial modes, all of which have meanings relative to each other. The man who grows his sideburns long is expressing something about his class and his age group. The man who lets his cheek whiskers grow in tufts or shaves his sideburns off is also projecting some part of a chosen self-image. All kinds of curious facial topiary are accepted provided that they have some pedigree within our cultural tradition. The associations of such variations as curled and waxed mustaches, Mexican revolutionary mustaches, pencil mustaches, and toothbrush mustaches are endlessly subtle and constantly being remade.

In the recent past we came to accept long flowing hair as a possible masculine alternative; with the passing of time our initial reactions of outrage have softened into acceptance. Men's long curls are now a sign of nostalgia for the sixties, the last quiver of hippie energy, which was never anything to be feared. By contrast, the man who completely shaves his head still shocks us. It is as if he is flaunting a violence that he has done to himself. Other men, hairless through no choice of their own, may have wigs on the National Health to hide their embarrassing nakedness. Western youths whose heads are shaven in accordance with the practice of oriental monastics will wear wigs when they go to badger people in airports because shaven heads are so alienating to our sensibilities. The man who shaves his head and does not cover it is indulging in a form of indecent exposure, the purpose of which, as usual, is intimidation.

The shaving of women's heads is considered so disfiguring that it seemed adequate punishment for women who collaborated with the Nazis in the Second World War, and yet there are many cultures whose women shave all or part of their heads and would feel dirty or unkempt if they did not. Girls who shave off all the hair except what grows on the crown of their heads are doing no more than the Turkana women of Kenya have always done, but by doing it in a society where such styles have never been seen, they defy the accepted norms and court rejection. The coxcomb and its variants, sometimes called the Mohawk or Mohican hairstyle, imitate the intimidating shapes of the advanced crests of fighting birds. A less daring version, for it can be tamed into smoothness when the wearer is in the haunts of the smooth, is the teased mop. The ferocity mimicked by the hairstyle is further expressed in the studded belts and armlets and earrings in the shape of a skull, but it is clearly a mere affectation. The camp aggressiveness of the display stands in inverse ratio to the social power wielded by the group. Their cultural uniformity is actually competitiveness and does not lead to solidarity.

In most societies which modify the body, the visible changes are outward signs of the fulfilment of the rites of passage. The acceptance of the newborn into the community at a naming ceremony or its equivalent may be marked by a ritual haircut, the shape of which may indicate his or her clan or totem. The approach of puberty may be signalled by circumcision or scarification or the adoption of a new hairstyle. The prelude to marriage may require further scarification or tattooing or fattening or a period of special body painting, while marriage itself may be signified by drastic changes in appearance, especially for women. The birth of children, achievement of elder status, or the death of a spouse bring the last changes. In classless societies where property is either held in common or kept to a minimum, all changes in status must involve changes in physical appearance. Where no one carries an identity card which will, say, permit him to drink in the company of adults, everyone who may must be distinguished by a sign. The achievement of these signs is one of the most important satisfactions of such societies. Before imperialists brought mirrors, such people could not confer the signs upon themselves: The recognition of a transition was given dramatic form by the ceremony of the conferring of signs in which the interested parties all acted as a group.

In Western society the outward signs of social status have withered into mere vestiges. Pubescent boys may live through intense dramas of hair cultivation, struggling for a mustache or bushy sideburns or simply longing to shave every day. Little girls may covet high heels and brassieres and long for the day that they can wear make-up, but the menarche will not be marked in any way: Marriageability will be signified only by the absence of an inconspicuous ring on the fourth finger of the left hand. In Jewish society, circumcision is still a rite of passage, but once the bar mitzvah is over, the initiate cannot be recognized by any other outward sign. Married women used to be expected to dress differently from girls: a pale echo of the sixteenth-century custom which required married women to wear closed bodices and hide their hair under a cap. This persisted into the twentieth century when married women were expected to wear hats on social occasions, but has now died out.

The disappearance of distinguishing marks of social status in industrial societies is not meaningless, nor can it be construed to mean that human beings have outgrown such childish things. It is an accurate reflection of the fact that social relationships, particularly kinship relations, have been and are under intense pressure from economic relationships. The one insignia that is worn, in the United States more than in Europe but the strengthening of the trend is apparent, is the insignia of the employer. The family is no longer the dominant group and human beings are no longer differentiated on the grounds of their status within it. Instead they are differentiated by their consumer behavior, employment status, income, and possessions: The contrasts are so striking that it is considered indiscreet and tasteless to flaunt them by display of wealth. Instead the degrees of difference are signaled, more or less subtly, by grooming and by some carefully chosen attributes; hints to those who know how to take them are conveyed by the watch,

10

the pen, the attaché case, the note case, the cuff links. Along with the indications of success are clues to other allegiances, the college ring, the lodge pin, the old school tie. Democracy and uniformity in outward appearance are necessitated by the extreme differentiation in economic circumstances, which might otherwise become a source of tension.

In tribal societies, where economic activity is static, limited as it is to the repetitive daily functions of survival, there is time to elaborate the paraphernalia of status considered in all but economic terms and immense satisfaction connected with doing so. The individual who proceeds through the stages all duly solemnized has conferred an elegance and order upon the struggle, and within that wider function there is scope for individual expression and aesthetic concerns.

The motives for Western beautification are very different. . . . People who are excluded from economic activity . . . cannot compensate by celebrating other forms of status for these have been eliminated. Unhappily, as the social roles which evolve out of family relationships ceased to command respect, the number of older people condemned to live for many years outside the sphere of economic activity in conditions of mere survival increased and will go on increasing. Among the displacement activities which this group must now concentrate on in order to beguile the time between retirement and the grave, there are a number connected with futile imitation of the group from which they have been excluded. As there is no prestige or power connected with being old, it is important to deny the aging process itself. Where once humans celebrated the achievement of seniority and longevity, they now invest as much energy or more in trying to resist the inevitable. Where hair coloring used to be done for fun, it is now done for camouflage.

A full head of strawberry blonde curls is only acquired by a sixty-year-old after regular orgies of dying, setting, and backcombing, all of which actually speed the degeneration of the scalp and the hair shaft. There is a good deal of pain involved as the dyes bite into sensitive old skin and the hot dryers tighten the hair, driving the pins still further into the old scalp. The ordeal is worth it if the sufferer sees herself rejuvenated by it; the suffering is an essential part of the prophylaxis, but it must be accompanied by words of tenderness and filial care from the torturers. We are not surprised to see the hairdresser as a shaman, hung about with amulets, his face suffused with long-suffering compassion. The payment of money for his services guarantees that the job has been well done; an old lady with a fifty-dollar hairstyle is still a person to be reckoned with. . . .

. . . We are in the midst of a cultural upheaval in which the body, which for aeons was a holy thing, its excretions and its orifices feared and revered, is becoming reified. It is becoming a toy, an asset, a commodity, an instrumentality for human will, and the pace of the change is much too fast. The intolerability of pictures of stainless steel meticulously carving out faces and breasts, isolating the unwanted and throwing it in the trash, tells us that we are still superstitious. We still suspect that the fantasy which is being imposed upon the body is less potent and less various than the body itself. Yet we cannot ease our anxiety by sneering, for we know the callousness which characterizes our treatment of the old and obese. We can understand why people who have the money will endure pain and risk death rather than go on living inside the bodies which bear the marks of their own history. Cosmetic surgery is the secular version of confession and absolution. It has taken the place of all our lost ceremonies of death and rebirth. It is reincarnation.

Most societies reject the grossly deformed. All societies have notions   15
of beauty and fitness to which they aspire: relatively non-neurotic societies tend to admire characteristics which are well-distributed among their people, because distance from the culturally recognized norm causes suffering. We are affected by our bodies just as our behavior marks them. Peculiar looking people tend to behave peculiarly. Criminologists have known for many years that cosmetic surgery may do more for a social delinquent than years of custody and psychiatric care, when it comes to rehabilitation.

Once we begin to sculpt the body to our own aesthetic requirements we enter a realm of shifting values to which there is no guide. In essence, beautification and mutilation are the same activity. The African women who practice genital mutilation do so primarily because they think the result is more attractive; the unreconstructed genitalia are disgusting to them. Very few Westerners really find the female genitalia beautiful, but most of them would be horrified, even nauseated, by the sight of an infibulated vagina. None of them, by contrast, would cry out in disgust at the sight of a mutilated penis, stripped of its foreskin; all of them would be unpleasantly affected by the sight of a sub-incised penis.

Some mutilations have an ulterior purpose; the biting off of little finger joints of the newborn by Aboriginal mothers may be a way of deflecting the attention of evil spirits who would covet a perfect child. The custom of branding sickly infants in India may incidentally eliminate the feebler ones before too much energy has been invested in their care, and even, perhaps, activate sluggish resistance to the pathogens in the environment. In any event, the brands are carefully placed. The endurance of pain, especially in poor communities where pain and discomfort are daily realities, is another important aspect of beautification/mutilation. Scarification is valued not only because it is symmetrically placed about the body and not only because it implies the achievement of new status, but because it hurts. Where survival is only achieved by constant effort, stoicism and willpower are immensely important. The young woman who lies unflinching while the circumciser grinds her clitoris off between two stones is proving that she will make a good wife, equal to all the anguish of child-bearing and daily toil, not only to the witnesses of her bravery, but more importantly, to herself.

Industrialized society is the first in which endurance of physical pain is not a condition of survival. We have identified pain as our enemy and have done our best to eradicate even its most manageable manifestations. Scars have no value for us and their aesthetic appeal has perished alongside their moral value. A few women might confess that they feel strangely drawn to men with scarred faces (or eye-patches or limps) but it is generally considered to be an aberrant taste. Yet, augmentation mammoplasty is no more after all than a raised scar. The great difference between ancient and modern beautification/mutilation procedures is that nowadays we must conceal the fact of the procedure itself. The association of sculpted breasts with pain is anaphrodisiac, so much so, that a man who guesses that what he is admiring was produced by a knife, may lose all interest. Some women may boast of their cosmetic operations, but this is a safety valve against the possibility that they will be found out.

Most mutilations which have been accepted as beautiful are so by consensus; historically the most astonishing distortions have been admired, necks so elongated that they could not hold up the head unless supported by brass rings, teeth filed and knocked out, lips stretched to accommodate large discs, ear-lobes stretched until they hung down in large loops. However *outré* the punks may appear they are the merest beginners in the arts of mutilation. The admiration of certain disfigurements is an important part of the process of self-definition: Contempt for the same practices is one of the ways in which other groups insist upon their separateness. We are not surprised to find the greatest contrasts in groups living side by side. When genetic equipment and economic status are both very similar, contrasting cultural practices become immensely important; they become the expression of the group's introverted altruism. In most tribal societies the attitude is more or less pluralistic; a group of labret wearers, for example, will simply define themselves as labret wearers, without making any attempt to impose labrets on others or to deride them for being without them. Western industrial society, deluded perhaps by its own vastness and uniformity, is not pluralistic, but utterly convinced that its own practices are the product of enlightenment and ought to be followed by all progressive peoples. Thus Western women, fully accoutred with nail polish (which is incompatible with manual work), high-heeled shoes (disastrous for the posture and hence the back, and quite unsuitable for walking long distances over bad roads), and brassieres (which imitate the shape of a pubescent non-lactating breast rather than the useful organs to be found in most of the world) denounce female circumcision, without the shadow of a suspicion that their behavior is absurd.

Yet within this bland but crushing orthodoxy there are spores of something different. Our unemployed young have reverted to tribal practices. They indulge in flamboyant mutilation/beautification which is not understood, let alone appreciated in our common judgment. Teenage daughters come to their parents' dinner parties covered with blue spots, with blue hair standing on end. Deviant groups cemented by shared ritual intoxication or guilt or ordeal or all of these are budding in our rotting inner cities, terrorizing us with raucous music and insulting doggerel. If they had the power to grow like a malignant organism and invade the whole of the body politic we might have reason to be afraid. Like millions of generations of body decorators before them, they have no economic activity beyond survival; they could be toughened by the necessity of existing on the little that society will mete out to them so that they accumulate the collective power to strike at its unprotected underbelly. Or they could fritter away their spare energy in intercommunal war, as gangs have always done. The body art of the urban deviant is unlike any which has appeared on earth before in that it has no socially constructed significance. There is . . . [no] . . . mutual decoration; no young warriors apply magical designs to each other's backs. No priests and witches or mothers and aunts confer new powers upon an initiate. The only human interactions we see are commercial. The manicurists, the cosmetologists, the surgeons, the hairdressers, the tattooists are all professionals. Between the dancer and the dance has been interposed the mirror; the clients have come to the professionals after long and lonely contemplation of the self which dissatisfies them. Individuals do not modify their bodies to please others or to clarify their relationship to others. Rather they inflict changes upon themselves in order to approximate to narcissistic needs which may have been projected on to putative others.

Inside the bodies they have reconstructed, the body builders live in-communicado. The illustrated men disappear behind designs imported from a highly structured alien culture into which they themselves could never be accepted. The body building, the tattooing, the cultivation of cockscombs, the driving of rings, bolts, barbs, and studs through labia, lobes, cartilage, nipples, foreskin are all displacement activities. A caged bird suffering from loneliness and sensory deprivation will turn upon it-self and pluck out all its feathers or peck off its own leg. Middle-aged women rejected by their children will turn to surgery, restlessly beautifying/mutilating to no purpose, and a good deal of their activity will be directed against their sexuality. The body builders will proceed until they have become epicene monsters, all body hair shaved off so that the light can catch the slick greased muscles. . . . One of the most potent symbols among all natural symbols is the breast, not only the fe-male breast but by extension the male simulacrum. Only groups doomed to extinction have ever attacked the nipples; cutting, piercing, and distorting them . . . is something hideously strange. . . . Attacks upon the genitalia and the secondary sexual characteristics are attacks upon the continuity of the species; they are only conceivable in lives which are confined to their own duration, on bodies which must be their own gratification, among human contacts which are fleeting and self-centered. . . .

The right to economic activity is no longer a right which our society can guarantee to everyone. We are on the brink of an era in which most people will be condemned to a life of enforced leisure and mere subsis-tence. It may very well be that these displacement activities will have to evolve into legitimate art forms involving a strong and healthy body dec-orated with skill, sophistication, and meaning. Perhaps human worker bees will some day be delighted by the displays of squads of human but-terflies bred and trained to dance the drab streets as living works of art. It would be a great pity if the dazzling tradition of human body art were to perish in a waste of dreary conformity on the one hand and neurotic self-distortion on the other.

EXPLORATIONS

1. According to Germaine Greer, what are the main reasons why a culture creates a custom of mutilating its members' bodies in a certain way?

2. How would you describe Greer's prose style in this essay? How do her style and tone compare with those of typical contemporary writing about fashion and physical appearance? (See, for instance, Natasha Singer's "The New Russian Dressing," p. 378.) How does Greer's style contribute to the impact of the points she is making?

3. Find two points where Greer draws her own conclusions about the goal or motive behind a group's (or a group member's) manipulation of physical appearance. On what kinds of evidence does she base her conclusions? Do you agree with her assessments? Why or why not?

CONNECTIONS

1. "Teenage daughters come to their parents' dinner parties covered with blue spots, with blue hair standing on end" (para. 20). According to Greer, what is the attitude of these girls toward their parents, and why? How does their attitude contrast with that of the girls in Susan Orlean's "Quinceañera" (p. 40)? What do you think are the main reasons for the difference?

2. How does Jill Ker Conway describe Australians' "inner landscape of the mind" (p. 7)? What evidence of Conway's view appears in "One Man's Mutilation Is Another Man's Beautification"?

3. Read Gerald Early's short description on page 392 of watching hairdressers at work. Compare Early's comments and questions with Greer's statements in the second half of her paragraph 20. What ideas are expressed by both writers? How would you expect Early to disagree with Greer's analysis?

ELABORATIONS

1. Do you agree with Greer's comments about shaved heads (paras. 6–7)? How have social attitudes toward shaved heads changed since she wrote this essay in 1986? Write your own essay describing and analyzing head-shaving in particular, or hair fashions in general, in the contemporary United States.

2. Find several places where Greer describes a current Western fashion. What techniques does she use to make a familiar practice sound like a strange tribal custom? For instance, what kind of vocabulary does she choose? What kind of syntax? Verbs? Pronouns? Does she make value judgments? If so, how are they expressed? Write an essay analyzing Greer's prose style and the effect of her stylistic choices on her essay's impact.

PAUL HARRISON

The Westernization of the World

Paul Harrison is a freelance writer and consultant based in London. He has traveled widely in Asia, Africa, and Latin America and has written extensively about population and the environment. He has contributed frequently to the *Guardian, New Society,* and *New Scientist,* and to publications of major United Nations agencies, such as the World Health Organization, the Food and Agriculture Organization, UNICEF, and the International Labor Organization. In 1990 and 1992 he was the principal researcher for the UN Population Fund's major annual report, *The State of World Population.* Harrison attended Manchester Grammar School and took master's degrees at Cambridge University and the London School of Economics. His interest in the Third World began in 1968 when he was lecturing in French at the University of Ife, Nigeria. Among his recent books are *The Greening of Africa* (1987), *The Third Revolution* (1992), and *Caring for the Future: Report of the Independent Commission on Population and Quality of Life* (1996).

"The Westernization of the World" comes from the second edition of Harrison's 1981 book *Inside the Third World,* reprinted with a revised postscript in 1987. Harrison based the book on research and travel between 1975 and 1980, visiting Sri Lanka, Upper Volta and the Ivory Coast, Colombia and Peru, Brazil, Indonesia and Singapore, India, Bangladesh, and Kenya. "In some ways it was a mad enterprise to attempt to cover so much ground," he admits. However, "The underdevelopment of countries and of human beings cannot be compartmentalized if it is to be fully grasped. It is a total situation, in which every element plays a part."

Like many commentators, Harrison refers to underdeveloped countries and their citizens collectively as the *Third World.* The term has more than one definition; typically it is applied to nations in Africa, Asia, and Latin America that are not heavily industrialized and have a low standard of living. Shiva Naipaul has noted ironically: "The exemplary Third World denizen . . . lives a hand-to-mouth existence, he is indifferent to the power struggles of the mighty ones, and he is dark-skinned." Naipaul adds, "To blandly subsume, say, Ethiopia, India, and Brazil under the one banner of Third Worldhood is as absurd and as denigrating as the old assertion that all Chinese look alike." Still, keeping in mind the dangers noted by Simone de Beauvoir of dividing humanity into "us" and "them" (see p. 445), we can use the concept of the Third World to examine, as Harrison does, certain tendencies shared by nations that are otherwise dissimilar.

> The bourgeoisie has, through its exploitation of the world market, given a cosmopolitan character to production and consumption in every country.
>
> – Karl Marx

In Singapore, Peking opera still lives, in the back streets. On Boat Quay, where great barges moor to unload rice from Thailand, raw rubber from Malaysia, or timber from Sumatra, I watched a troupe of traveling actors throw up a canvas-and-wood booth stage, paint on their white faces and lozenge eyes, and don their resplendent vermilion, ultramarine, and gold robes. Then, to raptured audiences of bent old women and little children with perfect circle faces, they enacted tales of feudal princes and magic birds and wars and tragic love affairs, sweeping their sleeves and singing in strange metallic voices.

The performance had been paid for by a local cultural society as part of a religious festival. A purple cloth temple had been erected on the quayside, painted papier-mâché sculptures were burning down like giant joss sticks, and middle-aged men were sharing out gifts to be distributed among members' families: red buckets, roast ducks, candies, and moon cakes. The son of the organizer, a fashionable young man in Italian shirt and gold-rimmed glasses, was looking on with amused benevolence. I asked him why only old people and children were watching the show.

"Young people don't like these operas," he said. "They are too old-fashioned. We would prefer to see a high-quality Western variety show, something like that."

He spoke for a whole generation. Go to almost any village in the Third World and you will find youths who scorn traditional dress and sport denims and T-shirts. Go into any bank and the tellers will be dressed as would their European counterparts; at night the manager will climb into his car and go home to watch TV in a home that would not stick out on a European or North American estate.[1] Every capital city in the world is getting to look like every other; it is Marshall McLuhan's global village, but the style is exclusively Western. And not just in consumer fashions: The mimicry extends to architecture, industrial technology, approaches to health care, education, and housing.

To the ethnocentric Westerner or the Westernized local, that may   5
seem the most natural thing in the world. That is modern life, they might think. That is the way it will all be one day. That is what development and economic growth are all about.

---

[1]Housing development. — ED.

Yet the dispassionate observer can only be puzzled by this growing world uniformity. Surely one should expect more diversity, more indigenous styles and models of development? Why is almost everyone following virtually the same European road? The Third World's obsession with the Western way of life has perverted development and is rapidly destroying good and bad in traditional cultures, flinging the baby out with the bathwater. It is the most totally pervasive example of what historians call cultural diffusion in the history of mankind.

Its origins, of course, lie in the colonial experience. European rule was something quite different from the general run of conquests. Previous invaders more often than not settled down in their new territories, interbred, and assimilated a good deal of local culture. Not so the Europeans. Some, like the Iberians[2] or the Dutch, were not averse to cohabitation with native women: unlike the British, they seemed free of purely racial prejudice. But all the Europeans suffered from the same cultural arrogance. Perhaps it is the peculiar self-righteousness of Pauline[3] Christianity that accounts for this trait. Whatever the cause, never a doubt entered their minds that native cultures could be in any way, materially, morally, or spiritually, superior to their own, and that the supposedly benighted inhabitants of the darker continents needed enlightening.

And so there grew up, alongside political and economic imperialism, that more insidious form of control — cultural imperialism. It conquered not just the bodies but the souls of its victims, turning them into willing accomplices.

Cultural imperialism began its conquest of the Third World with the indoctrination of an elite of local collaborators. The missionary schools sought to produce converts to Christianity who would go out and proselytize among their own people, helping to eradicate traditional culture. Later the government schools aimed to turn out a class of junior bureaucrats and lower military officers who would help to exploit and repress their own people. The British were subtle about this, since they wanted the natives, even the Anglicized among them, to keep their distance. The French, and the Portuguese in Africa, explicitly aimed at the "assimilation" of gifted natives, by which was meant their metamorphosis into model Frenchmen and Lusitanians,[4] distinguishable only by the tint of their skin.

---

[2]Spanish or Portuguese (i.e., from the Iberian peninsula). — ED.
[3]Relating to the writings and teachings of St. Paul. — ED.
[4]Portuguese. Lusitania was the Roman name for the part of the Iberian peninsula that is now Portugal. — ED.

The second channel of transmission was more indirect and volun-   10
tary. It worked by what sociologists call reference-group behavior, found
when someone copies the habits and life-style of a social group he
wishes to belong to, or to be classed with, and abandons those of his
own group. This happened in the West when the new rich of early
commerce and industry aped the nobility they secretly aspired to join.
Not surprisingly, the social climbers in the colonies started to mimic
their conquerors. The returned slaves who carried the first wave of
Westernization in West Africa[5] wore black woolen suits and starched
collars in the heat of the dry season. The new officer corps of India were
molded into what the Indian writer Nirad Chaudhuri has called "imitation, polo-playing English subalterns," complete with waxed mustaches
and peacock chests. The elite of Indians, adding their own caste-
consciousness to the class-consciousness of their rulers, became more
British than the British (and still are).

There was another psychological motive for adopting Western ways,
deriving from the arrogance and haughtiness of the colonialists. As the
Martiniquan political philosopher, Frantz Fanon, remarked, colonial
rule was an experience in racial humiliation. Practically every leader of
a newly independent state could recall some experience such as being
turned out of a club or manhandled on the street by whites, often of low
status. The local elite were made to feel ashamed of their color and of
their culture. "I begin to suffer from not being a white man," Fanon
wrote, "to the degree that the white man imposes discrimination on me,
makes me a colonized native, robs me of all worth, all individuality. . . .
Then I will quite simply try to make myself white: that is, I will compel
the white man to acknowledge that I am human." To this complex
Fanon attributes the colonized natives' constant preoccupation with at-
tracting the attention of the white man, becoming powerful like the
white man, proving at all costs that blacks too can be civilized. Given
the racism and culturism of the whites, this could only be done by succeeding in their terms, and by adopting their ways.

This desire to prove equality surely helps to explain why Ghana's
Nkrumah built the huge stadium and triumphal arch of Black Star
Square in Accra. Why the tiny native village of Ivory Coast president
Houphouët-Boigny has been graced with a four-lane motorway starting
and ending nowhere, a five-star hotel and ultramodern conference cen-
ter. Why Sukarno transformed Indonesia's capital, Jakarta, into an

---

[5]One of many plans for solving the problem of slavery in the United States was to send
freed slaves to Africa. The Republic of Liberia in West Africa was founded for this purpose
in 1822. — ED.

exercise in gigantism, scarred with six-lane highways and neofascist monuments in the most hideous taste. The aim was not only to show the old imperialists, but to impress other Third World leaders in the only way everyone would recognize: the Western way.

The influence of Western life-styles spread even to those few nations who escaped the colonial yoke. By the end of the nineteenth century, the elites of the entire non-Western world were taking Europe as their reference group. The progress of the virus can be followed visibly in a room of Topkapi, the Ottoman palace in Istanbul, where a sequence of showcases display the costumes worn by each successive sultan. They begin with kaftans and turbans. Slowly elements of Western military uniform creep in, until the last sultans are decked out in brocade, epaulettes, and cocked hats.

The root of the problem with nations that were never colonized, like Turkey, China, and Japan, was probably their consciousness of Western military superiority. The beating of these three powerful nations at the hands of the West was a humiliating, traumatic experience. For China and Japan, the encounter with the advanced military technology of the industrialized nations was as terrifying as an invasion of extraterrestrials. Europe's earlier discovery of the rest of the world had delivered a mild culture shock to her ethnocentric attitudes. The Orient's contact with Europe shook nations to the foundations, calling into question the roots of their civilizations and all the assumptions and institutions on which their lives were based.

In all three nations groups of Young Turks[6] grew up, believing that   15 their countries could successfully take on the West only if they adopted Western culture, institutions, and even clothing, for all these ingredients were somehow involved in the production of Western technology. As early as the 1840s, Chinese intellectuals were beginning to modify the ancient view that China was in all respects the greatest civilization in the world. The administrator Wei Yüan urged his countrymen to "learn the superior technology of the barbarians in order to control them." But the required changes could not be confined to the technical realm. Effectiveness in technology is the outcome of an entire social system. "Since we were knocked out by cannon balls," wrote M. Chiang, "naturally we became interested in them, thinking that by learning to make them we could strike back. From studying cannon balls we came to mechanical inventions which in turn led to political reforms, which led us again to the political philosophies of the West." The

---

[6]Members of an aggressive reform group. — ED.

republican revolution of 1911 attempted to modernize China, but her subjection to the West continued until another Young Turk, Mao Zedong, applied that alternative brand of Westernization: communism, though in a unique adaptation.

The Japanese were forced to open their border to Western goods in 1853, after a couple of centuries of total isolation. They had to rethink fast in order to survive. From 1867, the Meiji rulers Westernized Japan with astonishing speed, adopting Western science, technology, and even manners: short haircuts became the rule, ballroom dancing caught on, and *moningku* with *haikara* (morning coats and high collars) were worn. The transformation was so successful that by the 1970s the Japanese were trouncing the West at its own game. But they had won their economic independence at the cost of losing their cultural autonomy.

Turkey, defeated in the First World War, her immense empire in fragments, set about transforming herself under that compulsive and ruthless Westernizer, Kemal Atatürk. The Arabic script was abolished and replaced with the Roman alphabet. Kemal's strange exploits as a hatter will probably stand as the symbol of Westernization carried to absurd lengths. His biographer, Lord Kinross, relates that while traveling in the West as a young man, the future president had smarted under Western insults and condescension about the Turkish national hat, the fez. Later, he made the wearing of the fez a criminal offense. "The people of the Turkish republic," he said in a speech launching the new policy, "must prove that they are civilized and advanced persons in their outward respect also. . . . A civilized, international dress is worthy and appropriate for our nation and we will wear it. Boots or shoes on our feet, trousers on our legs, shirt and tie, jacket and waistcoat — and, of course, to complete these, a cover with a brim on our heads. I want to make this clear. This head covering is called a hat."

EXPLORATIONS

1. Early in his essay Paul Harrison asks the central question: "Why is almost everyone following virtually the same European road?" (para. 6). What are the characteristics of this "European road"? What are the origins of the specific examples the author cites?

2. What general cause, and what specific channels, does Harrison cite as responsible for the Third World's Westernization? What differences between Western newcomers and Third World natives seem to have most strongly affected relations between them?

3. "By the end of the nineteenth century," writes Harrison, "the elites of the entire non-Western world were taking Europe as their reference group" (para. 13). How does he explain the initial westward tilt of countries that were never colonized? What explanation does he suggest for their continuing interest in Western ways?

CONNECTIONS

1. In paragraph 10 Harrison discusses "reference-group behavior." What examples of this behavior can you find in Germaine Greer's "One Man's Mutilation Is Another Man's Beautification" (p. 65)? In Margaret Atwood's "A View from Canada" (p. 59)?

2. Harrison's subject, the Westernization of the world, leads him to focus on the impact of colonialism. How does his description of Indians at the end of paragraph 10 differ from the ways Salman Rushdie (p. 53) and Anita Desai (p. 4) describe their lives in India? Which of Harrison's ideas also appear in Rushdie's or Desai's recollections?

3. What does Harrison say in paragraph 7 about the policy of the Iberian (Spanish and Portuguese) colonizers toward the native peoples they met in the New World? Do you think Mario Vargas Llosa (p. 4) would agree? What does Vargas Llosa have to say about what Harrison calls "cultural imperialism"?

ELABORATIONS

1. Harrison focuses on Westernization in non-Western countries. What explanation (if any) does he offer for the spread of a single cultural trend all over Europe and North America? On the basis of Harrison's theories, plus evidence from other selections you have read, write an essay identifying causes and effects behind the West's homogeneity.

2. It has become fairly common for couples and individuals in the United States to adopt babies from Third World countries. In what ways does cross-cultural adoption benefit the child, the original and adoptive parents, and the child's original and adoptive homeland? What are the drawbacks of this practice? Write an argumentative essay defending or opposing cross-cultural adoption, or a process analysis essay advising the would-be parent(s) on how to protect the interests of all involved.

SPOTLIGHT:
MEXICO

Identifying Ourselves: *Skeletons are popular at Mexico City's fiestas.*

Latin America comprises those countries south of the United States where languages derived from Latin are spoken — Portuguese in Brazil, Spanish in the rest of South America, Central America, and Mexico. España ("Spain" in English) occupies most of the Iberian peninsula, with Portugal to its west and France to its east. Conquered by Rome around 200 B.C., the region was converted to Christianity by invading Visigoths, then to Islam by African Moors. In 1469, the kingdoms of Aragon and Castile were united by the marriage of Ferdinand II and Isabella I. Their victory over the last Moorish stronghold in Granada in 1492 extended their rule and completed Spain's return to Roman Catholicism. That same year, the discovery of America by Cristobal Colon (Christopher Columbus) launched the wave of exploration and conquest that won Spain its vast colonial empire. (See Chilean poet Pablo Neruda's comments on page 509.) Although Spain lost its American colonies in the 1800s, its language, religion, architecture, and descendants still pervade Latin America.

The United States' neighbor to the south has been populated since around 21,000 B.C. The great Olmec, Toltec, Mayan, and Aztec civilizations arose between A.D. 100 and A.D. 900. When Hernán Cortés and other explorers arrived from Spain in the 1500s, they conquered the ruling Aztecs and made Mexico a heavily exploited colony until a series of rebellions achieved independence in 1821. A republic was declared in 1823, followed by two emperors, several dictators, and a series of presidents. Although the government is officially democratic, one party — the Institutional Revolutionary Party (PRI) — has governed Mexico since 1929. "Mexico is a bureaucratic state halfway between capitalism and socialism," Octavio Paz has observed; "it is between democracy and dictatorship with a constitutional transfer of power, but also a president with absolute power and one-party rule."

Economic problems are pushing the country toward political reform. After an oil boom in the 1970s, Mexico's economy had declined severely by the mid-1980s. The presidency of Carlos Salinas de Gortari brought improvement after years of stagnation, as wages, job opportunities, and exports increased; however, most of the rural and much of the urban population remained poor, with many workers seeking jobs across the northern border. In the early 1990s, controversy arose over the North American Free Trade Agreement (NAFTA), aimed at lifting economic barriers between Mexico, Canada, and the United States. Soon after NAFTA passed, and Ernesto Zedillo Ponce de Leon took over the presidency, economic crisis struck. A belated devaluation of the peso revealed such flaws in Salinas's policies and Mexico's finances that the United States stepped in and backed a loan guarantee to stave off potential collapse, which could have reverberated worldwide. According to Carlos Fuentes, "the problem is political more than economic." He blames Mexico's lack of accountability and of checks and balances — "two terms that are common in U.S. public law . . . [but] are not even translatable into Spanish." While President Zedillo is persisting with market-based economic policies, he also has promised to break the bond between the president and the PRI; and the National Action Party (PAN) expects to contest the 2000 presidential election vigorously.

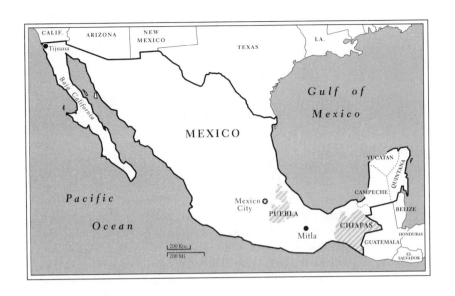

OCTAVIO PAZ

The Art of the Fiesta

Although Octavio Paz is represented here by an essay, he is also
known for his fiction, his art criticism, and his poetry. "Poetic activity is
revolutionary by nature," he has written, "a means of interior liberation." Paz was born in Mexico City in 1914. Educated at a Roman
Catholic school and the National University of Mexico, he founded an
avant-garde literary journal at age seventeen; at nineteen he published
his first book of poems. Four years later he went to Europe, where he
supported the Republican side in the Spanish Civil War, established
himself as a writer with another book of poems, and met prominent Sur-
realist poets in Paris. Back in Mexico Paz founded and edited several
literary reviews, including the journal *Vuelta* ("Return"), which he
started in 1976 and still publishes. In 1942 he married the writer Elena
Garro (see p. 93); they were later divorced. In 1950 Paz produced his famous study of Mexican character and culture, *El laberinto de la soledad*
(*The Labyrinth of Solitude: Life and Thought in Mexico*, 1961). "The
Art of the Fiesta" comes from the chapter "The Day of the Dead"; it
was translated from the Spanish by Lysander Kemp. After working for
the Mexican embassies in Paris and Japan, Paz served as Mexico's ambassador to India from 1962 to 1968, resigning over Mexico's brutal
treatment of student radicals. He has also lived in England, France, and
the United States, where he taught at Harvard University and at the
University of Texas. Following many other awards, Paz won the Nobel
Prize for literature in 1990.

The solitary Mexican loves fiestas and public gatherings. Any occasion for getting together will serve, any pretext to stop the flow of time
and commemorate men and events with festivals and ceremonies. We
are a ritual people, and this characteristic enriches both our imaginations and our sensibilities, which are equally sharp and alert. The art of
the fiesta has been debased almost everywhere else, but not in Mexico.
There are few places in the world where it is possible to take part in a
spectacle like our great religious fiestas with their violent primary colors, their bizarre costumes and dances, their fireworks and ceremonies,
and their inexhaustible welter of surprises: the fruit, candy, toys, and
other objects sold on these days in the plazas and open-air markets.

Our calendar is crowded with fiestas. There are certain days when the whole country, from the most remote villages to the largest cities, prays, shouts, feasts, gets drunk, and kills, in honor of the Virgin of Guadalupe or Benito Juárez. Each year on the fifteenth of September, at eleven o'clock at night, we celebrate the fiesta of the *Grito*[1] in all the plazas of the Republic, and the excited crowds actually shout for a whole hour . . . the better, perhaps, to remain silent for the rest of the year. During the days before and after the twelfth of December,[2] time comes to a full stop, and instead of pushing us toward a deceptive tomorrow that is always beyond our reach, offers us a complete and perfect today of dancing and revelry, of communion with the most ancient and secret Mexico. Time is no longer succession, and becomes what it originally was and is: the present, in which the past and future are reconciled.

But the fiestas which the Church and State provide for the country as a whole are not enough. The life of every city and village is ruled by a patron saint whose blessing is celebrated with devout regularity. Neighborhoods and trades also have their annual fiestas, their ceremonies and fairs. And each one of us — atheist, Catholic, or merely indifferent — has his own saint's day, which he observes every year. It is impossible to calculate how many fiestas we have and how much time and money we spend on them. I remember asking the mayor of a village near Mitla, several years ago, "What is the income of the village government?" "About 3,000 pesos a year. We are very poor. But the Governor and the Federal Government always help us to meet our expenses." "And how are the 3,000 pesos spent?" "Mostly on fiestas, señor. We are a small village, but we have two patron saints."

This reply is not surprising. Our poverty can be measured by the frequency and luxuriousness of our holidays. Wealthy countries have very few: There is neither the time nor the desire for them, and they are not necessary. The people have other things to do, and when they amuse themselves they do so in small groups. The modern masses are agglomerations of solitary individuals. On great occasions in Paris or New York, when the populace gathers in the squares or stadiums, the absence of people, in the sense of *a* people, is remarkable: There are couples and small groups, but they never form a living community in which the individual is at once dissolved and redeemed. But how could a poor Mexican live without the two or three annual fiestas that make up for his

---

[1]Padre Hidalgo's call-to-arms against Spain, 1810. — TRANS.
[2]Fiesta of the Virgin of Guadalupe. — TRANS.

poverty and misery? Fiestas are our only luxury. They replace, and are perhaps better than, the theater and vacations, Anglo-Saxon weekends and cocktail parties, the bourgeois reception, the Mediterranean café.

In all of these ceremonies — national or local, trade or family — the   5 Mexican opens out. They give him a chance to reveal himself and to converse with God, country, friends or relations. During these days the silent Mexican whistles, shouts, sings, shoots off fireworks, discharges his pistol into the air. He discharges his soul. And his shout, like the rockets we love so much, ascends to the heavens, explodes into green, red, blue, and white lights, and falls dizzily to earth with a trail of golden sparks. This is the night when friends who have not exchanged more than the prescribed courtesies for months get drunk together, trade confidences, weep over the same troubles, discover that they are brothers, and sometimes, to prove it, kill each other. The night is full of songs and loud cries. The lover wakes up his sweetheart with an orches- tra. There are jokes and conversations from balcony to balcony, side- walk to sidewalk. Nobody talks quietly. Hats fly in the air. Laughter and curses ring like silver pesos. Guitars are brought out. Now and then, it is true, the happiness ends badly, in quarrels, insults, pistol shots, stab- bings. But these too are part of the fiesta, for the Mexican does not seek amusement: He seeks to escape from himself, to leap over the wall of solitude that confines him during the rest of the year. All are possessed by violence and frenzy. Their souls explode like the colors and voices and emotions. Do they forget themselves and show their true faces? No- body knows. The important thing is to go out, open a way, get drunk on noise, people, colors. Mexico is celebrating a fiesta. And this fiesta, shot through with lightning and delirium, is the brilliant reverse to our si- lence and apathy, our reticence and gloom.

According to the interpretation of French sociologists, the fiesta is an excess, an expense. By means of this squandering the community pro- tects itself against the envy of the gods or of men. Sacrifices and offerings placate or buy off the gods and the patron saints. Wasting money and ex- pending energy affirms the community's wealth in both. This luxury is a proof of health, a show of abundance and power. Or a magic trap. For squandering is an effort to attract abundance by contagion. Money calls to money. When life is thrown away it increases; the orgy, which is sex- ual expenditure, is also a ceremony of regeneration; waste gives strength. New Year celebrations, in every culture, signify something beyond the mere observance of a date on the calendar. The day is a pause: Time is stopped, is actually annihilated. The rites that celebrate its death are in- tended to provoke its rebirth, because they mark not only the end of an old year but also the beginning of a new. Everything attracts its opposite.

The fiesta's function, then, is more utilitarian than we think: waste attracts or promotes wealth, and is an investment like any other, except that the returns on it cannot be measured or counted. What is sought is potency, life, health. In this sense the fiesta, like the gift and the offering, is one of the most ancient of economic forms.

This interpretation has always seemed to me to be incomplete. The fiesta is by nature sacred, literally or figuratively, and above all it is the advent of the unusual. It is governed by its own special rules, that set it apart from other days, and it has a logic, an ethic, and even an economy that are often in conflict with everyday norms. It all occurs in an enchanted world: Time is transformed to a mythical past or a total present; space, the scene of the fiesta, is turned into a gaily decorated world of its own; and the persons taking part cast off all human or social rank and become, for the moment, living images. And everything takes place as if it were not so, as if it were a dream. But whatever happens, our actions have a greater lightness, a different gravity. They take on other meanings and with them we contract new obligations. We throw down our burdens of time and reason.

In certain fiestas the very notion of order disappears. Chaos comes back and license rules. Anything is permitted: The customary hierarchies vanish, along with all social, sex, caste, and trade distinctions. Men disguise themselves as women, gentlemen as slaves, the poor as the rich. The army, the clergy, and the law are ridiculed. Obligatory sacrilege, ritual profanation is committed. Love becomes promiscuity. Sometimes the fiesta becomes a Black Mass. Regulations, habits, and customs are violated. Respectable people put away the dignified expressions and conservative clothes that isolate them, dress up in gaudy colors, hide behind a mask, and escape from themselves.

Therefore the fiesta is not only an excess, a ritual squandering of the goods painfully accumulated during the rest of the year; it is also a revolt, a sudden immersion in the formless, in pure being. By means of the fiesta society frees itself from the norms it has established. It ridicules its gods, its principles, and its laws: It denies its own self.

The fiesta is a revolution in the most literal sense of the word. In the 10 confusion that it generates, society is dissolved, is drowned, insofar as it is an organism ruled according to certain laws and principles. But it drowns in itself, in its own original chaos or liberty. Everything is united: good and evil, day and night, the sacred and the profane. Everything merges, loses shape and individuality and returns to the primordial mass. The fiesta is a cosmic experiment, an experiment in disorder, reuniting contradictory elements and principles in order to bring about a renascence of life. Ritual death promotes a rebirth; vomiting increases the appetite; the orgy, sterile in itself, renews the fertility of the mother or of the earth. The fiesta is a return to a remote and undifferentiated state, prenatal or presocial. It is a return that is also a beginning, in accordance with the dialectic that is inherent in social processes.

The group emerges purified and strengthened from this plunge into chaos. It has immersed itself in its own origins, in the womb from which it came. To express it in another way, the fiesta denies society as an organic system of differentiated forms and principles, but affirms it as a source of creative energy. It is a true "re-creation," the opposite of the "recreation" characterizing modern vacations, which do not entail any rites or ceremonies whatever and are as individualistic and sterile as the world that invented them.

Society communes with itself during the fiesta. Its members return to original chaos and freedom. Social structures break down and new relationships, unexpected rules, capricious hierarchies are created. In the general disorder everybody forgets himself and enters into otherwise forbidden situations and places. The bounds between audience and actors, officials and servants, are erased. Everybody takes part in the fiesta, everybody is caught up in its whirlwind. Whatever its mood, its character, its meaning, the fiesta is participation, and this trait distinguishes it from all other ceremonies and social phenomena. Lay or religious, orgy or saturnalia, the fiesta is a social act based on the full participation of all its celebrants.

Thanks to the fiesta the Mexican opens out, participates, communes with his fellows and with the values that give meaning to his religious or political existence. And it is significant that a country as sorrowful as ours should have so many and such joyous fiestas. Their frequency, their brilliance and excitement, the enthusiasm with which we take part, all suggest that without them we would explode. They free us, if only momentarily, from the thwarted impulses, the inflammable desires that we carry within us. But the Mexican fiesta is not merely a return to an original state of formless and normless liberty: The Mexican is not seeking to return, but to escape from himself, to exceed himself. Our fiestas are explosions. Life and death, joy and sorrow, music and mere noise are united, not to re-create or recognize themselves, but to swallow each other up. There is nothing so joyous as a Mexican fiesta, but there is also nothing so sorrowful. Fiesta night is also a night of mourning.

If we hide within ourselves in our daily lives, we discharge ourselves in the whirlwind of the fiesta. It is more than an opening out: We rend ourselves open. Everything — music, love, friendship — ends in tumult and violence. The frenzy of our festivals shows the extent to which our

solitude closes us off from communication with the world. We are familiar with delirium, with songs and shouts, with the monologue . . .
but not with the dialogue. Our fiestas, like our confidences, our loves,
our attempts to reorder our society, are violent breaks with the old or
the established. Each time we try to express ourselves we have to break
with ourselves. And the fiesta is only one example, perhaps the most
typical, of this violent break. It is not difficult to name others, equally
revealing: our games, which are always going to extremes, often mortal;
our profligate spending, the reverse of our timid investments and business enterprises; our confessions. The somber Mexican, closed up in
himself, suddenly explodes, tears open his breast and reveals himself,
though not without a certain complacency, and not without a stopping
place in the shameful or terrible mazes of his intimacy. We are not
frank, but our sincerity can reach extremes that horrify a European.
The explosive, dramatic, sometimes even suicidal manner in which we
strip ourselves, surrender ourselves, is evidence that something inhibits
and suffocates us. Something impedes us from being. And since we
cannot or dare not confront our own selves, we resort to the fiesta. It
fires us into the void; it is a drunken rapture that burns itself out, a pistol
shot in the air, a skyrocket.

EXPLORATIONS

1. For what kinds of occasions do Mexicans hold fiestas? According to Octavio
   Paz, how important to a fiesta is the occasion being celebrated? What does
   Paz suggest are the main reasons why Mexico has so many fiestas?

2. "There is nothing so joyous as a Mexican fiesta, but there is also nothing so
   sorrowful" (para. 13). What other paradoxes appear in Paz's essay? Why does
   he think fiestas are so full of them?

3. Have you ever been to a Mardi Gras festival? New Year's Eve in Times
   Square? Any other mass celebration in the United States? What aspects of
   such events in this country resemble the Mexican fiestas Paz describes?
   What aspects are different? To what extent do U.S. "fiestas" play the social
   role Paz assigns to Mexican fiestas?

CONNECTIONS

1. Does Paz regard the Mexican fiesta as having been Westernized in any of
   the ways Paul Harrison describes in "The Westernization of the World"
   (p. 76)? What evidence in "The Art of the Fiesta" supports your answer?

2. In the fiesta, Paz writes in paragraph 5, "the Mexican does not seek amusement: He seeks to escape from himself, to leap over the wall of solitude that
   confines him during the rest of the year." What comments in James Baldwin's "The New Lost Generation" (p. 18) suggest similar reasons for becoming an expatriate? Why do you think Paz's revelers and Baldwin's travelers
   choose different escape routes?

3. What observations about Mexicans appear in both Paz's essay and Alma
   Guillermoprieto's comments on page 7? How do these two writers' interpretations differ? How do you think Paz would explain the love of *ranchera*
   music described by Guillermoprieto?

ELENA GARRO

The Day We Were Dogs

The writer Elena Garro is better known in the Spanish-speaking world than in the United States. She was born in 1920 in Puebla, Mexico. While studying philosophy at the National University of Mexico (UNAM) and choreographing for the University Theater, she married Octavio Paz (see p. 86) and began working as a journalist. After her divorce from Paz, Garro lived in Spain, the United States, Mexico, and France, writing for various newspapers and producing several plays. Her best-known work is her award-winning novel *Los recuerdos del porvenir* (1963; *Recollections of Things to Come*, 1969), an early landmark in the literature of magic realism and a forerunner of such books as Gabriel García Márquez's *One Hundred Years of Solitude* (see p. 567). Her short-story collections include *La semana de colores* (1964) and *Andamos huyendo Lola* (1980). "The Day We Were Dogs" ("El dia que fuimos perros"), translated from the Spanish by Tona Wilson, comes from *La semana de colores*; it first appeared in English in *Contemporary Women Authors of Latin America: New Translations* (1983).

The day we were dogs was not just any day, even though it began the way every day begins. We awoke at six in the morning and knew that it was a day with two days inside it. Lying on her back, Eva opened her eyes and, without changing her position, looked at one day and looked at the other. I had opened mine just a few moments before and, so as not to see the vastness of the empty house, I was looking at her. Why had we not gone to Mexico City? I still do not know that. We asked to stay and no one opposed our wish. The day before, the hall was filled with suitcases: Everyone was fleeing the heat of August. Very early the suitcases left in a horse-drawn cart; on the table remained half-finished cups of coffee and the oatmeal sticking to the bowls. Advice and suggestions rained down upon the tiles in the hall. Eva and I watched them disdainfully. We were the mistresses of the patios, the gardens, the rooms. When we took possession of the house, a great weight fell upon us. What could we do with the archways, the windows, the doors, and the furniture? The day turned solid, the violet sky clouded over with dark papers, and fear settled into the pillars and the plants. In silence we wandered about the house and watched our hair become rags. We had nothing to do, no one to ask what to do. In the kitchen, the servants clustered around the hearth, to eat and doze. The beds were not made; no one watered the ferns or took the dirty cups off the dining room table. At dusk, the songs of the servants filled with crimes and sorrows, and the house sank into the day, like a rock in a deep gorge.

We awoke determined not to repeat the preceding day. The new day shone double and intact. Eva looked at the two parallel days that glowed like two lines drawn in the water. Then she studied the wall, where Christ was in his white tunic. Then she turned her eyes to the other picture, which showed the image of Buddha wrapped in his orange tunic, pensive, in the middle of a yellowish landscape. Between the two pictures that guarded her bed, Eva had hung a clipping from a newspaper, with a photograph in which a lady in a beret was sailing on a yacht. "Madame Kroupuskaia on the Neva" said the caption.

"I like Russians," said Eva, and she clapped her hands to call the servants. No one responded to her call. We looked at each other without surprise. Eva clapped her hands in one of the days and her claps did not reach the day of the kitchen.

"Let's sniff around," she said to me.

And she jumped up on my bed to look at me up close. Her blonde   5
hair covered her forehead. From my bed she jumped to the floor, put a finger to her lips and penetrated cautiously into the day that advanced parallel to the other. I followed her. No one. The day was alone, and it was as frightening as the other. The quiet trees, the rounded sky, green like a gentle meadow, without anyone either, without a horse, without a rider, abandoned. From the well rose the heat of August, which had caused the flight to Mexico City. Stretched out next to a tree was Toni. They had already chained him up. He looked at us attentively and we saw that he was in our day.

"Toni's good," said Eva and patted his open mouth.

Then she lay down next to him and I lay down on his other side.

"Did you already have breakfast, Toni?"

Toni didn't answer, only looked at us sadly. Eva got up and disappeared among the plants. She returned running and threw herself down next to Toni.

"I just told them to cook for three dogs and no people."   10

I didn't ask anything. Next to Toni the house had lost its weight. Two ants were walking on the ground of the day; an earthworm peeked out of a little hole, I touched it with my fingertip and it became a red ring. There were bits of leaves, little pieces of branches, tiny pebbles, and the black earth smelled of magnolia water. The other day was off to one

side. Toni, Eva, and I watched without fear its gigantic towers and stationary winds, purple and mulberry colored.

"You, what's your name going to be? Look for your dog name, I'm
looking for mine."

"I'm a dog?"

"Yes, we're dogs."

I accepted that and moved closer to Toni, who moved his head, dis-   15
gusted. I remembered that he was not going to go to heaven; I would
have the same fate. "Animals don't go to heaven." Our Lord Jesus
Christ had not put a place for dogs in heaven. Nor had Lord Buddha
put a place in Nirvana for dogs. In the house it was very important to be
good so we could go to heaven. We couldn't hoard things, nor kill animals; we were vegetarians and on Sundays we threw Sunday from the
balcony so someone could pick it up and we would learn not to keep
anything. We lived up to date. The people of the town spied around the
balconies of the house. "They're Spaniards," they said and looked at us
askance. We didn't know that we weren't from there because we were
going to heaven, either to one or the other: the white and blue or the
orange and yellow one. Now there wouldn't be a place for the three of
us in either of them. The alchemists, the Greeks, the anarchists, the ro-
mantics, the occultists, the Franciscans, and the Romans occupied the
library shelves and dinner-table conversations. The Evangelists, the
Vedas, and the poets had a place apart. For the dogs there was nowhere
but the foot of a tree. And afterwards? Afterwards we would be left lying
on the ground.

"I just found my name."

"Already?" Eva sat up, curious.

"Yes: Christ."

Eva looked at me enviously.

"Christ? That's a good dog name."   20

Eva rested her head on her forepaws and closed her eyes.

"I found mine too," she said, sitting up suddenly.

"What?"

"Buddha!"

"That's a very good dog name."   25

And Buddha lay down next to Toni and began to growl with pleasure.

No one came to visit the day of Toni, Christ, and Buddha. The
house was far away, within its other day. The chimes of the church
clock told nothing. The ground began to get very hot: The worms
crawled into their holes, the black beetles looked for moist places

underneath the stones, the ants cut acacia leaves, which they used as green sunshades. Where the dogs were, there was thirst. Buddha barked impatiently, asking for water, Toni imitated him, and a moment later Christ joined in the barking. On a distant path appeared the feet of Rutilio, in huaraches. He brought three bowls of water. Indifferently he put a bowl in front of Toni, looked at Christ and Buddha, and placed a bowl of water near each of their snouts. Rutilio patted the heads of the dogs, and they gratefully wagged their tails. It was difficult to drink water with your tongue. Later the old servant brought food in a pot and served it in a big crock. The dogs' rice had bones and meat. Christ and Buddha looked at each other, astonished: Weren't dogs vegetarians? Toni lifted his upper lip, growled fiercely through his white fangs, and quickly grabbed the chunks of meat. Christ and Buddha put their snouts in the crock and ate the rice moistened like gruel. Toni finished and drowsily watched his companions, who lapped up the rice. Later, they too rested on their forefeet. The sun beat down, the earth burned, and the dogs' food was heavy as a bag of rocks. They stayed sleeping in their day, separated from the day of the house. They were awakened by a blast that came from the other day. A long silence followed. Alert, they listened to the other afternoon. Another explosion, and the three dogs began running in the direction of the sound. Toni could not join in the race, because his chain stopped him close to the tree. Christ and Buddha jumped over the bushes in the direction of the gate.

"Where are you going, you wretched little brats?" Rutilio yelled at them, from the other day.

The dogs got to the gate; it was hard for them to open the door; the bolts were very high up. Finally they went out into the street, illuminated by the four o'clock sun. The street shone splendidly, like a fixed image. The stones glittered in the dust. There was nobody. Nobody but the two men bathed in blood, embraced in their struggle. Buddha sat down on the edge of the sidewalk and looked at them with eyes wide open. Christ settled down right next to Buddha and also looked at them with amazement. The men growled in the other day, "You'll see" . . . "Ayay! Son of a bitch!" Their smothered voices came from very far away. One restrained the hand of the one that held the pistol and with his free hand tattooed the other's chest with his knife. He was clasped to the body of the other, and, as though he hadn't enough strength, he slipped to the ground in the embrace. The man with the pistol stood firm in the splendid afternoon. His shirt and his white pants were soaked in blood. With a movement he freed his imprisoned hand and rested the pistol against the center of the forehead of his kneeling enemy. A dry sound divided the other afternoon in two, and opened a little hole in the forehead of the kneeling man. The man fell on his back and looked fixedly at the sky.

"Bastard!" yelled the man standing on the stones, while his legs con-   30 tinued to rain blood. Then he too raised his eyes to look at the same sky, and at the end of a few moments turned them on the dogs, who a couple of yards away, sitting on the edge of the sidewalk, stared at him open-mouthed.

Everything was still. The other afternoon got so high that down below the street was outside of it. In the distance appeared several men with rifles. They were, like all the men, dressed in white, with palm sombreros on their heads. They walked slowly. The tread of their huaraches sounded from very far away. In the street there were no trees to deaden the sound of the footsteps; only white walls, against which echoed, closer and closer, the steps, like the roll of the drums on a day of fiesta. The road stopped suddenly when they got to the wounded man.

"You killed him?"

"I sure did, ask the girls."

The men looked at the dogs.

"Did you see it?"   35

"Woof! Woof!" replied Buddha.

"Woof! Woof!" responded Christ.

"O.K. Take him away."

They took away the man and there remained no trace of him but the blood on the paving stones. He was writing his fate; the dogs read his bloody destiny and turned to look again at the dead man.

A time passed, and the door of the house remained open, and the   40 dogs, absorbed, sitting on the edge of the sidewalk, continued to look at the dead man. A fly appeared at the wound on his forehead, then cleaned its feet and moved to his hair. After an instant it returned to the forehead, looked at the wound, and again cleaned its feet. When the fly returned to the wound, a woman arrived and threw herself upon the dead man. But to him neither the fly nor the woman mattered. Unmoved, he continued to look at the sky. Other people came and bent down to see his eyes. It began to get dark and Buddha and Christ remained there, neither moving nor barking. They looked like two stray dogs and nobody paid any attention to them.

"Eva! Leli!" someone was calling from very high up. The dogs jumped, startled.

"Just wait till your parents get home! Just you wait and see!" Rutilio led them into the house. He placed a chair in the hallway, very close to the wall, and sat down to look at the dogs, who, lying at his feet, were watching him attentively. Candelaria brought a lighted paraffin lamp, and, strutting, returned to the kitchen. In a little while the songs flooded the house with mourning.

"It's your fault I can't go sing! . . . Wicked brats!" griped Rutilio.

Christ and Buddha listened to him from the other day. Rutilio, his chair, the lamp, and the dead man, they were all in the parallel day, separated from the other day by an invisible line.

"Just wait and see, the witches will come and suck your blood. They   45
say they love the blood of blondes. I'm going to tell Candelaria to leave the coals burning, so they can warm their calves. From the hearth they'll go straight up to your bed to enjoy themselves. It's what you deserve, for being wretches."

The hearth with the burning coals, Candelaria, Rutilio, the songs, and the witches, passed before the dogs' eyes like figures projected in another time. Rutilio's words circled through the hall without end and didn't touch them. On the floor of the day of the dogs, there were fat little bugs that were going to sleep. The sleepiness of the bugs was contagious and Christ and Buddha, curled up over their front paws, nodded.

"Supper time!"

They sat them down on the kitchen floor, in the circle of servants who were drinking alcohol and gave them a plate of beans with sausage. The dogs were falling asleep. Until yesterday they had still had oatmeal with milk for supper and the sausage made them feel queasy.

"Put them to bed, they're acting drunk!"

They put them both in the same bed, put out the lamp, and left. The   50
dogs slept in the other day, at the foot of the tree, with the chain around their necks, near the ants with their green sunshades and the red earthworms. After a short time they woke up, startled. The parallel day was there, sitting in the middle of the room. The walls were breathing burning coals; through the cracks the witches lurked, watching the blue veins of their temples. Everything was very dark. In one of the beds lay the dead man with his forehead open; at his side the man with the tattooed chest gushed blood. Very far away, at the back of the garden, slept the servants; Mexico City, with their parents and their brothers, who knew where that was? On the other hand, the other day was there, very close to them, without a bark, with its immobile dead man, in the immobile afternoon, with the enormous fly peering into the enormous wound and cleaning its feet. In sleep, without realizing it, we passed from one day to the other, and lost the day we were dogs.

"Don't be afraid, we're dogs . . ."

But Eva knew that it was no longer true. We had discovered that the heaven of men was not the same as the heaven of dogs.

The dogs did not share the crime with us.

EXPLORATIONS

1. How old would you say the narrator is in "The Day We Were Dogs"? What is her relationship to Eva? What other identifying information does Elena Garro supply about her two main characters? How does she supply it?

2. How is Garro's story affected by the dog names her characters choose? How would the story's impact change if the girls picked more common dog names?

3. At the end of the story the narrator says, "We had discovered that the heaven of men was not the same as the heaven of dogs." What does she mean?

CONNECTIONS

1. What is the immediate response of Garro's characters to the killing they witness? What are their later responses? How do you think Octavio Paz (p. 86) would explain their reactions?

2. If this story were set and written in the United States, how would the scene in paragraphs 28–38 be likely to change? According to Paz, what is typically Mexican about this scene, and why?

3. At what points in her story does Garro use the "fractured perceptions" described by Salman Rushdie in "The Broken Mirror" (see, for example, p. 56, para. 11)? How does this technique help her to represent childhood in a way that feels authentic?

CARLOS FUENTES

The Two Americas

Carlos Fuentes was born in Panama in 1928 to the family of a Mexican diplomat. Thanks to his father's career, Fuentes spent his childhood in various Latin American capitals as well as Washington, D.C. He studied law in both Mexico City and Geneva, Switzerland. In the 1950s he worked for the United Nations Information Center in Mexico City, won a prestigious writing fellowship, and published his first book of short stories. After cofounding the *Mexican Review of Literature*, he became director of international cultural relations for Mexico's Ministry of Foreign Affairs. Fuentes's first novel, *La región más transparente*, was published in 1958 (*Where the Air Is Clear*, 1960), followed four years later by the celebrated *La muerte de Artemio Cruz* (*The Death of Artemio Cruz*, 1964). Along with Mario Vargas Llosa of Peru (see p. 4) and Gabriel García Márquez of Colombia (see p. 567), among others, Fuentes triggered the eruption of Latin American literature known as "El Boom." Besides continuing to write, and teaching as a visiting writer at universities in Mexico, England, Paris, and the United States, he served as Mexico's ambassador to France from 1975 to 1977. However, his denunciation of U.S. intervention in Vietnam caused the State Department to refuse him a visa and impede his entry into the United States up through the late 1980s. Fuentes's books, particularly *El gringo viejo* (*The Old Gringo*, 1985), have won numerous international awards. Recent works include *The Buried Mirror: Reflections on Spain and the New World* (1992), a book and TV miniseries he wrote and narrated on the evolution of Hispanic culture, and *El naranjo, o los circulos del tiempo* (*The Orange Tree*, 1994), in which "The Two Americas" appears.

> . . . to give an account to the King and Queen of the things they saw, a thousand tongues would be insufficient; nor would the author's hands suffice to write about them, because they seemed enchanted . . .
>
> – Christopher Columbus, *Journal of the First Voyage*,
> from the extract made by Bartolomé de Las Casas

Fragments from the Diary of a Genoese Sailor

Today I landed on the enchanted beach. It was hot and the sun rose at an early hour. The radiance of the water was brighter than the light in the sky. No sea is more translucent, as green as the lemon juice my sailors craved, ravaged as they were by scurvy during the long voyage from the port of Palos. You can see all the way to the bottom, as if the surface of the water were a sheet of glass. The bottom is white sand, crisscrossed by fish of every color.

The storms shredded my sails. On August 3, we crossed the Saltes bar, and on September 6, we saw land for the last time when we left the port of Gomera in the Canaries. There were three caravels, but all that remains is the ship's boat I managed to save after the mutiny and massacre. I am the only survivor.

Only my eyes see this shore, only my feet walk it. I do what habit orders me to do. I get down on my knee and give thanks to a God who is certainly too busy with more important matters to think about me. I cross two old branches and invoke the sacrifice and benediction. I claim this land in the name of the Catholic Kings who will never set foot on it, and understand why they showed such magnanimity when they granted me possession of everything I might discover. They knew very well that without resources I couldn't dominate anything. I've reached these shores naked and poor. But what will they or I possess? What land is this? Where the hell am I?

Back in Genoa, my mother would say to me while I helped her stretch the huge sheets out to dry — while I imagined myself, even then, carried along by great sails to the far edges of the universe — "Son, stop dreaming. Why can't you be happy with what you can see and touch? Why do you always talk about things that don't exist?"

She was right. The pleasure of what I'm looking at should satisfy me. The white shore. The abrupt silence, so different from the deafening clamor of Genoa or Lisbon. The mild breezes and weather like Andalusia's in April. The purity of the air, with not one of the foul odors that plague the thronged ports of the Tyrrhenian Sea. Here only flocks of parrots darken the sky. And on the beaches I don't find the shit, the garbage, the bloody rags, the flies, and the rats of all the European cities. Here I find the snowy white horizons of purity, pearls as plentiful as the sand itself, turtles laying eggs, and beyond the beach, in successive ranks, a thick forest: palm trees near the beach and then, rising toward the mountains, thick groves of pine, oak, and strawberry trees. It's bliss just to look at them. And, on the highest peak in the world, an extremely high mountain crowned with snow, dominating the universe and exempted — I dare say it — from the furies of the universal flood. I have reached — can there be any doubt? — Paradise.

Is this what I wanted to find? I know my plan was to reach China and Japan. I always said that in the end we discover what we first imagine. So getting to Asia was only a metaphor for my will, or, if you prefer, of my sensuality. From the cradle, I had a carnal impression of the round-ness of the earth. My mother had two glorious breasts that I was so good at sucking that they quickly ran dry. She said she preferred washing and hanging out sheets to feeding such a voracious baby. One after another: that's how my Italian wet nurses came, each one milkier, rounder, than her predecessor, enjoyable, with their breasts capped off with delicious tips which for me came to represent, clearly, my vision of the world. Breast after breast, milk after milk, my eyes and my lips overflowed with the vision and savor of the globe.

First consequence: I always viewed the world as a pear, very round except where it comes to a point, where it is highest. Or like a very round ball, but, instead of a ball, like a woman's breast, with the nipple being the highest part and closest to heaven.

Second consequence: If someone told me I was insane and that an egg can't stand on its end, I would win the argument by smashing one end of the egg and standing it up. But my mind, in reality, was thinking about biting a nipple until the breast was empty of milk, until the wet nurse shrieked. In pleasure or in pain?

I'll never know.

That childhood of mine had a third consequence I'd better confess   10
right now. We Genoese are not taken very seriously. In Italy, there are different levels of seriousness. The Florentines give us Genoese no cre-dence. Of course, they see themselves as a nation of sober, calculating people with a good head for business. But the citizens of Ferrara view the Florentines as sordid, sinister, avaricious, full of deceit and tricks they use to get what they want and justify themselves in some fashion. The people of Ferrara prefer to be fixed and aristocratic, like classical medals and just as immutable and refined. Because they are (or feel) so superior, they do nothing to betray the image of their nobility and quickly fall into despair and suicide.

So, if the Ferrarese scorn the Florentines, and the Florentines scorn the Genoese, there's nothing left for us to do but despise the loud-mouthed, scummy, frivolous Neapolitans, who, in turn, have no way out but to heap filth on the sinister, murderous, dishonest Sicilians.

I want the readers of this diary, which I will soon toss into the sea, to understand what I've just said so that they will also understand my dramatic decision. A man of my country and my era had to suffer as many humiliations as he inflicted on others. As a Genoese, I was considered a visionary and a fraud in every court in Europe to which I brought my knowledge of navigation and my theories about the planet's mammary circumference. Fast-talking and proud, more full of fantasy than facts. That's how I was treated, whether in Paris, Rome, London, or the ports of the Hanseatic League. That's how Ferdinand and Isabella — I was told by the ubiquitous gossips — talked about me after my first visit. Which is why I moved to Lisbon: All the adventurers, dreamers, merchants, money-lenders, alchemists, and inventors of new worlds congregated in the Portuguese capital. There I could be one among many, be anything I wanted while I learned what I had to learn in order to embrace the round world, grab the universe by the teats, and suck its nipples until there wasn't a drop of milk left. I had a costly apprenticeship.

Yesterday I was approached by the first man I'd ever seen from these new lands. I was sleeping on the sand, exhausted by the last days of my voyage in the ship's boat, alone, guided only by my excellent knowledge of *the stars*. In my dream, actually a nightmare, appeared the terrible scenes of storms on the high seas, the despair of the sailors, scurvy, death, the mutiny, and finally the vile decision of the Pinzón brothers to return to Spain and abandon me in a boat with three casks of water, two bottles of spirits, a sack of seeds, and my trunk filled with curiosities: trumpery, red caps, and a secret compartment with paper, quill pens, and ink. They left me in dire straits: Yesterday I dreamed their toothless corpses passed by on a raft made of snakes.

I awaken, my lips covered with sand, like a second skin granted by the deepness of my sleep. First I see the sky and the fugitive procession of ravens and ducks, instantly blocked out by the circle of faces the color of the natives of the Canary Islands. They speak like birds, in a singsong, high-pitched language, and when they rise to take me by the armpits and stand me up, they reveal themselves totally naked before me.

They gave me water and led me to tentlike buildings where they gave me food I didn't recognize and let me rest.

Over the course of the following days, cared for and protected by these people, I regained my strength. I was amazed by these men and women unsullied by the evil of war, naked, very gentle, and without weapons. Their lands were extremely fertile and very well watered.

They led peaceful, happy lives. They slept in beds that swayed back and forth like cotton nets. They strolled through their villages carrying smoking coals they sucked with as great satisfaction as I had sucked breasts. They made very beautiful dugouts ninety-five palms long out of a single trunk that carried as many as one hundred and fifty people, and thus they communicated with other islands and the mainland, which they soon brought me to see.

Yes, I had reached Paradise, and I had only one problem: Should I communicate this discovery to my illustrious European patrons or not? Should I remain silent or announce my feat?

I wrote the appropriate letters so the astonished world would honor me and the monarchs of Europe would bow at my great deed. What lies didn't I tell? I knew the mercantile ambition and the boundless greed of my continent and the rest of the world, so I described lands full of gold and spices and mastic and rhubarb. After all, these discovery companies, whether English, Dutch, Spanish, or Portuguese, were paid to put salt and pepper on the tables of Europe. So I wrote that gold nuggets may be gathered like grains of wheat. King Solomon's mountains of gold are to be found here, safe from the waters of the flood, tall and resplendent, as if they were the breasts of creation.

Also, I was not ignorant of my contemporaries' need for fable, the metallic wrapping that would disguise and make palatable their lust for gold. Gold, yes, but hidden in deep mines by cannibals and fierce beasts. Pearls as well, but revealed by the song of sirens, sirens with three breasts — three. Transparent seas, but plied by sharks with two phalluses — folding phalluses. Prodigious islands, defended by amazons who receive men only once a year, who allow themselves to be made pregnant and each nine months send the male children back to their fathers, keeping only the girl children. Implacable with themselves, they cut off one breast, the better to shoot their arrows.

Now, I must admit that both my mythical outlandishness and my 20
very solid appreciation of the nobility of these savages masked the most painful experience of my life. Twenty years ago, I joined a Portuguese expedition to Africa, which turned out to be an infamous business of capturing blacks and then selling them. No one had ever seen greater cynicism. The black kings of the ivory coasts would hunt down and capture their own subjects, accusing them of rebellion and desertion. They would hand them over to Christian clergymen who would convert them and save their souls. The clergymen, in turn, would entrust them

to the kind care of the Portuguese slavers, who were to teach them trades and transport them to Europe.

I saw them sail from the ports of the Gulf of Guinea, where the Portuguese traders would arrive with shiploads of merchandise for the African kings, to exchange for their enslaved population — redeemed of course, by religion. The ships would empty of silks, percales, thrones, dishes, mirrors, views of the Ile de France, missals, and chamber pots; they would fill up with husbands separated from their wives — the women sent one place, the men elsewhere, their children similarly divided, and all thrown into crowded cargo holds with no place to move around, forced to shit and piss on top of one another, to touch only what was near them and to speak to others, mortally embracing them, who understood nothing. Has there ever been a race more humiliated, despised, subjected to the pure whim of cruelty than they?

I saw the ships sail out of the Gulf of Guinea, and now, here in my New World, I swore it would never happen again.

This was like the Golden Age the ancients evoke, which is how I recited it to my new friends from Antilia, who listened to me without understanding. After all, I was describing them and their time: first came the Golden Age, when man governed himself with uncorrupted reason and constantly sought the good. Not forced by punishment, not spurred on by fear, man used simple words and possessed a sincere soul. There was no need for law where there was no oppressor, no need for judges or courts. Or battlements, or trumpets, or swords to be forged, because everyone was ignorant of these two words: *yours* and *mine.*

Was it inevitable that the Iron Age come? Could I put it off? For how long?

I had reached the Golden Age. I embraced the noble savage. Was I   25 going to reveal his existence to Europeans? Was I going to deliver these sweet, naked people, devoid of malice, to slavery and death?

I decided to be silent and to stay among them for several reasons, using several strategies. I don't want the reader to think he's dealing with a fool: We Genoese may be liars but we aren't idiots.

I opened my trunk and found the hats and beads. It gave me pleasure to give them to my hosts, who enjoyed themselves immensely with the trinkets. But I asked myself: If my intention was to reach the court of the grand khan in Peking and the fabulous empire of Japan, whom did I think I was going to impress with this junk I picked up in the Puerto de Santa María market? The Chinese and the Japanese would have laughed at me. So, within my mammary, unconscious zone, I knew the truth: I would never reach Cathay because I didn't really want to reach

Cathay; I wanted to get to Paradise, and in Eden the only wealth is nakedness and unawareness. Perhaps that was my real dream. I carried it through. Now I would have to protect it.

I was helped by the most ironclad law of Portuguese navigation, the law of secrecy. The sailors who left Lisbon and Sagres had imposed a policy of secrecy at all costs, ordered by their Sebastianist, utopian monarchs. Any Portuguese captain (to say nothing of common sailors) who revealed the routes or the places they'd discovered would be hunted to the ends of the earth and, when found (which they would be, don't doubt it for a second), would be drawn and quartered. The heads, feet, and hands of traitors had been seen all along Portuguese routes, from Cape Verde to the Cape of Good Hope, from Mozambique to Macao. The Portuguese were implacable: If they encountered ships intruding in their sea-lanes, they had standing orders to sink them immediately.

I am availing myself of that absolute silence. I turn it inside out like a glove and use it for my own advantage. Absolute silence. Eternal secrecy. What became of the talkative, fantastical Genoese? Where did he really come from? Why, if he was Italian, did he write only in Spanish? But why doubt he was Italian when he himself (that is, I myself) wrote: I am a foreigner. But what did it mean in those days to be a foreigner? A Genoese was a foreigner to a Neapolitan, as was an Andalusian to a Catalan.

As if I had foreseen my destiny, I sowed minuscule confusions. In   30
Pontevedra, I left a false archive to drive the Galicians insane. No matter, their heads are a muddle of realism and fantasy. On the other hand, in Estremadura, where they never dream, I convinced people that I grew up in Plasencia, when in fact it was Piacenza. As for Majorca and Catalunia, well, I gave them the flesh of my flesh: my last name, that of the Holy Spirit, which abounds on those coasts. Corsica, which as yet produced no man of note, could claim me because of a lie I told to two drunken abbots when I passed through Bastia.

I fooled no one. The only thing about myself I put down in writing clearly is this:

> At a very tender age, I became a seafarer and have continued to be one until this very day. . . . For more than forty years I have been doing this work. Everything that until today has been sailed I have sailed; everywhere I have traveled. I have had business and conversation with wise folk, churchmen and laymen, Latins and Greeks, Jews and Moors, and with many others of other sects.
> My country is the sea.

▼ ▼ ▼

I threw the bottle with its pages of legend into the sea — all the lies about sirens and amazons, gold and pearls, leviathans and sharks. But I also told the truth about rivers and coasts, mountains and forests, arable land, fruit and fish, the noble beauty of the people, the existence of Paradise.

I disguised it in a name I heard here and created a special identity for it. The name was Antilia. The identity was intermittence; that is, the isle of Antilia would appear and disappear. One day, the sun would reveal it; the next, the mists would blot it out. It floated one day and sank the next. A tangible mirage, a fleeting reality between sleep and wakefulness, this land of Antilia was only visible, ultimately, for those who, like me as a child, could imagine it first.

I tossed the bottle with the legend into the sea, certain that no one would ever find it. If someone did, he would read in it the ravings of a madman. Led by my sweet friends to the place that would be my permanent residence, I told myself a truth that only now I can put on record.

This was the place: a freshwater gulf into which seven rivers emptied, 35 overwhelming the salt sea with their fresh force. A river is an eternal birth, renovation, perpetually renewed cleanliness and spirit, and the rivers of Antilia flowed into the gulf with a delightful, constant noise that dispelled the clamor of the Mediterranean alleys with the din of their peddlers, children, doorkeepers, rogues, street surgeons, butchers, trinket sellers, knife sellers, oil sellers, tinkers, bakers, skinners, and barbers. It also banished the silence of the night and its fear. The silence of imminent death.

Here they assigned me a hut and a hammock (the name of their woven beds). A tender woman, eager to please. A canoe for my little trips, and two young oarsmen to accompany me. Plenty of food, dorados from the sea and trout from the river, deer and turkey, papaya and custard apples. Out of my sack I took orange seeds, and together we planted them along the valleys and hillsides of the Gulf of Paradise. The trees grew better in Antilia than in Andalusia, with shiny leaves and fragrant flowers. I never saw better oranges, oranges that so resembled the sun they made the sun envious. I finally had a garden of perfect breasts, suckable, edible, renewable. I had conquered my own life. I was the eternal owner of my recovered youth. I was a boy without shame or nostalgia of being one. I could suck oranges until I died.

That's right, paradise. So I stayed there, liberated above all from the horrible need to explain a different reality to Europeans, a history for them inexplicable. How could Europe understand that there is a history different from the one it made or learned? A second history? How will

Europeans accept that the present is not only the heir of the past but the origin of the future? What a hideous responsibility. No one could stand it. Especially me.

I would have enough trouble eliminating all the lies about me and admitting that I'm not Catalan, Galician, Majorcan, or Genoese. I am a Sephardic Jew whose family fled Spain because of the usual persecutions: one more, one of so many, not the first and not the last . . .

The reader of these notes dedicated to chance will no doubt understand the reasons behind my silence, my abstention, my staying in Antilia. I wanted to attribute the care with which I was treated to my personal charm or to my empathy with those who received me. I paid no attention to the rumors that transformed me into the protagonist of a divine legend. Me, a bearded white god? Me, punctually returning to see if mankind had taken care of the earth I'd given them? I remembered the breasts of my wet nurses and took a big bite out of the orange that's always at my side, perennially renewed, almost my scepter.

From the top of my high, whitewashed belvedere, I see the length 40 and breadth of the lands and the confluence of the rivers, the gulf, and the sea. Seven rivers flow down, some calm and others torrential (including one waterfall), to fill the gulf, which, in turn, gently opens on to a sea protected from its own rage by coral reefs. My white house, cooled by the trade winds, dominates the orange groves and is defended by dozens of laurels. Behind me, the mountains whisper their names: pine and cypress, oak and strawberry. Royal eagles perch on the white summits; butterflies descend like another waterfall, half gold, half rain; all the birds in the world meet in this immaculate air, from cranes, macaws, and owls wearing black glasses to those I identify more by their looks than by their names: birds like witches with black ears, birds that unfold what look like huge parasols, others dressed in the red of princes of the Church, others with plantlike throats, woodpeckers and squirrel birds, birds with red beaks and doves with short beaks, birds that sound like trumpets and others that sound like clocks, jacamars and ant-eating birds who live off the abundance of those they consume. The permanent cry of the caracara bird presides over all: my earthbound falcon that has never flown but which, dragging itself over the earth, devours waste and in so doing redeems life.

Beyond the visible life of my earthly paradise is what sustains it, the minutiae of invisible life. The richness of animal life is obvious, and the crow, the ocelot, the tapir, and the ounce mark their paths through the jungle or the forest clearly. They would get lost without the guidance of the living odors that are the routes of the silence and the night. The araguato monkey, the armadillo, the jaguar, and the iguana are all guided by millions of invisible organisms that purge the water and the air of their daily poisons, just as the caracara falcon does it right before our eyes. The aroma of the jungle is dispelled by millions of hidden little bodies that are like the invisible light of the forest.

They await the night to move around and learn things. We wait for the dawn. I look at the enormous, downy ears of the gray-brown wolf that comes up to my door every night. Blood rushes into those ears and allows heat to escape. It's the symbol of life in the tropics, where everything is arranged for living well, provided we want to prolong life and respect its natural flow. But everything turns against us the instant we show hostility and try to dominate nature by harming it. The men and women of my new world know how to care for the earth. I tell them that from time to time, which is why they venerate and protect me, even if I'm not God.

I compare this life with the one I left behind in Europe and shudder. Cities buried in garbage, redeemed from time to time by fire, but immediately drowned in soot. Cities with visible intestines, crowned with feces, along whose gutters flow pus and urine, menstrual blood and vomit, useless semen and dead cats. Cities without light, narrow, cramped, where everything wanders, ghostlike, or nods off like a succubus. Beggars, thieves, the insane, multitudes talking to themselves, skulking rats, runaway dogs that return in packs, migraines, fevers, vertigoes, tremors, hard volcanoes of blood between the legs and in the armpits, a black pattern on the skin: Forty days of abstinence did not prevent forty million deaths in Europe. The cities were depopulated. Bands of looters came in to steal our possessions, and animals took over our beds. Our eyeballs burst. Our people were accused of poisoning wells. We were expelled from Spain.

Now I live in Paradise.

For how long? Sometimes I think about my family, about my scat-   45
tered people. Do I also have a family, a wife, children here in this new world? Possibly. To live in Paradise is to live without consequences. My loves pass over my skin and my memory like water through a filter. What's left is more sensation than memory. It's as if time hadn't passed since I reached these lands and took up residence in the white mansion with the orange trees.

I cultivate my own garden. My most immediate sensual pleasures occur in the orange grove — I look, touch, peel, bite, and swallow. So do the oldest of sensations: my mother, wet nurses, breasts, the sphere, the world, the egg . . .

If I want my personal story to have a collective resonance, I'll have to go beyond the breast-orange to the two memory objects I've always borne with me. One is the key to the ancestral house of my forefathers in the Toledo ghetto. Expelled from Spain by persecution, we never lost the language of Castile or the key to our home. It's passed from hand to hand. It's never been a cold key despite being made of metal. Too many Jewish palms, fingers, and fingertips have fondled it.

The other thing is a prayer. We Sephardic Jews all travel with it and nail it to the door of our closets. I do the same thing in Antilia. I've improvised a clothing chest that holds, like mementos, my old doublet, my jerkin, and my breeches — my New World friends have taught me to wear linen, smooth and soft, white and airy: a shirt and trousers, sandals. To the chest I've nailed the prayer of the Jewish émigrés, which goes like this:

> Mother Spain, you have been cruel to your Israelite children. You have persecuted and expelled us. We have left behind our houses, our lands, but not our memories. Despite your cruelty, we love you, Spain, and we long to return to you. One day you will receive your wandering children, you will open your arms to them, ask their forgiveness, and recognize our fidelity to your land. We shall return to our houses. This is the key. This is the prayer.

I recite it, and, almost like a satisfied desire, a memory returns to me of my disastrous arrival, shrieking like a caracara bird. I am sitting on my balcony at the first hour, doing what I do best: contemplating. The earliest breezes are blowing. The only thing missing is the sound of nightingales. I have recited the prayer of the Sephardic return to Spain. I don't know why, but I'm thinking about something that never worries me because I'm so used to it. Antilia is a land that appears and disappears periodically. I haven't discovered the laws that govern this mutability, and I prefer not knowing them. I'm afraid that knowing the calendar of appearances and disappearances would be something like knowing the date of our death beforehand.

I prefer doing what nature and the real time of life ordain. Contemplation and enjoyment. But this morning, surprisingly, a white bird flies by carrying the stalk of a bulrush, the kind of bird sailors see with pleasure because it doesn't sleep at sea; it's a sign land is near. The trade winds blow and the sea is as flat as a river. Crows, ducks, and a gannet pass over, fleeing to the southeast. Their haste alarms me. In a rare gesture, I stand up with a start as I see a kite floating high in the sky — a bird that makes gannets and other birds of prey vomit up their food and then eats it. It's a seabird, but doesn't land on the water, and never goes farther than twenty leagues out to sea.

I realize I'm looking at an event from the past. This is what I saw when I first arrived here. I try to dismiss this mirage and see what's happening today, but I can't distinguish between the two events. Another bird becomes visible in the sky. It comes closer, first barely a dot, then a brilliant star, so brilliant that it blinds me when I compare it to the sun. The bird descends toward the gulf. From its belly emerge two feet as huge as canoes, and, with a horrifying grunt that silences the terrified shrieking of the caracara, it settles on the water, raising a cloud of foam. ·

Everything becomes calm. The bird has doors and windows. It's an air house. A combination of Noah's ark and the Pegasus of mythology. The door opens and there appears, smiling, with teeth whose shine darkens that of the sun and of metal, a yellow man, just as my predecessor Marco Polo describes them. He's wearing glasses that add to the glare and is dressed in a strange fashion: He carries a small black case in one hand and wears crocodile-skin shoes.

He bows, boards a roaring boat lowered from the flying ship, and comes toward me.

Nothing surprises me. From the beginning, I disabused those who wanted to see in me a kind of garrulous, ignorant sailor. God gave me intelligence, and it flourished in the sailing world; of astrology it gave me a sufficiency, as it did of geometry and arithmetic; and ingenuity enough in my soul to draw spheres, and within them the cities, rivers, mountains, islands, and ports — all in their proper place.

Even if I possess these talents, I've grieved deeply (while never admit-   55 ting it) because I suspect I never reached Japan, as I'd wanted, but a new land. As a man of science, I had to confess its existence; as a political man, I had to deny it. Which is what I did, but that fatal morning in my story, when the small man in the light-gray suit as brilliant as the bird that brought him to me, with his black leather case in his hand and his crocodile shoes, smiled and introduced himself, I discovered the horrible truth: I hadn't reached Japan. Japan had reached me.

Surrounded by six people, four men and two women, who worked all sorts of contraptions, compasses perhaps, hourglasses, calipers, or chastity belts for all I knew, and who pointed disrespectfully at my face and voice, my visitor introduced himself simply as Mister Nomura.

His argument was direct, clear, and simple:

"We've been attentively and admiringly observing your custodianship of these Lands. Thanks to you, the world possesses an immaculate reserve of rivers, forests, flora and fauna, pristine beaches and uncon-

taminated fish. Congratulations, Cristóbal-san. We have respected your
isolation for a long time. Today the moment for you to share Paradise
with the rest of humanity has come."

"How did you find out . . . ?" I stammered.

"You did not reach Japan, but your bottle stuffed with manuscripts   60
did. We are patient. We've been waiting for the right moment. Your
Paradise — do you see? — would appear and disappear very frequently.
Expeditions sent out in the past never returned. We had to wait for a
long time, until we perfected the technology that would fix the presence of what we agreed to call the New World, locate it permanently,
despite its random, ultimately deceptive movements, despite the appearances and disappearances. I'm talking about radar, laser, ultra-
sound . . . I'm talking about high-definition screens."

"What is it you want?" I managed to say, in spite of my growing confusion.

"Your collaboration, Colombo-san. Be a team player. We only work
in teams. Cooperate and everything will turn out fine. Wa! Wa! Wa!
Conformity, Don Cristóbal," he said, prancing a bit and then standing
on tiptoe.

He smiled and sighed. "We meet at last. Well, better late than
never."

I signed more papers than I had during the Santa Fe capitulations
with Ferdinand and Isabella. Nomura and his army of Japanese lawyers
(the gulf filled up with yachts, ketches, and hydroplanes) forced me to
cede the beaches of Antilia to the Meiji Company which in turn sub-
contracted their development to the Amaterasu Company which in
turn ceded construction of hotels to the Minamoto Corporation which
contracted to buy tablecloths from Murasaki Designs, all towel-related
items from the Mishima Group, and soaps and perfumes from the
Tanizaki Agency, while foodstuffs would be supplied by Akutagawa Associates in combination with the Endo Group insofar as imported products were concerned and with the Obe Group insofar as domestic products were concerned, all of which would be processed on the island by
the Mizoguchi Corporation and transported to the hotels by Kurosawa
Transport Corporation. All of it would be procured by local employees
(what term do you think we should use for them: "aborigines," "natives," "indigenous peoples," "Antilleans"? We wouldn't want to hurt
anyone's feelings) who will prosper with the influx of tourists,
Columbus-san, and see their standard of living go through the roof. We
need tourist guides, drivers, bus lines, car rental agencies, pink jeeps,
and pleasure boats for the hotel guests. Which in turn will require high-

ways and everything tourists need strung out along them: motels, pizzerias, gas stations, and recognizable trademarks to make them feel at home, because tourists — it's the first thing you should know as Admiral of the Ocean Sea and president of the Paradise Administrative Council, Inc. — travel to feel they haven't left home.

He offered me some bitter tea: "Accordingly, we've given conces- 65 sions to very familiar trademarks. You should sign — right here, if you don't mind — private contracts with each one to avoid difficulties that might arise out of the antimonopoly law of the European Economic Community, which, I add to relieve your conscience, would never have accepted something as greedy as the 1503 Casa de Contratación in Seville."

Dazed, I signed the various contracts, including clauses relating to fried chicken and soda water, gas stations, motels, pizzerias, ice cream parlors, picture magazines, cigarettes, tires, supermarkets, cameras, cars, yachts, musical instruments, and a list of etceteras longer than the list of titles belonging to the monarchs of Spain for whom I had embarked on my voyage of discovery.

I felt my new world had been covered over by a spiderweb and that I was the poor fly captured at the center, impotent, because, as I've already said, living in Paradise was living without consequences.

"Don't worry. Work with the team. Work with the corporation. Don't ask who is going to be the owner of all this. No one. Everyone. Trust us: Your natives are going to live better than they ever did. And the world will thank you for the Last, the Supreme, the Most Exclusive Resort on the Planet, the New World, the Enchanted Beach Where You and Your Children Can Leave Behind Pollution, Crime, Urban Decay, and Enjoy a Pure Earth, PARADISE INC."

I want to shorten this. The landscape is changing. Night and day, an acid smoke flows down my throat. My eyes tear, even when I smile at the hyperactive Mister Nomura, my protector, who has placed at my service a team of samurai who guard me against the people who have threatened me or organized unions and protests. Not long ago they were my friends.

"Remember, Don Cristóbal. We are a corporation for the twenty-first 70 century. Speed and agility are our norms. We avoid offices and bureaucracies; we have no buildings or staff; we rent everything, and that's it. And when reporters ask you questions about the real owner of Paradise Inc., just say: No one. Everyone. Team spirit, Cristóbal-san, company loyalty, yoga every morning, Valium every night . . ."

Nomura pointed out that, far from being a restricted place, Paradise Inc. was open to all nations. It's true: I felt nostalgia looking at the old flags I'd left behind as they arrived on the airships with a horde of tourists eager to enjoy our immaculate waters and our pure air, the whiteness of our beaches and the virginity of our forests. TAP, Air France, Iberia, Lufthansa, Alitalia, BA . . . The colors of their insignia reminded me, with sweet bitterness, of the courts I'd wandered through, begging support for my enterprise. Now they were like the coats of arms decorating a herd of Pegasus in the field of the Pleiades.

Thousands and thousands of tourists came, and on October 12, dressed in my fifteenth-century clothes, I was paraded around on a float brought from the Carnival of Nice, surrounded by naked Indians (male and female). Now, it's hardly worth saying, all my clothing comes from Banana Republic. No one bothers me. I'm an institution.

But my nose vainly tries to sniff the invisible highways of the night, when thousands of hidden organisms used to perfume the air to guide the tapir, the deer, the ocelot, and the ounce. But I don't hear them anymore, don't smell them either. Only my gray-brown fox with pointy ears stays close with me. The heat of the tropics escapes through those palpitating white ears. The two of us look toward the orange groves that surround us. I wish the fox would understand: the grove, the animal, and I are survivors . . .

They don't let anyone near me. They've forced me to become fearful. From time to time, I exchange glances with a lanky, dark-skinned Indian girl who fixes my pink-sheeted bed and waters the orchids before leaving. Her eyes are not only wary but hostile and something worse: resentful.

One night, the young Indian maid doesn't show up. Annoyed, I'm   75
just about to protest. I realize a change has taken place. I become intolerant, comfortable, old . . . I open the netting that protects my hammock (I've retained that delightful custom from my original astonishment) and find stretched out in it a slim young woman the color of honey: stiff as a pencil, only the swaying of the hammock softens her. She introduces herself with verbal and gestural intensity as Ute Pinkernail, native of Darmstadt, Germany. She tells me she's managed to sneak in by taking the maid's place, that I'm very protected and don't know the truth. She stretches out her arms, wraps them around me, and whispers breathlessly, nervously into my ear: "There are six billion people on the planet, the big cities in the East and the West are about to disappear. Asphyxiation, garbage, and plague are burying them. They've fooled you. Your paradise is the last sewer for our narrow, packed, beggarly cities without light, without roofs, through which wan-

der thieves, madmen, crowds that talk to themselves, skulking rats, dogs in savage packs, migraines, fevers, vertigoes: a city in ruins, submerged in its own sewage, for the majority; for the smallest minority, there is another inaccessible city on the heights. Your island is the last sewer, you've carried out your destiny, you've enslaved and exterminated your people . . ."

She was unable to go on. The samurai came in shouting, jumping, brandishing submachine guns, violently pulling me away. My veranda was shrouded in dust and noise; everything was bathed in white light, and in one vast, simultaneous instant, the flamethrowers burned up my orange grove, a bayonet pierced the heart of my trained wolf, and Ute Pinkernail's breasts appeared before my astonished, desiring eyes. The girl's blood dripped through the weaving in the hammock . . .

To live in paradise is to live without consequences. Now I know I'm going to die, and ask permission to return to Spain. First, Mr. Nomura berated me: "You didn't act like a member of the team, Cristóbal-san. Well, what did you think, that you were going to be able to keep your paradise away from the laws of progress forever? You've got to realize that by preserving a paradise you were only magnifying a universal desire to invade it and enjoy it. Try to understand once and for all: There is no paradise without a Jacuzzi, champagne, a Porsche, and a discotheque. No paradise without french fries, hamburgers, sodas, and Neapolitan pizza. Something for everyone. You can't go around believing in the symbolism of your name, 'Christ-bearer, dove of the Holy Spirit.' Come back, fly away little dove, and carry your message: Sayonara, Christ; Paradise, Banzai! Wa! Wa! Wa! Conformity! The nail that sticks out will soon be hammered down."

On the Iberia flight, I'm treated like what I am, a venerable relic: Cristóbal Colón returning to Spain after a five-hundred-year absence. I'd lost all notion of time and space. Now, up in the sky, I recover them. Oh, how I enjoy seeing from up here the trace of my first voyage — in reverse: the oak-covered hills, the strawberry trees, the incredibly fertile soil all under cultivation, the canoes plying the gulf into which seven rivers empty, one of them in a smooth, milk-colored cascade. I look at the sea and the sirens, the leviathans and the amazons shooting their arrows at the sun. And flying over my burned-out orchard, I begin to sense the beaches with shit tides, bloody rags, flies and rats, the acrid sky, and the poisoned water. Will they put the blame for all this on the Jews and the Arabs before expelling them or exterminating them again?

I observe the flight of ducks and ravens, and I feel that our own ship is pushed along by soft trade winds on a variable sea — here it's as

smooth as glass; there, when we're anchored in the sargasso, it's sometimes as stormy as it was in the worst moments of the first voyage. I fly
near the stars and yet I see only one constellation as night falls. It's
made up of Ute Pinkernail's magnificent breasts, the teats I was never to
touch . . .

They serve me Freixenet champagne and they give me the magazine   80
Hola to read. I don't get the drift of the articles. They don't mean anything to me. I'm on my way back to Spain. I'm going home. In each
hand I carry the proof of my origin. In one hand, I clutch the orange
seeds. I want this fruit to survive the implacable exploitation of the island. In the other, I carry the frozen key to my ancestral home in
Toledo. I'll go back there to die: a stone house with a sagging roof, a
door made of creaking boards that hasn't been opened since the time of
my ancestors, the Jews expelled by pogroms and plagues, fear and
death, lies and hatred . . .

I silently recite the prayer nailed to my chest like a scapulary. I recite
it in the language the Jews of Spain kept alive during all eternity, so we
would not renounce our home and house:

> You, beloved Spain, we call Mother, and during all our lives we will not
> abandon your sweet language. Even though you exiled us like a step-
> mother from your breast, we will not cease to love you as a most holy
> land, the land where our fathers left their families buried and the ashes
> of thousands of their loved ones. For you we save our filial love, glorious
> nation; therefore we send you our glorious greeting.

I repeat the prayer, I squeeze the key, I caress the seeds, and I give
myself up to a vast sleep over the sea where time circulates like the currents, uniting and relating everything, yesterday's conquistadors and
today's, reconquests and counterconquests, besieged paradises, pinna-
cles and decadences, arrivals and departures, appearances and disappearances, utopias of memory and desire . . . The constant element in
this going back and forth is the painful movement of peoples, immigration, escape, hope, yesterday and today.

What shall I find when I return to Spain?

I shall open the door of my home again.

I shall plant the orange seed again.   85

EXPLORATIONS

1. What do you think are the meanings to Fuentes's title, "The Two Americas"?

2. What evidence in this story reveals the narrator's identity? What connections does Fuentes make between the narrator's name and his role in the story?

3. At what points do oranges (fruit, trees, seeds) appear in "The Two Americas"? What is their significance at each point?

CONNECTIONS

1. Disguises and pretending are central to both "The Two Americas" and "The Day We Were Dogs" (p. 93). How are they important in each story? What common results do they have in both stories?

2. What events and statements in "The Two Americas" are examples of points made by the Argentinian writer Julio Cortázar on page 3?

3. What events and statements in "The Two Americas" are examples of points made by the Peruvian writer Mario Vargas Llosa on page 4?

RICHARD RODRIGUEZ

Mexico's Children

Much of Richard Rodriguez's writing centers on the contrasts and contradictions of growing up in California as the son of Mexican immigrants. Born in San Francisco in 1944, he was called Ricardo and spoke only Spanish until he entered school. His parents were committed to his education despite the distance it put between him and them. With their support, Rodriguez went from private Roman Catholic schools in Sacramento to Stanford University, graduating in 1967; he received his M.A. from Columbia University, did graduate work at the University of California at Berkeley, and won a Fulbright fellowship to the Warburg Institute in London in 1972–1973. He turned down several teaching offers and held assorted jobs before settling into writing as a full-time occupation. Personal experience has made him skeptical of bilingual education and affirmative action policies, two of the many subjects he has addressed in his magazine features, essays for "The NewsHour" on PBS, and two memoirs. *Hunger of Memory: The Education of Richard Rodriguez* won critical praise in 1982; "Mexico's Children" comes from the chapter by that name in *Days of Obligation: An Argument with My Mexican Father* (1992). Rodriguez is also an associate editor with the Pacific News Service and a contributing editor for *Harper's* and the *Los Angeles Times*. He lives in San Francisco.

When I was a boy it was still possible for Mexican farmworkers in California to commute between the past and the future.

The past returned every October. The white sky clarified to blue and fog opened white fissures in the landscape.

After the tomatoes and the melons and the grapes had been picked, it was time for Mexicans to load up their cars and head back into Mexico for the winter.

The schoolteacher said aloud to my mother what a shame it was the Mexicans did that — took their children out of school.

Like wandering Jews, Mexicans had no true home but the tabernacle   5
of memory.

The schoolteacher was scandalized by what she took as the Mexicans' disregard of their children's future. The children failed their tests. They made no friends. What did it matter? Come November, they would be gone to some bright world that smelled like the cafeteria on Thursdays — Bean Days. Next spring they would be enrolled in some other school, in some other Valley town.

The schoolroom myth of America described an ocean — immigrants leaving behind several time zones and all the names for things.

Mexican-American memory described proximity. There are large Mexican-American populations in Seattle and Chicago and Kansas City, but the majority of Mexican-Americans live, where most have always lived, in the Southwestern United States, one or two hours from Mexico, which is within the possibility of recourse to Mexico or within the sound of her voice.

My father knew men in Sacramento who had walked up from Mexico.

There is confluence of earth. The cut of the land or its fold, the   10
bleaching sky, the swath of the wind, the length of shadows — all these suggested Mexico. Mitigated was the sense of dislocation otherwise familiar to immigrant experience.

By November the fog would thicken, the roads would be dangerous. Better to be off by late October. Families in old trucks and cars headed south down two-lane highways, past browning fields. Rolls of toilet paper streaming from rolled-down windows. After submitting themselves to the vegetable cycle of California for a season, these Mexicans were free. They were Mexicans! And what better thing to be?

HAIIII-EEE. HAI. HAI. HAI.

There is confluence of history.

Cities, rivers, mountains retain Spanish names. California was once Mexico.

The fog closes in, condenses, and drips day and night from the bare   15
limbs of trees. And my mother looks out the kitchen window and cannot see the neighbor's house.

Amnesia fixes the American regard of the past. I remember a graduate student at Columbia University during the Vietnam years; she might have been an ingenue out of Henry James. "After Vietnam, I'll never again believe that America is the good and pure country I once thought it to be," the young woman said.

Whereas Mexican-Americans have paid a price for the clarity of their past.

Consider my father: When he decided to apply for American citizenship, my father told no one, none of his friends, those men with whom he had come to this country looking for work. American citizenship would have seemed a betrayal of Mexico, a sin against memory. One afternoon, like a man with something to hide, my father slipped away. He went downtown to the Federal Building in Sacramento and disappeared into America.

Now memory takes her revenge on the son.

VETE PERO NO ME OLVIDES.   20

Go, but do not forget me, someone has written on the side of a building near the border in Tijuana.

Mexicans may know their souls are imperiled in America but they do not recognize the risk by its proper name.

Two Mexican teenagers say they are going to *los Estados Unidos* for a job. Nothing more.

For three or four generations now, Mexican villages have lived under the rumor of America, a rumor vaguer than paradise. America exists in thousands of maternal prayers and in thousands of pubescent dreams. Everyone knows someone who has been. Everyone knows someone who never came back.

What do you expect to find?   25

The answer is always an explanation for the journey: "I want money enough to be able to return to live with my family in Mexico."

Proofs of America's existence abound in Mexican villages — stereo equipment, for example, or broken-down cars — but these are things Americans picked up or put down, not America.

Mexicans know very little of the United States, though they have seen America, the TV show, and America, the movie. Mexico's preeminent poet, Octavio Paz, writes of the United States as an idea of no characteristic mansion or spice. Paz has traveled and taught in America, but his writings relegate America to ineluctability — a jut of optimism, an aerodynamic law.

To enter America, which is invisible, Mexicans must become invisible. Tonight, a summer night, 500 Mexicans will become invisible at 8:34 P.M. While they wait, they do not discuss Tom Paine or Thomas Jefferson or the Bill of Rights. Someone has an uncle in Los Angeles who knows a peach farmer near Tracy who always hires this time of year.

Compared with pulpy Mexico, grave Mexico, sandstone Mexico,   30
which takes the impression of time, the United States and its promise of the future must seem always hypothetical — occasion more than place.

I once had occasion to ask a middle-class Mexican what he admires about the United States (a provocative question because, according to Mexican history and proverb, there is nothing about the United States to admire). He found only one disembodied word: "organization."

When I pressed the man to anthropomorphize further he said, "Deliveries get made, phones are answered, brakes are repaired" (indirect constructions all, as if by the consent of unseen hands).

Coming from Mexico, a country that is so thoroughly *there*, where things are not necessarily different from when your father was your age, Mexicans are unable to puncture the abstraction. For Mexicans, even death is less abstract than America.

Mexican teenagers waiting along the levee in Tijuana are bound to be fooled by the United States because they do not yet realize the future will be as binding as the past. The American job will introduce the Mexican to an industry, an optimism, a solitude nowhere described in Mexico's theology.

How can two Mexican teenagers know this, clutching the paper bags their mamas packed for them this morning? The past is already the future, for the bags contain only a change of underwear. These two may have seen "Dallas" on TV and they may think they are privy to the logic and locution of America. But that is not the same thing as having twenty American dollars in their own pockets.

Mexico, mad mother. She still does not know what to make of our   35
leaving. For most of this century Mexico has seen her children flee the house of memory. During the Revolution 10 percent of the population picked up and moved to the United States; in the decades following the Revolution, Mexico has watched many more of her children cast their lots with the future; head north for work, for wages; north for life. Bad enough that so many left, worse that so many left her for the gringo.

America wanted cheap labor. American contractors reached down into Mexico for men to build America. Sons followed fathers north. It became a rite of passage for the poor Mexican male.

I will send for you or I will come home rich.

I would see them downtown on Sundays — men my age drunk in Plaza Park. I was still a boy at sixteen, but I was an American. At sixteen, I wrote a gossip column, "The Watchful Eye," for my school paper.

Or they would come into town on Monday nights for the wrestling matches or on Tuesday nights for boxing. They worked on ranches over in Yolo County. They were men with time on their hands. They were men without women. They were Mexicans without Mexico.

On Saturdays, Mexican men flooded the Western Union office,   40
where they sent money — money turned into humming wire and then turned back into money — all the way down into Mexico. America was a monastery. America was a vow of poverty. They kept themselves poor for Mexico.

Fidel, the janitor at church, lived over the garage at the rectory. Fidel spoke Spanish and was Mexican. He had a wife down there, people said; some said he had grown children. But too many years had passed and he didn't go back. Fidel had to do for himself. Fidel had a clean piece of linoleum on the floor; he had an iron bed; he had a table and a chair; he had a frying pan and a knife and a fork and a spoon. Everything else Fidel sent back to Mexico. Sometimes, on summer nights, I would see his head through the bars of the little window over the garage of the rectory.

My parents left Mexico in the twenties: she as a girl with her family; he as a young man, alone. To tell different stories. Two Mexicos. At some celebration — we went to so many when I was a boy — a man in the crowd filled his lungs with American air to crow over all, ¡VIVA MEXICO! Everyone cheered. My parents cheered. The band played louder. Why VIVA MEXICO? The country that had betrayed them? The country that had forced them to live elsewhere?

I remember standing in the doorway of my parents' empty bedroom.

Mexico was memory — not mine. Mexico was mysteriously both he and she, like this, like my parents' bed. And over my parents' bed floated the Virgin of Guadalupe in a dimestore frame. In its most potent guise, Mexico was a mother like this queen. Her lips curved like a little boat. *Tú. Tú.* The suspirate vowel. *Tú.* The ruby pendant. The lemon tree. The song of the dove. Breathed through the nose, perched on the lips.

Two voices, two pronouns were given me as a child, like good and   45
bad angels, like sweet and sour milks, like rank and clement weathers; one yielding, one austere.

In the sixteenth century, Spain bequeathed to Mexico two forms of address, two versions of "you": In Mexico there is *tú* and there is *usted*.

In Sacramento, California, everything outside our house was English, was "you" — hey you. My dog was you. My parents were you. The nuns were you. My best friend, my worst enemy was you. God was You.

Whereas the architecture of Mexico is the hardened shell of a Spanish distinction.

Treeless, open plazas abate at walls; walls yield to refreshment, to interior courtyards, to shuttered afternoons.

At the heart there is *tú* — the intimate voice — the familiar room in   50
a world full of rooms. *Tú* is the condition, not so much of knowing, as of being known; of being recognized. *Tú* belongs within the family. *Tú* is spoken to children and dogs, to priests; among lovers and drunken

friends; to servants; to statues; to the high court of heaven; to God Himself.

The shaded arcade yields once more to the plaza, to traffic and the light of day. *Usted*, the formal, the bloodless, the ornamental you, is spoken to the eyes of strangers. By servants to masters. *Usted* shows deference to propriety, to authority, to history. *Usted* is open to interpretation; therefore it is subject to corruption, a province of politicians. *Usted* is the language outside Eden.

In Mexico, one is most oneself in private. The very existence of *tú* must undermine the realm of *usted*. In America, one is most oneself in public.

In order to show you America I would have to take you out. I would take you to the restaurant — OPEN 24 HOURS — alongside a freeway, any freeway in the U.S.A. The waitress is a blond or a redhead — not the same color as her last job. She is divorced. Her eyebrows are jet-black migraines painted on, or relaxed, clownish domes of cinnamon brown. Morning and the bloom of youth are painted on her cheeks. She is at once antimaternal — the kind of woman you're not supposed to know — and supramaternal, the nurturer of lost boys.

She is the priestess of the short order, curator of the apple pie. She administers all the consolation of America. She has no illusions. She knows the score; she hands you the Bill of Rights printed on plastic, decorated with an heraldic tumble of French fries and drumsticks and steam.

Your table may yet be littered with bitten toast and spilled coffee and a dollar tip. Now you will see the greatness of America. As one complete gesture, the waitress pockets the tip, stacks dishes along one strong forearm, produces a damp rag soaked in lethe water, which she then passes over the Formica.   55

There! With that one swipe of the rag, the past has been obliterated. The Formica gleams like new. You can order anything you want.

If I were to show you Mexico, I would take you home; with the greatest reluctance I would take you home, where family snapshots crowd upon the mantel. For the Mexican, the past is firmly held from within. While outside, a few miles away in the American city, there is only loosening, unraveling; generations living apart. Old ladies living out their lives in fiercely flowered housedresses. Their sons are divorced; wear shorts, ride bikes; are not men, really; not really. Their granddaughters are not fresh, are not lovely or keen, are not even nice.

Seek the Mexican in the embrace of the family, where there is much noise. The family stands as a consolation, because in the certainty of generation there is protection against an uncertain future. At the center of this gravity the child is enshrined. He is not rock-a-bye baby at the very top of the family tree, as it is with American families. The child does not represent distance from the past, but reflux. She is not expected to fly away, to find herself. He is not expected to live his own life.

I will send for you or I will come home rich.

The culture of *tú* is guarded by the son, desired by the son, enforced by the son. Femininity is defined by the son as motherhood. Only a culture so cruel to the wife could sustain such a sentimental regard for *mamacita*. By contrast, much license is appropriated by the Mexican male. If the brother is taught to hover — he is guarding his sister's virginity — the adolescent male is otherwise, elsewhere, schooled in seduction. For the male as for the female, sexuality is expressed as parenthood. The male, by definition, is father. The husband is always a son.

It is not coincidental that American feminists have borrowed the Spanish word *macho* to name their American antithesis. But in English, the macho is publicly playful, boorish, counterdomestic. American macho is drag — the false type for the male — as Mae West is the false type for the female.

Machismo in Mexican Spanish is more akin to the Latin *gravitas*. The male is serious. The male provides. The Mexican male never abandons those who depend upon him. The male remembers.

Mexican *machismo*, like Mexican politics, needs its mise-en-scène. In fair Verona, in doublet and hose, it might yet play. The male code derives less from efficacy than from valor. *Machismo* is less an assertion of power or potency than it is a rite of chivalry.

The *macho* is not urbane Gilbert Roland or the good guy Lee Trevino; he is more like Bobby Chacon, the slight, leathery, middle-aged boxer, going twelve rounds the night after his wife commits suicide. The *macho* holds his own ground. There is sobriety in the male, and silence, too — a severe limit on emotional range. The male isn't weak. The male wins a Purple Heart or he turns wife beater. The male doesn't cry.

Men sing in Mexico. In song, the male can admit longing, pain, desire, weakness.

HAIII-EEEE.

A cry like a comet rises over the song. A cry like mock-weeping tickles the refrain of Mexican love songs. The cry is meant to encourage the balladeer — it is the raw edge of his sentiment. HAI-II-EEE. It is the man's sound. A ticklish arching of semen, a node wrung up a guitar string, until it bursts in a descending cascade of mockery. HAI. HAI.

HAI. The cry of the jackal under the moon, the whistle of the phallus, the maniacal song of the skull.

So it may well be Mama who first realizes the liberation of the American "you," the American pan-*usted*, the excalibur "I" which will deliver her from the Islamic cloister of Mexico. (*Tú*.)

EXPLORATIONS

1. What does Richard Rodriguez mean in his first sentence by "commute between the past and the future"? What does Rodriguez define as the past and why? What does he define as the future and why?

2. "Mexicans may know their souls are imperiled in America but they do not recognize the risk by its proper name" (para. 22). What is the risk Rodriguez refers to? What does he imply by calling it a risk to the soul?

3. How are the Spanish pronouns *tú* and *usted* used differently in Mexico? How does Rodriguez apply them to differences between Mexico and the United States?

CONNECTIONS

1. Which of Rodriguez's ideas about the United States match Carlos Fuentes's ideas about the modern world in "The Two Americas" (p. 100)? What qualities of the Antilia depicted by Fuentes also show up in Rodriguez's Mexico? Do you think Rodriguez's Mexico is more like Fuentes's Antilia before its discovery by the twentieth century, or after? Why?

2. Compare Rodriguez's view of the United States from Mexico with Margaret Atwood's view of the United States from Canada (p. 59). What ideas appear in both essays? What are the main differences?

3. What ideas about emigration from his homeland does Rodriguez share with James Baldwin in "The New Lost Generation" (p. 18)? Do you think Rodriguez considers the "Mexican teenagers waiting along the levee in Tijuana" (para. 33) to be part of a lost generation, as Baldwin uses the term? Why or why not?

INVESTIGATIONS

1. Susan Orlean in "Quinceañera" (p. 40), Octavio Paz in "The Art of the Fiesta" (p. 86), and Richard Rodriguez in "Mexico's Children" (p. 118) all mention the Virgin of Guadalupe. Using their references as a starting point,

find out more about Our Lady of Guadeloupe (as she is also called): Who she is, and how and why she became so important to Mexicans.

2. The headnote to this Spotlight quotes Octavio Paz: "Mexico is a bureaucratic state halfway between . . . democracy and dictatorship with a constitutional transfer of power, but also a president with absolute power and one-party rule." Investigate the history of Mexico's ruling political party, the Partido Revolucionario Institucional. Write an essay about the PRI's traditional power or its recent challenges from other parties, or both.

3. Paz's "The Art of the Fiesta" is excerpted from a longer essay, "The Day of the Dead" (*Dia de los Muertos*), which is the name of one of Mexico's best-known holidays and fiestas. Write an essay about this unique national celebration: its nature, history, symbolism, cultural role, local variations, counterparts in other countries, or all of these.

PART TWO

FAMILIES

Francine du Plessix Gray • Chang-Rae Lee • Frances Rose Besmer
Patricia Schroeder • Angela Davis • Anwar El-Sadat • Philip Roth
Susan C. McMillan • Paula Fomby • Judith Ortiz Cofer • Robert Bly
Ved Mehta • Norimitsu Onishi

MIRRORS: The United States

Louise Erdrich: *Foreword*
Henry Louis Gates Jr.: *Down to Cumberland*
Susan Cheever: *The Nanny Dilemma*
Nicholas Bromell: *Family Secrets*

WINDOWS: The World

Rigoberta Menchú: *Birth Ceremonies*
  (GUATEMALA)
Amos Oz: *If There Is Justice* (ISRAEL)
Frank McCourt: *Limerick Homecoming*
  (IRELAND)
Zlata Filipović: *Sarajevo Diary* (BOSNIA)

SPOTLIGHT: Japan

John David Morley: *Acquiring a Japanese
  Family*
Yukiko Tanaka: *Mothers' Children*
Kenzaburo Oe: *Japan, the Ambiguous, and
  Myself*
Kazuo Ishiguro: *A Family Supper*

What happened to the American family — the fraying effect of harassed working parents, the stranglehold of the media, the pressures of peer culture — is a theme much ranted about. Yet one aspect of what has happened has been overlooked: Kids . . . never seem to sit down to a proper meal at home anymore. This is not another pious harangue on "spiritual starvation"; this is about the fact that we may be witnessing the first generation in history that has not been required to participate in that primal rite of socialization, the family meal. The family meal is not only the core curriculum in the school of civilized discourse; it is also a set of protocols that curb our natural savagery and our animal greed, and cultivate a capacity for sharing and thoughtfulness.

— FRANCINE DU PLESSIX GRAY
The New Yorker, 1995

▼ ▼ ▼

My mother could whip up most anything, but during our first years of living in this country we ate only Korean foods. At my haranguelike behest, my mother set herself to learning how to cook exotic American dishes. . . . I was an insistent child, and, being my mother's firstborn, much too prized. . . . She reminded me daily that I was her sole son, her reason for living, and that if she were to lose me, either in body or spirit, she wished that God would mercifully smite her, strike her down like a weak branch.

In the traditional fashion, she was the house accountant, the maid, the launderer, the disciplinarian, the driver, the secretary, and, of course, the cook. She was also my first basketball coach. In South Korea, where girls' high-school basketball is a popular spectator sport, she had been a star, the point guard for the national high-school team that once won the all-Asia championships. . . .

It puzzled me how much she considered her own history to be immaterial, and if she never patently diminished herself, she was able to finesse a kind of self-removal by speaking of my father whenever she could.

— CHANG-RAE LEE
"Coming Home Again"
The New Yorker, 1995

▼ ▼ ▼

Foster parenting, like parenting one's own children, offers many valuable rewards, but monetary gain is not among them. . . . Providing room and board — three hots and a cot — is just for starters. Medical treatment for infections, lice, or delinquent immunizations plus shopping trips for clothes, a few toys, and favorite foods are immediate needs. Intangible requirements of patience and encouragement are just as important to help a child adjust to eating meals together at a table and sleeping alone in a bed. Food hoarding, biting, temper tantrums, and bed-wetting are common behaviors in dislocated children; depression is recognizable even in tiny babies. A place where the parents are neither drunk nor drugged, where a child is relieved of a surrogate parenting role, and where words rather than fists are used to satisfy wants and vent anger may indeed be safe and warm, but it may not feel at all like home. Once a child's initial anxieties are put to rest, other qualities — a sense of humor, freedom to talk and be listened to, interests in music, sports, or appropriate TV programs — can be nourished. . . .

Single parenthood, abandonment, sexual abuse, substance abuse, and violent behavior occur in all classes of our society; money, or lack of it, determines how these issues are handled. All parents whose children are placed in foster care have at least two things in common: poverty and failure. Among the poor, whatever genuine love and attachments may exist, they are often overwhelmed by the stigma of failure, notwithstanding the millions of dollars being spent on programs for "family reunification." . . . In our experience, few of the foster children who return to their own parents actually remain with them.

> — FRANCES ROSE BESMER
> "Foster Parenting: Something
> to Remember with Affection"
> *Mount Holyoke Alumnae Quarterly*, 1996

▼ ▼ ▼

Many people believe that those who "choose" to work don't deserve any assistance in their effort to balance work and family. They see the choice of working outside the home solely as a life-style decision and not as an economic issue. In fact, government statistics tell us that only one woman in ten will get through life with the option to decide whether she wants to work. The other nine will have to work. . . .

Modern-day economic realities have put pressures on the family that have not been levied on any other generation, and it is quite clear to me that the family unit is breaking down, in large part, because we don't give it any support. We do less than any other industrialized nation: In terms of tax breaks, we would do better raising thoroughbred dogs or horses than children.

> — PATRICIA SCHROEDER
> "From Star Wars to Child Care"
> *New Perspectives Quarterly*, 1990

▼ ▼ ▼

Much of the public debate in recent years about the breakdown of the African-American family has failed to acknowledge that the traditional nuclear family has never been the typical model of the black family. First of all, from the days of slavery to the present, both husband and wife have been compelled to work outside the home. Secondly, the predominant model in the African-American community has been the extended family, which has conferred important roles on grandmothers, grandfathers, aunts, uncles, and cousins. This expansive domestic environment has often been much healthier for the child and has functioned as a child-care system available to working parents.

The African-American family structure evolved out of the fusion of African extended-family traditions with the conditions imposed by slavery. During this era, the father was relegated to the negligible role of providing the "seed." In most cases, the name of the father was not even acknowledged but was subordinated to the mother's name. If, for example, the father's name was John, and the woman who bore his child was Mary, he would be called "Mary's John" — and his name would not even appear in the birth records. The slave family, as viewed by the slave owners, consisted solely of the mother and her children. This practice succeeded in annihilating the "family space" within which resistance to slavery could develop.

The slave community attempted to challenge this assault on the family by creating surrogate family members and by establishing naming practices which affirmed the place of the father, even though he was often sold away. The creativity with which African-American people improvised family connections is a cultural trait that has spanned the centuries.

– ANGELA DAVIS
"Child Care or Workfare"
New Perspectives Quarterly, 1990

▼ ▼ ▼

Everything made me happy in Mit Abul-Kum, my quiet village in the depths of the Nile Delta, even the cold water in the winter when we had to leave at dawn for the special canal that filled to overflowing for no more than two weeks, our "statutory" irrigation period, during which all land in the village had to be watered. . . . We worked together on one person's land for a whole day, then moved to another's, using any *tunbur* (Archimedean screw) that was available, regardless of who owned it. . . .

That kind of collective work — with and for other men, with no profit or any kind of individual reward in prospect — made me feel that I belonged not merely to my immediate family at home, or even to the big family of the village, but to something vaster and more significant: the land. It was that feeling that made me, on the way home at sunset, gaze at the evening scene with a rare warmth, recognizing an invisible bond of love and friendship with everything around me — the smoke rolling down the valley promising a delicious meal at the close of a village day, and a perfect calm and peace in the hearts of all.

That big, shady tree was made by God; He decreed it, and it came into being. These fresh green plants whose seeds we had ourselves sown could never have been there if God had not decreed it. This land on which I walked, the running water in the canal, indeed, everything around me was made by an overseeing God — a vast, mighty Being that watches and takes care of all, including me. Trees, seeds, and fruits were all, therefore, my fellows in existence; we all came out of the land and could never exist without it. The land is firm and tough, so all that belongs to it must be equally tough.

As these ideas floated in my young head, the echoes of a saying of my grandmother's became almost audible: "Nothing is as significant as your being a child of this land. Land is immortal, for it harbors the mysteries of creation."

– ANWAR EL-SADAT
In Search of Identity, 1977

▼ ▼ ▼

I knew only two boys in our neighborhood whose families were fatherless, and thought of them as no less blighted than the blind girl who attended our school for a while and had to be read to and shepherded everywhere. . . .

I knew no child whose family was divided by divorce. Outside of the movie magazines and the tabloid headlines, it didn't exist, certainly not among Jews like us. Jews didn't get divorced — not because divorce was forbidden by Jewish law but because that was the way they were. If Jewish fathers didn't come home drunk and beat their wives — and in our neighborhood, which was Jewry to me, I'd never heard of any who did — that too was because of the way they were. In our lore, the Jewish family was an inviolate haven against every form of menace, from personal isolation to gentile hostility. Regardless of internal friction and strife, it was assumed to be an indissoluble consolidation. *Hear, O Israel, the family is God, the family is One.*

Family indivisibility, the first commandment.

– PHILIP ROTH
The Facts, 1988

▼ ▼ ▼

131

While being married should certainly never be the sole qualifying factor in the ability to adopt, being unmarried should always be the sole disqualifying factor. The most basic, rudimentary instinct of any civilized society is to protect its young and to invest in the well-being of their future. By robbing a child of a two-gender upbringing, we are not only failing an individual child's future, but also failing to invest in the future of society.

> – SUSAN C. MCMILLAN
> "Neither Gays Nor Singles Should Adopt"
> *San Francisco Chronicle*, 1995

▼ ▼ ▼

The hardest part of having a gay mother was accepting homosexuality and all its consequences before I even knew what that involved. . . . I'm lucky to have been raised by people I genuinely like, and being a woman raised by women, I've not had the problems in relating to my parents that a man might have had. However, I've heard enough jokes and insults to know that people don't really believe the gay family exists in large numbers and turns out healthy, well-balanced children. It is time for society to expand the definition of family. While everyone can agree that the usual sit-com family is increasingly atypical, there is no description of what has evolved to replace it.

> – PAULA FOMBY
> "Why I'm Glad I Grew Up in a Gay Family"
> *Mother Jones*, 1991

▼ ▼ ▼

At three or four o'clock in the afternoon, the hour of *café con leche*, the women of my family gathered in Mamá's living room to speak of important things and to tell stories for the hundredth time, as if to each other, meant to be overheard by us young girls, their daughters. In Mamá's house (everyone called my grandmother Mamá) was a large parlor . . . furnished with several mahogany rocking chairs, acquired at the births of her children, and one intricately carved rocker that had passed down to Mamá at the death of her own mother. It was on these rockers that my mother, her sisters, and my grandmother sat on these afternoons of my childhood to tell their stories, teaching each other, and my cousin and me, what it was like to be a woman, more specifically, a Puerto Rican woman. They talked about life on the island, and life in *Los Nueva Yores*, their way of referring to the United States, from New York City to California: the other place, not home, all the same. They told real-life stories, though as I later learned, always embellishing them with a little or a lot of dramatic detail, and they told *cuentos*, the morality and cautionary tales told by the women in our family for generations: stories that became part of my subconscious as I grew up in two worlds, the tropical island and the cold city, and which would later surface in my dreams and in my poetry.

– JUDITH ORTIZ COFER
"*Casa:* A Partial Remembrance
of a Puerto Rican Childhood"
Silent Dancing, 1990

▼ ▼ ▼

Among the Hopis and other native Americans of the Southwest, the old men take the boy away at the age of twelve and bring him *down* into the all-male area of the kiva. He stays *down* there for six weeks, and does not see his mother again for a year and a half.

The fault of the nuclear family today isn't so much that it's crazy and full of double binds (that's true in communes and corporate offices too — in fact, in any group). The fault is that the old men outside the nuclear family no longer offer an effective way for the son to break his link with his parents without doing harm to himself.

The ancient societies believed that a boy becomes a man only through ritual and effort — only through the "active intervention of the older men". . . [who] welcome the younger man into the ancient, mythologized, instinctive male world.

– ROBERT BLY
Iron John, 1990

▼ ▼ ▼

Before we moved to Lahore, Daddyji had gone to Mussoorie, a hill station in the United Provinces, without telling us why he was going out of the Punjab. Now, several months after he made that trip, he gathered us around him in the drawing room at 11 Temple Road while Mamaji mysteriously hurried Sister Pom upstairs. He started talking as if we were all very small and he were conducting one of our "dinner-table-school" discussions. He said that by right and tradition the oldest daughter had to be given in marriage first, and that the ripe age for marriage was nineteen. He said that when a girl approached that age her parents, who had to take the initiative, made many inquiries and followed many leads. They investigated each young man and his family background, his relatives, his friends, his classmates, because it was important to know what kind of family the girl would be marrying into, what kind of company she would be expected to keep. . . . "That's why I said nothing to you children when I went to Mussoorie," he concluded. "I went to see a young man for Pom. She's already nineteen."

We were stunned. We have never really faced the idea that Sister Pom might get married and suddenly leave, I thought.

"We won't lose Pom, we'll get a new family member," Daddyji said, as if reading my thoughts.

Then all of us started talking at once. We wanted to know if Sister Pom had been told; if she'd agreed; whom she'd be marrying.

"Your mother has just taken Pom up to tell her," Daddyji said. "But she's a good girl. She will agree."

– VED MEHTA
The Ledge Between the Streams, 1982

▼ ▼ ▼

When Kathleen Kamatani married Robert DeMeulemeester this fall, their friends were somewhat startled when the Kamatani family yelled out the traditional Japanese cheer of "Banzai!" or "May you live 10,000 years!" Some of them had scarcely realized that Ms. Kamatani, who met her husband at the Columbia University Business School, was Japanese-American.

This made her mother, Fuji Kamatani, somewhat wistful since she had once sent her daughter to Japanese school in the hopes of imparting something lasting. But she was fully accepting of the marriage. All three of her daughters have married white men; intermarriage, she said, is simply a fact of life in Japanese-American culture, which has the highest intermarriage rate of any ethnic group in the country.

"Because we are not living in Japan, because we are living in America, we have accepted that our children will not marry Japanese," said Mrs. Kamatani, who was interned during World War II because of her ancestry. "As the second generation, being Japanese was the thing that held us together. Perhaps now there's nothing cohesive to hold us together any longer.". . .

After their release from the camps, Japanese-Americans were not permitted to return en masse to the West Coast towns that had been their homes. Instead, they fanned out across the country, and were discouraged by the Government from rebuilding their communities. . . .

Many Japanese-Americans agree that a positive legacy of the internment was to integrate them into mainstream American society, which contributed to the educational and professional achievements of the children of nisei. But the psychological scars were deep: Because their ancestry had singled them out and humiliated them, many nisei reacted by denying it. They did not teach their children Japanese, or send them to Saturday school, or even give them Japanese middle names. . . .

Today even most of the elderly do not speak Japanese. Instead, in many Japanese-American households, the use of Japanese is limited to a few words — like "nihongo," meaning the Japanese language, or "haku-jin," meaning "Caucasian" — sprinkled in English conversations.

– NORIMITSU ONISHI
"Japanese in America Looking
Beyond Past to Shape Future"
New York Times, 1995

EXPLORATIONS

1. Many of the observations you have just read mention "the breakdown of the family." What does this phrase mean? What causes do these commentators blame for the family's breakdown? How dangerous a problem do they think it is, and why?

2. Which commentators suggest that the two-parent nuclear family is not necessarily the best environment for bringing up children? What reasons do they give? Do you agree? Why or why not?

3. Anwar El-Sadat served as Egypt's president during a time of violent turmoil over Israel's right to exist on land that also was claimed by Palestinian Arabs. In both Sadat's childhood reminiscence (p. 130) and Philip Roth's comments about Jewish families (p. 131), what reasons are suggested for Middle Eastern Arabs' and Jews' resistance to giving up any land they regard as "theirs"?

4. How do the purposes and method of the induction ritual described by Robert Bly (p. 133) differ from those of the ritual described by Judith Ortiz Cofer (p. 132)? What similar functions are carried out by both rituals?

MIRRORS:
THE UNITED STATES

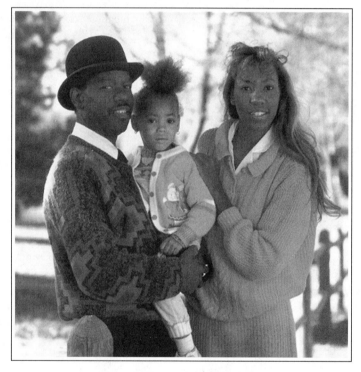

Families: *A young family enjoys a sunny day in the country.*

LOUISE ERDRICH

*Foreword**

The poet and novelist Karen Louise Erdrich (pronounced Er-drick) was born in 1954 in Little Falls, Minnesota, the oldest of seven children. Part German, part French, and part Turtle Mountain Chippewa, she grew up near a Sioux Indian reservation in Wahpeton, North Dakota. She met Michael Dorris (see p. 273) when she entered Dartmouth College in 1972 as a member of the first class to include women. After graduation Erdrich worked on a television documentary about the Northern Plains Indians, earned her master's degree at Johns Hopkins University, worked for the Boston Indian Council, waited tables, taught, wrote, and edited. In 1981 she came back to Dartmouth as a writer in residence, married Dorris, and became the mother of his three adopted children. Erdrich and Dorris since have had three more children together. They developed an equally collaborative approach to writing: He became the agent for her first novel, *Love Medicine* (1984), which won the National Book Critics Circle Award and has been translated into over eighteen languages; now each reads and revises everything the other writes. Erdrich's fourth novel, *The Bingo Palace* (1994), continues the adventures of her Chippewa characters from *Love Medicine* and *Tracks* (1988). "Foreword" introduces Dorris's autobiographical book *The Broken Cord* (1989), which dramatically publicized the impact of Fetal Alcohol Syndrome on their son Abel (referred to as "Adam" in this piece) and other children, particularly Native Americans. Abel was hit by a car and died at the age of twenty-three.

The snow fell deep today. February 4, 1988, two days before Michael and I are to leave for our first trip abroad together, ten days before Saint Valentine's holiday, which we will spend in Paris, fifteen days after Adam's twentieth birthday. This is no special day, it marks no breakthrough in Adam's life or in mine, it is a day held in suspension by the depth of snow, the silence, school closing, our seclusion in the country along a steep gravel road which no cars will dare use until the town plow goes through.

It is just a day when Adam had a seizure. His grandmother called and said that she could see, from out the window, Adam lying in the snow, having a seizure. He had fallen while shoveling the mailbox clear. Michael was at the door too, but I got out first because I had on sneakers. Jumping into the snow I felt a moment of obscure gratitude to Michael for letting me go to Adam's rescue. Though unacknowledged between us, these are the times when it is easy to be a parent to Adam. His seizures are increasingly grand mal now. And yet, unless he hurts himself in the fall, there is nothing to do but be a comforting presence, make sure he's turned on his side, breathing. I ran to Adam and I held him, spoke his name, told him I was there, used my most soothing tone. When he came back to consciousness I rose, propped him against me, and we stood to shake out his sleeves and the neck of his jacket.

A lone snowmobiler passed, then circled to make sure we were all right. I suppose we made a picture that could cause mild concern. We stood, propped together, hugging and breathing hard. Adam is taller than me, and usually much stronger. I held him around the waist with both arms and looked past his shoulder. The snow was still coming, drifting through the deep-branched pines. All around us there was such purity, a wet and electric silence. The air was warm and the snow already melting in my shoes.

It is easy to give the absolute, dramatic love that a definite physical problem requires, easy to stagger back, slipping, to take off Adam's boots and make sure he gets the right amount of medicine into his system.

It is easy to be the occasional, ministering angel. But it is not easy to   5
live day in and day out with a child disabled by Fetal Alcohol Syndrome or Fetal Alcohol Effect. This set of preventable birth defects is manifested in a variety of ways, but caused solely by alcohol in an unborn baby's developing body and brain. The U.S. Surgeon General's report for 1988 warned about the hazards of drinking while pregnant, and many doctors now say that since no level of alcohol has been established as safe for the fetus, the best policy to follow for nine months, longer if a mother nurses, is complete abstinence. . . . Every woman reacts differently to alcohol, depending on age, diet, and metabolism. However, drinking at the wrong time of development can cause facial and bodily abnormalities, as well as lower intelligence, and may also impair certain types of judgment, or alter behavior. Adam suffers all the symptoms that I've mentioned, to some degree. It's a lot of fate to play with for the sake of a moment's relaxation.

I never intended to be the mother of a child with problems. Who does? But when, after a year of marriage to their father, I legally adopted Adam, Sava, and Madeline — the three children *he* had adopted, years before, as a single parent — it simply happened. I've got less than the ordinary amount of patience, and for that reason I save all my admiration for those like Ken Kramberg, Adam's teacher, and others who work day in and day out with disability. I save it for my husband, Michael, who spent months of his life teaching Adam to tie his shoes. Living with Adam touches on my occupation only in the most peripheral ways; this is the first time I've ever written about him. I've never disguised him as a fictional character or consciously drawn on our experience together. It is, in fact, painful for a writer of fiction to write about actual events in one's personal life. . . .

Although he has no concern about us as professionals, neither pride nor the slightest trace of resentment, Adam takes pleasure when, as a family, our pictures have occasionally been in the paper. He sees Michael and me primarily in the roles to which we've assigned ourselves around the house. Michael is the laundryman, I am the cook. And beyond that, most important, we are the people who respond to him. In that way, though an adult, he is at the stage of a very young child who sees the world only as an extension of his or her will. Adam is the world, at least his version of it, and he knows us only as who we are when we enter his purview.

Because of this, there are ways Adam knows us better than we know ourselves, though it would be difficult for him to describe this knowledge. He knows our limits, and I, at least, hide my limits from myself, especially when I go beyond them, especially when it comes to anger. Sometimes it seems to me that from the beginning, in living with Adam, anger has been inextricable from love, and I've been as helpless before the one as before the other.

We were married, Michael, his three children, and I, on a slightly overcast October day in 1981. Adam was thirteen, and because he had not yet gone through puberty, he was small, about the size of a ten-year-old. He was not, and is not, a charming person, but he is generous, invariably kind-hearted, and therefore lovable. He had then, and still possesses, the gift — which is also a curse, given the realities of the world — of absolute, serene trust. He took our ceremony, in which we exchanged vows, literally. At the end of it we were pronounced husband, wife, and family by the same friend, a local judge, who would later formally petition for me to become the adoptive mother of Adam, Sava, and Madeline; then still later, as we painfully came to terms with certain truths, he helped us set up a lifelong provision for Adam in our wills. As Judge Daschbach pronounced the magic words, Adam turned to me with delight and said, "Mom!" not Louise. Now it was official. I melted. That trust was not to change a whit, until I changed it.

Ten months pass. We're at the dinner table. I've eaten, so have our other children. It's a good dinner, one of their favorites. Michael's gone. 10

Adam eats a bite then puts down his fork and sits before his plate. When I ask him to finish, he says, "But, Mom, I don't like this food."

"Yes, you do," I tell him. I'm used to a test or two from Adam when Michael is away, and these challenges are wearying, sometimes even maddening. But Adam has to know that I have the same rules as his father. He has to know, over and over and over. And Adam *does* like the food. I made it because he gobbled it down the week before and said he liked it, and I was happy.

"You have to eat or else you'll have a seizure in the morning," I tell him. This has proved to be true time and again. I am reasonable, firm, even patient at first, although I've said the same thing many times before. This is normal, Adam's way, just a test. I tell him again to finish.

"I don't like this food," he says again.

"Adam," I say, "you have to eat or you'll have a seizure."

He stares at me. Nothing.   . 15

Our younger children take their empty dishes to the sink. I wash them. Adam sits. Sava and Madeline go upstairs to play, and Adam sits. I check his forehead, think perhaps he's ill, but he is cool, and rather pleased with himself. He has now turned fourteen years old. But he still doesn't understand that, in addition to his medication, he must absorb so many calories every day or else he'll suffer an attack. The electricity in his brain will lash out, the impulses scattered and random.

"Eat up. I'm not kidding."

"I did," he says, the plate still full before him.

I simply point.

"I don't like this food," he says to me again.   20

I walk back to the cupboard. I slap a peanut butter sandwich together. He likes those. Maybe a concession on my part will satisfy him, maybe he'll eat, but when I put it on his plate he just looks at it.

I go into the next room. It is eight o'clock and I am in the middle of a book by Bruce Chatwin. There is more to life . . . but I'm responsible. I have to make him see that he's not just driving me crazy.

"Eat the sandwich . . ."

"I did." The sandwich is untouched.

"Eat the dinner . . ."   25

"I don't like this food."

"Okay then. Eat half."

He won't. He sits there. In his eyes there is an expression of stubborn triumph that boils me with the suddenness of frustration, dammed and suppressed, surfacing all at once.

"EAT!" I yell at him.

Histrionics, stamping feet, loud voices, usually impress him with the   30
serious nature of our feelings much more than the use of reason. But
not this time. There is no ordering, begging, or pleading that will make
him eat, even for his own good. And he is thin, so thin. His face is
gaunt, his ribs arch out of his sternum, his knees are big, bony, and his
calves and thighs straight as sticks. I don't want him to fall, to seize, to
hurt himself.

"Please . . . for me. Just do it."

He looks at me calmly.

"Just for me, okay?"

"I don't like this food."

The lid blows off. Nothing is left. If I can't help him to survive in the   35
simplest way, how can I be his mother?

"Don't eat then. And don't call me Mom!"

Then I walk away, shaken. I leave him sitting and he does not eat,
and the next morning he does have a seizure. He falls next to the aquarium, manages to grasp the table, and as his head bobs and his mouth
twists, I hold him, wait it out. It's still two days before Michael will arrive home and I don't believe that I can handle it and I don't know how
Michael has, but that is only a momentary surge of panic. Adam finally
rights himself. He changes his pants. He goes on with his day. He does
not connect the seizure with the lack of food: He won't. But he does
connect my words, I begin to notice. He does remember. From that
night on he starts calling me Louise, and I don't care. I'm glad of it at
first, and think it will blow over when we forgive and grow close again.
After all, he forgets most things.

But of all that I've told Adam, all the words of love, all the encour-
agements, the orders that I gave, assurances, explanations, and instructions, the only one he remembers with perfect, fixed comprehension,
even when I try to contradict it, even after months, is "Don't call me
Mom."

Adam calls me "Mother" or "Mom" now, but it took years of patience, of backsliding, and of self-control, it took Adam's father explaining and me explaining and rewarding with hugs when he made me feel
good, to get back to mother and son again. It took a long trip out west,
just the two of us. It took a summer of side-by-side work. We planted
thirty-five trees and one whole garden and a flower bed. We thinned the
strawberries, pruned the lilacs and forsythia. We played tic-tac-toe, then
Sorry. We lived together. And I gave up making him eat, or distanced

myself enough to put the medicine in his hand and walk away, and realize I can't protect him.

That's why I say it takes a certain fiber I don't truly possess to live and   40
work with a person obstinate to the core, yet a victim. Constant, nag-
ging insults to good sense eventually wear on the steel of the soul. Logic
that flies in the face of logic can madden one. In the years I've spent
with Adam, I have learned more about my limits than I ever wanted to
know. And yet, in spite of the ridiculous arguments, the life-and-death
battles over medication and the puny and wearying orders one must
give every day, in spite of pulling gloves onto the chapped, frost-bitten
hands of a nearly grown man and knowing he will shed them, once out
of sight, in the minus-thirty windchill of January, something mysterious
has flourished between us, a bond of absolute simplicity, love. That is,
unquestionably, the alpha and omega of our relationship, even now
that Adam has graduated to a somewhat more independent life.

But as I said, that love is inextricable from anger, and in loving
Adam, the anger is mostly directed elsewhere, for it is impossible to love
the sweetness, the inner light, the qualities that I trust in Adam, without
hating the fact that he will always be kept from fully expressing those aspects of himself because of his biological mother's drinking. He is a
Fetal Alcohol Effect victim. He'll always, all his life, be a lonely person.

I drank hard in my twenties and eventually got hepatitis. I was lucky.
Beyond an occasional glass of wine, I can't tolerate liquor anymore. But
from those early days, I understand the urge for alcohol, its physical
pull. I had formed an emotional bond with a special configuration of
chemicals, and I realize to this day the attraction of the relationship and
the immense difficulty in abandoning it.

Adam's mother never did let go. She died of alcohol poisoning, and
I'd feel sorrier for her, if we didn't have Adam. As it is, I only hope that
she died before she had a chance to produce another child with his
problems. I can't help but wish, too, that during her pregnancy, if she
couldn't be counseled or helped, she had been forced to abstain for
those crucial nine months. On some American Indian reservations, the
situation has grown so desperate that a jail internment during pregnancy has been the only answer possible in some cases. Some people . . .
have taken more drastic stands and even called for the forced steriliza-
tion of women who, after having previously blunted the lives of several
children like Adam, refuse to stop drinking while they're pregnant. This
will outrage some women, and men, good people who believe that it is
the right of individuals to put themselves in harm's way, that drinking is
a choice we make, that a person's liberty to court either happiness or despair is sacrosanct. I believed this, too, and yet the poignancy and frus-

tration of Adam's life has fed my doubts, has convinced me that some of my principles were smug, untested. After all, where is the measure of responsibility here? Where, exactly, is the demarcation between self-harm and child abuse? Gross negligence is nearly equal to intentional wrong, goes a legal maxim. Where do we draw the line?

The people who advocate forcing pregnant women to abstain from drinking come from within the communities dealing with a problem of nightmarish proportions. Still, this is very shaky ground. Once a woman decides to carry a child to term, to produce another human being, has she also the right to inflict on that person Adam's life? Because his mother drank, Adam is one of the earth's damaged. Did she have the right to take away Adam's curiosity, the right to take away the joy he could have felt at receiving a high math score, in reading a book, in wondering at the complexity and quirks of nature? Did she have the right to make him an outcast among children, to make him friendless, to make of his sexuality a problem more than a pleasure, to slit his brain, to give him violent seizures?

It seems to me, in the end, that she had no right to inflict such harm, 45 even from the depth of her own ignorance. Roman Catholicism defines two kinds of ignorance, vincible and invincible. Invincible ignorance is that state in which a person is unexposed to certain forms of knowledge. The other type of ignorance, vincible, is willed. It is a conscious turning away from truth. In either case, I don't think Adam's mother had the right to harm her, and our, son.

Knowing what I know now, I am sure that even when I drank hard, I would rather have been incarcerated for nine months and produce a normal child than bear a human being who would, for the rest of his or her life, be imprisoned by what I had done.

And for those still outraged at this position, those so sure, so secure, I say the same thing I say to those who would not allow a poor woman a safe abortion and yet have not themselves gone to adoption agencies and taken in the unplaceable children, the troubled, the unwanted:

If you don't agree with me, then please, go and sit beside the alcohol-affected while they try to learn how to add. My mother, Rita Erdrich, who works with disabled children at the Wahpeton Indian School, does this every day. Dry their frustrated tears. Fight for them in the society they don't understand. Tell them every simple thing they must know for survival, one million, two million, three million times. Hold their heads when they have unnecessary seizures and wipe the blood from their bitten lips. Force them to take medicine. Keep the damaged of the earth safe. Love them. Watch them grow up to sink into the easy mud of alcoholism. Suffer a crime they won't understand committing. Try to understand lack of remorse. As taxpayers, you are already paying for their jail terms, and footing the bills for expensive treatment and education. Be a victim yourself, beat your head against a world of brick, fail constantly. Then go back to the mother, face to face, and say again: "*It was your right.*"

When I am angriest, I mentally tear into Adam's mother. When I am saddest, I wish her, exhaustedly . . . but there is nowhere to wish her worse than the probable hell of her life and death. And yet, if I ever met her, I don't know what I'd do. Perhaps we'd both be resigned before this enormous lesson. It is almost impossible to hold another person responsible for so much hurt. Even though I know our son was half-starved, tied to the bars of his crib, removed by a welfare agency, I still think it must have been "society's fault." In public, when asked to comment on Native American issues, I am defensive. Yes, I say, there are terrible problems. It takes a long, long time to heal communities beaten by waves of conquest and disease. It takes a long time for people to heal themselves. Sometimes, it seems hopeless. Yet in places, it is happening. Tribal communities, most notably the Alkali Lake Band in Canada, are coming together, rejecting alcohol, re-embracing their own humanity, their own culture. These are tough people and they teach a valuable lesson: To whatever extent we can, we must take charge of our lives.

Yet, in loving Adam, we bow to fate. Few of his problems can be   50
solved or ultimately changed. So instead, Michael and I concentrate on only what we can control — our own reactions. If we can muster grace, joy, happiness in helping him confront and conquer the difficulties life presents . . . then we have received gifts. Adam has been deprived of giving so much else. . . .

Michael and I have a picture of our son. For some reason, in this photograph, taken on my grandfather's land in the Turtle Mountains of North Dakota, no defect is evident in Adam's stance or face. Although perhaps a knowing doctor could make the fetal alcohol diagnosis from his features, Adam's expression is intelligent and serene. He is smiling, his eyes are brilliant, and his brows are dark, sleek. There is no sign in this portrait that anything is lacking.

I look at this picture and think, "Here is the other Adam. The one our son would be if not for alcohol." Sometimes Michael and I imagine that we greet him, that we look into his eyes, and he into ours, for a long time and in that gaze we not only understand our son, but he also understands us. He has grown up to be a colleague, a peer, not a person who needs pity, protection, or special breaks. By the old reservation cabin where my mother was born, in front of the swirled wheat fields and woods of ancestral land, Adam stands expectantly, the full-hearted man he was meant to be. The world opens before him — so many doors, so much light. In this picture, he is ready to go forward with his life.

EXPLORATIONS

1. For Louise Erdrich, what is the hardest part of being Adam's mother? What is the most rewarding part?

2. "This is no special day," writes Erdrich in paragraph 1. What incident in this day would make it special for most other people? What is the effect of Erdrich's saying it isn't special for her and her family?

3. How would the impact of Erdrich's essay change if she stated that Adam is a victim of Fetal Alcohol Syndrome, and defined this problem, in her opening paragraph? Where does she give such information instead?

CONNECTIONS

1. By what steps did Erdrich's and Adam's family come into being? How do you think Erdrich would define *family*? Which observations on pages 128–135 imply a similar definition of *family*?

2. How do Erdrich and her husband deal with the problems of childcare mentioned by Frances Rose Besmer (p. 128) and Patricia Schroeder (p. 129)? As professional writers, what advantages and disadvantages have this couple created for themselves as parents?

3. Compare the household roles played by Chang-Rae Lee's mother (p. 128) with the roles Erdrich plays in "Foreword." How are they alike, and why? How are they different, and why?

ELABORATIONS

1. Choose one of the incidents Erdrich narrates in "Foreword" and rewrite it from Adam's point of view. Include whatever awareness you imagine Adam has of being affected by Fetal Alcohol Syndrome.

2. Several of the commentators on pages 128–135 mention meals as a central family ritual. What functions do they suggest that meals fulfill for a family and its members? Which of these functions (and what additional functions) can you identify in the dinner scene Erdrich describes on pages 139–141? Write an essay on the role of meals as a family ritual, drawing on these selections and your own experience for evidence.

HENRY LOUIS GATES JR.

Down to Cumberland

Henry Louis "Skip" Gates Jr. was born Louis Smith Gates in Piedmont, West Virginia, in 1950. He spent a year at Potomac State College before transferring to Yale University, from which he graduated summa cum laude with a degree in history. Gates changed his name to his father's, married, worked as a London correspondent for *Time* magazine, and received his Ph.D. in English from Cambridge University. After teaching at Yale, Cornell, and Duke Universities, Gates became a professor of English, chair of Afro-American Studies, and director of the W. E. B. DuBois Institute for Afro-American Research at Harvard University. He continues to write essays, features, and criticism for such publications as *Harper's, The New Yorker, The Village Voice,* and *The New York Times Book Review.* A member of numerous committees and professional associations, including the Council on Foreign Relations and the American Civil Liberties Union National Advisory Council, Gates holds honorary degrees from several American universities. His books include *The Signifying Monkey: Towards a Theory of African-American Literary Criticism* (1988), which won an American Book Award, and *Loose Canons: Notes on the Culture Wars* (1992). "Down to Cumberland" comes from his memoir *Colored People* (1994).

Because I lived in Piedmont, surrounded by my mother's brothers and sisters and dozens of their children, the Coleman family was familiar to me — all too familiar sometimes. And a contemptuous familiarity obtained between a few of Mama's brothers and me. The Gateses, on the other hand, lived in the mysterious world of Cumberland, Maryland, twenty-five miles, half a dozen shades of brown complexion, and as many grades of hair away. The rooms of their house had a certain worn and aging depth and the sort of dust-covered calm that suggested tradition. They drank beer and Scotch, played cards, read detective novels and traded them with each other, did crossword puzzles, and loved puns. Their favorite term of endearment was "Dummy."

The Colemans, by contrast, were the force of self-righteousness, teetotalers, non-smoking, non-gambling souls, who seemed to equate close-cropped, well-oiled hair and well-washed automobiles with the very purpose of life itself. One quickly realized that what one could or could not do "in front of Big Mom" was the ultimate mechanism for controlling the independent and the unruly.

Though I'd see my Coleman uncles, aunts, and cousins all together at our annual family reunions and Up the Hill at Big Mom's house on Christmas, I saw the Gateses all together on only two occasions in my childhood, and those were my grandparents' funerals.

I used to collect old photographs and paste them into albums. It was my first hobby; taking pictures was my second. I learned much of my family history, and especially the history of the Gateses, from old photographs. Daddy loved telling stories about his family, and I loved listening to them, mostly because they were so funny. The day that the photographs first came to life was the day of my grandfather's funeral.

Gateses never had family reunions and seemed to pride themselves   5
on that fact. But funerals served the same function. I was ten when Pop Gates died. Standing next to my dad, I misread his silent sobs, his quivering shoulders. I thought Daddy was *laughing* right there in front of the casket, right there in front of everybody. His pop *did* look funny, laid out as he was, white as the driven snow. Maybe he *was* white, I remember thinking.

Funny as my grandfather looked lying in the casket, I was glad that somebody had the good sense to laugh. Maybe that would loosen things up a little in that funeral home, what with Aunt Helen crying like crazy. So I started to giggle and looked up into Daddy's face, his eyes red and glassy with tears, as he broke down and sobbed real loud. My mouth flew open, and I squeezed his hand. He had been crying! I started to cry too. I was holding the hand of a man I didn't even know. And for the first time in my life, I felt sorry for him.

Years later, when Mama died, Daddy told me how proud he was of [my daughters] Maggie and Liza, crying at the funeral. He likes his emotions *signed*. I didn't even notice, to tell you the truth. I wanted to be the child that day.

We were laughing, Liza confessed much later that day. We didn't know *what* was going on, she said — we hardly knew Grams. When you all started crying we had started to laugh. Then we got scared and began to cry.

The crying was what Daddy saw. He appreciated it, was what he'd said. But of course I flashed back to old Pop Gates's funeral when I was ten and had done the same thing.

Pop Gates's funeral was the occasion at which I met my great-aunts,   10
Pop's three sisters, Pansy, Lettitia, and Maude, their husbands — a dentist, a pharmacist, and a painter — and some of their children. That was also the day I realized that death could be big business, because each

one had brought along a lawyer or a lawyer's opinion about Pop's will, and each of the three sisters sat occupying a corner of the living room, like battlements armed and well prepared to sustain a war. Only my dad seemed able to move from fort to castle to fort, like a neutral scout or the Secretary-General of the United Nations, trying to stall or prevent the outbreak of war.

That day was a revelation. Doctors and dentists, lawyers and pharmacists; Howard and Talladega, Harvard and Radcliffe — all of these careers and all of these schools were in my grandparents' living room that day, and each had a Gates face attached to it. It came as a shock to realize that these mythic characters in Daddy's tales were actual brown and tan and beige people. And refined. And well spoken. Obviously comfortable in the world. And they seemed to love my father's boys and seemed eager to hear tales of conquests ending with "straight A's." Yes, ma'am, a doctor, I said a hundred times. Maybe a brain surgeon. I'd seen that on "Ben Casey."

They wanted a chunk of the property, just their rightful share, mind you, plus a share of all that cash Pop Gates used to stash in his secret hiding place on, or around, or under, the porch. Not one penny more. I bet them niggers will be bumping into each other on Pop's back porch tonight in the dark, Daddy had said, laughing, in the car as we drove past the still segregated Barton's Dairy Restaurant on the road back to Piedmont. Tearing up the bricks, looking for Pop's money. But nobody ever claimed to have found it.

Pop Gates had been left the property and everything else when his parents died. He had been the only one who had stayed behind to work the farm and then to establish several businesses with his father. They prospered, too: as chimney stokers who would light up your furnaces just before dawn and haul away the ashes as chimney sweeps; a cleaning service with lots of workers, who tended the businesses on Main Street. A bit of this, a bit of that. Good returns on the sale of some of the property that Old Man Brady left to Jane Gates, the first and oldest Gates, a slave. They had done all right. Everything paid for, every deed unencumbered. Never use credit, Pop had told my daddy for as long as he could remember.

In the midst of all the family grief, I went down with Daddy, to help clear out his father's belongings. His mother, Nan — a wispy woman with a wicked wit — was in a fragile state, so we were all helping out. My grandfather kept lots and lots of scrapbooks, full of photographs and clippings and all sorts of memorabilia. Because they never had to move after 1882, they never threw anything away. They lived in a colored museum. Pop Gates also kept the family Bible, in the family for over a century, easy. Turning through the pages of the scrapbooks, past all sorts of clippings about Pop Gates's prized tulips and roses and the red and blue ribbons he had received for his tulips (his backyard looked like a botanical garden in summer, especially around the little rectangular goldfish pond banked with stone), we came across an obituary dated 1892. Its headline read as follows: DIED TODAY, JANE GATES, CITY. AN ESTIMABLE COLORED LADY. It was like stumbling onto the Rosetta Stone or Schliemann's uncovering Troy.

Jane Gates, as I've said, was the oldest Gates, our missing link with   15 Africa. We don't really know where in Africa she came from. But we do have a picture of her, a solid, brown-skinned woman with a midwife's cap on her head. That she was born in 1816 we know from the family Bible and from the obituary Daddy and I found.

In Pop's old trunk, we also found sepia photographs of all of Jane's children. Tall and thin, high cheekbones and light-yellow and cream colors, thin lips and "good hair." All of Jane's children were apparently fathered by one white man, the man who we think owned her. Supposedly his name was Brady, and he was an Irish property-owner who lived in Creasaptown, Maryland, just outside Cumberland. Jane's oldest son, Edward, was my great-grandfather. In his picture, he looked like a white man just as his son, Pop Gates, did. Maybe Brady loved her; maybe he just felt guilty; but sometime between the 1860 and 1870 censuses, Brady gave Jane a whole lot of land in western Maryland. Good land, too. The farm at Patterson's Creek has 200 of the most beautiful acres of bottomland you'll ever see. That's where Gates Point is, the highest site in Mineral County. Patterson's Creek, an offshoot of the South Branch of the Potomac River, runs right through the property, full of trout and bass. The bottomland is surrounded by hills and mountains, abounding with wild turkey and deer, squirrels and rabbits.

A white family bought the farm in the twenties when the Gateses moved into their city house, which they had bought in 1882. There were no pictures of the farm, but there were numerous photographs of a handsome woman dressed in white, standing outside a wooden gazebo, and I wondered who she might be.

That was Pop Gates's mother, my great-grandmother, a matriarchal terror, by everyone's account. She was a bitch, Daddy said coldly, peering down at her photo. Her name was Maude Fortune, and where she came from is anybody's guess. She loved to read, and she worshiped education. Sometime at the turn of the century, when Pop Gates was twenty-one, she decided to send her three daughters to Washington to get a formal education; she kept the boy at home to run the farm. He never forgave her or his three sisters (which is why they all brought

lawyers to their brother's funeral). Two went to Howard, the other to
Morgan. Two became teachers, the other a nurse. Daddy's grandma
read the newspaper to her husband out loud each night, and together as
a family they listened to the news on the radio. He read only with difficulty; when she got cataracts, they were forced to switch roles, with him
reading to her out loud at night. That was hell on everybody, Daddy
says. She loved Germans and German culture, and nicknamed Daddy
"Heinie," when he was born in 1913, despite the fact that a world war
was looming, and Germany would be fighting on the other side. She
became a socialist in 1919 and was the first colored person in Cumberland to subscribe to W. E. B. DuBois's *Crisis* magazine. She died a socialist. Her husband was a Lincoln Republican.

In 1890, Maude Gates founded St. Phillips Episcopal Church in
Cumberland; colored priests from Haiti and Jamaica were enlisted to
serve there. Maude's daughters' children did well: They all graduated
from college, from Howard to Harvard. Three generations at Howard,
including the board of trustees, two generations at Harvard, including
Harvard Law School. Three generations of dentists and three of doctors.
On her son's side, however, the story is a different one. His seven sons
all went to work at factories, although my daddy attended school in
New Jersey for a while. That was around the time that he had wanted to
be a priest. He was the head acolyte within his generation, the seventh
son, the golden boy on whose head grew Jesus Moss. His aunt Pansy,
who told me she had wanted to adopt him, had sent him up to Newark,
New Jersey, where he attended a predominantly Jewish school. Everyone there thought he was Jewish, until he went to school on Rosh
Hashanah. "Heinie," his teacher asked him, "what are you doing in
school today? It's Rosh Hashanah." "Rosh what?" Daddy replied. His
uncle Fred had passed for Jewish, had even married a Jewish woman.
He never contacted the family again. When Maude, his mother, died,
Pop Gates refused to contact him, his own brother. Passing is not regarded with great favor in our family.

Which may seem curious since, until a generation ago, most of the   20
Gateses qualified as octoroons — "light and bright and damn near
white," Daddy said, turning the pages of the photo album. My grandfather and his father looked like white people, and they married the light-
est black people they could find. Shit-colored niggers with Jesus Moss,
people used to say. No need to claim they were part Irish, part English,
part Dutch, part German, part anything, as my Coleman cousins and I
felt compelled to do when we were around white kids in school. No,
these people wore the complexity of their bloodlines on their faces and
on the crowns of their heads.

One day, Pop Gates had called Aunt Helen into the parlor and told her to take a bag of money over to Cumberland's main bank. Ask for Mr. Brady, he stressed. When she came home and handed him the receipt, he asked what Mr. Brady had said to her. He didn't say anything, she said, not after he asked me if I was a Gates. He just stared at me in a funny way.

He's your cousin, was all Pop Gates had said, and you remind him of his sister.

My father's generation, sensing a depletion of the gene pool, so it's been said, married the darkest Negroes they could find. Except for one brother, who liked white women and went crazy one day after he fell in love with the sales clerk in the Cumberland jewelry store where he worked in the back. So crazy he pulled a gun on his beloved's husband and ordered him to stay away from her, she was his woman now . . . then was taken straight to jail. A few of his brothers bailed him out. I remember the day that Daddy got his call from prison. Got to go and bail out my brother, he said, pushing his chair back from the kitchen table. Running that white woman again.

It was a day trip to visit Daddy's family, down to Cumberland. Daddy never learned to drive, so about once a month, on his day off, he, my brother Rocky, and I would take the yellow-and-orange Osgood bus from East Hampshire Street to Cumberland. We'd play "reading the signs" or "spotting the horses," and the person who saw the most horses won the prize that day. Learning how to spot phantom horses that nobody else could see was part of the art of the game, and the fun, especially if you could do it artfully.

We'd get off at Greene Street in Cumberland and begin the rounds, 25 house-hopping from one of Daddy's brothers to the next, starting with Nan's and Pop's house and ending up at Aunt Helen's and Uncle Bill's, before dropping in briefly to say goodbye to Nan again, since her house was closest to the bus stop. At lunchtime, we'd go downtown and across the tracks to Hammersmith's, a dark beer joint with a colored section, which served the best fried-fish sandwiches and french fries in the world. Daddy would drink a beer and spend a lot of time talking to his old buddies from Carver High School, the guys he used to be wild and crazy with. He'd tell the funniest stories about getting in trouble. He was *always* in some kind of trouble.

"I just didn't give a damn," he'd say. I don't think this was strictly true. But he was in trouble a lot, skipping school and playing hooky, and he loved to drink and to gamble.

A milk truck ran over his foot once when he was a boy, sitting on a curb watching the new electric scoreboard in downtown Cumberland.

Pop Gates's brother, Great-uncle Guy, a doctor in Washington, came up to Cumberland for the weekend. He unwrapped Daddy's foot slowly and carefully, took a good look at it, then said, "It's broken, all right," and proceeded to wrap it up again. Daddy says he thought that was funny even then, unlike all sorts of things that are funny only years later, when the pain stops hurting. They got $500 as settlement, which his father promptly borrowed to buy a new Ford Model T.

Years later, when he was dying, Pop Gates confessed how guilty he'd felt for not returning that money. All that time feeling guilty for taking settlement money from a twelve-year-old's smashed foot, which probably shouldn't have been on the road in the first place.

Daddy was particularly close to his sister Helen. Helen and he argued constantly, laughing and joking all the way. One of their recurrent topics of conversation was a bet they once had, which Daddy apparently lost, giving Aunt Helen an IOU. Daddy said that Helen was "old and dotty," that he hadn't lost that bet at all, and even if he had, where was the proof? Show me the piece of paper. No IOU, no money. Helen would busy herself calculating the compound interest on a twenty-five cent bet over a thirty-year period. Compounded *daily*. I'm a millionaire, she'd tell him, as long as you owe me. Years later, Helen found the Gates family Bible, which was falling apart, and she hauled it out to see if I knew how to get it fixed. I'd be happy to get it rebound, I said. As we leafed through its pages, yellowing and fragile, out fell a faded sheet of notepaper, which to everyone's astonishment read: "I.O.U. 25 cents. Signed, Heinie Gates, July 25, 1925." Daddy snatched that piece of paper and — it still pains me to relate — ripped it to shreds.

When I was going on fifteen, I had taken off school to attend the funeral of Daddy's favorite niece, Carolyn. She had been very beautiful and was just ten years older than I was. Though usually the funerals of the Gateses are reunions or parties, with cousins meeting cousins and everybody drinking and telling lies, being extra funny to heal the sadness, nobody did any of those things this time. Everyone was just sad and spent a lot of time crying, and whispering in corners.

Carolyn had left three small children, two girls and a boy, and a huge custody battle was about to erupt between her sister, Jane, and her jive-time husband, Ernie. That is the lyingest nigger on earth, Uncle Bill had said. He did lie a lot. There was the time that he unveiled all the trophies he had won in his hometown in Ohio, where he had been a great athlete. How impressed everybody had been — until the man who owned the trophy store asked Uncle Bob just what Ernie was going to do with all those awards he had bought.

No one seemed to know what Carolyn had died of. I heard about a brain tumor, then some sort of fever, then this, then that. People lied so much about it that they forgot which disease they had used the last time they discussed it. So finally, a week or so later, I asked Daddy what the truth was. He wasn't sure, he said, but one story was that she had been mutilated in an illegal abortion and had died from an infection. At the age of twenty-five.

Since the festive air that typified the Gates funerals I had attended was absent at hers, I could take my time and look around the cemetery. It was a graveyard full of Gateses, going back well over a hundred years. We were all buried there, under worn flat markers in the nineteenth century, medium-sized headstones later on. Even babies were there, like Daddy's seventh brother, Charles. I felt cloaked in the mantle of my family at that cemetery.

As I grew up, the family farm at Patterson's Creek in West Virginia gained in significance for me. Despite the fact that we no longer owned it, I visited it several times in my teens. Daddy and I used to walk all over it, reliving scenes from his memory. Things he had been telling my brother and me for years were brought to life here in the place where they had occurred. Like the cave we stumbled on, which, when we were kids, Daddy would say was full of gold coins. Whenever I heard "Ali Baba and the Forty Thieves," I'd think about our cave, and wonder if I'd stumble upon equally magic words. Daddy had shown me the very gate to the property where his father had bumped into Helen Redman one day, decided that she looked just like a little china doll, and begun to court her. The barn where Pop Gates's horse, Old Toag, had been hitched to the buggy still stood.

It was in the living room, with its stone fireplace, that Dr. Rayford 35 Logan had shown up one day from Washington to ask for Lettitia Gates's hand. Logan, who took the Ph.D. in history from Harvard, was a *gentleman*, Grandma declared. He was drafted during the war, went off to France in 1917, and decided to stay in Paris, where he felt free and a man. So Lettitia married Russell Carpenter instead. He used to call everybody "Chappy." Carpenter left Lettitia at the age of sixty-five and married a white woman who looked just like her. Like an old witch, Daddy would say. In the late 1970s, I met Rayford Logan, then a renowned historian, when we brought him to Yale to deliver an endowed lecture. He seemed astounded that I was Lettitia's descendant; he begged me for tales about her and asked me for her picture. His eyes said that he thought he'd stayed in Paris a bit too long.

EXPLORATIONS

1. Henry Louis Gates Jr. mentions several different generations of Gateses in "Down to Cumberland." Which characters in this essay are members of his own generation? His father's generation? His grandfather's generation? What other generations are represented, and by whom?

2. What occasions typically bring the author's father's family (the Gateses) together? What occasions typically bring his mother's family (the Colemans) together? Which branch of Gates's family is more like your family?

3. At what points in "Down to Cumberland" does Gates apparently feel closest to his family, and why?

CONNECTIONS

1. In "Foreword" (p. 137), what choice did Adam's birth mother make that greatly affected her son's life? What was the impact of that choice? Which of Gates's ancestors made choices that greatly affected their children's lives? What were the impacts of those choices?

2. Which of Angela Davis's comments on page 130 apply to the Gates family, and in what ways?

3. Reread the last paragraph of "Down to Cumberland." How do you think James Baldwin ("The New Lost Generation," p. 18) would explain Dr. Rayford Logan's emigration to Paris? How might he explain Logan's apparent regret for staying so long?

ELABORATIONS

1. Draw your family tree going back at least as far as your grandparents and farther if you can. Using all or part of "Down to Cumberland" as a model, write a short essay describing the people on your family tree.

2. Have you ever attended a family reunion? A funeral? Write an essay about a get-together in your own family, or one you have attended with some other family.

SUSAN CHEEVER

The Nanny Dilemma

As the daughter of novelist John Cheever, Susan Cheever grew up understanding that writing fiction was a craft, "doable by a human being"; but not until her thirties did she tackle it herself. Cheever was born in New York City in 1943 and graduated from Brown University. Her first marriage was to an editor, her second to a writer for *The New Yorker*, the magazine in which "The Nanny Dilemma" appeared as part of a 1995 essay called "The Nanny Track." Cheever has written nonfiction for much of her life. After teaching English for a few years after college, she became affiliated with *Queen* magazine in London, the *Tarrytown Daily News* in New York State, and *Newsweek*, where she began as religion editor and went on to the positions of life-style editor and writer. Cheever's first three novels appeared in the early 1980s, beginning with the autobiographical *Looking for Work* (1980). After her father died from cancer she continued the log she had kept during his illness and then sifted through his voluminous diaries, which "changed the whole way I looked at the world." Her revelations about this man she "had never known . . . had never understood" she shaped into the award-winning memoir *Home Before Dark* (1984). Cheever also pursued her curiosity about the doctors who had treated her father and incorporated her discoveries into a novel, *Doctors and Women* (1987). A past Steinberg Symposium Fellow and chair of the nonfiction panel for the National Book Awards, she continues to write fiction and nonfiction from her New York home.

Dominique came to New York eight years ago, but she says it would take a lifetime to figure out New Yorkers. We teach our kids that money can't buy love, and then we go right ahead and buy it for them — hiring strangers to love them, because we have more important things to do. "You are workaholics, that's for sure," she tells me, in the lilting island accent she uses for unpleasant truths. "It's work, work, work with you, and money, money, money. You analyze every little stupid thing, and then you run off to some therapist to get the answers." She shakes her head and laughs, fiddling with a red plastic Thunderzord my five-year-old son has left on the table. Strangest of all, she says, we super-smart New Yorkers are afraid of our children — afraid to say no, afraid to deny them anything that other kids have. "It's hard for the nannies to adjust to our New York way," says Eileen Stein, of Town & Country, an agency that has placed Dominique in several jobs. "Here children are the boss. The children run the home. The parents let the children do whatever they want."

If there's a good woman behind every great man, behind every great *woman* there's a good nanny. The restructuring of the American family has created a huge demand for childcare. According to a 1992 Department of Consumer Affairs report that calls the nanny-placement industry a "free-for-all," there are almost 400,000 children under thirteen in New York City whose parents both work, and fewer than 100,000 places for them in after-school and day-care programs. The demand for childcare at home has been met by an unregulated patchwork of agencies, a few experienced nannies, and thousands of immigrant women looking for jobs that require no training, no degrees, and, often, no papers. "It's hard to make a living back home," says Dominique, who came from Trinidad on a tourist visa when she was twenty, leaving behind a job that paid the equivalent of $130 a week. "Working here and sending money home is the only way I can take care of my family."

This collision of necessity and need is a disaster for working mothers, who have to find reliable childcare in an unreliable market, and for the nannies who work for them with no protection or guarantees. Many New York nannies are from the Caribbean — Trinidad, Jamaica, other islands of the West Indies — but there are thousands of Philippine, Irish, and South and Central American nannies, too. (A nanny is a full-time worker who lives in or out and is paid between $250 and $600 a week. A baby nurse lives in for twenty-four hours a day during the first weeks of an infant's life and gets $100 a day or more.) Usually, nannies arrive with visas that are valid for a few months. But finding a good legal nanny is so difficult that many families are willing to break the law. And agencies sometimes lie about the legal status of the nannies they place.

Dominique is lucky; she got her green card through one of the first families she worked for. But in eight years she has had eight jobs — some good, some bad, some ugly. These days, she lives in Brooklyn — like most nannies, she can't afford Manhattan rents — and works for a professional couple who live with their two children in a big postwar building on East 86th Street. She was worked in Greenwich Village (she loves it), on the Upper West Side (she hates it), and in the suburbs (trapped!). From 1992 to 1994, she worked for me, taking care of my two children. I had always thought of myself as the perfect employer; when I interviewed Dominique for this article — in which I have changed some names and identifying details — she gently set me straight.

Dominique's morning begins in the dark, in the heart of Brooklyn.   5
She switches on CD 101.9 radio and Channel 5 TV ("Good Day New
York"), and slides a worn Bible out from under her pillow. "Consider
the lilies of the field, how they grow," she reads. "They toil not, neither
do they spin." It's 6:08 A.M., and the temperature is thirty-six degrees.
There are tie-ups on the George Washington Bridge and ten-minute
delays on the Lexington Avenue line. "Take therefore no thought for
the morrow," she reads. "Sufficient unto the day is the evil thereof."
Her apartment, a studio that costs $504 a month, is sparsely furnished
with a glass-topped dining-room table and chairs from Workbench, and
a bed; Dominique would rather have no furniture than the tacky stuff
some of her friends crowd into their apartments. Next to the stereo system are neat piles of Toni Braxton and Luther Vandross tapes and the
eight-pound dumbbells that Dominique uses three or four times a
week — she does half an hour of lifting and twenty minutes of aerobics.
Out the window, beyond the fire escape, she can see the Sears sign over
near Flatbush Avenue and the outline of Canarsie out toward Jamaica
Bay. . . .

   Out on 86th Street, an icy wind is blowing off the East River. Dominique thinks of New York as home, but she'll never get used to how
cold it is here and the way night falls at 4 P.M. in the winter. She stops
to buy an orange and a Snapple. The people she works for eat out, and
their children live on sweet cereal, bread, boxed fruit juice, and peanut
butter and jelly that are premixed in the jar. Dominique nurses her
Snapple (guava or pink-grapefruit flavored) all day, eats the orange
when she's hungry, and tries to make herself a proper dinner when she
gets home. On a good night, she makes some curried chicken and
steams some broccoli. On a bad night, she stops at Burger King for a
shake. Now, shouldering her way through the crowds, she passes the
health-food store where the kids eat vegetarian pizza. She avoids looking in the windows of a new, expensive shoe store: She loves to buy shoes.

   At York Avenue, she turns away from her destination and goes
around the corner of 87th Street to St. Joseph's Church. Inside, she
crosses herself with holy water, lights a candle, and kneels near the
back, where stained-glass windows throw splashes of color on the whitewashed walls. It's almost eight o'clock. The people she works for are just
getting out of bed. But as she kneels Dominique daydreams for a
minute, remembering home: the big white-and-blue house in Valencia
where she lived after her mother married the small town's unofficial
mayor, Big Daddy Will Diamond. The candle is for her mother. She
also prays for her own eight-year-old daughter, Crystal, who lives in Valencia with Dominique's sister. Dominique hasn't seen her daughter in

three years. As she prays, she feels a familiar, sharp sadness about Crystal. Then she reminds herself that the money she is making will buy her daughter an education, so that she can get a stable job with good wages — *she* won't end up in New York taking care of other people's children.

When Dominique was growing up, she always knew she wasn't going to be a typical Trini girl — hanging out in Valencia, with its dead-end jobs, and girls who had children when *they* were still children. She was going a lot farther than Sangre Grande, the nearest big town, which everyone called Sandy Grandy. Dominique had an aunt who lived in London, but she favored New York. She saw "Saturday Night Fever" four times. Every Sunday she watched "Fame," the TV show starring the lucky kids at the New York School of Performing Arts, who stopped traffic with their dancing. Dominique loved to dance. She still does, turning up the volume and pulling down the shades and prancing alone around her little room. But now she knows that nothing stops New York traffic. "Take therefore no thought for the morrow . . ." she remembers as she crosses 86th Street to work. "Sufficient unto the day is the evil thereof."

Dominique smiles at the doorman and lets herself into the apartment. Suzanne is desperately jiggling the crying baby on one hip while she tries to make a peanut-butter-and-jelly sandwich. The dog is yapping. Emily, the five-year-old, is giggling and eating Froot Loops at the kitchen table. There's a puddle of milk on the floor. Suzanne's nightgown is stained with applesauce and instant coffee. Dominique says good morning; in response, Suzanne groans and hands her the baby. Dominique can hear the shower: Henry is getting ready for work.

It's a modern apartment, with lots of light, but it's crowded with furniture and unopened mover's boxes are piled in one corner. The kitchen counters are overflowing with dishes, and the cabinets are filled with paper plates and appliances that are still in bubble wrap. When Dominique took this job, six months ago, Suzanne explained that they had just moved in. Later, Dominique found out that they had "just moved in" in 1992; she has often heard Henry boast that they got the apartment for a great price in a buyer's market.

The baby screeches with delight and then grunts with satisfaction, 10
wiggling his whole body in Dominique's arms. Dominique kisses him on the top of his downy head and silently tells him to chill. She doesn't want Suzanne to be jealous. She doesn't like dealing with parents' jealousy of the bonds that she forms with their children. "They want us to be mother and father to these children," she says. "They're the ones

who brought the kids into the world, but then they don't have time to raise them. So the kids get attached to you, because you're the one who's always there. Then the parents get angry."

This is part of what Dominique and her friends call the attachment factor — one of the most intransigent problems of being a New York nanny. "The kids see you all the time, and they assume you are going to be part of their life," says Sally, an Irish nanny, who is Dominique's closest friend in the building. Sally has had three jobs in five years. Two years ago, she applied for a position with a rich, prominent New York family. When she was interviewed, she was told she would wear a uniform, would have to be available for traveling, and would never under any circumstances speak directly with the parents of the children she was caring for — the family had hired a liaison person for that. She took the job on East 86th Street instead.

"When you leave, the children can be devastated — and it can break your heart, too," Sally says. Nannies rarely get notice. Then, there's the problem of the hours, which seem to get more flexible (i.e., longer) the longer you work for a family. There's the problem of being asked to do work — dog walking, ironing, serving at dinner parties — that was not part of the job description and was not included in the original salary. And if the job can sometimes be too flexible the salary is often inflexible: Many employers count minutes and deduct dollars when a nanny is late. Sometimes nannies get farmed out to clean or babysit for their employers' friends, too. "When they act as if my services are their property — property they can lend out whenever they want — that really makes me feel bought," Sally says.

There is the problem of summers. Many families offer nannies a Hobson's choice: either go away with them and be trapped in some all-white resort (in nanny circles, the Hamptons is a synonym for Hell) or take token wages while they're gone. There is the problem of a family's dependence on their nanny. "Some weekends, they call me five or six times," Dominique says. "Basically, I'm on call around the clock. I feel like my life isn't mine even when I'm at home."

Many nannies wonder why their employers bothered to have children at all. "I see these women struggling between being the career person who gets self-esteem from her job and being the parent who really loves her children," Sally says. "But you shouldn't have kids if you're not ready to make adjustments. Sometimes it blows me away when I'll come in to work and there will be no milk and no cereal and no money for groceries. Two people without kids who eat out don't have to have groceries, but with kids you need to have something for them to eat."

Worst of all, being a nanny is a job with negative stability. When   15
children go to school — and in New York they sometimes go to school
at age two — the job begins to evaporate. Many New York children are
in school from 9 A.M. to 3 P.M. by the time they are five. Nannies have
to get along with their employers in a relationship that is in certain respects more intimate than a marriage. Sometimes they are treated like
servants; sometimes they are treated like best friends. They are required
to be completely reliable and completely discreet. They are asked to ignore drug problems. They must see no evil, hear no evil, speak no
evil — like the nanny in Jamaica Kincaid's novel *Lucy*, who walks in on
her employer licking the neck of his wife's best friend. (The intensity of
the connection between nannies, mothers, and children has attracted
storytellers from Homer — who made Odysseus' nurse the only woman
who could identify him — to Charlotte Brontë, who made her most
sympathetic heroine, Jane Eyre, a governess. The nanny canon also includes the evil Miss Jessel from Henry James's *The Turn of the Screw*,
the precursor to dozens of malignant child-care professionals, all acting
out a mother's worst fears — right up to *The Hand That Rocks the
Cradle*.)

Nannies want to be treated as professionals. Dominique's friend
Maria took a nanny-awareness class in Brooklyn last year. "The main
thing they told us was to be businesslike," she says. "Businesslike, businesslike! But it's hard to be businesslike when you're going into someone's house and taking care of their children." I heard one or two horror stories from the nannies I spoke to: an employer who would give a
reference only in exchange for sex; a man who left pornographic pictures around and watched the nanny's reactions; a woman who checked
the garbage to see what her children had eaten; another woman who
came home at 2 A.M. and broke all the windows in her apartment with a
heavy copper saucepan. But the real horrors are more subtle — employers who tell their nannies what to wear, employers who depend on
them so much that the nannies go to work even when they're sick. Sally
says, "I lie there in bed when I'm sick and I think, Did anyone get Lau-
rie's lunch? Do they know that it's library day? Do they know that she
has a play date with Joan after school? I might as well go to work." And
when a nanny leaves, it can be as devastating for the parents as it is for
the children.

"We could close down the city," says Myrtle Johnson, a child-care
veteran who works as a short-term baby nurse because she believes that
nannies always end up getting treated badly. "If we didn't go to work,
the mothers would go crazy, and they'd drive the husbands crazy, and
no one could work. If there's a garbage strike, the trash just lies there. If

there's a postal strike, the mail doesn't get delivered. But if the nannies were to strike it would be different. You can't just leave a baby around until there's someone ready to take care of it."

In twenty-five years as a baby nurse, Myrtle has traveled with families to Calgary (for the Olympics) and London (where she stayed at Claridge's), and has saved enough to buy a big brick house on Grant Avenue in the Bronx. In her kitchen there's a double Garland stove — the best. Upstairs, she has installed a pink-and-gold bathroom with a wicker basket of fluffy towels; it could fit right in on Park Avenue. But success hasn't changed her attitude. "The nannies are there for the duration," she says. "The employers get to think they own them, and it's just like anything else. You have a boyfriend, you do anything to keep him, you give him cocktails and lobsters. Then, when he marries you, it's no more cocktails and no more lobsters."

In the thirteen years I have been raising children in New York, I've employed three full-time nannies, supplemented by about a dozen babysitters. . . . Our generation has made a religion of parenting. Our mothers had Dr. Spock; we have books to fill a ten-foot shelf. They had a family doctor; we have pediatric endocrinologists who specialize in glandular disorders. We love our children passionately, and for me, at least, leaving them — for a week, or even for a day — is the hardest thing I've ever had to do. This makes the person who takes care of them in my absence both indispensable and somehow an agent of separation and doom — much more than a simple employee. In many families, where women take on most of the job of raising the children, along with doing their outside jobs, the nanny becomes the true significant other. It's the nanny who works with the mother to create a place where the children can thrive; the husband is at best an assistant to the team and at worst an obstacle to their aims. "It's a fragile situation," Sally says. "I have to come in every morning and assess the mood in the house and take up the slack. In these marriages, the mothers depend on us so that they can work, and the fathers sometimes get off scot-free — a lot of the time it's as if they didn't even have children." Dominique and Sally have decided that the perfect employer would be a single mother with one child.

Honesty and professionalism go a long way toward helping nannies 20
and families get along, but the circumstances of their employment will always be colored by our worst fears. The nannies know everything about us, and we know little about them. They come from alien cultures to fill our culture's most important job — raising our kids. We've decided to let other women take care of our children so that we can

give those children a better life. It's an excruciating decision, as the nannies know better than anyone. The truth is, we are more like our nannies than we realize — strung out between the old ways and the new, between the demands of money and the demands of love. They have chosen to give their children less mothering so that they can make more money, and so have we. There are bad nannies and good nannies, just as there are bad mothers and good mothers, but it's our similarities rather than our differences that make the situation so painful.

EXPLORATIONS

1. Judging from "The Nanny Dilemma," what characteristics do New York families share who hire nannies? How does their approach to the care of their children differ from Dominique's approach to the care of her child, and why?

2. What information does Susan Cheever supply about Dominique in her opening paragraph? How do we find out Dominique's occupation? When do we learn where she came from? How would Dominique's role in this essay change if she were fully introduced at the start?

3. According to Cheever, what are the benefits of the nanny system to New York working mothers? Fathers? Their children? Their nannies? Who else benefits and how?

CONNECTIONS

1. "Behind every great woman there's a good nanny" (para. 2). Judging from "Down to Cumberland" (p. 146), would anyone in the Gates family (past or present) agree with this statement? If so, who and why? If not, why not?

2. Which of the family models described in the epigraphs on pages 128–135 are closest to Dominique's family in Trinidad? In what ways?

3. How do you think Susan C. McMillan (p. 132) would respond to Cheever's portrait of working motherhood? How do you think Patricia Schroeder (p. 129) would respond?

ELABORATIONS

1. "We super-smart New Yorkers are afraid of our children" (para. 1). "Here children are the boss." Is this true? If so, why? Is it true of other families besides those Cheever describes? Write an essay analyzing why Cheever's de-

piction is accurate (or not) and recommending steps to change the situation, applying her comments either to the New Yorkers in her essay or to families whom you know.

2. How many ways are there to balance the demands of marriage, work, and childcare? What choices are best for the marriage? For the partners' professional development? For the children? Write an essay in which you either compare and contrast the options or argue for the plan you favor, using the essays in this chapter (and additional research, if you wish) as sources.

NICHOLAS BROMELL

Family Secrets

Nicholas Bromell describes his unorthodox childhood in the following essay, which appeared in the 1993 collection *Turning Toward
Home: Reflections on the Family*. Bromell graduated magna cum laude
from Amherst College in 1972. After completing the Radcliffe Publishing Procedures Course in Cambridge, Massachusetts, he worked for
Harvard University Press and later became editor-in-chief of *The Boston
Review*. Bromell was awarded a teaching fellowship at Stanford University and received his Ph.D. there in English and American literature.
Winning a Massachusetts Artists Foundation Fellowship in nonfiction
writing in 1987, he taught at Brandeis University, served as a preceptor
in the Public Policy Communications Program at Harvard's Kennedy
School of Government, and continued to publish essays, feature stories,
and journal articles in a variety of publications. He is now an assistant
professor of English and American literature at the University of Massachusetts, Amherst.

In *The Teachings of Don Juan*, Carlos Castaneda learns from his
Yaqui shaman that each person has his "spot" in the world, a place
where the strength of the earth wells up and protects him from the
demons of the psyche. But because of the work my father used to do, I
come from nowhere and have no spot. Often I feel I've built my life
atop an emptiness that could implode at any moment. It is, moreover,
an emptiness held firm by silence, by the untellable oddity of my childhood. My wife, who rolls her eyes when my most mundane childhood
stories play out in places such as Baghdad, Piraeus, Petra, or Shiraz,
doesn't believe that I am awed by her childhood in a small Catholic
parish on the South Side of Chicago. She can't understand that I envy
her because she is a *real* American — because she experienced a childhood other Americans recognize. We all try to make sense of our lives
by having stories to tell, and, like all narratives, these stories are subject
to conventions. The chief of these, in this country at least, is a prohibition against the exotic. A Southern boyhood, or a prep-school boyhood,
or an only-child boyhood might be interesting, but to be told, they must
be grounded in the ordinary. If the prep school is in Bogotá, or if the fa-

ther is a Rockefeller, the story becomes unreal and untellable. And if
the father is a spy — or, as he prefers to call himself, an intelligence officer — the story becomes untellable twice over. You grow up swearing
an oath of silence without knowing it and owing allegiance to an institution you will never see or know.

But now, after the demise of the Soviet Union and the war against
Iraq, I have come to realize that my childhood had a certain historical
specificity. It was, with more intensity than most, a Cold War childhood. Born precisely at midcentury, I was made to understand at a very
young age that somewhere, or rather everywhere, an immense silent
contest was being fought, that our side was locked in a struggle with another side, and that what was at stake was the very shape of the future.
Of course, every American child of my generation was born into a
world structured by this Manichaean paradigm — us against them,
good against evil — but when your father's daily work actually contributes to this struggle, it has a different, more intimate, meaning. Not
that my father was vocal about the Cold War. I never heard him say a
word against the Russians. But somehow we knew (I think probably
from our grandmother, his doting mother) that he did not work for
money, and that his work mattered in some deeper, stronger way that
could never be discussed.

When we were "home" in the United States, Dad left the house for
"work" in some unspecified "office" we never saw. Overseas, however,
his work was more visible, no matter how painstakingly he tried to conceal it. To me and my two brothers, the fact of what my father did was
the very ground we walked on, and the élan with which he and his colleagues conducted themselves was the air we breathed. For them,
World War II had never ended. They slipped out of flight jackets and
fatigues and into gray suits, but their new anonymity was even more lus-
trous than their celebrated role as soldiers. They were an elite. They
were a team. They knew one another, but no one knew them. On
spring weekends we took picnics to ancient ruins in the desert; while
the mothers scratched in the sand for shards and the men relaxed with
cold martinis poured from my parents' thermos, my brothers and I
scouted the hillocks and ravines, finally sneaking up behind the men,
listening to their deep laughter, their sudden moments of seriousness,
and unconsciously reproducing in our games of creeping and spying
the work a number of them performed out of their embassy offices.
Hearing their laughter in memory now, I feel that it perfectly expressed
the double life most of them led: one day, a relaxed picnic with the
family; the next, a trek in dusty Land Rovers deep into the wastes where
the oil pipelines ran; where a solitary coffeehouse marked the borders of

Iraq, Syria, and Jordan; where Arab armies engaged in maneuvers; where bedouin chieftains beckoned them into black-cloth tents for hot, sugary tea drunk from little glasses with gold rims.

My brothers and I came to accept certain announcements as plain matters of fact. Mother: "Your father won't be home tonight." Father: "I'm expecting visitors this afternoon; I want you all to stay outside the house until after five." One morning my older brother sprang from behind a door to scare our father, who instantly spun around, fists raised to strike, and then, ashen, explained that we were never, ever to jump out and scare him. And in order to make his prohibition convincing, he had to drop a corner of the curtain he kept between us and his profession. "In my job I have to worry that someone might want to sneak up behind me like that, and I have to be ready to defend myself," he explained gently. "I might hurt you before I could stop myself." Many years later, in another country, a team of men from the embassy came to our house with suitcases of electronics equipment, tripod-mounted antennas, headphones, and other gear, and my brothers and I were old enough to realize what they were doing — debugging our house. But we were hardly surprised. Without ever knowing that we knew, we had understood for some time that our father was a spy.

The silence of this acknowledged fact was the silence that legiti-   5 mated many other silences within our family. "There are certain things we don't talk about," we were told. "It would be better if you didn't mention to your friends where we went this weekend." I realize now how often we must have been part of my father's cover. When we went as a family to visit a man somewhere, and to drink sickly sweet rose water ("Drink a little to be polite!") on the terrace while he and my father conversed inside, we made quite a different impression on the neighbors than my father would have made arriving and entering the house alone. We were a family of conspirators. One afternoon my best friend saw all of us piling into an army helicopter that had landed in the fields near our house. The next day he confronted me with what he had seen, and I blithely denied it. Us? Piling into a helicopter? What on earth for? And because he had no one to corroborate the outrageous thing he had seen, my friend shook his head and soon disbelieved it himself. More than most other children, I think, I grew up seeing the world double. I saw not just the doubleness of adults pretending things to children but the doubleness of adults pretending things to one another. And knowing no other world, this seemed normal to me.

The Cold War, which was not a war, or not the war it pretended to be — a war of doubleness — was thus the architecture of my family and childhood. For middle-class Americans back home, and for children my age growing up in suburban neighborhoods of bikes and lawns and newspaper routes — things I knew about only from movies and old television shows — the Cold War was at most the sound of distant thunder. It came home to them only at moments — when Francis Gary Powers was shot down, when Nikita Khrushchev famously banged his shoe on a table at the United Nations. I found, when I entered college in 1968, that my new friends were shocked by revelations about American duplicity at home and abroad. My father and his colleagues had done their work too well. All their efforts at the front lines, keeping the enemy at bay, had preserved the American delusion that the world could be seen in terms of right and wrong, communism and democracy. That the United States had actually undermined democracies (in, for example, Iran) was incredible to my classmates. They had to rethink everything they knew, or thought they had known, about the world, about power, about history. I joined them in their expressions of outrage, I marched with them on Washington, but though I shared their disapproval of American policies I could not quite share their disgust and disappointment. I had been prepared, having known for as long as I could remember that things are seldom what they seem.

In 1957 we went overseas for the first time, sailing from New York on the S.S. *Excambian* and bound for Beirut. There we stayed briefly at the Hotel St. Georges, at that time the city's only luxury hotel, a faded, *fin de siècle* symbol of an era about to pass, and which my memory conflates with the "large, proud, rose-colored hotel" of F. Scott Fitzgerald's *Tender Is the Night*. The St. Georges, however, had no "bright tan prayer rug of a beach." The green Mediterranean thundered onto the rocks surrounding the great railed veranda that jutted into the sea. In the morning we ate in the shade of the hotel, spearing with tiny forks the scalloped butter pats nestled in their dewy serving dish and drinking dark hot chocolate from a pewter urn. In the evening, as the sky flushed to apricot over the water, children and their nannies were given license to run, skip, hide, play over the veranda. Then night fell and waiters circulated busily, setting out tables, lighting small lanterns. Long after our bedtime we boys crouched on our balcony, peering down at the grownups eating their dinner, listening to the murmur of their conversation mingling with the murmur of waves in the darkness beyond the lights.

My senses — the senses of a seven-year-old — absorbed everything. I was a roll of film stretched open beneath the summer sun. Every photon that hit me sank and stayed. Even today, when I happen to get a starched white napkin at a restaurant, the smell of fresh bread issuing miraculously from the fabric strips away the years and drops me, a boy,

into the morning shade of the veranda of the St. Georges. But these
memories are now more than ever evanescent sensations. Whether we
know it or not, in Brattleboro as much as in Beirut, history flows
through childhood the way light passes through the curtains of a bedroom. I see now that the rolls and butter I consumed on the veranda of
the St. Georges were not ahistorical fragments tumbling through the
empty space of time but precise embodiments of French colonialism,
which at that very moment was giving way to an American "presence."
The St. Georges itself is just such history writ large. It was named, of
course, for the warrior-saint whose lance speared the serpent of hea-
thenism and whose emblem accompanied thousands of Christian soldiers during the Crusades. Since the time we stayed there, it metamor-
phosed gradually into a modern but charmless hotel in the American
style. Later still, seized now by one and now by another militant faction,
it crumbled under twenty years of internecine warfare to a ghostly, but
miraculously functioning, ruin — like the city itself.

We flew from Beirut to Baghdad, where my father had been posted
to the embassy, and stepped out of the airplane into a heat so white and
thick that I gasped. Driving to what would be our house, I gazed stu-
pidly at the tall palm trees — I had never seen palms before — beneath
whose leaves hung clusters of what looked like enormous cockroaches
(dates, my mother explained). The car stopped at a pair of gates set in a
high mud wall. Twenty feet away, on a pile of refuse bulkier than the
car, two emaciated dogs lolled motionless, not even panting. The gates
swung open. This was "our" garden and that was "our" house. Inside,
we found the shutters closed, the hall dark as a cave. Huge fans turned
beneath immensely high ceilings. The American couple who had met
us at the airport introduced us to our cook, our houseboy, our nanny,
and our gardener. In low tones the American woman spoke reassuringly
to our mother. Then the grown-ups moved into the "library," where the
man mixed them drinks, and we boys were left alone to explore.

Looking back, I realize how young my parents were (in their early   10
thirties) and how innocent. All of this was as new to them as it was to us.
Still, I am astonished that they did not explain more to us. They had
just transported their children to a place that was as different as another
planet, and they simply let us loose in it. We were on our own, in-
structed only not to drink the water from the faucets and never to ask
the servants for anything. We ambled around the shadowy house,
touching, smelling, examining. In the library brown veins ran down the
walls, and the books we opened had tiny sand tunnels running through
them. Termites, my father explained. The kitchen cupboards were
stocked with foods we had never heard of: squash (not sodas), biscuits

(not crackers), sweets (not candies). Down in the basement we found the belongings, awaiting shipment, of the family we had replaced; surreptitiously, we pried into the boxes and lifted out treasures — chief among them a magnificent set of albums filled with huge, colorful stamps, most of them, if I remembered correctly, from the Belgian Congo, my father's predecessor's former post.

One evening a light rain fell. We stood at an open upstairs window and looked down over the garden wall at the street. Traffic had halted and Baghdadis ran out of the shops, hands uplifted, to touch and greet the spattering drops. Soon thereafter the days grew cooler at last; we began to play in the garden. Arranging our soldiers (all of them British lead soldiers with red uniforms and black beaver hats — the only kind available in the local stores) on fortifications we had built alongside the irrigation ditches, we stayed for hours in our smaller world that we could control and understand. Like all colonial children, we discovered the mysteries of servants' quarters — a small building behind the kitchen, occupied by our cook and houseboy. We learned enough Arabic to communicate brokenly, but more often we played our spying games on them, climbing into the trees near their door and watching them move back and forth from the kitchen to their quarters, understanding almost nothing of what they said but delighting in the mere fact of being unseen, unheard, and watching.

We had just begun to explore the world beyond our garden walls — riding our bikes to the British Council library one afternoon, where we watched Laurence Olivier in the film version of *Richard III* — when the mood of the city palpably changed. Winter dust storms blew out of the desert, and coated trees and streets and cars in a fine yellow dust that penetrated doors and shutters and blurred the glossy surface of the dining-room table. But more than the weather changed. One day our cook invited us to go with him to a hanging, and when my older brother went to ask our mother for permission, she slapped him before she could think or speak. When we drove down Al-Raschid Street, we began to notice more crowds, more speeches, more banners, more soldiers. The city seemed to turn in upon itself. Then we learned the word "curfew" when the government imposed one. At dusk merchants pulled down the metal grates in front of their shops and went home. Even the tiny corner store where we bought Mars bars and firecrackers closed before dark. Because we had diplomatic plates on our car, we were allowed to drive after dusk, and the city we passed through seemed to eye us through a thousand shuttered windows.

Then it happened. The army revolted. The young king whose face was familiar to us from the stamps we collected was shot in his palace.

We heard rumors that a mob chased two Americans into the Hilton Hotel, caught them in the lobby, dragged them outside, and tore them limb from limb. Tanks and armored cars squatted at the end of our street. My mother came into our room and told us to pick one book and one toy each. We were packing. We were leaving that night on a special plane. We learned two more words that day: "revolution" and "evacuation."

While my father remained with a small delegation in Iraq, we flew to Rome, where we stayed for three days at the luxurious Hassler Hotel before moving to a tiny pensione in a street of perpetual shadows. Through the open bedroom window there came the sounds and smells of that great city, waking us in the morning and lulling us to sleep at night. I was eight years old — listless, restless, perhaps irked by my father's double absence. One day at lunch I watched my mother open a fresh pack of cigarettes, then I covertly pocketed the slender strip of red cellophane she discarded in the ashtray. That afternoon, during siesta, in obedience to some inarticulate inner prompting, I walked down the hall to the pensione's only bathroom, tied one end of the red strip to the bolt of the lock, closed the door, and carefully pulled the strip back through, thereby locking the door from the outside. With a swift jerk I yanked most of the strip free, leaving nothing visible. Then I returned to our bedroom and told my incredulous brothers what I had done.

We waited. At four o'clock the pensione began to stir. Pans clattered   15 in the kitchen. The telephone rang in the vestibule. Footsteps padded by as people woke up and made their way to the bathroom. Gradually a murmur arose in the hall, and we drifted out to see what was the matter. A small crowd milled in front of the bathroom. Someone knocked, then thumped, then banged. Angry voices shouted in Italian. The proprietress emerged from the kitchen, straightened her apron, and knocked. No answer. She shouted. Finally they sent for a man who put a ladder against the wall of the building, climbed two stories, entered through the bathroom window, and opened the bathroom door to the angry, mystified crowd.

"*Ma chi è?*" cried the landlady, pouncing on the red strip dangling from the lock. At that point we thought it best to retire to our room, grateful that our father was not there to catch us in the act of imitating him.

We spent eight months in Rome without my father. Mother moved us into and out of a series of apartments with dysfunctional central heating. She found us a pretty English nanny named Nina whom I loved but who had an Italian boyfriend who was a pilot for a mercenary army fighting somewhere in Africa. Mother bought us matching flannel shorts and V-necked blue sweaters and took us out for dinner to small restaurants where the men made much of us and more of her — a beautiful young woman alone in Rome with her three boys. After the inevitable violinist had played the inevitable song that brought the inevitable tears to Mother's dark eyes, we walked home through the cobblestone streets, banging our heels on the manhole covers embossed with the letters S.P.Q.R.

S.P.Q.R.: *Senatus Populusque Romanus.* An empire once, a city now. Who can account for the influence that the vestiges of empire had on the historical consciousness of an eight-year-old American boy? At the time I understood nothing. But I absorbed, in the yellow Roman light, the knowledge that history is more than an aggregate of moments, of names of generals and dates of battles learned in school. History turns suddenly on a pivot. Whole orders of being pass away. No one tried to answer because I never asked the question that shadowed every monument and ruin we saw: What happened? But I felt that no gradual process of change could possibly connect the Arch of Constantine with the Fiats and Vespas swirling noisily beneath it. History must be dramatic, swift, inexplicable. And it is; the Cold War ended in three months, without a shot fired.

We were living in Maadi, a suburb of Cairo, when the Six-Day War between Israel and Egypt broke out in June of 1967. Egypt immediately severed diplomatic relations with the United States, and for the second time in my life I was evacuated, this time to Athens. Once again my father stayed behind to perform the invisible work that sustained us.

None of us really knows what he did for the next six months: He wrote one postcard, telling us that he went out a lot at night wearing the soft-soled shoes he jokingly called his "brothel creepers." Many years later, however, and after much wine, he uncharacteristically dropped the veil and let one story slip. On the night President Gamal Abdel Nasser announced he would resign, my father had needed to go out and visit certain "people" in various quarters of Cairo. The city was in upheaval. Distraught crowds roamed the streets, carrying placards of Nasser and crying out for vengeance against Israel and its chief ally, the United States. Around midnight, in a dark street of one of the city's poorer sections, my father turned a corner and found himself twenty yards away from just such a crowd. (He is recognizably American and speaks no Arabic.) Almost before he could move, he was surrounded. A young man seized him by the arms, and instead of resisting, my father took the young man's hand and guided his fingers to the skin under his own glasses. The man paused, stepped back, then turned and quieted the crowd. When he had finished, he put his arm around my father and guided him through the mass, which parted like the waters of the Red Sea. My father continued quietly on his way.

What had happened? On seeing the crowd, my father spat on his hands and rubbed them beneath his eyes. The moisture there convinced the young man that my father, like so many Egyptians, had been weeping with sorrow at the news that Nasser planned to resign. This is what the man had explained to the crowd and why they had let my father through.

An example of quick thinking, no doubt. But more than that. My father, I know, truly was saddened by Nasser's announcement; if he were a man capable of crying easily, he might have cried that night. He wasn't just tricking the crowd; he was feeling with them. But at the same time, this moment of communion with the people of Egypt was forced to be an act of duplicity. There will always be a need for subterfuge in foreign relations and in the gathering of intelligence, but during the Cold War these necessities became enshrined as virtues. And not just overseas. For many American men of my father' generation, the Cold War paradigm of interminable struggle against an implacable foe was just the most focused articulation of a general state of being. Unlike Vietnam veterans later, many men of my father's generation who returned home from war may not have had to deal with the shock of peace. There *was* no peace. A new war was nurtured into being, providing them a field in which to go on fighting — not just abroad but at home, where the ethos of conflict made the pursuit of success a cause, not just a fate. While the idea of capitalism had to be protected by cold warriors like my father, its actual triumph could be assured only by the unremitting and self-sacrificing struggle of corporate cadres back home — a struggle that has, they claim, paid off at last.

But now what? Thirty years ago, on a spring night in Washington, a man who was an intelligence officer stood with a martini in hand beside a charcoal grill, watching the coals glow. That afternoon, he had left a large office building, driven home anonymously, had doffed tie and jacket and rolled up his shirtsleeves. Now his sneakers rested lightly on the brick patio of a Georgetown garden, and his gaze, when he looked up at the pale spring sky, was at once vague and vigilant. We played at his feet, and he protected us. Inside the house his wife, our mother, made potato salad and placed plastic forks and paper plates on a tray to carry out to us.

Today my own young children take root and flourish in a small town in New England. Outside, sprawled on a chaise lounge and sipping wine as hamburgers cook, I protect them from nothing. Their horizon does not end at a wall topped with barbed wire but expands indefinitely. I realize now that I have tried to make my work the exact opposite of my father's. Against his commitment to silence I oppose my claims to speech — as a teacher and a writer. At the same time, though, I inevitably reproduce him — in manner, in temperament, and even in work. Closeted in my study, demanding a household of silence while I write, I may be as mysterious to my sons as my father was to his.

Constantine Cavafy's poem "Waiting for the Barbarians" asks: "And now, without the Barbarians, what is to become of us?/After all, those people were a kind of solution." The premise of the Cold War was a bipolar world, every nation allied with us or with our "enemies." For more than forty years the Cold War made this particular construction of reality more real than others. For many Americans — and I hope for my sons, whose shouts float up from the bottom of the garden — a choice has emerged: to view the world as a more complicated place, requiring subtler thinking and more varied partnerships; or to retrench behind a new polarity, peering over the battlements at the numerous, angry poor. Not, unfortunately, that these options necessarily exclude each other.

I rise to prod the hamburgers. The world is no longer two; it is many. But the boys have armed themselves anyway, I see. Hefting sticks, since we don't allow them toy guns, they stalk each other through the dusk. At their age, my brothers and I mowed down legions of Nazis and Commies. Watching my sons join the ancient hunt, I wonder: Who will be designated as their enemies?

EXPLORATIONS

1. According to Nicholas Bromell, what criteria define a real American childhood (para. 1)? Which of these criteria does his own childhood fail to meet? Do you agree with his definition? Why or why not?

2. At what points does Bromell's family seem most ordinary to other people? At what points does his family seem most ordinary to its members? What qualities create the impression of normality in each case?

3. What proper names does Bromell mention? How does he identify his family members? How does his use of names affect his essay?

CONNECTIONS

1. What do the New York children in "The Nanny Dilemma" (p. 155) have in common with Nicholas Bromell and his brothers in "Family Secrets"? When young New Yorkers grow up, would you expect them to recall their childhoods as "real American" by Bromell's definition (para. 1)? Why or why not?

2. Nicholas Bromell, like Louise Erdrich (p. 137), describes a family that centers on one member. Why is each family willing to do this? What are the positive and negative effects of this choice?

3. Bromell writes about having a "spot" in the world (para. 1). What elements in Anwar El-Sadat's description of his hometown (p. 130) evidently made Mit Abul-Kum feel like his "spot"?

ELABORATIONS

1. "History flows through childhood the way light passes through the curtains of a bedroom" (para. 8). What does Bromell mean by this? Think of some national or world event that occurred when you were younger, and recall the personal incidents and sensations you experienced in your own smaller world at the same time. Using Bromell's essay (or part of it) as a model, write your own essay about history flowing through childhood.

2. In his last four paragraphs, Bromell describes two parallel "real American childhood" scenes. Did your childhood include summer evenings of charcoal-grilled hamburgers and homemade potato salad? What family activities do you recall as most classic or typical? Write an essay describing your memories.

WINDOWS:
THE WORLD

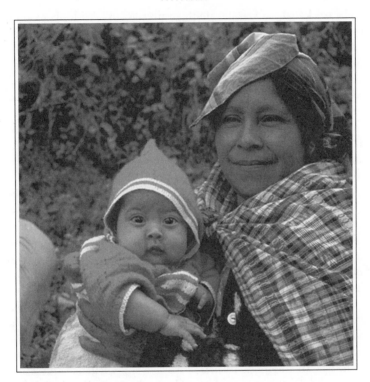

Families: *A mother holds a baby in a Guatemalan Indian village.*

RIGOBERTA MENCHÚ

Birth Ceremonies

The week that marked the 500th anniversary of Christopher Columbus's arrival in the New World also saw the Nobel Peace Prize awarded
to a thirty-three-year-old Central American Indian. Rigoberta Menchú
Tum is a Mayan of Guatemala's Quiché group. She grew up poor and
uneducated in the village of Chimel with her parents and ten brothers
and sisters. A migrant farm worker from the age of eight, she later became a live-in maid in Guatemala City, where she taught herself to
read and write Spanish. Her father, an organizing member of the Peasant Unity Committee, fought for property rights. In 1979 her sixteen-
year-old brother was kidnapped by Guatemalan soldiers, tortured for
two weeks, flayed, and burned alive with several other prisoners in front
of their families. The next year her father was killed when police
stormed the Spanish embassy his group was occupying and burned it.
Soon afterward, Menchú's mother was abducted, raped, and tortured
to death by soldiers. Menchú fled to Mexico City. There the Venezuelan writer Elisabeth Burgos-Debray helped her create her book *Me
llamo Rigoberta Menchú y asi me nacio la conciencia* ("I am named
Rigoberta Menchú and so my conscience was born"). "Birth Ceremonies" comes from the English translation by Ann Wright, *I, Rigoberta Menchú: An Indian Woman in Guatemala* (1984). Menchú has
since held several international posts and continues to work for peace
and reform.

The Mayan empire flourished in Mexico and Guatemala for a thousand years before Spanish conquistadors colonized the region. Famed
for their advances in medicine, mathematics, and astronomy, the Maya
left behind the great ruin of Tikal, still a source of pride to
Guatemalans. Although Indians remain a majority of the country's 10
million population, *ladinos* (Spanish speakers of mixed descent) are politically and economically dominant. The Central American states declared independence from Spain in 1821; the Republic of Guatemala
was established in 1839. Following the CIA-assisted overthrow of an
elected leftist government in 1954, a series of military governments gave
the country one of the hemisphere's worst human-rights records as well
as one of its longest-running civil wars: In the past forty years, well over
100,000 people have died. When President Alvaro Arzu Irigoyen was
elected in 1996, he ordered a purge of the military and police forces
which provoked a wave of murder, kidnapping, theft, and death threats.
However, Arzun vows to end both these forces' involvement in crime
and their impunity from punishment.

> Whoever may ask where we are, tell them what you know of
> us and nothing more.
>
> Learn to protect yourselves, by keeping our secret.
>
> – Popol Vuh[1]

In our community there is an elected representative, someone who is highly respected. He's not a king but someone whom the community looks up to like a father. In our village, my father and mother were the representatives. Well, then the whole community becomes the children of the woman who's elected. So a mother, on her first day of pregnancy, goes with her husband to tell these elected leaders that she's going to have a child, because the child will not only belong to them but to the whole community and must follow as far as he can our ancestors' traditions. The leaders then pledge the support of the community and say: "We will help you, we will be the child's second parents." They are known as *abuelos*, "grandparents" or "forefathers." The parents then ask the "grandparents" to help them find the child some godparents, so that if he's orphaned, he shouldn't be tempted by any of the bad habits our people sometimes fall into. So the "grandparents" and the parents choose the godparents together. It's also the custom for the pregnant mother's neighbors to visit her every day and take her little things, no matter how simple. They stay and talk to her, and she'll tell them all her problems.

Later, when she's in her seventh month, the mother introduces her baby to the natural world, as our customs tell her to. She goes out in the fields or walks over the hills. She also has to show her baby the kind of life she leads, so that if she gets up at three in the morning, does her chores and tends the animals, she does it all the more so when she's pregnant, conscious that the child is taking all this in. She talks to the child continuously from the first moment he's in her stomach, telling him how hard his life will be. It's as if the mother were a guide explaining things to a tourist. She'll say, for instance, "You must never abuse nature and you must live your life as honestly as I do." As she works in the fields, she tells her child all the little things about her work. It's a duty to her child that a mother must fulfill. And then, she also has to think of a way of hiding the baby's birth from her other children.

When her baby is born, the mother mustn't have her other children around her. The people present should be the husband, the village leaders, and the couple's parents. Three couples. The parents are often

---

[1]Sacred book of the Quiché Indian tribe.

away in other places, so if they can't be there, the husband's father and the wife's mother can perhaps make up one pair. If one of the village leaders can't come, one of them should be there to make up a couple with one of the parents. If none of the parents can come, some aunts and uncles should come to represent the family on both sides, because the child is to be part of the community. The birth of a new member is very significant for the community, as it belongs to the community, not just to the parents, and that's why three couples (but not just anybody) must be there to receive it. They explain that this child is the fruit of communal love. If the village leader is not a midwife as well, another midwife is called (it might be a grandmother) to receive the child. Our customs don't allow single women to see a birth. But it does happen in times of need. For instance, I was with my sister when she went into labor. Nobody else was at home. This was when we were being heavily persecuted. Well, I didn't exactly see, but I was there when the baby was born.

My mother was a midwife from when she was sixteen right up to her death at forty-three. She used to say that a woman hadn't the strength to push the baby out when she's lying down. So what she did with my sister was to hang a rope from the roof and pull her up, because my brother wasn't there to lift her up. My mother helped the baby out with my sister in that position. It's a scandal if an Indian woman goes to the hospital and gives birth there. None of our women would agree to that. Our ancestors would be shocked at many of the things which go on today. Family planning, for example. It's an insult to our culture and a way of swindling the people, to get money out of them.

This is part of the reserve that we've maintained to defend our customs and our culture. Indians have been very careful not to disclose any details of their communities, and the community does not allow them to talk about Indian things. I too must abide by this. This is because many religious people have come among us and drawn a false impression of the Indian world. We also find a *ladino* using Indian clothes very offensive. All this has meant that we keep a lot of things to ourselves and the community doesn't like us telling its secrets. This applies to all our customs. When the Catholic Action[2] arrived, for instance, everyone started going to mass and praying, but it's not their only religion, not the only way they have of expressing themselves. Anyway, when a baby is born, he's always baptized within the community before

---

[2]Association created in 1945 by Monsignor Rafael Gonzalez, to try and control the Indian fraternities of the *Altiplano*.

he's taken to church. Our people have taken Catholicism as just another channel of expression, not our one and only belief. Our people do
the same with other religions. The priests, monks, and nuns haven't
gained the people's confidence because so many of their things contradict our own customs. For instance, they say, "You have too much trust
in your elected leaders." But the village elects them *because* they trust
them, don't they? The priests say, "The trouble is you follow those sorcerers," and speak badly of them. But for our people this is like speaking
ill of their own fathers, and they lose faith in the priests. They say,
"Well, they're not from here, they can't understand our world." So
there's not much hope of winning our people's hearts.

To come back to the children, they aren't to know how the baby is
born. He's born somewhere hidden away and only the parents know
about it. They are told that a baby has arrived and that they can't see
their mother for eight days. Later on, the baby's companion, the placenta, that is, has to be burned at a special time. If the baby is born at
night, the placenta is burned at eight in the morning, and if he's born
in the afternoon, it'll be burned at five o'clock. This is out of respect for
both the baby and his companion. The placenta is not buried, because
the earth is the mother and the father of the child and mustn't be
abused by having the placenta buried in it. All these reasons are very
important for us. Either the placenta is burned on a log and the ashes
left there, or else it is put in the *temascal*. This is a stove which our
people use to make vapor baths. It's a small hut made of adobe and inside this hut is another one made of stone, and when we want to have a
bath, we light a fire to heat the stones, close the door, and throw water
on the stones to produce steam. Well, when the woman is about four
months pregnant, she starts taking these baths infused with evergreens,
pure natural aromas. There are many plants the community uses for
pregnant women, colds, headaches, and things like that. So the pregnant mother takes baths with plants prescribed for her by the midwife or
the village leader. The fields are full of plants whose names I don't
know in Spanish. Pregnant women use orange and peach leaves a lot
for bathing and there's another one we call Saint Mary's leaf which they
use. The mother needs these leaves and herbs to relax because she
won't be able to rest while she's pregnant since our women go on working just as hard in the fields. So after work, she takes this calming bath
so that she can sleep well, and the baby won't be harmed by her working hard. She's given medicines to take as well. And leaves to feed the
child. I believe that in practice (even if this isn't a scientific recommendation) these leaves work very well, because many of them contain vitamins. How else would women who endure hunger and hard work give

birth to healthy babies? I think that these plants have helped our people
survive.

The purity with which the child comes into the world is protected
for eight days. Our customs say that the newborn baby should be alone
with his mother in a special place for eight days, without any of her
other children. Her only visitors are the people who bring her food.
This is the baby's period of integration into the family; he very slowly
becomes a member of it. When the child is born, they kill a sheep and
there's a little fiesta just for the family. Then the neighbors start coming
to visit and bring presents. They either bring food for the mother or
something for the baby. The mother has to taste all the food her neighbors bring to show her appreciation for their kindness. After the eight
days are over, the family counts up how many visitors the mother had
and how many presents were received; things like eggs or food apart
from what was brought for the mother, or clothing, small animals, and
wood for the fire, or services like carrying water and chopping wood. If,
during the eight days, most of the community has called, this is very important, because it means that this child will have a lot of responsibility
toward his community when he grows up. The community takes over
all the household expenses for these eight days and the family spends
nothing.

After eight days, everything has been received, and another animal is
killed as recognition that the child's right to be alone with his mother is
over. All the mother's clothes, bedclothes, and everything she used during the birth are taken away by our elected leader and washed. She
can't wash them in the well, so no matter how far away the river is, they
must be carried and washed there. The baby's purity is washed away
and he's ready to learn the ways of humanity. The mother's bed is
moved to a part of the house which has first been washed with water
and lime. Lime is sacred. It strengthens the child's bones. I believe this
really is true. It gives a child strength to face the world. The mother has
a bath in the *temascal* and puts on clean clothes. Then the whole house
is cleaned. The child is also washed and dressed and put into the new
bed. Four candles are placed on the corners of the bed to represent the
four corners of the house and show him that this will be his home.
They symbolize the respect the child must have for his community, and
the responsibility he must feel toward it as a member of a household.
The candles are lit and give off an incense which incorporates the child
into the world he must live in. When the baby is born, his hands and
feet are bound to show him that they are sacred and must only be used
to work or do whatever nature meant them to do. They must never steal
or abuse the natural world, or show disrespect for any living thing.

After the eight days, his hands and feet are untied and he's now with his mother in the new bed. This means he opens the doors to the other members of the community, because neither the family or the community know him yet. Or rather, they weren't shown the baby when he was born. Now they can all come and kiss him. The neighbors bring another animal, and there's a big lunch in the new baby's house for all the community. This is to celebrate his integration "in the universe," as our parents used to say. Candles will be lit for him, and his candle becomes part of the candle of the whole community, which now has one more person, one more member. The whole community is at the ceremony, or at least, if not all of it, then some of it. Candles are lit to represent all the things which belong to the universe — earth, water, sun, and man — and the child's candle is put with them, together with incense (what we call *pom*) and lime — our sacred lime. Then the parents tell the baby of the suffering of the family he will be joining. With great feeling, they express their sorrow at bringing a child into the world to suffer. To us, suffering is our fate, and the child must be introduced to the sorrows and hardship, but he must learn that despite his suffering, he will be respectful and live through his pain. The child is then entrusted with the responsibility for his community and told to abide by its rules. After the ceremony comes the lunch, and then the neighbors go home. Now there is only the baptism to come.

When the baby is born, he's given a little bag with a garlic, a bit of 10 lime, salt, and tobacco in it to hang round his neck. Tobacco is important because it is a sacred plant for Indians. This all means that the child can ward off all the evil things in life. For us, bad things are like spirits, which exist only in our imagination. Something bad, for instance, would be if the child were to turn out to be a gossip — not sincere, truthful, and respectful, as a child should be. It also helps him collect together and preserve all our ancestors' things. That's more or less the idea of the bag — to keep him pure. The bag is put inside the four candles as well, and this represents the promise of the child when he grows up.

When the child is forty days old, there are more speeches, more promises on his behalf, and he becomes a full member of the community. This is his baptism. All the important people of the village are invited and they speak. The parents make a commitment. They promise to teach the child to keep the secrets of our people, so that our culture and customs will be preserved. The village leaders come and offer their experience, their example, and their knowledge of our ancestors. They explain how to preserve our traditions. Then, they promise to be responsible for the child, teach him as he grows up, and see that he follows in their ways. It's also something of a criticism of humanity, and of the many people who have forsaken their traditions. They say almost a prayer, asking that our traditions again enter the spirits of those who have forsaken them. Then, they evoke the names of our ancestors, like Tecun Umán and others who form part of the ceremony, as a kind of chant. They must be remembered as heroes of the Indian peoples. And then they say, . . . "Let no landowner extinguish all this, nor any rich man wipe out our customs. Let our children, be they workers or servants, respect and keep their secrets." The child is present for all of this, although he's all wrapped up and can scarcely be seen. He is told that he will eat maize,[3] and that, naturally, he is already made of maize because his mother ate it while he was forming in her stomach. He must respect the maize; even the grain of maize which has been thrown away, he must pick up. The child will multiply our race, he will replace all those who have died. From this moment, he takes on this responsibility, and is told to live as his "grandparents" have lived. The parents then reply that their child promises to accomplish all this. So, the village leaders and the parents both make promises on behalf of the child. It's his initiation into the community.

The ceremony is very important. It is also when the child is considered a child of God, our one father. We don't actually have the word God but that is what it is, because the one father is the only one we have. To reach this one father, the child must love beans, maize, the earth. The one father is the heart of the sky, that is, the sun. The sun is the father and our mother is the moon. She is a gentle mother. And she lights our way. Our people have many notions about the moon, and about the sun. They are the pillars of the universe.

When children reach ten years old, that's the moment when their parents and the village leaders talk to them again. They tell them that they will be young men and women and that one day they will be fathers and mothers. This is actually when they tell the child that he must never abuse his dignity, in the same way his ancestors never abused their dignity. It's also when they remind them that our ancestors were dishonored by the White Man, by colonization. But they don't tell them the way that it's written down in books, because the majority of Indians can't read or write, and don't even know that they have their own texts. No, they learn it through oral recommendations, the way it has been handed down through the generations. They are told that the Spaniards dishonored our ancestors' finest sons, and the most humble

---

[3]Corn. — ED.

of them. And it is to honor these humble people that we must keep our secrets. And no one except we Indians must know. They talk a lot about our ancestors. And the ten-years ceremony is also when our children are reminded that they must respect their elders, even though this is something their parents have been telling them ever since they were little. For example, if an old person is walking along the street, children should cross over to allow him to pass by. If any of us sees an elderly person, we are obliged to bow and greet him. Everyone does this, even the very youngest. We also show respect to pregnant women. Whenever we make food, we always keep some for any of our neighbors who are pregnant.

When little girls are born, the midwives pierce their ears at the same time as they tie their umbilical cords. The little bags around their necks and the thread used to tie their umbilical cord are both red. Red is very significant for us. It means heat, strength, all living things. It's linked to the sun, which for us is the channel to the one God, the heart of everything, of the universe. So red gives off heat and fire, and red things are supposed to give life to the child. At the same time, it asks him to respect living things too. There are no special clothes for the baby. We don't buy anything special beforehand but just use pieces of *corte*[4] to wrap him in.

When a male child is born, there are special celebrations, not because he's male but because of all the hard work and responsibility he'll have as a man. It's not that *machismo* doesn't exist among our people, but it doesn't present a problem for the community because it's so much part of our way of life. The male child is given an extra day alone with his mother. The usual custom is to celebrate a male child by killing a sheep or some chickens. Boys are given more, they get more food because their work is harder and they have more responsibility. At the same time, he is head of the household, not in the bad sense of the word, but because he is responsible for so many things. This doesn't mean girls aren't valued. Their work is hard too and there are other things that are due to them as mothers. Girls are valued because they are part of the earth, which gives us maize, beans, plants, and everything we live on. The earth is like a mother which multiplies life. So the girl child will multiply the life of our generation and of our ancestors whom we must respect. The girl and the boy are both integrated into the community in equally important ways; the two are interrelated

15

---

[4]Multicolored material that Guatemalan women use as a skirt. It is part of their traditional costume.

and compatible. Nevertheless, the community is always happier when a male child is born and the men feel much prouder. The customs, like the tying of the hands and feet, apply to both boys and girls.

Babies are breast-fed. It's much better than any other sort of food. But the important thing is the sense of community. It's something we all share. From the very first day, the baby belongs to the community, not only to the parents, and the baby must learn from all of us. . . . In fact, we behave just like bourgeois families in that, as soon as the baby is born, we're thinking of his education, of his well-being. But our people feel that the baby's school must be the community itself, that he must learn to live like all the rest of us. The tying of the hands at birth also symbolizes this; that no one should accumulate things the rest of the community does not have and he must know how to share, to have open hands. The mother must teach the baby to be generous. This way of thinking comes from poverty and suffering. Each child is taught to live like the fellow members of his community.

We never eat in front of pregnant women. You can only eat in front of a pregnant woman if you can offer something as well. The fear is that, otherwise, she might abort the baby or that the baby could suffer if she didn't have enough to eat. It doesn't matter whether you know her or not. The important thing is sharing. You have to treat a pregnant woman differently from other women because she is two people. You must treat her with respect so that she recognizes it and conveys this to the baby inside her. You instinctively think she's the image of the baby about to be born. So you love her. Another reason why you must stop and talk to a pregnant woman is because she doesn't have much chance to rest or enjoy herself. She's always worried and depressed. So when she stops and chats a bit, she can relax and feel some relief.

When the baby joins the community, with him in the circle of candles — together with his little red bag — he will have his hoe, his machete, his axe, and all the tools he will need in life. These will be his playthings. A little girl will have her washing board and all the things she will need when she grows up. She must learn the things of the house, to clean, to wash, and to sew her brothers' trousers, for example. The little boy must begin to live like a man, to be responsible and learn to love the work in the fields. The learning is done as a kind of game. When the parents do anything they always explain what it means. This includes learning prayers. This is very important to our people. The mother may say a prayer at any time. Before getting up in the morning, for instance, she thanks the day which is dawning because it might be a very important one for the family. Before lighting the fire, she blesses the wood because that fire is going to cook food for the whole family.

Since it's the little girl who is closest to her mother, she learns all of this. Before washing the *nixtamal*,[5] the woman blows on her hands and puts them in the *nixtamal*. She takes everything out and washes it well. She blows on her hands so that her work will bear fruit. She does it before she does the wash as well. She explains all these little details to her daughter, who learns by copying her. With the men it's the same. Before they start work every day, whatever hour of the morning it is, they greet the sun. They remove their hats and talk to the sun before starting work. Their sons learn to do it too, taking off their little hats to talk to the sun. Naturally, each ethnic group has its own forms of expression. Other groups have different customs from ours. The meaning of their weaving patterns, for example. We realize the others are different in some things, but the one thing we have in common is our culture. Our people are mainly peasants, but there are some people who buy and sell as well. They go into this after they've worked on the land. Sometimes when they come back from working in the *finca*,[6] instead of tending a little plot of land, they'll start a shop and look for a different sort of life. But if they're used to greeting the sun every morning, they still go on doing it. And they keep all their old customs. Every part of our culture comes from the earth. Our religion comes from the maize and bean harvests which are so vital to our community. So even if a man goes to try and make some money, he never forgets his culture springs from the earth.

As we grow up we have a series of obligations. Our parents teach us to be responsible, just as they have been responsible. The eldest son is responsible for the house. Whatever the father cannot correct is up to the eldest son to correct. He is like a second father to us all and is responsible for our upbringing. The mother is the one who is responsible for keeping an account of what the family eats and what she has to buy. When a child is ill, she has to get medicine. But the father has to solve a lot of problems too. And each one of us, as we grow up, has our own small area of responsibility. This comes from the promises made for the child when he is born, and from the continuity of our customs. The child can make the promise for himself when his parents have taught him to do it. The mother, who is closest to the children, does this, or sometimes the father. They talk to their children explaining what they have to do and what our ancestors used to do. They don't impose it as a law, but just give the example of what our ancestors have always done.

---

[5]Cauldron where the maize is cooked.
[6]Plantation, estate.

This is how we all learn our own small responsibilities. For example, the little girl begins by carrying water, and the little boy begins by tying up the dogs when the animals are brought into the yard at night, or by fetching a horse which has wandered off. Both girls and boys have their tasks and are told the reasons for doing them. They learn responsibility because if they don't do their little jobs well, their father has the right to scold them, or even beat them. So, they are very careful about learning to do their jobs well, but the parents are also very careful to explain exactly why the jobs have to be done. The little girl understands the reasons for everything her mother does. For example, when she puts a new earthenware pot on the fire for the first time, she hits it five times with a branch, so that it knows its job is to cook and so that it lasts. When the little girl asks, "Why did you do that?" her mother says, "So that it knows what its job is and does it well." When it's her turn to cook, the little girl does as her mother does. Again this is all bound up with our commitment to maintain our customs and pass on the secrets of our ancestors. The elected fathers of the community explain to us that all these things come down to us from our grandfathers and we must conserve them. Nearly everything we do today is based on what our ancestors did. This is the main purpose of our elected leader — to embody all the values handed down from our ancestors. He is the leader of the community, a father to all our children, and he must lead an exemplary life. Above all, he has a commitment to the whole community. Everything that is done today is done in memory of those who have passed on.

EXPLORATIONS

1. Besides recognizing biological parenthood, in what other ways do the Quiché Indians apply the concepts of mother and father?
2. What ceremonies mark the landmarks in a Quiché child's life, both before and after birth? What are the main purposes of these ceremonies?
3. What specific steps are taken by a Quiché baby's parents, and what steps are taken by others in the community, to make sure the child learns his or her responsibilities?

CONNECTIONS

1. What ideas about community and family are expressed by the rituals Menchú describes? What rituals (formal or informal) does Henry Louis Gates Jr. mention in "Down to Cumberland" (p. 146) that express similar ideas?

2. What are the similarities between the induction ceremonies described by Robert Bly (p. 133) and Judith Ortiz Cofer (p. 132) and those described by Menchú? What ideas mentioned by Michael Dorris on page 273 illuminate the problems Bly ascribes to contemporary U.S. nuclear families?

3. Judging from Ved Mehta's recollection on page 133, what ideas about family did his Indian parents share with Guatemalan Quiché parents? In what ways was Mehta's family more like one in the United States?

ELABORATIONS

1. In Quiché society, talismans are given to a child to "ward off all the evil things in life" (para. 10). What evil things are warded off in this way? What tactics are used in the United States to ward off similar (or different) evils? Write an essay classifying the dangers from which our culture tries to protect children, and the methods we use to do this.

2. How are Quiché children taught to regard their ancestors? Write a narrative or descriptive essay about the role of ancestors in your life or in your culture.

AMOS OZ

If There Is Justice

Born Amos Klausner in Jerusalem in 1939, Amos Oz belongs to the first generation of Israeli writers who are sabras (native born). His grandfather had fled anti-Semitism in Russia and Poland to help build an ideal Jewish state in Palestine. As a schoolchild Oz filled sandbags after the British departure in 1948. Four years later, as the fledgling state of Israel struggled to accommodate over a million refugees, Oz's mother committed suicide. Her son cast off his father's scholarly right-wing Zionism to become a peasant-soldier on Kibbutz Hulda, midway between Jerusalem (then half in Israel and half in Jordan) and Tel Aviv to the north. There Oz took his new last name, which means "strength" in Hebrew; worked in the cotton fields; studied socialism; and eventually was sent to Hebrew University in Jerusalem for his bachelor's degree. On his return he adopted the routine he followed until recently: teaching in the high school, doing assigned chores, spending time with his wife and three children, and writing stories and novels involving kibbutz life and ideals. Oz left Kibbutz Hulda for fellowships at Oxford and Hebrew Universities and a lecture tour of U.S. campuses and to fight in the Sinai Desert and Golan Heights in the 1967 and 1973 wars. The recipient of several international literary awards, he is a leader of Israel's Peace Now movement. Oz's most recent novels include *To Know a Woman* (1991) and *Fima* (1993).

"If There Is Justice" was translated from the Hebrew by Nicholas de Lange with assistance from the author. It comes from Oz's novel *Elsewhere, Perhaps*, which was published in Israel shortly before the Six-Day War in 1967. Oz served with Israeli armored divisions in that war, which ended in Israel's almost doubling its territory by occupying Syria's Golan Heights to the north, Jordan's West Bank to the east (including Jerusalem), and the Gaza Strip, formerly administered by Egypt, to the southeast. Before then, Israel consisted of roughly 8,000 square miles of land on the eastern Mediterranean coast, only a fifth of which is arable. Archaeological evidence documents a Hebrew kingdom in the region (known as Palestine) going back to about 1,000 B.C., the era of the biblical House of David. After World War I, victorious Britain and France divided up the Middle Eastern remnants of Turkey's Ottoman Empire. France was to control Syria and Lebanon, while Britain continued to dominate Egypt, Iraq, the newly created Transjordan, and Palestine (the southeastern Mediterranean coast). Their plans to make these territories independent were hampered in Palestine by the struggle for dominance between its Arab and Jewish populations. With World War II, and the Nazi slaughter of Jews, the need for an official Jewish homeland became urgent. After the war, Britain turned Palestine over to the United Nations, which in 1948 voted — over strong Arab protests — to create the state of Israel. Jews here always have been surrounded by Arabs: Israel currently is bounded on the north by Lebanon, on the east by Syria and Jordan, and on the southwest by Egypt. The conflict in this region is more than 3,000 years old (human habitation dates back at least 100,000 years); it has shaped both Amos Oz's writing and his homeland. For more background on Israel, see p. 713.

Rami Rimon came home for the weekend on leave.

His face was thinner. His skin had shrunk a little. His jaws seemed more prominent. The lines on his face were sharper. His mother's face struggling to get out. Fine creases ringed his mouth. The sun had etched wrinkles round his eyes. Twin furrows ran from his nose to the corners of his mouth.

He was wearing an impeccable greenish uniform, with his beret tucked in his pocket. His stout boots were shod with steel at toe and heel. His sleeves were rolled up to reveal hairy forearms, and his hands were covered with little scars. He was conscious of his manly appearance as he strode slowly across the yard with an air of studied indifference. The men and women he met greeted him warmly. He responded with an offhand nod. There were traces of gun grease under his fingernails, and his left elbow was dressed with a grubby bandage.

When the first tumult of hugs and kisses, received by Rami with a wavering smile, had died down, Fruma said:

"Well, you won't believe it, but I was just thinking of you the moment before you turned up. Mother's intuition." 5

Rami thought there was nothing strange in that. He had said in his letter that he would come on Friday afternoon, and she knew perfectly well what time the bus came. As he spoke, he put down his shabby kit bag, pulled his shirt outside his trousers, lit a cigarette, and laid a heavy hand on Fruma's shoulder.

"It's good to see you, Mom. I wanted to tell you that I'm really glad to see you again."

Fruma glanced at his dusty boots and said:

"You've lost so much weight."

Rami drew on his cigarette and asked about her health. 10

"Come inside and have a shower before dinner. You're all sweaty. Would you like a cold drink first? No. A warm drink would be better for you. Wait, though, the first thing is to take you along to the surgery. I want the nurse to have a look at your elbow."

Rami started to explain about the wound. It happened during a bayonet practice; the clumsy oaf of a section commander . . . but Fruma did not let him finish the story.

"There you go dropping your ash on the floor. I've just washed it in your honor. There are four ashtrays in the house, and you . . ."

Rami sat down in his filthy clothes on the clean white bedspread and kicked off his boots. Fruma rushed to fetch her husband's old slippers. Her eyes were dry, but she tried to turn her face away from her son to hide the look he disliked so much. Rami, however, pretended not to have seen that strained look, as of a dam about to burst. He lay back on the bed, looked up at the ceiling, drew the ashtray that Fruma had put in his hand closer to him, and blew out a puff of smoke.

"The day before yesterday we crossed a river on a rope bridge. Two   15 ropes stretched one above the other, one to walk on and the other to hold. With all our stuff on our backs, spade, blankets, gun, ammunition, the lot. Now, who do you suppose it was who lost his balance and fell in the water? The section commander! We all . . ."

Fruma eyed her son and exclaimed:

"You've lost at least ten pounds. Have you had any lunch? Where? No, you haven't. I'll dash across to the hall and get you something to eat. Just a snack — I'll make you a proper meal when you've had a rest. How about some raw carrot? It's very good for you. Are you sure? I can't force you. All right, then, have a shower and go to sleep. You can eat when you wake up. But perhaps I'd better take you to the surgery right away. Wait a minute. Here's a nice glass of orange juice. Don't argue, drink it."

"I jumped in the water and fished him out," Rami continued. "Then I had to dive in again to look for his rifle. Poor wretch! It was hilarious. It wasn't his first accident, though. Once, on an exercise . . ."

"You need some new socks. They're all falling apart," Fruma remarked as she pulled his dirty laundry out of the kit bag.

"Once, on an exercise, he fired his submachine gun by accident.   20 Nearly killed the battalion commander. He's the clumsiest fool you can imagine. You can tell what's he like from his name. He's called Zalman Zulman. I've written a song about him, and we sing it all day long. Listen."

"But they don't feed you there. And you didn't write every other day, as you promised. But I saw in the letter box that you wrote to Noga Harish. That's life. Your mother works her fingers to the bone, and some child comes and collects the honey. It doesn't matter now. There's something I must know: Did she answer your letter? No? Just as I thought. You don't know what she's like. It was just as well you ditched her. Everybody knows what she is. The mistress of a man who's old enough to be her grandfather. It's disgusting. Disgusting. Have you got enough razor blades? It's disgusting, I tell you."

"Is it true they're starting to work the Camel's Field? That's going to cause a flare-up, all right. Provided, of course, the powers that be don't get cold feet. You know, Jewish sentimentality, and all that. My buddies say . . ."

"Go and have a shower. The water's just right now. No, I heard every word. Test me. 'Jewish sentimentality.' There aren't many boys of your age with such an independent way of thinking. After your shower you can have a nap. Meanwhile, I'll ask the nurse to come here. That wound looks very nasty. You've got to have it seen to."

"By the way, Mom, did you say that she . . ."

"Yes, son?"   25

"All right. Never mind. It doesn't matter now."

"Tell me, tell me what you need. I'm not tired. I can do anything you want me to."

"No, thanks. I don't need anything. I just wanted to say something, but it's not important. It's irrelevant. I've forgotten. Stop running around. I can't bear it. We'll talk this evening. Meanwhile, you must have a rest, too."

"Me! I'll rest in my grave. I don't need to rest. I'm not tired. When you were a baby, you had something wrong with your ears. A chronic infection. There weren't any antibiotics then. You cried all night, night after night. You were in pain. And you've always been a sensitive boy. I rocked your cradle all night, night after night, and sang you songs. One does everything for children, without counting the cost. You won't repay me. You'll repay it to your own children. I won't be here any more, but you'll be a good father, because you're so sensitive. You don't think about rest when you're doing something for your children. How old were you then? You've forgotten all about it. It was the time when Yoash started going to school, so it must have been when you were eighteen months old. You were always a delicate child. Here am I rambling on, and you need to sleep. Go to sleep now."

"By the way, Mom, if you're going to the surgery could you bring me   30 some corn ointment. You won't forget, will you?"

At five o'clock Rami woke up, put on a clean white shirt and gray trousers, quietly helped himself to a snack, and then went to the basketball field. On the way he met Einav, limping awkwardly. She asked how he was. He said he was fine. She asked if it was a hard life. He said he was ready to face any hardship. She asked if his mother was pleased with him and answered her own question:

"Of course Fruma's pleased with you. You're so bronzed and handsome."

The field was floodlit, but the light was not noticeable in the bright twilight. The only living souls there were Oren's gang. Rami put his hands in his pockets and stood for a while without doing or saying anything. The Sabbath will go by. Empty. Without anything happening. With mother. Sticky. What do I need? A cigarette. That thin boy playing by himself over there in the corner is called Ido Zohar. Once I caught him sitting in the common room at night writing a poem. What was I saying? A cigarette.

Rami put the cigarette in his mouth and two planes roared by, shattering the Sabbatical calm, hidden in the twilight glow. The dying sun struck sparks off their fuselage. The metal shone back dazzlingly. In a flash Rami realized that they were not our planes. They had the enemy's marking on their wings. An excited shout burst from his throat.

"Theirs!"   35

Instinctively he looked down, just long enough to hear Oren's confused cry, but by the time he looked up again the drama was almost over. The enemy planes had turned tail and were fleeing from other planes that were approaching powerfully from the southwest, evidently trying to block their escape. Instantly, dark shapes fell through the air toward the orchards to the north. Both planes had jettisoned the spare fuel tanks fixed to their wings to speed their flight. Rami clenched his fists and growled through his teeth, "Let them have it." Before he had finished there was an answering burst of gunfire. Lightning flashed. After what seemed a long interval, there came a dull roll of thunder. The fate of the raid was settled in an instant. The enemy planes disappeared over the mountains, one of them trailing a cloud of white smoke mixed with gray. Their pursuers paused, circled the valley twice like angry hounds, then vanished into the darkening sky.

Oren shouted jubilantly:

"We hit one! We smashed one! We brought one down!"

And Rami Rimon, like a child, not like a soldier, hugged Oren Geva and exclaimed:

"I hope they burn! I hope they burn to death!"   40

He pounded Oren's ribs exultantly with his fists until Oren drew away groaning with pain. Rami was seized by demented joy.

▼ ▼ ▼

His joy accompanied him to the dining hall, where a spirit of noisy
excitement reigned. He made his way among the tables to where Noga
Harish stood in her best dress, looking at the notice board. He put his
hands on her shoulders and whispered in her ear:

"Well, silly girl, did you see or didn't you?"

Noga turned to face him with a condescending smile.

"Good Sabbath, Rami. You're very brown. It suits you. You look   45
happy."

"I . . . I saw it all. From beginning to end. I was up at the basketball
field. Suddenly I heard a noise to the east, and I realized at once that . . ."

"You're like my little brother. You're cute. You're happy."

These remarks encouraged Rami. He spoke up boldly:

"Shall we go outside? Will you come outside with me?"

Noga thought for a moment. Then she smiled inwardly, with her   50
eyes, not with her mouth.

"Why not?" she said.

"Come on then," said Rami, and took hold of her arm. Almost at
once he let it go.

When they were outside the dining hall, Noga said:

"Where shall we go?"

Strangely enough, at that moment Noga remembered something she   55
had forgotten: Rami's full name was Avraham. Avraham Rominov.

"Anywhere," Rami said. "Let's go."

Noga suggested they sit down on the yellow bench, facing the door
of the dining hall. Rami was embarrassed. People would see them
there, he said. And stare at them. And talk.

Noga smiled again, and again she asked calmly, "Why not?"

Rami could find no answer to her question. He crossed his legs, took
a cigarette out of his shirt pocket, tapped it three times on his match-
box, stuck it in the corner of his mouth, struck a match, shielded the
flame with both hands even though there was no wind, inhaled deeply
with half-closed eyes, blew out a long stream of smoke, and when all
this was done, lowered his eyes to the ground once more. Finally, he
gave her a sidelong glance and began:

"Well? What have you got to say for yourself?"   60

Noga replied that she hadn't been going to say anything. On the contrary, she thought it was he who was going to do the talking.

"Oh, nothing special. Just . . . What do you expect me to do?" he
suddenly burst out violently. "Spend the whole evening, the whole Sabbath, my whole leave with my mother, like some mother's darling?"

"Why not? She's missed you badly."

"Why not? Because . . . All right. I can see I bore you. Don't think I can't live without you. I can get on quite well without you. Do you think I can't?"

Noga said she was sure he could manage perfectly well without her.   65
They fell silent.

Hasia Ramigolski and Esther Klieger-Isarov came toward them, chatting in Yiddish and laughing. When they caught sight of Noga and Rami their conversation stopped dead. As they walked past, Hasia said:

"Good evening. Shabbat Shalom." She dwelt suggestively on the stressed syllables.

Rami grunted, but Noga smiled and said gently:

"A very good evening to you both."   70

Rami said nothing for a while. Then he murmured:

"Well?"

"I'm listening."

"I hear they're going to start working on the hill," Rami said. "There's going to be trouble."

"It's so pointless."   75

Rami quickly changed the subject. He told the story of his section commander who had fallen in the water trying to demonstrate how to cross a river on a rope bridge. He went on to say that it wasn't the poor fool's first accident. "Once, on an exercise, he accidentally fired his submachine gun and nearly killed the battalion commander. You can tell what he's like from his name. He's called Zalman Zulman, of all things. I've written a rhyme about him:

> "Zalman Zulman's full of fun,
> Always letting off his gun.
> Zalman Zulman lost his grip,
> Took an unexpected dip.
> Zalman Zulman . . ."

"Just a minute. Does he play an instrument?"

"Who?"

"Zalman. The man you were talking about. What's the matter with your elbow?"

"What's that got to do with it?" Rami asked indignantly.   80

"With what?"

"With what we were talking about."

"You were telling me about someone called Zalman. I asked if he played an instrument. You haven't answered my question."

"But I don't see what . . ."

"You're very brown. It suits you."   85

"It's hardly surprising. We train all day in the sun. Of course we get brown. Listen: We went on a fifty-mile route march, with all the kit, gun, pack, spade, and all at the trot. Eight of the people in my squad . . ."

"Chilly, don't you think?"

". . . collapsed on the way. And we had to carry them on stretchers. I . . ."

"I'm cold. Couldn't you finish the story tomorrow? If you don't mind terribly."

"What's the matter?" Rami considered, and then asked thickly,   90
"What's up? Is somebody waiting for you? Are you rushing off to . . . to keep an appointment?"

"Yes, I've got to take my father his dinner. He isn't well."

"What, again?" Rami asked absently. Noga explained that he had a pain in his chest and the doctor had ordered him to go to bed.

"Next week he's got to have an examination. That's all. Shall we meet here again tomorrow afternoon?"

Rami did not answer. He lit another cigarette and threw the lighted match away behind the bench. Noga said good night and started to go. Then she stopped, turned, and said:

"Don't smoke too much."   95

At that moment five steps separated them. Rami asked irritably why she should care whether he smoked a lot or a little. Noga ignored his question and said:

"You're very brown. It suits you. Good night."

Rami said nothing. He sat alone on the bench until the dancing started in the square, as it did every Friday night at a quarter past nine.

When it was over, shortly before midnight, he set off for his mother's room. He changed his course, however, because he met Dafna Isarov, who asked him if he was going home to bed already, and Rami thought he detected a sneer in her voice. So he turned off the path. His feet guided him toward the cow shed, where he had worked before he was called up. And as he walked he talked to himself.

This could never have happened to Yoash. It's happened to me,   100
though. Women understand only one language, brute force. But, as mother said, I was always a delicate child. Hell. Now they're laughing. Everybody wants something bad to happen to someone else so as to make life more interesting. It's like that everywhere; it's like that on the kibbutz and it's even like that in the army. You're a child you're a child you're a child. You're like my little brother. Maybe being brown does suit me, but it hasn't got me anywhere. She didn't insult me for once. She didn't even call me a horse. What did she do to me tonight, how

did she make fun of me? My Rami is a delicate, sensitive boy. I wish I
could die. That'd show them. I can bend this sprinkler with my bare
hands. That'll drive Theodor Herzl Goldring mad. I've got stronger
hands than Yoash. If only he weren't dead, I'd show him. Where am I
going? Walking around like some Jack looking for his Jill. Leaping on
the mountains, skipping in the hills, as that filthy old lecher would say.
People like that ought to be put down. Like Arabs. Punch him in the
face, he raises his hands to protect himself, you hit him in the stomach
and give him a kick for good measure. All over. Here we are at the cow
shed. Hey, Titan, good bull. Are you awake? Bulls sleep standing up because they can't lie down because of the iron ring. If they come to
slaughter you, Titan, don't let them. Don't give in. Show your mettle.
Don't be a ghetto bull. Give them a *corrida*. We mustn't give in without
a struggle. We must be strong and quick and light and violent like a jet
fighter. Swoop and dart and turn and soar like a knife flashing through
the sky like a fighter. A fighter is such a powerful thing. I could have
been a pilot, but Mother.

Strange that the moon is shining. The moon does strange things.
Changes things strangely. Changes the colors of things. Silver. My
Rami is a delicate sensitive child Rami writes poems like Izo Zohar he
loves nature hell he loves plants and animals hope they burn to death.
Her father has a pain in his chest. It's because of old Berger. Dirty old
man. Her father taught us a poem by Bialik once, called "The Slaughter," where it says that there is no justice in this world. It's true. It's a
ghetto poem, but it's true. He's lived his life, he's got grown-up children, he's found his niche. Why did he steal her from me? What have I
done to him? And she said I was brown and handsome. If I'm brown
and handsome, and he's old and fat, then why.

When I die, she'll know. It'll shatter her. The moon colors everything white. Silver. Listen, Noga, listen. I've also got a pain in my chest,
I'm also in pain, so why don't you. I make fun of Zalman Zulman, she
makes fun of me, they all make fun of me. It shows there isn't any justice in the world, only slaughter, Titan, worse than anything the Devil
could invent. That's from the same poem. The man who's being
slaughtered starts thinking about justice. The man who's slaughtering
him thinks only about violence. My mistake was not to use force on her.
Why, Titan, why didn't I use force, do you know why? I'll tell you. Because my Rami is a delicate boy curse them he loves nature hope they
burn he loves plants and animals filthy whores. That sounds like planes
overhead. It's after midnight. I love these planes, roaring along without
lights. There's going to be a big war. I'll die. Then they'll know.

The fish ponds. A light in Grisha's hut. A pressure lamp. I can hear Grisha's voice. In the boat. Shouting to his fishermen. He's been in three wars and he's come out alive.

Maybe Dafna, his daughter. Ridiculous. They'd laugh. What's in this filthy shed? Barrels. Sacks of fish food. The fishermen's supper. If they find me here. Grisha's belt. A pistol. It's a revolver. Fancy leaving a revolver in an empty shed. They'll be coming back to eat soon. They'll laugh, they'll laugh. They'll say I went for a walk to look for inspiration. I know how it works. It has a revolving drum with six chambers. You put a bullet in each chamber. After each shot the drum revolves and brings another bullet in line with the barrel. That's how the revolver works. Now let's see how Rami Rimon works. A trial. Without a judge. I'm the judge. Now let's begin.

Rami takes a bullet out of the leather holster, a yellow metal case containing a little brown metal projectile. First of all, he puts the bullet in his mouth. A sharp, metallic taste. Then he puts the bullet in one of the chambers. He spins the drum without looking, because luck must be blind. He puts the gun to his temple. The chances are five to one. He squeezes the trigger. A dry thud. Rami inserts a second bullet. Spins the blind drum. Four to two. Gun to temple. Squeezes. Dry thud. Maybe I'm being silly. We'll soon know, Judge. I'm not trying to kill myself. It's only an experiment. Up to five. A delicate sensitive child couldn't do this. A third bullet. Blind spin. Cold damp hand. I've touched something damp. If I can do this, I'm not a delicate sensitive child. Up to five. Gun to temple. Squeeze the trigger. Dry thud. I'm past halfway. Two more tries. Fourth bullet. Now the odds are against me. Now comes the test. Watch carefully, Judge. Spin. Slowly. The drum, slowly. Without looking. Slowly. Temple. You're crazy. But you're no coward. Slowly squeeze. It's cold here.

Now the fifth. Last one. Like an injection. Delicate sensitive child's trembling. Why? Nothing will happen because nothing's happened so far, even though according to the odds I should have died with the fourth bullet. Don't tremble, dear little delicate child who cried all night with earache, don't tremble, think of Grisha Isarov who's come out of three wars alive. Yoash wouldn't have trembled, because he was Yoash. Little ghetto boy, with a little cap and a gray coat and side curls. I want to know how many I. Not to kill myself. Four. That's enough. Madness to go on. No, we said five — five let it be. Don't change your mind, coward, don't lie, you said five, not four. Five let it be. Put the gun to your temple. Now squeeze, horse, squeeze, you're a ghetto child, you're a little boy, you're my little brother, squeeze. Wait a moment. I'm allowed to think first. Suppose I die here. She'll know. She'll know I wasn't joking. But they'll say "broken heart" they'll say "unrequited love" they'll say "emotional crisis." Sticky, very sticky. Hell. Squeeze. You won't feel a thing. A bullet in the brain is instant death. No time for pain. And afterward? Like plunging through the sky. An invisible fighter. It doesn't hurt. Perhaps I've already pressed the trigger and died perhaps when you die nothing changes. Other people see a corpse blood bones and you carry on as usual. I can try again. If I press the trigger, it's a sign I'm still alive. Afterward everything will be black and warm. When you die it's warm even though the body gets cold. Warm and safe like under a blanket in winter. And quiet. Squeeze. You've got a chance. Like when we used to play dice when I was little and sometimes I wanted very badly to throw a six and I threw a six. Now I want very badly to press the trigger but my finger won't press. Trembling. Careful you don't press it accidentally. Everything is different when the moon shines yellow. Can hear Grisha cursing next week we're going to the firing range that'll be interesting I'll be top of the class I'm an excellent shot now count up to three and shoot. Eyes open. No. Eyes closed. No. One, two , th- no. Up to ten. One, two, three, four, five, six, seven, eight, nine, t-.

But Rami Rimon did not try his luck the fifth time. He put down the revolver and went out into the fields and wandered about till his feet guided him back to the cow shed. Grisha won't notice. And if he does, he'll have a shock. I forgot to check the most important thing. I didn't look inside the gun to see what would have happened if I'd pressed the fifth time. Better not to know. Some things are better left undone.

A new thought occurred to Rami. It soothed him like a gentle caress. Not all men are born to be heroes. Maybe I wasn't born to be a hero. But in every man there's something special, something that isn't in other men. In my nature, for instance, there's a certain sensitivity. A capacity to suffer and feel pain. Perhaps I was born to be an artist, or even a doctor. Some women go for doctors and others go for artists. Men aren't all cast in the same mold. It's true. I'm not Yoash. But Yoash wasn't me. I've got some things he didn't have. A painter, perhaps.

It'll be morning soon. Planes in the sky. Sad Zalman Zulman's full of fun, always letting off his gun. Zalman Zulman lost his grip, took an unexpected dip. Zalman Zulman, whore like me, looking for justice in the w.c. Zalman Zulman go to bed, time to rest your weary head.

I composed the poem. I can abolish it. It's an abolished poem. 110

EXPLORATIONS

1. Who is Yoash? What can you tell about him from the story? What is his current significance to Rami? To Fruma?

2. What kind of person does Rami want to be, and what kind of person does he think he is? How has his self-image — the qualities he sees as desirable and undesirable in himself — evidently been affected by his role as a soldier? By living in a close-knit, war-oriented community?

3. What does Rami learn from his game of Russian roulette? Why does he start it? Why does he stop?

CONNECTIONS

1. According to Rigoberta Menchú in "Birth Ceremonies" (p. 176), how and from whom do Quiché children learn their role in the community? In "If There Is Justice," how and from whom has Rami Rimon evidently learned his role as a kibbutz member? How and from whom has he been learning his role as an adult Israeli?

2. "One does everything for children, without counting the cost," Fruma tells her son (para. 29). "You won't repay me. You'll repay it to your own children." What is generous and what is selfish about these statements? How would their meaning change and how would it stay the same if the statements were made by one of the parents in Susan Cheever's "The Nanny Dilemma" (p. 155)?

3. Compare Fruma's supervision of her son in "If There Is Justice" with Louise Erdrich's supervision of her son in "Foreword" (p. 137). In what ways does living on a kibbutz give Fruma more parental power and responsibility than Erdrich has? In what ways does living in a single-family home in a small American town give Erdrich more parental power and responsibility than Fruma has?

ELABORATIONS

1. Write an essay explaining Oz's story title, "If There Is Justice." What theme(s) does the title reflect? How do specific incidents, such as Rami's game of Russian roulette, exemplify or illuminate the story's larger theme(s)?

2. Reread Robert Bly's comments on page 133 on boys' initiation into manhood. In what ways does the Israeli culture in Oz's story meet and fail to meet the needs Bly discusses? How does Oz's definition of manhood seem to differ from Bly's? Look also at Judith Ortiz Cofer's (p. 132) and Michael Dorris's (p. 273) observations. Write an essay on an initiation rite (or the need for better initiation rites) in your family, religion, or community.

FRANK McCOURT

Limerick Homecoming

Francis McCourt was born in Brooklyn, New York, in 1930 after his poverty-stricken parents moved there from Ireland. When he was four years old, his family — still poor but now including four young sons — returned in desperation to the mother's hometown of Limerick. The following essay about that homecoming comes from McCourt's book *Angela's Ashes* (1996). McCourt returned to the United States at age nineteen and was drafted into the army. Although he never finished high school, he attended New York University on the G.I. Bill. After graduating in 1957 he began teaching in and around New York City, and in 1970 became an English teacher at the renowned Stuyvesant High School. In 1988 he retired to travel around the world with his brother Malachy and perform an autobiographical cabaret show they had developed, *A Couple of Blaguards*. He now lives and writes in New York City.

Eire, or the Republic of Ireland, occupies all of the island of Ireland except for six northern counties known as Ulster, which are part of the United Kingdom of Great Britian and Northern Ireland (U.K.). Ireland has been inhabited since the Stone Age. Around the fourth century B.C., Celts from the European mainland established a Gaelic civilization. St. Patrick brought Christianity in A.D. 432, and monasteries became centers of learning comparable to universities. In the twelfth century the Pope gave Ireland to Henry II of England, a bequest that persisted even after Henry VIII quit the Roman Catholic Church. In the 1600s, Protestants from Scotland began immigrating to Ulster and displacing Gaelic-speaking Catholics. In 1801 the Act of Union formally united England, Scotland, and Ireland. Nationalist uprisings led to the proclamation of an Irish republic in 1919 and its recognition three years later as the Irish Free State, a dominion of Great Britain. (Ulster voted to stay with the U.K.. Although the rest of Ireland is mostly Catholic, the North was by then mostly Protestant.) In 1949 the Republic of Ireland became official and left the British Commonwealth. Catholic resentment in Northern Ireland flared in 1968–1969 into demonstrations against housing, voting, and unemployment discrimination. As the outlawed Irish Republican Army (IRA) emerged as a militant force, Protestant paramilitary groups formed to oppose it. Turmoil continued until Britain agreed over Loyalist protests to give the Republic of Ireland a voice in governing Northern Ireland. In 1994 the IRA declared a ceasefire, and peace negotiations began between representatives of Britain, Ireland, Ulster, and the IRA; so far, progress has been erratic.

There she was on the platform at Limerick — Grandma, white hair, sour eyes, a black shawl, and no smile for my mother or any of us, even my brother Malachy, with his big smile and sweet white teeth. Mam pointed to Dad. This is my husband, she said, and Grandma nodded and looked away. She called two boys who were hanging around the railway station and paid them to carry the trunk. The boys had shaved heads, snotty noses, and no shoes and we followed them through the streets of Limerick. I asked Mam why they had no hair and she said their heads were shaved so that the lice would have no place to hide. Malachy said, What's a lice? and Mam said, Not lice. One of them is a louse. Grandma said, Will ye stop it! What kind o' talk is this? The boys whistled and laughed and trotted along as if they had shoes and Grandma told them, Stop that laughin' or 'tis droppin' an' breakin' that trunk ye'll be. They stopped the whistling and laughing and we followed them into a park with grass so green it dazzled you.

Dad carried the twins, Mam carried a bag in one hand and held Malachy's hand with the other. When she stopped every few minutes to catch her breath, Grandma said, Are you still smokin' them fags? Them fags will be the death of you. There's enough consumption in Limerick without people smokin' fags on top of it an' 'tis a rich man's foolishness.

Along the path through the park there were hundreds of flowers of different colors that excited the twins. Dad stopped and put Eugene and Oliver down. He said, Flowers, and the twins ran back and forth, pointing, trying to say "flowers." One of the boys with the trunk said, God, are they Americans? and Mam said, They are. They were born in New York. The boy said to the other boy, God, they're Americans. They put the trunk down and stared at us and we stared back at them till Grandma said, Are ye goin' to stand here all day lookin' at flowers an' gawkin' at each other? And we all moved on again, out of the park, down a narrow lane, and into another lane to Grandma's house.

There is a row of small houses on each side of the lane and Grandma lives in one of the small houses. Her kitchen has a shiny polished black iron range with a fire glowing in the grate. There is a picture on the wall by the range of a man with long brown hair and sad eyes. He is pointing to his chest, where there is a big heart with flames coming out of it. Mam tells us, That's the Sacred Heart of Jesus, and I want to know why the man's heart is on fire and why doesn't He throw water on it? Grandma says, Don't these children know anything about their religion? and Mam tells her it's different in America. Grandma says the Sacred Heart is everywhere and there's no excuse for that kind of ignorance.

There aren't enough chairs for everyone so I sit on the stairs with   5
my brothers to have some bread and tea. Dad and Mam sit at the table
and Grandma sits under the Sacred Heart. She says, I don't know
under God what I'm goin' to do with ye. There is no room in this
house. There isn't room for even one of ye.

Malachy says, Ye, ye, and starts to giggle and I say, Ye, ye, and the
twins say, Ye, ye, and we're laughing so hard we can hardly eat our
bread.

Grandma glares at us. What are ye laughin' at? There's nothin' to
laugh at in this house. Ye better behave yeerselves before I go over to ye.

She won't stop saying Ye, and now Malachy is helpless with laughter,
spewing out his bread and tea, his face turning red.

That night Mam's sister, Aunt Aggie, came home from her job in the
clothing factory. She was big and she had flaming-red hair. She was living in Grandma's because she had had a fight with her husband, Pa
Keating, who told her, when he had taken drink, You're a great fat cow,
go home to your mother. That's what Grandma told Mam and that's
why there was no room for us in Grandma's house. She had herself,
Aunt Aggie, and her son Pat, who was my uncle and who was out selling newspapers.

Grandma spread coats and rags on the floor of the little back room   10
and we slept there and in the morning Aunt Aggie came for her bicycle
telling us, Will ye mind yeerselves, will ye. Will ye get out of my way?

When she left, Malachy kept saying, Will ye mind yeerselves, will
ye? Will ye get out of the way, will ye? and I could hear Dad laughing
out in the kitchen till Grandma came down the stairs and he had to tell
Malachy be quiet.

That day Grandma and Mam went out and found a furnished room
on Windmill Street. Grandma paid the rent, ten shillings for two weeks.
She gave Mam money for food, loaned us a kettle, a pot, a frying pan,
knives and spoons, jam jars to be used for mugs, a blanket and a pillow.
She said that was all she could afford, that Dad would have to get up off
his arse, get a job, go on the dole, go for the charity at the St. Vincent
de Paul Society, or go on the relief.

The room had a fireplace where we could boil water for our tea or
for an egg in case we ever came into money. We had a table and three
chairs and a bed that Mam said was the biggest she had ever seen. It
didn't matter that there were six of us in the bed, we were together,
away from grandmothers, Malachy could say Ye, ye, ye, and we could
laugh as much as we liked.

Dad and Mam lay at the head of the bed, Malachy and I at the bottom, the twins wherever they could find comfort. In the moonlight I

could look up the length of the bed and see Dad still awake and when
Oliver cried in his sleep Dad reached for him and held him. Whisht,
he said. Whisht.

Then Eugene sat up, screaming, tearing at himself. Ah, ah, Mommy,   15
Mommy. Dad sat up. What? What's up, son? Eugene went on crying
and when Dad leaped from the bed and turned on the gaslight we saw
the fleas, leaping, jumping, fastened to our flesh. We slapped at them
and slapped but they hopped from body to body, hopping, biting. We
jumped from the bed, the twins crying, Mam moaning, Oh, Jesus, will
we have no rest! Dad poured water and salt into a jam jar and dabbed at
our bites. The salt burned, but he said we'd feel better soon.

Mam sat by the fireplace with the twins on her lap. Dad pulled on
his trousers and dragged the mattress off the bed and out to the street.
He filled the kettle and the pot with water, stood the mattress against
the wall, pounded it with a shoe, told me to keep pouring water on the
ground to drown the fleas dropping there. The Limerick moon was so
bright I could see bits of it shimmering in the water and I wanted to
scoop up moon bits, but how could I with the fleas leaping on my legs?

A man on a bicycle stopped and wanted to know why Dad was beating that mattress. Mother o' God, he said, I never heard such a cure for
fleas. Do you know that if a man could jump like a flea one leap would
take him halfway to the moon? The thing to do is this, When you go
back inside with that mattress stick it on the bed upside down and that
will confuse the little buggers. They won't know where they are and
they'll be biting the mattress or each other, which is the best cure of all.
They're a right bloody torment an' I should know for didn't I grow up in
Limerick, down in the Irish Town, an' the fleas there were so plentiful
an' forward they'd sit on the toe of your boot an' discuss Ireland's woeful
history with you. It is said there were no fleas in ancient Ireland, that
they were brought in by the English to drive us out of our wits entirely,
an' I wouldn't put it past the English.

Dad said, You wouldn't by any chance have a cigarette, would you?

A cigarette? Oh, sure, of course. Here you are. Aren't I nearly destroyed from the fags myself. The oul' hacking cough, you know. So
powerful it nearly knocks me off the bicycle. I can feel that cough stirring in me solar plexus an' workin' its way up through me entrails till
the next thing it takes off the top o' me head.

He wobbled away on his bicycle, a cigarette dangling from his mouth,   20
the cough racking his body. Dad said, Limerickmen talk too much. Come
on, we'll put this mattress back and see if there's any sleep in this night.

Eugene is sleeping under a coat on the bed. Dad sits by the fireplace
with Oliver on his lap. Oliver's cheeks are bright red and he's staring

into the dead fire. Mam puts her hand on his forehead. I think he has a fever, she says. I wish I had an onion and I'd boil it in milk and pepper. That's good for the fever. But even if I had what would I boil the milk on? We need coal for that fire.

She gives Dad the docket for the coal down the Dock Road. He takes me with him, but it's dark and all the coalyards are closed.

What are we going to do now, Dad?

I don't know, son.

Ahead of us, women in shawls and small children are picking up coal along the road.

There, Dad, there's coal.

Och, no, son, We won't pick coal off the road. We're not beggars.

He tells Mam the coalyards are closed and we'll have to drink milk and eat bread tonight, but when I tell her about the women on the road she passes Eugene to him.

If you're too grand to pick coal off the road I'll put on my coat and go down the Dock Road.

She gets a bag and takes Malachy and me with her. Beyond the Dock Road there is something wide and dark with lights glinting in it. Mam says that's the River Shannon. She says that's what she missed most of all in America, the River Shannon. The Hudson was lovely but the Shannon sings. I can't hear the song, but my mother does and that makes her happy. The other women are gone from the Dock Road and we search for the bits of coal that drop from lorries. Mam tells us gather anything that burns, coal, wood, cardboard, paper. She says, There are them that burn the horse droppings but we're not gone that low yet. When her bag is nearly full she says, Now we have to find an onion for Oliver. Malachy says he'll find one but she tells him, No, you don't find onions on the road, you get them in shops.

The minute he sees a shop he cries out, There's a shop, and runs in.

Oonyen, he says. Oonyen for Oliver.

Mam runs into the shop and tells the woman behind the counter, I'm sorry. The woman says, Lord, he's a dote. Is he an American or what?

Mam says he is. The woman smiles and shows two teeth, one on each side of her upper gum. A dote, she says, and look at them gorgeous goldy curls. And what is it he wants now? A sweet?

Ah, no, says Mam. An onion. I wanted to get an onion for my other child that's sick.

True for you, missus. You can't beat the onion boiled in milk. And look, little boy, here's a sweet for yourself and one for the other little boy, the brother, I suppose. And here's a nice onion for the sick child, missus.

Mam says, God bless you, ma'am, and her eyes are watery.

Dad is walking back and forth with Oliver in his arms and Eugene is playing on the floor with a pot and a spoon. Dad says, Did you get the onion?

I did, says Mam, and more. I got coal and the way of lighting it.

I knew you would. I said a prayer to St. Jude. He's my favorite saint,   40
patron of desperate cases.

I got the coal. I got the onion, no help from St. Jude.

Dad says, You shouldn't be picking up coal off the road like a common beggar. It isn't right. Bad example for the boys.

Then you should have sent St. Jude down the Dock Road.

Mam gets the fire going, cuts the onion in half, and drops it in boiling milk. She takes Oliver on her lap and tries to feed him, but he turns away and looks into the fire.

Ah, come on, love, she says. Good for you. Make you big and strong.   45

He tightens his mouth against the spoon. She puts the pot down, rocks him till he's asleep, lays him on the bed, and tells the rest of us to be quiet or she'll demolish us. She slices the other half of the onion and fries it in butter with slices of bread. She lets us sit on the floor around the fire where we eat the fried bread and sip at scalding sweet tea in jam jars.

The fire makes the room warm and with the flames dancing in the coal you can see faces and mountains and valleys and animals leaping. Eugene falls asleep on the floor and Dad lifts him to the bed beside Oliver. Mam puts the boiled-onion pot up on the mantelpiece for fear a mouse or a rat might be at it.

Soon we're all in bed and if there's the odd flea I don't mind because it's warm in the bed with the six of us and I love the glow of the fire the way it dances on the walls and ceiling and makes the room go red and black, red and black, till it dims to white and black and all you can hear is a little cry from Oliver turning in my mother's arms.

Dad is touching my shoulder. Come on, Francis, you have to take care of your little brothers.

Mam is slumped on the edge of the bed, making small crying sounds   50
like a bird. Grandma is pulling on her shawl. She says, I'll go down to Thompson the undertaker about the coffin and the carriage. The St. Vincent de Paul Society will surely pay for that, God knows.

Dad stands facing the wall over the fire, beating on his thighs with his fists, sighing, Och, och, och.

Dad frightens me with his Och, och, och, and Mam frightens me with her small bird sounds, and I don't know what to do, though I wonder if anyone will light the fire in the grate so that we can have tea and bread. If Dad would move away from the fireplace I could light the fire myself. All you need is paper, a few bits of coal or turf, and a match. He won't move so I try to go around his legs while he's beating on his thighs, but he notices me and wants to know why I'm trying to light the fire. I tell him we're all hungry and he lets out a crazy laugh. Hungry? he says. Och, Francis, your wee brother Oliver is dead.

He picks me up and hugs me so hard I cry out. Then Malachy cries, my mother cries, Dad cries, I cry, but Eugene stays quiet. Then Dad sniffles, We'll have a feast. Come on, Francis.

He carries me through the streets of Limerick and we go from shop to shop with him asking for food or anything they can give to a family that has two children dead in a year, one in America, one in Limerick, and in danger of losing three more for the want of food and drink. Most shopkeepers shake their heads.

Dad says he's glad to see the spirit of Christ alive in Limerick and   55
they tell him they don't need the likes of him with his Northern accent to be telling them about Christ and he should be ashamed of himself dragging a child around like that, like a common beggar, a tinker, a knacker.

A few shopkeepers give bread, potatoes, tins of beans and Dad says, We'll go home now and you boys can eat something, but we meet Uncle Pa Keating and he tells Dad he's very sorry for his troubles and would Dad like to have a pint in this pub here?

There are men sitting in this pub with great glasses of black stuff before them. They lift their glasses carefully and slowly drink. There is creamy white stuff on their lips which they lick with little sighs.

Uncle Pa says, Frankie, this is the pint. This is the staff of life. This is the best thing for nursing mothers and for those who are long weaned.

He laughs and Dad smiles and I laugh because I think that's what you're supposed to do when Uncle Pa says something. He doesn't laugh when he tells the other men about Oliver dying. The other men tip their hats to Dad. Sorry for your troubles, mister, and surely you'll have a pint.

Dad says yes to the pints and soon he's singing "Roddy McCorley"   60
and "Kevin Barry" and song after song I never heard before and crying over his lovely little girl, Margaret, that died in America and his little boy Oliver. It frightens me the way he yells and cries and sings and I wish I could be at home with my three brothers, no, my two brothers, and my mother.

The man behind the bar says to Dad, I think now, mister, you've had enough. We're sorry for your troubles but you have to take that child home to his mother that must be heartbroken by the fire.

Dad says, One, one more pint, just one, eh? and the man says no. Dad shakes his fist. I did me bit for Ireland, and when the man comes out and takes Dad's arm Dad tries to push him away.

Uncle Pa says, Come on now, stop the blackguarding. You have to go home to Angela. You have a funeral tomorrow and the lovely children waiting for you.

Dad wants to go to another place for a pint but Uncle Pa says he has no more money. Dad says he'll tell everyone his sorrows and they'll give him pints. Uncle Pa says that's a disgraceful thing to do and Dad cries on his shoulder. You're a good friend, he tells Uncle Pa. It's terrible, terrible, says Uncle Pa, but you'll get over this in time.

Dad straightens up and looks at him. Never, he says. Never.   65

Next day we rode to the hospital in a carriage with a horse. They put Oliver into a white box that came with us in the carriage and we took him to the graveyard. I did not like the jackdaws that perched on the trees and gravestones and I did not want to leave Oliver with them. I threw a rock at a jackdaw that waddled over toward Oliver's grave. Dad says I shouldn't throw rocks at jackdaws, they might be somebodies' souls. I didn't know what a soul was but I didn't ask him, because I didn't care. Oliver was dead and I hated jackdaws. I'd be a man someday and I'd come back with a bag of rocks and I'd leave the graveyard littered with dead jackdaws.

The morning after Oliver's burial Dad went to the Labour Exchange to sign and collect the week's dole, nineteen shillings and sixpence. He said he'd be home by noon, that he'd get coal and make a fire, that we'd have rashers and eggs and tea in honor of Oliver, that we might even have a sweet or two.

He wasn't home by noon, or one, or two, and we boiled and ate the few potatoes the shopkeepers had given us. He wasn't home anytime before the sun went down that day in May. There was no sign of him till we heard him, long after the pubs closed, rolling along Windmill Street, singing.

He stumbled into the room, hanging on to the wall. A snot oozed from his nose and he wiped it away with the back of his hand. He tried to speak. Zeeze shildren should be in bed. Lishen to me. Shildren go to bed.

Mam faced him. These children are hungry. Where's the dole   70
money?

She tried to stick her hands into his pockets but he pushed her away. Have reshpeck, he said. Reshpeck in front of shildren.

She struggled to get at his pockets. Where's the money? The children are hungry. You mad oul' bastard, did you drink all the money again? Just what you did in Brooklyn.

He blubbered, Och, poor Angela. And poor wee Margaret and poor wee Oliver.

He staggered to me and hugged me and I smelled the drink I used to smell in America. My face was wet from his tears and his spit and his snot and I was hungry and I didn't know what to say when he cried all over my head.

EXPLORATIONS

1. Who are the living members of Frank McCourt's family when they arrive in Ireland? When and how do we find out that there was another child in the family? How does the way this information is revealed affect its impact?

2. How do the readers of this essay learn that the narrator came to Limerick from America? How do other characters in the narrative learn where the McCourts came from?

3. At what points in "Limerick Homecoming" does McCourt write in the present tense? In the past tense? How does the essay's effect change when he changes tense?

CONNECTIONS

1. What role does patriotism play in the characters' lives in "Limerick Home-coming," and how does it affect them? What role does patriotism play in the characters' lives in Amos Oz's "If There Is Justice" (p. 188), and how does it affect them?

2. What role does religion play in the characters' lives in "Limerick Home-coming," and how does it affect them? What role does religion play in the characters' lives in "If There Is Justice," and how does it affect them?

3. Frances Rose Besmer writes about the impact of poverty and failure on families (p. 128). Which of her comments apply to the McCourt family, and in what way? What advantages do the McCourts have over the families Besmer describes?

ELABORATIONS

1. What are the strengths and weaknesses of the parents and other adults in "Limerick Homecoming"? What choices do they make that save the day or that lead to disaster? Pick at least one good choice and one bad one. Write an essay showing how each decision affected the family and projecting how things could have gone differently if the decision maker had chosen differently.

2. What rhetorical strategies does McCourt use in "Limerick Homecoming" to narrate events convincingly from a child's point of view? Write an essay identifying his tactics and describing their effects.

ZLATA FILIPOVIĆ

Sarajevo Diary

"Sarajevo Diary" is an excerpt from the diary begun by eleven-year-old Zlata Filipović in 1991 — the year Yugoslavia began disintegrating. Filipović was born in Sarajevo; her father, Malik, is a lawyer, and her mother, Alicia, is a biochemist. The family is not religious, and their heritage is mixed Croatian, Serbian, and Muslim. Zlata Filipović started her diary eight months before the Bosnian war began; she continued recording her experiences and impressions until October 1993. Two months later, she and her parents were transported in armored vehicles from their home to the Sarajevo airport, where they boarded a United Nations plane to Paris. UNICEF (an acronym for United Nations International Children's Emergency Fund) published part of the diary in Croat to win attention for the children of Sarajevo. The complete manuscript became an immediate bestseller in France, then in English-speaking countries after it was translated by Christina Pribichevich-Zoric as *Zlata's Diary: A Child's Life in Sarajevo* (1994). Universal Pictures bought the film rights for $1.4 million; Filipović toured the United States, spoke with President Clinton and U.S. senators, appeared on the *Today* show and the cover of *Newsweek*, and was widely hailed as "Bosnia's Anne Frank." Daunted, the Filipovićs pondered whether to leave Paris for Slovenia, or, if possible, Sarajevo.

At the time Zlata Filipović began writing, her hometown was the capital of Yugoslavia. This nation had been created after World War I out of former provinces of the Austro-Hungarian Empire plus the state of Montenegro. Invaded by Germany in 1941, it became the Socialist Federal Republic of Yugoslavia after World War II. The partisan fighter Josip Broz, known as Marshal Tito, suppressed the violent rivalry between political and ethnic groups by executing his main competitor and running the country's Communist government until he died in 1980. For the next decade the Party leadership and presidency rotated among the heads of Yugoslavia's six member republics (Serbia, Croatia, Slovenia, Bosnia-Herzegovina, Macedonia, and Montenegro) and the two autonomous provinces within Serbia (Vojvodina and Kosovo). But with the end of the Soviet Union and its domination of Eastern Europe, the Yugoslav union began disintegrating as member republics seceded. Belgrade remained the capital of Serbian-dominated Yugoslavia, where Communists (now renamed Socialists) retained power. Zagreb became the capital of largely Roman Catholic Croatia; and Sarajevo became the capital of largely Muslim Bosnia. The war Filipović describes began as a Serbian campaign to bring all territory occupied by ethnic Serbs under Serbian control, typically by expelling or killing any others living there — a policy known as "ethnic cleansing." The violence spread from Croatia into Bosnia, where an arms embargo and the intervention of UN peacekeepers did little to keep the Muslims from losing ground to the Serbs. A more active role by the United States led to UN air strikes against the Serbs and negotiations among the warring parties which produced the Dayton Peace Accord and an agreement to create a federation. As we go to press, it remains unclear whether any of these measures will yield lasting progress.

Monday, September 2, 1991. Behind me — a long, hot summer and the happy days of summer holidays; ahead of me — a new school year. I'm starting fifth grade. I'm looking forward to seeing my friends at school, to being together again. Some of them I haven't seen since the day the school bell rang, marking the end of term. I'm glad we'll be together again, and share all the worries and joys of going to school.

Mirna, Bojana, Marijana, Ivana, Maša, Azra, Minela, Nadža — we're all together again.

Thursday, September 19, 1991. Classes have also started at music school now. I go twice a week for piano and solfeggio. I'm continuing my tennis lessons. Oh yes, I've been moved up to the "older" group in tennis. Wednesdays I go to Auntie Mika's for English lessons. Tuesdays I have choir practice. Those are my responsibilities. I have six lessons every day, except Fridays. I'll survive . . .

Sunday, October 6, 1991. I'm watching the American Top 20 on MTV. I don't remember a thing, who's in what place.

I feel great because I've just eaten a "Four Seasons" PIZZA with ham, cheese, ketchup and mushrooms. It was yummy. Daddy bought it for me at Galija's (the pizzeria around the corner). Maybe that's why I didn't remember who took what place — I was too busy enjoying my pizza.

I've finished studying and tomorrow I can go to school BRAVELY, without being afraid of getting a bad grade. I deserve a good grade because I studied all weekend and I didn't even go out to play with my friends in the park. The weather is nice and we usually play "monkey in the middle," talk and go for walks. Basically, we have fun.

Saturday, October 19, 1991. Yesterday was a really awful day. We were ready to go to Jahorina (the most beautiful mountain in the world) for the weekend. But when I got home from school, I found my mother in tears and my father in uniform. I had a lump in my throat when Daddy said he had been called up by the police reserve. I hugged him, crying, and started begging him not to go, to stay at home. He said he had to go. Daddy went, and Mommy and I were left alone. Mommy cried and phoned friends and relatives. Everyone came immediately (Slobo, Doda, Keka, Mommy's brother Braco, Aunt Melica, there were so many I can't remember them all). They all came to console us and to offer their help. Keka took me to spend the night with Martina and Matea. When I woke up in the morning, Keka told me everything was all right and that Daddy would be home in two days.

I'm home now. Melica is staying with us and it looks as though everything will be all right. Daddy should be home the day after tomorrow. Thank God!

Tuesday, October 22, 1991.   Everything really does seem to have turned out all right. Daddy got back yesterday, on his birthday. He's off again tomorrow, and then every two days. He'll be on duty for ten hours each time. We'll just have to get used to it. I suppose it won't last for long. But, I don't know what it all means. Some reservists from Montenegro have entered Herzegovina. Why? For what? Politics, it seems, but I don't understand politics. After Slovenia and Croatia, are the winds of war now blowing toward Bosnia-Herzegovina??? No, that's impossible.

Wednesday, October 23, 1991.   There's a real war going on in   10
Dubrovnik. It's being badly shelled. People are in shelters, they have no water, no electricity, the phones aren't working. We see horrible pictures on TV. Mommy and Daddy are worried. Is it possible that such a beautiful town is being destroyed? Mommy and Daddy are especially fond of it. It was there, in the Ducal Palace, that they picked up a quill and wrote "YES" to spending the rest of their lives together. Mommy says it's the most beautiful town in the world and it mustn't be destroyed!!!

We're worried about Srdjan (my parents' best friend who lives and works in Dubrovnik, but his family is still in Sarajevo) and his parents. How are they coping with everything that's happening over there? Are they alive? We're trying to talk to him with the help of a ham radio, but it's not working. Bokica (Srdjan's wife) is miserable. Every attempt to get some news ends in failure. Dubrovnik is cut off from the rest of the world.

Thursday, November 14, 1991.   Daddy isn't going to the reserves anymore. Hooray!!! . . . Now we'll be able to go to Jahorina and Crnotina on weekends. But, gasoline has been a problem lately. Daddy often spends hours waiting in the line for gasoline, he goes outside of town to get it, and often comes home without getting the job done.

Together with Bokica we sent a package to Srdjan. We learned through the ham radio that they have nothing to eat. They have no water, Srdjan swapped a bottle of whisky for five liters of water. Eggs, apples, potatoes — the people of Dubrovnik can only dream about them.

War in Croatia, war in Dubrovnik, some reservists in Herzegovina. Mommy and Daddy keep watching the news on TV. They're worried. Mommy often cries looking at the terrible pictures on TV. They talk mostly politics with their friends. What is politics? I haven't got a clue. And I'm not really interested. I just finished watching "Midnight Caller" on TV.

Thursday, December 19, 1991.   Sarajevo has launched an appeal (on TV) called "Sarajevo Helps the Children of Dubrovnik." In Srdjan's parcel we put a nice New Year's present for him to give to some child in Dubrovnik. We made up a package of sweets, chocolates, vitamins, a doll, some books, pencils, notebooks — whatever we could manage, hoping to bring happiness to some innocent child who has been stopped by the war from going to school, playing, eating what he wants and enjoying his childhood. It's a nice little package. I hope it makes whoever gets it happy. That's the idea. I also wrote a New Year's card saying I hoped the war in Dubrovnik would end soon.

Thursday, March 5, 1992.   Oh God! Things are heating up in Sarajevo. On Sunday (March 1), a small group of armed civilians (as they say on TV) killed a Serbian wedding guest and wounded the priest. On March 2 (Monday) the whole city was full of barricades. There were "1,000" barricades. We didn't even have bread. At 6:00 people got fed up and went out into the streets. The procession set out from the cathedral. It went past the parliament building and made its way through the entire city. Several people were wounded at the Marshal Tito army barracks. People sang and cried "Bosnia, Bosnia," "Sarajevo, Sarajevo," "We'll live together" and "Come outside." Zdravko Grebo[1] said on the radio that history was in the making.

At about 8:00 we heard the bell of a streetcar. The first streetcar had passed through town and life got back to normal. People poured out into the streets hoping that nothing like that would ever happen again. We joined the peace procession. When we got home we had a quiet

15

---

[1]President of the Soros Foundation in Sarajevo and editor-in-chief of ZID, the independent radio station.

night's sleep. The next day everything was the same as before. Classes, music school . . . But in the evening, the news came that 3,000 Chetniks [Serbian nationalists] were coming from Pale[2] to attack Sarajevo, and first, Baščaršija [the old part of town]. Melica said that new barricades had been put up in front of her house and that they wouldn't be sleeping at home tonight. They went to Uncle Nedjad's place. Later there was a real fight on YUTEL TV. Radovan Karadžič [Bosnian Serb leader] and Alija Izetbegovič [President of Bosnia-Herzegovina] phoned in and started arguing. Then Goran Milič[3] got angry and made them agree to meet with some General Kukanjac.[4] Milič is great!!! Bravo!

On March 4 (Wednesday) the barricades were removed, the "kids" [a popular term for politicians] had come to some agreement. Great?!

That day our art teacher brought in a picture for our class-mistress (for March 8, Women's Day). We gave her the present, but she told us to go home. Something was wrong again! There was a panic. The girls started screaming and the boys quietly blinked their eyes. Daddy came home from work early that day too. But everything turned out OK. It's all too much!

Monday, March 30, 1992. Hey, Diary! You know what I think? Since 20
Anne Frank called her diary Kitty, maybe I could give you a name too.
What about:

ASFALTINA	PIDŽAMETA
ŠEFIKA	HIKMETA
ŠEVALA	MIMMY

or something else???
I'm thinking, thinking . . .
I've decided! I'm going to call you
MIMMY
All right, then, let's start.

Dear Mimmy,   25
It's almost half-term. We're all studying for our tests. Tomorrow we're supposed to go to a classical music concert at the Skenderija Hall. Our teacher says we shouldn't go because there will be 10,000 people, pardon me, children, there, and somebody might take us as hostages or plant a bomb in the concert hall. Mommy says I shouldn't go. So I won't.

Hey! You know who won the Yugovision Song Contest! EXTRA NENA!!!???

---

[2]Resort outside of Sarajevo, now headquarters of the Bosnian Serbs.
[3]A well-known newscaster on television, one of the founders of the YUTEL television station before the war.
[4]General of the then Yugoslav army, who was in Sarajevo when the war broke out.

I'm afraid to say this next thing. Melica says she heard at the hairdresser's that on Saturday, April 4, 1992, there's going to be BOOM — BOOM, BANG — BANG, CRASH Sarajevo. Translation: They're going to bomb Sarajevo.
Love,
Zlata

Saturday, April 4, 1992
Today is Bairam [a Muslim religious holiday]. There aren't many people in the streets. I guess it's fear of the stories about Sarajevo being bombed. But there's no bombing. It looks as though Mommy was right when she said it was all misinformation. Thank God!
Love you,
Zlata

Sunday, April 5, 1992
Dear Mimmy,
I'm trying to concentrate so I can do my homework (reading), but I simply can't. Something is going on in town. You can hear gunfire from the hills. Columns of people are spreading out from Dobrinja. They're trying to stop something, but they themselves don't know what. You can simply feel that something is coming, something very bad. On TV I see people in front of the B-H parliament building. The radio keeps playing the same song: "Sarajevo, My Love." That's all very nice, but my stomach is still in knots and I can't concentrate on my homework anymore.
  Mimmy, I'm afraid of WAR!!!
Zlata

30

Monday, April 6, 1992
Dear Mimmy,
Yesterday the people in front of the parliament tried peacefully to cross the Vrbanja bridge. But they were shot at. Who? How? Why? A girl, a medical student from Dubrovnik, was KILLED. Her blood spilled onto the bridge. In her final moments all she said was: "Is this Sarajevo?"
HORRIBLE, HORRIBLE HORRIBLE!
  NO ONE AND NOTHING HERE IS NORMAL!
  The Baščaršija has been destroyed! Those "fine gentlemen" from Pale fired on Baščaršija!
  Since yesterday people have been inside the B-H parliament. Some of them are standing outside, in front of it. We've moved my television set into the living room, so I watch Channel I on one TV and "Good Vibrations" on the other. Now they're shooting from the Holiday Inn,

killing people in front of the parliament. And Bokica is there with Vanja and Andrej. Oh, God!

Maybe we'll go to the cellar. You, Mimmy, will go with me, of   35 course. I'm desperate. The people in front of the parliament are desperate too. Mimmy, war is here. PEACE, NOW!

They say they're going to attack RTV Sarajevo [radio and TV center]. But they haven't. They've stopped shooting in our neighborhood. KNOCK! KNOCK! (I'm knocking on wood for good luck.)

WHEW! It was tough. Oh, God! They're shooting again!!!
Zlata

Thursday, April 9, 1992

Dear Mimmy,

I'm not going to school. All the schools in Sarajevo are closed. There's danger hiding in these hills above Sarajevo. But I think things are slowly calming down. The heavy shelling and explosions have stopped. There's occasional gunfire, but it quickly falls silent. Mommy and Daddy aren't going to work. They're buying food in huge quantities. Just in case, I guess. God forbid!

Still, it's very tense. Mommy is beside herself, Daddy tries to calm her down. Mommy has long conversations on the phone. She calls, other people call, the phone is in constant use.
Zlata

Saturday, April 18, 1992

Dear Mimmy,   40

There's shooting, shells are falling. This really is WAR. Mommy and Daddy are worried, they sit up until late at night, talking. They're wondering what to do, but it's hard to know. Whether to leave and split up, or stay here together. Keka wants to take me to Ohrid. Mommy can't make up her mind — she's constantly in tears. She tries to hide it from me, but I see everything. I see that things aren't good here. There's no peace. War has suddenly entered our town, our homes, our thoughts, our lives. It's terrible.

It's also terrible that Mommy has packed my suitcase.
Love,
Zlata

Monday, April 20, 1992

Dear Mimmy,

War is no joke, it seems. It destroys, kills, burns, separates, brings unhappiness. Terrible shells fell today on Baščaršija, the old town center. Terrible explosions. We went down into the cellar, the cold, dark, revolting cellar.

And ours isn't even all that safe. Mommy, Daddy, and I just stood there, holding on to one another in a corner that looked safe. Standing there in the dark, in the warmth of my parents' arms, I thought about leaving Sarajevo. Everybody is thinking about it, and so am I. I couldn't bear to go alone, to leave behind Mommy and Daddy, Grandma and Granddad. And going with just Mommy isn't any good either. The best would be for all three of us to go. But Daddy can't. So I've decided we should stay here together. Tomorrow I'll tell Keka that you have to be brave and stay with those you love and those who love you. I can't leave my parents, and I don't like the other idea of leaving my father behind alone either.
Your Zlata

Tuesday, April 21, 1992

Dear Mimmy,
It's horrible in Sarajevo today. Shells falling, people and children getting killed, shooting. We will probably spend the night in the cellar. Since ours isn't safe, we're going to our neighbors', the Bobars' house. The Bobar family consists of Grandma Mira, Auntie Boda, Uncle Žika (her husband), Maja and Bojana. When the shooting gets bad, Žika phones us and then we run across the yard, over the ladder and the table, into their building and finally knock at their door. Until just the other day we took the street, but there's shooting and it's not safe anymore. I'm getting ready to go to the cellar. I've packed my backpack with biscuits, juice, a deck of cards and a few other "things." I can still hear the cannon fire, and something that sounds like it.
Love you, Mimmy,
Zlata

Saturday, May 2, 1992

Dear Mimmy,
Today was truly, absolutely the worst day ever in Sarajevo. The shooting started around noon. Mommy and I moved into the hall. Daddy was in his office, under our apartment, at the time. We told him on the intercom to run quickly to the downstairs lobby where we'd meet him. We brought Cicko [Zlata's canary] with us. The gunfire was getting worse, and we couldn't get over the wall to the Bobars', so we ran down to our own cellar.

The cellar is ugly, dark, smelly. Mommy, who's terrified of mice, had 45 two fears to cope with. The three of us were in the same corner as the other day. We listened to the pounding shells, the shooting, the thundering noise overhead. We even heard planes. At one moment I realized that this awful cellar was the only place that could save our lives. Suddenly, it started to look almost warm and nice. It was the only way we could

defend ourselves against all this terrible shooting. We heard glass shattering in our street. Horrible. I put my fingers in my ears to block out the terrible sounds. I was worried about Cicko. We had left him behind in the
lobby. Would he catch cold there? Would something hit him? I was terribly hungry and thirsty. We had left our half-cooked lunch in the kitchen.

When the shooting died down a bit, Daddy ran over to the apartment
and brought us back some sandwiches. He said he could smell something
burning and that the phones weren't working. He brought our TV set down
to the cellar. That's when we learned that the main post office (near us) was
on fire and that they had kidnapped our President. At around 8:00 we went
back up to our apartment. Almost every window in our street was broken.
Ours were all right, thank God. I saw the post office in flames. A terrible
sight. The firefighters battled with the raging fire. Daddy took a few photos
of the post office being devoured by the flames. He said they wouldn't
come out because I had been fiddling with something on the camera. I was
sorry. The whole apartment smelled of the burning fire. God, and I used to
pass by there every day. It had just been done up. It was huge and beautiful,
and now it was being swallowed up by the flames. It was disappearing.
That's what this neighborhood of mine looks like, my Mimmy. I wonder
what it's like in other parts of town? I heard on the radio that it was awful
around the Eternal Flame. The place is knee-deep in glass. We're worried
about Grandma and Granddad. They live there. Tomorrow, if we can go
out, we'll see how they are. A terrible day. This has been the worst, most
awful day in my eleven-year-old life. I hope it will be the only one. Mommy
and Daddy are very edgy. I have to go to bed.
Ciao!
Zlata

Tuesday, May 5, 1992

Dear Mimmy,
The shooting seems to be dying down. I guess they've caused enough
misery, although I don't know why. It has something to do with politics.
I just hope the "kids" come to some agreement. Oh, if only they would,
so we could live and breathe as human beings again. The things that
have happened here these past few days are terrible. I want it to stop forever. PEACE! PEACE!

I didn't tell you, Mimmy, that we've rearranged things in the apartment.
My room and Mommy and Daddy's are too dangerous to be in. They face
the hills, which is where they're shooting from. If only you knew how
scared I am to go near the windows and into those rooms. So, we turned a
safe corner of the sitting room into a "bedroom." We sleep on mattresses on
the floor. It's strange and awful. But, it's safer that way. We've turned every-

thing around for safety. We put Cicko in the kitchen. He's safe there, although once the shooting starts there's nowhere safe except the cellar. I suppose all this will stop and we'll all go back to our usual places.
Ciao!
Zlata

Thursday, May 7, 1992

Dear Mimmy,
I was almost positive the war would stop, but today . . . Today a shell fell on the park in front of my house, the park where I used to play and sit with my girlfriends. A lot of people were hurt. From what I hear Jaca, Jaca's mother, Selma, Nina, our neighbor Dado, and who knows how many other people who happened to be there were wounded. Dado, Jaca, and her mother have come home from the hospital, Selma lost a kidney but I don't know how she is, because she's still in the hospital. AND NINA IS DEAD. A piece of shrapnel lodged in her brain and she died. She was such a sweet, nice little girl. We went to kindergarten together, and we used to play together in the park. Is it possible I'll never see Nina again? Nina, an innocent eleven-year-old little girl — the victim of a stupid war. I feel sad. I cry and wonder why? She didn't do anything. A disgusting war has destroyed a young child's life. Nina, I'll always remember you as a wonderful little girl.
Love, Mimmy,
Zlata

Sunday, May 17, 1992

50

Dear Mimmy,
It's now definite: There's no more school. The war has interrupted our lessons, closed down the schools, sent children to cellars instead of classrooms. They'll give us the grades we got at the end of last term. So I'll get a report card saying I've finished fifth grade.
Ciao!
Zlata

Wednesday, May 27, 1992

Dear Mimmy,
SLAUGHTER! MASSACRE! HORROR! CRIME! BLOOD! SCREAMS! TEARS! DESPAIR!
   That's what Vaso Miškin Street looks like today. Two shells exploded in the street and one in the market. Mommy was nearby at the time. She ran to Grandma and Granddad's. Daddy and I were beside ourselves because she hadn't come home. I saw some of it on TV but I still can't believe what

I actually saw. It's unbelievable. I've got a lump in my throat and a knot in my tummy. HORRIBLE. They're taking the wounded to the hospital. It's a madhouse. We kept going to the window hoping to see Mommy, but she wasn't back. They released a list of the dead and wounded. Daddy and I were tearing our hair out. We didn't know what had happened to her. Was she alive? At 4:00, Daddy decided to go and check the hospital. He got dressed, and I got ready to go to the Bobars', so as not to stay home alone. I looked out the window one more time and . . . I SAW MOMMY RUN-NING ACROSS THE BRIDGE. As she came into the house she started shaking and crying. Through her tears she told us how she had seen dis-membered bodies. All the neighbors came because they had been afraid for her. Thank God, Mommy is with us. Thank God.
A HORRIBLE DAY. UNFORGETTABLE.
HORRIBLE! HORRIBLE!
Your Zlata

Saturday, May 30, 1992

Dear Mimmy,
55
The City Maternity Hospital has burned down. I was born there. Hun-dreds of thousands of new babies, new residents of Sarajevo, won't have the luck to be born in this maternity hospital now. It was new. The fire devoured everything. The mothers and babies were saved. When the fire broke out two women were giving birth. The babies are alive. God, people get killed here, they die here, they disappear, things go up in flames here, and out of the flames, new lives are born.
Your Zlata

Friday, June 5, 1992

Dear Mimmy,
There's been no electricity for quite some time and we keep thinking about the food in the freezer. There's not much left as it is. It would be a pity for all of it to go bad. There's meat and vegetables and fruit. How can we save it?
Daddy found an old wood-burning stove in the attic. It's so old it looks funny. In the cellar we found some wood, put the stove outside in the yard, lit it and are trying to save the food from the refrigerator. We cooked everything, and joining forces with the Bobars, enjoyed our-selves. There was veal and chicken, squid, cherry strudel, meat and potato pies. All sorts of things. It's a pity, though, that we had to eat everything so quickly. We even overate. WE HAD A MEAT STROKE.
We washed down our refrigerators and freezers. Who knows when we'll be able to cook like this again. Food is becoming a big problem in

Sarajevo. There's nothing to buy, and even cigarettes and coffee are becoming a problem for grown-ups. The last reserves are being used up. God, are we going to go hungry to boot???
Zlata

Tuesday, June 16, 1992

Dear Mimmy,
Our windows are broken. All of them except the ones in my room. That's the result of the revolting shell that fell again on Zoka's jewelry shop, across the way from us. I was alone in the house at the time. Mommy and Daddy were down in the yard, getting lunch ready, and I had gone upstairs to set the table. Suddenly I heard a terrible bang and glass breaking. I was terrified and ran toward the hall. That same moment, Mommy and Daddy were at the door. Out of breath, worried, sweating and pale they hugged me and we ran to the cellar, because the shells usually come one after the other. When I realized what had happened, I started to cry and shake. Everybody tried to calm me down, but I was very upset. I barely managed to pull myself together.

We returned to the apartment to find the rooms full of glass and the windows broken. We cleared away the glass and put plastic sheeting over the windows. We had had a close shave with that shell and shrapnel. I picked up a piece of shrapnel and the tail end of a grenade, put them in a box and thanked God I had been in the kitchen, because I could have been hit . . . HORRIBLE! I don't know how often I've written that word. HORRIBLE. We've had too much horror. The days here are full of horror. Maybe we in Sarajevo could rename the day and call it horror, because that's really what it's like.
Love,
Zlata

Thursday, June 18, 1992

Dear Mimmy,
Today we heard some more sad, sad news. Our country house in Crnotina, a tower that's about 150 years old, has burned down. Like the post office, it disappeared in flames. I loved it so much. We spent last summer there. I had a wonderful time. I always looked forward to going there. We had redone it so nicely, bought new furniture, new rugs, put in new windows, given it all our love and warmth, and its beauty was our reward. It lived through so many wars, so many years and now it's gone. It has burned down to the ground. Our neighbors, Žiga, Meho, and Bečir were killed. That's even sadder. Vildana's house also burned down. All the houses burned down. Lots of people were killed. It's terribly sad news.

I keep asking why? What for? Who's to blame? I ask, but there's no answer. All I know is that we are living in misery. Yes, I know, politics is to blame for it all. I said I wasn't interested in politics, but in order to find out the answer I have to know something about it. They tell me only a few things. I'll probably find out and understand much more one day. Mommy and Daddy don't discuss politics with me. They probably think I'm too young or maybe they themselves don't know anything. They just keep telling me: This will pass — "it has to pass"????????
Your Zlata

Friday, July 3, 1992

Dear Mimmy,

Mommy goes to work at her new office. She goes if there's no shooting, but we never know when the shelling will start. It's dangerous to walk around town. It's especially dangerous to cross our bridge, because snipers shoot at you. You have to run across. Every time she goes out, Daddy and I go to the window to watch her run. Mommy says: "I didn't know the Miljacka (our river) was so wide. You run, and you run, and you run, and there's no end to the bridge." That's fear, Mimmy, fear that you'll be hit by something.

Daddy doesn't go to work. The two of us stay at home, waiting for Mommy. When the sirens go off we worry about how and when and if she'll get home. Oh, the relief when she walks in!

Neda came for lunch today. Afterward we played cards. Neda said   65
something about going to Zagreb. It made Mommy sad, because they've been friends since childhood. They grew up together, spent their whole lives together. I was sad too because I love her and I know she loves me.
Zlata

Sunday, July 5, 1992

Dear Mimmy,

I don't remember when I last left the house. It must be almost two months ago now. I really miss Grandma and Granddad. I used to go there every day, and now I haven't seen them for such a long time.

I spend my days in the house and in the cellar. That's my wartime childhood. And it's summer. Other children are vacationing on the seaside, in the mountains, swimming, sunbathing, enjoying themselves. God, what did I do to deserve being in a war, spending my days in a way that no child should. I feel caged. All I can see through the broken windows is the park in front of my house. Empty, deserted, no children, no joy. I hear the sound of shells, and everything around me smells of war. War is now my life. OOHHH, I can't stand it anymore! I want to scream and cry. I wish I could

play the piano at least, but I can't even do that because it's in "the dangerous room," where I'm not allowed. How long is this going to go on???
Zlata

Tuesday, July 7, 1992

Dear Mimmy,
There was no water yesterday, the day before or the day before that. It came at around 8:30 this morning and now, at 10:30, it's slowly disappearing again.

We filled whatever we could find with water and now have to save on the precious liquid. You have to save on everything in this war, including water and food.

Mommy is at work, Daddy is reading something, and I'm going to Bojana's because there's no shooting.

Tuesday, July 14, 1992

Dear Mimmy,
On July 8 we got a UN package. Humanitarian aid. Inside were 6 cans of beef, 5 cans of fish, 2 boxes of cheese, 3 kilos of detergent, 5 bars of soap, 2 kilos of sugar and 5 liters of cooking oil. All in all, a super package. But Daddy had to stand in line for four hours to get it.

Dobrinja has been liberated. They received UN packages there too.

We're waiting to hear what the Security Council has decided about military intervention in B-H.

The water and electricity went off the day before yesterday, July 12, and still aren't back.
Ciao!
Zlata

Monday, July 20, 1992

Dear Mimmy,
Since I'm in the house all the time, I watch the world through the window. Just a piece of the world.

There are lots of beautiful pedigree dogs roaming the streets. Their owners probably had to let them go because they couldn't feed them anymore. Sad. Yesterday I watched a cocker spaniel cross the bridge, not knowing which way to go. He was lost. He wanted to go forward, but then he stopped, turned around and looked back. He was probably looking for his master. Who knows whether his master is still alive? Even animals suffer here. Even they aren't spared by the war.
Ciao!
Zlata

Sunday, August 16, 1992

Dear Mimmy,
Daddy has a hernia. He's lost a lot of weight and carrying the water was too much for him. The doctor has told him that he mustn't lift anything heavy anymore. Mustn't? But somebody has to bring the water! Mommy will have to do it alone now. How will she manage?
Zlata

Tuesday, August 18, 1992

Dear Mimmy,
Mommy is carrying home the water. It's hard on her, but she has to do it. The water hasn't come back on. Nor has the electricity.
   I didn't tell you, Mimmy, but I've forgotten what it's like to have water pouring out of a tap, what it's like to shower. We use a jug now. The jug has replaced the shower. We wash dishes and clothes like in the Middle Ages. This war is taking us back to olden times. And we take it, we suffer it, but we don't know for how long?
Zlata

Tuesday, August 25, 1992

Dear Mimmy,   80
I go regularly to summer school. I like it. We're together. We don't think about the shelling or the war. Maja and Lela, who help our teacher Irena Vidovic, cheer us up. We write, we recite, we spend the hours together. It takes me back to the days before the war. I'm also glad to be able to go out into the street. True, it's not far away (200 meters from my house), but I've finally stepped outside. Daddy takes me. Children mustn't walk in the street alone in Sarajevo. I was already going stir crazy. And I "do" myself up, I wear something nice. I mustn't show off too much?
Ciao!
Zlata

Sunday, September 20, 1992

Dear Mimmy,
YIPPEE! I crossed the bridge today. Finally I got to go out too! I can hardly believe it. The bridge hasn't changed. But it's sad, sad because of the post office, which looks even sadder. It's in the same place, but it's not the same old post office. The fire has left its mark. It stands there like a witness to brutal destruction.
   The streets aren't the same, not many people are out, they're worried, sad, everybody rushing around with bowed heads. All the shop

windows have been broken and looted. My school was hit by a shell and its top floor destroyed. The theater was also hit by some disgusting shells, and it's wounded. An awful lot of wonderful old Sarajevo buildings have been wounded.

I went to see Grandma and Granddad. Oh, how we hugged and kissed! They cried with joy. They've lost weight and aged since I last saw them four months ago. They told me I had grown, that I was now a big girl. That's nature at work. Children grow, the elderly age. That's how it is with those of us who are still alive.

And there are lots and lots of people and children in Sarajevo who are no longer among the living. The war has claimed them. And all of them were innocent. Innocent victims of this disgusting war.

We ran into Marijana's mother. They didn't leave. They're alive and well. She told me that Ivana had gone to Zagreb — with a Jewish convoy.   85

We also went to see our friend Doda. She, too, was surprised when she saw me. She cried. She says I've grown. Slobo (her husband) was wounded, but he's all right now. There's no news of Dejan (her son). It makes me sad.

Dear Mimmy, I have something to confess to you. I dressed up. I put on that nice plaid outfit. My shoes were a bit tight, because my feet have grown, but I survived.

So, that was my encounter with the bridge, the post office, Grandma, Granddad, and with a wounded Sarajevo. If only the war would stop, the wounds would heal!

Ciao!

Zlata

Thursday, October 1, 1992

Dear Mimmy,

Spring has come and gone, summer has been and gone, and now it's autumn. October has started. And the war is still on. The days are getting shorter and colder. Soon we'll move the stove upstairs to the apartment. But how will we keep warm? God, is anyone thinking of us in Sarajevo? Are we going to start winter without electricity, water or gas, and with a war going on?

The "kids" are negotiating. Will they finally negotiate something?   90
Are they thinking about us when they negotiate, or are they just trying to outwit each other, and leave us to our fate?

Daddy has been checking the attic and cellar for wood. It looks to me as though part of the furniture is going to wind up in the stove if this keeps up until winter. It seems that nobody is thinking of us, that this madness is going to go on and on. We have no choice, we have to rely on ourselves, to take care of ourselves and find a way to fight off the oncoming winter.

Mommy came home from work in a state of shock today. Two of her colleagues came from Grbavica. It really is true that people are being expelled from there. There's no sign of Mommy's and Nedo's relatives or of Lalo. Nedo is going berserk.
Your Zlata

Thursday, November 19, 1992

Dear Mimmy,
Nothing new on the political front. They are adopting some resolutions, the "kids" are negotiating, and we are dying, freezing, starving, crying, parting with our friends, leaving our loved ones.

I keep wanting to explain these stupid politics to myself, because it seems to me that politics caused this war, making it our everyday reality. War has crossed out the day and replaced it with horror, and now horrors are unfolding instead of days. It looks to me as though these politics mean Serbs, Croats, and Muslims. But they are all people. They are all the same. They all look like people, there's no difference. They all have arms, legs, and heads, they walk and talk, but now there's "something" that wants to make them different.

Among my girlfriends, among our friends, in our family, there are Serbs   95
and Croats and Muslims. It's a mixed group and I never knew who was a Serb, a Croats, or a Muslim. Now politics has started meddling around. It has put an "S" on Serbs, an "M" on Muslims, and a "C" on Croats, it wants to separate them. And to do so it has chosen the worst, blackest pencil of all — the pencil of war which spells only misery and death.

Why is politics making us unhappy, separating us, when we our-selves know who is good and who isn't? We mix with the good, not with the bad. And among the good there are Serbs and Croats and Muslims, just as there are among the bad. I simply don't understand it. Of course, I'm "young," and politics are conducted by "grown-ups." But I think we "young" would do it better. We certainly wouldn't have chosen war.

The "kids" really are playing, which is why us kids are not playing, we are living in fear, we are suffering, we are not enjoying the sun and flowers, we are not enjoying our childhood. WE ARE CRYING.

A bit of philosophizing on my part, but I was alone and felt I could write this to you, Mimmy. You understand me. Fortunately, I've got you to talk to.
And now,
Love,
Zlata

EXPLORATIONS

1. What is Zlata Filipović's attitude toward politics when she starts keeping her diary? When and how does her attitude change?

2. In what ways do the Filipović family members try to maintain their normal prewar life as war closes in on them? What else do they do to keep up their spirits?

3. How would the impact of "Sarajevo Diary" be different if it opened after the war in Bosnia had already started? How did you react to the early (peacetime) entries when you read them? How did they affect your reaction to later entries?

CONNECTIONS

1. Zlata Filipović and Frank McCourt ("Limerick Homecoming," p. 200) both go through experiences that no one would wish on a child. How does each set of parents try to protect their child? In what ways do they succeed, in what ways do they fail, and why?

2. In what ways does Zlata Filipović's response to being involved in a war differ from the response of Rami Rimon in "If There Is Justice" (p. 188)? What differences in their circumstances and in themselves do you think are responsible for the contrast?

3. Does the Filipović family seem more like the self-contained nuclear family mentioned by Susan Cheever, Nicholas Bromell, Louise Erdrich, and others in Part Two, or the extended family mentioned by Judith Ortiz Cofer, Angela Davis, Anwar El-Sadat, and others? On what evidence do you base your answer? What are the pros and cons of the Filipovićs' kind of family?

ELABORATIONS

1. A diary can be a useful source of information for other kinds of autobiographical (or biographical) writing. Based on "Sarajevo Diary," and additional research if you wish, write an expository essay about the changes war causes in Zlata Filipović's life.

2. If a war had broken out around your childhood home, how would your family have responded? Imagine your town being bombed, familiar buildings destroyed, your water and electricity cut off, windows shattered, friends and neighbors wounded or killed. Write an essay about the steps you and the other members of your family would take to cope with the kinds of crisis described in "Sarajevo Diary."

SPOTLIGHT:
JAPAN

Families: *A Tokyo family dines together in a traditional tatami room.*

Japan is a 2,360-mile archipelago off Asia's east coast consisting of four main islands and over 3,000 smaller ones. The northernmost of the main islands, Hokkaido, is east of Russia; south of it is the largest island, Honshu, opposite the Korean peninsula, where many major cities are located. South of Honshu are Kyushu, which lies east of China, and Shikoku, on the Pacific Ocean side of the chain. Most of the country is hills and mountains, many of them dormant or active volcanoes. Paleolithic people may have occupied Japan as long as 30,000 years ago, when land bridges probably linked the islands with Korea. As an island nation, Japan might have become a seagoing power, but its shipbuilding and trade routes gave way in the early 1600s to the Tokugawa shogunate's policy of isolation. Christianity (which had been introduced in 1549) was banned, along with all Europeans except the Dutch.

The city of Nagasaki on the island of Kyushu was the only place even the
Dutch and Chinese were allowed to maintain trading posts. It was U.S.
Commodore Matthew C. Perry who forced the reopening of trade in 1854.
Japan was then still ruled by the shoguns, a series of military governors who
had held power since 1192. Before the shogunate came the empire, which
supposedly began in 660 B.C., and which reestablished itself in 1868 (the
Meiji Restoration). Under the young Meiji emperor, Japan began an aggressive campaign of expansion, clashing with China, then Russia, Korea, Germany, and finally the United States. At the outset of World War II, Japan allied with Germany and the other Axis powers. Its attack on Pearl Harbor in
Hawaii in 1941 led to its defeat four years later after the United States
dropped the world's first nuclear bombs on Hiroshima and Nagasaki. In its
postwar constitution Japan renounced the right to wage war and shifted law-
making authority to the Diet, or parliament. Today Emperor Akihito is
Japan's head of state in a parliamentary democracy led by a prime minister.
In 1993, a series of scandals and widespread corruption ended thirty-eight
years of one-party rule by the Liberal Democrats. So pervasive was the problem, and so important to the Japanese, that since 1989, five prime ministers
have been forced out of office. Japan's economic boom has slowed in recent
years along with the rest of the world economy, but the country has maintained an enviable growth rate. At the same time, more and more Japanese
have been objecting to the almost feudal expectations of many corporations
regarding long work hours, ever-increasing production rates, and the sacrifice
of employees' personal lives. Foreign residents resent Japan's traditional rigid
ethnic homogeneity; and women have been pressing for more varied professional and personal opportunities.

JOHN DAVID MORLEY

Acquiring a Japanese Family

John David Morley, the son of a British foreign officer, was born in
Singapore in 1948 and grew up speaking Malay. After a year in Ghana
(then the Gold Coast), he went to Britain for school in 1955. Morley
took a first-class honors degree from Oxford University in 1969 and
moved to Munich. His first job, however, was in Mexico, as tutor to the
children of Elizabeth Taylor and Richard Burton. Working in the
theatre in Germany had led him to develop an interest in the drama —
and later the general culture — of Japan. He taught himself Japanese
and went to Japan on a Japanese government scholarship, to study at
the Language Research Institute of Waseda University, Tokyo. "Acquiring a Japanese Family" comes from his semiautobiographical novel *Pictures from the Water Trade: Adventures of a Westerner in Japan* (1985).
Morley moved back to Germany (then West Germany) in time for the
fall of the Berlin Wall in 1989, which he covered from East Germany
for the *London Sunday Times*. Material gathered then appears in his
1996 novel *Destiny, or the Attraction of Affinities*. Morley worked as European coordinator for the Japanese Broadcasting Corporation from the
late 1970s–1980s. He has continued to write both fiction and nonfiction, including novels, film scripts, and articles for newspapers including the *London Times* and the *New York Times* as well as German publications. "From a professional point of view, living as an English writer
in a non-English–speaking country has been problematic," he writes;
but "At some time or other in my life I have been most places."

Boon did not like the Foreign Students Hall where it had been
arranged for him to live, and on the same evening he moved in he
decided he would move out. . . . But the decision that he did not
want to live there was one thing, finding somewhere else to stay was
quite another, and this in turn would have been impossible or at
least very difficult if he had not happened to meet Sugama a few
days after arriving in the country.

The introduction was arranged through a mutual acquaintance,
Yoshida, at the private university where Boon was taking language
courses and where Sugama was employed on the administrative staff.
They met one afternoon in the office of their acquaintance and inspected each other warily for ten minutes.

"Nice weather," said Boon facetiously as he shook hands with Sugama. Outside it was pouring with rain.

"Nice weather?" repeated Sugama doubtfully, glancing out of the window. "But it's raining."

It was not a good start.   5

Sugama had just moved into a new apartment. It was large enough for two, he said, and he was looking for someone to share the expenses. This straightforward information arrived laboriously, in bits and pieces, sandwiched between snippets of Sugama's personal history and vague professions of friendship, irritating to Boon, because at the time he felt they sounded merely sententious. All this passed back and forth between Sugama and Boon through the mouth of their mutual friend, as Boon understood almost no Japanese and Sugama's English, though well-intentioned, was for the most part impenetrable.

It made no odds to Boon where he lived or with whom. All he wanted was a Japanese-speaking environment in order to absorb the language as quickly as possible. He had asked for a family, but none was available.

One windy afternoon in mid-October the three of them met outside the gates of the university and set off to have a look at Sugama's new apartment. It was explained to Boon that cheap apartments in Tokyo were very hard to come by, the only reasonable accommodation available being confined to housing estates subsidized by the government. Boon wondered how a relatively prosperous bachelor like Sugama managed to qualify for government-subsidized housing. Sugama admitted that this was in fact only possible because his grandfather would also be living there. It was the first Boon had heard of the matter and he was rather taken aback.

It turned out, however, that the grandfather would "very seldom" be there — in fact, that he wouldn't live there at all. He would only be there on paper, he and his grandson constituting a "family." That was the point. "You must *say* he is there," said Sugama emphatically.

The grandfather lived a couple of hundred miles away, and although   10
he never once during the next two years set foot in the apartment he still managed to be the bane of Boon's life. A constant stream of representatives from charities, government agencies, and old people's clubs, on average one or two a month, came knocking on the door, asking to speak to grandfather. At first grandfather was simply "not in" or had "gone for a walk," but as time passed and the flow of visitors never faltered, Boon found himself having to resort to more drastic measures. Grandfather began to make long visits to his home in the country; he had not yet returned because he didn't feel up to making the journey;

his health gradually deteriorated. Finally Boon decided to have him in-
valided, and for a long time his condition remained "grave." On grandfather's behalf Boon received the condolences of all these visitors, and
occasionally even presents.

Two years later grandfather did in fact die. Boon was thus exoner-
ated, but in the meantime he had got to know grandfather well and had
become rather fond of him. He attended his funeral with mixed
feelings.

Sugama had acquired tenure of his government-subsidized apartment by a stroke of luck. He had won a ticket in a lottery. These apartments were much sought after, and in true Japanese style their distribution among hundreds of thousands of applicants was discreetly left to
fate. The typical tenant was a young couple with one or two children,
who would occupy the apartment for ten or fifteen years, often under
conditions of bleak frugality, in order to save money to buy a house. Although the rent was not immoderate, prices generally in Tokyo were
high, and it was a mystery to Boon how such people managed to live at
all. Among the lottery winners there were inevitably also those people
for whom the acquisition of an apartment was just a prize, an unexpected bonus, to be exploited as a financial investment. It was no problem for these nominal tenants to sublet their apartments at prices well
above the going rate.

Boon had never lived on a housing estate and his first view of the tall
concrete compound where over fifty thousand people lived did little to
reassure him. Thousands of winner families were accommodated in
about a dozen rectangular blocks, each between ten and fifteen stories
high, apparently in no way different (which disappointed Boon most of
all) from similar housing compounds in Birmingham or Berlin. He had
naively expected Japanese concrete to be different, to have a different
color, perhaps, or a more exotic shape.

But when Sugama let them into the apartment and Boon saw the interior he immediately took heart: this was unmistakably Japanese. Taking off their shoes in the tiny boxlike hall, the three of them padded reverently through the kitchen into the *tatami* rooms.

"Smell of fresh *tatami*," pronounced Sugama, wrinkling his nose.   15

Boon was ecstatic. Over the close-woven pale gold straw matting lay
a very faint greenish shimmer, sometimes perceptible and sometimes
not, apparently in response to infinitesimal shifts in the texture of the
falling light. The *tatami* was quite unlike a carpet or any other form of
floor covering he had ever seen. It seemed to be alive, humming with
colors he could sense rather than see, like a greening tree in the brief

interval between winter and spring. He stepped onto it and felt the fibers recoil, sinking under the weight of his feet, slowly and softly.

"You can see green?" asked Sugama, squatting down.

"Yes indeed."

"Fresh *tatami*. Smell of grass, green color. But not for long, few weeks only."

"What exactly is it?"   20

"Yes."

Boon turned to Yoshida and repeated the question, who in turn asked Sugama and conferred with him at great length.

"*Tatami* comes from *oritatamu*, which means to fold up. So it's a kind of matting you can fold up."

"Made of straw."

"Yes."   25

"How long does it last?"

Long consultation.

"He says this is not so good quality. Last maybe four, five years."

"And then what?"

"New *tatami*. Quite expensive, you see. But very practical."   30

The three *tatami* rooms were divided by a series of *fusuma*, sliding screens made of paper and light wood. These screens were decorated at the base with simple grass and flower motifs; a natural extension, it occurred to Boon, of the grasslike *tatami* laid out in between. Sugama explained that the *fusuma* were usually kept closed in winter, and in summer, in order to have "nice breeze," they could be removed altogether. He also showed Boon the *shoji*, a type of sliding screen similar to the *fusuma* but more simple: an open wooden grid covered on one side with semitransparent paper, primitive but rather beautiful. There was only one small section of *shoji* in the whole apartment; almost as a token, thought Boon, and he wondered why.

With the exception of a few one- and two-room apartments, every house that Boon ever visited in Japan was designed to incorporate these three common elements: *tatami, fusuma,* and *shoji.* In the houses of rich people the *tatami* might last longer, the *fusuma* decorations might be more costly, but the basic concept was the same. The interior design of all houses being much the same, it was not surprising to find certain similarities in the behavior and attitudes of the people who lived in them.

The most striking feature of the Japanese house was lack of privacy; the lack of individual, inviolable space. In winter, when the *fusuma* were kept closed, any sound above a whisper was clearly audible on the other side, and of course in summer they were usually removed altogether. It is impossible to live under such conditions for very long without a common household identity emerging which naturally takes precedence over individual wishes. This enforced family unity was still held up to Boon as an ideal, but in practice it was ambivalent, as much a yoke as a bond.

There was no such thing as the individual's private room, no bedroom, dining- or sitting-room as such, since in the traditional Japanese house there was no furniture determining that a room should be reserved for any particular function. A person slept in a room, for example, without thinking of it as a bedroom or as his room. In the morning his bedding would be rolled up and stored away in a cupboard; a small table known as the *kotatsu*, which could also be plugged into the mains to provide heating, was moved back into the center of the room and here the family ate, drank, worked, and relaxed for the rest of the day. Although it was becoming standard practice in modern Japan for children to have their own rooms, many middle-aged and nearly all older Japanese still lived in this way. They regarded themselves as "one flesh," their property as common to all; the *uchi* (household, home) was constituted according to a principle of indivisibility. The system of movable screens meant that the rooms could be used by all the family and for all purposes: walls were built round the *uchi*, not inside it.

Boon later discovered analogies between this concept of house and   35
the Japanese concept of self. The Japanese carried his house around in his mouth and produced it in everyday conversation, using the word *uchi* to mean "I," the representative of my house in the world outside. His self-awareness was naturally expressed as corporate individuality, hazy about quite what that included, very clear about what it did not. . . .

The almost wearying sameness about all the homes which Boon visited, despite differences in the wealth and status of their owners, prompted a rather unexpected conclusion: the classlessness of the Japanese house. The widespread use of traditional materials, the preservation of traditional structures, even if in such contracted forms as to have become merely symbolic, suggested a consensus about the basic requirements of daily life which was very remarkable, and which presumably held implications for Japanese society as a whole. Boon's insight into that society was acquired very slowly, after he had spent a great deal of time sitting on the *tatami* mats and looking through the sliding *fusuma* doors which had struck him as no more than pleasing curiosities on his first visit to a Japanese-style home.

Sugama, Yoshida, and Boon celebrated the new partnership at a restaurant in Shinjuku, and a week later Boon moved in.

The moment he entered the apartment a woman who was unexpectedly standing in the kitchen dropped down on her knees and prostrated herself in a deep bow, her forehead almost touching the floorboards, introducing herself with the words "*Irrashaimase. Sugama de gozaimasu . . .*"

Boon was extremely startled. He wondered whether he should do the same thing and decided not, compromising with a halfhearted bow which unfortunately the woman couldn't even see, because she had her face to the ground. She explained that she was *o-kaasan*, Sugama's mother.

Sugama had a way of springing surprises — or rather, he indicated his intentions so obtusely that Boon usually failed to realize what would happen until it was already in progress — and so for quite a while Boon assumed that there must have been a change in plan, that the mother had perhaps joined the household as a stand-in for the grandfather. He greeted her in fluent Japanese (he had been studying introductions for the past week) and promptly fell into unbroken silence, mitigated by the occasional appreciative nod. Boon for his part hardly understood a word of what Sugama's mother was saying but she, encouraged by the intelligible sounds he had initially produced, talked constantly for the best part of an hour, and by the time Sugama eventually arrived Boon had become resigned to the idea that his talkative mother was going to be a permanent resident. 40

The misunderstanding was swiftly ironed out. No, *o-kaasan* had only come up to Tokyo for a few days (from whatever angle of the compass one approached Tokyo the journey to the capital was described as an elevation) in order to help with the move.

Sugama's mother was a small, wiry woman in her late fifties. Her teeth protruded slightly; like most Japanese women, even those who had very good teeth, she covered her mouth with her hand whenever she laughed. She was a vivacious woman and laughed frequently, so one way and another, with all the cooking, cleaning, and sewing she also did during the next four days, her hands were kept continually busy. She was of slight build but very sound in lung, with the effect that when she laughed it resounded throughout her whole body, as if the laugh were more than the body could accommodate. Perhaps this laughter drew Boon's attention to a girlish quality she had about her, despite her age and a rather plain appearance. He often watched her working, and in the spare, effortless movements of a woman who has performed the same tasks so many times that not even the tiniest gesture is superfluous there was also something unexpectedly graceful.

On the far side of the *fusuma* Boon often heard them talking late into the night. Night after night she sawed away at him with her flinty, abrasive voice. In the mornings Sugama was moody, the atmosphere in the house increasingly tense. Boon was left guessing. Gradually, in the course of weeks and months, Sugama began to take him into his confidence, and in retrospect he learned what must have been the subject of those nightly conversations.

O-kaasan's most pressing concern was that her son, at the advanced age of twenty-eight, was still unmarried. Boon couldn't see what the fuss was about, but Sugama was slowly coming round to his mother's view, who was quite sure it was a disaster. "The wind blows hard," he announced mysteriously, apparently by way of explanation — Boon himself had to blow pretty hard to keep up with conversations on this level. He said it was up to Sugama to decide when and whether he wanted to get married. It wasn't anybody else's business. Sugama would clearly have liked to be able to agree with this facile advice and just as clearly he could not, entangled in a web of sentiment and duty of which Boon was wholly ignorant.

The promptings of filial duty which caused Sugama such heartache   45 and which to Boon were so alien demanded of Sugama a second, even more painful decision. He was the *chonan*, the eldest son, thereby inheriting the obligation not merely to provide for his aging parents but to live with them in the same house. There were two alternatives open to him. He could either bring his parents to live with him in Tokyo or he could return home to his province in the north. A house in Tokyo large enough to provide room for grandfather, parents, Sugama, and — sooner or later — a fourth-generation family was out of the question; on his present salary he would have to work for several lifetimes in order to pay for it. A one-way ticket home came a great deal cheaper, which was just as well, since the only job awaiting him at the other end would be poorly paid and with even poorer prospects. Such was the path of righteousness. . . .

O-kaasan had only just packed her bags and gone home when — as usual without any forewarning — Sugama turned up late one evening accompanied by an old man, his wife, and an enormous cardboard box. Boon was sitting in his pajamas eating noodles out of a saucepan when these unexpected visitors arrived. Consternation. The old lady caught sight of him and dropped her bag (very probably she had not been forewarned either), immediately prostrating herself on the floor in the deepest of deep bows, old-style obeisance with the added advantage of concealing momentary shock and embarrassment. The old man was no slouch either. Palms on the floor and fingers turned inwards he bobbed his head up and down several times in Boon's direction, apologizing profusely every time he came up for air. All this happened so quickly that the astonished Boon didn't even have the presence of mind to put down the saucepan he was holding, and he sat there in his pajamas uneasily aware that he was the most unworthy object of the visitors' attentions.

Sugama came forward rather sheepishly, stepping in cavalier fashion between the prone bodies on the kitchen floor, and explained who they were.

"My grandfather's brother — younger brother — and wife."

"Not your grandfather?" asked Boon doubtfully, always alert to the possibility of misunderstandings when Sugama ventured into English.

"No, no *not* my grandfather."   50

"Your *great*-uncle, then."

"Ah! Great-uncle? *Great* uncle?"

Sugama paused to digest this new word, mustering his ancient relative with pursed lips. It was clear what was passing through his mind.

Boon was still not reassured. He kept an eye on the ominous cardboard box, quite large enough to accommodate a third, perhaps enfeebled relative, and wondered what else was in store for him.

"What are they doing here?"   55

"Earthquake," said Sugama simply. Boon fetched his dictionary and Sugama, reverting to Japanese, sat down to explain the situation.

At about nine o'clock that evening his great-uncle had called him in his office (Sugama worked a late shift) with the startling news that a major earthquake was imminent. How did he know? His wife had told him so. How did she know? A fortune-teller she regularly visited and in whom she placed absolute confidence had seen it in his cards and crystal ball. She was terrified, and having personally experienced the Great Kanto Earthquake of 1923 in which over a hundred thousand people had died she was not taking any chances. Her fortune-teller couldn't predict exactly when the earthquake would occur, but it might be at any time within the next three days; the greatest likelihood of its occurrence was forecast for midnight on the following day. The two old people ran a little shop in the downtown area of Tokyo where many of the houses were flimsy wooden structures which tended to slump and collapse very easily, even without the encouragement of an earthquake. But their great-nephew, they heard, had just moved into a marvelous modern building that was supposed to be *earthquake-proof*. Could they come and stay for a few days? Of course, said Sugama. So without more ado they bundled their worldly goods into the largest available box and Sugama brought them over in a neighbor's truck.

As a matter of fact there had been a slight tremor the previous evening. It was Boon's first. He had been standing in the kitchen

helping himself to another glass of whiskey when the floor unaccountably began to sway and a set of irreproachable stainless steel ladles,
which until then had given him no cause for complaint, started rattling
menacingly on the kitchen wall. Boon had replaced the whiskey and
made himself a cup of tea instead.

Great-uncle and his wife knelt on the *tatami* listening to Sugama's
recital, wagging their heads and smiling from time to time, as if allowing that there was something rather droll about the situation, but also
wanting to be taken absolutely seriously. However, with every moment
they spent in the apartment this became increasingly hard to do, for the
eccentric old couple seemed to be guided by a mischievous genius —
they belonged to nature's blunderers, everything they touched turned to
farce. Their great-nephew had just finished his dramatic account when
there was a shrill call of *ohayo!* (Good morning) from the kitchen, and
all eyes turned to the neglected cardboard box.

"Oh dear! The poor thing!" crowed the old lady, getting up at once   60
and pattering over to the box. She pulled open the flap and gently lifted
out a bright yellow parrot. The indignant bird rapped her knuckles a
couple of times with the side of his beak and settled frostily on the tip of
her finger.

Sugama, Boon, the elderly couple, and the yellow parrot housed together for the next three days. Once he had provided his relatives with a
roof over their heads Sugama took no further interest in them and was
unaccountably busy for as long as they stayed there, leaving the house
earlier and returning later than usual. His prodigiously long working
hours impressed great-uncle and worried his wife, who took to preparing nutritious cold snacks for the laboring hero before retiring for the
night. Sugama did justice to these snacks with the same appetite he applied himself to his work, warding off their anxieties with careless
equanimity.

"You've got to hand it to him — he certainly works hard," said great-
uncle at breakfast one morning, just after Sugama had left the house.

"Ah," replied Boon noncommittally. He knew perfectly well that
Sugama's overtime was not spent at the office but at mah-jongg parlors
in Nakano and Takadanobaba.

In the meantime Boon was left to study the evacuees and the evacuees Boon with mutual curiosity. On the whole he had the impression
that they were rather disappointed in him. At first they looked at him as
if he had descended from another planet, but when it became obvious
that he was not going to live up to these expectations their interest declined into an attitude of gently reproachful familiarity. For Boon did
not sleep on a bed, he dispensed with bacon and egg, he knew nothing

about baseball, ate rice and drank green tea with relish, and was un-
pardonably fond of dried cuttlefish and raw squid, foods which foreigners were commonly supposed to regard with horror and loathing.
Altogether Boon was not as Boon should be, and they were rather
disconcerted.

This attitude — a national prejudice, really — that foreigners and 65
the Japanese way of life must almost as a matter of principle be wholly
incompatible was something Boon encountered time and again. Under
the cover of courtesy, of polite considerations for differences in tastes
and customs, many Japanese would gleefully reveal their own select
cabinet of horrors, confronting their guest with fermented bean curd or
prawns drowned in sake not as something he might care to sample but
as a kind of ethnological litmus test: If he found it indigestible and
swiftly turned green this would be taken by them as confirmation of
their own cultural and racial singularity. With barely concealed triumph the host would commiserate with his victim, invariably remarking
Yappari, nihonjin ja nai to . . . (Ah well, unless one is Japanese . . .). . . .

On the fateful morning great-uncle took cover under the *kotatsu* earlier than usual and sat tight for the rest of the day. His wife went about
her household tasks as briskly as ever, but when there was nothing left
for her to do and at last she knelt down beside great-uncle at the little
table it became evident how restless she really was. From time to time
she laid down her sewing, listened intently, sighed, and picked it up
again. As the evening wore on and the tension began to mount, Boon
couldn't resist cracking a few jokes, which great-uncle good-humoredly
deflected at his wife. It was only to set her mind at rest that they had
come to stay, he assured Boon. Women couldn't resist fortune-tellers,
but it was just a lot of nonsense after all; and for good measure he made
a few jokes himself at her expense. Boon was not deceived. Throughout
the evening great-uncle helped himself to the bottle of fine old malt
whiskey, originally intended as Sugama's present, much more liberally
than he otherwise did and by midnight he was in true fighting spirit, his
face shining with such particular splendor that his wife's attention was
diverted from the impending destruction of Tokyo to the threat of great-
uncle's imminent collapse.

There was no earthquake that night, but the old lady couldn't quite
believe this and for two more days she sat it out in her nephew's apartment waiting for the dust to clear. Sugama was dispatched, like a kind
of dove from Noah's Ark, to report on the state of the world, and it was
only after he had personally confirmed that the house in downtown
Tokyo was still in perfect order that she consented to their departure.
Boon particularly regretted the loss of the parrot, which spoke few

words of Japanese but those very frequently, thus improving his pronunciation of the language.

EXPLORATIONS

1. According to John David Morley, what are the two meanings of the Japanese term *uchi* (paras. 34–35)?

2. How are Sugama's obligations to the older members of his family different from those of most twenty-eight-year-olds in the United States?

3. Morley describes his experiences in Japan through the eyes of the fictional character Boon. What advantages do you think Morley gains from writing in the third person rather than the first person?

CONNECTIONS

1. In paragraph 33, Morley writes about "a common household identity emerging which naturally takes precedence over individual wishes." Why does war create such an identity for the Filipović family in "Sarajevo Diary" (p. 210)? In what specific ways does their household unity take precedence over individual wishes?

2. Reread Rigoberta Menchú's description of the Quiché Indians' attitude toward outsiders in paragraph 5 of "Birth Ceremonies" (p. 176). What similarities do you notice between her account and Morley's description of the Japanese response to outsiders?

3. What ideas about the role of family and the obligations of family members are shared by the Japanese family as Morley describes it and the Indian family as Ved Mehta describes it (p. 133), but not by most families in the United States?

YUKIKO TANAKA

Mothers' Children

Yukiko Tanaka is a professional writer and translator and the editor
of several collections of Japanese women's writing. "Mothers' Children" comes from her book *Contemporary Portraits of Japanese Women*
(1995). Tanaka was born during World War II near Yokohama, in what
was then a farming community and now is part of an industrial mega-
lopolis that sprawls from the outskirts of Tokyo almost to Mount Fuji.
"The first five years of my life belong to the war years," she writes in the
book's introduction. "My memory retains the sound of bombing aircraft
that shattered window panes and shrieking sirens telling us to evacuate
to a shelter." Their shelter was a cave in a nearby hill, where Tanaka enjoyed gathering with the neighbors. The habit of sharing persisted after
the war: Tanaka's mother bartered for food and opened their home to
the extended family. "She made everything we wore in those days —
dresses, trousers, slips, even underpants." Tanaka started school in
1947. As the family grew more prosperous, her mother became a forerunner of the "Education Mom" she describes in this selection. Although only 5 percent of Japanese women then attended college,
Tanaka studied at Tsuda College and went on to graduate school at the
University of Denver (Colorado). She returned to Japan in 1965, working as a clinical social worker in Yokohama and Tokyo. Four years later
she moved back to the United States. Over the next two decades, in between frequent trips to Japan, she married an American, had two children, and obtained a Ph.D. in comparative literature from the University of California at Los Angeles. She and her family went to Osaka to
live for one year in 1987; since their return, Tanaka has regarded herself
as an American. They now live in Seattle.

During the post–World War II era, Japanese popular films and songs
quite often depicted a mother who happily sacrifices herself for her
family; she denies her sexuality and lives only for her children. Quite
often fate has been unkind to her, and she is poor, with many struggles
with life. Considering the real hardship the Japanese experienced during the postwar period, this representation has an element of truth.
Mothers, many of whom were without their husbands, might indeed
not have been able to manage a decent life for their families unless they
denied their own desires. "Women are weak but mothers are strong," an

241

expression popular in those days, described the situation, which lasted until the beginning of the 1960s.

The common perception of motherhood in the next decade can be seen in one of the most popular songs of the era, *Konnichiwa Akachan* ("Hello, My Baby"). This song about a young mother admiring her baby celebrates motherhood in a nontraditional nuclear family. A time of rapid economic growth, the 1960s were also a time when the ideal of "my homism," or family centeredness, began to permeate urban middle-class families. The introduction of electrical appliances made work around the house easier, allowing mothers more free time to devote to their children, particularly to their education. Due to increasing Western influence, the English word "mama" began replacing the Japanese word, *ōkasan*. With husbands working harder than ever and away from home most of their waking hours, the psychological tie between mother and child was reinforced. A declining family fertility rate (1.54 in 1990 compared to 5.11 in 1926) strengthened this bond. This was the era when *kyōiku mama* (education moms) emerged.

One of the most popular songs of 1968, "Entrance Exam Blues," introduced "education moms" to the Japanese public as controlling, selfish women who lived their lives vicariously through their sons' academic achievement. The news media focused on the negative influence of these mothers upon their children and criticized them. According to sociologist Amano Masako, it was also around this time that Japanese mothers themselves began expressing a sense of loss of direction and of their lives being empty. Considering my own mother, I find a relationship between her strong interest in her children's education and the fact that she found herself, in the early 1950s, with free time, relieved of time-consuming chores around the house. Among the forerunners of the "education moms," however, she appears not to have had a clearly defined goal or ambition for herself, which some people seem to associate with "education moms." She simply had energy and time to spare, and, as is the case with most Japanese mothers, her children were her first concern.

Rapid and large-scale industrial development and a mass exodus of people from villages and small towns during the 1950s and early 1960s resulted in expansion of large industrial centers in Japan. This has presented new situations for mothers and their children. Although urbanization is a universal phenomenon of all industrial nations, the Japanese version produced more drastic problems because of its speed, which was roughly four times that of the United States. In order to accommodate this large flow of people, major cities constructed enormous residential complexes on their outskirts. Unlike similarly constructed communities in other countries, such as Britain, these complexes — *nyū taun* ("new town") as the Japanese call them — consist exclusively of apartment houses. Since no shops or offices were built in conjunction with the apartments, these new towns are also called *beddo taun* ("bed town"), a place where people return to sleep. The distance of these homes from the city centers has produced many problems.

Extreme and rapid urbanization meant that most mothers were rais- 5 ing their children in an environment entirely different from the one in which they themselves had been raised; they lacked the social networks that had existed for their mothers. A new mother might be left with books on child rearing and a couple of phone numbers to connect her to the outside, to people who could understand her problems and give advice.

Studying popular articles from magazines and newspapers during the 1970s, Amano found that mothers were now portrayed as if they were merciless "ogres"; it was around this time that infanticide began receiving attention from reporters as a newly emerging social pathology. A new type of child desertion began to be noticed around the same time; dead bodies were even found in such unheard-of places as coin lockers in train stations (in contrast to the backdoor of someone's house, as in the common practice of old days). Writing on this bizarre new form of child desertion, poet Kōra Rumiko composed a poem entitled "Koin rokā no kurayami" ("Darkness Inside the Coin Locker"); Sakamoto Ryū wrote a novel called *Koin rokā beibīzu* (*Coin Locker Babies*).

Because Japanese culture has traditionally emphasized the mother-child relationship and because people think that a mother "naturally" bonds with her child, rather than learning once she becomes a mother, cases of abusive mothers are seen as caused by a loss of basic human decency. This is evident in such a headline as "Maternal Instinct Gone Berserk" for an article reporting a case in which a mother killed her three-month-old baby so that she could go back to work and start saving money to buy a house. What is missing in some of these reporters' views is that, in an age when family life has been dramatically altered, some young mothers are having a great deal of difficulty, and their frustration is shared by more mothers than one might think.

One of my elderly woman acquaintances believes that a shift in the attitude toward procreation is related to many difficulties that Japanese mothers are facing today in raising children. In earlier times, children were simply born, but now they are "planned." Instead of perceiving children as future caretakers who will look after them in their old age, parents now produce offspring so that they can experience emotional satisfaction. My acquaintance claims that here is a source of Japanese parents' indulgence toward their children and their loss of control, resulting in various problems.

The life cycle of Japanese women has also changed, affecting the parent-child relationship. In 1940, the average number of years between a woman's marriage and the birth of her first child was three; by 1978, this interval had been reduced to thirteen months. The majority of women now have their first child during their first or second year of marriage, when they are barely adjusted to this major life change. Since a wide age gap between the first and second child is generally considered undesirable, mothers now have the second child at about age twenty-eight (in contrast to age thirty-five for their mothers, who did not mind spreading out their childbearing over a period of fifteen years).

As noted, the physical environment in which many Japanese mothers raise their children has changed greatly from that of earlier times as well. In 1987, I lived with my family in a neighborhood of one of the new towns on the outskirts of Osaka. Throughout our nine-month stay, I witnessed continuous urban development around us. Next to a nearby bamboo forest, more apartment buildings were being built; adjacent to newly laid concrete roads were still a few farmhouses with thatched roofs and small rice paddies between them. The feeling of artificiality and the lack of continuity that characterized this neighborhood seemed eerie. A woman I befriended confided that she felt "a strange aversion" to the next-door neighbors on both sides of her apartment unit. The knowledge that her neighbors, literally thousands of them, lived in a space of exactly the same size and floor plan had a strange effect on her psyche, she said. Physical proximity seemed, ironically, to work against the residents of the new town becoming close to their neighbors; during the nearly ten years my acquaintance had lived there, she had not made any good friends. The aversion described is related to living without any meaningful human network in enclosed spaces that are identified, for instance, as "building Q, unit 711." By 1985, 77 percent of the entire Japanese population lived in urban areas, and three-quarters of the urban population lived in the three major metropolitan areas that have several new towns.

After talking with quite a few mothers during my stay in Japan in 1987, I concluded that Japanese mothers, particularly younger mothers, perceive child rearing as a difficult task. In conjunction with a lack of adequate living space and the high cost of education, this perceived difficulty is a reason for limiting the desired number of children to one or two.

Japanese mothers today complete their childbearing within a little over three years after marriage. In terms of the mothers' extended life expectancy, the time spent on child rearing represents only a small portion of their lives. Even with the society's emphasis on motherhood, it is now much more difficult to be satisfied with simply being a mother, and many mothers are realizing this. For those who want to work outside the home, however, finding childcare is the biggest hurdle. Not uncommon in many societies, this difficulty is even greater in Japan, where child-care centers, most of which are public facilities, have inflexible hours, where there is usually a long commute between home and work, and where fathers are either unwilling or unable to share responsibility.

Consider the situation of my friend Kusunose Mikiko. The mother of two children, ages four and two, Mikiko, who works at an advertising firm in central Tokyo, leaves home around 7:30; she drops her children at day care on her way to the station, arriving at work by 9:00. She cannot make it to the day-care center to collect the children before it closes at 6:00, so she has hired a woman to do this for her and to stay with the children until she gets home, which is around 8:00 at night. Her husband, a computer programmer, cannot help because he leaves home even earlier than Mikiko and returns home around midnight. The cost of childcare, including hiring the woman, is not small — almost half of Mikiko's salary.

My friend, however, is lucky because she has found a public day-care facility that can take both of her children. The availability of such day care, with relatively small fees and supervision by the municipal government, depends upon one's geographical location; in order to qualify for such day care, mothers often have to go through a lot of red tape. Furthermore, since these facilities close at 6:00 (partly in order to protect the women who work there, but also on the grounds that keeping children longer than eight hours is not desirable), they do not fully meet the needs of mothers who have full-time jobs like Mikiko's.

What about private day care? Kawashima Shizuyo, the author of a 15 book entitled *Yami ni tadayou kodomotachi* (*Children Drifting in the Darkness*) found out the reality of one kind. At a *bebī hoteru*, or baby's hotel, children and infants may be kept until after midnight, sometimes overnight. Often situated inside a high-rise building on a neon-lit street, sandwiched between a bar and a mahjong parlor, *bebī hoteru* are called "hotels" because they offer round-the-clock care. Many who avail themselves of these "hotels" are bar hostesses; some places have contracts with nightclubs, which advertise the availability of childcare when recruiting hostesses.

The number of baby hotels mushroomed throughout Japan during the 1970s, although most Japanese learned about their existence only through television news reports of various accidental deaths of the children in these hotels, mostly caused by suffocation. Reports on these accidents, the poor conditions (up to twenty children looked after by one or two adults), and the long hours the children were being kept there appalled viewers. The reporters pointed out that, despite Japan's Child Welfare Law (which makes it clear that the government, along with parents, has a responsibility to provide adequate care and protection), the government has permitted a private industry to fill a void by insisting on the view that institutional care is undesirable for the young child. Investigation followed the news reports, and regulations governing baby hotels were written. According to Kawashima, however, there seems to have been little improvement.

In 1987, I saw one of these baby hotels in downtown Osaka, located amid restaurants, bars, and nightclubs. The children's colorful drawings, pasted on the windows, looked incongruous against the bright neon, but, in an age when women's employment has increased and diversified, a facility like this, with its great flexibility, is naturally appealing. According to a 1980 study, about half of the mothers who used baby hotels worked in order to support themselves and their children. In Kawashima's book are dozens of photos. One shows a young girl, wide awake on a top bunk bed, waiting for her mother to pick her up while all the other children sleep; another shows a sign reading "Mother for Rent."

Considering education the key to the production of highly skilled, well-disciplined workers who support a nation's economic growth, U.S. news media have repeatedly reported how well the Japanese educational system works. Reporters point out that, in international comparisons, Japanese students score high not only in fields that require rote memory, but in areas like science as well. Some observers conclude that Japanese students are well educated because they spend more days at school (sixty more days a year than American children). Others assume that the Japanese educational system works because Japanese society is more homogeneous, and uniformity in teaching is maintained. Uniformity, it is true, is achieved through the use of a limited number of textbooks approved by the Ministry of Education; the national government also exerts a great deal of influence on curriculum development.

Yet another view suggests that the key to Japanese success in education is the high regard the Japanese have for the profession of teaching. Although there has been a definite corrosion in this attitude in recent years, regard still exists to a great extent. Moreover, Japanese primary and secondary school teachers tend to see themselves as engaged in a process they refer to as "life guidance." I witnessed this "life guidance" firsthand, when I sent my two children to public school in Osaka in 1987. For instance, during school lunch (compulsory during the first six years of public school), the teacher made sure that students ate all of their food — the teaching of a good habit; at a parent-teacher conference, my third-grade daughter's teacher expressed interest in my disciplinary approach at home. Home visits by teachers are part of their job, so that they can understand their students in their family environments. In other words, teachers are concerned with their student both in and out of school, and they expect a great deal of parental participation.

All of this said, however, there is no doubt that a very important key   20
to high academic performance among Japanese students lies in a fierce competition they undergo, willingly or unwillingly, and the efforts of mothers to support and encourage their children to be winners. It is true, as Edwin Reischauer has pointed out, that the importance of preparing for the required entrance examinations (for both high school and the university) helps explain the seriousness with which the Japanese approach education.

The case of Kumiko and her mother, a friend of mine, is typical of ninth-grade students in Japan. Never very studious and busy with her school band, Kumiko did not do too much entrance exam preparation until six months before she was to take the exams to enter a high school. Then she began to study very hard. Every day she studied for a few hours after school and again after dinner, until she went to bed at 10:00; she then got up at 3:30 the next morning to study some more. Since her alarm could not completely wake her up, she enlisted the help of her willing mother, who, after waking Kumiko, returned to bed. During the two weeks of winter break, Kumiko also went all day to a *juku*, a cram school. She told me that her classmates stopped talking about their favorite television programs as the entrance exam date approached and instead shared information on the test and how to solve difficult math problems.[1]

With its focus on helping children pass entrance examinations, the *juku* features motivational techniques and more advanced teaching than does regular school. During a 1983 visit to Japan, I discovered how widespread the practice of sending children to *juku* had become. Cramming schools had become so popular, I was told, that those who did not attend one had problems finding playmates after regular school.

---

[1]Even though 97 percent of children now attend high school — compared to 50 percent in my day, some thirty years ago — high school education in Japan is not compulsory, and entrance exams are required to attend.

Children now also start *juku* earlier, sometimes during the fourth grade. *Juku* are run by private enterprise and are costly; some mothers take a part-time job so that they can afford the expense.

In Japan today, it is considered the mother's responsibility to see that her children do well at school and are prepared to receive an optimal education. Hence, the mother encourages, scolds, bribes, and does anything else that might help her child study. Unlike American mothers, who tend to see their role in their child's achievement as limited, perhaps because they believe that the key component is the child's innate ability to learn, Japanese mothers emphasize effort as most important for success.

I observed how far this effort to help their children succeed can go with an old friend, Toda Akiko. The mother of a fifth-grade boy at the time I visited her in 1987, Akiko told me of her educational plan for her son. The Todas live in Miyazaki, a remote town on Kyushu, where Akiko's husband teaches at a university, but Akiko has a plan to move to Tokyo with her son within a few years. She claims that the best high schools in the country are found only in a few big cities and that her husband, an unusually self-sufficient man for a Japanese husband, will not mind being left behind. Until then, during school breaks, Akiko has been accompanying her son on two-hour plane trips to Tokyo, so that he can attend one of the more prestigious *juku* there.

Akiko does not consider herself an "education mom," for the term   25
has been used in the recent past to describe mothers who pressure their children — mostly sons — into unreasonable study habits. As the leader of a women's volunteer organization, she has other interests besides being a mother. In her calm description of the realities of competition in Japan's educational system, I did not detect any traces of the obsessiveness of an egocentric mother who lives her life vicariously through her son. Nonetheless, when we met to talk about old times, Akiko showed me a few geometry problems she had helped her fifth-grader with the night before. I could see then that preparing for the examination is not a task for a child alone. Clearly more is expected of Japanese children now than when Akiko and I were primary school students thirty-five years ago — or of the majority of American children of comparable age today.

I see another dimension to Japanese educational competition. The degree of sacrifice that Japanese parents are willing to make so that their children receive the best possible education can be understood more fully if education is seen clearly as an investment. If one asks Japanese parents what they consider the most important investment for the future, many will answer "children." In their minds, the child's (mainly the son's) secure financial future, with lifetime employment in a large and well-established firm, is equivalent to their own future security.

The same perspective is reflected in the parents' preferences for their children's future careers. Many parents want their sons to go into engineering (30 percent, in one study) and government work (19 percent), two of the most promising and secure fields. Both because of the traditional emphasis on filial responsibility and because social welfare provisions in Japan have long been paltry and subject to the vicissitudes of the country's economy, many Japanese expect that their children — sons in most cases — will take care of them, if necessary, in their old age. Parental expectations for their children's future careers often differ according to the gender of the child, likewise manifesting the view of education as an investment.

Education at pre-college levels has become quite expensive in Japan in the past few decades, due to the practice of sending students to *juku* and hiring private tutors, as well as to the increased popularity of private schools. The average annual cost of high school education (both public and private) in 1983, for instance, was as much as 210,000 yen ($1,680). Many households put aside a good portion of their year-end bonuses (often equivalent to three months' salary) either to cover their children's educational expenses or to save for the future, instead of spending the money for pleasure and the enrichment of their present lives. This practice perhaps is related to the high level of personal savings among the Japanese. Couples have also been opting to have fewer children so that they can afford the "right" education for them.

Many Japanese are disturbed by what they consider to be excessive educational competition, accompanied by parents' pouring money into their children's education. Despite the criticism, however, the majority continue to feel that they have no choice. The villain, they say, is the *gakureki shakai*, or diploma-oriented society. The dramatic increase in interest in higher education, however, seems inevitable; it partially reflects changes in the Japanese economy — the very rapid shift from manufacturing to high-tech and other industries that require higher education. College education is more important now than even a decade ago. Thus, despite the rising cost of education at all levels, the desire of Japanese parents to provide their children with higher education has steadily increased. One poll has shown that as many as 79 percent of them want their sons (24 percent for daughters) to receive a four-year college education. Although many new colleges have opened in the past few decades, this level of parental expectation is not matched by educational resources. Hence, high competition rates.

A mother who wants her child to succeed — as most do — will con-   30
tinue to sacrifice not only money but much personal time and effort to
support the child's "examination years." A friend of mine, a professional
woman, recently told me in a letter that she plans to cut back her hours
of work to help her daughter pass her high school exams. I do not expect a lessening of this maternal fervor in Japanese mothers in the coming years.

EXPLORATIONS

1. According to Yukiko Tanaka, what changes has the Japanese mother's popular image undergone since World War II? What does Tanaka believe are the
   main factors behind these changes?
2. What role does Tanaka describe Japanese fathers as playing in their families? What clues in her essay reveal the priorities of Japanese husbands?
3. Which of Tanaka's comments indicate that she is writing mainly about a
   particular Japanese socioeconomic group? Besides their attitudes toward education, what are this group's characteristics?

CONNECTIONS

1. "Many Japanese expect that their children — sons in most cases — will take
   care of them, if necessary, in their old age" (para. 27). What details does
   John David Morley supply about this traditional expectation in "Acquiring a
   Japanese Family" (p. 230)?
2. Reread U.S. Representative Patricia Schroeder's comments on childcare
   and economic pressure on families (p. 129). What evidence in "Mothers'
   Children" suggests that Japanese families face the same problems? What
   statements by Schroeder and Tanaka suggest that the Japanese and U.S.
   governments have taken similar positions on this issue?
3. According to Tanaka, how do Japanese families commonly address the
   problems Rep. Schroeder describes? How are their solutions different from
   those of the New Yorkers described by Susan Cheever in "The Nanny
   Dilemma" (p. 155)? What appear to be the reasons for the differences?

KENZABURO OE

Japan, the Ambiguous, and Myself

"I was born in a small village in the valley on Shikoku Island, surrounded by virgin forests," says Kenzaburo Oe. "Our ancestors in the valley have always believed that we have our own myth, our own traditional culture, which we should preserve."[1] In this respect Oe recognizes a kinship with such U.S. writers as William Faulkner, Flannery O'Connor, and Toni Morrison (see p. 544). Oe's mountain village on the smallest and most rural of Japan's four major islands is Ose, where he was born in 1935, the third of seven children. He received his B.A. degree in French literature from the University of Tokyo in 1959; by that time he had already won two literary prizes. Oe's first novel, *Warera no jidai* (1959, *Our Times*) shocked contemporary Japanese critics, as did his next three novels. Meanwhile, Oe married Yukari Itami and became the father of a son, Hikari, with a congenital cranial abnormality. As he notes in the following excerpt from his 1994 Nobel Prize acceptance speech, his life and his writing changed focus at that point. A cycle of narratives from 1964 to 1976, beginning with "Sora no kaibutsu aguwee" ("Aghwee the Sky Monster"), explored father-son relationships. Oe's many novels and essay collections have won worldwide praise and numerous awards. He has traveled and lectured in Europe, Australia, Latin America, and the United States, and has been a writer-in-residence at the Colegio de Mexico and the University of California at Berkeley. Besides Hikari, now a successful composer, Oe and his wife have another son and a daughter; they live in Tokyo.

During the last catastrophic World War, I was a little boy and lived in a remote, wooded valley on Shikoku Island in the Japanese archipelago, thousands of miles away from here [Sweden]. At that time there were two books that I was really fascinated by: *The Adventures of Huckleberry Finn* and *The Wonderful Adventures of Nils.*[2] The whole world was then engulfed by waves of horror. By reading *Huckleberry Finn* I felt I was able to justify my habit of going into the mountain forest at night and sleeping among the trees with a sense of security that I could never find indoors.

---

[1]*The Georgia Review*, Winter 1995, p. 835; translated by Michiko Niikuni Wilson.
[2]*The Adventures of Huckleberry Finn*, by Mark Twain (U.S., 1835–1910); *The Wonderful Adventures of Nils*, by Selma Lagerlöf (Sweden, 1858–1940).

The hero of *The Wonderful Adventures of Nils* is transformed into a tiny creature who understands the language of birds and sets out on an exciting journey. I derived from the story a variety of sensuous pleasures. Firstly, living as I was in a deeply wooded area in Shikoku just as my ancestors had done long before, I found it gave me the conviction, at once innocent and unwavering, that this world and my way of life there offered me real freedom. Secondly, I felt sympathetic and identified with Nils, a naughty child who, while traveling across Sweden, collaborating with and fighting for the wild geese, grows into a different character, still innocent, yet full of confidence as well as modesty. But my greatest pleasure came from the words Nils uses when he at last comes home, and I felt purified and uplifted as if speaking with him when he says to his parents (in the French translation): "'Maman, Papa! Je suis grand, je suis de nouveau un homme!'" ("Mother, Father! I'm a big boy, I'm a human being again!")

I was fascinated by the phrase "je suis de nouveau un homme!" in particular. As I grew up, I was to suffer continual hardships in different but related realms of life — in my family, in my relationship to Japanese society, and in my general way of living in the latter half of the twentieth century. I have survived by representing these sufferings of mine in the form of the novel. In that process I have found myself repeating, almost sighing, "je suis de nouveau un homme!" Speaking in this personal vein might seem perhaps inappropriate to this place and to this occasion. However, allow me to say that the fundamental method of my writing has always been to start from personal matters and then to link them with society, the state, and the world in general. I hope you will forgive me for talking about these personal things a little longer.

Half a century ago, while living in the depths of that forest, I read *The Wonderful Adventures of Nils* and felt within it two prophecies. One was that I might one day be able to understand the language of birds. The other was that I might one day fly off with my beloved wild geese — preferably to Scandinavia.

After I got married, the first child born to us was mentally handi-   5
capped. We named him Hikari, meaning "light" in Japanese. As a baby he responded only to the chirping of wild birds and never to human voices. One summer when he was six years old we were staying at our country cottage. He heard a pair of water rails calling from the lake beyond a grove, and with the voice of a commentator on a recording of birdsong he said: "Those are water rails." These were the first words that my son had ever uttered. It was from then on that my wife and I began communicating verbally with him.

Hikari now works at a vocational training center for the handi-capped, an institution based on ideas learned from Sweden. In the mean-time he has been composing works of music. Birds were the things that occasioned and mediated his composition of human music. On my be-half Hikari has thus fulfilled the prophecy that I might one day under-stand the language of birds. I must also say that my life would have been impossible but for my wife with her abundant female strength and wisdom. She has been the very incarnation of Akka, the leader of Nils's wild geese. Together we have flown to Stockholm, and so the second of the prophecies has also, to my great delight, now been realized.

Yasunari Kawabata, the first Japanese writer to stand on this platform as a Nobel laureate for literature, delivered a lecture entitled "Japan, the Beautiful, and Myself." It was at once very beautiful and very vague. I use the word "vague" as an equivalent of the Japanese *aimaina*, itself a word open to several interpretations. The kind of vagueness that Kawa-bata deliberately adopted is implied even in the title of his lecture, with the use of the Japanese particle *no* (literally "of") linking "Myself" and "Beautiful Japan." One way of reading it is "myself as a part of beautiful Japan," the *no* indicating the relationship of the noun following it to the noun preceding it as one of possession or attachment. It can also be un-derstood as "beautiful Japan and myself," the particle in this case link-ing the two nouns in apposition, which is how they appear in the Eng-lish title of Kawabata's lecture as translated by Professor Edward Seidensticker, one of the most eminent American specialists in Japa-nese literature. His expert translation — "Japan, the beautiful, *and* my-self" — is that of a *traduttore* (translator) and in no way a *traditore* (traitor).

Under that title Kawabata talked about a unique kind of mysticism which is found not only in Japanese thought but also more widely in Oriental philosophy. By "unique" I mean here a tendency toward Zen Buddhism. Even as a twentieth-century writer Kawabata identified his own mentality with that affirmed in poems written by medieval Zen monks. Most of these poems are concerned with the linguistic impossi-bility of telling the truth. Words, according to such poems, are confined within closed shells, and the reader cannot expect them ever to emerge, to get through to us. Instead, to understand or respond to Zen poems one must abandon oneself and willingly enter into the closed shells of those words.

Why did Kawabata boldly decide to read those very esoteric poems in Japanese before the audience in Stockholm? I look back almost with nostalgia on the straightforward courage he attained toward the end of

his distinguished career which enabled him to make such a confession
of his faith. Kawabata had been an artistic pilgrim for decades during
which he produced a series of masterpieces. After those years of pilgrimage, it was only by talking of his fascination with poetry that baffled any
attempt fully to understand it that he was able to talk about "Japan, the
Beautiful, and Myself"; in other words, about the world he lived in and
the literature he created.

It is noteworthy, too, that Kawabata concluded his lecture as follows: 10

> My works have been described as works of emptiness, but it is not to be
> taken for the nihilism of the West. The spiritual foundation would seem
> to be quite different. Dogen entitled his poem about the seasons "Innate
> Reality," and even as he sang of the beauty of the seasons he was deeply
> immersed in Zen.
>
> (Translation by Edward Seidensticker)

Here also I detect a brave and straightforward self-assertion. Not only
did Kawabata identify himself as belonging essentially to the tradition of
Zen philosophy and aesthetic sensibility pervading the classical literature of the Orient, but he went out of his way to differentiate emptiness
as an attribute of his works from the nihilism of the West. By doing so
he was wholeheartedly addressing the coming generations of mankind
in whom Alfred Nobel placed his hope and faith.

To tell the truth, however, instead of my compatriot who stood here
twenty-six years ago, I feel more spiritual affinity with the Irish poet
William Butler Yeats, who was awarded a Nobel Prize for Literature
seventy-one years ago when he was about the same age as me. Of course
I make no claim to being in the same rank as that poetic genius; I am
merely a humble follower living in a country far removed from his. But
as William Blake, whose work Yeats reevaluated and restored to the
high place it holds in this century, once wrote: "Across Europe & Asia
to China & Japan like lightenings."

During the last few years I have been engaged in writing a trilogy
which I wish to be the culmination of my literary activities. So far the
first two parts have been published, and I have recently finished writing
the third and final part. It is entitled in Japanese *A Flaming Green Tree*.
I am indebted for this title to a stanza from one of Yeats's important
poems, "Vacillation":

> A tree there is that from its topmost bough
> Is half all glittering flame and half all green
> Abounding foliage moistened with the dew. . . .
>
> ("Vacillation," 11–13)

My trilogy, in fact, is permeated by the influence of Yeats's work as a whole.

On the occasion of his winning the Nobel Prize the Irish Senate proposed a motion to congratulate him, which contained the following sentences: 15

> . . . the recognition which the nation has gained, as a prominent contributor to the world's culture, through his success . . . a race that hitherto had not been accepted into the comity of nations. . . .

> Our civilization will be assessed on the name of Senator Yeats. Coming at a time when there was a regular wave of destruction [and] hatred of beauty . . . it is a very happy and welcome thing. . . . [T]here will always be the danger that there may be a stampeding of people who are sufficiently removed from insanity in enthusiasm for destruction.
> (The Nobel Prize: Congratulations to Senator Yeats)

Yeats is the writer in whose wake I would like to follow. I would like to do so for the sake of another nation that has now been "accepted into the comity of nations" not on account of literature or philosophy but for its technology in electronic engineering and its manufacture of motorcars. Also I would like to do so as a citizen of a nation that in the recent past was stampeded into "insanity in enthusiasm for destruction" both on its own soil and on that of neighboring nations.

As someone living in present-day Japan and sharing bitter memories of the past, I cannot join Kawabata in saying "Japan, the Beautiful, and Myself." A moment ago I referred to the "vagueness" of the title and content of his lecture. In the rest of my own lecture I would like to use the word "ambiguous," in accordance with the distinction made by the eminent British poet Kathleen Raine, who once said of Blake that he was not so much vague as ambiguous. It is only in terms of "Japan, the Ambiguous, and Myself" that I can talk about myself.

After a hundred and twenty years of modernization since the opening up of the country, contemporary Japan is split between two opposite poles of ambiguity. This ambiguity, which is so powerful and penetrating that it divides both the state and its people, and affects me as a writer like a deep-felt scar, is evident in various ways. The modernization of Japan was oriented toward learning from and imitating the West, yet the country is situated in Asia and has firmly maintained its traditional culture. The ambiguous orientation of Japan drove the country into the position of an invader in Asia, and resulted in its isolation from other Asian nations not only politically but also socially and culturally. And even in the West, to which its culture was supposedly quite open, it has long remained inscrutable or only partially understood.

In the history of modern Japanese literature, the writers most sincere in their awareness of a mission were the "postwar school" of writers who came onto the literary scene deeply wounded by the catastrophe of war yet full of hope for a rebirth. They tried with great pain to make up for the atrocities committed by Japanese military forces in Asia, as well as to bridge the profound gaps that existed not only between the developed nations of the West and Japan but also between African and Latin American countries and Japan. Only by doing so did they think that they could seek with some humility reconciliation with the rest of the world. It has always been my aspiration to cling to the very end of the line of that literary tradition inherited from those writers.

The present nation of Japan and its people cannot but be ambiva- [20] lent. The Second World War came right in the middle of the process of modernization, a war that was brought about by the very aberration of that process itself. Defeat in this conflict fifty years ago created an opportunity for Japan, as the aggressor, to attempt a rebirth out of the great misery and suffering that the "postwar school" of writers depicted in their work. The moral props for a nation aspiring to this goal were the idea of democracy and the determination never to wage a war again — a resolve adopted not by innocent people but people stained by their own history of territorial invasion. Those moral props mattered also in regard to the victims of the nuclear weapons that were used for the first time in Hiroshima and Nagasaki, and for the survivors and their offspring affected by radioactivity (including tens of thousands of those whose mother tongue is Korean).

In recent years there have been criticisms leveled against Japan suggesting that it should offer more military support to the United Nations forces and thereby play a more active role in the keeping and restoration of peace in various parts of the world. Our hearts sink whenever we hear these comments. After the Second World War it was a categorical imperative for Japan to renounce war forever as a central article of the new constitution. The Japanese chose, after their painful experiences, the principle of permanent peace as the moral basis for their rebirth.

I believe that this principle can best be understood in the West, with its long tradition of tolerance for conscientious objection to military service. In Japan itself there have all along been attempts by some people to remove the article about renunciation of war from the constitution, and for this purpose they have taken every opportunity to make use of pressure from abroad. But to remove the principle of permanent peace would be an act of betrayal toward the people of Asia and the victims of the bombs dropped on Hiroshima and Nagasaki. It is not difficult for me as a writer to imagine the outcome.

The prewar Japanese constitution, which posited an absolute power transcending the principle of democracy, was sustained by a degree of support from the general public. Even though our new constitution is already half a century old, there is still a popular feeling of support for the old one, which lives on in some quarters as something more substantial than mere nostalgia. If Japan were to institutionalize a principle other than the one to which we have adhered for the last fifty years, the determination we made in the postwar ruins of our collapsed effort at modernization — that determination of ours to establish the concept of universal humanity — would come to nothing. Speaking as an ordinary individual, this is the specter that rises before me.

What I call Japan's "ambiguity" in this lecture is a kind of chronic disease that has been prevalent throughout this modern age. Japan's economic prosperity is not free from it either, accompanied as it is by all kinds of potential dangers in terms of the structure of the world economy and environmental conservation. The "ambiguity" in this respect seems to be accelerating. It may be more obvious to the critical eyes of the world at large than to us in our own country. At the nadir of postwar poverty we found a resilience to endure it, never losing our hope of recovery. It may sound curious to say so, but we seem to have no less resilience in enduring our anxiety about the future of the present tremendous prosperity. And a new situation now seems to be arising in which Japan's wealth assumes a growing share of the potential power of both production and consumption in Asia as a whole.

I am a writer who wishes to create serious works of literature distinct   25
from those novels which are mere reflections of the vast consumer culture of Tokyo and the subcultures of the world at large. My profession — my "habit of being" (in Flannery O'Connor's words) — is that of the novelist who, as Auden described him, must:

> . . . , among the Just
> Be just, among the Filthy filthy too,
> And in his own weak person, if he can,
> Must suffer dully all the wrongs of Man.
> ("The Novelist," 12–14)

What, as a writer, do I see as the sort of character we Japanese should seek to have? Among the words that George Orwell often used to describe the traits he admired in people was "decent," along with "humane" and "sane." This deceptively simple term stands in stark contrast to the "ambiguous" of my own characterization, a contrast matched by the wide discrepancy between how the Japanese actually appear to others and how they would like to appear to them.

Orwell, I hope, would not have objected to my using the word "decent" as a synonym of the French *humaniste*, because both terms have in common the qualities of tolerance and humanity. In the past, Japan too had some pioneers who tried hard to build up the "decent" or "humanistic" side of ourselves. One such person was the late Professor Kazuo Watanabe, a scholar of French Renaissance literature and thought. Surrounded by the insane patriotic ardor of Japan on the eve and in the throes of the Second World War, Watanabe had a lonely dream of grafting the humanistic view of man onto the traditional Japanese sense of beauty and sensitivity to nature, which fortunately had not been entirely eradicated. (I hasten to add that Watanabe's conception of beauty and nature was different from that of Kawabata as expressed in his "Japan, the Beautiful, and Myself.") The way Japan had tried to construct a modern state modeled on the West was a disaster. In ways different from yet partly corresponding to that process, Japanese intellectuals tried to bridge the gap between the West and their own country at its deepest level. It must have been an arduous task but also one that sometimes brimmed with satisfaction. . . .

As someone influenced by [Watanabe's] thought, I wish my work as a novelist to help both those who express themselves in words and their readers to overcome their own sufferings and the sufferings of their time, and to cure their souls of their wounds. I have said that I am split between the opposite poles of an ambiguity characteristic of the Japanese. The pain this involves I have tried to remove by means of literature. I can only hope and pray that my fellow Japanese will in time recover from it too.

If you will allow me to mention him again, my son Hikari was awakened by the voices of birds to the music of Bach and Mozart, eventually composing his own works. The little pieces that he first produced had a radiant freshness and delight in them; they seemed like dew glittering on leaves of grass. The word "innocence" is composed of *in* and *nocere*, or, "not to hurt." Hikari's music was in this sense a natural effusion of the composer's own innocence.

As Hikari went on to produce more works, I began to hear in his   30
music also "the voice of a crying and dark soul." Handicapped though he was, his hard-won "habit of being" — composing — acquired a growing maturity of technique and a deepening of conception. That in turn enabled him to discover in the depth of his heart a mass of dark sorrow which until then he had been unable to express.

"The voice of a crying and dark soul" is beautiful, and the act of setting it to music cures him of this sorrow, becoming an act of recovery. His music, moreover, has been widely accepted as one that cures and restores other listeners as well. In this I find grounds for believing in the wondrous healing power of art.

There is no firm proof of this belief of mine, but "weak person" though I am, with the aid of this unverifiable belief, I would like to "suffer dully all the wrongs" accumulated throughout this century as a result of the uncontrolled development of inhuman technology. As one with a peripheral, marginal, off-center existence in the world, I would like to continue to seek — with what I hope is a modest, decent, humanistic contribution of my own — ways to be of some use in the cure and reconciliation of mankind.

EXPLORATIONS

1. What does Kenzaburo Oe mean by ambiguity? What specific ambiguities does he cite in contemporary Japan?

2. At what points and in what ways is Oe's lecture itself ambiguous? Cite at least two ambiguous statements, and analyze the meanings implied in each one.

3. What are the reasons why Oe's comments about his family are an appropriate way to start and end his lecture?

CONNECTIONS

1. How is Oe's depiction of his family similar to the popular image of the Japanese family Yukiko Tanaka describes in "Mothers' Children" (p. 241)?

2. Kenzaburo Oe and John David Morley (p. 230) both describe the Japanese perception of Westerners' perception of the Japanese. In what ways do their descriptions match? In what ways do they differ, and why?

3. Reread Oe's paragraphs 26–28 about his son Hikari. After reading Louise Erdrich's "Foreword" (p. 137) (and other selections in this chapter), what "mass of dark sorrow" do you think it is that Hikari seeks to express in his music?

KAZUO ISHIGURO

A Family Supper

Kazuo Ishiguro was born in Nagasaki, Japan, in 1954, less than a decade after the United States dropped an atomic bomb on the city to end World War II. When he was six years old his family moved to England, where he has lived ever since. Ishiguro studied at the University of Kent in Canterbury and the University of East Anglia. At the age of twenty-five he won recognition for some early writing anthologized in a collection of stories by promising young authors. His first novel, *A Pale View of Hills* (1982), won the Royal Society of Literature's Winifred Holtby Prize; his second novel, *An Artist of the Floating World* (1986), was named Whitbread Book of the Year. His third novel, *The Remains of the Day* (1989), won Britain's highest literary award, the Booker Prize, and was subsequently made into a film starring Anthony Hopkins and Emma Thompson. Ishiguro visited the United States on the publication of *The Unconsoled* (1995); he lives in London. His story "A Family Supper" first appeared in 1990.

Fugu is a fish caught off the Pacific shores of Japan. The fish has held a special significance for me ever since my mother died after eating one. The poison resides in the sex glands of the fish, inside two fragile bags. These bags must be removed with caution when preparing the fish, for any clumsiness will result in the poison leaking into the veins. Regrettably, it is not easy to tell whether or not this operation has been carried out successfully. The proof is, as it were, in the eating.

Fugu poisoning is hideously painful and almost always fatal. If the fish has been eaten during the evening, the victim is usually overtaken by pain during his sleep. He rolls about in agony for a few hours and is dead by morning. The fish became extremely popular in Japan after the war. Until stricter regulations were imposed, it was all the rage to perform the hazardous gutting operation in one's own kitchen, then to invite neighbors and friends round for the feast.

At the time of my mother's death, I was living in California. My relationship with my parents had become somewhat strained around that period and consequently I did not learn of the circumstances of her death until I returned to Tokyo two years later. Apparently, my mother had always refused to eat fugu, but on this particular occasion she had made an exception, having been invited by an old school friend whom she was

260

anxious not to offend. It was my father who supplied me with the details as we drove from the airport to his house in the Kamakura district. When we finally arrived, it was nearing the end of a sunny autumn day.

"Did you eat on the plane?" my father asked. We were sitting on the tatami floor of his tearoom.

"They gave me a light snack."   5

"You must be hungry. We'll eat as soon as Kikuko arrives."

My father was a formidable-looking man with a large stony jaw and furious black eyebrows. I think now, in retrospect, that he much resembled [Chinese Communist leader] Chou En-lai, although he would not have cherished such a comparison, being particularly proud of the pure samurai blood that ran in the family. His general presence was not one that encouraged relaxed conversation; neither were things helped much by his odd way of stating each remark as if it were the concluding one. In fact, as I sat opposite him that afternoon, a boyhood memory came back to me of the time he had struck me several times around the head for "chattering like an old woman." Inevitably, our conversation since my arrival at the airport had been punctuated by long pauses.

"I'm sorry to hear about the firm," I said when neither of us had spoken for some time. He nodded gravely.

"In fact, the story didn't end there," he said. "After the firm's collapse, Watanabe killed himself. He didn't wish to live with the disgrace."

"I see."   10

"We were partners for seventeen years. A man of principle and honor. I respected him very much."

"Will you go into business again?" I asked.

"I am . . . in retirement. I'm too old to involve myself in new ventures now. Business these days has become so different. Dealing with foreigners. Doing things their way. I don't understand how we've come to this. Neither did Watanabe." He sighed. "A fine man. A man of principle."

The tearoom looked out over the garden. From where I sat I could make out the ancient well that as a child I had believed to be haunted It was just visible now through the thick foliage. The sun had sunk low and much of the garden had fallen into shadow.

"I'm glad in any case that you've decided to come back," my father   15
said. "More than a short visit, I hope."

"I'm not sure what my plans will be."

"I, for one, am prepared to forget the past. Your mother, too, was always ready to welcome you back — upset as she was by your behavior."

"I appreciate your sympathy. As I say, I'm not sure what my plans are."

"I've come to believe now that there were no evil intentions in your mind," my father continued. "You were swayed by certain . . . influences. Like so many others."

"Perhaps we should forget it, as you suggest."   20

"As you will. More tea?"

Just then a girl's voice came echoing through the house.

"At last." My father rose to his feet. "Kikuko has arrived."

Despite our difference in years, my sister and I had always been close. Seeing me again seemed to make her excessively excited, and for a while she did nothing but giggle nervously. But she calmed down somewhat when my father started to question her about Osaka and her university. She answered him with short, formal replies. She in turn asked me a few questions, but she seemed inhibited by the fear that her questions might lead to awkward topics. After a while, the conversation had become even sparser than prior to Kikuko's arrival. Then my father stood up, saying: "I must attend to the supper. Please excuse me for being burdened by such matters. Kikuko will look after you."

My sister relaxed quite visibly once he had left the room. Within a   25
few minutes, she was chatting freely about her friends in Osaka and about her classes at university. Then quite suddenly she decided we should walk in the garden and went striding out onto the veranda. We put on some straw sandals that had been left along the veranda rail and stepped out into the garden. The light in the garden had grown very dim.

"I've been dying for a smoke for the last half hour," she said, lighting a cigarette.

"Then why didn't you smoke?"

She made a furtive gesture back toward the house, then grinned mischievously.

"Oh, I see," I said.

"Guess what? I've got a boyfriend now."   30

"Oh, yes?"

"Except I'm wondering what to do. I haven't made up my mind yet."

"Quite understandable."

"You see, he's making plans to go to America. He wants me to go with him as soon as I finish studying."

"I see. And you want to go to America?"   35

"If we go, we're going to hitchhike." Kikuko waved a thumb in front of my face. "People say it's dangerous, but I've done it in Osaka and it's fine."

"I see. So what is it you're unsure about?"

We were following a narrow path that wound through the shrubs and finished by the old well. As we walked, Kikuko persisted in taking unnecessarily theatrical puffs on her cigarette.

"Well, I've got lots of friends now in Osaka. I like it there. I'm not sure I want to leave them all behind just yet. And Suichi . . . I like him, but I'm not sure I want to spend so much time with him. Do you understand?"

"Oh, perfectly." 40

She grinned again, then skipped on ahead of me until she had reached the well. "Do you remember," she said as I came walking up to her, "how you used to say this well was haunted?"

"Yes, I remember."

We both peered over the side.

"Mother always told me it was the old woman from the vegetable store you'd seen that night," she said. "But I never believed her and never came out here alone."

"Mother used to tell me that too. She even told me once the old 45 woman had confessed to being the ghost. Apparently, she'd been taking a shortcut through our garden. I imagine she had some trouble clambering over these walls."

Kikuko gave a giggle. She then turned her back to the well, casting her gaze about the garden.

"Mother never really blamed you, you know," she said, in a new voice. I remained silent. "She always used to say to me how it was their fault, hers and Father's, for not bringing you up correctly. She used to tell me how much more careful they'd been with me, and that's why I was so good." She looked up and the mischievous grin had returned to her face. "Poor Mother," she said.

"Yes. Poor Mother."

"Are you going back to California?"

"I don't know. I'll have to see." 50

"What happened to . . . to her? To Vicki?"

"That's all finished with," I said. "There's nothing much left for me now in California."

"Do you think I ought to go there?"

"Why not? I don't know. You'll probably like it." I glanced toward the house. "Perhaps we'd better go in soon. Father might need a hand with the supper."

But my sister was once more peering down into the well. "I can't see 55 any ghosts," she said. Her voice echoed a little.

"Is Father very upset about his firm collapsing?"

"Don't know. You never can tell with Father." Then suddenly she straightened up and turned to me. "Did he tell you about old Watanabe? What he did?"

"I heard he committed suicide."

"Well, that wasn't all. He took his whole family with him. His wife and his two little girls."

"Oh, yes?"   60

"Those two beautiful little girls. He turned on the gas while they were all asleep. Then he cut his stomach with a meat knife."

"Yes, Father was just telling me how Watanabe was a man of principle."

"Sick." My sister turned back to the well.

"Careful. You'll fall right in."

"I can't see any ghost," she said. "You were lying to me all that time."   65

"But I never said it lived down the well."

"Where is it then?"

We both looked around at the trees and shrubs. The daylight had almost gone. Eventually I pointed to a small clearing some ten yards away.

"Just there I saw it. Just there."

We stared at the spot.   70

"What did it look like?"

"I couldn't see very well. It was dark."

"But you must have seen something."

"It was an old woman. She was just standing there, watching me."

We kept staring at the spot as if mesmerized.   75

"She was wearing a white kimono," I said. "Some of her hair came undone. It was blowing around a little."

Kikuko pushed her elbow against my arm. "Oh, be quiet. You're trying to frighten me all over again." She trod on the remains of her cigarette, then for a brief moment stood regarding it with a perplexed expression. She kicked some pine needles over it, then once more displayed her grin. "Let's see if supper's ready," she said.

We found my father in the kitchen. He gave us a quick glance, then carried on with what he was doing.

"Father's become quite a chef since he's had to manage on his own," Kikuko said with a laugh.

He turned and looked at my sister coldly. "Hardly a skill I'm proud 80
of," he said. "Kikuko, come here and help."

For some moments my sister did not move. Then she stepped forward and took an apron hanging from a drawer.

"Just these vegetables need cooking now," he said to her. "The rest just needs watching." Then he looked up and regarded me strangely for some seconds. "I expect you want to look around the house," he said eventually. He put down the chopsticks he had been holding. "It's a long time since you've seen it."

As we left the kitchen I glanced toward Kikuko, but her back was turned.

"She's a good girl," my father said.

I followed my father from room to room. I had forgotten how large the house was. A panel would slide open and another room would appear. But the rooms were all startlingly empty. In one of the rooms the lights did not come on, and we stared at the stark walls and tatami in the pale light that came from the windows.

"This house it too large for a man to live in alone," my father said. "I don't have much use for most of these rooms now."

But eventually my father opened the door to a room packed full of books and papers. There were flowers in vases and pictures on the walls. Then I noticed something on a low table in the corner of the room. I came nearer and saw it was a plastic model of a battleship, the kind constructed by children. It had been placed on some newspaper; scattered around it were assorted pieces of gray plastic.

My father gave a laugh. He came up to the table and picked up the model.

"Since the firm folded," he said, "I have a little more time on my hands." He laughed again, rather strangely. For a moment his face looked almost gentle. "A little more time."

"That seems odd," I said. "You were always so busy."

"Too busy, perhaps." He looked at me with a small smile. "Perhaps I should have been a more attentive father."

I laughed. He went on contemplating his battleship. Then he looked up. "I hadn't meant to tell you this, but perhaps it's best that I do. It's my belief that your mother's death was no accident. She had many worries. And some disappointments."

We both gazed at the plastic battleship.

"Surely," I said eventually, "my mother didn't expect me to live here forever."

"Obviously you don't see. You don't see how it is for some parents. Not only must they lose their children, they must lose them to things they don't understand." He spun the battleship in his fingers. "These little gunboats here could have been better glued, don't you think?"

"Perhaps. I think it looks fine."

"During the war I spent some time on a ship rather like this. But my ambition was always the air force. I figured it like this: If your ship was struck by the enemy, all you could do was struggle in the water hoping for a lifeline. But in an airplane — well, there was always the final weapon." He put the model back onto the table. "I don't suppose you believe in war."

"Not particularly."

He cast an eye around the room. "Supper should be ready by now," he said. "You must be hungry."

Supper was waiting in a dimly lit room next to the kitchen. The only   100
source of light was a big lantern that hung over the table, casting the rest of the room in shadow. We bowed to each other before starting the meal.

There was little conversation. When I made some polite comment about the food, Kikuko giggled a little. Her earlier nervousness seemed to have returned to her. My father did not speak for several minutes. Finally he said:

"It must feel strange for you, being back in Japan."

"Yes, it is a little strange."

"Already, perhaps, you regret leaving America."

"A little. Not so much. I didn't leave behind much. Just some empty   105
rooms."

"I see."

I glanced across the table. My father's face looked stony and forbidding in the half-light. We ate on in silence.

Then my eye caught something at the back of the room. At first I continued eating, then my hands became still. The others noticed and looked at me. I went on gazing into the darkness past my father's shoulder.

"Who is that? In that photograph there?"

"Which photograph?" My father turned slightly, trying to follow   110
my gaze.

"The lowest one. The old woman in the white kimono."

My father put down his chopsticks. He looked first at the photograph, then at me.

"Your mother." His voice had become very hard. "Can't you recognize your own mother?"

"My mother. You see, it's dark. I can't see it very well."

No one spoke for a few seconds, then Kikuko rose to her feet. She   115
took the photograph down from the wall, came back to the table, and gave it to me.

"She looks a lot older," I said.

"It was taken shortly before her death," said my father.

"It was dark. I couldn't see very well."

I looked up and noticed my father holding out a hand. I gave him the photograph. He looked at it intently, then held it toward Kikuko. Obediently, my sister rose to her feet once more and returned the picture to the wall.

There was a large pot left unopened at the center of the table. When Kikuko had seated herself again, my father reached forward and lifted the lid. A cloud of steam rose up and curled toward the lantern. He pushed the pot a little toward me.

"You must be hungry," he said. One side of his face had fallen into shadow.

"Thank you." I reached forward with my chopsticks. The steam was almost scalding. "What is it?"

"Fish."

"It smells very good."

In the soup were strips of fish that had curled almost into balls. I picked one out and brought it to my bowl.

"Help yourself. There's plenty."

"Thank you." I took a little more, then pushed the pot toward my father. I watched him take several pieces to his bowl. Then we both watched as Kikuko served herself.

My father bowed slightly. "You must be hungry," he said again. He took some fish to his mouth and started to eat. Then I, too, chose a piece and put it in my mouth. It felt soft, quite fleshy against my tongue.

The three of us ate in silence. Several minutes went by. My father lifted the lid and once more steam rose up. We all reached forward and helped ourselves.

"Here," I said to my father, "you have this last piece."

"Thank you."

When we had finished the meal, my father stretched out his arms and yawned with an air of satisfaction. "Kikuko," he said, "prepare a pot of tea, please."

My sister looked at him, then left the room without comment. My father stood up.

"Let's retire to the other room. It's rather warm in here."

I got to my feet and followed him into the tearoom. The large sliding windows had been left open, bringing in a breeze from the garden. For a while we sat in silence.

"Father," I said, finally.

"Yes?"

"Kikuko tells me Watanabe-san took his whole family with him."

My father lowered his eyes and nodded. For some moments he seemed deep in thought. "Watanabe was very devoted to his work," he said at last. "The collapse of the firm was a great blow to him. I fear it must have weakened his judgment."

"You think what he did . . . it was a mistake?"   140

"Why, of course. Do you see it otherwise?"

"No, no. Of course not."

"There are other things besides work," my father said.

"Yes."

We fell silent again. The sound of locusts came in from the garden. I   145
looked out into the darkness. The well was no longer visible.

"What do you think you will do now?" my father asked. "Will you stay in Japan for a while?"

"To be honest, I hadn't thought that far ahead."

"If you wish to stay here, I mean here in this house, you would be very welcome. That is, if you don't mind living with an old man."

"Thank you. I'll have to think about it."

I gazed out once more into the darkness.   150

"But of course," said my father, "this house is so dreary now. You'll no doubt return to America before long."

"Perhaps. I don't know yet."

"No doubt you will."

For some time my father seemed to be studying the back of his hands. Then he looked up and sighed.

"Kikuko is due to complete her studies next spring," he said. "Per-   155
haps she will want to come home then. She's a good girl."

"Perhaps she will."

"Things will improve then."

"Yes, I'm sure they will."

We fell silent once more, waiting for Kikuko to bring the tea.

EXPLORATIONS

1. How would the impact of "A Family Supper" change without the opening section (paras. 1–3) on fugu? How would it change without the father's comments about his business partner (paras. 9–13 and 139–142)?

2. In what ways does Kazuo Ishiguro supply information about the relationships between the various members of the narrator's family in "A Family Supper"? Which sources of this information do you find most believable?

3. What are the effects of Ishiguro's telling this story from the first-person viewpoint of a participant instead of the third-person viewpoint of an outside observer?

CONNECTIONS

1. In what ways does "A Family Supper" exemplify the ambiguity described by Kenzaburo Oe in his Nobel Prize lecture (p. 251)?

2. What descriptions does Ishiguro supply of the house in which the story takes place? Having read John David Morley's "Acquiring a Japanese Family" (p. 230), what more do you know about the house than Ishiguro tells us?

3. Recall the information given by Morley and by Yukiko Tanaka in "Mothers' Children" (p. 241) about Japanese parents' expectations of their children. What hopes do you think the narrator's parents in "A Family Supper" had for him as their oldest son that he has failed to meet? What hopes did Oe and his wife probably have that their son Hikari has failed to meet? How have these two families dealt differently with their thwarted hopes?

INVESTIGATIONS

1. In "Mothers' Children," Yukiko Tanaka traces some of the difficulties of contemporary Japanese mothers to their having children sooner and closer together than their mothers did (para. 8). Have mothers in the United States followed this pattern? Do women in all or most U.S. subcultures start bearing children at about the same age, and do they have approximately the same number of children the same distance apart? Investigate these trends and statistics and write a research paper comparing U.S. childbearing patterns with the Japanese patterns Tanaka describes.

2. "To understand or respond to Zen poems one must abandon oneself and willingly enter into the closed shells of those words." Reread Kenzaburo Oe's comments on Zen poems in paragraph 8 of "Japan, the Ambiguous, and Myself." In what ways must a listener (or reader) approach Oe's lecture in the same way as a Zen poem? How is his lecture, like those poems, "concerned with the linguistic impossibility of telling the truth"? Write an essay exploring the link between the literary traditions Oe cites and the theme of ambiguity as expressed in both the form and the substance of his lecture.

3. In what ways does Kazuo Ishiguro's "A Family Supper" exemplify the Japanese literary and social concepts described by Kenzaburo Oe in "Japan, the Ambiguous, and Myself"? In what ways does Ishiguro's story reflect the Western consciousness of a writer who moved from Japan to England at age six? Write an essay analyzing the mixture of traditions in "A Family Supper."

PART THREE

TURNING POINTS

Clive Barker • Bob Seger • Gail Sheehy • Michael Dorris
Gloria Anzaldúa • Günter Grass • Aleksandr Solzhenitsyn
Malcolm X with Alex Haley • Sven Birkerts • Alexander Theroux
Kit R. Roane • Anonymous

MIRRORS: The United States

Maya Angelou: *Mary*
Annie Dillard: *Flying*
Andre Dubus: *Imperiled Men*
Richard Ford: *Optimists*

WINDOWS: The World

Sophronia Liu: *So Tsi-fai* (TAIWAN)
Liliana Heker: *The Stolen Party*
(ARGENTINA)
Amitav Ghosh: *The Ghosts of Mrs. Gandhi*
(INDIA)
Nadine Gordimer: *Where Do Whites Fit In?*
(SOUTH AFRICA)

SPOTLIGHT: Russia

Vladimir Nabokov: *From* Speak, Memory
Joseph Brodsky: *Less than One*
Galina Dutkina: *Sovs, Hacks, and
Freeloaders*
Natasha Singer: *The New Russian Dressing*

As a child you are given dream time as part of your fictional life. Into your hands go the books of dream travel, Dorothy's dream travel, the Darling family's dream travel in *Peter Pan*, the children of Narnia. You're given books in which children with whom you identify take journeys which are essentially dream journeys. They are to places in which the fantastical not only happens, but is commonplace. Alice falls down a hole, the Darling children take flight, the tornado picks up Dorothy's house. These children are removed and taken to a place which is essentially a place of dreams.

And then, at the age of five or something like that, they start to teach you the gross national product of Chile. And you're left thinking, Wait! What happened to Oz and Never-Never Land and Narnia? Are they no longer relevant? One of the things you're taught is No! they are no longer relevant. They are, as it were, a sweet introduction to the business of living. And now comes the real stuff — so get on with it.

> – CLIVE BARKER
> *Writers Dreaming*
> (Naomi Epel, ed.), 1993

▼ ▼ ▼

I wish I didn't know now what I didn't know then.

> – BOB SEGER
> "Against the Wind"
> *Against the Wind*, 1980

▼ ▼ ▼

After eighteen, we begin Pulling Up Roots in earnest. College, military service, and short-term travels are all customary vehicles our society provides for the first round trips between family and a base of one's own. In the attempt to separate our view of the world from our family's view, despite vigorous protestations to the contrary — "I know exactly what I want!" — we cast about for any beliefs we can call our own. And in the process of testing those beliefs we are often drawn to fads, preferably those most mysterious and inaccessible to our parents. . . .

A stormy passage through the Pulling Up Roots years will probably facilitate the normal progression of the adult life cycle. If one doesn't have an identity crisis at this point, it will erupt during a later transition, when the penalties may be harder to bear.

> – GAIL SHEEHY
> *Passages*, 1974

▼ ▼ ▼

In most cultures, adulthood is equated with self-reliance and responsibility, yet often Americans do not achieve this status until we are in our late twenties or early thirties — virtually the entire average lifespan of a person in a traditional non-Western society. We tend to treat prolonged adolescence as a warm-up for real life, as a wobbly suspension bridge between childhood and legal maturity. Whereas a nineteenth-century Cheyenne or Lakota teenager was expected to alter self-conception in a split-second vision, we often meander through an analogous rite of passage for more than a decade — through high school, college, graduate school.

Though he had never before traveled alone outside his village, the Plains Indian male was expected at puberty to venture solo into the wilderness. There he had to fend for and sustain himself while avoiding the menace of unknown dangers, and there he had absolutely to remain until something happened that would transform him. Every human being, these tribes believed, was entitled to at least one moment of personal, enabling insight.

Anthropology proposes feasible psychological explanations for why this flash was eventually triggered: Fear, fatigue, reliance on strange foods, the anguish of loneliness, stress, and the expectation of ultimate success all contributed to a state of receptivity. Every sense was quickened, altered to perceive deep meaning, until at last the interpretation of an unusual event — a dream, a chance encounter, or an unexpected vista — reverberated with metaphor. Through this unique prism, abstractly preserved in a vivid memory or song, a boy caught foresight of both his adult persona and of his vocation, the two inextricably entwined.

– MICHAEL DORRIS
"Life Stories"
Antaeus, 1989

▼ ▼ ▼

Coyolxhauqui was the Aztec moon goddess; her brother Huitzilopochtli dismembered her. He started human sacrifice and she was the first. In taking the risk to make a work, to write that poem or story or theoretical piece, you may feel like the moon goddess — like you are jumping off the temple steps or off a cliff. You land at the bottom and you're broken in pieces. At this stage your work is shit, it doesn't say anything. But the next step in the creative process is picking up the pieces and moving them around — restructuring that broken body of Coyolxhauqui. You don't put her together in the same way; you end up with something new, and something has changed in you because of going through this struggle. You end up not quite the same person that you were. And the viewer or reader of your piece also undergoes a change of consciousness, moving from a before to an after. That traversal I call the *nepantla* stage — between the worlds.

I see what's happening to our country in the same way; we're going through a stage of being pulled apart. We're trying to recompose the nation — recreate it. A person who is undergoing therapy for a trauma like incest or assault is doing the same thing, and so is a mathematician or a scientist trying to figure out new theories.

– GLORIA ANZALDÚA
"Afterthoughts"
Utne Reader, 1996

▼ ▼ ▼

In May 1945[, w]hen I was seventeen years of age, living with a hundred thousand others in an American prison camp out under the open sky, in a foxhole, I was famished, and because of this I focused, with a cunning born of hunger, exclusively on survival — otherwise I had not a clear notion in my head. Rendered stupid by dogma and accordingly fixated on lofty goals: This was the state in which the Third Reich released me and many of my generation from our oaths of loyalty. "The flag is superior to death" was one of its life-denying certainties.

All this stupidity resulted not only from a schooling knocked full of holes by the war — when I reached fifteen, my time as Luftwaffe helper began, which I mistakenly welcomed as liberation from school — it was, rather, an overarching stupidity, one that transcended difference of class and religion, one that was nourished by German complacency. Its ideological slogans usually began with "We Germans are . . . ," "To be German means . . . ," and, finally, "A German would never . . ."

This last-quoted rule lasted even beyond the capitulation of the Greater German Reich and took on the stubborn force of incorrigibility. For when I, with many of my generation — leaving aside our fathers and mothers for now — was confronted with the results of the crimes for which Germans were responsible, crimes that would be summed up in the image of *Auschwitz*, I said: Impossible. I said to myself and to others, and others said to themselves and to me: "Germans would never do a thing like that."

– GÜNTER GRASS
"Writing After Auschwitz"
Two States — One Nation?, 1990

▼ ▼ ▼

. . . Woe to that nationality whose literature is cut short by forcible interference. This is no mere simple violation of "freedom of the press." This is a closing up, a locking up, of the national heart, amputation of the national memory. That nationality has no memory of its own self. It is deprived of its spiritual unity. And even though compatriots apparently speak the same language, they suddenly cease to understand one another. Whole speechless generations are born and die off who do not tell each other about themselves, nor speak about themselves to their descendants. If such literary geniuses as Akhmatova and Zamyatin are immured alive throughout their lifetimes, condemned right up to the grave to create in silence, without hearing a reverberation from what they have written, this is not only their own personal misfortune but a sorrow for all nationalities, and a danger for all nations.

And, in certain cases, for all humanity as well: that is, when, as a result of such silence, the whole of HISTORY ceases to be understood.

— ALEKSANDR SOLZHENITSYN
"The Nobel Lecture in Literature," 1972

▼ ▼ ▼

I had come to the Norfolk Prison Colony still going through only book-reading motions. Pretty soon, I would have quit even these motions, unless I had received the motivation that I did.

I saw that the best thing I could do was get hold of a dictionary — to study, to learn some words. I was lucky enough to reason also that I should try to improve my penmanship. It was sad. I couldn't even write in a straight line. It was both ideas together that moved me to request a dictionary along with some tablets and pencils from the Norfolk Prison Colony school.

. . . I started copying what eventually became the entire dictionary. It went a lot faster after so much practice helped me to pick up handwriting speed. Between what I wrote in my tablet, and writing letters, during the rest of my time in prison I would guess I wrote a million words.

I suppose it was inevitable that as my word-base broadened, I could for the first time pick up a book and read and now begin to understand what the book was saying. Anyone who has read a great deal can imagine the new world that opened. Let me tell you something: From then until I left that prison, in every free moment I had, if I was not reading in the library, I was reading on my bunk. You couldn't have gotten me out of books with a wedge. . . . Months passed without my even thinking about being imprisoned. In fact, up to then, I never had been so truly free in my life. . . .

I have often reflected upon the new vistas that reading opened to me. I knew right there in prison that reading had changed forever the course of my life. As I see it today, the ability to read awoke inside me some long dormant craving to be mentally alive. I certainly wasn't seeking any degree, the way a college confers a status symbol upon its students. My homemade education gave me, with every additional book that I read, a little bit more sensitivity to the deafness, dumbness, and blindness that was afflicting the black race in America. Not long ago, an English writer telephoned me from London, asking questions. One was, "What's your alma mater?" I told him, "Books." You will never catch me with a free fifteen minutes in which I'm not studying something I feel might be able to help the black man.

– MALCOLM X with ALEX HALEY
"Learning to Read"
The Autobiography of Malcolm X, 1964

▼ ▼ ▼

When we look at the large-scale shift to an electronic culture, looking as if at a time-lapse motion study, we can see not only how our situation has come about but also how it is in our nature that it should have. At every step — this is clear — we trade for ease. And ease is what quickly swallows up the initial strangeness of a new medium or tool. Moreover, each accommodation paves the way for the next. The telegraph must have seemed to its first users a surpassingly strange device, but its new-fangledness was overridden by its usefulness. Once we had accepted the idea of mechanical transmission over distances, the path was clear for the telephone. Again, a monumental transformation: turn select digits on a dial and hear the voice of another human being. And on it goes, the inventions coming gradually, one by one, allowing society to adapt. We mastered the telephone, the television with its few networks running black-and-white programs. And although no law required citizens to own or use either, these technologies did in a remarkably short time achieve near total saturation.

We are, then, accustomed to the process; we take the step that will enlarge our reach, simplify our communication, and abbreviate our physical involvement in some task or chore. The difference between the epoch of early modernity and the present is — to simplify drastically — that formerly the body had time to accept the graft, the new organ, whereas now we are hurtling forward willy-nilly, assuming that if a technology is connected with communications or information processing it must be good, we must need it. I never cease to be astonished at what a mere two decades have brought us. Consider the evidence. Since the early 1970s we have seen the arrival of — we have accepted, deemed all but indispensable — personal computers, laptops, telephone-answering machines, calling cards, fax machines, cellular phones, VCRs, modems, Nintendo games, E-mail, voice mail, camcorders, and CD players. Very quickly, with almost no pause between increments, these circuit-driven tools and entertainments have moved into our lives, and with a minimum rippling of the waters, really — which, of course, makes them seem natural, even inevitable. Which perhaps they are. Marshall McLuhan called improvements of this sort "extensions of man," and this is their secret. We embrace them because they seem a part of us, an enhancement. They don't seem to challenge our power so much as add to it.

I am startled, though, by how little we are debating the deeper philosophical ramifications. We talk up a storm when it comes to policy issues — who should have jurisdiction, what rates may be charged — and there is great fascination in some quarters with the practical minutiae of functioning, compatibility, and so on. But why do we hear so few people asking whether we might not *ourselves* be changing, and whether the changes are necessarily for the good?

> — SVEN BIRKERTS
> "The Electronic Hive"
> *Harper's*, May 1994

▼ ▼ ▼

"I want to be what I was when I wanted to be what I am now."
> — ALEXANDER THEROUX
> *Darconville's Cat*, 1981

▼ ▼ ▼

Amina Brka, fourteen, returned this week to a world she had only seen on television and read about in letters from home. This was her country, but it bore little resemblance to the one she had left nearly four years ago. Much of its beauty had been burned or mangled under the barrage of war, and when she rode into Sarajevo, she was surprised that anything was left at all.

"It's not as bad as I had pictured it," Amina said as she tussled with new school books on her first day of class here. "My visions were much worse. And from the pictures I saw on television, with all the grenades thrown from the mountains, I thought Sarajevo had been flattened."

Amina, who is Muslim, is one of more than 300 pupils returning after a long hiatus; peace is expected to bring many more. They enter a situation both familiar and strange to them. They are forced to pick up survival skills from others and cull the reality from the stories they hear on the streets. . . .

There is much to cull from the ruins. In her class, children described famine. Their teachers recalled months when shelling was so heavy that children never left their basements, and the false moments of calm that always ended in massacre. On some of these days, teachers said, children watched their parents blown apart, then went out to play without shedding a tear in public.

"The shocking thing is their understanding of death," said Casar Jadranka, a general studies teacher. "Normal people are shocked by death. These kids take it lightly."

"It's just no big deal anymore," said Spaho Sanin, fourteen, as he lounged in the back of a chilly chemistry class. "A girl in our class found a gun and blew her head off last week and an old woman hanged herself in her closet just a while ago.

"There have been a lot of people killed during the war and I believe there has been a suicide in every building in the city," he added. "People are just not normal anymore."

– KIT R. ROANE
"For Bosnian Schoolgirl
an Uneasy Homecoming"
New York Times, 1995

▼ ▼ ▼

A gigantic queue in front of the American Embassy. Today, the 36,124th person has been placed on the waiting list. The majority are Muscovites, but many have come from other cities — Tashkent, Kiev, Zhitomir, Vilnius, Novosibirsk, Kishinev. I, too, am standing here waiting for what everyone else is waiting for: an application to leave permanently for the United States. . . .

The reason I am leaving is not because there is no meat, sugar, boots, soap, cigarettes, almost nothing in the country. And not even because the reward for any work is unimaginably small. Of course, all of that is terribly humiliating, creates bad blood, and probably even shortens our life spans. But no, that's not why I'm leaving.

I'm not fleeing; I'm being evicted. For me it's not emigration but rather evacuation. I don't feel like a rat abandoning a sinking ship so much as a dog driven away by its evil master. And all those silent people in front of the American Embassy? Somehow one doesn't see in their faces even the slightest anticipation of joy at the prospect of a heavenly life in a utopia where there are no problems with meat and soap, where the feet of each inhabitant are shod, I imagine, in no fewer than ten pairs of boots. These emigrants are anything but the dregs of society. For the most part, they are quite cultured people, and well dressed — some even have cars. What's driving them into exile? What can they be looking for there?

That's easily explained. They share one disadvantage that makes them unfit to live in the country in which they were born. They are Jews. I, too, am Jewish. My passport says so. Though, in all honesty, I have always felt I was as much Russian as Jewish. Not anymore, because now I live in a country where the "Jewish Question" exists. Now I know I am a Jew, since those splendid lads of Pamyat [the right-wing, nationalist movement] have promised to squash my kind like bedbugs; because the pensioner in the adjacent house regularly recommends we scram to Israel; because when I drag a drunken women from the street, passersby make it immediately clear to me that we alone have led the Russian people to drink. Suddenly, there is a certain "we" of which I am a part.

> — ANONYMOUS
> "Evicted: A Russian Jew's Story (Again)"
> *Harper's*, 1991

EXPLORATIONS

1. How are the lines from Bob Seger's song "Against the Wind" (p. 272) and Alexander Theroux's novel *Darconville's Cat* (p. 277) similar and different in meaning? What other epigraphs for this chapter contain either or both of these ideas, and how do Seger's and Theroux's ideas apply to each writer's circumstances?

2. Which of the preceding epigraphs show individuals dramatically changed by political changes, and in what ways? Which epigraphs suggest that individuals can make political changes, and in what ways? Which epigraphs show individuals acting to change themselves, and in what ways?

3. Compare Kit R. Roane's description of postwar Sarajevo with the wartime description in Zlata Filipović's "Sarajevo Diary" (p. 210). Judging from these two accounts, and also the epigraphs by Günter Grass (p. 274) and Aleksandr Solzhenitsyn (p. 275), what do you think are the reasons why "these kids take[death] lightly" and "there has been a suicide in every building in the city" (Roane, p. 278)?

MIRRORS:
THE UNITED STATES

Turning Points: *A stunt flyer arcs over Seattle's Seafair Festival.*

MAYA ANGELOU

Mary

Maya Angelou came to nationwide attention in 1993 when President Clinton asked her to compose an original poem ("On the Pulse of Morning"), which she delivered at his inauguration. In 1995 Angelou starred in the film *How to Make an American Quilt*. She was already known to television audiences for her performance in Alex Haley's serial "Roots," for which she received an Emmy Award nomination.

At the time "Mary" took place, Angelou was still going by her birth name, Marguerite Johnson. Born in St. Louis, Missouri, in 1928, by the age of sixteen she had survived rape, the breakup of her family, and unwed motherhood. (The rapist was her mother's friend Mr. Freeman, who was tried, convicted, and later found beaten to death — the sequence of events Angelou refers to in paragraph 21.) Support from her mother and her brother, Bailey, helped to keep her going through five years in which she never spoke. She later became a dancer, appeared in several plays (including a twenty-two-nation tour of *Porgy and Bess*), worked with the Harlem Writers' Guild, lived in Ghana, and produced a series on Africa for the Public Broadcasting System. Angelou has been awarded numerous honorary doctorates and, at the request of Martin Luther King Jr., served as a coordinator for the Southern Christian Leadership Conference. President Ford appointed her to the Bicentennial Commission and President Carter to the Commission of International Woman's Year. The author of six books of poetry, various songs and musical scores, and several plays and screenplays, Angelou is best known for her five-volume autobiography. "Mary" comes from the first volume, *I Know Why the Caged Bird Sings* (1970), which recounts her childhood in Stamps, Arkansas. She currently lives in North Carolina, where she holds a lifetime chair in American Studies at Wake Forest University.

Recently a white woman from Texas, who would quickly describe herself as a liberal, asked me about my hometown. When I told her that in Stamps my grandmother had owned the only Negro general merchandise store since the turn of the century, she exclaimed, "Why, you were a debutante." Ridiculous and even ludicrous. But Negro girls in small Southern towns, whether poverty-stricken or just munching along on a few of life's necessities, were given as extensive and irrelevant preparations for adulthood as rich white girls shown in magazines. Admittedly the training was not the same. While white girls learned to waltz and sit gracefully with a tea cup balanced on their knees, we were lagging behind, learning the mid-Victorian values with very little money to indulge them. (Come and see Edna Lomax spending the money she made picking cotton on five balls of ecru tatting thread. Her fingers are bound to snag the work and she'll have to repeat the stitches time and time again. But she knows that when she buys the thread.)

We were required to embroider and I had trunkfuls of colorful dish-towels, pillowcases, runners, and handkerchiefs to my credit. I mastered the art of crocheting and tatting, and there was a lifetime's supply of dainty doilies that would never be used in sacheted dresser drawers. It went without saying that all girls could iron and wash, but the finer touches around the home, like setting a table with real silver, baking roasts, and cooking vegetables without meat, had to be learned else-where. Usually at the source of those habits. During my tenth year, a white woman's kitchen became my finishing school.

Mrs. Viola Cullinan was a plump woman who lived in a three-bedroom house somewhere behind the post office. She was singularly unattractive until she smiled, and then the lines around her eyes and mouth which made her look perpetually dirty disappeared, and her face looked like the mask of an impish elf. She usually rested her smile until late afternoon when her women friends dropped in and Miss Glory, the cook, served them cold drinks on the closed-in porch.

The exactness of her house was inhuman. This glass went here and only here. That cup had its place and it was an act of impudent rebel-lion to place it anywhere else. At twelve o'clock the table was set. At 12:15 Mrs. Cullinan sat down to dinner (whether her husband had ar-rived or not). At 12:16 Miss Glory brought out the food.

It took me a week to learn the difference between a salad plate, a   5
bread plate, and a dessert plate.

Mrs. Cullinan kept up the tradition of her wealthy parents. She was from Virginia. Miss Glory, who was a descendant of slaves that had worked for the Cullinans, told me her history. She had married beneath her (according to Miss Glory). Her husband's family hadn't had their money very long and what they had "didn't 'mount to much."

As ugly as she was, I thought privately, she was lucky to get a hus-band above or beneath her station. But Miss Glory wouldn't let me say a thing against her mistress. She was very patient with me, however, over the housework. She explained the dishware, silverware, and ser-vants' bells.

The large round bowl in which soup was served wasn't a soup bowl, it was a tureen. There were goblets, sherbet glasses, ice-cream glasses, wine glasses, green glass coffee cups with matching saucers, and water glasses. I had a glass to drink from, and it sat with Miss Glory's on a separate shelf from the others. Soup spoons, gravy boat, butter knives, salad forks, and carving platter were additions to my vocabulary and in fact almost represented a new language. I was fascinated with the novelty, with the fluttering Mrs. Cullinan and her Alice-in-Wonderland house.

Her husband remains, in my memory, undefined. I lumped him with all the other white men that I had ever seen and tried not to see.

On our way home one evening, Miss Glory told me that Mrs. Culli-   10
nan couldn't have children. She said that she was too delicate-boned. It was hard to imagine bones at all under those layers of fat. Miss Glory went on to say that the doctor had taken out all her lady organs. I reasoned that a pig's organs included the lungs, heart, and liver, so if Mrs. Cullinan was walking around without those essentials, it explained why she drank alcohol out of unmarked bottles. She was keeping herself embalmed.

When I spoke to Bailey about it, he agreed that I was right, but he also informed me that Mr. Cullinan had two daughters by a colored lady and that I knew them very well. He added that the girls were the spitting image of their father. I was unable to remember what he looked like, although I had just left him a few hours before, but I thought of the Coleman girls. They were very light-skinned and certainly didn't look very much like their mother (no one ever mentioned Mr. Coleman).

My pity for Mrs. Cullinan preceded me the next morning like the Cheshire cat's smile. Those girls, who could have been her daughters, were beautiful. They didn't have to straighten their hair. Even when they were caught in the rain, their braids still hung down straight like tamed snakes. Their mouths were pouty little cupid's bows. Mrs. Cullinan didn't know what she missed. Or maybe she did. Poor Mrs. Cullinan.

For weeks after, I arrived early, left late, and tried very hard to make up for her barrenness. If she had had her own children, she wouldn't have had to ask me to run a thousand errands from her back door to the back door of her friends. Poor old Mrs. Cullinan.

Then one evening Miss Glory told me to serve the ladies on the porch. After I set the tray down and turned toward the kitchen, one of the women asked, "What's your name, girl?" It was the speckled-faced one. Mrs. Cullinan said, "She doesn't talk much. Her name's Margaret."

"Is she dumb?"   15

"No. As I understand it, she can talk when she wants to but she's usually quiet as a little mouse. Aren't you, Margaret?"

I smiled at her. Poor thing. No organs and couldn't even pronounce my name correctly.

"She's a sweet little thing, though."

"Well, that may be, but the name's too long. I'd never bother myself. I'd call her Mary if I was you."

I fumed into the kitchen. That horrible woman would never have   20
the chance to call me Mary because if I was starving I'd never work for her. I decided I wouldn't pee on her if her heart was on fire. Giggles drifted in off the porch and into Miss Glory's pots. I wondered what they could be laughing about.

Whitefolks were so strange. Could they be talking about me? Everybody knew that they stuck together better than the Negroes did. It was possible that Mrs. Cullinan had friends in St. Louis who heard about a girl from Stamps being in court and wrote to tell her. Maybe she knew about Mr. Freeman.

My lunch was in my mouth a second time and I went outside and relieved myself on the bed of four-o'clocks. Miss Glory thought I might be coming down with something and told me to go on home, that Momma would give me some herb tea, and she'd explain to her mistress.

I realized how foolish I was being before I reached the pond. Of course Mrs. Cullinan didn't know. Otherwise she wouldn't have given me the two nice dresses that Momma cut down, and she certainly wouldn't have called me a "sweet little thing." My stomach felt fine, and I didn't mention anything to Momma.

That evening I decided to write a poem on being white, fat, old, and without children. It was going to be a tragic ballad. I would have to watch her carefully to capture the essence of her loneliness and pain.

The very next day, she called me by the wrong name. Miss Glory   25
and I were washing up the lunch dishes when Mrs. Cullinan came to the doorway. "Mary?"

Miss Glory asked, "Who?"

Mrs. Cullinan, sagging a little, knew and I knew. "I want Mary to go down to Mrs. Randall's and take her some soup. She's not been feeling well for a few days."

Miss Glory's face was a wonder to see. "You mean Margaret, ma'am. Her name's Margaret."

"That's too long. She's Mary from now on. Heat that soup from last night and put it in the china tureen and, Mary, I want you to carry it carefully."

Every person I knew had a hellish horror of being "called out of his   30
name." It was a dangerous practice to call a Negro anything that could

be loosely construed as insulting because of the centuries of their having been called niggers, jigs, dinges, blackbirds, crows, boots, and spooks.

Miss Glory had a fleeting second of feeling sorry for me. Then as she handed me the hot tureen she said, "Don't mind, don't pay that no mind. Sticks and stones may break your bones, but words . . . You know, I been working for her for twenty years."

She held the back door open for me. "Twenty years. I wasn't much older than you. My name used to be Hallelujah. That's what Ma named me, but my mistress give me 'Glory,' and it stuck. I likes it better too."

I was in the little path that ran behind the houses when Miss Glory shouted, "It's shorter too."

For a few seconds it was a tossup over whether I would laugh (imagine being named Hallelujah) or cry (imagine letting some white woman rename you for her convenience). My anger saved me from either outburst. I had to quit the job, but the problem was going to be how to do it. Momma wouldn't allow me to quit for just any reason.

"She's a peach. That woman is a real peach." Mrs. Randall's maid 35 was talking as she took the soup from me, and I wondered what her name used to be and what she answered to now.

For a week I looked into Mrs. Cullinan's face as she called me Mary. She ignored my coming late and leaving early. Miss Glory was a little annoyed because I had begun to leave egg yolk on the dishes and wasn't putting much heart in polishing the silver. I hoped that she would complain to our boss, but she didn't.

Then Bailey solved my dilemma. He had me describe the contents of the cupboard and the particular plates she liked best. Her favorite piece was a casserole shaped like a fish and the green glass coffee cups. I kept his instructions in mind, so on the next day when Miss Glory was hanging out clothes and I had again been told to serve the old biddies on the porch, I dropped the empty serving tray. When I heard Mrs. Cullinan scream, "Mary!" I picked up the casserole and two of the green glass cups in readiness. As she rounded the kitchen door I let them fall on the tiled floor.

I could never absolutely describe to Bailey what happened next, because each time I got to the part where she fell on the floor and screwed up her ugly face to cry, we burst out laughing. She actually wobbled around on the floor and picked up shards of the cups and cried, "Oh, Momma. Oh, dear Gawd. It's Momma's china from Virginia. Oh, Momma, I sorry."

Miss Glory came running in from the yard and the women from the porch crowded around. Miss Glory was almost as broken up as her mistress. "You mean to say she broke our Virginia dishes? What we gone do?"

Mrs. Cullinan cried louder, "That clumsy nigger. Clumsy little black nigger." 40

Old speckled-face leaned down and asked, "Who did it, Viola? Was it Mary? Who did it?"

Everything was happening so fast I can't remember whether her action preceded her words, but I know that Mrs. Cullinan said, "Her name's Margaret, goddamn it, her name's Margaret!" And she threw a wedge of the broken plate at me. It could have been the hysteria which put her aim off, but the flying crockery caught Miss Glory right over her ear and she started screaming.

I left the front door wide open so all the neighbors could hear.

Mrs. Cullinan was right about one thing. My name wasn't Mary.

EXPLORATIONS

1. When Maya Angelou first goes to work for Mrs. Cullinan, what is her attitude toward her employer? At what points does her attitude change, in what ways, and for what reasons?

2. What reason does Angelou give for a black person's horror of being "called out of his name" (para. 30)? Why does she find her change of name so offensive?

3. In paragraph 24, young Marguerite decides "to write a poem on being white, fat, old, and without children." Why do you think she wanted to do this? What personal goals does Angelou seem to have achieved by writing about Mrs. Cullinan in her autobiography?

CONNECTIONS

1. How does Angelou's reaction to being renamed by Mrs. Cullinan illustrate the creative process Gloria Anzaldúa describes on page 273? What specific comments by Anzaldúa apply to the events (internal as well as overt) in "Mary"?

2. In what ways does Angelou's Southern girlhood in the 1930s resemble Henry Louis Gates Jr.'s Southern boyhood twenty years later (p. 146)? What are the main reasons for the differences?

3. In paragraphs 1–2 Angelou compares the "extensive and irrelevant preparations for adulthood" of Negro and white girls in her hometown. How do these two sets of preparations compare with the preparations described by

Susan Orlean in "Quinceañera" (p. 40)? In each case, what kind of adulthood are the girls being prepared for? What aspects of their training are especially relevant and irrelevant to the futures they face?

ELABORATIONS

1. How old were you when you first worked for money? What do you remember of your reactions to the job, the people involved, and having an income? What were the sources of conflict? Using "Mary" as a model, write an essay about your recollections.

2. In paragraph 4 Angelou describes the "inhuman" exactness of Mrs. Cullinan's house: glasses precisely placed, meals precisely scheduled. Do you know anyone who is so demanding? Is there any aspect of your life — the way you arrange your desk, a recipe you prepare, specialized clothing you put on for some activity — that is so exact? Write a descriptive or process analysis essay about your experience with exactness.

ANNIE DILLARD

Flying

The poet and essayist Annie Dillard was born Annie Doak in Pitts-
burgh in 1945. While attending Hollins College near Roanoke, Virginia, she married her writing teacher, Richard Dillard. She also fell in
love with the Blue Ridge landscape and wrote her master's thesis on
Henry David Thoreau's *Walden*. A serious illness in 1971 persuaded
Dillard to pursue her affinity with nature and her interest in spirituality:
She lived by Tinker Creek for a year, observing, writing, and reading.
The result was her Pulitzer-Prize–winning book *Pilgrim at Tinker Creek*
(1974). In 1975 Dillard moved to Washington State, becoming a
scholar-in-residence at Western Washington University in Bellingham
and living on Puget Sound. It was during this period she met the stunt
pilot Dave Rahm, whom she writes about in "Flying." Dillard came east
again in 1979 as a professor and later a writer-in-residence at Wesleyan
University in Middletown, Connecticut. She currently spends winters
there and summers on Cape Cod with her third husband, Robert D.
Richardson Jr., a Thoreau biographer, and daughter Rosie. Dillard has
produced a dozen volumes of poetry, essays, and fiction, including *Encounters with Chinese Writers* (1984), on her experiences as part of a
cultural exchange between the United States and China. "Flying"
comes from her 1989 book *The Writing Life*.

Dave Rahm lived in Bellingham, Washington, north of Seattle.
Bellingham, a harbor town, lies between the San Juan Islands in Haro
Strait and the alpine North Cascade Mountains. I lived there between
stints on the island. Dave Rahm was a stunt pilot, the air's own genius.

In 1975, with a newcomer's willingness to try anything once, I attended the Bellingham Air Show. The Bellingham airport was a wide
clearing in a forest of tall Douglas firs; its runways suited small planes. It
was June. People wearing blue or tan zipped jackets stood loosely on
the concrete walkways and runways outside the coffee shop. At that lati-
tude in June, you stayed outside because you could, even most of the
night, if you could think up something to do. The sky did not darken
until ten o'clock or so, and it never got very dark. Your life parted and
opened in the sunlight. You tossed your dark winter routines, thought
up mad projects, and improvised everything from hour to hour. Being a

stunt pilot seemed the most reasonable thing in the world; you could wave your arms in the air all day and all night, and sleep next winter.

I saw from the ground a dozen stunt pilots; the air show scheduled them one after the other, for an hour of aerobatics. Each pilot took up his or her plane and performed a batch of tricks. They were precise and impressive. They flew upside down, and straightened out; they did barrel rolls, and straightened out; they drilled through dives and spins, and landed gently on a far runway.

For the end of the day, separated from all other performances of every sort, the air show director had scheduled a program titled "DAVE RAHM." The leaflet said that Rahm was a geologist who taught at Western Washington University. He had flown for King Hussein in Jordan. A tall man in the crowd told me Hussein had seen Rahm fly on a visit the king made to the United States; he had invited him to Jordan to perform at ceremonies. Hussein was a pilot, too. "Hussein thought he was the greatest thing in the world."

Idly, paying scant attention, I saw a medium-sized, rugged man 5 dressed in brown leather, all begoggled, climb in a black biplane's open cockpit. The plane was a Bücker Jungman, built in the thirties. I saw a tall, dark-haired woman seize a propeller tip at the plane's nose and yank it down till the engine caught. He was off; he climbed high over the airport in his biplane, very high until he was barely visible as a mote, and then seemed to fall down the air, diving headlong, and streaming beauty in spirals behind him.

The black plane dropped spinning, and flattened out spinning the other way; it began to carve the air into forms that built wildly and musically on each other and never ended. Reluctantly, I started paying attention. Rahm drew high above the world an inexhaustibly glorious line; it piled over our heads in loops and arabesques. It was like a Saul Steinberg fantasy; the plane was the pen. Like Steinberg's contracting and billowing pen line, the line Rahm spun moved to form new, punning shapes from the edges of the old. Like a Klee line, it smattered the sky with landscapes and systems.

The air show announcer hushed. He had been squawking all day, and now he quit. The crowd stilled. Even the children watched dumbstruck as the slow, black biplane buzzed its way around the air. Rahm made beauty with his whole body; it was pure pattern, and you could watch it happen. The plane moved every way a line can move, and it controlled three dimensions, so the line carved massive and subtle slits in the air like sculptures. The plane looped the loop, seeming to arch its back like a gymnast; it stalled, dropped, and spun out of it climbing; it spiraled and knifed west on one side's wings and back east on another; it turned cartwheels, which must be physically impossible; it played with its own line like a cat with yarn. How did the pilot know where in the air he was? If he got lost, the ground would swat him.

Rahm did everything his plane could do: tailspins, four-point rolls, flat spins, figure 8's, snap rolls, and hammerheads. He did pirouettes on the plane's tail. The other pilots could do these stunts, too, skillfully, one at a time. But Rahm used the plane inexhaustibly, like a brush marking thin air.

His was pure energy and naked spirit. I have thought about it for years. Rahm's line unrolled in time. Like music, it split the bulging rim of the future along its seam. It pried out the present. We watchers waited for the split-second curve of beauty in the present to reveal itself. The human pilot, Dave Rahm, worked in the cockpit right at the plane's nose; his very body tore into the future for us and reeled it down upon us like a curling peel.

Like any fine artist, he controlled the tension of the audience's long-   10
ing. You desired, unwittingly, a certain kind of roll or climb, or a return to a certain portion of the air, and he fulfilled your hope slantingly, like a poet, or evaded it until you thought you would burst, and then ful- filled it surprisingly, so you gasped and cried out.

The oddest, most exhilarating and exhausting thing was this: He never quit. The music had no periods, no rests or endings; the poetry's beautiful sentence never ended; the line had no finish; the sculptured forms piled overhead, one into another without surcease. Who could breathe, in a world where rhythm itself had no periods?

It had taken me several minutes to understand what an extraordinary thing I was seeing. Rahm kept all that embellished space in mind at once. For another twenty minutes I watched the beauty unroll and grow more fantastic and unlikely before my eyes. Now Rahm brought the plane down slidingly, and just in time, for I thought I would snap from the effort to compass and remember the line's long intelligence; I could not add another curve. He brought the plane down on a far run- way. After a pause, I saw him step out, an ordinary man, and make his way back to the terminal.

The show was over. It was late. Just as I turned from the runway, something caught my eye and made me laugh. It was a swallow, a blue- green swallow, having its own air show, apparently inspired by Rahm. The swallow climbed high over the runway, held its wings oddly, tipped them, and rolled down the air in loops. The inspired swallow. I always want to paint, too, after I see the Rembrandts. The blue-green swallow tumbled precisely, and caught itself and flew up again as if excited, and looped down again, the way swallows do, but tensely, holding its body carefully still. It was a stunt swallow.

I went home and thought about Rahm's performance that night, and the next day, and the next.

I had thought I knew my way around beauty a little bit. I knew I   15
had devoted a good part of my life to it, memorizing poetry and focusing my attention on complexity of rhythm in particular, on force, movement, repetition, and surprise, in both poetry and prose. Now I had stood among dandelions between two asphalt runways in Bellingham, Washington, and begun learning about beauty. Even the Boston Museum of Fine Arts was never more inspiring than this small northwestern airport on this time-killing Sunday afternoon in June. Nothing on earth is more gladdening than knowing we must roll up our sleeves and move back the boundaries of the humanly possible once more.

EXPLORATIONS

1. What reasons does Annie Dillard give for attending the Bellingham Air Show? How do her reasons for going affect our expectations about what she will see there? What other observations in paragraphs 2–5 help shape our expectations?

2. How would the impact of "Flying" change if Dillard did not compare Dave Rahm with visual and literary artists? What other techniques besides analogy does she use to make her depiction of Rahm's performance as vivid as possible?

3. What are the crucial differences between Rahm's artistry as a pilot and the artistry of the earthbound creators with whom Dillard compares him? Why do you think she chooses not to call attention to these differences?

CONNECTIONS

1. Where and how does Dillard foreshadow her personal turning point at the Bellingham Air Show? Where and how does Maya Angelou (p. 281) foreshadow her personal turning point in "Mary"? What is the impact of these hints at what is to come?

2. What point do you think Clive Barker (p. 272) is making about places of dreams? How do his observations apply to "Flying"? What evidence in Dillard's essay suggests whether she would agree with him?

3. Michael Dorris writes, "Every human being, these tribes believed, was entitled to at least one moment of personal, enabling insight" (p. 273). What does Annie Dillard have to say in "Flying" about the value of such moments?

ELABORATIONS

1. Flying is an ability human beings covet, dream of, strive for, and fear. Write an essay about some aspect of the role flying has played in history or in your own life.

2. In her description of the swallow imitating the stunt pilot (para. 13), Dillard empathizes: "I always want to paint, too, after I see the Rembrandts." What models have you watched that made you want to imitate their brilliance? When you play music or sports, or draw or write or cook, are you inspired by a memory of someone whose work you admire? Write an essay either about such a hero's performance or about your efforts to emulate it.

ANDRE DUBUS

Imperiled Men

Andre Dubus (pronounced de-*buse*) was born in 1936 in Lake
Charles, Louisiana. After graduating from McNeese State College in
1958 he became a lieutenant in the U.S. Marine Corps. Experiences
such as the one he describes in "Imperiled Men" provoked him into becoming a writer; he left the Marines as a captain in 1964 to study for his
M.F.A. at the University of Iowa's legendary Writers' Workshop.
Dubus's first novel, *The Lieutenant*, appeared in 1967. He is best
known for his short stories, however, which have appeared in numerous
periodicals and in more than half a dozen collected volumes. Dubus
taught fiction and writing at Bradford College in Massachusetts from
1966–1984, won a writing fellowship from the National Endowment
for the Arts in 1985, and has continued to publish fiction and nonfiction in the *Sewanee Review, The New Yorker, Ploughshares*, and elsewhere. Among other events, his life was altered by a 1986 auto accident
in which he lost a leg, and by a 1988 five-year MacArthur Fellowship.
He lives in northeastern Massachusetts. "Imperiled Men" first appeared in *Harper's* in June 1993, shortly after President Clinton drew
heated opposition for trying to lift the ban on gay men and lesbians in
the military.

He was a navy pilot in World War II and in Korea, and when I knew
him in 1961 for a few months before he killed himself he was the Commander of the Air Group aboard the USS *Ranger*, an aircraft carrier,
and we called him by the acronym CAG. He shot himself with his .38
revolver because two investigators from the Office of Naval Intelligence
came aboard ship while we were anchored off Iwakuni in Japan and
gave the ship's captain a written report of their investigation of CAG's
erotic life. CAG was a much-decorated combat pilot, and his duty as a
commander was one of great responsibility. The ship's executive officer,
also a commander, summoned CAG to his office, where the two investigators were, and told him that his choices were to face a general court-
martial or to resign from the navy. Less than half an hour later CAG
was dead in his stateroom. His body was flown to the United States; we
were told that he did not have a family, and I do not know where he was
buried. There was a memorial service aboard ship, but I do not remember it; I only remember a general sadness like mist in the passageways.

I did not really know him. I was a first lieutenant then, a career marine; two years later I would resign and become a teacher. On the *Ranger* I was with the marine detachment; we guarded the planes' nuclear weapons stored below decks, ran the brig, and manned one of the antiaircraft gun mounts. We were fifty or so enlisted men and two officers among a ship's crew of about 3,000 officers and men. The Air Group was not included in the ship's company. They came aboard with their planes for our seven-month deployment in the western Pacific. I do not remember the numbers of pilots and bombardier-navigators, mechanics and flight controllers, and men who worked on the flight deck, but there were plenty of all, and day and night you could hear planes catapulting off the front of the deck and landing on its rear.

The flight deck was 1,052 feet long, the ship weighed 81,000 tons fully loaded, and I rarely felt its motion. I came aboard in May for a year of duty, and in August we left our port in San Francisco Bay and headed for Japan. I had driven my wife and three young children home to Louisiana, where they would stay during the seven months I was at sea, and every day I longed for them. One night on the voyage across the Pacific I sat in the wardroom drinking coffee with a lieutenant commander at one of the long tables covered with white linen. The wardroom was open all night because men were always working. The lieutenant commander told me that Soviet submarines tracked us, they recorded the sound of our propellers and could not be fooled by the sound of a decoy ship's propellers, and that they even came into San Francisco Bay to do this; our submarines did the same with Soviet carriers. He said that every time we tried in training exercises to evade even our own submarines we could not do it, and our destroyers could not track and stop them. He said, "So if the whistle blows we'll get a nuclear fish up our ass in the first thirty minutes. Our job is to get the birds in the air before that. They're going to Moscow."

"Where will they land afterward?"

"They won't. They know that."   5

The voyage to Japan was five or six weeks long because we did not go directly to Japan; the pilots flew air operations. Combat units are always trained for war, but these men who flew planes, and the men in orange suits and ear protectors who worked on the flight deck during landings and takeoffs, were engaging in something not at all as playful as marine field exercises generally were. They were imperiled. One pilot told me that from his fighter-bomber in the sky the flight deck looked like an aspirin tablet. On the passage to Japan I became friendly with some pilots drinking coffee in the wardroom, and I knew what CAG looked like because he was CAG. He had dark skin and alert eyes, and he walked proudly. Then in Japan I sometimes drank with young pilots. I was a robust twenty-five-year-old, one of two marine officers aboard ship, and I did not want to be outdone at anything by anyone. But I could not stay with the pilots; I had to leave them in the bar, drinking and talking and laughing, and make my way back to the ship to sleep and wake with a hangover. Next day the pilots flew; if we did not go to sea, they flew from a base on land. Once I asked one of them how he did it.

"The pure oxygen. Soon as you put on the mask, your head clears."

It was not simply the oxygen, and I did not understand any of these wild, brave, and very efficient men until years later when I read Tom Wolfe's *The Right Stuff.*

It was on that same tour that I saw another pilot die. I worked below decks with the marine detachment, but that warm gray afternoon the entire ship was in a simulated condition of war, and my part was to stand four hours of watch in a small turret high above the ship. I could move the turret in a circular way by pressing a button, and I looked through binoculars for planes or ships in the 180-degree arc of our port side. On the flight deck planes were taking off; four could do this in quick sequence. Two catapults launched planes straight off the front of the ship, and quickly they rose and climbed. The third and fourth catapults were on the port side where the flight deck angled sharply out to the left, short of the bow. From my turret I looked down at the ship's bridge and the flight deck. A helicopter flew low near the ship, and planes were taking off. On the deck were men in orange suits and ear protectors; on both sides of the ship, just beneath the flight deck, were nets for these men to jump into, to save themselves from being killed by a landing plane that veered or skidded or crashed. One night I'd inspected a marine guarding a plane on the flight deck; we had a sentry there because the plane carried a nuclear bomb. I stepped from a hatch into the absolute darkness of a night at sea and into a strong wind that lifted my body with each step. I was afraid it would lift me off the deck and hurl me into the sea, where I would tread water in that great expanse and depth while the ship went on its way; tomorrow they would learn that I was missing. I found the plane and the marine; he stood with one arm around that cable that held the wing to the deck.

In the turret I was facing aft when it happened: Men in orange were   10
at the rear of the flight deck, then they sprinted forward, and I rotated my turret toward the bow and saw a plane in the gray sea and an orange-suited pilot lying facedown in the water, his parachute floating beyond his head, moving toward the rear of the ship. The plane had dropped off the port deck and now water covered its wing, then its cockpit, and it sank. The pilot was behind the ship; his limbs did not move, his face

was in the sea, and his parachute was filling with water and starting to
sink. The helicopter hovered low and a sailor on a rope descended from
it; he wore orange, and I watched him coming down and the pilot floating and the parachute sinking beneath the waves. There was still some
length of parachute line remaining when the sailor reached the pilot;
he grabbed him; then the parachute lines tightened their pull and drew
the pilot down. There was only the sea now beneath the sailor on the
rope. Then he ascended.

I shared a stateroom with a navy lieutenant, an officer of medical administration, a very tall and strong man from Oklahoma. He had been
an enlisted man, had once been a corpsman aboard a submarine operating off the coast of the Soviet Union, and one night their periscope
was spotted, destroyers came after them, and they dived and sat at the
bottom and listened by sonar to the destroyers' sonar trying to find
them. He told me about the sailor who had tried to save the pilot. In the
dispensary they gave him brandy, and the sailor wept and said he was
trained to do that job, and this was his first time, and he had failed. Of
course he had not failed. No man could lift another man attached to a
parachute filled with water. Some people said the helicopter had not
stayed close enough to the ship while the planes were taking off. Some
said the pilot was probably already dead; his plane dropped from the
ship, and he ejected himself high into the air, but not high enough for
his parachute to ease his fall. This was all talk about the mathematics of
violent death; the pilot was killed because he flew airplanes from a ship
at sea.
He was a lieutenant commander, and I knew his face and name. As
he was being catapulted, his landing gear on the left side broke off and
his plane skidded into the sea. He was married; his widow had been
married before, also to a pilot who was killed in a crash. I wondered if it
were her bad luck to meet only men who flew; years later I believed that
whatever in their spirits made these men fly also drew her to them.

I first spoke to CAG at the officers' club at the navy base in Yokosuka.
The officers of the Air Group hosted a party for the officers of the ship's
company. We wore civilian suits and ties, and gathered at the club to
drink. There were no women. The party was a matter of protocol, probably a tradition among pilots and the officers of carriers; for us young officers it meant getting happily drunk. I was doing this with pilots at the
bar when one of them said, "Let's throw CAG into the pond."
He grinned at me, as I looked to my left at the small shallow pond
with pretty fish in it; then I looked past the pond at CAG, sitting on a

soft leather chair, a drink in his hand, talking quietly with two or three other commanders sitting in soft leather chairs. All the pilots with me were grinning and saying yes, and the image of us lifting CAG from his chair and dropping him into the water gave me joy, and I put my drink on the bar and said, "Let's *go*."

I ran across the room to the CAG, grabbed the lapels of his coat, 15 jerked him up from his chair, and saw his drink spill onto his suit; then I fell backward to the floor, still holding his lapels, and pulled him down on top of me. There was no one else with me. He was not angry yet, but I was a frightened fool. I released his lapels and turned my head and looked back at the laughing pilots. Out of my vision the party was loud, hundreds of drinking officers who had not seen this, and CAG sounded only puzzled when he said, "What's going on?"

He stood and brushed at the drink on his suit, watching me get up from the floor. I stood not quite at attention but not at ease either. I said, "Sir, I'm Marine Lieutenant Dubus. Your pilots fooled me." I nodded toward them at the bar, and CAG smiled. "They said, 'Let's throw CAG into the pond.' But, sir, the joke was on me."

He was still smiling.

"I'm very sorry, sir."

"That's all right, Lieutenant."

"Can I get the Commander another drink, sir?" 20

"Sure," he said, and told me what he was drinking, and I got it from the bar, where the pilots were red-faced and happy, and brought it to CAG, who was sitting in his chair again with the other commanders. He smiled and thanked me, and the commanders smiled; then I returned to the young pilots and we all laughed.

Until a few months later, on the day when he killed himself, the only words I spoke to CAG after the party were greetings. One night I saw him sitting with a woman in the officers' club, and I wished him good evening. A few times I saw him in the ship's passageways; I recognized him seconds before the features of his face were clear: He had a graceful, athletic stride that dipped his shoulders. I saluted and said, "Good morning, sir" or "Good afternoon, sir." He smiled as he returned my salute and greeting, his eyes and voice mirthful, and I knew that he was seeing me again pulling him out of his chair and down to the floor, then standing to explain myself and apologize. I liked being a memory that gave him sudden and passing amusement.

On a warm sunlit day we were anchored off Iwakuni, and I planned to go with other crew members on a bus to Hiroshima. I put on civilian clothes and went down the ladder to the boat that would take us ashore. I was not happily going to Hiroshima; I was going because I was an

American, and I felt that I should look at it and be in it. I found a seat on the rocking boat, then saw CAG in civilian clothes coming down the ladder. There were a few seats remaining, and he chose the one next to me. He asked me where I was going, then said he was going to Hiroshima, too. I was relieved and grateful; while CAG was flying planes in World War II, I was a boy buying savings stamps and bringing scrap metal to school. On the bus he would talk to me about war, and in Hiroshima I would walk with him and look with him, and his seasoned steps and eyes would steady mine. Then from the ship above us the officer of the deck called down, "CAG?"

CAG turned and looked up at him, a lieutenant junior grade in white cap and short-sleeved shirt and trousers.

"Sir, the executive officer would like to see you."   25

I do not remember what CAG said to me. I only remember my disappointment when he told the boat's officer to go ashore without him. All I saw in CAG's face was the look of a man called from rest back to his job. He climbed the ladder, and soon the boat pulled away.

Perhaps when I reached Hiroshima CAG was already dead; I do not remember the ruins at ground zero or what I saw in the museum. I walked and looked, and stood for a long time at a low arch with an open space at the ground, and in that space was a stone box that held the names of all who died on the day of the bombing and all who had died since because of the bomb. That night I ate dinner alone, then rode the boat back to the ship, went to my empty room, climbed to my upper bunk, and slept for only a while, till the quiet voice of my roommate woke me: "The body will be flown to Okinawa."

I looked at him standing at his desk and speaking into the telephone.

"Yes. A .38 in the temple. Yes."

I turned on my reading lamp and watched him put the phone down.   30
He was sad, and he looked at me. I said, "Did someone commit suicide?"

"CAG."

"CAG?"

I sat up.

"The ONI investigated him."

Then I knew what I had not known I knew, and I said, "Was he a ho-   35
mosexual?"

"Yes."

My roommate told me the executive officer had summoned CAG to his office, shown him the report, and told him that he could either resign or face a general court-martial. Then CAG went to his room. Fifteen minutes later the executive officer phoned him; when he did not answer, the executive officer and the investigators ran to his room. He was on his bunk, shot in the right temple, his pilot's .38 revolver in his hand. His eyelids fluttered; he was unconscious but still alive, and he died from bleeding.

"They *ran?*" I said. "They *ran* to his room?"

Ten years later one of my shipmates came to visit me in Massachusetts; we had been civilians for a long time. In my kitchen we were drinking beer, and he said, "I couldn't tell you this aboard ship, because I worked in the legal office. They called CAG back from that boat you were on because he knew the ONI was aboard. His plane was on the ground at the base of Iwakuni. They were afraid he was going to fly it and crash into the sea and they'd lose the plane."

All 3,000 of the ship's crew did not mourn. Not every one of the hundreds of men in the Air Group mourned. But the shock was general and hundreds of men did mourn, and each morning we woke to it, and it was in our talk in the wardroom and in the passageways. In the closed air of the ship it touched us, and it lived above us on the flight deck and in the sky. One night at sea a young pilot came to my room; his face was sunburned and sad. We sat in desk chairs, and he said, "The morale is very bad now. The whole Group. It's just shot." 40

"Did y'all know about him?"

"We all knew. We didn't care. We would have followed him into hell."

Yes, they would have followed him; they were ready every day and every night to fly with him from a doomed ship and follow him to Moscow, to perish in their brilliant passion.

EXPLORATIONS

1. What meaning does Andre Dubus specify in his essay for its title, "Imperiled Men"? What other meanings for this title does the essay imply?

2. What is the effect of Dubus's choice not to name any of the characters in his essay but himself? What kinds of information does he give us about CAG and the other people aboard the *Ranger?* What is his opinion of CAG? How can you tell?

3. What point is Dubus making with his repeated question (para. 38), "'They *ran?*' I said. 'They *ran* to his room?'" What is the impact of giving this question a paragraph to itself? How does the next paragraph amplify Dubus's point?

CONNECTIONS

1. Like Annie Dillard (p. 288) and Maya Angelou (p. 281), Dubus gives us advance warning of the central event in his narrative. How do you think the impact of "Imperiled Men" would change if we did not know about CAG's suicide until it happens?

2. After reading "Imperiled Men" and "Flying," what do you think Dillard might add to Dubus's explanation of pilots' attraction to flying and drinking (paras. 6–8 and 13–21) and a woman's attraction to pilots (para. 12)?

3. Why do you think CAG shot himself? Why do you think the girl in Kit R. Roane's epigraph on Sarajevo shot herself (p. 277)? How much do you think their wartime surroundings and exposure to other deaths affected each of these suicides? On what evidence do you base your answer?

ELABORATIONS

1. "Imperiled Men" appeared in *Harper's* shortly after President Clinton tried unsuccessfully to lift the ban on gay men and women serving in the U.S. armed forces. What is the nation's current policy on gays in the military? What do you think our policy should be, and why? Write an essay explaining and supporting your decision.

2. Dubus's drunken attempt to throw CAG into the pond (paras. 13–22), although embarrassing at the time, had unexpected positive effects. Have you ever played a trick on someone that backfired? What were the results? Have you ever done something unkind (or been the victim of unkindness) that ultimately produced a better understanding between you and the other person involved? Recall such an experience and write an essay about it.

RICHARD FORD

Optimists

Born in Jackson, Mississippi, in 1944, Richard Ford eschews the label "Southern writer"; he has lived all over the United States. Ford credits his childhood dyslexia with teaching him to attend closely to words. Another influence was living across the street from the writer Eudora Welty (see p. 531). After his father had a heart attack, Ford spent long periods at the hotel run by his grandparents in Arkansas. At eighteen, after his father died, he went to work for the Missouri Pacific Railroad. He enrolled in 1962 at Michigan State University, taught for a year, then applied to join the Arkansas State Police but enlisted instead in the U.S. Marine Corps. Discharged with hepatitis, Ford tried law school in Missouri before moving to New York to marry Kristina Hensley and become a writer. For a while he worked for *American Druggist* magazine; then he and Hensley moved to California, where he earned his M.F.A. degree at the University of California at Irvine in 1970. Although two of his short stories finally were published in New Zealand, lack of success in the United States prodded him to switch to a novel: *A Piece of My Heart* (1976). He supported himself with lectureships (University of Michigan, Princeton University, Williams College), grants (Guggenheim Foundation, National Endowment for the Arts), and sportswriting until his third novel, *The Sportswriter* (1986), won critical acclaim. The story collection *Rock Springs*, in which "Optimists" appears, followed the next year. In 1996 Ford's reputation was clinched when his novel *Independence Day* (1995) won both the PEN/Faulkner Award for Fiction and the Pulitzer Prize.

All of this that I am about to tell you happened when I was only fifteen years old, in 1959, the year my parents were divorced, the year when my father killed a man and went to prison for it, the year I left home and school, told a lie about my age to fool the army, and then did not come back. The year, in other words, when life changed for all of us and forever — ended, really, in a way none of us could ever have imagined in our most brilliant dreams of life.

My father was named Roy Brinson, and he worked on the Great Northern Railway, in Great Falls, Montana. He was a switch-engine fireman, and when he could not hold that job on the seniority list he worked the extra-board as a hostler, or as a hostler's helper, shunting engines through the yard, onto and off the freight trains that went south and east. He was thirty-seven or thirty-eight years old in 1959, a small, young-appearing man, with dark-blue eyes. The railroad was a job he liked, because it paid high wages and the work was not hard, and because you could take off days when you wanted to, or even months, and have no one to ask you questions. It was a union shop, and there were people who looked out for you when your back was turned. "It's a workingman's paradise," my father would say, and then laugh.

My mother did not work then, though she *had* worked — at waitressing and in the bars in town — and she had liked working. My father thought, though, that Great Falls was coming to be a rougher town than it had been when he grew up there, a town going downhill, like its name, and that my mother should be at home more, because I was at an age when trouble came easily. We lived in a rented two-story house on Edith Street, close to the freight yards and the Missouri River, a house where from my window at night I could hear the engines as they sat, throbbing, could see their lights move along the dark rails. My mother was at home most of her time, reading or watching television or cooking meals, though sometimes she would go out to movies in the afternoon, or would go to the Y.W.C.A. and swim in the indoor pool. Where she was from — in Havre, Montana, much farther north — there was never such a thing as a pool indoors, and she thought that to swim in the winter, with snow on the ground and the wind howling, was the greatest luxury. And she would come home late in the afternoon, with her brown hair wet and her face flushed, and in high spirits, saying she felt freer.

The night that I want to tell about happened in November. It was not then a good time for railroads — not in Montana especially — and for firemen not at all, anywhere. It was the featherbedding time, and everyone knew, including my father, that they would all of them eventually lose their jobs, though no one knew exactly when or who would go first, or, clearly, what the future would be. My father had been hired out for ten years, and had worked on coal-burners and oil-burners out of Forsythe, Montana, on the Sheridan spur. But he was still young in the job and low on the list, and he felt that when the cut came young heads would go first. "They'll do something for us, but it might not be enough," he said, and I had heard him say that other times — in the kitchen, with my mother, or out in front, working on his motorcycle, or with me, fishing the whitefish flats up the Missouri. But I do not know if he truly thought that or in fact had any reason to think it. He was an optimist. Both of them were optimists, I think.

I know that by the end of summer in that year he had stopped taking days off to fish, had stopped going out along the coulee rims to spot deer. He worked more then and was gone more, and he talked more about work when he was home: about what the union said on this subject and that, about court cases in Washington, D.C., a place I knew nothing of, and about injuries and illnesses to men he knew that threatened their livelihoods and by association threatened his own — threatened, he must've felt, our whole life.

Because my mother swam at the Y.W.C.A. she had met people there and made friends. One was a large woman named Esther, who came home with her once and drank coffee in the kitchen and talked about her boyfriend and laughed out loud for a long time, though I never saw her again. And another was a woman named Penny Mitchell, whose husband, Boyd, worked for the Red Cross in Great Falls and had an office upstairs in the building with the Y.W.C.A., and with whom my mother would sometimes play canasta on the nights my father worked late. They would set up a card table in the living room, the three of them, and drink and eat sandwiches until midnight. And I would lie in bed with my radio tuned low to the Calgary station, listening to a hockey match beamed out over the great empty prairie, and could hear the cards snap and laughter downstairs, and later I would hear footsteps leaving, hear the door shut, the dishes rattle in the sink, cabinets close. And in a while the door to my room would open and the light would fall inside, and my mother would set a chair back in. I could see her silhouette. She would always say, "Go back to sleep, Frank." And then the door would shut again, and I would almost always go to sleep in a minute.

It was on a night that Penny and Boyd Mitchell were in our house that trouble came about. My father had been working his regular bid-in job on the switch engine, plus a helper's job off the extra-board — a practice that was illegal by the railroad's rules but ignored by the union, who could see bad times coming and knew there would be nothing to help it when they came, and so would let men work if they wanted to. I was in the kitchen, eating a sandwich alone at the table, and my mother was in the living room playing cards with Penny and Boyd Mitchell. They were drinking vodka and eating the other sandwiches my mother had made, when I heard my father's motorcycle outside in the dark. It was eight o'clock at night, and I knew he wasn't expected home until midnight.

"Roy's home," I heard my mother say. "I hear Roy. That's wonderful." I heard chairs scrape and glasses tap.

"Maybe he'll want to play," Penny Mitchell said. "We can play four hands."

I went to the kitchen door and stood looking through the dining   10
room at the front door. I don't think I knew something was wrong, but I think I knew something was unusual, something I would want to know about firsthand.

My mother was standing beside the card table when my father came inside. She was smiling. But I have never seen a look on a man's face that was like the look on my father's face at that moment. He looked wild. His eyes were wild. His whole face was. It was cold outside, and the wind was coming up, and he had ridden home from the train yard in only his flannel shirt. His face was red, and his hair was strewn about his bare head, and I remember his fists were clenched white, as if there was no blood in them at all.

"My God," my mother said. "What is it, Roy? You look crazy." She turned and looked at me, and I knew she was thinking that this was something I might not need to see. But she didn't say anything. She just looked back at my father, stepped toward him and touched his hand, where he must've been the coldest. Penny and Boyd Mitchell sat at the card table, looking up. Boyd Mitchell was smiling for some reason.

"Something awful happened," my father said. He reached and took a corduroy jacket off the coat nail and put it on, right in the living room, then sat down on the couch and hugged his arms. His face seemed to get redder then. He was wearing black steel-toe boots, the boots he wore every day, and I stared at them and felt how cold he must be, even in his own house. I did not come any closer.

"Roy, what is it?" my mother said, and she sat down beside him on the couch and held his hand in both of hers.

My father looked at Boyd Mitchell and at his wife, as if he hadn't   15
known they were in the room until then. He did not know them very well, and I thought he might tell them to get out, but he didn't.

"I saw a man be killed tonight," he said to my mother, then shook his head and looked down. He said, "We were pushing into that old hump yard on Ninth Avenue. A cut of coal cars. It wasn't even an hour ago. I was looking out my side, the way you do when you push out a curve. And I could see this one open boxcar in the cut, which isn't unusual. Only this guy was in it and was trying to get off, sitting in the door, scooting. I guess he was a hobo. Those cars had come in from Glasgow tonight. And just the second he started to go off, the whole cut buckled up. It's one thing that'll happen. But he lost his balance just when he hit the gravel, and he fell backwards underneath. I looked right at him.

And one set of trucks rolled right over his foot." My father looked at my mother then. "It hit his foot," he said.

"My God," my mother said, and looked down at her lap.

My father squinted. "But then he moved, he sort of bucked himself like he was trying to get away. He didn't yell, and I could see his face. I'll never forget that. He didn't look scared, he just looked like a man doing something that was hard for him to do. He looked like he was concentrating on something. But when he bucked he pushed back, and the other trucks caught his hand." My father looked at his own hands then, and made fists out of them and squeezed them.

"What did you do?" my mother said. She looked terrified.

"I yelled out. And Sherman stopped pushing. But it wasn't that fast." 20

"Did you do anything then?" Boyd Mitchell said.

"I got down," my father said, "and I went up there. But here's a man cut in three pieces in front of me. What can you do? You can't do very much. I squatted down and touched his good hand. And it was like ice. His eyes were open and roaming all up in the sky."

"Did he say anything?" my mother said.

"He said, 'Where am I today?' And I said to him, 'It's all right, bud, you're in Montana. You'll be all right.' Though, my God — he wasn't. I took my jacket off and put it over him. I didn't want him to see what had happened."

"You should've put tourniquets on," Boyd Mitchell said gruffly. 25
"That could've helped. That could've saved his life."

My father looked at Boyd Mitchell then as if he had forgotten he was there and was surprised that he spoke. "I don't know about that," he said. "I don't know anything about those things. He was already dead. A boxcar had run over him. He was breathing, but he was already dead to me."

"That's only for a licensed doctor to decide," Boyd Mitchell said. "You're morally obligated to do all you can." And I could tell from his tone of voice that he did not like my father. He hardly knew him, but he did not like him. I had no idea why. Boyd Mitchell was a big, husky, red-faced man with curly hair — handsome in a way, but with a big belly — and I knew only that he worked for the Red Cross, and that my mother was a friend of his wife's, and maybe of his, and that they played cards when my father was gone.

My father looked at my mother in a way I knew was angry. "Why have you got these people over here now, Dorothy? They don't have any business here."

"Maybe that's right," Penny Mitchell said, and she put down her hand of cards and stood up at the table. My mother looked around the room, as though an odd noise had occurred inside of it and she couldn't find the source.

"Somebody definitely should've done something," Boyd Mitchell   30 said, and he leaned forward on the table toward my father. "That's all there is to say." He was shaking his head no. "That man didn't have to die." Boyd Mitchell clasped his big hands on top of the playing cards and stared at my father. "The unions'll cover this up, too, I guess, won't they? That's what happens in these things."

My father stood up then, and his face looked wide, though it still looked young. He looked like a young man who had been scolded and wasn't sure how he should act. "You get out of here," he said in a loud voice. "My God. What a thing to say. I don't even know you."

"I know you, though," Boyd Mitchell said angrily. "You're another featherbedder. You aren't good to do anything. You can't even help a dying man. You're bad for this country, and you won't last."

"Boyd, my goodness," Penny Mitchell said. "Don't say that. Don't say that to him."

Boyd Mitchell glared up at his wife. "I'll say anything I want to," he said. "And he'll listen, because he's helpless. He can't do anything."

"Stand up," my father said. "Just stand up on your feet." His fists   35 were clenched again.

"All right, I will," Boyd Mitchell said. He glanced up at his wife again. And I realized then that Boyd Mitchell was drunk, and it was possible that he did not even know what he was saying, or what had happened, and that words just got loose from him this way, and anybody who knew him knew it. Only my father didn't. He only knew what had been said.

Boyd Mitchell stood up and put his hands in his pockets. He was much taller than my father. He had on a white Western shirt and whipcords and cowboy boots and was wearing a big silver wristwatch. "All right," he said. "Now I'm standing up. What's supposed to happen?" He weaved a little. I saw that.

And my father hit Boyd Mitchell then, hit him from across the card table, hit him with his right hand, square into the chest — not a lunging blow, just a hard, hitting blow that threw my father off balance and made him make a chuffing sound with his mouth. Boyd Mitchell groaned, "Oh," and fell down immediately, his big, thick, heavy body hitting the floor already doubled over. And the sound of him hitting the floor in our house was like no sound I had ever heard before. It was the sound of a man's body hitting the floor, and it was only that. In my life I have heard it many other times, in hotel rooms and in bars, and it is one you do not want to hear.

You can hit a man in a lot of ways, I know that, and I knew that then, because my father had told me. You can hit a man to insult him, or you can hit a man to bloody him, or to knock him down, or to lay him out. Or you can hit a man to kill him. Hit him that hard. And that is how my father hit Boyd Mitchell — as hard as he could, in the chest, and not in the face, the way someone might think who didn't know about it.

"Oh my God," Penny Mitchell said. Boyd Mitchell was lying on his side in front of the TV, and she had gotten down on her knees beside him. "Boyd," she said. "Are you hurt? Oh, look at this. Stay where you are, Boyd. Stay on the floor."

"Now, then. All right," my father said. "Now. All right." He was standing against the wall, over to the side of where he had been when he hit Boyd Mitchell from across the card table. The light was bright in the room, and my father's eyes were wide and touring around. He seemed out of breath and both his fists were clenched, and I could feel his heart beating in my own chest. "All right, now, you son of a bitch," my father said, and loudly. I don't think he was even talking to Boyd Mitchell. He was just saying words that came out of him.

"Roy," my mother said calmly. "Boyd's hurt now. He's hurt." She was just looking down at Boyd Mitchell. I don't think she knew what to do.

"Oh, no," Penny Mitchell said in an excited voice. "Look up, Boyd. Look up at Penny. You've been hurt." She had her hands flat on Boyd Mitchell's chest, and her skinny shoulders close to him. She wasn't crying, but I think she was hysterical and couldn't cry.

All this had taken only five minutes, maybe even less time. I had never even left the kitchen door. And for that reason I walked out into the room where my father and mother were, and where Boyd and Penny Mitchell were both of them on the floor. I looked down at Boyd Mitchell, at his face. I wanted to see what had happened to him. His eyes had cast back up into their sockets. His mouth was open, and I could see his pink tongue inside. He was breathing heavy breaths, and his fingers — the fingers on both of his hands — were moving, moving in the way a man would move them if he was nervous or anxious about something. I think he was dead then, and I think even Penny Mitchell knew he was dead, because she was saying, "Oh please, please, please, Boyd."

That is when my mother called the police, and I think it is when my father opened the front door and stepped out into the night.

All that happened next is what you would expect to happen. Boyd Mitchell's chest quit breathing in a minute, and he turned pale and

cold and began to look dead right on our living-room floor. He made a
noise in his throat once, and Penny Mitchell cried out, and my mother
got down on her knees and held Penny's shoulders while she cried.
Then my mother made Penny get up and go into the bedroom — hers
and my father's — and lie on the bed. Then she and I sat in the brightly
lit living room, with Boyd Mitchell dead on the floor, and simply
looked at each other — maybe for ten minutes, maybe for twenty. I
don't know what my mother could've been thinking at the time, because she did not say. She did not ask about my father. She did not tell
me to leave the room. Maybe she thought about the rest of her life then
and what that might be like after tonight. Or maybe she thought this:
that people can do the worst things they are capable of doing and in the
end the world comes back to normal. Possibly, she was just waiting for
something normal to begin to happen again. That would make sense,
given her particular character.

Though what I thought myself, sitting in that room with Boyd
Mitchell dead, I remember very well, because I have thought it other
times, and to a degree I began to date my real life from that moment
and that thought. It is this: that situations have possibilities in them, and
we only have to be present to be involved. Tonight was a very bad one.
But how were we to know it would turn out this way until it was too late
and we had all been changed forever? I realized, though, that trouble,
real trouble, was something to be avoided, inasmuch as once it has
passed by, you have only yourself to answer to, even if, as I was, you are
the cause of nothing.

In a little while, the police arrived to our house. First one and then
two more cars with their red lights turning in the street. Lights were on
in the neighbors' houses, and people came out and stood in the cold in
their front yards watching — people I didn't know and who didn't know
us. "It's a circus now," my mother said to me when we looked through
the window. "We'll have to move somewhere else. They won't let us
alone."

An ambulance came, and Boyd Mitchell was taken away on a
stretcher, under a sheet. Penny Mitchell came out of the bedroom and
went with them, though she did not say anything to my mother, or to
anybody, just got in a police car and left into the dark.

Two policemen came inside, and one asked my mother some ques-   50
tions in the living room, while the other one asked me questions in the
kitchen. He wanted to know what I had seen, and I told him. I said
Boyd Mitchell had cursed at my father for some reason I didn't know,
then had stood up and tried to hit him, and that my father had pushed
Boyd and that was all. He asked me if my father was a violent man, and

I said no. He asked if my father had a girlfriend, and I said no. He asked if my mother and father had ever fought, and I said no. He asked me if I loved my mother and father, and I said I did. And then that was all.

I went out into the living room then, and my mother was there, and when the police left we stood at the front door, and there was my father outside, standing by the open door of a police car. He had on handcuffs. And for some reason he wasn't wearing a shirt or his corduroy jacket but was bare-chested in the cold night, holding his shirt behind him. His hair looked wet to me. I heard a policeman say, "Roy, you're going to catch cold," and then my father say, "I wish I was a long way from here right now. China maybe." He smiled at the policeman. I don't think he ever saw us watching, or if he did he didn't want to admit it. And neither of us did anything, because the police had him, and when that is the case there is nothing you can do to help.

All this happened by ten o'clock. At midnight my mother and I drove down to the city jail and got my father out. I stayed in the car while my mother went in — sat and watched the high windows of the jail, which were behind wire mesh and bars. Yellow lights were on there, and I could hear voices and see figures move past the lights, and twice someone called out, "Hello, hello. Marie, are you with me?" And then it was quiet, except for the cars that drove slowly past ours.

On the ride home, my mother drove and my father sat and stared out at the big electrical stacks by the river, and the lights of houses on the other side, in Black Eagle. He had on a checked shirt someone inside had given him, and his hair was neatly combed. No one said anything, but I did not understand why the police would put anyone in jail because he had killed a man and in two hours let him out again. It was a mystery to me, even though I wanted him to be out and for our life to resume, and even though I did not see any way it could and, in fact, already knew it never would.

Inside our house, all the lights were burning when we got back. It was one o'clock and there were still lights in some neighbors' houses. I could see a man at the window across the street, both of his hands to the glass, watching out, watching us.

My mother went into the kitchen, and I could hear her running 55 water for coffee and taking down cups. My father stood in the middle of the living room and looked around, looking at the chairs, at the card table with cards still on it, at the open doorways to the other rooms. It was as if he had forgotten his own house and now saw it again and didn't like it.

"I don't feel I know what he had against me," my father said. He said this to me, but he said it to anyone, too. "You'd think you'd know what a man had against you, wouldn't you, Frank?"

"Yes," I said. "I would." We were both just standing there, my father and I, in the lighted room there. We were not about to do anything.

"I want us to be happy here now," my father said. "I want us to enjoy life. I don't hold anything against anybody. Do you believe that?"

"I believe that," I said. My father looked at me with his dark-blue eyes and frowned. And for the first time I wished my father had not done what he did but had gone about things differently. I saw him as a man who made mistakes, as a man who could hurt people, ruin lives, risk their happiness. A man who did not understand enough. He was like a gambler, though I did not even know what it meant to be a gambler then.

"It's such a quickly changing time now," my father said. My mother,   60
who had come into the kitchen doorway, stood looking at us. She had on a flowered pink apron, and was standing where I had stood earlier that night. She was looking at my father and at me as if we were one person. "Don't you think it is, Dorothy?" he said. "All this turmoil. Everything just flying by. Look what's happened here."

My mother seemed very certain about things then, very precise. "You should've controlled yourself more," she said. "That's all."

"I know that," my father said. "I'm sorry. I lost control over my mind. I didn't expect to ruin things, but now I think I have. It was all wrong."

My father picked up the vodka bottle, unscrewed the cap and took a big swallow, then put the bottle back down. He had seen two men killed tonight. Who could've blamed him?

"When I was in jail tonight," he said, staring at a picture on the wall, a picture by the door to the hallway. He was just talking again. "There was a man in the cell with me. And I've never been in jail before, not even when I was a kid. But this man said to me tonight, 'I can tell you've never been in jail before just by the way you stand up straight. Other people don't stand that way. They stoop. You don't belong in jail. You stand up too straight.'" My father looked back at the vodka bottle as if he wanted to drink more out of it, but he only looked at it. "Bad things happen," he said, and he let his open hands tap against his legs like clappers against a bell. "Maybe he was in love with you, Dorothy," he said. "Maybe that's what the trouble was."

And what I did then was stare at the picture on the wall, the picture   65
my father had been staring at — a picture I had seen every day. Probably I had seen it a thousand times. It was two people with a baby on a beach. A man and a woman sitting in the sand with an ocean behind.

They were smiling at the camera, wearing bathing suits. In all the times I had seen it I'd thought that it was a picture in which I was the baby and the two people were my parents. But I realized as I stood there that it was not me at all; it was my father who was the child in the picture, and the parents there were his parents — two people I'd never known, and who were dead — and the picture was so much older than I'd thought it was. I wondered why I hadn't known that before, hadn't understood it for myself, hadn't always known it. Not even that it mattered. What mattered was, I felt, that my father had fallen down now, as much as the man he had watched fall beneath the train just hours before. And I was as helpless to do anything as he had been. I wanted to tell him that I loved him, but for some reason I did not.

Later in the night, I lay in my bed with the radio playing, listening to news that was far away, in Calgary and in Saskatoon, and even farther, in Regina and Winnipeg — cold, dark cities I knew I would never see in my life. My window was raised above the sill, and for a long time I had sat and looked out, hearing my parents talk softly down below, hearing their footsteps, hearing my father's steel-toed boots strike the floor, and then their bedsprings squeeze and then be quiet. From out across the sliding river I could hear trucks — stock trucks and grain trucks heading toward Idaho, or down toward Helena, or into the train yards where my father hostled engines. The neighborhood houses were dark again. My father's motorcycle sat in the yard, and out of the night air I felt I could hear even the falls themselves, could hear every sound of them, sounds that found me and whirled and filled my room — could even feel them, cold and wintry, so that warmth seemed like a possibility I would never know again.

After a time then my mother came in my room. The light fell on my bed, and she set a chair inside. I could see that she was looking at me. She closed the door, came and turned off my radio, then took her chair to the window, closed it, and sat so that I could see her face silhouetted against the street light. She lit a cigarette and did not look at me, still cold under the covers of my bed.

"How do you feel, Frank?" she said, smoking her cigarette.

"I feel all right," I said.

"Do you think your house is a terrible house now?"

"No," I said.

"I hope not," my mother said. "Don't feel it is. Don't hold anything against anyone. Poor Boyd. He's gone."

"Why do you think that happened?" I said, though I didn't think she would answer, and wondered if I even wanted to know.

70

My mother blew smoke against the window glass, then sat and breathed. "He must've seen something in your father he just hated. I don't know what it is. Who knows? Maybe your father felt the same way." She shook her head and looked out into the street-lamp light. "I remember once," she said. "I was still in Havre, in the thirties. We were living in a motel my father part-owned out Highway 2, and my mother was around then, but wasn't having any of us. My father had this big woman named Judy Belknap as his girlfriend. She was Assiniboin. Just some squaw. But we used to go on nature tours when he couldn't put up with me anymore. She'd take me way up above the Milk River. All this stuff she knew about, animals and plants and ferns — she'd tell me all that. And once we were sitting watching some gadwall ducks on the ice where a creek had made a little turnout. It was getting colder, just like now. And Judy just all at once stood up and clapped. Just clapped her hands. And all these ducks got up, all except for one that stayed on the ice, where its feet were frozen, I guess. It didn't even try to fly. It just sat. And Judy said to me, 'It's just a coincidence, Dottie. It's wildlife. Some always get left back.' And that seemed to leave her satisfied for some reason. We walked back to the car after that. So," my mother said. "Maybe that's what this is. Just a coincidence."

She raised the window again, dropped her cigarette out, blew the last 75 smoke from her throat, and said, "Go to sleep, Frank. You'll be all right. We'll all survive this. Be an optimist."

When I was asleep that night, I dreamed. And what I dreamed was of a plane crashing, a bomber dropping out of the frozen sky, bouncing as it hit the icy river, sliding and turning on the ice, its wings like knives, and coming into our house, where we were sleeping, levelling everything. And when I sat up in bed I could hear a dog in the yard, its collar jingling, and I could hear my father crying, "Boo-hoo-hoo, boo-hoo-hoo" — like that, quietly — though afterward I could never be sure if I heard him crying in just that way or if all of it was a dream, a dream I wished I never had.

The most important things in your life can change so suddenly, so unrecoverably, that you can forget even the most important of them and their connections, you are so taken up by the chanciness of all that's happened and by all that could and will happen next. I now no longer remember the exact year of my father's birth, or how old he was when I last saw him, or even when that last time took place. When you're young, these things seem unforgettable and at the heart of everything. But they slide away and are gone when you are not so young.

My father went to Deer Lodge prison and stayed five months for killing Boyd Mitchell by accident, for using too much force to hit him. In Montana you cannot simply kill a man in your living room and walk off free from it, and what I remember is that my father pleaded no contest, the same as guilty.

My mother and I lived in our house for the months he was gone. But when he came out and went back on the railroad as a switchman the two of them argued about things, about her wanting us to go someplace else to live — California and Seattle were mentioned. And then they separated, and she moved out. And after that I moved out by joining the Army and adding years to my age, which was sixteen then.

I know about my father only that after a time he began to live a life 80 that he himself would never have believed. He fell off the railroad, divorced my mother, who would now and then resurface in his life. Drinking was involved in that, and gambling, embezzling money, even carrying a pistol, is what I heard. I was apart from all of it. And when you are the age I was then, and loose on the world and alone, you can get along better than at almost any other time, because it's a novelty, and you can act directly for what you want, and you can think that being alone will not last forever. All I know of my father, finally, is that he was once in Laramie, Wyoming, and not in good shape, and then he simply disappeared from view.

A month ago I saw my mother. I was buying groceries at a drive-in store by the interstate in Anaconda, Montana, not far from Deer Lodge itself, where my father had been. It had been fifteen years, I think, since I had seen her, though I am forty-three years old now, and possibly it was longer. But when I saw her I walked across the store to where she was and I said, "Hello, Dorothy. It's Frank."

She looked at me and smiled and said, "Oh, Frank. How are you? I haven't seen you in a long time. I'm glad to see you now, though." She was dressed in blue jeans and boots and a Western shirt, and she looked like a woman who could be sixty years old. Her hair was tied back and she looked pretty, though I think she had been drinking. It was ten o'clock in the morning.

There was a man standing near her, holding a basket of groceries, and she turned to him and said, "Dick, come here and meet my son, Frank. We haven't seen each other in a long time. This is Dick Spivey, Frank."

I shook hands with Dick Spivey, who was a man younger than my mother but older than me — a tall, thin-faced man with coarse blue-black hair — and who was wearing Western boots like hers. "Let me say a word to Frank, Dick," my mother said, and she put her hand on Dick's wrist and squeezed it and smiled at him. And he walked up toward the checkout to pay for his groceries.

"So. What are you doing now, Frank?" my mother said, and put her hand on my wrist the way she had on Dick Spivey's, but held it there. "These years," she said.   85

"I've been down in Rock Springs, on the coal boom," I said. "I'll probably go back down there."

"And I guess you're married, too."

"I was," I said. "But not right now."

"That's fine," she said. "You look fine." She smiled at me. "You'll never get anything fixed just right. That's your mother's word. Your father and I had a marriage made in Havre — that was our joke about us. We used to laugh about it. You didn't know that, of course. You were too young. A lot of it was just wrong."

"It's a long time ago," I said. "I don't know about that."   90

"I remember those times very well," my mother said. "They were happy enough times. I guess something *was* in the air, wasn't there? Your father was so jumpy. And Boyd got so mad, just all of a sudden. There was some hopelessness to it, I suppose. All that union business. We were the last to understand any of it, of course. We were trying to be decent people."

"That's right," I said. And I believed that was true of them.

"I still like to swim," my mother said. She ran her fingers through the back of her hair, as if it were wet. She smiled at me again. "It still makes me feel freer."

"Good," I said. "I'm happy to hear that."

"Do you ever see your dad?"   95

"No," I said. "I never do."

"I don't either," my mother said. "You just reminded me of him." She looked at Dick Spivey, who was standing at the front window, holding his sack of groceries, looking out at the parking lot. It was March, and some small bits of snow were falling onto the cars in the lot. He didn't seem in any hurry. "Maybe I didn't appreciate your father enough," she said. "Who knows? Maybe we weren't even made for each other. Losing your love is the worst thing, and that's what we did." I didn't answer her, but I knew what she meant, and that it was true. "I wish we knew each other better, Frank," my mother said to me. She looked down, and I think she may have blushed. "We have our deep feelings, though, don't we? Both of us."

"Yes," I said. "We do."

"So. I'm going out now," my mother said. "Frank." She squeezed my wrist, and walked away through the checkout and into the parking lot, with Dick Spivey carrying their groceries beside her.

But when I had bought my own groceries and paid, and gone out to 100 my car and started up, I saw Dick Spivey's green Chevrolet drive back into the lot and stop, and watched my mother get out and hurry across the snow to where I was, so that for a moment we faced each other through the open window.

"Did you ever think," my mother said, snow freezing in her hair, "did you ever think back then that I was in love with Boyd Mitchell? Anything like that? Did you ever?"

"No," I said. "I didn't."

"No, well, I wasn't," she said. "Boyd was in love with Penny. I was in love with Roy. That's how things were. I want you to know it. You have to believe that. Do you?"

"Yes," I said. "I believe you."

And she bent down and kissed my cheek through the open window 105 and touched my face with both her hands, held me for a moment that seemed like a long time, before she turned away, finally, and left me there alone.

EXPLORATIONS

1. From the point of view of this story's narrator, what is an optimist? Who are the optimists of the title? How can you tell?

2. What evidence in the story indicates whether the narrator regards himself as an optimist? What evidence indicates whether he regards being an optimist as good, bad, or neutral?

3. At what points in "Optimists" does the action pause as the narrator looks backward and forward in time? What conclusions does he draw at each point about the connections between past, present, and future?

CONNECTIONS

1. Compare the significance of unexpected death in "Optimists" and "Imperiled Men" (p. 293). Within each selection, who is most affected by the death or deaths that occur? Which death do you think is most tragic, and why?

2. In what sense does Bob Seger's line "I wish I didn't know now what I didn't know then" (p. 272) apply to the narrator of "Optimists"?

3. In what ways does the narrator's family in the last section of "Optimists" (paras. 77–103) resemble the narrator's family in Kazuo Ishiguro's "A Family Supper" (p. 260)? What important differences do you notice?

ELABORATIONS

1. In paragraph 1, the narrator lists a series of events that happened in the same year. After reading all of "Optimists," what do you think are the relationships between these events? Find each event where it takes place in the story and figure out what factors — obvious and not so obvious — caused it to happen. Write an essay about "Optimists" analyzing what author Richard Ford has to say about the ways events shape people, the ways people shape events, and the ways events shape other events. Which chain of connections do you think Ford (or, at least, his narrator) regards as most important, and why?

2. "And for the first time I wished my father had not done what he did . . ." states the narrator in paragraph 59. "I saw him as a man who made mistakes . . . a man who did not understand enough." Write a narrative essay about a turning point in your own life when you recognized that an older person you looked up to was in fact a fallible, flawed human being. What were the circumstances? What were your reactions?

WINDOWS:
THE WORLD

Turning Points: *An Indian mob waves weapons during a dispute.*

SOPHRONIA LIU

So Tsi-fai

Born in Hong Kong in 1953, Sophronia Liu came to the United States to study at the age of twenty. Some of her family are still in Hong Kong; others now live in the United States, Canada, and England. Liu received a bachelor's degree in English and French, and a master's degree in English, from the University of South Dakota. She taught composition at the University of Minnesota while working toward her Ph.D. in English. A resident of Minneapolis–St. Paul for the past thirteen years, she is an educational consultant for Asian-American Literature Designs and conducts teacher-training workshops for the Minnesota Center for Arts Education. In the fall of 1990 Liu returned to Hong Kong to do research for a program she was developing for Asian-American students; she plans to spend the winter of 1996–1997 there as well. For the past three years Liu has been writing, directing, and performing in theater productions: She is a founding member of the theatrical group Asian-American Renaissance and has been active in Theatre Mu. She is also a professional interpreter and translator and a trained T'ai Chi instructor. "So Tsi-fai" was written in response to a class assignment and originally appeared in the Minnesota feminist publication *Hurricane Alice*.

Hong Kong, where Liu attended The Little Flower's School with So Tsi-fai, is a British Crown colony at the mouth of China's Pearl River. Its nucleus is Hong Kong Island, which Britain acquired from China in 1841. Most of the colony's 409 square miles consist of other Chinese territory held by Britain on a ninety-nine-year lease. Hong Kong's population of over five million includes fewer than 20,000 British; it absorbed more than a million Chinese refugees after Mao's Communists won the mainland in 1949. In 1985 China and Britain agreed that Hong Kong will revert to China in 1997, when the lease expires, but will be allowed to keep its social, economic, and legal system for fifty years after that. In the meantime, the British governor has been strengthening the colony's democratic institutions, while Hong Kong (meaning "fragrant harbor") remains a thriving capitalist port.

Voices, images, scenes from the past — twenty-three years ago, when I was in sixth grade:

"Let us bow our heads in silent prayer for the soul of So Tsi-fai. Let us pray for God's forgiveness for this boy's rash taking of his own life . . ."

Sister Marie (Mung Gu-liang). My sixth-grade English teacher. Missionary nun from Paris. Principal of The Little Flower's School. Disciplinarian, perfectionist, authority figure: awesome and awful in my ten-year-old eyes.

"I don't need any supper. I have drunk enough insecticide." So Tsi-fai. My fourteen-year-old classmate. Daredevil; good-for-nothing lazy-bones (according to Mung Gu-liang). Bright black eyes, disheveled hair, defiant sneer, creased and greasy uniform, dirty hands, careless walk, shuffling feet. Standing in the corner for being late, for forgetting his homework, for talking in class, for using foul language. ("Shame on you! Go wash your mouth with soap!" Mung Gu-liang's sharp command. He did, and came back with a grin.) So Tsi-fai: Sticking his tongue out behind Mung Gu-liang's back, passing secret notes to his friends, kept behind after school, sent to the Principal's office for repeated offense. So Tsi-fai: incorrigible, hopeless, and without hope.

It was a Monday in late November when we heard of his death, returning to school after the weekend with our parents' signatures on our midterm reports. So Tsi-fai also showed his report to his father, we were told later. He flunked three out of the fourteen subjects: English Grammar, Arithmetic, and Chinese Dictation. He missed each one by one to three marks. That wasn't so bad. But he was a hopeless case. Overaged, stubborn, and uncooperative; a repeated offender of school rules, scourge of all teachers; who was going to give him a lenient passing grade? Besides, being a few months over the maximum age — fourteen — for sixth graders, he wasn't even allowed to sit for the Secondary School Entrance Exam.

All sixth graders in Hong Kong had to pass the SSE before they   5
could obtain a seat in secondary school. In 1964 when I took the exam, there were more than 20,000 candidates. About 7,000 of us passed: 4,000 were sent to government and subsidized schools, the other 3,000 to private and grant-in-aid schools. I came in around no. 2,000; I was lucky. Without the public exam, there would be no secondary school for So Tsi-fai. His future was sealed.

Looking at the report card with three red marks on it, his father was furious. So Tsi-fai was the oldest son. There were three younger children. His father was a vegetable farmer with a few plots of land in Wong Juk-hang, by the sea. His mother worked in a local factory. So Tsi-fai helped in the fields, cooked for the family, and washed his own clothes. ("Filthy, dirty boy!" gasped Mung Gu-liang. "Grime behind the ears, black rims on the fingernails, dirty collar, crumpled shirt. Why doesn't your mother iron your shirt?") Both his parents were illiterate. So Tsi-fai was their biggest hope: He made it to the sixth grade.

Who woke him up for school every morning and had breakfast waiting for him? Nobody. ("Time for school! Get up! Eat your rice!" Ah Ma nagged and screamed. The aroma of steamed rice and Chinese sausages spread all over the house. "Drink your tea! Eat your oranges! Wash your face! And remember to wash behind your ears!") And who helped So Tsi-fai do his homework? Nobody. Did he have older brothers like mine who knew all about the arithmetic of rowing a boat against the currents or with the currents, how to count the feet of chickens and rabbits in the same cage, the present perfect continuous tense of "to live" and the future perfect tense of "to succeed"? None. Nil. So Tsi-fai was a lost cause.

I came first in both terms that year, the star pupil. So Tsi-fai was one of the last in the class: He was lazy; he didn't care. Or did he?

When his father scolded him, So Tsi-fai left the house. When he showed up again, late for supper, he announced, "I don't need any supper. I have drunk enough insecticide." Just like another one of his practical jokes. The insecticide was stored in the field for his father's vegetables. He was rushed to the hospital; dead upon arrival.

"He gulped for a last breath and was gone," an uncle told us at the   10
funeral. "But his eyes wouldn't shut. So I said in his ear, 'You go now and rest in peace.' And I smoothed my hand over his eyelids. His face was all purple."

His face was still purple when we saw him in his coffin. Eyes shut tight, nostrils dilated and white as if fire and anger might shoot out, any minute.

In class that Monday morning, Sister Marie led us in prayer. "Let us pray that God will forgive him for his sins." We said the Lord's Prayer and the Hail Mary. We bowed our heads. I sat in my chair, frozen and dazed, thinking of the deadly chill in the morgue, the smell of disinfectant, ether, and dead flesh.

"Bang!" went a gust of wind, forcing open a leaf of the double door leading to the back balcony. "Flap, flap, flap." The door swung in the wind. We could see the treetops by the hillside rustling to and fro against a pale blue sky. An imperceptible presence had drifted in with the wind. The same careless walk and shuffling feet, the same daredevil air — except that the eyes were lusterless, dripping blood; the tongue hanging out, gasping for air. As usual, he was late. But he had come back to claim his place.

"I died a tragic death," his voice said. "I have as much right as you to be here. This is my seat." We heard him; we knew he was back.

. . . So Tsi-fai: Standing in the corner for being late, for forgetting his   15
homework, for talking in class, for using foul language. So Tsi-fai: palm
outstretched, chest sticking out, holding his breath: "Tat. Tat. Tat."
Down came the teacher's wooden ruler, twenty times on each hand.
Never batting an eyelash: then back to facing the wall in the corner by
the door. So Tsi-fai: grimy shirt, disheveled hair, defiant sneer. So Tsi-
fai. Incorrigible, hopeless, and without hope.

   The girls in front gasped and shrank back in their chairs. Mung Gu-
liang went to the door, held the doorknob in one hand, poked her head
out, and peered into the empty balcony. Then, with a determined jerk,
she pulled the door shut. Quickly crossing herself, she returned to the
teacher's desk. Her black cross swung upon the front of her gray habit as
she hurried across the room. "Don't be silly!" she scolded the frightened girls in the front row.

   What really happened? After all these years, my mind is still haunted
by this scene. What happened to So Tsi-fai? What happened to me?
What happened to all of us that year in sixth grade, when we were green
and young and ready to fling our arms out for the world? All of a sudden, death claimed one of us and he was gone.

   Who arbitrates between life and death? Who decides which life is
worth preserving and prospering, and which to nip in its bud? How did
it happen that I, at ten, turned out to be the star pupil, the lucky one,
while my friend, a peasant's son, was shoveled under the heap and lost
forever? How could it happen that this world would close off a young
boy's life at fourteen just because he was poor, undisciplined, and
lacked the training and support to pass his exams? What really
happened?

   Today, twenty-three years later, So Tsi-fai's ghost still haunts me. "I
died a tragic death. I have as much right as you to be here. This is my
seat." The voice I heard twenty-three years ago in my sixth-grade classroom follows me in my dreams. Is there anything I can do to lay it to
rest?

EXPLORATIONS

1. How do you think Sophronia Liu regarded So Tsi-fai before his death? How
   did her view change after his suicide? How can you tell? What other attitudes did Liu evidently reexamine and alter at that point?

2. Whom and what does Liu blame for So Tsi-fai's suicide? What preventive
   measures does her story suggest to protect other students from a similar fate?

Judging from Liu's narrative, what changes in Hong Kong's social and educational institutions do you think would help students like So Tsi-fai?

3. Liu's first three paragraphs consist almost entirely of incomplete sentences. How does she use these sentence fragments to establish her essay's central conflict? At what points does she use complete sentences? What is their effect?

CONNECTIONS

1. How are So Tsi-fai's reasons for committing suicide similar to CAG's in Andre Dubus's "Imperiled Men" (p. 293)? How did the futures differ that these two characters could not bear to face?

2. Like So Tsi-fai, Sugama in John David Morley's "Acquiring a Japanese Family" (p. 230) is his parents' oldest son. What dilemma does this status create for Sugama? What dilemma does it create for So Tsi-fai?

3. Reread paragraphs 1–13 of "The New Lost Generation" (p. 18). What apparently prompted James Baldwin's friend to commit suicide? How did his death affect Baldwin? What comments by So Tsi-fai's ghost in Liu's story might have been made by Baldwin's friend? How does Liu's response to suicide resemble Baldwin's?

ELABORATIONS

1. What is the role of Mung Gu-liang/Sister Marie in "So Tsi-fai"? Do you think the nun would agree with Liu's assessment of what happened? How might her memory and interpretation of these events differ from Liu's? Write a narrative or argumentative version of So Tsi-fai's story from Mung Gu-liang's point of view.

2. When you were in elementary school, who were the outcasts in your class and why? If you recall one student in particular who was regarded as "different," write an essay describing him or her and narrating some of the incidents that set him or her apart. If your class consisted of two or more distinct groups, write an essay classifying these groups according to their special characteristics and their behavior toward each other. In either case, how has your attitude toward the "outcasts" changed?

LILIANA HEKER

The Stolen Party

Argentine writer Liliana Heker published her highly regarded first volume of short stories, *Those Who Beheld the Burning Bush*, while still in her teens. As editor in chief of the literary magazine *El Ornitorrinco* ("The platypus"), Heker kept open a national forum for writers throughout the years of Argentina's chaotic and bloody military dictatorships. From the late 1960s through 1982 she and others debated about the proper role of a writer in a strife-torn, oppressed society. The late Argentine novelist Julio Cortázar (see p. 3), living in Paris, defended his role as a writer in exile, while Heker took a position similar to Nadine Gordimer's in South Africa (see p. 344): "To be heard, we must shout from within." Heker's second novel, *Zona de Clivage*, was published in 1988 and won the Buenos Aires Municipal Prize. "The Stolen Party," first published in 1982, was translated from the Spanish by Alberto Manguel for his anthology *Other Fires* (1985). It has since become the title story of Heker's most recent short-story collection in English (1994).

Four times the size of Texas, Argentina occupies most of South America's southern tip. When the first Spanish settlers appeared in the early 1500s, nomadic Indians roamed the pampas. By the late 1800s nearly all of them had been killed, making room for the influx of Europeans who today are 97 percent of the population. Argentina had won independence from Spain in 1819; by the century's end it was the most prosperous, educated, and industrialized Latin American nation. Military dictatorships and coups have dominated this century, however. Aside from General Juan Perón, elected president from 1946 to 1955 and again in 1973, most regimes have been nasty, brutish, and short-lived. Argentina's failed attempt to take the Islas Malvinas (Falkland Islands) from Great Britain in 1982 led to the first general election since Perón's, which established a democratic government in this economically beleaguered nation. Political and military jockeying for power continued throughout the 1980s. Despite opposition from former military officers and some of his fellow Peronists, President Carlos Menem's aggressive economic policies slowed inflation and the budget deficit; however, the trade deficit, foreign debt, and the gap between rich and poor kept widening, provoking political shifts and constitutional reform by the mid-nineties.

As soon as she arrived she went straight to the kitchen to see if the monkey was there. It was: What a relief! She wouldn't have liked to admit that her mother had been right. *Monkeys at a birthday?* her mother had sneered. *Get away with you, believing any nonsense you're told!* She was cross, but not because of the monkey, the girl thought; it's just because of the party.

"I don't like you going," she told her. "It's a rich people's party."

"Rich people go to Heaven too," said the girl, who studied religion at school.

"Get away with Heaven," said the mother. "The problem with you, young lady, is that you like to fart higher than your ass."

The girl didn't approve of the way her mother spoke. She was barely   5
nine, and one of the best in her class.

"I'm going because I've been invited," she said. "And I've been invited because Luciana is my friend. So there."

"Ah yes, your friend," her mother grumbled. She paused. "Listen, Rosaura," she said at last. "That one's not your friend. You know what you are to them? The maid's daughter, that's what."

Rosaura blinked hard: She wasn't going to cry. Then she yelled: "Shut up! You know nothing about being friends!"

Every afternoon she used to go to Luciana's house and they would both finish their homework while Rosaura's mother did the cleaning. They had their tea in the kitchen and they told each other secrets. Rosaura loved everything in the big house, and she also loved the people who lived there.

"I'm going because it will be the most lovely party in the whole   10
world, Luciana told me it would. There will be a magician, and he will bring a monkey and everything."

The mother swung around to take a good look at her child, and pompously put her hands on her hips.

"Monkeys at a birthday?" she said. "Get away with you, believing any nonsense you're told!"

Rosaura was deeply offended. She thought it unfair of her mother to accuse other people of being liars simply because they were rich. Rosaura too wanted to be rich, of course. If one day she managed to live in a beautiful palace, would her mother stop loving her? She felt very sad. She wanted to go to that party more than anything else in the world.

"I'll die if I don't go," she whispered, almost without moving her lips.

And she wasn't sure whether she had been heard, but on the morn-   15
ing of the party she discovered that her mother had starched her Christmas dress. And in the afternoon, after washing her hair, her mother

rinsed it in apple vinegar so that it would be all nice and shiny. Before going out, Rosaura admired herself in the mirror, with her white dress and glossy hair, and thought she looked terribly pretty.

Señora Ines also seemed to notice. As soon as she saw her, she said: "How lovely you look today, Rosaura."

Rosaura gave her starched skirt a slight toss with her hands and walked into the party with a firm step. She said hello to Luciana and asked about the monkey. Luciana put on a secretive look and whispered into Rosaura's ear: "He's in the kitchen. But don't tell anyone, because it's a surprise."

Rosaura wanted to make sure. Carefully she entered the kitchen and there she saw it: deep in thought, inside its cage. It looked so funny that the girl stood there for a while, watching it, and later, every so often, she would slip out of the party unseen and go and admire it. Rosaura was the only one allowed into the kitchen. Señora Ines had said: "You yes, but not the others, they're much too boisterous, they might break something." Rosaura had never broken anything. She even managed the jug of orange juice, carrying it from the kitchen into the dining room. She held it carefully and didn't spill a single drop. And Señora Ines had said: "Are you sure you can manage a jug as big as that?" Of course she could manage. She wasn't a butterfingers, like the others. Like that blonde girl with the bow in her hair. As soon as she saw Rosaura, the girl with the bow had said:

"And you? Who are you?"   20

"I'm a friend of Luciana," said Rosaura.

"No," said the girl with the bow, "you are not a friend of Luciana because I'm her cousin and I know all her friends. And I don't know you."

"So what," said Rosaura. "I come here every afternoon with my mother and we do our homework together."

"You and your mother do your homework together?" asked the girl, laughing.

"I and Luciana do our homework together," said Rosaura, very seri-   25
ously.

The girl with the bow shrugged her shoulders.

"That's not being friends," she said. "Do you go to school together?"

"No."

"So where do you know her from?" said the girl, getting impatient.

Rosaura remembered her mother's words perfectly. She took a deep   30
breath.

"I'm the daughter of the employee," she said.

Her mother had said very clearly: "If someone asks, you say you're the daughter of the employee; that's all." She also told her to add: "And proud of it." But Rosaura thought that never in her life would she dare say something of the sort.

"What employee?" said the girl with the bow. "Employee in a shop?"

"No," said Rosaura angrily. "My mother doesn't sell anything in any shop, so there."

"So how come she's an employee?" said the girl with the bow.   35

Just then Señora Ines arrived saying *shh shh*, and asked Rosaura if she wouldn't mind helping serve out the hotdogs, as she knew the house so much better than the others.

"See?" said Rosaura to the girl with the bow, and when no one was looking she kicked her in the shin.

Apart from the girl with the bow, all the others were delightful. The one she liked best was Luciana, with her golden birthday crown; and then the boys. Rosaura won the sack race, and nobody managed to catch her when they played tag. When they split into two teams to play charades, all the boys wanted her for their side. Rosaura felt she had never been so happy in all her life.

But the best was still to come. The best came after Luciana blew out the candles. First the cake. Señora Ines had asked her to help pass the cake around, and Rosaura had enjoyed the task immensely, because everyone called out to her, shouting "Me, me!" Rosaura remembered a story in which there was a queen who had the power of life or death over her subjects. She had always loved that, having the power of life or death. To Luciana and the boys she gave the largest pieces, and to the girl with the bow she gave a slice so thin one could see through it.

After the cake came the magician, tall and bony, with a fine red   40
cape. A true magician: He could untie handkerchiefs by blowing on them and make a chain with links that had no openings. He could guess what cards were pulled out from a pack, and the monkey was his assistant. He called the monkey "partner." "Let's see here, partner," he would say, "turn over a card." And, "Don't run away, partner: Time to work now."

The final trick was wonderful. One of the children had to hold the monkey in his arms and the magician said he would make him disappear.

"What, the boy?" they all shouted.

"No, the monkey!" shouted back the magician.

Rosaura thought that this was truly the most amusing party in the whole world.

The magician asked a small fat boy to come and help, but the small   45
fat boy got frightened almost at once and dropped the monkey on the

floor. The magician picked him up carefully, whispered something in his ear, and the monkey nodded almost as if he understood.

"You mustn't be so unmanly, my friend," the magician said to the fat boy.

"What's unmanly?" said the fat boy.

The magician turned around as if to look for spies.

"A sissy," said the magician. "Go sit down."

Then he stared at all the faces, one by one. Rosaura felt her heart 50 tremble.

"You, with the Spanish eyes," said the magician. And everyone saw that he was pointing at her.

She wasn't afraid. Neither holding the monkey, nor when the magician made him vanish; not even when, at the end, the magician flung his red cape over Rosaura's head and uttered a few magic words . . . and the monkey reappeared, chattering happily, in her arms. The children clapped furiously. And before Rosaura returned to her seat, the magician said:

"Thank you very much, my little countess."

She was so pleased with the compliment that a while later, when her mother came to fetch her, that was the first thing she told her.

"I helped the magician and he said to me, 'Thank you very much, 55 my little countess.'"

It was strange because up to then Rosaura had thought that she was angry with her mother. All along Rosaura had imagined that she would say to her: "See that the monkey wasn't a lie?" But instead she was so thrilled that she told her mother all about the wonderful magician.

Her mother tapped her on the head and said: "So now we're a countess!"

But one could see that she was beaming.

And now they both stood in the entrance, because a moment ago Señora Ines, smiling, had said: "Please wait here a second."

Her mother suddenly seemed worried. 60

"What is it?" she asked Rosaura.

"What is what?" said Rosaura. "It's nothing; she just wants to get the presents for those who are leaving, see?"

She pointed at the fat boy and at a girl with pigtails who were also waiting there, next to their mothers. And she explained about the presents. She knew, because she had been watching those who left before her. When one of the girls was about to leave, Señora Ines would give her a bracelet. When a boy left, Señora Ines gave him a yo-yo. Rosaura preferred the yo-yo because it sparkled, but she didn't mention that to her mother. Her mother might have said: "So why don't you ask for one, you blockhead?" That's what her mother was like. Rosaura didn't feel like explaining that she'd be horribly ashamed to be the odd one out. Instead she said:

"I was the best-behaved at the party."

And she said no more because Señora Ines came out into the hall   65
with two bags, one pink and one blue.

First she went up to the fat boy, gave him a yo-yo out of the blue bag, and the fat boy left with his mother. Then she went up to the girl and gave her a bracelet out of the pink bag, and the girl with the pigtails left as well.

Finally she came up to Rosaura and her mother. She had a big smile on her face and Rosaura liked that. Señora Ines looked down at her, then looked up at her mother, and then said something that made Rosaura proud:

"What a marvelous daughter you have, Herminia."

For an instant, Rosaura thought that she'd give her two presents: the bracelet and the yo-yo. Señora Ines bent down as if about to look for something. Rosaura also leaned forward, stretching out her arm. But she never completed the movement.

Señora Ines didn't look in the pink bag. Nor did she look in the blue   70
bag. Instead she rummaged in her purse. In her hand appeared two bills.

"You really and truly earned this," she said handing them over. "Thank you for all your help, my pet."

Rosaura felt her arms stiffen, stick close to her body, and then she noticed her mother's hand on her shoulder. Instinctively she pressed herself against her mother's body. That was all. Except her eyes. Rosaura's eyes had a cold, clear look that fixed itself on Señora Ines's face.

Señora Ines, motionless, stood there with her hand outstretched. As if she didn't dare draw it back. As if the slightest change might shatter an infinitely delicate balance.

EXPLORATIONS

1. In what senses is Luciana's birthday party a stolen party?

2. At the end of "The Stolen Party," what is the intended message of Señora Ines's gift to Rosaura? What message does Rosaura draw from the gift? What changes occur in the characters' perceptions of each other, and of themselves, in the story's last two paragraphs?

3. Rosaura has a number of standards for judging people — more specifically, for measuring herself against others. For example, in paragraph 5: "The girl

didn't approve of the way her mother spoke. She was barely nine, and one of the best in her class." Find at least four other points in the story when Rosaura makes a comparative judgment. How well does she fare in her own estimation? What do you learn about Rosaura as a character from these judgments?

CONNECTIONS

1. Both Sophronia Liu's "So Tsi-fai" (p. 318) and "The Stolen Party" focus on young people who represent, to themselves or their families or both, ambitions higher than their present circumstances. What disadvantages do So Tsi-fai and Rosaura share? Why does Rosaura appear likely to succeed where So Tsi-fai fails?

2. What similarities do you notice between Rosaura's situation and that of Maya Angelou in "Mary" (p. 281)? How are these two girls' problems, and the solutions they choose, different?

3. What seem to be the goals of Luciana's mother for her daughter's birthday party? How do her goals differ from Luciana's? What seem to be the goals of the mothers in charge of the *quinceañera* in Susan Orlean's "Quinceañera" (p. 40)? How would you guess their goals differ from their daughters?

ELABORATIONS

1. The characters in "The Stolen Party" — particularly the two mother-daughter pairs — all have different concepts of the extent to which they control their own destinies. Write an essay classifying these concepts: Describe each mother's and daughter's sense of herself as a social actor; identify the factors she views as conferring or limiting her power, such as age, intelligence, and social class; and cite the evidence in the story that supports your conclusions.

2. Several writers in this book, including Liliana Heker in "The Stolen Party," Maya Angelou in "Mary," Richard Ford in "Optimists," and James Baldwin in "The New Lost Generation," are concerned with the suffering that comes when youthful innocence ends. In what ways is this suffering due to the young person's ignorance? In what ways is it due to ignorance on the part of the more powerful adults whose world the young person is entering? Write an essay discussing whether and how parents can protect their children from suffering as they enter adulthood. Use evidence from selections such as Heker's, Angelou's, Ford's, and Baldwin's to support your ideas.

AMITAV GHOSH

The Ghosts of Mrs. Gandhi

Amitav Ghosh was born in 1956 in Calcutta, India, the son of a
Hindu diplomat. After completing his M.A. at Delhi University in 1978,
he went to England to study for his doctorate in social anthropology at
Oxford University. A discovery there altered his plans: Among the papers of a group of 12th-century Jewish Tunisians, transferred to Oxford's
archives from a Cairo synagogue, he found references to a local merchant and his Indian slave. Ghosh became so intrigued that he studied
Arabic at the Institut Bourgui des Langues Vivantes in Tunis, enrolled
at the University of Alexandria, and lived among Egyptian farmers in
the village of Lataifa. After completing his Ph.D. at Oxford in 1982 he
returned to India. Having worked as a reporter and editor for *Indian Express*, Ghosh turned seriously to writing fiction; he also became a lecturer in the sociology department at Delhi University. His first novel,
The Circle of Reason, was published in 1986, followed by *The Shadow
Lines* in 1988. That year he also made another trip to Lataifa. Ghosh's
novel *In an Antique Land* (1993) describes his experiences there, in
chapters alternating with his reconstruction of the medieval story of the
merchant and slave — a strategy that reflects his admiration for Herman
Melville's novel *Moby Dick*. "The Ghosts of Mrs. Gandhi," which took
him almost as long to write, appeared in *The New Yorker* in July 1995.

With a third of the area of the United States, India has three times its
population. Indian civilization is among the world's oldest, dating back
more than 5,000 years. Conquerors around 1500 B.C. laid the foundations of the caste system, a hereditary class structure comprising the
Brahman (priests and scholars), the Kshatriya (warriors and rulers), the
Vaisya or Bania (farmers and merchants), and the Sudra (peasants and
laborers); below these were the now illegal Untouchables, who performed the most menial tasks. A thousand years later, Buddhism originated in India. European traders discovered this South Asian peninsula
in the sixteenth century. By 1820, the British had wrested power from
the native rajas, ruling in alliance with the Sikhs, a religious minority
who controlled the north. After World War I, Mohandas Gandhi (called
Mahatma, "great soul") led his people in nonviolent resistance and civil
disobedience. When the region won independence in 1947, it was partitioned into two nations: India (mostly Hindu) and Pakistan (mostly
Muslim). From then until 1989, India's central family was that of its
first prime minister, Jawaharlal Nehru, whose daughter Indira Gandhi
(no relation to Mohandas) succeeded him and was in turn succeeded by

her son Rajiv. The Nehru-Gandhi dynasty ended when Rajiv Gandhi
lost the November 1989 election and was assassinated while campaigning two years later. His successors have faced an electorate that is more
assertive and more impatient, a new divergence between state and society, increasing clashes between Hindus, Sikhs, and Muslims, and ongoing tensions between India and its neighbors, particularly Pakistan.

Nowhere else in the world did the year 1984 fulfill its apocalyptic
portents as it did in India. Separatist violence in the Punjab; the military attack on the great Sikh temple of Amritsar; the assassination of the
Prime Minister, Mrs. Indira Gandhi; riots in several cities; the gas disaster in Bhopal — and the events followed relentlessly on each other.
There were days in 1984 when it took courage to open the New Delhi
papers in the morning.

Of the year's many catastrophes, the sectarian violence following
Mrs. Gandhi's death had the greatest effect on my life. Looking back, I
see that the experiences of that period were profoundly important to my
development as a writer; so much so that I have never attempted to
write about them until now.

At the time, I was living in a part of New Delhi called Defence
Colony — a neighborhood of large, labyrinthine houses, with little self-
contained warrens of servants' rooms tucked away on rooftops and
above garages. When I lived there, those rooms had come to house a
floating population of the young and straitened — journalists, copywrit-
ers, minor executives, and university people like myself. We battened
upon this wealthy enclave like mites in a honeycomb, spreading from
rooftop to rooftop, our ramshackle lives curtained from our landlords by
chiffon-draped washing lines and thickets of TV aerials.

I was twenty-eight. The city I considered home was Calcutta, but
New Delhi was where I had spent all my adult life except for a few years
away in England and Egypt. I had returned to India two years before,
upon completing a doctorate at Oxford, and recently found a teaching
job at Delhi University. But it was in the privacy of my baking rooftop
hutch that my real life was lived. I was writing my first novel, in the classic fashion, perched in a garret.

On the morning of October 31st, the day of Mrs. Gandhi's death, I   5
caught a bus to Delhi University, as usual, at about half past nine. From
where I lived, it took an hour and a half: a long commute, but not an
exceptional one for New Delhi. The assassination had occurred shortly
before, just a few miles away, but I had no knowledge of this when I

boarded the bus. Nor did I notice anything untoward at any point during the ninety-minute journey. But the news, traveling by word of mouth, raced my bus to the university.

When I walked into the grounds, I saw not the usual boisterous, Frisbee-throwing crowd of students but small groups of people standing intently around transistor radios. A young man detached himself from one of the huddles and approached me, his mouth twisted into the tight-lipped knowing smile that seems always to accompany the gambit "Have you heard . . . ?"

The campus was humming, he said. No one knew for sure, but it was being said that Mrs. Gandhi had been shot. The word was that she had been assassinated by two Sikh bodyguards, in revenge for her having sent troops to raid the Sikhs' Golden Temple of Amritsar earlier that year.

Just before stepping into the lecture room, I heard a report on All India Radio, the national network: Mrs. Gandhi has been rushed to hospital after an attempted assassination.

Nothing stopped: The momentum of the daily routine carried things forward. I went into a classroom and began my lecture, but not many students had shown up and those who had were distracted and distant; there was a lot of fidgeting.

Halfway through the class, I looked out through the room's single,   10 slit-like window. The sunlight lay bright on the lawn below and on the trees beyond. It was the time of year when Delhi was at its best, crisp and cool, its abundant greenery freshly watered by the recently re-treated monsoons, its skies washed sparkling clean. By the time I turned back, I had forgotten what I was saying and had to reach for my notes.

My unsteadiness surprised me. I was not an uncritical admirer of Mrs. Gandhi. Her brief period of semi-dictatorial rule in the mid-seventies was still alive in my memory. But the ghastliness of her murder was a sudden reminder of the very real qualities that had been taken for granted: her fortitude, her dignity, her physical courage, her endurance.

Yet it was not just grief I felt at that moment. Rather, it was a sense of something slipping loose, of a mooring coming untied somewhere within.

The first reliable report of Mrs. Gandhi's death was broadcast from Karachi, by Pakistan's official radio network, at around 1:30 P.M. On All India Radio, regular broadcasts had been replaced by music.

I left the university in the late afternoon with a friend, Hari Sen, who lived at the other end of the city. I needed to make a long-distance phone call, and he had offered to let me use his family's telephone.

To get to Hari's house, we had to change buses at Connaught Place,   15 the elegant circular arcade that lies at the geographical heart of Delhi, linking the old city with the new. As the bus swung around the periphery of the arcade, I noticed that the shops, stalls, and eateries were beginning to shut down, even though it was still afternoon.

Our next bus was not quite full, which was unusual. Just as it was pulling out, a man ran out of an office and jumped on. He was middle-aged and dressed in shirt and trousers, evidently an employee in one of the nearby government buildings. He was a Sikh, but I scarcely noticed this at the time.

He probably jumped on without giving the matter any thought, this being his regular, daily bus. But, as it happened, on this day no choice could have been more unfortunate, for the route of the bus went past the hospital when Indira Gandhi's body then lay. Certain loyalists in her party had begun inciting the crowds gathered there to seek revenge. The motorcade of Giani Zail Singh, the President of the Republic, a Sikh, had already been attacked by a mob.

None of this was known to us then, and we would never have suspected it: Violence had never been directed at the Sikhs in Delhi.

As the bus made its way down New Delhi's broad, tree-lined avenues, official-looking cars, with outriders and escorts, overtook us, speeding toward the hospital. As we drew nearer, it became evident that a large number of people had gathered there. But this was no ordinary crowd: It seemed to consist mostly of red-eyed young men in half-unbuttoned shirts. It was now that I noticed that my Sikh fellow-passenger was showing signs of increasing anxiety, sometimes standing to look out, sometimes glancing out the door. It was too late to get off the bus; thugs were everywhere.

The bands of young men grew more and more menacing as we ap-   20 proached the hospital. There was a watchfulness about them; some were armed with steel rods and bicycle chains; others had fanned out across the busy road and were stopping cars and buses.

A stout woman in a sari sitting across the aisle from me was the first to understand what was going on. Rising to her feet, she gestured urgently to the Sikh, who was sitting hunched in his seat. She hissed at him in Hindi, telling him to get down and keep out of sight.

The man started in surprise and squeezed himself into the narrow footspace between the seats. Minutes later, our bus was intercepted by a group of young men wearing bright, sharp synthetics. Several had bicycle chains wrapped around their wrists. They ran along beside the bus as it slowed to a halt. We heard them call out to the driver through the open door, asking if there were any Sikhs on the bus.

The driver shook his head. No, he said, there were no Sikhs on the bus.

A few rows ahead of me, the crouching, turbaned figure had gone completely still.

Outside, some of the young men were jumping up to look through   25
the windows, asking if there were any Sikhs on the bus. There was no anger in their voices; that was the most chilling thing of all.

No, someone said, and immediately other voices picked up the refrain. Soon all the passengers were shaking their heads and saying, No, no, let us go now, we have to get home.

Eventually, the thugs stepped back and waved us through.

Nobody said a word as we sped away down Ring Road.

Hari Sen lived in one of New Delhi's recently developed residential colonies. It was called Safdarjang Enclave, and it was neatly and solidly middle-class, a neighborhood of aspirations rather than opulence. Like most such New Delhi suburbs, the area had a mixed population: Sikhs were well represented.

A long street ran from end to end of the neighborhood, like the spine   30
of a comb, with parallel side streets running off it. Hari lived at the end of one of those streets, in a fairly typical, big, one-story bungalow. The house next door, however, was much grander and uncharacteristically daring in design. An angular structure, it was perched rakishly on stilts. Mr. Bawa, the owner, was an elderly Sikh who had spent a long time abroad, working with various international organizations. For several years, he had resided in Southeast Asia; thus the stilts.

Hari lived with his family in a household so large and eccentric that it had come to be known among his friends as Macondo, after Gabriel García Márquez's magical village. On this occasion, however, only his mother and teenage sister were at home. I decided to stay over.

It was a very bright morning. When I stepped into the sunshine, I came upon a sight that I could never have imagined. In every direction, columns of smoke rose slowly into a limpid sky. Sikh houses and businesses were burning. The fires were so carefully targeted that they created an effect quite different from that of a general conflagration: It was like looking upward into the vault of some vast pillared hall.

The columns of smoke increased in number even as I stood outside watching. Some fires were burning a short distance away. I spoke to a passerby and learned that several nearby Sikh houses had been looted and set on fire that morning. The mob had started at the far end of the colony and was working its way in our direction. Hindus and Muslims who had sheltered or defended Sikhs were also being attacked; their houses, too, were being looted and burned.

It was still and quiet, eerily so. The usual sounds of rush-hour traffic were absent. But every so often we heard a speeding car or a motorcycle on the main street. Later, we discovered that these mysterious speeding vehicles were instrumental in directing the carnage that was taking place. Protected by certain politicians, "organizers" were zooming around the city, assembling "mobs" and transporting them to Sikh-owned houses and shops.

Apparently, the transportation was provided free. A civil-rights report   35 published shortly afterward stated that this phase of the violence "began with the arrival of groups of armed young people in tempo vans, scooters, motorcycles, or trucks," and went on to say, "With cans of petrol they went around the localities and systematically set fire to Sikh houses, shops, and gurdwaras. . . . The targets were primarily young Sikhs. They were dragged out, beaten up, and then burnt alive. . . . In all the affected spots, a calculated attempt to terrorize the people was evident in the common tendency among the assailants to burn alive the Sikhs on public roads."

Fire was everywhere; it was the day's motif. Throughout the city, Sikh houses were being looted and then set on fire, often with their occupants still inside.

A survivor — a woman who lost her husband and three sons — offered the following account to Veena Das, a Delhi sociologist: "Some people, the neighbors, one of my relatives, said it would be better if we hid in an abandoned house nearby. So my husband took our three sons and hid there. We locked the house from outside, but there was treachery in people's hearts. Someone must have told the crowd. They baited him to come out. Then they poured kerosene on that house. They burnt them alive. When I went there that night, the bodies of my sons were on the loft — huddled together."

Over the next few days, some 2,500 people died in Delhi alone. Thousands more died in other cities. The total death toll will never be known. The dead were overwhelmingly Sikh men. Entire neighborhoods were gutted; tens of thousands of people were left homeless.

Like many other members of my generation, I grew up believing that mass slaughter of the kind that accompanied the Partition of India and Pakistan, in 1947, could never happen again. But that morning, in the city of Delhi, the violence had reached the same level of intensity.

As Hari and I stood staring into the smoke-streaked sky, Mrs. Sen,   40
Hari's mother, was thinking about matters closer at hand. She was
about fifty, a tall, graceful woman with a gentle, soft-spoken manner. In
an understated way, she was also deeply religious, a devout Hindu.
When she heard what was happening, she picked up the phone and
called Mr. and Mrs. Bawa, the elderly Sikh couple next door, to let
them know that they were welcome to come over. She met with an unexpected response: an awkward silence. Mrs. Bawa thought she was joking, and wasn't sure whether to be amused or not.

Toward midday, Mrs. Sen received a phone call: The mob was now
in the immediate neighborhood, advancing systematically from street to
street. Hari decided that it was time to go over and have a talk with the
Bawas. I went along.

Mr. Bawa proved to be a small, slight man. Although he was casually
dressed, his turban was neatly tied and his beard was carefully combed
and bound. He was puzzled by our visit. After a polite greeting, he
asked what he could do for us. It fell to Hari to explain.

Mr. Bawa had heard about Indira Gandhi's assassination, of course,
and he knew that there had been some trouble. But he could not understand why these "disturbances" should impinge on him or his wife.
He had no more sympathy for the Sikh terrorists than we did; his revulsion at the assassination was, if anything, even greater than ours. Not
only was his commitment to India and the Indian state absolute but it
was evident from his bearing that he belonged to the country's ruling
élite.

How do you explain to someone who has spent a lifetime cocooned
in privilege that a potentially terminal rent has appeared in the wrap-
pings? We found ourselves faltering. Mr. Bawa could not bring himself
to believe that a mob might attack him.

By the time we left, it was Mr. Bawa who was mouthing reassur-   45
ances. He sent us off with jovial pats on our backs. He did not actually
say "Buck up," but his manner said it for him.

We were confident that the government would soon act to stop
the violence. In India, there is a drill associated with civil disturbances: A curfew is declared; paramilitary units are deployed; in extreme cases, the Army marches to the stricken areas. No city in India
is better equipped to perform this drill than New Delhi, with its huge
security apparatus. We later learned that in some cities — Calcutta,
for example — the state authorities did act promptly to prevent violence. But in New Delhi — and in much of northern India — hour
followed hour without response. Every few minutes, we turned to
the radio, hoping to hear that the Army had been ordered out. All

we heard was mournful music and descriptions of Mrs. Gandhi's
lying in state; of the comings and goings of dignitaries, foreign and
national. The bulletins could have been messages from another
planet.

As the afternoon progressed, we continued to hear reports of the
mob's steady advance. Before long, it had reached the next alley: We
could hear the voices; the smoke was everywhere. There was still no
sign of the Army or the police.

Hari again called Mr. Bawa, and now, with the flames visible from
his windows, he was more receptive. He agreed to come over with his
wife, just for a short while. But there was a problem: How? The two
properties were separated by a shoulder-high wall, so it was impossible
to walk from one house to the other except along the street.

I spotted a few of the thugs already at the end of the street. We
could hear the occasional motorcycle, cruising slowly up and down.
The Bawas could not risk stepping out into the street. They would
be seen: The sun had dipped low in the sky, but it was still light. Mr.
Bawa balked at the thought of climbing over the wall: It seemed an
insuperable obstacle at his age. But eventually Hari persuaded him to
try.

We went to wait for them at the back of the Sens' house — in a spot   50
that was well sheltered from the street. The mob seemed terrifyingly
close, the Bawas reckless in their tardiness. A long time passed before
the elderly couple finally appeared, hurrying toward us.

Mr. Bawa had changed before leaving the house: He was neatly
dressed, dapper, even — in blazer and cravat. Mrs. Bawa, a small, ma-
tronly woman, was dressed in a *salwar* and *kameez*. Their cook was with
them, and it was with his assistance that they made it over the wall. The
cook, who was Hindu, then returned to stand guard.

Hari led the Bawas into the drawing room, where Mrs. Sen was waiting, dressed in a chiffon sari. The room was large and well appointed,
its walls hung with a rare and beautiful set of miniatures. With the curtains now drawn and the lamps lit, it was warm and welcoming. But all
that lay between us and the mob in the street was a row of curtained
French windows and a garden wall.

Mrs. Sen greeted the elderly couple with folded hands as they came
in. The three seated themselves in an intimate circle, and soon a silver
tea tray appeared. Instantly, all constraint evaporated, and, to the tin-
kling of porcelain, the conversation turned to the staples of New Delhi
drawing-room chatter.

I could not bring myself to sit down. I stood in the corridor, distracted, looking outside through the front entrance.

A couple of scouts on motorcycles had drawn up next door. They   55
had dismounted and were inspecting the house, walking in among the
concrete stilts, looking up into the house. Somehow they got wind of
the cook's presence and called him out.

The cook was very frightened. He was surrounded by thugs thrusting
knives in his face and shouting questions. It was dark, and some were
carrying kerosene torches. Wasn't it true, they shouted, that his employers were Sikhs? Where were they? Were they hiding inside? Who
owned the house — Hindus or Sikhs?

Hari and I hid behind the wall between the two houses and listened
to the interrogation. Our fates depended on this lone, frightened man.
We had no idea what he would do: of how secure the Bawas were of his
loyalties, or whether he might seek revenge for some past slight by revealing their whereabouts. If he did, both houses would burn.

Although stuttering in terror, the cook held his own. Yes, he said, yes,
his employers were Sikhs, but they'd left town; there was no one in the
house. No, the house didn't belong to them; they were renting from a
Hindu.

He succeeded in persuading most of the thugs, but a few eyed the
surrounding houses suspiciously. Some appeared at the steel gates in
front of us, rattling the bars.

We went up and positioned ourselves at the gates. I remember a   60
strange sense of disconnection as I walked down the driveway, as
though I were watching myself from somewhere very distant.

We took hold of the gates and shouted back: Get away! You have no
business here! There's no one inside! The house is empty!

To our surprise, they began to drift away, one by one.

Just before this, I had stepped into the house to see how Mrs. Sen
and the Bawas were faring. The thugs were clearly audible in the lamp-
lit drawing room; only a thin curtain shielded the interior from their
view.

My memory of what I saw in the drawing room is uncannily vivid.
Mrs. Sen had a slight smile on her face as she poured a cup of tea for
Mr. Bawa. Beside her, Mrs. Bawa, in a firm, unwavering voice, was
comparing the domestic help situations in New Delhi and Manila.

I was awed by their courage.   65

The next morning, I heard about a protest that was being organized
at the large compound of a relief agency. When I arrived, a meeting
was already under way, a gathering of seventy or eighty people.

The mood was somber. Some of the people spoke of neighborhoods
that had been taken over by vengeful mobs. They described countless

murders — mainly by setting the victims alight — as well as terrible destruction: the burning of Sikh temples, the looting of Sikh schools, the razing of Sikh homes and shops. The violence was worse than I had imagined. It was decided that the most effective initial tactic would be to march into one of the badly affected neighborhoods and confront the rioters directly.

The group had grown to about 150 men and women, among them Swami Agnivesh, a Hindu ascetic; Ravi Chopra, a scientist and environmentalist; and a handful of opposition politicians, including Chandra Shekhar, who became Prime Minister for a brief period several years later.

The group was pitifully small by the standards of a city where crowds of several hundred thousand were routinely mustered for political activities. Nevertheless, the members rose to their feet and began to march.

Years before, I had read a passage by V. S. Naipaul which has stayed   70
with me ever since. I have never been able to find it again, so this account is from memory. In his incomparable prose Naipaul describes a demonstration. He is in a hotel room, somewhere in Africa or South America; he looks down and sees people marching past. To his surprise, the sight fills him with an obscure longing, a kind of melancholy; he is aware of a wish to go out, to join, to merge his concerns with theirs. Yet he knows he never will; it is simply not in his nature to join crowds.

For many years, I read everything of Naipaul's I could lay my hands on; I couldn't have enough of him. I read him with the intimate, appalled attention that one reserves for one's most skillful interlocutors. It was he who first made it possible for me to think of myself as a writer, working in English.

I remembered that passage because I believed that I, too, was not a joiner, and in Naipaul's pitiless mirror I thought I had seen an aspect of myself rendered visible. Yet as this forlorn little group marched out of the shelter of the compound I did not hesitate for a moment: Without a second thought, I joined.

The march headed first for Lajpat Nagar, a busy commercial area a mile or so away. I knew the area. Though it was in New Delhi, its streets resembled the older parts of the city, where small, cramped shops tended to spill out onto the footpaths.

We were shouting slogans as we marched: hoary Gandhian staples of peace and brotherhood from half a century before. Then, suddenly, we were confronted with a starkly familiar spectacle, an image of twentieth-century urban horror: burned-out cars, their ransacked interiors visible through smashed windows; debris and rubble everywhere. Blackened pots had been strewn along the street. A cinema had been gutted, and the charred faces of film stars stared out at us from half-burned posters.

As I think back to that march, my memory breaks down, details dis-   75
solve. I recently telephoned some friends who had been there. Their
memories are similar to mine in only one respect: They, too, clung to
one scene while successfully ridding their minds of the rest.

The scene my memory preserved is of a moment when it seemed inevitable that we would be attacked.

Rounding a corner, we found ourselves facing a crowd that was
larger and more determined-looking than any other crowds we had encountered. On each previous occasion, we had prevailed by marching
at the thugs and engaging them directly, in dialogues that turned
quickly into extended shouting matches. In every instance, we had
succeeded in facing them down. But this particular mob was intent
on confrontation. As its members advanced on us, brandishing knives
and steel rods, we stopped. Our voices grew louder as they came toward
us; a kind of rapture descended on us, exhilaration in anticipation of a
climax. We braced for the attack, leaning forward as though into a
wind.

And then something happened that I have never completely understood. Nothing was said; there was no signal, nor was there any break in
the rhythm of our chanting. But suddenly all the women in our
group — and the women made up more than half of the group's numbers — stepped out and surrounded the men; their saris and *kameezes*
became a thin, fluttering barrier, a wall around us. They turned to face
the approaching men, challenging them, daring them to attack.

The thugs took a few more steps toward us and then faltered, confused. A moment later, they were gone.

. . .The Bosnian writer Dzevad Karahasan, in a remarkable essay   80
called "Literature and War" (published last year in his collection *Sarajevo, Exodus of a City*), makes a startling connection between modern
literary aesthetics and the contemporary world's indifference to violence: "The decision to perceive literally everything as an aesthetic phenomenon — completely sidestepping questions about goodness and
truth — is an artistic decision. That decision started in the realm of art,
and went on to become characteristic of the contemporary world."

When I went back to my desk in November of 1984, I found myself
confronting decisions about writing that I had never faced before. How
was I to write about what I had seen without reducing it to a mere spectacle? My next novel was bound to be influenced by my experiences,
but I could see no way of writing directly about those events without recreating them as a panorama of violence — "an aesthetic phenomenon," as Karahasan was to call it. At the time, the idea seemed obscene

and futile; of much greater importance were factual reports of the testimony of the victims. But these were already being done by people who were, I knew, more competent that I could be.

Within a few months, I started my novel, which I eventually called *The Shadow Lines* — a book that led me backward in time, to earlier memories of riots, ones witnessed in childhood. It became a book not about any one event but about the meaning of such events and their effects on the individuals who live through them.

And until now I have never really written about what I saw in November of 1984. I am not alone: Several others who took part in that march went on to publish books, yet nobody, as far as I know, has ever written about it except in passing.

There are good reasons for this, not least the politics of the situation, which leave so little room for the writer. The riots were generated by a cycle of violence, involving the terrorists in the Punjab, on the one hand, and the Indian government, on the other. To write carelessly, in such a way as to appear to endorse terrorism or repression, can add easily to the problem: In such incendiary circumstances, words cost lives, and it is only appropriate that those who deal in words should pay scrupulous attention to what they say. It is only appropriate that they should find themselves inhibited.

But there is also a simpler explanation. Before I could set down a   85
word, I had to resolve a dilemma, between being a writer and being a citizen. As a writer, I had only one obvious subject: the violence. From the news report, or the latest film or novel, we have come to expect the bloody detail or the elegantly staged conflagration that closes a chapter or effects a climax. But it is worth asking if the very obviousness of this subject arises out of our modern conventions of representation; within the dominant aesthetic of our time — the aesthetic of what Karahasan calls "indifference" — it is all too easy to present violence as an apocalyptic spectacle, while the resistance to it can as easily figure as mere sentimentality, or, worse, as pathetic or absurd.

Writers don't join crowds — Naipaul and so many others teach us that. But what do you do when the constitutional authority fails to act? You join and in joining bear all the responsibilities and obligations and guilt that joining represents. My experience of the violence was overwhelmingly and memorably of the resistance to it. When I think of the women staring down the mob, I am not filled with a writerly wonder. I am reminded of my gratitude for being saved from injury. What I saw at first hand — and not merely on that march but on the bus, in Hari's house, in [a refugee] compound that filled with essential goods — was not the horror of violence but the affirmation of humanity: In each case, I witnessed the risks that perfectly ordinary people were willing to take for one another.

When I now read descriptions of troubled parts of the world, in which violence appears primordial and inevitable, a fate to which masses of people are largely resigned, I find myself asking, Is that all there was to it? Or is it possible that the authors of these descriptions failed to find a form — or a style or a voice or a plot — that could accommodate both violence *and* the civilized, willed response to it?

The truth is that the commonest response to violence is one of repugnance, and that a significant number of people everywhere try to oppose it in whatever ways they can. That these efforts so rarely appear in accounts of violence is not surprising: They are too undramatic. For those who participate in them, they are often hard to write about for the very reasons that so long delayed my own account of 1984.

"Let us not fool ourselves," Karahasan writes. "The world is written first — the holy books say that it was created in words — and all that happens in it, happens in language first."

It is when we think of the world the aesthetic of indifference might   90
bring into being that we recognize the urgency of remembering the stories we have not written.

EXPLORATIONS

1. In paragraph 11 Amitav Ghosh gives a brief description of Indian Prime Minister Indira Gandhi. How do the qualities he mentions relate to his essay's title? Who or what are the "ghosts"?

2. What specific incidents in the wake of Gandhi's assassination are turning points for Ghosh? How is he changed by each incident?

3. Which other characters in Ghosh's narrative are changed by the events he describes, and in what ways?

CONNECTIONS

1. Mr. and Mrs. Bawa in "The Ghosts of Mrs. Gandhi," like Señora Ines and Luciana in "The Stolen Party" (p. 323), have "spent a lifetime cocooned in privilege" (para. 44). How does that fact cause each of these characters to make a naive and unrealistic choice? Which choices pay off, and why? Which ones do not pay off, and why?

2. In what ways is the Sikhs' predicament in "The Ghosts of Mrs. Gandhi" similar to that of the Muslims in "Sarajevo Diary" (p. 210)? In what ways are these two groups' predicaments different?

3. Ghosh quotes the Bosnian writer Dzevad Karahasan on "the decision to perceive literally everything as an aesthetic phenomenon — completely sidestepping questions about goodness and truth" (para. 80). How does Karahasan's (and Ghosh's) point apply to the story James Baldwin relates in paragraphs 1–13 of "The New Lost Generation" (p. 18)?

ELABORATIONS

1. "The Ghosts of Mrs. Gandhi," Liliana Heker's "The Stolen Party" (p. 323), Zlata Filipović's "Sarajevo Diary" (p. 210), and several other selections in this book show people clinging to the belief that their environment is safe and friendly despite mounting evidence to the contrary. At what point does faith become folly? On the other hand, at what point does caution become paranoia? Is it worse to live in ignorance or in fear? Choose two or more selections that raise these issues. Write an essay in which you either address these questions, using the characters' experiences as evidence for your conclusions, or compare and contrast the characters' reasons for trusting in their security, the signs that this security is illusory, the points at which the characters should and do realize that they are in danger, and the price they would pay for reaching that realization sooner (or later).

2. "It is when we think of the world the aesthetic of indifference might bring into being that we recognize the urgency of remembering the stories we have not written" (para. 90). What does Ghosh mean? Have you ever read (or seen on television) a true story that you felt should not have been written and made public? Have you ever had an experience like Ghosh's, one that you couldn't forget but also couldn't write about? How does Ghosh's statement about the aesthetic of indifference, and the points he makes leading up to it, apply to life in the contemporary United States? Write an essay arguing for or against Ghosh's declaration on the basis of your own experience and beliefs.

NADINE GORDIMER

Where Do Whites Fit In?

Born in a small gold-mining town in South Africa in 1923, Nadine
Gordimer is an outspoken civil libertarian who has always believed that
change in her country's policies is best spurred from within. Her writing — much of it focusing on the impact of apartheid on South Africans — is renowned around the world. Gordimer started writing in
childhood; she was educated at a convent school and Witwatersrand
University but gives most credit to her local library. Her novels, short
stories, and essays have won her numerous awards and honorary degrees.
She has contributed to many American magazines, including *The New
Yorker, Harper's, The Atlantic Monthly,* and *The New York Review of
Books,* as well as taught creative writing at Columbia University's Graduate School of the Arts. In 1978 she was elected an honorary member of
the American Academy and Institute of Arts and Letters; in 1991 she became the first South African to win the Nobel Prize for literature.
Gordimer currently lives with her family in Johannesburg. Her novels
include *The Conservationist* (1974), *July's People* (1981), *A Sport of Nature* (1987), and *None to Accompany Me* (1994). In her 1995 book *Writing and Being,* drawn from a lecture series at Harvard University, she
considers not only her fellow South African writers but Naguib Mahfouz of Egypt (see p. 480), Chinua Achebe of Nigeria (see p. 599), and
Amos Oz of Israel (see p. 188). The book's final sentences make a fitting
postscript for "Where Do Whites Fit In?" (which first appeared in 1959
in *Twentieth Century*): "My country is the world, whole, a synthesis. I
am no longer a colonial. I may now speak of 'my people.'"

Covering Africa's southern tip, the Republic of South Africa is about
twice the size of Texas. The region's Khoisan tribes — formerly known
as Bushmen and Hottentots — had been joined by Bantus from the
north by the time Dutch settlers arrived in the seventeenth century.
Racial and political conflicts began when the British seized the Cape of
Good Hope in 1806. At that time many Dutch moved north and
founded two new republics, the Transvaal and the Orange Free State,
displacing native Khoisan and Bantu tribes. Whites of Dutch descent
became known as Afrikaners and their language as Afrikaans. They and
their white compatriots kept political control by means of *apartheid,* a
policy of racial separation that severely limited blacks' access to jobs,
housing, income, and influence. Asians (mostly Indians) and Coloureds
(those of mixed descent) also were shut out of power, but less repres-
sively than the majority black population. Conflict intensified when diamonds and gold were discovered in the late 1800s. The ensuing Anglo-

Boer (British versus Dutch) War was won by the British, who created the Union of South Africa in 1910. In 1948 apartheid became official, legally enforcing racially separate development and residential areas. In 1961, with only whites allowed to vote, South African voters withdrew their nation from the British Commonwealth; in the late 1980s, Asians and Coloureds received the right to vote (with restrictions), and laws banning interracial marriage were repealed. In 1994, after decades of pressure from Nelson Mandela and other members of the African National Congress (ANC), as well as an international community of allies including writers like Gordimer, free multiracial elections were held in South Africa for the first time. Mandela became president; for more information on him and his country, see page 688.

Where do whites fit in in the New Africa? *Nowhere,* I'm inclined to say, in my gloomier and least courageous moods; and I do believe that it is true that even the gentlest and most westernized Africans would like the emotional idea of the continent entirely without the complication of the presence of the white man for a generation or two. But *nowhere,* as an answer for us whites, is in the same category as remarks like *What's the use of living?* in the face of threat of atomic radiation. We are living; we are in Africa. *Nowhere* is the desire to avoid painful processes and accept an ultimate and final solution (which doesn't exist in the continuous process that is life itself); the desire to have over and done with; the death wish, if not of the body, at least of the spirit.

For if we're going to fit in at all in the new Africa, it's going to be sideways, where-we-can, wherever-they'll-shift-up-for-us. This will not be comfortable; indeed, it will be hardest of all for those of us (I am one myself) who want to belong in the new Africa as we never could in the old, where our skin-color labeled us as oppressors to the blacks and our views labeled us as traitors to the whites. We want merely to be ordinary members of a multi-colored, any-colored society, freed both of the privileges and the guilt of the white sins of our fathers. This seems to us perfectly reasonable and possible and, in terms of reason, it is. But belonging to a society implies two factors which are outside reason: the desire to belong, on the one part, and acceptance, on the other part. The new Africa may, with luck, grant us our legal rights, full citizenship, and the vote, but I don't think it will accept us in the way we're hankering after. If ever, it will take the confidence of several generations of jealous independence before Africa will feel that she can let us belong.

There is nothing so damaging to the ego as an emotional rebuff of this kind. (More bearable by far the hate-engendered hate that the apartheiders must expect.) And you don't have to be particularly thin-skinned in order to feel this rebuff coming in Africa. Africans are prick-ling with the desire to be off on their own; the very fact that you wel-come the new Africa almost as fervently as they do seems an intrusion in itself. They have had so much of us — let's not go through the whole list again, from tear-gas and taxes to brotherly advice — that all they crave is to have no part of us.

You'll understand that I'm not speaking in economic or even polit-ical, but purely in human or, if you prefer it, psychological terms. For the purposes of what I have to say it may be true that in South Africa, for example, foreign capital and skills would have to be retained, in order to keep the mines and industry going, by wide concessions given by any black independent government with its head screwed on the right way. But the fact that we might go on living in our comfortable houses in the suburbs of Johannesburg under a black republic just as we do under a white near-republic, does not mean that we should feel ourselves accepted as part of the homogeneous society of the new Africa. For a long time to come any white South African must expect to find any black man, from any African territory, considered by the black South African as more of a brother than the white South African him-self. No personal bonds of loyalty, friendship, or even love will change this; it is a nationalism of the heart that has been brought about by suf-fering. There is no share in it we can hope to have. I for one can read this already in the faces, voices, and eloquently regretful but firm hand-clasps of my own African friends.

Make no mistake, those moderate African political leaders who offer   5
us whites — with sincerity, I believe — full participation in the new life of Africa offer us only the tangibles of existence. The intangibles that make up emotional participation and the sense of belonging cannot be legislated for.

What are we to do? Shall we go? Shall we leave Africa? For those small white communities who are truly foreign to the African territories in which they live, "sent out" from a homeland in Europe for a spell of duty on administrative jobs or as representatives of commercial firms, there can't be much question of staying on. But in those territories, such as South Africa and the Rhodesias, where there is a sizable and set-tled white population whose *home* is Africa, there is no easy answer; sometimes, it seems no answer at all. I do not attempt to speak, of course, for the stubborn mass that will continue, like a Napoleon in a madhouse, to see itself as the undisputed master and make no attempt to consider the reality of living another role. I do not even try to guess what will happen to them; what *can* happen to them in a situation that they find unthinkable. I can only fear that events will deal with them grimly, as events usually do with people who refuse to think. I speak for people like myself, who think almost too much about the whole business and hope to arrive at an honest answer, without self-pity for the whites or sentiment about the blacks.

Some of us in South Africa want to leave; a few of us have gone already. And certainly, when one comes to Europe on a visit, one becomes a little uneasy at the number of friends (well-informed friends with a good perspective on the swerves and lurches of the way the world is going) who take one aside and ask whether one isn't planning to leave Africa? Which brings me to the reasons why some people have left and why these friends in Europe think one should pack up, too. A few have left because they cannot bear the guilt and ugliness of the white man's easy lot here; a few have left because they are afraid of the black man; and most, I should say, have left because of a combination of the two. I doubt if any consciously have left for the long-term reason I have elaborated here — the growing unwelcomeness of the white man in Africa. Yet I feel that if the white man's lot were to become no better and no worse than anyone else's tomorrow and the fear of violence at the hands of the black man (which we all have) were to have been brought to the test and disproved, unwelcomeness might still remain as the factor that would, in the end, decide many of us to give up our home and quit Africa.

I myself fluctuate between the desire to be gone — to find a society for myself where my white skin will have no bearing on my place in the community — and a terrible, obstinate, and fearful desire to stay. I feel the one desire with my head and the other with my guts. I know that there must be many others who feel as I do, and who realize that generally the head is the more sensible guide of the two. Those of us who stay will need to have the use of our heads in order to sustain the emotional decision that home is not necessarily where you belong ethnogenically, but rather the place you were born to, the faces you first saw around you, and the elements of the situation among your fellow men in which you found yourself and with which you have been struggling, politically, personally, or artistically, all your life.

The white man who wants to fit in in the new Africa must learn a number of hard things. He'd do well to regard himself as an immigrant to a new country; somewhere he has never lived before, but to whose life he has committed himself. He'll have to forget the old impulses to leadership, and the temptation to give advice backed by the experience and culture of Western civilization — Africa is going through a stage when it passionately prefers its own mistakes to successes (or mistakes) that are not its own. This is an absolutely necessary stage in all political, sociological, and spiritual growth, but it is an uncomfortable and disillusioning one to live through. And giving up the impulse to advise and interfere and offer to resume responsibility may not be as easy as we whites think. Even those of us who don't want to be boss (or *baas*, rather) have become used to being bossy. We've been used to assuming leadership or at least tutorship, even if it's only been in liberal campaigns to secure the rights of the Africans to vote and speak for themselves. Out of our very concern to see Africans make a go of the new Africa, we may — indeed, I know we shall — be tempted to offer guidance when we haven't been consulted. The facts that we'll be well-meaning and that the advice may be good and badly-needed do not count; the sooner we drum that into our egos the better. What counts is the need of Africa to acquire confidence through the experience of picking itself up, dusting itself down, and starting all over again; and the quickening marvel of often getting things right into the bargain.

It's hard to sit quiet when you think you can tell how a problem may   10
be solved or a goal accomplished, but it may be even harder to give help without recriminations or, worse, smugness when it is sought. If we want to fit in anywhere in Africa, that is what we'll have to teach ourselves to do; answer up, cheerfully and willingly, when we're called upon and shut up when we're not. Already I notice that the only really happy whites I know in Africa — the only ones who are at peace with themselves over their place in the community — are some South African friends of mine who have gone to live in Ghana, and who have an educational job to do on contract from the government. They are living as equals among the Africans, they have no say in the affairs of the country for the Africans to resent, and they are contributing something useful and welcome to the development of Africa. In other words, they are in the position of foreign experts, employed at the government's pleasure. I can positively feel my fellow-whites in Africa swelling with indignance at this extreme picture of the white man's future life on the continent; and it makes me feel rather indignant myself. But I think we've got to accept the home truth of the picture, whether we like it or not, and whether or not what we see there seems fair. All that the new Africa will really want from us will be what we can give as "foreign experts" — the technical, scientific, and cultural knowledge that white civilization has acquired many hundreds of years before black civilization, and on which, whether the Africans like it or not, their own aspirations are based.

I suppose we may get over being a minority minority instead of the majority minority we've been used to being all these past years, but I don't know whether that valuable change of attitude will actually bring us much nearer the integration we seek. Will intermarriage help us? It would, of course, on a large scale, but personally I don't believe that it will happen on a large scale in Africa. Intermarriage has always been regarded as a social stigma by whites, even in those territories where, unlike South Africa, it is not actually a crime, but I have never been able to find out whether, among blacks, it is regarded as a stigma or a step up in the world. (Most whites assume it is regarded as a deeply desired privilege, of course.) I know that, for example, in South Africa many Africans who are not Bechuanas, and have nothing whatever to do with the people of Bechuanaland, have on their walls a picture of Ruth and Seretse Khama.[1] It is difficult to say whether this means that they take pride in the fact that a white woman chose to marry an important African, or whether the picture simply gives them a chance to identify themselves with the ex-chief's successful defiance of white taboo and authority.

Once the social stigma is removed — in the new Africa marriage with an African will be marrying into the ruling class, remember, and no one can measure how much of color-prejudice is purely class-prejudice, in a country where there has been a great gap between the living standards of black and white — and once (in the case of South Africa) there are no legal disabilities in mixed marriages, I think that intermarriage will increase at two extreme levels of the social scale, but scarcely at all in between. Intellectuals will intermarry because they feel closer to intellectuals, whatever their race or color, than to the mass, and the humbler and poorly-adjusted fringes of both the black and white masses, who have not found acceptance in their own societies, will intermarry in order to find a home somewhere — if not within the confines of their own background, then in someone else's. But I don't think we can hope for intermarriage on an effective scale between ordinary people, and I shouldn't be surprised if independent black Africa frowned upon it, in an unofficial but firm way. Especially in a country like South Africa, where there might remain whites in sufficiently large numbers to create an unease at the possibility that they might try to close their hands once again on those possessions of power from which their fingers had been prised back one by one. It is quite likely that there will be a social stigma, among ordinary people whose sense of nationalism is well stoked up, attached to marrying whites; it may be considered un-African. (Nkrumah[2] has set the official precedent already, by choosing not a Ruth Williams, but a girl who "belongs" to the continent — a bride from Nasser's Egypt.) If white numbers do not dwindle

---

[1]Seretse Khama, who became president of Botswana (formerly Bechuanaland) after it gained independence from Britain (see p. 431) married Englishwoman Ruth Williams. — ED.
[2]Kwame Nkrumah was the first president of independent Ghana. — ED.

in those areas of the continent which are heavily white-populated, and there is integration in schools and universities and no discrimination against white children, the picture will change in a few generations, of course. I do not see those young people as likely to regard parental race prejudice on either side as anything but fuddy-duddy. But will the whites remain, stick it out anywhere in Africa in sufficient numbers for this to come about? Isn't it much more likely that they will dwindle to small, socially isolated communities, whites in the diaspora?

If one will always have to feel white first, and African second, it would be better not to stay on in Africa. It would not be worth it for this. Yet, although I claim no mystique about Africa, I fear that like one of those oxen I sometimes read about in the Sunday papers, I might, dumped somewhere else and kindly treated, continually plod blindly back to where I came from.

EXPLORATIONS

1. What is Nadine Gordimer's first answer to the question "Where Do Whites Fit In?" How would you summarize her real answer to this question? What are the effects of her starting with a more extreme answer than she ends up with?

2. For Gordimer, what is the critical factor in deciding whether to stay in South Africa or leave? What evidence in her essay suggests that she sees the same factor as critical to South Africa's future success under black rule?

3. What is Gordimer's definition of "African" in this essay? What term or terms does she use for people in her own racial and national group? How does her usage bolster her essay's thesis?

CONNECTIONS

1. After reading Amitav Ghosh's "The Ghosts of Mrs. Gandhi" (p. 330), what kind of turning point do you think Gordimer is trying to prevent in South Africa? What are the potential advantages of her asking "Where Do Whites Fit In?" while whites still controlled South Africa's government and society?

2. In paragraphs 8–9 Gordimer discusses the need in the new Africa for the former ruling class to resist the temptation "to offer guidance when we haven't been consulted." How do her observations here apply to Rosaura's mother in Liliana Heker's "The Stolen Party" (p. 323)? Does Rosaura's mother follow Gordimer's advice? What are the results?

3. Compare Gordimer's arguments for and against leaving Africa with James Baldwin's arguments for and against emigrating from the United States to Europe (p. 18). What points do both writers make? What points does Baldwin make about the problems that follow emigration which probably would affect Gordimer and other white ex-Africans?

ELABORATIONS

1. Many of Gordimer's observations in "Where Do Whites Fit In?" could be applied to other groups besides white South Africans: mothers of newly married sons, for instance, or officers at a formerly all-male military academy. Choose some group that has lost its former exclusivity or dominance and write an essay redirecting Gordimer's ideas and recommendations to that group.
2. ". . . Home is not necessarily where you belong ethnogenically, but rather the place you were born to, the faces you first saw around you, and the elements of the situation among your fellow men in which you found yourself and with which you have been struggling, politically, personally, or artistically, all your life" (para. 8). What are these "faces" and "elements" for Gordimer? How does her definition of home apply to Anwar El-Sadat's Mit Abul-Kum (p. 130)? To Amy Tan's San Francisco in "Two Kinds" (p. 28)? To Henry Louis Gates Jr.'s West Virginia in "Down to Cumberland" (p. 146)? Write an essay expanding on Gordimer's definition of home, drawing evidence either from these and other selections or from your own experience.

SPOTLIGHT:
RUSSIA

▲▲▲▲▲▲▲▲▲▲
▼▼▼▼▼▼▼▼▼▼

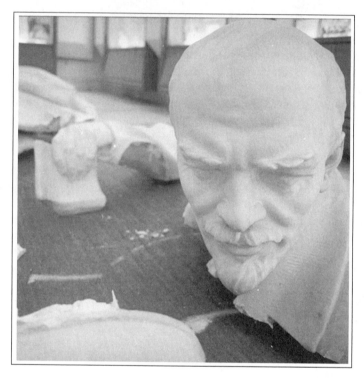

Turning Points: *Lenin watches as the Lenin Museum is dismantled.*

Since the Union of Soviet Socialist Republics (USSR) broke up in 1991, the largest of its twelve member states, Russia, remains the world's biggest country. The USSR — or Soviet Union — was formed in 1922 after the Russian Revolution of 1917 toppled Russia's last hereditary czar, and the Bolshevik Revolution felled his successors. "When, at the end of the year, [Nikolai] Lenin took over, the Bolsheviks immediately subordinated everything to the retention of power," Vladimir Nabokov wrote in *Speak, Memory*, "and a regime of bloodshed, concentration camps, and hostages entered upon its stupendous career." Religion was squelched; St. Petersburg, where both Nabokov and Joseph Brodsky were born, was renamed Leningrad. Czar Peter the Great had built the city with similar arrogance, relocating Russia's capital from Moscow to the Baltic Coast. His ancestor Ivan the Terrible had proclaimed himself the first czar (a title derived from the Roman *caesar*) in 1547. Western ideas and modernization spread across Russia during the nineteenth and twentieth centuries, but the political system remained feudal. The czars' downfall was triggered by Russia's war losses against Japan in 1904, and climaxed when workers' strikes in 1917 escalated into revolution.

Lenin, the first Soviet president, died in 1924, and Joseph Stalin took over. Stalin forcibly established a Communist system of centralized economic planning, collectivized agriculture, and state-owned land. Brodsky describes in "Less than One" how pervasively Stalin's government dominated the Soviet Union. By the time Stalin died in 1953, after World War II, postwar rivalry between communism and capitalism had pitted the USSR and United States against each other in a "cold war." That forty-year arms race overloaded an already topheavy economy to the point of collapse. When Mikhail Gorbachev became president in 1985, he introduced policies of *perestroika* (restructuring) and *glasnost* (openness) which included reorganizing the government, holding competitive elections, and ultimately, in 1991, dissolving both the Communist Party and the Soviet Union itself. Economic chaos followed, as Galina Dutkina and Natasha Singer describe in "Sovs, Hacks, and Freeloaders" and "The New Russian Dressing." Anti-Semitism also erupted: Although Jews periodically had been persecuted in Russia over their thousand-year history there, such practices were technically illegal under communism. Gorbachev, who increased freedom of expression for both Jews and anti-Semites, soon was replaced by President Boris Yeltsin, who in 1996 fought off a strong Communist challenge to win reelection to a second term.

VLADIMIR NABOKOV

From Speak, Memory

Vladimir Nabokov was born into an aristocratic Russian family in St. Petersburg in 1899. His father, a leader of a liberal democratic party in czarist Russia, took the family to England after the 1917 revolution, where Nabokov entered Cambridge University. Shortly before he graduated, his father was assassinated in Berlin while shielding another man. Already writing in English as well as Russian, Nabokov spent the next eighteen years in Germany and France. From poetry and translations he expanded to drama and screenplays, settling on fiction as his preferred form. Within three years in Berlin he published his first short story and his first novel (*Mashenka,* 1926; in English, *Mary,* 1970) and married Vera Slonim. They and their son, Dmitri, lived in happy poverty while Nabokov hunted butterflies, produced scientific papers on insects, and created increasingly intricate and unorthodox novels. In 1940 they emigrated to the United States, where Nabokov continued his insect research at Harvard University and taught Russian literature at Wellesley College. The same year Nabokov became an American citizen (1945), his older brother, Sergei, died in a Nazi concentration camp. *Lolita* (1955), his first best-seller, debuted in Paris after being refused by U.S. publishers. It finally appeared here three years later and was filmed by Stanley Kubrick in 1962, when *Pale Fire* was published in New York. Nabokov and his wife meanwhile had moved to Switzerland; he died there in 1977. Subsequent books include *Lectures on Literature* (1980), *The Enchanter* (1986), and *The Stories of Vladimir Nabokov* (1995), edited by his son, Dmitri. The following essay comes from his autobiography, *Speak, Memory* (1966).

The reactionary press never ceased to attack my father's party, and I had got quite used to the more or less vulgar cartoons which appeared from time to time — my father and Milyukov handing over Saint Russia on a plate to World Jewry and that sort of thing. But one day, in the winter of 1911 I believe, the most powerful of the Rightist newspapers employed a shady journalist to concoct a scurrilous piece containing insinuations that my father could not let pass. Since the well-known rascality of the actual author made him "non-duelable" (*neduelesposobnïy,* as the Russian dueling code had it), my father called out the somewhat less disreputable editor of the paper in which the article had appeared.

A Russian duel was a much more serious affair than the conventional Parisian variety. It took the editor several days to make up his mind whether or not to accept the challenge. On the last of these days, a Monday, I went, as usual, to school. In consequence of my not reading the newspapers, I was absolutely ignorant of the whole thing. Sometime during the day I became aware that a magazine opened at a certain page was passing from hand to hand and causing titters. A well-timed swoop put me in possession of what proved to be the latest copy of a cheap weekly containing a lurid account of my father's challenge, with idiotic comments on the choice of weapons he had offered his foe. Sly digs were taken at his having reverted to a feudal custom that he had criticized in his own writings. There was also a good deal about the number of his servants and the number of his suits. I found out that he had chosen for second his brother-in-law, Admiral Kolomeytsev, a hero of the Japanese war. During the battle of Tsushima, this uncle of mine, then holding the rank of captain, had managed to bring his destroyer alongside the burning flagship and save the naval commander-in-chief.

After classes, I ascertained that the magazine belonged to one of my best friends. I charged him with betrayal and mockery. In the ensuing fight, he crashed backward into a desk, catching his foot in a joint and breaking his ankle. He was laid up for a month, but gallantly concealed from his family and from our teachers my share in the matter.

The pang of seeing him carried downstairs was lost in my general misery. For some reason or other, no car came to fetch me that day, and during the cold, dreary, incredibly slow drive home in a hired sleigh I had ample time to think matters over. Now I understood why, the day before, my mother had been so little with me and had not come down to dinner. I also understood what special coaching Thernant, a still finer *maître d'armes* than Loustalot, had of late been giving my father. What would his adversary choose, I kept asking myself — the blade or the bullet? Or had the choice already been made? Carefully, I took the beloved, the familiar, the richly alive image of my father fencing and tried to transfer the image, minus the mask and the padding, to the dueling ground, in some barn or riding school. I visualized him and his adversary, both bare-chested, black-trousered, in furious battle, their energetic movements marked by that strange awkwardness which even the most elegant swordsmen cannot avoid in a real encounter. The picture was so repulsive, so vividly did I feel the ripeness and nakedness of a madly pulsating heart about to be pierced, that I found myself hoping for what seemed momentarily a more abstract weapon. But soon I was in even deeper distress.

As the sleigh crept along Nevski Avenue, where blurry lights swam in
the gathering dusk, I thought of the heavy black Browning my father
kept in the upper right-hand drawer of his desk. I knew that pistol as
well as I knew all the other, more salient, things in his study; the *objets
d'art* of crystal or veined stone, fashionable in those days; the glinting
family photographs; the huge, mellowly illuminated Perugino; the
small, honey-bright Dutch oils; and, right over the desk, the rose-and-
haze pastel portrait of my mother by Bakst: The artist had drawn her
face in three-quarter view, wonderfully bringing out its delicate features
— the upward sweep of the ash-colored hair (it had grayed when she
was in her twenties), the pure curve of her forehead, the dove-blue eyes,
the graceful line of the neck.

When I urged the old, rag-doll-like driver to go faster, he would
merely lean to one side with a special half-circular movement of his
arm, so as to make his horse believe he was about to produce the short
whip he kept in the leg of his right felt boot; and that would be sufficient for the shaggy little hack to make as vague a show of speeding up
as the driver had made of getting out his *knutishko*. In the almost hallu-
cinatory state that our snow-muffled ride engendered, I refought all the
famous duels a Russian boy knew so well. I saw Pushkin, mortally wounded at the first fire, grimly sit up to discharge his pistol at d'Anthès.
I saw Lermontov smile as he faced Martïnov. I saw stout Sobinov
in the part of Lenski crash down and send his weapon flying into the orchestra. No Russian writer of any repute had failed to describe *une ren-
contre*, a hostile meeting, always of course of the classical *duel à volonté*
type (not the ludicrous back-to-back-march-face-about-bang-bang performance of movie and cartoon fame). Among several prominent families, there had been tragic deaths on the dueling ground in more or less
recent years. Slowly my dreamy sleigh drove up Morskaya Street, and
slowly dim silhouettes of duelists advanced upon each other and leveled their pistols and fired — at the crack of dawn, in damp glades of
old country estates, on bleak military training grounds, or in the driving
snow between two rows of fir trees.

And behind it all there was yet a very special emotional abyss that I
was desperately trying to skirt, lest I burst into a tempest of tears, and
this was the tender friendship underlying my respect for my father; the
charm of our perfect accord; the Wimbledon matches we followed in
the London papers; the chess problems we solved; the Pushkin iambics
that rolled off his tongue so triumphantly whenever I mentioned some
minor poet of the day. Our relationship was marked by that habitual exchange of homespun nonsense, comically garbled words, proposed imi-
tations of supposed intonations, and all those private jokes which is the

secret code of happy families. With all that he was extremely strict in matters of conduct and given to biting remarks when cross with a child or servant, but his inherent humanity was too great to allow his rebuke to Osip for laying out the wrong shirt to be really offensive, just as a first-hand knowledge of a boy's pride tempered the harshness of reproval and resulted in sudden forgiveness. Thus I was more puzzled than pleased one day when upon learning that I had deliberately slashed my leg just above the knee with a razor (I still bear the scar) in order to avoid a recitation in class for which I was unprepared, he seemed unable to work up any real wrath; and his subsequent admission of a parallel transgression in his own boyhood rewarded me for not withholding the truth.

I remembered that summer afternoon (which already then seemed long ago although actually only four or five years had passed) when he had burst into my room, grabbed my net, shot down the veranda steps — and presently was strolling back holding between finger and thumb the rare and magnificent female of the Russian Poplar Admirable that he had seen baking on an aspen leaf from the balcony of his study. I remembered our long bicycle rides along the smooth Luga highway and the efficient way in which — mighty-calved, knickerbock-ered, tweed-coated, checker-capped — he would accomplish the mounting of his high-saddled "Dux," which his valet would bring up to the porch as if it were a palfrey. Surveying the state of its polish, my father would pull on his suede gloves and test under Osip's anxious eye whether the tires were sufficiently tight. Then he would grip the handlebars, place his left foot on a metallic peg jutting at the rear end of the frame, push off with his right foot on the other side of the hind wheel and after three or four such propelments (with the bicycle now set in motion), leisurely translate his right leg into pedal position, move up his left, and settle down on the saddle.

At last I was home, and immediately upon entering the vestibule I became aware of loud, cheerful voices. With the opportuneness of dream arrangements, my uncle the Admiral was coming downstairs. From the red-carpeted landing above, where an armless Greek woman of marble presided over a malachite bowl for visiting cards, my parents were still speaking to him, and as he came down the steps, he looked up with a laugh and slapped the balustrade with the gloves he had in his hand. I knew at once that there would be no duel, that the challenge had been met by an apology, that all was right. I brushed past my uncle and reached the landing. I saw my mother's serene everyday face, but I could not look at my father. And then it happened: My heart welled in me like that wave on which the *Buynïy* rose when her captain brought her alongside the burning *Suvorov*, and I had no handkerchief, and ten years were to pass before a certain night in 1922, at a public lecture in Berlin, when my father shielded the lecturer (his old friend Milyukov) from the bullets of two Russian Fascists and, while vigorously knocking down one of the assassins, was fatally shot by the other. But no shadow was cast by that future event upon the bright stairs of our St. Petersburg house; the large, cool hand resting on my head did not quaver, and several lines of play in a difficult chess composition were not blended yet on the board.

EXPLORATIONS

1. What is Nabokov's central realization during his sleigh ride home from school? What does he realize when he arrives home? What phrases in the last paragraph reveal his response to these realizations?

2. What does Nabokov learn about life and about himself between the beginning and end of the selection? What additional insights are contributed by his adult self as narrator?

3. Nabokov's central metaphor — the duel faced by his father — is echoed throughout his essay. What examples can you find of combat between two opponents? Of duel-related imagery?

CONNECTIONS

1. Compare the ways Nabokov's essay and Sophronia Liu's "So Tsi-fai" (p. 318) make use of an untimely death. How do these writers' purposes appear to be the same and also different? How would the impact of Nabokov's reminiscences change if he structured his essay more like Liu's? What does he gain or lose (or both) by focusing on a near miss rather than the more dramatic death that followed it a decade later?

2. Both Liliana Heker's "The Stolen Party" (p. 323) and Nabokov's essay feature wealthy families. What evidence in Heker's story characterizes Luciana as a spoiled child? What evidence in Nabokov's narrative characterizes him as spoiled? What does Heker perceive as the disadvantages to children of having wealthy parents? Aside from material comforts, what does Nabokov perceive as the advantages?

3. What does Nabokov mean by his final clause: "and several lines of play in a difficult chess composition were not blended yet on the board"? In what sense is he making the same point as Alexander Theroux's line, "I want to be what I was when I wanted to be what I am now" (p. 277)?

JOSEPH BRODSKY

Less than One

The poet and essayist Iosif Alexandrovich Brodsky was born in 1940 in what was then Leningrad, USSR, but is now and was originally St. Petersburg, Russia. In the following excerpt from his 1976 essay "Less than One," he describes attending school there. After walking out in 1956, he worked as a stoker, sailor, metalworker, photographer, geologist's assistant, hospital morgue attendant, and farm laborer. He also learned English and Polish, partly by reading poets such as John Donne, W. H. Auden, and Czeslaw Milosz. Brodsky began publishing his own poems and translations in the mid-1960s, but only outside the Soviet Union. There he was charged with "parasitism" — writing poetry without academic qualifications instead of doing honest work for the motherland — and sentenced to five years' hard labor. (Protests from other artists reduced his time to eighteen months.) In this essay Brodsky alludes to the anti-Semitism that already had cost his father his position in the Russian navy. Now, when he was invited to immigrate to Israel, the Soviet government urged him to go. He refused, but he was exiled anyway in 1972 and took refuge in the United States. Brodsky taught and wrote at the University of Michigan and Queens College before becoming a U.S. citizen and accepting a chair in literature at Mount Holyoke College. His books include *Elegy to John Donne and Other Poems* (1967), *Chast'rechi: Stikhotvoreniia, 1972–1976* (1977; *A Part of Speech*, 1980), and the essay collections *Less than One* (1984) and *On Grief and Reason* (1996). Among his many international awards and honors were a MacArthur Fellowship in 1981 and the Nobel Prize for literature in 1987. Brodsky died in New York of a heart attack in 1996; he was 55.

As failures go, attempting to recall the past is like trying to grasp the meaning of existence. Both make one feel like a baby clutching at a basketball: One's palms keep sliding off.

I remember rather little of my life and what I do remember is of small consequence. Most of the thoughts I now recall as having been interesting to me owe their significance to the time when they occurred. If any do not, they have no doubt been expressed much better by someone else. A writer's biography is in his twists of language. I remember, for instance, that when I was about ten or eleven it occurred to me that Marx's dictum that "existence conditions consciousness" was true only for as long as it takes consciousness to acquire the art of estrangement; thereafter, consciousness is on its own and can both condition and ignore existence. At that age, this was surely a discovery — but one hardly worth recording, and surely it had been better stated by others. And does it really matter who first cracked the mental cuneiform of which "existence conditions consciousness" is a perfect example?

So I am writing all this not in order to set the record straight (there is no such record, and even if there is, it is an insignificant one and thus not yet distorted), but mostly for the usual reason why a writer writes — to give or to get a boost from the language, this time from a foreign one. The little I remember becomes even more diminished by being recollected in English.

For the beginning I had better trust my birth certificate, which states that I was born on May 24, 1940, in Leningrad, Russia, much as I abhor this name for the city which long ago the ordinary people nicknamed simply "Peter" — from Petersburg. There is an old two-liner:

> *The sides of people*
> *Are rubbed by Old Peter.*

In the national experience, the city is definitely Leningrad; in the growing vulgarity of its content, it becomes Leningrad more and more. Besides, as a word, "Leningrad" to a Russian ear already sounds as neutral as the word "construction" or "sausage." And yet I'd rather call it "Peter," for I remember this city at a time when it didn't look like "Leningrad" — right after the war. Gray, pale-green façades with bullet and shrapnel cavities; endless, empty streets, with few passersby and light traffic; almost a starved look with, as a result, more definite and, if you wish, nobler features. A lean, hard face with the abstract glitter of its river reflected in the eyes of its hollow windows. A survivor cannot be named after Lenin.

Those magnificent pockmarked façades behind which — among old   5
pianos, worn-out rugs, dusty paintings in heavy bronze frames, leftovers of furniture (chairs least of all) consumed by the iron stoves during the siege — a faint life was beginning to glimmer. And I remember, as I passed these façades on my way to school, being completely absorbed in imagining what was going on in those rooms with the old, billowy wallpaper. I must say that from these façades and porticoes — classical, modern, eclectic, with their columns, pilasters, and plastered heads of

mythic animals or people — from their ornaments and caryatids holding up the balconies, from the torsos in the niches of their entrances, I have learned more about the history of our world than I subsequently have from any book. Greece, Rome, Egypt — all of them were there, and all were chipped by artillery shells during the bombardments. And from the gray, reflecting river flowing down to the Baltic, with an occasional tugboat in the midst of it struggling against the current, I have learned more about infinity and stoicism than from mathematics and Zeno.

All that had very little to do with Lenin, whom, I suppose, I began to despise even when I was in the first grade — not so much because of his political philosophy or practice, about which at the age of seven I knew very little, but because of his omnipresent images which plagued almost every textbook, every class wall, postage stamps, money, and whatnot, depicting the man at various ages and stages of his life. There was baby Lenin, looking like a cherub in his blond curls. Then Lenin in his twenties and thirties, bald and uptight, with that meaningless expression on his face which could be mistaken for anything, preferably a sense of purpose. This face in some way haunts every Russian and suggests some sort of standard for human appearance because it is utterly lacking in character. (Perhaps because there is nothing specific in that face it suggests many possibilities.) Then there was an oldish Lenin, balder, with his wedge-like beard, in his three-piece dark suit, sometimes smiling, but most often addressing the "masses" from the top of an armored car or from the podium of some party congress, with a hand outstretched in the air.

There were also variants: Lenin in his worker's cap, with a carnation pinned to his lapel; in a vest, sitting in his study, writing or reading; on a lakeside stump, scribbling his April Theses, or some other nonsense, al fresco. Ultimately, Lenin in a paramilitary jacket on a garden bench next to Stalin, who was the only one to surpass Lenin in the ubiquitousness of his printed images. But Stalin was then alive, while Lenin was dead and, if only because of that, "good" because he belonged to the past — i.e., was sponsored by both history and nature. Whereas Stalin was sponsored only by nature, or the other way around.

I think that coming to ignore those pictures was my first lesson in switching off, my first attempt at estrangement. There were more to follow; in fact, the rest of my life can be viewed as a nonstop avoidance of its most importunate aspects. I must say, I went quite far in that direction; perhaps too far. Anything that bore a suggestion of repetitiveness became compromised and subject to removal. That included phrases, trees, certain types of people, sometimes even physical pain; it affected many of my relationships. In a way, I am grateful to Lenin. Whatever there was in plenitude I immediately regarded as some sort of propaganda. This attitude, I think, made for an awful acceleration through the thicket of events, with an accompanying superficiality.

I don't believe for a moment that all the clues to character are to be found in childhood. For about three generations Russians have been living in communal apartments and cramped rooms, and our parents made love while we pretended to be asleep. Then there was a war, starvation, absent or mutilated fathers, horny mothers, official lies at school and unofficial ones at home. Hard winters, ugly clothes, public exposé of our wet sheets in summer camps, and citations of such matters in front of others. Then the red flag would flutter on the mast of camp. So what? All this militarization of childhood, all the menacing idiocy, erotic tension (at ten we all lusted for our female teachers) had not affected our ethics much, or our aesthetics — or our ability to love and suffer. I recall these things not because I think that they are the keys to the subconscious, or certainly not out of nostalgia for my childhood. I recall them because I have never done so before, because I want some of those things to stay — at least on paper. Also, because looking backward is more rewarding than its opposite. Tomorrow is just less attractive than yesterday. For some reason, the past doesn't radiate such immense monotony as the future does. Because of its plenitude, the future is propaganda. So is grass.

The real history of consciousness starts with one's first lie. I happen   10
to remember mine. It was in a school library when I had to fill out an application for membership. The fifth blank was of course "nationality." I was seven years old and knew very well that I was a Jew, but I told the attendant that I didn't know. With dubious glee she suggested that I go home and ask my parents. I never returned to that library, although I did become a member of many others which had the same application forms. I wasn't ashamed of being a Jew, nor was I scared of admitting it. In the class ledger our names, the names of our parents, home addresses, and nationalities were registered in full detail, and from time to time a teacher would "forget" the ledger on the desk in the classroom during breaks. Then, like vultures, we would fall upon those pages; everyone in my class knew that I was a Jew. But seven-year-old boys don't make good anti-Semites. Besides, I was fairly strong for my age, and the fists were what mattered most then. I was ashamed of the word "Jew" itself — in Russian, "*yevrei*" — regardless of its connotations.

A word's fate depends on the variety of its contexts, on the frequency of its usage. In printed Russian "*yevrei*" appears nearly as seldom as, say, "mediastinum" or "gennel" in American English. In fact, it also has something like the status of a four-letter word or like a name for VD. When one is seven one's vocabulary proves sufficient to acknowledge this word's rarity, and it is utterly unpleasant to identify oneself with it; somehow it goes against one's sense of prosody. I remember that I always felt a lot easier with a Russian equivalent of "kike" — "*zhyd*" (pronounced like André Gide): It was clearly offensive and thereby meaningless, not loaded with allusions. A one-syllable word can't do much in Russian. But when suffixes are applied, or endings, or prefixes, then feathers fly. All this is not to say that I suffered as a Jew at that tender age; it's simply to say that my first lie had to do with my identity.

Not a bad start. As for anti-Semitism as such, I didn't care much about it because it came mostly from teachers: It seemed innate to their negative part in our lives; it had to be coped with like low marks. If I had been a Roman Catholic, I would have wished most of them in Hell. True, some teachers were better than others; but since all were masters of our immediate lives, we didn't bother to distinguish. Nor did they try to distinguish among their little slaves, and even the most ardent anti-Semitic remarks bore an air of impersonal inertia. Somehow, I never was capable of taking seriously any verbal assault on me, especially from people of such a disparate age group. I guess the diatribes my parents used to deliver against me tempered me very well. Besides, some teachers were Jews themselves, and I dreaded them no less than I did the pure-blooded Russians.

This is just one example of the trimming of the self that — along with the language itself, where verbs and nouns change places as freely as one dares to have them do so — bred in us such an overpowering sense of ambivalence that in ten years we ended up with a willpower in no way superior to a seaweed's. Four years in the army (into which men were drafted at the age of nineteen) completed the process of total surrender to the state. Obedience would become both first and second nature.

If one had brains, one would certainly try to outsmart the system by devising all kinds of detours, arranging shady deals with one's superiors, piling up lies and pulling the strings of one's semi-nepotic connections. This would become a full-time job. Yet one was constantly aware that the web one had woven was a web of lies, and in spite of the degree of success or your sense of humor, you'd despise yourself. That is the ultimate triumph of the system: Whether you beat it or join it, you feel

equally guilty. The national belief is — as the proverb has it — that
there is no Evil without a grain of Good in it and presumably vice versa.

Ambivalence, I think, is the chief characteristic of my nation. There   15
isn't a Russian executioner who isn't scared of turning victim one day,
nor is there the sorriest victim who would acknowledge (if only to himself) a mental ability to become an executioner. Our immediate history
has provided well for both. There is some wisdom in this. One might
even think that this ambivalence *is* wisdom, that life itself is neither
good nor bad, but arbitrary. Perhaps our literature stresses the good
cause so remarkably because this cause is challenged so well. If this emphasis were simply doublethink, that would be fine; but it grates on the
instincts. This kind of ambivalence, I think, is precisely that "blessed
news" which the East, having little else to offer, is about to impose on
the rest of the world. And the world looks ripe for it.

The world's destiny aside, the only way for a boy to fight his imminent lot would be to go off the track. This was hard to do because of
your parents, and because you yourself were quite frightened of the unknown. Most of all, because it made you different from the majority,
and you got it with your mother's milk that the majority is right. A certain lack of concern is required, and unconcerned I was. As I remember
my quitting school at the age of fifteen, it wasn't so much a conscious
choice as a gut reaction. I simply couldn't stand certain faces in my
class — of some of my classmates, but mostly of teachers. And so one
winter morning, for no apparent reason, I rose up in the middle of the
session and made my melodramatic exit through the school gate, knowing clearly that I'd never be back. Of the emotions overpowering me at
that moment, I remember only a general disgust with myself for being
too young and letting so many things boss me around. Also, there was
that vague but happy sensation of escape, of a sunny street without end.

The main thing, I suppose, was the change of exterior. In a centralized state all rooms look alike: The office of my school's principal was
an exact replica of the interrogation chambers I began to frequent some
five years later. The same wooden panels, desks, chairs — a paradise for
carpenters. The same portraits of our founders, Lenin, Stalin, members
of the Politburo, and Maxim Gorky (the founder of Soviet literature) if
it was a school, or Felix Dzerzhinsky (the founder of the Soviet Secret
Police) if it was an interrogation chamber.

Often, though, Dzerzhinsky — "Iron Felix" or "Knight of the Revolution," as propaganda has it — would decorate the principal's wall as
well, because the man had glided into the system of education from the
heights of the KGB. And those stuccoed walls of my classrooms, with
their blue horizontal stripe at eye level, running unfailingly across the

whole country, like the line of an infinite common denominator: in halls, hospitals, factories, prisons, corridors of communal apartments. The only place I didn't encounter it was in wooden peasant huts.

This decor was as maddening as it was omnipresent, and how many times in my life would I catch myself peering mindlessly at this blue two-inch-wide stripe, taking it sometimes for a sea horizon, sometimes for an embodiment of nothingness itself. It was too abstract to mean anything. From the floor up to the level of your eyes a wall covered with rat-gray or greenish paint, and this blue stripe topping it off; above it would be the virginally white stucco. Nobody ever asked why it was there. Nobody could have answered. It was just there, a border line, a divider between gray and white, below and above. They were not colors themselves but hints of colors, which might be interrupted only by alternating patches of brown: doors. Closed, half open. And through the half-open door you could see another room with the same distinction of gray and white marked by the blue stripe. Plus a portrait of Lenin and a world map.

It was nice to leave the Kafkaesque cosmos, although even then — or   20
so it seems — I sort of knew that I was trading six for half a dozen. I knew that any other building I was going to enter would look the same, for buildings are where we are doomed to carry on anyhow. Still, I felt that I had to go. The financial situation in our family was grim: We existed mostly on my mother's salary, because my father, after being discharged from the navy in accordance with some seraphic ruling that Jews should not hold substantial military ranks, had a hard time finding a job. Of course, my parents would have managed without my contribution; they would have preferred that I finish school. I knew that, and yet I told myself that I had to help my family. It was almost a lie, but this way it looked better, and by that time I had already learned to like lies for precisely this "almost-ness" which sharpens the outline of truth: After all, truth ends where lies start. That's what a boy learned in school and it proved to be more useful than algebra.

EXPLORATIONS

1. In paragraph 2 Joseph Brodsky quotes a dictum of Karl Marx: "Existence conditions consciousness." What does it mean? What does Brodsky mean by countering that once consciousness "acquire[s] the art of estrangement . . . [it] can both condition and ignore existence"? How does his own life show Brodsky's point in action?

2. Why do you think the Soviet government displayed pictures of Lenin every-where (paras. 7–8)? How were citizens meant to react to these "omnipresent images"? How did Brodsky react to them?

3. What information does Brodsky give us about himself in "Less than One" that helps to explain why he quit school at age fifteen?

CONNECTIONS

1. The experiences Vladimir Nabokov recalls in the excerpt from *Speak, Memory* (p. 354) took place in 1911, before the Russian Revolution; Brodsky's experi-ences in "Less than One" took place after World War II, almost half a century later. Comparing these two writers' recollections of St. Petersburg/Leningrad, what resemblances can you find? What are the most striking con-trasts?

2. In "Mary" (p. 281), Maya Angelou describes her reaction to her boss's changing her name. What is Brodsky's response to the Soviets' changing the name of his city, and why?

3. Compare Brodsky's attitude toward the Soviet Union with the attitude ex-pressed in "Evicted: A Russian Jew's Story (Again)," excerpted on page 278. How are these two writers' viewpoints alike and different? What factors do you think may be responsible for the differences?

GALINA DUTKINA

Sovs, Hacks, and Freeloaders

Galina Dutkina is a member of the Russian Union of Journalists and the Union of Translators. She has worked at Raduga Publishers and Radio Moscow and is currently working in Moscow as a journalist and lecturer on Japanese culture and literature. She is the author of *Mysterious Moscow: The Diary of Galya* (1992). "Sovs, Hacks, and Freeloaders," translated by Catherine A. Fitzpatrick, comes from her book *Moscow Days: Life and Hard Times in the New Russia* (1996), as does this biographical note.

Much has been written about Russia, this "mystery wrapped in an enigma." Oh, the inscrutable profundity of the Russian East, this fusion of Europe and Asia, so fascinating to the philosophers and writers! Many have tried to unravel the mystery hidden in the soul of Russia. But it is only at first glance that Russia is unique, great, and unified. In reality there are many Russias, like fantastic parallel universes. The fate of a specific individual depends solely upon which of these Russias he has been destined to inhabit, whether the country of harsh submission or the country of unlimited freedom of spirit; the country of angelic holiness or of beastly profanity; in the Russia of geniuses, or of the faceless masses. Perhaps some will find such a cocktail of philosophy and science fiction strange, but isn't this monstrous brew in itself peculiar, this blend of such terribly contradictory features in one nation? For even after solving the riddle concealed within the soul of Russia, we still come up against a brick wall. How could such a strange creature arise — like the mythological Chinese *qilin* — with the body of a deer, the horn of a unicorn, the neck of a wolf, the tail of a bull, and the hooves of a horse? . . .

Long ago, an ice age killed off the dinosaurs but other carnivores and herbivores who were more nimble and adaptable to the new conditions flourished. Likewise, the thawing of the cold war era saw the end of *homo Sovieticus*. In the time since, what sort of beasts have emerged in Russia in place of the old dinosaurs? And who are these reptiles who have multiplied now under the tender sun of "freedom" granted by perestroika and reform?

We all have lived for so many years in proximity to the zone — and some right in it — that now it turns out that practically the whole country speaks the slang of prisons, labor camps, and criminals. Many of these words, like other coarse language, sully the formerly great and pure Russian language, and are alternately humorous and horrifying. Sometimes the uninitiated cannot guess the secret, hidden meaning in familiar-sounding words, but like the three wheels, the three pillars, or the three cornerstones upon which rests the world, there are three all-encompassing words upon which the universe of the post-Soviet psychology is upheld: *sovok, khaltura,* and *khalyava.* Unlike *sputnik* or *glasnost,* these Russian terms are not known to the foreign reader, and even a specialist in Russian culture would most likely find it difficult to explain them completely. Nevertheless, these three words define with greatest accuracy the psychology of the post-Soviet citizen and the moral climate in Russia today.

The slang of the prisons, labor camps, and underworld of the Stalinist zone defined the word *sovok,* or *sov,* in two ways. First, as *Sovetskaya vlast,* Soviet power or government, and secondly as *Sovetskiy Soyuz,* the Soviet Union. (The very sound of the word conveys a pejorative nuance because its homonym means "scoop" or "dustpan," a thing used to pick up garbage.) Now *sovok* is defined differently. A sov is generally a person raised in the traditions of socialist egalitarian ideology, with all the resultant personality traits (including a slavish attitude toward authority). In other words, *homo Sovieticus* was a sov. Strictly speaking, all of us — and perhaps even our children — are to some extent still sovs, but a classic, 100-percent sov stands out immediately. Still a sov is not necessarily a worker or peasant. A sov can just as easily be (or not be) someone in any profession or social group, from a janitor to a professor, from a writer to a pig tender, from the faceless masses to the ruling elite.

The habit of slavery was programmed into the Russian character   5 from the time of the Mongolian-Tatar Yoke, and was reinforced in the years of cheerless serfdom. Normally a slave will work only under the fear of reprisal. As soon as the reins are slackened even a little bit, he tries to shirk his job and crawl off to the side. Thus we came to know the charms of Andropov's campaign for labor discipline in the 1980s. Any policeman or auxiliary had the full right to demand to see the identification of people sitting in cafes, restaurants, or movie theaters or even just walking down the street, and to expect an explanation for why they were not at their jobs in the middle of the workday. Official reports to places of employment were written against "violators" who were unable to come up with convincing reasons; sometimes this even led to their dismissal. Then Gorbachev's perestroika and the reforms of Yegor

Gaidar and Anatoly Chubais[1] opened up untold prospects for the aggressively indolent. They bestowed those sov loafers with ample opportunities for hackwork and freeloading.

Nowadays — thanks to the reform! — lazy and irresponsible sovs no longer have to tremble with fear when they skip work. Work-shirkers have no reason to be afraid that they will be kicked out of Moscow under the criminal-code article penalizing "malicious parasitism," or failure to hold a job. Because now work is no longer obligatory, and in order to live well you don't even have to steal and murder. Why go to such extremes when there are such wonderful methods available as hackwork and freeloading! Now it is legalized and approved on a national scale. Have fun, people!

Khaltura is defined as "work on the side for extra earnings" and also (more accurately) "careless work performed haphazardly, hastily." *Khalyava* is defined as "receiving something for nothing, for free." . . .

Take the typical Russian fairy tale in which an unwashed, uncombed, loafing bum named Ivan the Fool sits on top of a big stove of the sort that typically used to grace Russian homes. He is too lazy even to climb down to the floor, whereas his elder brothers labor by the sweat of their brows, earning a good living. Suddenly Ivan jumps off the stove and scurries out of the cabin to catch a magic fish who will grant him three wishes. Or a magic horse named Sivkaburka appears, and Ivan blows in his ear, spits three times and — presto, change-o — he has beat everyone, turned himself into a handsome rich man, and even won the tsar's daughter and half the tsardom to boot!

In the more than half a century of socialist egalitarianism, with a free crust of bread guaranteed to everyone, and with free (although poor) health care, housing, and public education, the habit of parasitism has irreversibly corrupted the Russian people. Thus millions of Russian television viewers have found endless Mexican soap operas to their taste, where the heroes, wilting under the blows of cruel fate for the whole series, are inevitably brought fortune in the end. The popularity of these shows has not only surpassed all Soviet and Western film masterpieces, literary scenarios following the formula of these sagas have become more cherished by the ordinary Russian than even the works of Pushkin, Lermontov, Gogol, Tolstoy, and Chekhov taken together — I won't even mention Dostoyevsky, who requires particular mental and emotional effort to read. These seeds from across the ocean fell on fertile ground and yielded abundant fruits — they bred new Ivan the Fool types by the millions, who dream of their own personal Firebird of Fortune.

---

[1]Yegor Gaidar headed President Yeltsin's economic reform team; Anatoly Chubais was minister of privatization, then deputy prime minister. — ED.

When he began his privatization games, Anatoly Chubais solemnly   10
vowed to create a class of property owners in Russia. Later, however, he
renounced his promise, just as Peter denied Christ. It turned out, as he
said, that "we had never set ourselves the task of making each citizen a
property owner; the chief task of privatization was to provide each person the opportunity to become a property owner!" An invisible sleight
of hand (or tongue) — and the rabbit disappears from the hat.

After taking away their entire life's savings in a day, the state
solemnly awarded each citizen a slip of paper called a voucher, which
symbolized his or her portion of the national product. At the time the
little piece of paper was worth 10,000 rubles. Now it's worth a little
more, but even so, when converted to dollars, it is humiliatingly, ridicu-
lously tiny — less than five dollars. A logical question arises: Who arro-
gated to themselves all these odd portions of the national wealth that
supposedly belonged to a nonexistent class of property owners? Who,
for example, decided that Beryozka, the Moscow store, is valued more
than the entire Far Eastern fleet? Psychologically, the result of all these
childish games with scraps of paper, investment funds, and ridiculous
dividends is terrifying. Instead of the declared class of property owners
who were to become the bulwark of a civilized state, Russia has got a
rather well-established class of freeloaders.

Let us take a look at the television screen glowing in virtually every
home. There's an irritating series of commercials that keeps flickering
on the screen, interrupting the movies and the interesting shows for ten
to fifteen minutes at a time. The leitmotif is unchanging: how to make
big money. For nothing.

. . . Two members of the intelligentsia, a father and son trying to
look like intellectuals, are sitting on a bank fishing in the pouring rain.
The son suddenly says dreamily, "*That's* the way to do it!" "What?" the
father asks, puzzled. "Why, don't you see?" the son says in surprise.
"We're sitting here and our money's working for us!" Then both of
them drop their fishing rods and begin punching the buttons on their
calculators like crazy men. This is a commercial for the Telemarket
Company, which is supposedly investing in the creation of an integrated Russian communications system, but actually is bilking the public out of their money.

Of course these numerous financial companies and the dozens —
hundreds — of other such fraudulent operations have no government
license for such activity. Just like their investors, they have something
else — a relentless, passionate desire to get rich quickly and easily.

Most likely some of the commercial producers realize, after all, how 15
amoral they and their investors might appear, because sometimes "justifying" dialogue like this comes along:

"You're an idler, Lyonya, a freeloader," says the worker, Ivan, the
brother of Lyonya Golubkov. "I've been breaking my back for my whole
life and never have earned anything and here you are raking in money
for nothing. You freeloader!"

"I'm not a freeloader, I'm a partner," says Lyonya indignantly.

In the next commercial in the series both brothers are already traveling together to the world soccer championship in America — from
which it follows that after racking his brains, brother Ivan finally realized that being a "partner" was easier and simpler than being an honest
working stiff. The television viewer, already green with envy, is then finished off: The two brothers are shown dancing with Victoria Ruffo, the
Mexican star who plays the main character in the extremely popular
soap *Simply Maria*. "Maria" flashes an artificial smile and, like a
windup doll, keeps giving the same answer to all the questions: "Si, si!"
But the viewer is in ecstasy at the sight. Indeed, among all the commercials, first prize unquestioningly goes to the MMM Joint Stock Company and its creation — "the mirror of Russian reform" — the half-
prole, half-bum, but now prospering investor, Lyonya Golubkov.

In developed countries a person who has a lot of money becomes an
investor, but in Russia it's all backward. Those who don't have any
money at all dream of becoming investors. And no wonder! Because
sweet-talking Alisa the Fox and Bazilio the Cat promise as much as a
1,600 percent annual return. The interest is automatically compounded on the principle, much to the envy of the rest of the world,
where a 6 percent annual yield is an almost incredible figure.

There is a boom in private investment in Russia now. Millions of 20
"partners" are investing their pennies (and sometimes quite respectable
sums) in stocks, certificates of deposit, foreign currency, and other securities, dreaming of becoming millionaires within a few months. Not
only is honest labor no longer respected; working fair and square has
somehow become shameful and stupid. Poverty corrupts no less than
wealth, especially if it turns into a dream of freeloading where sponging
becomes the only panacea.

But are we worse off than we were before in the days before perestroika? After all, in the old days the ordinary citizen didn't exactly eat
sandwiches with red caviar every day and drink imported beer. But the
essence of the tragedy of the ordinary consumer can be expressed in
one sentence: We are not just suffering inflation, but a radical alter-
ation of the price structure. The darned thing about it is that in this

chaos it is very hard for us to adapt and to figure out where we stand. I will cite a concrete example from my personal life.

After graduating from Moscow State University, my husband and I became young specialists, as they were called (something like trainees) — I as an editor at Moscow Radio and he as a consultant at the All-Union Copyright Agency (VAAP), both with knowledge of Japanese and English, with degrees in history. Together we earned 240 rubles per month. Even with our parents paying for the apartment, giving us clothing, buying furniture, and kicking in money and groceries, we did not have enough to live on. At the end of each month we regularly bummed twenty or thirty rubles from our friends and acquaintances and returned the debt on payday on the first of the following month. After five years we had "grown up" to earning a total of 400 rubles a month, plus my honoraria for articles and literary translations, so that within a year without particular strain we could save up for a used car.

Workers, especially skilled ones, earned a fairly decent wage. Engineers of various types and junior scientific researchers in academic institutions lived far more modestly, but as far as I recall even they did not groan as much as they do now. University professors, on the other hand, and government ministers received 500 to 600 rubles per month, and enjoyed an entirely comfortable, almost luxurious social life, taking off on foreign trips every year and inviting a full house of guests to their homes every week. Their housing was practically free, along with health care and education — the quality wasn't important. And I am not even mentioning the nomenklatura,[2] who had long since been living solidly "under communism."

Now the pyramid has been turned upside down, and those who were on top suddenly find themselves on the bottom. Students who never graduated from college, working part-time in commercial firms, get up to $200 a month for "petty expenses" (almost double the country's average wages). Meanwhile their parents, employed at state-subsidized organizations, do not collect their wages for months at a time due to the cash shortage. Even when they finally do get their pay, it is so small that they sometimes don't even manage to bring it home — they spend it all on the way. Yesterday's proud professors go around in torn jackets humbly begging for grants from foreign universities, whereas the blockheads who were expelled for academic failure five years ago are now the geniuses of the political and financial world. Yesterday's scam artists are

---

[2]The original *nomenklatura* in the Soviet system were the party-approved personnel in top party, state, and economic posts. The term has come to mean privileged officials of various types in Russia. — TRANS.

now the cream of society, and yesterday's cream has gone sour and become the stinking dregs of society. Only the nomenklatura — both the old and the new — have hung on to their interests.

On the whole, it is difficult to compare the current situation with the old days; still, one small but substantial nuance reveals the essence of the change. For decades the state took our "surplus product," so of course most Russians were never rich. But through persistent, slavish labor people still somehow managed to put away some savings for their retirement — and for death, for a coffin and a set of fine clothes in which to be laid out. We were not rich then, but everything, especially food, was cheaper. By economizing on food, even families with very modest means could allow themselves to buy a set of furniture (sometimes two or three), certainly a television, a refrigerator, a washing machine, and a vacuum cleaner. Almost the entire middle class and a good share of the skilled workers had dachas[3] (with their accompanying free plots of earth, which were distributed at the place of employment) and cars. People were able to acquire all these things because they cost almost next to nothing by world standards. Nobody was concerned about how these low prices were achieved — by selling off natural resources such as timber. The government feared popular discontent and tried to maintain the low prices and required selection of goods in stores until the very last moment, when the mechanism of the economy finally sprung loose.

Those were the days of universal freeloading, a government of handouts. Therefore, relatively poor as they were, people grew accustomed during the years of Soviet rule to not noticing their poverty, and were kept in an illusion of relative prosperity. Now people have had to part with all those cherished illusions along with their habit of hanging on the government's neck (because the state raised them, fed them, educated them, provided them with shoes and clothing — and did not leave them without work!). The state — that very same caring state — not only rudely and roughly awoke people from their sweet dreams, it in fact robbed them with the liberalization of prices and endless monetary reforms. It took away their savings, their relative prosperity, their vacations, and their confidence in the future.

We go to bed at night and wake up every morning with one unpleasant thought: What will become of us tomorrow if . . . This "if" has countless possible variations, each more horrible than the next.

But for now we thoughtlessly spend all our money (since it's useless

25

---

[3]Vacation cottages. — ED.

to save it) on food and pretty rags, like feasting during the plague. Meanwhile the old necessities in our apartments are aging, rusting, or disintegrating. It is unthinkable now to buy new furniture, a television, refrigerator, or vacuum cleaner. Our rundown, ancient automobiles have to last out the century. What will be left when all of these finally die? Will our walls be bare? And what will become of a person who dies within those bare walls, without even enough savings for a funeral? A polyethylene bag and a spot in a common grave?

Admittedly we have always been relatively poor in the material sense but now we have been pushed into a poverty of spirit. After my friend's husband died of cancer her son entered the medical institute, solemnly vowing that he would save people from such a torturous death. He graduated with honors, interned for a year in England, and received wonderful commendations. Eight years passed. The salaries of doctors fell to among the lowest in society. Thus our genius doctor, after spending a year living off the salary of his wife who worked in a commercial firm, took up buying and reselling children's clothing.

Another of my acquaintances, a former designer, rented a little store   30 and spent the summer selling vegetables. In the end he was barely able to cover his rent, and racketeers who quickly appeared on the scene threatened to take away even this amount. Thus the failed merchant dropped everything in a panic and has been hiding out for several months in a friend's apartment.

A neighbor of mine, a professional artist (and quite a good one) who had exhibited her works at international shows, no longer paints. She is occupied with far more important business now: having invested all her earnings in stocks, she now spends weeks standing in lines to collect her dividends in time.

Who are these people — a new lumpen[4] or simply freeloaders? It is not an easy question. Some people dig garden beds and grow berries and vegetables to sell. Others stand outside the metro or in the passageways and outside stores selling cigarettes, salami, and vodka. Still others are out hawking their wares at flea markets. They steal a little, sell a little, deal a little — in short, they find a way to live by puttering about.

Moscow is literally swarming with such self-styled vendors. The same is true of other cities in Russia. . . . Although these people have chopped off their old roots, they have not grown new ones. They cannot become real merchants because they don't have their own stores, vending places, or wholesale outlets. They have no regular customers nor their own business. All of this "retail" is haphazard — someone buys something a little cheaper, sells it for a little more, and either spends

[4]The disenfranchised, uprooted members of the proletariat (laboring class).

the difference or puts it back into circulation. They do not pay taxes and no one registers them — except perhaps the mafia, which has long arms and a big appetite. They have no legal status or defense. Such commerce cannot guarantee reliable and safe earnings. And if you take into account the bribes (and the beatings) from the police and the racketeers, at times they are worse off than when they started. Nevertheless, half of Russia is selling. And half of Russia is buying. Nobody is producing. In 1993, 42 percent of the retail trade went through "shuttlers" who travel abroad to buy goods to resell, through private persons, or through unregistered companies.

All of this comprises the so-called "gray" economy. It is gray because essentially all the products sold are contraband. Forty-two percent of retail a year — that's an enormous figure! Let us imagine how these figures could coincide with the percentages of Russians who are "below the poverty line." Perhaps this is the reason that no one is fainting and falling down from hunger even though they do not receive their wages for months, or receive far less than the minimum living standard? People have found a second niche for themselves: extra earnings in the shadow economy.

The most amazing thing is that this is not merely a means of survival,   35
a way of preventing death by starvation, a temporary phenomenon. No one even dreams of returning to their old lives when things settle down. These people find their new mode of existence quite to their taste because they don't have to put any labor into such vending. They do not have to do anything or produce anything. They do not have to work with their hands or their head. All that is required is to stand next to their wares and name a price. Zero effort. You buy, you sell, you get money. It used to be illegal, now it's allowed. It is a mixture of hackwork and freeloading sanctioned by the government. And if you don't feel like standing out in the freezing cold, there is something even simpler: invest money in stocks and securities. True, for the sake of collecting your dividends, you have to get yourself crushed in lines, but that's almost a form of entertainment.

Of course, not all of these people turned to vending because of the traditional Russian idleness — many of them were driven to it from desperation. After all, when you're paid pennies or nothing at all and you have hungry children at home, most likely you are willing to do almost anything. Most likely.

The reform began more than four years ago. Perestroika, which actually started everything, also took about three years. All together it has been about seven years. How could Russian society reach such a state in such a short time? How could our social ties break so easily, and the moral foundations crumble? The answer is clear: The ties were unstable to begin with and the foundations were extremely shaky. Today's lumpens did not arise out of a vacuum — they were bred from yesterday's marginals.

It is enough to recall what happened to Russia at the turn of the century to understand that truly ideal conditions were created here for the emergence of enormous masses of marginals, these "interim people," and their ensuing lumpenization. First came World War I, then the October Revolution of 1917, then the Civil War and emigration. Next came War Communism, collectivization, and industrialization. This enormous country occupying one-sixth of the earth's land surface bubbled like an enormous pot, mixing millions and millions of people in frenzied vortexes, disrupting customary ties, sweeping masses of people like grains of sand in the sea from one place to another. Stalin's purges, the forced resettlement of peoples, and World War II only finished off the dissolution of social ties. Through all this, the best of the best perished, the very ones who had stood out from the gray masses.

Already by the time of the Khrushchev-Brezhnev era there existed in the USSR a special "ghetto" subculture, as scholars called it, with a new type of déclassé loafer who remained within the framework of his social group. In the perestroika and reform eras the formation of this sociopsychological type was completed. Now a new pyramid of power has been created, and those who have come up from the bottom, yesterday's bums and loafers, have carried the psychology of the freeloader to the top — and to all segments of the new society.

Freeloaders are ruled by the psychology of the mob. The Russian   40 mob, ordinarily an extremely passive swamp, has an inert but terrible strength and needs a leader. If the mob is swayed or stirred, if the dangerous wave is skillfully raised, it is capable of washing over, drowning, and sweeping away everything in its path. Just as happened in 1917.

EXPLORATIONS

1. What is a *sov*? Out of the information Galina Dutkina supplies in paragraphs 4–6 and elsewhere in "Sovs, Hacks, and Freeloaders," define and describe a *sov* in your own words.

2. What are Dutkina's chief complaints about the old Soviet government's policies and its impact on the Russian people? What explanation does she offer for its failings?

3. In what ways does Dutkina think the current political and economic system in Russia is better and worse than the Soviet system? What explanation does she offer for its failings, and what remedies does she suggest?

CONNECTIONS

1. What similar complaints against Soviet communism are voiced by Dutkina in "Sovs, Hacks, and Freeloaders" and by Joseph Brodsky in "Less than One" (p. 359)? What statements in Dutkina's essay suggest that she would agree with Brodsky's ideas in paragraph 2 about Marx's dictum and the antidote for it?

2. In his excerpt from *Speak, Memory* (p. 354), how does Vladimir Nabokov depict the West's influence on Russia? Cite specific examples. In "Sovs, Hacks, and Freeloaders," how does Dutkina depict the West's influence on Russia? Cite specific examples.

3. Reread the last paragraph of Dutkina's essay. Based on these and her other statements, how do you think Dutkina would explain the anti-Semitism described in the anonymous epigraph on page 278?

NATASHA SINGER

The New Russian Dressing

Since journalist Natasha Singer moved to Russia to become the Moscow bureau chief of the New York–based Jewish weekly the *Forward* three years ago, she has learned Russian ("from taxi drivers and watermelon sellers") and visited more than twenty countries in Eastern Europe. She also spent two months dining, clubbing, and shopping with the Russian elite for "The New Russian Dressing." "Moscow today is like Chicago in the twenties, Berlin before World War II, and Wall Street in the 80s," she says. Singer was born in Boston in 1966; she grew up there and in London and Paris. She graduated from Brown University in 1987 and received her master's degree from Boston University in 1990. Her work has appeared in *Vogue, Elle,* and *Islands* magazines, the *Los Angeles Times,* the *International Herald Tribune, USA Today,* the *European,* the *Providence Journal,* and the *Boston Phoenix.* Singer is now working full time on a book about her adopted city, tentatively titled *My Moscow.* "But I like to think of it as Bonfire of the Muscovites." Her remarks and a slightly longer version of this essay appeared in *Vogue* in October 1995.

The camouflage-clad troops stationed in front of Moscow's President Hotel were hoarse from trying to sort out a traffic jam of green Jaguars and red Jeep Cherokees. So they gave up shouting and used their spit-shined AK-47s to direct the crush of imported vehicles.

Several young women in butterfly-print Versace suits with matching scarves climbed out of a BMW; others clutched their black-and-gold Versace handbags like heirlooms already bequeathed to their kin. A jewelry dealer in a red satin Alberta Ferretti gown with rhinestone buckles alighted from a limousine. Big black Mercedeses disgorged bankers and businesswomen sporting the latest Russian ear accessory: the mobile phone.

Guests squirmed for a glimpse of the evening's main attraction, supermodel Nadja Auermann, who was here, down the street from the Kremlin, to help judge the Elite Model Look of 1995, an international modeling contest. But the most passionate glances were reserved for socialite Olga Sloutsker, in a tight pink Vivienne Westwood vest, whose deep décolletage left half of the room swooning.

For Sloutsker, the thirty-year-old president of the World Fitness Corporation, which owns Russia's trendiest gyms, supermodels are already passé, as is Versace and perhaps even Chanel. "Several years ago, I was crazy about Chanel. I bought suits, evening dresses, purses, everything. But now everybody here is wearing it, so I buy only pieces," she said. Between canapés, Sloutsker found time to place an order with Almaz, the jewelry emporium, for a large emerald. Since I'd seen her wear only Cartier, I was surprised she wanted a domestic gem.

"Cartier is for day wear," she told me, tugging at a heavy gold charm   5 bracelet at her wrist. "For serious jewelry, I buy at Franklin Adler in Geneva. Now I want a twelve-carat emerald, a good-quality stone. I'll work hard for it. I'll be greedy," she said in self-parody. "I'll ask my husband to give it to me."

But Vladimir Sloutsker, an oil man, almost didn't live to foot the bill. The next morning, assassins used a radio-controlled antipersonnel mine lodged in a chestnut tree in front of the Sloutskers' apartment to flatten Vladimir's white Chevrolet jeep. The blast blew out six stories of the apartment building's windows and pockmarked the car with forty-seven craters. The chauffeur and a bodyguard suffered serious injury. Vladimir, standing several feet away, survived unscathed.

"Terrorist acts happen all over the world against highly placed people; they just happen more often now in Russia," Sloutsker said several days later when she called me from the South of France, where she recently bought a villa, en route to the couture shows in Paris. The couple returned to Moscow the next week, having purchased a bombproof "presidential Chevrolet limousine, the kind President Clinton uses" in his motorcade.

In the new Moscow, where you are nothing without a Cartier watch, a Moschino bag, and a Filofax, accessories are expensive, but life is cheap.

After seventy years of a Soviet-induced product drought, Russians are shopping like mad. Until a few years ago there was, as Elite's press director, Xavier Moreau, recalls, "no lipstick, no shoes, no perfume, no dresses, no money, nothing, nothing, nothing." Now, suddenly, there is everything. A Versace emporium and a Laura Biagiotti boutique. Christian Dior outlets and Estée Lauder counters. An abundance of personal trainers and plastic surgeons. Maxim's, with $1,400 wines on the menu. Cellular phones galore (a necessary antidote to the dysfunctional public-phone service). A Jacques Dessange studio and several Wella salons. The state department store, G.U.M., now houses Benetton, Yves

Rocher, Revlon, Reebok, and Galeries Lafayette. You've come a long way, Masha.

Like Wall Street in the 1980s or California during the Gold Rush,   10
Moscow is fast becoming a hub for a new generation of new rich. The
.01 percent of the population — about 15,000 bankers, brokers, import-
export dealers, computer entrepreneurs, and gangsters — that forms
Russia's *haute société* is in the throes of a grab-buying binge that has the
feel of wholesale gluttony after consumer starvation. And the new capi-
talists (or the New Russians, as the local press has dubbed them, pejora-
tively) are casting about for historical models of style and wealth, recalling 1914, when Russia held the largest gold reserves in the world. Like
its aristocratic antecedents, this new nobility wants only the best,
whether it be sneakers, sports cars, or swimming pools for new country
estates. The current Cartier craze is a throwback to the turn of the century, when Pierre Cartier himself visited Russia, sparking a frenzy
among the aristocracy. In fashion, the penchant for having it all often
translates into a one-designer-only look. A Muscovite might wear all
Chanel one day — from shoes to perfume to jewelry — and all Escada
the next.

In a decade or two, if Russia's economy and political system work out
their kinks, the gulf between Russia's poor, who earn a minimum wage
of twelve dollars a month, and Russia's rich, who can spend twelve dollars for a cup of coffee, may narrow. Right now, however, in Russia's
overheated economy, entrepreneurs can make millions by taking advantage of gray areas in the laws. But with hitmen regularly targeting
prominent businessmen, the fear of losing everything tomorrow —
either at the hands of gangs or because of the wildly fluctuating economy — is breeding a buy-it-now decadence that hasn't been seen in
Russia since the czarist era. Moscow's wealthy women have made a vocation of competitive opulence — whether they are redecorating summer cottages in all-Empire interiors, draping themselves in couture
ballgowns, or watching their boyfriends lose $100,000 at blackjack ta-
bles in well-appointed casinos. The Russian capital has turned itself
into a mecca for carpe diem consumers.

On a Monday afternoon, Galina Grishena, twenty-two, spent $3,000
at the Moscow Trading House, a new designer-only boutique that takes
up two floors of an entire city block, in downtown Moscow. Ignoring
the sections devoted to Jil Sander and Claude Montana — the only
such sales racks in Moscow — she homed in on the separate wing devoted to Gianni Versace, selecting pieces from his latest Istante collection. On Tuesday afternoon, she spent $1,000 more at the same address

and instantly acquired the status of most-favored Trading House customer. The manager, recognizing a surefire designer junkie, offered her an espresso at the boutique's bar. On Wednesday, she was back. Wearing the black spandex glitter Istante dress and matching high-heeled sandals she had acquired the day before, Grishena wanted to inspect a suit she had put on hold.

Except for her stately poise, Grishena, with her long blonde hair and pale blue eyes, could pass for a California girl. Her considerable disposable income (she says she can spend $8,000 in a shopping spree) comes from her husband, a computer and high-tech importer. Grishena recently started modeling "as a hobby." Although Prada, Escada, Féraud, and Armani hang in her closet, Versace is her favorite, and she values her prized holdings like a collector.

"I have everything Versace — the bags, the boots, watch, sunglasses. I have coats, a leather coat, a leather jacket, and a white leather suit," she says as she tries on a pair of glittering Istante sandals. Grishena lives by the unwritten Moscow fashion rule that forbids mixing and matching designers. "The Cartier sunglasses go with the Cartier watch; the Versace watch goes with the Versace sunglasses," she instructs.

For Grishena, part of the allure of prêt-à-porter labels lies in the attention from the sales staff. "I want not only to buy what I need but to buy it in a nice environment. In a Russian store, no one helps you; you have to wait in long lines; and if you ask too many questions or try on too many things, the staff gets irritated," she says as she waits for a salesgirl to find her a matching purse.

Grishena — who made more appearances at the store Thursday and Friday and spent another $1,200 — is a typical Trading House client (regular customers spend $10,000 to $50,000 a month, sometimes in cash), but she hasn't always lived in such high style. She and her husband both grew up poor in an industrial town outside of Moscow. They married at the outset of his career because she found him "smart, solid, and sober," and he admired her housekeeping skills. Several years later, with his computer business booming, and their young son packed off to vacation with his grandmothers in Italy, she has more than enough time and money to indulge her passion for clothes.

Alas, the matching purse Grishena wanted today is out of stock, so she decides to try the Versace boutique across town. She reaches into the little black Versace shopping bag that habitually holds her mobile phone and Filofax, and pulls out a walkie-talkie.

"Sasha, come in; Sasha, over," she calls to her chauffeur, who pulls up her new black Range Rover. This is a precautionary measure against the possibility of auto theft, robbery, and kidnapping; her husband travels around town with two bodyguards. From boutique door to car door is about the biggest glimpse of the street Grishena gets these days.

The Versace boutique takes precautions, too; two armed men stand guard at the door, deciding who qualifies for a shopping spree. It's difficult, however, to determine their admission criteria. We are immediately invited in — the entire staff knows Grishena by name — but so are two young toughs with Makarov pistols stuffed down their jeans.

The luxurious boutique is about as lush an oasis as one can find in   20
Moscow. A decorator gone mad with the Midas touch has blanketed the entire interior with gold. While Versace boutiques all over the world are characterized by the same unabashed glitz, the Moscow shop seems particularly incongruous set against the backdrop of Russian privation. But for Grishena, the boutique is as familiar as her walk-in closet, and she arrives with the assurance of a queen entering her throne room.

"Versace is bright and attention-getting, and I don't want to be lost in the crowd," she says. "I know in America, women wear more comfortable clothes. I know it's not practical to go to our country house in high heels, but I do it because it's beautiful. Our rich women now do not want to be modest," she says.

With so many Versace vixens around town, shopping is ultra-competitive. "People are mad for Versace. It's like an infection," says store manager Stanislav Sukharev, sitting in a gold-and-black upholstered chair. He sees some loyal customers daily. They get dressed and "come to Versace every morning as if they were going to work. We are their job," he says.

"In a month we will run out of stock, and then," he predicts, surveying the half-empty racks of evening gowns, "people will start demanding to buy the display windows, even the clothes off the salesgirls. It has happened before. It will happen again."

Moscow spendaholics also do their shopping at Sadko Arcade, a cinder-block version of a suburban strip mall. Here, in the province of MaxMara suits, Fogal hose, Wedgwood china, Cacharel for kids, Maserati cars, and a Charles Jourdan boutique, there are no Nintendo arcades and sullen, gum-chewing teens. The Moscow mall rat is another species entirely. Take Irina Iretskaya, a tall, willowy college student with the graceful gait and upright posture of a ballerina.

Iretskaya is already world-weary at twenty. Her long ebony hair   25
pulled back in a tight knot, she plunks herself down in a booth at the Swiss Confectionary Cafe, where I have been waiting for three hours. It's 4:00 P.M. and Iretskaya has only just tumbled out of bed, haggard

from a night of heavy partying. "We danced until 7:00 A.M. It was Trance Night at Titanic [her favorite club], and everybody was on drugs," she says with Holly Golightly blitheness from behind a pair of Fendi sunglasses.

By day, Iretskaya is a student a the formidable Institute for Foreign Relations, the Russian equivalent of the Fletcher School of Law and Diplomacy; in the evenings, she studies for her MBA at the American University program here. Iretskaya's life has changed considerably since she met her businessman boyfriend several months ago. Midnight usually finds them in the intimate green-marble salon of Eldorado, a hip Italian restaurant. They greet dawn in one of a handful of trendy nightclubs. The two also travel extensively. On a recent trip to New York, Iretskaya discovered designer labels and acquired pieces from Donna Karan, Jean Paul Gaultier, Calvin Klein, Yves Saint Laurent, and Karl Lagerfeld. "My boyfriend is a wealthy man, and when we go shopping together, for sure he buys all my clothes," she says as Moscow teenagers in three-inch heels and metallic leather skirts clatter by our booth.

Being young, winsome, and long of limb always has attracted hard currency, but in today's Russia beauty carries exponential value. Still, Iretskaya's stunning sloe-eyed looks can be deceiving. She's studying corporate finance and intends to be a banker. Asked about Russian commerce, she rattles off a detailed list of banks and subdivisions, commenting on their capital and lending rates.

Iretskaya relishes the political and economic changes that will make her fortunes fairer than those of the preceding generation. She is too young, she says proudly, to remember standing in lines, acknowledging, "I already have much more opportunity than my mother had. She worked for the Foreign Ministry and traveled a lot, but she was always short of money. I'm sure it was unpleasant for her to see that life abroad was great but she couldn't afford it."

. . . As is true of elites the world over, New Russians inhabit a parallel universe — one that rarely collides with the world of ordinary Russians. . . . On a recent Friday morning, Olga Sloutsker, who owns four World Class Health Clubs, enters her kitchen in a puffy white monogrammed robe from the Grand Hôtel du Cap Ferrat near Nice. Setting her mobile phone down by her coffee cup, she harangues her maid: "How could you buy this! I asked for nonfat yogurt, and this is extra-fat yogurt!" Sloutsker, whose entrée extends to the top echelons of Moscow politics and society, lives life in Russia's precarious fast lane. "Either you live abroad, make normal money, and live a normal life," she says, "or you live here, make big money, and are nervous."

Sloutsker's lifestyle has changed radically since the mid-1980s, when   30
she was on the Soviet national fencing team. On their first trip abroad,
to Finland, teammates sold tins of caviar so they would have enough
money to buy clothes. Now Sloutsker collects Russian paintings, antiques, and Empire furnishings and travels abroad to do her shopping.
"In New York, at Chanel, they call me when something I might like
comes in. At Barneys, I have Bella in the Alaïa department. To buy
shoes, I go to Bergdorf Goodman, to the Manolo Blahnik department.
Frederic Fekkai does my hair," she says.

By early evening, the parking lot of World Class is bloated with
chauffeurs and bodyguards calling one another on mobile phones from
Mercedes 600s, Volvos, and government-issued black Volgas. World
Class is not only the premier workout joint in Moscow, it's a combination Royalton and Harvard Club, where top bankers, traders, publishers, brokers, models, and politicians sweat together on gleaming new
LifeCircuit machines. It's a place where women put on makeup before
they do aerobics, where less fortunate souls can languish at the bottom
of the six-month waiting list for years. Here, Sloutsker works out with
her personal trainer, the formidable Ludmilla Popovskaya, a pentathlon
champion. "Today you will run three kilometers," the redhead announces to Sloutsker, turning on the Tunturi treadmill. Nearby, models
from the Red Stars agency are panting on StairMasters, and the world
champion female bodybuilder, Yulia Stefanovich, works the bench press.

"I forbid Olga to take calls while working out. If the phone rings
and it's one of her friends, I won't let her talk," Popovskaya says while
her boss sweats at the chest press. But Sloutsker's cellular phone rings
incessantly with calls from business associates, tanning-bed suppliers
from abroad, and queries from employees at her new health club in
St. Petersburg.

A man in a Reebok shorts-and-T-shirt set deposits his barbell on a
mat to answer his mobile phone. "For another $250 million, we can
own the oil business in Kazakhstan," he says curtly and returns to his
weights.

For the Russian leisure class, sports have become serious business.
The greens at the Moscow Country Club, designed by internationally
renowned course designer Robert Trent Jones Jr., have made golf widows of Russian industrialists' wives. The leading Russian business magazine recently ran a spread on "Yachting in Russia: Riding the Crest of
the Wave," discussing where to buy, outfit, dock, or charter a vessel in
Moscow. The sports craze is good news for Sloutsker. "When we
opened two years ago, 20 percent of the clientele were Russian. Now

80 percent are Russian," she says. "We used to have four aerobics classes a day. Now we have them every hour."

After a long day of meetings with business associates and government   35
bureaucrats, a spot check at the construction site of her new house on the Moscow River, and a quick facial, Sloutsker relaxes at Titanic, for the moment Moscow's hottest club. At 2:00 A.M. she's dressed down, in Levi's jeans, white Comme des Garçons T-shirt, white leather Rifat Ozbek blazer, and Hermès belt. But the Versace brigade here is fully armed with leather jackets, evening bags, and sunglasses with heavy gold logos sending across the dance floor their unmistakable message, which is not so much "I'm cool" as "I'm wearing $400 on my head."

The Soviet Union always had a hip bohemian class, but the hyper-groomed clubgoers here are something entirely new, a clique of nascent Beautiful People who would do Studio 54 proud. Anyone who is anyone in Moscow, be she poseur or spectator, is at Titanic tonight. Here is Galina Grishena, who drove over at 3:00 A.M. in her day-old silver Mercedes C280 with the sun roof open and the radio at full blast. Striding past the railings across Titanic's upper decks in a sexy white leather Versace miniskirt, her blonde hair pulled back by Mary Quant–style flower barrettes, she looks every inch a James Bond girl. Here, too, is Irina Iretskaya, in a little black sleeveless Donna Karan sheath, thumping to too much techno with her boyfriend and her friends from the Institute. And here is Olga Sloutsker, tired from pumping iron and tired of explaining Russian taste.

"People don't understand why Russians want to have the best; best cars, best clothes, best holidays in the best hotels," she says. "Even in olden times, visitors to Russia were shocked at the sight of merchants eating mountains of caviar and drinking champagne out of ladies' slippers. Maybe we just have this in our character.

"Maybe sometimes we look cheap and not stylish and we don't know how to communicate, but we are learning," she continues, "and I think maybe in ten years we will be quite sophisticated.

"Come on," she adds, relinquishing for the first time in fifteen hours her beloved mobile phone. "We're going to dance."

EXPLORATIONS

1. What are the meanings of Natasha Singer's title, "The New Russian Dressing"? What does this title imply about Singer's attitude toward the subjects of her essay? What elements in the essay reflect the same attitude?

2. What appear to be the top status symbols for New Russian women? For New Russian men? What messages do these symbols communicate, and to whom?

3. What contrast does Singer establish in her opening paragraph? Where else in her essay does she reinforce that contrast? What is its point?

CONNECTIONS

1. In "Sovs, Hacks, and Freeloaders" (p. 367), Galina Dutkina writes, "For now we thoughtlessly spend all our money (since it's useless to save it) on food and pretty rags" (para. 28). Who are the "we" in Dutkina's statement? Do they "thoughtlessly spend" for the same reasons as the New Russians in Singer's essay? How can you tell?

2. In "Less than One" (p. 359), Joseph Brodsky writes, "Anything that bore a suggestion of repetitiveness became compromised and subject to removal" (para. 9). In what way do the characters in "The New Russian Dressing" share Brodsky's nonconformity? How is theirs different from his, and why?

3. According to Singer, "the New Russians . . . are casting about for historical models of style and wealth, recalling 1914" (para. 10). In what ways do the Sloutskers and others seem to be emulating old Russians such as Vladimir Nabokov's family as he describes them in the excerpt from *Speak, Memory* (p. 354)? What other models do you think the New Russians are copying?

INVESTIGATIONS

1. Since the Soviet Union dissolved in 1990, Russian politics and history have been in a state of upheaval (see headnote, p. 352). Choose one of the developments raised in "Spotlight: Russia," such as the widening income gap between rich and poor (Singer, p. 378, and Dutkina, p. 367); anti-Semitism (Brodsky, p. 359, and Anonymous, p. 278); or the influence of the West (all). Research your choice and write an essay summarizing your findings and conclusions.

2. In his 1987 Nobel Prize lecture Joseph Brodsky wrote, "Aesthetics is the mother of ethics. The categories of 'good' and 'bad' are, first and foremost,

aesthetic ones. . . . A man with taste, particularly with literary taste, is less susceptible to the refrains and the rhythmical incantations peculiar to any version of political demagogy. . . . The more substantial an individual's aesthetic experience is, the sounder his taste, the sharper his moral focus, the freer — though not necessarily the happier — he is." Compare Brodsky's statements with those of Dzevad Karahasan quoted by Amitav Ghosh in paragraph 80, page 340. Who is right? Brodsky? Karahasan? Both? Write an essay on the link between ethics and aesthetics, particularly in relation to political conflicts. Support your position with evidence from selections in this book.

3. In the second paragraph of Nabokov's essay from *Speak, Memory* (p. 354), he shifts from exposition (explaining what circumstances drew his father into a duel) to narrative (telling how he found out about it). With typical unconventionality, Nabokov peppers the active part of his story with inactive verbs: some of them passive ("digs were taken") and some intransitive ("a magazine . . . was passing from hand to hand"). Why do writers usually prefer action-oriented verbs for a narrative scene? What does Nabokov convey by his verb choices? Rewrite the narrative section of this paragraph, from "Sometime during the day" to "number of his suits," using stronger, more active verbs. (For example: "A well-timed swoop put me in possession of" might become "I grabbed.") Then write a short evaluation of the scene's change in impact.

PART FOUR

OPPOSITE SEXES

Paula Gunn Allen • David Friedman • Joe Kane • Rose Weitz
Gerald Early • Population Communications International
Camille Paglia • Lawrence Wright • Dympna Ugwu-Oju
Violeta Chamorro • Miriam Cooke

MIRRORS: The United States
John Updike: *The Disposable Rocket*
Sam Keen: *Man and WOMAN*
Deborah Tannen: *How Male and Female
    Students Use Language Differently*
Leslie Marmon Silko: *Yellow Woman*

WINDOWS: The World

Marjorie Shostak: *Nisa's Marriage*
    (BOTSWANA)
Nikos Kazantzakis: *The Isle of Aphrodite*
    (GREECE)
Simone de Beauvoir: *Woman as Other*
    (FRANCE)
Alberto Moravia: *The Chase* (ITALY)

SPOTLIGHT: The Islamic Middle East
Diana Abu-Jaber: *In Flight* (JORDAN)
Naila Minai: *Women in Early Islam* (ARABIA)
Naguib Mahfouz: *A Day for Saying Goodbye*
    (EGYPT)
Unni Wikan: *The Xanith: A Third Gender
    Role?* (OMAN)

An American Indian woman is primarily defined by her tribal identity. In her eyes, her destiny is necessarily that of her people, and her sense of herself as a woman is first and foremost prescribed by her tribe. The definitions of woman's roles are as diverse as tribal cultures in the Americas. In some she is devalued, in others she wields considerable power. In some she is a familial/clan adjunct, in some she is as close to autonomous as her economic circumstances and psychological traits permit. But in no tribal definitions is she perceived in the same way as are women in Western industrial and postindustrial cultures.

In the West, few images of women form part of the cultural mythos, and these are largely sexually charged. Among Christians, the Madonna is the female prototype, and she is portrayed as essentially passive: Her contribution is simply that of birthing. Little else is attributed to her, and she certainly possesses few of the characteristics that are attributed to mythic figures among the Indian tribes. This image is countered (rather than balanced) by the witch-goddess/whore characteristics designed to reinforce cultural beliefs about women, as well as Western adversarial and dualistic perceptions of reality.

The tribes see women variously, but they do not question the power of femininity. Sometimes they see women as fearful, sometimes peaceful, sometimes omnipotent and omniscient, but they never portray women as mindless, helpless, simple, or oppressed. And while the women in a given tribe, clan, or band may be all these things, the individual woman is provided with a variety of images of women from the interconnected supernatural, natural, and social worlds she lives in.

> – PAULA GUNN ALLEN
> "Where I Come from Is Like This"
> *The Sacred Hoop*, 1986

▼ ▼ ▼

The Sioux have a name for the rite of passage the rest of us call becoming a man.

They call it "The Big Impossible."

And the rest of us are only now learning how right they are.

A century after the death of Sitting Bull, today's male finds himself perplexed, confused, and frustrated by the requirements of masculinity. This befuddlement is so great, in fact, that many men have dropped out of the process completely. If becoming a man really is as dubious a proposition as the Sioux believe, these dropouts wonder what's the point in trying. Instead of failing to be a man, why not succeed at some-

390

thing equally rewarding (at least to males), definitely easier, and — why deny it — a lot more fun?

The heck with being a man. The '90s male would rather be a guy.

Unlike a man, a guy is far less interested in the serious ramifications of manhood, such as becoming a parent or sustaining a meaningful career. He is, in fact, far less interested in the serious ramifications of anything. And that certainly includes finding his lost manhood in the woods while banging on a drum.

According to Dave Barry, the Robert Bly of the Guy Movement and author of the best-seller *Dave Barry's Complete Guide to Guys*, guys share certain primal characteristics:

- They like neat stuff, especially if it's expensive and more powerful than necessary.
- They like to scratch, even in public. Especially in public.
- They like pointless challenges.
- They do not have a rigid, well-defined moral code — least of all about sex.
- They have a Noogie Gene.
- They are not great at communicating intimate feelings — assuming they have any, which is not a smart assumption.
- And, most of all, they like hanging out with other guys.

In fact, there's probably a guy inside all men just waiting to burst out — the more inopportune the moment, the better.

> – DAVID FRIEDMAN
> "The 'Guy' Thing"
> *Newsday*, 1995

▼ ▼ ▼

Women have begun to ascend — *have* ascended — into roles of power and prestige once reserved for men. No corresponding change in acceptable roles has occurred for men. . . .

Come on, admit it: When you meet an ambitious, successful woman, and the man in her life is not an achiever of equal note, you figure him for a wimp, don't you? And your judgment of him is far more severe than your judgment of her would be if the situation were reversed. If there is no new role for men in a world where women are rising, men will just be that much more reluctant to give up the roles they already have.

> – JOE KANE
> "Star Wars: How Men Are Coping
> with Female Success"
> *Ms.*, 1985

. . . Whereas lesbians threaten the status quo by refusing to accept their inferior position as women, gay males may threaten it even more by appearing to reject their privileged status as men.

> – ROSE WEITZ
> "What Price Independence?"
> *Women: A Feminist Perspective,* 1984

▼ ▼ ▼

What did I see as a boy when I passed the large black beauty shop on Broad and South Streets in Philadelphia where the name of its owner, Adele Reese, commanded such respect or provoked such jealousy? What did I see there but a long row of black women dressed immaculately in white tunics, washing and styling the hair of other black women. That was a sign of what culture, of what set of politics? The sheen of those straightened heads, the entire enterprise of the making of black feminine beauty: Was it an enactment of a degradation inspired by a bitter inferiority or was it a womanly laying on of hands where black women were, in their way, helping themselves to live through and transcend their degradation?

> – GERALD EARLY
> "Life With Daughters: Watching
> the Miss America Pageant"
> *Kenyon Review,* 1992

▼ ▼ ▼

In addition to more "traditional" abuses of women, domestic violence in developing countries is often rooted in deeply entrenched cultural attitudes and practices. In India, "bride burning" by family members or in-laws is a well-known practice; official police records show that 4,835 women were killed in 1990 because of their families' failure to meet demands for money and goods. In greater Bombay, one of every five deaths among women aged fifteen to forty-four was listed as a case of "accidental burning." Female infanticide is an old and widely practiced form of family violence in Asia, where girls are often killed within a few days of birth. In South Asia, according to one survey, 58 percent of known female infanticide was committed by feeding babies the poisonous sap of a plant or by choking them by lodging rice hulls soaked in milk in their throats. The culturally dictated practice of genital mutilation of young girls, obligatory in much of the Middle East and Africa and in some Asian countries, has been carried to the United States and Canada by immigrants. Globally, at least 2 million girls a year experience the violence demanded by their societies and approved by their families. And every day, there are 6,000 new cases — or five girls genitally mutilated every minute. As for "traditional" family violence against women, in Costa Rica 95 percent of pregnant hospital clients under fifteen were found to be incest victims. At a police station in São Paulo, Brazil, 70 percent of all reported cases of violence against women took place in the home. Similarly, in Santiago, Chile, some 75 percent of all assault-related injuries of women were caused by family members. In a hospital in Peru, researchers found 90 percent of young mothers twelve to sixteen years old were victims of rape, often by a father, stepfather, or other close relative. Violence during pregnancy is a major reason for miscarriage. A Mexico City sampling found 20 percent of battered women reported blows to the stomach by their partners.

– POPULATION COMMUNICATIONS INTERNATIONAL
Focus on Women: Violence Against Women, 1995

▼ ▼ ▼

The sexes are at war. Men must struggle for identity against the overwhelming power of their mothers. Women have menstruation to tell them they are women. Men must do or risk something to be men. Men become masculine only when other men say they are. Having sex with a woman is one way a boy becomes a man.

College men are at their hormonal peak. They have just left their mothers and are questing for their male identity. In groups, they are dangerous. A woman going to a fraternity party is walking into Testosterone Flats, full of prickly cacti and blazing guns. If she goes, she should be armed with resolute alertness. She should arrive with girlfriends and leave with them. A girl who lets herself get dead drunk at a fraternity party is a fool. A girl who goes upstairs alone with a brother at a fraternity party is an idiot. Feminists call this "blaming the victim." I call it common sense. . . .

Aggression and eroticism are deeply intertwined. Hunt, pursuit, and capture are biologically programmed into male sexuality. Generation after generation, men must be educated, refined, and ethically persuaded away from their tendency toward anarchy and brutishness. Society is not the enemy, as feminism ignorantly claims. Society is woman's protection against rape.

– CAMILLE PAGLIA
Sex, Art, and American Culture, 1992

▼ ▼ ▼

Is it possible that of the two genders nature created, one is nearly perfect and the other is badly flawed? Well, yes, say the psychobiologists.

Unlike women, who carry two X chromosomes, men have an X and a Y. The latter has relatively little genetic information except for the gene that makes us men. A woman who has a recessive gene on one X chromosome might have a countering dominant gene on the other. That's not true for men, who are therefore more vulnerable to biological and environmental insults, as well as more prone to certain behavioral tendencies that may be genetically predetermined. Although male hormones (called androgens) don't cause violent criminal or sexual behavior, they apparently create an inclination in that direction. . . . Androgens are associated with a number of other male traits (in humans as well as animals), including assertive sexual behavior, status-related aggression, spatial reasoning, territoriality, pain tolerance, tenacity, transient bonding, sensation seeking, and predatory behavior. Obviously, this list posts many of the most common female complaints about men, and yet androgens make a man a man; one can't separate maleness from characteristic male traits.

. . . Anyone looking at men today should be able to see that they are confused and full of despair. It's not just our place in society or the family that we are struggling for; we're fighting against our own natures. We didn't create the instincts that make us aggressive, that make us value action over consensus, that make us more inclined toward strength than sympathy. Nature and human history have rewarded those qualities and in turn have created the kind of people men are. Moreover, these competitive qualities have been necessary for the survival of the species, and despite the debate over masculinity, they are still valued today.

– LAWRENCE WRIGHT
Texas Monthly, 1992

▼ ▼ ▼

An Ibo woman has very little personal identity, even if she lives in the United States and has success in her career. Our culture takes very little pride in a woman's accomplishment. At an Ibo gathering a woman is more likely to be asked whose wife or mother she is before she is asked her name or what she does for a living. If the woman is accomplished but unmarried, people will say, "But where is she going with all that success?" Ibos cling to the adage that a woman is worth nothing unless she's married and has children.

I am as guilty as any other Ibo woman living in the United States in perpetuating this. Professionally, I am more successful than the majority of Ibo men I've met in this country, yet when we gather for a party, usually to celebrate a marriage or a birth, I join the women in the kitchen to prepare food and serve the men. I remember to curtsy just so before the older men, looking away to avoid meeting their eyes. I glow with pride when other men tease my husband about his "good wife.". . .

Hundreds of thousands of women from the Third World and other traditional societies share my experience. We straddle two cultures, cultures that are often in opposition. Mainstream America, the culture we embrace in our professional lives, dictates that we be assertive and independent — like men. Our traditional culture, dictated by religion and years of socialization, demands that we be docile and content in our roles as mothers and wives — careers or not.

– DYMPNA UGWU-OJU
New York Times Magazine, 1993

▼ ▼ ▼

As you know, certain studies show that women traditionally lead by means of reconciliation, interrelations, and persuasion, considering the fact that society has traditionally counted on the women to keep the family together, while men usually lead through control and intimidation. When women entered the fields of politics and business, they brought with them the moral values they had learned from home. These values have shown good results; I dare say they have even shown better results than did the traditional model created by men. . . . I think it is time that male leaders look to women leaders as role models. They will find that persuasion brings better results than confrontation. And, finally, they will realize that, when dealing with the nations of the world, reconciliation unites people and allows them to work together for the benefit of all.

– VIOLETA CHAMORRO
Women World Leaders
(Laura A. Lizwood), 1995

▼ ▼ ▼

In the American imagination, the harem, far from being a historical institution, where veiled wives eked out a miserable existence under the harsh rule of a domestic despot, is a living and exotic fantasy made reality. Unfortunately, such a stereotype is reinforced by a superficial glance at the societies of the Arabian Peninsula, where the Bedouin *burqa* (the black face covering with apertures for the eyes) and the *batula* (the beaklike mask made of polished indigo-impregnated cloth that resembles leather, or even metal) further enhance the alien image of Muslim women. . . .

Although the countries of the Arabian Peninsula never discarded the veil, other Muslim countries, such as Egypt, Lebanon, Syria, Iraq, Iran,

Turkey, and Pakistan did. At some point, usually around the time of independence, the veil became a bone of contention, and it was officially rejected. However, during the past two decades, some sectors of the female population have been reveiling. . . . This new political veil, akin to a nun's habit, does not hark back to some previous traditional modest dress. It is called the *ziyy islami,* to be distinguished from the *hijab,* which is the umbrella term used for the veil whatever the local cultural variations may be. The women wearing the *ziyy islami* have made a political decision; they have proclaimed a new identity within a religious framework. . . .

Veiling was favored by men because it guaranteed possession and prestige while claiming to be the ultimate mark of respect for something that had to be protected. Protection, however, has several possible meanings: It may connote concern for the woman's safety or it may indicate anxiety about the woman's sexuality — in which case it is the men who are being protected. In either case, of primary concern is the safeguarding of honor, the man's honor. As Fatima Mernissi says, virginity does seem to be a game that men play with each other, women merely serving as "silent intermediaries."

– MIRIAM COOKE
"The Veil Does Not Prevent
Women from Working"
The World and I, 1991

EXPLORATIONS

1. Rose Weitz alludes to the "inferior position" of women and "privileged status" of men. Which of the other writers of these epigraphs regard women as occupying an inferior position, and in what ways? Which writers regard men as having a privileged status, and in what ways?

2. Which writers of these epigraphs depict women as having a privileged status, and in what ways? Which writers regard men as occupying an inferior position, and in what ways?

3. David Friedman, Camille Paglia, Lawrence Wright, and Violeta Chamorro write about what men are like. What points do some or all of these commentators agree on? What points do they disagree on? In what respects do you agree and disagree with them?

4. Paula Gunn Allen, Gerald Early, Dympna Ugwu-Oju, and Violeta Chamorro write about what women are like. What points do some or all of these commentators agree on? What points do they disagree on? In what respects do you agree and disagree with them?

MIRRORS:
THE UNITED STATES

▲▲▲▲▲▲▲▲▲▲
▼▼▼▼▼▼▼▼▼▼

Opposite Sexes: *Tennis players discuss a singles game across the net.*

JOHN UPDIKE

The Disposable Rocket

John Updike credits his mother for encouraging him early to write. Today he is one of the most prolific and respected authors in the United States, having published more than a dozen each of novels, short story collections, and volumes of poetry, as well as several plays and children's books. Also a noted critic, Updike has won most of this country's major literary prizes, including the National Book Award, American Book Award, and Pulitzer Prize. He was born in Shillington, Pennsylvania, in 1932. After graduating summa cum laude from Harvard University, he studied in Oxford, England, at the Ruskin School of Drawing and Fine Arts. Among Updike's best-known works are *Rabbit, Run* (1960), the first of four novels about a small-town Pennsylvania car salesman; *Couples* (1968), a chronicle of suburban infidelities; and *The Witches of Eastwick* (1984), which became the basis for a motion picture. His most recent novel is *In the Beauty of the Lilies* (1996). Updike is highly regarded for, among other things, his sharp observation of manners and mores, his vivid descriptions, and his grapplings with the Christian dilemmas of faith, passion, and evil (see p. 504). A member of the American Academy, he lives with his wife Martha north of Boston. "The Disposable Rocket" originally appeared in the Michigan Quarterly Review (1994).

Inhabiting a male body is like having a bank account; as long as it's healthy, you don't think much about it. Compared to the female body, it is a low-maintenance proposition: a shower now and then, trim the fingernails every ten days, a haircut once a month. Oh yes, shaving — scraping or buzzing away at your face every morning. Byron, in *Don Juan*, thought the repeated nuisance of shaving balanced out the periodic agony, for females, of childbirth. Woman are, his lines tell us,

> Condemn'd to child-bed, as men for their sins
> Have shaving too entail'd upon their chins, —

> A daily plague, which in the aggregate
> May average on the whole with parturition.

From the standpoint of reproduction, the male body is a delivery system, as the female is a mazy device for retention. Once the delivery is made, men feel a faint but distinct falling-off of interest. Yet against the enduring female heroics of birth and nurture should be set the male's superhuman frenzy to deliver his goods: He vaults walls, skips sleep, risks wallet, health, and his political future all to ram home his seed into the gut of the chosen woman. The sense of the chase lives in him as the key to life. His body is, like a delivery rocket that falls away in space, a disposable means. Men put their bodies at risk to experience the release from gravity.

When my tenancy of a male body was fairly new — of six or so years' duration — I used to jump and fall just for the joy of it. Falling — backwards, or down stairs — became a specialty of mine, an attention-getting stunt I was still practicing into my thirties, at suburban parties. Falling is, after all, a kind of flying, though of briefer duration than would be ideal. My impulse to hurl myself from high windows and the edges of cliffs belongs to my body, not my mind, which resists the siren call of the chasm with all its might; the interior struggle knocks the wind from my lungs and tightens my scrotum and gives any trip to Europe, with its Alps, castle parapets, and gargoyled cathedral lookouts, a flavor of nightmare. Falling, strangely, no longer figures in my dreams, as it often did when I was a boy and my subconscious was more honest with me. An airplane, that necessary evil, turns the earth into a map so quickly the brain turns aloof and calm; still, I marvel that there is no end of young men willing to become jet pilots.

Any accounting of male-female differences must include the male's superior recklessness, a drive not, I think, toward death, as the darker feminist cosmogonies would have it, but to test the limits, to see what the traffic will bear — a kind of mechanic's curiosity. The number of men who do lasting damage to their young bodies is striking; war and car accidents aside, secondary-school sports, with the approval of parents and the encouragement of brutish coaches, take a fearful toll of skulls and knees. We were made for combat, back in the postsimian, East-African days, and the bumping, the whacking, the breathlessness, the pain-smothering adrenaline rush form a cumbersome and unfashionable bliss, but bliss nevertheless. Take your body to the edge, and see if it flies.

The male sense of space must differ from that of the female, who has such interesting, active, and significant inner space. The space that interests men is outer. The fly ball high against the sky, the long pass spiraling overhead, the jet fighter like a scarcely visible pinpoint nozzle laying down its vapor trail at forty thousand feet, the gazelle haunch flickering just beyond arrow-reach, the uncountable stars sprinkled on their great black wheel, the horizon, the mountaintop, the quasar —

these bring portents with them and awaken a sense of relation with the invisible, with the empty. The ideal male body is taut with lines of potential force, a diagram extending outward; the ideal female body curves around centers of repose. Of course, no one is ideal, and the sexes are somewhat androgynous subdivisions of a species: Diana the huntress is a more trendy body type nowadays than languid, overweight Venus, and polymorphous Dionysius poses for more underwear ads than Mars. Relatively, though, men's bodies, however elegant, are designed for covering territory, for moving on.

An erection, too, defies gravity, flirts with it precariously. It extends   5
the diagram of outward direction into downright detachability — objective in the case of the sperm, subjective in the case of the testicles and penis. Men's bodies, at this juncture, feel only partly theirs; a demon of sorts has been attached to their lower torsos, whose performance is erratic and whose errands seem, at times, ridiculous. It is like having a (much) smaller brother toward whom you feel both fond and impatient; if he is you, it is you in curiously simplified and ignoble form. This sense, of the male body being two of them, is acknowledged in verbal love play and erotic writing, where the penis is playfully given a pet name, an individuation not even the rarest rapture grants a vagina. Here, where maleness gathers to a quintessence of itself, there can be no insincerity, there can be no hiding; for sheer nakedness, there is nothing like a hopeful phallus; its aggressive shape is indivisible from its tender-skinned vulnerability. The act of intercourse, from the point of view of a consenting female, has an element of mothering, of enwrapment, of merciful concealment, even. The male body, for this interval, is tucked out of harm's way.

To inhabit a male body, then, is to feel somewhat detached from it. It is not an enemy, but not entirely a friend. Our being seems to lie not in cells and muscles but in the traces that our thoughts and actions inscribe on the air. The male body skims the surface of nature's deeps wherein the blood and pain and mysterious cravings of women perpetuate the species. Participating less in nature's processes than the female body, the male body gives the impression — false — of being exempt from time. Its powers of strength and reach descend in early adolescence, along with acne and sweaty feet, and depart, in imperceptible increments, after thirty or so. It surprises me to discover, when I remove my shoes and socks, the same paper-white, hairless ankles that struck me as pathetic when I observed them on my father. I felt betrayed when, in some tumble of touch football twenty years ago, I heard my tibia snap; and when, between two reading engagements in Cleveland, my appendix tried to burst; and when, the other day, not for the first time, there arose to my nostrils out of my own body the musty attic smell my grandfather's body had.

A man's body does not betray its tenant as rapidly as a woman's. Never as fine and lovely, it has less distance to fall; what rugged beauty it has is wrinkleproof. It keeps its capability of procreation indecently long. Unless intense athletic demands are made upon it, the thing serves well enough to sixty, which is my age now. From here on, it's chancy. There are no breasts or ovaries to admit cancer to the male body, but the prostate, that awkwardly located little source of seminal fluid, shows the strain of sexual function with fits of hysterical cell replication, and all that male-bonding beer and potato chips add up in the coronary arteries. A writer, whose physical equipment can be minimal as long as it gets him to the desk, the lectern, and New York City once in a while, cannot but be grateful to his body, especially to his eyes, those tender and intricate sites where the brain extrudes from the skull, and to his hands, which hold the pen or tap the keyboard. His body has been, not himself exactly, but a close pal, pot-bellied and balding like most of his other pals now. A man and his body are like a boy and the buddy who has a driver's license and the use of his father's car for the evening; one goes along, gratefully, for the ride.

EXPLORATIONS

1. Where in "The Disposable Rocket" does John Updike use the analogy of his title, and in what ways does he apply it? In what additional way is the analogy implied in his essay's last paragraphs?

2. What is the central comparison–contrast in this essay? Where and how does Updike introduce it? How does he change the terms of the comparison in his opening paragraph?

3. What additional comparisons and analogies appear in "The Disposable Rocket"? Find at least six. In this essay, what advantages does Updike gain by leaning more heavily on comparison than on other techniques such as description and abstract explanation?

CONNECTIONS

1. What point about male sexuality is made by both John Updike and Camille Paglia (p. 393)? How do they interpret the same point differently?

2. In his first paragraph on page 393, Lawrence Wright lists some male traits associated with androgens. Which of the same traits does Updike refer or allude to? Which ones does Updike treat more positively than Wright, and in what ways?

3. What does Updike say about flying? Which of his comments do you think apply to the pilots Andre Dubus describes in "Imperiled Men" (p. 293)? To Dave Rahm, the stunt pilot in Annie Dillard's "Flying" (p. 288)?

ELABORATIONS

1. What does it mean to you to be whichever gender you are? How has your concept of maleness or femaleness changed over the course of your life? What gender-related traits do you enjoy most and least? What traits do you mind the most and envy the most in the opposite sex? Keeping in mind John Updike's use of comparison and contrast, write your own essay addressing some or all of these questions.

2. Updike mentions dreams of falling, akin to dreams of flying. What dreams have you had that involve these or similar physical sensations? How did such dreams relate to your waking life? Write an essay either describing your dreams and your reaction to them, or explaining how your dreams helped you to understand real events.

SAM KEEN

Man and WOMAN

Sam Keen graduated from Ursinus College in 1953 and holds advanced degrees from Harvard Divinity School and Princeton University. After completing his Ph.D. at Princeton he taught philosophy of religion at Louisville Presbyterian Theological Seminary from 1962 to 1968 before becoming a contributing editor for *Psychology Today* magazine. His writing and teaching have explored religion, philosophy, and psychology at the grass-roots level; his first book to attract significant attention was *Apology for Wonder* (1969), in which he looks at the role of wonder in the approach of children and ancient societies to the world. Over the next two decades Keen continued to lecture, consult, and lead groups at colleges, corporations, and a variety of other institutions all over the United States, as well as to write books and magazine features. In 1987 he collaborated on a public-television documentary based on his book *Faces of the Enemy* (1986). Keen's best-known book is *Fire in the Belly: On Being a Man* (1991), which gave him the status of a leader (along with Robert Bly; see p. 133) of the men's movement. "Man and WOMAN" comes from the introduction to *Fire in the Belly*. Keen's latest book is *Hymns to an Unknown God* (1994). He lives in Sonoma, California, with his wife and daughters.

One of the major tasks of manhood is to explore the unconscious feelings that surround our various images of WOMAN, to dispel false mystification, to dissolve the vague sense of threat and fear, and finally to learn to respect and love the strangeness of womankind. It may be useful to think about sexual-spiritual maturation — the journey of manhood — as a process of changing WOMAN into women into Jane (or one certain woman), of learning to see members of the opposite sex not as archetypes or members of a class but as individuals. It is the WOMAN in our heads, more than the women in our beds or boardrooms, who causes most of our problems. And these archetypical creatures — goddesses, bitches, angels, Madonnas, castrators, witches, Gypsy maidens, earth mothers — must be exorcised from our minds and hearts before we can learn to love women. So long as our house is haunted by the ghost of WOMAN we can never live gracefully with any woman. If we continue to deny that she lives in the shadows she will continue to have power over us.

A man's journey in relationship to WOMAN involves three stages. In the beginning he is sunk deep in an unconscious relationship with a falsely mystified figure who is composed of unreal opposites: virgin-whore, nurturer-devouring mother, goddess-demon. To grow from man-child into man, in the second stage, he must take leave of WOMAN and wander for a long time in the wild and sweet world of men. Finally, when he has learned to love his own manhood, he may return to the everyday world to love an ordinary woman.

In the first stage of his journey, or so long as he remains unconscious, the trinity that secretly controls man is: WOMAN as goddess and creatrix, WOMAN as mother and matrix, and WOMAN as erotic-spiritual power.

WOMAN *as Goddess and Creatrix*

Woman was, is, and always will be goddess and creatrix. She is the womb from which we sprang, the ground of our being. Feminists who argue that goddess-worship historically preceded the notion of God as father are certainly correct. What they fail to see is that the goddess, since her historical dethronement, has remained alive and well, and continues to exert power from deep in the hidden recesses of the male psyche. Granted, she has been sentenced to remain in a kind of internal exile, under house arrest, but her power is obvious from the efforts spent to keep her imprisoned.

As our source, the goddess is both historically and psychologically primary. She has been an inevitable symbol of divinity since the beginning of time and remains a sacred presence in the timeless dimension of every psyche. The earliest images we have of WOMAN and divinity are one and the same, stone figurines such as the so-called Venus of Willendorph — women without faces or feet, with ponderous breasts and prominent vulvas. When we look at these early icons of mother-goddesses it doesn't require much empathy to imagine the overwhelming sense of awe men experienced at woman's capacity to give birth. She was at once the revelation and the incarnation of creativity. Her womb was of the same substance as the fruitful earth. She was Mother Nature.

In explaining the continuing power of WOMAN as creatrix over men, psychologists have often reduced the mystery of gender to a matter of "penis envy" or "womb envy." But to name the awe we feel in the presence of the opposite sex "envy" is mean and mistaken. Call it "womb awe" or even "womb worship," but it is not simple envy.

I don't remember ever wanting to be a woman. But each of the three times I have been present at the birth of one of my children I have been overwhelmed by a sense of reverence. As the event of birth approached, the delivery room was bathed in a transcendent light and transformed into a stage for a cosmic drama. It was, quite suddenly, the first day of creation; the Goddess was giving birth to a world. When Jessamyn, my last child, was born, the doctors had to attend to Jananne, my wife. I took off my shirt, put the baby next to my body, and walked and sang her welcome into the world. In that hour all my accomplishments — books I had written, works of will and imagination, small monuments to my immortality — shrank into insignificance. Like men since the beginning of time I wondered: What can I ever create that will equal the magnificence of this new life?

As creatrix, WOMAN addresses an inescapable challenge to a man to justify his existence. She gives birth to meaning out of her body. Biology alone assures her of a destiny, of making a significant contribution to the ongoing drama of life. A man responds to her challenge by simulating creation, by making, fabricating, and inventing artifacts. But while she creates naturally and literally, he creates only artificially and metaphorically. She creates from her corpus; he invents a "corporation," a fictitious legal body with endowed rights of a natural person. Her creation sustains the eternal cycle of nature. Each of his artifacts contributes to making history a series of unrepeatable events. (Sometimes I imagine that the hidden intent of technology is to create a perfect mechanical baby — an automobile, a machine that moves by itself, is capable of perpetual motion, is fed its daily bottle of petroleum, and has its pollution diapered.) In response to the power of the goddess, man creates himself in the image of a god he imagines has fabricated the world like a craftsman working with a blueprint to shape matter into meaningful objects. Much of the meaning men attribute to their work is a response to the question posed to us by WOMAN'S capacity to give life.

WOMAN *as Mother and Matrix*

WOMAN, in her second aspect as mother and matrix, is food, everlasting arms, teacher of language and philosophy, the horizon within which we live and move and have our being. To paraphrase an old hymn, She is "so high you can't get over her, so low you can't get under her, so wide you can't get around her." She exists; therefore I am.

Within the warp of her womb our bodies are woven — flesh of her flesh. Within the woof of her arms our minds, spirits, and visions of the world are braided together. She is teacher of the categories by which we will understand ourselves. Her face was our first mirror. A newborn is programmed for immediate face recognition and will spend 90 percent of its waking time focused on the mother. The changing pattern of her face — her smile, her frown, the joy or sadness in her eyes — is the infant's barometer of reality. If she smiles I am good. If she is angry I am bad. There was terror in her disapproving glance, and bliss when her face shone upon us.

Consider the fundamental categories of our emotional and intellec-   10
tual life that we learn before we are weaned. At the breast we learn: desire, satisfaction, disappointment, anger, fear, authority, expectation, judgment. Little wonder that Hindu philosophers identify WOMAN with Maya — illusion — as well as nurturance. Her body is our first information system. If she is warm and sensuous and loves to hold us, we learn that the world is supported by trustworthy and everlasting arms. If she is tense and unhappy we learn the world is fearful and filled with nameless dangers.

WOMAN, as the mother, continues to have enormous power over our adult lives because her most important lessons are taught wordlessly. She shapes us before we understand language, and therefore her influence is hidden from our adult consciousness. Her instructions remain within us like posthypnotic suggestion. Imagine that long ago your mother wrote and inserted the software disk that preprogrammed your life. She etched the script for your life, inserted a philosophy-of-life program, on the blank pages of your mind. This set of instructions remains in the archaic layers of your psyche and continues to shape your perceptions and feelings well into adulthood. The language in which she wrote is as cryptic and difficult to decipher as ancient hieroglyphics, and yet to break the spell she has woven you must learn to decipher these early messages and bring the wordless information and misinformation into the light of consciousness.

In the degree that Mother remains a shadow presence in the life of a man, he will see himself and all women as if reflected in Mother's eyes. He will perform for them as he performed for her, fearing displeasure, courting approval. The size of his ego and the size of his cock will be determined by what he sees in the mirror she holds. And all the while he will imagine that her judgments are those of the flesh-and-blood women in his life. Just like the song says, he will "marry a girl just like the girl that married dear old Dad," and will love and hate her accordingly. Almost inevitably, men marry Mother unless they have undertaken the long struggle to recognize and exorcise WOMAN from their psyches.

Modern men bear a special burden in relationship to Mother; our task of separation is more difficult than that of traditional men. For most modern sons, Mother is a problem that needs to be solved and we find it difficult to break the symbiotic bond.

Freud said that the first major crisis in a boy's life was severing his attachment to his mother and identifying with his father. In the gospel according to Freud, every boy wants to possess and sleep with his mother and displace his powerful father. But he fears being castrated or killed by the father (a fear substantiated by his observation that women and little girls lack, and therefore must have lost, the penis). About the age of six the son learns to live by the ancient adage, "If you can't beat them, join them." He renounces his desire to be his mother's lover and makes common cause with his enemy — the father. This successful resolution of the Oedipus complex, like ancient initiation rites, involves identification with power, authority, and the values of the father and the male establishment.

If this classical drama of separation from Mother and the initiation of   15
the son by the father sounds strange to our ears it is because the world has changed. Since the industrial revolution, the son is more likely to have remained mama's boy than to have identified with any powerful male authority. The powerful father has been all but replaced by the powerful mother.

Dad is no longer present to teach his sons how to be men. More than any other single factor, this absence of the father from the modern family is what presently disturbs the relationship between mothers and their sons and therefore between men and women, husbands and wives. Where once there was a father, there is now a vacuum. Dad belongs more to the world of work than to the family. He is, or was until recently, the provider, but he is gone from the home most of the time. Someone, using what I call SWAG statistics (Scientific Wild-Ass Guess) has estimated that prior to World War I men spent four hours a day with their children, between World War I and World War II two hours, and since World War II twenty minutes.

There are many variations on the modern mother-son theme, but in some degree most sons were forced to step into the role of husband and lover to their mother. As a friend told me: "Mother made me into the husband my father never was. I was the listener, the helper, the ally in hard times. In a sense I became the man of the house. I was super-responsible, so I never really got a chance to be a kid." While the love between mother and son seldom becomes literally incestuous, it becomes too close for comfort. Rollo May, in a conversation with me, characterized the problem of the son who is too close to his mother as the opposite of that which Freud presented. "The dilemma of the modern son is that he *wins* the Oedipal battle against the father and gets Mother. And then he doesn't know what to do with her because she overwhelms him."

Ambivalence is the consequence of the modern mother-son relationship. The son experiences the mother as nearly omnipotent. She works outside the home, manages the household, and provides for his daily needs. But he learns from the rhetoric and values of the surrounding society that women are less important than men, that childrearing is an inferior task, that men have real power and authority, and that what counts is success in the public arena of business and politics. So the son is faced with a tragic, schizophrenic choice. If he is to become a man and play a role in the "real" world, he must deny his visceral knowledge of the goodness of Mother's caring power and join the male conspiracy to "keep women in their place," in the missionary position, beneath men.

Meanwhile the son must develop various strategies to deal with the power of Mother. He may surrender, becoming mama's boy, and devote his life to pleasing her, and later his wife or lover. If he takes this tack his relationships with women will be dominated by the desire to perform well, to gain approval, and to avoid female anger or rejection. Or he may take an opposite course and reduce females to either servants or sex objects. The Don Juan male constantly tries to prove his potency by seduction and conquest. The more violent man who is obsessed with pornography or rape is compelled to demean and take revenge of woman in order to deny her power over him.

To be free from and for women, to discover the unique ground of [20] manhood, a man must take leave of Motherland.

WOMAN *as Erotic-Spiritual Power*

The third aspect of WOMAN is as an irresistible erotic-spiritual force. She is the magnet, and men the iron filings that lie within her field.

It is difficult to give this aspect of WOMAN a familiar name because Western mythology, philosophy, and psychology have never acknowledged its reality. Once, men and women assumed that the goddess controlled all things that flow and ebb — the waxing and waning moon, the rise and fall of tide and phallus. But ever since God became Father, and men have considered themselves the lords over nature (and women), we have defined man as active and WOMAN as reactive. Consequently, we have never developed a language that does justice to WOMAN'S erotic-spiritual power.

In Eastern mythology, notions of gender are reversed. The female principle is seen as active and the male as responsive. Among human beings, lions, and other members of the animal kingdom, the female of the species sends out her invitations on the wind and commands the male's response. He may think he initiates, but her sexual perfumes (pheromones) and inspiring image influence him to action. She is the prime mover, the divine eros, whose power draws him to her. As Joseph Campbell points out,[1] the term *Shakti* in Hindu mythology names the energy or active power of a male divinity that is embodied in his spouse. "Every wife is her husband's Shakti and every beloved woman her lover's. Beatrice was Dante's. Carried further still: The word connotes female spiritual power in general, as manifest, for instance, in the radiance of beauty, or on the elemental level in the sheer power of the female sex to work effects on the male."

To detect this important aspect of men's experience of WOMAN that our language or philosophy of gender does not name or honor, we have to look at the angelic and demonic extremes of men's sexuality — the ways in which WOMAN figures in the imaginations of artists and rapists.

For many creative men WOMAN is the muse and inspiration for   25 their work. She possesses a semidivine power to call forth their creativity. Without her inspiration they cannot paint, write, or manage. She is the anima, the spirit and soul of a man. Without her a man is only will and intellect and blind force.

At the opposite end of the spectrum the rapist confesses the same experience of the irresistible erotic power of WOMAN. His defense is inevitably: "She tempted me. She wanted it. She seduced me." For a moment, put aside the correct response to such deluded excuses, which is that it is *not* the victim's fault, and consider the raw unconscious experience of WOMAN that underlies rape no less than the inspiration of the artist. In both cases, she is experienced as the active, initiatory power.

When we consider how most "civilized" men have repressed their experience of the power of WOMAN as goddess, mother, and erotic-spiritual motivator, it is easy to understand the reasons that lie in back of

---

[1]Joseph Campbell and M. J. Abadie, *The Mythic Image* (Princeton, N.J.: Princeton University Press, 1981).

the history of men's cruelty to women. We fear, therefore deny, therefore demean, therefore (try to) control the power of WOMAN. There is
no need here to rehearse the routine insults and gynocidal hatreds of
men toward women. Mary Daly, Susan Griffin, and other feminist
thinkers have traced this painful history in brilliant and convincing
fashion.

As men we need to recollect our experience, reown our repressed
knowledge of the power of WOMAN, and cease establishing our manhood in reactionary ways. If we do not, we will continue to be workers
desperately trying to produce trinkets that will equal WOMAN'S creativity, macho men who confuse swagger with independence, studs
who anxiously perform for Mother's eyes hoping to win enough ap-
plause to satisfy a fragile ego, warriors and rapists who do violence to a
feminine power they cannot control and therefore fear.

So long as we define ourselves by our reactions to unconscious images of WOMAN we remain in exile from the true mystery and power
of manhood.

EXPLORATIONS

1. What point of view does author Sam Keen use in "Man and WOMAN"?
What is his intended audience? How can you tell? Where in this selection
does Keen's personal experience play a role, and what role does it play?

2. What does Keen mean by WOMAN? What does he believe is the usual relationship between men and women before "sexual-spiritual maturation —
the journey of manhood" (para. 1)? What does he believe is the ideal relationship between men and women after this maturation journey?

3. On what kinds of information does Keen base his statements about
WOMAN? What sources does he cite? On what basis do you think Keen expects readers to accept his statements?

CONNECTIONS

1. According to Keen, what three aspects of WOMAN comprise "the trinity
that secretly controls man" (para. 3)? How do you think Keen would classify
John Updike's depiction of women in "The Disposable Rocket" (p. 398)?
How do you think Updike would respond to Keen's trinity?

2. How does Paula Gunn Allen summarize Western images of women
(p. 390)? In what ways does Keen's description of WOMAN match Allen's

summary? How would you expect Allen's recommendations to men regarding women to be like and unlike Keen's?

3. "The heck with being a man," writes David Friedman (p. 390). "The '90s male would rather be a guy." After reading "Man and WOMAN," what reasons can you suggest why some men feel this way? How do you think Keen would respond to Friedman?

ELABORATIONS

1. Choose one of the historic or religious references in "Man and WOMAN" that interests you, such as the ancient tradition of goddess worship (paras. 4–5) or the psychoanalytic theory of penis envy (para. 6), and find out enough about it to write an essay on it.

2. Write an essay about either WOMAN or MAN from your own sex's point of view. You may want to use "Man and WOMAN" as a structural or stylistic model, or you may want to write an argument critiquing or rebutting Keen's ideas.

DEBORAH TANNEN

How Male and Female Students Use Language Differently

The youngest of three daughters, Deborah Tannen was born in Brooklyn, New York, in 1945. At age seven a case of mumps damaged her hearing — a problem she suspects made her unusually attentive to people's conversational styles. Tannen graduated from Hunter College High School and in 1966 from Harpur College. After a stint as an insurance claims adjuster, she traveled to Europe, where she worked in Crete teaching English as a second language and in Athens as an instructor at the Hellenic-American Union. Returning to the United States, Tannen received her M.A. in English literature from Wayne State University. She taught in New Jersey and New York, then returned to school, where she switched her focus to linguistics. With a Ph.D. from the University of California at Berkeley, she joined the faculty at Georgetown University in 1979; she still holds the title of University Professor there.

Tannen had published many scholarly articles and two books before winning popular attention with *That's Not What I Meant!: How Conversational Style Makes or Breaks Your Relations with Others* (1986). Readers' response led her to follow up with the best-seller *You Just Don't Understand: Women and Men in Conversation* (1990), which by 1994 had sold nearly 2 million copies and been translated into eighteen languages. Ever since, Tannen's teaching and writing have been interspersed with media and lecture appearances. She has served on a variety of editorial boards and advisory panels and won numerous awards while continuing to edit and write books. Her recent work includes poetry and a play, as well as *Talking from 9 to 5: How Women's and Men's Conversational Styles Affect Who Gets Heard, Who Gets Credit, and What Gets Done at Work* (1995). "How Male and Female Students Use Language Differently" first appeared in 1991 in the *Chronicle of Higher Education.* Tannen and her husband live in Washington, D.C., and New York.

When I researched and wrote my book *You Just Don't Understand: Women and Men in Conversation*, the furthest thing from my mind was reevaluating my teaching strategies. But that has been one of the direct benefits of having written the book.

412

The primary focus of my linguistic research always has been the language of everyday conversation. One facet of this is conversational style: how different regional, ethnic, and class backgrounds, as well as age and gender, result in different ways of using language to communicate. *You Just Don't Understand* is about the conversational styles of women and men. As I gained more insight into typically male and female ways of using language, I began to suspect some of the causes of the troubling facts that women who go to single-sex schools do better in later life, and that when young women sit next to young men in classrooms, the males talk more. This is not to say that all men talk in class, nor that no women do. It is simply that a greater percentage of discussion time is taken by men's voices.

The research of sociologists and anthropologists such as Janet Lever, Marjorie Harness Goodwin, and Donna Eder has shown that girls and boys learn to use language differently in their sex-separate peer groups. Typically, a girl has a best friend with whom she sits and talks, frequently telling secrets. It's the telling of secrets, the fact and the way that they talk to each other, that makes them best friends. For boys, activities are central: Their best friends are the ones they do things with. Boys also tend to play in larger groups that are hierarchical. High-status boys give orders and push low-status boys around. So boys are expected to use language to seize center stage: by exhibiting their skill, displaying their knowledge, and challenging and resisting challenges.

These patterns have stunning implications for classroom interaction. Most faculty members assume that participating in class discussion is a necessary part of successful performance. Yet speaking in a classroom is more congenial to boys' language experience than to girls', since it entails putting oneself forward in front of a large group of people, many of whom are strangers and at least one of whom is sure to judge speakers' knowledge and intelligence by their verbal display.

Another aspect of many classrooms that makes them more hospitable   5 to most men than to most women is the use of debate-like formats as a learning tool. Our educational system, as Walter Ong argues persuasively in his book *Fighting for Life* (Cornell University Press, 1981), is fundamentally male in that the pursuit of knowledge is believed to be achieved by ritual opposition: public display followed by argument and challenge. Father Ong demonstrates that ritual opposition — what he calls "adversativeness" or "agonism" — is fundamental to the way most males approach almost any activity. (Consider, for example, the little boy who shows he likes a little girl by pulling her braids and shoving her.) But ritual opposition is antithetical to the way most females learn and like to interact. It is not that females don't fight, but that they don't fight for fun. They don't *ritualize* opposition.

Anthropologists working in widely disparate parts of the world have found contrasting verbal rituals for women and men. Women in completely unrelated cultures (for example, Greece and Bali) engage in ritual laments: spontaneously produced rhyming couplets that express their pain, for example, over the loss of loved ones. Men do not take part in laments. They have their own, very different verbal ritual: a contest, a war of words in which they vie with each other to devise clever insults.

When discussing these phenomena with a colleague, I commented that I see these two styles in American conversation: Many women bond by talking about troubles, and many men bond by exchanging playful insults and put-downs, and other sorts of verbal sparring. He exclaimed: "I never thought of this, but that's the way I teach: I have students read an article, and then I invite them to tear it apart. After we've torn it to shreds, we talk about how to build a better model."

This contrasts sharply with the way I teach: I open the discussion of readings by asking, "What did you find useful in this? What can we use in our own theory building and our own methods?" I note what I see as weaknesses in the author's approach, but I also point out that the writer's discipline and purposes might be different from ours. Finally, I offer personal anecdotes illustrating the phenomena under discussion and praise students' anecdotes as well as their critical acumen.

These different teaching styles must make our classrooms wildly different places and hospitable to different students. Male students are more likely to be comfortable attacking the readings and might find the inclusion of personal anecdotes irrelevant and "soft." Women are more likely to resist discussion they perceive as hostile, and, indeed, it is women in my classes who are most likely to offer personal anecdotes.

A colleague who read my book commented that he had always taken   10
for granted that the best way to deal with students' comments is to challenge them; this, he felt it was self-evident, sharpens their minds and helps them develop debating skills. But he had noticed that women were relatively silent in his classes, so he decided to try beginning discussion with relatively open-ended questions and letting comments go unchallenged. He found, to his amazement and satisfaction, that more women began to speak up.

Though some of the women in his class clearly liked this better, perhaps some of the men liked it less. One young man in my class wrote in a questionnaire about a history professor who gave students questions to think about and called on people to answer them: "He would then play devil's advocate . . . i.e., he debated us. . . . That class *really* sharpened me intellectually. . . . We as students do need to know how to defend ourselves." This young man valued the experience of being attacked and challenged publicly. Many, if not most, women would shrink from such "challenge," experiencing it as public humiliation.

A professor at Hamilton College told me of a young man who was upset because he felt his class presentation had been a failure. The professor was puzzled because he had observed that class members had listened attentively and agreed with the student's observations. It turned out that it was this very agreement that the student interpreted as failure: Since no one had engaged his ideas by arguing with him, he felt they had found them unworthy of attention.

So one reason men speak in class more than women is that many of them find the "public" classroom setting more conducive to speaking, whereas most women are more comfortable speaking in private to a small group of people they know well. A second reason is that men are more likely to be comfortable with the debatelike form that discussion may take. Yet another reason is the different attitudes toward speaking in class that typify women and men.

Students who speak frequently in class, many of whom are men, assume that it is their job to think of contributions and try to get the floor to express them. But many women monitor their participation not only to get the floor but to avoid getting it. Women students in my class tell me that if they have spoken up once or twice, they hold back for the rest of the class because they don't want to dominate. If they have spoken a lot one week, they will remain silent the next. These different ethics of participation are, of course, unstated, so those who speak freely assume that those who remain silent have nothing to say, and those who are reining themselves in assume that the big talkers are selfish and hoggish.

When I looked around my classes, I could see these differing ethics   15 and habits at work. For example, my graduate class in analyzing conversation had twenty students, eleven women and nine men. Of the men, four were foreign students: two Japanese, one Chinese, and one Syrian. With the exception of the three Asian men, all the men spoke in class at least occasionally. The biggest talker in the class was a woman, but there were also five women who never spoke at all, only one of whom was Japanese. I decided to try something different.

I broke the class into small groups to discuss the issues raised in the readings and to analyze their own conversational transcripts. I devised three ways of dividing the students into groups: one by the degree program they were in, one by gender, and one by conversational style, as closely as I could guess it. This meant that when the class was grouped according to conversational style, I put Asian students together, fast talk-ers together, and quiet students together. The class split into groups six times during the semester, so they met in each grouping twice. I told students to regard the groups as examples of interactional data and to note the different ways they participated in the different groups. Toward the end of the term, I gave them a questionnaire asking about their class and group participation.

I could see plainly from my observation of the groups at work that women who never opened their mouths in class were talking away in the small groups. In fact, the Japanese woman commented that she found it particularly hard to contribute to the all-woman group she was in because "I was overwhelmed by how talkative the female students were in the female-only group." This is particularly revealing because it highlights that the same person who can be "oppressed" into silence in one context can become the talkative "oppressor" in another. No one's conversational style is absolute; everyone's style changes in response to the context and others' styles.

Some of the students (seven) said they preferred the same-gender groups; others preferred the same-style groups. In answer to the question "Would you have liked to speak in class more than you did?" six of the seven who said yes were women; the one man was Japanese. Most star-tlingly, this response did not come only from quiet women; it came from women who had indicated they had spoken in class never, rarely, some-times, and often. Of the eleven students who said the amount they had spoken was fine, seven were men. Of the four women who checked "fine," two added qualifications indicating it wasn't completely fine: One wrote in "maybe more," and one wrote, "I have an urge to participate but often feel I should have something more interesting/relevant/wonderful/ intelligent to say!!"

I counted my experiment a success. Everyone in the class found the small groups interesting, and no one indicated he or she would have preferred that the class not break into groups. Perhaps most instructive, however, was the fact that the experience of breaking into groups, and of talking about participation in class, raised everyone's awareness about classroom participation. After we had talked about it, some of the qui-etest women in the class made a few voluntary contributions, though sometimes I had to ensure their participation by interrupting the stu-dents who were exuberantly speaking out.

Americans are often proud that they discount the significance of cul-   20 tural differences: "We are all individuals," many people boast. Ignoring such issues as gender and ethnicity becomes a source of pride: "I treat everyone the same." But treating people the same is not equal treatment if they are not the same.

The classroom is a different environment for those who feel comfortable putting themselves forward in a group than it is for those who find the prospect of doing so chastening, or even terrifying. When a professor asks, "Are there any questions?" students who can formulate statements the fastest have the greatest opportunity to respond. Those who need significant time to do so have not really been given a chance at all, since by the time they are ready to speak, someone else has the floor.

In a class where some students speak out without raising hands, those who feel they must raise their hands and wait to be recognized do not have equal opportunity to speak. Telling them to feel free to jump in will not make them feel free; one's sense of timing, of one's rights and obligations in a classroom, are automatic, learned over years of interaction. They may be changed over time, with motivation and effort, but they cannot be changed on the spot. And everyone assumes his or her own way is best. When I asked my students how the class could be changed to make it easier for them to speak more, the most talkative woman said she would prefer it if no one had to raise hands, and a foreign student said he wished people would raise their hands and wait to be recognized.

My experience in this class has convinced me that small-group interaction should be part of any class that is not a small seminar. I also am convinced that having the students become observers of their own interaction is a crucial part of their education. Talking about ways of talking in class makes students aware that their ways of talking affect other students, that the motivations they impute to others may not truly reflect others' motives, and that the behaviors they assume to be self-evidently right are not universal norms.

The goal of complete equal opportunity in class may not be attainable, but realizing that one monolithic classroom-participation structure is not equal opportunity is itself a powerful motivation to find more diverse methods to serve diverse students — and every classroom is diverse.

EXPLORATIONS

1. According to Deborah Tannen, what is the main difference between women's and men's use of language in social groups? How does this difference affect their use of language in classrooms?

2. On what sources does Tannen base her statements? Which kinds of evidence in her essay did you find most convincing, and why?

3. According to Tannen, what factors besides students' gender affect who speaks out the most in class? In what ways do your college classes match (or not) Tannen's depiction?

CONNECTIONS

1. What does Tannen say about the ways women and men influence each other's behavior in the classroom? After reading "Man and WOMAN" (p. 403), what do you think Sam Keen would say about male and female students' influence on each other's tendency to speak, argue, or be silent in class? What do you think Camille Paglia (p. 393) might add?

2. What does Dympna Ugwu-Oju's description of being an Ibo woman in the United States (p. 394) have in common with Tannen's description of male and female styles of communication? What explanation would you expect Ugwu-Oju to offer for the ethnic differences in communication style that Tannen noticed in her class?

3. What are the parallels between Tannen's observations and those of Violeta Chamorro (p. 395)? Given that Chamorro is the president of Nicaragua and the widow of a political activist, what are the probable sources for her statements?

ELABORATIONS

1. What happens to conversational style when women and men leave the classroom? Choose one or more selections from this book that show members of both sexes interacting in ways Tannen describes: Frank McCourt's "Limerick Homecoming" (p. 200), Kazuo Ishiguro's "A Family Supper" (p.260), Richard Ford's "Optimists" (p. 301), Amitav Ghosh's "The Ghosts of Mrs. Ghandi" (p. 330). Write an essay applying Tannen's ideas to other situations besides the ones she considers. You may use evidence from your chosen selection(s) to support Tannen's conclusions or to dispute them.

2. Which of the factors Tannen mentions have the most effect on your participation in class? What other factors do you find significant that Tannen does not mention? Write an essay describing the ideal class structure. Explain how and why you believe it would be effective, using examples from your own experience.

LESLIE MARMON SILKO

Yellow Woman

The novelist and poet Leslie Marmon Silko was born in Albuquerque, New Mexico, in 1948. Part Laguna Pueblo, part Mexican, and part Anglo, she grew up on the Laguna Pueblo Reservation in the shadow of Mt. Taylor, legendary home of the ka'tsina spirits that appear in Pueblo and Hopi mythology. In the matrilineal Pueblo culture, houses and land are generally owned and passed down through the women. Work and family life overlap and involve everyone. So, says Silko, "The kinds of things that cause white upper-middle-class women to flee the home for a while to escape or get away from domination and powerlessness and inferior status, *vis-à-vis* the husband, . . . they're not operating at all." Silko graduated summa cum laude from the University of New Mexico in 1969, the same year she wrote "Yellow Woman." After teaching at Navajo Community College in Arizona, she moved to Ketchikan, Alaska, where she would later set the title story for her collection *Storyteller* (1981). Returning to the Southwest, she taught at the University of New Mexico and at the University of Arizona, Tucson, where she has been a professor of English since 1978. Silko's stories have appeared in a variety of magazines and collections. Among her writing awards is a 1983 MacArthur Foundation Fellowship. Her highly praised novel *Ceremony* (1977), the first novel published by a Native American woman, is regarded as a landmark in American fiction. Her most recent book is *Yellow Woman and a Beauty of the Spirit: Essays on Native American Life Today* (1996).

I

My thigh clung to his with dampness, and I watched the sun rising up through the tamaracks and willows. The small brown water birds came to the river and hopped across the mud, leaving brown scratches in the alkali-white crust. They bathed in the river silently. I could hear the water, almost at our feet where the narrow fast channel bubbled and washed green ragged moss and fern leaves. I looked at him beside me, rolled in the red blanket on the white river sand. I cleaned the sand out of the cracks between my toes, squinting because the sun was above the willow trees. I looked at him for the last time, sleeping on the white river sand.

I felt hungry and followed the river south the way we had come the afternoon before, following our footprints that were already blurred by lizard tracks and bug trails. The horses were still lying down, and the black one whinnied when he saw me but he did not get up — maybe it was because the corral was made out of thick cedar branches and the horses had not yet felt the sun like I had. I tried to look beyond the pale red mesas to the pueblo. I knew it was there, even if I could not see it, on the sand rock hill above the river, the same river that moved past me now and had reflected the moon last night.

The horse felt warm underneath me. He shook his head and pawed the sand. The bay whinnied and leaned against the gate trying to follow, and I remembered him asleep on the red blanket beside the river. I slid off the horse and tied him close to the other horse. I walked north with the river again, and the white sand broke loose in footprints over footprints.

"Wake up."

He moved in the blanket and turned his face to me with his eyes still   5
closed. I knelt down to touch him.

"I'm leaving."

He smiled now, eyes still closed. "You are coming with me, remember?" He sat up now with his bare dark chest and belly in the sun.

"Where?"

"To my place."

"And will I come back?"   10

He pulled his pants on. I walked away from him, feeling him behind me and smelling the willows.

"Yellow Woman," he said.

I turned to face him. "Who are you?" I asked.

He laughed and knelt on the low, sandy bank, washing his face in the river. "Last night you guessed my name, and you knew why I had come."

I stared past him at the shallow moving water and tried to remember   15
the night, but I could only see the moon in the water and remember his warmth around me.

"But I only said that you were him and that I was Yellow Woman — I'm not really her — I have my own name and I come from the pueblo on the other side of the mesa. Your name is Silva and you are a stranger I met by the river yesterday afternoon."

He laughed softly. "What happened yesterday has nothing to do with what you will do today, Yellow Woman."

"I know — that's what I'm saying — the old stories about the ka'tsina spirit and Yellow Woman can't mean us."

My old grandpa liked to tell those stories best. There is one about Badger and Coyote who went hunting and were gone all day, and when the sun was going down they found a house. There was a girl living there alone, and she had light hair and eyes and she told them that they could sleep with her. Coyote wanted to be with her all night so he sent Badger into a prairie-dog hole, telling him he thought he saw something in it. As soon as Badger crawled in, Coyote blocked up the entrance with rocks and hurried back to Yellow Woman.

"Come here," he said gently.   20

He touched my neck and I moved close to him to feel his breathing and to hear his heart. I was wondering if Yellow Woman had known who she was — if she knew that she would become part of the stories. Maybe she'd had another name that her husband and relatives called her so that only the ka'tsina from the north and the storytellers would know her as Yellow Woman. But I didn't go on; I felt him all around me, pushing me down into the white river sand.

Yellow Woman went away with the spirit from the north and lived with him and his relatives. She was gone for a long time, but then one day she came back and she brought twin boys.

"Do you know the story?"

"What story?" He smiled and pulled me close to him as he said this. I was afraid lying there on the red blanket. All I could know was the way he felt, warm, damp, his body beside me. This is the way it happens in the stories, I was thinking, with no thought beyond the moment she meets the ka'tsina spirit and they go.

"I don't have to go. What they tell in stories was real only then, back   25
in time immemorial, like they say."

He stood up and pointed at my clothes tangled in the blanket. "Let's go," he said.

I walked beside him, breathing hard because he walked fast, his hand around my wrist. I had stopped trying to pull away from him, because his hand felt cool and the sun was high, drying the river bed into alkali. I will see someone, eventually I will see someone, and then I will be certain that he is only a man — some man from nearby — and I will be sure that I am not Yellow Woman. Because she is from out of time past and I live now and I've been to school and there are highways and pickup trucks that Yellow Woman never saw.

It was an easy ride north on horseback. I watched the change from the cottonwood trees along the river to the junipers that brushed past us in the foothills, and finally there were only piñons, and when I looked

up at the rim of the mountain plateau I could see pine trees growing on
the edge. Once I stopped to look down, but the pale sandstone had disappeared and the river was gone and the dark lava hills were all around.
He touched my hand, not speaking, but always singing softly a mountain song and looking into my eyes.

I felt hungry and wondered what they were doing at home now —
my mother, my grandmother, my husband, and the baby. Cooking
breakfast, saying, "Where did she go? — maybe kidnaped," and Al
going to the tribal police with the details: "She went walking along the
river."

The house was made with black lava rock and red mud. It was high   30
above the spreading miles of arroyos and long mesas. I smelled a mountain smell of pitch and buck brush. I stood there beside the black horse,
looking down on the small, dim country we had passed, and I shivered.

"Yellow Woman, come inside where it's warm."

II

He lit a fire in the stove. It was an old stove with a round belly and an
enamel coffeepot on top. There was only the stove, some faded Navajo
blankets, and a bedroll and cardboard box. The floor was made of
smooth adobe plaster, and there was one small window facing east. He
pointed at the box.

"There's some potatoes and the frying pan." He sat on the floor with
his arms around his knees pulling them close to his chest and he
watched me fry the potatoes. I didn't mind him watching me because
he was always watching me — he had been watching me since I came
upon him sitting on the river bank trimming leaves from a willow twig
with his knife. We ate from the pan and he wiped the grease from his
fingers on his Levi's.

"Have you brought women here before?" He smiled and kept chewing, so I said, "Do you always use the same tricks?"

"What tricks?" He looked at me like he didn't understand.   35

"The story about being a ka'tsina from the mountains. The story
about Yellow Woman."

Silva was silent; his face was calm.

"I don't believe it. Those stories couldn't happen now," I said.

He shook his head and said softly, "But someday they will talk about
us, and they will say, 'Those two lived long ago when things like that
happened.'"

He stood up and went out. I ate the rest of the potatoes and thought 40
about things — about the noise the stove was making and the sound of
the mountain wind outside. I remembered yesterday and the day before, and then I went outside.

I walked past the corral to the edge where the narrow trail cut
through the black rim rock. I was standing in the sky with nothing
around me but the wind that came down from the blue mountain peak
behind me. I could see faint mountain images in the distance miles
across the vast spread of mesas and valleys and plains. I wondered who
was over there to feel the mountain wind on those sheer blue edges —
who walks on the pine needles in those blue mountains.

"Can you see the pueblo?" Silva was standing behind me.

I shook my head. "We're too far away."

"From here I can see the world." He stepped out on the edge. "The
Navajo reservation begins over there." He pointed to the east. "The
Pueblo boundaries are over here." He looked below us to the south,
where the narrow trail seemed to come from. "The Texans have their
ranches over there, starting with that valley, the Concho Valley. The
Mexicans run some cattle over there too."

"Do you ever work for them?" 45

"I steal from them," Silva answered. The sun was dropping behind
us and shadows were filling the land below. I turned away from the
edge that dropped forever into the valleys below.

"I'm cold," I said; "I'm going inside." I started wondering about this
man who could speak the Pueblo language so well but who lived on a
mountain and rustled cattle. I decided that this man Silva must be
Navajo, because Pueblo men didn't do things like that.

"You must be a Navajo."

Silva shook his head gently. "Little Yellow Woman," he said, "you
never give up, do you? I have told you who I am. The Navajo people
know me, too." He knelt down and unrolled the bedroll and spread the
extra blankets out on a piece of canvas. The sun was down, and the only
light in the house came from outside — the dim orange light from sun-
down.

I stood there and waited for him to crawl under the blankets. 50

"What are you waiting for?" he said, and I lay down beside him. He
undressed me slowly like the night before beside the river — kissing my
face gently and running his hands up and down my belly and legs. He
took off my pants and then he laughed.

"Why are you laughing?"

"You are breathing so hard."

I pulled away from him and turned my back to him.

He pulled me around and pinned me down with his arms and chest.   55
"You don't understand, do you, little Yellow Woman? You will do what
I want."

And again he was all around me with his skin slippery against mine,
and I was afraid because I understood that his strength could hurt me. I
lay underneath him and I knew that he could destroy me. But later,
while he slept beside me, I touched his face and I had a feeling — the
kind of feeling for him that overcame me that morning along the river.
I kissed him on the forehead and he reached out for me.

When I woke up in the morning he was gone. It gave me a strange
feeling because for a long time I sat there on the blankets and looked
around the little house for some object of his — some proof that he had
been there or maybe that he was coming back. Only the blankets and
the cardboard box remained. The .30–30 that had been leaning in the
corner was gone, and so was the knife I had used the night before. He
was gone, and I had my chance to go now. But first I had to eat, because I knew it would be a long walk home.

I found some dried apricots in the cardboard box, and I sat down on
a rock at the edge of the plateau rim. There was no wind and the sun
warmed me. I was surrounded by silence. I drowsed with apricots in my
mouth, and I didn't believe that there were highways or railroads or
cattle to steal.

When I woke up, I stared down at my feet in the black mountain
dirt. Little black ants were swarming over the pine needles around my
foot. They must have smelled the apricots. I thought about my family
far below me. They would be wondering about me, because this had
never happened to me before. The tribal police would file a report. But
if old Grandpa weren't dead he would tell them what happened — he
would laugh and say, "Stolen by a ka'tsina, a mountain spirit. She'll
come home — they usually do." There are enough of them to handle
things. My mother and grandmother will raise the baby like they raised
me. Al will find someone else, and they will go on like before, except
that there will be a story about the day I disappeared while I was walking along the river. Silva had come for me; he said he had. I did not decide to go. I just went. Moonflowers blossom in the sand hills before
dawn, just as I followed him. That's what I was thinking as I wandered
along the trail through the pine trees.

It was noon when I got back. When I saw the stone house I remem-   60
bered that I had meant to go home. But that didn't seem important anymore, maybe because there were little blue flowers growing in the
meadow behind the stone house and the gray squirrels were playing in
the pines next to the house. The horses were standing in the corral, and

there was a beef carcass hanging on the shady side of a big pine in front of the house. Flies buzzed around the clotted blood that hung from the carcass. Silva was washing his hands in a bucket full of water. He must have heard me coming because he spoke to me without turning to face me.

"I've been waiting for you."

"I went walking in the big pine trees."

I looked into the bucket full of bloody water with brown-and-white animal hairs floating in it. Silva stood there letting his hand drip, examining me intently.

"Are you coming with me?"

"Where?" I asked him.   65

"To sell the meat in Marquez."

"If you're sure it's O.K."

"I wouldn't ask you if it wasn't," he answered.

He sloshed the water around in the bucket before he dumped it out and set the bucket upside down near the door. I followed him to the corral and watched him saddle the horses. Even beside the horses he looked tall, and I asked him again if he wasn't Navajo. He didn't say anything; he just shook his head and kept cinching up the saddle.

"But Navajos are tall."   70

"Get on the horse," he said, "and let's go."

The last thing he did before we started down the steep trail was to grab the .30–30 from the corner. He slid the rifle into the scabbard that hung from his saddle.

"Do they ever try to catch you?" I asked.

"They don't know who I am."

"Then why did you bring the rifle?"   75

"Because we are going to Marquez where the Mexicans live."

III

The trail leveled out on a narrow ridge that was steep on both sides like an animal spine. On one side I could see where the trail went around the rocky gray hills and disappeared into the southeast where the pale sandrock mesas stood in the distance near my home. On the other side was a trail that went west, and as I looked far into the distance I thought I saw the little town. But Silva said no, that I was looking in the wrong place, that I just thought I saw houses. After that I quit looking off into the distance; it was hot and the wildflowers were closing up their deep-yellow petals. Only the waxy cactus flowers bloomed in the bright sun, and I saw every color that a cactus blossom can be; the white ones and the red ones were still buds, but the purple and the yellow were blossoms, open full and the most beautiful of all.

Silva saw him before I did. The white man was riding a big gray horse, coming up the trail toward us. He was traveling fast and the gray horse's feet sent rocks rolling off the trail into the dry tumbleweeds. Silva motioned for me to stop and we watched the white man. He didn't see us right away, but finally his horse whinnied at our horses and he stopped. He looked at us briefly before he loped the gray horse across the three hundred yards that separated us. He stopped his horse in front of Silva, and his young fat face was shadowed by the brim of his hat. He didn't look mad, but his small, pale eyes moved from the blood-soaked gunny sacks hanging from my saddle to Silva's face and then back to my face.

"Where did you get the fresh meat?" the white man asked.

"I've been hunting," Silva said, and when he shifted his weight in the   80
saddle the leather creaked.

"The hell you have, Indian. You've been rustling cattle. We've been looking for the thief for a long time."

The rancher was fat, and sweat began to soak through his white cowboy shirt and the wet cloth stuck to the thick rolls of belly fat. He almost seemed to be panting from the exertion of talking, and he smelled rancid, maybe because Silva scared him.

Silva turned to me and smiled. "Go back up the mountain, Yellow Woman."

The white man got angry when he heard Silva speak in a language he couldn't understand. "Don't try anything, Indian. Just keep riding to Marquez. We'll call the state police from there."

The rancher must have been unarmed because he was very fright-   85
ened and if he had a gun he would have pulled it out then. I turned my horse around and the rancher yelled, "Stop!" I looked at Silva for an instant and there was something ancient and dark — something I could feel in my stomach — in his eyes, and when I glanced at his hand I saw his finger on the trigger of the .30–30 that was still in the saddle scabbard. I slapped my horse across the flank and the sacks of raw meat swung against my knees as the horse leaped up the trail. It was hard to keep my balance, and once I thought I felt the saddle slipping backward; it was because of this that I could not look back.

I didn't stop until I reached the ridge where the trail forked. The horse was breathing deep gasps and there was a dark film of sweat on its

neck. I looked down in the direction I had come from, but I couldn't
see the place. I waited. The wind came up and pushed warm air past
me. I looked up at the sky, pale blue and full of thin clouds and fading
vapor trails left by jets.

I think four shots were fired — I remember hearing four hollow explosions that reminded me of deer hunting. There could have been
more shots after that, but I couldn't have heard them because my horse
was running again and the loose rocks were making too much noise as
they scattered around his feet.

Horses have a hard time running downhill, but I went that way instead of uphill to the mountain because I thought it was safer. I felt better with the horse running southeast past the round gray hills that were
covered with cedar trees and black lava rock. When I got to the plain in
the distance I could see the dark green patches of tamaracks that grew
along the river; and beyond the river I could see the beginning of the
pale sandrock mesas. I stopped the horse and looked back to see if anyone was coming; then I got off the horse and turned the horse around,
wondering if it would go back to its corral under the pines on the
mountain. It looked back at me for a moment and then plucked a
mouthful of green tumbleweeds before it trotted back up the trail with
its ears pointed forward, carrying its head daintily to one side to avoid
stepping on the dragging reins. When the horse disappeared over the
last hill, the gunny sacks full of meat were still swinging and bouncing.

IV

I walked toward the river on a wood-hauler's road that I knew would
eventually lead to the paved road. I was thinking about waiting beside
the road for someone to drive by, but by the time I got to the pavement
I had decided it wasn't very far to walk if I followed the river back the
way Silva and I had come.

The river water tasted good, and I sat in the shade under a cluster of   90
silvery willows. I thought about Silva, and I felt sad at leaving him; still,
there was something strange about him, and I tried to figure it out all
the way back home.

I came back to the place on the river bank where he had been sitting
the first time I saw him. The green willow leaves that he had trimmed
from the branch were still lying there, wilted in the sand. I saw the
leaves and I wanted to go back to him — to kiss him and to touch
him — but the mountains were too far away now. And I told myself,

because I believe it, he will come back sometime and be waiting again by the river.

I followed the path up from the river into the village. The sun was getting low, and I could smell supper cooking when I got to the screen door of my house. I could hear their voices inside — my mother was telling my grandmother how to fix the Jell-O and my husband, Al, was playing with the baby. I decided to tell them that some Navajo had kidnaped me, but I was sorry that old Grandpa wasn't alive to hear my story because it was the Yellow Woman stories he liked to tell best.

EXPLORATIONS

1. Does the narrator of this story believe that she and Silva really are the ka'tsina and Yellow Woman? How can you tell? What are her reasons for wanting to believe this?

2. From whose viewpoint do we get to know Silva? What are his outstanding qualities? How is our image of him different from the image expressed by the white man who appears in paragraph 78?

3. At what points in "Yellow Woman" does the narrator state her feelings directly? In what other ways are her feelings revealed?

CONNECTIONS

1. "It's the telling of secrets, the fact and the way that they talk to each other, that makes [girls] best friends," writes Deborah Tannen in "How Male and Female Students Use Language Differently" (p. 412, para. 3). "Boys are expected to use language to seize center stage: by exhibiting their skill, displaying their knowledge, and challenging and resisting challenges." What examples of these contrasting styles appear in "Yellow Woman"?

2. Which of the categories in Sam Keen's "Man and WOMAN" (p. 403) does Yellow Woman fall into and why? How does Silko's depiction of her differ from Keen's female images? What is the impact of Silko's including a male as well as a female mythical character in her story?

3. Reread Paula Gunn Allen's observations about the way an American Indian woman defines her identity (p. 390). Combining this information with what Silko supplies, why do you think the narrator of "Yellow Woman" leaves her home and family to go off with Silva? Why does she return at the end of the story?

ELABORATIONS

1. People, especially lovers, often compare themselves and each other with fictional (or nonfictional) characters in order to see their behavior more clearly. For the narrator of "Yellow Woman," Pueblo stories supplied models. The narrator's mother in Amy Tan's "Two Kinds" (p. 28) compared her daughter with Shirley Temple and other child performers. Where do your models come from? *Romeo and Juliet?* "The Simpsons"? Write an essay either about a specific experience that made you feel like a dramatic character or about the most popular sources of models in contemporary society.

2. What clues in "Yellow Woman" suggest that Silva may have given the narrator an excuse to make a break she had been considering for some time? Write a narrative essay about a dramatic change made by you or someone you know. Identify both the event(s) that triggered the change and the long-standing circumstances that paved the way for it.

WINDOWS: THE WORLD

▲▲▲▲▲▲▲▲▲▲
▼▼▼▼▼▼▼▼▼▼

Opposite Sexes: *A not-quite-secret embrace between Roman columns.*

MARJORIE SHOSTAK

Nisa's Marriage

"Nisa's Marriage" comes from Marjorie Shostak's 1981 book *Nisa: The Life and Words of a !Kung Woman*, based on Shostak's two and a half years among the !Kung San of Botswana. (The ! indicates a clicking sound.) At the time she was a research assistant on the Harvard Kalahari Desert Project, having previously received a bachelor's degree in English literature from Brooklyn College. Shostak, born in 1945, now teaches anthropology at Emory University in Atlanta. Her most recent book, coauthored with S. Boyd Eaton and Melvin Konner, is *The Paleolithic Prescription: A Program of Diet and Exercise and a Design for Living.* In 1989 Shostak returned to Botswana and met up with Nisa, who was then in her mid-sixties. Shostak is writing a book about their visit.

In her introduction to *Nisa*, Shostak writes: "Nisa is a member of one of the last remaining traditional gatherer-hunter societies, a group calling themselves the *Zhun/twasi,* the 'real people,' who currently live in isolated areas of Botswana, Angola, and Namibia. . . . They are also known as the !Kung Bushmen, the !Kung San, or simply the !Kung. They are short — averaging about five feet in height — lean, muscular, and, for Africa, light-skinned. They have high cheekbones and rather Oriental-looking eyes." Population biologists call these people Khoisan, from *Khoi,* the group previously known as Hottentots, and *San,* the group known as Bushmen, who together were the original inhabitants of South Africa (see pp. 344 and 688). Botswana, Nisa's homeland, gained its name and independence in 1966 after eighty years as the British protectorate of Bechuanaland. The !Kung live on the edges of the Kalahari Desert, which occupies much of Botswana's center and southwest.

Shostak describes meeting Nisa, who was then close to fifty years old: "Nisa wore an old blanket loosely draped over the remnants of a faded, flower-print dress, sizes too big. . . . [She] was all activity: Constantly in motion, her face expressive, she spoke fast and was at once strong and surprisingly coquettish." In the following excerpt, the events Nisa describes took place more than thirty-five years earlier, just as she entered puberty.

The day of the wedding, everyone was there. All of Tashay's friends were sitting around, laughing and laughing. His younger brother said, "Tashay, you're too old. Get out of the way so I can marry her. Give her to me." And his nephew said, "Uncle, you're already old. Now, let *me* marry her." They were all sitting around, talking like that. They all wanted me.

I went to my mother's hut and sat there. I was wearing lots of beads and my hair was completely covered and full with ornaments.

That night there was another dance. We danced, and some people fell asleep and others kept dancing. In the early morning, Tashay and his relatives went back to their camp; we went into our huts to sleep. When morning was late in the sky, they came back. They stayed around and then his parents said, "Because we are only staying a short while — tomorrow, let's start building the marriage hut."

The next day they started. There were lots of people there — Tashay's mother, my mother, and my aunt worked on the hut; everyone else sat around, talking. Late in the day, the young men went and brought Tashay to the finished hut. They set him down beside it and stayed there with him, sitting around the fire.

I was still at my mother's hut. I heard them tell two of my friends to go and bring me to the hut. I thought, "Oohh . . . I'll run away." When they came for me, they couldn't find me. They said, "Where did Nisa go? Did she run away? It's getting dark. Doesn't she know that things may bite and kill her?" My father said, "Go tell Nisa that if this is what she's going to do, I'll hit her and she won't run away again. What made her want to run away, anyway?"

I was already far off in the bush. They came looking for me. I heard them calling, "Nisa . . . Nisa . . ." I sat down at the base of a tree. Then I heard Nukha, "Nisa . . . Nisao . . . my friend . . . a hyena's out there . . . things will bite and kill you . . . come back . . . Nisa . . . Nisao . . ."

When Nukha finally saw me, I started to run. She ran after me, chasing me, and finally caught me. She called out to the others, "Hey! Nisa's here! Everyone, come! Help me! Take Nisa, she's here!"

They came and brought me back. Then they laid me down inside the hut. I cried and cried. People told me, "A man is not something that kills you; he is someone who marries you, who becomes like your father or your older brother. He kills animals and gives you things to eat. Even tomorrow, while you are crying, Tashay may kill an animal. But when he returns, he won't give you any meat; only he will eat. Beads, too. He will get beads but he won't give them to you. Why are you so afraid of your husband and what are you crying about?"

I listened and was quiet. Later, we went to sleep. Tashay lay down beside the opening of the hut, near the fire, and I lay down inside; he thought I might try and run away again. He covered himself with a blanket and slept.

While it was dark, I woke up. I sat up. I thought, "How am I going to   10
jump over him? How can I get out and go to mother's hut to sleep beside her?" I looked at him sleeping. Then came other thoughts, other
thoughts in the middle of the night, "Eh . . . this person has just married me . . ." and I lay down again. But I kept thinking, "Why did
people give me this man in marriage? The older people say he is a good
person, yet . . ."

I lay there and didn't move. The rain came beating down. It fell
steadily and kept falling. Finally, I slept. Much later dawn broke.

In the morning, Tashay got up and sat by the fire. I was so frightened
I just lay there, waiting for him to leave. When he went to urinate, I
went and sat down inside my mother's hut.

That day, all his relatives came to our new hut — his mother, his father, his brothers . . . everyone! They all came. They said, "Go tell Nisa
she should come and her in-laws will put the marriage oil on her. Can
you see her sitting over there? Why isn't she coming so we can put the
oil on her in her new hut?"

I refused to go. They kept calling for me until finally, my older
brother said, "Uhn uhn. Nisa, if you act like this, I'll hit you. Now, get
up and go over there. Sit over there so they can put the oil on you."

I still refused and just sat there. My older brother grabbed a switch   15
from a nearby tree and started coming toward me. I got up. I was afraid.
I followed him to where the others were sitting. Tashay's mother
rubbed the oil on me and my aunt rubbed it on Tashay.

Then they left and it was just Tashay and me. . . .

That Zhun/twa, that Tashay, he really caused me pain.

Soon after we were married, he took me from my parents' village to
live at his parents' village. At first my family came and lived with us, but
then one day they left, left me with Tashay and his parents. That's when
I started to cry. Tashay said, "Before your mother left, you weren't crying. Why didn't you tell me you wanted to go with them? We could have
followed along." I said, "I was afraid of you. That's why I didn't tell you."

But I still wanted to be with my mother, so later that day, I ran away.
I ran as fast as I could until I finally caught up with them. When my
mother saw me she said, "Someday a hyena is going to kill this child in
the bush. She's followed us. Here she is!" I walked with them back to
their village and lived with them a while.

A long time passed. One day Tashay left and came to us. When I saw   20
him, I started to cry. He said, "Get up. We're going back." I said, "Why
does this person keep following me? Do I own him that he follows me

everywhere?" My father said, "You're crazy. A woman follows her husband when he comes for her. What are you just sitting here for?"

Tashay took me with him and I didn't really refuse. We continued to live at his village and then we all went and lived at another water hole. By then, I knew that I was no longer living with my mother. I had left my family to follow my husband.

We lived and lived and then, one day, my heart started to throb and my head hurt; I was very sick. My father came to visit and went into a medicinal trance to try and cure me. When I was better, he left and I stayed behind.

After Tashay and I had been living together for a long time, we started to like each other with our hearts and began living nicely together. It was really only after we had lived together for a long time that he touched my genitals. By then, my breasts were already big.

We were staying in my parents' village the night he first had sex with me and I didn't really refuse. I agreed, just a little, and he lay with me. But the next morning, I was sore. I took some leaves and wound them around my waist, but I continued to feel pain. I thought, "Ooo . . . what has he done to my insides that they feel this way?"

I went over to my mother and said, "That person, last night . . . I'm only a child, but last night he had sex with me. Move over and let me eat with you. We'll eat and then we'll move away. Mother . . . mother . . ." 25

My mother turned to my father and said, "Get up, get a switch and hit this child. She's ruining us. Get up and find something to hit her with." I thought, "What? Did I say something wrong?"

My father went to find a switch. I got up and ran to my aunt's hut. I sat there and thought, "What was so bad? How come I talked about something yet . . . is that something so terrible?"

My father said to my aunt, "Tell Nisa to come back here so I can beat her. The things this young girl talks about could crack open the insides of her ears."

My mother said, "This child, her talk is terrible. As I am now, I would stick myself with a poison arrow; but my skin itself fears and that's why I won't do it. But if she continues to talk like that, I will!"

They wanted me to like my husband and not to refuse him. My mother told me that when a man sleeps with his wife, she doesn't tell; it's a private thing. 30

I got up and walked away from them. I was trembling, "Ehn . . . nn . . . nn . . ." I looked at my genitals and thought, "Oh, this person . . . yesterday he took me and now my genitals are ruined!" I took some water and washed my genitals, washed and washed.

Because, when my genitals first started to develop, I was afraid. I'd look at them and cry and think something was wrong with them. But people told me, "Nothing's wrong. That's what you yourself are like."

I also thought that an older person, an adult like my husband, would tear me apart, that his penis would be so big that he would hurt me. Because I hadn't known older men. I had only played sex play with little boys. Then, when Tashay did sleep with me and it hurt, that's when I refused. That's also when I told. But people didn't yell at him, they only yelled at me, and I was ashamed.

That evening, we lay down again. But this time, before he came in, I took a leather strap, held my leather apron tightly against my legs, tied the strap around my genitals, and then tied it to the hut's frame. I was afraid he'd tear me open and I didn't want him to take me again.

The two of us lay there and after a long time, he touched me. When 35 he touched my stomach, he felt the leather strap. He felt around to see what it was. He said, "What is this woman doing? Last night she lay with me so nicely when I came to her. Why has she tied her genitals up this way? What is she refusing to give me?"

He sat me up and said, "Nisa . . . Nisa . . . what happened? Why are you doing this?" I didn't answer. He said, "What are you so afraid of that you had to tie up your genitals?" I said, "Uhn, uhn. I'm not afraid of anything." He said, "No, now tell me. In the name of what you did, I'm asking you."

Then he said, "What do you think you're doing when you do something like this? When you lie down with me, a Zhun/twa like yourself, it's not as though you were lying with another, a stranger. We are both Zhun/twasi, yet you tied yourself up!"

I said, "I refuse to lie down with anyone who wants to take my genitals. Last night you had sex with me and today my insides hurt. That's why I've tied myself up and that's why you won't take me again."

He said, "Untie the strap. Do you see me as someone who kills people? Am I going to eat you? No, I'm not going to kill you, but I have married you and want to make love to you. Do you think I married you thinking I wouldn't make love to you? Did you think we would just live beside each other? Do you know any man who has married a woman and who just lives beside her without having sex with her?"

I said, "I don't care. I don't want sex. Today my insides hurt and I 40 refuse." He said, "Mm, today you will just lie there, but tomorrow, I will take you. If you refuse, I'll pry your legs open and take you by force."

He untied the strap and said, "If this is what use you put this to, I'm going to destroy it." He took his knife and cut it into small pieces. Then he put me down beside him. He didn't touch me; he knew I was afraid. Then we went to sleep.

The next day we got up, did things, and ate things. When we returned to our hut that night, we lay down again. That's when he forced himself on me. He held my legs and I struggled against him. But I knew he would have sex with me and I thought, "This isn't helping me at all. This man, if he takes me by force, he'll really hurt me. So I'll just lie here, lie still and let him look for the food he wants. But I still don't know what kind of food I have because even if he eats he won't be full."[1]

So I stopped fighting and just lay there. He did his work and that time it didn't hurt so much. Then he lay down and slept.

After that, we just lived. I began to like him and he didn't bother me again, he didn't try to have sex with me. Many months passed — those of the rainy season, those of the winter season, and those of the hot season. He just left me alone and I grew up and started to understand about things. Because before that, I hadn't really known about men. . . .

We continued to live and it was as if I was already an adult. Because, beginning to menstruate makes you think about things. Only then did I bring myself to understand, only then did I begin to be a woman.

When Tashay wanted to lie with me, I no longer refused. We just had sex together, one day and then another. In the morning, I'd get up and sit beside our hut and I wouldn't tell. I'd think, "My husband is indeed my husband now. What people told me, that my husband is mine, is true."

We lived and lived, the two of us, together, and after a while I started to really like him and then, to love him. I had finally grown up and had learned how to love. I thought, "A man has sex with you. Yes, that's what a man does. I had thought that perhaps he didn't."

We lived on and I loved him and he loved me. I loved him the way a young adult knows how to love; I just *loved* him. Whenever he went away and I stayed behind, I'd miss him. I'd think, "Oh, when is my husband ever coming home? How come he's been gone so long?" I'd miss him and want him. When he'd come back my heart would be happy, "Eh, hey! My husband left and once again has come back."

We lived and when he wanted me, I didn't refuse; he just lay with me. I thought, "Why had I been so concerned about my genitals? They aren't that important, after all. So why was I refusing them?"

I thought that and gave myself to him, gave and gave. We lay with each other and my breasts were very large. I was becoming a woman.

45

50

---

[1]Food and eating are universally used by the !Kung as metaphors for sex. However, they claim no knowledge or practice of oral-genital contact.

EXPLORATIONS

1. Judging from "Nisa's Marriage," what specific rituals are part of a Zhun/twasi wedding? What is the practical or symbolic (or both) purpose of each ritual?

2. What facts can you glean about the Zhun/twasi way of life from "Nisa's Marriage"? What appears to be the group's main food source? What dangers do they fear? What images in their speech reflect these basic elements of their existence?

3. When Nisa runs home to her mother after having sex with her husband, her mother says, "As I am now, I would stick myself with a poison arrow; but my skin itself fears and that's why I won't do it. But if she continues to talk like that, I will!" (para. 29). What does she mean? How might an American mother express the same sentiments?

CONNECTIONS

1. What ideas about relations between the sexes appear in both "Nisa's Marriage" and Leslie Marmon Silko's "Yellow Woman" (p. 419)? What cues in "Yellow Woman" suggest a longing on the narrator's part to return to an older, simpler culture (more like the Zhun/twasi) than her present home?

2. What incidents in "Nisa's Marriage" show women and men using language in contrasting ways, and for contrasting purposes, in a pattern similar to the one Deborah Tannen describes (p. 412)? What practical advantages do gender-differentiated verbal styles have for the Zhun/twasi?

3. After reading "Nisa's Marriage," look back at John Updike's "The Disposable Rocket" (p. 398). Which of Updike's ideas about the male body seem rooted in contemporary Western culture? Which ideas also appear among the Zhun/twasi?

ELABORATIONS

1. "Nisa's Marriage" illustrates a very different approach to sexuality from that of Western cultures. List all the rules you can identify that govern marriage, sexual intercourse, and gender roles among the Zhun/twasi. What needs of the society shape its sexual rules? Write an essay comparing and contrasting social needs and sexual rules among the Zhun/twasi with those you are familiar with as an American.

2. Nisa's last sentence is: "I was becoming a woman." What does she mean? How does her definition of *woman* compare with others you have encountered in this chapter? Write an essay about the ways different cultures or groups define manhood and womanhood, and the reasons why their definitions differ.

NIKOS KAZANTZAKIS

The Isle of Aphrodite

A novelist, poet, essayist, playwright, travel writer, and translator, Nikos Kazantzakis is best known in the United States for his novel *Zorba the Greek* (1952; *Bios kai politeia tou Alexi Zorba*, 1946), which also became a motion picture (1964) and Broadway musical (1968). Kazantzakis was born into a peasant farming family on the island of Crete in 1883. In 1897 the Cretans revolted against Turkish rule, and the family fled to the Greek island of Naxos. At a monastery there Kazantzakis studied languages and Western philosophy, as well as the Christian preoccupation with the mystery of existence. In 1906 he earned a law degree from the University of Athens, published his first novella, and moved to France. He continued to travel, write, and study; later he also worked for the Greek government. Kazantzakis wrote in the spoken (demotic) form of Greek rather than the customary literary form. He was nearly excommunicated from the Greek Orthodox Church for portraying it unfavorably in his novel *The Greek Passion* (*Ho Christos xanastavronetai*, 1954). A series of controversial novels culminated with *The Last Temptation of Christ* (1960; *Ho teleftaios peirasmos*, 1955; motion picture, 1988). When Kazantzakis died from leukemia in Germany in 1957, the Church refused him a burial Mass in Greece, so he was buried where he was born, in Iraklion, Crete. "The Isle of Aphrodite" comes from his essay collection *Journeying* (1961), translated from the Greek by Themi and Theodora Vasils.

Iraklion is named for the mythical hero Hercules, whose twelve labors included mastering a Cretan bull terrorizing the court of King Minos. Minos's palace — built around 1600 B.C. — also housed the labyrinth devised by Daedalus and Icarus to hide the monstrous Minotaur. Excavated in this century, it contained lavish frescoes, pottery, jewelry, the earliest form of written Greek, and indoor plumbing. The Athenian prince Theseus overthrew Minos, winning Crete for his father, King Aegeus (namesake of the Aegean Sea). Over the next thousand years Athens became a hub of Mediterranean civilization, the birthplace of democracy, theater, and Western philosophy. Rome conquered Greece between 150 and 100 B.C. In the mid-1400s the Turks took over; and in 1827 Greece won independence. George I became king in 1863 and reigned for fifty-seven years, during which Crete and other Aegean islands shifted from Turkish back to Greek control. The monarchy was re-placed by a republic in 1923, followed by a series of military dictatorships, another brief monarchy, a briefer republic, and finally, in 1967, a civilian government. In 1981 Greece joined the European Community.

Cyprus is indeed the native land of Aphrodite. Never have I seen an island with so much fertility or breathed air so saturated with perilous sweet persuasions. In the late afternoon when the sun goes down and the gentle breeze blows in from the sea, soft languor overtakes me — drowsiness and sweetness. And when the small children spill out on the seashore, their hands filled with jasmine, and the little caïques[1] sway lightly in the sea, to right and left, my heart breaks loose and surrenders like the Pandemos Aphrodite.[2]

Here you live incessantly what elsewhere you feel only in rare moments of torpor. You feel it slowly as it penetrates deeply, like the scent of jasmine. "Thought is an effort that goes contrary to the direction of life. The lifting of the soul, the vigilance of the mind, the charge toward the heights, all are the great ancestral sins against the will of God."

The other day while I was still wandering over the mountains of Judea I could hear a contrary relentless cry coming up from the entire land. "Let the hand be severed that it may glorify the Lord. Let the leg be severed that it may dance eternally." The sand trembled and the peaks of the mountains smoldered in the heat of the sun. A harsh god, without water, without a tree, without a woman, walked by, and you could feel the bones in your skull caving in. All of life leaped through the fevered brain like a battle cry.

And now Cyprus reposes in the middle of the open sea, singing softly like a Siren,[3] soothing my troubled head after the abrasive journey through the Judean mountains beyond. We sailed across the narrow sea and in one night passed from Jehovah's camp to the bed of Aphrodite. I was going from Famagusta to Larnaca and from Larnaca to Limassol, all the while getting closer to that holy spot in the sea at Paphos,[4] that fickle, indestructible liquid element in whose foam this feminine mask of mystery was born.

I could clearly feel the two great torrents struggling within me: The 5 one pushes toward harmony, patience, and gentleness. It functions with ease, without effort, following only the natural order of things. You throw a stone up high and for a second you force it against its will; but quickly it joyfully falls again. You toss a thought in the air but the thought quickly tires, it becomes impatient in the empty air and falls back to earth and settles with the soil. The other force is, it would seem,

---

[1]Small sailboats. — ED.
[2]The earthly goddess of carnal love.
[3]A mythical sea nymph who lured sailors to destruction by singing. — ED.
[4]The ancient city sacred to Aphrodite, on the western tip of Cyprus. Aphrodite's birth from sea foam is believed to have occurred at Paphos.

contrary to nature. An unbelievable absurdity. It wants to conquer weight, abolish sleep, and, with the lash, prod the universe upward.

To which of these two forces shall I conform and say: "This is my will," and finally be able with certainty to distinguish good from evil and impose a hierarchy on virtues and passions?

These were my thoughts on the morning I set out from Limassol for Paphos. By noon we were driving through jagged, uninteresting scenery. Carob trees, low mountains, red earth. Now and then a blossoming pomegranate tree unfolded along the way and flickered like flames in the noonday whiteness. Here and there two or three olive trees swayed gently and tamed the landscape.

We passed a dry riverbed blooming with oleander. A small owl was roosting on a stone bridge on the road, motionless, half blinded, and paralyzed by the intense light. The landscape was gradually growing gentler. We drove through a village brimming with orchards — the apricots were glimmering like gold on the trees and hulking clusters of loquats shone through the dark thick leaves.

Women began emerging on their doorsteps, plump and heavily dressed. Several men in the coffeehouses turned their heads as we drove by, the others continued their card playing with a passion. A young girl carrying on her shoulder a large round jug that was painted with primitive black designs stepped out of our way, frightened, and took refuge on a large rock. But as I smiled, her face lit up as though the sun shone on it.

The automobile stopped.   10

"What's your name?" I asked the girl.

I waited for her to say "Aphrodite" but she replied:

"Maria."

"And is Paphos still far from here?"

The girl looked flustered; she didn't understand what I was saying.   15

"You mean Kouklia,[5] my boy," broke in an old woman. "You mean Kouklia, where you'll find the palace of the Mistress of the Oleanders. It's there, right behind the carob tree."

"And why do they call it Kouklia, ma'am?"

"What? Don't you know? They find dolls there, my boy; little clay women. Here, dig, and you'll find some, too. You're a lord,[6] aren't you?"

---

[5]Kouklia is the new town built on the site of old Paphos.

[6]Since [the eighteenth-century British archaeologist] Lord Elgin, the villagers, accustomed to English lords excavating their landscape, assumed all strangers interested in antiquities were English lords.

"And what do they do with these little women?"

"How should I know? Some say they're gods, others say they're [20] devils. Who can tell the difference?"

"What does religion say?"

"What can our poor religion say? Do you think it knows everything?"

The chauffeur was in a hurry so the conversation ended. We passed the village and soon the sea stretched out to our left, again, infinite, deep blue, foamy. And suddenly, as I turned to the right, I saw on the peak of a low hill, far from the road, the ruins of an open, multiwindowed fortress. I knew it was the renowned main temple of Aphrodite. I looked around at the outlines of the mountain, the sea, the small plain where the worshipers must have camped. I tried to isolate this enclave of the much-beloved, full-breasted goddess and relive the vision that once existed here. But, as so often happens to me, my heart was unmoved and unreceptive to all these fleshless fantasies.

The chauffeur stopped in front of a taverna on the road and called out:

"*Kyria* Kalliopi!"[7]   [25]

The small door of the taverna opened quickly and the proprietress came out and stood on the doorstep.

I shall never forget her. Tall, full-bodied with ample buttocks, about thirty years old, this smiling, coquettish, earthy, all-enchanting Aphrodite filled the doorway with her presence. The chauffeur looked at her, sighed softly, and stroked his youthful mustache.

"Come here," he called. "Are you afraid?"

She laughed and stepped down from her threshold, chuckling. I eagerly cocked my ear to hear the conversation.

"Tomorrow I want you to make me two okas of your best *loukoumia*,"[8]   [30] the chauffeur said.

"Twenty-four *grosia*,"[9] answered the woman, sobering. "Nothing less."

"Eighteen."

"Twenty-four."

The man looked at her for a moment; he sighed again.

"All right," he said. "Twenty-four? Twenty-four!"   [35]

---

[7]*Kyria*: Mrs.; *Kalliopi* (or *Calliope*): The legendary Muse who presided over epic poetry. — ED.

[8]A jellylike, gummy confection sprinkled with powdered sugar, known as Turkish delight.

[9]About 3 cents. — ED.

The bargaining ended. The entire landscape took on an unexpected sweetness. This little trifling dialogue had excited my heart. The great temple, all the inspiration of the renowned landscape, the memories, the historical profundity, were unable to move me, but this small human moment resurrected in a flash all of Aphrodite in me.

Thus, joyously, I set out and began the slow climb up the sacred hill.

The thyme, the daffodils, poppies, all the familiar elements one encounters on a Greek mountainside, were there. A young shepherd, goats, sheep dogs, an innocent downy newborn donkey that was frisking about, still looking at the world with surprise.

The sun was finally setting, the shadows were lengthening and touching the earth, the Star of Aphrodite was glittering, playing, and twirling in the sky as I entered the deserted temple of the "Mistress." I entered quietly, without excitement, as though I were entering my house. I sat on a rock, thinking of nothing, making no effort at thought. I was gently tired, gently happy, and settled comfortably on the rock. Gradually I began to look at some insects that were chasing each other in the air, intermittently flitting from plant to plant, and I listened to the brittle metallic sound of their wings.

Suddenly, as I was observing the insects, a mysterious fear overtook   40
me. At first I couldn't comprehend the cause, but slowly, with dread, I understood. Engrossed as I was in the insects I remembered, at first dimly, but later more vividly, a frightful sight I had seen in my adolescent years.

One afternoon as I was wandering through a dry riverbed I saw two insects mating under a plane tree leaf. They were two green, willowy, charming little "ponies of the Virgin." I approached them slowly, holding my breath. But suddenly I stopped short, stunned: the male, small and weak, was on top, struggling to consummate its sacred duty; and with horror I saw that its head was missing. The female was calmly chewing it and when she finished she slowly turned and cut off the neck and then she cut off the breast of the male who was clamped tightly over her still pulsating . . .

This terrifying scene suddenly bolted out of the ruins before me. Tonight blue lightning rips through and illumines my heart.

The full-breasted goddess lifts her veil. The breath of the unfathomable is more obvious to plants and animals than it is to man. They, faithful and naked, follow the great Cry. To them, love and death are identical. When we see them headless and chestless, struggling to defeat death by giving birth, we recognize with awe the same Cry within us. The giddiness, the certainty of death; and yet, above this is the joy, the madness in death, and the lunge for immortality . . .

It was finally dark. An old man had been watching me from the opposite hill and had come down. He was standing behind me for a long time but did not dare approach but now, as he saw me getting up, he reached out his hand.

"Sir, I've brought you an antique to buy."   45

He put a small stone in my hand; I looked at it but could not discern what it portrayed. The old man lit a match. Now I could make out the sculptured head of a woman with a war helmet. And as I kept turning the little stone around, I noticed that the upper part of the helmet portrayed the upside-down head of a warrior. I suddenly recalled Ares, and shuddered to see Aphrodite wearing the male thus, as an ornament on her head. I hastily returned the ring stone to the old man.

"Go," I said with involuntary curtness. "I don't like it."

That night I slept at a small hotel nearby. At dawn I had a dream: I was holding a rose, the blackest of roses, in my palm. And as I held it I could feel it slowly, voraciously, silently, eating away at my hand.

EXPLORATIONS

1. What deities and what places are represented by the two opposing torrents or forces described in paragraphs 5–6? What are the differences between them? What use does Nikos Kazantzakis make of gender in this opening section?

2. What is the meaning of the dream in Kazantzakis's last paragraph? How has he prepared us to interpret his dream?

3. What religion does Kazantzakis apparently belong to? Cite evidence from his essay.

CONNECTIONS

1. What similar strategy do Kazantzakis and Leslie Marmon Silko use to begin "The Isle of Aphrodite" and "Yellow Woman" (p. 419)? How is this strategy appropriate for a piece of writing in which sex is important?

2. Which of Sam Keen's three images of WOMAN from "Man and WOMAN" (p. 403) can you identify in "The Isle of Aphrodite," and where do they appear? How do you think Keen would interpret Kazantzakis's fearful visions in paragraphs 40–48?

3. Reread Kazantzakis's paragraphs 40–48. What does this view of relations between the sexes have in common with the view Camille Paglia expresses (p. 393)? How are Kazantzakis's and Paglia's views different?

ELABORATIONS

1. Compare Kazantzakis's description of two opposing torrents in paragraphs
   1–6, particularly paragraph 5, with John Updike's description of the male
   versus the female body in "The Disposable Rocket" (p. 398). In what ways
   do they overlap? What additional meanings besides sexual ones does
   Kazantzakis intend? How does he answer his own question, "To which of
   these two forces shall I conform . . . ?" Write an essay translating Kazantzakis's metaphors into more literal language, analyzing the question he is really asking, and explaining his answer.

2. Both Kazantzakis in "The Isle of Aphrodite" and Carlos Fuentes in "The
   Two Americas" (p. 100) consider an ancient culture and a modern one
   built on the same site. What are each writer's purposes, concerns, and beliefs? How are their stylistic choices alike and different? Write an essay comparing and contrasting the two essays.

SIMONE DE BEAUVOIR

Woman as Other

Simone de Beauvoir was born in Paris in 1908 and lived there most of her life, though her interests and influence were worldwide. Having a devout Catholic mother and an agnostic father who practiced law and was involved in amateur theater encouraged her to think for herself. She vowed early to be a writer rather than a wife. True to her plan, Beauvoir is best known for her feminist fiction and nonfiction and for her lifelong relationship with the existentialist philosopher and writer Jean-Paul Sartre. She was twenty when she met Sartre while studying at the Sorbonne. The two never married, lived together, or viewed their liaison as exclusive, but they worked closely together and kept apartments in the same building until Sartre's death in 1980. Beauvoir's several memoirs chronicle her social and political development; her novels examine existentialist ideas and sometimes their proponents as well. *The Mandarins* (1954), based on her affair with American novelist Nelson Algren, won the prestigious Prix Goncourt. Beauvoir's most famous work is the international best-seller *The Second Sex* (1952; *Le deuxième sexe*, 1949), translated from the French by H. M. Parshley, from which "Woman as Other" is taken. A vigorous and compassionate champion of antiestablishment causes, Beauvoir died in Paris in 1986.

Although France was settled by the Parisii in the third century B.C., the French celebrated their bicentennial in 1989. Bastille Day, July 14, marks the date in 1789 when outraged citizens stormed Paris's notorious Bastille prison and launched the Revolution, which ended nearly a thousand years of monarchy. King Louis XVI was beheaded by the guillotine in 1793, followed by his queen, the extravagant and unpopular Marie Antoinette. After a two-year orgy of executions and a short-lived republic, Napoleon Bonaparte ruled as emperor from 1804 to 1815. After him came a series of republics and the brief Second Empire, culminating in the Fifth Republic, which holds power today. During World War II, France was occupied by Germany. Having accumulated worldwide colonies during the centuries of European expansion, France withdrew in the 1950s from Indochina, Morocco, and Tunisia, and subsequently from most of its other African territories. France also withdrew most of its troops in 1966 from the North Atlantic Treaty Organization (NATO). A founding member of the European Community, France continues to play a significant political, economic, and cultural role in Europe and the world.

What is a woman?

To state the question is, to me, to suggest, at once, a preliminary answer. The fact that I ask it is in itself significant. A man would never get the notion of writing a book on the peculiar situation of the human male. But if I wish to define myself, I must first of all say: "I am a woman"; on this truth must be based all further discussion. A man never begins by presenting himself as an individual of a certain sex; it goes without saying that he is a man. The terms *masculine* and *feminine* are used symmetrically only as a matter of form, as on legal papers. In actuality the relation of the two sexes is not quite like that of two electrical poles, for man represents both the positive and the neutral, as is indicated by the common use of *man* to designate human beings in general; whereas woman represents only the negative, defined by limiting criteria, without reciprocity. In the midst of an abstract discussion it is vexing to hear a man say: "You think thus and so because you are a woman"; but I know that my only defense is to reply: "I think thus and so because it is true," thereby removing my subjective self from the argument. It would be out of the question to reply: "And you think the contrary because you are a man," for it is understood that the fact of being a man is no peculiarity. A man is in the right in being a man; it is the woman who is in the wrong. It amounts to this: Just as for the ancients there was an absolute vertical with reference to which the oblique was defined, so there is an absolute human type, the masculine. Woman has ovaries, a uterus; these peculiarities imprison her in her subjectivity, circumscribe her within the limits of her own nature. It is often said that she thinks with her glands. Man superbly ignores the fact that his anatomy also includes glands, such as the testicles, and that they secrete hormones. He thinks of his body as a direct and normal connection with the world, which he believes he apprehends objectively, whereas he regards the body of woman as a hindrance, a prison, weighed down by everything peculiar to it. "The female is a female by virtue of a certain *lack* of qualities," said Aristotle; "we should regard the female nature as afflicted with a natural defectiveness." And St. Thomas for his part pronounced woman to be an "imperfect man," an "incidental" being. This is symbolized in Genesis where Eve is depicted as made from what Bossuet called "a supernumerary bone" of Adam.

Thus humanity is male and man defines woman not in herself but as relative to him; she is not regarded as an autonomous being. Michelet writes: "Woman, the relative being. . . ." And Benda is most positive in his *Rapport d'Uriel*: "The body of man makes sense in itself quite apart from that of woman, whereas the latter seems wanting in significance by itself. . . . Man can think of himself without woman. She cannot think of herself without man." And she is simply what man decrees; thus she is called "the sex," by which is meant that she appears essentially to the male as a sexual being. For him she is sex — absolute sex, no less. She is defined and differentiated with reference to man and not he with reference to her; she is the incidental, the inessential as opposed to the essential. He is the Subject, he is the Absolute — she is the Other.

The category of the *Other* is as primordial as consciousness itself. In the most primitive societies, in the most ancient mythologies, one finds the expression of a duality — that of the Self and the Other. This duality was not originally attached to the division of the sexes; it was not dependent upon any empirical facts. It is revealed in such works as that of Granet on Chinese thought and those of Dumézil on the East Indies and Rome. The feminine element was at first no more involved in such pairs as Varuna-Mitra, Uranus-Zeus, Sun-Moon, and Day-Night than it was in the contrasts between Good and Evil, lucky and unlucky auspices, right and left, God and Lucifer. Otherness is a fundamental category of human thought.

Thus it is that no group ever sets itself up as the One without at once setting up the Other over against itself. If three travelers chance to occupy the same compartment, that is enough to make vaguely hostile "others" out of all the rest of the passengers on the train. In small-town eyes all persons not belonging to the village are "strangers" and suspect; to the native of a country all who inhabit other countries are "foreigners"; Jews are "different" for the anti-Semite, Negroes are "inferior" for American racists, aborigines are "natives" for colonists, proletarians are the "lower class" for the privileged.

Lévi-Strauss, at the end of a profound work on the various forms of primitive societies, reaches the following conclusion: "Passage from the state of Nature to the state of Culture is marked by man's ability to view biological relations as a series of contrasts; duality, alternation, opposition, and symmetry, whether under definite or vague forms, constitute not so much phenomena to be explained as fundamental and immediately given data of social reality." These phenomena would be incomprehensible if in fact human society were simply a *Mitsein* or fellowship based on solidarity and friendliness. Things become clear, on the contrary, if, following Hegel, we find in consciousness itself a fundamental hostility toward every other consciousness; the subject can be posed only in being opposed — he sets himself up as the essential, as opposed to the other, the inessential, the object.

But the other consciousness, the other ego, sets up a reciprocal claim. The native traveling abroad is shocked to find himself in turn

5

regarded as a "stranger" by the natives of neighboring countries. As a matter of fact, wars, festivals, trading, treaties, and contests among tribes, nations, and classes tend to deprive the concept *Other* of its absolute sense and to make manifest its relativity; willy-nilly, individuals and groups are forced to realize the reciprocity of their relations. How is it, then, that this reciprocity has not been recognized between the sexes, that one of the contrasting terms is set up as the sole essential, denying any relativity in regard to its correlative and defining the latter as pure otherness? Why is it that women do not dispute male sovereignty? No subject will readily volunteer to become the object, the inessential; it is not the Other who, in defining himself as the Other, establishes the One. The Other is posed as such by the One in defining himself as the One. But if the Other is not to regain the status of being the One, he must be submissive enough to accept this alien point of view. Whence comes this submission in the case of woman?

There are, to be sure, other cases in which a certain category has been able to dominate another completely for a time. Very often this privilege depends upon inequality of numbers — the majority imposes its rule upon the minority or persecutes it. But women are not a minority, like the American Negroes or the Jews; there are as many women as men on earth. Again, the two groups concerned have often been originally independent; they may have been formerly unaware of each other's existence, or perhaps they recognized each other's autonomy. But a historical event has resulted in the subjugation of the weaker by the stronger. The scattering of the Jews, the introduction of slavery into America, the conquests of imperialism are examples in point. In these cases the oppressed retained at least the memory of former days; they possessed in common a past, a tradition, sometimes a religion or a culture.

The parallel drawn by Bebel between women and the proletariat is valid in that neither ever formed a minority or a separate collective unit of mankind. And instead of a single historical event it is in both cases a historical development that explains their status as a class and accounts for the membership of *particular individuals* in that class. But proletarians have not always existed, whereas there have always been women. They are women in virtue of their anatomy and physiology. Throughout history they have always been subordinated to men, and hence their dependency is not the result of a historical event or a social change — it was not something that *occurred*. The reason why otherness in this case seems to be an absolute is in part that it lacks the contingent or incidental nature of historical facts. A condition brought about at a certain time can be abolished at some other time, as the Negroes of Haiti and others have proved; but it might seem that a natural condition is beyond the possibility of change. In truth, however, the nature of things is no more immutably given, once for all, than is historical reality. If woman seems to be the inessential which never becomes the essential, it is because she herself fails to bring about this change. Proletarians say "We"; Negroes also. Regarding themselves as subjects, they transform the bourgeois, the whites, into "others." But women do not say "We," except at some congress of feminists or similar formal demonstration; men say "women," and women use the same word in referring to themselves. They do not authentically assume a subjective attitude. The proletarians have accomplished the revolution in Russia, the Negroes in Haiti, the Indochinese are battling for it in Indochina; but the women's effort has never been anything more than a symbolic agitation. They have gained only what men have been willing to grant; they have taken nothing, they have only received.

The reason for this is that women lack concrete means for organizing   10
themselves into a unit which can stand face to face with the correlative unit. They have no past, no history, no religion of their own; and they have no such solidarity of work and interest as that of the proletariat. They are not even promiscuously herded together in the way that creates community feeling among the American Negroes, the ghetto Jews, the workers of Saint-Denis, or the factory hands of Renault. They live dispersed among the males, attached through residence, housework, economic condition, and social standing to certain men — fathers or husbands — more firmly than they are to other women. If they belong to the bourgeoisie, they feel solidarity with men of that class, not with proletarian women; if they are white, their allegiance is to white men, not to Negro women. The proletariat can propose to massacre the ruling class, and a sufficiently fanatical Jew or Negro might dream of getting sole possession of the atomic bomb and making humanity wholly Jewish or black; but woman cannot even dream of exterminating the males. The bond that unites her to her oppressors is not comparable to any other. The division of the sexes is a biological fact, not an event in human history. Male and female stand opposed within a primordial *Mitsein*, and woman has not broken it. The couple is a fundamental unity with its two halves riveted together, and the cleavage of society along the line of sex is impossible. Here is to be found the basic trait of woman: She is the Other in a totality of which the two components are necessary to one another.

One could suppose that this reciprocity might have facilitated the liberation of woman. When Hercules sat at the feet of Omphale and helped with her spinning, his desire for her held him captive; but why did she fail to gain a lasting power? To revenge herself on Jason, Medea killed their children; and this grim legend would seem to suggest that she might have obtained a formidable influence over him through his love for his offspring. In *Lysistrata* Aristophanes gaily depicts a band of women who joined forces to gain social ends through the sexual needs of their men; but this is only a play. In the legend of the Sabine women, the latter soon abandoned their plan of remaining sterile to punish their ravishers. In truth woman has not been socially emancipated through man's need — sexual desire and the desire for offspring — which makes the male dependent for satisfaction upon the female.

Master and slave, also, are united by a reciprocal need, in this case economic, which does not liberate the slave. In the relation of master to slave the master does not make a point of the need that he has for the other; he has in his grasp the power of satisfying this need through his own action; whereas the slave, in his dependent condition, his hope and fear, is quite conscious of the need he has for his master. Even if the need is at bottom equally urgent for both, it always works in favor of the oppressor and against the oppressed. That is why the liberation of the working class, for example, has been slow.

Now, woman has always been man's dependent, if not his slave; the two sexes have never shared the world in equality. And even today woman is heavily handicapped, though her situation is beginning to change. Almost nowhere is her legal status the same as man's, and frequently it is much to her disadvantage. Even when her rights are legally recognized in the abstract, long-standing custom prevents their full expression in the mores. In the economic sphere men and women can almost be said to make up two castes; other things being equal, the former hold the better jobs, get higher wages, and have more opportunity for success than their new competitors. In industry and politics men have a great many more positions and they monopolize the most important posts. In addition to all this, they enjoy a traditional prestige that the education of children tends in every way to support, for the present enshrines the past — and in the past all history has been made by men. At the present time, when women are beginning to take part in the affairs of the world, it is still a world that belongs to men — they have no doubt of it at all and women have scarcely any. To decline to be the Other, to refuse to be a party to the deal — this would be for women to renounce all the advantages conferred upon them by their alliance with the superior caste. Man-the-sovereign will provide woman-the-liege with material protection and will undertake the moral justification of her existence; thus she can evade at once both economic risk and the metaphysical risk of a liberty in which ends and aims must be contrived without assistance. Indeed, along with the ethical urge of each individual to affirm his subjective existence, there is also the temptation to forgo liberty and become a thing. This is an inauspicious road, for he who takes it — passive, lost, ruined — becomes henceforth the creature of another's will, frustrated in his transcendence and deprived of every value. But it is an easy road; on it one avoids the strain involved in undertaking an authentic existence. When man makes of woman the *Other*, he may, then, expect her to manifest deep-seated tendencies toward complicity. Thus, woman may fail to lay claim to the status of subject because she lacks definite resources, because she feels the necessary bond that ties her to man regardless of reciprocity, and because she is often very well pleased with her role as the *Other*.

EXPLORATIONS

1. "Woman as Other" was originally published as part of *The Second Sex* in 1949. Which, if any, of Simone de Beauvoir's observations about women's status have been invalidated since then by political and social changes? Which of the problems she mentions are live issues in our society today?

2. What emotionally loaded words, phrases, and sentences indicate that Beauvoir is presenting an argument in "Woman as Other"? Who is her intended audience? To what extent, and for what reasons, do you think she expects part or all of her audience to resist the case she is making?

3. What kinds of sources does Beauvoir cite? In what ways would her essay gain or lose impact if she included quotations from interviews with individual women and men? In what ways would it gain or lose impact if she cut all references to outside sources?

CONNECTIONS

1. Which points made by Beauvoir in "Woman as Other" are illustrated in Nikos Kazantzakis's "The Isle of Aphrodite" (p. 438)? Give specific references from both selections.

2. What evidence in Leslie Marmon Silko's "Yellow Woman" (p. 419) shows the narrator perceiving herself as defined by or dependent on men, in the way Beauvoir describes? What evidence shows Silko's narrator holding views that contradict Beauvoir's?

3. Which comments in Sam Keen's "Man and WOMAN" (p. 403) show men viewing women as "Other"? Which comments recommend ways to overcome the problems Beauvoir describes?

ELABORATIONS

1. Beauvoir notes that male glands affect men's thinking as much as female glands affect women's thinking. How do the writers of the epigraphs on 390–396 apply this idea? On the basis of their observations, Beauvoir's, and Deborah Tannen's in "How Male and Female Students Use Language Differently" (p. 412), write a cause-and-effect essay about the relationship (or absence of a relationship) between gender and attitudes.

2. "What is a woman?" asks Beauvoir in her opening paragraph. She goes on: "If I wish to define myself, I must first of all say: 'I am a woman.'" Already she is letting her readers know that her choice of *definition* as the form for her inquiry has a political as well as a rhetorical basis. That is, she is not simply defining woman, as her opening question implies; she is examining a definition of woman imposed by men. The same tactic can be applied to any issue in which a preexisting definition is crucial to the argument. Choose such an issue that interests you — for instance, What is a drug? or What is military defense? Write a definition essay exploring the issue by examining the tacit definitions that underlie it.

ALBERTO MORAVIA

The Chase

Alberto Moravia has been called the first existentialist novelist in
Italy — a forerunner of Jean-Paul Sartre and Albert Camus in France.
Moravia is best known in the United States for the films that have been
based on his work: Michelangelo Antonioni's *L'Avventura* (1961), Jean-
Luc Godard's *Le Mépris* (*Contempt*, 1965), and Bernardo Bertolucci's
The Conformist (1970). The film of *Conjugal Love* (1949) was directed
by Moravia's wife, Dacia Maraini. Born Alberto Pincherle in Rome in
1907, Moravia had little formal schooling but was taught to read English, French, and German by governesses and earned a high school
diploma. He began his first novel at age sixteen while in a sanatorium
for the tuberculosis he had contracted when he was nine; he considered
his long illness a major influence on his career. Moravia's novels, stories, and scripts are too numerous to list. Many of them, including his
1987 novel *The Voyeur*, are available in English. "The Chase," translated from the Italian in 1969 by Angus Davidson, is from the story collection *Command, and I Will Obey You*. Moravia also represented Italy
in the European Parliament as of 1984. He died in 1990.

Italy, a boot-shaped peninsula across the Mediterranean Sea from
Libya, has been occupied since the Stone Age. Its political heyday was
the Roman Empire, which by A.D. 180 ruled from Britain to Africa to
Persia (now Iran). The Roman civilization fell to barbarian invaders in
the fourth and fifth centuries but left as a legacy its capital city, alphabet,
roads, laws, and arts. The United Nations Educational, Scientific, and
Cultural Organization (UNESCO) estimates that half of the world's cultural heritage has come from Italy, which still houses much of the finest
architecture, sculpture, painting, and other visual arts in Europe.

Italy remained politically fragmented until the 1860s, when it united
under a parliament and king. In 1922 Fascist dictator Benito Mussolini
took over the government, proclaiming Victor Emmanuel III emperor
and subsequently joining Germany in World War II. After Fascism was
overthrown in 1943, Italy declared war on Germany and Japan. Mussolini was killed in 1946, and the monarchy was voted out. Democratic
postwar governments have tended to be short-lived. However, Italy was a
founding member of the European Community and continues to have
a thriving market economy. Recently the government has cracked down
on the Mafia, or Cosa Nostra, the multinational criminal organization
based on the Italian island of Sicily; although arrests and prosecutions
proceed, some officials have been murdered by the mob and others im-
plicated in a web of political and corporate corruption.

I have never been a sportsman — or, rather, I have been a sportsman only once, and that was the first and last time. I was a child, and one day, for some reason or other, I found myself together with my father, who was holding a gun in his hand, behind a bush, watching a bird that had perched on a branch not very far away. It was a large, gray bird — or perhaps it was brown — with a long — or perhaps a short — beak; I don't remember. I only remember what I felt at that moment as I looked at it. It was like watching an animal whose vitality was rendered more intense by the very fact of my watching it and of the animal's not knowing that I was watching it.

At that moment, I say, the notion of wildness entered my mind, never again to leave it: Everything is wild which is autonomous and unpredictable and does not depend upon us. Then all of a sudden there was an explosion; I could no longer see the bird and I thought it had flown away. But my father was leading the way, walking in front of me through the undergrowth. Finally he stooped down, picked up something, and put it in my hand. I was aware of something warm and soft and I lowered my eyes: There was the bird in the palm of my hand, its dangling, shattered head crowned with a plume of already-thickening blood. I burst into tears and dropped the corpse on the ground, and that was the end of my shooting experience.

I thought again of this remote episode in my life this very day after watching my wife, for the first and also the last time, as she was walking through the streets of the city. But let us take things in order.

What had my wife been like; what was she like now? She once had been, to put it briefly, "wild" — that is, entirely autonomous and unpredictable; latterly she had become "tame" — that is, predictable and dependent. For a long time she had been like the bird that, on that far-off morning in my childhood, I had seen perching on the bough; latterly, I am sorry to say, she had become like a hen about which one knows everything in advance — how it moves, how it eats, how it lays eggs, how it sleeps, and so on.

Nevertheless I would not wish anyone to think that my wife's wildness   5 consisted of an uncouth, rough, rebellious character. Apart from being extremely beautiful, she is the gentlest, politest, most discreet person in the world. Rather her wildness consisted of the air of charming unpredictability, of independence in her way of living, with which during the first years of our marriage she acted in my presence, both at home and abroad. Wildness signified intimacy, privacy, secrecy. Yes, my wife as she sat in front of her dressing table, her eyes fixed on the looking glass, passing the hairbrush with a repeated motion over her long, loose hair, was just as wild as the solitary quail hopping forward along a sun-filled furrow or the furtive fox coming out into a clearing and stopping to look around before running on. She was wild because I, as I looked at her, could never manage to foresee when she would give a last stroke with the hair-

brush and rise and come toward me; wild to such a degree that sometimes when I went into our bedroom the smell of her, floating in the air,
would have something of the acrid quality of a wild beast's lair.

Gradually she became less wild, tamer. I had had a fox, a quail, in
the house, as I have said; then one day I realized that I had a hen. What
effect does a hen have on someone who watches it? It has the effect of
being, so to speak, an automaton in the form of a bird; automatic are
the brief, rapid steps with which it moves about; automatic its hard,
terse pecking; automatic the glance of the round eyes in its head that
nods and turns; automatic its ready crouching down under the cock; automatic the dropping of the egg wherever it may be and the cry with
which it announces that the egg has been laid. Good-bye to the fox;
good-bye to the quail. And her smell — this no longer brought to my
mind, in any way, the innocent odor of a wild animal; rather I detected
in it the chemical suavity of some ordinary French perfume.

Our flat is on the first floor of a big building in a modern quarter of
the town; our windows look out on a square in which there is a small
public garden, the haunt of nurses and children and dogs. One day I was
standing at the window, looking in a melancholy way at the garden. My
wife, shortly before, had dressed to go out; and once again, watching her,
I had noticed the irrevocable and, so to speak, invisible character of her
gestures and personality: something which gave one the feeling of a
thing already seen and already done and which therefore evaded even
the most determined observation. And now, as I stood looking at the garden and at the same time wondering why the adorable wildness of former times had so completely disappeared, suddenly my wife came into
my range of vision as she walked quickly across the garden in the direction of the bus stop. I watched her and then I almost jumped for joy; in a
movement she was making to pull down a fold of her narrow skirt and
smooth it over her thigh with the tips of her long, sharp nails, in this
movement I recognized the wildness that in the past had made me love
her. It was only an instant, but in that instant I said to myself: She's become wild again because she's convinced that I am not there and am not
watching her. Then I left the window and rushed out.

But I did not join her at the bus stop; I felt that I must not allow myself to
be seen. Instead I hurried to my car, which was standing nearby, got in, and
waited. A bus came and she got in together with some other people; the bus
started off again and I began following it. Then there came back to me the
memory of that one shooting expedition in which I had taken part as a
child, and I saw that the bus was the undergrowth with its bushes and trees,
my wife the bird perching on the bough while I, unseen, watched it living
before my eyes. And the whole town, during this pursuit, became, as

though by magic, a fact of nature like the countryside: The houses were hills, the streets valleys, the vehicles hedges and woods, and even the passersby on the pavements had something unpredictable and autonomous — that is, wild — about them. And in my mouth, behind my clenched teeth, there was the acrid, metallic taste of gunfire; and my eyes, usually listless and wandering, had become sharp, watchful, attentive.

These eyes were fixed intently upon the exit door when the bus came to the end of its run. A number of people got out, and then I saw my wife getting out. Once again I recognized, in the manner in which she broke free of the crowd and started off toward a neighboring street, the wildness that pleased me so much. I jumped out of the car and started following her.

She was walking in front of me, ignorant of my presence, a tall   10
woman with an elegant figure, long-legged, narrow-hipped, broadbacked, her brown hair falling on her shoulders.

Men turned around as she went past; perhaps they were aware of what I myself was now sensing with an intensity that quickened the beating of my heart and took my breath away: the unrestricted, steadily increasing, irresistible character of her mysterious wildness.

She walked hurriedly, having evidently some purpose in view, and even the fact that she had a purpose of which I was ignorant added to her wildness; I did not know where she was going, just as on that far-off morning I had not known what the bird perching on the bough was about to do. Moreover I thought the gradual, steady increase in this quality of wildness came partly from the fact that as she drew nearer to the object of this mysterious walk there was an increase in her — how shall I express it? — of biological tension, of existential excitement, of vital effervescence. Then, unexpectedly, with the suddenness of a film, her purpose was revealed.

A fair-haired young man in a leather jacket and a pair of corduroy trousers was leaning against the wall of a house in that ancient, narrow street. He was idly smoking as he looked in front of him. But as my wife passed close to him, he threw away his cigarette with a decisive gesture, took a step forward, and seized her arm. I was expecting her to rebuff him, to move away from him, but nothing happened: Evidently obeying the rules of some kind of erotic ritual, she went on walking beside the young man. Then after a few steps, with a movement that confirmed her own complicity, she put her arm around her companion's waist and he put his around her.

I understood then that this unknown man who took such liberties with my wife was also attracted by wildness. And so, instead of making a conventional appointment with her, instead of meeting in a café with a handshake, a falsely friendly and respectful welcome, he had preferred, by agreement with her, to take her by surprise — or, rather, to pretend to do so — while she was apparently taking a walk on her own account.

All this I perceived by intuition, noticing that at the very moment when he stepped forward and took her arm her wildness had, so to speak, given an upward bound. It was years since I had seen my wife so alive, but alas, the source of this life could not be traced to me.

They walked on thus entwined and then, without any preliminaries, just like two wild animals, they did an unexpected thing: They went into one of the dark doorways in order to kiss. I stopped and watched them from a distance, peering into the darkness of the entrance. My wife was turned away from me and was bending back with the pressure of his body, her hair hanging free. I looked at that long, thick mane of brown hair, which as she leaned back fell free of her shoulders, and I felt at that moment her vitality reached its diapason, just as happens with wild animals when they couple and their customary wildness is redoubled by the violence of love. I watched for a long time and then, since the kiss went on and on and in fact seemed to be prolonged beyond the limits of my power of endurance, I saw that I would have to intervene.

I would have to go forward, seize my wife by the arm — or actually by that hair, which hung down and conveyed so well the feeling of feminine passivity — then hurl myself with clenched fists upon the blond young man. After this encounter I would carry off my wife, weeping, mortified, ashamed, while I was raging and brokenhearted, upbraiding her and pouring scorn upon her.

But what else would this intervention amount to but the shot my father fired at that free, unknowing bird as it perched on the bough? The disorder and confusion, the mortification, the shame, that would follow would irreparably destroy the rare and precious moment of wildness that I was witnessing inside the dark doorway. It was true that this wildness was directed against me; but I had to remember that wildness, always and everywhere, is directed against everything and everybody. After the scene of my intervention it might be possible for me to regain control of my wife, but I should find her shattered and lifeless in my arms like the bird that my father placed in my hand so that I might throw it into the shooting bag.

The kiss went on and on: Well, it was a kiss of passion — that could not be denied. I waited until they finished, until they came out of the doorway, until they walked on again still linked together. Then I turned back.

EXPLORATIONS

1. What are the functions of the long opening section of "The Chase"? What role does the narrator assign himself here in relation to the adult male world? How would the story's impact change without this section?

2. At what point(s) in "The Chase" does the narrator recall his childhood hunting incident again? How is his role different now from the first time he mentioned the incident? How does the narrator vacillate between roles at the end of the story, and what role does he finally choose for himself?

3. Reread Alberto Moravia's last sentence; then look back at his third paragraph. What do you conclude that the narrator has done, and intends to do, after the point when the story ends? In what way is he himself adopting qualities he prizes in his wife? What effects does he apparently expect this behavior to have on his marriage?

CONNECTIONS

1. What evidence in "The Chase" confirms Simone de Beauvoir's contention in "Woman as Other" (p. 445) that men perceive women as Other? How does Moravia's narrator feel about his wife's "otherness"? What can you deduce from the story about his wife's view of their situation?

2. Like "The Chase," Leslie Marmon Silko's "Yellow Woman" (p. 419) is a first-person story about a woman who temporarily leaves her husband for another man. Which of these marriages do you think is more likely to continue successfully after the wife returns home, and why?

3. In what ways is the narrator's revelation in "The Chase" similar to the narrator's revelation in "The Isle of Aphrodite" (p. 438)?

ELABORATIONS

1. Near the end of "The Chase" the narrator observes, "Wildness, always and everywhere, is directed against everything and everybody" (para. 17). What does he mean? Do you agree? What other aspects of life are affected by wildness as Moravia defines it? Write an essay arguing for or against Moravia's statement, or examining a specific human action (e.g., putting animals in zoos or destroying ancient forests) to which his statement applies.

2. In the first section of "The Chase," Moravia's narrator speaks as if he knows his wife as completely as a farmer knows his hens. In the second section, he discovers that he does not know her so well after all. Think of a situation in which you based your expectations about another person on an image — perhaps an idealized social role, such as mother, grandfather, friend, or fiancé. How did you come to realize that the person was not as predictable as you thought? Write a narrative essay about the incident(s) that changed your attitude.

SPOTLIGHT:
THE ISLAMIC MIDD

▲▲▲▲▲▲▲▲▲▲
▼▼▼▼▼▼▼▼▼▼

Opposite Sexes: *Medallions decorate a Palestinian woman's traditional hooded mask.*

The Islamic religion originated in what is now Saudi Arabia, as Naila Minai describes in "Women in Early Islam." The name Islam means submission — that is, submission to the will of God (*Allah* in Arabic). Adherents of Islam are Muslims. The world's second largest religion (after Roman Catholicism), Islam is dominant in every country of the Middle East except the Jewish state of Israel. From the ancient centers of Mecca and Medina it spread throughout Arabia — the peninsula that now comprises Oman, Yemen, South Yemen, the United Arab Emirates, Qatar, Kuwait, Bahrain, and several neutral zones as well as the much larger Kingdom of Saudi Arabia. Powerful not only because of its size but because of its vast oil and gas deposits, Saudi Arabia is an absolute monarchy based on the Sharia (Islamic

459

as revealed in the Koran (the holy book) and the Hadith (teachings and sayings of the prophet Muhammad). After Muhammad united the Arabs in the seventh century, his followers created an empire stretching from Africa through the Middle East which lasted until the Turks invaded during the sixteenth and seventeenth centuries. It was King Ibn Saud, however, who in the early 1900s forged the union of emirates that today bears his name.

North of the Arabian peninsula are four more members of the Arab League: the Islamic nations of Jordan, Syria, Lebanon, and Iraq. Turkey to the north and Iran to the East also are Islamic by religion but have ethnically distinct populations from Arabia. West of Arabia, across the Red Sea in northern Africa, are the Arab League members Egypt, Sudan, Libya, Tunisia, Algeria, and Morocco, all predominantly Islamic and generally counted as Arab nations.

The selections that follow come from three different parts of the Islamic Middle East. Diana Abu-Jaber's "In Flight" takes place in Jordan; Unni Wikan's "The Xanith: A Third Gender Role?" in Oman; and Naguib Mahfouz's "A Day for Saying Goodbye" in Egypt. Naila Minai's "Women in Early Islam" centers on Arabia, particularly Saudi Arabia, but relates to the entire region.

The nation we call Jordan calls itself Urdunn; its official name is Al-Mamlaka al-Urduniya al-Hashimiya. Formerly a region of nomadic Bedouin tribes, this largely desert country has become heavily populated with Palestinians since Israel was created. Much biblical history took place here; over the centuries, Jordan's corridor location has made it a target for the Roman, Byzantine, and Ottoman empires as well as the Christian Crusaders. After World War II Jordan was part of the British protectorate of Palestine (see p. 188). The emirate of Trans-Jordan gradually passed from British control into the hands of a Bedouin-descended monarchy; in 1946 it became the "Hashemite Kingdom of Trans-Jordan." At present a prime minister and parliament share authority with the king.

Oman became an important Mesopotamian market and sea power over 2,000 years ago. For most of its history, its long seacoast and strategic location at the mouth of the Persian Gulf have made it prey to invaders from Persia, Mongolia, Arabia, and Europe. Oman was controlled by Portugal for 150 years before the Imam Nasir bin Murshid and his son took over, uniting African and Asian territories. British influence in the nineteenth century re-divided and redominated the country — which was discovered to have valuable oil and gas fields — until 1955. Today the former Sultanate of Muscat is the capital of the former Imamate of Oman, the two officially joined as Sultanatu Oman. Although it now has an elected parliament, Oman's sultan is an absolute monarch. The country's assets have not alleviated its widespread poverty and illiteracy, as two-thirds of the national budget goes to defense. Sohar (or Suhar), the site of Unni Wikan's "The Xanith: A Third Gender Role?", is a small city near Oman's northern tip.

Egypt is one of the world's oldest civilizations, dating back some 6,000 years. Its official name is Al-Jumhuria Misr al-Arabia, or Misr for short. Most of its people have always lived along the Nile River, a fertile strip surrounded by deserts. Libyan and Sudanese-descended pharaohs built its famous pyramids and Sphinx long before Athenians built the Parthenon. The Nile delta seaport of Alexandria (Al-Iskandariyah) was an economic and cultural center for centuries B.C. when traders, scholars, and would-be conquerors crisscrossed the Mediterranean Sea between Greece, Crete, Rome, and North Africa. By the time of Cleopatra, when Julius Caesar was emperor of Rome, Egypt was losing its ascendancy. Arabs migrated into the country, bringing their language and their Islamic religion. During the Renaissance Egypt again became a center of trade and culture, this time with Cairo (Al-Gahirah) as its capital. Successively dominated by the Crusaders, the Turks, and the French and British, Egyptians shook off colonial rule in the 1950s, spurred by their fierce opposition to the creation of Israel. The efforts of President Anwar Sadat (see p. 130) to modernize his country hit a predictable nerve: Sadat tried to strengthen Egypt's foreign ties to bolster its economy, and his 1973 attack on Israel was followed by a diplomatic visit to Jerusalem. He was assassinated in 1981. His successor, President Hosni Mubarak, has continued working with the West to improve the economy and normalize relations with Israel. Mubarak easily won reelection in 1993, but Islamic fundamentalists are pressing for major shifts in policy.

DIANA ABU-JABER

In Flight

Diana Abu-Jaber was born in 1959 in Syracuse, New York, to parents who had immigrated from Jordan. "In Flight" comes from her forthcoming second novel, *Memories of Birth*. When this excerpt appeared in the Left Bank book Borders & Boundaries (1993), Abu-Jaber commented, "The gist of the story comes from my grandmother who was an amazing role model. She married my grandfather at age fourteen and had seventeen children. When she moved into the desert with my grandfather, who was a descendant of Bedouins, she built one of the first libraries in Jordan in her home because so many people brought books to her." Abu-Jaber's stories have been published in *Story and Kenyon Review*, among other publications; her first novel was *Arabian Jazz* (1993). She graduated from the State University of New York at Oswego in 1980 and received her Ph.D. from SUNY Binghamton in 1986. For several years she taught creative writing and Third World and Middle Eastern culture and literature at the University of Oregon in Eugene. After a year in Jordan doing research for *Memories of Birth*, in 1996 she moved to Portland State University, where she teaches fiction writing and a course on first-generation minority writers.

I was a baby at the time, maybe five years old. I remember walking and walking, movement without rest. We were crossing land whose name and nature were changing under our feet, part of a mosaic: the *nakbeh*, tragedy. I don't know how it was that we and the few women with us broke from the others, but we found ourselves following the boundary of the Jordan River, as if to delay our real departure — from native soil — as long as possible. I believe now that we were trapped in our own flight, as any species may be when they are dying: the raptors that refuse to mate, the American buffalo that lie down and will not eat. We might have been the last of our people for all we knew. We waded the hip-high grass of the riverbanks. Then, after perhaps a week of this wandering, we came to cutaway escarpments, shining bands of salt rimming the Dead Sea and freezing the earth.

At that place we crossed a wooden bridge that people would tell me later was not there, that it had been destroyed by Romans or Turks. They tell me, impossible, there has never been a bridge there. But it rises from memory in perfect clarity: stone joints, planked floor, grass stuffed between the cracks. We crossed from desolation into desolation, and when I turned to see where we had just come from, the bridge disappeared back into the landscape, and I felt the salt air fill my throat and mouth and etch into my heart.

We were not lost; that implies there was a way to go, a place to be lost from. We were homeless. We wandered at times in great circles. We tore the leaves from the trees to eat, and sometimes peeled the tender bark. I ate grass and dirt and winged beetles. As we walked away from the river we moved toward the desert, until the day we woke and it glittered under us in a plain of light, crystal white as the ocean.

That was the day the men found us. There were three of them on camels, swords tilted carelessly toward the sky, their animals drifting long, delicate legs under fur and rugs. The men were also wrapped up, heads bound in red and white. The desert stretched behind them, tufted with sparse grass, rock rising straight up in places like towers. They looked at us for what felt like a long time. I remember that long watching, their silence, that opal land, the white desert. A place that has never left my nights since then without some twist of dream.

"Here's some more," one man said. 5

The others nodded, as if they already knew us. In town we had called these sorts of men the *ruhhal*, wanderers.

The man touched his eyes then offered my mother his hand. "We ask respectfully that you come to live with us."

We followed them; sometimes I walked, other times I was carried upon a camel's undulating back. The land opened to us in cliffs and valleys, blue nooks and canyons. Their camp was hard to see through the yellow slant of sun. Light reflected from their sheep and the tents made of goat hairs, everything beaten to yellow. A black burro grazed by the edge of the grounds. Beyond that, we saw the shoulders of the *djebels* rising into the distance, folding mountains.

The *sitti*, matriarch of the tribe, emerged wreathed in black. Her face was tattooed over the chin, cheeks, and brow, and the eyes of the baby she held were blacked with kohl for the visitors. The other women came, and their arms were filled with leaves and flowers, as if they had known, perhaps even before we did, that we were coming, as if the desert floor murmured to them, bringing our footsteps over the land. They came, white veils lifting from their hair, arms filled, telling us, "Welcome, welcome, *assalamu alaikum*, you are home, at last, you are home again."

We lived with the Huwyatat Bedouins for a month. It was a time that 10 my mother would later say was the happiest in her life, as if she had lived all her previous life with a cord tied about her waist. In the desert, the knot had broken and she went free.

"We know about the wanderings of marked men," said Sitti Jasmine. "For whom no land is home and against whom all hands are turned. Then there are nomads like us, who make the earth their home."

Jeneva, a woman who had come with us and had seen her home burned down, said, "You say that as if this desert *was* the whole world. You don't know what you're talking about. You don't know there are people out there, somewhere on the other side of the river right now, who will name your desert after their grandfathers, tell you that you never lived there, that the centuries were hallucinations, and that you will certainly never live here again."

One little girl said, "I'll take my daddy's pistol and shoot them!"

Sitti hushed her, gathering the child into her lap, and said to Jeneva, "If white-eyes come from all around to my desert, doesn't that prove my point? That this is land like any other on earth? When a man puts a name and draws his lines down on a piece of land, what foolishness. Those lines and words are invisible. Only in men's minds do these things exist. The Bedouin understand this. We walk and we know the joy in movement, in following the natural inclinations of the territory. We're content because the earth confirms that we're alive."

I remember a month of walking, of coming to campsites that dotted   15
the earth, oases of stone walls and fountains, centuries stained. The Huwyatat would draw in their camel herds, set the black-haired sheets across the walls, and let the smell of coffee and cardamom rise, arabesques of smoke turning in the air. Sometimes we moved alongside an old railway line, where the camels wandered to graze between its tracks. We walked from *ouadi* to *ouadi*, the watering holes of valleys, muddy and flat in a white-scorched land or springing through green-terraced country. We carried embroidery, spun sheets and carpets, and listened to the clink of Roman coins and gold bands around the women's arms.

I also remember the absence in my mother's eyes as she gave herself to the march. The fact of movement and the company of others, I now believe, was what sustained her. Her eyes changed forever, imprinted with the image of a disappearing landscape, but I know the Bedouins gave something inviolable to us. In our first days of travel, I saw an oasis that was like a lake; the water was vast, and as we came closer I saw that its surface was alive, that it moved and formed itself in pieces from the air. Then I realized that these pieces of lake and air were birds. Their wings shattered the air and their cries were layers of song, trebling, croaking, shrilling, musical and ornate, overlaid like the layers of Bedouin embroidery. That memory of bird song and flight was to return to me throughout my life.

The Bedouins lived lightly, leaving just the imprint of their feet, their gathering hands, and the camels' soft mouths to mark their passing. They were easy, too, with command, relying upon the elders, especially Sitti Jasmine, her skin brown as a tree stump and traced over. On the rare occasion that we met a visitor — once a falconer, another time, *journalists* from Britain — the men would cry out, *Alan wa sahlan!* Be twice welcomed! My tent, they said, is certainly your tent. And coffee, black, crude, and sugary, would be put before them. The falconer showed us how his bird sat on his leather glove, just a thread around the bird's talons and a tasseled hood over the bird's eyes like a too-large turban. The journalists had Sitti Jasmine speak into a whirring box. Their questions went round in circles, like men lost in the desert:

> Where do you travel?
> What do you eat?
> Where will you go next?

They pushed some buttons and we heard Sitti Jasmine's voice creak forth from under a cloud of whispery noises and repeat her answers. She clapped her hands together then and said in English, "You have jinnis in your boxes!" Then she turned to the rest of us and, grabbing her five-year-old granddaughter, said in Arabic, "But this one, big-ears, can repeat that trick in clearer voice and with extra commentary added in."

We came to a place that stretched beyond my mind's outlines: pillars, veined, footed, and engraved, some sunken almost completely in fields of yellow wild flower. There were stone-swept avenues that turned into plazas, stone altars, and theaters open to the air. We walked through carved archways, light-shot openings, where the men demonstrated how those before us had positioned weapons or leaned out into the night, charting stars. The Huwyatat unfurled their carpets and moored them between pillars. Among the ruins, the smell of coffee was rich as earth.

From this place we passed single file, along ridges and between   20
mountain crevices barely as wide as a camel's hips, places where the stone was hooked in a thousand places like piles of skulls, down a trail crusted in the earth. At the end of the trail we walked between the sides of two stone faces, set shoulder to shoulder. Siq, our leader's snow-white camel, swung its head back once, then we turned into a brilliant basin. Before us, pink and white, satiny as a girl's thigh, intricate as a heart, a facade emerged from the rock face.

I and the other children ran up before the riders to the beauty standing out of the rock. Its columns and archways were delicately hued as
rose petals, and above those, atop the elaborate portico, there was an
urn intricate as Aladdin's lamp. One of the men leveled his rifle at it.

"There's no gold in there, you fool," the leader said.

The other man put down his gun, shrugged, and said, "One never
knows."

We walked along the clearing, and the leader pointed out other
columns and openings, some just tracery along the rocks, sketches of
palaces, others opened into rooms cut by shadows or dark and watery,
swimming with bands of pink, blue, and ochre. Everything was silent,
even the camels' feet seemed to walk in pools of silence. The dust in
the air was still. The running children made no sound. Outside an
archway, I found a fallen stone man; he had wild waves of hair and
beard, empty eyes, and lips parted in silent command.

Birds skittered across the air, hectoring and wheeling. I stood by the   25
toppled stone head and seemed to see time moving up the weathered
stone walk. I ran to look for my mother and found her in the farthest
room with her hand on the back of the leader's son, Ibn Abdel, the
young man who had first found us. Her other hand was pressed between his shoulder blades as they sank down onto a rush mat. I quickly
walked away.

We moved on again. One night we saw the silhouettes of riders on a
djebel crest just ahead. Their cloaks unfurled like wings and we could
see the black strokes of their rifles against the sky. I was terrified and
began calling for my mother, only to have another woman tell me to
hush. The children spoke of spirits, but one of the elders whispered,
"No ghosts, unfortunately. These are only men."

Our men had begun shifting on their horses, taking the lead and un-
sheathing swords. We continued advancing as a group until they gestured for us to hang back. I felt my mother's hands encircle my waist.

A shot tore the sky from the crest over the length of the valley, then
another, illuminating the rifle points. The Huwyatat men spurred their
horses, their snake-limbed Arabs charging up the hillside, moonlight
catching their flanks. The women stood and cried out, rippling their
voices. They set up a ululation of war that rose, full and eerie as a
ghost's lament, a ziggurat of sound.

We could see that our challengers were outnumbered. As the Huwyatat neared the hilltop, only a small band rode forward. The rifles had
been used only to announce war, and the men drew swords that shone
with the moon, blades clashing as we lost sight of the men in the dark. I
remember flashes of metal, hooves, but most of all, I remember that

keening song without words or end, with all the courage of a battle dance.

In the morning, the Huwyatat had taken the bodies of two chal- 30 lengers; the rest had been spared and fled. The men were from the Ahl el-Jabal tribe, enemies in a nearly forgotten blood feud, the women said. Other Huwyatat said the men were not lost but renegades, camel thieves, real criminals. Ibn Abdel came to me with a child's gold ring that he had found on the body of the man he had killed. "Perhaps this will fit you," he said. "This is probably from one of their young victims."

"Or perhaps it was a keepsake from his own child," another man said.

That night my mother tugged the ring off my finger and flung it into the sky.

Not long after that night my mother took me away from the other children. I had learned their games as well as their work, and I had learned to speak exactly as they did. My mother went to Ibn Abdel and said, "My daughter is getting to be savage like wild thorns, and this is not the kind of life I had hoped for her."

Sitti Jasmine, who also sat in the tent said, "It is exactly the kind of life she should have. She has fresh *leben* every day from the goat's milk, she learns the language of the desert wind and the paths of the stars. She has several grandmothers and grandfathers, many guides and pro-tectors, playmates and cousins. She has daily contact with the beauty and health of animals, an understanding of mirages and visions, of Allah's munificent voice, of the bounty of spirit and the clean warmth of goat-hair blankets. Our life is the most perfect life, the most pleasing to God. So tell me, what sort of life is it that you had in mind for her?"

My mother squatted on the beaten floor, her brow tipped to her 35 knees. At last she lifted her head and said, "This is not the life that *I* was born to. I can't keep moving like you. I need a place to stay in, even if it's a strange place. And I'm beginning to feel like I'll never be able to find myself again unless I stay still. I've been cut loose from my home and family. Sometimes I feel like my spirit has been lost over this desert of yours."

Ibn Abdel said, "I'm sorry, but for all of us. If you leave I will be los-ing a wife and daughter."

That week we came to an encampment, a collection of tents, corru-gated metal, trash, wire. So different from the tidy camps of the Huwy-atat, it looked as if it had been brought in and deposited by a circular wind. The eyes of the inhabitants were drops of lead that fell through me.

"The *mish ism*," the Huwyatat women murmured, "no names."

We gave them skins full of yoghurt, pistachios, figs, pressed apricot, and thyme, layer upon layer of the crackling leaves.

Ahlan, ahlan, they said, eyes lowered, peace be upon you, God bless   40
you, bless your hand.

Through it all the Bedouins held their faces averted. The Huwyatat women made gestures against the evil eye and fingered the charms that dangled from their necks.

"We found them here last Ramadan," Ibn Abdel said. "Like you, wandering like baby goats, blind to the signs of the earth, sand, and stars. These people were also separated the way you were. They were our first sign of the new white-eyes. But I talk too much. It is written, it is better to bless than to curse."

My mother held my hand, and we walked through the camp, through scraps of metal, a torn doll, the husks of food. Men squatted at their coffeepots over curds of black coffee, their clothes in tatters looking as if they'd shredded them with their own fingers. Their Arabic was shredded, the words flew into fragments of thought. I remembered the migratory birds at the first oasis we'd traveled to. I saw the torn wing of an ibis as it rose, low and uneven along the reeds, the movement of longing, dispersal, its cry the cry of dead souls.

The women clustered around us and talked about the taking of their village: soldiers marching in, doors and windows slamming open, bullets pinning corpses against buildings, men cut down at the knees, the sound of tanks. Those my mother and I saw at the camp had run for their lives, grabbing small possessions and running, and had come to this place, to Beit el Sala'am, they called it, to contemplate misery.

"Children died too?" I asked.   45

An old woman with the face of Sitti Jasmine grabbed my hand with both of hers. She was hurting me, but I couldn't pull away. "I had fourteen children!" she said. "Now they spin around the air above my head, trying to reenter my womb. I call to them, come back! They try to enter my ears and eyes and mouth, but there isn't room."

That night I slept in Sitti Jasmine's bed, and I dreamed of a man who looked familiar. He was calling my name, which broke into three parts.

This was how we began our life at Beit el Sala'am camp, and how I ended my life out of time with the Huwyatat Bedouin. I begged them not to leave us. And when it was time for them to go, Sitti Jasmine tried to hide me in one of the camels' back pouches. But Ibn Abdel came and returned me to my mother. For the short time I lived among the Bedouin, I was lifted out of the stream of things and I saw how the earth, sky, and all things in it functioned together, each part of the world a part of the movement through and into it, and the movement of the Bedouin was the movement of the world, intrepid, caught in the winding tails of the spirits, the white, whipped edge of a sheet in the wind.

EXPLORATIONS

1. According to Diana Abu-Jaber, what is the pattern of Bedouin life? What jobs evidently belong to women among the Huwyatat? What jobs belong to men?

2. "We carried embroidery, spun sheets and carpets, and listened to the clink of Roman coins and gold bands around the women's arms" (para. 15). What appear to be the functions of these various objects in the Bedouins' lives? What other possessions are essential to the group and why?

3. British journalists ask Sitti Jasmine, "Where do you travel? What do you eat? Where will you go next?" (para. 17). What answers to these questions can you glean from the story? Which questions are not important to the Huwyatat, and why not?

CONNECTIONS

1. The narrator of Alberto Moravia's "The Chase" observes: "Everything is wild which is autonomous and unpredictable and does not depend upon us" (p. 454, para. 2). What is this character's attitude toward wildness? Which characters in "In Flight" have a similar attitude, and how do they express it?

2. In "Woman as Other" Simone de Beauvoir writes that "no group ever sets itself up as the One without at once setting up the Other over against itself" (p. 447, para. 5). What "others" appear in "In Flight"? How do the Huwyatat respond to them? What factors seem to determine which response a given "other" group gets from these Bedouins?

3. "In Flight" and Leslie Marmon Silko's "Yellow Woman" (p. 419) both depict a young mother taking up with a strange man and then leaving him to return to a more familiar situation. What similar and contrasting ideas do these two stories express about romance, sexuality, gender roles, family bonds, home, and responsibility?

NAILA MINAI

Women in Early Islam

Naila Minai was born in Japan and grew up in Turkey and many other countries of the Middle East. "My Turkish-Tatar grandmother was tutored at home, married a polygamous man, and has never discarded her head veil," she writes. "My mother never wore the veil, studied in schools close to home, and settled down as a housewife in a monogamous marriage. I left my family as a teenager to study in the United States and Europe, where I hitchhiked from country to country . . . eventually making a solo trip across the Sahara." Minai's flight took her to the Sorbonne in Paris and the University of California, Berkeley, where she received her degrees in literature and biology. She has worked as a UN correspondent and has continued to travel widely as a free-lance journalist. "Women in Early Islam" comes from her 1981 book *Women in Islam*. She currently divides her time between the United States and her extended family in the Middle and Far East.

Khadija, an attractive forty-year-old Arabian widow, ran a flourishing caravan business in Mecca in the seventh century A.D., and was courted by the most eligible men of her society. But she had eyes only for an intelligent and hardworking twenty-five-year-old in her employ named Muhammad. "What does she see in a penniless ex-shepherd?" her scandalized aristocratic family whispered among themselves. Accustomed to having her way, however, Khadija proposed to Muhammad and married him. Until her death some twenty-five years later, her marriage was much more than the conventional Cinderella story in reverse, for Khadija not only bore six children while comanaging her business with her husband, but also advised and financed him in his struggle to found Islam, which grew to be one of the major religions of the world.

It was a religion that concerned itself heavil y with women's rights, in a surprisingly contemporary manner. A woman was to be educated and allowed to earn and manage her income. She was to be recognized as legal heir to her father's property along with her brother. Her rights in marriage were also clearly spelled out: She was entitled to sexual satisfaction as well as economic support. Nor was divorce to consist any longer of merely throwing the wife out of the house without paying her financial compensation.

This feminist bill of rights filled an urgent need. Meccans in the seventh century were in transition from a tribal to an urban way of life. As their town grew into a cosmopolitan center of trade, kinship solidarity had deteriorated, but municipal laws had not yet been fully established to protect the citizens. Women were particularly vulnerable, their rights closely linked with the tribal way of life their people had known before renouncing nomadism to settle in Mecca around A.D. 400. In nomadic communities of the desert a woman was not equal to a man. During famine a female could be killed at birth to increase her brother's food supply. However, if she managed to reach adulthood she had a better status in the desert than in the city, largely because her labors were indispensable to her clan's survival in the harsh environment. While the men protected the encampment and engaged in trade, she looked after the herds and produced the items to be traded — meat, wool, yogurt, and cheese, all of which bought weapons and grains as well as other essentials. As a breadwinner the tribal woman enjoyed considerable political clout. Even if she did not always participate in council meetings, she made her views known. Only a fool refused to heed his womenfolk and risked antagonizing a good half of his tribe, with whom he had to live in the close confines of the camp and caravan.

If tribal discord was uncomfortable in the best of circumstances, it was catastrophic during the battles that broke out frequently among the clans over pasture and watering rights or to avenge heroes slain by the enemy. With the battlefront so close to home, a woman was needed as a nurse, cheerleader, and even soldier. She was sometimes captured and ransomed or sold into slavery. If her tribesmen could not pay her captors the required number of camels in ransom, they valiantly stormed the enemy's camp to rescue her. These were men brought up on recitations of epic poems about brave warriors who rescued fair damsels in distress. Poets and poetesses of the tribe kept chivalry alive, constantly singing praises of heroism among their people and condemning cowardliness and disloyalty. No one who wanted a respectable place in his tribe could afford to ignore the ubiquitous "Greek chorus," for life without honor was worse than death to a nomad, who could not survive as an outcast in the desert.

Marriage customs varied from tribe to tribe, but the most popular were those that tended to maintain the woman's independence, if only incidentally, by having her remain within her family circle after marriage. If the husband was a close relative, the couple set up a conjugal tent near both of their parents. A husband who was not kin merely visited her at her home. In some clans women could be married to several visiting husbands at the same time. When the wife bore a child, she simply summoned her husbands and announced which of them she believed to be the child's father. Her decision was law. Actually, it did not matter greatly who the biological father was, since children of such unions belonged to the matrilineal family and were supported by communal property administered by her brothers or maternal uncles.

Life in the desert was so hard and precarious that some of the most impoverished tribes renounced nomadism to submit to a less independent existence in towns. Muhammad's ancestors, a segment of the Kinanah tribe, were among them. They settled down at the crossroads of important caravan routes in the place which is now Mecca, and prospered as middlemen under the new name of Quraysh. Their great wealth and power undoubtedly helped their deities extend their spiritual influence far beyond Mecca's boundaries and make Kaaba, their sanctuary, the most important shrine in central Arabia. As keepers of the shrine the leading Quraysh families grew immeasurably rich, but the wealth was not equitably distributed. As survival no longer depended on communal sharing and on women's contributing equally to the family budget, Meccans became more interested in lucrative business connections than in kinship ties. Glaring socioeconomic differences — unknown among nomads — emerged. Women lost their rights and their security.

If brothers went their separate ways, their sister who continued to live with them after marriage lost her home unless one of them took her and her children under his protection. A woman could not automatically count on her brothers to assume this duty, for with the rise of individualism the patrilineal form of marriage, which had coexisted with other marital arrangements in seventh-century Mecca, was gaining popularity. A self-made man tended to prefer leaving his property to his own sons, which sharpened his interest in ensuring that his wife bore only his children. The best way to guarantee this was to have her live under close supervision in his house. The woman thus lost her personal freedom, but the security she gained from the marital arrangement was precarious at best in the absence of protective state laws. Not only did she have to live at her in-laws' mercy, she could be thrown out of the house on her husband's whim. Khadija escaped such a fate because she was independently wealthy and belonged to one of the most powerful families of the Quraysh — a fact that must have helped her significantly to multiply her fortune.

It was against such a backdrop of urban problems that Islam was born. Even though Muhammad lived happily and comfortably with his rich wife, he continued to identify with the poor and the dispossessed of Mecca, pondering the conditions that spawned them. He himself had been orphaned in early childhood and passed on from one relative to another. Since his guardians were from the poor and neglected branch of the Quraysh, Muhammad earned his keep as a shepherd from a very early age. But he was luckier than other orphans, for he at least had a place in loving homes and eventually got a good job with Khadija's caravan, which allowed him to travel widely in the Middle East.

These journeys had a direct bearing on his spiritual growth and gave focus to his social concerns by exposing him to Christian monks and well-educated Jewish merchants. They intrigued him, for they seemed to have put into practice a monotheistic faith which a few Meccans of the educated circles were beginning to discuss. How did the Christian God inspire such diverse nationalities to worship Him alone? How did the Judaic God manage to unite widely dispersed Semitic groups under one set of laws which provided for the protection of women and children even in large cities? The astral deities that Muhammad's people inherited from their nomadic ancestors demanded offerings but gave nothing in return. After discussions with people of various faiths, Muhammad sought the ultimate solution to his community's problems in the solitude of a cave on Mount Hiraa overlooking Mecca, where he often retreated in his spare moments, with Khadija or by himself.

While meditating alone one day in the cave, Muhammad heard a voice which he believed to be the angel Gabriel's. "Proclaim in the name of thy Lord and Cherisher who created, created man out of a clot of congealed blood" (Quran,[1] surah [chapter] 96, verses 1–2), it said, pointing out that there was only one God and that man must serve Him alone. When Muhammad recovered from his ecstasy, he ran back, shaken, and described his experience to his wife. Having shared his spiritual struggles, Khadija understood that her husband had received a call to serve the one God whom the Christians and the Jews also worshiped. Bewildered and confused, Muhammad went on with his daily work in the city and occasional meditations on Mount Hiraa. Again the voice commanded him to tell his people about the one omnipotent God, who would welcome believers into heaven and cast wicked people into hell. With Khadija's repeated encouragement, Muhammad finally accepted his prophetic call and devoted the rest of his life to preaching God's word as the new religion of Islam (which means "submission [to the will of God]"). Converts to it were called Muslims ("those who submit"). They were not to be called Muhammadans, because they did not worship Muhammad, who was merely a human

10

---

[1]Variation of Koran, the sacred text of Islam. — ED.

messenger for the one God. Though invisible and immortal, this God was named Allah after the Zeus of the old Meccan pantheon.

Numerous revelations that Muhammad received from Allah throughout his life were compiled shortly after his death into the Muslim bible, named the Quran, which formed the basis for the Shariah, or Islamic law. A supplement to it was provided by the Hadith, or Muhammad's words, which were recorded over many years as his survivors and their descendants remembered them. Despite the exotic Arabic words in which it is couched, Islam's message is similar in its essentials to the one promulgated by Judaism and Christianity, and can be summed up by the Ten Commandments. *Allah*, after all, is but the Arabic name for the God worshiped by both Jews and Christians. But the rituals differed. Muhammad required his followers to obey the commandments through the practice of five specific rituals, called the pillars of Islam. A Muslim must (1) profess faith in one God; (2) pray to Him; (3) give alms to the poor; (4) fast during Ramadan, the month in the lunar calendar during which Muhammad received his first revelation; and (5) go on a pilgrimage to Mecca at least once in his lifetime (if he can afford to do so) to pay respects to the birthplace of Islam and reinforce the spirit of fellowship with Muslims from all over the world. Although these laws preached fairness and charity among all mankind, God — through Muhammad — preferred to establish specific guidelines to protect the interests of women.

Once he had united enough people under Allah to make a viable community, Muhammad devoted an impressive number of his sermons to women's rights. In doing so, however, he did not attempt to fight the irreversible tide of urbanization. Nor did he condemn the trend toward patrimonial families, although they often abused women. Too shrewd a politician to antagonize Mecca's powerful patriarchs, he introduced a bill of rights for women which would not only ensure their protection under patriarchy but also reinforce the system itself so that it would stand as a minitribe against the rest of the world.

He did this mainly by providing for women's economic rights in marriage in such a way that they had a financial stake in the system which constantly threatened to erode their independence. Upon marriage a man had to pay his bride a dowry, which was to be her nest egg against divorce or widowhood. While married to him, she could manage the dowry and all other personal income in any way that she pleased, exclusively for her own benefit, and will them to her children and husband upon her death. In her lifetime she did not have to spend her money on herself, or her children for that matter, since only the man was responsible for supporting his family. If the woman stayed married to her husband until his death, she also inherited part of his property. While her share was less than her children's, she was assured of being supported by her sons in widowhood. By the same line of reasoning, her inheritance from her father was half that of her brother's: Her husband supported her, whereas her brother had to support his wife. The daughter's right to inherit tended to divide the patriarch's wealth, but the problem was customarily solved by having her marry a paternal first cousin. Failing that, the inheritance became a part of yet another Muslim family in the same tribe of Islam, united through faith rather than kinship. In either case, a Muslim woman with neither a paid occupation nor an inheritance enjoyed a modicum of financial independence, at the price of her submission to a patriarchal form of marriage.

But she was to be allowed to choose her own spouse, according to the Hadith: "None, not even the father or the sovereign, can lawfully contract in marriage an adult woman of sound mind without her permission, whether she be a virgin or not." This freedom was to be assured by a law that required the dowry to be paid to the bride herself. Since the parents were not to pocket it, as they often did before Islam, they were presumably above being "bought." But the brides' freedom remained largely theoretical, since most of them were barely ten years old when engaged to be married for the first time. Aysha, whom Muhammad married after Khadija's death, was only about six or seven years old when she was betrothed and about ten when she moved into her husband's house with her toys. Muhammad was not playing legal tricks on women, however. He did revoke the parents' choice of mate when their daughters complained to him about it. Although parents were to be honored and obeyed, he made it clear that the grown-up daughter was to be respected as an individual — so much so that the marriage contract could be tailored to her specific needs: The bride could impose conditions on her contract. A cooperative wife, he pointed out, was the best foundation for a stable marriage.

Though Muhammad repeatedly preached compassion and love as   15
the most important bonds of marriage, he also gave men financial enticements to keep the family together. The husband was allowed to pay only a part of the dowry upon marriage, with the balance payable upon divorce. If the dowry was large enough, the arrangement deterred the husband from throwing out his wife without substantial cause. In fact, under Islam he could no longer just throw her out. He had to pay her not only the balance of the dowry but also "maintenance on a reasonable scale" (Quran 2:241). He was also to support her through the ensuing *idda*, the three months of chastity which the Shariah asked her to

observe in order to determine whether she was carrying his child. If pregnant, she was to be helped until she delivered and had nursed the infant to the point where he could be cared for by the husband's family. All of her children remained under the paternal roof. In a patriarchal society where men were not eager to support others' children or to provide employment for women, the child custody law assured children a decent home and enabled the divorcée to remarry more easily, but even an independently wealthy woman was forbidden to walk out of her husband's home with her children.

Any sexual behavior that would weaken the patriarchal system was strongly discouraged or made illegal. If the custom of taking a visiting husband was frowned upon, her taking more than one at a time was condemned as adultery, which was punishable by whipping. Although men were also forbidden to sow wild oats, they could marry up to four wives and have as many concubines as they could afford. This law may have been partly a concession by Muhammad to the widely accepted custom among wealthy urban men, but he also saw it as a way to attach surplus women to the men's households for their own protection as well as to maintain social order. Due to frequent intertribal warfare and attacks on the merchants' caravans, women always outnumbered men. The conflict became increasingly serious as Muhammad's following grew large enough to threaten the purse and the prestige of the families who amassed fortunes from pilgrims to the Kaaba. So vicious were the attacks that in A.D. 622, after Khadija died, Muhammad moved his budding Muslim community to Medina, an agricultural community without important shrines that would be threatened by Allah. Moreover, the perpetually quarreling clans of Medina welcomed Muhammad because of his reputation as a just man and a skillful arbitrator.

Muhammad succeeded brilliantly in settling the clans' differences and won a prominent place in Medina. This made Meccans even more determined to destroy him before he built up an alliance against them. Violent battles between the Muslims and the Meccans followed. Alliances and betrayals by various tribal factions during each battle engendered more battles, which decimated the Muslim community. The number of widows mounted to such catastrophic proportions after the battle fought at Uhud, near Medina, that God sent a message officially condoning polygamy: "Marry women of your choice, two, or three, or four." But He added, "If you fear that you cannot treat them equitably, marry only one" (3:3). A polygamous husband was required to distribute not only material goods but also sexual attention equally among his wives, for sexual satisfaction, according to Muhammad, was every woman's conjugal right. Besides, a sexually unsatisfied wife was believed to be a threat to her family's stability, as she was likely to seek satisfaction elsewhere.

Unmarried men and women also posed a threat to Muhammad's scheme of social order, which may be one reason why he frowned upon monasticism. Sexual instincts were natural, he reasoned, and therefore would eventually seek fulfillment in adultery[2] unless channeled into legitimate marriage. Wives and husbands were thus necessary for each other's spiritual salvation. "The curse of God be upon those women who remain unwed and say they will never marry," he said, "and a man who does not marry is none of mine."

Though the Quran abolished the ancient custom of stoning adulteresses to death and called instead for public whipping — a hundred lashes administered to male and female offenders alike — Muhammad knew that the sexual double standard would single out women as targets of slander. After a bitter personal experience, he hastened to build safety features into his antiadultery and antifornication laws.

One day Aysha was left behind inadvertently by Muhammad's cara-   20
van when she stepped away to look for a necklace that she had lost. She was brought back to the caravan the following morning by a man many years younger than her middle-aged husband, which set tongues wagging. Even Ali, Muhammad's trusted cousin and son-in-law, cast doubt on her reputation. The Prophet's faith in his wife was severely shaken. Aysha was finally saved when her husband fell into a trance, which indicated that he was receiving a message from God. Relief spread over his face. God had vouched for her innocence. The "affair of the slander," as it came to be known, was closed. Four witnesses were henceforth required to condemn women of adultery, as against only two for business transactions and murder cases. Moreover, false witnesses were to be whipped publicly.

Other than false witnesses, violators of women's rights were not punished on this earth. The law would catch up with them in the next world, where they would be cast into the fire (an idea borrowed from the Christians). The good, on the other hand, would reside forever in a heavenly oasis with cool springs in shady palm groves where their every whim would be served by lovely dark-eyed houris. Like the Christian preachers who promised believers a heaven with pearly gates and haloed creatures floating about on white clouds, Muhammad merely presented images that would spell bliss to the common man. Though he did not specify who was going to serve the deserving

[2]Here *adultery* refers to premarital as well as extramarital sex.

women, probably for fear of offending their husbands, Muhammad
guaranteed a place for them in paradise. Women had the same religious duties as men, and their souls were absolutely equal in God's
eyes, with not even the responsibility for original sin weighing upon
them. Islam rejects the idea of original sin altogether, claiming that
every child is born pure. Nor does the Quran single out Eve as the
cause of man's fall (though folklore in various parts of the Middle East
does condemn her). According to the Quran, Allah tells both Adam
and Eve not to eat the apple. "Then did Satan make them slip from
the Garden" (2:36). Allah scolds them both equally, but promises
mercy and guidance when they repent.

Muhammad's decision to rely on each man's conscience to fulfill his
Islamic obligation toward women reflected a realistic approach to legis-
lation. He seems to have recognized how far he could carry his reforms
without losing his constituents' support. In a city where women had
neither economic nor political weight, men would take only so much
earthly punishment for disregarding her rights. By the same token, they
would not entirely give up their old prerogative of divorcing their wives
for any cause without answering to a third party, or pay them more than
comfortably affordable compensation. Muhammad therefore struck a
compromise in his laws, but repeatedly emphasized the spirit of kindness and respect for women which was implied in them. . . .

The unspecified rights that women had enjoyed during Muhammad's time were chipped away gradually. But the meticulously detailed
laws on marital and financial rights were too specific to be ignored entirely, and gave women a modicum of security and independence in
the patriarchal family, which survived as a minitribe in the sprawling
empire. Within the family circle women exerted considerable influence, not only on their men but also on the blossoming of Arab culture
in the Middle Ages. An exceptional few followed Aysha's example and
ruled the caliphs and their empire, which spread Islam to lands and
peoples far beyond the Arabian peninsula.

EXPLORATIONS

1. According to Naila Minai, what were the main responsibilities, privileges,
   and dangers of being female in a nomadic tribe?

2. How did Muhammad's marriage to Khadija contribute to the founding of
   Islam? How did his marriage to Aysha contribute to the religion's rules?

3. What is the effect of Minai's opening her essay with a romantic anecdote? What elements in this first paragraph were presumably added by the author rather than drawn from source documents? How would you evaluate the balance she has struck between human interest and historical accuracy?

CONNECTIONS

1. Diana Abu-Jaber's "In Flight" (p. 462) takes place in what is now Jordan in the early 1900s. What evidence in that story matches Minai's observations in paragraphs 3–4 about women's roles in nomadic Arabian tribes 1,500 years earlier? Why do you think nomadic life was so similar in such different times and places?

2. What rules governing sexuality and marriage among Muslims also appear among the Zhun/twasi as described in "Nisa's Marriage" (p. 431) by Marjorie Shostak? What explanations does Minai offer for these rules in Arabia that also may explain them in Botswana?

3. Look back at Ved Mehta's epigraph on page 133. In what ways do the Hindu concepts of male and female rights and responsibilities he describes resemble those of Islam? What aspects of both cultures' definition of sex roles illustrate points made by Simone de Beauvoir in "Woman as Other" (p. 445)?

NAGUIB MAHFOUZ

A Day for Saying Goodbye

Egypt's (and the Arab world's) only Nobel laureate for literature, Naguib Mahfouz, was born in Cairo in 1911. "I am the son of two civilizations that at a certain age in history formed a happy marriage," he said in his 1988 Nobel lecture. "The first of these, seven thousand years old, is the Pharaonic civilization; the second, one thousand four hundred years old, is the Islamic one." Maufouz graduated from the University of Cairo in 1934 and did postgraduate work there in philosophy. A prolific writer, he began publishing in 1939 and continued to produce short stories and novels while working for the newspaper *Al-Ahram* and for the Egyptian government. Most of his government jobs involved the arts; his last position, which he left in 1971, was as a consultant for cinema affairs to the Ministry of Culture. Until his 1988 Nobel Prize, very little of Mahfouz's work was available in English, although his portraits of Cairo and its people (nearly all his writing is set there) have been compared to Charles Dickens's depictions of London. In the Arab world, his best-known novels are his critically acclaimed "Cairo Trilogy" of 1956 and 1957. His books occasionally have been banned in Islamic countries for political reasons, as when he supported the 1979 peace treaty between Egypt and Israel. The chaos and contradictions that fill Mahfouz's writing came unexpectedly to life when a stranger with a knife attacked him in 1994. At age eighty-two he weathered five hours of surgery and later returned home with his wife and daughters. His most recent novel to appear in the United States is the retranslated *Children of the Alley* (1996; *Children of Gebelaawi*, 1981), which was originally serialized in Egypt in 1959 and published in Lebanon in 1967. "A Day for Saying Goodbye" comes from *The Time and the Place and Other Stories* (1991); it was translated by Denys Johnson-Davies.

Life was going on with all its clamor, just as though nothing had happened. Every human being embraces his own secret, possesses it on his own. I cannot be the only one. If the inclinations of the inner self were to assume concrete form, crimes and acts of heroism would be rife. For myself, the experience has come to an end, all because of a blind impulse. Nothing remains but a farewell outing.

At the crossroads, emotions flare up, memories are resurrected. How great is my distress! An extraordinary strength is required to control myself, otherwise the moments of saying goodbye will disappear. Look and enjoy everything, move from place to place, for in every corner there is some forgotten happiness that you must bring to mind. What a crushing blow, filled with bitterness, fury, and hate! I have plunged headlong recklessly, quite oblivious of the consequences. A life that was not bad has been scattered to the winds. Look and remember, be happy, then be sad. For reasons there is not time to enumerate, the angel turned into a devil. How often decay afflicts everything that is good! Love had been uprooted from my heart and it had turned to stone. Let us ignore all that in the short time that remains. What a crushing blow! Of what significance was it?

Port Said Street stirs under an umbrella of white autumnal clouds. The fumes that rise from my chest darken the beauty of things. The nostalgic beckonings from the distant past rap at the doors of my heart. My feet drag me to pay a visit to my sister. Her calm pallid face gazes at me from behind the door. It lights up with happiness. "A rare and unexpected pleasure at this early hour," she says.

She went off to make the coffee, and I sat down to wait in the living room. Our parents and brothers and sisters, who had passed away, looked down at me from their photographs hanging above the tables. No one was left to me except this widowed sister who, being childless, had given her abundant love to me and to Samira and Gamal. Had I come here to commit my son and daughter to her care? She returned with the coffee. She wore a white dressing gown. "Why didn't you go to the office?"

"I took the day off because I felt out of sorts."   5

"You don't look well — is it a cold?"

"Yes."

"Don't neglect yourself."

My face had begun to betray me. What, I wondered, was now happening in my unhappy flat?

"Yesterday Samira and Gamal paid me a visit."   10

"They love you just as you love them."

"And how is Seham?"

What an innocent question!

"She's fine."

"Haven't things got better between you?"   15

"I don't think so."

"I'm always nice to her but I feel she's uneasy with me."

I was seized with grief and kept silent.

"The times we live in need patience and wisdom."

I wanted to ask her to look after Samira and Gamal, but how to do   20
so? Later she would realize the import of my visit. Would Samira and
Gamal forgive me for what I had done? How great is my distress!

"What if I went with you now to the doctor's?"

"That's not necessary, Siddiqa. I've got to go and do certain jobs."

"How can I be sure you're all right?"

"I'll visit you tomorrow."

Tomorrow? Once again I am walking in the street. Look and enjoy,   25
and move from place to place. The Sporting Club beach is solitary, devoid of human beings, the waves clapping out their summons and no
one answering. The heart beats under the tightly closed envelope of
worries. The moment she emerged from the water with her slim body,
the skin tinged by the sun's gossamer, she wrapped herself in her beach
robe and hurried to the cabin to seat herself by her parents' feet. I was
walking by, in shorts, and our eyes met. I was pervaded by a sensation of
pleasure to which my heart responded. A voice called to me, and I answered and thus found myself in her company, for the person who had
called was her uncle, a colleague of mine in the firm. We were introduced, and some casual conversation between us followed — but how
enjoyable it was! Moments of sheer unadulterated happiness, moments
that were not to be repeated, moments that refused to be repeated. Now
they circle around my heart in the form of a passing yearning that has
its warm existence despite the fact that the threads that one day bound
them to reality have been torn apart. And her saying that day, "You've a
good heart and that is something beyond price." Was it true? Who,
then, was it who said that there was no one more vile and despicable
than you? And who was it who said that the Lord had created you to torture her and make her miserable? Love should have risen up and stood
against the disparities of temperament, but it was the disparities that
had put an end to love. Each of us had been stubborn, we had each had
as our slogan All or nothing. You were crazy about inane outward appearances and would shout at me saying I was retarded. In terror
Samira and Gamal would take refuge in their rooms. How greatly we
had harmed them! The love between us had suffered hour by hour and
day by day till it breathed its last. It had been choked in the hubbub of
continuing arguments, quarrels, and exchanges of abuse. Yet it was in
this outdoor café, in this actual corner, that I had disclosed to her uncle
my admiration for her.

"Though she hasn't been to university, she is well-educated. Her father had his own policy. After completing her secondary education, the
girl was prepared by him for being a housewife, in view of her being sufficiently well provided for."

"That's very convenient," I had said.

He had invited us both to dinner at Santa Lucia, and afterward we had met in the Pelican Garden. The days of courtship, of dreams and impeccable behavior. I hear a beautiful, rapturous tune, though all the strings on which it was played have been broken. What a crushing blow! What is happening in the flat now? Why isn't life made up of perpetual days of courtship? Oh, the masks of lies we hide behind! A salutary method of knowing oneself is indispensable.

"Mr. Mustafa Ibrahim?"

I looked at the man who was calling my name and found him to be an inspector at the firm, no doubt on his way to work. "Hullo, Amr Bey."

"On holiday?"

"Slightly unwell."

"It's only too clear. Would you like me to give you a lift somewhere?"

"No thanks."

He was perhaps the first witness. No, my neighbor the doctor had already seen me as I left the flat. Had he noticed anything unusual? The concierge had seen me too. That was of no importance. I had never thought of making my escape. I would be waiting until the end. Had it not been for my final eagerness to say goodbye, I would have gone by myself.

It was not possible to discard life of my own accord. It had been wrenched from me by force. I had never sought this ending. I had still five years to go before I was fifty. Despite the suffering, life was sweet. Seham had not been able to make it hateful to me. Should I visit Samira and Gamal at the College of Science? They had left without my seeing them, and I had not foreseen what had occurred. I would not find the courage to look them in the eye. It pained me to leave them to their fate. I could imagine them knocking at the door and their mother not hastening to open it. The day would leave its mark until the end of life. And if they cursed me, they would be entitled to do so.

When would I put my grief behind me and dedicate myself to saying goodbye? Look and enjoy, and move from place to place. The market. The day we walked in the market to make our purchases. A man with a bride feels that he is about to take possession of the world itself, feels that happiness may be anything in the world — but not like methylated spirit that just evaporates. With love I say, "To San Giovanni." And she says joyfully, "I'll phone Mummy."

Graciousness, sweetness, and angelic gentleness during our first days together. When and how had the new Seham made her appearance? After becoming a mother, but not at any precisely definable time. How had the sensation of dashed hopes taken control of me? Samira once said, "How quickly and violently you become angry, Father." And I once admitted to Seham, "I may forget myself when I get angry, but it's always for a good reason."

"And for no reason. It's a misunderstanding."

"You squander our life on trivialities."   40

"Trivialities? You don't understand life."

"You're autocratic. You set no store by reason. What you have in your head must come about regardless of anything."

"Had I respected your opinions we would have been in a real mess."

Look and enjoy, and move from place to place. Abu Qir is the ideal summer resort. Let's have a fish lunch. Fill your stomach and stimulate it with some white wine. We sat together at this place, and here we taught Samira and Gamal to swim when they were young. It is said that despair is one of the two states of rest. Would it not have been better to divorce her?

"Divorce me and set me free."   45

"I'd like nothing better, if it weren't for my concern for Samira and Gamal."

"You should rather have some concern for yourself and realize that you're an unbearable person."

The truth is that I often wished for your death. However, the fates are not in my hand. Any hardships are easy to bear alongside the hellfire of my hatred. We exchange hatred without making a secret of it. After exchanging the most awful and cruel words, how is it that I am able to partake of my food with appetite? Truly, despair possesses a happiness that is not to be underrated. From the radio issued the song "I, the torment, and your love," and my heart trembled. It was a song I came to love greatly during that fraudulent month of honeymoon. How is it that happiness vanishes after being stronger than existence itself? It is dispersed from the heart and attaches itself to the atmosphere of places after its starting point has been erased. Then, like a bird, it alights on dry ground, adorning it with the embroidery of its wings for several seconds. *I, the torment, and your love* — and this crushing blow.

Perhaps it was the day that, in your madness, you hurled yourself at Samira. In fear I pushed you from her, and you fell and hit your head. There gleamed in your eyes an inhuman look that spat out poison. "I hate you."

"So what?"   50

"I hate you until death."

"Go to hell."

"Once my heart is disturbed how impossible for it to become cloud-less!"

It is, unfortunately, the truth. O you with the black heart that found no way to apologize or make up or be amiable. After that no conversation took place between us other than about necessities and the household budget. Vengeance became mingled with the cost of living. The spring of compassion ran dry. As with a prisoner, my dreams revolved around escape. The desires of my heart dried up, and desolation closed over it. And all the while she behaved like a free woman, going and coming without permission or even letting me know. Silence enveloped her, and she uttered no word unless she had to. Pride encompassed her secret, and she complained of me to no one but my sister Siddiqa. When Siddiqa did not do what Seham expected, but sought to make peace between us, she hated her in turn. She said that it was not the madness of one man but a madness running in the family.

Seizing the opportunity of being alone with Samira and Gamal, I   55
asked their opinion of what they had seen of our situation. "Your situation is not a happy one, Father," Gamal had said. "It's like the situation of our country, or even worse, and I'm planning to emigrate at the first opportunity."

I know his recalcitrance well, but as for Samira, she is a sensible girl, religious and modern at one and the same time, and yet she said, "I'm sorry, Father, but neither on your side nor on hers is there any tolerance."

"I was defending you, Samira."

"I wish you hadn't done so. She would have made it up with me after an hour, but you get angry so quickly, Father."

"But she's unreasonable."

"Our whole home is unreasonable."   60

"I chose you to be a judge."

"No, I'm in no way entitled to be that."

"I have found no comfort from either of you."

To which Gamal said, "We have no comfort for you or for ourselves."

If these two have not loved me as I have loved them, then what good   65
do I wish for in this existence? Ah, look and enjoy, and move from place to place. As for the life that is being lost, live the moment that you are in and forget the past completely. Take your fill, for you will not see again that which you are leaving. Every moment is the last. From a world with which I am not satiated and whose pleasures I have not

renounced, a world that has been snatched from me in a hasty outburst of anger. Which of these streets has not seen us together? Or has not seen our whole family, with Samira and Gamal going ahead of us? Was there no way of repairing the discord?

The cruelest punishment is having to bid farewell to Alexandria in the splendor of its white autumn — and in the prime of mature manhood. And here is the silent sea on the other side of Abu Qir, and together we sing, "O for the bliss you are in, my heart." In a dialogue of song between two watchful hearts. With Samira and Gamal breathlessly counting the number of fishing boats at anchor above the moon's sparkling reflections. Is a single day sufficient for making a tour of the landmarks of a quarter of a century? Why do we not record the sweet avowals at the time so that they may be of benefit to us in the hour of dryness? Memories are as numerous as the leaves of the trees, and the period of time remaining is as short as happiness. Happiness, when it presents itself, dispels awareness, and double-crosses us when it vanishes.

And who have I to bring me together with Dawlat? There is no possibility of that today. And were it possible it would only make matters worse and compromise me prematurely. And what is the point of pretending to a love that is nonexistent? Despair is what pushed me into it. She never stopped hinting at marriage, without caring about the fate of Samira and Gamal. It is not love but rather a whim of revenge. If only I had halted there and not crossed over to the fatal blow.

As evening falls, the search for me no doubt intensifies. So let me wait in Asteria, the place I love best of all for passing the evening. The meeting place of families, lovers, and rosy dreams. Beer and a light supper. Perhaps I shall be the only one by myself. Forgive me, Samira. Forgive me, Gamal. I had met the morning with a sincere and open heart, but anger hurls us into the path of perils. I entreated that the hour might be put back by just one minute. And when the violent tensions had vanished, nothing was left but despair with its icy, tongue-tied face. I undertook this farewell excursion with death sometimes following at my back, sometimes preceding me. Life has been abbreviated into hours, and I have understood life more than at any time past. How happy are the people around me, and were they to know my secret they would be happier still! Amiably, the waiter asks me, "Where's Madam?"

"She's out of town," I answer with hidden dejection.

There was no time left. Soon two or more men would approach me. 70 "You are Mustafa Ibrahim?"

"Yes sir."

"Would you be good enough to come with us?"

I answer with total calm. "I was waiting for you."

EXPLORATIONS

1. What event has led the narrator of this story to spend his day saying good-bye? When and how did you know what that event is? What did you first guess it was, and why?

2. The narrator introduces his wife in paragraph 25 without naming her. How did you realize whom he was thinking about? Where else in the story does the narrator mix emotional declarations and the introduction of new characters in the same paragraph? What is the impact of Naguib Mahfouz's use of this technique?

3. Who is the "Dawlat" the narrator introduces in paragraph 67, and how can you tell? What effect does she have on the story?

CONNECTIONS

1. What elements in "A Day for Saying Goodbye" reflect the Islamic and Arab aspects of Egypt's heritage described by Naila Minai in "Women in Early Islam" (p. 470)? What elements in the story reflect the Christian and Western aspects of Egypt's heritage?

2. In what ways does Mahfouz's narrator define his wife as "other" as Simone de Beauvoir uses that term in "Woman as Other" (p. 445)? Reread Beauvoir's last paragraph. Which of her reasons why women accept the role of "other" seem to apply to Seham?

3. What factors brought together this story's narrator and his future wife? In which cultures you have read about in this book would those factors be considered a suitable basis for marriage? (Cite specific selections.) What factors do you think this couple overlooked that might have helped their marriage to succeed?

UNNI WIKAN

The Xanith: *A Third Gender Role?*

"I was born and grew up way above the Arctic Circle in the land of
the Midnight Sun," writes the Norwegian anthropologist Unni Wikan.
"In those days, we had neither TV, trains, nor planes up North, so it was
a remote but splendid place to live. But I kept gazing at the blue mountains, wondering what lay beyond. My first glimpse of the big wide
world was at seventeen when I came as an exchange student to Wellesley, Massachusetts. Since then, my life has been one of travel. I love my
work, anthropology, and have spent years living in Egypt, Oman, Bali,
and Bhutan besides traveling in much of the world. I have also written
several books about those places, like *Behind the Veil in Arabia: Women
in Oman* [1982]; *Life Among the Poor in Cairo* [1980]; and *Managing
Turbulent Hearts: A Balinese Formula for Living* [1990]. Because I believe the world needs generalists, not just specialists, I have chosen to
work in diverse fields: poverty research, gender issues, cultural studies,
and medical and psychological anthropology. I have also worked with
the UN in the developing world, and on critical social issues in Norway.
A firm believer in the power of ideas to change the world, I love teaching (I am a professor at the University of Oslo), and also lecturing to the
general public. To reach out I make ample use of the media (radio, TV,
newspapers)." Wikan supplied this autobiography to the student
newsletter at Harvard University's Leverett House when she was a Resident Tutor there in 1995–1996. Besides her stint at Harvard, where she
held the positions of Visiting Scholar in the Department of Anthropology and Guest Lecturer in the Department of Social Medicine, Wikan
has been a Visiting Professor at Johns Hopkins University and at
L'École des Hautes Études in Paris. She was born in Norway in 1944;
she grew up in Harstad and received her Ph.D. from the University of
Oslo in 1980. Her most recent book is *Tomorrow God Willing: Self-
made Destinies in Cairo* (1996). "The Xanith: A Third Gender Role?"
comes from *Behind the Veil in Arabia.*

Any discussion of the social roles of the sexes in Sohar would be incomplete without detailed attention also to a special kind of person,
known locally as *xanith* and, for many purposes, regarded by Soharis as
neither man nor woman. In English, one might call such persons male
transvestites or transsexuals. The way they are conceptualized in Sohar
and the way they function in that society, they cannot lightly be dis-

488

missed as aberrant or deviant individuals, but are better understood, as far as I can judge, as having a truly distinct, third gender role. The existence of such a triad of gender roles — woman, man, and *xanith* — provides an unusually productive opportunity to explore more thoroughly the basic properties and preconditions of male and female roles as they are conceptualized in Sohar. . . .[1]

The word *xanith* carries the sense of effeminate, impotent, soft. Although anatomically male, *xaniths* speak of themselves with emphasis and pride as "women." They are socially classified with women with respect to the strict rules of segregation. According to the estimates of informants, in 1976 there were about sixty *xaniths* in Sohar, as well as an unknown number of men who had been *xaniths* previously, but no longer were. In other words, well above one in every fifty males has a past or present history as a *xanith*. In the following I shall seek to develop a role analysis that does not see the *xanith* in artificial isolation, but confronts the role in the context of the reciprocal roles of man and woman, and the basic constitution of social persons and relationships in this society.

To perform such an analysis, I need to describe both how people classify and think about each other, and how they act and interact. I shall try to show how the conceptualization of each role in the triad reflects the existence of the other two, and how the realization of any one role in behavior presupposes, and is dependent on, the existence and activities of both the other roles. In this manner, I mean to use the role of the *xanith* as a key to answer the following questions: What is the basis for the Sohari conceptualization of sex and gender identity? What insight does this provide into the construction of male and female roles in Sohar, and into fundamental values and premises in Omani society?

Let me first describe some of the concrete behavior enacted by *xaniths* by describing the process by which I myself discovered them. I had completed four months of field work when one day a friend of mine asked me to go visiting with her. Observing the rules of decency, we made our way through the back streets away from the market, where we met a man, dressed in a pink *dishdasha*, with whom my friend stopped to talk. I was highly astonished, as no decent woman — and I had every reason to believe my friend was one — stops to talk with a man in the street. So I reasoned he must be her very close male relative.

---

[1]After I had completed this manuscript, Dr. Frank H. Stewart kindly alerted me to references in the anthropological literature to transvestism, both male and female, among the Marsh Arabs of Iraq. I acknowledge that other references may also have been made, but I have not been in a position to check the literature systematically.

But their interaction did not follow the pattern I had learned to expect across sex lines, she was too lively and informal, their interaction too intimate. I began to suspect my friend's virtue. Could the man be her secret lover? No sooner had we left him than she identified him. "That one is a *xanith*," she said. In the twenty-minute walk that followed, she pointed out four more. They all wore pastel-colored *dishdashas*, walked with a swaying gait, and reeked of perfume. I recognized one as a man who had been singing with the women at a wedding I had recently attended. And my friend explained that all men who join women singing at weddings are *xaniths*. Another was identified as the brother of a man who had offered to be our servant — an offer we turned down precisely because of this man's disturbingly effeminate manners. And my friend explained that all male servants (except for slaves) are *xaniths*, that all *xaniths* are homosexual prostitutes, and that it is quite common for several brothers to partake of such an identity. Another bizarre experience now became intelligible: At a wedding celebration, on the wedding night, when no male other than the bridegroom himself may see the bride's face, I was witness to a man casually making his way into the bride's seclusion chamber and peeping behind her veil! But no one in the audience took offense. Later that night, the same man ate with the women at the wedding meal, where men and women are strictly segregated. At the time, I took him to be a half-wit; that was the only reason I could find for such deviant behavior to be accepted. The man's strangely effeminate manners and high-pitched voice, giving him a rather clownish appearance, lent further credence to my interpretation. I then realized that he, as well as the five men we had met that day, were transvestites or transsexuals.

This incident also serves to highlight problems of discovery and interpretation in field work which are made acute in a strictly sex-segregated society like Oman. I wonder whether persons corresponding to *xaniths* who have not previously been reported in the anthropological literature on the Middle East may not indeed be found some places there, but have escaped notice because the vast majority of field workers have been men. Barred from informal contact with the women, the male anthropologist might miss the crucial clues to the transvestite/transsexual phenomenon. He is likely to meet some effeminate men whom he will recognize as homosexuals (as we did our would-be servant), and others who will strike him as half-wits (like some Omani male singers). The fact that *xaniths* do not assume full female clothing would also give credence to the above interpretations. But the essential feature of the phenomenon — persons who are anatomically male, but act effeminately and move freely amongst

5

women behind purdah — would easily escape the male anthropolo-gist, for the forums and arenas where this interaction takes place are inaccessible to him.

A brief comparative perspective and clarification of terms is helpful at this point. The term *transvestite*, by which such phenomena have gener-ally been known in the anthropological literature, means, etymologically, cross-dressing, and it has come to refer to the act of dressing in the clothes of the opposite sex. The classical anthropological case is the *berdache* of the Plains Indians — men who dressed like women, performed women's work, and married men (Lowie, *The Crow Indians*. New York: Rinehart & Co., 1935). However, it is not easy to assess, in the anthropological record, the cross-cultural distribution of transvestites, for they are often simply referred to as homosexuals; and homosexuality again is usually equated with a high degree of effeminacy in males. But we know un-equivocally that, in a few societies, a transvestite role was a fully institu-tionalized part of traditional life, as for example, the Koniag of Alaska, Tanala of Madagascar, Mesakin of Nuba, and Chukchee of Siberia. However, I have not been able to find evidence that these institutions are practiced today with their traditional vitality.

On the Batinah coast of Oman, on the contrary, *xanith*s are an inte-gral part of the local social organization and very much in evidence. As we have seen, they cannot be said to wear either female or male cloth-ing, but have distinctive dress of their own. But Soharis believe that if *xanith*s had the option, they would choose to dress like women. In the event, they are forbidden to do so, as we shall soon see. Does this then mean that they are to be understood most truly as "transvestites"?

The term *transsexual* was first introduced by D. O. Cauldwell in 1949. It became well known after the publication of Harry Benjamin's book *The Transsexual Phenomenon* in 1966. Prior to 1949, transsexuals had always been labeled as transvestites — a term introduced sometime around the turn of the century (Dr. John Money, personal communication). Dr. Ben-jamin's significant discovery was that men who impersonate women can derive extremely different feelings of subjective identity from the act: For some, impersonating women is a way to bolster their subjectively cherished identity as a *male*; for others, it is the way to escape from an undesired male identity and *become* a woman. The transvestite achieves his purpose through the secret fetishistic sexual pleasure he derives from female cloth-ing. There seems to be an emerging consensus in psychiatric and sociolog-ical literature today to regard this kind of person as a transvestite. [Robert J. Stoller, an] authority on the topic, writes, for instance: "For these men, not only are their penises the source of the greatest erotic pleasure, but they also consider themselves men, not just males. Transsexuals, on the other hand,

are *never* found to be fetishistic. They have no capacity for episodes of un-
remarkably masculine appearance. They do not grow out of their femininity. They do not work in masculine professions" ("The Term 'Transvestism'," *Arch. Gen. Psychiatry.* 1971, p. 231).

According to this usage, it is probable that the Omani *xaniths* are
better classified as transsexuals rather than as transvestites in that they
claim to be women, not men; they never truly grow out of their femininity; and they are assumed by women to resemble themselves in basic
sexual attitudes. However, *xaniths* are also clearly analogues to the cases
described in traditional anthropological literature as "transvestites" and
should be seen in this comparative perspective. Finally, the question remains whether a *xanith* can be illuminated by being classified as either
a transvestite or a transsexual? As Dr. Money has lucidly observed (personal communication): "In an area of the world where there is no local
vernacular or differential diagnostic terminology for men who impersonate women, one has the same problem as existed in Europe and
America before the middle nineteenth century. The Omani *xaniths*
have only one way of expressing themselves, and that is as *xaniths* and
not as either transvestites or transsexuals." In the following, therefore, I
shall stick to Omani terminology.

As I have pointed out, the population of Sohar contains not only ap-   10
proximately sixty *xaniths*, but also an unknown number of *former
xaniths*. A male's career as a "woman" may have several alternative ter-
minations: (1) The man may be a woman for some years, whereupon
he reverts to being a man for the rest of his life; (2) he may live as a
woman until old age; (3) he may become a woman, return to being a
man, again become a woman, and so forth. To us it would appear obvious that the decisive criterion by which men and women are distinguished is anatomical, and that it is only through hormonal change and
surgical modification that one's sex and gender role are changed. Omanis
apparently hold a fundamentally different view. But it should be emphasized that this potential for change is a characteristic of males only.
Omani females, on the contrary, retain female identity throughout life.
I shall return to the reasons for this contrast between the possible careers of men and women.

Let me now turn to a description of the role that we seek to understand. Its character as an intermediate role is most clearly shown in
counterpoint to male and female roles.

Women wear *burqas*[2] before all marriageable males. They need not
wear them before *xaniths* and slaves, because they, in their own words,

---

[2]*burqa*: A facial mask made of black cotton.

do not feel shy before them. The *xanith*, on the other hand, is not allowed to wear the *burqa*, or any other female clothing. His clothes are intermediate between male and female: He wears the *dishdasha*, the ankle-length shirt of the male, but with the swung waist of the female dress. Male clothing is white; females wear patterned cloth in bright colors; *xaniths* wear unpatterned cloth in pastel colors. Men cut their hair short, women wear theirs long, *xaniths* medium long. Men comb their hair backward away from the face, women comb theirs diagonally forward from a central part, *xaniths* comb theirs forward from a side part, and they oil it heavily in the style of women. Both men and women cover their head; *xaniths* go bareheaded. Men always have their arms covered; women may be uncovered from elbow to wrist in private, but never in public (the specific Koranic injunction on this point makes it clear that the arm above the wrist is regarded as erotic and intimate); *xaniths* characteristically expose their lower arms in public. Perfume is used by both sexes, especially at festive occasions and during intercourse. The *xanith* is generally heavily perfumed, and he uses much make-up to draw attention to himself. This is also achieved by his affected swaying gait, emphasized by the close-fitting garments. His sweet falsetto voice and facial expressions and movements also closely mimic those of women. If *xaniths* wore female clothing, I doubt that it would in many instances be possible to see that they are, anatomically speaking, male and not female. The *xanith*'s appearance is judged by the standards of female beauty: white skin, shiny black hair, large eyes, and full cheeks. Some *xaniths* fulfill these ideals so well that women may express great admiration for their physical beauty.

Eating cooked food together represents a degree of intimacy second only to intercourse and physical fondling. Only in the privacy of the elementary family do men and women eat together; and Omanis are so shy about eating that host and guest, even when they are of the same sex, normally do not eat major meals (as contrasted to coffee, sweets, and fruit) together. Whenever food is offered in public, for example, at weddings, *xaniths* eat with the women.

Women are secluded in their homes and must have the husband's permission to go visiting family or friends. The *xanith*, in contrast, moves about freely; but like women, he stays at home in the evenings, whereas men may spend their time in clubs and cafés.

Division of labor follows sex lines. Housework is women's work. The 15 *xanith* does housework in his own home and is often complimented and flattered for excelling women in his cooking, home decoration, and neatness. He may also take employment as a domestic servant, which no woman or freeman can be induced to do.[3] By this employment he supports himself, as a man must. But wherever tasks are allocated by sex, the *xanith* goes with the women. At weddings, women sing, while the men are musicians; *xanith*s are praised as the best singers. By appearing together with the women singers at weddings, the *xanith* broadcasts his status to a wide public. These performances characteristically serve as occasions to announce in public a change of identity from man to *xanith*. Thus, during my field work, there was a sheikh's son — a married man and the father of three children — who suddenly appeared at a wedding singing with the women. The audience was in no doubt as to the meanings of this act, and one woman of my acquaintance later remarked: "Imagine, the son of a sheikh, married to a pretty woman with very white skin, and yet he turns *xanith!*"

Women are legally minors and must be represented by a guardian. *Xanith*s represent themselves, as do all sane men. Legally speaking, they retain male status.

What then does the *xanith* mean by saying, as he explicitly does, that he is a woman, and why is he socially classified and treated as a woman in situations where sex differences are important? He was born an ordinary boy and acted and was treated as a normal boy until he started his career as a prostitute, commonly at the age of twelve or thirteen. Why then is he classified as a *xanith* — a person with a distinctive gender identity — and not merely as a male homosexual prostitute?

Let us observe closely the process by which the *xanith* returns to a male identity in order to search for an answer to this question. The change from *xanith* to man takes place in connection with marriage. But the critical criterion is more explicit than this: The *xanith* must demonstrate, as must every normal bridegroom, that he can perform intercourse in the male role. Among Sohari Arabs, the marriage celebration has a customary form so that consummation is publicly verified. Intercourse takes place between the spouses in private; but next morning, the groom must document his potency in one of two ways: by handing over a bloodstained handkerchief, which also serves as a proof of the bride's honor, to the bride's attendant (*mikobra*), or by raising an outcry, which spreads like wildfire, and lodging a complaint to the bride's father, and maybe also the Wali, because the bride was not a virgin, and he has been deceived.

If neither event takes place, the impotence of the groom is revealed by default. This will cause grave concern among the bride's family and

---

[3]In Oman domestic employment is taken only by young boys, *xanith*s, or ex-slaves — before all of whom women may discard their *burqas*.

nervous suspense among the wedding guests. . . . The essential point here is simply that such a groom's adequacy as a man is in doubt. Conversely, the *xanith* who does deflower the bride becomes, like every other successful bridegroom, a *man*.

From this moment, all women must observe the rules of modesty   20 and segregation before him,[4] always wear the *burqa*, never speak to him, never let him step into the compound when the husband is absent. Women stress that this does not pose difficulties. The *xanith* himself changes overnight into a responsible man, maintaining the proper distance and, in turn, protecting his own wife as would any other man. In other words, the *xanith* has been transformed from a harmless friend to a compromising potential sexual partner.[5]

But in all his demeanor — facial expressions, voice, laughter, movements — a *xanith* will reveal his past: His femininity remains conspicuous. I consequently expressed pity to some female friends for the poor woman who has such a "woman" for a husband; I felt she could not possibly respect him.[6] "No-no," they corrected me — *of course* she would respect him and love him. He had proved his potency; so he is a *man*.

Here, then, may be the key to an understanding of the gender system in Sohar. It is the sexual act, not the sexual organs, which is fundamentally constitutive of gender. A man who acts as a woman sexually *is* a woman socially. And there is no confusion possible in this culture between the male and female role in intercourse: The man "enters," the woman "receives"; the man is active, the woman is passive. Behavior, and not anatomy, is the basis for the Omani conceptualization of gender identity.

Consequently, the man who enters into a homosexual relationship in the active role in no way endangers his male identity, whereas the passive, receiving homosexual partner cannot possibly be conceptualized as a man. Therefore, in Oman, all homosexual prostitutes are ascribed the status of *xanith*.

Such conceptualizations also imply that a person with female sexual organs is a *maiden* (*bint*) until she has intercourse. At that moment, she

---

[4]A *xanith* groom-to-be usually stops his prostitute activities a few weeks prior to marriage.

[5]As their motive for an eventual marriage, *xanith*s give the desire for security in sickness and old age. Only a wife can be expected to be a faithful nurse and companion. Significantly, however, our best *xanith* informant, a femininely beautiful seventeen-year-old boy, did not realize the full implications of marriage for his gender identity. He was definite that he would be able to continue his informal relationship with women after marriage, arguing that he was to women like both a father and a mother. This is out of the question in Omani society, but his belief may serve as a significant measure of the *xanith*'s own confused identity.

[6]*Xanith*s fetch their brides from far away, and marriages are negotiated by intermediaries, so the bride's family will be uninformed about the groom's irregular background.

becomes a *woman* (*horma*). A spinster, no matter how old, remains a girl, a maiden.

Yet Omanis recognize, as do all other peoples in the world, the fundamental, undeniable character of anatomical sex. Girl and boy, female and male, are identities ascribed at birth. This is one reason why the Omani homosexual prostitute becomes a *xanith*, treated *as if* he were a woman. Yet he is referred to in the masculine grammatical gender, and he is forbidden to dress in women's clothes, for reasons we shall return to shortly. Attempts by *xaniths* to appear dressed as women have taken place, but *xaniths* were punished by imprisonment and flogging. But because the *xanith* must be fitted in somewhere in a society based on a fundamental dichotomization of the sexes, he is placed with those whom he resembles most: in this society, with women.

It is consistent with these conceptualizations that, in the absence of sexual activity, anatomical sex reasserts itself as the basis for classification. When in old age a *xanith* loses his attraction and stops his trade, he is assimilated to the old-man (*agoz*) category. From the few cases I came across, my impression is that such men tend to avoid large public occasions, where the issue of their gender identity would arise.

Most societies regard sexual organs as the ultimate criterion for gender identity. It is fascinating to speculate over the origin of the *xanith* status in Oman. Did it emerge through a clarification of the male role, whereby Omani men declared, "You act like a woman; you do not belong among us"? Or was it the *xaniths* themselves who wished to be women and progressively transgressed the gender boundary? The fact that *xaniths* cluster in groups of brothers suggests the existence of developmental causes for their motivation. Or the motive may be . . . a desire to escape from the exacting demands of the Omani male role. But, in either case, why is the *xanith* not seen as a threat to the virtue of women and thus constrained by the men? Physically, there is no denying that he has male organs. Yet, considering the lack of safeguards observed, it is true to say that he is treated as a eunuch. And, as far as I know, no documentary sources are available that might illuminate the origin of the Omani *xanith* status.

Every role, however, also has a sociological origin, which may be identified in synchronic and consequently potentially far more adequate data. That a role once was created does not explain its continued existence: It must be perpetuated, re-created anew every day in the sense that some persons must choose to realize it, and others acknowledge it, as part of their daily life — whether in admiration, disgust, contempt, or indifference. In how they relate to the role encumbent, they also reveal something of themselves and their values. The institutionalized role of the *xanith* in Oman in 1976 is therefore a clear expression of basic premises and values in that culture today.

As regards the question of what makes some males choose to become *xaniths*, we may distinguish two kinds of data that can illuminate it: people's own understanding of the nature of the *xanith* and his relationships, and why he seeks such an identity, or, on the other hand, objective, distinctive features, which an investigator may identify in the background, situation, or person of acknowledged *xaniths*.

The folk understanding of why some young boys turn into *xaniths* is 30 deceptively simple. Men say that when young boys at puberty start being curious and exploring sexual matters, they may "come to do that thing" together, and then the boy "who lies underneath" may discover that he likes it. If so, he "comes to want it," and, as the Soharis say, "An egg that is once broken can never be put back together," "Water that has been spilt can not be put back again."

Thus the homosexual activity of the *xanith* is seen by others as a compulsion: degrading to the person, but springing from his inner nature. Although it is performed for payment of money, its cause is emphatically not seen as economic need stemming from poverty. Indeed, informants insist that old *xaniths* who are no longer able to attract customers will end up paying men to serve them.

In the limited material I have been able to obtain, I have been unable to identify any clear social or economic factors effecting recruitment to the *xanith* role. Cases are found in all ethnic groups; they show a considerable range of class and wealth in family background. There is nothing remarkable, to the outsider, about the homes in which they grow up. Closer investigations, however, might uncover some such factors.

Homosexual practices and relationships, of course, have a certain frequency in most, if not all, societies. And, in that sense, there is nothing remarkable about their occurrence in Sohar. Our interest focuses on the crystallization of the distinctive category of *xanith* whereby the passive party to male homosexuality is institutionalized as a recognized role and, for general social purposes, treated as if he constituted a third gender. Are there identifiable factors in the Omani conceptualization of sexuality and sexual relations which give rise to this?

We might go part of the way in answering this question by comparing the role of the *xanith* with that of males practicing homosexuality elsewhere in the Middle East. Homosexual practice is a common and recognized phenomenon in many Middle Eastern cultures, often in the form of an institutionalized practice whereby older men seek sexual satisfaction with younger boys. But this homosexual relationship generally has two qualities that make it fundamentally different from

that practiced in Oman. First, it is part of a deep friendship or love relationship between two men, which has qualities, it is often claimed, of
being purer and more beautiful than love between man and woman.
Such relationships are also said to develop sometimes in Sohar, but
very infrequently, and those who enter into them will try to conceal
them from others. Neither party to such a relationship is regarded as a
xanith. Second, both parties play both the active and the passive sexual
role — either simultaneously or through time. In contrast, there is
nothing in the Omani *xanith*'s behavior which is represented as pure
or beautiful; and he does not seek sexual release for himself. Indeed,
till he has proved otherwise (most?) people doubt that he is capable of
having an erection.[7] Like a fallen woman, he simply sells his body to
men in return for money: He is a common prostitute.

Herein lies the other component, I will argue, of the explanation   35
why the *xanith* emerges as an intermediate gender role, rather than representing an irregular pattern of recruitment to the female role. The
xanith is treated as if he were a woman, and, for many critical purposes,
he is classified with women, but he is not allowed to become completely assimilated to the category by wearing female dress. This is not
because he is anatomically a male, but because he is sociologically
something that no Omani woman should be: a prostitute. For such a
person to dress like a woman would be to dishonor womanhood. The
woman's purity and virtue are an axiom. Officially, there is no such
thing as female prostitution. (In practice it exists, but in a concealed
form.) By his mere existence, the *xanith* defines the essence of womanhood; he moves as an ugly duckling among the beautiful and throws
them into relief. Through him, the pure and virtuous character of
women may be conceptualized. One may speculate whether this aspect
of the female role would be so clarified, were it not for him.

According to this hypothesis, it would be difficult to maintain a conception of women as simultaneously pure and sexually active, if some
among them were publicly acknowledged also to serve as prostitutes. If
the public view, however, is that prostitution is an act of *xaniths*,
whereas women are not associated with the moral decay that prostitu-

---

[7]Women were definite that *xaniths* who were prostitutes on a large scale (*waegid
xanith*) were incapable of performing intercourse in the male role. However, one popular
xanith whom we interviewed was equally definite that he could, though he had never
tried, arguing that he knew several men who had practiced on an even larger scale than
himself, yet had been potent. When I reported this view to some female friends, they cate-
gorically rejected it. To their understanding, there is an antithesis between performance in
the male and the female sexual role; true bisexuality cannot be imagined. Therefore, if an
ex-*xanith* proved potent, the modest extent of his activities would thus be proved ex post
facto.

tion represents, then women may be conceptualized as pure and virtuous *in* their sexual role. *Womanhood* is thereby left uncontaminated by such vices, even though individual women may be involved. Indeed, the term by which women refer to the activities of female prostitutes (that is, women who are not merely unfaithful for love, but have sexual relations with several men) is *yitxannith*, the active verbal form of *xanith*.

The x*anith* thus illuminates major components of the female role in Sohar. But he can also serve us in a broader purpose, as a key to the understanding of basic features of Sohari culture and society, and the fundamental premises on which interaction in this society is based.

Homosexual prostitution is regarded as shameful in Oman; and all forms of sexual aberration and deviance are sinful according to religion. Boys who show homosexual tendencies in their early teens are severely punished by anguished parents and threatened with eviction from home. So far, reactions in Oman are as one might expect in our society. But the further course of development is so distinctly Omani that any feeling of similarity disappears.

If the deviant will not conform in our society, we tend to respond with moral indignation, but with no organizational adjustments. He is disgusting and despicable, a violation of our sense of modesty and a threat to public morality. Strong sanctions force him to disguise his deviance and practice it covertly. But because we do not wish to face up to him, we also fail to take cognizance of his distinctive character. As a result, we construct a social order where men and women who are sexually attracted by members of their *own* sex nonetheless are enjoined to mix freely with them in situations where *we* observe rules of sexual modesty, such as public baths and toilets.

Omanis, on the other hand, draw the consequences of the fact that 40 the sexual deviant cannot be suppressed. He is acknowledged and reclassified as a *xanith* and left in peace to practice his deviance. The condition is simply that he establish his little brothel under a separate roof; he must rent a date-palm hut for himself. But this may be located anywhere in town, and it is not shameful to sublet to him.

This reaction to the sexual deviant is a natural consequence of the basic Omani view of life: The world is imperfect; people are created with dissimilar natures and are likewise imperfect. It is up to every person to behave as correctly — that is, tactfully, politely, hospitably, morally, and amicably — as possible in all the different encounters in which he or she engages, rather than to demand such things of others. To blame, criticize, or sanction those who fall short of such ideals is to be tactless and leads to loss of esteem. The world contains mothers who do not love their children, children who do not honor their parents, wives who deceive their husbands, men who act sexually like women . . . and it is not for me to judge or sanction them, unless the person has offended me in the particular relationship I have to him. It is up to the husband to control and punish his wife, the parents, their children, the state — if it so chooses — the sexual deviant. The rest of us are not involved — on the contrary, we are under an obligation always to be tactful and hospitable to people. . . .

EXPLORATIONS

1. According to Unni Wikan, how does a boy in Sohar become a *xanith*? How does a *xanith* become a man? What valuable social tasks are performed by *xaniths*?

2. To Soharis "it is the sexual *act*, not the sexual organs, which is fundamentally constitutive of gender" (para. 22). What does Wikan mean by this? How and why is the social status of *xaniths* in Sohar different from the status of homosexuals in the United States?

3. Which of the social rules governing the behavior and appearance of women and of men in Sohar would seem bizarre to most Westerners? Which of the reasons Wikan gives for those rules would strike most Westerners as bizarre?

CONNECTIONS

1. "The woman's purity and virtue are an axiom" (para. 35). What kind of stereotype does this axiom represent? What observations in Naguib Mahfouz's "A Day for Saying Goodbye" (p. 480) point to the existence of a similar stereotype? What evidence in Mahfouz's story suggests that such axioms and stereotypes create unrealistic expectations for both men and women? In what ways do the Soharis' rules against close contact between the sexes protect them against disappointment?

2. As Wikan describes the Soharis, they are quite open about categorizing women as "other." What specific statements by Simone de Beauvoir in "Woman as Other" (p. 445) are illustrated by what specific practices mentioned in "The *Xanith*: A Third Gender Role?"

3. Rose Weitz writes, "Whereas lesbians threaten the status quo by refusing to accept their inferior position as women, gay males may threaten it even more by appearing to reject their privileged status as men" (p. 392). Does the evidence in "The *Xanith*: A Third Gender Role?" suggest that this statement applies in Sohar? Why or why not? How would you expect lesbians to

find their position easier or harder (or both) in Sohar than in the United States?

▲▲▲▲▲▲▲▲▲▲
▼▼▼▼▼▼▼▼▼▼

INVESTIGATIONS

1. Although Islam is prominent in every Arab country, not all Islamic countries are Arab, and different Arab countries — as well as different groups within some countries — favor different forms of Islam. Choose a country in the Islamic Middle East and write a research-based essay about the roles of religion in its political and social structure, including its history and its relations with other countries.

2. Unni Wikan's "The *Xanith*: A Third Gender Role?" and Naila Minai's "Women in Early Islam" (p. 470), as well as Miriam Cooke's epigraph on page 395, contain some information on dress codes in the Islamic Middle East. In which countries do women wear concealing clothing, and what kinds? Do they dress the same way at home as in public? How specific are the rules for men, and what happens to violators? To what extent are clothing choices dictated by age? Social class? Educational level? Religious beliefs? Personal taste? See what you can find out, and write an essay about your discoveries.

3. Many Muslims live outside the Middle East, including some in the United States. How did Islam come to this country? How large is its following here? Among what demographic groups is it most popular? Have the rules and practices of Islam changed over time in the same ways here as in the Middle East? Write either an expository essay about Islam in the United States or a comparison-contrast essay about Islam in different countries.

The fairest thing we can experience is the mysterious. It is the fundamental emotion which stands at the cradle of true art and true science. He who knows it not and can no longer wonder, no longer feel amazement, is as good as dead, a snuffed-out candle. It was the experience of mystery — even if mixed with fear — that engendered religion. A knowledge of the existence of something we cannot penetrate, of the manifestations of the profoundest reason and the most radiant beauty, which are only accessible to our reason in their most elementary forms — it is this knowledge and this emotion that constitute the truly religious attitude; in this sense, and in this alone, I am a deeply religious man.

— ALBERT EINSTEIN
The World As I See It, 1956

▼ ▼ ▼

The word "spirituality" comes, by way of "spirit," from the Latin verb for the act of breathing, *spirare.* Spirit, then, is the principle of life within us, our invisible essence. A parallel derivation took a rather different turn in French, becoming the noun *esprit,* which came to signify the mind, the rarefied human gift of understanding. In English the word remains brainless, and it has diminished over the decreasingly metaphysical decades to a semi-comic ghost, as when we say "evil spirits," which are not to be confused with spirits of alcohol or turpentine. The concept of spirituality retains connotations of the volatile, the impalpable, the immaterial, the dispensable. . . . Pressed, I would define spirituality as the shadow of light humanity casts as it moves through the darkness of everything that can be explained. I think of Buddha's smile and Einstein's halo of hair. I think of birthday parties. I think of common politeness, and the breathtaking attempt to imagine what someone else is feeling. I think of spirit lamps.

— JOHN UPDIKE
Odd Jobs: Essays and Criticism, 1991

▼ ▼ ▼

Once, when we were living in London, and I was very sick, I had a mystical vision. That is, I "had" a "mystical vision" — the heart sinks: such pretension — or something resembling one. A fever-dream, let's call it. It impressed me enormously and impresses me still, though I've long since lost the capacity to see it with my mind's eye, or even, I suppose, to believe in it. There is a statute of limitations on "mystical visions" as on romantic love.

I was very sick, and I imagined my life as a thread, a thread of breath, or heartbeat, or pulse, or light, yes it was light, radiant light, I was burn-

504

ing with fever and I ascended to that plane of serenity that might be mistaken for (or *is*, in fact) Nirvana, where I had a waking dream of uncanny lucidity —

My body is a tall column of light and heat.

My body is not "I" but "it."

My body is not one but many.

My body, which "I" inhabit, is inhabited as well by other creatures, unknown to me, imperceptible — the smallest of them mere sparks of light.

My body, which I perceive as substance, is in fact an organization of infinitely complex, overlapping, imbricated structures, radiant light their manifestation, the "body" a tall column of light and blood-heat, a temporary agreement among atoms, like a high-rise building with numberless rooms, corridors, corners, elevator shafts, windows. . . . In this fantastical structure the "I" is deluded as to its sovereignty, let alone its autonomy in the (outside) world; the most astonishing secret is that the "I" doesn't exist! — but it behaves as if it does, as if it were one and not many.

In any case, without the "I" the tall column of light and heat would die, and the microscopic life-particles would die with it . . . will die with it. The "I," which doesn't exist, is everything.

— JOYCE CAROL OATES
"Against Nature," 1986

▼ ▼ ▼

In a sense, the history of man is the story of the struggle between good and evil. All of the great religions have recognized a tension at the very core of the universe. Hinduism, for instance, calls this tension a conflict between illusion and reality; Zoroastrianism, a conflict between the god of light and the god of darkness; and traditional Judaism and Christianity, a conflict between God and Satan. Each realizes that in the midst of the upward thrust of goodness there is the downward pull of evil.

— MARTIN LUTHER KING JR.
Strength to Love, 1963

▼ ▼ ▼

Since I was a little girl, I have puzzled over some of the teachings of the Koran. In adolescence, a number of questions came to mind. Why are some of the references to women an incitement to violence against them? Who are the seven *houris* promised to each true Muslim in paradise? Who are the women slaves or prisoners of war men can keep as courtesans? Do I have a place in the Muslim paradise? If the seven, ten, 46,000 houris — the number of houris given to each man very according to the interpretation — promised to true Muslim men, are not Muslim women, then who are they? If they are not women believers then I have no place in Muslim paradise.

What is this Islam that promises paradise to the true Muslim? There are many "Islams" in the Muslim world based on different interpretations and applications of the Koran and Hadith. . . . However, in the Islamic world today, and among Islamic minorities in the West, there is what Salman Rushdie has described as "Already Existing Islam," with "granite, heartless certainties," stifling Muslim societies. Between us and Allah stand the self-appointed clerics who claim to be the sole defenders of the Islamic faith, and who use "holier than thou" techniques to politicize Islam beyond recognition.

. . . But if there is no place for me in the Muslim paradise of others, then I have my own vision of that paradise: the Islam of eleventh-century Andalucía, or how I imagine it to have been. Imagination is respected by this Islam, which the Arab bearer of art and science to medieval Europe. Translators of Greek and Persian books were not stabbed, but rather given gold equal in weight to the books they had translated. The Islam of Andalucía, sure of its identity, was open to other cultures and influences. This was an Islam committed to the pursuit of knowledge and literacy with all their consequences. Burning books was alien to it.

— FADIA FAQIR
New Statesman and Society, 1992

▼ ▼ ▼

In the nearly two weeks since the Vatican inaugurated its own electronic hookup, more than a million people have logged on to http://www.vatican.va/ — a new computer address that promises to be the next bully pulpit for a Pope who has already established himself as a television star and best-selling author. . . . "I don't know if this is a prayer line or not, but I figure this is the closest I'll get to the Vatican and to asking the Pope to say a prayer for my father-in-law," said an American named Richard. Another said that knowing the Pope was on the Internet gave him "a feeling of being close to God." . . . To date, the Vatican has received 1,200 personal messages from seventy-one countries, many from the United States, most of them addressed to the Pope himself. Dr. Joaquín Navarro-Valls, chief spokesman for the Vatican, said the Pope had seen only a sampling and would send out a single standard reply, offering his greetings and promising his prayers. . . . But the message traffic has already been an eye-opener for the Vatican. "It has been a little bit revealing of the difference between what we think people think about religious matters, and what they really think," Dr. Navarro-Valls said. "We can theorize and conceptualize, but this way, we see what really preoccupies them."

– CELESTINE BOHLEN
"Pope John Paul @ Vatican:
How Many Angels Can Dance . . . ?"
New York Times, 1996

▼ ▼ ▼

The vast majority of Americans share a respect for certain fundamental traits of character: honesty, compassion, courage, and perseverance. These are virtues. But because children are not born with this knowledge, they need to learn what these virtues are. We can help them gain a grasp and appreciation of these traits by giving children material to read about them. We can invite our students to discern the moral dimensions of stories, of historical events, of famous lives. There are many wonderful stories of virtue and vice with which our children should be familiar. . . .

First, these stories, unlike courses in "moral reasoning," give children some specific reference points. Our literature and history are a rich quarry of moral literacy. . . .

Second, these stories and others like them are fascinating to children. . . . Nothing in recent years, on television or anywhere else, has improved on a good story that begins "Once upon a time . . ."

Third, these stories help anchor our children in their culture, its history and traditions. Moorings and anchors come in handy in life; moral anchors and moorings have never been more necessary.

Fourth, in teaching these stories we engage in an act of renewal. We welcome our children to a common world, a world of shared ideals, to the community of moral persons. In that common world we invite them to the continuing task of preserving the principles, the ideals, and the notions of goodness and greatness we hold dear.

– WILLIAM J. BENNETT
The Book of Virtues, 1993

▼ ▼ ▼

A lot of people think of storytelling as something that is done at bedtime — that it is something that is done for small children. When I use the term "storytelling," I include a far wider range of telling activity. I also do not limit storytelling to simply old stories, but to again go back to the original view of creation, which sees that it is all part of a whole; we do not differentiate or fragment stories and experiences. In the beginning, Tséitsínako, Thought Woman, thought of all these things, and all of these things are held together as one holds many things together in a single thought. . . .

The storytelling always includes the audience and the listeners, and, in fact, a great deal of the story is believed to be inside the listener, and the storyteller's role is to draw the story out of the listeners. This kind of shared experience grows out of a strong community base. The storytelling goes on and continues from generation to generation.

The Origin story functions basically as a maker of our identity — with the story we know who we are. We are the Lagunas. This is where we came from. We came this way. We came by this place. And so from the time you are very young, you hear these stories, so that when you go out into the wider world, when one asks who you are, or where you came from, you immediately know: We are the people who came down from the north. We are the people of these stories. It continues down into clans so that you are not just talking about Laguna Pueblo people, you are talking about your own clan. Within the clans there are stories which identify the clan.

In the Creation story, Antelope says that he will help knock a hole in the earth so that the people can come up, out into the next world. Antelope tries and tries, and he uses his hooves and is unable to break through; and it is then that Badger says, "Let me help you." And Badger very patiently uses his claws and digs a way through, bringing the people into the world. When the Badger clan people think of themselves, or when the Antelope people think of themselves, it is as people who are of *this* story, and this is *our* place, and we fit into the very beginning when the people first came, before we began our journey south.

— Leslie Marmon Silko
"Language and Literature from a Pueblo
Indian Perspective," 1979

▼ ▼ ▼

From ancient times, it was the custom in each Irish village to start the Celtic New Year on November 1 with storytelling every night until May brought the summer back. Only in the dark of evening could tales be spun — it was unlucky to tell stories during the day. The "magic casements" could be flung open only at night; it was dangerous for fantastic Otherworldly goings-on to invade the normalcy of day.

. . . For centuries, many of these fireside tales were the property of the Celtic aristocracy, recited in hall or battle-camp by men of the highest rank, known as *filidh*. These were members of a learned order within the privileged class, guardians of an oral-based culture and living repositories of its history and mythology. They underwent at least twelve

508

years of intensive training in developing memory and concentration, and learned literally hundreds of stories and verses, histories, and genealogies. A *fili*'s repertoire had to include tales of Destructions, Cattle Raids, Courtships, Battles, Deaths, Feasts, Adventures in the Otherworld, Elopements, and Visions. He was a composer, too, who had mastered the art of crafting verse in intricate metrical forms.

Such a long education was rewarded well: On graduating, a *fili* wore a cloak of crimson and yellow feathers, and carried a golden rod. Each year he received twenty-one cows, food for himself and twenty attendants. He could keep six horses and two dogs, and was granted immunity from arrest for any crime save treason or murder.

– MARA FREEMAN
"Word of Skill"
Parabola, 1995

▼ ▼ ▼

The function of literature is sacramental in the sense that when we go to a book that is a work of art, to a book of poems that we admire, we go privately; we don't go collectively. We go in quiet, we go in silence, and we go in respect that may turn into awe and certainly may reconfirm beliefs. . . . The value of an individual reading a particular work of art, I think, is a wider thing, eventually, than something that evaporates and is evanescent like a football game or a quiz show. That's part of our consumption of stuff — you know, it's part of our digestion. It's not to be taken any more seriously than, say, a sandwich is to be taken seriously. On the other hand, if we transform that sandwich into a communion wafer . . . Without being pompous and overreligious, that is exactly the kind of feeling you may have reading a great poem: that you have taken a wafer and something has happened within you.

– DEREK WALCOTT
The Georgia Review, 1995

▼ ▼ ▼

. . . What a great language I have, it's a fine language we inherited from the fierce conquistadors . . . They strode over the giant cordilleras, over the rugged Americas, hunting for potatoes, sausages, beans, black tobacco, gold, corn, fried eggs, with a voracious appetite not found in the world since then . . . They swallowed up everything, religions, pyramids, tribes, idolatries just like the ones they brought along in their huge sacks . . . Wherever they went, they razed the land . . . But words fell like pebbles out of the boots of the barbarians, out of their beards, their helmets, their horseshoes, luminous words that were left glittering

here . . . our language. We came up losers . . . We came up winners
. . . They carried off the gold and left us the gold . . . They carried everything off and left us everything . . . They left us words.

– PABLO NERUDA
"Lost in the City"
Memoirs, 1976

▼ ▼ ▼

Nigeria contains several of the world's oldest continuous cultures, including the Yoruba, the Ibo, and the Hausa, peoples with rich artistic
and literary heritages, whose separate greatness has yet to cohere —
thirty-five years after independence — into the great nation that the
sum of its parts promised in 1960. It came as no surprise that Africa's
first Nobel Laureate, Wole Soyinka, hails from the Yoruba, a people so
much like the Greeks, with a centuries-old tradition of education and
political participation. A people with a literary, religious, and mythological tradition as densely metaphorical as it is deeply lyrical, built around
the Ife Oracle, similar to the Delphic Oracle of the Greeks, yet still
functioning and regularly consulted today. . . .

Divided by rivers into a "Y," thirds dominated respectively by the
Yoruba (west), the Hausa and Fulani (north), and the Ibo (east), democracy in Nigeria arrived stillborn, in large part because the British selected the Hausa, whose feudal government most closely mirrored
Britain's monarchical system, as their logical heirs. The tensions between the largely Christian south (Yoruba and Ibo) and the Muslim
north would make continuing neocolonial economic control fairly easy.

The results have been brilliant: Muslim factions have dominated
each successive junta and have profited enormously from Nigeria's oil
wealth and from allowing their country to be used as a pivotal conduit
for drug trafficking. [General Sani] Abacha, who is said to have played
central roles in each recent coup, is widely thought to be a billionaire.

– HENRY LOUIS GATES JR.
"Kernel of Light"
The New Republic, 1995

EXPLORATIONS

1. Albert Einstein links religion to "the experience of mystery . . . A knowledge
   of the existence of something we cannot penetrate"; Martin Luther King Jr.
   notes the conflict between opposites at the heart of religion. How do these

two ideas appear in John Updike's definition of spirituality? In Derek Walcott's comments on the sacramental aspect of literature?

2. King writes, "In the midst of the upward thrust of goodness there is the downward pull of evil." What concepts of good and evil can you identify in Fadia Faqir's examination of Islam? In William J. Bennett's discussion of virtue? In Pablo Neruda's lines about the Spanish conquistadors in America?

3. Compare William J. Bennett's, Leslie Marmon Silko's, and Mara Freeman's observations about the functions of storytelling. What shared views appear in these selections? How does the role of the storyteller differ for Bennett's "majority of Americans," Silko's Lagunas, and Freeman's Celts?

4. In what ways and for what reasons would you expect professional writers, such as Updike, Oates, Silko, Walcott, and Neruda, to be more alert and receptive than most other people to experiences involving myth, ritual, and magic? How and why would you expect professional writers to be more resistant to such experiences than most other people?

MIRRORS:
THE UNITED STATES

▲▲▲▲▲▲▲▲▲▲
▼▼▼▼▼▼▼▼▼▼

Myth, Ritual, and Magic: *An archeological dig uncovers the bones of an Apache Indian.*

DAVID ABRAM

Making Magic

Ecologist, writer, and free-lance magician David Abram was born on Long Island, New York, in 1957. After graduating summa cum laude from Wesleyan University in Connecticut, he received his Ph.D. in philosophy from the State University of New York at Stony Brook. Abram took up magic in high school and began performing professionally during his first year at college. In 1980 he was awarded a Watson Fellowship for a year's research among tribal healers in Indonesia, Nepal, and Sri Lanka. "Making Magic" grew out of his South Asian travels; it was first published in *Parabola* (1982) and excerpted in the *Utne Reader* (1988). Abram's articles on ecological perception and indigenous cultures have appeared in *The Ecologist, Journal of Environmental Ethics, Orion,* and *Wild Earth.* He has taught at various universities and lectured extensively on the Gaia hypothesis, which holds that the earth's atmosphere is being modulated by all of the earth's organisms acting collectively. Abram lives in New Mexico. He is the author of *The Spell of the Sensuous: Perception and Language in a More-Than-Human World* (1996).

Bali, where most of the following adventures took place, is one of 13,500 islands that make up the Republic of Indonesia. Bali's rich artistic and religious traditions migrated here from nearby Java in the fifteenth century, when that island's Hindu Majapahit dynasty fled from Muslim invaders. Today, Bali's temples, music and dance, masks, and paintings attract tourists, as does its dramatic landscape of beaches and mountains, jungles and rice paddies. Bali became part of Indonesia — along with Java, Sumatra, most of Borneo, and part of New Guinea, among others — in 1945. For hundreds of years before that, the islands' natural resources and location, south of the Philippines and north of Australia, drew European traders. First the Portuguese dominated, then the Dutch. In 1824 the British and Dutch split their holdings in the region, then known as the East Indies. The southern Dutch East Indies declared independence in 1945 as Indonesia, after being occupied by Japan through World War II. The northern British East Indies evolved into part of the Federation of Malaya, now Malaysia.

They told me I had powers.

Powers? I had been a magician for seven years, performing steadily back in the States, entertaining in clubs and restaurants throughout the country, yet I had never heard anyone mention powers. To be sure, once or twice a season I was rebuked by some spectator fresh out of Bible school for "doing the work of Satan," but the more customary refrain was: "How did you do that?" Every evening in the clubs: "How? How did *that* happen?" "C'mon, tell us — how does that work?"

"I don't know," I took to saying, mostly out of boredom, yet also because I felt there was a grain of truth in that statement, because there was some aspect of my sleight-of-hand tricks that mystified even me. It was not something I could experience when rehearsing alone, at home, or when practicing my sleights before a mirror. But when I would stand before my audience, letting my fingers run through one of their routines with some borrowed coins, and I'd see the spectators' eyes slowly widening with astonishment, well, there was something astonishing about that for me as well, although I was unable to say just what it was.

When I received a fellowship to support a year's research on the intertwining of magic and medicine in Asia, I thought I might have a chance to explore the secrets that lay hidden within my own magic, or at least to discern what mysteries my magic had in common with the magic used in traditional cultures not merely for entertainment, but for healing, fortification, and transformation. I was intending to use my skills as a Western sleight-of-hand magician to gain access to the native practitioners and their rituals — I would approach them not as an academic researcher, not as an anthropologist or sociologist, but as a magician in my own right, and in this manner would explore the relation between ritual and transformation from the inside.

As it turned out, this method worked well — at first almost too well,   5 for the potency my magic tricks took on in rural Asia brought some alarming difficulties. In the interior of Sri Lanka, where I began my quest, I was rather too open with my skills; anxious to get a sense of the local attitude toward magic, I began performing on village street corners much as I had three years earlier while journeying as a street magician through Europe. But these were different streets, much more worn and dusty than those concrete thoroughfares, reeking with smells of incense and elephants, frequented as much by gods and demons as by the human inhabitants of the island. Less than a week after I began plucking handkerchiefs from the air, "the young magician from the West" was known throughout the country. Huge crowds followed me wherever I went, and I was constantly approached by people in the grip of disease, by the blind and crippled, all asking me to cure them with my powers. What a frightful, saddening position to be in! When, like a fool, I attempted to show that my magic feats were but illusions accomplished by dexterous manipulations, I only insulted these people —

clearly, to them, I was using clumsy explanations to disguise and hide my real powers. I fled Sri Lanka after only three weeks, suffering from a severe case of ethical paradox, determined to begin my work afresh in Indonesia, where I would above all keep my magic more to myself.

It was five months later — after carefully immersing myself in the Indonesian island universe, observing and recording the patterns of culture, while slowly, inadvertently, slipping into those patterns myself — that I first allowed myself a chance to explore the more unusual possibilities of my position. For five months I had been true to my resolve, keeping my magic much more "up my sleeve" than I had in Sri Lanka — waiting for just the right moment to make something impossible happen, and performing for only a few people at a time, perhaps in a tea stall or while sauntering past the rice paddies. In this manner I slowly and much more surely wove my way into the animist fabric of the society. I had the sense that I was becoming known in the region, but in a more subtle and curious manner than before — here and there I had begun to hear stories about a Westerner, glimpsed on the far side of the island, who actually had access to the invisible world, to the spirits.

Gradually I had been contacted by a number of *dukuns*, or sorcerers, often in some clandestine manner, through a child or a friend, and asked to visit them in their homes. The initial meetings had been strained, sometimes frightening, for these practitioners felt their status threatened by a stranger who could so easily produce shells from the air or make knives vanish between his hands. And I in return felt threatened by the resultant antagonism — I did not want these magicians to view me as their competitor, for I knew the incredible power of the imagination and had no wish to be the victim of any dark spells. (When I came down with a nightmarish case of malaria, I was sure, in my delirium, that I had brought it upon myself by offending a particular sorcerer.) As the months unfolded, I had learned not to shy away from these tensions, but to work with them. I had become adept at transforming the initial antagonism into some sort of mutual respect, at times into a real sense of camaraderie. I had lived with a sorcerer-healer in Java and traded magic with a *balian tapakan*, or spirit medium, in Bali, both of whom were convinced that my presence in their household enhanced their own access to the gods and accentuated their power as healers. But that is another story.

On a certain early monsoon day I sat in a rice stall in a small fishing village on the coast of Bali, shielding myself from the afternoon rain. Munching my rice, I stared out at a steamy, emerald landscape — with the rainy season finally breaking overhead, all the Balinese greens were beginning to leak into the air. Inside, the old woman was serving rice across the wooden slab of a counter to two solemn fishermen; in the corner of the hut three others were laughing and conversing in low Balinese. The downpour outside stopped abruptly; now other sounds — dogs fighting in the distance, someone singing.

I stood up to pay the woman, counting out the correct number of coins and reaching across to drop them into her hand. I opened my fingers — the coins were not there! The woman and I looked at each other, astonished. I turned my empty hands over several times, looked on the dirt floor behind me, then reached under my rice bowl and found the coins. Feigning relief, I took them up and reached across to hand them to the bewildered woman — except that the coins were missing once again when I opened my fist. By now the men in the corner had stopped talking and the two at the counter had paused in the middle of their meal, watching as I became more and more annoyed, searching the floor and the bench without finding my money. One of the fishermen suggested that I look under my bowl again. I lifted it up, but the coins were not there. Upset, I stared at the others. One of them backed slowly into the street. I shrugged my shoulders sadly at the woman, then caught sight of the two half-filled rice bowls resting in front of the other men at the counter. I motioned hesitantly for one of the fishermen to lift up his bowl. He looked around at the others, then gingerly raised one edge of the bowl — there they were! The coins glittered on the palmwood as the fishermen began shouting at each other, incredulous. The old woman was doubled over with laughter.

The man who had uncovered the coins stared at me long and hard.   10
As the others drifted out onto the street, still shouting, this man shoved his rice aside, leaned over to me, and asked, in Indonesian, if I would be so kind as to accompany him to meet his family. Something urgent in his voice intrigued me; I nodded. He paid the old woman, who clapped me on the shoulder as we left, and led me down the street toward the beach. He turned off to the right before reaching the sand, and I followed him through the rice paddies, balancing like a tightrope-walker on one of the dikes that separate the flooded squares. To our left the village spread itself out along the shore: A young woman nursed an infant, smoke rose from cooking fires, three pigs rummaged through a pile of rags and wood. The man turned to the left between two paddies and led me through a makeshift gate into his family compound. Children were playing. He motioned me inside one of the two buildings — his brother lived in the other, he explained — where a young woman sat with a child on her lap. Before I could make a formal greeting, the fisherman pushed his wife and child out the door, slinging a blanket over the doorway and another over the window. He sat me down in the

dark, offered a Javanese cigarette, lit one for himself, then sat down cross-legged on the floor next to me. He gripped my ankle as he began to explain his situation. He spoke quickly, in broken Indonesian, which was good, since I could never have followed his story had he spoken so quickly in Balinese.

Essentially what he had to say was this: that he was a poor and ignorant fisherman blessed with a loving wife and many children, and that despite his steady and enthusiastic propitiation of the local gods and ancestors, he had been unable to catch any fish for the last six months. This was especially upsetting since before that time he had been one of the most successful fishermen in the village. He said it was evident to everyone in the village that his present difficulties were the result of some left-handed magic; clearly a demon had been induced by some sorcery to take up residence in the hull of his fishing boat, and was now frightening the fish away from his nets. Furthermore, he knew that another fisherman in the village had secretly obtained a certain talisman from a priest, a magic shell that made this other man's boat fill up with fish whenever he took it out on the water. And so perhaps I, who obviously knew about such things and had some powers of my own, would be willing to work some special magic on *his* boat so that he could once again catch enough fish to feed his family.

Now, it was clear that this man was both honest and in earnest (his grip on my poor ankle had increased considerably), but I had been in this position before, and though less disconcerted by it than I had been five months earlier, I was still reluctant to play very deeply within the dream-space of a culture that was not my own. And so I explained to Gedé (one of his many names) that my magic was only good for things like making coins vanish or causing fruit to appear (I plucked a ripe banana out of the darkness, making him laugh), that my magic was useless when it came to really practical matters. Besides, I told him, I had never worked with fish, but was sure (since they could breathe underwater and all) that their own powers were even more potent than mine; if a demon was frightening them away, he or she was certainly beyond my influence. Gedé nodded in agreement, released my ankle, and changed the subject. After a few minutes he led me to the doorway and thanked me for coming.

I felt sure I had convinced him with my excuses. But perhaps I had failed to take into account the Balinese habit of self-effacement before accepting praise (*Saya bodoh,* "I am stupid," any Balinese healer will reply when told that he or she is skillful), including, apparently, the praise and respect implied in being offered a difficult task. Unaware, I walked along the beach toward the little bamboo hut I had procured for the night. As the sun sank into the land, the moon rose from the ocean, pale white, nearly full. In the distance, between the rising and the lowering, sat the great volcano, silently looming on the horizon.

That night I had difficulty falling asleep. A weird symphony of chirping crickets accompanied the chorus of frogs gurgling in unison outside my hut. Sometimes this loud music stopped all at once — leaving only the faint lapping of waves and the afternoon rain dripping off the night leaves.

Toward midnight I was awakened by a persistent tapping at the window. I stumbled to my feet and lifted the thin slab of wood — there was Gedé, grinning nervously. He hissed that we must attempt the magic now, while the others were asleep. In an instant I understood the situation — that Gedé was not taking no for an answer, or rather that he had taken my refusal as an acceptance — and I found myself, oddly enough, giving in to the challenge this time without hesitation. Wrapping a sarong around myself, I recalled the dream from which Gedé's tapping had awakened me: I had been back in the States, performing strange, hypnotic magic for sea monsters in a nightclub that was actually an aquarium. Just before waking, I had heard one monster applauding; his clapping had become the tapping at my window. Now, looking around hastily for something to use, I grabbed an empty Coke bottle I had tossed in the corner, then, on an inspiration, dug in my backpack for some flashpaper I'd brought from the States. (Flashpaper, a common tool of the stage magician, is thin paper that has been soaked in a magnesium solution. When crumpled and ignited, it goes up in a sudden bright flash, leaving no ashes behind — wonderful stuff.) I shoved the flashpaper into a fold in my sarong and, gripping the Coke bottle, hurried outside where Gedé was fidgeting anxiously. When he saw me, he turned and led the way down to the beach.

We walked quickly along the water's edge to where the boats were resting on the sand, their long, painted hulls gleaming in the moonglow. As we walked, Gedé whispered to me that the fishermen don't go out fishing on nights when the moon is full or nearly full, since the fish can then see the nets. Only on such a night as this could we accomplish the magic in secret, while the other fishermen slept. He stopped before a sleek blue and white boat, somewhat longer than most of the others, and motioned for me to help him. We lifted the bamboo outriggers and slid the craft into the dark water. I hopped back onto the beach and scooped my Coke bottle full of the black, volcanic sand, then waded back out and climbed into the boat with Gedé. Really a long dugout canoe with limbs — the two bamboo outriggers and a short, roughhewn mast near the bow — it rested on the swells while Gedé unrolled

15

a white triangle of sail and hoisted it from a beam on the mast. The breeze rose up and the boat glided silently into the night. Overhead, the moon drifted behind a cloud and set the whole cloud glowing. The volcano, luminous, watched and waited.

In the Balinese universe, the volcano provides a sort of gateway to and from the upper world, the world of the ancestors, of the gods. The sea, meanwhile, provides passage to the lower world of demons; these destructive forces are known to reside in the black depths of the waters that surround the island. Consequently, those islanders who live near the shore, and especially the fishermen who make their living on the water, are a highly nervous and wary bunch, and they partake even more than the average Balinese of the animistic rites and ceremonies of protection for which the island is famous. At this point in my journey I was only beginning to sense what I would later see clearly: that while the magicians of all traditional cultures are working fundamentally toward the same mystery, the magic of each culture takes its structure from the particular clues of the region, that is, from the particular powers of earth to be found only there — whether volcanoes, or wind, or ocean, or desert — for magic evolves from the land.

The wind shifted, became cooler. I moved close to where Gedé sat in the stern guiding the rudder, and asked him why it was so necessary for us to work in secret. "So other fishermen not jealous," he explained softly. He lit himself a cigarette. After some time I turned away from him and slipped a piece of flashpaper, crumpled, into the mouth of the Coke bottle. The beach was a thin silver line in the distance. I told Gedé that I thought we were out far enough for the magic to take effect, and he agreed. As I took down the sail, I wedged the rest of the flashpaper under a splinter near the top of the mast. Gedé heaved an anchor over the side, then settled back into the stern, watching me carefully.

How to improvise an exorcism? I leaned with my back against the mast, emptying my mind of thoughts, feeling the rock and sway of this tiny boat on the night waters. Small waves slapped against the hull, angrily at first, then softer, more playful, curious. Gradually something regular established itself — the swaying took on a rhythm, a steady rock and roll that grew in intensity as my body gave in to the dance. Phosphorescent algae glimmered like stars around me. The boat became a planet, and I leaned with my back against the axis of the world, a tree with roots in the ocean and branches in the sky, tilting, turning.

Without losing the rhythm, I began to move toward the rear of the boat, keeping it rocking, swinging the bottle of black sand around myself in circles, from one hand to the other. When I reached Gedé I took the cigarette from his hand, puffed on it deeply once or twice, then

20

touched the lit end to the mouth of the bottle. A white flash of fire exploded from the bottle with a "Whooshh," propelled by the pressure inside, a wild spirit lunging for air.

Gedé sat bolt upright, with his arms quivering, grasping the sides of the hull. I motioned for him to cup his hands, he did so, and I tipped the bottle down, pouring a small mound of spirit-sand onto his fingers. There were little platforms affixed symmetrically around the hull, platforms upon which Gedé, when fishing, would place his lanterns to coax the fish up from the depths. I moved around to each of them, nine in all, the cardinal points of this drifting planet, and carefully anointed each one with a mound of sand. I then sat down in the bottom of the carved-out hull and planted my hands against the wood, against the inside of that hollowed-out tree, waiting to make contact with whatever malevolent presence slumbered beneath the chiseled surface. I felt the need for a sound, for some chant to keep the rhythm, but I could think of nothing appropriate, until a bit of Jewish liturgy sprang to my lips from somewhere, perhaps from my own initiation at age thirteen. I sang softly. The planet heaved and creaked, the hollow tree rolled from side to side, the upright tree with roots in the sea swung like a pendulum against moon-edged clouds.

At some point the moon itself rolled out from a cloud pocket and the whole mood shifted — sharp shadows slid back and forth across the wood. Somewhere inside me another planet turned; I began to feel slightly sick. I stood up and began weaving from one side of the boat to the other, sweeping the mounds of sand off the platforms. When I came to the fisherman, I reached into the sky above him and produced another cigarette, already lit, from the dark. I felt a fever flushing my forehead and cheeks. I held the cigarette first to his mouth, then to my own, and we each took a puff on it. I held my breath, walked back rather dizzily, and blew a long line of smoke from the bottom to the top of the mast.

Then I touched the cigarette to the paper wedged in up among the invisible branches. A rush of flame shot into the sky. Instantly I felt better — the fever was gone, the turning stopped, the little boat rocked on the waves. I turned to Gedé and nodded. A wide grin broke across his face and he tossed the sand, still cupped in his hands, over his head into the water. We drew anchor, hoisted the sail, and tacked back to the village with Gedé singing gaily at the rudder.

I had to leave the coast the next day to begin work with a healer in the interior, but I promised Gedé I would return in a month or so to check on the results of my impromptu exorcism.

Five weeks later I returned, with mounting trepidation, to the fishing   25
village. I found Gedé waiting for me with open arms. I was introduced
to his family, presented with gifts, and stuffed with food. The magic had
been successful. The fishing business was thriving, as was apparent
from the new gate and the new building Gedé had built to house the
family kitchen. After the meal Gedé took me aside to tell me of his new
ideas, projects he could accomplish if only he had a little magic help. I
backed off gracefully, paid my respects, and left the village, feeling
elated and strange.

I am scribbling the last words of this story at a table in the small Vermont nightclub where I have been performing magic this winter.
Tonight I was doing mostly card magic, with some handkerchiefs and
coin stuff thrown in for good measure. Some hours ago a woman
grabbed my arm. "How?" she gasped. "How did you do that?"

"I really don't know," I told her.

I think there's something honest in that.

EXPLORATIONS

1. What statements in David Abram's essay suggest that he regards his magic as
   tricks and illusions? What statements suggest that he thinks there is more to it?

2. What is the goal of Abram's travels in Asia? What questions is he investigating, and what answers does he glean in Bali? How does the purpose for
   which he uses magic change on this trip, and how does he react to the
   change?

3. What role is played by descriptive and expository passages about the narrator's Balinese surroundings (see, for instance, paras. 14 and 17)? How would
   the essay's impact change without such passages?

CONNECTIONS

1. "When I came down with a nightmarish case of malaria, I was sure, in my
   delirium, that I had brought it upon myself by offending a particular sorcerer" (para. 7). Compare Abram's change of attitude once he got well with
   Joyce Carol Oates's (p. 504). Why do you think both writers are skeptical
   now about the insights they had while they were ill? What evidence in each
   selection suggests that the writer's skepticism is not wholehearted?

2. The fisherman Gedé tells Abram that "we must attempt the magic now,
   while the others were asleep," and Abram goes along with him (para. 15).

What reasons are given in "Making Magic" for their working by night? What other possible reason is given by Mara Freeman (p. 508)?

3. Like Abram in "Making Magic," Nikos Kazantzakis in "The Isle of Aphrodite" (p. 438) is a foreigner exploring a place and its people's traditional beliefs. How and why are Abram's and Kazantzakis's investigatory approaches similar? How and why are they different?

ELABORATIONS

1. An American reading about Gedé's boat being hexed by a demon while another fisherman's boat is protected by a talisman might classify this information as superstition. What is superstition? How do we draw the line between believing in demons and believing in atoms? Why is refusing a food because it is taboo different from refusing a food because it has invisible germs? Write an essay defining superstition as you see it, using your experience, selections in this book, and outside research (if desired) for evidence.

2. Reread Jill Ker Conway's comments on page 7 and compare them with Abram's observations in paragraph 17. Look also at what Leslie Marmon Silko writes about the Laguna Pueblo people and their component clans in the Southwestern United States (p. 507). In what ways is the culture you live in shaped by its landscape and history? Using Conway's, Abram's, and Silko's ideas as guidelines, and noting also William J. Bennett's remarks about the role of stories in acculturating children (p. 506), write an essay about your cultural identity.

JOSEPH BRUCHAC

Digging into Your Heart

Not until adulthood did Joseph Bruchac III learn that the grandfather who reared him in the Adirondack foothills of New York State was an Abenaki Indian. Today Bruchac is a member of the Abenaki Nation, carrying the name Gahnegohheyoh ("the good mind"). He was born in 1942 in Saratoga Springs, New York. At Cornell University he was active in civil rights and the antiwar movement; after receiving his master's degree from Syracuse University in 1966, he went to Ghana, West Africa, "to teach — but more than that to be taught." Returning to the United States in 1969, he did graduate work at the State University of New York at Albany while teaching creative writing and African and black literatures at Skidmore College. He also started editing and publishing the *Greenfield Review* in Greenfield Center, New York, where he now lives. Bruchac's first book of poetry, *Indian Mountain and Other Poems*, appeared in 1971. The next year he began teaching creative writing at Comstock Prison; in 1975 he received his Ph.D. from Union Graduate School. A winner of numerous grants, fellowships, and writing awards, Bruchac has contributed poems, essays, and stories to hundreds of periodicals and dozens of collections. His writing about Native American traditions draws on first-hand experience as well as formal and informal research. Among his many books are *Thirteen Moons on Turtle's Back*, chosen as a 1993 Notable Children's Book in the Language Arts, and the novels *Dawn Land* (1993) and *Long River* (1995). "Digging into Your Heart" first appeared in the Winter 1994 issue of *Parabola*.

A traditional Wabanaki story tells of four men who make a difficult journey to visit Gluskap, the powerful ancient being who did many things to make the earth a better place for his human "grandchildren" before he retired to an island shrouded in a magical mist created by the tobacco smoke from his pipe.

Each of the men has a wish and Gluskap grants those wishes. He gives each one a pouch and tells them not to open them until they are within their own lodges. Three of those wishes, however, are selfish ones and bring about ironic consequences. Not only that, the first three men are so eager to get their heart's desire that they each open their pouches before they reach their homes. The man who wishes to be taller than all others becomes a tree; the one who wishes never to die becomes a stone; the one who wishes to have more possessions than anyone else receives so many things that they sink his canoe, and he is drowned. Only the fourth man, who wishes to be able to help his people, waits until he is in his lodge before looking in his pouch. It is empty, but when he opens it, good thoughts come into his mind and he finds within his own heart that which was formerly hidden from him. In one version of the story, he discovers the knowledge needed to be a better hunter, in another he finds the knowledge needed to show his people the right ways to live.

This story, like a Seneca story about Handsome Lake, teaches about the power of wishes and actions: to desire things which benefit only yourself will eventually result in your own downfall; to wish something which will bring good to your people will produce good results for everyone. In June of 1800, at a time when the Seneca people had lost most of their land and were deep in despair, on the verge of losing everything else, the prophet Handsome Lake was given a vision by three messengers as he lay in an alcoholic coma. The vision was intended to guide him and his people back from the brink of destruction. As the messengers took him along the sky road of the Milky Way, pointing out the evils which his people must avoid, one of the sights he was shown illustrated the results of such wrong desires:

> Now they said to him
> "We will pause here
> in order for you to see."
>
> And as he watched,
> he saw a large woman
> sitting there.
> She was grasping frantically
> at all the things
> within her reach
> and because of her great size
> she could not stand.
> That was what he saw.
>
> Then they asked him
> "What did you see?"
>
> He answered
> "It is hard to say.
> I saw a woman of great size,
> snatching at all that was about her.
> It seemed she could not rise."

5

Then the messengers answered,
"It is true.
What you saw was the evil of greed,
She cannot stand
and will remain thus forever.

Thus it will always be with those
who think more of the things of earth
than of this new world above.
They cannot stand upon the heaven road."

The story of the four wishes also illustrates the virtue of patience and   10
the necessity of following the instructions of elders. As a result, the man
who waits receives what he desires — something not material, but
knowledge, found by looking into his heart. There is a word in the Cree
language which describes the place that knowledge and stories come
from — *achimoona*, "the sacred place within." The Micmac people
speak of the "great man inside," a spiritual being within each person's
heart who will provide good guidance if heeded.

Although more than 400 very different Native cultures and languages are found within the North American continent, the lessons of
that Wabanaki story seem to hold true for all Native traditions. Father
Claude Chauchetiere, who was a priest at the Mohawk mission of Kahnawake (near present-day Montreal), wrote the following (which was
collected in the *Jesuit Relations* and later published in 1981 in the *Narrative of the Mission of Sault St. Louis, 1667–1685*):

We see in these savages the fine roots of human nature which are entirely corrupted in civilized nations . . . Living in common, without disputes, content with little, guiltless of avarice . . .

The context which this interpretation of the Wabanaki story of the
four wishes creates helps us see into the heart of the Mohegan elder
Gladys Tantaquidgeon's tale of frustrated treasure seekers:
Sometime around 1900, Burrill Fielding [Gladys' uncle] had the
same dream three nights in a row — a sure sign that the dream was going
to come true. In it, he found himself walking at midnight in the old
Shantup burying ground near the river. Each time he came to a stand of
three white birches near a flat rock. In the dream, he knew that was the
place to dig. Finally, after the third time he had the dream, he asked
Henry Dolbeare, another Mohegan, to go with him that night to the spot
he had seen. They took their shovels with them and, sure enough, they

found the stand of birches and the flat rock. It was close to midnight. They
started to dig, neither one of them saying a word, because to speak when
you were digging for a treasure would make that treasure go away. The
bright light of a full moon shone down on them as they dug, and soon
Fielding's shovel struck a wooden, hollow-sounding object. Just at that
moment, something big and black jumped down into the hole between
them. Both men let out a yell, dropped their shovels and ran away as fast as
they could. When Fielding finally got up the courage to come back —
several days later in the middle of the day — he found the shovels resting
on the rock and the hole they had dug was filled in.

"Uncle Burrill," Gladys Tantaquidgeon said, "never went digging at
midnight again!"

There are, of course, many elements in this story which appear to   15
come directly from Western folklore. The themes of buried treasures
and murdered men whose ghosts become supernatural guardians are familiar ones in both European-American and European traditions. As
William S. Simmons points out in *Spirit of the New England Tribes, Indian History and Folklore, 1620–1984*:

> The treasure story is a category of folk narrative that is widespread and
> particularly well represented in historic American, West European,
> Caribbean, and Latin American oral traditions. The stories are not in-
> digenous to the New England Indians, and none were recorded among
> them until the twentieth century . . .
>
> The Euro-American treasure legend usually involves pirates who bury
> their ill-gotten wealth and kill one of their crew, whose ghost guards the
> chest or kettle filled with gold.[1]

The coast of Connecticut where the Mohegan people live was a familiar place for such notorious pirates as Captain Kidd, and many sites,
including one particular area up the Thames River close to the present-
day Mohegan community, have been said to be places where he buried
his treasure. For centuries now people have looked for that treasure.
Poe's famous story, "The Gold Bug," is one of the best-known literary
treatments of that theme and takes place in roughly the same landscape.

But the Mohegan story of Captain Kidd's treasure, though it may
seem familiar, has a different slant. The point of Poe's tale is the figur-
ing out of a mystery: Wealth comes to the treasure seekers as a result of
their intellectual puzzle-solving — and their defiling of a pirate grave.
In the Mohegan tale, the knowledge of the treasure's location is arrived

---

[1]William S. Simmons, *Spirit of the New England Tribes, Indian History and Folklore,
1620–1984* (Hanover, N.H.: University Press of New England, 1986).

at through purely supernatural means — a dream vision. And just when the two Mohegan men are about to uncover the treasure, it is taken away from them under equally mystical circumstances.

Another tale of pirate treasure is told by the Wampanoag people. Written down in 1934 by Mrs. Frederick Gardner, herself a Mashpee Wampanoag, it tells the story of Hannah Screecham, a Wampanoag woman who befriended the pirates and helped them in the burial of their treasure and the accompanying murder of the sailors who would guard those gold-filled graves. But then, when Hannah went to dig up some of that treasure for herself, she was strangled by the ghosts of the murdered men.

The messages held in a story of seeking pirate treasure may be quite   20
different when the tale is told as part of the traditions of a Native American people, even when that story is told in a way which seems completely in line with European-American traditions. It is not just the *how* of the story's telling, it is also the *why*.

Bearing in mind what happened in the traditional story of the four wishes, in the more modern tales of failed quests for buried pirate treasure we can understand that desire for personal, selfish gain dooms the seeker to, at best, failure and, at worst, destruction. But there is another message which is held in these stories, one that is so much a part of the consciousness of all Native peoples of North and South America that we sometimes forget that European Americans do not share or understand this point of view, this feeling which Native peoples have about "buried treasure," about gold and graves.

In contrast to the tradition in pirate legends of burying someone else with your gold — gold which you plan to dig up and use at a later time (the eighteenth-century equivalent of an IRA?) — the Native traditions of the Americas frequently included interring material possessions as "grave goods" to go in spirit with the deceased person into the next life. The idea of digging up those grave goods was an abomination, whether they were gold ornaments to wear, or baskets filled with corn to feed the spirit. Yet the thoughtless digging up of such graves by less-than-professional "archaeologists," "pot-hunters," and fortune seekers continues to this day. Wampanoag traditions indicate that when the ill-prepared Pilgrims of the Plymouth Colony arrived in Massachusetts, the Native people watched them for some time before deciding whether or not to approach them. One of the Wampanoags, Squanto (who was clearly a man of a forgiving nature, having just made his way back to Massachusetts after being taken some years before to Europe as a slave by another group of Englishmen), finally made the fateful decision to assist them, although many of the others urged him not to do so. They had observed the Pilgrims digging up

Indian graves to obtain the baskets of corn buried there as food for the
dead, something even a starving Native would never have done.

Throughout the Americas, there are still stories told of lost Indian gold,
from the Seven Cities of Cibola in the American Southwest to the South
American tale of El Dorado — the lake where a fabled "chief" would
coat his body with gold and then wash it off in the waters as a sacrifice.
Even the Adirondack mountains of New York State have one such tale. It
is said (in a story which seems to have originated with Jed Rossman, a tall
tale teller who worked for years at Adirondack Loj in the heart of the
High Peaks) that there is a hidden cave filled with Indian treasure on the
side of Mount Colden. That cave can only be seen when standing on another peak at midnight under a full moon in the month of August. But
the ghost of a giant Indian guards the treasure in that cave, which was
brought there by Kahnawake Mohawk and St. Francis Abenaki Indians
on their way back north after a raid in 1690 on Schenectady.

Whether such stories hold a grain of truth or not, they illustrate the
popular mindset concerning "Indian treasures": It does not matter if
those treasures are grave goods or sacrifices to the spirits. Quite simply,
that hidden wealth, placed by Native people to rest forever in the breast
of the earth, is there for the taking. And, until quite recently, much of
the archaeological community felt the same about the wealth of knowledge to be uncovered in Native graves — it was there for the taking. Although it has long been illegal to dig up the graves of non-Natives, finding and exhuming Native remains was standard practice throughout the
last four centuries and in a number of American states is still legal. As
Dean R. Snow notes in his book *The Archaeology of North America*:

> For a long time American archaeology has involved Europeans or their de-
> scendants as scholars and American Indians as subjects. Fortunately, this
> situation has begun to change as some Indians have become archaeologists
> and some non-Indian sites have become the subject of excavation . . .
>
> Unfortunately, people calling themselves archaeologists have angered   25
> both Indians and legitimate archaeologists by looting burials and other
> sites for fun and profit. Even professional archaeologists have sometimes
> contributed to the misunderstanding by showing less sensitivity toward
> Indian burial sites than they would toward their own.[2]

The repatriation to Native peoples of the remains of their ancestors
who were dug up by "scientific researchers" is a very new phenomenon.
Some Native communities, like my own Abenaki people, believe that

---

[2]Dean R. Snow, *The Archaeology of North America* (New York: Chelsea House, 1989).

bad luck has come to both white and Indian communities as a result of those ancestors not being placed back to rest. Yet even those enlightened non-Native people who have agreed to return human remains still find it hard to understand that the "grave goods" are also supposed to be returned so that the journey to the spirit world can be continued in the proper way. I recall a meeting in the 1980s (which the Abenaki Nation has on videotape) in which several hours were spent trying to explain that point to a group of people from the University of Vermont who were unable to understand why the return of the bones alone was not enough. Thus, we may also hear Gladys Tantaquidgeon's story of the failed treasure hunt — and such legends as that of Hannah Screecham — as teaching tales and a response to that long-standing European passion for grave-robbing. The dead, and whatever has been sent with them to the next world, must be left in peace. Those who do not heed that injunction will find themselves confronted by guardians from the spirit world. No one, Indian or non-Indian, should disturb Indian graves, and Native people should not fall into the trap of the avaricious thinking which sometimes seems to characterize European cultures.

The 1990s have brought a further irony to the locale of that first story I told: Where European Americans once sought out Captain Kidd's buried millions, crowds now flock to Indian-run casinos all over the United States. Because of current federal laws which recognize the "sovereign" status of Native lands, gambling operations are legal on Indian reservations and hundreds of casinos have been constructed and are bringing new wealth to Native communities — among them are the Mashuntucket Pequots and the Mohegans. With that new wealth — and all of the dangers of corruption brought by such sudden riches — flowing into those previously impoverished Native communities, the tale of the four wishes and the stories of search for pirate treasure may take on new meaning for Native communities. Understanding that meaning may help them make the right wishes, help them remember that the only place to dig for the true treasure is in your heart.

EXPLORATIONS

1. What is the message of the first two Native American stories Joseph Bruchac tells? What is the message of the next two stories? What third, more practical message does Bruchac convey in the last third of his essay by connecting those first two messages?

2. What advice does Bruchac give (directly or indirectly) to Native American readers of "Digging into Your Heart"? What details in the essay seem meant to appeal particularly to those readers?

3. What advice does Bruchac give (directly or indirectly) to European-American readers of "Digging into Your Heart"? What details in the essay seem meant to appeal particularly to those readers?

CONNECTIONS

1. When magical events take place in David Abram's "Making Magic" (p. 513), who causes them and why? When magical events take place in the Native American stories retold by Bruchac, who causes them and why?

2. Reread Leslie Marmon Silko's explanation of storytelling among the Laguna (p. 507). Which of her points are applied in the Native American stories Bruchac tells? Which of her points are applied in Bruchac's essay itself?

3. Which of William J. Bennett's reasons for telling stories do you think Bruchac would agree with, and why? How and why do you think Bruchac would disagree with Bennett?

ELABORATIONS

1. What argument does Bruchac present in "Digging into Your Heart"? Where does his thesis appear? How does he state and support his points? Write an essay reorganizing the information and ideas in this selection into a more typical argumentative format.

2. What stories did your parents or other family members tell or read to you as a child that have influenced your sense of who you are, what your heritage is, how to behave, or all of these? Has the effect of these stories on you been positive, negative, or both? Write an essay answering these questions.

EUDORA WELTY

Fairy Tale of the Natchez Trace

The novelist, essayist, critic, and short-story writer Eudora Welty's most recent award was the Legion of Honor, France's highest distinction. Her first award was a Guggenheim fellowship in 1942; others include the O. Henry Award (in 1942, 1943, and 1968); the William Dean Howells Medal of the American Academy of Arts and Letters (1955, for *The Ponder Heart*); the National Institute of Arts and Letters Gold Medal for fiction writing (1972); the Pulitzer Prize in fiction (1973, for *The Optimist's Daughter*); the National Medal for Literature (1980); the Presidential Medal of Freedom (1980); the American Book Award (1981, for *The Collected Stories of Eudora Welty*, and 1984, for *One Writer's Beginnings*); and the National Medal of Arts (1987).

Welty was born in 1909 in Jackson, the capital of Mississippi; she still lives in a house her father built there in 1925. She attended the Mississippi State College for Women but completed her B.A. degree at the University of Wisconsin in 1929. Urged toward a more practical career than writing, she spent a year studying advertising at the Columbia University Graduate School of Business. In New York City the Harlem Renaissance was in full swing; Welty went dancing at Harlem jazz clubs, saw plays, and every Sunday visited the Metropolitan Museum of Art. Her father's death brought Welty home in 1931. She worked for local newspapers and a radio station, then traveled around Mississippi reporting, interviewing, and photographing for the Works Progress Administration (WPA). Although her photographs were not published until much later (*One Time, One Place: Mississippi in the Depression: A Snapshot Album*, 1971), she wove her observations into short stories which began appearing in print in the mid-1930s. Following her first story collection (*A Curtain of Green*, 1941) came her critically acclaimed novella *The Robber Bridegroom* (1942). Welty explains that book's origins in "Fairy Tale of the Natchez Trace," a talk she gave to the Mississippi Historical Society and published in *The Eye of the Story* (1978). In the essay she mentions that southern Mississippi belonged to Spain 200 years ago, having been claimed by Hernando de Soto and held (despite counterclaims from France, Britain, and the United States) until 1810. She describes the Natchez Trace, two miles from the Mississippi River, as "that old buffalo trail where travelers passed along and were set upon by the bandits and the Indians and torn apart by the wild animals."

The Robber Bridegroom, my second book, was my first novel — or novella — and different from the fiction I'd done before or was yet to do in exactly this respect: It did not spring from the present-day world, from life I could see around me, from human activities I might run into every day. My fictional characters are always imaginary — but the characters of *The Robber Bridegroom* are peculiarly so.

The novel is set in the Natchez country of the late eighteenth century, in the declining days of Spanish rule. It opens like this:

> It was the close of day when a boat touched Rodney's Landing on the Mississippi River, and Clement Musgrove, an innocent planter, with a bag of gold and many presents, disembarked. He had made the voyage from New Orleans in safety, his tobacco had been sold for a fair price to the King's men. In Rodney he had a horse stabled against his return, and he meant to spend the night there at an inn, for the way home through the wilderness was beset with dangers.
>
> As his foot touched shore, the sun sank into the river the color of blood, and at once a wind sprang up and covered the sky with black, yellow, and green clouds the size of whales, which moved across the face of the moon. The river was covered with foam, and against the landing the boats strained in the waves and strained again. River and bluff gave off alike a leaf-green light, and from the water's edge the red torches lining the Landing-under-the-Hill and climbing the bluff to the town stirred and blew to the left and right. There were sounds of rushing and flying, from the flourish of carriages hurrying through the streets after dark, from the bellowing throats of the flatboatmen, and from the wilderness itself, which lifted and drew itself in the wind, and pressed its savage breath even closer to the little galleries of Rodney, and caused a bell to turn over in one of the steeples, and shook the fort and dropped a tree over the racetrack.
>
> Holding his bag of gold in his hand, Clement made for the first inn   5 he saw under the hill. It was all lighted up and full of the sounds of singing.[1]

In the first sentence, there is one word in particular that may have signaled to the reader the kind of story that this is *not.* It is the word "innocent." Used to describe Clement Musgrove's character — and the only description allotted to him — "innocent" has nothing to do with the historical point of view; and it shines like a cautionary blinker to what lies on the road ahead.

---

[1] All excerpts are from Welty's *The Robber Bridegroom*; see headnote. – ED.

In *The Robber Bridegroom*, the elements of wilderness and pioneer settlements, flatboats and river trade, the Natchez Trace and all its life, including the Indians and the bandits, are all to come together. The story is laid in an actual place, traces of which still exist, and in historical times — which, all of you need no reminding, have been well recorded. And you historians and scholars would be the first to recognize that this is not a *historical* historical novel.

The Robber Bridegroom does not fit anywhere that I know of into that pattern, which conventionally tends to be grand and to run to length. Nor was fitting into the pattern ever its aim. It *is* a story laid in and around Rodney just before 1798 — but you had better now meet all the characters.

Clement Musgrove, on this opening night at the Rodney inn, draws two strangers for bedfellows, which was not uncommon. However, the two strangers *are*. Here speaks one of them:

> "I'm an alligator!" yelled the flatboatman, and began to flail his   10
> mighty arms through the air. "I'm a he-bull and a he-rattlesnake and a
> he-alligator all in one! I've beat up so many flatboatmen and thrown
> them in the river I haven't kept a count since the Flood, and I'm a lover
> of women like you'll never see again . . . I can outrun, out-hop, out-
> jump, throw down, drag out, and lick any man in the country! . . . I can
> pick up a grown man by the neck in each hand and hold him out at
> arm's length, and often do, too . . . I eat a whole cow at one time, and fol-
> low her up with a live sheep if it's Sunday . . . I only laugh at the Indians,
> and I can carry a dozen oxen on my back at one time, and as for pigs, I
> tie them in a bunch and hang them to my belt!"

As you have recognized, the innocent planter has for one bedfellow Mike Fink, the legendary folk hero. And for the other? We see a young man: "brawny and six feet tall, dressed up like a New Orleans dandy, with his short coat knotted about him capewise . . . His heavy yellow locks hung over his forehead and down to his shoulders . . . When he removed his cloak, there was a little dirk hid in the knot."

And so it's a night of wondering who will succeed in robbing or murdering whom, but Jamie Lockhart establishes himself as the hero to the innocent planter by saving his life, and to us as a bandit at the same time. "We shall surely meet again," says Jamie to Clement as they part. It's surer than history! Knotting the sleeves of his coat about his shoulders, Jamie takes up a Raven in his fingers, which speaks boding words:

> "Turn back, my bonny,
> Turn away home."

Jamie Lockhart's Raven — though I have let him avail himself of it from the possession of Mike Fink — has really got here from the same place Jamie did: the fairy tale. The Robber Bridegroom, the double character of the title, owes his existence on the one side to history — the history of the Natchez Trace outlaws — and on the other side to the Brothers Grimm.

It is not only the character of our hero that partakes of the fairy tale. Mike Fink, in his bragging just now, might have been speaking the words of Jack the Giant Killer. And here is the planter Clement Musgrove telling Jamie the story of his wife Salome:

> "There on the land which the King of Spain granted to me," said Clement, "I built a little hut to begin with. But when my first tobacco was sold on the market, Salome, my new wife, entreated me in the night to build a better house, like the nearest settler's, and so I did . . .
>
> "'Clement,' Salome would say, 'I want a gig to drive in to Rodney.' 'Let us wait another year,' said I. 'Nonsense!' So there would be a gig. Next, 'Clement, I want a row of silver dishes to stand on the shelf.' 'But my dear wife, how can we be sure of the food to go in them?' And the merchants, you know, have us at their mercy. Nevertheless, my next purchase off the Liverpool ship was not a new wrought-iron plow, but the silver dishes. And it did seem that whatever I asked of the land I planted on, I would be given, when she told me to ask, and there was no limit to its favors."
>
> "How is your fortune now?" asked Jamie, leaning forward on his two elbows.
>
> "Well, before long a little gallery with four posts appeared across the front of my house, and we were sitting there in the evening; and new slaves sent out with axes were felling more trees, and indigo and tobacco were growing nearer and nearer to the river there under the black shadow of the forest. Then in one of the years she made me try cotton, and my fortune was made."

15

You'll be reminded of a story in Grimm, "The Fisherman and His Wife." The Fisherman, because he kindly returned to the sea a magic Flounder he'd caught, is offered his wish; and his wife sends him to the Flounder again and again to have a new wish granted: From living in a pot, she wants to rise to be owner of a cottage, then owner of a castle, then king, then emperor, then pope, and then the Lord Almighty — at which the Flounder loses his patience.

> "Next year," said Salome, and she shaded her eagle eye with her eagle claw, and scanned the lands from east to west, "we must cut down more

of the forest, and stretch away the fields until we grow twice as much of everything. Twice as much indigo, twice as much cotton, twice as much tobacco. For the land is there for the taking, and I say, if it can be taken, take it."

"To encompass so much as that is greedy," said Clement. "It would   20
take too much of time and the heart's energy."

"All the same, you must add it on," said Salome. "If we have this much, we can have more."

"Are you not satisfied already?" asked her husband.

"Satisfied!" cried Salome. "Never, until we have got rid of this house which is little better than a Kentuckian's cabin, with its puncheon floor, and can live in a mansion at least five stories high, with an observatory of the river on top of that, with twenty-two Corinthian columns to hold up the roof."

"My poor wife, you are ahead of yourself," said Clement.

(The reason she's ahead of herself, as you will know, is that she's de-   25
scribing Windsor Castle, out from Port Gibson, which did not get built until 1861.)

I think it's become clear that it was by no accident that I made our local history and the legend and the fairy tale into working equivalents in the story I came to write. It was my firm intention to bind them together. And the intention further directed that beyond the innocent planter, the greedy second wife, the adventurous robber, the story needed its beautiful maiden. Of these, as we know, there were plenty in that part of the world: They were known as "the Rodney heiresses." Rosamond is beautiful and young and unwed, with a devoted father and a wicked stepmother, and she is also an heiress. We see her first leaning from her window to sing a lovesick ballad out to the waiting air, "truly a beautiful golden-haired girl, locked in the room by her stepmother for singing, and still singing on." And Rosamond "did not mean to tell anything but the truth, but when she opened her mouth in answer to a question, the lies would simply fall out like diamonds and pearls." So she has every fairy-tale property. Diamonds and pearls normally fall from the lips of fairy-tale maidens because they can speak nothing but what is truthful and pure — otherwise, the result is snakes and toads — but Rosamond is a romantic girl, not a wicked one, and the lies she's given to telling are simply a Rodney girl's daydreams, not intended to do any harm: perfectly good pearls.

In several other ways her fairy-tale character has ironic modifications. Jamie Lockhart and Rosamond meet for the first time when he, now as the robber with his face disguised in berry juice, rides up to her in the woods to rob her of her fine clothes: Clement's present from New

Orleans, a wonderful gown with a long train, is what she's wearing out to pick herbs.

When he has the gown —

> Then she stood in front of Jamie in her cotton petticoats, two deep, and he said, "Off with the smocks, girl, and be quick . . . Now off with the rest."
>
> "God help me," said Rosamond, who had sometimes imagined such a   30 thing happening, and knew what to say. "Were you born of woman? For the sake of your poor mother, who may be dead in her grave, like mine, I pray you to leave me with my underbody."

Jamie will do no such thing, and —

> Rosamond, who had imagined such things happening in the world, and what she would do if they did, readily reached up and pulled the pins out of her hair, and down fell the long golden locks, almost to the ground, but not quite, for she was very young yet."

Jamie, as he gathered up the gold hairpins from France, asks politely —

> "Which would you rather? Shall I kill you with my little dirk, to save your name, or will you go home naked?"
>
> "Why, sir, life is sweet," said Rosamond, looking straight at him through the two curtains of her hair, "and before I would die on the point of your sword, I would go home naked any day."

The fairy-tale daughter, as we see, is also the child of her times, a straightforward little pioneer herself.

Jamie has to come a second time in order to steal Rosamond herself.   35 He sweeps her up as she carries in the milk from the barn and gallops away with her on his horse. "So smoothly did they travel that not a single drop was spilled." As I read somewhere in the history books, "It was the habit of the day for heiresses to disappear."

And so the circle is joined: Jamie Lockhart the New Orleans dandy is besought by Clement Musgrove to find his lost daughter Rosamond, and Jamie Lockhart the bandit is already her enamored kidnapper. And neither lover knows who the other is.

The title of the novel is the title of the fairy tale; and it may be appropriate at this point to recall the original story of the Robber Bridegroom to mind.

In Grimm, a maiden becomes engaged to a man, and preceding her wedding day goes to his house to surprise him with a visit. There, no one seems to be at home. Only a bird speaks to her. This bird says —

he's more explicit than my Raven — "Turn back, turn back, young maiden dear, 'Tis a murderer's house you enter here." On she goes. An old old woman kept prisoner deep in the lower part of the house gives the maiden the further news that her bridegroom and his gang are cannibals and make a habit of eating young girls like her. The bride-to-be hides behind a cask to await the robbers' return, and just as my Rosamond at length will do, she sees, in place of herself, another young girl dragged in to be their victim. Grimm relates: "They gave her wine to drink, three glasses full, one glass of white wine, one glass of red, and a glass of yellow, and with this her heart burst in twain." (Rosamond is given only her stepmother's poisonous insinuations.) Thereupon the robbers "cut her beautiful body in pieces and strewed salt thereon." The little finger flies out and falls into the maiden's bosom. And so with Rosamond. Only, in my story it is not Jamie's own self whom Rosamond sees perform this act of monstrosity — it's his terrible, and real-life, counterpart, the Little Harpe — who might have done it.

Nothing has stopped the maiden yet, in the very sinister tale of Grimm's, and after this revelation she goes right ahead with the wedding. And then afterward, at the feast, she has her turn: She tells the bridegroom the whole story of her visit to the house and what she saw, saying disingenuously at every stage, "My darling, I only dreamt this," until she reaches the part about the finger. "It fell in my bosom," she says, "— and here it is!" She holds it up for all present to see, and the wedding guests hold the bridegroom fast and "deliver him over to justice."

Whereas all that Rosamond is frightened into doing, after what she   40
sees in the robbers' house, is making a direct investigation on her own. After she and Jamie are in bed and he falls asleep, she washes off those berry stains.

Jamie's berry stains, the disguise in which he carries on his work, in which he kidnaps Rosamond, and in which he has continued to keep his identity secret from her after she joins him in the robbers' house (he never lets her see his face unwashed) are conventional in Mississippi history (the bandit Mason blacked his face as a disguise) and still more widely in song and story. Bandits, adventurers, lovers, and gods have the disguise in common. But girls always fall for taking it off. Psyche, in the fable, held a candle over Cupid's sleeping face — a god who only came in the dark — then let a drop of hot wax fall, and up he jumped, away he flew. Rosamond tries a mixture — her witch of a stepmother gives her the recipe, which concludes with a recipe's magic words, "It can't fail" — and she makes her version of the classic mistake.

In my novel, Jamie rises out of his bed, waked up by having his face washed.

> "Goodbye," he said. "For you did not trust me, and did not love me, for you wanted only to know who I am. Now I cannot stay in the house with you."
>
> And going straight to the window, he climbed out through it and in another moment was gone.
>
> Then Rosamond tried to follow and climbed out after him, but she   45
> fell in the dust.
>
> At the same moment, she felt the stirring within her that sent her a fresh piece of news.
>
> And finally a cloud went over the moon, and all was dark night.

Actually, the fairy tale exceeds my story in horror. But even so, it isn't so much worse than what really went on during those frontier times, is it? History tells us worse things than fairy tales do. People were scalped. Babies had their brains dashed out against tree trunks or were thrown into boiling oil when the Indians made their captures. Slavery was the order on the plantations. The Natchez Trace outlaws eviscerated their victims and rolled their bodies downhill, filled with stones, into the Mississippi River. War, bloodshed, massacre were all part of the times. In my story, I transposed these horrors — along with the felicities that also prevailed — into the element I thought suited both just as well, or better — the fairy tale. The line between history and fairy tale is not always clear, as *The Robber Bridegroom* along the way points out. And it was not from the two elements taken alone but from their interplay that my story, as I hope, takes on its own headlong life.

In the strivings and carryings-on of the day, there was also, you must agree, an element of comedy. Every period has its parodists and clowns. In *The Robber Bridegroom*, Goat and his mother and flock of sisters are the clowns — folk clowns. They go scrambling about at the heels of the purposeful, and live by making sly bargains and asking "What's in it for me?" — cashing in on other people's troubles. (You could almost accuse me of unearthing some of the collateral forerunners of the family Snopes.)

Goat, who has through mutual attraction become the familiar of   50
Rosamond's wicked stepmother, is out to do her bidding one day when he comes upon a certain robber sitting out in front of his cave, and salutes him. This robber —

> blinked his eyes and smiled, for nothing pleased him on a fine day like a lack of brains. "Come here," he said, "I will give you work to do."

"Gladly," replied Goat, "but I am already working for another, a very rich lady who wants me to see that her step-daughter is well kidnapped by a bandit. But I don't see why a young fellow like me could not take care of two commissions at once."

"That is the way to talk," said the Little Harpe. "You will come up in the world."

For of course, you will have had in mind the real-life bandits of the day, and here is the sample. The historical Little Harpe is hiding out correctly here, very close to Rodney. He is in possession — again correctly — of the head of his brother, the Big Harpe, which he keeps in a trunk. He can always turn it in and claim the reward on it — it's like money in the savings bank.

The Little Harpe is in the novel right along with Jamie Lockhart; a side story develops in clownish parallel to Jamie and Rosamond's story: a ludicrous affair of hapless kidnapping and mistaken identity between the Little Harpe and Goat's oldest sister with a sack over her head.

For while Jamie Lockhart leads a double life by hero's necessity, clearly this isn't the only aspect of duality in the novel. Crucial, or comical, scenes of mistaken identity take place more or less regularly as the story unwinds. There's a doubleness in respect to identity that runs in a strong thread through all the wild happenings — indeed, this thread is their connection, and everything that happens hangs upon it. I spun that thread out of the times. Life was so full, so excessively charged with energy in those days, when nothing seemed impossible in the Natchez country, that leading one life hardly provided scope enough for it all. In the doubleness there was narrative truth that I felt the times themselves had justified.

Of the story's climax, it's sufficient to say that all the elements are caught up in one whirl together, in which identities and disguises and counter-disguises, stratagems and plans and deceits and betrayals and gestures heroic and desperate all at one time come into play.

I think I've proved my claim that mine was not a *historical* historical novel. *The Robber Bridegroom*, from the start, took another direction: Instead of burying itself deep in historical fact, it flew up, like a cuckoo, and alighted in the borrowed nest of fantasy.

Fantasy, like any other form of fiction, must have its validity. Fantasy is no good unless the seed it springs up from is a truth, a truth about human beings. The validity of my novel has to lie in the human motivations apparent alike in the history of a time and in the timeless fairy tale. In whatever form these emerge, they speak out of the same aspirations —

to love, to conquer, to outwit and overcome the enemy, to reach the goal in view. And, in the end, to find out what we all wish to find out, exactly who we are and who the other fellow is, and what we are doing here all together.

Subservient to the needs of the fantasy, the characters may take on an exaggerated size. But to whatever scale they are drawn, they are each and every one human beings at the core. Even Little Harpe. When Jamie puts an end to him after a terrible battle that lasts all night, "the Little Harpe, with a wound in his heart, heaved a deep sigh and a tear came out of his eye, for he hated to give up his life as badly as the harmless deer in the wood."

In correct historical detail, the end of the Little Harpe was having 60 his own head stuck on a pole. My reading tells me that the heads of Little Harpe and one of his partners, brought in for reward, were mounted on poles at the north and south ends of the town of Old Greenville where the Natchez Trace went by — I can't recall if it's certain who was responsible. Naturally, in *The Robber Bridegroom*, the Robber Bridegroom himself alone is responsible. It's necessary that Jamie Lockhart kill his evil counterpart, the Little Harpe, for the sake of Jamie Lockhart's future and that of his love, Rosamond; for as the novel ends — and this is the only ending possible — the hero is to be a robber no longer.

But of course, the Robber Bridegroom's pursuit of a double life was (like his subsequent renouncement of it) by hero's necessity. On the one occasion when Rosamond manages to leave the robbers' house for a visit home, Clement, her father, says to her:

> "If being a bandit were his breadth and scope, I should find him and kill him for sure. But since in addition he loves my daughter, he must be not one man but two, and I should be afraid of killing the second. For all things are double, and this should keep us from taking liberties with the outside world, and acting too quickly to finish things off . . . And perhaps after the riding and robbing and burning and assault is over with this man you love, he will step out of it all like a beastly skin, and surprise you with his gentleness. For this reason, I will wait and see; but it breaks my heart not to have seen with my own eyes what door you are walking into and what your life has turned out to be.

Clement, for his good prophecy, gets his wish. Several years later (enough for the steamboat to have been invented), on a trip to the New Orleans market, he goes walking about, and this is the way the novel ends:

New Orleans was the most marvelous city in the Spanish country or anywhere else on the river. Beauty and vice and every delight possible to the soul and body stood hospitably, and usually together, in every doorway and beneath every palmetto by day and lighted torch by night. A shutter opened, and a flower bloomed. The very atmosphere was nothing but aerial spice, the very walls were sugar cane, the very clouds hung as golden as bananas in the sky. But Clement Musgrove was a man who could have walked the streets of Bagdad without sending a second glance overhead at the Magic Carpet, or heard the tambourines of the angels in Paradise without dancing a step, or had his choice of the fruits of the Garden of Eden without making up his mind. For he was an innocent of the wilderness, and a planter of Rodney's Landing, and this was his good.

So, holding a bag of money in his hand, he went to the docks to de- 65 part . . . And as he was putting his foot on the gangplank, he felt a touch at his sleeve, and there stood his daughter Rosamond, more beautiful than ever, and dressed in a beautiful, rich, white gown.

Then how they embraced, for they had thought each other dead and gone.

"Father!" she said. "Look, this wonderful place is my home now, and I am happy again!"

And before the boat could leave, she told him that Jamie Lockhart was now no longer a bandit but a gentleman of the world in New Orleans, respected by all that knew him, a rich merchant in fact. All his wild ways had been shed like a skin, and he could not be kinder to her than he was. They were the parents of beautiful twins, one of whom was named Clementine, and they lived in a beautiful house of marble and cypress wood on the shores of Lake Pontchartrain, with a hundred slaves, and often went boating with other merchants and their wives, the ladies reclining under a blue silk canopy; and they sailed sometimes out on the ocean to look at the pirates' galleons. They had all they wanted in the world, and now that she had found her father still alive, everything was well. Of course, she said at the end, she did sometimes miss the house in the wood, and even the rough-and-tumble of their old life when he used to scorn her for her curiosity. But the city was splendid, she said; it was the place to live.

"Is all this true, Rosamond, or is it a lie?" said Clement.

"It is the truth," she said, and they held the boat while she took him to 70 see for himself, and it was all true but the blue canopy.

Then the yellow-haired Jamie ran and took him by the hand, and for the first time thanked him for his daughter. And as for him, the outward transfer from bandit to merchant had been almost too easy to count it a change at all, and he was enjoying all the same success he had ever had. But now, in his heart Jamie knew that he was a hero and had always been one, only with the power to look both ways and to see a thing from all sides.

Then Rosamond prepared her father a little box lunch with her own hands. She asked him to come and stay with them, but he would not.

"Goodbye," they told each other. "God bless you."

So I present them all — the characters of *The Robber Bridegroom* — to you historians in order that you may claim them. They're fanciful, overcharged with high spirits, perhaps, and running out of bounds when advisable or necessary, some of them demented — but they are legitimate. For they're children of their time, and fathered, rather proudly, by its spirit. If I carried out well enough my strongest intentions, fantasy does not take precedence over that spirit, but serves the better to show it forth. It partakes, in a direct way possible to fantasy alone, of the mood and tempo and drive of those challenging times, in the wild and romantic beauty of that place.

Some of the novel's reviewers called it a dream. I think it more accurate to call it an awakening to a dear native land and its own story of early life, made and offered by a novelist's imagination in exuberance and joy.   75

EXPLORATIONS

1. Early in "Fairy Tale of the Natchez Trace," Eudora Welty calls attention to the word "innocent" (para. 6). What other words and phrases in her first quoted passage from *The Robber Bridegroom* (paras. 3–5) foreshadow trouble ahead?

2. Welty identifies some aspects of *The Robber Bridegroom* as coming from local history. What other countries or cultures besides the Natchez area does she mention as sources?

3. What historic reasons does Welty give for the dualities in *The Robber Bridegroom*? What are the dramatic advantages of this doubleness?

CONNECTIONS

1. In paragraphs 13–24, Welty quotes a disagreement between Clement Musgrove and his wife Salome. What would Joseph Bruchac (p. 523) say about the message behind Salome's ambitions in this fairy tale?

2. Reread William J. Bennett's (p. 506) and Leslie Marmon Silko's (p. 507) statements about the purposes of storytelling. Which of the purposes they mention are evidently important to Welty?

3. When Jamie, the Robber Bridegroom, wakes up because Rosamond has washed his face, he flees: "For you did not trust me, and did not love me, for you wanted only to know who I am" (para. 43). How and why does Rosamond respond differently to her lover's mysterious identity from the narrator in Leslie Marmon Silko's "Yellow Woman" (p. 419)?

ELABORATIONS

1. According to Welty, the validity of a fairy tale comes from the validity of its human motivations: "to love, to conquer, to outwit and overcome the enemy, to reach the goal in view" (para. 58). Choose a story you enjoyed reading in this book. Using "Fairy Tale of the Natchez Trace" as a model, write a brief literary analysis of it, showing where and how it includes these motivations.

2. In *The Robber Bridegroom*, Welty weaves threads of various myths, local legends, and facts into a fairy tale. "History tells us worse things than fairy tales do," she reminds us. "People were scalped. Babies had their brains dashed out against tree trunks . . ." (para. 48). What violent, tragic, or glorious events are part of your community's history? With local facts and legends for a starting point, write your own short fairy tale.

TONI MORRISON

From Beloved

The first African-American to receive the Nobel Prize for literature,
Toni Morrison was born Chloe Anthony Wofford in Lorain, Ohio, in
1931. Growing up during the Depression and World War II, she started
working at age twelve but still managed to graduate from high school
with honors. She received her bachelor's degree from Howard University in 1953 and her master's from Cornell University in 1955. After
teaching at Texas Southern University she returned to Howard, where
she met and married Jamaican architect Harold Morrison. Her efforts to
juggle marriage, an academic career, writing, and motherhood ended in
divorce in 1964. Moving to New York with her two sons, Morrison became an editor for Random House. For twenty years she worked on
both sides of the publishing fence: Her novel *The Bluest Eye* appeared
in 1969, followed by *Sula* in 1973 and the even more successful *Song of
Solomon* in 1977. Meanwhile, she periodically lectured and taught at
such universities as Cambridge, Harvard, and Princeton (where she is
the Robert F. Goheen Professor of Humanities).

Morrison's novel *Beloved* (1987), from which the following chapter
comes, won the Pulitzer Prize for fiction and the Robert F. Kennedy
Award. It also paved the way for her 1993 Nobel Prize for literature,
which followed her publication in 1992 of the novel *Jazz*, the essay collection *Playing in the Dark: Whiteness and the Literary Imagination*, and
the edited volume *Race-ing Justice, En-Gendering Power*. "Myth . . . has
enormous effect on my own imagination," she commented at a 1995
panel discussion in Atlanta. "I am perhaps enchanted still by enchant-
ment and by what used to be called superstition and magic. But those
words are very small for what . . . I'm looking for, which is just a way in
which to describe and recreate the enhanced life, life as in an upper register that comes from one's very close association with the world that we
already inhabit."

124 was spiteful. Full of a baby's venom. The women in the house
knew it and so did the children. For years each put up with the spite in
his own way, but by 1873 Sethe and her daughter Denver were its only
victims. The grandmother, Baby Suggs, was dead, and the sons,
Howard and Buglar, had run away by the time they were thirteen years
old — as soon as merely looking in a mirror shattered it (that was the

signal for Buglar); as soon as two tiny hand prints appeared in the cake (that was it for Howard). Neither boy waited to see more; another kettleful of chickpeas smoking in a heap on the floor; soda crackers crumbled, and strewn in a line next to the doorsill. Nor did they wait for one of the relief periods: the weeks, months even, when nothing was disturbed. No. Each one fled at once — the moment the house committed what was for him the one insult not to be borne or witnessed a second time. Within two months, in the dead of winter, leaving their grandmother, Baby Suggs; Sethe, their mother; and their little sister, Denver, all by themselves in the gray and white house on Bluestone Road. It didn't have a number then, because Cincinnati didn't stretch that far. In fact, Ohio had been calling itself a state only seventy years when first one brother and then the next stuffed quilt packing into his hat, snatched up his shoes, and crept away from the lively spite the house had for them.

Baby Suggs didn't even raise her head. From her sickbed she heard them go but that wasn't the reason she lay still. It was a wonder to her that her grandsons had taken so long to realize that every house wasn't like the one on Bluestone Road. Suspended between the nastiness of life and the meanness of the dead, she couldn't get interested in leaving life or living it, let alone the fright of two creeping-off boys. Her past had been like her present — intolerable — and since she knew death was anything but forgetfulness, she used the little energy left her for pondering color.

"Bring a little lavender in, if you got any. Pink, if you don't."

And Sethe would oblige her with anything from fabric to her own tongue. Winter in Ohio was especially rough if you had an appetite for color. Sky provided the only drama, and counting on a Cincinnati horizon for life's principal joy was reckless indeed. So Sethe and the girl Denver did what they could, and what the house permitted, for her. Together they waged a perfunctory battle against the outrageous behavior of that place; against turned-over slop jars, smacks on the behind, and gusts of sour air. For they understood the source of the outrage as well as they knew the source of light.

Baby Suggs died shortly after the brothers left, with no interest whatsoever in their leave-taking or hers, and right afterward Sethe and Denver decided to end the persecution by calling forth the ghost that tried them so. Perhaps a conversation, they thought, an exchange of views or something would help. So they held hands and said, "Come on. Come on. You may as well just come on."

The sideboard took a step forward but nothing else did.

"Grandma Baby must be stopping it," said Denver. She was ten and still mad at Baby Suggs for dying.

Sethe opened her eyes. "I doubt that," she said.

"Then why don't it come?"

"You forgetting how little it is," said her mother. "She wasn't even 10
two years old when she died. Too little to understand. Too little to talk
much even."

"Maybe she don't want to understand," said Denver.

"Maybe. But if she'd only come, I could make it clear to her." Sethe
released her daughter's hand and together they pushed the sideboard
back against the wall. Outside a driver whipped his horse into the gal-
lop local people felt necessary when they passed 124.

"For a baby she throws a powerful spell," said Denver.

"No more powerful than the way I loved her," Sethe answered and
there it was again. The welcoming cool of unchiseled headstones; the
one she selected to lean against on tiptoe, her knees wide open as any
grave. Pink as a fingernail it was, and sprinkled with glittering chips.
Ten minutes, he said. You got ten minutes I'll do it for free.

Ten minutes for seven letters. With another ten could she have got- 15
ten "Dearly" too? She had not thought to ask him and it bothered her
still that it might have been possible — that for twenty minutes, a half
hour, say, she could have had the whole thing, every word she heard
the preacher say at the funeral (and all there was to say, surely) engraved on her baby's headstone: Dearly Beloved. But what she got, settled for, was the one word that mattered. She thought it would be
enough, rutting among the headstones with the engraver, his young son
looking on, the anger in his face so old; the appetite in it quite new.
That should certainly be enough. Enough to answer one more
preacher, one more abolitionist and a town full of disgust.

Counting on the stillness of her own soul, she had forgotten the
other one: the soul of her baby girl. Who would have thought that a
little old baby could harbor so much rage? Rutting among the stones
under the eyes of the engraver's son was not enough. Not only did she
have to live out her years in a house palsied by the baby's fury at having
its throat cut, but those ten minutes she spent pressed up against dawn-
colored stone studded with star chips, her knees wide open as the grave,
were longer than life, more alive, more pulsating than the baby blood
that soaked her fingers like oil.

"We could move," she suggested once to her mother-in-law.

"What'd be the point?" asked Baby Suggs. "Not a house in the country ain't packed to its rafters with some dead Negro's grief. We lucky this
ghost is a baby. My husband's spirit was to come back in here? or yours?
Don't talk to me. You lucky. You got three left. Three pulling at your
skirts and just one raising hell from the other side. Be thankful, why

don't you? I had eight. Every one of them gone away from me. Four taken, four chased, and all, I expect, worrying somebody's house into evil." Baby Suggs rubbed her eyebrows. "My first-born. All I can remember of her is how she loved the burned bottom of bread. Can you beat that? Eight children and that's all I remember."

"That's all you let yourself remember," Sethe had told her, but she was down to one herself — one alive, that is — the boys chased off by the dead one, and her memory of Buglar was fading fast. Howard at least had a head shape nobody could forget. As for the rest, she worked hard to remember as close to nothing as was safe. Unfortunately her brain was devious. She might be hurrying across a field, running practically, to get to the pump quickly and rinse the chamomile sap from her legs. Nothing else would be in her mind. The picture of the men coming to nurse her was as lifeless as the nerves in her back where the skin buckled like a washboard. Nor was there the faintest scent of ink or the cherry gum and oak bark from which it was made. Nothing. Just the breeze cooling her face as she rushed toward water. And then sopping the chamomile away with pump water and rags, her mind fixed on getting every last bit of sap off — on her carelessness in taking a shortcut across the field just to save a half mile, and not noticing how high the weeds had grown until the itching was all the way to her knees. Then something. The plash of water, the sight of her shoes and stockings awry on the path where she had flung them; or Here Boy lapping in the puddle near her feet, and suddenly there was Sweet Home rolling, rolling, rolling out before her eyes, and although there was not a leaf on that farm that did not make her want to scream, it rolled itself out before her in shameless beauty. It never looked as terrible as it was and it made her wonder if hell was a pretty place too. Fire and brimstone all right, but hidden in lacy groves. Boys hanging from the most beautiful sycamores in the world. It shamed her — remembering the wonderful soughing trees rather than the boys. Try as she might to make it otherwise, the sycamores beat out the children every time and she could not forgive her memory for that.

When the last of the chamomile was gone, she went around to the front of the house, collecting her shoes and stockings on the way. As if to punish her further for her terrible memory, sitting on the porch not forty feet away was Paul D, the last of the Sweet Home men. And although she could never mistake his face for another's, she said, "Is that you?"

"What's left." He stood up and smiled. "How you been, girl, besides barefoot?"

When she laughed it came out loose and young. "Messed up my legs back yonder. Chamomile."

He made a face as though tasting a teaspoon of something bitter. "I don't want to even hear 'bout it. Always did hate that stuff."

Sethe balled up her stockings and jammed them into her pocket. "Come on in."

"Porch is fine, Sethe. Cool out here." He sat back down and looked   25
at the meadow on the other side of the road, knowing the eagerness he felt would be in his eyes.

"Eighteen years," she said softly.

"Eighteen," he repeated. "And I swear I been walking every one of em. Mind if I join you?" He nodded toward her feet and began unlacing his shoes.

"You want to soak them? Let me get you a basin of water." She moved closer to him to enter the house.

"No, uh uh. Can't baby feet. A whole lot more tramping they got to do."

"You can't leave right away, Paul D. You got to stay awhile."   30

"Well, long enough to see Baby Suggs, anyway. Where is she?"

"Dead."

"Aw no. When?"

"Eight years now. Almost nine."

"Was it hard? I hope she didn't die hard."   35

Sethe shook her head. "Soft as cream. Being alive was the hard part. Sorry you missed her though. Is that what you came by for?"

"That's some of what I came for. The rest is you. But if all the truth be known, I go anywhere these days. Anywhere they let me sit down."

"You looking good."

"Devil's confusion. He lets me look good long as I feel bad." He looked at her and the word "bad" took on another meaning.

Sethe smiled. This is the way they were — had been. All of the   40
Sweet Home men, before and after Halle, treated her to a mild brotherly flirtation, so subtle you had to scratch for it.

Except for a heap more hair and some waiting in his eyes, he looked the way he had in Kentucky. Peachstone skin; straight-backed. For a man with an immobile face it was amazing how ready it was to smile, or blaze or be sorry with you. As though all you had to do was get his attention and right away he produced the feeling you were feeling. With less than a blink, his face seemed to change — underneath it lay the activity.

"I wouldn't have to ask about him, would I? You'd tell me if there was anything to tell, wouldn't you?" Sethe looked down at her feet and saw again the sycamores.

"I'd tell you. Sure I'd tell you. I don't know any more now than I did then." Except for the churn, he thought, and you don't need to know that. "You must think he's still alive."

"No. I think he's dead. It's not being sure that keeps him alive."

"What did Baby Suggs think?"   45

"Same, but to listen to her, all her children is dead. Claimed she felt each one go the very day and hour."

"When she say Halle went?"

"Eighteen fifty-five. The day my baby was born."

"You had that baby, didn't you? Never thought you'd make it." He chuckled. "Running off pregnant."

"Had to. Couldn't be no waiting." She lowered her head and   50 thought, as he did, how unlikely it was that she had made it. And if it hadn't been for that girl looking for velvet, she never would have.

"All by yourself too." He was proud of her and annoyed by her. Proud she had done it; annoyed that she had not needed Halle or him in the doing.

"Almost by myself. Not all by myself. A whitegirl helped me."

"Then she helped herself too, God bless her."

"You could stay the night, Paul D."

"You don't sound too steady in the offer."   55

Sethe glanced beyond his shoulder toward the closed door. "Oh it's truly meant. I just hope you'll pardon my house. Come on in. Talk to Denver while I cook you something."

Paul D tied his shoes together, hung them over his shoulder and followed her through the door straight into a pool of red and undulating light that locked him where he stood.

"You got company?" he whispered, frowning.

"Off and on," said Sethe.

"Good God." He backed out the door onto the porch. "What kind of   60 evil you got in here?"

"It's not evil, just sad. Come on. Just step through."

He looked at her then, closely. Closer than he had when she first rounded the house on wet and shining legs, holding her shoes and stockings up in one hand, her skirts in the other. Halle's girl — the one with iron eyes and backbone to match. He had never seen her hair in Kentucky. And though her face was eighteen years older than when last he saw her, it was softer now. Because of her hair. A face too still for comfort; irises the same color as her skin, which, in that still face, used to make him think of a mask with mercifully punched-out eyes. Halle's woman. Pregnant every year including the year she sat by the fire telling him she was going to run. Her three children she had already packed into a wagonload of others in a caravan of Negroes crossing the river. They were to be left with Halle's mother near Cincinnati. Even in that tiny shack, leaning so close to the fire you could smell the heat in her dress, her eyes did not pick up a flicker of light. They were like two wells into which he had trouble gazing. Even punched out they needed to be covered, lidded, marked with some sign to warn folks of what that emptiness held. So he looked instead at the fire while she told him, because her husband was not there for the telling. Mr. Garner was dead and his wife had a lump in her neck the size of a sweet potato and unable to speak to anyone. She leaned as close to the fire as her pregnant belly allowed and told him, Paul D, the last of the Sweet Home men.

There had been six of them who belonged to the farm, Sethe the only female. Mrs. Garner, crying like a baby, had sold his brother to pay off the debts that surfaced the minute she was widowed. Then schoolteacher arrived to put things in order. But what he did broke three more Sweet Home men and punched the glittering iron out of Sethe's eyes, leaving two open wells that did not reflect firelight.

Now the iron was back but the face, softened by hair, made him trust her enough to step inside her door smack into a pool of pulsing red light.

She was right. It was sad. Walking through it, a wave of grief soaked   65
him so thoroughly he wanted to cry. It seemed a long way to the normal light surrounding the table, but he made it — dry-eyed and lucky.

"You said she died soft. Soft as cream," he reminded her.

"That's not Baby Suggs," she said.

"Who then?"

"My daughter. The one I sent ahead with the boys."

"She didn't live?"   70

"No. The one I was carrying when I run away is all I got left. Boys gone too. Both of em walked off just before Baby Suggs died."

Paul D looked at the spot where the grief had soaked him. The red was gone but a kind of weeping clung to the air where it had been.

Probably best, he thought. If a Negro got legs he ought to use them. Sit down too long, somebody will figure out a way to tie them up. Still . . . if her boys were gone . . .

"No man? You here by yourself?"

"Me and Denver," she said.   75

"That all right by you?"

"That's all right by me."

She saw his skepticism and went on. "I cook at a restaurant in town. And I sew a little on the sly."

Paul D smiled then, remembering the bedding dress. Sethe was thirteen when she came to Sweet Home and already iron-eyed. She was a timely present for Mrs. Garner who had lost Baby Suggs to her husband's high principles. The five Sweet Home men looked at the new girl and decided to let her be. They were young and so sick with the absence of women they had taken to calves. Yet they let the iron-eyed girl be, so she could choose in spite of the fact that each one would have beaten the others to mush to have her. It took her a year to choose — a long, tough year of thrashing on pallets eaten up with dreams of her. A year of yearning, when rape seemed the solitary gift of life. The restraint they had exercised possible only because they were Sweet Home men — the ones Mr. Garner bragged about while other farmers shook their heads in warning at the phrase.

"Y'all got boys," he told them. "Young boys, old boys, picky boys,   80
stroppin boys. Now at Sweet Home, my niggers is men every one of em.
Bought em thataway, raised em thataway. Men every one."

"Beg to differ, Garner. Ain't no nigger men."

"Not if you scared, they ain't." Garner's smile was wide. "But if you a man yourself, you'll want your niggers to be men too."

"I wouldn't have no nigger men round my wife."

It was the reaction Garner loved and waited for. "Neither would I," he said. "Neither would I," and there was always a pause before the neighbor, or stranger, or peddler, or brother-in-law or whoever it was got the meaning. Then a fierce argument, sometimes a fight, and Garner came home bruised and pleased, having demonstrated one more time what a real Kentuckian was: one tough enough and smart enough to make and call his own niggers men.

And so they were: Paul D Garner, Paul F Garner, Paul A Garner,   85
Halle Suggs and Sixo, the wild man. All in their twenties, minus women, fucking cows, dreaming of rape, thrashing on pallets, rubbing their thighs and waiting for the new girl — the one who took Baby Suggs' place after Halle bought her with five years of Sundays. Maybe that was why she chose him. A twenty-year-old man so in love with his mother he gave up five years of Sabbaths just to see her sit down for a change was a serious recommendation.

She waited a year. And the Sweet Home men abused cows while they waited with her. She chose Halle and for their first bedding she sewed herself a dress on the sly.

"Won't you stay on awhile? Can't nobody catch up on eighteen years in a day."

Out of the dimness of the room in which they sat, a white staircase climbed toward the blue-and-white wallpaper of the second floor. Paul D could see just the beginning of the paper; discreet flecks of yellow sprinkled among a blizzard of snowdrops all backed by blue. The luminous

white of the railing and steps kept him glancing toward it. Every sense he
had told him the air above the stairwell was charmed and very thin. But
the girl who walked down out of that air was round and brown with the
face of an alert doll.

Paul D looked at the girl and then at Sethe who smiled saying, "Here
she is my Denver. This is Paul D, honey, from Sweet Home."

"Good morning, Mr. D."   90

"Garner, baby. Paul D Garner."

"Yes sir."

"Glad to get a look at you. Last time I saw your mama, you were
pushing out the front of her dress."

"Still is," Sethe smiled, "provided she can get in it."

Denver stood on the bottom step and was suddenly hot and shy. It   95
had been a long time since anybody (good-willed whitewoman,
preacher, speaker or newspaperman) sat at their table, their sympathetic
voices called liar by the revulsion in their eyes. For twelve years, long
before Grandma Baby died, there had been no visitors of any sort and
certainly no friends. No coloredpeople. Certainly no hazelnut man
with too long hair and no notebook, no charcoal, no oranges, no questions. Someone her mother wanted to talk to and would even consider
talking to while barefoot. Looking, in fact acting, like a girl instead of
the quiet, queenly woman Denver had known all her life. The one who
never looked away, who when a man got stomped to death by a mare
right in front of Sawyer's restaurant did not look away; and when a sow
began eating her own litter did not look away then either. And when
the baby's spirit picked up Here Boy and slammed him into the wall
hard enough to break two of his legs and dislocate his eye, so hard he
went into convulsions and chewed up his tongue, still her mother had
not looked away. She had taken a hammer, knocked the dog unconscious, wiped away the blood and saliva, pushed his eye back in his
head and set his leg bones. He recovered, mute and off-balance, more
because of his untrustworthy eye than his bent legs, and winter, summer, drizzle or dry, nothing could persuade him to enter the house
again.

Now here was this woman with the presence of mind to repair a dog
gone savage with pain rocking her crossed ankles and looking away
from her own daughter's body. As though the size of it was more than
vision could bear. And neither she nor he had on shoes. Hot, shy, now
Denver was lonely. All that leaving: first her brothers, then her grandmother — serious losses since there were no children willing to circle
her in a game or hang by their knees from her porch railing. None of

that had mattered as long as her mother did not look away as she was doing now, making Denver long, downright *long*, for a sign of spite from the baby ghost.

"She's a fine-looking young lady," said Paul D. "Fine-looking. Got her daddy's sweet face."

"You know my father?"

"Knew him. Knew him well."

"Did he, Ma'am?" Denver fought an urge to realign her affection.   100

"Of course he knew your daddy. I told you, he's from Sweet Home."

Denver sat down on the bottom step. There was nowhere else gracefully to go. They were a twosome, saying "Your daddy" and "Sweet Home" in a way that made it clear both belonged to them and not to her. That her own father's absence was not hers. Once the absence had belonged to Grandma Baby — a son, deeply mourned because he was the one who had bought her out of there. Then it was her mother's absent husband. Now it was this hazelnut stranger's absent friend. Only those who knew him ("knew him well") could claim his absence for themselves. Just as only those who lived in Sweet Home could remember it, whisper it and glance sideways at one another while they did. Again she wished for the baby ghost — its anger thrilling her now where it used to wear her out. Wear her out.

"We have a ghost in here," she said, and it worked. They were not a twosome anymore. Her mother left off swinging her feet and being girl-ish. Memory of Sweet Home dropped away from the eyes of the man she was being girlish for. He looked quickly up the lightning-white stairs behind her.

"So I hear," he said. "But sad, your mama said. Not evil."

"No sir," said Denver, "not evil. But not sad either."   105

"What then?"

"Rebuked. Lonely and rebuked."

"Is that right?" Paul D turned to Sethe.

"I don't know about lonely," said Denver's mother. "Mad, maybe, but I don't see how it could be lonely spending every minute with us like it does."

"Must be something you got it wants."   110

Sethe shrugged. "It's just a baby."

"My sister," said Denver. "She died in this house."

Paul D scratched the hair under his jaw. "Reminds me of that head-less bride back behind Sweet Home. Remember that, Sethe? Used to roam them woods regular."

"How could I forget? Worrisome . . ."

"How come everybody run off from Sweet Home can't stop talking 115 about it? Look like if it was so sweet you would have stayed."

"Girl, who you talking to?"

Paul D laughed. "True, true. She's right, Sethe. It wasn't sweet and it sure wasn't home." He shook his head.

"But it's where we were," said Sethe. "All together. Comes back whether we want it to or not." She shivered a little. A light ripple of skin on her arm, which she caressed back into sleep. "Denver," she said, "start up that stove. Can't have a friend stop by and don't feed him."

"Don't go to any trouble on my account," Paul D said.

"Bread ain't trouble. The rest I brought back from where I work. 120 Least I can do, cooking from dawn to noon, is bring dinner home. You got any objections to pike?"

"If he don't object to me I don't object to him."

At it again, thought Denver. Her back to them, she jostled the kindlin and almost lost the fire. "Why don't you spend the night, Mr. Garner? You and Ma'am can talk about Sweet Home all night long."

Sethe took two swift steps to the stove, but before she could yank Denver's collar, the girl leaned forward and began to cry.

"What is the matter with you? I never knew you to behave this way."

"Leave her be," said Paul D. "I'm a stranger to her." 125

"That's just it. She got no cause to act up with a stranger. Oh baby, what is it? Did something happen?"

But Denver was shaking now and sobbing so she could not speak. The tears she had not shed for nine years wetting her far too womanly breasts.

"I can't no more. I can't no more."

"Can't what? What can't you?"

"I can't live here. I don't know where to go or what to do, but I can't 130 live here. Nobody speaks to us. Nobody comes by. Boys don't like me. Girls don't either."

"Honey, honey."

"What's she talking 'bout nobody speaks to you?" asked Paul D.

"It's the house. People don't —"

"It's not! It's not the house. It's us! And it's you!"

"Denver!" 135

"Leave off, Sethe. It's hard for a young girl living in a haunted house. That can't be easy."

"It's easier than some other things."

"Think, Sethe. I'm a grown man with nothing new left to see or do and I'm telling you it ain't easy. Maybe you all ought to move. Who owns this house?"

Over Denver's shoulder Sethe shot Paul D a look of snow. "What you care?"

"They won't let you leave?" 140

"No."

"Sethe."

"No moving. No leaving. It's all right the way it is."

"You going to tell me it's all right with this child half out of her mind?"

Something in the house braced, and in the listening quiet that fol- 145 lowed Sethe spoke.

"I got a tree on my back and a haint in my house, and nothing in between but the daughter I am holding in my arms. No more running — from nothing. I will never run from another thing on this earth. I took one journey and I paid for the ticket, but let me tell you something, Paul D Garner: it cost too much! Do you hear me? It cost too much. Now sit down and eat with us or leave us be."

Paul D fished in his vest for a little pouch of tobacco — concentrating on its contents and the knot of its string while Sethe led Denver into the keeping room that opened off the large room he was sitting in. He had no smoking papers, so he fiddled with the pouch and listened through the open door to Sethe quieting her daughter. When she came back she avoided his look and went straight to a small table next to the stove. Her back was to him and he could see all the hair he wanted without the distraction of her face.

"What tree on your back?"

"Huh." Sethe put a bowl on the table and reached under it for flour.

"What tree on your back? Is something growing on your back? I 150 don't see nothing growing on your back."

"It's there all the same."

"Who told you that?"

"Whitegirl. That's what she called it. I've never seen it and never will. But that's what she said it looked like. A chokecherry tree. Trunk, branches, and even leaves. Tiny little chokecherry leaves. But that was eighteen years ago. Could have cherries now for all I know."

Sethe took a little spit from the tip of her tongue with her forefinger. Quickly, lightly she touched the stove. Then she trailed her fingers through the flour, parting, separating small hills and ridges of it, looking for mites. Finding none, she poured soda and salt into the crease of her folded hand and tossed both into the flour. Then she reached into a can and scooped half a handful of lard. Deftly she squeezed the flour through it, then with her left hand sprinkling water, she formed the dough.

"I had milk," she said. "I was pregnant with Denver but I had milk 155
for my baby girl. I hadn't stopped nursing her when I sent her on ahead with Howard and Buglar."

Now she rolled the dough out with a wooden pin. "Anybody could smell me long before he saw me. And when he saw me he'd see the drops of it on the front of my dress. Nothing I could do about that. All I knew was I had to get my milk to my baby girl. Nobody was going to nurse her like me. Nobody was going to get it to her fast enough, or take it away when she had enough and didn't know it. Nobody knew that she couldn't pass her air if you held her up on your shoulder, only if she was lying on my knees. Nobody knew that but me and nobody had her milk but me. I told that to the women in the wagon. Told them to put sugar water in cloth to suck from so when I got there in a few days she wouldn't have forgot me. The milk would be there and I would be there with it."

"Men don't know nothing much," said Paul D, tucking his pouch back into his vest pocket, "but they do know a suckling can't be away from its mother for long."

"Then they know what it's like to send your children off when your breasts are full."

"We was talking 'bout a tree, Sethe."

"After I left you, those boys came in and took my milk. That's what 160
they came in there for. Held me down and took it. I told Mrs. Garner on em. She had that lump and couldn't speak but her eyes rolled out tears. Them boys found out I told on em. Schoolteacher made one open up my back, and when it closed it made a tree. It grows there still."

"They used cowhide on you?"

"And they took my milk."

"They beat you and you was pregnant?"

"And they took my milk!"

The fat white circles of dough lined the pan in rows. Once more 165
Sethe touched a wet forefinger to the stove. She opened the oven door and slid the pan of biscuits in. As she raised up from the heat she felt Paul D behind her and his hands under her breasts. She straightened up and knew, but could not feel, that his cheek was pressing into the branches of her chokecherry tree.

Not even trying, he had become the kind of man who could walk into a house and make the women cry. Because with him, in his pres-

ence, they could. There was something blessed in his manner.
Women saw him and wanted to weep — to tell him that their chest
hurt and their knees did too. Strong women and wise saw him and
told him things they only told each other: that way past the Change of
Life, desire in them had suddenly become enormous, greedy, more
savage than when they were fifteen, and that it embarrassed them and
made them sad; that secretly they longed to die — to be quit of it —
that sleep was more precious to them than any waking day. Young
girls sidled up to him to confess or describe how well-dressed the visi-
tations were that had followed them straight from their dreams.
Therefore, although he did not understand why this was so, he was
not surprised when Denver dripped tears into the stovefire. Nor, fifteen minutes later, after telling him about her stolen milk, her mother
wept as well. Behind her, bending down, his body an arc of kindness,
he held her breasts in the palms of his hands. He rubbed his cheek on
her back and learned that way her sorrow, the roots of it; its wide
trunk and intricate branches. Raising his fingers to the hooks of her
dress, he knew without seeing them or hearing any sigh that the tears
were coming fast. And when the top of her dress was around her hips
and he saw the sculpture her back had become, like the decorative
work of an ironsmith too passionate for display, he could think but not
say, "Aw, Lord, girl." And he would tolerate no peace until he had
touched every ridge and leaf of it with his mouth, none of which
Sethe could feel because her back skin had been dead for years. What
she knew was that the responsibility for her breasts, at last, was in
somebody else's hands.

Would there be a little space, she wondered, a little time, some way
to hold off eventfulness, to push busyness into the corners of the room
and just stand there a minute or two, naked from shoulder blade to
waist, relieved of the weight of her breasts, smelling the stolen milk
again and the pleasure of baking bread? Maybe this one time she could
stop dead still in the middle of a cooking meal — not even leave the
stove — and feel the hurt her back ought to. Trust things and remember things because the last of the Sweet Home men was there to catch
her if she sank?

The stove didn't shudder as it adjusted to its heat. Denver wasn't stirring in the next room. The pulse of red light hadn't come on and Paul
D had not trembled since 1856 and then for eighty-three days in a row.
Locked up and chained down, his hands shook so bad he couldn't
smoke or even scratch properly. Now he was trembling again but in the
legs this time. It took him a while to realize that his legs were not shaking because of worry, but because the floorboards were and the grind-

ing, shoving floor was only part of it. The house itself was pitching. Sethe slid to the floor and struggled to get back into her dress. While down on all fours, as though she were holding her house down on the ground, Denver burst from the keeping room, terror in her eyes, a vague smile on her lips.

"God damn it! Hush up!" Paul D was shouting, falling, reaching for anchor. "Leave the place alone! Get the hell out!" A table rushed toward him and he grabbed its leg. Somehow he managed to stand at an angle and, holding the table by two legs, he bashed it about, wrecking everything, screaming back at the screaming house. "You want to fight, come on! God damn it! She got enough without you. She got enough!"

The quaking slowed to an occasional lurch, but Paul D did not stop 170 whipping the table around until everything was rock quiet. Sweating and breathing hard, he leaned against the wall in the space the sideboard left. Sethe was still crouched next to the stove, clutching her salvaged shoes to her chest. The three of them, Sethe, Denver, and Paul D, breathed to the same beat, like one tired person. Another breathing was just as tired.

It was gone. Denver wandered through the silence to the stove. She ashed over the fire and pulled the pan of biscuits from the oven. The jelly cupboard was on its back, its contents lying in a heap in the corner of the bottom shelf. She took out a jar, and, looking around for a plate, found half of one by the door. These things she carried out to the porch steps, where she sat down.

The two of them had gone up there. Stepping lightly, easy-footed, they had climbed the white stairs, leaving her down below. She pried the wire from the top of the jar and then the lid. Under it was cloth and under that a thin cake of wax. She removed it all and coaxed the jelly onto one half of the half a plate. She took a biscuit and pulled off its black top. Smoke curled from the soft white insides.

She missed her brothers. Buglar and Howard would be twenty-two and twenty-three now. Although they had been polite to her during the quiet time and gave her the whole top of the bed, she remembered how it was before: the pleasure they had sitting clustered on the white stairs — she between the knees of Howard or Buglar — while they made up die-witch! stories with proven ways of killing her dead. And Baby Suggs telling her things in the keeping room. She smelled like bark in the day and leaves at night, and Denver would not sleep in her old room after her brothers ran away.

Now her mother was upstairs with the man who had gotten rid of the only other company she had. Denver dipped a bit of bread into the jelly. Slowly, methodically, miserably she ate it.

EXPLORATIONS

1. In this opening chapter to her novel *Beloved*, much of Toni Morrison's exposition is indirect. Who are the three living characters in the present, and how are they related to each other? Who is Halle, and how is he related to each of them?

2. "Now at Sweet Home, my niggers is men every one of em," Mr. Garner brags. "Bought em thataway, raised em thataway" (para. 80). How are these statements contradictory? What is the impact of that contradiction on the men he refers to?

3. How would the opening to this story change if Toni Morrison used the word "haunted" instead of "spiteful" in her first sentence? What point is she making about the ghost's significance? How does the choice of "spiteful" rather than "haunted" relate to Denver's later statements, "It's not the house. It's us! And it's you!" (para. 134)?

CONNECTIONS

1. In "Fairy Tale of the Natchez Trace" (p. 531), Eudora Welty points out that the word "innocent" early in her novel *The Robber Bridegroom* "shines like a cautionary blinker to what lies on the road ahead" (p. 532). What cautionary blinker appears in the second sentence of *Beloved*? Why does it stand out as unusual? What horror does it warn us about?

2. Like Joseph Bruchac's "Digging into Your Heart" (p. 523), *Beloved* contains different messages for different audiences. What do you think are Morrison's intended audiences, and what messages are they likely to draw from this chapter? What specific aspects of *Beloved* seem meant to appeal to each audience?

3. "When the Antelope people think of themselves," writes Leslie Marmon Silko, "it is as people who are of *this* story, and this is *our* place, and we fit into the very beginning when the people first came . . ." (p. 508). In what ways do these ideas apply to Morrison's story?

ELABORATIONS

1. In "Fairy Tale of the Natchez Trace," Eudora Welty describes mixing local history with other historical facts and legends to create *The Robber Bridegroom*. With Welty's essay as a model, write a short literary analysis of this

chapter from *Beloved* showing how Toni Morrison has used a similar strategy to combine her own set of ingredients into a different kind of story.

2. Choose some aspect of Morrison's opening chapter that interests you — for instance, the impact of slavery in the United States, how plantations operated in Kentucky, the history of Cincinnati, the pros and cons of living in an extended family, the effects of a baby's death on a family, or the role of ghost stories in American folklore. Find out more about it and write an expository essay based on your discoveries.

WINDOWS:
THE WORLD

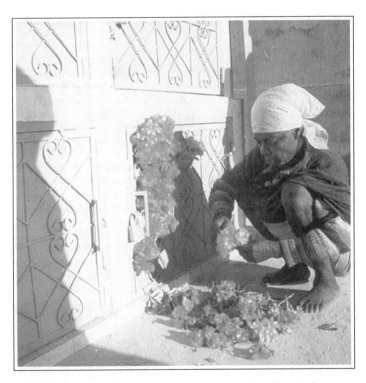

Myth, Ritual, and Magic: *A woman lays flowers beside a tomb on Haiti's Day of the Dead.*

ES'KIA MPHAHLELE

African Literature: What Tradition?

Es'kia Mphahlele (pronounced m-fa-lay-lay) was born Ezekiel Mphahlele in South Africa in 1919. He grew up in the capital city of Pretoria and received his B.A. with honors from the University of South Africa. Although he was banned from teaching in 1952 for protesting the segregationist Bantu Education Act, Mphahlele completed his master's degree and served as fiction editor for a Johannesburg magazine before leaving the country in 1957. In Paris he became director of African programs for the International Association for Cultural Freedom. Moving to the United States, he received his Ph.D. from the University of Denver and taught in the English department there; he also has taught at the University of Pennsylvania and in Kenya, Nigeria, and Zambia. Mphahlele returned to South Africa in 1977. "There is a force I call the tyranny of place," he has said; "the kind of unrelenting hold a place has on a person that gives him the motivation to write and a style." Even though his books were banned under apartheid, he taught and became head of African Literature at the University of the Witwatersrand (he is now a Professor Emeritus). Mphahlele has published story collections, works of criticism, novels, and a children's book; his essays have appeared in numerous journals. His autobiographical novel *The Wanderers* was designated Best African Novel of 1968–1969. "African Literature: What Tradition?" comes from a longer essay by the same title which originally appeared in the *Denver Quarterly*.

For more information on South Africa, see pages 344 and 688.

It all started when Africa was shanghaied into the history of the West in the late nineteenth century. What were we coming into? — a long line of continuity going back some 9,000 years since the civilizations of the great river valleys of the Nile, the Tigris and Euphrates, the Indus, and the Hwang-ho had launched man on a long intellectual quest. We had been discovered by an aggressive Western culture which was never going to let us be. Nor could we cease following the neon lights — or has it been a will o' the wisp? Time will tell. Perhaps Hegelian historical determinism will have it that it is as it should be: How could Africa be left out of it all indefinitely?

And so here I am, an ambivalent character. But I'm nothing of the oversimplified and sensationalized Hollywood version of a man of two worlds. It is not as if I were pinned on a rock, my legs stretched in opposite directions. Education sets up conflicts but also reconciles them in degrees that depend on the subject's innate personality equipment. It seems to me a writer in an African setting must possess this equipment and must strive toward some workable reconciliation inside himself. It is an agonizing journey. It can also be humiliating to feel that one has continually to be reassessing oneself with reference to the long line of tradition he has entered — the tradition of the West. How else? I have assimilated the only education the West had to offer me. I was brought up on European history and literature and religion and made to identify with European heroes while African heroes were being discredited, except those that became Christians or signed away their land and freedom, and African gods were being smoked out. I later rejected Christianity. And yet I could not return to ancestral worship in any overt way. But this does not invalidate my ancestors for me. Deep down there inside my agnostic self, I feel a reverence for them.

The majority of writers in Africa, I venture to say, are attached in a detached manner to one indigenous religion or another. They are not involved in its ritual, but they look at it with reverence. When, in their full consciousness, they have found themselves Christian — which can often just mean baptized — they have not adopted churchianity. Because our whole education system in Africa has been mission-ridden right from the beginning, and the white minister was supposed by the government or commercial or school-board employer to know the "native," you had always to produce a testimonial signed by a white church minister when you were applying for a job. Not even black ministers could speak for you. If you wanted to go out for further studies, you knew where to find St. Peter. The black minister himself required testimonials from one of his white brethren, never from another black minister. So we called ourselves Christians; we entered "Christian" on the line against an item that asked for it on all the multiplicity of forms, just in order to save ourselves the trouble of explaining and therefore failing to go through the gates. In independent Africa, we are luckily able to trust fellow blacks who vouch for us and others. And you can almost see the Christian veneer peeling off because it has nothing to do with conscience. . . .

By far the larger part of Africa is still traditionally minded in varying degrees. The whole dialogue around tradition is an intellectual one. The parents of people of my generation, although they may be urbanized, are still close to tradition. They worry a great deal about the way in which we break loose at one point and ignore some elements of tradition. Each time an African mother sends a child to high school, it is like giving birth to him all over again. She knows she is yielding something. Dialogue between her and the child decreases and eventually stays on the level of basic essentials: our needs, our family relations, family life, which must continue more or less normally, whatever else around us may progressively be reduced to abstractions or gadgets. It is no less excruciating for the young man who stands in this kind of relationship with his parents. But he can reconcile himself to it — the very educational process that wrenches him from his moorings helps him to arrange a harmonization within himself.

The parent will often moan and complain to him about the awkward distance he has reached away from tradition. But it is never a reprimand; it is an indulgent complaint. Because, I think, the parents are always aware that this whole business of education does not of itself engage you in an activity that expressly subverts the morals of the family, the clan, or of the tribe. They are aware of the many situations around them that require an education to cope with them. The benefits of tradition are abstract, and the parents' own thinking has not been stagnant while the whole landscape around them has been changing, while the white man's government has been impinging on their way of life over several decades. And the benefits of a modern education are tangible, real.

I have always asked myself what it is in one's formal education that leads to the rupture, to the ever-widening gulf between one and one's parents and one's community. You recognize the alphabet, then words, and then you can extract meaning from many sentences in a row. With that shock of recognition, words leap into life in front of you. They set your mind on fire; longings and desires you would never have known are released and seem to whirl around in currents that explode into other currents: something like what you see in a glass flask of water that you have on a naked flame to observe the movement of heat in liquid. From then on, one must not stop. Yet it is not something one can take for granted in an African context, because to start at all is not inevitable: Education is not compulsory, and the financial cost of it is immense.

In your higher education, you assimilate patterns of thought, argument, and so on from an alien culture in an alien language; they become your own. Of course you cannot help using your African setting as your field of reference; you cannot help going out of the queue of Western orientation now and again to consult those of your people who are not physically in it. You try to express their philosophy in a European language whose allegory, metaphor, and so on are alien to the spirit of that philosophy: something that can best be understood in terms of allegory and metaphor that are centered heavily on human relationships and external nature. All the same, you are in the queue, and you belong not only to an African community but also to a worldwide intellectual or worldwide economic community, or both. This is why communication becomes difficult, sometimes impossible between your people who are still not tuned into Western intellectual systems and yourself. Your mind operates in a foreign language, even while you are actually talking your mother tongue, at the moment you are engaged in your profession. You try hard to find correspondences and you realize there are only a few superficial ones: You have to try to *make* most of them. In the pure sciences, which are universally applicable, the correspondences are numerous; there is no problem.

Indigenous languages that have only recently become literary, that is, only since the church missions established presses in Africa, seem to have relied more and more heavily on the spoken word, so that gesture, facial expression, inflection of voice became vital equipment in communication. Language became almost a ritual in itself, and metaphor and symbol became a matter of art and device. Metaphor became a sacred thing if it had descended from usage in earlier times; when an elder, in a traditional court case, prefaced a proverb or aphorism or metaphor by saying, "Our elders say . . ." his audience listened with profound reverence. Notice the present tense in "our elders *say*. . . ." Because his elders would be the ancestors, who are still present with us in spirit. You can imagine what confusion prevails in a modern law court when a witness or the accused operate in metaphor and glory in the sensuousness of the spoken word quite irrelevant to the argument at hand. Ask any magistrate or prosecutor or lawyer in a differentiated Western-type society whether they find a court trial a sensuous activity, and hear what they say. Even the rhetoric that a lawyer may indulge in is primarily a thing of the brain rather than of the heart. In African languages, activities overlap a great deal, and there are no sharp dividing lines between various functions.

All that I have said so far has been an attempt to indicate the relative distances between tradition and the present — some shifting, others freezing, some thawing, others again presenting formidable barriers. And we are living in a situation in which the past and the present live side by side, because the past is not just a segment in time to think *back* upon: We can see it in living communities. We need to appreciate these distances if we are to understand what the African writer is about. He is part of the whole pattern.

EXPLORATIONS

1. As an African writer, to what "two worlds" does Es'kia Mphahlele belong? What choices does his dual heritage force him to make?

2. Why does Mphahlele perceive education as so crucial an issue for African writers? What price do they pay for it? What happens if they refuse to pay that price?

3. "The whole dialogue around tradition is an intellectual one," writes Mphahlele (para. 4). Cite three or four passages that show him to be part of the Western intellectual tradition. What passages show that he also belongs to the African tradition, in which speakers "operate in metaphor and glory in the sensuousness of the spoken word" (para. 8)?

CONNECTIONS

1. What similarities appear in Mphahlele's recollections of white-run South Africa and Toni Morrison's re-creation of the antebellum United States (p. 544)? How are the problems and the possible solutions alike and different in these two situations?

2. "Africa was shanghaied into the history of the West" (para. 1). In what ways does Joseph Bruchac's "Digging into Your Heart" (p. 523) suggest Native Americans were similarly shanghaied? Which customs or values of his native culture does each writer believe should be preserved, and why? What aspects of Westernization is each writer willing or eager to accept, and why?

3. "Words leap into life in front of you. They set your mind on fire. . . ." Compare Mphahlele's reflections in paragraph 6 with the excerpts from Pablo Neruda's memoir on page 509 and Malcom X's autobiography on page 275. What inner conflicts does each man express about words, and why?

ELABORATIONS

1. "I have always asked myself," writes Mphahlele, "what it is in one's formal education that leads to the rupture, to the ever-widening gulf between one and one's parents and one's community" (para. 6). Write a cause-and-effect essay that addresses this question, using "Tradition and the African Writer," other selections in this book, and your own experience as sources.

2. "The benefits of tradition are abstract," writes Mphahlele. "The benefits of a modern education are tangible, real" (para. 5). What does he mean? Looking at your own role in the world as an adult, what have you gained (or do you hope to gain) from your education? From the tradition(s) in which you grew up? Write an essay classifying or contrasting the benefits to you of your education and heritage.

GABRIEL GARCÍA MÁRQUEZ

Dreams for Hire

"It bothers me that the people of the United States have appropriated the word *America* as if *they* were the only Americans," Gabriel García Márquez told an interviewer shortly before he won the 1982 Nobel Prize for literature. A devotee of North American fiction, García Márquez was for a time prevented from entering the United States because he had worked for the Cuban news agency in New York in 1961. His old friendship with Fidel Castro, he says, is based on a shared love of literature and fish recipes. Born in the Caribbean coastal village of Aracataca, Colombia, in 1928, García Márquez grew up listening to his grandfather's tales of war and politics and his grandmother's stories of the supernatural. Out of this mix came the fictional town of Macondo (named for a nearby banana plantation), the setting for much of his fiction. García Márquez studied at the Universidad Nacional in Bogotá, Colombia's capital; he left to be a journalist, traveling to other parts of South America, the United States, and Europe, and began writing short stories. Recognition came with his 1961 novella *El coronel no tiene quien le escriba* (*No One Writes to the Colonel*, 1968), during the flowering of Latin American literature referred to as "El Boom." But it was *Cien años de soledad* (1967; *One Hundred Years of Solitude*, 1970) that made him famous, selling more than 10 million copies in more than thirty languages. García Márquez's fusion of naturalism and fantasy has given him a central place in the genre known as magic realism. Among his other novels are *Crónica de una muerte anunciada* (1981; *Chronicle of a Death Foretold*, 1982), which prompted the Nobel Prize; *El amor en los tiempos de cólera* (1985; *Love in the Time of Cholera*, 1988); and *Del amor y otros demonios* (1994; *Of Love and Other Demons*, 1995). "Dreams for Hire," translated from the Spanish by Nick Caistor, appeared in the Autumn 1992 volume of *Granta*.

The Panama-Colombia border is where Central and South America meet. Colombia thus is the only South American country with both a Caribbean and a Pacific coast. The national language is Spanish, and 97 percent of Colombians are Roman Catholic. Ethnically a majority are mestizos (mixed Spanish and Indian). Like Panama, Venezuela, and Ecuador, Colombia was ruled by Spain as part of New Granada from the 1500s until Simón Bolívar led the region to independence (1819–1824) and became its first president. (Venezuela and Ecuador broke away ten years later; Panama followed in 1903.) Although Colombia is one of the continent's longest-lived democracies, its history has been turbulent. Struggles for power between Liberal and Conservative parties often have erupted into literal battles and coups d'état, including the nationwide War of a Thousand Days (1899–1902); the 1928 "banana massacre" of striking United Fruit Company workers by government troops (depicted in *One Hundred Years of Solitude*); and *la violencia* ("the violence"), a decade of rioting and civil war following a 1948 political assassination. Today, strife between Colombia's government and its drug cartels exacerbates the country's economic and social problems.

Cuba comprises one large and several small islands 135 miles off Florida's southern tip. Christopher Columbus claimed it for Spain in 1492; its native Arawak Indians soon died off from enslavement, slaughter, and disease. After the Spanish-American War, Spain freed Cuba (1899) and the United States occupied it, withdrawing its troops in 1902 but remaining a force in the economy. In 1958 Fidel Castro and a guerrilla army, including Argentine physician Ernesto "Che" Guevara, overthrew dictator Fulgencio Batista. Allying with the Soviet Union, Castro nationalized foreign-owned businesses and instituted many Soviet-style changes. The United States responded with a trade embargo which, coupled with the breakup of the Soviet Union in 1991 and the collapse of the Communist Bloc in Europe, has hamstrung Cuba's economy.

At nine o'clock in the morning, while we were having breakfast on the terrace of the Hotel Riviera in Havana, a terrifying wave appeared out of nowhere — the day was sunny and calm — and came crashing upon us. It lifted the cars that had been passing along the sea front, as well as several others that had been parked nearby, and tossed them into the air, smashing one into the side of our hotel. It was like an explosion of dynamite, spreading panic up and down the twenty floors of our building and transforming the lobby into a pile of broken glass, where many of the hotel guests were hurled through the air like the furniture. Several were wounded in the hail of glass shards. It must have been a tidal wave of monumental size: The hotel is protected from the sea by a wall and the wide two-way avenue that passes before it, but the wave had erupted with such force that it obliterated the glass lobby.

Cuban volunteers, with the help of the local fire brigade, set to sweeping up the damage, and in less than six hours, after closing off the hotel's sea front entrance and opening up an alternative, everything was back to normal. Throughout the morning no one paid any attention to the car that had been smashed against the wall of the hotel, believing it had been among the vehicles parked along the avenue. But by the time it was eventually removed by a crane, the body of a woman was discovered inside, moored to the driving seat by her seat belt. The blow had been so great that there wasn't a bone in her body which was left unbroken. Her face was messy and unrecognizable, her ankle boots had burst at the seams, her clothes were in tatters. But there was a ring, still worn on her finger, which remained intact: It was made in the shape of a serpent and had emeralds for eyes. The police established that she was the housekeeper for the new Portuguese ambassador and his wife. In fact she had arrived with them only fifteen days before and had that morning left for the market in their new car. Her name meant nothing to me when I read about the incident in the papers, but I was intrigued by that ring, made in the shape of a serpent with emeralds for its eyes. I was, unfortunately, unable to find out on which finger the ring had been worn.

It was an essential detail: I feared that this woman might be someone I knew and whom I would never forget, even though I never learned her real name. She, too, had a ring made in the shape of a serpent, with emeralds for its eyes, but she always wore it on the first finger of her right hand, which was unusual, especially then. I had met her forty-six years ago in Vienna, eating sausages and boiled potatoes and drinking beer straight from the barrel, in a tavern frequented by Latin American students. I had arrived from Rome that morning, and I still recall that first impression made by her ample opera-singer's bosom, the drooping fox tails gathered around the collar of her coat, and that Egyptian ring made in the shape of a serpent. She spoke a rudimentary Spanish, in a breathless shopkeeper's accent, and I assumed that she must be Austrian, the only one at that long wooden table. I was wrong: She had been born in Colombia and between the wars had traveled to Austria to study music and singing. When I met her she must have been around thirty, and she had begun aging before her time. Even so, she was magical; and, also, among the most fearsome people I've ever met.

At that time — the late forties — Vienna was nothing more than an ancient imperial city that history had reduced to a remote provincial capital, located between the two irreconcilable worlds left by the Second World War, a paradise for the black market and international espionage. I couldn't imagine surroundings better suited to my fugitive compatriot, who went on eating in the students' tavern on the corner only out of nostalgia for her roots, because she had more than enough money to buy the whole place, its diners included. She never told us her real name; we always referred to her by the German tongue twister that the Latin American students in Vienna had invented for her: Frau Frida. No sooner had we been introduced than I committed the fortuitous imprudence of asking her how she came to find herself in a part of

the world so distant and different from the windy heights of the Quin-
dio region in Colombia. She replied matter-of-factly, "I hire myself out
to dream."

That was her profession. She was the third of eleven children of a   5
prosperous shopkeeper from the old region of Caldas, and by the time
she learned to speak, she had established the habit of telling all her
dreams before breakfast, when, she said, her powers of premonition
were at their most pure. At the age of seven, she dreamt that one of her
brothers had been swept away by a raging torrent. The mother, simply
out of a nervous superstitiousness, refused to allow her son to do what
he most enjoyed, swimming in the local gorge. But Frau Frida had already developed her own system of interpreting her prophecies.

"What the dream means," she explained, "is not that he is going to
drown, but that he mustn't eat sweets."

The interpretation amounted to a terrible punishment, especially for
a five-year-old boy who could not imagine life without his Sunday
treats. But the mother, convinced of her daughter's divinatory powers,
ensured that her injunction was adhered to. Unfortunately, following a
moment's inattention, the son choked on a gob-stopper that he had
been eating in secret, and it proved impossible to save him.

Frau Frida had never thought that it would be possible to earn a living from her talent until life took her by the scruff of the neck and, during a harsh Viennese winter, she rang the bell of the first house where
she wanted to live, and, when asked what she could do, offered the
simple reply: "I dream." After only a brief explanation, the lady of the
house took her on, at a wage that was little more than pocket money,
but with a decent room and three meals a day. Above all, there was a
breakfast, the time when the members of the family sat down to learn
their immediate destinies: the father, a sophisticated *rentier;*[1] the
mother, a jolly woman with a passion for Romantic chamber music;
and the two children, aged eleven and nine. All of them were religious
and therefore susceptible to archaic superstitions, and they were delighted to welcome Frau Frida into their home, on the sole condition
that every day she revealed the family's destiny through her dreams.

She did well, especially during the war years that followed, when reality was more sinister than any nightmare. At the breakfast table every
morning, she alone decided what each member of the family was to do
that day, and how it was to be done, until eventually her prognostica-
tions became the house's sole voice of authority. Her domination of the
family was absolute: Even the slightest sigh was made on her orders.

---

[1]Someone of independent means. — ED.

The father had died just prior to my stay in Vienna, and he had had the good grace to leave Frau Frida a part of his fortune, again on the condition that she continued dreaming for the family until she was unable to dream any more.

I spent a month in Vienna, living the frugal life of a student while 10 waiting for money which never arrived. The unexpected and generous visits that Frau Frida paid to our tavern were like fiestas in our otherwise penurious regime. One night, the powerful smell of beer about us, she whispered something in my ear with such conviction that I found it impossible to ignore.

"I came here specially to tell you that last night I saw you in my dreams," she said. "You must leave Vienna at once and not come back here for at least five years."

Such was her conviction that I was put, that same night, on the last train for Rome. I was so shaken that I have since come to believe that I survived a disaster I never encountered. To this day I have not set foot in Vienna again.

Before the incident in Havana I met up with Frau Frida once more, in Barcelona, in an encounter so unexpected that it seemed to me especially mysterious. It was the day that Pablo Neruda set foot on Spanish soil for the first time since the [Spanish] Civil War, during a stopover on a long sea journey to Valparaiso in Chile.[2] He spent the morning with us, big game hunting in the antiquarian bookshops, buying eventually a faded book with torn covers for which he paid what must have been the equivalent of two months' salary for the Chilean consulate in Rangoon. He lumbered along like a rheumatic elephant, showing a childlike interest in the internal workings of every object he came across. The world always appeared to him as a giant clockwork toy.

I have never known anyone who approximated so closely the received idea of a Renaissance Pope — that mixture of gluttony and refinement — who even against his will, would dominate and preside over any table. Matilde, his wife, wrapped him in a bib which looked more like an apron from a barbershop than a napkin from a restaurant, but it was the only way to prevent him from being bathed in sauces. That day Neruda ate three lobsters in their entirety, dismembering them with the precision of a surgeon, while concurrently devouring everyone else's dishes with his eyes, until he was unable to resist picking from each plate, with a relish and an appetite that everyone found contagious: clams from Galicia, barnacle geese from

---

[2]See page 509. Neruda was living in Spain when the war broke out, after working at the Chilean consulate in Rangoon, Burma; later he frequently returned to Spain. — ED.

Cantabria, prawns from Alicante, swordfish from the Costa Brava. All the while he was talking, just like the French, about other culinary delights, especially the prehistoric shellfish of Chile that were his heart's favorite. And then suddenly he stopped eating, pricked up his ears like the antennae of a lobster, and whispered to me: "There's someone behind me who keeps staring at me."

I looked over his shoulder. It was true. Behind him, three tables   15
back, a woman, unabashed in an old-fashioned felt hat and a purple scarf, was slowly chewing her food with her eyes fixed on Neruda. I recognized her at once. She was older and bigger, but it was her, with the ring made in the form of a serpent on her first finger.

She had traveled from Naples on the same boat as the Nerudas, but they had not met on board. We asked her to join us for coffee, and I invited her to talk about her dreams, if only to entertain the poet. But the poet would have none of it, declaring outright that he did not believe in the divination of dreams.

"Only poetry is clairvoyant," he said.

After lunch, and the inevitable walk along the Ramblas, I deliberately fell in with Frau Frida so that we could renew our acquaintance without the others hearing. She told me that she had sold her properties in Austria and, having retired to Porto, in Portugal, was now living in a house that she described as a fake castle perched on a cliff from where she could see the whole Atlantic as far as America. It was clear, although she didn't say as much explicitly, that, from one dream to another, she had ended up in possession of the entire fortune of her once unlikely Viennese employers. Even so, I remained unimpressed, only because I had always thought that her dreams were no more than a contrivance to make ends meet. I told her as much.

She laughed her mocking laugh. "You're as shameless as ever," she said. The rest of our group had now stopped to wait for Neruda who was speaking in Chilean slang to the parrots in the bird market. When we renewed our conversation, Frau Frida had changed the subject.

"By the way," she said, "you can go back to Vienna if you like."   20

I then realized that thirteen years had passed since we first met.

"Even if your dreams aren't true, I will never return," I told her, "just in case."

At three o'clock we parted in order to accompany Neruda to his sacred siesta, which he took at our house, following a number of solemn preparatory rituals that, for some reason, reminded me of the Japanese tea ceremony. Windows had to be opened, others closed — an exact temperature was essential — and only a certain kind of light from only a certain direction could be tolerated. And then: an absolute silence.

Neruda fell asleep at once, waking ten minutes later, like children do, when we expected it least. He appeared in the living room, refreshed, the monogram of the pillow case impressed on his check.

"I dreamt of that woman who dreams," he said.

Matilde asked him to tell us about the dream.   25

"I dreamt she was dreaming of me," he said.

"That sounds like Borges," I said.

He looked at me, crestfallen. "Has he already written it?"

"If he hasn't, he's bound to write it one day," I said. "It'll be one of his labyrinths."

As soon as Neruda was back on board ship at six that afternoon, he   30
said his farewells to us, went to sit at an out-of-the-way table, and began writing verses with the same pen of green ink that he had been using to draw flowers, fish, and birds in the dedications he signed in his own books. With the first announcement to disembark, we sought out Frau Frida and found her finally on the tourist deck just as we were about to give up. She, too, had just woken from a siesta.

"I dreamt of your poet," she told us.

Astonished, I asked her to tell me about the dream.

"I dreamt he was dreaming about me," she said, and my look of disbelief confused her. "What do you expect? Sometimes among all the dreams there has to be one that bears no relation to real life."

I never saw or thought about her again until I heard about the ring made in the form of a serpent on the finger of the woman who died in the sea disaster at the Hotel Riviera. I could not resist asking the Portuguese ambassador about it when we met up a few months later at a diplomatic reception.

The ambassador spoke of her with enthusiasm and tremendous ad-   35
miration. "You can't imagine how extraordinary she was," he said. "You would have been unable to resist wanting to write a story about her." And he continued in the same spirit, on and on, with some occasional, surprising details, but without an end in sight.

"Tell me then," I said finally, interrupting him, "what exactly did she do?"

"Nothing," he replied, with a shrug of resignation. "She was a dreamer."

EXPLORATIONS

1. In what ways does Gabriel García Márquez express skepticism of Frau Frida's dreams? In what ways does he express credulity? How does the poet Pablo Neruda react to her, and why?

2. In what ways do the structure, content, and style of "Dreams for Hire" make it seem more like a short story than an essay? What aspects of the piece remind us that it is a factual account?

3. In what ways is the last sentence of "Dreams for Hire" ambiguous? How would the narrative's impact change if the Portuguese ambassador explicitly answered the questions García Márquez has raised?

CONNECTIONS

1. Es'kia Mphahlele writes: "You belong not only to an African community but also to a worldwide intellectual or worldwide economic community, or both. This is why communication becomes difficult, sometimes impossible between your people who are still not tuned into Western intellectual systems and yourself" (p. 565). How does Frau Frida link people from different communities in "Dreams for Hire"? How does she serve as a dividing line or litmus test?

2. What are the similarities between Frau Frida's line of work and David Abram's in "Making Magic" (p. 513)? How do Frau Frida and Abram differ in their attitudes toward their work? What attitudes do they share, and why?

3. What similar reactions to dream revelations are expressed by García Márquez and by Joyce Carol Oates (p. 504)? Which writer places more importance on explaining — finding rational reasons for — the seeming power of dreams? What are some likely reasons for that contrast?

ELABORATIONS

1. To analyze the art of Gabriel García Márquez is a task beyond the most ambitious critic; but we can learn a lot about writing by studying his craft. For instance, how does he use the literary device of a quest to create purpose, momentum, and suspense in this essay? Whose quest is it, and what is its object? What incidents begin and end it? What adventures along the way maintain our curiosity? Write an essay analyzing García Márquez's use of a quest as his central thread in "Dreams for Hire."

2. Have your dreams ever come true? Have you learned anything from dreams about yourself or your relationships with other people? What are your beliefs about the nature and purposes of dreams? Write an essay defining or classifying dreams or narrating an experience involving a powerful dream.

ISABEL ALLENDE

Clarisa

Isabel Allende (pronounced ah-*yen*-day) was born in 1942 in Lima, Peru, where her father was stationed as a diplomat. The family traveled extensively: Allende discovered *The Thousand and One Nights* at age twelve in Beirut, Lebanon. Back home in Chile, she completed high school in the capital city of Santiago and got a job with the Food and Agriculture Organization (FAO) of the United Nations. Allende became a journalist when she had to fill television time for the FAO. She won a fellowship to study radio and television in Belgium; in Chile she continued to work in television and wrote plays and a magazine column. In 1970 her uncle, Dr. Salvador Allende Gossens, became president — the first Marxist-Leninist freely elected by a non-Communist country. Three years later he was ousted and killed in a U.S.-backed military coup led by Augusto Pinochet Ugarte, who ran a brutally repressive right-wing dictatorship until 1990. Isabel Allende and her family fled to Venezuela, where she switched from journalism to fiction. "To lose Chile and all of my past because of the military coup and being forced into exile pushed me to write *The House of the Spirits* [1985; *La casa de los espiritus*, 1982]. The loss of political innocence, when I became aware of the disappeared, the tortured, the dead, the brutal repression throughout Latin America, impelled me to write *Of Love and Shadows* [1987; *De amor y de sombra*, 1984]. *The Infinite Plan* [1993; *El Plan Infinito*] was inspired by the love of my present husband." So Allende told an interviewer for Barcelona's "La Vanguardia" in 1994 at her home in California. Her latest book, *Paula*, began as a letter to her daughter who was in a coma from a rare (and ultimately fatal) illness. "Clarisa," translated by Margaret Sayers Peden, comes from *The Stories of Eva Luna* (1991; *Cuentos de Eva Luna*, 1989), a book of tales supposedly spun Scheherezade-fashion by the heroine of Allende's novel *Eva Luna* (1987, 1988).

Chile is a long strip of seacoast that runs along western South America from Peru and Bolivia to the continent's southern tip. The Andes Mountains divide it on the east from Argentina. Spain took northern Chile from the native Incas in the mid-1500s; the southern Araucanian Indians held out for another three centuries. Chile won its independence in the early 1800s under José de San Martín and Bernardo O'Higgins, who became its first dictator. A constitution adopted in 1925 brought democracy, which lasted until the overthrow of President Allende. Under a new constitution in 1980, dictator Pinochet became president for an eight-year term. At its end he was forced to hold a plebiscite which rejected his bid to stay in power. In January 1990, Pinochet finally stepped down. His elected successors have sought to balance the need to investigate and punish past brutalities with the need for national reconciliation, as well as to continue strengthening Chile's economy.

Clarisa was born before the city had electricity, she lived to see the television coverage of the first astronaut levitating on the moon, and she died of amazement when the Pope came for a visit and was met in the streets by homosexuals dressed up as nuns. She had spent her childhood among pots of ferns and corridors lighted by oil lamps. Days went by slowly in those times. Clarisa never adjusted to the fits and starts of today's time; she always seemed to have been captured in the sepia tints of a nineteenth-century portrait. I suppose that once she had had a virginal waist, a graceful bearing, and a profile worthy of a medallion, but by the time I met her she was already a rather bizarre old woman with shoulders rounded into two gentle humps and with white hair coiled around a sebaceous cyst the size of a pigeon egg crowning her noble head. She had a profound, shrewd gaze that could penetrate the most hidden evil and return unscathed. Over the course of a long lifetime she had come to be considered a saint, and after she died many people placed her photograph on the family altar along with other venerable images to ask her aid in minor difficulties, even though her reputation for being a miracle worker is not recognized by the Vatican and undoubtedly never will be. Her miraculous works are unpredictable: She does not heal the blind, like Santa Lucia, or find husbands for spinsters, like St. Anthony, but they say she helps a person through a hangover, or problems with the draft, or a siege of loneliness. Her wonders are humble and improbable, but as necessary as the spectacular marvels worked by cathedral saints.

I met Clarisa when I was an adolescent working as a servant in the house of La Señora, a lady of the night, as Clarisa called women of her occupation. Even then she was distilled almost to pure spirit; I thought at any minute she might rise from the floor and fly out the window. She had the hands of a healer, and people who could not pay a doctor, or were disillusioned with traditional science, waited in line for her to relieve their pain or console them in their bad fortune. My *patrona* used to call her to come lay her hands on her back. In the process, Clarisa would rummage about in La Señora's soul with the hope of turning her life around and leading her along the paths of righteousness — paths my employer was in no hurry to travel, since that direction would have unalterably affected her commercial enterprise. Clarisa would apply the curative warmth of the palms of her hands for ten or fifteen minutes, depending on the intensity of the pain, and then accept a glass of fruit juice as payment for her services. Sitting face to face in the kitchen, the two women would have their chat about human and divine topics, my *patrona* more on the human side and Clarisa more on the divine, never straining tolerance nor abusing good manners. Later, when I found a different job, I lost sight of Clarisa until we met once again some twenty years later and reestablished a friendship that has lasted to this day, overcoming the many obstacles that lay in our way, including death, which has put a slight crimp in the ease of our communications.

Even in the times when age had slowed her former missionary zeal, Clarisa persevered steadfastly in her good works, sometimes even against the will of the beneficiaries — as in the case of the pimps on Calle República, who had to bear the mortification of the public harangues that good lady delivered in her unwavering determination to redeem them. Clarisa gave everything she owned to the needy. As a rule she had only the clothes on her back, and toward the end of her life it was difficult to find a person any poorer than she. Charity had become a two-way street, and you seldom could tell who was giving and who was receiving.

She lived in an old rundown three-story house; some rooms were empty but some she rented as a storehouse for a saloon, so that the rancid stench of cheap liquor always hung in the air. She had never moved from the dwelling she had inherited from her parents because it reminded her of an aristocratic past, and also because for more than forty years her husband had buried himself alive in a room at the back of the patio. He had been a judge in a remote province, an office he had carried out with dignity until the birth of his second child, when disillusion robbed him of the will to accept his fate, and like a mole he had taken refuge in the malodorous cave of his room. He emerged only rarely, a scurrying shadow, and opened the door only to hand out his chamber pot and collect the food his wife left for him every day. He communicated with her by means of notes written in his perfect calligraphy and by knocks on the door — two for yes and three for no. Through the walls of his room you could hear asthmatic hacking and an occasional longshoreman's curse intended for whom, no one never knew.

"Poor man, I pray that God will soon call him to His side, and he will take his place in the heavenly choir," Clarisa would sigh without a   5 suspicion of irony. The opportune passing of her husband, however, was one grace Divine Providence never granted, for he has survived to the present day. He must be a hundred by now, unless he has already died and the coughs and the curses we hear are only echoes from the past.

Clarisa married him because he was the first person to ask her, and also because her parents thought that a judge would be the best possible match. She left the sober comfort of her paternal hearth and reconciled herself to the avarice and vulgarity of her husband with no thought of a better fate. The only time she was ever heard to utter a nostalgic comment about the refinements of her past was in regard to a grand piano that had enchanted her as a little girl. That is how we learned of her love for music and much later, when she was an old woman, a group of us who were her friends gave her a modest piano. It had been sixty years since she had been anywhere near a keyboard, but she sat down on the piano stool and played, by memory and without hesitation, a Chopin nocturne.

A year or so after the marriage to the judge, she gave birth to an albino daughter, who as soon as she began to walk accompanied her mother to church. The tiny creature was so dazzled by the pageantry of the liturgy that she began pulling down drapes to "play bishop," and soon the only game that interested her was imitating the ecclesiastical ritual, chanting in a Latin of her own invention. She was hopelessly retarded; her only words were spoken in an unknown tongue, she drooled incessantly, and she suffered uncontrollable attacks during which she had to be tied like a circus animal to prevent her from chewing the furniture and attacking guests. With puberty, however, she grew more tractable, and helped her mother around the house. The second child was born into the world totally devoid of curiosity and bearing gentle Asian features; the only skill he ever mastered was riding a bicycle, but it was of little benefit to him since his mother never dared let him out of the house. He spent his life pedaling in the patio on a stationary bicycle mounted on a music stand.

Her children's abnormality never affected Clarisa's unalterable optimism. She considered them pure souls immune to evil, and all her relations with them were marked by affection. Her greatest concern was to save them from earthly suffering, and she often asked herself who would look after them when she was gone. The father, in contrast, never spoke of them, and used the pretext of his retarded children to wallow in shame, abandon his career, his friends, even fresh air, and entomb himself in his room, copying newspapers with monklike patience in a series of stenographic notebooks. Meanwhile, his wife spent the last

cent of her dowry, and her inheritance, and took on all kinds of jobs to
support the family. In her own poverty, she never turned her back to the
poverty of others, and even in the most difficult periods of her life she
continued her works of mercy.

Clarisa had a boundless understanding of human weaknesses. One
night when she was sitting in her room sewing, her white head bent
over her work, she heard unusual noises in the house. She got up to see
what they might be, but got no farther than the doorway, where she ran
into a man who held a knife to her throat and threatened, "Quiet, you
whore, or I'll slash your throat."

"This isn't the place you want, son. The ladies of the night are across   10
the street, there where you hear the music."

"Don't try to be funny, this is a robbery."

"What did you say?" Clarisa smiled, incredulous. "And what are you
going to steal from me?"

"Sit down in that chair. I'm going to tie you up."

"I won't do it, son. I'm old enough to be your mother. Where's your
respect?"

"Sit *down,* I said!"   15

"And don't shout, you'll frighten my husband, and he's not at all
well. By the way, put that knife down, you might hurt someone," said
Clarisa.

"Listen, lady, I came here to rob you," the flustered robber muttered.

"Well, there's not going to be any robbery. I will not let you commit
a sin. I'll *give* you some money of my own will. You won't be taking it
from me, is that clear? I'm giving it to you." She went to her purse and
took out all the money for the rest of the week. "That's all I have. We're
quite poor, as you see. Come into the kitchen, now, and I'll set the
kettle to boil."

The man put away his knife and followed her, money in hand. Clarisa brewed tea for both of them, served the last cookies in the house,
and invited him to sit with her in the living room.

"Wherever did you get the notion to rob a poor old woman like me?"   20

The thief told her he had been watching her for days; he knew that
she lived alone and thought there must be something of value in that big
old house. It was his first crime, he said; he had four children, he was out
of a job, and he could not go home another night with empty hands.
Clarisa pointed out that he was taking too great a risk, that he might not
only be arrested but was putting his immortal soul in danger — although
in truth she doubted that God would punish him with hell, the worst
might be a while in purgatory, as long, of course, as he repented and
did not do it again. She offered to add him to her list of wards and

promised she would not bring charges against him. As they said goodbye, they kissed each other on the cheek. For the next ten years, until
Clarisa died, she received a small gift at Christmastime through the
mail.

Not all Clarisa's dealings were with the indigent; she also knew
people of note, women of breeding, wealthy businessmen, bankers, and
public figures, whom she visited seeking aid for the needy, with never a
thought for how she might be received. One day she presented herself
in the office of Congressman Diego Cienfuegos, known for his incendiary speeches and for being one of the few incorruptible politicians in
the nation, which did not prevent his rising to the rank of Minister and
earning a place in history books as the intellectual father of an important peace treaty. In those days Clarisa was still young, and rather timid,
but she already had the unflagging determination that characterized
her old age. She went to the Congressman to ask him to use his influence to procure a new modern refrigerator for the Teresian Sisters. The
man stared at her in amazement, questioning why he should aid his
ideological enemies.

"Because in their dining room the Little Sisters feed a hundred children a day a free meal, and almost all of them are children of the Communists and evangelicals who vote for you," Clarisa replied mildly.

That was the beginning of a discreet friendship that was to cost the
politician many sleepless nights and many donations. With the same ir-
refutable logic, Clarisa obtained scholarships for young atheists from
the Jesuits, used clothing for neighborhood prostitutes from the League
of Catholic Dames, musical instruments for a Hebrew choir from the
German Institute, and funds for alcohol rehabilitation programs from
viniculturists.

Neither the husband interred in the mausoleum of his room nor the   25
debilitating hours of her daily labors prevented Clarisa's becoming
pregnant again. The midwife advised her that in all probability she
would give birth to another abnormal child, but Clarisa mollified her
with the argument that God maintains a certain equilibrium in the universe, and just as He creates some things twisted, He creates others
straight; for every virtue there is a sin, for every joy an affliction, for
every evil a good, and on and on, for as the wheel of life turns through
the centuries, everything evens out. The pendulum swings back and
forth with inexorable precision, she said.

Clarisa passed her pregnancy in leisure, and in the proper time gave
birth to her third child. The baby was born at home with the help of the
midwife and in the agreeable company of the two inoffensive and smiling retarded children who passed the hours at their games, one spout-

ing gibberish in her bishop's robe and the other pedaling nowhere on his stationary bicycle. With this birth the scales tipped in the direction needed to preserve the harmony of Creation, and a grateful mother offered her breast to a strong boy with wise eyes and firm hands. Fourteen months later Clarisa gave birth to a second son with the same characteristics.

"These two boys will grow up healthy and help me take care of their brother and sister," she said with conviction, faithful to her theory of compensation; and that is how it was, the younger children grew straight as reeds and were gifted with kindness and goodness.

Somehow Clarisa managed to support the four children without any help from her husband and without injuring her family pride by accepting charity for herself. Few were aware of her financial straits. With the same tenacity with which she spent late nights sewing rag dolls and baking wedding cakes to sell, she battled the deterioration of her house when the walls began to sweat a greenish mist. She instilled in the two younger children her principles of good humor and generosity with such splendid results that in the following years they were always beside her caring for their older siblings, until the day the retarded brother and sister accidentally locked themselves in the bathroom and a leaking gas pipe transported them gently to a better world.

When the Pope made his visit, Clarisa was not quite eighty, although it was difficult to calculate her exact age; she had added years out of vanity, simply to hear people say how well preserved she was for the ninety-five years she claimed. She had more than enough spirit, but her body was failing; she could barely totter through the streets, where in any case she lost her way, she had no appetite, and finally was eating only flowers and honey. Her spirit was detaching itself from her body at the same pace her wings germinated, but the preparations for the papal visit rekindled her enthusiasm for the adventures of this earth. She was not content to watch the spectacle on television because she had a deep distrust of that apparatus. She was convinced that even the astronaut on the moon was a sham filmed in some Hollywood studio, the same kind of lies they practiced in those stories where the protagonists love or die and then a week later reappear with the same faces but a new destiny. Clarisa wanted to see the pontiff with her own eyes, not on a screen where some actor was costumed in the Pope's robes. That was how I found myself accompanying her to cheer the Pope as he rode through the streets. After a couple of hours fighting the throngs of faithful and vendors of candles and T-shirts and religious prints and plastic saints, we caught sight of the Holy Father, magnificent in his portable glass cage, a white porpoise in an aquarium. Clarisa fell to her knees, in danger of being crushed by fanatics and the Pope's police escort. Just at the instant when the Pope was but a stone's throw away, a rare spectacle surged from a side street: a group of men in nun's habits, their faces garishly painted, waving posters in favor of abortion, divorce, sodomy, and the right of women to the priesthood. Clarisa dug through her purse with a trembling hand, found her eyeglasses, and set them on her nose to assure herself she was not suffering a hallucination.

She paled. "It's time to go, daughter. I've already seen too much."   30

She was so undone that to distract her I offered to buy her a hair from the Pope's head, but she did not want it without a guarantee of authenticity. According to a socialist newspaperman, there were enough capillary relics offered for sale to stuff a couple of pillows.

"I'm an old woman, and I no longer understand the world, daughter. We'd best go home."

She was exhausted when she reached the house, with the din of the bells and cheering still ringing in her temples. I went to the kitchen to prepare some soup for the judge and heat water to brew her a cup of chamomile tea, in hopes it would have a calming effect. As I waited for the tea, Clarisa, with a melancholy face, put everything in order and served her last plate of food to her husband. She set the tray on the floor and for the first time in forty years knocked on his door.

"How many times have I told you not to bother me," the judge protested in a reedy voice.

"I'm sorry, dear, I just wanted to tell you that I'm going to die."   35
"When?"
"On Friday."
"Very well." The door did not open.

Clarisa called her sons to tell them about her imminent death, and then took to her bed. Her bedroom was a large dark room with pieces of heavy carved mahogany furniture that would never become antiques because somewhere along the way they had broken down. On her dresser sat a crystal urn containing an astoundingly realistic wax Baby Jesus, rosy as an infant fresh from its bath.

"I'd like for you to have the Baby, Eva. I know you'll take care of Him."   40
"You're not going to die. Don't frighten me this way."

"You need to keep Him in the shade, if the sun strikes Him, He'll melt. He's lasted almost a century, and will last another if you protect Him from the heat."

I combed her meringue hair high on her head, tied it with a ribbon, and then sat down to accompany her through this crisis, not knowing exactly what it was. The moment was totally free of sentimentality, as if in fact she was not dying but suffering from a slight cold.

"We should call a priest now, don't you think, child?"

"But Clarisa, what sins can you have?" 45

"Life is long, and there's more than enough time for evil, God willing."

"But you'll go straight to heaven — that is, if heaven exists."

"Of course it exists, but it's not certain they'll let me in. They're very strict there," she murmured. And after a long pause, she added, "When I think over my trespasses, there was one that was very grave . . ."

I shivered, terrified that this old woman with the aureole of a saint was going to tell me that she had intentionally dispatched her retarded children to facilitate divine justice, or that she did not believe in God and had devoted herself to doing good in this world only because the scales had assigned her the role of compensating for the evil of others, an evil that was unimportant anyway since everything is part of the same infinite process. But Clarisa confessed nothing so dramatic to me. She turned toward the window and told me, blushing, that she had not fulfilled her conjugal duties.

"What does that mean?" I asked. 50

"Well, I mean I did not satisfy my husband's carnal desires, you understand?"

"No."

"If you refuse your husband your body, and he falls into the temptation of seeking solace with another woman, you bear that moral responsibility."

"I see. The judge fornicates, and the sin is yours."

"No, no. I think it would be both our sins. . . . I would have to look it 55 up."

"And the husband has the same obligation to his wife?"

"What?"

"I mean, if you had had another man, would your husband share the blame?"

"Wherever did you get an idea like that, child!" She stared at me in disbelief.

"Don't worry, because if your worst sin was that you slighted the 60 judge, I'm sure God will see the joke."

"I don't think God is very amused by such things."

"But Clarisa, to doubt divine perfection *would* be a great sin."

She seemed in such good health that I could not imagine her dying, but I supposed that, unlike us simple mortals, saints have the power to die unafraid and in full control of their faculties. Her reputation was so solid that many claimed to have seen a circle of light around her head and to have heard celestial music in her presence, and so I was not

surprised when I undressed her to put on her nightgown to find two in-
flamed bumps on her shoulders, as if her pair of great angel wings were
about to erupt.

The rumor of Clarisa's coming death spread rapidly. Her children
and I had to marshal an unending line of people who came to seek her
intervention in heaven for various favors, or simply to say goodbye.
Many expected that at the last moment a significant miracle would
occur, such as, the odor of rancid bottles that pervaded the house would
be transformed into the perfume of camelias, or beams of consolation
would shine forth from her body. Among the visitors was her friend the
robber, who had not mended his ways but instead become a true professional. He sat beside the dying woman's bed and recounted his es-
capades without a hint of repentance.

"Things are going really well. I rob only upper-class homes now. I   65
steal from the rich, and that's no sin. I've never had to use violence, and
I work clean, like a true gentleman," he boasted.

"I will have to pray a long time for you, my son."

"Pray on, Grandmother. It won't do me any harm."

La Señora came, too, distressed to be saying goodbye to her beloved
friend, and bringing a flower crown and almond-paste sweets as her
contribution to the death vigil. My former patrona did not know me,
but I had no trouble recognizing her despite her girth, her wig, and the
outrageous plastic shoes printed with gold stars. To offset the thief, she
came to tell Clarisa that her advice had fallen upon fertile ground, and
that she was now a respectable Christian.

"Tell Saint Peter that, so he'll take my name from his black book,"
was her plea.

"What a terrible disappointment for all these good people if instead   70
of going to heaven I end up in the cauldrons of hell," Clarisa said after I
was finally able to close the door and let her rest for a while.

"If that happens, no one down here is going to know, Clarisa."

"Thank heavens for that!"

From early dawn on Friday a crowd gathered outside in the street, and
only her two sons' vigilance prevented the faithful from carrying off relics,
from strips of paper off the walls to articles of the saint's meager wardrobe.
Clarisa was failing before our eyes and, for the first time, she showed signs
of taking her own death seriously. About ten that morning, a blue automobile with Congressional plates stopped before the house. The chauffeur
helped an old man climb from the back seat; the crowds recognized him
immediately. It was *don* Diego Cienfuegos, whom decades of public service had made a national hero. Clarisa's sons came out to greet him, and
accompanied him in his laborious ascent to the second floor. When Clar-

isa saw him in the doorway, she became quite animated; the color returned to her cheeks and the shine to her eyes.

"Please, clear everyone out of the room and leave us alone," she whispered in my ear.

Twenty minutes later the door opened and *don* Diego Cienfuegos departed, feet dragging, eyes teary, bowed and crippled, but smiling. Clarisa's sons, who were waiting in the hall, again took his arms to steady him, and seeing them there together I confirmed something that had crossed my mind before. The three men had the same bearing, the same profile, the same deliberate assurance, the same wise eyes and firm hands.

I waited until they were downstairs, and went back to my friend's room. As I arranged her pillows, I saw that she, like her visitor, was weeping with a certain rejoicing.

"*Don* Diego was your grave sin, wasn't he?" I murmured.

"That wasn't a sin, child, just a little boost to help God balance out the scales of destiny. You see how well it worked out, because my two weak children had two strong brothers to look after them."

Clarisa died that night, without suffering. Cancer, the doctor diagnosed, when he saw the buds of her wings; saintliness, proclaimed the throngs bearing candles and flowers; astonishment, say I, because I was with her when the Pope came to visit.

EXPLORATIONS

1. A skilled writer sets out to work immediately creating a story's world. How does the first paragraph of "Clarisa" transport us into the world where the story takes place? How does that world differ from ours? What facts in Clarisa's world (as Isabel Allende develops it throughout her story) are superstitions in ours? What facts in our world are superstitions in Clarisa's?

2. In paragraph 2 the narrator says that her friendship with Clarisa "has lasted to this day, overcoming the many obstacles that lay in our way, including death, which has put a slight crimp in the ease of our communications." What other statements by the narrator over the course of "Clarisa" refer to improbabilities as realities? How do these statements affect the story's impact?

3. When Clarisa is pregnant with her third child, what is her stated reason for believing the baby will be normal? What is her unstated reason? Why is it appropriate that her husband sired the children he did, "one spouting gibberish in her bishop's robe and the other pedaling nowhere on his stationary bicycle" (para. 26)?

CONNECTIONS

1. Gabriel García Márquez writes of the Viennese family who first employed Frau Frida in "Dreams for Hire" (p. 567): "All of them were religious and therefore susceptible to archaic superstitions" (para. 8). What evidence of this connection between religion and superstition appears in "Clarisa"? What evidence in each of these two selections indicates the writer's attitude toward religious and superstitious beliefs?

2. In *Beloved* (p. 544), what evidence indicates whether we as readers are meant to believe in the ghost in Sethe's house? Aside from location and other external trappings, how is the world of *Beloved* similar to and different from that of "Clarisa"? What strategies does Toni Morrison use to place us in her characters' world that are similar to Allende's strategies?

3. Compare Martin Luther King Jr.'s observations on page 505 with Clarisa's argument in paragraph 25. What ideas appear in both selections? How do these two commentators apparently differ in their attitudes toward evil?

ELABORATIONS

1. Isabel Allende, like Gabriel García Márquez, writes in the tradition called magic realism, treating phenomena such as ghosts and miracles as matter-of-factly as any other events. Find out more about magic realism, particularly in Latin American literature. Write an essay defining the term and showing how Allende's story "Clarisa" and García Márquez's essay "Dreams for Hire" exemplify it.

2. Reread Allende's description of the Pope's visit in paragraph 29. What improbable details does she treat realistically? What real (albeit fictional) details does she distort so that they seem bizarre and unreal? What techniques does she use to accomplish these reversals? Describe some event you have attended or experienced, using similar techniques to distort and reverse reality.

GINO DEL GUERCIO

The Secrets of Haiti's Living Dead

Gino Del Guercio is currently an independent filmmaker specializing in science, medicine, and technology. Born in New York City in 1958, he graduated from Brown University in 1980. For the next four years he worked for United Press International (UPI), where he was a national science writer when he wrote "The Secrets of Haiti's Living Dead." A former MACY fellow at Boston's public television station WGBH, Del Guercio left there in 1989 for Boston Science Communications, Inc. The next year he added an adjunct professorship at Boston University to his diverse occupations. He has written numerous magazine and newspaper articles for the *New York Times, Boston Globe, Washington Post,* and *Los Angeles Times,* among other publications. His documentaries have appeared on PBS, the Discovery Channel, and Arts & Entertainment, as well as won him the CINE Golden Eagle, the Director's Prize from the International Scientific Film Festival. The following article on Wade Davis's investigation of Haiti's zombies and voodoo (or vodoun) first appeared in *Harvard Magazine* in 1986. Davis was then a doctoral student at Harvard University; his book *The Serpent and the Rainbow* (1988) later became the basis for a movie by the same name. After returning to the United States, Davis became a research associate in ethnobotany at the New York Botanical Garden.

The Caribbean island of Hispaniola, like Cuba to the northwest, came to European notice after Christopher Columbus landed there in 1492. Spain and France both colonized it, and in 1697 they divided it. France's western third was Haiti; Spain's eastern two-thirds would become the Dominican Republic. Both powers brought in African slaves to work their sugar plantations as the native Arawak Indians died off. Soon slaves in Haiti vastly outnumbered landowners. In 1791, former slave Toussaint L'Ouverture led a rebellion that lasted twelve years and produced the world's first black republic as well as the first independent state in Latin America (see para. 15). Political strife continued, however. The United States responded by occupying Haiti in 1915; even after withdrawing its troops, it remained influential, supporting a 1957 coup by François "Papa Doc" Duvalier. Dictators Papa Doc and his son Jean-Claude, or "Baby Doc," demolished Haiti's economy and Haitians' civil rights with the help of voodoo and their repressive military force, the Tontons-Macoutes. In 1985, mounting protests forced Baby Doc to flee the country. Haiti vacillated between military and civilian rule until pressure from the United States and United Nations compelled the withdrawal of General Raoul Cedras and reinstated democratically elected President Jean-Bertrand Aristide. In 1996 Aristide's term expired and, as agreed, he turned over the presidency to his elected successor and close friend Rene Preval.

Five years ago, a man walked into l'Estère, a village in central Haiti, approached a peasant woman named Angelina Narcisse, and identified himself as her brother Clairvius. If he had not introduced himself using a boyhood nickname and mentioned facts that only intimate family members knew, she would not have believed him. Because, eighteen years earlier, Angelina had stood in a small cemetery north of her village and watched as her brother Clairvius was buried.

The man told Angelina he remembered that night well. He knew when he was lowered into his grave because he was fully conscious, although he could not speak or move. As the earth was thrown over his coffin, he felt as if he were floating over the grave. The scar on his right cheek, he said, was caused by a nail driven through his casket.

The night he was buried, he told Angelina, a voodoo priest raised him from the grave. He was beaten with a sisal whip and carried off to a sugar plantation in northern Haiti where, with other zombies, he was forced to work as a slave. Only with the death of the zombie master were they able to escape, and Narcisse eventually returned home.

Legend has it that zombies are the living dead, raised from their graves and animated by malevolent voodoo sorcerers, usually for some evil purpose. Most Haitians believe in zombies, and Narcisse's claim is not unique. At about the same time he reappeared, in 1980, two women turned up in other villages saying they were zombies. In the same year, in northern Haiti, the local peasants claimed to have found a group of zombies wandering aimlessly in the fields.

But Narcisse's case was different in one crucial respect; it was documented. His death had been recorded by doctors at the American-directed Schweitzer Hospital in Deschapelles. On April 30, 1962, hospital records show, Narcisse walked into the hospital's emergency room spitting up blood. He was feverish and full of aches. His doctors could not diagnose his illness, and his symptoms grew steadily worse. Three days after he entered the hospital, according to the records, he died. The attending physicians, an American among them, signed his death certificate. His body was placed in cold storage for twenty hours, and

then he was buried. He said he remembered hearing his doctors pronounce him dead while his sister wept at his bedside.

At the Centre de Psychiatrie et Neurologie in Port-au-Prince, Dr.
Lamarque Douyon, a Haitian-born, Canadian-trained psychiatrist, has
been systematically investigating all reports of zombies since 1961.
Though convinced zombies were real, he had been unable to find a
scientific explanation for the phenomenon. He did not believe zombies were people raised from the dead, but that did not make them any
less interesting. He speculated that victims were only made to *look*
dead, probably by means of a drug that dramatically slowed metabolism. The victim was buried, dug up within a few hours, and somehow
reawakened.

The Narcisse case provided Douyon with evidence strong enough to
warrant a request for assistance from colleagues in New York. Douyon
wanted to find an ethnobotanist, a traditional-medicines expert, who
could track down the zombie potion he was sure existed. Aware of the
medical potential of a drug that could dramatically lower metabolism, a
group organized by the late Dr. Nathan Kline — a New York psychiatrist and pioneer in the field of psychopharmacology — raised the funds
necessary to send someone to investigate.

The search for that someone led to the Harvard Botanical Museum,
one of the world's foremost institutes of ethnobiology. Its director,
Richard Evans Schultes, Jeffrey Professor of Biology, had spent thirteen
years in the tropics studying native medicines. Some of his best-known
work is the investigation of curare, the substance used by nomadic
people of the Amazon to poison their darts. Refined into a powerful
muscle relaxant called D-tubocurarine, it is now an essential component of the anesthesia used during almost all surgery.

Schultes would have been a natural for the Haitian investigation, but
he was too busy. He recommended an other Harvard ethnobotanist for
the assignment, Wade Davis, a twenty-eight-year-old Canadian pursuing a doctorate in biology.

Davis grew up in the tall pine forests of British Columbia and en- 10
tered Harvard in 1971, influenced by a *Life* magazine story on the student strike of 1969. Before Harvard, the only Americans he had known
were draft dodgers, who seemed very exotic. "I used to fight forest fires
with them," Davis says. "Like everybody else, I thought America was
where it was at. And I wanted to go to Harvard because of that *Life*
article. When I got there, I realized it wasn't quite what I had in mind."

Davis took a course from Schultes, and when he decided to go to
South America to study plants, he approached his professor for guid-

ance. "He was an extraordinary figure," Davis remembers. "He was a man who had done it all. He had lived alone for years in the Amazon." Schultes sent Davis to the rain forest with two letters of introduction and two pieces of advice: wear a pith helmet and try ayahuasca, a powerful hallucinogenic vine. During that expedition and others, Davis proved himself an "outstanding field man," says his mentor. Now, in early 1982, Schultes called him into his office and asked if he had plans for spring break.

"I always took to Schultes's assignments like a plant takes to water," says Davis, tall and blond, with inquisitive blue eyes. "Whatever Schultes told me to do, I did. His letters of introduction opened up a whole new world." This time the world was Haiti.

Davis knew nothing about the Caribbean island — and nothing about African traditions, which serve as Haiti's cultural basis. He certainly did not believe in zombies. "I thought it was a lark," he says now.

Davis landed in Haiti a week after his conversation with Schultes, armed with a hypothesis about how the zombie drug — if it existed — might be made. Setting out to explore, he discovered a country materially impoverished, but rich in culture and mystery. He was impressed by the cohesion of Haitian society; he found none of the crime, social disorder, and rampant drug and alcohol abuse so common in many of the other Caribbean islands. The cultural wealth and cohesion, he believes, spring from the country's turbulent history.

During the French occupation of the late eighteenth century,   15 370,000 African-born slaves were imported to Haiti between 1780 and 1790. In 1791, the black population launched one of the few successful slave revolts in history, forming secret societies and overcoming first the French plantation owners and then a detachment of troops from Napoleon's army, sent to quell the revolt. For the next 100 years Haiti was the only independent black republic in the Caribbean, populated by people who did not forget their African heritage. "You can almost argue that Haiti is more African than Africa," Davis says. "When the west coast of Africa was being disrupted by colonialism and the slave trade, Haiti was essentially left alone. The amalgam of beliefs in Haiti is unique, but it's very, very African."

Davis discovered that the vast majority of Haitian peasants practice voodoo, a sophisticated religion with African roots. Says Davis, "It was immediately obvious that the stereotypes of voodoo weren't true. Going around the countryside, I found clues to a whole complex social world." Vodounists believe that they communicate directly with, indeed are often possessed by, the many spirits who populate the everyday world. Vodoun society is a system of education, law, and medicine; it embodies a code of ethics that regulates social behavior. In rural areas, secret vodoun societies, much like those found on the west coast of Africa, are as much or more in control of everyday life as the Haitian government.

Although most outsiders dismissed the zombie phenomenon as folklore, some early investigators, convinced of its reality, tried to find a scientific explanation. The few who sought a zombie drug failed. Nathan Kline, who helped finance Davis's expedition, had searched unsuccessfully, as had Lamarque Douyon, the Haitian psychiatrist. Zora Neale Hurston, an American black woman, may have come closest. An anthropological pioneer, she went to Haiti in the Thirties, studied vodoun society, and wrote a book on the subject, *Tell My Horse*, first published in 1938. She knew about the secret societies and was convinced zombies were real, but if a powder existed, she too failed to obtain it.

Davis obtained a sample in a few weeks.

He arrived in Haiti with the names of several contacts. A BBC reporter familiar with the Narcisse case had suggested that he talk with Marcel Pierre. Pierre owned the Eagle Bar, a bordello in the city of Saint Marc. He was also a voodoo sorcerer and had supplied the BBC with a physiologically active powder of unknown ingredients. Davis found him willing to negotiate. He told Pierre he was a representative of "powerful but anonymous interests in New York," willing to pay generously for the priest's services, provided no questions were asked. Pierre agreed to be helpful for what Davis will only say was a "sizable sum." Davis spent a day watching Pierre gather the ingredients — including human bones — and grind them together with mortar and pestle. However, from his knowledge of poison, Davis knew immediately that nothing in the formula could produce the powerful effects of zombification.

Three weeks later, Davis went back to the Eagle Bar, where he found 20 Pierre sitting with three associates. Davis challenged him. He called him a charlatan. Enraged, the priest gave him a second vial, claiming that this was the real poison. Davis pretended to pour the powder into his palm and rub it into his skin. "You're a dead man," Pierre told him, and he might have been, because this powder proved to be genuine. But, as the substance had not actually touched his skin, Davis was able to maintain his bravado, and Pierre was impressed. He agreed to make the poison and show Davis how it was done.

The powder, which Davis keeps in a small vial, looks like dry black dirt. It contains parts of toads, sea worms, lizards, tarantulas, and human bones. (To obtain the last ingredient, he and Pierre unearthed a child's grave on a nocturnal trip to the cemetery.) The poison is rubbed into the victim's skin. Within hours he begins to feel nauseated and has difficulty breathing. A pins-and-needles sensation afflicts his arms and legs, then progresses to the whole body. The subject becomes paralyzed; his lips turn blue for lack of oxygen. Quickly — sometimes within six hours — his metabolism is lowered to a level almost indistinguishable from death.

As Davis discovered, making the poison is an inexact science. Ingredients varied in the five samples he eventually acquired, although the active agents were always the same. And the poison came with no guarantee. Davis speculates that sometimes instead of merely paralyzing the victim, the compound kills him. Sometimes the victim suffocates in the coffin before he can be resurrected. But clearly the potion works well enough often enough to make zombies more than a figment of Haitian imagination.

Analysis of the powder produced another surprise. "When I went down to Haiti originally," says Davis, "my hypothesis was that the formula would contain *concombre zombi*, the 'zombie's cucumber,' which is a *Datura* plant. I thought somehow *Datura* was used in putting people down." *Datura* is a powerful psychoactive plant, found in West Africa as well as other tropical areas and used there in ritual as well as criminal activities. Davis had found *Datura* growing in Haiti. Its popular name suggested the plant was used in creating zombies.

But, says Davis, "there were a lot of problems with the *Datura* hypothesis. Partly it was a question of how the drug was administered. *Datura* would cause a stupor in huge doses, but it just wouldn't produce the kind of immobility that was key. These people had to appear dead, and there aren't many drugs that will do that."

One of the ingredients Pierre included in the second formula was a   25
dried fish, a species of puffer or blowfish, common to most parts of the world. It gets its name from its ability to fill itself with water and swell to several times its normal size when threatened by predators. Many of these fish contain a powerful poison known as tetrodotoxin. One of the most powerful nonprotein poisons known to man, tetrodotoxin turned up in every sample of zombie powder that Davis acquired.

Numerous well-documented accounts of puffer fish poisoning exist, but the most famous accounts come from the Orient, where *fugu* fish, a species of puffer, is considered a delicacy. In Japan, special chefs are licensed to prepare *fugu*. The chef removes enough poison to make the fish nonlethal, yet enough remains to create exhilarating physiological effects — tingles up and down the spine, mild prickling of the tongue and the lips, euphoria. Several dozen Japanese die each year, having bitten off more than they should have.

"When I got a hold of the formula and saw it was the *fugu* fish, that suddenly threw open the whole Japanese literature," says Davis. Case histories of *fugu* poisoning read like accounts of zombification. Victims remain conscious but unable to speak or move. A man who had "died" after eating *fugu* recovered seven days later in the morgue. Several summers ago, another Japanese poisoned by *fugu* revived after he was nailed into his coffin. "Almost all of Narcisse's symptoms correlated. Even strange things such as the fact that he said he was conscious and could hear himself pronounced dead. Stuff that I thought had to be magic, that seemed crazy. But, in fact, that is what people who get *fugu*-fish poisoning experience."

Davis was certain he had solved the mystery. But far from being the end of his investigation, identifying the poison was, in fact, the starting point. "The drug alone didn't make zombies," he explains. "Japanese victims of puffer-fish poisoning don't become zombies, they become poison victims. All the drug could do was set someone up for a whole series of psychological pressures that would be rooted in the culture. I wanted to know why zombification was going on," he says.

He sought a cultural answer, an explanation rooted in the structure and beliefs of Haitian society. Was zombification simply a random criminal activity? He thought not. He had discovered that Clairvius Narcisse and "Ti Femme," a second victim he had interviewed, were village pariahs. Ti Femme was regarded as a thief. Narcisse had abandoned his children and deprived his brother of land that was rightfully his. Equally suggestive, Narcisse claimed that his aggrieved brother had sold him to a *bokor*, a voodoo priest who dealt in black magic; he made cryptic reference to having been tried and found guilty by the "masters of the land."

Gathering poisons from various parts of the country, Davis had come 30 into direct contact with the vodoun secret societies. Returning to the anthropological literature on Haiti and pursuing his contacts with informants, Davis came to understand the social matrix within which zombies were created.

Davis's investigations uncovered the importance of the secret societies. These groups trace their origins to the bands of escaped slaves that organized the revolt against the French in the late eighteenth century. Open to both men and women, the societies control specific territories of the country. Their meetings take place at night, and in many rural parts of Haiti the drums and wild celebrations that characterize the gatherings can be heard for miles.

Davis believes that secret societies are responsible for policing their communities, and the threat of zombification is one way they maintain order. Says Davis, "Zombification has a material basis, but it also has a societal logic." To the uninitiated, the practice may appear a random criminal activity, but in rural vodoun society, it is exactly the opposite — a sanction imposed by recognized authorities, a form of capital punishment. For rural Haitians, zombification is an even more severe punishment than death, because it deprives the subject of his most valued possessions: his free will and independence.

The vodounists believe that when a person dies, his spirit splits into several different parts. If a priest is powerful enough, the spiritual aspect that controls a person's character and individuality, known as *ti bon ange*, the "good little angel," can be captured and the corporeal aspect, deprived of its will, held as a slave.

From studying the medical literature on tetrodotoxin poisoning, Davis discovered that if a victim survives the first few hours of the poisoning, he is likely to recover fully from the ordeal. The subject simply revives spontaneously. But zombies remain without will, in a trance-like state, a condition vodounists attribute to the power of the priest. Davis thinks it possible that the psychological trauma of zombification may be augmented by *Datura* or some other drug; he thinks zombies may be fed a *Datura* paste that accentuates their disorientation. Still, he puts the material basis of zombification in perspective: "Tetrodotoxin and *Datura* are only templates on which cultural forces and beliefs may be amplified a thousand times."

Davis has not been able to discover how prevalent zombification is in   35
Haiti. "How many zombies there are is not the question," he says. He compares it to capital punishment in the United States: "It doesn't really matter how many people are electrocuted, as long as it's a possibility." As a sanction in Haiti, the fear is not of zombies, it's of becoming one.

Davis attributes his success in solving the zombie mystery to his approach. He went to Haiti with an open mind and immersed himself in the culture. "My intuition unhindered by biases served me well," he says. "I didn't make any judgments." He combined this attitude with what he had learned earlier from his experiences in the Amazon. "Schultes's lesson is to go and live with the Indians as an Indian." Davis was able to participate in the vodoun society to a surprising degree, eventually even penetrating one of the Bizango societies and dancing in their nocturnal rituals. His appreciation of Haitian culture is apparent. "Everybody asks me how did a white person get this information? To ask the question means you don't understand Haitians — they don't judge you by the color of your skin."

As a result of the exotic nature of his discoveries, Davis has gained a certain notoriety. . . . He has already finished writing a popular account of his adventures . . . called *The Serpent and the Rainbow,* after the serpent that vodounists believe created the earth and the rainbow spirit it married. Film rights have already been optioned; in October Davis went back to Haiti with a screenwriter. But Davis takes the notoriety in stride. "All this attention is funny," he says. "For years, not just me, but all Schultes's students have had extraordinary adventures in the line of work. The adventure is not the end point, it's just along the way of getting the data. At the Botanical Museum, Schultes created a world unto itself. We didn't think we were doing anything above the ordinary. I still don't think we do. And you know," he adds, "the Haiti episode does not begin to compare to what others have accomplished — particularly Schultes himself."

EXPLORATIONS

1. What is the principal source of the information in "The Secrets of Haiti's Living Dead"? What kinds of evidence does Gino Del Guercio supply to convince readers of his source's credibility?

2. "Tetrodotoxin and *Datura* are only templates on which cultural forces and beliefs may be amplified a thousand times" (para. 34). What does this statement mean?

3. "Vodoun society is a system of education, law, and medicine; it embodies a code of ethics that regulates social behavior" (para. 16). Why do you think this report, and other investigations of voodoo, tend to focus on zombies and on identifying a zombie drug more than on these social aspects?

CONNECTIONS

1. In paragraphs 28–34 and elsewhere in this essay, Del Guercio alludes to the power of people's beliefs to make things happen that seem scientifically impossible. What examples appear in Isabel Allende's "Clarisa" of beliefs exerting such power (p. 575)? Does Del Guercio's description of the voodoo religion's role in maintaining social order also apply to the Roman Catholic religion in "Clarisa"? Why or why not?

2. In paragraphs 4–6 of "Making Magic" (p. 513), David Abram describes his approach to investigating magic in Asia. How are his purposes, methods, and preparation different from Wade Davis's in Haiti? How are they similar? What are the advantages and disadvantages of each man's approach?

3. "For rural Haitians, zombification is an even more severe punishment than death, because it deprives the subject of his most valued possessions: his free

will and independence" (para. 32). These Haitians, like the characters in Toni Morrison's *Beloved* (p. 544), are descended from enslaved Africans. What evidence in *Beloved* suggests that its African-American characters value free will and independence as highly as the Haitians do?

ELABORATIONS

1. After reading "The Secrets of Haiti's Living Dead," do you believe you understand how zombification works? Look up more information on the subject, including other investigators' reports, critiques of Wade Davis's work, and reviews of his books. Write a short research paper on voodoo and zombies.

2. In paragraph 15 Del Guercio summarizes the history of Africans in Haiti. Find out more about Toussaint L'Ouverture, who led the Haitian slaves' successful revolt against the French planters, and write an essay about him or the revolt or both. Or, imagine what the United States would be like if African slaves had revolted successfully against Southern plantation owners, and write a fictional essay on that topic.

SPOTLIGHT:
NIGERIA

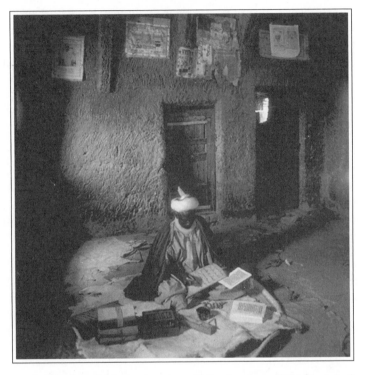

Myth, Ritual, and Magic: *A turbaned Nigerian imam (Muslim priest) reads the Koran in a temple.*

The Federal Republic of Nigeria, which lies in the large curve of Africa's western coast, is a nation of many tribes and 125 million people. Three of its more than 400 languages — Hausa, Igbo (or Ibo), and Yoruba — are used by about half the population; the official language is English. As Henry Louis Gates Jr. notes (p. 510), Nigeria has a rich artistic and literary heritage as well as rich natural resources. Its early cultures date back to at least 700 B.C., and the Yoruba people (in the southwest) had developed advanced urban social and political systems by the eleventh century. Starting in the thirteenth century, the increasingly Islamic Hausa states (in the north) became a center for the slave trade, and the main source of eunuchs (castrated men) to guard harems in other Islamic countries. Portuguese and British slavers began arriving in southern Nigeria 200 years later, followed by Christian missionaries.

In 1861 the British seized the capital port city of Lagos during an antislavery campaign and gradually extended their control over the country. Nigeria won back its independence in 1960 and is now a republic within the British Commonwealth.

The tribal tradition, however, made centralized democratic government difficult. In 1967, an Igbo region in Eastern Nigeria tried to secede as the Republic of Biafra (see p. 599). As the oil industry developed, ethnic rivalries and military power intensified. General Ibrahim Babangida, who became president in a 1985 coup, promised to return Nigeria to civilian rule in 1992. He first postponed the elections, then declared them invalid after the apparent victory of Muslim Yoruba Chief Moshood Abiola. Abiola fled to London; Britain and the United States suspended economic aid; demonstrations broke out in Lagos. Babangida resigned under pressure and new elections were scheduled. Abiola returned home to a warm welcome, which prompted Defense Minister Sani Abacha to stage a coup, proclaim himself Nigeria's new leader, and imprison Abiola along with dozens of other supporters of democracy. Several of Abacha's "hostages," as Wole Soyinka calls them, are from Soyinka's hometown of Abeokuta, including Abiola himself and Dr. Beko Ransome-Kuti, whose mother was also a political activist until soldiers threw her out of a window in 1977. "The policy of the Abacha regime is murder by installment," Soyinka bitterly told *The Guardian* in 1994. A year later, despite international protests, Abacha hanged nine Ogoni environmentalists, including the poet and novelist Ken Saro-Wiwa (see p. 510).

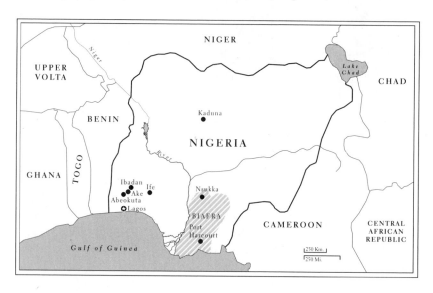

598

CHINUA ACHEBE

The Song of Ourselves

One of the foremost contemporary African writers, Albert Chinualu-mogu Achebe was born in the Igbo (or Ibo) village of Ogidi, Nigeria, in 1930. His father was a teacher for the Church Missionary Society who screened the family from the tribal beliefs and festivities around them. Achebe attended a government-run secondary school modeled on those in England, where the Igbo storytelling tradition interwove with Dickens, Swift, and Shakespeare. After studying at University College in Ibadan, he graduated from London University in 1953. He vowed to become a writer, shortened his name, and published several stories before going to work for the Nigerian Broadcasting Company as a producer and later director. In 1959 Achebe's first novel appeared: *Things Fall Apart*, which has sold over 2 million copies in forty-five languages. The book depicts an Igbo village in the late 1880s, just before Nigeria became a British colony. His next novel, *No Longer at Ease*, examines the clash between an Igbo upbringing and a Western education and lifestyle; it appeared in 1960, the year Nigeria became an independent entity within the British Commonwealth. Achebe turned to writing essays and poetry and joined the University of Nigeria, Nsukka, as a senior research fellow in 1966. The following year Eastern Nigeria, his tribal homeland, proclaimed itself the Republic of Biafra. Civil war followed, with casualties of over a million — including many Biafrans (mostly Igbos) who starved despite international relief efforts. In 1970 the secessionists capitulated. Achebe, who had been active on Biafra's side, began editing *Okike: An African Journal of New Writing* the next year. Since then he has taught at the universities of Massachusetts and Connecticut; published essays, poetry, stories, and children's literature; and won dozens of international awards and honorary degrees. His long-awaited fifth novel, *Anthills of the Savannah*, appeared in 1987. He lives in Nsukka, where he is a professor emeritus at the university and continues to accept worldwide invitations as a visiting writer and lecturer. "The Song of Ourselves" comes from a talk he gave on London television, reprinted in 1990 in *New Statesman and Society* magazine.

Just under two years ago, I was one of a dozen or so foreign guests at a writers' symposium in Dublin. The general theme chosen, I believe, by the novelist Anthony Cronin, was "Literature as celebration." Some of my colleagues appeared to have difficulty with that subject.

For my part, I found it almost perfect; it rendered in a simple form of words a truth about art which accorded with my traditional inheritance and satisfied my personal taste. A kind columnist referred to me as the man who invented African literature. I took the opportunity given me at the symposium to dissociate myself from that well-meant but blasphemous characterization. My refusal was due rather to an artistic taboo among my people the Igbo of Nigeria, a prohibition — on pain of being finished off rather quickly by the gods — from laying a proprietary hand on even the smallest item in that communal enterprise in creativity.

I offer this to you as one illustration of my pre-colonial inheritance — of art as celebration of my reality; of art in its social dimension; of the creative potential in all of us and of the need to exercise this latent energy again and again in artistic expression and communal, cooperative enterprises.

Now I come to my colonial inheritance. To call my colonial experience an inheritance may surprise some people. But everything is grist to the mill of the artist. True, one grain may differ from another in its powers of nourishment; still, we must accord appropriate recognition to every grain that comes our way.

It is not my intention to engage in a detailed evaluation of the colonial experience, but merely to ask what possibility, what encouragement there was in this episode of our history for the celebration of our own world, for the singing of the song of ourselves, in the din of an insistent world and song of others.

Colonization may indeed be a very complex affair, but one thing is certain; you do not walk in, seize the land, the person, the history of another, and then sit back and compose hymns of praise in his honor. To do that would amount to calling yourself a bandit; and you don't want to do that. So what do you do? You construct very elaborate excuses for your action. You say, for instance, that the man in question is worthless and quite unfit to manage himself or his affairs. If there are valuable things like gold or diamonds which you are carting away from this territory, you proceed to prove that he doesn't own them in the real sense of the word — that he and they just happened to be lying around the same place when you arrived. Finally, if the worse comes to the worst, you may even be prepared to question whether such as he can be, like you, fully human. From denying the presence of a man standing there before you, you end up questioning his very humanity.

In the colonial situation, *presence* was the critical question, the crucial word. Its denial was the keynote of colonialist ideology.

Question: Were there people there?

Answer: Well . . . not really, you know people of sorts, perhaps, but not as you and I understand the word.

From the period of the slave trade, through the age of colonization to the present day, the catalog of what Africa and Africans have been said not to have or not to be is a pretty extensive list. Churchmen at some point wondered about the soul itself. Did the black man have a soul? Lesser attributes such as culture and religion were debated extensively by others and generally ruled out as far as Africa was concerned. African history seemed unimaginable except perhaps for a few marginal places like Ethiopia, where Gibbon tells us of a short burst of activity followed from the seventh century by 1,000 years in which she fell into a deep sleep, "forgetful of the world by whom she was forgot," to use his own famous phrase.

A habit of generosity to Africa has not grown since Gibbon's time; on   10 the contrary, it seems to have diminished. If we shift our focus from history to literature we find the same hardening of attitude.

In *The Tempest*, Caliban is not specifically African; but he is the quintessential colonial subject created by Shakespeare's genius at the very onset of Europe's Age of Expansion. To begin with, Caliban knew not his own meaning but "wouldst gabble like a thing most brutish." However, Shakespeare restores humanity to him in many little ways, but especially by giving him not just speech but great poetry to speak before the play's end. Contrast this with Joseph Conrad's *Heart of Darkness* 300 years later. His Calibans make "a violent babble of uncouth sounds" and go on making it right through the novel.

So these African creatures have no soul, no religion, no culture, no history, no human speech, no IQ. Any wonder then that they should be subjected by those who are endowed with these human gifts?

A character in John Buchan's colonial novel *Prester John* says:

> I knew then the meaning of the white man's duty. He has to take all the risks. . . . That is the difference between white and black, the gift of responsibility, the power of being in a little way a king, and so long as we know and practice it we will rule not in Africa alone but wherever there are dark men who live only for their bellies.

John Buchan, by the way, was a very senior colonial administrator and novelist. One suspects he knew his terrain. So let us add to our long list of absences this last item — the absence of responsibility. If we add up all the absences reported from Africa, our grand total would equal one great absence of the Human Mind and Spirit.

I am not quite certain whether all the fieldworkers who reported these absences genuinely believed their report or whether it was some kind of make-believe, the kind of alibi we might expect a man arraigned for a serious crime to put together. It is significant, for example, that the moment when churchmen began to worry and doubt the existence of the black man's soul was the same moment when the black man's body was fetching high prices in the market place.

On the other hand, these reporters may well have believed their own stories — such was the complex nature of the imperial vocation. The picture of Africa and Africans which they carried in their minds did not grow there adventitiously, but was planted and watered by careful mental and educational husbandry. In an important study, Philip Curtin tells us that Europe's image of Africa which began to emerge in the 1870s was:

> found in children's books, in Sunday school tracts, in the popular press. Its major affirmations were the "common knowledge" of the educated classes. Thereafter, when new generations of explorers and administrators went to Africa, they went with a prior impression of what they would find. Most often, they found it . . .

Conrad's *Heart of Darkness*, first published in 1899, portrays Africa as a place where the wandering European may discover that the dark impulses and unspeakable appetites he has suppressed and forgotten through ages of civilization may spring into life again in answer to Africa's free and triumphant savagery. In one striking passage, Conrad reveals a very interesting aspect of the question of presence. It is the scene where a French gunboat is sitting on the water and firing rockets into the mainland. Conrad's intention, high minded as usual, is to show the futility of Europe's action in Africa:

> Pop would go one of the six-inch guns; a small flame would dart and vanish, a tiny projectile would give a feeble screech — and nothing happened. Nothing could happen. There was a touch of insanity in the proceeding.

About sanity I cannot speak. But futility, good heavens, no! By that crazy act of shelling the bush, France managed to acquire an empire in West and Equatorial Africa nine to ten times its own size. Whether there was method in the madness or not, there was profit, quite definitely.

Conrad was giving vent to one popular conceit that Europe's devastation of Africa left no mark on the victim. Africa is presumed to pursue its dark, mysterious ways and destiny untouched by explorations and expeditions. Sometimes Africa as an anthropomorphic personage steps out of the shadows and physically annihilates the invasion — which of course adds a touch of suspense and even tragedy to Europe's enterprise. One of the best images in *Heart of Darkness* is of a boat going upstream and the forest stepping across to bar its return. Note, however, that it is the African forest that takes the action: The Africans themselves are absent.

Contrast Conrad's episode of the French gunboat with the rendering of an analogous incident in *Ambiguous Adventure*, a powerful novel of colonization by the Muslim writer Cheikh Hamidou Kane, from Senegal — a country colonized by the French. Conrad insists on the futility of the bombardment but also the absence of human response to it. Cheikh Hamidou Kane, standing as it were at the explosive end of the trajectory, tells a different story. The words are those of the Most Royal Lady, a member of the Diallobe aristocracy:

> A hundred years ago our grandfather, along with all the inhabitants of
> this countryside, was awakened one morning by an uproar arising from
> the river. He took his gun and, followed by all the elite of the region, he
> flung himself upon the newcomers. His heart was intrepid and to him
> the value of liberty was greater than the value of life. Our grandfather,
> and the elite of the country with him, was defeated. Why? How? Only
> the newcomers know. We must ask them: We must go to learn from
> them the art of conquering without being in the right.

Conrad portrays a void, Hamidou Kane celebrates a human presence and a heroic struggle.

The difference is very clear. You might say *that* difference was the very reason the African writer came into being. His story had been told for him and he found the telling quite unsatisfactory. I went to a good school modeled on British public schools. I read lots of English books there; *Treasure Island* and *Gulliver's Travels* and *Prisoner of Zenda*, and *Oliver Twist* and *Tom Brown's School Days* and such books in their dozens. But I also encountered Ryder Haggard and John Buchan and the rest, and their "African" books.

I did not see myself as an African to begin with. I took sides with the white men against the savages. In other words, I went through my first level of schooling thinking I was of the party of the white man in his hair-raising adventures and narrow escapes. The white man was good and reasonable and intelligent and courageous. The savages arrayed against him were sinister and stupid or, at the most, cunning. I hated their guts.

But a time came when I reached the appropriate age and realized   20
that these writers had pulled a fast one on me! I was not on Marlowe's
boat steaming up the Congo in *Heart of Darkness*. I was one of those
strange beings jumping up and down on the river bank, making horrid
faces.

That was when I said no, and realized that stories are not innocent;
that they can be used to put you in the wrong crowd, in the party of the
man who has come to dispossess you.

And talking of dispossession, what about language itself? Does my
writing in the language of my colonizer not amount to acquiescing in
the ultimate dispossession? This is a big and complex matter I cannot
go into fully here. Let me simply say that when at the age of thirteen I
went to that school modeled after British public schools, it was not only
English literature that I encountered there. I came in contact also for
the first time in my life with many boys of my own age who did not
speak my Igbo language. And they were not foreigners, but fellow Nigerians. We lived in the same dormitories, attended the same morning assembly and classes, and gathered in the same playing fields. To be able
to do all that we had to put away our different mother tongues and communicate in the language of our colonizers. This paradox was not peculiar to Nigeria. It happened in every colony where the British put diverse people together under one administration.

Some of my colleagues, finding this too awkward, have tried to
rewrite their story into a straightforward case of oppression by presenting a happy monolingual African childhood brusquely disrupted by the
imposition of a domineering foreign language. This historical fantasy
demands that we throw out the English language in order to restore linguistic justice and self-respect to ourselves.

My position is that anyone who feels unable to write in English
should follow their desires. But they must not take liberties with our history. It is simply not true that the English forced us to learn their language. On the contrary, British colonial policy in Africa and elsewhere
emphasized again and again its preference for native languages. We see
remnants of that preference today in the Bantustan policies of South
Africa. We chose English not because the British desired it, but because
having tacitly accepted the new nationalities into which colonialism
had grouped us, we needed its language to transact our business, including the business of overthrowing colonialism itself in the fullness of
time.

Now, that does not mean that our indigenous languages should now   25
be neglected. It does mean that these languages must coexist and interact with the newcomer now and in the foreseeable future. For me, it is

not *either* English or Igbo, it is *both*. Twenty-one years ago when Christopher Okigbo, our finest poet, fell in the Biafran battlefield, I wrote for him one of the best poems I have ever written, in the Igbo language, in the form of a traditional dirge sung by his age-grade. Fifteen years ago I wrote a different kind of poem, in English, to commemorate the passing away of the Angolan poet and President, Agostinho Neto.

It is inevitable, I believe, to see the emergence of modern African literature as a return of celebration. It is tempting to say that this literature came to put people back into Africa. But that would be wrong because people never left Africa except in the guilty imagination of Africa's antagonists.

EXPLORATIONS

1. What general reasons and what specific reasons does Chinua Achebe give for endorsing the idea of "literature as celebration"?

2. According to Achebe, what myth did European colonizers create to justify their conquest of Africa? What kinds of evidence does he rely on to convince his audience (which is largely European) that it was a myth?

3. According to Achebe, what myth have some of his fellow African writers created as an argument against writing in English? What is his response? How does his view apply to Africa in general as well as to Nigeria specifically?

CONNECTIONS

1. What does Achebe see as the advantages and disadvantages of his British-style education? How do his conclusions compare with Es'kia Mphahlele's in "Tradition and the African Writer" (p. 562)? What techniques or devices does Achebe use in his essay that Mphahlele mentions as typically African?

2. What statements by Achebe in this essay match observations by Pablo Neruda on page 509? In terms of language, how was Africa's colonial experience different from Latin America's, and how has it left a different legacy?

3. Compare Achebe's recollections of his school days with Margaret Atwood's in "A View from Canada" (p. 59). How was each child influenced by English literature and history? How and why did each child's concept of his or her place in the world change?

WOLE SOYINKA

Nigerian Childhood

Playwright, poet, novelist, and critic Wole Soyinka (pronounced *woh*-leh shoy-*yin*-ka) won the 1986 Nobel Prize for literature. He was born Akinwande Oluwole Soyinka near Abeokuta, Nigeria, in 1934. Educated in Ibadan, Nigeria, and at Leeds University in England, he studied theater in London and had a number of plays produced there. Returning to Ibadan, Soyinka became co-editor of the literary journal *Black Orpheus* and was instrumental in the development of a Nigerian theater. His career was interrupted by two years in prison for allegedly supporting Biafra's secession from Nigeria (see p. 599). Soyinka has taught drama and comparative literature at the universities of Ibadan, Lagos, and Ife in Nigeria, and at Cambridge and Cornell universities. He holds the French title of Commander of the Legion of Honor, the traditional Yoruba chieftaincy title Akogun (Warlord) of Isara, and several honorary degrees; his awards include England's prestigious John Whiting Drama Prize. His plays have appeared in theaters around the world, including Ife, London, Stratford, New York, and Chicago. Soyinka chairs the editorial board of the influential international journal *Transition*. A vocal opponent of the brutal regime of General Sani Abacha (see p. 598), he fled from Nigeria to Paris in 1994 when "we learned that plans to turn me into the next high-profile hostage had reached the state of execution." His most recent books are *Art, Dialogue, and Outrage: Essays on Literature and Culture* (1994) and *The Open Sorrow of a Continent: A Personal Narrative of the Nigerian Crisis* (1996). "Nigerian Childhood" comes from his 1981 autobiography *Aké: The Years of Childhood*. It takes place about twenty years before the end of British rule. At that time Soyinka lived with his father, here called Essay, the headmaster of the Anglican Girls' School in the town of Aké; his mother, called Wild Christian; and his sister Tinu. "Bishop Ajayi Crowther" is Samuel Ajayi Crowther: Enslaved in 1821, freed and educated by the British, he became the first black African bishop of the Anglican church.

If I lay across the lawn before our house, face upwards to the sky, my head towards BishopsCourt, each spread-out leg would point to the inner compounds of Lower Parsonage. Half of the Anglican Girls' School occupied one of these lower spaces, the other half had taken over BishopsCourt. The lower area contained the school's junior class-

606

rooms, a dormitory, a small fruit garden of pawpaws, guava, some bamboo, and wild undergrowth. There were always snails to be found in the rainy season. In the other lower compound was the mission bookseller, a shriveled man with a serene wife on whose ample back we all, at one time or the other, slept or reviewed the world. His compound became a short cut to the road that led to Ibarà, Lafenwá, or Igbèin and its Grammar School over which Ransome-Kuti presided and lived with his family. The bookseller's compound contained the only well in the parsonage; in the dry season, his place was never empty. And his soil appeared to produce the only coconut trees.

BishopsCourt, of Upper Parsonage, is no more. Bishop Ajayi Crowther would sometimes emerge from the cluster of hydrangea and bougainvillea, a gnomic face with popping eyes whose formal photograph had first stared at us from the frontispiece of his life history. He had lived, the teacher said, in BishopsCourt and from that moment, he peered out from among the creeping plants whenever I passed by the house on an errand to our Great Aunt, Mrs. Lijadu. BishopsCourt had become a boarding house for the girls' school and an extra playground for us during the holidays. The Bishop sat, silently, on the bench beneath the wooden porch over the entrance, his robes twined through and through with the lengthening tendrils of the bougainvillea. I moved closer when his eyes turned to sockets. My mind wandered then to another photograph in which he wore a clerical suit with waistcoat and I wondered what he really kept at the end of the silver chain that vanished into the pocket. He grinned and said, Come nearer, I'll show you. As I moved towards the porch he drew on the chain until he had lifted out a wholly round pocket watch that gleamed of solid silver. He pressed a button and the lid opened, revealing, not the glass and the face dial but a deep cloudfilled space. Then, he winked one eye, and it fell from his face into the bowl of the watch. He snapped back the lid, nodded again and his head went bald, his teeth disappeared, and the skin pulled backward till the whitened cheekbones were exposed. Then he stood up and, tucking the watch back into the waistcoat pocket, moved a step towards me. I fled homewards.

BishopsCourt appeared sometimes to want to rival the Canon's house. It looked a houseboat despite its guard of whitewashed stones and luxuriant flowers, its wooden fretwork frontage almost wholly immersed in bougainvillea. And it was shadowed also by those omnipresent rocks from whose clefts tall, stout-boled trees miraculously grew. Clouds gathered and the rocks merged into their accustomed gray turbulence, then the trees were carried to and fro until they stayed suspended over Bishops-Court. This happened only in heavy storms. BishopsCourt, unlike the

Canon's house, did not actually border the rocks or the woods. The girls'
playing fields separated them and we knew that this buffer had always
been there. Obviously bishops were not inclined to challenge the spirits.
Only the vicars could. That Bishop Ajayi Crowther frightened me out of
that compound by his strange transformations only confirmed that the
Bishops, once they were dead, joined the world of spirits and ghosts. I
could not see the Canon decaying like that in front of my eyes, nor the
Rev. J. J. who had once occupied that house, many years before, when
my mother was still like us. J. J. Ransome-Kuti had actually ordered back
several ghommids[1] in his lifetime; my mother confirmed it. She was his
grandniece and, before she came to live at our house, she had lived in the
Rev. J. J.'s household. Her brother Sanya also lived there and he was acknowledged by all to be an *òrò*,[2] which made him at home in the woods,
even at night. On one occasion, however, he must have gone too far.

"They had visited us before," she said, "to complain. Mind you, they
wouldn't actually come into the compound, they stood far off at the
edge, where the woods ended. Their leader, the one who spoke, emitted
wild sparks from a head that seemed to be an entire ball of embers —
no, I'm mixing up two occasions — that was the second time when he
chased us home. The first time, they had merely sent an emissary. He
was quite dark, short and swarthy. He came right to the backyard and
stood there while he ordered us to call the Reverend.

"It was as if Uncle had been expecting the visit. He came out of the   5
house and asked him what he wanted. We all huddled in the kitchen,
peeping out."

"What was his voice like? Did he speak like an *egúngún?*"[3]

"I'm coming to it. This man, well, I suppose one should call him a
man. He wasn't quite human, we could see that. Much too large a
head, and he kept his eyes on the ground. So, he said he had come to
report us. They didn't mind our coming to the woods, even at night, but
we were to stay off any area beyond the rocks and that clump of bamboo
by the stream."

"Well, what did Uncle say? And you haven't said what his voice was
like."

Tinu turned her elder sister's eye on me. "Let Mama finish the
story."

"You want to know everything. All right, he spoke just like your fa-   10
ther. Are you satisfied?"

---

[1] Wood spirits. — ED.
[2] A kind of tree demon.
[3] Spirit of a dead ancestor. — ED.

I did not believe that but I let it pass. "Go on. What did Grand Uncle do?"

"He called everyone together and wanted us to keep away from the place."

"And yet you went back!"

"Well, you know your Uncle Sanya. He was angry. For one thing the best snails are on the other side of that stream. So he continued to complain that those *òrò* were just being selfish, and he was going to show them who he was. Well, he did. About a week later he led us back. And he was right you know. We gathered a full basket and a half of the biggest snails you ever saw. Well, by this time we had all forgotten about the warning, there was plenty of moonlight and anyway, I've told you Sanya is an *òrò* himself. . . ."

"But why? He looks normal like you and us."   15

"You won't understand yet. Anyway, he is *òrò*. So with him we felt quite safe. Until suddenly this sort of light, like a ball of fire, began to glow in the distance. Even while it was still far we kept hearing voices, as if a lot of people around us were grumbling the same words together. They were saying something like, 'You stubborn, stiff-necked children, we've warned you and warned you but you just won't listen. . . .'"

Wild Christian looked above our heads, frowning to recollect the better. "One can't even say, 'they.' It was only this figure of fire that I saw and he was still very distant. Yet I heard him distinctly, as if he had many mouths which were pressed against my ears. Every moment, the fireball loomed larger and larger."

"What did Uncle Sanya do? Did he fight him?"

"*Sanya wo ni yen?* He was the first to break and run. *Bo o ló o yă mi, o di kítìpà kítìpà!*[4] No one remembered all those fat snails. That *iwin*[5] followed us all the way to the house. Our screams had arrived long before us and the whole household was — well, you can imagine the turmoil. Uncle had already dashed down the stairs and was in the backyard. We ran past him while he went out to meet the creature. This time that *iwin* actually passed the line of the woods, he continued as if he meant to chase us right into the house, you know, he wasn't running, just pursuing us steadily." We waited. This was it! Wild Christian mused while we remained in suspense. Then she breathed deeply and shook her head with a strange sadness.

"The period of faith is gone. There was faith among our early Chris-   20 tians, real faith, not just church-going and hymn-singing. Faith.

---

[4]If you aren't moving, get out of my way!
[5]A ghommid; a wood sprite which is also believed to live in the ground.

Igbàgbó. And it is out of that faith that real power comes. Uncle stood there like a rock, he held out his Bible and ordered, 'Go back! Go back to that forest which is your home. Back, I said, in the name of God.' Hm. And that was it. The creature simply turned and fled, those sparks falling off faster and faster until there was just a faint glow receding into the woods." She sighed. "Of course, after prayers that evening, there was the price to be paid. Six of the best on every one's back. Sanya got twelve. And we all cut grass every day for the next week."

I could not help feeling that the fright should have sufficed as punishment. Her eyes gazing in the direction of the square house, Wild Christian nonetheless appeared to sense what was going on in my mind. She added, "Faith and — Discipline. That is what made those early believers. Psheeaw! God doesn't make them like that any more. When I think of that one who now occupies that house . . ."

Then she appeared to recall herself to our presence. "What are you both still sitting here for? Isn't it time for your evening bath? Lawanle!" "Auntie" Lawanle replied "Ma" from a distant part of the house. Before she appeared I reminded Wild Christian, "But you haven't told us why Uncle Sanya is *òrò.*"

She shrugged, "He is. I saw it with my own eyes."

We both clamored, "When? When?"

She smiled, "You won't understand. But I'll tell you about it some   25
other time. Or let him tell you himself next time he is here."

"You mean you saw him turn into an *òrò?*"

Lawanle came in just then and she prepared to hand us over. "Isn't it time for these children's bath?"

I pleaded, "No, wait Auntie Lawanle," knowing it was a waste of time. She had already gripped us both, one arm each. I shouted back, "Was Bishop Crowther an *òrò?*"

Wild Christian laughed. "What next are you going to ask? Oh I see. They have taught you about him in Sunday school have they?"

"I saw him." I pulled back at the door, forcing Lawanle to stop. "I see   30
him all the time. He comes and sits under the porch of the Girls' School. I've seen him when crossing the compound to Auntie Mrs. Lijadu."

"All right," sighed Wild Christian. "Go and have your bath."

"He hides among the bougainvillea. . . ." Lawanle dragged me out of hearing.

Later that evening, she told us the rest of the story. On that occasion, Rev. J. J. was away on one of his many mission tours. He traveled a lot, on foot and on bicycle, keeping in touch with all the branches of his diocese and spreading the Word of God. There was frequent opposition but nothing deterred him. One frightening experience occurred in one of the villages in Ijebu. He had been warned not to preach on a particular day, which was the day for an *egúngún* outing, but he persisted and held a service. The *egúngún* procession passed while the service was in progress and, using his ancestral voice, called on the preacher to stop at once, disperse his people, and come out to pay obeisance. Rev. J. J. ignored him. The *egúngún* then left, taking his followers with him but, on passing the main door, he tapped on it with his wand, three times. Hardly had the last member of his procession left the church premises than the building collapsed. The walls simply fell down and the roof disintegrated. Miraculously however, the walls fell outwards while the roof supports fell among the aisles or flew outwards — anywhere but on the congregation itself. Rev. J. J. calmed the worshippers, paused in his preaching to render a thanksgiving prayer, then continued his sermon.

Perhaps this was what Wild Christian meant by Faith. And this tended to confuse things because, after all, the *egúngún* did make the church building collapse. Wild Christian made no attempt to explain how that happened, so the feat tended to be of the same order of Faith which moved mountains or enabled Wild Christian to pour ground-nut oil from a broad-rimmed bowl into an empty bottle without spilling a drop. She had the strange habit of sighing with a kind of rapture, crediting her steadiness of hand to Faith and thanking God. If however the basin slipped and she lost a drop or two, she murmured that her sins had become heavy and that she needed to pray more.

If Rev. J. J. had Faith, however, he also appeared to have Stubborn- 35 ness in common with our Uncle Sanya. Stubbornness was one of the earliest sins we easily recognized, and no matter how much Wild Christian tried to explain the Rev. J. J. preaching on the *egúngún*'s outing day, despite warnings, it sounded much like stubbornness. As for Uncle Sanya there was no doubt about his own case; hardly did the Rev. J. J. pedal out of sight on his pastoral duties than he was off into the woods on one pretext or the other, and making for the very areas which the *òrò* had declared out of bounds. Mushrooms and snails were the real goals, with the gathering of firewood used as the dutiful excuse.

Even Sanya had however stopped venturing into the woods at night, accepting the fact that it was far too risky; daytime and early dusk carried little danger as most wood spirits only came out at night. Mother told us that on this occasion she and Sanya had been picking mushrooms, separated by only a few clumps of bushes. She could hear his movements quite clearly, indeed, they took the precaution of staying very close together.

Suddenly, she said, she heard Sanya's voice talking animatedly with someone. After listening for some time she called out his name but he did not respond. There was no voice apart from his, yet he appeared to be chatting in friendly, excited tones with some other person. So she peeped through the bushes and there was Uncle Sanya seated on the ground chattering away to no one that she could see. She tried to penetrate the surrounding bushes with her gaze but the woods remained empty except for the two of them. And then her eyes came to rest on his basket.

It was something she had observed before, she said. It was the same, no matter how many of the children in the household went to gather snails, berries, or whatever, Sanya would spend most of the time playing and climbing rocks and trees. He would wander off by himself, leaving his basket anywhere. And yet, whenever they prepared to return home, his basket was always fuller than the others'. This time was no different. She came closer, startling our Uncle, who snapped off his chatter and pretended to be hunting snails in the undergrowth.

Mother said that she was frightened. The basket was filled to the brim, impossibly bursting. She was also discouraged, so she picked up her near empty basket and insisted that they return home at once. She led the way but after some distance, when she looked back, Sanya appeared to be trying to follow her but was being prevented, as if he was being pulled back by invisible hands. From time to time he would snatch forward his arm and snap,

"Leave me alone. Can't you see I have to go home? I said I have to   40
go."

She broke into a run and Sanya did the same. They ran all the way home.

That evening, Sanya took ill. He broke into a sweat, tossed on his mat all night, and muttered to himself. By the following day the household was thoroughly frightened. His forehead was burning to the touch and no one could get a coherent word out of him. Finally, an elderly woman, one of J. J.'s converts, turned up at the house on a routine visit. When she learnt of Sanya's condition, she nodded wisely and acted like one who knew exactly what to do. Having first found out what things he last did before his illness, she summoned my mother and questioned her. She told her everything while the old woman kept on nodding with understanding. Then she gave instructions:

"I want a basket of *àgìdi*, containing fifty wraps. Then prepare some *èkuru* in a large bowl. Make sure the *èkuru* stew is prepared with plenty of locust bean and crayfish. It must smell as appetizing as possible."

The children were dispersed in various directions, some to the market to obtain the *àgìdi*, others to begin grinding the beans for the amount of *èkuru* which was needed to accompany fifty wraps of *àgìdi*. The children's mouths watered, assuming at once that this was to be an appeasement feast, a *sàarà*[6] for some offended spirits.

When all was prepared, however, the old woman took everything to 45 Sanya's sickroom, plus a pot of cold water and cups, locked the door on him, and ordered everybody away.

"Just go about your normal business and don't go anywhere near the room. If you want your brother to recover, do as I say. Don't attempt to speak to him and don't peep through the keyhole."

She locked the windows too and went herself to a distant end of the courtyard where she could monitor the movements of the children. She dozed off soon after, however, so that mother and the other children were able to glue their ears to the door and windows, even if they could not see the invalid himself. Uncle Sanya sounded as if he was no longer alone. They heard him saying things like:

"Behave yourself, there is enough for everybody. All right you take this, have an extra wrap . . . Open your mouth . . . here . . . you don't have to fight over that bit, here's another piece of crayfish . . . behave, I said . . ."

And they would hear what sounded like the slapping of wrists, a scrape of dishes on the ground, or water slopping into a cup.

When the woman judged it was time, which was well after dusk, 50 nearly six hours after Sanya was first locked up, she went and opened the door. There was Sanya fast asleep but, this time, very peacefully. She touched his forehead and appeared to be satisfied by the change. The household who had crowded in with her had no interest in Sanya however. All they could see, with astonished faces, were the scattered leaves of fifty wraps of *àgìdi*, with the contents gone, a large empty dish which was earlier filled with *èkuru*, and a water pot nearly empty.

No, there was no question about it, our Uncle Sanya was an *òrò*; Wild Christian had seen and heard proofs of it many times over. His companions were obviously the more benevolent type or he would have come to serious harm on more than one occasion, J. J.'s protecting Faith notwithstanding.

---

[6]An offering, food shared out as offering.

EXPLORATIONS

1. What is the relationship in Wole Soyinka's family between Anglican religious beliefs and traditional African magic? At what points in "Nigerian Childhood" do parents use each of these belief systems to control or teach children? At what points do the children's beliefs guide them toward "good" behavior?

2. "Stubbornness was one of the earliest sins we easily recognized," writes Soyinka in paragraph 35. What other virtues, failings, and rules of behavior have these children evidently been taught? Cite specific evidence for your conclusions.

3. What aspects of Soyinka's narrative make it clear that he was an adult when he wrote "Nigerian Childhood"? What passages indicate that he is telling his story from a child's rather than an adult's point of view?

CONNECTIONS

1. Several times in "The Song of Ourselves" (p. 599), Chinua Achebe refers to Europeans' doubting whether Africans had souls. How does "Nigerian Childhood" remind us that not all Europeans shared that doubt? What form did their interest take in Africans' souls?

2. Es'kia Mphahlele mentions in "African Literature: What Tradition?" (p. 562) the reverence given to someone in a traditional law court who quotes a saying handed down from the elders: "Because his elders would be the ancestors, who are still present with us in spirit" (para. 8). What evidence of this statement appears in Soyinka's memoir?

3. Isabel Allende's "Clarisa" (p. 575), John David Morley's "Acquiring a Japanese Family" (p. 230), and Soyinka's "Nigerian Childhood" all depict characters with beliefs that most people in the United States would regard as superstitious. What similarity do you notice between Allende's, Morley's, and Soyinka's way of handling these beliefs? How does the author's approach affect your response to his or her characters' superstitions?

J. F. ADE AJAYI

On the Politics of Being Mortal

Jacob Festus Adeniyi Ajayi was born in 1929 in Ikole-Ekiti. He attended Higher College, Lagos, and graduated from the University of Ibadan in 1951. Like Chinua Achebe and Wole Soyinka, he followed the custom of continuing his education in England, receiving an advanced degree in history from the University of Leicester and a Ph.D. from King's College, London. When he returned to Nigeria, Ajayi joined the faculty of the University of Ibadan; he became a full professor in 1963 and continued in that position until he retired in 1989. He has served on several commissions and boards, including the United Nations University Council, which he chaired in 1976–1977. Besides editing or contributing to a number of books and journals related to African history, Ajayi wrote *Yoruba Warfare in the Nineteenth Century* (with Robert Smith; 1961), *Milestones in Nigerian History* (1962), and *A Patriot to the Core: Samuel Ajayi Crowther* (1992), among others. "On the Politics of Being Mortal" appeared in slightly longer form in Issue 59 of *Transition* in 1993.

Burial Rites

Not counting my student days, 1947–1951, I have spent my life on university campuses in Nigeria, both at Ibadan and at Lagos. These are residential universities where faculty, staff, students, workers, and their families live, and they have, inevitably, become communities, with a multicultural ethos of their own. Often enough, we have had to arrange funerals. The University of Ibadan has its own cemetery, while a public cemetery lies close to the gates of the University of Lagos.

In the 1960s, when the expatriate community was still large, a professor of obstetrics and gynecology died at the University of Ibadan at the age of fifty. He had been very popular, and many women on campus, both Nigerian and expatriate, were his patients. He had not been much of a churchgoer, and there was some awkwardness about arranging a secular funeral for him. He was of South African–Indian origin but had completed his medical education in Britain, and his wife was English.

His cousin, who was a professor of pediatrics at the university, took charge of the arrangements until the brother of the deceased flew in from South Africa. The body lay in state in the main auditorium to allow students and friends to pay their last respects; it was then moved to the chapel. During the service, the chaplain said a few words to console the family and the university community; and his brother, on behalf of the family, thanked the community for the outpouring of grief and concern. After the deceased's interment in the university cemetery, his friends retired to his house to console the widow. To relieve the tension, someone started serving drinks. Another got the bright idea to play some music and get people, including the widow, to dance, on the grounds that the good-hearted professor would not have wished for gloom at his funeral.

Contrast the situation if the deceased were a Nigerian professor, with the extended family based 150 miles away. The family would be contacted immediately, and they would be responsible for arranging the details of the funeral in consultation with the widow. If the deceased were Muslim, prayers would be said, he would be interred as soon as possible, usually in the family compound, and traditional rites would follow, especially at the eight- and fortieth-day prayers. If Christian, even if not a regular churchgoer, it would at once be assumed that the funeral would embrace elements of both the Christian and the traditional customary rites. For the practicing Traditionalist, church services would of course be dispensed with. Otherwise, there would be a service of songs at his campus residence on Thursday. On Friday, his body would lie in state in the auditorium for a couple of hours, then would be moved for the farewell service in the chapel. His body would then be taken to his hometown for the traditional wake-keeping that Friday night.

The basic aim of the rites is to get the family and the community to accept the fact of his death. Various age-grades and other associations to which he belonged in the community or the church would come to pay their respects with appropriate rites, but it would be predominantly an affair of the extended family. His *oriki* would be chanted again and again. These are praise-verses embodying elements from the different segments of the extended family, thus indicating his connections, and yet in their unique conjunction signifying his individual identity. The body might be laid in state on Saturday morning for the general public to pay its respects. There would then be a service in the home church, followed by a party. The traditional ceremonies would usually go on until the eighth day before the widow could return to campus, and she would have to observe a period of mourning. An essential feature of the ceremonies is that the different branches of the extended family get together and the children get to know them. Formal meetings are held to deliberate on the implications of the death for the family and what adjustments have to be made because of it. . . .

It seems obvious that the awkwardness in the arrangements for the   5
burial of the professor of obstetrics arose partly from the concept of a secular funeral, and partly from the fact that, though of Indian origin, he was British, from a Western culture that feels ill at ease in dealing with death. Some scholars argue that this "pornography" of death is a phenomenon of the twentieth century; others argue that the fear of death, or, rather, the fear of extinction, is a fundamental component of Western thought that can be traced back at least to the seventeenth century, and that it is the decline of active religion that has highlighted the problem in the twentieth century.

Let me emphasize that the situation in Nigeria is far from static. Some fundamentalist Christians would like to play down the traditional aspects and use the victory of Christ over death as an excuse for denying the reality of death. There was recently the funeral of a forty-year-old man whose widow was not allowed to show grief as that might imply that she doubted that her late husband was happier with Jesus. (It is worth noting that most Nigerian Christians would argue that the message of the Resurrection is the conquest, not the denial, of death.) There was also the case of the prominent politician with socialist connections. When he died three years ago, his followers regarded him as irreplaceable. He was embalmed like Lenin, and was to be put on show to the public once a month. His birthday, rather than the date of his death, continues to be celebrated as was customary before his death. Funeral parlors have not caught on yet in Nigeria, but a number of wealthy people around the politician's part of the country seem to be competing in the design and construction of spectacular mausoleums. Accessible land for cemeteries is already hard to find in crowded cities like Lagos, but cremation remains "unthinkable."

The Politics of Being Mortal

It is, of course, no longer true that the subject of death is treated with silence or avoidance in the Western world. Diseases like cancer and AIDS — even more forcibly than Hiroshima and the stockpiling of nuclear arms or the threat of global warming — have made the spectacle of the dying unavoidable, and have thus brought the subject of death into focus. Nevertheless, the consensus among scholars is that the prevalent attitude in the Western world remains that of denial.

People make wills and take out life insurance, talk metaphorically of "dying at base" or "sudden death" on the sports field; but they try not to get too emotionally involved in the physical reality of their own mortality, or in the awareness that death sets a limit and makes a change. Death is seen as a challenge to science and technology, an obstacle to be conquered — an attitude that the Indian prime minister recently described as the arrogance of Western science seeking to master rather than to work with nature. Daily reports of violence and death on television serve as a vaccine that immunizes us against the reality of death. As my daughter tells her mother whenever she flinches as the gangster on TV pulls the trigger: "Relax, mum, it is only a film." Not so for my old aunt, who still cannot bear to look at a videotape of someone she knows is now dead. And how does one react to the televised holocaust: Does it help to bring home the reality of the terror, or does it just make the unthinkable comprehensible? In January 1986, all eyes were glued on the Challenger space shuttle carrying an amiable schoolteacher as the first civilian in space. When it exploded, many were emotionally involved because it was not just a report on TV, but a real-life situation with which they personally identified.

Alfred G. Killilea's *The Politics of Being Mortal* apparently grew out of that national trauma. He sees the denial of death as a fundamental aspect of American culture, and he tries to show how important it is to overcome it. He argues that it is important within the context of secular American culture to accept the limitations that death sets, and to find meaning in life — not in unlimited competition and accumulation, but in touching the lives of others for good. As of the time of its publication by the University Press of Kentucky in 1988, he seems to me to have the most comprehensive survey of the literature and of the issues involved.

Of the many writers who analyze the denial of death in American culture and feel comfortable with it or positively justify it, he singles out Ernest Becker as the most dramatic. . . . Becker argues in *Escape from Evil* [that] culture has the sacred duty to provide citizens with the opportunity to seek importance, significance, and durability, to "raise men above nature, to assure them in some ways their lives count in the universe more than merely physical things count. . . . The thing that connects money with the domain of the sacred is its power. . . . It abolishes one's likeness to others."

. . . Where Becker justifies the denial of death with the need to find   10
meaning in life through the competition for money and power, Killilea suggests restraining the competition and violence by facing up to the reality of death, and by accepting the finiteness of human mortality as an

opportunity to find a new basis for the meaning of life. . . . Rather than look outside secular Western culture for alternative paradigms, however, Killilea digs deeper into the philosophical roots of the democratic capitalist society, back to John Locke, where he finds the direct link between the denial of death and the labor theory of value. The solution then becomes easy: The fundamental change needed in Western thought is to accept mortality, curb the unrestrained appetite for competition and acquisition, and promote the meaning of life by reaching out to others through love.

A Critique

I do not know how this work was received by the American public or what impact it has made. It seems to me, however, to be largely a restatement of welfarism. In looking only inward for a solution to the problem he so clearly stated, Killilea encountered two main difficulties, one of which he was aware of, and the other of which apparently eluded him. Since the problem of death is usually discussed in the context of religion, he was anxious to find a solution that is compatible with the secular basis of American culture. This did not prove too difficult since his welfarism, I believe, is based on the Protestant ethic that has generally been accepted as compatible with the secularism of American society. Objections might come from fundamentalists on the Right who reject secularism, especially on matters touching the meaning of life and immortality, and from atheists who find American secularism religiously based to an uncomfortable degree; but we are not concerned here with such possible objections.

The more formidable problem that Killilea encounters, in my view, is that the social and community consciousness and sense of interdependence from which he wants his readers to derive new meaning in life is not only compatible with but actually reaffirms individualism. "Besides being necessary for gaining a perspective on life," he says, "finiteness establishes each person's uniqueness." He agrees with [Jacques] Choron that the consciousness of death "goes hand in hand with human individualization, with the establishment of single individualities," and he relies on biology to clinch the argument, quoting Victor Frankel:

> [T]he inner limits only add to the meaning of man's life. If all men were perfect, then every individual would be replaceable by anyone else. From the very imperfection of men follows the indispensability and

inexchangeability of each individual; for each is imperfect in his own fashion. No man is universally gifted; but the bias of the individual makes for his uniqueness.

But Killilea goes further than that and seems to confuse the nature of society with that of the individual. He sees society as the individual writ large: "Just as society could not survive without death," he says, "the same paradox applies to the individual." He apparently does not see that it is the individual that dies, not society. He notes that the nearness of death heightens a willingness to share and thus shatters "the charade of heroic individualism." But he does not acknowledge that the interest of the individual may not always be compatible with that of the group, presumably because he fears the authoritarianism that might arise from the interest of the individual being sacrificed to that of the group. Thus, it seems to me that his welfarism has failed to resolve the crucial issue of how the interest of the unique individual is to fit into the overall interest of society. And yet it is in resolving the tension, not only between unique individuals, but also between society and the individual, that the individual can find fulfillment and meaning in life. It is in the context of society that death can "establish the uniqueness of the individual." In the Protestant ethic on which Killilea's welfarism is based, while the doctrine of individual responsibility to God has usually been emphasized, the other part of the commandment — to love your neighbor as yourself — has more often than not been played down.

Killilea wrote before the collapse of the Soviet Union. He mentions that the denial of death was just as rampant in the Soviet Union as in the United States, but he does not discuss socialism as a distinct component of Western thought. He therefore does not discuss the socialist viewpoint that, in order to challenge the notion that competition and unlimited acquisition give meaning to life, we also need to question the doctrine of individualism within the capitalist system.

The neglect of the socialist viewpoint may also be the same reason why he does not discuss the idea of progress as a fundamental doctrine in Western thought, comparable to Locke's theory of labor value in encouraging the arrogance of science, unlimited acquisition, and the denial of death. This idea was particularly strong in the nineteenth century, when it was reinforced by the theories of evolution and of Marx's dialectical materialism. Then, the idea of progress tended to ignore the biological argument that no individual is perfect, and that it is imperfection which provides a basis for explaining change and adaptation both in nature and in human society. It is because of such individual imperfection that, while the perpetuity of society can be presumed, cumulative change and unlimited progress in a rectilinear fashion cannot.

An African Perspective

Perhaps in the same sense that we have been discussing Western   15
thought as a unified concept, we can also, at least by way of contrast, talk of an African perspective as a unified body of ideas — provided we do not lose sight of the generalizations and approximations involved in both the concepts and in the activity of contrasting. The African perspective seems to me to offer rather more satisfactory solutions to some of the issues that Killilea tries to confront, and should be relevant in the more global approach to humanistic scholarship that we seek. This perspective can be gleaned from the studies of aging in Africa, the concept of "continuity" in African thought, the structuring of African societies by generations, and recent critiques of modernization as a Western-based paradigm for development in Africa.

Largely because of the involvement of the International Federation on Aging and the World Council of Churches, the Presidential Commission on the Problems of Aging, set up a few years ago, has generated some comparative studies in Zaire, Kenya, Nigeria, and Ghana. The dominant view in those reports can be summed up in the words of Masamba, an American-trained physician from Zaire:

> Even though they were sometimes feared by the younger generations, the elderly were respected and integrated into communal life. No one was seen as a burden or simply a "productive unit." Older persons played a special role in educating and socializing the young. . . . My father's own personal growth enabled him to maintain his integrity in the face of deteriorating health and approaching death. His example was especially important to his children and grandchildren, and helped them to understand the meaning of life and change.

The aged were able to contemplate death with composure and without fear, and by their example teach their offspring about the meaning of life and change, because to them death did not mean extinction. Although death marked their finiteness as individuals in this world, they regarded it as only a transition to enable them to join the ancestors and as such to continue to live in the life of the society. As K. O. Dike and I put it in an article on African historiography in the International Encyclopaedia of the Social Sciences published in 1968: "A belief in the continuity of life, a life after death, and a community of interest

between the living, the dead, and the generations yet unborn is fundamental to all African religious, social, and political life." This basic doctrine of the continuity of life and death, we argued, can be traced back
to the ancient Egyptians: "The essence of the Horus myth was that the
dead, particularly the kings, continued to influence the life of the living
by affecting the annual inundations of the Nile and the germination of
crops. A good deal of Egyptian religion revolved around the commemoration of the dead." What different African societies have made of this
basic doctrine over the centuries is an important part of the intellectual
history of Africa that we may never know except vaguely. Early Christianity in North Africa and in the Nile valley did not seem to have had
much difficulty reconciling the concept of the veneration of ancestors
with the doctrine of life after death and the practice of the veneration of
saints. This survives today in Coptic Christian worship in Egypt and in
the Orthodox Church in Ethiopia. With its emphasis on the unques-
tioning acceptance of death as the will of Allah, Islam was generally
more hostile than early Christianity to the cult of the ancestors. It has
been suggested that it is for this reason that the sufi orders and mysticism have dominated Islam in Africa; the veneration of ancestors has
thus been subsumed under the veneration of the founders of the sufi orders and of other holy men.

The nineteenth-century evangelical movement, which was responsible for spreading Christianity in much of sub-Saharan Africa through
both Protestant and Roman Catholic missionaries, was hostile to the
idolatry involved in ancestor worship. At the same time, attempts to indigenize Christianity have usually involved finding a basis of accommodation between the Christian belief in life after death and the African
veneration of ancestors. One approach has been to argue that the Christian doctrine of the resurrection of the spirits of the dead at the second
coming of Christ leaves some room for traditional beliefs as to what
happens to the ancestors in the meantime.

Another approach is to emphasize that the veneration of ancestors is
not an act of worship but of respect, with no more religious connotation
than is involved in prostrating to elders in their lifetime. Thus, while
some Christians frown at the pouring of libation as tending toward worship and idolatry, others treat it purely as a formality, a matter of culture
and custom with no more worship than is involved, for example, in laying flowers on the grave or lighting a candle in the church. Even
among the adherents of the traditional religions, few people today still
believe that the ancestors come to visit the living once a year in the
form of masquerades. Rather, egúngún and similar carnivals are taken,
like the Mexican Feast for the Dead, as festivals at which only the living

gather to commemorate the dead, or the living dead as some prefer to call them. Many Africans find comfort in such acts of commemoration and communication with the spirits of the dead, and overcome the fear of death as extinction, whether such acts are formal and religious, or merely symbolic and customary.

What needs to be emphasized is that neither Islam nor Christianity has been able completely to eradicate this belief of Africans in the continuity of life and death as a fundamental view of history. Even now, it is difficult for most Africans to conceptualize history, as in Western society, as something that has gone past and is now behind us. Rather, we face the ancestors who have gone ahead of us, and we picture generations yet unborn as those coming behind us. As Boubou Hama and Kizerbo have expressed the matter:

> Traditional African time includes and incorporates eternity in both directions. Bygone generations are not lost to the present. In their own way they remain contemporary, and as influential as they were during their lifetime, if not more so. In these circumstances, causality operates in a forward direction, of course, from past to present and from present to future, not only through the influence of bygone facts and events, but through a direct intervention which can operate in any direction. When Mansa Musa, Emperor of Mali (1312–1332), sent an ambassador to the king of Yatenga asking him to be converted to Islam, the Mossi ruler answered that he would have to consult his ancestors before making such a decision.

The fear of what the ancestors will say has remained an important sanction constraining the action of the living; and it is the greater proximity of the elders to the ancestors that is responsible, at least in part, for the fear of the elderly by the younger generations to which Masamba refers.

In this continuous flow, the passage of time is reckoned in terms of a [20] succession of generations, and, in the predominantly nonliterate societies, this forms the basis of chronology and periodization. There is much interest, of course, in genealogies. In some societies, there are set patterns to follow in naming one's children after one's parents and grandparents, and this helps to keep track of the generations. In most African societies, age-sets were formally constituted by gender periodically in ceremonies linked to puberty rites, made into associations with their own officers and regulations. This could be every three, five, or six years, so that a succession of age-sets constituted a generation. An individual participated in the life of the community not only through his or her lineage but, sometimes even more effectively, through the age-set association. Different tasks were assigned according to the age of the members of the age-set: maintenance of roads and markets, sanitation, care of the shrines, defense, judicial proceedings, administration. In the noncentralized societies, the age-set associations were important factors in coordination, cutting across lineages and extended families. Even in centralized societies, where the rulers had built up administrative systems separate from the lineages and age-set associations, they still found the associations useful for facilitating effective participation of the members in decision-making. This was the more so where, as was often the case, the age-set associations became the mechanism for recruiting people into the army and determining their location in the normal formations. Without doubt, the age-set associations were an important mechanism for fostering group feeling across lineage loyalties and affinities, and for mobilizing the whole community according to age in the traditional societies in Africa.

The age-set associations were also important in managing conflict between the generations and were thus a major factor making for change in traditional societies. Conflict was inherent between the generations at both the societal level and at the level of individual, interpersonal relations within the family. At the societal level, there was conflict between the age-set of the elders who made final decisions on matters concerning the whole community — disputes between lineages and between age-set associations; and matters of external relations such as defense, war, and peace — and the age-sets of the younger people who did most of the production and the fighting. The most frequent area of conflict, however, tended to be within the extended family, which was the basic economic unit. The head of the family often had the last say in the management of the family property, the most important being land. For example, he controlled the arrangements for the marriage of the younger women as well as access to the resources that the younger men required to be able to marry and [have] their own farms. In many African societies, there were practices and taboos to anticipate and structurally control generational conflict. For example, among the Luo, there were taboos forbidding father and married son to sleep under the same roof; among the Mossi, taboos regulating access of the grown eldest son to his father; and among the Bakongo, taboos prohibiting mother and daughter-in-law from using the same toilet.

Today, the age-set associations are rarely formally constituted; they survive largely as anthropological curiosities rather than as active principles for broadening the basis of participation and involvement in the life of the group. Many decry their neglect; others treat them as part of the static, backward-looking Africa that they are anxious to be rid of, while they continue to search for development on the basis of foreign ideologies. Because of European conquest and colonial rule, Europeans have for a long time set the agenda for development in Africa. African values have been under pressure not only from Christianity, but also from imported paradigms of development such as Europeanization, Westernization, modernization, and now democratization.

And yet it needs to be said that African development cannot proceed far on the basis of paradigms of development such as Marxist or capitalist ideologies imposed from above. African leaders can be expected to plan and make meaningful choices only on the basis of improved appreciation of African values. The view that African values reflected a static society was part of the myth propagated by colonialism. African cultures did not encourage the aggressive individualism of the West; rather, they tried to reconcile respect for the uniqueness of the individual with the communal interest of the group. The societies looked forward to the ancestors; their interest in looking backward was to protect their heritage in the interest of generations yet unborn, the kind of interest that is now being fostered in the West with the newly found concern for the environment.

The conflict of generations, if properly understood, should at least add something to the theory of the class struggle as a way of understanding how change takes place in history. Let us note that, for a community that sees itself as a group of households or extended families, the class struggle does not cut across society in a horizontal manner, but rather vertically unites the poorer households against the richer. By contrast, the generational gap cuts across every household. . . .

I am not claiming that all we need do to promote stability and development in Africa is to revive the generational structuring of society and the veneration of ancestors. But I am suggesting that we are not doing, and are not likely to do, any better by merely abandoning these and promoting the individualism and the class structure of Western society. 25

Neither am I claiming that American society will solve the problems raised by Killilea merely by constituting age-set associations and venerating the dead. But I do suggest that there exist, even in Western thought, ideas such as the continuity of life and afterlife that can be used to modify the rigidities of the doctrines of individualism, the class struggle, and unlimited progress.

Above all, what I am trying to say is that humanistic inquiry must stress the uniqueness of each individual person and each culture without negating the commonality of the human condition. We must continue to stress the uniqueness of our individual cultural identities without denying the richness of our cultural diversities. With all our diversity, however, an essential definition of the human condition is that we shall all die. It is this common mortality that makes us kin. Without death, there can be no life; the seed that will germinate must first die. We need not fear or be despondent about this. As the Tiv[1] put it, "When the mushroom dies, the mushroom tribe lives on."

EXPLORATIONS

1. What aspects of the funeral he describes in paragraph 2 does J. F. Ade Ajayi evidently regard as inappropriate, and why? Which specific words and phrases convey his disapproval?

2. According to Ajayi, what is the prevalent attitude toward death in the Western world? What Western recommendations to change this attitude does he cite?

3. According to Ajayi, what is the prevalent attitude toward death in Africa? What advantages does the African attitude have over the Western one?

CONNECTIONS

1. "Attempts to indigenize Christianity have usually involved finding a basis of accommodation between the Christian belief in life after death and the African veneration of ancestors" (para. 17). What examples of such accommodations appear in Wole Soyinka's "Nigerian Childhood" (p. 606)? Which of the bases for accommodation Ajayi offers here do you think fits Soyinka's examples best, and why?

2. In "The Song of Ourselves" (p. 599), Chinua Achebe calls the statement that he invented African literature "blasphemous" (para. 1). Why? What ideas in "On the Politics of Being Mortal" help to explain Achebe's reaction more fully?

3. What ideas that Ajayi cites as African also appear in Joseph Bruchac's "Digging into Your Heart" (p. 523)?

---

[1]The Tiv: a Nigerian tribe — ED.

BUCHI EMECHETA

Ona

Florence Onye Buchi Emecheta has lived in London since 1962, but she is known as a Nigerian writer, both for her historical novels set there and for her rarity as a successful female Nigerian (or, for that matter, African) author. Emecheta was born in Yaba, a small village near Lagos, in 1944. Orphaned as a child, she grew up under the protection of her father's sister. This Ibo aunt's stories about the family's origins and ancestors persuaded Emecheta to be a storyteller when she grew up. She got a scholarship to the Methodist Girls' High School, then at age sixteen married a man she had been betrothed to five years earlier. After having two children, she and her husband went to England so he could continue his education. Emecheta bore three more children despite poverty and abuse; but when her husband burned the manuscript of her first book, she left him. Every morning she wrote before caring for the children, scrubbing floors for money, and studying. For a while she worked as a library officer at the British Museum, then as a youth worker and sociologist. Emecheta received her bachelor's degree in sociology with honors from the University of London in 1972. That year she also published *In the Ditch*, a collection of columns she had written in the form of a diary for the *New Statesman*. She began traveling as a writer and lecturer; her stops in the United States included Pennsylvania State University, the University of Illinois, and the University of California at Los Angeles. Meanwhile, she wrote a series of novels focusing particularly on Nigerian women, both before and after independence, including the autobiographical *Second-Class Citizen* (1974), *The Slave Girl: A Novel* (1977), and *The Joys of Motherhood* (1979), from which "Ona" is taken. Emecheta also has written children's books; an autobiography, *Head Above Water* (1984); and a play, *A Kind of Marriage*, which was produced on BBC television. Her most recent novel is *Kehinde* (1994).

Nwokocha Agbadi was a very wealthy local chief. He was a great wrestler, and was glib and gifted in oratory. His speeches were highly spiced with sharp anecdotes and thoughtful proverbs. He was taller than most and, since he was born in an age when physical prowess determined one's role in life, people naturally accepted him as a leader. Like most handsome men who are aware of their charismatic image, he had

627

many women in his time. Whenever they raided a neighboring village, Agbadi was sure to come back with the best-looking women. He had a soft spot for those from big houses, daughters of chiefs and rich men. He knew from experience that such women had an extra confidence and sauciness even in captivity. And that type of arrogance, which even captivity could not diminish, seemed to excite some wicked trait in him. In his young days, a woman who gave in to a man without first fighting for her honor was never respected. To regard a woman who is quiet and timid as desirable was something that came after his time, with Christianity and other changes. Most of the women Nwokocha Agbadi chose as his wives and even slaves were those who could match his arrogance, his biting sarcasm, his painful jokes, and also, when the mood called, his human tenderness.

He married a few women in the traditional sense, but as he watched each of them sink into domesticity and motherhood he was soon bored and would go further afield for some other exciting, tall and proud female. This predilection of his extended to his mistresses as well.

Agbadi was from Ogboli, a village of people who, legend said, had lived in that part of what is now Ibuza before the Eastern Ibo people from Isu came and settled there with them. . . . Two of Agbadi's wives came from Ibuza, two from his own village of Ogboli, three were slaves he had captured during his wanderings; and he also had two mistresses.

One of these mistresses was a very beautiful young woman who managed to combine stubbornness with arrogance. So stubborn was she that she refused to live with Agbadi. Men being what they are, he preferred spending his free time with her, with this woman who enjoyed humiliating him by refusing to be his wife. Many a night she would send him away, saying she did not feel like having anything to do with him, even though Agbadi was not supposed to be the kind of man women should say such things to. But she refused to be dazzled by his wealth, his name, or his handsomeness. People said that Nwokocha Agbadi spent all his life on this earth courting Ona.

Ona was Agbadi's name for her, not the name originally given to her. 5
Her father was a chief, too, and Agbadi had seen her as a child following her father about. People used to find it strange that a chief like Obi Umunna would go about unashamedly pulling a tiny toddler with him. But her father told people that his little girl was his ornament. Agbadi then said, jokingly, "Why don't you wear her around your neck, like an *ona*, a 'priceless jewel'?" People had laughed. But the name stuck. It never occurred to him that he would be one of the men to ask for her when she grew up. Her father, despite having several wives, had few children, and in fact no living son at all, but Ona grew to fill her father's

expectation. He had maintained that she must never marry; his daughter was never going to stoop to any man. She was free to have men, however, and if she bore a son, he would take her father's name, thereby rectifying the omission nature had made.

She was of medium height, and had skin like that of half-ripe palm nuts, smooth, light coffee in color. Her hair, closely cropped, fitted her skull like a hat atop a head that seemed to be thrust out of her shoulders by a strong, long, powerful neck. When she walked, her expensive waist-beads, made of the best coral, murmured, and for men raised in that culture, who knew the sound of each bead, this added to her allurement. She had been used all her life to walking in bush paths, so she knew the tricks of avoiding thorns, using the balls of her feet rather than putting her full weight on her soles. This gave her movement the air of a mysterious and yet exciting cat. She had a trick of pointing her chin forward, as if she saw with it instead of her eyes, which were black-rimmed and seemed sunken into her head. Like most of her people, she had little patience for walking, and as she ran, in the same way as young girls would run to the stream or run out of their homesteads to find out what was going on, she would cup her hands to support her breasts, which swung with bare health. She seldom wore any tops, neither did she tie her lappa over her breasts like the old women. But she had many waist lappas, and expensive changes of coral beads for her neck and waist. Greenish-black tattoos stood out richly against her brown skin. Though she was always scantily dressed, she frequently made people aware of being a conservative, haughty presence, cold as steel and remote as any woman royally born. When she sat, and curled her long legs together in feminine modesty, one knew that she had style, this only daughter of Obi Umunna.

Nwokocha Agbadi would not have minded sending all his wives away just to live with this one woman. But that was not to be. People said she had had him bewitched, that she had a kind of power over him; what person in his right mind would leave his big spacious household and women who were willing to worship and serve him in all things to go after a rude, egocentric woman who had been spoiled by her father? This story gained credence particularly when Agbadi's young wives showed signs of sexual neglect. He would be reminded to do his duty by them, then when they became pregnant he would not be seen in their huts until the time came for him to mate them again. But whenever he returned from his many wanderings he would go and stay with his Ona.

It was during one rainy season that Nwokocha Agbadi went to hunt some elephants which he and his age-group knew would be crossing the bush marshes called Ude. He came too near one of the heavy creatures on this occasion, and that single slip almost led to a terrible disaster. He was thrown with a mighty tusk into a nearby wild sugar-cane bush and he landed in the bubbly black mud. The animal was so enraged that, uncharacteristically for a big elephant, it chased after him blindly, bellowing like a great locomotive, so that the very ground seemed about to give way at its heavy approach. Agbadi reacted quickly. He was pinned to the sugar-cane bush unable to move his body, nonetheless with a practiced hand he aimed his spear and threw it under the belly of the angry animal. It roared, but still made a determined assault on Agbadi, almost tearing his arm from his shoulder, attacking him with a fury increased by the painful spear under it. The elephant roared and fell, but not before it had wounded Agbadi so badly that he himself suspected he was nearing his end. The other hunters, hearing the commotion, rushed to the scene and quickly finished off the elephant, which was still very alive and kicking furiously. They saw Nwokocha Agbadi bleeding to death. His shoulder bone was thrust out of his skin, and the elephant's tusks had indented his side. The men gathered and with bamboo splints tied the twisted shoulder, though they could do little about the bleeding side; judging from the pool of blood that was fast forming around him, they doubted that he would last long. Agbadi soon passed out and it seemed to all that he had died. The oldest man of the group took his *otuogwu* cloth which he had left in a dry hilly place by the stream, rolled Agbadi in it as if he were a dead person, then the anxious hunters carried him in a bigger bamboo crate which they had quickly constructed, and made their way gradually and sadly home.

The procession of dignified men emerging from the belly of the bush into the town was a moving spectacle. It was obvious to those farmers on their way to their lands that something was very wrong, but if they suspected the truth, they could not yet show grief: Nwokocha Agbadi was not only a chief but an important one, therefore the disclosure of his death would have to comply with certain cultural laws — there must be gun shots, and two or three goats must be slaughtered before the announcement. Anyone who started grieving before the official proclamation would be made to pay fines equivalent to three goats. So people watched the hunters' approach in awe, wondering who it was that had been so mummified. Women and children ran from their homesteads to witness the sight, and observant people noticed that the only chief missing among the returning hunters was Nwokocha Agbadi. His carriers were followed by four hefty male slaves dragging the dead elephant, groaning and sweating with the weight of the beast. People knew then that Agbadi had either been badly wounded or killed while hunting the elephant! Word circulated in whispers.

When Ona heard of it, the more vulnerable personality underneath her daily steely mask came out. She dashed out from where she was sitting by her father and soon caught up with the carriers.

"Tell me, please say something, is my lover dead?" she asked anxiously as she galloped after them on the balls of her feet, her waist-beads rumbling to the rhythm of her movements.

She held on first to this man, asking the same question, then to that one, begging him to say something. She pestered Agbadi's closest and oldest friend Obi Idayi, so much that he lost his temper. He had ignored her for some time, and never had any love for this wild uncontrolled woman. He did not know what Agbadi found in her. Now he stopped in his heavy stride and snapped,

"In life you tortured him, teased him with your body. Now that he is dead, you cry for his manhood."

Ona was stunned. She held her hands over her head and spoke like someone hypnotized: "It can't be. It just can't be."

Some older women standing by hushed her, saying, "He may be your lover, girl, but don't forget that he is Nwokocha Agbadi. Watch your tongue."

With fear and apprehension lightening her brain, Ona followed the carriers to Ogboli.

Agbadi was placed in the center of his courtyard. The medicine man was able to detect a very faint life in him, although his breathing was toilsome and indicated that he was a dying man. They had to massage his heart into activity again. All his wives were shooed away, but Ona fought and clawed to be allowed to stay and would let no one touch Agbadi except herself. His people did not much like her, yet they respected her as the only woman who could make Agbadi really happy, so the medicine man let her attend to him. So frightened was she in the aftermath of the accident that, together with the men sitting around Agbadi, she forgot that food was meant to be eaten and that night was meant for sleep.

Goats were slaughtered every day to appease Agbadi's *chi*; others were left alive by river banks and at Ude to appease the other gods. The thought of going home never occurred to Ona, not even on the fourth day. Nor did her possessive father call for her, for he understood her plight; hers were civilized people and they trusted her. For the first time, she realized how attached she was to this man Nwokocha Agbadi, though he was cruel in his imperiousness. His tongue was biting like the edge of a circumcision blade. He ruled his family and children as if he were a god. Yet he gave her his love without reservation, and she en-joyed it; she suspected, however, that her fate would be the same as that of his other women should she consent to become one of his wives. No, maybe the best way to keep his love was not to let that happen. But if he were to die now . . . God, she would will herself death too! All the same, she would rather have her tongue pulled out of her head than let that beast of a man know how much she cared. That, she decided, would be his lot for being so domineering and having such a foul temper. She watched over him closely and told herself that she would go if he should start showing signs of being on the mend.

On the fifth day he opened his eyes without any help from the medi-cine man. Ona was so surprised that she simply stared back at him. Her first impulsive act was to scream her joy; then she remembered her self-control. Agbadi looked at her for a split second, his eyes unfocused. For that small time, he looked so dependent that Ona felt like gathering him in her arms and singing to him, as one would do to a baby. He started to chew the side of his mouth, a habit of his which she knew from experi-ence was normally the prelude to a hurtful remark. He looked at her sit-ting there cross-legged beside him, one of her knees almost touching his head which was supported by a wooden head-rest. He said nothing but his sharp mind had taken in the whole situation. Still biting the corner of his lower lip, he allowed his eyes to wander over her from head to toe. Then he simply rolled away and closed his eyes again. She did not doubt that the light in the open courtyard where he was lying was too strong for his eyes, since he had not opened them for five long days, but she had not missed his look of derision. What a way to thank her for all her help!

She did not tell anyone that Agbadi had regained consciousness; she   20 watched hopefully, yet with fear, for further signs of recovery. That evening while she was trying to ease the bamboo splints that had been fixed to straighten his shoulder, two men had to hold his strong long legs to prevent him from kicking. He groaned in pain, and she was told to mop up the fresh blood oozing from the wound. She heard herself saying, "You have borne the pain like a man. The bones are set now; you only have the wound, and this will heal in a day or two."

Agbadi's eyes flew open, and this time they were clear and evil. His white teeth flashed in a sardonic smile. He chuckled wickedly, then said roughly, "What would you have done without your lover, Ona?"

"If you don't stop talking that way, I shall throw this calabash of med-icine at you and walk out of here back to my father's compound. You're much better now, judging from the sharpness of your tongue."

Her eyes burned with hot tears, but she controlled and never shed them, sensing that nothing would please her lover more than to see her face awash with tears of frustration. She got up from Agbadi's goatskin rug and began to make her way out of the compound.

"You can't go now. You have to finish what you started," Agbadi observed.

She whirled around. "Who is going to stop me? Who dares to stop me? You?" she wailed, very near to hysteria. "Bah! You think you have the right to play God, just because you are Agbadi? You have your wives — they can look after you. You have your slaves — let them mop up your stinking blood!"

"My wives are too much in love with me to stand by and see me in pain. I need a heartless woman like you . . . a woman whose heart is made of stone to stay and watch men remove my splints and not drown me with tears. I will die if you go."

"You will die if I go?" Ona sneered, jutting her pointed chin into the air and throwing back her head in feigned amusement. "A statement like that coming from the great Agbadi! So you are just an ordinary person after all — no, not an ordinary man but a spoiled child who cries when his mother leaves him. Nwokocha Agbadi, hurry up and die, because I'm going back to my father's compound. My heart is not made of stone but I would rather die than let it soften for the likes of you."

"I did not say I am dying because you are so indispensable . . ." This was followed by his low, mocking laughter. He was joined by his close friend Idayi, and they seemed to be enjoying her discomfiture.

Then Idayi coughed gently. "Look, Agbadi," he warned, "if you don't stop chuckling you'll start to bleed again. As for you, our Ona, you have lain there by him these five days, when he had lost his power of speech. Now that he can talk, you want him to kneel down and say 'thank you,' eh?"

"Yes, why not? Haven't I done enough for that? I left my father's compound to come here —"

"I didn't ask you to come, remember," Agbadi put in, determined to be the proud hunter till death.

"Oh, you have nerve!"

"All right, all right," Idayi intervened again, seeing that Ona was becoming more and more angry. If her self-control was allowed to snap she might well throw the calabash as she threatened. "In a day or two he will get better, Ona. Then you can go back to your people. We are grateful to you and to your father, I assure you. If Agbadi were to lower himself to thank you, I am sure you would stop caring for him. You need a man, Ona, not a snail. We all know you. For a while I thought we were losing our giant forever. Well, don't worry, he is still too weak to bother any woman for many days, but what he needs is the comfort of your nearness, though he won't admit it. The sun is going down now; he needs to be brought his blood meal, if you want him to heal properly," Idayi said with his usual studied calmness.

Ona went to do as she was told, thinking to herself how unfair it was that Agbadi should accuse her of having a heart of stone. How else could she behave since she could not marry him? Because her father had no son, she had been dedicated to the gods to produce children in his name, not that of any husband. Oh, how torn she was between two men: She had to be loyal to her father, as well as to her lover Agbadi.

There were many friends and well-wishers in Agbadi's compound 35 when she brought the meal from the medicine man's hut, knelt down, and silently began to feed Agbadi.

Then the familiar salutation "He who keeps peace" could be heard from people outside, and Ona knew that her father Obi Umunna had come to pay Agbadi a visit. Agbadi looked at her in silent appeal and the message was clear: He did not want her to leave yet.

"How can you be so strong and yet so soft, Agbadi?" she asked him in a low voice so that the well-wishers would not hear.

In answer, he simply smiled noncommittally.

Obi Umunna approached and said airily: "So how is the lucky man? You are very lucky, my friend. Bring your best drink and kola nuts and let us pray for long life and thank your *chi* for rescuing you."

"You are right," Idayi agreed. "I was just telling your daughter that 40 for a while we thought we would lose him. But, my friend, I hope you are not here to take her home. She is not ready yet."

"And how is my Ona?" Obi Umunna asked after watching her for a few moments.

"He who keeps peace," she replied, "I am being well looked after, Father."

"Good; but remember that you are not married to Agbadi. I don't want his money. You must come home as soon as he is better."

"Why do you not turn her into a man?" Agbadi said bitingly. "Clinging to your daughter as if —"

"I am not here to argue with you, Agbadi; you are sick. And we have 45 gone through this argument so many times before. My daughter will marry no one."

Ona purposely spooned some of the meal near Agbadi's nose, as a way of telling him not to insult her father in her presence.

Agbadi coughed and remarked: "A daughter who you have not even taught how to feed a sick man . . ."

"Oh, Agbadi!" Ona gasped.

"Kola nut and palm wine are here," Idayi said as one of Agbadi's children brought in the wooden tray with refreshments. "Let us pray to our ancestors."

Being the oldest man in the courtyard, Idayi said the prayers. He 50 prayed to the almighty Olisa to cure his good friend Nwokocha Agbadi and begged him to give them all good health. Agbadi lay silently on his back on the goatskin, sometimes gazing at the bamboo ceiling, sometimes letting out grunts in agreement with the many prayers being said. For most of the time his eyes were closed, and the sweat on his matted chest had to be mopped with cold water time and time again.

Agbadi had slept so much in the day that, now he was feeling better, he was finding it difficult to sleep the night through. He must have dozed for a while, nonetheless, for when he opened his eyes, the whole compound was quiet. Cool night air blew in through the open roof window and he could hear his goats grunting. He heard a light breathing nearby on a separate goatskin. Now he remembered — Ona was lying beside him. He watched her bare breasts rising and falling as she breathed, and noted with amusement how she made sure to stay as far away from him as possible, though in unconscious defiance, like everything else she did, her leg was thrust out so that it was almost touching him. "The heartless bitch," he thought, "I will teach her." He winced as his still-sore shoulder protested, but he managed to turn fully on to his side and gazed his fill at her. To think that in that proud head, held high even in sleep, and to think that in those breasts, two beautiful firm mounds on her chest looking like calabashes turned upside-down, there was some tenderness was momentarily incredible to him. He felt himself burn.

Then the anger came to him again as he remembered how many times this young woman had teased and demeaned him sexually. He felt like jumping on her, clawing at her, hurting her. Then again the thought that she needed him and was there just for his sake came uppermost in his mind and won against the vengeful impulse. He found himself rolling towards her, giving her nipples gentle lover's bites, letting his tongue glide down the hollow in the center of her breasts and then back again. He caressed her thigh with his good hand, moving to her small night lappa and fingering her coral waist-beads. Ona gasped and opened her eyes. She wanted to scream. But Agbadi was faster, more experienced. He slid on his belly, like a big black snake, and covered her mouth with his. He did not let her mouth free for a very long time. She struggled fiercely like a trapped animal, but Agbadi was becoming himself again. He was still weak, but not weak enough to ignore his desire. He worked on her, breaking down all her resistance. He stroked and explored with his perfect hand, banking heavily on the fact that Ona was a woman, a mature woman, who had had him many a time. And he was right. Her struggling and kicking lessened. She started to moan and groan instead, like a woman in labor. He kept on, and would not let go, so masterful was he in this art. He knew he had reduced her to longing and craving for him. He knew he had won. He wanted her completely humiliated in her burning desire. And Ona knew. So she tried to counteract her feelings in the only way she guessed would not give her away.

"I know you are too ill to take me," she murmured.

"No, my Ona, I am waiting for you to be ready."

She felt like screaming to let free the burning of her body. How   55
could one's body betray one so? She should have got up and run out, but something was holding her there; she did not know what and she did not care. She wanted to be relieved of the fire inside her. "Please, I am in pain."

"Yes," came his confident reply. "I want you to be."

She melted and could say no more. She wept and the sobs she was trying to suppress shook her whole being. He felt it, chuckled, and remarked thickly, "Please, Ona, don't wake the whole household."

Either she did not hear, or he wanted her to do just that, for he gave her two painful bites in between her breasts, and she in desperation clawed at him, and was grateful when at last she felt him inside her.

He came deceptively gently, and so unprepared was she for the passionate thrust which followed that she screamed, so piercingly she was even surprised at her own voice: "Agbadi, you are splitting me in two!"

Suddenly the whole courtyard seemed to be filled with moving   60
people. A voice, a male voice, which later she recognized to be that of Agbadi's friend Obi Idayi, shouted from the corner of the open courtyard: "Agbadi! Agbadi! Are you all right?"

Again came that low laughter Ona loved and yet loathed so much. "I am fine, my friend. You go to sleep. I am only giving my woman her pleasures."

Grunting like an excited animal with a helpless prey, he left her abruptly, still unsatiated, and rolled painfully to the other side of the goatskin. Having hurt her on purpose for the benefit of his people sleeping in the courtyard, he had had his satisfaction.

She hated him at that moment. "All this show just for your people, Agbadi?" she whispered. Unable to help herself, she began to cry quietly.

Then he was sorry for her. He moved her closer to him and, letting her curl up to him, encouraged her to get the bitterness off her chest.

He felt her hot tears flowing, but he said nothing, just went on tracing the contours of those offending nipples.

Agbadi's senior wife, Agunwa, became ill that very night. Some said later that she sacrificed herself for her husband; but a few had noticed that it was bad for her morale to hear her husband giving pleasure to another woman in the same courtyard where she slept, and to such a woman who openly treated the man they all worshipped so badly. A woman who was troublesome and impetuous, who had the audacity to fight with her man before letting him have her: a bad woman.

Agbadi and Ona were still sleeping the following morning when the alarm was raised by one of the children.

"Wake up, Father, wake up! Our mother is having a seizure."

"What?" Agbadi barked. "What is the matter with her? She was all right last night." Momentarily he forgot himself and made as if to get up; Ona, wide awake now, restrained him. "Damn this shoulder," he grumbled. "But what is the matter with Agunwa?"

"That's what we are trying to find out," said the reassuring voice of Idayi, who had been keeping vigil over his friend.

"Lie still, Agbadi," other voices advised.

He watched helplessly as they took his senior wife away to her hut in her own part of the compound. "Send her my medicine man. What is the matter with the woman?" he fumed.

Soon his friend came from Agunwa's hut and told him. "Your chief wife is very ill. Your *dibia* is doing all he can for her, but I don't think she will survive."

"Why, Idayi, why at this time?"

"Nobody knows when their time will come. Your wife Agunwa is no exception. The strain of your illness . . . since the day we brought you back from Ude, she has watched over you from that corner of your courtyard. She was even here last night."

"Oh, come, my friend. What are you trying to tell me? She's my chief wife, I took her to Udo the day I became an Obi. She is the mother of my grown sons. You are wrong, Idayi, to suggest she might be sore or bitter just because last night with Ona I amused myself a little. Agunwa is too mature to mind that. Why, if she behaved like that what kind of example would that be to the younger wives?"

"You talk of last night as only a little amusement. But it kept all of us awake. You and your Ona woke the very dead . . ."

Goats and hens were sacrificed in an attempt to save Agunwa. When, on the eighteenth day, Agbadi was able to get up and move about with the help of one of his male slaves and a stick, the first place he visited was his senior wife's hut. He was shocked to see her. She was too far gone to even know of his presence.

He looked around and saw two of his grown sons watching him. "Your mother is a good woman. So unobtrusive, so quiet. I don't know who else will help me keep an eye on those young wives of mine, and see to the smooth running of my household."

Two days later, Agunwa died and Agbadi sent a big cow to her people to announce her death. Having died a "complete woman," she was to be buried in her husband's compound.

"Make sure that her slave and her cooking things go with her. We   80 must all mourn her."

Ona moved about like a quiet wife. She knew that people blamed her for Agunwa's death though no one had the courage to say so openly. That night, after she had given Agbadi his meal and helped his men rub life into his stiff side and shoulder, she curled up to him and asked: "Would you like me to go now? My father will be worrying, wondering what your people are saying."

"And what are my people saying, woman? That I took my mistress in my own courtyard, and that I take her every night as I see fit? Is that it? Haven't I got enough to worry about without you adding your bit? Go to sleep, Ona, you're tired and you don't look too well to me. Tomorrow is going to be a busy day. The burial of a chief's wife is not a small thing in Ibuza."

The funeral dancing and feasting started very early in the morning and went on throughout the day. Different groups of people came and went and had to be entertained. In the evening it was time to put Agunwa in her grave. All the things that she would need in her after-life were gathered and arranged in her wooden coffin which was made of the best mahogany Agbadi could find. Then her personal slave was ceremoniously called in a loud voice by the medicine man: She must be laid inside the grave first. A good slave was supposed to jump into the grave willingly, happy to accompany her mistress; but this young and beautiful woman did not wish to die yet.

She kept begging for her life, much to the annoyance of many of the men standing around. The women stood far off for this was a custom they found revolting. The poor slave was pushed into the shallow grave, but she struggled out, fighting and pleading, appealing to her owner Agbadi.

Then Agbadi's eldest son cried in anger: "So my mother does not   85 even deserve a decent burial? Now we are not to send her slave down with her, just because the girl is beautiful?" So saying, he gave the woman a sharp blow with the head of the cutlass he was carrying. "Go down like a good slave!" he shouted.

"Stop that at once!" Agbadi roared, limping up to his son. "What do you call this, bravery? You make my stomach turn."

The slave woman turned her eyes, now glazed with approaching death, towards him. "Thank you for this kindness, Nwokocha the son of Agbadi. I shall come back to your household, but as a legitimate daughter. I shall come back . . ."

Another relative gave her a final blow to the head, and at last she fell into the grave, silenced for ever. As her blood spurted, splashing the men standing round, there was a piercing scream from the group of mourning women standing a little way off. But it was not their feelings for the dead woman that caused this reaction, Agbadi saw; they were holding Ona up.

"Now what is happening?" Agbadi said hoarsely. "My friend Idayi, take the burial kola nut and finish the ceremony. I think Umunna's daughter Ona wants to die on me, too. She has been ill all day, I don't know why. I must take her inside." He limped over to her with his stick as fast as he could.

Ona was lain on a goatskin in Agbadi's courtyard while the medicine   90
man went on praying and performing in the center of the compound. For a while that night Ona went hot and cold, but before dawn it was clear that although the illness was tiring and weakening her she could bear it. Agbadi's early fear had been that it might be *iba*, the malaria which killed anyone in a short time.

Obi Umunna came in the morning and said to Agbadi without preamble: "I think there is something in your family killing everyone. First you barely escaped death, then your Agunwa was taken, now my healthy daughter who came to look after you —"

"My friend, if you were not an Obi like me, and not Ona's father, I would tell you a few home truths. If she is ill because of a curse in my household, would it not be right for you to leave her with me until she gets better? I will look after her myself."

Over the next few days Agbadi's practiced eyes noted the pattern of the sickness, and he said to Ona one morning as she sat beside him, "Ona, the daughter of Umunna, I think I am making you into a mother. You are carrying our love child."

He said it so lightly that she was too surprised to say a word.

"Well, it is true. What are you going to say to your father?"   95

"Oh, please, Agbadi, don't take my joy away. You know I like staying here with you, but I am my father's daughter. He has no son. Your house is full of children. Please, Nwokocha the son of Agbadi, your bravery is known afar and so is your tenderness. Don't complicate this for me — the greatest joy of my life."

"But what of me? You and your father are using me as a tool to get what you wanted."

"We did not force you, remember," Ona said, anger rising in her. "Is it my fault that you decided to treat me as a wife and not a lover? You knew of my father's determination before you came to me. We did not use you. You used me, yet I don't regret it. If you want to regret it, well, that is up to you."

"So when are you leaving me?" Agbadi asked eventually.

"As soon as I feel stronger. You are getting better every day, ready to go back to your farm."   100

"Forget about my farm. Hurry up and get well, and go back to your shameless father."

"Don't call him names," she cried, and felt very weak.

"You see, you won't even allow yourself to be a woman. You are in the first weeks of motherhood, and all you can do is to think like a man, raising male issue for your father, just because he cannot do it himself."

"I am not going to quarrel with you," Ona declared.

That day, for the first time since the accident, Agbadi went to his   105 farm, much to everybody's surprise. "I want to see how the work is going," he replied to questions people put to him.

Ona felt lonely during his absence. But she sent word to her father to come for her the next day.

On that last night, she tried to reason with Agbadi, but he gave her his stiff back. "All right," she said in compromise, "my father wants a son and you have many sons. But you do not have a girl yet. Since my father will not accept any bride price from you, if I have a son he will belong to my father, but if a girl, she will be yours. That is the best I can do for you both."

They made it up before morning, Agbadi being tender and loving the rest of the night.

The next day, the women from Obi Umunna's compound came with presents for Agbadi's household. They were all very polite to each other, and Ona was relieved to note that her father had not come; she could not stand another argument between the two men, though she supposed she should regard herself as lucky for two men to want to own her.

Nwokocha Agbadi visited her often in her hut, and slept there many   110 an Eke night when he did not have to go to the farm or hunting. People had thought that after a while he would get fed up with her, but that was not so. Each parting was painful, just as if they were young people playing by the moonlight.

Some days when he could not come to her, she knew he was with his other wives. Being Agbadi, however, he never talked about them to her, and she respected him for it. It was on such a night that she came into labor. She cried quietly as she agonized alone through the long hours of darkness. Only when the pain became unbearable did she enlist the help of the women in her father's compound.

Her baby daughter was very merciful to her. "She simply glided into the world," the women around told her.

Ona was dazed with happiness. Agbadi had won, she thought to herself, at the same time feeling pity for her poor father.

Agbadi came the very second day and was visibly overjoyed. "Well, you have done well, Ona. A daughter, eh?"

He bent down and peeped at the day-old child wrapped and kept 115 warm by the fireside and remarked: "This child is priceless, more than twenty bags of cowries. I think that should really be her name, because she is a beauty and she is mine. Yes, 'Nnu Ego': twenty bags of cowries."

He called in the men who came with him and they brought enough yams and drinks to last Ona a long time, for custom did not allow him to go near her again until after twenty-five days.

Obi Umunna came in and for a while the two men toasted and prayed for the happiness of the new child.

"Did Ona tell you of our compromise? She agreed that if she bore a baby girl, she would be mine, if a boy, he would be yours," Agbadi said coolly.

"That may be true, my friend. I am not a man who can take seriously talks lovers have on their love mat. She was your guest, and you were a sick man then."

"What are you trying to say, Umunna? That your daughter should 120 go back on her promise?"

"She is a woman so I don't see why not. However, because she is my daughter, I am not asking her to violate her word. Yes, the baby is yours, but my daughter remains here. I have not accepted any money from you."

"How much do you want for her? What else do you expect? Is it her fault that you have no son?" Agbadi was beginning to roar like the wild animals he was wont to hunt and kill.

"Please, please, aren't you two happy that I have survived the birth? It seems nobody is interested in that part of it. I made a promise to Agbadi, yes; but, dear Agbadi, I am still my father's daughter. Since he has not taken a bride price from you, do you think it would be right for me to stay with you permanently? You know our custom does not permit it. I am still my father's daughter," Ona intoned sadly.

Agbadi drew himself up from the mud pavement where he had been sitting and said, "I have never forced a woman to come to me. Never, and I am not going to start now. The only women I captured were slaves. All my wives are happy to be such. You want to stay with your father? So be it." And he left alone.

For months, Ona did not see Agbadi. She heard from people that he 125
more or less lived in thick, swampy Ude where game was plentiful. Ona
missed him, yet she knew that, according to the way things were, she
was doing the right thing.

A year after the birth of Nnu Ego, Obi Umunna died, and Ona cried
for days for him, especially as he had gone without her producing the
wanted son. Agbadi relented when he heard of it, for he knew how
close Ona was to her father.

For over two years, he persisted in trying to persuade her to come
and live in his compound. "You are no longer bound by your father's
hopes. He is dead. But we are still living. Come and stay with me. You
are all alone here among your extended relatives. Please, Ona, don't let
us waste our lives longing for each other."

"You know my father would not have liked it, so stop talking like
that, Agbadi. I refuse to be intimidated by your wealth and your position."

Yet Agbadi went on visiting his Ona.

Nnu Ego was the apple of her parents' eyes. She was a beautiful 130
child, fair-skinned like the women from the Aboh and Itsekiri areas. At
her birth it was noticed that there was a lump on her head, which in
due course was covered with thick, curly, black hair. But suddenly one
evening she started to suffer from a strange headache that held her head
and shoulder together. In panic, Ona sent for Agbadi who came tearing
down from Ogboli with a *dibia*.

The *dibia* touched the child's head and drew in his breath, feeling
how much hotter the lump was than the rest of her body. He quickly set
to work, arranging his pieces of kola nut and snail shells and cowries on
the mud floor. He soon went into a trance and began to speak in a far-
off voice, strange and unnatural: "This child is the slave woman who
died with your senior wife Agunwa. She promised to come back as a
daughter. Now here she is. That is why the child has the fair skin of the
water people, and the painful lump on her head is from the beating
your men gave her before she fell into the grave. She will always have
trouble with that head. If she has a fortunate life, the head will not play
up. But if she is unhappy, it will trouble her both physically and emotionally. My advice is that you go and appease the slave woman."

"Ona, you must leave this place," Agbadi ordered, "you have to leave
your father's house, otherwise I am taking my daughter from you. She
can't worship her *chi* from a foreign place; she must be where her *chi* is
until all the sacrifices have been made."

So Ona finally had to leave her people, not because she allowed her
love for Agbadi to rule her actions but because she wanted the safety of

her child. As soon as they arrived at Ogboli, Nnu Ego got better. The slave woman was properly buried in a separate grave, and an image of her was made for Nnu Ego to carry with her.

Soon after that, Ona became pregnant again. From the very beginning she was ill, so that it was not a surprise to Agbadi's household when she came into premature labor. After the birth, Ona was weak but her head was clear. She knew she was dying.

"Agbadi," she called hoarsely, "you see that I was not destined to live 135 with you. But you are stubborn, my father was stubborn, and I am stubborn too. Please don't mourn me for long; and see that however much you love our daughter Nnu Ego you allow her to have a life of her own, a husband if she wants one. Allow her to be a woman."

Not long after this, Ona died; and her weak newborn son followed her only a day later. So all Nwokocha Agbadi had to remind him of his great passion for Ona was their daughter, Nnu Ego.

EXPLORATIONS

1. Buchi Emecheta remarks in paragraph 1 of "Ona" that in Nwokocha Agbadi's time, "physical prowess determined one's role in life." Why? What specific tasks and demands in the story make physical prowess crucial? Besides telling us what they look like, how does Emecheta establish Agbadi's and Ona's prowess?

2. After listing Agbadi's qualities, Emecheta concludes: "people naturally accepted him as a leader." Find at least four other places in "Ona" where the tribe or its myths are cited in this way as the source of information, authority, or both. Would these phrases work as well in a Western story? Why or why not?

3. What activities in "Ona" involve rituals that would be regarded in the United States as unnecessary? What appear to be the benefits of these rituals?

CONNECTIONS

1. J. F. Ade Ajayi notes in "On the Politics of Being Mortal" (p. 615) that "the interest of the individual may not always be compatible with that of the group" (para. 12). According to Ajayi, how do African and Western views differ as to whose interest comes first? What aspects of the romance between Agbadi and Ona (and others' reaction to it) illustrate the African view?

2. At the beginning of "Ona," Emecheta establishes Nwokocha Agbadi's credentials: He was a wealthy chief, a great wrestler, "and was glib and gifted in

oratory. His speeches were highly spiced with sharp anecdotes and thought-ful proverbs." What does Es'kia Mphahlele say about language in "African Literature: What Tradition?" (p. 562) that explains why Emecheta puts so much emphasis on her hero's oratorical skills?

3. Reread Dympna Ugwu-Oju's comments on page 394 about the traditional role of an Ibo wife. What examples of her statements appear in "Ona"?

INVESTIGATIONS

1. Chinua Achebe in "The Song of Ourselves" (p. 599) and Henry Louis Gates Jr. in his epigraph on page 510 comment on the ways British colonial policy has shaped Nigeria's identity. Wole Soyinka's "Nigerian Childhood" (p. 606) illustrates the influence of the Church of England; now in exile in London, Soyinka also has written frequently and passionately about his country's tangled political past and present. Look up some of the other work of the writers in this chapter, add any further research you care to do, and write an essay on the pros or cons or both of Nigeria's "colonial inheritance."

2. News coverage in the West of Nigeria's recent history has been dominated by the violence, repression, and corruption of General Sani Abacha's military regime. However, as Henry Louis Gates Jr. notes, this is a country with not just one but several rich artistic, literary, and religious heritages. Writers not represented in this chapter include the late poets Christopher Okigbo and Ken Saro-Wiwa, the novelist Ben Okri, and the poet Odia Ofeimun, among others. Besides the Ife Oracle Gates mentions, Soyinka's hometown of Abeokuta is dominated by Olumo Rock, where sacrifices still are performed weekly to over 400 Yoruba deities. Find out more about what is going on now in Nigeria and write an essay on some aspect of (or person in) its current events that interests you.

3. Wole Soyinka's "Nigerian Childhood" (p. 606), Toni Morrison's *Beloved* (p. 544), and Sophronia Liu's "So Tsi-fai" (p. 318) all describe encounters with ghosts. What roles do these ghosts play in their respective narratives? How are their dramatic functions different? How does the culture each ghost comes from affect its method of appearing and its reasons for appearing? Write an essay comparing and contrasting these ghosts, bolstering your exploration with additional research as necessary.

PART SIX

INSTITUTIONS AND INDIVIDUALS

Marilynne Robinson • Vine Deloria Jr. and Clifford M. Lytle
Nader Mousavizadeh • Haunani-Kay Trask • Robert Reich
Saul Bellow • Ted Koppel • David Guterson • Octavio Paz
bell hooks • Nuala O'Faolain • Population Communications International
Susan Sontag • Thomas L. Friedman

MIRRORS: The United States

Grace Paley: *Six Days: Some Rememberings*
Cornel West: *Race Matters*
Neil Postman: *Future Shlock*
T. Coraghessan Boyle: *Top of the Food
  Chain*

WINDOWS: The World

Nelson Mandela: *Black Man in a White
  Court* (SOUTH AFRICA)
Aung San Suu Kyi: *Freedom from Fear*
  (BURMA)
Fay Weldon: *Down the Clinical Disco*
  (GREAT BRITAIN)
David Grossman: *Israeli Arab, Israeli Jew* .
  (ISRAEL)

SPOTLIGHT: China

Anchee Min: *The Fall of Autumn Leaves*
Fang Lizhi: *Thoughts on Reform*
Orville Schell: *Fang Lizhi*
Jianying Zha: *Yearnings*

Ever since the Cold War ended, America has acted like a defeated nation. We've turned against our institutions as if they had failed us, as if we were the victims of some great fraud lately and suddenly revealed to us. In a period dominated by people who call themselves conservatives, our own national past is never invoked; conservatism has come to mean loyalty to an ideology called capitalism, which is neither named nor implied in once-authoritative documents such as the Constitution.

It is as if the long struggle had taken place not between real cultures and societies but between two economic theories — capitalism and communism — even though neither theory had ever been realized in pure form. . . .

Granting that our success in the Cold War is deeply equivocal — everlasting harm has been suffered by both sides, and the consequences of the Soviet collapse seem potentially very fearsome — the plain fact is that insofar as the Cold War tested our social cohesiveness and our economic vitality, these attributes did not fail us.

>   – MARILYNNE ROBINSON
>   "Modern Victorians Dressing Politics
>   in the Costumes of History"
>   *Harper's*, 1995

▼ ▼ ▼

The most profound and persistent element that distinguishes Indian ways of governing from European-American forms is the very simple fact that non-Indians have tended to write down and record all the principles and procedures that they believe essential to the formation and operation of a government. The Indians, on the other hand, benefiting from a religious, cultural, social, and economic homogeneity in their tribal societies, have not found it necessary to formalize their political institutions by describing them in a document. In addition, at least with the American experience, citizenship has been a means by which diverse peoples were brought into a relatively homogeneous social whole, and in order to ensure good citizenship, the principles of government have been taught so that newcomers to society can adapt themselves to the rules and regulations under which everyone has agreed to live. Within an Indian tribal society, on the other hand, the simple fact of being born establishes both citizenship and, as the individual grows, a homogeneity of purpose and outlook. Customs, rituals, and traditions are a natural part of life, and individuals grow into an acceptance of them, eliminating the need for formal articulation of the rules of Indian tribal society.

> – VINE DELORIA JR. and CLIFFORD M. LYTLE
> *The Native Within: The Past and Future
> of American Indian Sovereignty,* 1984

▼ ▼ ▼

This New Year's Eve in Denmark, as on every New Year's Eve that I can recall, one ritual of respect was re-enacted, one moment of reflection allowed before the revelries and the all-too-ritualized cheers of new beginnings could start. We had all gathered, about twenty or so old friends at a house in the country, surrounded by the snows of Denmark's first white Christmas in over ten years. Though none of us is exceedingly royalist, we had dropped everything in order to crowd around the television at precisely 6 P.M. for the Queen's New Year's address. It struck me, with my Americanized sensibilities (I have lived here for the past seven years but grew up in Denmark), as a remarkable moment in the life of a modern nation: The entire waking population tuning in, not for entertainment or pleasure or shock, but to be addressed by the monarch. . . .

What does it mean, though, that all of Denmark halts to hear the Queen's words? It doesn't mean that Danes are observing a royal tradition for the sake of tradition, but that they are renewing a tradition year after year, of their own free will. And, more importantly, it means that the Queen and the royal household have grasped a central irony of the constitutional monarchy. An institution as fundamentally undemocratic and unmeritocratic as royal authority can only be sustained, in the modern age, by the most fundamentally democratic and meritocratic conditions of individual ability and achievement. That is to say, only by winning over the people through dignity and charisma and exemplary behavior — by winning their approval — can a monarch earn what he or she in other times was born to: their allegiance.

> – NADER MOUSAVIZADEH
> "Copenhagen Diarist: The Royal We"
> *The New Republic,* 1996

▼ ▼ ▼

From the earliest days of Western contact my people told their guests that *no one* owned the land. The land — like the air and the sea — was for all to use and share as their birthright. Our chiefs were *stewards* of the land; they could not own or privately possess the land any more than they could sell it.

But the *haole* insisted on characterizing our chiefs as feudal landlords and our people as serfs. Thus, a European term which described a European practice founded on the European concept of private property — feudalism — was imposed upon a people halfway around the world from Europe and vastly different from her in every conceivable way. . . . Land tenure changes instituted by Americans and in line with current Western notions of private property were then made to appear beneficial to the Hawaiians. But in practice, such changes benefited the *haole*, who alienated the people from the land, taking it for themselves.

> – HAUNANI-KAY TRASK
> "From a Native Daughter"
> *The American Indian and the Problem of History*, 1987

▼ ▼ ▼

Last year, the top fifth of working Americans took home more money than the other four-fifths put together — the highest portion in postwar history. . . . In many cities and towns, the wealthy have in effect withdrawn their dollars from the support of the public spaces and institutions shared by all and dedicated the savings to their own private services. As public parks and playgrounds deteriorate, there is a proliferation of private health clubs, golf clubs, tennis clubs, skating clubs, and every other type of recreational association in which costs are shared among members. Condominiums and the omnipresent residential communities dun their members to undertake work that financially strapped local governments can no longer afford to do well — maintaining roads, mending sidewalks, pruning trees, repairing street lights, cleaning swimming pools, paying for lifeguards, and, notably, hiring security guards to protect life and property. (The number of private security guards in the United States now exceeds the number of public police officers.)

Of course, wealthier Americans have been withdrawing into their own neighborhoods and clubs for generations. But the new secession is more dramatic because the highest earners now inhabit a different economy from other Americans. The new elite is linked by jet, modem, fax, satellite, and fiber-optic cable to the great commercial and recreational centers of the world, but it is not particularly connected to the rest of the nation.

> – ROBERT REICH
> "The Global Elite"
> *New York Times Magazine*, 1991

There is simply too much to think about. It is hopeless — too many kinds of special preparation are required. In electronics, in economics, in social analysis, in history, in psychology, in international politics, most of us are, given the oceanic proliferating complexity of things, paralyzed by the very suggestion that we assume responsibility for so much. This is what makes packaged opinion so attractive.

It is here that the representatives of knowledge come in — the pundits, the anchormen, the specialist guests of talk shows. What used to be called an exchange of views has become "dialogue," and "dialogue" has been invested with a certain sanctity. Actually, it bears no resemblance to any form of real communication.

> – SAUL BELLOW
> "There Is Simply Too Much
> to Think About"
> *It All Adds Up*, 1994

▼ ▼ ▼

Let us give a name to that sandwich that my colleagues and I produce on television. Let us call it, for want of a better name, McThought. Just as the McDonald's hamburger has a vast distribution, so, too, does the McThought that is disseminated on television. Just as an increasingly large share of our population in this country is deriving its physical sustenance from McDonald's hamburgers, so, too, I fear, that an ever increasing number of people in this country are drawing their intellectual sustenance from television.

> – TED KOPPEL
> *Georgia Review*, 1995

▼ ▼ ▼

Professional sport, it seems fair to say, is a primary expression of the American character at the end of the twentieth century. Like money, it is something we love, a first waking thought and a chronic passion, as well as a vast sector of the economy, a wellspring for contemporary myth and totem, and a media phenomenon of the highest order. Our sports can fend off the brute facts of existence, temporarily arrest the sadness of life, briefly shroud the inevitability of death, and provide the happy illusion of meaning through long, enchanted afternoons. The elation of games can hold us spellbound until finally we are forced to accept their endings, and then we are spent and returned to life, rendered hollow or exuberantly fulfilled, but always afterward cognizant of the real world, with its bits of peanut shell under our shoes and the dark hint of rain to the west. In short, nothing about our national life is quite so national as sport is. Sport is a language we all speak. Sport is a mirror. Sport is life. Through sport we might know ourselves.

– DAVID GUTERSON
Harper's, 1994

▼ ▼ ▼

Literature has always been the product of a small group of writers and a small group of readers. I think the great difference between the past and modern times is not the *number* of people who read good books — these people have always been the minority — but the *kind* of people. In the time of Dante, the clerics and politicians, the directors of society, read poetry. In the Renaissance, you may recall, all the kings used to write poetry, some bad, some good, but poetry was popular in the upper class. With democracy, something changed, and the first one to notice this was Tocqueville, who saw very clearly that in the United States something new had appeared: the masses. The daily food for the masses became the newspapers, television, and other things.

It's useful to have television; it is useful to have newspapers; it is also useful to have good books. The problem is finding the right readers.

– OCTAVIO PAZ
Georgia Review, 1995

▼ ▼ ▼

In our society's cultural representations, poverty is characterized as negative. Why do people assume that a young woman like my sister A., who is on welfare and does not have a job all the time, couldn't use that time to create? We tend to see the realm of creativity as a class-bound world where those who inhabit a certain class position (a position that frees them from experiences of suffering and pain) are better situated to be artists. This is ironic. We forget about the relationship of Van Gogh's poverty to his painting. We use language that delegitimizes suffering: "You don't have to be starving artists in the garret." While that statement is true, we would not want to disallow, forget, or disremember the relationship of those particular forms of suffering to the art that is produced.

It is essential to restore to each life a respect for creativity and artistic production, no matter our class background. The great power of art is that all people can create. Despite deprivation, the imagination is not bound by limitations of class, race, or gender.

– bell hooks
"The Other Side"
Utne Reader, 1994

▼ ▼ ▼

I don't know who the Irish Republican Army (IRA) men and women mix with. If there are any IRA people in the little village in the west of Ireland where I was when the Canary Wharf bomb went off, they must have noticed the heartfelt grief that was the only reaction. . . .

The ordinary person in the South just doesn't see why the IRA feels justified in going on killing. But I suppose we don't matter to them. It seems that people outside their own people have no reality for them. If they cared for the intricate mystery of hundreds of human beings hurrying through a railway station after a day's work, they wouldn't send glass and brick and metal crashing and screaming into their innocent faces.

Who does the IRA think Irish nationalists in the South sympathize with — them or the office workers going home from work? Why would there be any sympathy with the project of murdering English people?

– NUALA O'FAOLAIN
"A Dialogue of the Deaf"
The Irish Times, 1996

▼ ▼ ▼

It wasn't the first time, but China's decision to prohibit dogs on its territory effective July 31 of this year sent shudders down the spines of many a pet owner. Nevertheless, the government, citing a burgeoning canine population that is a major environmental burden, defended the measure. China's capital, Beijing, has almost 200,000 dogs, and nationwide, there are over 100,000,000 — about one dog for every eleven persons. The dogs eat up fifteen tons of food per year, enough to feed 40 million Chinese. While a human being consumes the equivalent of half a kilo of cereal per day, dogs eat more than double that. It is estimated that 7 percent of the country's grain production goes "to the dogs." The government attempted the ban in 1994, but it was difficult to impose the rule in the Year of the Dog.

The prohibition does allow for some exemptions: Any dog measuring under 36 cm (14 inches) is allowed, as well as all Pekinese, a species long accorded almost reverential status in China. Those whose dogs meet the requirements must shell out U.S. $460 a year, approximately triple the wages of an employee working in a large city, in exchange for a medallion tag for the pet and an embossed registration certificate. For many, the only solution is having the dog shipped out of the country or killed. "We are going to be very strict with this new law," says Cho Wong Pu, head of the Dog Propaganda Unit in Beijing. "We have a duty to protect people and maintain social order and to clean up the environment. This law is deeply welcomed by the masses."

– POPULATION COMMUNICATIONS
INTERNATIONAL, 1995

For a long time almost all influential foreign scholarship and thinking about China started from the assumption that China was an essentially collectivist society with no indigenous tradition of individual rights. Hence, Sinologists argued, we shouldn't expect a real movement for democracy and for individual rights as these are understood in the West to emerge in China. This double-standard thinking about China reflects the general decline of universalist moral and political standards — of Enlightenment values — in the past generation. There is an increasing reluctance to apply a single standard of political justice, of freedom, and of individual rights and of democracy. The usual justifications for this reluctance are that it is "colonialist" (the label used by people on the left) or "Euro-centric" (the label used both by multiculturalist academics and by businessmen, who talk admiringly of authoritarian "Confucian cultures") to expect or to want non-European peoples to have "our" values. My own view is that it is precisely the reluctance to apply these standards — as if "we" in the European and the neo-European countries need them, but the Chinese and the peoples of Africa don't — that is colonialist and condescending.

– SUSAN SONTAG
New York Review of Books, 1996

▼ ▼ ▼

Like one of the great sea powers of old, Microsoft today controls access to the modern lanes of communication. Microsoft operating systems run 85 percent of the world's personal computers. Microsoft doesn't need Washington to open doors for it because foreign governments are begging Microsoft to come in and translate Windows 95 into their languages, so they can get on the information highway. . . . China has the greatest potential, not just because it has 1.2 billion people but because its birth control policies restricting every family to one child mean there are often two sets of grandparents and two parents — that is six adults — saving to buy a computer and software for each kid.

[Redmond, WA, executive Steve] Ballmer says Japan is just now taking off for Microsoft products, while Israel is so far advanced it has one of the few Microsoft development centers outside Redmond. But Microsoft's hottest market in the Middle East is Saudi Arabia. Iran and Egypt are nil, but India and Brazil are booming. The one European democracy that is slipping is France. Says Mr. Ballmer: "I don't want to say [France] has fallen behind," but "the penetration of PC's relative to population was quite high in France. That's not true anymore." . . .

While Microsoft is a coldblooded economic giant, its technology, along with that of its competitors, can foster democracy in ways G.M.

never could. Its software is making it possible for individuals to communicate horizontally, through the Internet, across international boundaries, and to create groups and information pools that are outside all government authority. To take full advantage of that software, societies have to become more open, deregulated, and interactive. Says Mr. Ballmer: "Once you let people on the Internet, the control aspects are reasonably out the window."

– THOMAS L. FRIEDMAN
New York Times, 1995

EXPLORATIONS

1. Marilynne Robinson writes: "We've turned against our institutions as if they had failed us" (p. 646). What are some specific examples of the institutions Americans have recently turned against, and which segments of American society have done the rejecting? According to Nuala O'Faolain (p. 651), what groups in Northern Ireland are rejecting which of their institutions, and why? Judging from Nader Mousavizadeh's comments on Denmark's monarchy (p. 647), why haven't Danes rejected this national institution?

2. Vine Deloria Jr. and Clifford M. Lytle briefly describe the way citizenship works in the United States. Which of the "rules and regulations under which everyone has agreed to live" (p. 646) does Robert Reich accuse the wealthiest Americans of rejecting (p. 648)? How do you think Reich would respond to Marilynne Robinson's contention that "our social cohesiveness and our economic vitality" have not failed us? How do you think Deloria and Lytle would respond?

3. Bell hooks asks, "Why do people assume that a young woman like my sister A., who is on welfare and does not have a job all the time, couldn't use that time to create?" (p. 650) What do you think is the answer to this question? Do you agree with hooks that to "inhabit a certain class position . . . frees [people] from experiences of suffering and pain"? Why or why not?

4. What is Haunani-Kay Trask's opinion (p. 647) about Westerners imposing their ideas about social structure on Hawaii, and why? What is Susan Sontag's opinion (p. 652) about Westerners imposing their ideas about social structure on China, and why? Which of their views do you agree with, and why?

MIRRORS:
THE UNITED STATES

▲▲▲▲▲▲▲▲▲▲
▼▼▼▼▼▼▼▼▼▼

Institutions and Individuals: *The exit is out of reach from a jail cell.*

GRACE PALEY

Six Days: Some Rememberings

Poet and short-story writer Grace Paley was born in New York City's borough of the Bronx in 1922. She studied at Hunter College and New York University. Married twice and the mother of two children, Paley has described herself as "a typist, a housewife, and a writer" as well as "a somewhat combative pacifist and cooperative anarchist." She has taught at Columbia and Syracuse universities, Dartmouth and Sarah Lawrence colleges, and the City College of New York. The winner of several writing awards, Paley also has been a faculty member and writer in residence at numerous writers' workshops, including the Fine Arts Work Center in Provincetown, Massachusetts; the Prague Summer Writers' Workshop; and Art Workshop International in Assisi, Italy. Many of the stories in her collections, which include *The Little Disturbances of Man* (1959), *Enormous Changes at the Last Minute* (1974), and *Later the Same Day* (1985), reflect her experience as a female Jewish New Yorker. Paley told an interviewer for *Threepenny Review* in 1996, "You don't have to love your cultural roots, but you have to recognize them in some way. They are the sounds that were always in your ear." Her poetry appears in the prose and poetry collection *Long Walks and Intimate Talks* (1991) and in *New and Collected Poems* (1992). In 1989, governor Mario Cuomo declared Paley the first official New York State Writer. Her most recent book, "The Collected Stories" (1994), was nominated for the National Book Award. "Six Days: Some Rememberings" first appeared in the *Alaska Quarterly Review* (1995).

I was in jail. I had been sentenced to six days in the Women's House of Detention, a fourteen-story prison right in the middle of Greenwich Village, my own neighborhood. This happened during the American War in Vietnam, I have forgotten which important year of the famous sixties. The civil disobedience for which I was paying a small penalty probably consisted of sitting down to impede or slow some military parade.

I was surprised at the sentence. Others had been given two days or dismissed. I think the judge was particularly angry with me. After all, I was not a kid. He thought I was old enough to know better, a forty-five-year-old woman, a mother and teacher. I ought to be too busy to waste time on causes I couldn't possibly understand.

I was herded with about twenty other women, about 90 percent black and Puerto Rican, into the bullpen, an odd name for a women's holding facility. There, through someone else's lawyer, I received a note from home, telling me that since I'd chosen to spend the first week of July in jail, my son would probably not go to summer camp, because I had neglected to raise the money I'd promised. I read this note and burst into tears, real running-down-the-cheek tears. It was true: Thinking about other people's grown boys, I had betrayed my little son. The summer, starting that day, July 1, stood up before me day after day, the steaming city streets, the after-work crowded city pool.

I guess I attracted some attention. You — you white girl you — you never been arrested before? A black woman about a head taller than I put her arm on my shoulder. — It ain't so bad. What's your time sugar? I gotta do three years. You huh?

Six days.   5

Six days? What the fuck for?

I explained, sniffling, embarrassed.

You got six days for sitting down in front of a horse? Cop on the horse? Horse step on you? Jesus in hell, cops gettin crazier and stupider and meaner. Maybe we get you out.

No, no, I said. I wasn't crying because of that. I didn't want her to think I was scared. I wasn't. She paid no attention. Shoving a couple of women aside — Don't stand in front of me, bitch. Move over. What you looking at? — she took hold of the bars of our cage, commenced to bang on them, shook them mightily, screaming — Hear me now, you motherfuckers, you grotty pigs, get this housewife out of here! She returned to comfort me. — Six days in this low-down hole for sitting in front of a horse!

Before we were distributed among our cells, we were dressed in a   10
kind of nurse's aide scrub uniform, blue or green, a little too large or a little too small. We had had to submit to a physical in which all our hiding places were investigated for drugs. These examinations were not too difficult, mostly because a young woman named Andrea Dworkin had fought them, refused a grosser, more painful examination some months earlier. She had been arrested protesting the war in front of the U.S. Mission to the UN. I had been there too, but I don't think I was arrested that day. She was mocked for that determined struggle at the Women's House, as she had been for other braveries, but according to the women I questioned, certain humiliating, perhaps sadistic customs had ended — for that period at least.

My cellmate was a beautiful young woman, twenty-three years old, a prostitute who'd never been arrested before. She was nervous, but she had been given the name of an important long-termer. She explained in a businesslike way that she *was* beautiful, and would need protection. She'd be O.K. once she found that woman. In the two days we spent together, she tried *not* to talk to the other women on our cell block. She said they were mostly street whores and addicts. She would never be on the street. Her man wouldn't allow it anyway.

I slept well for some reason, probably the hard mattress. I don't seem to mind where I am. Also I must tell you, I could look out the window at the end of our corridor and see my children or their friends, on their way to music lessons or Greenwich House pottery. Looking slantwise I could see right into Sutter's Bakery, then on the corner of Tenth Street. These were my neighbors at coffee and cake.

Sometimes the cell block was open, but not our twelve cells. Other times the reverse. Visitors came by: They were prisoners, detainees not yet sentenced. They seemed to have a strolling freedom, though several, unsentenced, unable to make bail, had been there for months. One woman peering into the cells stopped when she saw me. Grace! Hi! I knew her from the neighborhood, maybe the park, couldn't really remember her name.

What are you in for? I asked.

Oh nothing — well a stupid drug bust. I don't even use — oh well   15 forget it. I've been here six weeks. They keep putting the trial off. Are you O.K.?

Then I complained. I had planned not to complain about anything while living among people who'd be here in these clanging cells a long time; it didn't seem right. But I said, I don't have anything to read and they took away my pen and I don't have paper.

Oh you'll get all that eventually, she said. Keep asking.

Well they have all my hairpins. I'm a mess.

No no she said, you're O.K. You look nice.

(A couple of years later, the war continuing, I was arrested in Wash-   20 ington. My hair was still quite long. I wore it in a kind of bun on top of my head. My hairpins gone, my hair straggled wildly every which way. Muriel Rukeyser, arrested that day along with about thirty other women, made the same generous sisterly remark. No no Grace, love you with your hair down, you really ought to always wear it this way.)

The very next morning, my friend brought me *The Collected Writings of William Carlos Williams.* — These O.K.?

God! O.K. — Yes!

My trial is coming up tomorrow, she said. I think I'm getting off with time already done. Over done. See you around?

That afternoon, my cellmate came for her things — I'm moving to the fourth floor. Working in the kitchen. Couldn't be better. We were sitting outside our cells, she wanted me to know something. She'd already told me, but said it again. — I still can't believe it. This creep, this guy, this cop, he waits he just waits till he's fucked and fine, pulls his pants up, pays me, and arrests me. It's not legal. It's not. My man's so mad, he'd like to kill *me*, but he's not that kind of — he's not a criminal type, *my* man. She never said the word pimp. Maybe no one did. Maybe that was our word.

I had made friends with some of the women in the cells across the   25 aisle. How can I say "made friends." I just sat and spoke when spoken to, I was at school. I answered questions — simple ones. Why would I do such a fool thing on purpose? How old were my children? My man any good? Then, you live around the corner? That was a good idea, Evelyn said, to have a prison in your own neighborhood, so you could keep in touch, yelling out the window. As in fact we were able to do right here and now, calling and being called from Sixth Avenue, by mothers, children, boyfriends.

About the children: One woman took me aside. Her daughter was brilliant, she was in Hunter High School, had taken a test. No she hardly ever saw her, but she wasn't a whore — it was the drugs. Her daughter was ashamed, the grandmother, the father's mother made the child ashamed. When she got out in six months it would be different. This made Evelyn and Rita, right across from my cell, laugh. Different, I swear. Different. Laughing. But she *could* make it, I said. Then they really laughed. Their first laugh was a bare giggle compared to these convulsive roars. Change her ways? That dumb bitch Ha!!

Another woman, Helen, the only other white woman on the cell block, wanted to talk to me. She wanted me to know that she was not only white but Jewish. She came from Brighton Beach. Her father, he should rest in peace, thank God, was dead. Her arms were covered with puncture marks almost like sleeve patterns. But she needed to talk to me, because I was Jewish (I'd been asked by Rita and Evelyn — was I Irish? No, Jewish. Oh, they answered). She walked me to the barred window that looked down on West Tenth Street. She said, How come you so friends with those black whores? You don't hardly talk to me. I said I liked them, but I liked her too. She said, If you knew them for true, you wouldn't like them. They nothing but street whores. You know, once I was friends with them. We done a lot of things together, I knew them fifteen years Evy and Rita maybe twenty, I been in the streets with them, side by side, Amsterdam, Lenox, West Harlem; in bad weather we covered each other. Then one day along come Malcolm X and they don't know me no more, they ain't talking to me. You too white. I ain't all that white. Twenty years. They ain't talking.

My friend Myrt called one day, that is called from the street, called — Grace Grace. I heard and ran to the window. A policeman, the regular beat cop, was addressing her. She looked up, then walked away before I could yell my answer. Later on she told me that he'd said, I don't think Grace would appreciate you calling her name out like that.

What a mistake! For years, going to the park with my children, or simply walking down Sixth Avenue on a summer night past the Women's House, we would often have to thread our way through whole families calling up — bellowing, screaming to the third, seventh, tenth floor, to figures, shadows behind bars and screened windows — How you feeling? Here's Glena. She got big. Mami mami you like my dress? We gettin you out baby. New lawyer come by.

And the replies, among which I was privileged to live for a few days — 30 shouted down. — You lookin beautiful. What he say? Fuck you James. I got a chance? Bye bye. Come next week.

Then the guards, the heavy clanking of cell doors. Keys. Night.

I still had no pen or paper despite the great history of prison literature. I was suffering a kind of frustration, a sickness in the way claustrophobia is a sickness — this paper-and-penlessness was a terrible pain in the area of my heart, a nausea. I was surprised.

In the evening, at lights out (a little like the army or on good days a strict, unpleasant camp), women called softly from their cells. Rita hey Rita sing that song — Come on sister sing. A few more importunings and then Rita in the cell diagonal to mine would begin with a ballad. A song about two women and a man. It was familiar to everyone but me. The two women were prison sweethearts. The man was her outside lover. One woman, the singer, was being paroled. The ballad told her sorrow about having been parted from him when she was sentenced, now she would leave her loved woman after three years. There were about twenty stanzas of joy and grief.

Well, I was so angry not to have pen and paper to get some of it down that I lost it all — all but the sorrowful plot. Of course she had this long song in her head, and in the next few nights she sang and chanted others, sometimes with a small chorus.

Which is how I finally understood that I didn't lack pen and paper 35 but my own memorizing mind. It had been given away with a hundred poems, called rote learning, old-fashioned, backward, an enemy of creative thinking, a great human gift, disowned.

Now there's a garden where the Women's House of Detention once stood. A green place, safely fenced in, with protected daffodils and tulips; roses bloom in it too, sometimes into November.

The big women's warehouse and its barred blind windows have been removed from Greenwich Village's affluent throat. I was sorry when it happened; the bricks came roaring down, great trucks carried them away.

I have always agreed with Rita and Evelyn that if there are prisons, they ought to be in the neighborhood, near a subway — not way out in distant suburbs, where families have to take cars, buses, ferries, trains, and the population that considers itself innocent forgets, denies, chooses to never know that there is a whole huge country of the bad and the unlucky and the self-hurters, a country with a population greater than that of many nations in our world.

EXPLORATIONS

1. What is Grace Paley's attitude toward being in jail? What are the effects of her not describing her feelings explicitly? What cues in "Six Days: Some Rememberings" reveal her reactions to the experience?

2. How do Paley's choices not to use quotation marks and not to identify speakers in the usual way suit the setting of her narrative? What other stylistic choices does she make that are appropriate to this memoir, and why are they appropriate?

3. "That was a good idea, Evelyn said, to have a prison in your own neighborhood, so you could keep in touch, yelling out the window" (para. 25). What are some likely reasons why this prison later was moved out of Paley's Greenwich Village neighborhood in downtown New York City? Why was Paley "sorry when it happened" (para. 37)?

CONNECTIONS

1. Vine Deloria Jr. and Clifford M. Lytle note that non-Indians tend to write down all the principles and procedures of their government, while Indians have not found this necessary (p. 646). How is this non-Indian habit reflected in Marilynne Robinson's epigraph (p. 646)? How is it echoed in Paley's essay? After comparing Paley's and Deloria's and Lytle's comments, what advantages can you see in an oral tradition that relies on memory, and what advantages can you see in a record-keeping tradition?

2. Reread the epigraphs by Octavio Paz (p. 650), bell hooks (p. 650), Derek Walcott (p. 509), and Malcolm X (p. 275). What do you think were the

prison's reasons for taking away Grace Paley's pen and not giving her paper or books? What are the disadvantages of this policy?

3. Salman Rushdie writes in "The Broken Mirror" about the partial and fragmentary nature of memory (p. 53). How does Paley alert us from the start of her essay that her memory of her six days in the Women's House of Detention is fragmented in the way Rushdie describes?

ELABORATIONS

1. Simone de Beauvoir in "Woman as Other" (p. 445) and Chinua Achebe in "The Song of Ourselves" (p. 599) write about some of the ways one person may decide that another person does not deserve to be treated as a fellow human being. How does being sent to jail change someone's standing and deserts? Are the annoyances Paley describes in "Six Days: Some Rememberings" reasonable ways for prison employees to treat prisoners? For prisoners to treat each other? If so, why? If not, why not? Use these three selections and others in this book, as well as outside references if you wish, to write an essay on "prisoners as other."

2. A number of internationally known writers have been jailed for political reasons, including some represented in this book: Wole Soyinka in Nigeria and Joseph Brodsky in the Soviet Union, for instance. Choose two such writers from different countries and write an essay comparing and contrasting their experiences: the governmental policies that sent them to prison, their situation while serving time, the impact of their clash with the government on their work and vice versa.

CORNEL WEST

Race Matters

The scholar, theologian, and activist Cornel West was born in Tulsa, Oklahoma, in 1953. His family moved around before settling in Sacramento, California. The Baptist church, in which his grandfather had been a preacher, taught him early lessons about faith and commitment; from the nearby Black Panthers he learned the value of community-based political action. At the age of eight, West read a biography of Theodore Roosevelt — a fellow asthmatic — and decided he too would go to Harvard University. He graduated from Harvard magna cum laude at twenty. After receiving his M.A. in 1975 and his Ph.D. in 1980 from Princeton University, he joined Princeton's faculty, where he became Professor of Religion and Director of Afro-American Studies in 1988. West's books include *Post-Analytic Philosophy* (1985), *Prophetic Fragments* (1988), and, with bell hooks (see p. 650), *Breaking Bread* (1991). "Race Matters" comes from the introduction to his 1993 book by that title, a best-seller which inspired profiles of West in both *Time* and *Newsweek*. He is currently Professor of Afro-American Studies and the Philosophy of Religion at Harvard University. With department chair Henry Louis Gates Jr. (see p. 146), West recently finished writing *The Future of the Race*. He lives near Boston with his wife, Elleni, a social worker from Addis Ababa, Ethiopia, and their son, Clifton.

Since the beginning of the nation, white Americans have suffered from a deep inner uncertainty as to who they really are. One of the ways that has been used to simplify the answer has been to seize upon the presence of black Americans and use them as a marker, a symbol of limits, a metaphor for the "outsider." Many whites could look at the social position of blacks and feel that color formed an easy and reliable gauge for determining to what extent one was or was not American.

Perhaps that is why one of the first epithets that many European immigrants learned when they got off the boat was the term "nigger" — it made them feel instantly American. But this is tricky magic. Despite his racial difference and social status, something indisputably American about Negroes not only raised doubts about the white man's value system but aroused the troubling suspicion that whatever else the true American is, he is also somehow black.

–Ralph Ellison
"What America Would Be Like without Blacks" (1970)

What happened in Los Angeles in April of 1992 was neither a race riot nor a class rebellion. Rather, this monumental upheaval was a multi-racial, trans-class, and largely male display of justified social rage. For all its ugly, xenophobic resentment, its air of adolescent carnival, and its downright barbaric behavior, it signified the sense of powerlessness in American society. Glib attempts to reduce its meaning to the pathologies of the black underclass, the criminal actions of hoodlums, or the political revolt of the oppressed urban masses miss the mark. Of those arrested, only 36 percent were black, more than a third had full-time jobs, and most claimed to shun political affiliation. What we witnessed in Los Angeles was the consequence of a lethal linkage of economic decline, cultural decay, and political lethargy in American life. Race was the visible catalyst, not the underlying cause.

The meaning of the earthshaking events in Los Angeles is difficult to grasp because most of us remain trapped in the narrow framework of the dominant liberal and conservative views of race in America, which with its worn-out vocabulary leaves us intellectually debilitated, morally disempowered, and personally depressed. The astonishing disappearance of the event from public dialogue is testimony to just how painful and distressing a serious engagement with race is. Our truncated public discussions of race suppress the best of who and what we are as a people because they fail to confront the complexity of the issue in a candid and critical manner. The predictable pitting of liberals against conservatives, Great Society Democrats against self-help Republicans, reinforces intellectual parochialism and political paralysis.

The liberal notion that more government programs can solve racial problems is simplistic — precisely because it focuses *solely* on the economic dimension. And the conservative idea that what is needed is a change in the moral behavior of poor black urban dwellers (especially poor black men, who, they say, should stay married, support their children, and stop committing so much crime) highlights immoral actions while ignoring public responsibility for the immoral circumstances that haunt our fellow citizens.

The common denominator of these views of race is that each still sees black people as a "problem people," in the words of Dorothy I. Height, president of the National Council of Negro Women, rather than as fellow American citizens with problems. Her words echo the poignant "unasked question" of W. E. B. Du Bois, who, in *The Souls of Black Folk* (1903), wrote:

> They approach me in a half-hesitant sort of way, eye me curiously or compassionately, and then instead of saying directly, How does it feel to

be a problem? they say, I know an excellent colored man in my town. . . .
Do not these Southern outrages make your blood boil? At these I smile,
or am interested, or reduce the boiling to a simmer, as the occasion may
require. To the real question, How does it feel to be a problem? I answer
seldom a word.

Nearly a century later, we confine discussions about race in America to
the "problems" black people pose for whites, rather than consider what
this way of viewing black people reveals about us as a nation.

This paralyzing framework encourages liberals to relieve their guilty   5
consciences by supporting public funds directed at "the problems"; but
at the same time, reluctant to exercise principled criticism of black
people, liberals deny them the freedom to err. Similarly, conservatives
blame the "problems" on black people themselves — and thereby render black social misery invisible or unworthy of public attention.

Hence, for liberals, black people are to be "included" and "integrated" into "our" society and culture, while for conservatives they are
to be "well behaved" and "worthy of acceptance" by "our" way of life.
Both fail to see that the presence and predicaments of black people are
neither additions to nor defections from American life, but rather *constitutive elements of that life.*

To engage in a serious discussion of race in America, we must begin
not with the problems of black people but with the flaws of American
society — flaws rooted in historic inequalities and longstanding cultural
stereotypes. How we set up the terms for discussing racial issues shapes
our perception and response to these issues. As long as black people are
viewed as a "them," the burden falls on blacks to do all the "cultural"
and "moral" work necessary for healthy race relations. The implication is
that only certain Americans can define what it means to be American —
and the rest must simply "fit in."

The emergence of strong black-nationalist sentiments among blacks,
especially among young people, is a revolt against this sense of having to
"fit in." The variety of black-nationalist ideologies, from the moderate
views of Supreme Court Justice Clarence Thomas in his youth to those
of Louis Farrakhan today, rest upon a fundamental truth: White America has been historically weak-willed in ensuring racial justice and has
continued to resist fully accepting the humanity of blacks. As long as
double standards and differential treatment abound — as long as the rap
performer Ice-T is harshly condemned while former Los Angeles Police
Chief Daryl F. Gates's antiblack comments are received in polite silence, as long as Dr. Leonard Jeffries's anti-Semitic statements are met

with vitriolic outrage while presidential candidate Patrick J. Buchanan's anti-Semitism receives a genteel response — black nationalisms will thrive.

Afrocentrism, a contemporary species of black nationalism, is a gallant yet misguided attempt to define an African identity in a white society perceived to be hostile. It is gallant because it puts black doings and sufferings, not white anxieties and fears, at the center of discussion. It is misguided because — out of fear of cultural hybridization and through silence on the issue of class, retrograde views on black women, gay men, and lesbians, and a reluctance to link race to the common good — it reinforces the narrow discussions about race.

To establish a new framework, we need to begin with a frank acknowledgment of the basic humanness and Americanness of each of us. And we must acknowledge that as a people — *E Pluribus Unum* — we are on a slippery slope toward economic strife, social turmoil, and cultural chaos. If we go down, we go down together. The Los Angeles upheaval forced us to see not only that we are not connected in ways we would like to be but also, in a more profound sense, that this failure to connect binds us even more tightly together. The paradox of race in America is that our common destiny is more pronounced and imperiled precisely when our divisions are deeper. The Civil War and its legacy speak loudly here. And our divisions are growing deeper. Today, 86 percent of white suburban Americans live in neighborhoods that are less than 1 percent black, meaning that the prospects for the country depend largely on how its cities fare in the hands of a suburban electorate. There is no escape from our interracial interdependence, yet enforced racial hierarchy dooms us as a nation to collective paranoia and hysteria — the unmaking of any democratic order.

The verdict in the Rodney King case, which sparked the incidents in Los Angeles, was perceived to be wrong by the vast majority of Americans. But whites have often failed to acknowledge the widespread mistreatment of black people, especially black men, by law enforcement agencies, which helped ignite the spark. The verdict was merely the occasion for deep-seated rage to come to the surface. This rage is fed by the "silent" depression ravaging the country — in which real weekly wages of all American workers since 1973 have declined nearly 20 percent, while at the same time wealth has been upwardly distributed.

The exodus of stable industrial jobs from urban centers to cheaper labor markets here and abroad, housing policies that have created "chocolate cities and vanilla suburbs" (to use the popular musical artist George Clinton's memorable phrase), white fear of black crime, and the urban influx of poor Spanish-speaking and Asian immigrants — all have helped erode the tax base of American cities just as the federal government has cut its support and programs. The result is unemployment, hunger, homelessness, and sickness for millions.

And a pervasive spiritual impoverishment grows. The collapse of meaning in life — the eclipse of hope and absence of love of self and others, the breakdown of family and neighborhood bonds — leads to the social deracination and cultural denudement of urban dwellers, especially children. We have created rootless, dangling people with little link to the supportive networks — family, friends, school — that sustain some sense of purpose in life. We have witnessed the collapse of the spiritual communities that in the past helped Americans face despair, disease, and death and that transmit through the generations dignity and decency, excellence and elegance.

The result is lives of what we might call "random nows," of fortuitous and fleeting moments preoccupied with "getting over" — with acquiring pleasure, property, and power by any means necessary. (This is not what Malcolm X meant by this famous phrase.) Postmodern culture is more and more a market culture dominated by gangster mentalities and self-destructive wantonness. This culture engulfs all of us — yet its impact on the disadvantaged is devastating, resulting in extreme violence in everyday life. Sexual violence against women and homicidal assaults by young black men on one another are only the most obvious signs of this empty quest for pleasure, property, and power.

Last, this rage is fueled by a political atmosphere in which images,   15
not ideas, dominate, where politicians spend more time raising money than debating issues. The functions of parties have been displaced by public polls, and politicians behave less as thermostats that determine the climate of opinion than as thermometers registering the public mood. American politics has been rocked by an unleashing of greed among opportunistic public officials — who have followed the lead of their counterparts in the private sphere, where, as of 1989, 1 percent of the population owned 37 percent of the wealth and 10 percent owned 86 percent of the wealth — leading to a profound cynicism and pessimism among the citizenry.

And given the way in which the Republican Party since 1968 has appealed to popular xenophobic images — playing the black, female, and homophobic cards to realign the electorate along race, sex, and sexual-orientation lines — it is no surprise that the notion that we are all part of one garment of destiny is discredited. Appeals to special interests rather than to public interests reinforce this polarization. The Los Angeles upheaval was an expression of utter fragmentation by a powerless citizenry that includes not just the poor but all of us.

What is to be done? How do we capture a new spirit and vision to meet the challenges of the postindustrial city, postmodern culture, and postparty politics?

First, we must admit that the most valuable sources for help, hope, and power consist of ourselves and our common history. As in the ages of Lincoln, Roosevelt, and King, we must look to new frameworks and languages to understand our multilayered crisis and overcome our deep malaise.

Second, we must focus our attention on the public square — the common good that undergirds our national and global destinies. The vitality of any public square ultimately depends on how much we *care* about the quality of our lives together. The neglect of our public infrastructure, for example — our water and sewage systems, bridges, tunnels, highways, subways, and streets — reflects not only our myopic economic policies, which impede productivity, but also the low priority we place on our common life.

The tragic plight of our children clearly reveals our deep disregard for public well-being. About one out of every five children in this country lives in poverty, including one out of every two black children and two out of five Hispanic children. Most of our children — neglected by overburdened parents and bombarded by the market values of profit-hungry corporations — are ill-equipped to live lives of spiritual and cultural quality. Faced with these facts, how do we expect ever to constitute a vibrant society? 20

One essential step is some form of large-scale public intervention to ensure access to basic social goods — housing, food, health care, education, child care, and jobs. We must invigorate the common good with a mixture of government, business, and labor that does not follow any existing blueprint. After a period in which the private sphere has been sacralized and the public square gutted, the temptation is to make a fetish of the public square. We need to resist such dogmatic swings.

Last, the major challenge is to meet the need to generate new leadership. The paucity of courageous leaders — so apparent in the response to the events in Los Angeles — requires that we look beyond the same elites and voices that recycle the older frameworks. We need leaders — neither saints nor sparkling television personalities — who can situate themselves within a larger historical narrative of this country and our world, who can grasp the complex dynamics of our peoplehood and imagine a future grounded in the best of our past, yet who are attuned to the frightening obstacles that now perplex us. Our ideals of freedom, democracy, and equality must be invoked to invigorate all of us, especially the landless, propertyless, and luckless. Only a visionary leadership that can motivate "the better angels of our nature," as Lincoln said, and activate possibilities for a freer, more efficient, and stable America — only that leadership deserves cultivation and support.

This new leadership must be grounded in grass-roots organizing that highlights democratic accountability. Whoever *our* leaders will be as we approach the twenty-first century, their challenge will be to help Americans determine whether a genuine multiracial democracy can be created and sustained in an era of global economy and a moment of xenophobic frenzy.

Let us hope and pray that the vast intelligence, imagination, humor, and courage of Americans will not fail us. Either we learn a new language of empathy and compassion, or the fire this time will consume us all.

EXPLORATIONS

1. When Cornel West refers to *we* and *us*, whom does he mean? How does the meaning of these pronouns change in paragraph 6 when he puts them in quotation marks? How does West's use of the first person plural reinforce his essay's thesis?

2. "The paradox of race in America is that our common destiny is more pronounced and imperiled precisely when our divisions are deeper" (para. 10). Why, according to West, is this so?

3. Whom does West blame for the problems he describes? To whom does he assign responsibility for solving them? Cite evidence for your answers.

CONNECTIONS

1. What similarities and differences between the characters in Grace Paley's "Six Days: Some Rememberings" (p. 655) create alliances and enmities inside the Women's House of Detention? What roles does race play in that enforced community?

2. What points does West make that are also made by Robert Reich (p. 648)? What points does Reich make that West omits? What impact does West believe the economic and social trends he and Reich describe have had on the country?

3. West writes in paragraphs 13–14 about Americans' spiritual impoverishment. Which of his comments accord with J. F. Ade Ajayi's diagnosis of Westerners' problems in "On the Politics of Being Mortal" (p. 615)? What advice do you think Ajayi would give West's audience?

ELABORATIONS

1. What does the Latin phrase *E Pluribus Unum* mean (para. 10), where did it come from, and what is its significance to the United States? What did Malcolm X mean by his famous phrase "by any means necessary" (para. 14)? When and why did Abraham Lincoln invoke "the better angels of our nature" (para. 22)? Whom is West quoting in his conclusion, "or the fire this time will consume us all" (para. 24), and what was the context of the original reference? Choose one or more of these phrases and write an essay about its or their place in American political and social history.

2. In "Where Do Whites Fit In?" (p. 344), Nadine Gordimer anticipated some of the problems South Africans would face when their racially divided society became legally united. Which of these problems did American whites and blacks face after the Civil War? Which ones have been solved, and how? What solutions did the United States try unsuccessfully? Which problems still face Americans today? Write an essay comparing and contrasting the challenges in post-apartheid South Africa as Gordimer describes them with the challenges in the contemporary United States as Cornel West describes them.

NEIL POSTMAN

Future Shlock

Neil Postman has distinguished himself as a social critic, writer, educator, and communications theorist since the 1960s. Born in Brooklyn, New York, he started young. "When I went to Dodgers games with my father and brothers," he recently told a *School Library Journal* interviewer, "I would come home and immediately write up the game as if I were a sportswriter for the *Daily News*." Postman's early work focused on language and education. With such books as *Teaching as a Subversive Activity* (1969) and *The Soft Revolution: A Student Handbook for Turning Schools Around* (1971), both coauthored with Charles Weingartner, he became known as an advocate of radical education reform. For ten years he was editor of *Et Cetera*, the journal of general semantics. As television has played an increasingly central role in American culture, Postman has critically analyzed its impact not only on what information is available but on how we receive and understand information. Many of his twenty-some books, including *Amusing Ourselves to Death* (1986) and *How to Watch TV News* (with TV newsman Steve Powers, 1992), explore these issues. "Future Shlock" comes from his 1988 book *Conscientious Objections: Stirring Up Trouble About Language, Technology, and Education*. A former elementary and high school teacher, he has recently returned to his old preoccupations with the critically acclaimed *The End of Education: Redefining the Value of Schools* (1995). Postman is currently chair of the Department of Culture and Communications at New York University's School of Education; he also serves on the editorial board of *The Nation* magazine. He lives in Flushing, New York.

Sometime about the middle of 1963, my colleague Charles Weingartner and I delivered in tandem an address to the National Council of Teachers of English. In that address we used the phrase future shock *as a way of describing the social paralysis induced by rapid technological change. To my knowledge, Weingartner and I were the first people ever to use it in a public forum. Of course, neither Weingartner nor I had the brains to write a book called* Future Shock, *and all due credit must go to Alvin Toffler for having recognized a good phrase when one came along.*

I mention this here not to lament lost royalties but to explain why I now feel entitled to subvert the phrase. Having been among the first to trouble the public about future shock, I may be permitted to be among the first to trouble the public about future shlock.

Future shlock is the name I give to a cultural condition characterized by the rapid erosion of collective intelligence. Future shlock is the aftermath of future shock. Whereas future shock results in confused, indecisive, and psychically uprooted people, future shlock produces a massive class of mediocre people.

Human intelligence is among the most fragile things in nature. It doesn't take much to distract it, suppress it, or even annihilate it. In this century, we have had some lethal examples of how easily and quickly intelligence can be defeated by any one of its several nemeses: ignorance, superstition, moral fervor, cruelty, cowardice, neglect. In the late 1920s, for example, Germany was, by any measure, the most literate, cultured nation in the world. Its legendary seats of learning attracted scholars from every corner. Its philosophers, social critics, and scientists were of the first rank; its humane traditions an inspiration to less favored nations. But by the mid-1930s — that is, in less than ten years — this cathedral of human reason had been transformed into a cesspool of barbaric irrationality. Many of the most intelligent products of German culture were forced to flee — for example, Einstein, Freud, Karl Jaspers, Thomas Mann, and Stefan Zweig. Even worse, those who remained were either forced to submit their minds to the sovereignty of primitive superstition, or — worse still — willingly did so: Konrad Lorenz, Werner Heisenberg, Martin Heidegger, Gerhardt Hauptmann. On May 10, 1933, a huge bonfire was kindled in Berlin and the books of Marcel Proust, André Gide, Émile Zola, Jack London, Upton Sinclair, and a hundred others were committed to the flames, amid shouts of idiot delight. By 1936, Joseph Paul Goebbels, Germany's minister of propaganda, was issuing a proclamation which began with the following words: "Because this year has not brought an improvement in art criticism, I forbid once and for all the continuance of art criticism in its past form, effective as of today." By 1936, there was no one left in Germany who had the brains or courage to object.

Exactly why the Germans banished intelligence is a vast and largely unanswered question. I have never been persuaded that the desperate economic depression that afflicted Germany in the 1920s adequately explains what happened. To quote Aristotle: "Men do not become tyrants in order to keep warm." Neither do they become stupid — at least not *that* stupid. But the matter need not trouble us here. I offer the German case only as the most striking example of the fragility of human intelligence. My focus here is the United States in our own time, and I wish to worry you about the rapid erosion of our own intelligence. If you are confident that such a thing cannot happen, your confidence is misplaced, I believe, but it is understandable.

After all, the United States is one of the few countries in the world founded by intellectuals — men of wide learning, of extraordinary rhetorical powers, of deep faith in reason. And although we have had our moods of anti-intellectualism, few people have been more generous in support of intelligence and learning than Americans. It was the United States that initiated the experiment in mass education that is, even today, the envy of the world. It was America's churches that laid the foundation of our admirable system of higher education; it was the Land-Grant Act of 1862 that made possible our great state universities; and it is to America that scholars and writers have fled when freedom of the intellect became impossible in their own nations. This is why the great historian of American civilization Henry Steele Commager called America "the Empire of Reason." But Commager was referring to the United States of the eighteenth and nineteenth centuries. What term he would use for America today, I cannot say. Yet he has observed, as others have, a change, a precipitous decline in our valuation of intelligence, in our uses of language, in the disciplines of logic and reason, in our capacity to attend to complexity. Perhaps he would agree with me that the Empire of Reason is, in fact, gone, and that the most apt term for America today is the Empire of Shlock.

In any case, this is what I wish to call to your notice: the frightening displacement of serious, intelligent public discourse in American culture by the imagery and triviality of what may be called show business. I do not see the decline of intelligent discourse in America leading to the barbarisms that flourished in Germany, of course. No scholars, I believe, will ever need to flee America. There will be no bonfires to burn books. And I cannot imagine any proclamations forbidding once and for all art criticism, or any other kind of criticism. But this is not a cause for complacency, let alone celebration. A culture does not have to force scholars to flee to render them impotent. A culture does not have to burn books to assure that they will not be read. And a culture does not need a minister of propaganda issuing proclamations to silence criticism. There are other ways to achieve stupidity, and it appears that, as in so many other things, there is a distinctly American way.

To explain what I am getting at, I find it helpful to refer to two films,   5
which taken together embody the main lines of my argument. The first film is of recent vintage and is called *The Gods Must Be Crazy*. It is about a tribal people who live in the Kalahari Desert plains of southern Africa, and what happens to their culture when it is invaded by an

empty Coca-Cola bottle tossed from the window of a small plane passing overhead. The bottle lands in the middle of the village and is construed by these gentle people to be a gift from the gods, for they not only have never seen a bottle before but have never seen glass either. The people are almost immediately charmed by the gift, and not only because of its novelty. The bottle, it turns out, has multiple uses, chief among them the intriguing music it makes when one blows into it.

But gradually a change takes place in the tribe. The bottle becomes an irresistible preoccupation. Looking at it, holding it, thinking of things to do with it displace other activities once thought essential. But more than this, the Coke bottle is the only thing these people have ever seen of which there is only one of its kind. And so those who do not have it try to get it from the one who does. And the one who does refuses to give it up. Jealousy, greed, and even violence enter the scene, and come very close to destroying the harmony that has characterized their culture for a thousand years. The people begin to love their bottle more than they love themselves, and are saved only when the leader of the tribe, convinced that the gods must be crazy, returns the bottle to the gods by throwing it off the top of a mountain.

The film is great fun and it is also wise, mainly because it is about a subject as relevant to people in Chicago or Los Angeles or New York as it is to those of the Kalahari Desert. It raises two questions of extreme importance to our situation: How does a culture change when new technologies are introduced to it? And is it always desirable for a culture to accommodate itself to the demands of new technologies? The leader of the Kalahari tribe is forced to confront these questions in a way that Americans have refused to do. And because his vision is not obstructed by a belief in what Americans call "technological progress," he is able with minimal discomfort to decide that the songs of the Coke bottle are not so alluring that they are worth admitting envy, egotism, and greed to a serene culture.

The second film relevant to my argument was made in 1967. It is Mel Brooks's first film, *The Producers*. *The Producers* is a rather raucous comedy that has at its center a painful joke: An unscrupulous theatrical producer has figured out that it is relatively easy to turn a buck by producing a play that fails. All one has to do is induce dozens of backers to invest in the play by promising them exorbitant percentages of its profits. When the play fails, there being no profits to disperse, the producer walks away with thousands of dollars that can never be claimed. Of course, the central problem he must solve is to make sure that his play is a disastrous failure. And so he hits upon an excellent idea: He will take the most tragic and grotesque story of our century — the rise of Adolf Hitler — and make it into a musical.

Because the producer is only a crook and not a fool, he assumes that the stupidity of making a musical on this theme will be immediately grasped by audiences and that they will leave the theater in dumbfounded rage. So he calls his play *Springtime for Hitler*, which is also the name of its most important song. The song begins with the words:

> Springtime for Hitler and Germany;
> Winter for Poland and France.

The melody is catchy, and when the song is sung it is accompanied   10
by a happy chorus line. (One must understand, of course, that *Springtime for Hitler* is no spoof of Hitler, as was, for example, Charlie Chaplin's *The Great Dictator*. The play is instead a kind of denial of Hitler in song and dance; as if to say, it was all in fun.)

The ending of the movie is predictable. The audience loves the play and leaves the theater humming *Springtime for Hitler*. The musical becomes a great hit. The producer ends up in jail, his joke having turned back on him. But Brooks's point is that the joke is on us. Although the film was made years before a movie actor became president of the United States, Brooks was making a kind of prophecy about that — namely, that the producers of American culture will increasingly turn our history, politics, religion, commerce, and education into forms of entertainment, and that we will become as a result a trivial people, incapable of coping with complexity, ambiguity, uncertainty, perhaps even reality. We will become, in a phrase, a people amused into stupidity.

For those readers who are not inclined to take Mel Brooks as seriously as I do, let me remind you that the prophecy I attribute here to Brooks was, in fact, made many years before by a more formidable social critic than he. I refer to Aldous Huxley, who wrote *Brave New World* at the time that the modern monuments to intellectual stupidity were taking shape: nazism in Germany, fascism in Italy, communism in Russia. But Huxley was not concerned in his book with such naked and crude forms of intellectual suicide. He saw beyond them, and mostly, I must add, he saw America. To be more specific, he foresaw that the greatest threat to the intelligence and humane creativity of our culture would not come from Big Brother and ministries of propaganda, or gulags and concentration camps. He prophesied, if I may put it this way, that there is tyranny lurking in a Coca-Cola bottle; that we could be ruined not by what we fear and hate but by what we welcome and love, by what we construe to be a gift from the gods.

And in case anyone missed his point in 1932, Huxley wrote *Brave New World Revisited* twenty years later. By then, George Orwell's *1984* had been published, and it was inevitable that Huxley would compare Orwell's book with his own. The difference, he said, is that in Orwell's book people are controlled by inflicting pain. In *Brave New World*, they are controlled by inflicting pleasure.

The Coke bottle that has fallen in our midst is a corporation of dazzling technologies whose forms turn all serious public business into a kind of *Springtime for Hitler* musical. Television is the principal instrument of this disaster, in part because it is the medium Americans most dearly love, and in part because it has become the command center of our culture. Americans turn to television not only for their light entertainment but for their news, their weather, their politics, their religion, their history — all of which may be said to be their serious entertainment. The light entertainment is not the problem. The least dangerous things on television are its junk. What I am talking about is television's preemption of our culture's most serious business. It would be merely banal to say that television presents us with entertaining subject matter. It is quite another thing to say that on television all subject matter is presented as entertaining. And that is how television brings ruin to any intelligent understanding of public affairs.

Political campaigns, for example, are now conducted largely in the   15
form of television commercials. Candidates forgo precision, complexity, substance — in some cases, language itself — for the arts of show business: music, imagery, celebrities, theatrics. Indeed, political figures have become so good at this, and so accustomed to it, that they do television commercials even when they are not campaigning. . . . Even worse, political figures appear on variety shows, soap operas, and sitcoms. George McGovern, Ralph Nader, Ed Koch, and Jesse Jackson have all hosted "Saturday Night Live." Henry Kissinger and former president Gerald Ford have done cameo roles on "Dynasty." [Former Massachusetts officials] Tip O'Neill and Governor Michael Dukakis have appeared on "Cheers." Richard Nixon did a short stint on "Laugh-In." The late senator from Illinois, Everett Dirksen, was on "What's My Line?," a prophetic question if ever there was one. What *is* the line of these people? Or, more precisely, *where* is the line that one ought to be able to draw between politics and entertainment? I would suggest that television has annihilated it. . . .

But politics is only one arena in which serious language has been displaced by the arts of show business. We have all seen how religion is packaged on television, as a kind of Las Vegas stage show, devoid of ritual, sacrality, and tradition. Today's electronic preachers are in no way like America's evangelicals of the past. Men like Jonathan Edwards, Charles Finney, and George Whiteside were preachers of theological depth, authentic learning, and great expository power. Electronic preachers such as Jimmy Swaggart, Jim Bakker, and Jerry Falwell are merely performers who exploit television's visual power and their own charisma for the greater glory of themselves.

We have also seen "Sesame Street" and other educational shows in which the demands of entertainment take precedence over the rigors of learning. And we well know how American businessmen, working under the assumption that potential customers require amusement rather than facts, use music, dance, comedy, cartoons, and celebrities to sell their products.

Even our daily news, which for most Americans means television news, is packaged as a kind of show, featuring handsome news readers, exciting music, and dynamic film footage. Most especially, film footage. When there is no film footage, there is no story. Stranger still, commercials may appear anywhere in a news story — before, after, or in the middle. This reduces all events to trivialities, sources of public entertainment and little more. After all, how serious can a bombing in Lebanon be if it is shown to us prefaced by a happy United Airlines commercial and summarized by a Calvin Klein jeans commercial? Indeed, television newscasters have added to our grammar a new part of speech — what may be called the "Now . . . this" conjunction, a conjunction that does not connect two things but disconnects them. When newscasters say, "Now . . . this," they mean to indicate that what you have just heard or seen has no relevance to what you are about to hear or see. There is no murder so brutal, no political blunder so costly, no bombing so devastating that it cannot be erased from our minds by a newscaster saying, "Now . . . this." He means that you have thought long enough on the matter (let us say, for forty seconds) and you must now give your attention to a commercial. Such a situation is not "the news." It is merely a daily version of *Springtime for Hitler*, and in my opinion accounts for the fact that Americans are among the most ill-informed people in the world. To be sure, we know *of* many things; but we know *about* very little.

To provide some verification of this, I conducted a survey a few years back on the subject of the Iranian hostage crisis. I chose this subject because it was alluded to on television *every day for more than a year.* I did not ask my subjects for their opinions about the hostage situation. I am not interested in opinion polls; I am interested in knowledge polls. The questions I asked were simple and did not require deep knowledge. For example, Where is Iran? What language do the Iranians speak? Where did the Shah come from? What religion do the Iranians practice, and

what are its basic tenets? What does *Ayatollah* mean? I found that almost everybody knew practically nothing about Iran. And those who did
know something said they had learned it from *Newsweek* or *Time* or the
New York Times. Television, in other words, is not the great information
machine. It is the great disinformation machine. A most nerve-racking
confirmation of this came some time ago during an interview with the
producer and the writer of the TV mini-series "Peter the Great." Defending the historical inaccuracies in the drama — which included a
fabricated meeting between Peter and Sir Isaac Newton — the producer said that no one would watch a dry, historically faithful biography. The writer added that it is better for audiences to learn something
that is untrue, if it is entertaining, than not to learn anything at all. And
just to put some icing on the cake, the actor who played Peter, Maxi-
milian Schell, remarked that he does not believe in historical truth and
therefore sees no reason to pursue it.

   I do not mean to say that the trivialization of American public dis-   20
course is all accomplished on television. Rather, television is the paradigm for all our attempts at public communication. It conditions our
minds to apprehend the world through fragmented pictures and forces
other media to orient themselves in that direction. You know the standard question we put to people who have difficulty understanding even
simple language: We ask them impatiently, "Do I have to draw a picture for you?" Well, it appears that, like it or not, our culture will draw
pictures for us, will explain the world to us in pictures. As a medium for
conducting public business, language has receded in importance; it has
been moved to the periphery of culture and has been replaced at the
center by the entertaining visual image.

   Please understand that I am making no criticism of the visual arts in
general. That criticism is made by God, not by me. You will remember
that in His Second Commandment, God explicitly states that "Thou
shalt not make unto thee any graven image, nor any likeness of anything that is in Heaven above, or that is in the earth beneath, or the waters beneath the earth." I have always felt that God was taking a rather
extreme position on this, as is His way. As for myself, I am arguing from
the standpoint of a symbolic relativist. Forms of communication are
neither good nor bad in themselves. They become good or bad depending on their relationship to other symbols and on the functions they are
made to serve within a social order. When a culture becomes overloaded with pictures; when logic and rhetoric lose their binding authority; when historical truth becomes irrelevant; when the spoken or written word is distrusted or makes demands on our attention that we are
incapable of giving; when our politics, history, education, religion,

public information, and commerce are expressed largely in visual imagery rather than words, then a culture is in serious jeopardy.

Neither do I make a complaint against entertainment. As an old song has it, life is not a highway strewn with flowers. The sight of a few blossoms here and there may make our journey a trifle more endurable. But in America, the least amusing people are our professional entertainers. In our present situation, our preachers, entrepreneurs, politicians, teachers, and journalists are committed to entertaining us through media that do not lend themselves to serious, complex discourse. But these producers of our culture are not to be blamed. They, like the rest of us, believe in the supremacy of technological progress. It has never occurred to us that the gods might be crazy. And even if it did, there is no mountaintop from which we can return what is dangerous to us.

We would do well to keep in mind that there are two ways in which the spirit of a culture may be degraded. In the first — the Orwellian — culture becomes a prison. This was the way of the Nazis, and it appears to be the way of the Russians.[1] In the second — the Huxleyan — culture becomes a burlesque. This appears to be the way of the Americans. What Huxley teaches is that in the Age of Advanced Technology, spiritual devastation is more likely to come from an enemy with a smiling countenance than from one whose face exudes suspicion and hate. In the Huxleyan prophecy, Big Brother does not watch us, by his choice; we watch him, by ours. When a culture becomes distracted by trivia; when political and social life are redefined as a perpetual round of entertainments; when public conversation becomes a form of baby talk; when a people become, in short, an audience and their public business a vaudeville act, then — Huxley argued — a nation finds itself at risk and culture-death is a clear possibility. I agree.

EXPLORATIONS

1. What political developments are the context for Postman's opening description of Germany (paras. 1–2)? Where and how else does he refer to the same developments? How do these multiple references encourage us, as readers, "to take Mel Brooks as seriously as I do" (para. 12)?

2. At what points does Postman address the reader directly? What is the effect of these shifts into the second person ("you")? What is the effect of his frequent use of the first person singular ("I")? The first person plural ("we")?

---

[1]That is, the Soviet Union. — ED.

3. In what ways does Postman use entertainment to make his case? Is his essay a contradiction of his own argument? Why or why not?

CONNECTIONS

1. In "Race Matters" (p. 662), Cornel West accuses, "Our truncated public discussions of race suppress the best of who and what we are as a people because they fail to confront the complexity of the issue in a candid and critical manner" (para. 2). What factors does West blame for this failing? Compare the message Postman cites in Mel Brooks's film *The Producers*, "that the producers of American culture will increasingly turn our history, politics, religion, commerce, and education into forms of entertainment, and that we will become as a result a trivial people, incapable of coping with complexity, ambiguity, uncertainty, perhaps even reality" (para. 11). What evidence suggests that the problem Postman diagnoses may be responsible for the problem West diagnoses?

2. Compare the role of the Coke bottle in Postman's summary of the film *The Gods Must Be Crazy* (paras. 5–7) with the role of the Coke bottle in David Abram's "Making Magic" (p. 513, paras. 15–21). In what sense does Abram's "impromptu exorcism" illustrate the American tendency cited by Postman to "turn our history, politics, religion, commerce, and education into forms of entertainment"? In what sense is Abram's exorcism (and his trip to Asia) an effort to reverse this trend?

3. "No scholars, I believe, will ever need to flee America. . . . [But] a culture does not have to force scholars to flee to render them impotent" (para. 4). What development in American culture is Postman condemning? Judging from "The New Lost Generation" (p. 18), would James Baldwin agree? What do you think Baldwin would add to Postman's argument?

ELABORATIONS

1. Neil Postman makes his case by encouraging the reader to draw conclusions from evidence; sometimes he does not state his point directly. Go through "Future Shlock" and identify the thesis of each paragraph. Then write a brief essay incorporating these thesis statements into a shorter and more explicit version of Postman's argument.

2. Postman wrote "Future Shlock" during Ronald Reagan's presidency. Has the evolution of American culture since then confirmed or contradicted his diagnosis? Write an update of "Future Shlock" using more recent evidence to argue for or against Postman's position.

T. CORAGHESSAN BOYLE

Top of the Food Chain

T. Coraghessan Boyle (pronounced co-*rag*-a-san) was born Thomas John Boyle in Peekskill, New York, in 1948. He changed his middle name at age seventeen but is still known as Tom. A music student at the State University of New York (SUNY) at Potsdam, he graduated in 1970 and became a high school teacher. In the meantime he had discovered a flair for writing. After his first story was published, Boyle applied to Iowa University's legendary Writers' Workshop. He received his Ph.D. in 1977 and went to teach at the University of Southern California, where he is now a professor of creative writing. His first collection, *The Descent of Man* — titled for a story about a woman in love with a brilliant chimpanzee — appeared in 1979; his first novel, *Water Music*, which follows an explorer and a con man across Africa, came two years later. All of Boyle's books erupt with imagination and stylistic pyrotechnics. *The Road to Wellville* (1993), about an eccentric cereal magnate's sanitarium, later became a movie. "Top of the Food Chain" comes from his 1994 story collection *Without a Hero*. Boyle's most recent novel is *The Tortilla Curtain* (1995), a tale of clashing cultures in Los Angeles, a hundred miles from the quiet town where the author lives with his wife and three children.

The thing was, we had a little problem with the insect vector there, and believe me, your tamer stuff, your Malathion and pyrethrum and the rest of the so-called environmentally safe products didn't begin to make a dent in it, not a dent, I mean it was utterly useless — we might as well have been spraying with Chanel Number 5 for all the good it did. And you've got to realize these people were literally covered with insects day and night — and the fact that they hardly wore any clothes just compounded the problem. Picture if you can, gentlemen, a naked little two-year-old boy so black with flies and mosquitoes it looks like he's wearing long johns, or the young mother so racked with the malarial shakes she can't even lift a diet Coke to her lips — it was pathetic, just pathetic, like something out of the Dark Ages. . . . Well, anyway, the decision was made to go with DDT. In the short term. Just to get the situation under control, you understand.

Yes, that's right, Senator, *DDT*: Dichlorodiphenyltrichloroethane.

Yes, I'm well aware of that fact, sir. But just because *we* banned it domestically, under pressure from the birdwatching contingent and the hopheads down at the EPA, it doesn't necessarily follow that the rest of the world — especially the developing world — is about to jump on the bandwagon. And that's the key word here, Senator: *developing*. You've got to realize this is Borneo we're talking about here, not Port Townsend or Enumclaw. These people don't know from square one about sanitation, disease control, pest eradication — or even personal hygiene, if you want to come right down to it. It rains a hundred and twenty inches a year, minimum. They dig up roots in the jungle. They've still got headhunters along the Rajang River, for god's sake.

And please don't forget they *asked* us to come in there, practically begged us — and not only the World Health Organization, but the Sultan of Brunei and the government of Sarawak too. We did what we could to accommodate them and reach our objective in the shortest period of time and by the most direct and effective means. We went to the air. Obviously. And no one could have foreseen the consequences, no one, not even if we'd gone out and generated a hundred environmental-impact statements — it was just one of those things, a freak occurrence, and there's no defense against that. Not that I know of, anyway. . . .

Caterpillars? Yes, Senator, that's correct. That was the first sign: 5 caterpillars.

But let me backtrack a minute here. You see, out in the bush they have these roofs made of thatched palm leaves — you'll see them in the towns too, even in Bintulu or Brunei — and they're really pretty effective, you'd be surprised. A hundred and twenty inches of rain, they've got to figure a way to keep it out of the hut, and for centuries, this was it. Palm leaves. Well, it was about a month after we sprayed for the final time and I'm sitting at my desk in the trailer thinking about the drainage project at Kuching, enjoying the fact that for the first time in maybe a year I'm not smearing mosquitoes all over the back of my neck, when there's a knock at the door. It's this elderly gentleman, tattooed from head to toe, dressed only in a pair of running shorts — they love those shorts, by the way, the shiny material and the tight machine-stitching, the whole country, men and women and children, they can't get enough of them. . . . Anyway, he's the headman of the local village and he's very excited, something about the roofs — *atap*, they call them. That's all he can say, *atap, atap,* over and over again.

It's raining, of course. It's always raining. So I shrug into my rain slicker, start up the 4X4 and go have a look. Sure enough, all the *atap* roofs are collapsing, not only in his village, but throughout the target area. The people are all huddled there in their running shorts, looking pretty miserable, and one after another the roofs keep falling in, it's bewildering, and gradually I realize the headman's diatribe has begun to feature a new term I was unfamiliar with at the time — the word for caterpillar, as it turns out, in the Iban dialect. But who was to make the connection between three passes with the crop duster and all these staved-in roofs?

Our people finally sorted it out a couple weeks later. The chemical, which, by the way, cut down the number of mosquitoes exponentially, had the unfortunate side effect of killing off this little wasp — I've got the scientific name for it somewhere in my report here, if you're interested — that preyed on a the of caterpillar that in turn ate palm leaves. Well, with the wasps gone, the caterpillars hatched out with nothing to keep them in check and chewed the roofs to pieces, and that was unfortunate, we admit it, and we had a real cost overrun on replacing those roofs with tin . . . but the people were happier, I think, in the long run, because let's face it, no matter how tightly you weave those palm leaves, they're just not going to keep out the water like tin. Of course, nothing's perfect, and we had a lot of complaints about the rain drumming on the panels, people unable to sleep and what-have-you. . . .

Yes, sir, that's correct — the flies were next.

Well, you've got to understand the magnitude of the fly problem in Borneo, there's nothing like it here to compare it with, except maybe a garbage strike in New York. Every minute of every day you've got flies everywhere, up your nose, in your mouth, your ears, your eyes, flies in your rice, your Coke, your Singapore sling and your gin rickey. It's enough to drive you to distraction, not to mention the diseases these things carry, from dysentery to typhoid to cholera and back round the loop again. And once the mosquito population was down, the flies seemed to breed up to fill in the gap — Borneo wouldn't be Borneo without some damned insect blackening the air.

Of course, this was before our people had tracked down the problem with the caterpillars and the wasps and all of that, and so we figured we'd had a big success with the mosquitoes, why not a series of ground sweeps, mount a fogger in the back of a Suzuki Brat and sanitize the huts, not to mention the open sewers, which as you know are nothing but a breeding ground for flies, chiggers, and biting insects of every sort. At least it was an error of commission rather than omission. At least we were trying.

I watched the flies go down myself. One day they were so thick in the trailer I couldn't even *find* my paperwork, let alone attempt to get

10

through it, and the next they were collecting on the windows, bumbling around like they were drunk. A day later they were gone. Just like that. From a million flies in the trailer to none. . . .

Well, no one could have foreseen that, Senator.

The geckos ate the flies, yes. You're all familiar with geckos, I assume, gentlemen? These are the lizards you've seen during your trips to Hawaii, very colorful, patrolling the houses for roaches and flies, almost like pets, but of course they're wild animals, never lose sight of that, and just about as unsanitary as anything I can think of, except maybe flies.

Yes, well don't forget, sir, we're viewing this with twenty-twenty hindsight, but at the time no one gave a thought to geckos or what they ate — they were just another fact of life in the tropics. Mosquitoes, lizards, scorpions, leeches — you name it, they've got it. When the flies began piling up on the windowsills like drift, naturally the geckos feasted on them, stuffing themselves till they looked like sausages crawling up the walls. Where before they moved so fast you could never be sure you'd seen them, now they waddled across the floor, laid around in the corners, clung to the air vents like magnets — and even then no one paid much attention to them till they started turning belly-up in the streets. Believe me, we confirmed a lot of things there about the buildup of these products as you move up the food chain and the efficacy — or lack thereof — of certain methods, no doubt about that. . . .

The cats? That's where it got sticky, really sticky. You see, nobody really lost any sleep over a pile of dead lizards — though we did the tests routinely and the tests confirmed what we'd expected, that is, the product had been concentrated in the geckos because of the sheer number of contaminated flies they consumed. But lizards are one thing and cats are another. These people really have an affection for their cats — no house, no hut, no matter how primitive, is without at least a couple of them. Mangy-looking things, long-legged and scrawny, maybe, not at all the sort of animal you'd see here, but there it was: They loved their cats. Because the cats were functional, you understand — without them, the place would have been swimming in rodents inside of a week.

You're right there, Senator, yes — that's exactly what happened.

You see, the cats had a field day with these feeble geckos — you can imagine, if any of you have ever owned a cat, the kind of joy these animals must have experienced to see their nemesis, this ultra-quick lizard, and it's just barely creeping across the floor like a bug. Well, to make a long story short, the cats ate up every dead and dying gecko in the country, from snout to tail, and then the cats began to die . . . which to my

15

Institutions and Individuals

mind would have been no great loss if it wasn't for the rats. Suddenly there were rats everywhere — you couldn't drive down the street without running over half-a-dozen of them at a time. They fouled the grain supplies, fell in the wells and died, bit infants as they slept in their cradles. But that wasn't the worst, not by a long shot. No, things really went down the tube after that. Within the month we were getting scattered reports of bubonic plague, and of course we tracked them all down and made sure the people got a round of treatment with antibiotics, but we still lost a few and the rats kept coming. . . .

It was my plan, yes. I was brainstorming one night, rats scuttling all over the trailer like something out of a cheap horror film, the villagers in a panic over the threat of the plague and the stream of nonstop hysterical reports from the interior — people were turning black, swelling up and bursting, that sort of thing — well, as I say, I came up with a plan, a stopgap, not perfect, not cheap; but at this juncture, I'm sure you'll agree, something had to be implemented.

We wound up going as far as Australia for some of the cats, cleaning out the SPCA facilities and what-have-you, though we rounded most of them up in Indonesia and Singapore — approximately fourteen thousand in all. And yes, it cost us — cost us upfront purchase money and aircraft fuel and pilots' overtime and all the rest of it — but we really felt there was no alternative. It was like all nature had turned against us.

And yet still, all things considered, we made a lot of friends for the U.S.A. the day we dropped those cats, and you should have seen them, gentlemen, the little parachutes and harnesses we'd tricked up, fourteen thousand of them, cats in every color of the rainbow, cats with one ear, no ears, half a tail, three-legged cats, cats that could have taken pride of show in Springfield, Massachusetts, and all of them twirling down out of the sky like great big oversized snowflakes. . . .

It was something. It was really something.

Of course, you've all seen the reports. There were other factors we hadn't counted on, adverse conditions in the paddies and manioc fields — we don't to this day know what predatory species were inadvertently killed off by the initial sprayings, it's just a mystery — but the weevils and whatnot took a pretty heavy toll on the crops that year, and by the time we dropped the cats, well, the people were pretty hungry, and I suppose it was inevitable that we lost a good proportion of them right then and there. But we've got a CARE program going there now, and something hit the rat population — we still don't know what, a virus, we think — and the geckos, they tell me, are making a comeback.

So what I'm saying is, it could be worse, and to every cloud a silver lining, wouldn't you agree, gentlemen?

EXPLORATIONS

1. Who is speaking in "Top of the Food Chain," to whom, and why? How can you tell? Where is the story taking place, and where did the narrated events happen?

2. What stylistic choices on T. Coraghessan Boyle's part make it clear that "Top of the Food Chain" is being spoken, not written, by the narrator? Identify at least three. What is the impact of Boyle's presenting his story this way?

3. Who are "these people" (paras. 1 and 3)? What is the narrator's professional relationship to them? What is his attitude toward them, and how can you tell? Who are "our people" (paras. 8 and 11)? What is his attitude toward them, and how can you tell? Who are "gentlemen" (para. 1)? What is his attitude toward them, and how can you tell?

CONNECTIONS

1. Neil Postman mentions in "Future Shlock" (p. 670) "how easily and quickly intelligence can be defeated by any one of its several nemeses: ignorance, superstition, moral fervor, cruelty, cowardice, neglect" (para. 1). Which of these nemeses appear in "Top of the Food Chain," and where?

2. Cornel West refers in "Race Matters" (p. 662) to "a political atmosphere [in the United States] in which images, not ideas, dominate," and he accuses both public and private officials of greed and opportunism (para. 15). What specific evidence in "Top of the Food Chain" suggests that Boyle agrees with these accusations?

3. What is the food chain? What happens to it in Boyle's story? Reread the epigraph on page 651 about China's ban on dogs. What rationale is offered by the officials involved? What unanticipated effects might this law have on the food chain?

ELABORATIONS

1. Imagine you are a presidential aide attending the session Boyle describes in "Top of the Food Chain." Write a summary of the session for your boss, who has a press conference tomorrow about this foreign relations snafu. In essay form, cover "what, when, where, why, and who": that is, summarize

the problems that prompted intervention, the actions that were taken, who made what decisions, and any other information the president will need to know.

2. Find out about DDT. What does it do? When and why was it banned in the United States? Is it still manufactured here? If so, for what purposes? What has replaced it? Has the replacement been successful? Write your own essay — satirical or straightforward — about this chemical.

WINDOWS:
THE WORLD

Institutions and Individuals: *Aung San Suu Kyi gives one of her*
famous speeches in Burma.

NELSON MANDELA

Black Man in a White Court

In February 1990 the world celebrated Nelson Mandela's release from a South African prison after twenty-seven years. In April 1994 it celebrated his election as his country's first black president. Nelson Rolihlahla Mandela was born in 1918 to one of the royal families of the Transkei, the eldest son of a Tembu chief. He ran away to Johannesburg to escape an arranged tribal marriage; there he studied arts by correspondence and law at the University of Witwatersrand. With his law partner, Oliver Tambo, Mandela became active in the then illegal African National Congress (ANC), whose mission Tambo has described as "the African struggle against the most powerful adversary in Africa: a highly industrialized, well-armed State manned by a fanatical group of White men determined to defend their privilege and their prejudice, and aided by the complicity of American, British, West German, and Japanese investment in the most profitable system of oppression on the continent."

When an all-white referendum voted to declare South Africa a Nationalist Republic in 1961 (see p. 344), Mandela called a general strike to dramatize black opposition. He left his home, family, and office to live as a political outlaw, nicknamed "the Black Pimpernel." In 1962 he was betrayed by an informer, arrested, tried, and sentenced to three years in prison for leading the strike and for leaving the country illegally. "Black Man in a White Court" is an excerpt from his trial, reprinted in his book *No Easy Walk to Freedom* (1965). From his cell Mandela became a defendant in the notorious Rivonia Trial, accused of sabotage and conspiracy to overthrow the government by force. He and six codefendants were sentenced to life in prison.

The growing worldwide human rights movement increased international pressure on the South African government, which made such concessions as allowing Asians and Coloreds (but not blacks) to vote and repealing laws banning interracial marriage. The slow pace and limited scope of change fueled protest inside and outside South Africa, some of it violent, to the point that the government barred foreign news media from covering disruption. Popular pressure in the United States led many organizations to divest their holdings of stock in South African companies. After years of worldwide economic and political protest, President P. W. Botha was replaced by the more liberal F. W. De Klerk. Within months De Klerk met with Mandela in prison, unbanned the ANC and the Communist Party, desegregated beaches, limited detention without trial, lifted restrictions on the media, dismantled the repressive state security management system, and released seven other jailed ANC leaders before freeing Mandela. The two men began negotiating immediately for full political rights for black South Africans. In 1993 Mandela and De Klerk won the Nobel Peace Prize. The following year Mandela won the presidency in South Africa's first election open to all races. Besides opposition from conservative whites, including the neo-Nazi Afrikaner Resistance Movement (AWB), the ANC faced opposition from the Zulu Inkatha, supporters of Chief Mangosuthu Buthelezi. De Klerk served in the new government for two years before resigning. Progress toward economic and social justice has been expectedly slow; but Mandela remains the world's most respected head of state.

For more background on South Africa, see page 344.

"Black Man in a White Court"
First Court Statement, 1962

Extracts from the court record of the trial of Mandela held in the Old Synagogue court, Pretoria, from October 15 to November 7, 1962. Mandela was accused on two counts, that of inciting persons to strike illegally (during the 1961 stay-at-home) and that of leaving the country without a valid passport. He conducted his own defense.

Mandela: Your Worship, before I plead to the charge, there are one or two points I would like to raise.

Firstly, Your Worship will recall that this matter was postponed last Monday at my request until today, to enable counsel to make the arrangements to be available here today.[1] Although counsel is now available, after consultation with him and my attorneys, I have elected to conduct my own defense. Some time during the progress of these proceedings, I hope to be able to indicate that this case is a trial of the aspirations of the African people, and because of that I thought it proper to conduct my own defense. Nevertheless, I have decided to retain the services of counsel, who will be here throughout these

---

[1]Mandela had applied for a remand, because the trial had two-and-a-half months previously been scheduled to take place in the Johannesburg Regional Court, where Mandela had arranged for his defense by advocate Joe Slovo. During the weekend before it opened, however, it was suddenly switched to Pretoria — and Slovo was restricted by a government banning order to the magisterial district of Johannesburg.

proceedings, and I also would like my attorney to be available in the course of these proceedings as well, but subject to that I will conduct my own defense.

The second point I would like to raise is an application which is addressed to Your Worship. Now at the outset, I want to make it perfectly clear that the remarks I am going to make are not addressed to Your Worship in his personal capacity, nor are they intended to reflect upon the integrity of the court. I hold Your Worship in high esteem and I do not for one single moment doubt your sense of fairness and justice. I must also mention that nothing I am going to raise in this application is intended to reflect against the prosecutor in his personal capacity.

The point I wish to raise in my argument is based not on personal considerations, but on important questions that go beyond the scope of this present trial. I might also mention that in the course of this application I am frequently going to refer to the white man and the white people. I want at once to make it clear that I am no racialist, and I detest racialism, because I regard it as a barbaric thing, whether it comes from a black man or from a white man. The terminology that I am going to employ will be compelled on me by the nature of the application I am making.

I want to apply for Your Worship's recusal[2] from this case. I challenge the right of this court to hear my case on two grounds.   5

Firstly, I challenge it because I fear that I will not be given a fair and proper trial. Secondly, I consider myself neither legally nor morally bound to obey laws made by a parliament in which I have no representation.

In a political trial such as this one, which involves a clash of the aspirations of the African people and those of whites, the country's courts, as presently constituted, cannot be impartial and fair.

In such cases, whites are interested parties. To have a white judicial officer presiding, however high his esteem, and however strong his sense of fairness and justice, is to make whites judges in their own case.

It is improper and against the elementary principles of justice to entrust whites with cases involving the denial by them of basic human rights to the African people.

What sort of justice is this that enables the aggrieved to sit in judg-   10
ment over those against whom they have laid a charge?

A judiciary controlled entirely by whites and enforcing laws enacted by a white parliament in which Africans have no representation — laws which in most cases are passed in the face of unanimous opposition from Africans —

---

[2]Withdrawal from the case on grounds of prejudice.

Magistrate: I am wondering whether I shouldn't interfere with you at this stage, Mr. Mandela. Aren't we going beyond the scope of the proceedings? After all is said and done, there is only one court today and that is the white man's court. There is no other court. What purpose does it serve you to make an application when there is only one court, as you know yourself? What court do you wish to be tried by?

Mandela: Well, Your Worship, firstly I would like Your Worship to bear in mind that in a series of cases our courts have laid it down that the right of a litigant to ask for a recusal of a judicial officer is an extremely important right, which must be given full protection by the court, as long as that right is exercised honestly. Now I honestly have apprehensions, as I am going to demonstrate just now, that this unfair discrimination throughout my life has been responsible for very grave injustices, and I am going to contend that that race discrimination which outside this court has been responsible for all my troubles, I fear in this court is going to do me the same injustice. Now Your Worship may disagree with that, but Your Worship is perfectly entitled, in fact, obliged to listen to me and because of that I feel that Your Worship —

Magistrate: I would like to listen, but I would like you to give me the grounds for your application for me to recuse myself.

Mandela: Well, these are the grounds, I am developing them, sir. If 15 Your Worship will give me time —

Magistrate: I don't wish to go out of the scope of the proceedings.

Mandela: — Of the scope of the application. I am within the scope of the application, because I am putting forward grounds which in my opinion are likely not to give me a fair and proper trial.

Magistrate: Anyway proceed.

Mandela: As Your Worship pleases. I was developing the point that a judiciary controlled entirely by whites and enforcing laws enacted by a white parliament in which we have no representation, laws which in most cases are passed in the face of unanimous opposition from Africans, cannot be regarded as an impartial tribunal in a political trial where an African stands as an accused.

The Universal Declaration of Human Rights provides that all men 20 are equal before the law, and are entitled without any discrimination to equal protection of the law. In May 1951, Dr. D. F. Malan, then prime minister, told the Union parliament that this provision of the declaration applies in this country. Similar statements have been made on numerous occasions in the past by prominent whites in this country, including judges and magistrates. But the real truth is that there is in fact no equality before the law whatsoever as far as our people are concerned, and statements to the contrary are definitely incorrect and misleading.

It is true that an African who is charged in a court of law enjoys, on the surface, the same rights and privileges as an accused who is white insofar as the conduct of this trial is concerned. He is governed by the same rules of procedure and evidence as apply to a white accused. But it would be grossly inaccurate to conclude from this fact that an African consequently enjoys equality before the law.

In its proper meaning equality before the law means the right to participate in the making of the laws by which one is governed, a constitution which guarantees democratic rights to all sections of the population, the right to approach the court for protection or relief in the case of the violation of rights guaranteed in the constitution, and the right to take part in the administration of justice as judges, magistrates, attorneys-general, law advisers, and similar positions.

In the absence of these safeguards the phrase "equality before the law," insofar as it is intended to apply to us, is meaningless and misleading. All the rights and privileges to which I have referred are monopolized by whites, and we enjoy none of them.

The white man makes all the laws, he drags us before his courts and accuses us, and he sits in judgment over us.

It is fit and proper to raise the question sharply, What is this rigid   25
color bar in the administration of justice? Why is it that in this courtroom I face a white magistrate, am confronted by a white prosecutor, and escorted into the dock by a white orderly? Can anyone honestly and seriously suggest that in this type of atmosphere the scales of justice are evenly balanced?

Why is it that no African in the history of this country has ever had the honor of being tried by his own kith and kin, by his own flesh and blood?

I will tell Your Worship why: The real purpose of this rigid color bar is to ensure that the justice dispersed by the courts should conform to the policy of the country, however much that policy might be in conflict with the norms of justice accepted in judiciaries throughout the civilized world.

I feel oppressed by the atmosphere of white domination that lurks all around in this courtroom. Somehow this atmosphere calls to mind the inhuman injustices caused to my people outside this courtroom by this same white domination.

It reminds me that I am voteless because there is a parliament in this country that is white-controlled. I am without land because the white minority has taken a lion's share of my country and forced me to oc-

cupy poverty-stricken reserves, overpopulated and overstocked. We are
ravaged by starvation and disease . . .

Magistrate: What has that got to do with the case, Mr. Mandela?　　　30

Mandela: With the last point, sir, it hangs together, if Your Worship
will give me the chance to develop it.

Magistrate: You have been developing it for quite a while now, and I
feel you are going beyond the scope of your application.

Mandela: Your Worship, this to me is an extremely important
ground which the court must consider.

Magistrate: I fully realize your position, Mr. Mandela, but you must
confine yourself to the application and not go beyond it. I don't want to
know about starvation. That in my view has got nothing to do with the
case at the present moment.

Mandela: Well, Your Worship has already raised the point that here　　35
in this country there is only a white court. What is the point of all this?
Now if I can demonstrate to Your Worship that outside this courtroom
race discrimination has been used in such a way as to deprive me of my
rights, not to treat me fairly, certainly this is a relevant fact from which
to infer that wherever race discrimination is practiced, this will be the
same result, and this is the only reason why I am using this point.

Magistrate: I am afraid that I will have to interrupt you, and you will
have to confine yourself to the reasons, the real reasons for asking me to
recuse myself.

Mandela: Your Worship, the next point which I want to make is this:
I raise the question, how can I be expected to believe that this same
racial discrimination which has been the cause of so much injustice
and suffering right through the years should now operate here to give
me a fair and open trial? Is there no danger that an African accused may
regard the courts not as impartial tribunals, dispensing justice without
fear or favor, but as instruments used by the white man to punish those
amongst us who clamor for deliverance from the fiery furnace of white
rule? I have grave fears that this system of justice may enable the guilty
to drag the innocent before the courts. It enables the unjust to prose-
cute and demand vengeance against the just. It may tend to lower the
standards of fairness and justice applied in the country's courts by white
judicial officers to black litigants. This is the first ground for this application: that I will not receive a fair and proper trial.

The second ground of my objection is that I consider myself neither
morally nor legally obliged to obey laws made by a parliament in which
I am not represented.

That the will of the people is the basis of the authority of government is a principle universally acknowledged as sacred throughout the

civilized world, and constitutes the basic foundations of freedom and justice. It is understandable why citizens, who have the vote as well as the right to direct representation in the country's governing bodies, should be morally and legally bound by the laws governing the country.

It should be equally understandable why we, as Africans, should 40 adopt the attitude that we are neither morally nor legally bound to obey laws which we have not made, nor can we be expected to have confidence in courts which enforce such laws.

I am aware that in many cases of this nature in the past, South African courts have upheld the right of the African people to work for democratic changes. Some of our judicial officers have even openly criticized the policy which refuses to acknowledge that all men are born free and equal, and fearlessly condemned the denial of opportunities to our people.

But such exceptions exist in spite of, not because of, the grotesque system of justice that has been built up in this country. These exceptions furnish yet another proof that even among the country's whites there are honest men whose sense of fairness and justice revolts against the cruelty perpetrated by their own white brothers to our people.

The existence of genuine democratic values among some of the country's whites in the judiciary, however slender they may be, is welcomed by me. But I have no illusions about the significance of this fact, healthy a sign as it might be. Such honest and upright whites are few and they have certainly not succeeded in convincing the vast majority of the rest of the white population that white supremacy leads to dangers and disaster.

However, it would be a hopeless commandant who relied for his victories on the few soldiers in the enemy camp who sympathize with his cause. A competent general pins his faith on the superior striking power he commands and on the justness of his cause which he must pursue uncompromisingly to the bitter end.

I hate race discrimination most intensely and in all its manifestations. I 45 have fought it all during my life; I fight it now, and will do so until the end of my days. Even though I now happen to be tried by one whose opinion I hold in high esteem, I detest most violently the setup that surrounds me here. It makes me feel that I am a black man in a white man's court. This should not be. I should feel perfectly at ease and at home with the assurance that I am being tried by a fellow South African who does not regard me as an inferior, entitled to a special type of justice.

This is not the type of atmosphere most conducive to feelings of security and confidence in the impartiality of a court.

The court might reply to this part of my argument by assuring me that it will try my case fairly and without fear or favor, that in deciding whether or not I am guilty of the offense charged by the state, the court will not be influenced by the color of my skin or by any other improper motive.

That might well be so. But such a reply would completely miss the point of my argument.

As already indicated, my objection is not directed to Your Worship in his personal capacity, nor is it intended to reflect upon the integrity of the court. My objection is based upon the fact that our courts, as presently constituted, create grave doubts in the minds of an African accused, whether he will receive a fair and proper trial.

This doubt springs from objective facts relating to the practice of un- 50 fair discrimination against the black man in the constitution of the country's courts. Such doubts cannot be allayed by mere verbal assurances from a presiding officer, however sincere such assurances might be. There is only one way, and one way only, of allaying such doubts, namely, by removing unfair discrimination in judicial appointments. This is my first difficulty.

I have yet another difficulty about similar assurances Your Worship might give. Broadly speaking, Africans and whites in this country have no common standard of fairness, morality, and ethics, and it would be very difficult to determine on my part what standard of fairness and justice Your Worship has in mind.

In their relationship with us, South African whites regard it as fair and just to pursue policies which have outraged the conscience of mankind and of honest and upright men throughout the civilized world. They suppress our aspirations, bar our way to freedom, and deny us opportunities to promote our moral and material progress, to secure ourselves from fear and want. All the good things of life are reserved for the white folk and we blacks are expected to be content to nourish our bodies with such pieces of food as drop from the tables of men with white skins. This is the white man's standard of justice and fairness. Herein lies his conception of ethics. Whatever he himself may say in his defense, the white man's moral standards in this country must be judged by the extent to which he has condemned the vast majority of its inhabitants to serfdom and inferiority.

We, on the other hand, regard the struggle against color discrimination and for the pursuit of freedom and happiness as the highest aspiration of all men. Through bitter experience, we have learned to regard the white man as a harsh and merciless type of human being whose contempt for our rights, and whose utter indifference to the promotion of our welfare, makes his assurances to us absolutely meaningless and hypocritical.

I have the hope and confidence that Your Worship will not hear this objection lightly nor regard it as frivolous. I have decided to speak frankly and honestly because the injustice I have referred to contains the seeds of an extremely dangerous situation for our country and I make no threat when I say that unless these wrongs are remedied without delay, we might well find that even plain talk before the country's courts is too timid a method to draw the attention of the country to our political demands.

Finally, I need only to say that the courts have said that the possibil-   55
ity of bias and not actual bias is all that needs be proved to ground an application of this nature. In this application I have merely referred to certain objective facts, from which I submit that the possibility be inferred that I will not receive a fair and proper trial.

Magistrate: Mr. Prosecutor, have you anything to say?

Prosecutor: Very briefly, Your Worship, I just wish to point out that there are certain legal grounds upon which an accused person is entitled to apply for the recusal of a judicial officer from the case in which he is to be tried. I submit that the accused's application is not based on one of those principles, and I ask the court to reject it.

Magistrate: [to Mandela] Your application is dismissed. Will you now plead to your charges?

Mandela: I plead *not guilty* to both charges, to all the charges.

EXPLORATIONS

1. What application is Nelson Mandela making to the court in this argument? What two grounds does he give for his application? What appears to be the true purpose of his application? Is he successful? Why or why not?

2. Does the court seriously consider Mandela's application? What statements by Mandela and by the judge are the basis for your answer?

3. In what ways does Mandela emphasize that, as a lawyer, he is part of the same elite group as the judge and prosecutor? How does his stressing that point strengthen the impact of his speech?

CONNECTIONS

1. In the quotation by Ralph Ellison that opens Cornel West's "Race Matters" (p. 662), substitute the word "African" for "American." How do Ellison's re-

marks apply to the problems Nelson Mandela outlines in "Black Man in a White Court"?

2. Like Nadine Gordimer in "Where Do Whites Fit In?" (p. 344), Mandela refers to *Africans* and *whites* in paragraphs 8–12 and elsewhere rather than to *black South Africans* and *white South Africans*. What is the effect of this usage? What comments in Mandela's paragraphs 2, 7, and 45 illuminate his choice of words?

3. How do Shelby Steele's comments about innocence on page 5 apply to the relationship between blacks and whites described by Mandela, and to Mandela's strategy in court?

ELABORATIONS

1. Look closely at the transcript and background notes for "Black Man in a White Court." In what sense has the white South African government stacked the deck so that Mandela cannot win? How does Mandela use this stacked deck to set up a situation in which he cannot lose? Write a classification essay analyzing the various political agendas and strategies represented in this trial, and identifying winners and losers.

2. What statements about men and women in Simone de Beauvoir's "Woman as Other" (p. 445) express points made about white and black South Africans in "Black Man in a White Court"? Based on Beauvoir's discussion of the "Other," Mandela's transcript, Cornel West's "Race Matters" (p. 662), Chinua Achebe's "The Song of Ourselves" (p. 599), Es'kia Mphahlele's "African Literature: What Tradition?" (p. 562), Toni Morrison's chapter from *Beloved* (p. 544), and any epigraphs you find useful, write an essay analyzing the causes and effects of racism.

AUNG SAN SUU KYI

Freedom from Fear

Aung San Suu Kyi (pronounced ong son su chi) was awarded the Nobel Peace Prize in 1991 for her work on behalf of peace, dignity, and freedom in her native Burma. Newspapers around the world had published her essay "Freedom from Fear" to honor the European Parliament's awarding Suu Kyi the 1990 Sakharov Prize for Freedom of Thought. Her husband, Harvard professor Michael Aris, reprinted it in his 1991 collection of her writings, *Freedom from Fear*. In his introduction Aris wrote:

> From her earliest childhood, Suu has been deeply preoccupied with the question of what she might do to help her people. She never for a minute forgot that she was the daughter of Burma's national hero, Aung San. It was he who led the struggle for independence from British colonial rule and from the Japanese occupation. Trained by the Japanese during the Second World War, he and his associates among the legendary "Thirty Comrades" entered Burma with the invading Japanese army who promised independence. When that promise proved false he went underground to lead the resistance with the Burma Independence Army he had created. He assisted the reinvading Allies, and after the war negotiated with Clement Attlee's Labour government for final independence. But he and practically his entire cabinet in the provisional government were gunned down on 19 July 1947, just a few months before the transfer of power. A jealous political rival masterminded the assassination.
>
> Suu, who was born on 19 July 1945, has only the dimmest recollections of her father. However, everything she has learned about him inclined her to believe in his selfless courage and his vision of a free and democratic Burma.

The independent Union of Burma — southeast Asia's second-largest nation after Indonesia — became official in 1948. In 1962, General Ne Win took control in a military coup; he ruled until 1988. That year Aung San Suu Kyi was living with her husband and sons in Oxford, England, working on her doctoral thesis for London University. She returned to Burma when her mother had a stroke. Ne Win announced that he was resigning, but his promised referendum on Burma's political future never took place. Instead his party continued its brutal regime of coercion, torture, and murder. "Suu's house quickly became the main center of political activity in the country," Aris writes:

> Three heads of state were forced by the people's movement to resign in quick succession, though ultimate power remained vested

in the military officers loyal to Ne Win. The army controlled by
those officers finally staged a coup on 18 September and brought
in their State Law and Order Restoration Council (SLORC).
They reiterated the promise of free and fair elections while clearing the streets with gunfire. Suu and her close associates promptly
formed their party, the National League for Democracy [NLD].
Public enthusiasm for the NLD led SLORC to confine Suu Kyi under
house arrest after an assassination attempt failed. For six years she was
surrounded by guards and barbed wire, unable to go out, make phone
calls, or receive visitors. A 1990 election, which the NLD won in a land-
slide, was set aside. When SLORC yielded to international pressure and
released Suu Kyi in 1995, she began giving weekly speeches from her
gate to thousands of people. As we go to press, SLORC (which renamed
the country Myanmar) has stepped up its arrests and persecution of
NLD members, but has failed to stop Aung San Suu Kyi.

It is not power that corrupts but fear. Fear of losing power corrupts
those who wield it and fear of the scourge of power corrupts those who
are subject to it. Most Burmese are familiar with the four *a-gati*, the
four kinds of corruption. *Chanda-gati*, corruption induced by desire, is
deviation from the right path in pursuit of bribes or for the sake of those
one loves. *Dosa-gati* is taking the wrong path to spite those against
whom one bears ill will, and *moga-gati* is aberration due to ignorance.
But perhaps the worst of the four is *bhaya-gati*, for not only does *bhaya*,
fear, stifle and slowly destroy all sense of right and wrong, it so often lies
at the root of the other three kinds of corruption.

Just as *chanda-gati*, when not the result of sheer avarice, can be
caused by fear of want or fear of losing the goodwill of those one loves,
so fear of being surpassed, humiliated, or injured in some way can provide the impetus for ill will. And it would be difficult to dispel ignorance unless there is freedom to pursue the truth unfettered by fear.
With so close a relationship between fear and corruption it is little wonder that in any society where fear is rife corruption in all forms becomes
deeply entrenched.

Public dissatisfaction with economic hardships has been seen as the
chief cause of the movement for democracy in Burma, sparked off by
the student demonstrations in 1988. It is true that years of incoherent
policies, inept official measures, burgeoning inflation, and falling real
income had turned the country into an economic shambles. But it was
more than the difficulties of eking out a barely acceptable standard of
living that had eroded the patience of a traditionally good-natured,

quiescent people — it was also the humiliation of a way of life disfig-
ured by corruption and fear. The students were protesting not just
against the death of their comrades but against the denial of their right
to life by a totalitarian regime which deprived the present of meaning-
fulness and held out no hope for the future. And because the students'
protests articulated the frustrations of the people at large, the demonstrations quickly grew into a nationwide movement. Some of its keenest
supporters were businessmen who had developed the skills and the contacts necessary not only to survive but to prosper within the system. But
their affluence offered them no genuine sense of security or fulfillment,
and they could not but see that if they and their fellow citizens, regardless of economic status, were to achieve a worthwhile existence, an accountable administration was at least a necessary if not a sufficient condition. The people of Burma had wearied of a precarious state of passive
apprehension where they were "as water in the cupped hands" of the
powers that be.

> Emerald cool we may be
> As water in cupped hands
> But oh that we might be
> As splinters of glass
> In cupped hands.

Glass splinters, the smallest with its sharp, glinting power to defend itself against hands that try to crush, could be seen as a vivid symbol of
the spark of courage that is an essential attribute of those who would
free themselves from the grip of oppression. Bogyoke Aung San regarded himself as a revolutionary and searched tirelessly for answers to
the problems that beset Burma during her times of trial. He exhorted
the people to develop courage: "Don't just depend on the courage and
intrepidity of others. Each and every one of you must make sacrifices to
become a hero possessed of courage and intrepidity. Then only shall we
all be able to enjoy true freedom."

  The effort necessary to remain uncorrupted in an environment   5
where fear is an integral part of everyday existence is not immediately
apparent to those fortunate enough to live in states governed by the rule
of law. Just laws do not merely prevent corruption by meting out impartial punishment to offenders. They also help to create a society in
which people can fulfill the basic requirements necessary for the preservation of human dignity without recourse to corrupt practices. Where
there are no such laws, the burden of upholding the principles of justice and common decency falls on the ordinary people. It is the cumu-

lative effect of their sustained effort and steady endurance which will change a nation where reason and conscience are warped by fear into one where legal rules exist to promote man's desire for harmony and justice while restraining the less desirable destructive traits in his nature.

In an age when immense technological advances have created lethal weapons which could be, and are, used by the powerful and the unprincipled to dominate the weak and the helpless, there is a compelling need for a closer relationship between politics and ethics at both the national and international levels. The Universal Declaration of Human Rights of the United Nations proclaims that "every individual and every organ of society" should strive to promote the basic rights and freedoms to which all human beings regardless of race, nationality, or religion are entitled. But as long as there are governments whose authority is founded on coercion rather than on the mandate of the people, and interest groups which place short-term profits above long-term peace and prosperity, concerted international action to protect and promote human rights will remain at best a partially realized struggle. There will continue to be arenas of struggle where victims of oppression have to draw on their own inner resources to defend their inalienable rights as members of the human family.

The quintessential revolution is that of the spirit, born of an intellectual conviction of the need for change in those mental attitudes and values which shape the course of a nation's development. A revolution which aims merely at changing official policies and institutions with a view to an improvement in material conditions has little chance of genuine success. Without a revolution of the spirit, the forces which produced the iniquities of the old order would continue to be operative, posing a constant threat to the process of reform and regeneration. It is not enough merely to call for freedom, democracy, and human rights. There has to be a united determination to persevere in the struggle, to make sacrifices in the name of enduring truths, to resist the corrupting influences of desire, ill will, ignorance, and fear.

Saints, it has been said, are the sinners who go on trying. So free men are the oppressed who go on trying and who in the process make themselves fit to bear the responsibilities and to uphold the disciplines which will maintain a free society. Among the basic freedoms to which men aspire that their lives might be full and uncramped, freedom from fear stands out as both a means and an end. A people who would build a nation in which strong, democratic institutions are firmly established as a guarantee against state-induced power must first learn to liberate their own minds from apathy and fear.

Always one to practice what he preached, Aung San himself constantly demonstrated courage — not just the physical sort but the kind that enabled him to speak the truth, to stand by his word, to accept criticism, to admit his faults, to correct his mistakes, to respect the opposition, to parley with the enemy, and to let people be the judge of his worthiness as a leader. It is for such moral courage that he will always be loved and respected in Burma — not merely as a warrior hero but as the inspiration and conscience of the nation. The words used by Jawaharlal Nehru to describe Mahatma Gandhi could well be applied to Aung San: "The essence of his teaching was fearlessness and truth, and action allied to these, always keeping the welfare of the masses in view."

Gandhi, that great apostle of nonviolence, and Aung San, the   10
founder of a national army, were very different personalities, but as there is an inevitable sameness about the challenges of authoritarian rule anywhere at any time, so there is a similarity in the intrinsic qualities of those who rise up to meet the challenge. Nehru, who considered the instillation of courage in the people of India one of Gandhi's greatest achievements, was a political modernist, but as he assessed the needs for a twentieth-century movement for independence, he found himself looking back to the philosophy of ancient India: "The greatest gift for an individual or a nation . . . was *abhaya*, fearlessness, not merely bodily courage but absence of fear from the mind."

Fearlessness may be a gift but perhaps more precious is the courage acquired through endeavor, courage that comes from cultivating the habit of refusing to let fear dictate one's actions, courage that could be described as "grace under pressure" — grace which is renewed repeatedly in the face of harsh, unremitting pressure.

Within a system which denies the existence of basic human rights, fear tends to be the order of the day. Fear of imprisonment, fear of torture, fear of death, fear of losing friends, family, property or means of livelihood, fear of poverty, fear of isolation, fear of failure. A most insidious form of fear is that which masquerades as common sense or even wisdom, condemning as foolish, reckless, insignificant, or futile the small, daily acts of courage which help to preserve man's self-respect and inherent human dignity. It is not easy for a people conditioned by fear under the iron rule of the principle that might is right to free themselves from the enervating miasma of fear. Yet even under the most crushing state machinery courage rises up again and again, for fear is not the natural state of civilized man.

The wellspring of courage and endurance in the face of unbridled power is generally a firm belief in the sanctity of ethical principles combined with a historical sense that despite all setbacks the condition of man is set on an ultimate course for both spiritual and material advancement. It is his capacity for self-improvement and self-redemption which most distinguishes man from the mere brute. At the root of human responsibility is the concept of perfection, the urge to achieve it, the intelligence to find a path towards it, and the will to follow that path if not to the end at least the distance needed to rise above individual limitations and environmental impediments. It is man's vision of a world fit for rational, civilized humanity which leads him to dare and to suffer to build societies free from want and fear. Concepts such as truth, justice, and compassion cannot be dismissed as trite when these are often the only bulwarks which stand against ruthless power.

EXPLORATIONS

1. Who appears to be the intended audience for this essay? How can you tell? What impact does Aung San Suu Kyi seem to hope her words will have on her audience?

2. What picture does Suu Kyi paint of her country's government? What picture does she paint of its people? How do her portraits contrast with the way the government wants the Burmese people to think of it and to think of themselves?

3. How does Suu Kyi suggest that the current political and social conditions, which she opposes, are abnormal, and the conditions she is arguing for are normal and customary? What are the advantages of taking this position?

CONNECTIONS

1. What similar arguments are made by Suu Kyi in "Freedom from Fear" and Nelson Mandela in "Black Man in a White Court" (p. 688)? What are the important differences in their political circumstances, their intended audiences, and their messages?

2. Susan Sontag argues that Westerners' "reluctance to apply a single standard of political justice, of freedom, and of individual rights and of democracy . . . is colonialist and condescending" (p. 652). In "On the Politics of Being Mortal" (p. 615), J. F. Ade Ajayi argues that "African development cannot proceed far on the basis of paradigms of development . . . imposed from above [but] only on the basis of improved appreciation of African values" (p. 625). How are these two views contradictory? In "Freedom from Fear," where and how does Suu Kyi express each view?

3. "Just laws . . . help to create a society in which people can fulfill the basic requirements necessary for the preservation of human dignity without re-course to corrupt practices" (para. 4). What examples does Galina Dutkina give in "Sovs, Hacks, and Freeloaders" (p. 367) of unjust laws, damaged human dignity, and corrupt practices? Does Dutkina see these phenomena as linked in the same way Suu Kyi does? How can you tell?

ELABORATIONS

1. "Fear is not the natural state of civilized man" (para. 10). How do you think Suu Kyi is defining "civilized man"? What exactly is it about civilization that frees people from fear? If you agree with Suu Kyi's statement, write an essay explaining it as concretely as you can; if not, write an essay arguing against it.

2. Suu Kyi describes her father's courage: "The kind that enabled him to speak the truth, to stand by his word, to accept criticism, to admit his faults, to cor-rect his mistakes, to respect the opposition, to parley with the enemy, and to let people be the judge of his worthiness as a leader" (para. 9). Is this how you would define courage? If so, write an essay classifying the challenges in your own life, and your responses to them, according to the items in Suu Kyi's list. If not, write an essay defining courage as you see it.

FAY WELDON

Down the Clinical Disco

Fay Weldon was born Franklin Birkinshaw in 1931 in Worcester-shire, England. Her family moved to New Zealand soon afterward; her father, a physician, and her mother, a writer, divorced a few years later. Weldon spent most of her youth among women, attending the Girls' High School in Christchurch, then a convent school in London, where she lived with her mother, sister, and grandmother. She received her master's degree in economics and psychology from St. Andrews University at age twenty. Weldon married a schoolmaster twenty-five years older than she, had a son, divorced, and began writing novels. For money she worked in the Foreign Office, then as a market researcher for the *Daily Mirror*, and then as an advertising copywriter. In 1960 she married Ron Weldon, with whom she has had three more sons. Her first novel was published in 1967: *The Fat Woman's Joke* (U.S. title, *And the Wife Ran Away*, 1968). Continuing to write fiction, she also branched into television scripts, plays, radio plays, and nonfiction. Weldon is best known in the United States for her novel *The Life and Loves of a She-Devil* (1983), which was made into an award-winning television serial by the British Broadcasting Company (1986) and a motion picture, *She-Devil*, starring Meryl Streep and Roseanne (1989). The first woman ever to head the prestigious Booker Prize panel (1983), Weldon is currently a contributing editor for *Allure* magazine. Her most recent novels are *Trouble* (1993) and *Splitting* (1995). She lives in Shepton Mallet, Somerset, and keeps a house in London. "Down the Clinical Disco" comes from her short story collection *Moon Over Minneapolis* (1991).

The United Kingdom of Great Britain and Northern Ireland is a constitutional monarchy currently headed by Queen Elizabeth II and run by a prime minister and a parliament comprising the hereditary House of Lords and elected House of Commons. Slightly smaller than Oregon, it has commanded an empire that at various times included Australia and parts of Europe, North America, Asia, Africa, and Antarctica. The present United Kingdom consists of England, Scotland, and Wales on the island of Great Britain, and the six Irish counties that make up Northern Ireland (see p. 200); among its dominions are the Channel Islands, the Isle of Man, Gibraltar, the British West Indies, Bermuda, the Falklands, and several other South Atlantic islands. Geologically, Britain was part of the European continent until about 6000 B.C. The Romans conquered it in A.D. 43; after they withdrew in 410, Jutes, Angles, and Saxons raided and invaded from what are now

Scandinavia and Germany. The Norman Conquest of 1066 subjugated England to France and blended its Anglo-Saxon language with French to produce English. England and France vied for power over the next several centuries, with Scotland in and out of the fray. Henry VIII split off the Church of England from the Roman Catholic Church in 1534; his daughter Elizabeth I saw England established as a world naval power. She was succeeded by James VI of Scotland, who as James I of England united the two countries in 1603. The age of exploration and empire followed, peaking in the 1800s under Queen Victoria. In the twentieth century, independence movements have reversed British expansion. Although a victor in both world wars, Britain sustained heavy damage, and the rise of air power made its sea power less critical. The United Kingdom was a founding member of NATO and the Common Market and is a cornerstone of the European Community.

You never know where you'll meet your own true love. I met mine down the clinical disco. That's him over there, the thin guy with the jeans, the navy jumper,[1] and the red woolly cap. He looks pretty much like anyone else, don't you think? That's hard work on his part, not to mention mine, but we got there in the end. Do you want a drink? Gin? Tonic? Fine. I'll just have an orange juice. I don't drink. Got to be careful. You never know who's watching. They're everywhere. Sorry, forget I said that. Even a joke can be paranoia. Do you like my hair? That's a golden gloss rinse. Not my style really; I have this scar down my cheek: See, if I turn to the light? A good short crop is what suits me best, always has been: I suppose I've got what you'd call a strong face. Oops, sorry, dear, didn't mean to spill your gin; it's the heels. I do my best but I can never quite manage stilettos. But it's an ill wind; anyone watching would think I'm ever so slightly tipsy, and that's normal, isn't it. It is not absolutely A-okay not to drink alcohol. On the obsessive side. *Darling, of course there are people watching.*

Let me tell you about the clinical disco while Eddie finishes his game of darts. He hates darts but darts are what men do in pubs, okay? The clinical disco is what they have once a month at Broadmoor. (Yes, that place. Broadmoor. The secure hospital for the criminally insane.) You didn't know they had women there? They do. One woman to every nine men. They often don't look all that like women when they go in

---

[1]Sweater. — ED.

but they sure as hell look like them when (and if, if, if, if, if, if) they go out.

How did I get to be in there? You really want to know? I'd been having this crummy time at home and this crummy time at work. I was pregnant and married to this guy I loved, God knows why, in retrospect, but I did, only he fancied my mother, and he got her pregnant too — while I was out at work — did you know women can get pregnant at fifty? He didn't, she didn't, I didn't — but she was! My mum said he only married me to be near her anyway and I was the one who ought to have an abortion. So I did. It went wrong and messed me up inside, so I couldn't have babies, and my mum said what did it matter, I was a lesbian anyway, just look at me. I got the scar in a road accident, in case you're wondering. And I thought what the hell, who wants a man, who wants a mother, and walked out on them. And I was working at the Royal Opera House for this man who was a real pain, and you know how these places get: The dramas and the rows and the overwork and the underpay and the show must go on though you're dropping dead. Dropping dead babies. No, I'm not crying. What do you think I am, a depressive? I'm as normal as the next person.

What I did was set fire to the office. Just an impulse. I was having these terrible pains and he made me work late. He said it was my fault Der Rosenkavalier's wig didn't fit; he said I'd make his opera house a laughingstock: The wig slipped and the *New York Times* noticed and jeered. But it wasn't my fault about the wig: Wardrobe had put the message through to props, not administration. And I sat in front of the VDU[2] — the union is against them; they cause infertility in women but what employer's going to worry about a thing like that — they'd prefer everyone childless any day — and thought about my husband and my mum, five months pregnant, and lit a cigarette. I'd given up smoking for a whole year but this business at home had made me start again. Have you ever had an abortion at five months? No? Not many have.

How's your drink? How's Eddie getting on with the darts? Started another game? That's A-okay, that's fine by me, that's normal. 5

So what were we saying, Linda? Oh yes, arson. That's what they called it. I just moved my cigarette lighter under the curtains and they went up, whoosh, and they caught some kind of soundproof ceiling infill they use these days instead of plaster. Up it all went. Whoosh again. Four hundred pounds' worth of damage. Or so they said. If you ask me, they were glad of the excuse to redecorate.

---

[2]Video display unit; a computer monitor. — ED.

Like a fool, instead of lying and just saying it was an accident, I said
I'd done it on purpose, I was glad I had, opera was a waste of public
funds, and working late a waste of my life. That was before I got to
court. The solicitor[3] laddie warned me off. He said arson was no laughing matter, they came down very hard on arson. I thought a fine, perhaps; he said no, prison. Years not months.

You know my mum didn't even come to the hearing? She had a
baby girl. I thought there might be something wrong with it, my mum
being so old, but there wasn't. Perhaps the father being so young made
up for it.

There was a barrister chappie. He said look you've been upset, you
are upset, all this business at home. The thing for you to do is plead insane; we'll get you sent to Broadmoor, it's the best place in the country
for psychiatric care, they'll have you right in the head in no time. Otherwise it's Holloway, and that's all strip cells and major tranquilizers,
and not so much of a short sharp shock as a long sharp shock. Years, it
could be, arson.

So that's what I did, I pleaded insane, and got an indefinite sentence,   10
which meant into Broadmoor until such time as I was cured and safe to
be let out into the world again. I never was unsafe. You know what one of
those famous opera singers said when she heard what I'd done? "Good for
Philly," she said. "Best thing that could possibly happen: the whole place
razed to the ground." Only of course it wasn't razed to the ground, there
was just one room already in need of redecoration slightly blackened.
When did I realize I'd made a mistake? The minute I saw Broadmoor: a
great black pile; the second I got into this reception room. There were
three women nurses in there, standing around a bath of hot water; great
hefty women, and male nurses too, and they were talking and laughing.
Well, not exactly laughing, but an Inside equivalent; a sort of heavy
grunting ha-ha-ha they manage, halfway between sex and hate. They
didn't even look at me as I came in. I was terrified, you can imagine. One
of them said "strip" over her shoulder and I just stood there not believing
it. So she barked "strip" again, so I took off a cardigan and my shoes, and
then one of them just ripped everything off me and pushed my legs apart
and yanked out a Tampax — sorry about this, Linda — and threw it in a
bin and dunked me in the bath without even seeing me. Do you know
what's worse than being naked and seen by strangers, including men
strangers? It's being naked and unseen, because you don't even count as a
woman. Why men? In case the women patients are uncontrollable. The
bath was dirty. So were the nurses. I asked for a sanitary towel but no one

---

[3]Solicitor: a consulting lawyer. A barrister (para. 9) is a courtroom lawyer. — ED.

replied. I don't know if they were being cruel: I don't think they thought that what came out of my mouth were words. Well I was mad, wasn't I? That's why I was there. I was mad because I was a patient, I was wicked because I was prisoner; they were sane because they were nurses and good because they could go home after work.

Linda, is that guy over there in the suit watching? No? You're sure?

They didn't go far, mind you, most of them. They lived, breathed, slept The Hospital. Whole families of nurses live in houses at the foot of the great Broadmoor wall. They intermarry. Complain about one and you find you're talking to the cousin, aunt, lover, or best friend of the complainee. You learn to shut up; you learn to smile. I was a tea bag for the whole of one day and I never stopped smiling from dawn to dusk. That's right, I was a tea bag. Nurse Kelly put a wooden frame around my shoulders and hung a piece of gauze front and back and said, "You be a tea bag all day," so I was. How we all laughed. Why did he want me to be a tea bag? It was his little joke. They get bored, you see. They look to the patients for entertainment.

Treatment? Linda, I saw one psychiatrist six times and I was there three years. The men do better. They have rehabilitation programs, Ping-Pong, carpentry, and we all get videos. Only the men get to choose the video and they always choose blue films. They have to choose them to show they're normal, and the women have to choose not to see them to show the same. You have to be normal to get out. Sister[4] in the ward fills in the report cards. She's the one who decides whether or not you're sane enough to go before the Parole Committee. The trouble is, she's not so sane herself. She's more institutionalized than the patients.

Eddie, come and join us! How was your game? You won? Better not do that too often. You don't want to be seen as an overachiever. This is Linda, I'm telling her how we met. At the clinical disco. Shall we do a little dance, just the pair of us, in the middle of everything and everyone, just to celebrate being out? No, you're right, that would be just plain mad. Eddie and I love each other, Linda, we met at the clinical disco, down Broadmoor way. Who knows, the doctor may have been wrong about me not having babies; stranger things happen. My mum ran out on my ex, leaving him to look after the baby; he came to visit me in Broadmoor once and asked me to go back to him, but I wouldn't. Sister put me back for that: A proper woman wants to go back to her husband, even though he's her little sister's father. And after he'd gone I cried. You must never cry in Broadmoor. It means you're depressed;

---

[4]Head nurse. — ED.

and that's the worst madness of all. The staff all love it in there, and think you're really crazy if you don't. I guess they get kind of offended if you cry. So it's on with the lipstick and smile, smile, smile, though everyone around you is ballooning with largactyl and barking like the dogs they think they are.

I tell you something, Linda, these places are madhouses. Never, 15 never plead the balance of your mind is disturbed in court: Get a prison sentence and relax, and wait for time to pass and one day you'll be free. Once you're in a secure hospital, you may never get out at all, and they fill the women up with so many tranquilizers, you may never be fit to. The drugs give you brain damage. But I reckon I'm all right; my hands tremble a bit, and my mouth twitches sometimes, but it's not too bad. And I'm still *me*, aren't I. Eddie's fine — they don't give men so much, sometimes none at all. Only you never know what's in the tea. But you can't be seen not drinking it, because that's paranoia.

Eddie says I should sue the barrister, with his fine talk of therapy and treatment in Broadmoor, but I reckon I won't. Once you've been in you're never safe. They can pop you back inside if you cause any trouble at all, and they're the ones who decide what trouble is. So we keep our mouths shut and our noses clean, we ex-inmates of Broadmoor.

Are you sure that man's not watching? Is there something wrong with us? Eddie? You're not wearing your earring, are you? Turn your head. No, that's all right. We look just like everyone else. Don't we? Is my lipstick smudged? Christ, I hate wearing it. It makes my eyes look small.

At the clinical disco! They hold them at Broadmoor every month. Lots of the men in there are sex offenders, rapists, mass murderers, torturers, child abusers, flashers. The staff like to see how they're getting on, how they react to the opposite sex, and on the morning of the disco Sister turns up and says "you go" and "you" and "you" and of course you can't say no, no matter how scared you are. Because you're supposed to want to dance. And the male staff gee up the men — hey, look at those titties! Wouldn't you like to look up *that* skirt — and stand by looking forward to the trouble, a bit of living porno, better than a blue film any day. And they gee up the women too: Wow, there's a handsome hunk of male; and you have to act interested, because that's normal: If they think you're a lezzie you never get out. And the men have to act interested, but not too interested. Eddie and I met at the clinical disco, acting just gently interested. Eddie felt up my titties, and I rubbed myself against him and the staff watched and all of a sudden he said "Hey, I mean really," and I said "Hi," and he said "Sorry about this, keep smiling," and I said, "Ditto, what are you in for?" and he said "I got a job as a woman teacher. Six little girls framed me. But I love teaching, not little girls. There was just no job for a man," and I believed him; nobody else ever had. And I told him about my mum and my ex, and he seemed to understand. Didn't you, Eddie! That's love, you see. Love at first sight. You're just on the other person's side, and if you can find someone else like that about you, everything falls into place. We were both out in three months. It didn't matter for once if I wore lipstick, it didn't matter to him if he had to watch blue films: You stop thinking that acting sane is driving you mad: You don't have not to cry because you stop wanting to cry: The barking and howling and screeching stop worrying you; I guess when you're in love you're just happy so they have to turn you out; because your being happy shows them up. If you're happy, what does sane or insane mean, what are their lives all about? They can't bear to see it.

Linda, it's been great meeting you. Eddie and I are off home now. I've talked too much. Sorry. When we're our side of our front door I scrub off the makeup and get into jeans and he gets into drag, and we're ourselves, and we just hope no one comes knocking on the door to say, hey that's not normal, back to Broadmoor, but I reckon love's a talisman. If we hold on to that we'll be okay.

EXPLORATIONS

1. Who is the narrator of this story? To whom is she speaking? Where does the story take place?

2. Why does the story's narrator believe she has to act normal? Who defines and enforces normality? What are the criteria?

3. What characters in "Down the Clinical Disco" behave abnormally — that is, dysfunctionally — and in what ways? What social and political institutions encourage their behavior?

CONNECTIONS

1. How is "Down the Clinical Disco" similar in form and theme to T. Coraghessan Boyle's "Top of the Food Chain" (p. 680)? To whom is the narrator of each story speaking and why? In what ways do these two narrators' contrasting speaking styles suit their identities? Their goals?

2. What parallels can you find between the experience of Weldon's English narrator in Broadmoor and Grace Paley's experience in a New York prison

in "Six Days: Some Rememberings" (p. 655)? What are some notable differences?

3. What statements by Simone de Beauvoir in "Woman as Other" (p. 445) apply to the narrator's interactions with other characters in "Down the Clinical Disco"? How is it in the interest of an institution such as Broadmoor to define inmates as "other"?

ELABORATIONS

1. "Down the Clinical Disco" is full of institutions and individuals that fail to carry out their assigned functions. Write a comparison-contrast essay examining these contradictions — for instance, the official purpose of the clinical disco at Broadmoor versus the role it actually plays for patients and staff. What point is conveyed by these contradictions?

2. Look closely at the techniques Weldon uses to tell her story in the form of a monologue. How does she change scenes and time frames? What is the effect of the questions at the beginning of some paragraphs? What other functions are served by the invisible character, Linda? Choose an incident in your life, such as a clash with authority, and write about it in the same monologue form Weldon uses.

DAVID GROSSMAN

Israeli Arab, Israeli Jew

Widely regarded as one of Israel's most gifted writers, David Grossman was born in Jerusalem in 1954 and graduated from Hebrew University. His first novel, *Hiyukh ha-gedi* (1983; *The Smile of the Lamb*,
1991) won the Israeli Publisher's Association Prize for best novel in
1985. Other national and international awards have honored his several
children's books, two more novels, two volumes of nonfiction, and a
play. Grossman also has worked as a journalist for Kol Israel (Israeli
Radio). He wrote *Ha Zeman ha-tsahov* (1987; *The Yellow Wind*, 1988)
after interviewing Jews and Palestinians living in the West Bank for the
news weekly *Koteret Rashit*. "Israeli Arab, Israeli Jew" comes from his
1992 book *Hanochachim hanifkadim* (*Sleeping on a Wire: Conversations with Palestinians in Israel*), translated from the Hebrew by Haim
Watzman. Grossman's most recent novel to appear in the United States
is *Sefer hadikduk hapnimi* (1992; *The Book of Intimate Grammar*,
1994).

When Israel became independent in 1948, most of the Arab Palestinians living there fled or were evicted, while five Arab armies tried to
destroy the new nation. By the war's end only 156,000 Arabs remained
in Israel. Tensions flared in 1967 into the Six Day War, which ended
with Israel not only intact but in control of the rest of Palestine, previously managed by Syria, Jordan, and Egypt (see p. 188). A new attack on
Israel by Syria and Egypt in 1973 brought the United States into the
picture as a mediator. An Arab summit conference the next year recognized the Palestine Liberation Organization (PLO) under Yasir Arafat
as the sole legitimate representative of the Palestinian people — that is,
the Arab Palestinians living in the West Bank and Gaza Strip, now occupied by Israel. Israel's refusal to negotiate with the PLO and its policy
of building settlements in the occupied territories increased Arab resentment, Palestinian resistance, and Israeli reprisals. The Israeli government treated the grass-roots violence of the intifada — an uprising of
Palestinians against the troops whom they regard as an army of occupation — as a terrorist campaign. However, the hundreds of Palestinian
casualties inside and outside Israeli-run refugee camps focused worldwide attention on the PLO's demand for an independent Palestinian
state.

In 1993 Israel and the PLO officially recognized each other's legitimacy and agreed that Israel would cede control of the Gaza Strip and
the West Bank town of Jericho to the Palestinians. Progress toward
peace has been slowed by continuing tension on both sides, in particu-

lar the 1996 assassination of Israeli Prime Minister Yitzhak Rabin of the leftist Labor Party and his replacement by Benjamin Netanyahu of the more conservative Likud Party.

Today about 900,000 Arabs live in Israel — a sixth of the population. Although the country's Declaration of Independence promises them "full and equal citizenship" and "appropriate representation," discrimination is rampant. David Grossman notes that Israel has never had an Arab cabinet minister, Supreme Court justice, or director-general of a large company; only 3 out of 1,000 employees in the Ministry of Justice are Arabs; and although Arabs farm 17 percent of agricultural land, they get only 2.4 percent of the water.

For more background on Israel, see page 188.

"You see the wall there, by the bank?" Mohammed Kiwan swings his swivel chair around and points. "There they wrote, in big letters, 'Death to the Arabs.' And next to it, 'A good Arab is a dead Arab.' And that in the heart of the fair city of Hadera,[1] straight across from my office window. Fine, so the day they wrote it I call the Hadera municipality and tell them, Hey, guys, right across from my nice little office they're hanging me! So please, come clean it up. Ten days passed and they didn't come to wash it off. The graffiti pricks me in the back. When did they come? When we brought the press into it; within a day the mayor had ordered the graffiti cleaned up."

He is an attorney, lives in Um Elfahm, works in Hadera. At the beginning of the 1960s he had been a teacher — "an educator," he corrects me — and was fired because of his political activity. At the time Kiwan was active in the Nasserist[2] nationalist movement, Al-Ard. In 1965, after Al-Ard was outlawed, he was among the founders of Sons of the Village, a radical Palestinian movement whose aim was to fight for an improvement in the status of the Arabs in Israel. "We called it Abna el-Balad, because *balad* means both 'village' and 'homeland.' It's the unfortunate villager as opposed to the snobbish rich. It's the common man, Voltaire's Candide. I always look for that man. Among you [Jews] and among us. I'd like to get to the Candides among you, too. But your communications media are blocked to us. How many times have they interviewed an Arab on a television talk show? Despite the fact that

---

[1]Hadera lies on Israel's northern Mediterranean coast, Um Elfahm about fifteen miles inland on the border of the disputed West Bank. — ED.

[2]Gamal Abdel Nasser, Egypt's president from 1956 to 1970, favored Arab nationalism and opposed Israel's existence. — ED.

we're nearly 20 percent of the population and talk, God knows, just like you. Where's equality of opportunity? We're always shouting, but no one hears. They don't allow us to reach you. Here, two months ago I saw this guy Jojo from Ashdod[3] on television, the one on the beach. What a wise and simple man! What common sense and humanity! I wrote him an open letter, for the newspaper, and called to him: 'I, Mohammed, am searching for Jojo from Ashdod.' The paper, of course, would not print it. So I'm still looking for those Jojos."

"It's not that complicated," I told him. "Let's drive down to see him."

It wasn't all that simple, either. Jojo Abutbul lives in Ashdod, Mohammed Kiwan in Um Elfahm. Who should go to whom? "Tell him we'll meet halfway," Kiwan suggested. "What do you mean halfway?" Abutbul grumbled. "I've got to be in my restaurant on the beach every day, tell him to come here." I mediated, shuttle diplomacy by telephone, one day, another day, until Kiwan finally gave in; after all, he wanted to talk to Jojo, and if Jojo won't come to Mohammed, Mohammed will go to the beach.

On a hot summer's day, at Jojo's café-restaurant, The West Coast,   5 under the palm branches spread over the roof, the two sat facing each other. The restaurant loudspeakers played American music, the beach slumbered beyond. Jojo took a pack of cigarettes out of his pocket. Mohammed took out his pack. They lit their own, relaxed, and Jojo, the host, began.

"When we lived in Morocco, my mother had an Arab housemaid. She nursed me. That is, I grew up with her. I drank her milk. Let's say that when you go to sleep your life is a kind of box that you have to deposit with someone for safekeeping. That's an allegory. My mother would have had no problem handing that box, my life, over to her Arab neighbor. What I mean is that even when it was really a matter of life itself, the trust was so great that it was possible to place my life in her hands.

"So I — I don't have any preconceptions about you. An Arab is a human being. An Arab has a soul. I once talked about the pain. Fifteen get killed in the territories and they put it in small print in the newspaper. A Jew gets killed in an attack and it's on the front page! Why do they make distinctions when it comes to pain? If today I take my cigarette and put it out on Mohammed's hand, and take a cigarette and put it out on my hand, you'll measure the same force and feel exactly the same pain. Emotion. Love. Concern. Your son. These are things that

---

[3]Mediterranean port south of Tel Aviv. — ED.

weren't given to us by the Likud or the Labor Party. Not by Judaism or Islam. I lost a son. I know what pain is. And that woman in Ramallah or Nablus,[4] and don't think I'm justifying in any way their stone-throwing, but he's dead. She feels the same pain I felt when my son drowned in the sea. Pain can't be divided; its force can't be measured, because of its relation to a particular person.

"So I ask you, Mohammed, where do we want to get to? Are you satisfied with your plate, your bed, your house, or are you satisfied only with my plate, my bed, my wife, and my children? On the other hand, when a Jewish guy tells me he wants security here, you know? Security has no bounds! You can put a ground-to-air missile on every square meter. Will that give you security? Tomorrow some Ahmed won't come and knife you? So where's my security and where's Mohammed's security? So that's what we have to talk about today, me and you — what are we willing to give each other? And I'm certain that if the two of us sit down and talk, we can finish off all the problems in two minutes."

Mohammed listened quietly, nodding all the while. When Jojo finished talking, he said, "First I want to tell you that I'm glad I came to meet you. We don't know each other. I saw you one time on television and I had the impression that you are a person with healthy natural instincts and a love of life, and I felt that this person is really looking for a way to live together. I'm happy that the minute we met you said that we can solve all the problems straight off in two minutes. So the only question is: What work will that leave you, Grossman?"

We laughed, and drank our first cup of coffee. The beach was still   10
empty — only a few new immigrants from Russia cooking in the sun.

"Before we solve all the problems in two minutes," I said, "maybe we could clarify the most basic concepts, so that we'll know if we're talking about the same thing. What do you, Mohammed, call this country, the one Jojo calls Israel?"

"As far as I'm concerned," Mohammed said, "it's always Palestine. I don't care if Jojo calls it Israel. Jojo has the right to live here as an individual and as a nation, and my right as a Palestinian is to live in Palestine, as an individual and as a nation, with the right of self-determination for the Palestinian people. That's the basic principle, and I'm convinced Jojo will agree with me."

"I agree 100 percent," Jojo confirmed, "but you accept that this is also the Jewish state, right?"

---

[4]Palestinian towns in the West Bank. — ED.

"As far as I'm concerned, Israel can call itself whatever it wants." Mohammed smiled. "If it's just a semantic problem, I don't care. But if it means — like now — that it's a Jewish state with all the privileges and laws that discriminate in favor of the Jews, then other questions arise that I don't agree with."

Jojo stiffened. "Let's get this straight. I, as a Jew, have no country other than Israel. I have to have one country that will be mine. I, Jojo Abutbul, was born Jewish. I did not decide that. I didn't have a store where I could take from whatever shelf I wanted. I was born Jewish. I deserve a place somewhere in the world to live the way I want, yes or no?"

"Ah . . . with regard to that question, you formulated it in a very difficult way."

"I did not!" Jojo cried. "That's a question from the gut, not from the head!"

"Look, Jojo," Mohammed said, getting a little more serious. "Before you came from Morocco, I was here."

"I'm not kicking you out!"

"One second, give me a second. This pretty, sparkling Ashdod of yours, just for your information, even after the country was established in 1948, there were still Arabs here and in Ashkelon, and Israel expelled them in accordance with the infamous Plan D.[5] Now you're alive and you exist, and you have this country, and I'm not challenging your right to a country, but according to what you say, 'I'm here, I don't have anywhere else to go,' ditto as regards the Palestinians — they have nowhere else to go — "

"I agree with you," Jojo cut him off. "But just a minute! I can help you with something that I don't know if you know. I say that having the Law of Return[6] only for Jews — that's racist! I'm not hiding that! But I ask you, Mohammed, you have the option of getting up tomorrow and moving to Jordan, Egypt, Syria, Lebanon — all those are Arab countries. But here I'm saying to you, in addition to all twenty-two of those countries, I'm saying to you, here I'm going to build another country for you, completely Palestinian, in Gaza and the West Bank. Wait a minute! You don't have to take your things and move there. Understand! As far as I'm concerned, you are a citizen of the State of Israel, with all your rights! But by this act that I'm making, do you accept that

[5]Plan D was the first strategic plan of the IDF [Israeli Defense Force] in 1948 to occupy towns and villages populated by Arabs, in lands assigned by the UN partition to the Jewish state. — ED.
[6]The Law of Return gives every Jew the right to immigrate to Israel. — ED.

Israel is *my* country? You can live in it, but under my conditions, my government, my laws. And if I should want to live in your country, it will be under your laws and your government and your conditions. Can you live with that?"

"You and I, Jojo, when we're aware of those discriminatory, racist laws, and we both fight for their repeal by the legislature . . ."

Jojo: "You're not answering me! Say yes or no!"

Mohammed breathes deeply: "If you don't recognize my right to full equality here, I won't recognize your right."

"No, no, you don't understand." Jojo smiles uncomfortably. "I'm say-   25
ing this: You and I want a divorce. You've been married to me for forty-three years. I love you, you're my soul, everything. I don't want to live with you! Let's get divorced. What do you want as a dowry?"

"I'm not asking for a dowry. We really married against our wills. Not out of love. But today we're sailing on this sea in the same boat."

"And I own the sea."

"I don't agree that you own the sea!"

"But I'm the strong one! If I want, I can come today as Prime Minister Jojo and make a law — Whoever doesn't accept Israeli citizenship in the Jewish state — the *Jewish* state! — gets put in a car and taken away. Can you do anything to stop me? Nothing. Cry, scream until tomorrow!"

It's only Mohammed's mouth that is smiling at Jojo now. "First, Jojo,   30
my friend, inside, in my heart, I don't feel that you are in control and that you have power. I don't feel that I'm inferior to you. True, you now have strength and power, but I am among those who believe that power changes hands. I'm a minority under you, but you are a minority under me, in the Arab Middle East. I have no feelings of inferiority with regard to you. I was born here. I have the strongest possible links with this homeland. I don't feel that I'm a guest of yours. I sometimes feel, if I may be presumptuous, that you are a guest of mine, and that I accept you because I want to be realistic. That is, the Jewish people's starting point, that they're doing me a favor when they let me live in Um Elfahm, is mistaken. Look, in Um Elfahm we had 140,000 dunams[7] of land before Israel was established, and then the Knesset[8] came and made all kinds of laws and confiscated from Israel's Arab citizens 1,200,000 dunams all at once. Today two kibbutzim and a moshav[9] sit

---

[7]One dunam equals 1,000 square meters or about one-quarter of an acre. — ED.
[8]Israeli parliament. — ED.
[9]Jewish settlements. — ED.

on Um Elfahm's land. On our land! Another thing, 92 percent of Israel's land is state land. If this country really recognizes me as part of it, then I should have a proportional part of that 92 percent of the country. Do you understand why I'm shouting? Because when you tell me that you're doing me a favor by accepting me here, you have to look at things from my point of view, and then you'll begin to understand what kinds of huge concessions Palestinians are making today when they offer two states side by side. But if after the Palestinian state comes into being you come and rescind the discriminatory laws, if with regard to the Law of Return, for instance — "

"But here I'm not arguing with you," Jojo stops him. "The Law of Return has to apply to everyone."

Mohammed raises a finger. "In other words, you agree that the Arabs who were expelled from Ashdod can come back to live in Ashdod?"

"Yes! They can buy a house the way I do! I'm not giving them any privileges!"

Mohammed: "Allow me! You're saying that this country, this future country of ours, will agree that every man in the world who wants to live in it can?"

Jojo: "Suits me!"   35

"Even if some miserable Kurd from Iraq or Turkey wants to live with you in Ashdod?"

"I've got no problem with that. If, if, *if*. If he promises to serve in my army, to be loyal to the *Jewish* state and not betray it. To fight together with me against whoever wants to take this country from the both of us, even to fight against Syria with me!"

"But it should be clear to you," Kiwan says, "that if there's total equality here, the country won't have its Jewish character anymore."

"Why won't it?" Jojo asks in horror. "It has to have! There'll be maximum equality, as much as possible! But subject to this being a *Jewish* country!"

"Then it's not real equality! Then the Jews have extra rights because   40 of their Jewish birth! Then it's no longer Mohammed's country!"

"Just like in Syria there are extra rights for Arabs, as opposed to Jews!"

"Look, if you come at me with something like that" — Mohammed raised his thick, hoarse voice for the first time — "let me tell you that my counterdemand is just as purely racist — have the Palestinian state include all parts of Israel in which there are Palestinians! Give me the Galilee and the Triangle!"

"I'm ready to! I'm ready to give them to you, if — *if* you give me Nablus and Hebron, where I once lived!"

"Hey!"

"Why 'hey'? Why not? Don't you see you're talking out of both sides   45
of your mouth? Do Jews live in Hebron today? They do! Abraham lived
there two thousand years ago? He did! Listen to me, Mohammed." Jojo
sat back in his chair, lit two cigarettes in his mouth, pulled on both, and
passed one over to Mohammed. "For years you butchered and exiled
us, and for years we've butchered and exiled you. What I'm saying is
this: We have two possibilities. Either we can talk nice and act bad, or
talk bad and act nice. In other words, I, according to the way I see
things, I prefer to get the dirt out of my mouth. Let's sit in a room and
argue for twenty hours; I'll tell you you're garbage, you're crap, and you
tell me the same thing, but in the end you and I get up with a clean
heart, and we have no more demands, and we've divided up all the
property between us, but for always! Finished!"

"I agree with you on that. But understand one thing, that the minute
we repeal all the privileges Jews get here, this country will stop being a
Jewish country and will become the country of the people who live in it."

"People, what people?" Jojo slaps his forehead with an open palm.
"Is England a country of its people? Is Syria a country of its people?
England is the country of the English, and Syria is the country of the
Syrians. And you, if you live in Israel, will live in the country of the Is-
raelis, as an Arab minority in the country of the Jews!"

Their faces are now close to each other. Their hands, waving excitedly, hit one another, and at times intertwine for a moment. Both are
solidly built, with black hair and tough faces. Both look older than they
are. Mohammed is about fifty, balding a bit, more careful with his
words. Every so often he throws out a bit of legal jargon at Jojo in a
lawyerly tone, looking at him over his glasses, putting on a tolerant and
didactic expression. It drives Jojo crazy.

Jojo, thirty-eight, is in a blue undershirt and shorts. His sunglasses remain glued to his forehead even when he jumps up in indignation. He
has lived on the beach since he was four years old — "Everything I
know about life is from the sea." In his youth he was a violent criminal,
terrorizing this beach until he won himself a place and was pacified.
Ever since his appearance on television, politicians from all parties have
been courting him, and he, "even though I've been Likud from my
mother's womb," meets with them all, listens, gives advice — lively,
heart-winning, knowing well that they all think that through him they
have gained a direct linkup to "the people's voice." His face has infinite
expressions, and he talks in a very loud voice, at a shout, taking control
of the conversation, hyperemotional, undulating like a cat across the
table from Mohammed, ambushing words and arguments. He manages

the entire beach as he debates — giving advice to a young soccer player who approaches him, giving a contribution to a needy family, trading secrets with a party activist — a one-man band.

The two minutes passed. The conversation lasted close to four hours, 50 and in the process it slowly became clear to both sides how much trouble they were having bridging the gap between them. It was easy for the onlooker to realize that, despite the goodwill, their first line of defense was also their last. Jojo would never give up Israel as the Jewish state; Mohammed would never retreat from his goal of full equal rights with Jojo — that is, that Israel be "a country of its citizens" and not "the country of the Jewish people."

As this became apparent, the two of them became impatient, trying to catch hold of each other, to put it into other words, words that would circumvent an abyss. They did not want the victor in this confrontation to be familiar political differences. They wanted victory to go to those nameless things whose potency and insistence could be felt when Jojo's and Mohammed's faces came close together — that same link of expression and warmth, the mirror dialogue of mimicry, and the hidden thing that synchronized the two of them, as in a ceremonial warriors' dance. It was easy to imagine them changing roles and arguing, in an opposite state of affairs — each one making the other's points with the same fervor.

Mohammed: "The truth, Jojo: You too have suffered discrimination during your life in Israel, right?"

"Suffered?" Jojo guffaws. "I *grew up* on discrimination. I grew up on inequality. I grew up with the word *Moroccan*. I grew up with everything you've felt. Compared with the Ashkenazim,[10] I was discriminated against here, too."

"So you are the first one who should understand the violent response of the Palestinians in the territories, and the desire of the Arabs in Israel for equality."

"No, no," Jojo rebuffed him. "Me, my whole outlook now is against 55 violence. Ask why. Because all violence brings counterviolence. Mohammed tells me, 'You're strong in your country and weak in the Middle East.' But the Arabs are strong in the Middle East and weak in the world. The world, pal, is built like a ladder. For every strong man there's someone stronger than him, and what we're talking about is not how to be strong but how to reach an understanding. So that I can turn my back to you and sleep peacefully, and you the same. Look,

---

[10]Jews of European origin or descent. — ED.

Mohammed, for instance, wanted to be a lawyer. The country didn't try to trip him up, he went and learned law . . ."

"It certainly did try to trip me up!" Mohammed shot him down. "I'll give you a simple example. When I was studying they put me, in my second year, before exams, on house arrest, to keep me from passing the exams. I stayed at home for an entire year just for having quote unquote 'dared to protest' the injustices we spoke of before."

"But you studied and finished and became a lawyer, right? They didn't even give me the option you had! That is, between Jojo and Mohammed, Jojo was the one more discriminated against!"

"Look, Jojo. The Sephardim[11] were discriminated against and are still discriminated against. When I was in school, it hurt me to see that less than 1 percent of the students in the university were Arabs, and the same for the Sephardim!"

"Not only in the university! Also in the officer corps, and in the government!"

"It's very interesting how and why they block cooperation between   60
the Sephardim and the Arabs here, even though, from a theoretical point of view, logic says that both of us, the underdogs, should work together. Let me remind you that here in your Ashdod the government — indirectly but deliberately — uses the Sephardim against us, and when there's an Arab attack against Israelis, it's you who go out to beat up the poor Arab laborers! You, the Sephardim! In my opinion, the response of the Sephardim, so hostile to the Arabs, derives first from them not having been given an education. They were not given a chance to study. They're a simple, unsophisticated public, and when the newspaper headlines and the radio stir them up — and that's directed very well from above — that public gets hot and blows up. Second — discrimination. You and I, Jojo, both our groups get screwed here in this country, because of the historical reality that the early waves of immigration were Ashkenazim, and after a period of hardship here, they became the ones who eat the cream. Then you became disadvantaged, and it's well known that the disadvantaged — it's very simple — wants to compensate himself by discriminating against others."

"I don't agree!" Jojo jumped up from his seat. "Take the most extreme anti-Arab movements we have, Kahane and the Moledet Party who want to transfer all the Arabs out of Israel, in all their hierarchies you'll hardly find a single Sephardi! The entire leadership is Ashkenazim! Americans! So tell me, how can that be? Where's your theory?

---

[11]Jews of Mediterranean or Middle Eastern origin or descent. — ED.

Listen to me, Mohammed, don't go looking for university explanations. When it's a matter of life or death, there aren't any Ashkenazim and there aren't any Sephardim. Everyone comes together. Just as an Arab from Sudan hates me when I send my army into Lebanon, we're all against you when you butcher one of us. And precisely because you and I have the same mentality, you should understand that, and I'll explain to you: Our behavior, Mohammed, will be different from Grossman's in many ways, different from the Ashkenazi's. If he has a guest who comes in and talks to his wife, it won't bother him at all. If a guest comes and talks with my wife, he'll never enter my house again! That means with us, with you and with me, my wife, and to put it more generally, my honor, is a higher priority than my work, before everything. With the Ashkenazi, no. First his work, first advancement. With us, a guest comes to my house, even if two hours beforehand he ran over my son, the minute he comes to my house, first I welcome him in. I'll get him afterward — but that's separate. Our commitment is to honor. Our mentality all plays accompaniment to the first violin — our honor. And I, Jojo Abutbul, don't hate Arabs, but I would make a law that every Arab who throws a stone in the intifada should be shot. Because for me the act of throwing a stone is not just throwing a stone. I'm not afraid of a stone!" Jojo shouts, the veins in his neck bulging. "But with me, in Morocco, who do you throw stones at? At a dog! At a snake! It insults me! I'm not his dog, not his snake! And don't forget, Mohammed, that same stone you throw at us today, we grew up with it, we remember it!"

Kiwan's face went sour. "First of all, the Israeli public — and you, I'm very sorry to say, are a part of it — doesn't understand what the intifada is. You don't understand the pathetic state of the people there, how bitterness built up to the point that — how did that writer of yours, S. Yizhar, put it — 'a nation rose up.' People had no way to remain silent any longer, so they used the stone. Not, God forbid, to insult you! They are certainly not treating you like a dog, God forbid. An Arab will also throw a stone at another Arab. It's simply the only tool he has to make the world hear him! . . ."

The conversation was interrupted for a moment. One of the workers from the restaurant came up to Jojo to ask him something. He was limping a bit. Jojo introduced him to us as Uzi. "Actually," Jojo explained, "his name is Awad. I changed it to Uzi. Easier for him, easier for me." A deep, heavy glance curdled for a long moment between Mohammed Kiwan and Uzi. "He doesn't feel comfortable either when I call him Awad in front of people. Look at him, Mohammed. He lives in Gaza, and because he had good relations with Jews, your friends there put two bullets through his legs." Jojo sent the man off and resumed his flood of words. . . . "Here, in Israel, you and I will live in equality. According to the laws we make together. We are not allowed to decide to take the law into our own hands. If you or I start deciding which laws to obey, it will start today with the law about military service in the territories, tomorrow it will be the income tax law, and the day after it will be the law about how many wives I can have. You have to understand what the real meaning of democracy is. It's in your interest to understand, because you want democracy in the country you'll have someday. Democracy is that if I don't agree with the law I don't have a choice! And I want to hear from you now an answer to one question about all this — you, as a citizen here in the State of Israel: Will the Palestinian state, when it is established, satisfy you for good?"

Mohammed: "I accept that, with two of my reservations. That I have my basic rights, and then there's the last little problem that remains, my national identity."

Jojo leaned over at him suspiciously. "What's that? What did you say?"   65

Mohammed studied his fingers. "Give me recognition as a national minority. In other words, internal autonomy. In Israel. For the Arabs here."

"Oho!" Jojo erupts. "Hello, trouble! So now you've made me another problem — that you know in advance you're looking for as a problem, not a solution! Very nice! And here, from the start I've been telling you, Listen, let's the two of us bake two cakes. When it comes to how much flour, how many eggs we'll put in — about all that I'm willing to ask your advice. But the minute we've baked the two cakes, don't eat mine! And you, Mohammed, you should understand from your nature and I'm also appealing to your logic and your sense of justice — you can't take part of *mine* once I've given you yours! You got your country and flag and leadership, so leave me alone with my country and flag and leadership!" . . .

Jojo is again surging forward, and Mohammed's lips are already moving, mumbling his prepared answer, and it is already manifestly clear how each argument lights a long wick of memories with the other, running swiftly down the fuse of painful wounds. You can see how in each segment of their conversation the entire conflict is reborn, from its shell made of yesterday's newspapers back to Sarah the matriarch saying, "Cast out this bondwoman and her son: for the son of this bondwoman shall not be heir with my son, with Isaac."[12] And in the background —

---

[12]From the Biblical story of Abraham the patriarch, Genesis 21:10. — ED.

the sea, which also, you may recall, was once assigned a role in the conflict. "You're still not answering me about that, Mohammed, and time is running out. Think about it now and tell me yes or no, in one sentence; it has to be only one sentence, from the guts; you've got a problem, Mohammed, maybe because you're a lawyer, you send it from the guts to the brain and then to the mouth, and the whole time I've been talking to you out of my nature. Will you, Mohammed, recognize without any challenge my right to one Jewish state? Yes or no?"

Mohammed laughs. "Look, my dear Jojo, from the cumulative experience of the Arabs in Israel . . ."

"He's being a lawyer again."   70

"Just a minute. Listen to me. After the Palestinian state is created, we'll still have a problem with you. Our land. Our education. Our definition as a national minority here. Our national symbols. I'm coming out of all this, and in the most democratic way possible trying to change the situation, trying to convince you — not violently — that my good is your good. That we, the Arabs in Israel, will be a kind of, a canton, we ourselves will manage the — "

"Canton?!" Jojo burst out, from the heart. "Now you've killed me! Now you've actually created a state within a state!"

"Just a canton," Mohammed Kiwan blurted out, "a small kind of authority . . ."

"A canton is a state within a state!" Jojo Abutbul repeated.

"Switzerland, for instance, is one country and it has cantons in it!"   75

"So you know what?" Jojo banged his fist in his hand. "I'll keep the whole West Bank and Gaza under my control, and I'll make cantons there! You decide what canton you want to live in!"

"I want to explain to you, Jojo, that autonomy, or a form of self-administration, call it whatever you want, does not diminish your future State of Israel; it can even augment it and be helpful to solve all the problems now, and not to leave any wounds under the skin, because I don't want to reach a situation where ten years from now, because of the country's discrimination against me, there will be an internal intifada."

"So there can be an intifada of Ethiopian Jews, too, and an intifada of Russians, and of the oppressed Moroccans, too! So we should make a Moroccan canton? Listen, Mohammed, what you're actually saying is that a man like the Transferist is right. Gandhi says, I'll transfer out the Arabs, by consent or by force, but when I finish there will be only Jews here. That way I prevent any wounds under the skin! Then there'll be one wound, one earth-shattering scream, but that will finish it off and it will be healthier for everyone! You live with all your brothers in your

Palestinian state. You won't have double identities, you won't have a problem that you need ten words to explain who you are, Arab, Israeli, Palestinian, Muslim, and I won't have any problems either with citizens that threaten me constantly with an intifada."

Mohammed's face paled. "If you are such a racist and ignorant man that you think, like Gandhi, that in the twentieth century it's possible to transfer nations, then please. I think it will fail."

Jojo: "I'm against it! But now you're coming and scaring me, and not 80 leaving me a choice!"

"People aren't sheep to be taken to slaughter!" Mohammed shouted. "They'll oppose the transfer! There will be more bloodshed here!"

"Then 200,000 were killed and the problem was solved!" Jojo came back with a shout. "Then 400,000 were killed! But with that we've solved it for good!"

"But you already know from historical experience that that won't solve the problem! There will be a new problem!"

They pound the table furiously, shouting without listening. Two families of Russian immigrants, who might very well have arrived only a couple of days before, watch them in astonishment. They certainly have no conception how much this debate touches on them and their children. When Mohammed gets up for a moment to make a phone call, Jojo turns to me in amazement: "So there's a problem here that will never be solved! So whoever is strong will live! There's no other choice. Our leaders apparently know this problem. That's one of the things we don't know as citizens. . . . So we're back at square one with them again. We're in a round room without corners. No one can sit in his own corner; wherever you sit there's no corner. . . ." He whistles in amazement. "So it really has to be clear in the peace agreement that we solve this problem finally, and this is the last opportunity. If the PLO is Mohammed's sole representative, the PLO will have to commit itself to not having any more claims on the Galilee. We'll be sorry if that's not in the peace agreement." He rose, then sat down. "And even though I've been arguing until today that peace is the thing Israel needs most urgently, now I'll oppose it! With that kind of peace I'd rather not have it! Because then I didn't heal a wound, I only covered it up, and underneath, the wound will continue to become infected. Then my situation will be that much worse, because I've already handed over my best cards, Nablus and Hebron . . . very interesting . . . and he's honest, Mohammed, he's speaking sincerely. Someone will have to give way here, no arguing that. . . . I'm starting to understand what's happening here. . . . I've discovered a point of view that I, as an Israeli, never knew about."

Mohammed returns, sitting down heavily opposite him. Jojo turns to 85
him with a now quiet, slightly wounded voice. "I always thought that
you and I were equal. You and I — part of the map. Sure there are
problems, sure there isn't complete equality, but we try to attain it. You
are an Israeli Arab, I don't interfere with your feelings or with your religion, and I'll try to help you as much as I can, so that your son will go to
a good school, so that he has a future here like my son. I was ready to
put my shoulders level with yours. *But* to reach a state where one day
you'll want to set up a state within a state? I don't care what you call
it — canton, self-administration, the Autonomous Region of the
Galilee. I, Jojo Abutbul, would be making myself a misery that I never
thought of! So Jojo Abutbul is sitting and thinking that if that's the case,
maybe Gandhi and Sharon[13] really know what I didn't know and what
you knew."

Mohammed's face isn't what it was before, either. With a weariness
much greater than that caused by the conversation itself he says, "Link-
ing my ideas and Gandhi's is very strange. Because if I wanted to be like
Gandhi in my opinions and demands, I would have to say, 'Transfer the
entire Jewish state of Israel! Abutbul will go to Morocco, the one from
Russia will return to Russia, the one from Romania will return to Romania.' But what I'm trying to explain to my friend Jojo, unfortunately not
with any great success — "

"No, no, you really succeeded! God help me if I understood right
what I understood!"

They sat and talked for a few more minutes, repeating their indict-
ments and marveling at one another, trying to find a crack in the round,
cornerless wall. Afterward Mohammed told of the classroom where his
son studies, "in a four-meter-by-four-meter storage room, and in the
winter, for there to be enough light, the teacher has to leave the door
open."

"The country should be ashamed of itself," Jojo said. "It hurts me, it
wounds my pride in my country, I won't accept it."

Mohammed continued to recount the daily hardships and harass- 90
ments he endured as an Arab, problems deriving from the law and an
abuse whose source was deeper. He told of a Jewish boy who had come
up to him on the Netanya beach when he was there with his two small
children and demanded that he, Mohammed, leave "because you're
polluting our beach." Jojo listened. Before they parted, in an effort to

---

[13]Ariel Sharon (pronounced "sha-*rone*"), a vocal advocate of building Jewish settlements in the occupied territories. — ED.

smooth over — in retrospect — the sting left by the conversation, a clumsy effort but still heartwarming in its magnanimity, Jojo tried to put the best possible face on Kiwan's demand for autonomy. "If we want Mohammed and his people to be loyal Israeli citizens," he said, "first we have to be loyal to them. That means we can't take what little remains to them: their honor, their pride, the little that a man needs in order to live. We won't think only of what we want from them, we'll also think of what they want from us. They're part of us. And if there's a Palestinian state next to the Jewish state, and Mohammed has the right to choose where to live and he decides to live here anyway, that will be to our benefit, it will bring us honor that he feels good and equal here. And when a man like Mohammed comes and says that he wants that, autonomy, his canton, he, in my opinion, doesn't really mean it. He wants security. He wants a way to defend himself. That's what he means when he asks for a canton. He actually wants a lot less than that — equality."

Mohammed Kiwan accepted the hand proffered him. It seemed to me that Jojo's moving gesture was more important to him — at that moment — than standing his ideological ground. Maybe Jojo really had understood Mohammed's intent. I don't know. "Maybe, as Jojo said with great justice," Kiwan responded, "it may well be that the ideas I raised with regard to the canton were raised as a kind of shield, as the result of the cumulative and very bitter experience of the way the government here has behaved to the Arab population. But for me the most important part of this meeting was that I met Jojo the man. I felt in a very human way Jojo's willingness to understand me, to identify with my suffering, and I leave here exhilarated, not because of what we said, but because of the sublime values of man and humanity. I always believed that every human being is, when it comes down to it, human. The stigmas, the labels Jew, Arab — this conversation proved that they are as important as an onionskin. And just for that I'm happy I came."

The two of them stood, exhausted from the conversation, and then, in an impulse of the moment, embraced.

EXPLORATIONS

1. Why does Mohammed Kiwan want to meet "Jojo from Ashdod"? What common ground do these two men share?

2. What is the impact of David Grossman's choice to refer to Jojo Abutbul and Mohammed Kiwan by their first names? How would the essay's impact

change if Grossman used their last names instead, or used designations such as "the restaurateur" and "the lawyer" or "the Arab" and "the Jew"?

3. Jojo often uses metaphors and analogies to make his points. What are the positive effects of this technique on the discussion? What are the negative effects?

CONNECTIONS

1. What examples can you find in "Israeli Arab, Israeli Jew" that support Aung San Suu Kyi's statement in "Freedom from Fear" (p. 698), "Fear of losing power corrupts those who wield it and fear of the scourge of power corrupts those who are subject to it" (para. 1)? What kinds of fear do Mohammed and Jojo express? What kinds of corruption have resulted from Israeli Arabs' and Jews' fears?

2. What parallels can you see between the ethnic tension in Israel and in South Africa during apartheid? What statements by Nelson Mandela in "Black Man in a White Court" (p. 688) could be applied to Israel's problems, and in what way? What recommendations by Mandela and by Nadine Gordimer in "Where Do Whites Fit In?" (p. 344) might help resolve those problems?

3. What role does religion play in the argument between Jojo Abutbul and Mohammed Kiwan? Reread Naila Minai's "Women in Early Islam" (p. 470) and Amos Oz's "If There Is Justice" (p. 188). What other factors besides their belief in and approach to God have fueled the historic hostility between Jews and Arabs in the Middle East?

ELABORATIONS

1. "Israeli Arab, Israeli Jew" takes the form of a dialogue between Mohammed Kiwan and Jojo Abutbul. Go through the essay and record these two men's central and supporting arguments. Reread, too, Amos Oz's "If There Is Justice" (p. 188) and Anwar El-Sadat's epigraph (p. 130). Based on the facts and opinions presented in these selections, what solution (if any) can you recommend for the problems they discuss? Write a comparison-contrast or argumentative essay about the status of Arabs in Israel, drawing on additional research to support points on which you or these characters have more opinion than fact.

2. Among their other differences, Jojo Abutbul and Mohammed Kiwan are divided by the ways they think and express themselves. Look closely at each man's style of speaking — for instance, his use of data, imagery, comparison, and historical allusions. Write an essay comparing their styles and indicating how their rhetorical differences affect their response to each other.

SPOTLIGHT:
CHINA

▲▲▲▲▲▲▲▲▲▲
▼▼▼▼▼▼▼▼▼▼

Institutions and Individuals: *During Mao's regime, members of a Peking Opera company climb a mountain to work and study with the peasants for whom they also perform.*

Chinese civilization dates back some 5,000 years. The writing system used there today was created around 2,200 years ago, three centuries after Confucius laid some of the philosophical foundations of Chinese society. Unlike most of the world's other cultures, China's was unified early enough — thanks partly to strong emperors — to pass from generation to generation for centuries. Neither cultural advances nor the Great Wall, however, could keep out Mongolian invaders: From 1276 to 1368, China was ruled by Genghis Khan and his grandson Kublai Khan. The next unwelcome barbarians were traders from Portugal, Britain, and elsewhere in Europe a hundred years later. When China tried to stop the British from bringing in opium from India, Britain launched the Opium Wars. Defeated, China lost territory to Japan as well. But outsiders had brought ideas as well as drugs, weapons, and demands; and nationalists began allying to expel the interlopers. In 1911 Sun Yat-sen rallied other generals and proclaimed a republic. A decade later, a tiny group in Shanghai launched the Chinese Communist Party.

At first the Communists allied with Chiang Kai-Shek's Kuomintang (KMT) nationalists, but in 1927 the KMT slaughtered thousands of Communist leaders. Mao Zedong began organizing a peasant army which traveled for over a year to evade the KMT — his famous Long March. The two parties joined again to repel the Japanese in the 1940s but split after World War II. In 1949 Chairman Mao became head of the People's Republic of China. The victorious Maoists forced the U.S.-backed KMT into exile on Taiwan and began restructuring China's economy on the Soviet model: Private property was turned over to collectives, and central planning replaced markets.

The Communist Party's goals were ambitious, its tactics drastic, and its impact often tragic. The Hundred Flowers Movement toward openness in the mid-1950s was followed by the repressive Anti-Rightist Movement, in which many of those who had spoken out (such as Fang Lizhi, p. 754) were expelled and punished. During the Great Leap Forward, launched in 1958, hundreds of millions of people were put to work on large industrial projects and over 40 million starved to death. In 1966 the decade-long Cultural Revolution began, glorifying workers, peasants, and soldiers and purging "bourgeois" intellectuals and officials — including Deng Xiaoping, who would become Mao's successor. During this period, when every family had to include a peasant, Anchee Min (p. 732) was sent to labor on a remote collective farm.

After Mao's death in 1976, backlash against the Cultural Revolution — a pet project of Mao's wife, Jiang Quing — swept Jiang and her three top comrades, the "Gang of Four," out of power and into prison. In contrast to his predecessors, Deng recognized the country's need for intellectuals as well as

731

for workers, peasants, and soldiers. He took steps to open China to the outside world, countering Mao's dogmatic socialism with remarks like "Black cat, white cat — it's a good cat if it catches mice." Living and working conditions remained harsh by Western standards. Still, progress toward greater political freedom and a more market-driven economy gave China the reputation of a model for Communist reform until the spring of 1989. For weeks, students gathered in Beijing's Tienanmen Square to demonstrate for faster-paced and wider-ranging reforms. In June the army dispersed them, killing hundreds — perhaps thousands — of unarmed protesters. Deng's government has fended off Western reprisal by continuing to loosen restrictions on free enterprise and trade while insisting on Chinese sovereignty. As age and illness recently have sidelined Deng, a new regime and changing policies may be imminent.

A note on names: People's names in China normally are in reverse order from those in the West. For example, Fang Lizhi's family name (Fang) comes first and his given name (Lizhi) comes last. Both Anchee Min and Jianying Zha, in publishing their books in English, have chosen to switch their names from Chinese to English format, which we preserve here.

ANCHEE MIN

The Fall of Autumn Leaves

Anchee Min, whose given name (Anchee) means Jade of Peace, was born in 1957 in Shanghai, China. "The Fall of Autumn Leaves" comes from her memoir *Red Azalea* (1994), a chilling narrative of growing up under the omnipotent, arbitrary regime of Chairman Mao Zedong. This selection takes place when Min still lived with her parents, brother, and sisters (named Space Conqueror, Blooming, and Coral). Later, as the oldest child, she had to fulfill the Cultural Revolution's requirement for her family to include a peasant. At age seventeen she was sent to Red Fire Farm, a huge collective near the East China Sea. Sharing a small dirt-floored room with seven other young women, watching her friend Little Green attacked by leeches in the rice paddies and by jealous co-workers at Party meetings, Min's ideological enthusiasm began to fade. When Little Green was caught with a lover, forced to accuse him of rape (for which he was executed) and to undergo "intensive mind rebrushing," she lost her sanity and Min lost her Communist faith. Her only refuge on the unproductive farm was an increasingly close relationship with her company commander, Yan Sheng: "Yan, as in discipline; Sheng, as in victory." As informants closed in on the two women, Min was miraculously rescued by emissaries from Comrade Jiang Quing, the wife of Chairman Mao, who sought a heroine for Jiang Ching's latest Communist opera film. Although Min lost the role, she did become a set clerk at the film studio. After six years in that tedious job, she was helped by a friend to attend the School of the Art Institute in Chicago. A story she wrote there about Red Fire Farm was published in *Granta* in 1992. From that springboard Min got a lucrative contract for *Red Azalea*. She still lives in Chicago; her second book is the novel *Katherine* (1995).

In school Mao's books were our texts. I was the head of the class on the history of the Communist Party of China. To me, history meant how proletarians won over the reactionaries. Western history was a history of capitalist exploitation. We hung portraits of Marx, Engels, Lenin, and Stalin next to Mao in our classrooms. Each morning we bowed to them as well as bowing to Mao, praying for a long, long life for him. My sisters copied my compositions. My compositions were collected slogans. I always began with this: "The East wind is blowing, the fighting drum is beating. Who is afraid in the world today? It is not the people who are afraid of American imperialists. It is the American imperialists who are afraid of the people." Those phrases won me prizes. Space Conqueror looked up to me as if I were a magician. For me, compositions were nothing; it was abacus competitions that were difficult. I wrote compositions for my brother and sisters, but I felt I had not much in common with the children. I felt like an adult. I longed for challenges. I was at the school day and night promoting communism, making revolution by painting slogans on walls and boards. I led my schoolmates in collecting pennies. We wanted to donate the pennies to the starving children in America. We were proud of what we did. We were sure that we were making red dots on the world's map. We were fighting for the final peace of the planet. Not for a day did I not feel heroic. I was the opera.

I was asked to attend the school's Revolutionary Committee meeting. It was 1970 and I was thirteen years old. I discussed how to carry on the Cultural Revolution at our Long Happiness Elementary School with the committee people, the true revolutionaries. When I raised my hand and said I would like to speak, my face would no longer flush. I knew what I was talking about. Phrases from *People's Daily* and *Red Flag* magazine poured out of my mouth. My speeches were filled with an impassioned and noble spirit. I was honored. In the early seventies my being a head of the Little Red Guards at school brought our family honor. My award certificates were my mother's pride, although she never hung them on the wall. My name was constantly mentioned by the school authority and praised as "Study Mao Thoughts Activist," "Mao's Good Child," and "Student of Excellences." Whenever I would speak through a microphone in the school's broadcasting station, my sisters and brother would be listening in their classrooms and their classmates would look at them with admiration and envy.

The school's new Party secretary, a man named Chain, was a worker's representative from the Shanghai Shipping Factory. He was about fifty years old, extremely thin, like a bamboo stick. He taught me how to hold political meetings. He liked to say, We have to let our little general play a full role in the Cultural Revolution and give full scope to the initiative of the Little Red Guards. He told me not to be afraid of things that I did not understand. You must learn to think like this, he said. If the earth stops spinning, I'll continue to spin.

It was the first week of November when Secretary Chain called me in. He told me excitedly that the committee had finally dug out a hidden class enemy, an American spy. He said, We are going to have a meeting against her, a rally which two thousand people will be attending. You will be the student representative to speak against her. I asked who it was. Wrinkling his eyebrows, the secretary pronounced a shocking name. It was Autumn Leaves, my teacher. I thought I heard Secretary Chain wrong. But he nodded at me slowly, confirming that I heard him exactly right.

I sat down. I actually dropped down on the chair. My legs all of a   5
sudden lost their strength.

Autumn Leaves was a thin, middle-aged lady and was seriously nearsighted. She wore a dark pair of glasses and had a hoarse voice and a short temper. She loved Chinese, mathematics, and music. The first day she stepped into the classroom, she asked all the students if any of us could tell what her name Autumn Leaves meant. No one was able to figure it out. Then she explained it. She said that there was a famous poem written in the Tang Dynasty about autumn leaves. It praised the beauty and significance of the falling leaves. It said that when a leaf fell naturally, it symbolized a full life. The touch of the ground meant the transformation of a ripe leaf to fresh mud. It fertilized the seeds through the winter. Its pregnancy came to term with the next spring. She said that we were her spring.

She was an energetic teacher who never seemed to be tired of teaching. Her methods were unique. One moment she raised her arms to shoulder level and stretched them out to the sides, making herself look like a cross when explaining infinity; the next moment she spoke with a strong Hunan accent when explaining where a poet was from. Once she completely lost her voice while trying to explain geometric progression to me. When she finally made me understand, she laughed silently like a mute with her arms dancing in the air. When I thanked her, she said that she was glad that I was serious about learning. She set me up as the example for our class and then the entire grade. When she knew that I wanted to improve my Chinese, she brought me her own books to read. She was this way with all her students. One day when it was raining hard after class, she gave students her raincoat, rain shoes, and her umbrella as they went home. She herself went home wet. The next day she had a fever, but she came to class and struggled on, despite her fever. By the time she finished her lecture, she had lost her voice again. There was no way I could picture Autumn Leaves as an American spy.

As if reading my mind, Secretary Chain smiled and asked me if I had ever heard the phrase "Raging flames refine the real gold." I shook my head. He said, It is time for you to test yourself out to see whether you are a real revolutionary or an armchair revolutionary. He recited a Mao quotation: "To have a revolution is not like having a dinner party, not like painting a pretty picture or making embroidery. It is not that easy and relaxing. Revolution is an insurrection in which one class over-throws the other with violent force."

I found my words were blocked by my stiff tongue. I kept saying, Autumn Leaves is my teacher. Secretary Chain suggested that we work on my problem. He lit a cigarette and told me the fable of "A Wolf in Sheep's Skin." He said Autumn Leaves was the wolf. He told me that Autumn Leaves' father was a Chinese American who was still living in America. Autumn Leaves was born and educated in America. Secretary Chain said, The capitalist sent his daughter back to China to educate our children. Don't you see this as problematic?

For the next two hours Secretary Chain convinced me that Autumn   10
Leaves was a secret agent of the imperialists and was using teaching as a weapon to destroy our minds. Secretary Chain asked whether I would tolerate that. Of course not, I said. No one can pull our proletarians back to the old society. Good, said Secretary Chain, tapping my shoulders. He said he knew I would be a sharp spear for the Party. I raised my head and said, Secretary, please tell me what to do. He said, Write a speech. I asked what I should write. He said, Tell the masses how you were mentally poisoned. I said that I did not quite understand the words "mentally poisoned." Secretary Chain said, You are not mature enough to understand that yet. He then asked me to give an opinion on what kind of person I thought Autumn Leaves was. I told him the truth.

Secretary Chain laughed loudly at me. He said that I had already become a victim of the spy who had almost killed me with the skill of the wolf who killed the sheep, leaving no trace of blood. He punched his fist on the table and said loudly, That in itself is wonderful material to be discussed! I felt awkward. He stopped laughing and said, You shouldn't be discouraged by your immaturity.

He made me feel disappointed in myself. Let me help you, he suggested. He asked me the name of the books she loaned me. *An Old Man of Invention*, I began to recall, *The Little Mermaid*, and *Snow White*. He asked for the author's name. I said it was something like Andersen.

Secretary Chain suddenly raised his hand in the air and furrowed his brow. He said, Stop, this is it. Who is Andersen? An old foreign man, I guess, I replied. What were his fairy tales about? About lives of princes, princesses, and little people. What does Andersen do now? he asked. I do not know, I replied.

Look how careless you are! Secretary Chain almost yelled at me. He could be a foreign spy! Taking out a little glass vial, Secretary Chain put a few pills into his mouth. He explained that it was the medicine for his liver pain. He said his liver was hurting badly, but he could not tell his doctor about this because he would be hospitalized immediately. He said his pain was getting worse, but he could not afford to waste a second in the hospital. How can I disappoint Chairman Mao, who put his trust in people like us, the working class, the class that was once even lower than the pigs and dogs before Liberation?

His face was turning purple. I suggested that he take a rest. He waved   15
me to go on as he pressed his liver with his hands to endure the pain. He told me that he did not have much schooling. His parents died of hunger when he was five. His brother and little sister were thrown into the sea after they died of cholera. He was sold to a child dealer for fifteen pounds of rice. He became a child worker in a shipping factory in Shanghai and was beaten often by the owner. After the Liberation he joined the Party and was sent to a workers' night school. He said, I owe our Party a great deal and I haven't worked hard enough to show my appreciation.

I looked at him and was touched. His pain seemed to be increasing. His fingers pressed against his liver harder, but he refused to rest. You know, we found Autumn Leaves' diary and it had a paragraph about you, he said. What . . . what did she say about me? I became nervous. She said that you were one of the very few children who were educable. She put quotation marks around "educable." Can you think of what that means? Without waiting for my reply, Secretary Chain concluded, It was obvious that Autumn Leaves thought that you could be educated into her type, her father's type, the imperialists' type. He pointed out that the purpose of writing this diary was to present it to her American boss as proof of her success as a spy.

My world turned upside down. I felt deeply hurt and used. Secretary Chain asked me whether I was aware of the fact that I was set up as a model by Autumn Leaves to influence the others. Her goal is to make you all *betray* communism! I felt the guilt and anger. I said to Secretary Chain that I would speak tomorrow. He nodded at me. He said, Our Party trusts you and Mao would be very proud of you.

Pull out the hidden class enemy, the American spy Autumn Leaves! Expose her under the bare sun! the crowd shouted as soon as the meeting started. I was sitting on the stage on one of the risers. Two strong men escorted Autumn Leaves onto the stage facing the crowd of 2,000 people, including her students and colleagues. Her arms were twisted behind her. She was almost unrecognizable. Only a few days had passed since I had seen her, but it seemed as though she had aged ten years. Her hair had suddenly turned gray. Her face was colorless. A rectangular board reading "Down with American Spy" hung from her neck. Two men forced her to bow to Mao's portrait three times. One of the men bent her left arm very hard and said, Beg Chairman Mao for forgiveness now! Autumn Leaves refused to say the words. The two men bent her arms up backward. They bent her harder. Autumn Leaves' face contorted in pain and then her mouth moved. She said the words and the men let her loose.

My mouth was terribly dry. It was hard to bear what I saw. The string of the heavy board seemed to cut into Autumn Leaves' skin. I forgot what I was supposed to do — to lead the crowd to shout the slogans — until Secretary Chain came to remind me of my duty.

Long live the great proletarian dictatorship! I shouted, following the slogan menu. I was getting more and more scared when I saw Autumn Leaves struggling with the two men who had been trying to press her head toward the floor while she tried to face the sky. When her eyeglasses fell off, I saw her eyes close tightly.

Secretary Chain shouted at her. The crowd shouted, Confess! Confess! Secretary Chain took the microphone and said that the masses would not have much patience. By acting this way Autumn Leaves was digging her own grave.

Autumn Leaves kept silent. When kicked hard, she said that she had nothing to confess. She said she was innocent. Our Party never accuses anyone who is innocent, said Secretary Chain, and yet the Party would never allow a class enemy to slip away from the net of the proletarian dictatorship. He said now it was time to demonstrate that Autumn Leaves was a criminal. He nodded at me and turned to the crowd. He said, Let's have the victim speak out!

I stood up and felt dizzy. The crowd began clapping their hands. The sunlight was dazzlingly bright and was hurting my eyes. My vision became blurred and I saw a million bees wheeling in front of me sounding like helicopters. As the crowd kept clapping, I moved to the front of the stage. I stopped in front of the microphone. Taking out the speech I had written last night, I suddenly felt a need to speak with my parents. I had not gone home but slept in the classroom on the table with other Little Red Guards. Five of us wrote the speech. I regretted not having my parents go over the speech with me. I took a deep breath. My fingers were shaking and would not obey in turning the pages.

Don't be afraid, we are all with you, Secretary Chain said in my ear as he came to adjust the height of the microphone. He placed a cup of

water in front of me. I took the water and drank it down in one breath. I
felt a little better. I began to read.

I read to the crowd that Autumn Leaves was the wolf in sheep's skin.   25
I took out the books she loaned me and showed them to the crowd. As I
was delivering my speech, I saw from the corner of my eye that Autumn
Leaves had turned her head in my direction. She was murmuring. I became nervous but managed to continue. Comrades, I said, now I understand why Autumn Leaves was so kind to me. She was trying to turn
me into an enemy of our country, and a running dog of the imperialists!
I read on.

There was some slogan-shouting, during which I glanced secretly at
Autumn Leaves. She was breathing hard and was about to fall. I stood,
my limbs turning cold. I tried to remove my eyes from Autumn Leaves,
but she caught them. I was terrified when I saw her staring at me without her eyeglasses. Her eyes looked like two Ping-Pong balls that almost
popped out of her eye sockets.

The crowd shouted, Confess! Confess! Autumn Leaves began to
speak slowly to the crowd with her hoarse voice. She said that she
would never want to turn any of her students into the country's enemy.
She broke into tears. Why would I? she repeated again and again. She
was losing her voice. She began to swing her head trying to project her
words, but no sound came out. She swung her head again making an
effort to let her words out. She said that her father loved this country
and that was the reason she came back to teach. Both her father and she
believed in education. Spy? What are you talking about? Where did
you get this idea? She looked at me.

If the enemy doesn't surrender, let's boil her, fry her and burn her to
death! Secretary Chain shouted. The crowd followed, shouting and
waving their fists. Secretary Chain signaled for me to go on. But I was
trembling too hard to continue. Secretary Chain walked to the microphone from the back of the stage. He took over the microphone. He
told the crowd that this was a class enemy's live performance. It had
given us an opportunity to learn how deceitful an enemy could be. Can
we allow her to go on like this? No! the crowd shouted.

Secretary Chain was ordering Autumn Leaves to shut up and accept
the criticism of the revolutionary masses with a correct attitude. Autumn Leaves said that she could not accept any untrue facts. Autumn
Leaves said that a young girl such as I should not be used by someone
with an evil intention.

You underestimated our Little Red Guard's political awareness, Sec-   30
retary Chain said with a scornful laugh. Autumn Leaves demanded to
speak to me. Secretary Chain told her to go ahead. He said that as a

thorough-going dialectical materialist he never underestimated the role of teachers by negative example.

As the crowd quieted down, Autumn Leaves squatted on her heels to seek her glasses on the floor. When she put her glasses back on, she started to question me. I was scared. I did not expect that she would talk to me so seriously. My terror turned into fury. I wanted to get away. I said, How dare you put me in such a spot to be questioned like a reactionary? You had used me in the past to serve the imperialists; now you want to use me to get away from the criticism? It would be a shame if I lost to you!

Autumn Leaves called my name and asked if I really believed that she was an enemy of the country. If I did not think so, could I tell her who assigned me to do the speech. She said she wanted the truth. She said Chairman Mao always liked to have children show their honesty. She asked me with the exact same tone she used when she helped me with my homework. Her eyes were demanding me to focus on them. I could not bear looking at her eyes. They had looked at me when the magic of mathematics was explained; they had looked at me when the beautiful Little Mermaid story was told. When I won the first place in the Calculation-with-Abacus Competition, they had looked at me with joy; when I was ill, they had looked at me with sympathy and love. I had not realized the true value of what all this meant to me until I lost it forever that day at the meeting.

I heard people shouting at me. My head felt like a boiling teapot. Autumn Leaves' eyes behind the thick glasses now were like gun barrels shooting at me with fire. Just be honest! her hoarse voice raised to its extreme. I turned to Secretary Chain. He nodded at me as if to say, Are you going to lose to an enemy? He was smiling scornfully. Think about the snake, he said.

Yes, the snake, I remembered. It was a story Mao told in his book. It was about a peasant who found a frozen snake lying in his path on a snowy day. The snake had the most beautiful skin the peasant had ever seen. He felt sorry for her and decided to save her life. He picked up the snake and put her into his jacket to warm her with the heat of his body. Soon the snake woke up and felt hungry. She bit her savior. The peasant died. Our Chairman's point is, Secretary Chain said as he ended the story, to our enemy, we must be absolutely cruel and merciless.

I turned to look at the wall-sized portrait of Mao. It was mounted on 35 the back of the stage. The Chairman's eyes looked like two swinging lanterns. I was reminded of my duty. I must fight against anyone who dared to oppose Mao's teaching. The shouting of the slogans encouraged me.

Show us your standpoint — Secretary Chain passed me the microphone. I did not know why I was crying. I heard myself calling for my parents as I took the microphone. I said Mama, Papa, where are you? The crowd waved their angry fists at me and shouted, Down! Down! Down! I was so scared, scared of losing Secretary Chain's trust, and scared of not being able to denounce Autumn Leaves. Finally, I gathered all my strength and yelled hysterically at Autumn Leaves with tears in my throat: Yes, yes, yes, I do believe that you poisoned me; and I do believe that you are a true enemy! Your dirty tricks will have no more effect on me! If you dare to try them on me again, I'll shut you up! I'll use a needle to stitch your lips together!

I was never forgiven. Even after twenty-some years. After the Revolution was over. It was after my begging for forgiveness, I heard the familiar hoarse voice say, I am very sorry, I don't remember you. I don't think I ever had you as my student.

It was at that meeting I learned the meaning of the word "betrayal" as well as "punishment." Indeed, I was too young then, yet one is never too young to have vanity. When my parents learned about the meeting from Blooming, Coral, and Space Conqueror, they were terrified. They talked about disowning me. My mother said, I am a teacher too. How would you like to have my student do the same to me? She shut me out of the house for six hours. She said being my mother made her ashamed.

I wrote what my mother asked of me a thousand times. It was an old teaching passed down since Confucius. It said, Do not treat others how you yourself would not like to be treated. My mother demanded I copy it on rice paper using ink and a brush pen. She said, I want to carve this phrase in your mind. You are not my child if you ever disobey this teaching.

EXPLORATIONS

1. What are the Communist Party's accusations against Autumn Leaves? What are the grounds for these accusations? What evidence does Anchee Min present about Autumn Leaves that belies the accusations?

2. What slogans and analogies does Secretary Chain use to denounce Autumn Leaves? Why are these an effective tool for convincing young Anchee Min?

3. Min's mother makes her write "an old teaching passed down since Confucius. It said, Do not treat others how you yourself would not like to be treated." What forms does this saying take in the United States, and what

source or sources do we credit for it? How else does Min's mother try to make her understand what she has done wrong?

CONNECTIONS

1. Reread Marilynne Robinson's comments about Americans' tendency to confuse our culture and society with our economic system (p. 646). In what ways do the Communist characters in "The Fall of Autumn Leaves" make a similar mistake? Which of their actions and ideas are clearly Chinese rather than Communist?

2. In what ways do the Communist slogans quoted by Min resemble the McThought described by Ted Koppel (p. 649)? How does each of these forms of communication suit the society that uses it? How does Thomas L. Friedman (p. 652) suggest that the slogans of Mao's China are becoming obsolete?

3. In "The Song of Ourselves" (p. 599) Chinua Achebe mentions the shock of reading European novels and realizing that from the writers' viewpoint, he did not belong with their white heroes but rather with the savages in the jungle. How did you react when you read Min's denunciation of "American imperialists"? Judging from this essay, what qualities did the Chinese impute to Americans during Chairman Mao's regime?

FANG LIZHI

Thoughts on Reform

Using the Westernized form of his name, L. Z. Fang, the astrophysicist Fang Lizhi has published widely in scientific journals throughout the world. "Thoughts on Reform" comes from a speech by that name which Fang gave at Zhejiang University (nicknamed Zheda) in 1985. It was published in his collection *Bringing Down the Great Wall: Writings on Science, Culture, and Democracy in China* (1990). The book's editor and principal translator, James H. Williams, notes, "This talk was severely criticized by Communist Party officials for suggesting that Marxist economic beliefs be reappraised." Biographical information on Fang Lizhi appears in the following selection, "Fang Lizhi," by Orville Schell (p. 754). Besides his teaching and administrative posts in China, Fang has been a visiting professor at universities in Cambridge, Kyoto, Rome, and Princeton; a member of several international physics organizations; and chairman of the commission on astrophysics of the International Union of Pure and Applied Physics in Paris. Since coming to the United States he has held the position of Professor of Astrophysics at the Institute for Advanced Study in Princeton, New Jersey.

How are we to reform our society? Of course I can't answer this completely, but one thing that is clearly indispensable is science and technology. Way back in the May Fourth period, the battle cry was to save the nation through "science and democracy." So today I'll start with science, and wend my way on into democracy.

You're all familiar with the official slogan "Stress Knowledge, Stress Talent," which basically means "Stress Science and Technology." Most of you probably couldn't care less about such injunctions; you've all been subjected to the usual platitudes. But today I want to ask if we really know how these things interact? There is no shortage of theory, but how many of our problems have actually been solved? How great is the gap between our theory and our practice? And what does it mean when I say that science and technology have much broader implications than simply their economic roles?

We are always hearing that China is *economically* backward, and it is in this context that the example of science and technology inevitably comes up. But let's be a little more specific about the problems. During our work conference on science and technology, Comrade Song Jian[1] reported some numbers: In a study of per-capita GNP in 126 countries around the world, China was rated "among the last twenty-odd nations." You may think this is bad, but it is even worse that the word "odd" was used! Obviously we don't even know where we rank among the last twenty countries. According to this report, per-capita GNP (in U.S. dollars) is $11,000 in Japan, $13,000 in the United States, and $17,000 in Switzerland. That means the per-capita GNP of China is only one twenty-seventh that of Japan, one thirty-third that of the United States, and one forty-third that of Switzerland. In Shanghai, per-capita GNP is $2,300. Thus, the average productivity of five Shanghai citizens is equivalent to that of one American. Of course, Shanghai happens to be the most productive region in China, a real "singularity" [in physics parlance]. But what about the nine provinces where per-capita GNP is below $100? These nine represent nearly one-third of our thirty provinces. Individually, they are probably comparable to Chad, which ranked last on the list of 126 countries. It is under these sobering circumstances that we must exert our utmost efforts over the next fifty years to develop the Chinese economy. This is the situation that those working in industry, including many of you, will face.

Nevertheless, what I want to emphasize is that the reasons for "stressing knowledge and talent," which is to say, science and technology, are not merely economic. To bring about real changes in our national circumstances, we must look beyond economics. While it is true that the economy is important — and we are putting a great effort into expanding ours — economic growth alone is not the answer. The role of knowledge, and science, and educated individuals goes far beyond economics. In China we habitually refer to science and technology simply as "forces of production," as means of dealing with technical problems. But I think this is wrong, and that there is more to it than that. The rise of Western society is intimately linked to the influence of modern science on economics, on politics, on thought and culture in general. In the West, science and technology have affected all aspects of development, not just bits and pieces of it.

What do I mean by "development"? We all know that the United States, Japan, and Western European countries are developed countries, but how would we define development in a general sense? If we relied on official pronouncements from China, we would have to say that a developed country is one in which per-capita GNP is a few

---

[1]Director of the State Science and Technology Commission, China's highest policy-making body in the science and technology arena.

thousand U.S. dollars per year. But this simple definition is wrong, or at least incomplete. For instance, there are several countries with a high per-capita GNP that are not generally regarded as developed. In the Arab world there is plenty of oil, and the per-capita GNP is high. In Kuwait, for example, it is $10,000. But these countries depend on outside technology and personnel to exploit the petroleum resources, and they just sit there and collect the money. South America also has several countries, such as Colombia and Brazil, with GNP in excess of $1,000 per capita, but which cannot be considered developed.

Coming back to our own situation, the goal of quadrupling GNP by the year 2000 may be regarded as one kind of milestone for development, but it is not sufficient: We may reach it and still fall short in other ways. Economics is not the only mark of development. In the countries I mentioned, the economy has improved but other things have not. There are many other factors which rule out calling these countries developed, such as political corruption, inequitable distribution of wealth, and social unrest. If we emphasize only the quadrupling of GNP without regard to how we get there, we may find ourselves taking not a shortcut to development but a path to oblivion.

Consider the case of Brazil. The economy of Brazil took off within a relatively short time, but Brazil is far from being a fully developed country. Last year I visited Rio de Janeiro, and on the surface it looks very prosperous. The Brazilian economy boomed after the government borrowed heavily to build factories. But from my own observations, and from talking with Brazilians, it seems to me that life there is highly unstable. The annual inflation rate is 220 percent. I have been to hotels in many countries, and usually the hotel bill is paid upon checking out. But I stayed in Brazil for two weeks and had a brand new experience. At the end of the first week, a bill was brought to me with a note — an ultimatum, really — that said if the balance wasn't paid within twenty-four hours, the rates would go up. The owner was not trying to give me a hard time, but he was forced to do this because of inflation. He either had to collect his bills week by week, or else face losing a lot of money. Most of us have never experienced inflation, and we don't understand what it's like to live under such conditions, where you can literally see the prices rise from one week to the next. But there is little security in such a life. An economy built on foreign debt is not something we want for China.

It is also possible to fashion an economy by other dubious means. Last year I went to Colombia, where per-capita GNP has risen to more than $3,000 through drug trafficking — Colombia makes perhaps $8 billion a year from drugs. The drug trade is everywhere. Although the newspapers fume about suppressing drugs, and the government tries to police the trade, most of these efforts are only for show. Last year the government destroyed one drug center, but the real reason it did so was that the center was also used as a guerrilla base. Inflation is not so serious in Colombia, but the disparity in wealth is extreme, with classes of virtual slaves.

At one point I visited Cartagena, a small city in northern Colombia that enjoys a drug-based prosperity. (In Colombia we heard of all kinds of ways of delivering drugs, including direct air drops to the United States. Of course the United States has a good radar system, but the smugglers have developed a new technique to defeat it: The smuggler's plane flies so closely behind a commercial airliner that it can't be distinguished on the radar screen. The "Cartagena technique" thus helps to maintain the prosperity of the town.) I have encountered many different lifestyles in my time, but in Cartagena I lived for a few days in the manner of an aristocracy. I do not mean simply a very luxurious life, but rather one in which I was attended by slaves. No blacks were allowed in the hotel where my colleagues and I stayed. Coming back from the beach one day, we bought some food from a stand run by local black residents. We had no money with us, so they followed us back to the hotel to collect. However, they were not allowed inside — they had to wait by the door for us to come outside and pay them. This is a master-slave relationship, extremely unequal. A society such as this may have a high GNP, but it is by no means developed.

These examples illustrate why economic growth is not the only indicator of progress. Progress must be all-around. So what, then, *is* the definition of development? Well, that's still not clear, at least not to me. But many people would agree that one of the best criteria of development is education. The differences between developed and developing countries in terms of educational levels are quite clear, unlike the case with GNP. Education is widely available in developed countries and not so in developing countries. Illiteracy is high in places like South America and the Arab world, where the rate of illiteracy is not 1 or 2 percent, but is more likely to be 20, 30, or 40 percent. Here the contrast with the developed nations, such as those in North America, Western Europe, and Japan, is clear; they have promoted education to the extent that illiteracy is not much of a problem. In China, economic underdevelopment is an obvious shortcoming, but educational underdevelopment is even more serious. Our low level of culture generally is a primary reason for our lack of development in other spheres.

I won't repeat the stories we are always being told, about how lack of education causes problems in industry and high technology. But I would like to cite one highly symbolic example of how low our cultural level is. On June 16 of last year, the *People's Daily* ran an article, "Deep Friendship in the Water City," about the visit of Premier Zhao Ziyang to Venice. When Premier Zhao met the mayor of Venice, the latter presented him with an old map. Zhao asked: "Was this map made before or after the time of Copernicus?" Of course Copernicus is a great historical figure, whose discoveries marked a new era in our understanding of the universe, and he did study in Italy. Premier Zhao's question was properly asked. The mayor answered that the map was produced after the time of Copernicus. Premier Zhao then made a blunder: "Oh yes, were it not for Copernicus, we still wouldn't know that the earth is round." But all of us know that the greatest contribution of Copernicus is the heliocentric theory, which states that the earth revolves around the sun. The idea of a round earth is completely different from the heliocentric theory. That the earth is round has been known since the time of the Greeks, who even measured its radius. I've been to Italy twice since this event, and Italians have let me know that this gaffe was a diplomatic failing on our part, and demonstrated a low level of general knowledge. Responsibility for this blunder can't be laid solely at the feet of Premier Zhao, who presumably never studied the history of astronomy. But no one else caught the mistake either, neither the translators who accompanied him, nor the newspaper reporters who filed the story, nor the editorial staff of the *People's Daily*; and in their ignorance they enthusiastically reported this *faux pas* as an interesting anecdote.

You're all laughing, but I think it must be the laughter of embarrassment at our backwardness. Whether or not people know who said the earth is round and who said it revolves around the sun may be irrelevant to the economy, but it says something important about a culture. That is my point. If we look only at the technical aspects of science, only at its economic role — important though it may be — we will miss something essential. As I said to the physics department yesterday, physics is more than a basis for technology; it is a cornerstone of modern thought. Physics has been instrumental in the growth of human knowledge to its present stage. Development involves progress not only in the material realm but in the human realm as well. Even with the most advanced technology, without intelligent and civilized citizens no society will become "developed," and any attempt at reform will surely fail.

Why is China so backward today in so many aspects? If we take the long view, we can blame our feudal history. But if we look at the more recent past, the problem has been the orthodoxy that has held sway for the last thirty years. Since 1957, numerous anti-intellectual political campaigns have been waged, fostering suspicion and hatred of learning. From the Anti-Rightist Campaign to the Cultural Revolution, these pogroms seemed bent on eradicating any kind of intellectual endeavor. This is one immediate reason why China's intellectual standards are so low. Moreover, although there has been some superficial acknowledgment of the importance of learning, and of the need for science and technology, things have not really changed all that much. Why?

In my opinion, the animosity toward culture and learning found in these movements originated with the ideas of Comrade Mao Zedong, which were enshrined as orthodox beliefs. His erroneous theories continue to haunt us today. If you really want to promote respect for learning and do something about backwardness, then you have to address Comrade Mao's mistakes, which were many. Let me mention just a few.

In 1958 Mao began his misguided policy of "making intellectuals more like laborers." This was followed by his formula "the humble are the wisest, the high and mighty are the most foolish." Mao was never explicit about who the "high and mighty" in this equation were — although such terms were generally reserved for intellectuals — and on one level there is some truth to this expression. But what Mao meant was this: The more people know, the more stupid they are, and the less they know, the smarter they are. This sentiment was made increasingly explicit as time went on. During the Cultural Revolution, the most enthusiastic statement Mao made about the usefulness of education was, "Nevertheless, we still need education in the sciences and engineering." The implication of this remark is that education is a borderline issue — to have it is fine, but not to have it is fine, too. Such opinions still exert a powerful influence; they have by no means disappeared. There are some places where these attitudes have changed, but in many other places they still govern the treatment of knowledge and potential talent and skilled personnel. If this situation doesn't change, I think our reforms will have little chance of succeeding.

At our work conference, people cited numerous examples of how little respect there is for knowledge. A comrade from Shanghai told of a brain surgeon there who is paid less than a barber; it seems that he who takes care of the inside of the head gets less respect that he who takes care of the outside! You hear about such cases all the time, so I won't bother relating any more of them to you. But the inverted economic status of intellectuals is clearly a function of their inverted political status. The idea that the more you know, and the more complex the task you perform, the less you get paid, is totally inconsistent with the principles of socialism. This being the case, how could such a situation have developed? And why has it still not been seriously addressed and dealt with? I think that this problem has its origins in ideas. Whenever Mao Zedong spoke about intellectuals, it was in the context of "solidarity with the masses," "reform through labor," and "reeducation." Considering this background, I think that if you want to change the status of intellectuals, you will first have to make a theoretical case for what their place in our society ought to be.

Let me try to make such a case. You can read something like it in the recently released draft report on "Reform of the Science and Technology System,"[2] which I helped to prepare. In working on revisions of this report earlier this year, I argued that the position of intellectuals in our society must rest on a solid foundation in Marxist theory. So what is their place? At one time, of course, they were the "stinking ninth category," but lately they've gone up in the world; they are now "old number three," just below workers and peasants! At this point, let me say that I am opposed to dividing society up into a hierarchy of classes. I'm utterly against it. But be that as it may, if someone wants to argue seriously about which class should occupy the first rank, I'll give them an argument.

Let's start from a premise that all of us will recognize: that science is a "force of production." Not only is it a force of production, it is the most advanced one. No one would deny this; we are busily employing science and technology to improve the other areas of production. On whose skills do these most advanced forces of production depend? Well, on those who specialize in science and technology, namely educated people, the intellectuals. So what place should they occupy in society?

According to the standard Marxist argument, industrial workers are the most advanced element of society, the vanguard of the working class. Why? Because at the time of Marx, industry — coal, steel, vehicles — was seen to drive the whole economy, to set the pace for all other kinds of production. Those on whose skills and labor industry depends — namely, industrial workers — were thus considered the most advanced element of the working class. This is all classical Marxist theory, so far; now let me just borrow the methodology. What is today's most advanced force of production? Science and technology. And on whose skills and labor is science and technology dependent? Intellectu-

---

[2]A landmark document issued on March 13, 1985, by the Communist Party Central Committee, which mandated sweeping changes in the organization and funding of research and the diffusion of technology into the general economy.

als'! It is therefore apparent that intellectuals are not only *members* of
the working class, but that they are the very vanguard of the working
class! And yet we assign to society's most functional element the very
lowest rank — this is irrational! I think this argument stands up, not
only in terms of its logic — which is unassailable — but also in terms of
the facts.

We know that as society evolves, different classes arise, flourish, and   20
finally decline. The first great class was pastoral nomads, who were in
turn replaced by farmers as settled agriculture developed. When capitalist industry arose, farming populations declined. In the United States,
farmers now make up less than 1 percent of the population and no
longer play a dominant role in society. More recently still, even the industrial workforce in developed countries has declined. The traditional
heavy industries that require manual labor, such as coal, steel, chemicals, and automobiles, are now called "sunset" industries. Their day is
passing. The United States is doing all it can to export these industries
to developing countries; it no longer wants to encourage this smoke-
belching, water-fouling manufacturing at home. The recent accident in
Bhopal, India, illustrates this point.[3] Fewer people are working in these
"sunset" industries, and their importance to the economy is declining.
On the other hand, the need for workers with technical expertise is
growing constantly. In the United States there are now more white-
collar workers than blue-collar workers. It is the educated class that is
on the rise.

Even in our country, there has been a significant drop in the agricultural population; many peasants have gone to the cities to start businesses and open shops. As the economy grows, we will also see an eventual decline in the number of industrial workers; if we don't, it will
show that we have not become developed. I have already said that I deplore the ranking of different classes. But if you insist on doing it, I say
intellectuals should be put at the top. Mao's idea of "making intellectuals more like laborers" was completely mistaken. Intellectuals are already laborers, the ones whose labor holds the most promise for the future. Instead, it is "making laborers more intellectual" that we need to
emphasize.

The document on science and technology reform does not include
this argument *per se*, because it would have offended people. But if you
look at section nine, it contains the following language: "Scientific and

---

[3]In 1985, toxic gases leaked from a Union Carbide plant in Bhopal, India, killed thousands of people, and injured over 150,000. — ED.

technological personnel are the pathbreakers for new forces of production." You should all get a good grip on these words and not let them go; they are the basis of the kind of argument I just made. It will take a struggle to make our society change its views of intellectuals. It is by no means a sure thing that intellectuals are going to be allowed to play a leading role.

There is much more to the role of intellectuals than their inputs to production; they constitute an important force for social progress through the medium of thought and culture. I've discussed this point with Europeans, who tell me that far from being sequestered inside the science and technology sector, intellectuals in Europe have a far-reaching impact on all of society. Recent history illustrates this point. Prior to World War II, from Napoleon to Bismarck to Hitler, Europe was frequently at war, owing to a variety of causes, economic and otherwise. Now, however, Western Europe is virtually united. There are no armed conflicts between the nations, and even the borders between them are disappearing. During the past six or seven years I have visited Italy every year, and each time I've gone to the border crossing with France to take a look. When I first went, there were still guardhouses, barriers, and police. By the year before last, all these signs of territorial division had disappeared. In their place was a small bilingual road sign: *Italia* this way, *France* that way. The concept of national boundaries is fading fast, especially among the core countries of the European community, such as Italy, France, and Switzerland.

It is hard to conceive of these countries going to war with each other. How was such a state of affairs achieved? Was it brought about by politicians? In the end, no doubt, politicians must have signed their names to agreements. But the formation of a collective psychology that perceived the welfare of Europe as lying in community and cooperation, rather than in divisions and barriers, was not accomplished by politicians so much as by physicists. (There are, by the way, also nonphysicists who share this view!) It was something initiated by physicists that first suggested to Europeans that their common fate rested on cooperation, namely the establishment of CERN, the nuclear research center in Geneva. This was a first for postwar Europe, a place where scientists of all nationalities could work together for common ends, and its influence on society has been substantial.

We know that physicists do not have high political standing in China, nor are they particularly influential within our society; this is a consequence of the way our culture has developed. But the same is not true in Europe, where physics is part and parcel of their history. Especially after the atomic bomb brought World War II to a rapid close, the evident power of physics bestowed immense prestige on the physics community. Thus, the fact that physicists chose to cooperate was a great stimulus for all of Europe, prompting public opinion in favor of European cooperation in other areas.

So, intellectuals are a progressive force in production, and they can be a progressive force in society as well. If we do not play this role in China, the country will be headed for future setbacks instead of down the path of reform. This is the duty we face as Chinese intellectuals, and it is a heavy one. But without our efforts, the myriad problems that face China, both social and technical, will not be resolved, and China's attempts at reform will certainly be abortive.

I don't know if the authorities here at Zheda have let you in on this or not, but if they haven't, I will tell you a little secret. At the beginning of this semester I received a dispatch from my superiors instructing university presidents not to let the students create disturbances. So I went to the Keda students and told them, "We hope you don't create any disturbances!" This order was a consequence of the student protests that took place on several dozen campuses before the Spring Festival [Chinese New Year]. These included not only Beijing University and Beijing Normal University, but also local schools such as Nanjing University, where the trouble started. The immediate cause was probably bad food in the cafeterias; some of the students joked that they were joining the "fight against hunger." So, what I told the Keda students openly was this: "What is important here are your reasons for protesting. If you really want to make trouble, I can't stop you. But if you don't have a good cause, then it doesn't matter whether I try to stop you or not, because the protests will fizzle out by themselves." My suggestion was that they get together and think about the root causes of the things they were unhappy about. For instance, you may complain that your cafeteria food is lousy. I have no doubt that it is — it certainly is at Keda. I have been in academia for decades and have yet to hear a student praise dining-hall food. But the real issue is not so much the quality of the food as the price, which seems to rise from week to week. There must be reasons for this, and so what I challenged the students to do is think about the underlying problems and come up with some concrete solutions. This is our responsibility as educated people, to come up with solutions. If protests will solve the problem, then protest. If protests won't solve the problem, then go back to the drawing board and think of new approaches.

Some comrades are scared to death of student protests. Not that other people don't share some of the same viewpoints as the students, or that professors aren't affected by rising prices. We are. But students are much more accustomed to expressing their opinions directly: "Look, damn it, you've raised your prices again." To me, this just means that students are sensitive to what's going on in society, which I think is extremely valuable. We need to take advantage of this kind of concern in order to go out and solve our country's problems.

Student protests demonstrate the sensitivity of Chinese intellectuals, and show that they could play the same kind of catalytic role that the establishment of CERN played in Europe. If there is unrest among the students, the question we should be asking is "Why?" And we need to look for the root causes, not just for superficial reasons like the rising price of cafeteria food. Prices indicate much more than a change from thirty cents to thirty-five cents; they are a barometer of social conditions. At the conference on science and technology reform, the general assessment of the reforms was not an optimistic one, even though this conclusion was not exactly blazoned across the newspaper headlines. But I want to tell you this: We are still facing problems of an enormous magnitude, and if we do not resolve them, the hopes for successful reform may vanish like a soap bubble.

EXPLORATIONS

1. How does Fang Lizhi define "development"? What does he think China needs to do to become more developed?

2. Why does Fang regard Premier Zhao's gaffe in Italy as a symptom of Chinese backwardness (paras. 11–12)? If a high American official made such a faux pas, what do you think the reaction would be from the media? From the public? If Premier Zhao had made his remarks in the United States, what do you think the reaction would be?

3. On what evidence and reasoning does Fang base his statement that intellectuals "are the very vanguard of the working class" (para. 19)? Do you agree that "this argument stands up, not only in terms of its logic . . . but also in terms of the facts"?

CONNECTIONS

1. What evidence can you find in Anchee Min's "The Fall of Autumn Leaves" (p. 732) for Fang's statements about Chairman Mao (paras. 14–16)? What evidence can you find in "Thoughts on Reform" that the Communist party's policy of treating Mao as a deity, described by Min in paragraph 1 and elsewhere, had a powerful and lasting impact on China?

2. In paragraphs 18–20 Fang talks about China's "dividing society up into a hierarchy of classes" in which "industrial workers are the most advanced element of society." In what ways is society in the United States divided into a
   hierarchy of classes? What group (if any) is regarded in this country as "the
   most advanced element of society"? According to Robert Reich (p. 648),
   who is at the top of the American hierarchy and why?

3. Compare Chairman Mao's policy toward intellectuals as Fang describes it
   (para. 15) with the American way to achieve stupidity as Neil Postman describes it in "Future Shlock" (p. 670, para. 4). What is each writer's theory
   about the reasons why respect for learning has declined in his country?
   What does each writer see as the dangers of this decline? Do you agree with
   either or both? Why or why not?

ORVILLE SCHELL

Fang Lizhi

"Nine-tenths of good journalism is writing a piece over and over until you get it right," Orville Schell recently told an interviewer for the San Francisco *Examiner*. Born in New York City in 1940, Schell graduated magna cum laude from Harvard University in 1962 and then spent several years in the Far East studying Chinese. Along with his graduate work at National Taiwan University, he served as Asian correspondent for the *Atlantic, Look, Harper's*, the *New Republic*, the *Boston Globe*, and the San Francisco *Chronicle*. In 1964–1965 he worked for the Ford Foundation's Indonesia field office in Djakarta. Returning to the United States, Schell received a master's degree from the University of California at Berkeley in 1967. Since then he has written for *The New Yorker, Rolling Stone, Life, Look*, the *Atlantic*, and many other publications. He has also written a series of books on China, including "*Watch Out for the Foreign Guests!*" (1980), *Discos and Democracy* (1988), and *Mandate of Heaven: A New Generation of Entrepreneurs, Dissidents, Bohemians, and Technocrats Lays Claim to China's Future* (1994). "I write about China because it is an alternative," he once commented. "It shows that there are indeed utterly different ways to do things." "Fang Lizhi" comes from Schell's introduction to Fang's 1990 book *Bringing Down the Great Wall* (see p. 742). The recipient of several fellowships, including a Guggenheim, Schell was program consultant for the Emmy-winning CBS *60 Minutes* report "Made in China." In 1996 he became dean of the Graduate School of Journalism at the University of California at Berkeley.

When I returned to Beijing in the fall of 1986, after an absence of six months, it was hard not to feel disoriented by the sudden change in political climate. During the previous spring and summer, political and intellectual life had begun to thaw to an extent unprecedented since the Chinese Communist Party had come to power in 1949. Following on the heels of a bold program of economic reform and of opening up to the outside world, which China's paramount leader, Deng Xiaoping, had launched in 1978, this relaxation of Party control over economic, intellectual, and political life had filled the Chinese with a heady new sense of possibility. The increasing tolerance of individualism and freedom of expression reflected the surprising but growing conviction among China's new generation of reform-minded leaders that their country would not be successful in its efforts to modernize unless some dramatic way could be found to re-energize its people and win their willing participation in a new drive toward economic development. Political reform and democratization became their new rallying cries. But to the older, hard-line Maoists, who had spent their lives fighting for a very different kind of revolution — one that stressed centralization and Party discipline, rather than individual initiative and democracy — this latest wave of reform appeared as at best an unwelcome disruption and at worst a dangerous form of apostasy. While young reformers watched enthusiastically as official publications began to bloom with articles advocating freedom of speech and the press, the separation of governmental powers, and the protection of human rights, and as intellectuals publicly called for the democratization of almost all aspects of Chinese life, revolutionary hard-liners looked on with displeasure, waiting for an auspicious moment to counterattack.

A deep wariness of speaking too freely had been burned into many senior intellectuals by the crackdowns that had, with a horrifying regularity, terminated all previous interludes of liberalism in Chinese Communist history. While it was true that fall that the boundaries of acceptable political discourse were broader than ever, most intellectuals nonetheless prudently continued to try to stay within the elusive margins of Party tolerance. But there were a few who, seemingly without regard for these margins or their futures, dared speak out openly. The most vocal of these was a fifty-two-year-old astrophysicist of international stature named Fang Lizhi, who very quickly became renowned throughout China for his forceful calls for democracy and his forthrightness in publicly saying what he believed.

When I first met Fang, in his Beijing apartment in the fall of 1987, what impressed me about him first was his good cheer and guilelessness. He laughed easily — an infectious laugh that spiraled spontaneously into something like a whinny, carrying everything with it in a burst of unpremeditated mirthfulness. He was dressed simply, in a knit shirt, a tweed coat, and permanent-press slacks. Tortoiseshell glasses gave him a slightly owlish look. He made an initial impression of ordinariness — until, that is, he began to talk. Then I instantly sensed that I was in the presence of a man of not only keen intelligence and conviction but of intellectual boldness. The longer I was with him, the more this quality struck me. Far from being a studied posture adopted as a means of appearing to resist intimidation, Fang's fearlessness appeared deeply rooted in his personality, which in spite of its manifest self-confidence betrayed no suggestion of arrogance. Seldom have I met a man who, although at the center of an intense and dangerous national controversy — the Communist Party had laid the blame for the student demonstrations of the previous winter on his frequent speeches to student groups, in which he openly advocated Western democracy — so lacked the kind of polemical energy that often makes zealots of a lesser kind shrill and self-justifying. Although Fang obviously cared deeply about the cause of democracy in China, he was not one to thrust his views upon anyone; and although he had been politically persecuted throughout much of his life, there was no hint of rancor or resentment in his politics. What he was for was so much ascendant over what he was against that the notion of enemies seemed quite alien to his intellectual, political, and emotional vocabulary.

What made being with him strangely uncharacteristic of so many other experiences in China was his complete lack of the self-censorship that renders many other Chinese intellectuals of his generation incapable of speaking their minds. Without overriding his thoughts and feelings with the usual subtle (and frequently unconscious) genuflections to the official political line of the moment, Fang spoke so openly about what he was thinking and what he believed that one had to suppress the urge to warn him of the dangers of such candor. Although such warnings were, in fact, coming from many quarters, Fang seemed impervious to them. "Everything I have ever said is open," he told me, "I have nothing to hide. And since I have already said everything that I believe many times in public, what is the point of trying to hide things now, in private?"

Fang's life began in Beijing in 1936, when he was born into the family of a postal clerk from the city of Hangzhou. He entered Beijing University (Beida) in 1952, as a student of theoretical and nuclear physics, and although he quickly distinguished himself as an unusually capable scientist, politics soon began to attract him. His first recorded brush with political dissent occurred one February day in 1955, during the founding meeting of the university chapter of the Communist Youth League (an organization that arranges political and recreational activities for young people and that anyone who intends to become a Party member must join). The league branch secretary from the physics department had been addressing the gathering, in the auditorium of Beida's administration building, and had just begun discussing the role of the league in stimulating idealism among China's youth when Fang Lizhi, then a nineteen-year-old student, dashed up onto the stage, indicating his desire to speak.

"Some of us students in the physics department thought the meeting was too dull, just a lot of formalistic speeches, so we decided to liven things up a bit," Fang once remembered. "When it came time for our branch secretary to speak, he let me express my opinion, since I had the loudest voice." Taking over the stage from the secretary, Fang redirected the discussion to the more general subject of the Chinese educational system. "I said that this kind of meeting was completely meaningless. I asked what kind of people it was that we were turning out when what we should have been doing was training people to think independently. Just having the Three Goods [good health, good study practices, and good work] is such a depressing concept and hardly enough to motivate anyone! After I spoke, the meeting fell into complete disorder."

"The next day the Party committee secretary, who was the top person in charge of ideological work for students at Beijing University, spoke all day. He said that although independent thinking was, of course, all well and good, students should settle down and study."

In spite of his attraction to politics, Fang did in fact settle down to study, earning straight As at Beida. There he met his future wife, Li Shuxian, who was a fellow student in the physics department, which she ultimately joined as a faculty member. In 1956, at the age of twenty, Fang graduated from Beida and was assigned work at the Chinese Academy of Sciences' Institute of Modern Physics. But a year later the Anti-Rightist Movement began, and Chinese intellectuals who had spoken up during the previous Hundred Flowers Movement were ruthlessly persecuted. Because he had written a lengthy memorial on the need to reform China's educational system so that politics would not stifle scientific research, Fang was severely criticized. Unlike many other intellectuals under pressure, he refused to recant his alleged misdeeds and was expelled from the Party in 1958.

"For a long time after the Anti-Rightist Movement, I continued to believe in communism," Fang told me at one of our first meetings. "Even after I was expelled from the Party, I continued to have faith in Chairman Mao and believed that it must have been I who was wrong."

Wrong or not, as a promising young scientist he was greatly needed 10 by China in its early efforts to industrialize and was allowed to keep his position at the Institute of Modern Physics. He was ultimately even sent to help organize a new department of physics at the University of Science and Technology (Kexue Jishu Daxue, or Keda for short), which was just then being set up in Beijing. During the next few years, while teaching classes in quantum mechanics and electromagnetics, Fang also conducted research on solid-state and laser physics. Despite his previous political troubles, and because of his obvious talent in his field, in 1963 he was promoted to the position of lecturer.

But no sooner had Fang's life and career begun to resume a more normal course than the Cultural Revolution broke out, and like so many other Chinese intellectuals in 1966, Fang once more ran afoul of politics. This time he was "struggled against," branded a "reactionary," and incarcerated in a *niupeng,* or "cow shed" — a form of solitary confinement used by the Red Guards for intellectuals of the so-called "stinking ninth category," who were often dubbed "cow spirits." After a year's imprisonment he was released and "sent down" to the countryside in Anhui Province to work both in a mine and on a railroad. Here, because of the paucity of scientific books available to him, he was forced to change the focus of his scholarly work and to concentrate on the study of relativity and theoretical astrophysics.

"I had only one book with me — the Soviet physicist Lev Landau's *Classical Theory of Fields,*" Fang told me. "For six months I did nothing but read this book over and over again. It was this curious happenstance alone that caused me to switch fields from solid-state physics to cosmology."

But there was another equally important change brewing in his life. "It was then that I began to feel that perhaps Mao was not so good for the country," he remembered. "But because at the time most of us intellectuals still believed in communism, we were left with a difficult question: If not Mao, whom should we follow? There was, of course, no one else, and he was the embodiment of all idealism.

"After the Cultural Revolution started, everything became much clearer. I realized that the Party had not been telling the truth, that they had in fact been deceiving people, and that I should not believe them anymore. You see, a sense of duty, responsibility, and loyalty to the country had been inculcated within me as a youth, but what I saw around me made me feel that the leaders weren't similarly concerned about the country and weren't shouldering responsibility for its people."

In 1969, when the Academy of Sciences began to move several of the undergraduate departments of Keda from Beijing to the provincial capital of Hefei, in Anhui Province, Fang, along with several dozen other academics who had been stigmatized with rightist labels, was exiled with them. In Hefei, Fang began to study and teach astrophysics, but because of the political cloud hanging over him, he was able to publish the results of his research only under a pseudonym. 15

His full rehabilitation did not come about until 1978, two years after the fall of the Gang of Four. At this time he regained his Party membership and received tenure at Keda, shortly thereafter becoming China's youngest full professor. The next few years were perhaps his most creative, from a scientific point of view. Fang, who was increasingly interested in the cosmology of the early universe, began to publish frequently on this subject, now under his own name. (By 1986 he had more than 130 articles to his credit.) In 1980 his popularity at Keda led to his being elected director of the fundamental physics department, with more than 90 percent of the faculty's 120 votes. However, his political outspokenness and progressive views on education continued to cause the Party to distrust him. Because of secret reports from a fellow professor impugning his political reliability, Fang, though nominated several times, was rejected for the post of vice president of the University of Science and Technology.

What was ultimately to have the profoundest political impact on Fang were his readings in politics and his travels abroad, which became possible as a result of Deng Xiaoping's open-door policy. In 1978 Fang left China for the first time, to attend a conference on relativistic astrophysics in Munich. Subsequent trips took him to the Vatican, for a cosmology conference; to Bogotá, Colombia, for another conference; to Italy, as a visiting professor at the University of Rome; to England, as a senior visiting fellow at the Institute of Astronomy at the University of Cambridge; to Japan, as a visiting professor at Kyoto University's Research Institute for Fundamental Physics; and finally to the United States, where he was in residence at the Institute for Advanced Study, in Princeton, from March through July of 1986. These trips abroad were to influence deeply the way that Fang looked at both the Chinese socialist system and the role of intellectuals within it.

In spite of many years of political harassment and periodic near-total isolation from the world scientific community, Fang had now become one of the very few scientists from the People's Republic ever to have received such international scientific attention and acclaim. What made Fang even more unusual was his interest in education, philosophy, and politics — interests that grew out of his conviction that in any truly creative mind, science and philosophy, of which he took politics to be an extension, were indissolubly bound together. Just as scientific research was a way of bearing witness to truths about the natural world, so, Fang believed, intellectual and political inquiry were ways of bearing witness to truths about the political and social world.

In 1984 Fang Lizhi was finally promoted to the position of vice president of the University of Science and Technology, and Guan Weiyan, a colleague in physics, was appointed president. Clearly, Fang's star was now rising.

The next year the Ministry of Education issued a report, "The Reform of China's Educational Structure," calling for dramatic changes   20 in the country's university system. It recommended that administrators be elected to top positions by committees of academics, rather than being appointed by the Party. Encouraged by the report, Fang and Guan designed and proposed a radical plan to redistribute power horizontally at Keda. . . . To foster openness and engender a more cosmopolitan academic atmosphere, they also sought to establish as much contact as possible with the outside world. By the end of 1986 more than 900 faculty members and students from Keda had been sent abroad to visit, lecture, and study, more than 200 foreign scholars had visited Keda, and exchange programs had been set up with educational institutions in the United States, Japan, Britain, Italy, and France. . . .

So successful were Fang and Guan's reforms at Keda that the official Party newspaper, the *People's Daily*, which was itself caught up in China's new dalliance with democratic thinking, ran a series of five articles in October and November of 1986, describing them in the most adulatory way, which was tantamount to giving them the Party's seal of approval. In fact, the writer, Lu Fang, was so impressed by what he had seen at Keda that from the very first sentence of the first article he seemed unable to control his enthusiasm. Instead of reciting a litany of facts and statistics to introduce his subject, as this genre of news feature often calls for, he dove right in and gushed, "During my trip to Keda, everywhere I breathed the air of democracy." Lu went on to praise the openness and "unconstrained atmosphere" of this university in which students and faculty worked openly together.

Still mindful during those halcyon days of democratic dialogue that even the warmest political climate in China can suddenly frost over, the *People's Daily* published another article that fall asking rhetorically if it was not a concern that the radical experiments in educational reform at Keda might someday be branded as "wholesale Westernization," a derogatory phrase used by Party hard-liners to describe any overtly Western phenomenon. "Perhaps someone will bring up the question," the article admitted, before going on to answer itself. "In applying a system of 'separate and balanced powers' to run a college, is there not always some danger of being suspected of imitating Western capitalism? But the methods used at Keda are actually in accordance with the directions of Party Central regarding the 'practical application of democratization to every aspect of social life.' They are in accordance with the Constitution, which prescribes academic freedom. It [democracy] is not something that is being 'sneaked in the back door' here. We should have no suspicion about that."

The effect of these articles in the *People's Daily* was both to publicly transform Keda into a post-Mao model university and to elevate Guan and Fang to the status of semi-official heroes. . . .

Early that winter, just as Fang and many other Chinese intellectuals began evincing some sense of hope that China might succeed after all in evolving politically toward greater democratization, a series of events that no one had anticipated erupted. Beginning in Hefei, at Fang's own university, on December 5, and ending in Beijing on January 1, twenty large Chinese cities were suddenly racked by demonstrations in which students demanded a speedup in political reform. Tens of thousands of protesters flooded the streets of urban China carrying placards and banners emblazoned with such slogans as "No Democratization," "No Modernization," and "Government of the People, by the People, and for the People." Dreary campuses became festooned with wall posters proclaiming such anti-Party sentiments as "I Have a Dream, a Dream of Freedom. I Have a Dream of Democracy. I Have a Dream of Life Endowed with Human Rights. May the Day Come When All These Are More Than Dreams."

Alarmed by the specter of political chaos, the Party reflexively acted   25
not only to quell the disturbances, but to locate and root out their causes. Urged on by Maoist hard-liners, for whom the student uprising had been the embodiment of their worst fears about reform, the Party launched a swift counterattack.

On January 12 Zhou Guangzhao, a member of the Central Committee of the Chinese Communist Pary and the vice president of the Chinese Academy of Sciences, summoned the Keda faculty to a special meeting. In the very center of the front row of the large meeting hall were two conspicuously empty seats. When the room fell silent, Zhou Guangzhao announced that the Party Central Committee and the State Council had decided to remove Guan Weiyan, the president of the university, and Fang Lizhi, the vice president, from office and to reassign them, respectively, to the Institute of Physics and the Beijing Observatory, both in the capital.

After announcing this coup, Zhou Guangzhao accused Fang of having "disseminated many erroneous statements reflecting 'bourgeois liberalization'" and of having departed from the Four Cardinal Principles (i.e., adherence to the socialist road, to the people's democratic dictatorship, to the leadership of the Communist Party, and to Marxist–Leninist–Mao Zedong Thought). He continued his attack by saying that Fang's "ideas of running the school by attempting to shake off the Party leadership and departing from the socialist road had resulted in extremely nasty consequences for Keda. These erroneous ideas were fully revealed in the recent disturbance created by students of this university."

Over the next few days endless articles in the official press railed against Fang. These attacks were so relentless, repetitive, and overblown that it sometimes seemed as if the Party despaired of convincing even its own members, not to mention other intellectuals, of the righteousness of its actions, except by the sheer force and volume of its rhetoric. Any lingering uncertainties about whether the orders for Fang's ouster had come from the very top of the Party were dispelled when, a day after Fang's dismissal, Deng Xiaoping himself denounced Fang Lizhi, along with writers Liu Binyan and Wang Ruowang, by name during a meeting with Noboru Takeshita, then the Secretary General of the Japanese Liberal-Democratic Party, and soon to become Japan's Premier.

The Fang Lizhi affair quickly became a cause célèbre in China. Within days of his dismissal, members of the foreign press and the diplomatic community in Beijing were referring to him as "China's Sakharov." Chinese intellectuals, even those who did not completely agree with Fang's uncompromising vision of democracy for their country, applauded him for his unwavering boldness. The Party, desperate to stem this hagiographic treatment of Fang, was relentless in its media campaign against him. Even the *People's Daily*, which only two months earlier had lionized Fang and Guan for having created a model university at Keda, now blamed and ridiculed them, claiming that by "waving the banner of running universities in a democratic way" they were actually only "passing fish eyes off as pearls" and letting "vulcanized copper masquerade as gold." This was certainly not the first time that a Chinese publication had been forced to reverse itself — and surely there are few kinds of intellectual debasement worse than the forced repudiation by a writer or an editor of passionately held and publicly expressed beliefs — to keep its political position parallel to the flip-flopping Party line.

Fang's outspoken espousal of democracy and human rights had put   30
the Party in a difficult bind. Having vigorously tried to cultivate intellectuals at various times during the previous years with ever wider calls for ever greater freedom and democracy, it now seemed bent on persecuting them again in a way that could not but remind them of the Anti-Rightist Movement, which had followed Mao's call for the Hundred Flowers Movement, in the mid-1950s. Sometimes it appeared as if the Party, unable to find the "golden mean" (*zhongyong*) — the middle way revered by classical Chinese political philosophers — hoped at

least to create an optical illusion of moderation by oscillating back and forth rapidly between the extremes, alternately coddling and punishing its intellectuals. When, some months later, I asked Fang if he believed that democratization could ever take place in China under such conditions, he replied prophetically, "In China the concept of democratization has often been nothing more than a poker chip in what is really a game of power. Maybe there are still a few idealistic leaders, but on the whole most are preoccupied with the struggle for power, and they use such concepts as democracy as just another means of defeating their opponents. One side will say, 'I stand for reform and you don't, so you shouldn't be here!' The other will say, 'No! Reform is wrong, so you shouldn't be here!' In the end it is the Chinese people who suffer, because they get used as playthings.". . .

In January 1989 Fang electrified Chinese intellectuals by writing a personal letter to Deng Xiaoping in which he called on him to release all political prisoners, including the celebrated Democracy Wall Movement activist, Wei Jingsheng. Wei had been in jail since 1979 for, in the words of the Party, "openly agitating for the overthrow of the government of the dictatorship of the proletariat and the socialist system in China." Fang's simple but audacious act presaged a whole series of open petitions from other members of the intelligentsia that called for more freedom of expression, and helped usher in a period of open criticism against the Party that was unprecedented in recent Chinese history.

The groundswell of dissident energy reached a crescendo of sorts when President George Bush arrived in Beijing at the end of February 1989. He left home with the mistaken impression that he could fly into China from Japan on a whistlestop tour, throw a U.S. anchor windward against the upcoming Sino-Soviet summit scheduled for May by glad-handing Deng Xiaoping and other high-ranking Chinese leaders, and then, without grappling with the thorny issue of democracy and human rights in China, leave a day and a half later. But things did not quite work out that way. Just as Fang and Li were about to arrive at the Great Wall Hotel to attend a farewell presidential barbecue, to which they had been invited, their car was stopped by Chinese security police. They were not only denied entrance to the banquet but, bizarrely, forced out into the streets to wander through Beijing on foot for several hours in the dark with a phalanx of Public Security Bureau plainclothesmen trailing after them.

Appearing at a mass press conference later that night before hundreds of members of the Western media who had been accompanying George Bush on his trip, Fang not only protested his own exclusion from the U.S. presidential dinner but eloquently raised the larger question of human rights abuses in China in a way that no Chinese had before. Appearing on television screens and on the front pages of newspapers around the world, Fang instantly became China's first celebrity dissident, as well as a great embarrassment to the Chinese government.

Ironically, when the student democracy movement finally did erupt into street protests in April of 1989, Fang and his wife were virtual bystanders. They played no part in organizing any of the demonstrations, made no grand pronouncements, and, indeed, never even went to Tienanmen Square. Instead, they remained at home in their Beijing apartment watching television, receiving friends, giving interviews to foreign journalists, and biding their time. They kept a deliberately low profile to avoid giving the Party any excuse for branding the movement as their own manipulation, a presumption that conspiracy-minded hard-line leaders had been too eager to make in 1987.

"I am sure what I have been doing and saying has had a strong influence on what the students think, and, of course, we support what they are doing," Fang told me just before martial law was declared in May. "But neither they nor I want to give the government any pretext for saying that I am the hand in the glove. The truth is that I have had no organizational role at all in these demonstrations. This movement was completely spontaneous and self-supporting." 35

But it was a measure of Fang's intellectual influence that he was nonetheless blamed as being at the center of a "very small group of people" responsible for bringing about this "counterrevolutionary rebellion." Ironically, like the mythological Hydra of Lerna, which grew two new heads each time one was severed, every time the Party lambasted Fang, far from being diminished, his renown only seemed to increase.

Even when, fearing for his life after the June Fourth massacre, Fang reluctantly sought refuge with his wife in the American Embassy in Beijing, his renown did not cease to grow. Although trapped in a nether region between China and the outside world, he continued to do scientific research, to read, to write, and to bide his time until the uncertain moment of his release. But still hoping to besmirch his name, the Chinese government launched a massive propaganda campaign against him. They accused him of "counterrevolutionary propaganda and instigation," officially labeled him "the scum of intelligentsia," and even issued a warrant for his arrest. . . .

As negotiations between the United States and China dragged on over the next seven months, Fang and Li made no further public utterance. But the Bush administration's conviction that political silence was the best way to aid negotiations for his release did appear to make Fang somewhat uneasy. In a personal letter written at the beginning of June 1990, just before a new flurry of discussions finally led to their release, Fang expressed a keen awareness of his responsibility to continue speaking out even as he felt temporarily compelled to restrain himself.

"We know we have a responsibility and obligation to say something about China's present and future, especially now at the time of the Tienanmen incident's anniversary," he wrote. But, acknowledging that the continuing negotiations still made it awkward for him to make provocative statements, he admitted that he found it "very hard to find a balance between these two opinions."

During the beginning of Fang and Li's tenure in the U.S. Embassy, 40 the Chinese government was seemingly implacable in its demands that these "criminals" be handed over so that they could be "dealt with according to Chinese law." The only circumstance under which they appeared willing even to consider release was if Fang and Li would make public admissions of guilt.

"In the beginning the Chinese government insistently demanded that we admit our guilt and express a desire to reform," Fang recounted after his release. "Of course, we refused."

But once China had passed the anniversary of the Beijing massacre without any incidents, their hard-line negotiating position began to change as more hard-line leaders seemed to conclude that it was now in the interest of their country to resolve the bedeviling matter of Fang and Li so that relations with the outside world could begin to be normalized again. It was not long before negotiations with the United States began to center on a face-saving device for resolving the matter.

In May a perfect opportunity presented itself when Fang reported experiencing some minor heart palpitations. Although he was checked out by a Western doctor who found no serious medical problems, and although Fang himself later dismissed his chest pains as being the result of "drinking too much coffee," U.S. negotiators were not so quick to dismiss the matter. After news of how Fang was "stricken" had been leaked in Washington to the San Francisco *Examiner,* where it quickly garnered a front-page headline reading, "China Dissident Suffers Heart Attack," the year-long deadlock began to break in the Beijing negotiations.

On June 25, 1990, Fang and Li left the U.S. Embassy and flew to England, where he was to take up residence at the Institute of Astronomy, Cambridge University. When I met with Fang there, I was struck by how he had succeeded in keeping his intellectual clarity and political balance, when the world around him had been changing with such unpredictable and often frightening rapidity.

"If circumstances allow I will go immediately back to China to make 45 whatever contributions I can, because I can only really function there," he said matter-of-factly, as if, having barely had time to confront the present, he had already decided about the future.

Asked whether he thought his final departure from China was a victory or a failure, he replied with his usual unpolemical candor: "It is hard to say. It is a victory in the sense that the Chinese government finally had to let me out because they were under pressure. But it can also be seen as a failure because I have left my own country, my colleagues, and also many of my acquaintances and friends, and naturally my effectiveness will now be marked by this."

Then, as if he did not wish to seem too gloomy about the situation, he recounted a list of other Chinese leaders, including Kang Youwei, Liang Qichao, and Sun Yatsen, who in the past had succeeded in having considerable impact on the course of Chinese history from abroad. When asked if he did not feel a certain ambivalence at having escaped China while so many other nameless and faceless people remained trapped, many under detention and in jail, Fang acknowledged that the thing he was most concerned about was that "there are still so many people in prison. This is the most urgent matter, and one that I regard as my moral responsibility. China's record of human rights is, of course, very bad. As to human rights activities, in these I will participate directly."

Admitting that China was very different from Eastern Europe, he said that he nonetheless believed that "democratization is the trend of the modern world," and expressed a faith that finally China too would progress in this direction. "To say that one cannot have democracy because one has not had it in the past, is a point of view contrary to history."

When pressed on how he intended to respond to those many Chinese democracy movement activists who had been waiting for his release with such high hopes for guidance, Fang seemed to bridle at the presumption that he could or should become more than a "spiritual" leader.

"If Chinese are waiting for the appearance of a superhero, I am not 50 that man," he said emphatically. "Moreover, I think that this expectation is in itself an unhealthy one. Chinese too easily tend to put all their hopes on the next leader, only to become disillusioned. I do not mean that I want to avoid my responsibility, because I do feel a responsibility, especially after my experience during these last few years. But that does not mean that I want to be a leader."

What then would Fang advise those who look to him for leadership to do?

"If you ask me what should happen next in China . . . well, it's very difficult for me to answer," he said tentatively.

EXPLORATIONS

1. Orville Schell's impression on meeting Fang Lizhi was of "a man of not only keen intelligence and conviction but of intellectual boldness" (para. 3). How has each of these qualities contributed to Fang's success as an astrophysicist, as a teacher, and as a political leader?

2. Which policies of Chairman Mao Zedong and the Communist Party during the 1950s and 1960s hindered Fang's professional progress? Which Party policies helped his progress?

3. According to Schell, what are the key beliefs for which Fang was harassed, punished, and finally exiled? Judging from what you have read about China, why were Fang's beliefs so threatening to the Communist Party?

CONNECTIONS

1. How does Schell think international travel influenced Fang? In speaking to a student audience in "Thoughts on Reform" (p. 742), how does Fang say that international travel influenced him?

2. Schell mentions how impressed he was by Fang's fearlessness. According to Aung San Suu Kyi in "Freedom from Fear" (p. 698), why is fearlessness such an admirable trait? In what respects does Fang's specific experience support (or not) Aung San Suu Kyi's general statements?

3. How does Nader Mousavizadeh explain the Danish monarchy's success (p. 647)? How does his explanation apply to the policies of "China's new generation of reform-minded leaders" as Schell describes them in his first paragraph?

JIANYING ZHA

Yearnings

"Born and raised in Beijing, I grew up in the chaotic years of the Cultural Revolution, and was among the first lucky batch to obtain a college education right afterward," writes Jianying Zha. "I arrived on the campus of Beijing University straight from a year of 'reeducation' farm labor with the peasants. In 1981, I came to America at the age of twenty-one, and after five and a half years of graduate school in South Carolina and New York, I went back to China in 1987 with a dissertation grant and hopes of reconnecting with my roots. In the following two years of living there, I started a moderately successful career writing Chinese fiction, and became increasingly involved in China's lively cultural trends and intellectual circles. By the time the students arrived in Tienanmen, I was coediting an elite Beijing magazine with a group of high-profile Chinese writers and working at a temporary job at the *New York Times*'s Beijing bureau.

"Tienanmen brought all that to a halt. After witnessing the June 4th massacre, I returned to the United States. Since then, my working life has been spent in both China and America. Since 1990, my job as a China program coordinator at an independent research center in Chicago [the Center for Transcultural Studies] has enabled me to visit China regularly. I have been able to stay in my mother's apartment in Beijing for weeks, sometimes months, in order to conduct research and interviews. In the past two years, I've been writing a regular column of commentary on Beijing for a leading Hong Kong monthly. I am married to a Chinese-American and have made a home in Chicago while writing in both Chinese and English."

These biographical notes come from the introduction to Zha's book *China Pop: How Soap Operas, Tabloids, and Bestsellers are Transforming a Culture* (1995). "Yearnings" is excerpted from the chapter by that name in *China Pop*.

Teacher Bei is a buxom, sixty-three-year-old retired elementary school teacher who lives in a prefabricated apartment in the east side of Beijing. I call her "Teacher Bei," instead of "Aunt Bei" as Chinese normally call somebody her age, because of a warning from the friend who introduced us: It is very important, he said, to make her feel that she belongs to the educated class and is someone with culture. Teacher Bei was so pleased by our visit and got to talking so much that she skipped her nap and made a big pot of tea. She made us a delicious lunch in her spotless, drab living room, but she herself only nibbled. "I haven't had such a good time since *Yearning*," she admitted.

She says she has always been prone to depression. She has a history of breakdowns — the first one when she was twenty-five and married off against her will. Maybe this is why she always finds the gloom of Beijing's harsh winters so difficult. Last year, though, she didn't mind the winter because *Yearning* was on television just about every night. Two stations were showing it on different evenings, and she watched them both. "A good show gets better the second time," she says. She would shop, clean, wash, cook, and do what she could for herself and her husband (which was not that much at all), then get ready for the evening. She has two sons, both married, living away. They only drop by once in a while. "They are good children, as filial and respectful as anybody's, but they're always busy and have their own families to worry about now," Teacher Bei tells me stoically, not wanting to complain about what is obvious in her old age: the boredom, the emptiness, the marriage that never would have lasted were it not for the children.

Her husband, old Tang, is a railway engineer, half deaf from an accident but still working part-time. They have long lived in separate rooms; nowadays they hardly talk to each other. But in the months when *Yearning* was on, their household was almost conjugal. Every evening at 6:30, Tang would arrive from work and find dinner ready on a tray and his wife settled into a puffy lounge chair in front of the television, ready for *Yearning*. He would join her, sitting doggedly through the show, his eyes fixed on the screen even though half of the dialogue was lost on him. "It was bliss," Teacher Bei admits, sounding wistful. "Why can't they make a show like that more often? I guess it must be hard to come up with a story so complicated and gripping."

Yearning was a fifty-part Chinese television serial, in a genre that the Chinese television people call "indoor drama" because it is mostly shot with studio-made indoor scenes. The Chinese title, *Kewang*, literally means "a desire like thirst." Desire is a central theme of the show, which covers the lives of two Beijing families during the years of the Cultural Revolution and the eighties reforms. In normal times, according to normal social customs in China, they are not the kind of families who would care much to mix or socialize with one another: The Lius are simple workers living in a traditional courtyard house, whereas the Wangs are sophisticated intellectuals living in a modern apartment. However, the Cultural Revolution struck a heavy blow to the Wang family's fortunes, creating a chance for their son, a forlorn, sappy, soft young man of the type the Chinese call a "Little White Face," to meet the daughter of the Liu family. Of course, they get married, not out of love so much as a desire for the qualities of the opposite class: he for the simplicities of a heart of gold, she for the charm of being "cultured." From there on, despite the omnipresent Chairman Mao portraits on the walls of both homes, the Cultural Revolution and larger political events remain a blurry, underexamined background. Instead, the show focuses on daily family life and various romantic relationships.

At the heart of the story is Huifang, daughter of the Liu family, whose saintly presence quietly dominates and holds the moral high ground above the clatter of worldly events. Also central to the drama is a little girl whom the Liu family accidentally picks up: Huifang raises her through all manner of hardship, only to find out that she is the baby abandoned by the Wang family. Huifang is forever patient, kind, and giving — what Americans would call a goody-goody — yet she has the worst luck in the world. By the end of the show, she is divorced from her ungrateful husband, hit by a car, paralyzed and bedridden, and has to give back the adopted daughter so dear to her. In the true spirit of a long, drawn-out melodrama, *Yearning* entices its viewers with a fairly convoluted plot, conveniently linked by unlikely twists and turns, a good dose of tearjerking scenes, and a large gallery of characters from a broad spectrum of life.

There was little advertising for *Yearning* when it first aired in Nanjing in November 1990. The first few episodes attracted little attention, but by the end of the month just about anybody who cared anything about what's happening in China knew that the country was in for a "*Yearning* craze." By January 1991, all the major television stations had picked up the show. The number of stations quickly climbed to over 100, and the reception rate was unusually high. In the greater Beijing area, for instance, the rating was 27 percent, surpassing all previous foreign hits. In Yanshan, an oil and chemical industrial town with a population of over 100,000, the audience share was a stunning 98 percent.

Thousands of letters and phone calls flooded the stations daily. Demands were made with a good deal of fervor: People wanted *Yearning* on their television every night, and as many episodes as possible. Those who missed the earlier portion begged for a replay. Startled networks responded quickly. The time slot for the show increased, and reruns began even before the first run had ended — which helped to fan the flames and give the show more publicity. In some heavily populated cities such as Nanjing and Wuhan, the streets were deserted whenever *Yearning* was on. A department store in Hubei province broke its sales record: Over 1,500 television sets were sold while *Yearning* was on the air. In Wuhan, a scheduled power cut occurred in the middle of one episode; instead of sitting in the dark or going to bed as they had always done, an angry crowd surrounded the power plant and put so much pressure on the mayor that he ordered the power back on immediately.

People talked about *Yearning* everywhere — in the crowded commuter buses, on the streets, in the factories, offices, stores, and at family dinner tables. You could hear people humming the show's theme music in the narrow, deep lanes of Beijing and Nanjing. The audio track was packaged quickly into eighteen cassette versions, all of which sold like hot cakes. By the time the crew took its promotion tour for the show around the country, the main actors were already household names and the crew was mobbed by huge crowds everywhere. In some instances, the crew's arrival caused monumental traffic jams, de facto strikes, and work stoppages.

According to one report, the crew received such a spectacular welcome in Nanjing that the only other comparable turnout in the history of the city was when Chairman Mao first visited there decades ago. Fans waved banners and posters, some wept openly in front of the main actress, who had become, for them, a symbol of the virtuous victim; some even threatened to beat up the main actor, the embodiment of the selfish villain. Male viewers said that they yearned for a wife like Huifang; female viewers said that she was like a lovely sister to them. Everybody said that *Yearning* had brought out the best in them and made them understand better what it meant to be Chinese and how deeply rooted they all were in the Chinese values of family and human relations — and how all of this made them yearn for *Yearning* every night.

The press also jumped in. All sorts of stories about the series were   10 rushed into print in every possible form: behind-the-scenes reports, on-the-spot interviews, profiles, special columns, analytical essays, letters from the audience, statements from the writers and actors. For months, the promotions raged on fantastically, heating up a public already gripped by the show. Amid the flood of literature on *Yearning*, a 300-page book topped all others: From collecting the pieces to editing, laying it out, printing, and binding, the entire book was processed in sixteen days. And how could a title like *The Shock Waves of Yearning*, with a glossy cover photo of the demurely smiling star, fail to stop the heart of a *Yearning* fan browsing at a bookstall?

Such excitement had not stirred in China since Tienanmen.

By the time Teacher Bei was watching *Yearning* for the second time (it was soon to be shown a third time, and she along with many others would watch it a third time), a certain standing member of the Politburo was also watching it at home. On January 8, 1991, this Politburo member, Comrade Li Ruihuan — who had risen from his first job as a carpenter to become overseer of national ideology — met with the *Yearning* crew. It was in a reception room inside Zhongnanhai, the Chinese Communist Party headquarters, nuzzled against the red walls of the Forbidden Palace.

Li Ruihuan was clearly in a very good mood. He congratulated the crew on its success and called it "a worthy model for our literary and artistic workers." It is a lesson for us, he said, that a television drama depicting ordinary life could elicit such a warm *and* positive response from society. It tells us that an artistic work must entertain first, or it is useless to talk about educating people with it. The influence we exert must be subtle, imperceptible, and the people should be influenced without being conscious of it. In order to make the socialist principles and moral virtues acceptable to the broad masses, we must learn to use the forms that the masses favor. What he meant by socialist principles and moral virtues was "new types of human relations" — honesty, tolerance, harmony, and mutual help among the people. These, he said, were precisely what *Yearning* had portrayed so well.

On the following day, all the major Chinese newspapers reported Li's remarks on the front page.

Li Ruihuan had been assigned the job of ideology control right after   15
the massacre at Tienanmen. It was an important promotion because, in the Chinese Communist Party's brutal history of power struggles, ideology was deployed like the army: Both were used as weapons of control and intensely fought over. Intellectuals, writers, and artists were watchful, for here was the new boss of the political campaigns and the ideological policies that had the power to advance or destroy their careers, to still their pens, even to rob them of their livelihoods. The promotion of Li Ruihuan, the well-liked mayor of Tianjin with a reputation of being a down-to-earth, no-nonsense man on economic matters, was itself a significant political signal.

The mechanism of control in these areas is extremely complex. The centralized party structure has its people in every small office, building itself up level by level all the way to the central party committee. But in the last ten years, it has been weakened from both within and without: Independent research associations, political and artistic salons, and joint ventures that crisscross institutions and countries had grown and provided the Chinese with something like an alternative, parallel structure. Still, nobody seemed to doubt that Li, at the top rung of the party structure, would be a most valuable player in the game. He was called into a Beijing fraught with tension, where the victorious but nervous hard-liners were trying to reclaim as many controlling posts as possible after the crackdown at Tienanmen.

Li surprised everyone with his first move. With energy, spunk, and a good deal of charisma, he launched a campaign against pornography. He went everywhere, and everywhere he went he talked about "sweeping out the pornographic literature and trade poisoning our society." His speeches were filled with a conviction that pornography was the chief evil of bourgeois liberalism and the chief object of his rectification campaign. He vowed to stamp out pornography and called on every leader to join him in this important battle. Other issues tended to sound abstract or muddled in Li's speeches — obscured by the heated antipornography rhetoric. The hard-liners didn't know what to say about this, since pornography was definitely a disease of Western liberalism and bourgeois decadence, and antipornography was surely a politically correct line. The intellectuals smiled knowingly and relaxed a little. Seasoned by decades of party campaigns, Chinese intellectuals, especially those above thirty-five, possess a keen political consciousness: They can read between the lines of a party document or a party leader's speech — which to an outsider or novice in Chinese politics may seem like dull, standard party lines worded in dull, standard party jargon — and detect at a glance signs of a new political shift. Even at private gatherings, discussing and speculating on the latest party policies is a perverse fixation among elder, educated Chinese. As for the ideologically minded cadres at various levels, the correct interpretation and response to signals and messages from above is an automatic reflex. Some intellectuals began to find Li quite appealing, for a politician; some even worried that his style might be a bit too flamboyant, too bold, that such a style would backfire all too easily, that he wouldn't last very long — there had been plenty of instances like this in the history of Chinese Communist Party politics.

Others who saw in the former carpenter a born statesman, shrewd and crafty in the games of politics, liked to cite a widely known story about Li Ruihuan's actions during the critical period of the students' movement in 1989. The students of Tianjin, a big city only two hours away from Beijing by train, had been agitated by the hunger strike on Tienanmen Square and wanted to join forces. Many other cities were already swept up by local student demonstrations. Li Ruihuan, then mayor of Tianjin, quietly offered free train fares to those who wanted to go to Beijing. With the stream of students flowing to Beijing — to rock someone else's boat — and his conciliatory speeches about the importance of keeping up Tianjin's economic production, Li managed to preserve peace in his own territory. There were also other rumors about

Li's personal friendship with Deng, for whom Li had made home furniture with his own hands. This is playing politics Chinese style: With clever maneuvers and personal ties, you can go far, sometimes very far, in China's political arena.

Whatever Li Ruihuan's political prospects might be, he was a powerful figure and his words carried a formidable weight among the intelligentsia. Thus, the fact that Li Ruihuan had so graced *Yearning* with his warm endorsement seemed to indicate that the top leadership was well disposed toward the show. The large number of party VIPs accompanying Li to the Zhongnanhai reception included even leaders from the Beijing municipal party committee, a notoriously conservative bastion much hated for its active role in cracking down on the students at Tienanmen. Among them was Li Tieying, the education chief in the Politburo, whose image had been tarnished among educated Chinese because he took a firm stance alongside the hard-liners when the students went on their hunger strike. Li Tieying, as the papers reported the following day, used the occasion to talk about the need for "an in-depth campaign against cynicism about our country." Of course, he himself was hardly exempt from the charge of cynicism, after an embarrassing incident on television a few days after the Tienanmen massacre. It was one of those public political performances for politics: Li Tieying had been conducting a group of school children through a famous propaganda song, "Socialism Is Good," but the camera, fixing on his face, revealed that the conductor himself couldn't sing the song. His vaguely moving lips didn't match the words: A sinister ritual had been turned into a laughable farce.

Despite all the standard propaganda lines, however, the general tone 20 of the reception was clearly conciliatory, for Li Ruihuan's was the dominant voice. Li's remarks, highlighted in some papers by boldface print, were punctuated by telltale words like "harmony," "unity," "tolerance," and "prosperity." He kept saying things like: "Under socialism, everybody shares the same fundamental interests." Any Chinese with a degree of political sensitivity could see what was going on: Li was using *Yearning* to push his moderate line, to imply the need for political relief. While the hard-liners had been drumming about deepening the campaign of repression, using phrases like "live-or-die ideological struggles" to describe the post-Tienanmen situation, here was Li Ruihuan saying, basically, "Comrades, let's look at the bright side of the picture, let's focus on positive values."

When *Yearning* was first televised, some of China's writers and intellectuals tuned in too. At least here was something watchable, some of it even enjoyable. True, the story slowed down and the lines got repetitive, but the plot was absorbing enough, the tone not too didactic, and there was even some decent acting. The Wang family — and the intellectuals in general — didn't come out too well, but there was no need to take it so seriously. After all, it was only a soap opera. Their innocent enjoyment didn't last too long, though, because it soon became clear that *Yearning* was not being seen as simple lighthearted entertainment. Apart from the enthusiasm of the general public, officials from every level were following Li Ruihuan's cue and showering praises on the show. "They were wrapping the show up in a royal robe," a writer later told me. There was no question that the series was being exploited by a wide spectrum of officials, all of them lauding an aspect of the show to justify their particular approach to politics, or to illustrate their own theory of the Chinese national character.

The person who led the cheers within the literary community was a Mongolian by the name of Marlaqinfu, author of several undistinguished novels in the fifties and at the time party chief of the Chinese Writers Association. He dashed off an essay gloating over the public enthusiasm for *Yearning* as if it had been his personal victory. The show's success was living proof, declared Marlaqinfu, of how socialist realism is still vital in China and, what was more, how literature and art prosper after bourgeois influences have been cleaned away.

This kind of touting, so obviously opportunistic, was nevertheless joined by some other writers' more earnest, heartfelt appreciation of *Yearning*. These were the writers who, in the initial thaw after the Cultural Revolution, had won fame overnight, when a newly liberated literature assumed the prodigious role of moral spokesman for a people long silenced, and when writers became celebrities on the basis of a single "taboo-breaking," "truth-telling" story. Most of their works, though serious and courageous, had no style to speak of, let alone any breathtaking technique; they practiced a tiresome realism lacking the sophistication and depth that marked the great works of classical Chinese fiction and European realism. In the ensuing years, several waves of younger writers exploded onto the scene, dazzling the reader with their stylistic and narrative energy. They spearheaded an avant-garde movement infatuated with style, especially the styles of Western modernism. Their drive for new styles so overwhelmed literary circles that, suddenly, all previous writings seemed unimaginative, outdated, and irrelevant. In the meantime, nurtured by economic reform, commercial publishing was booming. It wasn't much of a fight: The majority of readers didn't have to be won over by sensational reportage and easy, entertaining materials — they rejoiced in them. Snubbed by elite critics and dropped by the general public, a great number of "outdated," "serious" writers, their memory of yesterday's glory still fresh, either had gone on producing works that were thoroughly ignored, or had stopped writing completely.

It was not surprising, then, that *Yearning*'s phenomenal success should excite them. As they saw it, here was a work done in a manner of good old realism, a show that depicted unambiguous, solid characters, gave them authentic, down-to-earth dialogue, followed an absorbing plot, and involved the audience emotionally with the dramatic fate of the characters. And it worked! The audience laughed and cried with it! What could be more precious, more satisfying to a writer than such a vital reaction? Chen Jiangong, a Beijing writer whose fiction was rather popular in the early eighties and who has been suffering a creative block since then, sounded almost grateful in a rave review of *Yearning*: In his view, the series owed its success to the good literary quality of its script — and by "good literary quality" he meant the solid creation of lifelike characters, from which Chinese writers had strayed. He was voicing the frustrations of an entire generation of writers for whom the popularity of *Yearning* had stirred the hope that perhaps their writing careers were not over yet.

Those who considered themselves members of the literary avant- 25 garde, on the other hand, regarded *Yearning* with unreserved disgust. In their eyes, everything about the show was offensive — its official status of "model product" and "campaign fruit," its crude, derogatory portrayal of the intellectuals, its vulgar, melodramatic style, and its celebration, in the service of party politics, of old Chinese values such as self-sacrifice and endurance (versus modern, Western values such as individualism and initiative). Beyond their antagonism toward the government — and they would have found whatever the current regime promoted repulsive, even if it were promoted by a moderate politician such as Li Ruihuan — the contempt for mass culture ran quite deep in the minds of these elite and elitist intellectuals. Most of them never bothered to watch *Yearning*; it was enough to condemn the show by its reputation, and for its success.

Yet in their sneer one could easily detect a certain embarrassment. After all, *Yearning* had been a great showcase for the state: The Chinese people may have followed the students and the elite intellectuals to Tienanmen Square, but now these same people were suddenly reunited with the government. Their love of *Yearning* stood in jarring contrast to their indifference toward the avant-garde scene, which by this time was suffering a rapid, cheerless deterioration: Works continued to be published, but the movement had lost its steam, and nobody seemed to care. Another disconcerting thing about the series was that one of its seven script writers, Wang Shuo, happened to be a young novelist who was not only tremendously popular among urban youths and common folk in Beijing but also respected, if grudgingly, by many elite critics. Puzzled by this man's role in Yearning, one such critic could not refrain from telling me that Wang Shuo was merely "playing" with television, earning a few easy bucks, and that he could not be responsible for such a gross product. "What about Zheng Wanlong?" I asked — about another widely acclaimed writer who was involved in developing the script. The critic's face fell. He was not at all ready to absolve Zheng the way he tried to excuse Wang. Frowning, he said coldly: "Oh, *he* sold out. I have no respect for writers like that. It's unforgivable." . . .

Zheng Wanlong now says that the whole thing was absurd. "What do you think my friends in exile would think of me getting mixed up in a model TV serial?" he asked me from behind the shroud of thick smoke from four hours of his chain-smoking. A fortyish, dark-skinned man, Zheng never went to college and had been a model factory worker and a low-level party bureaucrat until his fiction began to win critical acclaim ten years ago. A number of the critics who praised his fiction live in exile now. Since I knew some of them, and knew what they would say, I hesitated. He said, "Wouldn't they say that I have totally degenerated?" Without waiting for my reply, he shrugged and said: "Well, all my life, throughout my writing career, I have never degenerated. Let me taste just once what it feels like to degenerate."

In fact, the success of Yearning has transformed not only Zheng's image among his intellectual friends but, even more miraculously, his political fate. It was widely suspected that Zheng had something to do with organizing demonstrations and petitions in May 1989 — even that he had held up huge banners on the front lines. Serious trouble was in store for him. After the military crackdown on June 4, 1989, the Party moved on to a pervasive campaign of "facts verification." Every party member, especially in Beijing, was required to report his or her own activities during the democracy movement — whether one had gone to the Square, marched or signed any petitions, whether one had been sympathetic toward the movement, and what one thinks of it now, if one's "level of thinking and understanding" has improved after studying Deng's speeches and party documents regarding the "counterrevolutionary rebellion," and so on. This process of "facts verification" is normally referred in Chinese conversation as *jiang qing chu*, "making things clear"; but when an investigation deals with a million people on the streets, and thousands daily on the world's largest square, there is really no way to make things clear at all. Many people simply denied that they had done anything in May and June — and, anyway, they said, now they were taking the "correct stance" alongside the Party. In most such cases, so long as nobody came up with hard proof to the contrary, that was the end of it.

A friend of mine, a college teacher who had marched, designed humorous posters, and written slogans, flatly denied everything he had done. "You see, I was lying, and they probably knew I was lying, but they didn't mind my lies," he told me glibly, with no trace of shame or guilt on his face. "It saved me some trouble, and it saved them some work, so both sides are happy, and both sides are cynical. Thirty years ago the party wanted us to believe in it, now the party just wants us to *say* that we believe in it. And, what's more, so long as they need us intellectuals to do some work, they'd rather close one eye and pretend that things weren't really that bad."

Zheng, however, could not disentangle himself quite so easily. What with certain complications about his signature on a certain petition, and his status as a prominent writer and vice editor in chief of a large publishing house, it was not so easy to "close one eye" to him. So when things didn't become "clear," a special task force was formed, its task being to interrogate him daily. Members of this task force consisted of various political work cadres from the security and personnel divisions of Zheng's publishing house; among the perks they received was a car put at their disposal. The investigation went on for almost a year. For months, Zheng had to answer meticulous questions about everything — for instance, where had he been on a certain hour of a certain day, with whom, for how long, by what type of vehicle he had gotten there, and what he did there, what he saw, and so on and so forth. "That's when you find how inadequate your own memory is and how much they know about you," Zheng now says, smiling. "Well, they know much more than you think. For example, I said that on a certain morning around 9:00 I had left home by bicycle. One of them would be taking this down in his notebook, while the other checked *his* notebook and frowned: 'Are you sure about this?' he would say this looking into my eyes. 'According to our record here, you left at 8:15 that morning by bus.' That's the sort of thing that puts you in a cold sweat and makes your head throb, trying to recall every fucking little detail." In order not to complicate the situation and get more people entangled, Zheng simply stopped visiting or receiving friends. He also stopped writing letters and making phone calls. "Now I know what it means to be a hermit in a big city," he said, shaking his head, and laughed cheerfully.

Zheng can laugh, though, because his year of bad luck has turned into a new round of celebrity with *Yearning*. When his name appeared as a group of official censors screened the working copy, one of them asked if this Zheng was the writer from the publishing house; when this was confirmed, the official looked thoughtful for a moment, but the screening went on without further questions. From that moment on, the investigation of Zheng fizzled out. Since then, journalists have been flocking to Zheng's apartment and interrogating him about his role in the series. Because of *Yearning,* anything he says has news value and will find its way into a deliciously gossipy story; reporters reverently quote casual remarks he makes about writing, not because they care about his views on such things, but because of the fan club–like curiosity the show has inspired. One Beijing writer told me when I arrived there, "For a whole year Zheng was a criminal hiding in his hole; now he's once more a *xiang bo bo*" — a piece of sweet bread, which in Beijing slang refers to somebody who is hotly pursued. Zheng, though, says, "It's absurd," shaking his head, visibly pleased and a bit dazed by the turn of things for him. "First I felt like a hunted dog — then all of a sudden the search light switched, but I'm still a hunted dog!"

EXPLORATIONS

1. Why do the Chinese people say they liked *Yearning* so much? What other reasons does Jianying Zha suggest for the show's popularity?

2. Which parts of the political endorsement *Yearning* received (paras. 12–14) might a TV show in the United States receive from a high official? What parts are distinctly Chinese? How do the Chinese apparently see the role of television differently from Americans?

3. Zha writes that the comments on *Yearning* by Li Ruihuan, China's overseer of national ideology, "carried a formidable weight among the intelligentsia" (para. 19). Why? Who are the intelligentsia, according to Zha? How does Li's approval of the show potentially affect them?

CONNECTIONS

1. How does Zheng Wanlong's experience as a politically active writer (para. 22) parallel Fang Lizhi's experience as a politically active physicist as Orville Schell describes it (p. 754)? How and why have things gone differently for Zheng and Fang?

2. In "Thoughts on Reform" (p. 742), Fang Lizhi advises university students about protesting bad cafeteria food. In "Yearning," Zha describes an angry crowd surrounding the Wuhan power plant to bring their favorite TV show

back on the air. In what ways does the Wuhan protest support (or not) Fang's advice?

3. Compare "Yearnings" with Neil Postman's "Future Shlock" (p. 670). Does television as a medium of mass communication pose the same dangers to Chinese society as Postman believes it does to American society? Why or why not?

INVESTIGATIONS

1. There are several references in "Spotlight: China" to the Tienanmen Square demonstrations and massacre. Find out more about that pivotal series of events. Combine your research with what you have learned about China from this book to write an essay about Tienanmen: What conditions led up to it, what happened there in the spring of 1989, and what the consequences have been.

2. After World War II, Senator Joseph McCarthy led the United States government in a search for Communists which is often described as a witch hunt. Do some research on the McCarthy hearings, their causes, and their impact. Write an essay comparing and contrasting the American government's stance against communism with the Chinese government's stance against Westernization.

3. Galina Dutkina's "Sovs, Hacks, and Freeloaders" (p. 367) and Natasha Singer's "The New Russian Dressing" (p. 378) describe some of the dramatic changes in Russian society since the Cold War ended. How has China's political strategy as a Communist power differed from the now-defunct Soviet Union's? Which trends in Russia are also taking place in China, and why? Which ones are not, and why not? Using "Spotlight: Russia" and "Spotlight: China" as sources, write an essay comparing and contrasting the course of political and cultural events in these two nations.

Acknowledgments (continued from page iv)

Diane Abu-Jaber, "In Flight," from *Memories of Birth*. Originally appeared in *Left Bank No. 5*: "Borders and Boundaries." Reprinted by permission of the author.

Chinua Achebe, "The Song of Ourselves," from *New Statesman & Society* (February 9, 1990). Copyright © 1990 by Statesman and Nation Publishing Company Ltd. (UK). Reprinted by permission of the publishers.

J. F. Ade Ajayi, "On the Politics of Being Mortal," from *Transition* 59. Reprinted by permission of the author.

Isabel Allende, "Clarisa," from *The Stories of Eva Luna*, translated from the Spanish by Margaret Sayers Peden. Copyright © 1989 by Isabel Allende. English translation copyright © 1991 by Macmillan Publishing Company. Reprinted by permission of Scribner, a division of Simon & Schuster, Inc., and Key Porter Books.

Maya Angelou, "Mary" (editor's title), from *I Know Why the Caged Bird Sings*. Copyright © 1969 by Maya Angelou. Reprinted by permission of Random House, Inc.

Margaret Atwood, "A View from Canada," from *Second Words*. Copyright © 1982 by O. W. Todd, Ltd. Reprinted by permission of the author, c/o the Phoebe Larmore Literary Agency.

James Baldwin, "The New Lost Generation," from *The Price of the Ticket* (New York: St. Martin's Press, 1985). Originally published in *Esquire* (July 1961). Copyright © 1961 by James Baldwin. Reprinted by permission of The James Baldwin Estate.

Sven Birkerts, "The Electronic Home" (excerpt), from *Harper's* (1994). Copyright © 1994 by *Harper's* magazine. Reprinted by permission of *Harper's*.

T. Coraghessan Boyle, "Top of the Food Chain," from *Without a Hero*. Originally published in *Harper's*. Copyright © 1994 by T. Coraghessan Boyle. Reprinted by permission of Viking Penguin, a division of Penguin Books USA, Inc.

Joseph Brodsky, "Less than One" (excerpt), from *Less than One: Selected Essays*. Copyright © 1986 by Joseph Brodsky. Reprinted by permission of Farrar, Straus & Giroux, Inc.

Nicholas Bromell, "Family Secrets," from Katharine Whittemore and Ilena Silverman, eds., *Turning Toward Home: Reflections on the Family* from *Harper's* magazine. Originally appeared in *Harper's* (July 1992). Copyright © 1992 by *Harper's* magazine. Reprinted by permission of *Harper's*.

Joseph Bruchac, "Digging into Your Heart," from *Parabola* (Winter 1994). Copyright © 1994 by Joseph Bruchac. Reprinted by permission of Barbara S. Kouts Agency.

Susan Cheever, "The Nanny Dilemma" (editor's title; excerpted from "The Nanny Track"), from *The New Yorker* (March 6, 1995). Copyright © 1995 by Susan Cheever. Reprinted by permission of The Wylie Agency.

Simone de Beauvoir, "Women as Other," from *The Second Sex*, translated by H. M. Parshley. Copyright © 1952 and renewed © 1980 by Alfred A. Knopf, Inc. Reprinted by permission of the publishers.

Gino Del Guercio "The Secrets of Haiti's Living Dead," from *Harvard Magazine* (January/February 1986). Copyright © 1986 by *Harvard Magazine*, Inc. Reprinted by permission of the author.

Annie Dillard, "Flying" (editor's title), from *The Writing Life*. Copyright © 1989 by Annie Dillard. Reprinted by permission of HarperCollins Publishers, Inc.

Andre Dubus, "Imperiled Men," from *Harper's* (June 1993). Copyright © 1993 by *Harper's* magazine. Reprinted by permission of *Harper's*.

Galina Dutkina, "Sovs, Hacks, and Freeloaders," from *Moscow Days*. Copyright © 1996 by Galina Dutkina. English translation copyright © 1996 by Kodansha America, Inc. All rights reserved. Reprinted by permission of Kodansha America, Inc.

Buchi Emecheta, "Ona" (editor's title; excerpted from "The Mother's Mother"), from *The Joys of Motherhood*. Copyright © 1979 by Buchi Emecheta. Reprinted by permission of the author.

Louise Erdrich, "Foreword," from *The Broken Cord* by Michael Dorris. Copyright ©

1989 by Michael Dorris. Reprinted by permission of HarperCollins Publishers, Inc.

Fang Lizhi, "Thoughts on Reform," (excerpt) from *Bringing Down the Great Wall*, translated by James H. Williams. Copyright © 1990 by Alfred A. Knopf, Inc. Reprinted by permission of the publishers.

Zlata Filipović, excerpts from *Zlata's Diary*. English translation copyright © 1994 by Robert Laffont/Fixot. Reprinted by permission of Viking Penguin, a division of Penguin Books USA, Inc.

Richard Ford, "Optimists," from *The New Yorker* (March 30, 1987). Copyright © 1987 by Richard Ford. Reprinted by permission of International Creative Management.

Carlos Fuentes, "The Two Americas," translated by Alfred MacAdam from *The Orange Tree*. Copyright © 1994 by Carlos Fuentes. Reprinted by permission of Farrar, Straus & Giroux, Inc.

Gabriel García Márquez, "Dreams for Hire," from *Strange Pilgrims: Twelve Stories*, translated from the Spanish by Nick Caistor. Originally from *Granta* (Autumn 1992). Copyright © 1992 by Gabriel García Márquez. Reprinted by permission.

Elena Garro, "The Day We Were Dogs," translated by Tona Wilson from *Contemporary Authors of Latin America: New Translations*, edited by Doris Meyer and Margarite Fernandez-Olmos. Copyright © 1983 by Brooklyn College Press. Reprinted by permission of Margarite Fernandez-Olmos and Doris Meyer.

Henry Louis Gates Jr., "Down to Cumberland," from *Colored People*. Copyright © 1994 by Henry Louis Gates Jr. Reprinted by permission of Alfred A. Knopf, Inc.

Amitav Ghosh, "The Ghosts of Mrs. Gandhi" (excerpt), from *The New Yorker* (July 17, 1995). Copyright © 1995 by Amitav Ghosh. Reprinted by permission of the Karpfinger Agency.

Nadine Gordimer, "Where Do Whites Fit In?" from *Twentieth-Century* 155, No. 986 (April 1959). Copyright © 1959 by Nadine Gordimer. Reprinted by permission of A. P. Watt, Ltd., on behalf of Felix Licensing BV.

Germaine Greer, "One Man's Mutilation Is Another Man's Beautification," from *The Madwoman's Underclothes*. Copyright © 1986 by Germaine Greer. Reprinted by permission of Grove/Atlantic, Inc., and Picador Books, Ltd.

David Grossman, "Israeli Arab, Israeli Jew," from *Sleeping on a Wire*, translated by Haim Watzman. Copyright © 1993 by David Grossman. English translation copyright © 1993 by Haim Watzman. Reprinted by permission of Farrar, Straus & Giroux, Inc.

Paul Harrison, "The Westernization of the World," from *Inside the Third World: The Anatomy of Poverty, Second Edition* (London: Penguin Books, 1981). Copyright © 1981 by Paul Harrison. Reprinted by permission of Peters, Fraser & Dunlop Group, Ltd.

Liliana Heker, "The Stolen Party," from *Other Fires: Short Fiction by Latin American Women*, edited and translated by Alberto Manguel. Copyright © 1982 by Liliana Heker. Translation copyright © 1986 by Alberto Manguel. Reprinted by permission of the author and Clarkson N. Potter, a division of Crown Publishers, Inc.

Kazuo Ishiguro, "A Family Supper," from *Firebird 2* (London: Penguin Books, 1982). Copyright © 1982 by Kazuo Ishiguro. Reprinted by permission of The Estate of Kazuo Ishiguro, c/o Rogers, Coleridge & White Ltd., 20 Powis Mews, London W11 1JN, UK.

Nikos Kazantzakis, "The Isle of Aphrodite," from *Journeying*, translated by Themi Vasils and Theodora Vasils. Copyright © 1975 by Nikos Kazantzakis. English translation copyright © 1975 by Themi Vasils and Theodora Vasils. Reprinted by permission of Little, Brown and Company.

Sam Keen, "Man and WOMAN" (editor's title), from *Fire in the Belly*. Copyright © 1991 by Sam Keen. Reprinted by permission of Bantam Books, a division of Bantam Doubleday Dell Publishing Group, Inc.

Aung San Suu Kyi, "Freedom from Fear," from *Freedom from Fear,* translated by Michael Aris. English translation copyright © 1991 by Aung San Suu Kyi and Michael Aris. Reprinted by permission of Viking Penguin, a division of Penguin Books USA, Inc.

Sophronia Liu, "So Tsi-fai," from *Hurricane Alice 2,* No. 4 (Fall 1986). Copyright © 1986 by Sophronia Liu. Reprinted by permission of the author.

Naguib Mahfouz, "A Day for Saying Goodbye," from *The Time and the Place and Other Stories,* selected and translated by Denys Johnson-Davies. Copyright © 1991 by the American University in Cairo Press. Reprinted by permission of Doubleday, a division of Bantam Doubleday Dell Publishing Group, Inc.

Nelson Mandela, "Black Man in a White Court," from *Mandela: No Easy Walk to Freedom.* Reprinted by permission of Heinemann Publishers Oxford.

Frank McCourt, "Limerick Homecoming" (editor's title; excerpted from "Sorry for Your Troubles"), from *The New Yorker* (June 10, 1996). Copyright © 1996 by Frank McCourt. Reprinted by permission of the author and Simon & Schuster, Inc.

Anchee Min, "The Fall of Autumn Leaves" (editor's title), from *Red Azalea.* Copyright © 1994 by Anchee Min. Reprinted by permission of Pantheon Books, a division of Random House, Inc.

Naila Minai, "Women in Early Islam," from *Women in Islam.* Copyright © 1988 by Naila Minai. Reprinted by permission of the author.

Alberto Moravia, "The Chase" (originally titled "Una Cosa è una Cosa"), from *Command and I Will Obey You* by Alberto Moravia. English translation copyright © 1967 by Gruppo Editoriale Fabbri, Bompiani, Sonzogno, Etas Spa. Reprinted by permission.

John David Morley, "Acquiring a Japanese Family," from *Pictures from the Water Trade: Adventures of a Westerner in Japan* (Boston: Atlantic Monthly Press, 1985). Copyright © 1985 by John David Morley. Reprinted by permission of A. P. Watt, Ltd., on behalf of the author.

Toni Morrison, excerpt from *Beloved* (New York: Alfred A. Knopf, 1987). Copyright © 1987 by Toni Morrison. Reprinted by permission of the author and International Creative Management.

Es'kia Mphahlele, "African Literature: What Tradition?" from *Voices in the Whirlwind and Other Essays* by Ezekiel Mphahlele. Originally appeared in *Denver Quarterly.* Copyright © 1972 by Ezekiel Mphahlele. Reprinted by permission of Hill and Wang, a division of Farrar, Straus & Giroux, Inc.

Vladimir Nabokov, excerpt from *Speak, Memory: An Autobiography Revisited.* Copyright © 1967 by Vladimir Nabokov. Copyright © 1989 by the Estate of Vladimir Nabokov. Reprinted by permission of Alfred A. Knopf, Inc.

Kenzaburo Oe, "Japan, the Ambiguous, and Myself," (excerpt) from *Japan, the Ambiguous, and Myself: The Nobel Prize Speech and Other Lectures.* Published by Kodansha International, Ltd., 1995. Nobel Prize lecture copyright © 1994 by The Nobel Foundation. Reprinted by permission of The Nobel Foundation and Kodansha International, Ltd. All rights reserved.

Norimitsu Onishi, "Japanese in America Looking Beyond Past to Shape Future," (excerpt) from *The New York Times* (December 25, 1995). Copyright © 1995 by The New Times Company. Reprinted by permission of *The New York Times.*

Susan Orlean, "Quinceañera" from *Saturday Night.* Copyright © 1990 by Susan Orlean. Reprinted by permission of Alfred A. Knopf, Inc.

Amos Oz, "If There Is Justice," from *Elsewhere, Perhaps.* Copyright © 1966 by Sifriat Poalim. English translation copyright © 1973 by Harcourt Brace & Company. Reprinted by permission of the publishers.

Grace Paley, "Six Days: Some Rememberings," from *Best American Essays 1995.* Originally published in *Alaska Quarterly Review.* Copyright © 1995 by Grace Paley. Reprinted by permission of Elaine Markson Literary Agency.

GEOGRAPHICAL INDEX

Africa

Asia

Australia

Europe

INDEX OF
AUTHORS AND TITLES

former Yugoslavia

AUSTRIA
HUNGARY
SLOVENIA
CROATIA
ROMANIA
BOSNIA
AND
HERZEGOVINA
SERBIA
BULGARIA
Sarajevo
ITALY
Adriatic Sea
MACEDONIA
Tyrrhenian
Sea
ALBANIA
GREECE

RUSSIA

MONGOLIA

NOR
KOR

CHINA

SOUT
KOR

UNITED KINGDOM
OF GREAT BRITAIN
AND
NORTHERN IRELAND

GERMANY POLAND
CZECH REPUBLIC
SLOVAK REPUBLIC

IRELAND

FRANCE

See Inset

Genoa

TURKEY

PORTUGAL

SPAIN
Toledo
ANDALUSIA

GREECE

IRAN

TIBET

Lisbon
Palos
Seville

Mediterranean
Sea

ITALY
CYPRUS
ISRAEL

SYRIA

IRAQ

PAKISTAN

New
Delhi

LAOS

TAI

CANARY
ISLANDS

MOROCCO

TUNISIA

JORDAN

INDIA

BURMA

HO
KO

ALGERIA

LIBYA

EGYPT

SAUDI
ARABIA

OMAN

THAILAND

VIE

CAMBODIA

NIGERIA

SINGAPORE

INDONES

GHANA
Gulf of
Guinea

KENYA

INDIAN OCEAN

ATLANTIC

OCEAN

ANGOLA

NAMIBIA

BOTSWANA

SOUTH
AFRICA

In the interest of visual clarity and simplicity, only
countries treated in the selections are labeled on
this map.

Making
CONTACT

Readings from Home and Abroad

C A R O L   J .   V E R B U R G

Resources for Teaching

MAKING CONTACT

READINGS FROM HOME AND ABROAD

PREPARED BY

Nancy Hurrelbrinck

Charlottesville, Virginia

BEDFORD BOOKS   **BOSTON**

For information, write: Bedford Books, 75 Arlington Street, Boston, MA 02116
(617-426-7440)

ISBN: 0–312–15005–9

Instructors who have adopted *Making Contact: Readings from Home and Abroad* as a
textbook for a course are authorized to duplicate portions of this manual for their students.

PREFACE

We are often told that today's students are less interested in other cultures and contemporary history than past students, but the experience of instructors who have used *Ourselves Among Others*, out of which *Making Contact* grew, suggests otherwise. First, many of our students come from multicultural backgrounds within the United States or from foreign homelands. The selections in this reader provide a chance for such students to find themselves recognized for their unique contributions and the alternative points of view they can provide. Second, instructors report that students browse through this reader, finding writings of particular interest to them, and request that they be included in class assignments. Students are motivated enough by the subject matter to want to share in the shaping of class discussion and assignments. The primary purpose of this text is to help students develop as writers, and students who are interested and involved will engage more readily both with the selections in hand and with their responses to them. A further benefit of this work will become apparent as students become more aware of and better informed about other peoples and cultures. They will unconsciously absorb a great deal of geography, history, and political knowledge that should help them prepare for life in the twenty-first century.

However, many instructors using *Making Contact* think of themselves primarily as teachers of writing and literature. They do not necessarily have real expertise in other disciplines. Some might question whether the lack of a specialized background makes it difficult for an instructor to approach these texts. Our answer is that these essays and short stories, which have headnotes and background information provided, are very accessible. Students and instructors encounter these texts together, and they can focus on the ideas under discussion without needing to rely on additional facts. The discussions generated by these texts do not focus on "right" or "wrong" answers; rather, the texts and the questions following encourage readers to explore the relationships between ideas.

This manual is designed to guide instructors through the maze of new material presented in the text, providing assistance in both planning and implementing the course. Used in conjunction with the text, the manual should temper the apprehension accompanying any new venture, and it also should provide instructors, even those who have used this approach in the past, with suggestions for ways of thinking about and teaching the selections. In particular, the manual includes the following:

An introduction, exploring teaching possibilities and providing suggestions for getting the course off the ground;

Brief introductions to each part, suggesting various combinations and subthemes and listing corresponding readings from more familiar American and European authors;

Biographical notes for epigraph authors;

Discussion of all Explorations and Connections questions, paying particular attention to possible student reaction to more controversial pieces;

Geographical information about, and Web sites relevant to, the Spotlight countries;

Carefully structured additional questions following the same pattern for each part, including journal suggestions, imitation of forms, short essay assignments, research of current related topics, and further research into cultures represented in selections;

Suggested syllabi, adapting the text to different types of courses;

A rhetorical index, pointing out those selections that make use of particular organizing strategies;

A chart of rhetorical writing assignments in the text;

Additional resources, including an index to headnote information and a concise list of reference materials to facilitate research into other cultures;

A list of film, video, and audiocassette resources.

Working with *Making Contact* provides a challenge: There are always pitfalls involved when we leave familiar territory behind. But using this manual as a road map, both students and instructors should discover that when we explore it thoroughly, the foreign territory isn't all that unfamiliar. And the people — well, now and then we can make contact with others.

I gratefully acknowledge the work of my predecessors, Kathleen Shine Cain (who prepared the manual for the first edition of *Ourselves Among Others*), Marilyn Rye (who prepared the second edition manual), and Alice Adams and David London (who prepared the third edition manual).

CONTENTS

Contents

Contents

INTRODUCTION

Making Contact can be adapted to courses using a number of approaches. As a thematic reader, it is well suited to an introductory writing course or a standard reading- and research-oriented second-semester composition course. But its flexibility allows its use in several other types of courses as well: Instructors who focus on rhetorical analysis will find a variety of personae, tones, organizational strategies, and stylistic techniques represented in these selections. The manual includes a rhetorical index designed to assist instructors in choosing examples of various forms. The Chart of Rhetorical Assignments (p. 139) lists "Elaborations," the text's writing assignments, according to the particular rhetorical strategy the students are encouraged to use in their essays. In addition, questions in the text focus on style, emphasizing the profound effects realized by seemingly inconsequential choices. Several questions on Boyle's "Top of the Food Chain," for instance, focus on diction and voice; a question on Márquez's "Dreams for Hire" focuses on tone. After answering the questions in Liu's "So Tsi-fai," students should become aware of the use of varied sentence construction to suggest changes in the narrator's point of view. A question on Orlean's "Quinceañera" will help students recognize the uses of interview as a method of research. These represent only a few of the stylistic questions found in the text.

Those who focus on writing across the disciplines will find selections by journalists (Orlean, Singer, Del Guercio), anthropologists (Wikan, Shostak, Minai), political figures (Aung San Suu Kyi, Mandela, Menchú), and literary figures (Tan, Paz, Rushdie), among others. For those who focus primarily on personal writing, numerous models are available (for example, Soyinka's "Nigerian Childhood," Erdrich's "Adam," Paley's "Six Days"). The writing suggestions accompanying these and other selections offer a variety of personal essay assignments. Instructors who want to integrate creative literature with nonfiction will find a number of short stories and excerpts from longer works (identified in the table of contents) to compare with the essays in the book.

Finally, these readings work well when used in conjunction with a longer text. For example, instructors could ask students to consider the topic of coming of age in selections by Shostak, Oz, and the novel *Upon This Mountain,* by Timothy Wangusa. Students can see how the role of women is defined in different societies according to Silko, Menchú, and Wikan and then examine the role of women in longer works such as Chinua Achebe's *Things Fall Apart.* Other possibilities for longer texts are *Hunger of Memory,* by Richard Rodriguez; *Chronicle of a Death Foretold,* by Gabriel García Márquez; *I Shall Not be Moved,* by Maya Angelou; *In Good Faith,* by Salman Rushdie; *Tracks,* by Louise Erdrich; and *The Bluest Eye,* by Toni Morrison.

Making Contact is also adaptable to various teaching techniques. The discussion questions following each selection can be assigned as homework, in-class writing, or as collaborative assignments for small group discussion. When the last technique is used, comparisons between group responses, especially to "Connections" questions, should make for enlightening discussion when the class convenes as a whole.

Introduction

Regardless of the focus or teaching approach, however, it is probably best to acknowledge the foreignness of this material immediately. Most college students are still at a stage when differences are perceived as threatening, and in recent years a tendency toward xenophobia has emerged in the United States. Perhaps one of the best ways to chip away at prejudices is to discuss different cultures and values represented by the class. A logical next step would be to look at other cultures' views of the United States, re-examining a familiar subject from unfamiliar viewpoints. The opening section, "Identifying Ourselves," should jolt students out of complacent views of their own society and result in some lively discussion. Also, it should allow students to broaden their horizons and become more tolerant of differences, so when they move to subjects in the following sections they will be less judgmental and more open-minded.

Instructors can follow "Identifying Ourselves" with any section, but because students usually respond well when moving from familiar to less familiar ground, instructors may want to begin with "Families" or "Turning Points." These parts provide ample opportunities for students to draw on their own experiences and to consider the experiences of others by comparing them with their own.

If students explore the idea of the family early in the course, they can use different types of writing to help them think about a familiar concept in unfamiliar cultures. Depending on the approach adopted, students may be asked to write in their journals, compose a paper, or discuss in small groups their views on family. Possible topics include "Rules and Regulations for Living in the Family," "Ethnic (or Religious) Influences on the Family," "Relationships Between Members of the Family," and "Expectations Within the Family." Each topic is broad enough for the instructor to adapt to a particular class or for students to narrow themselves. The purpose of the assignment is threefold: One, in discussing their responses, students should discover some unusual customs among people they consider to be similar to themselves; two, they should discover familiar customs among people they regard as different; and three, after examining these customs, they should come to the conclusion that neither the similarities nor the differences are impenetrable barriers to a larger world. These revelations will become useful to students as they attempt to understand a wide range of customs during the semester. As they discuss and analyze the origins of family patterns, values, and relationships, students should lose some of their suspicion of things foreign.

Once students have been introduced to the idea of differences, the instructor should continue the course as he or she wishes. Several possible syllabi, designed to adapt the text to a variety of approaches, are included at the end of the instructor's manual (p. 133).

Part One

IDENTIFYING OURSELVES

INTRODUCTION

High schools throughout the country have been using a multicultural approach in English and History classes for several years, so you might begin this section by asking students about their previous experiences. What have they learned? What interests them most about the intersections between cultures? To what extent have they explored their own cultural roots and current milieu? Do their families uphold any cultural traditions that have shaped their own identities? What is the mix of cultures in their college or university?

The essays and short stories in this section provide a mosaic of approaches to studying cultural identity. Some pieces offer a particularized account of a struggle for identity, whereas others address the issue in broader terms, querying the meaning of sushi tacos or the global omnipresence of Western architecture. Students should respond especially well to Tan's story about a child's struggle with a parent, to Orlean's essay about teenage Latinas celebrating their culture (and themselves!), and to Greer's essay about how people announce their identities through their physical appearance.

Possible subthemes in this section are the effect of U.S. culture on other cultures' identities (Atwood, Harrison, Fuentes, and Rodriguez), the effect of being an expatriate (Baldwin, Rushdie, Tan), how family affects identity (Orlean, Tan), and religious traditions that maintain cultural identity (Paz, Orlean).

Instructors may wish to consult the following works in preparing related selections in *Making Contact*:

Essays

James Baldwin, "Stranger in the Village*" (Notes of a Native Son*, Dial Press, 1955)
Alex Haley, "My Furthest-Back-Person — 'The African'" (*New York Times*, July 16, 1972)
Maxine Hong Kingston, "No Name Woman" (*The Woman Warrior*, Knopf, 1976)
George Orwell, "Shooting an Elephant" (*Shooting an Elephant and Other Essays*, Harcourt, 1950)
Richard Rodriguez, "Aria" (*American Scholar*, Winter 1981; *Hunger of Memory*, David R. Godine, 1982)

Short Stories

Toni Cade Bambara, "The Lesson" (*Gorilla, My Love*, Random House, 1972)
Ralph Ellison, "Flying Home" (*Cross-Section*, ed. Edwin Seaver, Fischer Pub. Co., 1944)
Louise Erdrich, "American Horse" (1983; in *Imagining America*, ed. Wesley Brown and Amy Ling, Persea, 1991)
Franz Kafka, "The Metamorphosis" (*The Penal Colony*, Schocken, 1948)

D. H. Lawrence, "The Blind Man" (*The Complete Short Stories*, Vol. 2, Penguin, 1976)
Flannery O'Connor, "The Displaced Person" (*Complete Stories*, Farrar, Straus, 1971)
Frank O'Connor, "Guests of the Nation" (*Collected Stories*, Knopf, 1981)
Philip Roth, "Conversion of the Jews" (*Goodbye, Columbus*, Houghton Mifflin, 1959)

BIOGRAPHICAL NOTES ON EPIGRAPH AUTHORS

1. Richard Rayner, born in Yorkshire, England, now lives in Los Angeles. His books include *Los Angeles Without a Map* and *The Elephant*. He is a frequent contributor to *Granta*, the *New York Times Magazine*, and other publications.

2. African-American novelist, editor, essayist, and senior lecturer at the University of California, Berkeley, Ishmael Reed is known for his satiric wit and his use of motifs from black folklore to parody genre fiction such as westerns and mysteries. His books include *Flight to Canada* (1976), a farcical treatment of slavery, and *Japanese by Spring* (1993), a satiric account of academics posturing over multiculturalism.

3. Julio Cortázar (1914–1984), an Argentine writer who spent the second half of his life in Paris, published several luminous novels and collections of short stories. His works include *Bestiario* (1951), *Hopscotch* (1963), *62: A Model Kit* (1972), *A Change of Light* (1980), and *We Love Glenda So Much* (1983).

4. Anita Desai was born in 1937 in India to a German mother and an Indian father. She's the author of numerous novels and collections of stories, including *Baumgartner's Bombay*, a novel exploring that city's cultural mix. She currently teaches writing at Mt. Holyoke College and serves as a member of the Advisory Board for English in New Delhi.

5. Roger Rosenblatt is a contributing writer for the *New York Times Magazine* and the *New Republic* and appears as a regular essayist on PBS's "NewsHour with Jim Lehrer." He is the author of five books and the winner of a number of awards for print and television. His book *Children of War*, an account of young people growing up in modern war zones from Northern Ireland to the Middle East and Cambodia, won the 1983 Robert F. Kennedy Book Prize.

6. Born in Peru in 1936, Mario Vargas Llosa has taught at universities in England and the United States; has written several novels, including *Conversation in the Cathedral* and *The War of the End of the World*; has worked as a journalist in Peru and Paris; has won awards for his fiction and journalism; and, in 1990, ran for Peru's presidency.

7. Shelby Steele teaches English at San Jose State University. In 1990, he published a much discussed collection of essays, *The Content of Our Character: A New Vision of Race in America*.

8. Over four decades, Adrienne Rich has written fifteen books of poetry, moving from traditional, formalist poems to visionary expressions of feminist anger. *Diving into the Wreck* was co-winner of the National Book Award for Poetry and *An Atlas of the Difficult World* was a finalist for the National Book Award and the National Book Critics Circle Award. In 1994, Rich was named a MacArthur Fellow. Her most recent work, *Dark Fields of the Republic: Poems 1991–1995*, deepens and extends her exploration of how patriotic culture has endangered democracy and love.

9. Molly Ivins is a former reporter for the *New York Times* and is currently a contributing writer for *Esquire*, the *Atlantic*, *The Nation*, *Harper's*, and *Mother Jones*. She's the author of *Molly Ivins Can't Say that, Can She?*

10. Jill Ker Conway was born in Australia in 1934 on a sheep ranch. Since she emigrated to the United States in 1960, she has written a number of books on women's roles in American history. Recently she edited an anthology titled *The Politics of Women's Education* (1993). She currently teaches at MIT.

11. Alma Guillermoprieto is a journalist and dancer. Her novel *Samba* (1991) explores the history and culture of black Brazilians, focusing on their participation in Rio Carnival.

Explorations

1. This question raises the important issue of terminology: What should we call people who live in Spanish-speaking countries in the Americas? Is a Huaorani Indian who speaks no Spanish and lives by Stone-Age technology in the Ecuadorian Amazon a "Latin American"? Are Mexicans North Americans? Of the writers presented here, the following are North Americans: Richard Rayner, Ishmael Reed, Anita Desai, Roger Rosenblatt, Shelby Steele, Adrienne Rich, Molly Ivins, Jill Ker Conway, and Alma Guillermoprieto. Julio Cortázar and Mario Vargas Llosa could be called South Americans or Latin Americans.

2. The writers use a number of criteria other than nationality to identify themselves. Rayner is concerned with how long his ancestors stayed in one place — he's just moved, but he comes from stable stock. Reed wishes to challenge a monolithic understanding of American cultural identity by acknowledging non-Western cultural contributions. He notes that some of what is considered European has actually been borrowed from Turkey, Japan, Africa, and the Pacific Northwest. Cortázar sees an advantage in writing from what he considers an acultural and self-reliant perspective. He and other Latin American writers can reject identification with a political system and a readership that have betrayed them; they are free to create their own tradition of writing instead of building on an existing one. Desai uses languages as reference points for her identity: German was her "mother tongue"; Hindi was the language of her friends and neighbors in Delhi; and English was the language of her school, hence her literary language. Rosenblatt's "Enrique" also views language as an important part of cultural identity; he wants his sons to learn in English, because he hopes they will adapt to life in America. Llosa identifies with his forbears, insisting on the importance of seeing the ways in which his generation resembles them, rather than blaming them for his generation's ills. Steele sees identification in America split along racial lines. He views the racial struggle in America as a way that blacks and whites have come to see themselves as innocent: whites using innocence as a way to justify slavery and blacks using it as a way of overcoming years of hardships. Innocence, claims Steele, can be used to bargain for power. Rich wonders whether to identify herself as a Jewish lesbian so as to disavow her "southern gentile white woman's culpability." Ivins sees sexual orientation — which is not chosen — as a means of identification. Conway identifies with the myths arising from her forbears' relationship with the land; the "Great Drought" still haunts her, although her land is fertile. And Guillermoprieto identifies with *ranchera* music, which captures a sense of drama and pathos that seems to be vanishing from daily life.

3. In trying to characterize Rayner's neighbor, students are likely to confront their own biases; students might assume the neighbor would define an American as a white person of European descent whose family has lived in this country for at least three generations

3

(given that she regards Rayner's second-generation child as an immigrant). Reed would probably define an American as someone who encounters elements of a wide variety of cultures in his or her daily life. You might encourage students to come up with their own definitions, placing themselves somewhere on the continuum between Rayner's neighbor and Reed; you could take a quick survey by going around the room and having everyone say which views they identify with (this is a good method for getting everyone in the class to participate).

4. Students may balk a little at the complexity of this question, so it represents a good opportunity to show them how to break a difficult question down into its simpler components. Both writers argue that people in power need to relinquish the sense of their own innocence and take responsibility for the ways in which they oppress another group: Llosa wants Westernized Latin Americans to stop blaming those who colonized their countries (their own forbears) for current social injustices and to see what they can do to improve conditions for their Indian compatriots. Steele wants whites to relinquish the myth of their own superiority that gives them a hidden investment in perpetuating racism. The two differ thus: Llosa's people in power want to see themselves as innocents mistreated by the original colonizers rather than as a group currently mistreating Indians (whom he depicts as completely innocent). But Steele depicts those in power as aware that they lack innocence and willing to bargain for it with the group they oppress.

MIRRORS:
THE UNITED STATES

WALKER PERCY, A Short Quiz (p. 10)

Explorations

1. Percy's offering such a variety of ways to define the self suggests that the way one chooses to define oneself is more indicative of one's identity than the content of one's definition. Percy's thesis is that, paradoxically, although we spend more time getting to know ourselves than anyone or anything else, we find ourselves almost unknowable. Despite the proliferation of tools — astrology, religion, psychology, window reflections, science, art, government, work, play — we are at a loss to say who we really are.

2. By using a quiz format that uses the second person, Percy creates a light, playful tone for a traditionally weighty subject, adding emphasis to his claim of uncertainty about the nature of the self and involving the reader in the essay. The quiz also points ironically to the hugeness of the question, because a quiz is generally regarded as a test with quick, easy answers. By asking questions rather than making statements, Percy points to the complexity of the issues he discusses, as well as to the impossibility of providing succinct answers to the questions.

3. Students will probably need help understanding several elements in this list; you might want to put the list on the board, asking which items need explanation, and then draw on classmembers' knowledge and experience. If the class draws a blank on any items on the list, a good short research assignment would be to have students research the

4

item on the Internet, using a search engine like Metacrawler (http://www. metacrawler. com) or Alta Vista (http://www.altavista.digital.com).

Connections

1. The United States's "cultural bouillabaisse" status gives Americans a great sense of freedom to be whomever they choose, but it also gives us a less stable basis for determining our identities than that available to someone living in a more homogenous culture. Someone from a culture with only one race, religion, and philosophy (that is, one ideology) would probably find the quiz perplexing, if not offensive, because it presumes a postmodern audience that is skeptical about the possibility of fixed truths.

2. Of the various concepts of self presented by Percy, "the lost self" most closely approximates Rich's situation: her efforts to dissociate herself from her "southern gentile white woman's culpability" (p. 6) serve, in Percy's words, only to "tighten the bondage and distance the self even farther from the very world it wishes to inhabit as its homeland" (para. 38). The more distance we gain from ourselves through understanding our potential for multiple identities, the less chance we have of inhabiting any one of them.

3. Of the epigraph writers, Richard Rayner would probably agree with Percy's characterization of the United States as "a free and affluent society." Roger Rosenblatt might disagree on the grounds that Enrique's children's ability to perform in school may be compromised by peer pressure, and Shelby Steele might argue that racial issues prevent either blacks or whites from feeling free and restrict blacks' access to affluence.

JAMES BALDWIN, The New Lost Generation (p. 18)

Explorations

1. In the opening section of the essay, Baldwin conveys that he is an African-American who, at age 22, was a Socialist living in New York, a poet who did not believe in love, a man who had worked as a laborer and fought his landlord, and a man who believed the world despised him and who had decided he would despise it back. The last of these is most central to his essay: When he lived in Paris, Baldwin discovered that the French didn't necessarily relish his presence, thinking of all Americans as "children" (para. 24). Baldwin's sense of alienation followed him across the Atlantic, making Paris seem like a "large, inconvenient, indifferent city" (22), just as New York had been "fearfully hostile" (12). In other words, "voyagers discover that the world can never be larger than the person that is in the world" (21).

2. Baldwin left the United States because he feared that being black in America might have killed him, spiritually if not physically, just as it had led his friend to suicide. In Europe, he hoped to find freedom from racism and other forms of social oppression, as well as cheap studio apartments and goodwill, both of which the GIs had used up by the time he arrived. Living in Paris initially afforded him a sense of community with other expatriates, who gathered to gripe over their deprivations and who "walked . . . 'in friendly groups of five thousand'" (25). But Baldwin was shocked to miss some things he had taken for granted in the United States, such as a warm hotel room, toilet paper, the privilege of having friends visit him in his room.

3.　Baldwin uses "you" when discussing those aspects of Paris that disappointed him. When he talks about the landlords' attitudes toward "you," he both generalizes his experience and invites the reader to step into his shoes. His use of "one" provides a good opportunity to introduce the concept of irony; Baldwin uses it to show how, when he was younger, he tended to universalize his concerns, because it embarrassed him to admit that he missed his comforts: "One wondered how people, meaning, above all, oneself, could possibly do without them [the things one had fled from]" (22).

Connections

1.　Students will probably find this question quite difficult, so you might want to have a discussion about Percy's notion of "the lost self." How can one be "cut loose and imprisoned" (p. 15) by freedom? You might ask how Baldwin's reactions to Paris suggest that he still feels tied to American culture; because, for all that Baldwin believes he has found a place where he can be absolutely faithful to his own vision, he and his fellow "voyagers discover that the world can never be larger than the person that is in the world" (para. 21). Percy might explain Baldwin's emigration to Paris as a desire to free himself from racist U.S. culture — a move that might serve only to help Baldwin see how much of that racism he has internalized.

2.　Rayner, unlike Baldwin, sees himself fitting into the diverse racial makeup of America. Whereas Baldwin flees racial oppression and injustice, Rayner's only complaint is the casual remark of a neighbor, with whom he eventually becomes friends. Rayner is content to work within the fabric of a country he sees as vibrant and generous. Because Rayner is English and fits into the Anglo-Saxon majority in this country, and because he came to a later America than the one Baldwin left, he is accepted in ways Baldwin was not.

3.　Steele claims that blacks used the innocence that accrued during their long subjugation to seize power from whites via the Civil Rights movement. Although Baldwin and his friend perceive themselves as spotlessly innocent, they don't regard that innocence as a source of power.

AMY TAN, Two Kinds (p. 28)

Explorations

1.　Students will find it easy to come up with several meanings for the story's title. One of the most obvious meanings is revealed late in the story, when Jing-mei's mother shouts "Only two kinds of daughters. . . . Those who are obedient and those who follow their own mind!" (para. 74). The mother's denial that Jing-mei could be obedient in some ways and independent in others reflects the all-or-nothing thinking that affects every aspect of her relationship with Jing-mei. The mother believes that one is either a genius or "not trying." Initially, Jing-mei accepts her mother's view and thinks that she "would soon become *perfect*" (10). At times Jing-mei views herself as divided into two kinds — the prodigy and the failure. This interpretation of "two kinds" is reinforced by the contrast between Jing-mei and Waverly, who tells Jing-mei, "You aren't a genius like me" (61). But Jing-mei has already had a moment when she sees herself as "angry, powerful" (19). She realizes that the "prodigy side" of her is someone who can resist her mother. This doesn't resolve the conflicts embedded in the idea that there are "two kinds of daughters," but it is an important step toward integrating herself. Only much later, as an

6

adult, can Jing-mei resolve the conflicts she and her mother battled over. In the closing paragraph, Jing-mei returns to the idea of "two kinds" when she looks back at "Pleading Child," the music she tried to play at the recital, and sees that opposite it is another piece, "Perfectly Contented." She recognizes that "they were two halves of the same song," a realization that helps her put to rest the conflicts between her mother and herself.

2. The primary goal of Jing-mei Woo's mother is to make her daughter become a prodigy. Most of her actions during the story show that her life focuses on this goal. She constantly watches television or combs magazines for stories about prodigies to see which possibilities are open to her daughter (4, 12). She drills Jing-mei every evening. Finally, she exchanges cleaning chores for piano lessons and scrapes together money to buy a secondhand piano. Although students may find the mother a domineering and repellent figure, understanding her motivations will help them see the issue of meeting parental expectations from alternate points of view. The mother sees America as a magical place where anyone can be whatever she wants to be: rich, famous, a prodigy (1, 2). From her point of view, she is asking her daughter to achieve a very reasonable goal that will help Jing-mei experience a happier life than she herself has known.

3. After only one reading, students will probably interpret this story as an example of mother-daughter or parent-child conflict. However, thoughtful students who reread it will notice that the narrator herself has different feelings about being a child prodigy. Because she often shares her mother's feelings, abandoning them only after she feels incapable of meeting her mother's expectations, the conflict between Jing-mei and her mother could be interpreted as an externalization of Jing-mei's own inner struggle. At first she is "just as excited as [her] mother, maybe even more so" (9). Her parents will adore her (10). But she also is anxious that the prodigy in her will disappear (11) and she will turn out to be an ordinary person. Her failure to succeed at her mother's examinations confirms her sense of being ordinary and makes her lose faith in the possibility of becoming a genius. At that point, she says, "something inside of me began to die" (18).

Connections

1. Baldwin's comment reflects on the process of maturation and separation necessary to transform a youth into an autonomous and self-reliant individual. Jing-mei finds a delightful freedom in the realization that her piano teacher is not attentive enough to catch her mistakes, so she can play however she likes, so long as she keeps up the rhythm. She continues to accept her own vision as she frustrates her mother's dreams, not getting straight As or becoming class president or getting into Stanford or even finishing college. As she puts it, "I could only be me" (para. 80).

2. Tan's narrator would probably see herself as "the autonomous self" that is "free to pursue its own destiny without God" (p. 16) or an overbearing mother. The narrator's mother might prefer for her daughter to emulate "the role-taking self" (p. 15), perhaps the "feminine-doll-girl" who devotes herself to trying to please others.

3. "Two Kinds" dramatizes adolescent rebellion found in many (all?) cultures, but it seems more poignant in the context of an immigrant family. Enrique has moved to the United States seeking greater economic opportunities, but that doesn't mean his sons will share his dreams anymore than Jing-mei did her mother's. Enrique's sons may be particularly vulnerable to losing their dedication, because their peers at school aren't concerned with achievement. If any of your students are second-generation Americans, you might

7

launch a good discussion by asking how they believe their parents' expectations might differ from those of nonimmigrant parents.

SUSAN ORLEAN, Quinceañera (p. 40)

Explorations

1. Students may have some trouble understanding how Azteca Plaza, the formal-wear shopping center where parents shop for the gowns their fifteen-year-old daughters will wear to their quinceañeras, represents the dual nature of the Hispanic culture in Phoenix. They may find it easier if they begin by considering the dual meanings of "plaza." A plaza is a traditional outdoor marketplace and central meeting place, but it also denotes a modern shopping center. Mexico's native Aztec culture predated the European-derived Hispanic culture brought by Cortés in the sixteenth century; Hispanics simultaneously superseded and mixed with Aztecs in Mexico as European-Americans have done with Mexican-Americans in the southwestern United States.

2. Quinceañeras were originally meant to mark a girl's initiation into womanhood and society and to affirm her commitment to the Catholic Church (para. 1). Students will find plenty of evidence that quinceañeras still serve as a social debut. Whether the event is held for an individual girl or for groups of girls, it brings the community together to recognize the girls' passage from childhood to young womanhood. But some members of the Hispanic community are concerned that quinceañeras no longer serve as a meaningful religious rite. One of Orlean's informants tells her that the ethnic and religious significance of the quinceañera is irrelevent to today's young people (5). Father Sotelo tells Orlean that the quinceañera has become an empty ceremony (7). Some girls seem to regard the event as an opportunity simply to be the center of attention at a fancy party, and some parents seem to consider that it is their duty to go into debt to sponsor the most opulent party possible. Father Sotelo believes that the event should be primarily a religious celebration, hence his unwillingness to give masses for girls who are not religious or obedient to church doctrine. Father Peacock, on the other hand, believes that the church should work to meet people on their own terms (12) and to help them come together to celebrate family and community in any way they choose. Students will be able to come up with many reasons for the changes that have taken place in the ceremony since its Mexican origins. Most of these reasons may have to do with the impact of Anglo culture, which could be viewed as a threat to traditional values. The new de-emphasis on the religious aspects of the event, the modern gowns the girls wear, the mix of Mexican music with rock 'n' roll (27), and the emphasis on spending extravagantly to impress others are all changes that might be put down to the negative influence of Anglo values.

3. Orlean's selection of sources is so broad that most students will have trouble thinking of other sources she might have included. She observes firsthand Azteca Plaza, the Vesta Club quinceañeras mass, and the country club party that follows. She interviews adult community members who are involved in planning quinceañeras and two priests, Father Peacock and Father Sotelo, who have very different opinions of the meaning of the quinceañera celebration. She consults Father Sotelo's guidebook (6), written for girls who want to celebrate the mass, and she watches videotapes of quinceañera masses with Father Peacock (11). There are four sources, however, she does not cite directly. She includes no library research on the origins, history, or role of quinceañeras. She

does not consult the elderly, who might have participated in earlier quinceañeras and have a better grasp of changes that have taken place, nor speak with Mexican nationals, who could comment on the ethnic significance of the celebration. And finally, she does not interview any of the sixteen girls who are taking part in the quinceañera she attends. This last omission is especially curious because the event is for them.

Connections

1. You might want to begin by asking students what constitutes a community, because the factors fostering it in "Two Kinds" are not clearly identifiable; rather, it's evident in the sense that Jing-mei and her parents care about how other members of the Joy Luck Club and the larger community view them, that they know the people in their building well enough to know the piano teacher on the first floor, or that they have community events in the church hall. In "Quinceañera," there seem to be several subcommunities within the Hispanic community, based on class and religion. The upper-class group on which the essay focuses is putting on a quinceañera party sponsored by the Vesta Club, an organization for Hispanic college graduates. This quinceañera has a more religious tone than some, as the girls have gone to Father Sotelo's required classes and retreats. Less religious and/or well-off people are more likely to have the quinceañera performed by Father Peacock, who accepts all applicants, even those who rarely set foot in a church.

2. In "Two Kinds," the performance seems to be more for the parents' benefit than for the children's — Jing-mei's mother is looking for a chance to show off her daughter to the community. Jing-mei is excited about her lace bow, frilly dress, and curtsey, but she is too young to have thought about the effect her inept playing might have. The girls celebrating their quinceañera are also excited about their outfits, but their performance is religious as well as social. Old enough to care how the community views them, they attend classes and a retreat to prepare for the mass as well as practice their waltz for the party afterward. Both events represent a chance to be the center of attention at a big social gathering. For their parents, the quinceañera is a chance to celebrate their daughters, bring their communities together, reaffirm their heritage, and relive their own youth.

3. Orlean would probably apply Percy's definition of "the diverted self" to the subjects of her essay, because she depicts them as devoted to enjoying themselves. The subjects themselves might prefer to be identified in terms of "the role-playing self," because they're dutiful daughters, or "the Christian self," because they are ostensibly participating in a religious ritual.

WINDOWS:
THE WORLD

SALMAN RUSHDIE, The Broken Mirror (p. 53)

Explorations

1. Students may be better able to explore the dual meaning of the mirror if they first consider how Rushdie compares the old black-and-white photograph of his father's

9

home with the house he sees when he visits it. His vision of his past, like the photograph, is apparently stable and fixed. When he sees the house in person, he is "assaulted by colors," and the vividness of his new vision forces him to consider how partial — how "monochromatic" — his former vision of his childhood had been (para. 2). In paragraph 6, Rushdie mentions that the narrator for his book *Midnight's Children* has a "fallible memory . . . and his vision is fragmentary." He generalizes from the narrator to expatriated Indian writers, asserting that they cannot reflect an intact vision of India because they are working with "broken mirrors, some of whose fragments have been irretrievably lost" (6). This is, however, a valuable way of viewing the past and of viewing India. Rushdie argues, in regard to his own partial memories of images from India, that "fragmentation made trivial things seem like symbols, and the mundane acquired numinous qualities" (8).

2. Reflecting on his childhood in India and his later life in the West, Rushdie believes that "it's my present that is foreign, and that the past is home" (1). Nevertheless, his Western influences affect his vision of India and his childhood. He makes reference in the first paragraph to British writer L. P. Hartley while he is exploring the idea of a foreign present and later refers to John Fowles, another British writer, on the topic of whole versus partial vision (11). He wrote *Midnight's Children* in North London, a fact that caused him to consider how his life in the West changed his vision of India (5). Western influences affect his memories of India in more direct ways as well; Rushdie recalls seeing as a child billboards and ads for Western products (7). Rushdie makes two biblical references, the first when he alludes to Lot's wife in paragraph 4 and the second in the conclusion, when he addresses the issue of Western influences directly, by calling up an image of the expatriated Indian writer as "fallen" — an image that derives from Christianity (12).

3. Although Rushdie distinguishes between the Western and Indian parts of his identity in historical terms, as when he writes that "the past is a foreign country" (1), his strongest statements about expatriate Indian writers have to do with the mix of cultures they represent: "Our identity is at once plural and partial" (12). He considers his "ambiguous and shifting" position between cultures potentially productive. Rushdie wants to reclaim his Indian past (2, 3), but he also realizes that his life in the West has given him a grounding in worldwide (particularly European) literature and a perspective on India that is unavailable to those who remained there.

Connections

1. This question should help students understand Baldwin's predicament, if they haven't already. Both writers appreciate the enlarged vision of a dual perspective, and the impossibility of escaping from one's origins. Rushdie comes from a privileged background; his family sent him to England for a superior education. When he thinks of India, his main concern is the inadequacy of his memory and the imprecision with which his writing represents his homeland. By contrast, Baldwin left the United States because he perceived it as a hostile environment for blacks, especially black writers, and believed he could only realize his own vision outside of the country. He is less concerned with accurate recall than with understanding.

2. Rushdie claims that "human beings do not perceive things whole; we are . . . capable only of fractured perceptions. Partial beings, in all the senses of that phrase" (para. 11), echoing Percy's argument that the self defies definition, most of all from itself. Although Rushdie notes that expatriates have been "forced by cultural displacement to accept the

provisional nature of all truths" (11), he describes this as having perhaps "had modernism forced upon us" (11), implying that, like Percy, he sees alienation as the modern condition.

3. Desai agrees with Rushdie that describing India is a complicated matter, but she has a different angle: whereas he doubts the fidelity of his memory, she doubts that any statement about India can hold true for its many diverse regions. She would probably agree with Rushdie that Indian writers can only look back at their country through guilt-tinted spectacles, because she also expresses frustration at her inability to represent the country precisely: "Which [fragment of India] do I claim as mine? All and none" (p. 3).

MARGARET ATWOOD, A View from Canada (p. 59)

Explorations

1. Margaret Atwood sums up her youthful view of Americans when she recalls her shock at realizing Canada "was owned by the kind of people who carried tin boats across portages and didn't burn their garbage" (para. 4). Earlier still, she sums up her attitude this way: "Americans were wimps who had a lot of money but did not know what they were doing" (1). Students may come up with a variety of examples from the text that reveal Atwood's current view of the "typical American." Atwood describes the United States as an isolationist nation (10, 11) and points out that Americans always try to take their American life-style with them when they travel internationally (12). Perhaps the most telling statement Atwood makes is that "Americans experience themselves, individually, as small toads in the biggest and most powerful puddle in the world" (13). She recognizes that Americans experience "a sense of power [that] comes from identifying with the puddle." At the same time, her image suggests that the size and power of their own country make Americans feel small and swallowed up by it. Atwood begins to indicate a problem with Canadian self-image when she comments on the lingering effects of British colonialism, for instance, the fact that British history was taught in schools in preference to Canadian history (2, 3). However, Atwood points out the positive aspects of the Canadian outlook (although with some irony) when she writes that "Canada, having somehow become an expert at compromise, was the mediator" between Britain and the United States. Canadians are far more interested in international relations than are Americans (10). According to Atwood, Canadians realize they are not isolated from the world at large (11, 12). But they also think of their country as "a small sinking *Titanic* squashed between two icebergs" (11), a comment Atwood supports with the example of the Canadian politician who said that Canada walks in the footsteps of the United States (13).

2. Students will need help identifying the subtle indications that "A View from Canada" was written as a speech: the conversational and often jocular tone, frequent use of short phrases, and departures from formal diction ("hamburgers, cokes, and rock music surrounded you" [12]) are not obtrusive. However, it is obvious in paragraph 14 that Atwood is giving a speech, and that her audience is American, when she says, "south of you you have Mexico and south of us we have you" (15).

3. Students will be able to locate many places where Atwood uses humor, but it is important to point out that Atwood's humor can be ironic, with a serious and often barbed comment buried in it. The vision, in the first paragraph, of American ineptitude

exemplified in Atwood's portrait of Americans portaging a metal boat ("Typically American, we thought, as they ricocheted off yet another tree") offers not only a view of Americans as slapstick incompetents but also suggests that Canadians underestimated the ability of Americans to colonize Canada with money and cultural influence. Atwood recalls the sharp-edged humor of her first example in paragraph 4, when she says Canadians woke up in the sixties to realize their country was owned by incompetents. Lighter uses of humor include Atwood's wry comments on her own history: "I know it's hard to believe in view of my youthful appearance, but when I was a child there was no television" (5); "By this time I wanted to be a writer, and you can see it would be a dilemma . . . how could one be a writer and somehow manage to avoid having to become British and dead?" (7).

Connections

1. At some points in the essay, Atwood seems to take pride in her compatriots' cosmopolitanism and flexibility — Canadian newspapers cover international news, and, when Canadians live in India, they eat Indian food. But she also complains about the Canada of her youth, where British literature and history were learned at school and American comic books and pop music were imbibed after school; she believes present day Canada is "always comparing itself to the wrong thing" (para. 13). Atwood believes that Canadians' tendency to compare themselves to the United States hinders their capacity to appreciate what a "peaceful, happy, and prosperous" country they inhabit.

2. Atwood attended schools that were "bastions of the British Empire" (2), and Desai went to a British school; hence, both grew up learning British culture at school and another culture — American or Indian — outside of school.

3. No. Whereas Rayner and Reed emphasize Americans' diversity, Atwood describes them as non-Canadian buffoons who don't know how to behave in the woods, who try to take their comforts wherever they go, and who show little interest in international news. This question might launch a good discussion about how the United States and its citizens are generally viewed by outsiders and how misconceptions about Americans arise.

GERMAINE GREER, One Man's Mutilation Is Another Man's Beautification (p. 65)

Explorations

1. According to Greer, societies tend to admire characteristics that are "well-distributed among their people, because distance from the culturally recognized norm causes suffering" (para. 15). However, mutilation can serve several functions other than allowing a person to conform to the norm; in Western cultures, women wear heels, lipstick, nail polish, and bras to express the idea that women's principle pursuits are sexual attraction and vicarious leisure. In many societies, bodies are modified as part of a rite of passage: Puberty may be marked by circumcision, scarification, or the adoption of a new hairstyle. Underscoring much of Greer's discussion is the point that bodily modification signifies one's role in the culture; tattooed, pierced teens express their sense of alienation rather than their place in the social order.

2. Greer's style is more formal and academic than most fashion writing, and at the same time, witty and sarcastic. She turns a sharp eye on her subjects, questioning their motives

and supplying her own often unflattering explanations for their efforts at beauty. Whereas typical fashion writers express admiration for their subjects, never questioning the worth of their efforts, Greer questions her subjects' every gesture. The effect is to make all humans' efforts to beautify themselves seem arbitrary and somewhat foolish. Because Greer's tone is so distinct, a good exercise would be to have students rewrite a paragraph in a neutral voice.

3. It shouldn't be hard for students to find places where Greer draws her own conclusions about the goal or motive behind a group's behavior, because she does this throughout the essay. For instance, when she claims that "the rejection of traditional modes of hair management has less to do with convenience and common sense than with the desire to break out of the confinement of the group" (3), she ignores a number of quite sensible explanations for having an unconventional hairstyle. Or, her insistence that a man who shaves his head is "flaunting a violence he has done to himself" (6) seems exceedingly harsh. When discussing those who visit hairdressers or tattooists, she explains they "have come to the professionals after long and lonely contemplation of the self which dissatisfies them" (20): How could she know? Opinionated as she is, Greer makes a powerful argument here; you might ask students to describe how she uses evidence to prove her claims.

Connections

1. You might engage students with this question by asking what they believe the less conventional dressers on campus are trying to communicate to the world. According to Greer, teenagers come to their parents' dinner parties covered with blue spots because they want to assert their deviance from their parents' habits and beliefs. In contrast, the girls in Orlean's essay want to please their parents (or at least to avoid alienating them), because their parents are throwing a huge, expensive party in their honor. Yet the girls assert their individuality by choosing dresses in a variety of styles.

2. Conway uses the phrase "inner landscape of the mind" (p. 7) when discussing how farmers in Coorain tended to focus more on the occasional droughts than the many fertile seasons, because the droughts made such an impression on them. Likewise, Greer sees her subjects as incapable of thinking independently of their culture. Hence, it used to be the family or clan that determined one's social role, but now it is "consumer behaviour, employment status, income, and possessions" (para. 10). Our "inner landscape" is crowded with billboards of models in expensive clothes and laboriously applied makeup, trying to make us feel something is lacking in our own presentation.

3. Both writers observe the degree to which people will undergo painful machinations to achieve a certain look, whether they are black women straightening their hair with a burning hot comb or middle-aged women with polished nails and high heels. You might ask students if they believe Greer's argument is limited to a particular race or class when she discusses contemporary practices. Early's angle is a lot more positive than Greer's. Greer describes the women's activities as a kind of self-torture, like a lonely bird pecking off its own leg, whereas Early sees the hair straightening as a female bonding ritual, one of the mysteries of women he'll never understand.

PAUL HARRISON, The Westernization of the World (p. 76)

Explorations

1. The "European road" Harrison mentions is characterized by a worship of technology (especially military), a preoccupation with highways and large buildings, an infatuation with Western dress, and a rejection of traditional culture (note the opening anecdote). His examples, ranging from the bank manager's television (para. 4) to the Ivory Coast's four-lane highway going nowhere and Jakarta's "neo-fascist monuments" (12), are all traceable to a desire to impress others in the Third World with one's own successful adoption of Western ways.

2. That the general cause of the Third World's Westernization is European colonization should be readily apparent to all students. But recognizing the three specific channels through which Westernization was realized will take careful reading. Some students may point immediately to the political, economic, and cultural imperialism mentioned in paragraph 8, failing to realize that the article doesn't discuss political and economic factors. Cultural imperialism itself is the subject of the selection, and the channels are identified in paragraphs 9, 10, and 11 as the "indoctrination [by the colonial powers] of an elite of local collaborators"; the existence in the native population of "reference-group behavior," or imitation of the behavior of the elite group; and the practice of racial humiliation "deriving from the arrogance and haughtiness of the colonialists." Harrison cites self-righteous Pauline Christianity, cultural arrogance, racial prejudice, and the possession of power as the critical factors in the colonialist attitude and a total lack of the same among the natives as the reasons for the success of Westernization. The natives had no sense of their own value with which to fend off the assault of European influence.

3. Harrison cites "consciousness of Western military superiority" (14) as the primary force behind Westernization of noncolonial nations. The overwhelming desire to compete militarily with the European powers resulted in far-reaching social, economic, and political changes in these societies. Also important, according to Harrison, is the pervading racial prejudice of the West, leading some of the "Young Turks" who gained power in the noncolonial societies to further emulate European culture. Now that they've cast their lot with the West, a return to their own traditions would be extremely difficult. His observation that "contact with Europe shook nations to the foundations, calling into question the roots of their civilizations and all the assumptions and institutions on which their lives were based" (14) makes it quite clear that there is no turning back once Western culture has been embraced. Students may also point out his observation on the cultural price Japan has paid to become one of the leading industrial nations (16).

Connections

1. Greer's essay is filled with examples of conformist behavior, but students may confuse this with reference-group behavior, so you might want to make sure they understand Harrison's use of this sociological concept before proceeding with the question. The following examples of reference-group behavior appear in Greer's essay: women all over the world have adopted Western conventions such as high heels, lipstick, nail polish, and bras; aging women dye their hair or have plastic surgery in hopes of looking younger in a culture where old means obsolete; teenagers dye their hair, pierce their bodies, and terrorize people with "raucous music and insulting doggerel" (p. 73). With respect to Atwood, students may initially assume that as a Canadian she identified with the United States and wanted to adopt its culture; this is clearly not the case (aside from

her minor interest in comic books from the United States), because her pride in her Canadian heritage and identity is obvious throughout the essay. She does note, however, that this heritage and identity have English roots, as did her early literary aspirations. She also mentions the Canadians who spent time in India where the Canadians, who "are good at fitting in, partly because they can't afford to do otherwise" (p. 63), adopted Indian customs and learned about India. In contrast, visitors from the United States reject reference-group behavior: "if they can't stay in America they take it with them" (p. 63).

2. Students should note that Harrison is discussing India's new officer corps (para. 13) and other elites, whereas Rushdie and Desai are discussing the India of their childhoods, not a phase of life when one is usually class conscious. Rushdie describes memories of conversations and streets and billboards, whereas Desai depicts the diversity of languages she grew up with — German, Hindi, and English. Yet both writers' pieces reveal the British colonial influence: Rushdie attended an elite British-style private school until he left India to continue school in England; he seems soaked in British culture. Desai went to a school run by British missionaries, so English became her literary language.

3. Harrison claims that the Dutch and the Iberians were free of racial prejudice and mixed with the native women they colonized. Vargas Llosa would probably differ on some points but not on all: he argues that present-day Westernized Latin Americans are "behaving toward the Indians during the nineteenth and twentieth centuries as the Spaniards behaved toward the Aztecs and the Incas, and sometimes even worse" (p. 5). Although Vargas Llosa gives the impression that the colonizers mistreated the natives, he also points out that the Indians were systematically exterminated, not during the colony, but during the republic.

SPOTLIGHT:
MEXICO

ADDITIONAL INFORMATION ON COUNTRY

Environment: Located in the southernmost portion of North America, Mexico is mostly mountainous. Its ranges include the Eastern Sierra Madre on the Gulf of Mexico, the southern Sierra Madre, the Sierra Neovolcanica Transversal in the central part of the country, and the Western Sierra Madre on the Pacific side. Mexico's climate ranges from tropical rainy conditions in the southeast to arid desert in the north to a mild climate in the central plateau, where most of the population lives. Such climatic diversity gives Mexico a great variety of vegetation, including rainforests in the southeastern zone and temperate forests on the slopes of the Sierra Neovolcanica, both important economic centers.

Demographics: Resulting from the cultural and ethnic integration between native Indian groups and Spanish colonizers, Mexico's 88 million people are currently 60 percent mestizo (a mixture of Indian and European), 30 percent Amerindian, 9 percent white, and 1 percent other. Additionally, approximately 7 million Mexicans live in the south of the United States.

Religion: Mexico has no official religion, but almost 90 percent of the population is Roman Catholic. About 5 percent is Protestant, and their numbers are growing, particularly among the evangelical sects.

Education: Literacy is 90 percent for males, 85 percent for females. Nearly 100 percent of Mexicans attend primary school, about 56 percent attend secondary school, and about 1.5 percent attend college.

The Day of the Dead, described in Paz's essay, can be traced to the festivities held during the Aztec month of Miccailhuitontli, ritually presided over by the goddess Mictecacihuatl (Lady of the Dead) and dedicated to children and the dead. Originally, the holiday fell at the end of July, but in the postconquest era it was moved by Spanish priests so that it coincided with the Christian holiday of All Hallows Eve at the beginning of November in a vain effort to transform it from a pagan to a Christian celebration.

To celebrate this holiday, families visit the graves of their close kin, decorate them with flowers, and have a picnic. Families remember the departed by telling stories about them. But the occasion is far from morbid: because of the warm social environment, the colorful setting, and the abundance of food, drink, and good company, this celebration of the living and dead represents an important social ritual for recognizing the cycle of life and death that is human existence.

The Day of the Dead can range from a family supper with special bread and skeleton-shaped cookies, to an important cultural event with definite social and economic responsibilities for participants, to a religious observance featuring actual worship of the dead. In general, the more urban the locale, the less religious and cultural importance is attached to the holiday, whereas the more rural and Indian the locality, the greater its significance.

OCTAVIO PAZ, The Art of the Fiesta (p. 86)

Explorations

1. Mexico has nationwide fiestas honoring saints or military anniversaries; individual cities and villages have fiestas for their particular saints or occasions, often financed by the federal government; even neighborhoods and trades have annual fiestas, ceremonies, and fairs. According to Paz, the fiesta's *raison d'être* matters little; rather, Mexicans are hungry for opportunities to "open out," to whistle, shout, sing, talk loudly, get drunk, shoot off fireworks, and discharge their pistols and their souls into the air (para. 5). Paz makes the fiesta sound like an emotional escape valve for a people who are generally withdrawn and impassive. In an economic sense, the fiesta functions as a gift or an offering. Although its economic returns are not traceable, "waste attracts or promotes wealth," because "when life is thrown away it increases," according to some French sociologists (6). You might ask students how Paz's discussion of the fiesta's economic component might explain why Father Peacock in Susan Orlean's essay said he would rather see poor people spend money on quinceañeras than on material goods.

2. Other paradoxes surrounding the fiesta include the remark made by the mayor of a small village that meant "our poverty can be measured by the frequency and luxuriousness of our holidays" (4); that friends who have barely spoken get drunk and weep together (5); that license rules: "men disguise themselves as women, gentlemen as slaves, the poor as the rich" (8). The fiesta is both joyous and sorrowful, an occasion for tears as well as laughter. Paz believes the fiesta's many paradoxes derive from one essential to the Mexican temperament: "We are not frank, but our sincerity can reach extremes that horrify a European" (14).

16

3.   Freshman college students are notorious for being mild-mannered creatures by weekday and bacchanalian revelers by weekend night, so they shouldn't have trouble with the first part of the question. But they may have a harder time explaining how U.S. festivals differ from Mexican ones. You might ask to what extent a festival's social role depends on the coherence of the community celebrating it. That is, what is the difference between Mardi Gras and a saint's day in a country where everyone is Catholic? To what extent does a group's homogeneity contribute to the importance of its festivals? Is there the same need for a means to cut loose in a culture that already places so much emphasis on individual freedom?

Connections

1.   Paz does not regard the Mexican fiesta as having been Westernized in the ways Paul Harrison describes. Paz asserts that "the art of the fiesta has been debased almost everywhere else, but not in Mexico" (para. 1), later explaining that Mexicans' poverty "can be measured by the frequency and luxuriousness of our holidays" (4). Whereas citizens in wealthier Western countries prefer to gather in small groups, even on great occasions, "they never form a living community in which the individual is at once dissolved and redeemed" (4). Fiestas "replace, and are perhaps better than, the theater and vacations, Anglo-Saxon weekends and cocktail parties, the bourgeois reception, the Mediterranean cafe" (4).

2.   In the final paragraph of his essay, Baldwin explains how Europe liberated artists from the need to secure public approval, a process that "puts a premium on mediocrity and has all but slaughtered any concept of excellence" (26). With no escape valve within the culture, artists must leave for a place where they can find their own visions. Paz's revelers needn't travel, because their escape route is built into their culture.

3.   Both Paz and Guillermoprieto observe that Mexicans love to weep at parties and that they have a special relationship with death. But they appear to differ regarding the extent to which Mexicans have responded to Western influences. According to Guillermoprieto, Mexicans live much like other Westerners — "hardly anyone knows anymore what it is to live on a ranch or to die of passion" — and *ranchera* music is one of the few outlets Mexicans have to become their essentially mournful selves (p. 8). Because Paz does not believe Mexicans have lost their intimate connection with death, he would probably see *ranchera* music as one more emotional escape valve, along with fiestas and wakes.

ELENA GARRO, The Day We Were Dogs (p. 93)

Explorations

1.   Students are likely to find this story difficult, but starting with these basic questions should help them get oriented. You might want to trace the story's plot on the board, getting students to supply the details. The narrator, Leli, is probably between six and ten years old; she is Eva's sister (they live in the same house, sleep in the same room); she believes everything she has been told about heaven (people go to either a blue and white [Christian] one or a yellow and orange [Buddhist] one, but dogs can go to neither); the sisters have blond hair; the neighbors say of their family, "they are Spaniards"; their family has gone to Mexico City for the day to escape the heat; the girls

have remained home with the servants. The narrator does not make a point of giving readers background information; rather, the information emerges as she remembers the events of the day, and readers are challenged to construct a coherent plot for themselves.

2. Christ and Buddha are familiar figures to the girls, insofar as their images hang over the girls' beds, and the girls know they don't allow dogs into heaven or Nirvana. Hence, if it is important in their house to be good so they can go to heaven, then becoming dogs named Buddha and Christ allows them to be outlaws and kings simultaneously. More common dog names would not have helped to illustrate the sense of impotence the girls feel when their family is away.

3. Students may find this question difficult, so you might break it down into smaller questions: What is the heaven of dogs? It's the day the girls spend as dogs named Buddha and Christ. What is the heaven of men? Eva and Leli had thought it was a place where you were rewarded for being good, but seeing the dead men with the fly buzzing around their wounds shows them the harsh reality of death. Whereas the heaven of dogs was something they could create for themselves, the heaven of men is one of "immobile dead men, in the immobile afternoon, with the enormous fly peering into the enormous wound" (para. 50).

Connections

1. The girls' immediate response to the killing is to sit at the edge of the sidewalk and look at the men with wide eyes and open mouths. Later, they still sit by the curb, "neither moving nor barking" (para. 40). But when they wake in the night and realize that the dead men are in the room with them, they're frightened: "the walls were breathing burning coals; through the cracks the witches lurked, watching the blue veins of their temples. . . . Very far away, at the back of the garden, slept the servants" (50). Paz might explain the girls' immediate reaction thus: "the somber Mexican, closed up in himself, suddenly explodes, tears open his breast and reveals himself" (p. 91) when the appropriate moment arises. Paz is discussing how Mexicans respond to a fiesta, but his words might also describe Mexicans' response to death. On the one hand, "the Mexican . . . is familiar with death. . . ." True, there is perhaps as much fear in his attitude as in that of others, but at least death is not hidden away: he looks at it "face to face." Yet, the way the girls try to distance themselves from the death, creating a separate day for the activities of everyone else at the house, might be explained by Paz's remark that, though Mexicans' relations with death are intimate, they are empty of meaning.

2. This is a difficult question; you will get many different answers to it depending on your students' experiences with violence. You might ask if the girls' reaction is similar to the way girls from the United States would react. They don't fear the fighting men. In a U.S. story, the murder might be described more explicitly. And the forthright admission of guilt — "You killed him?" "I sure did . . ." (32, 33) — doesn't seem characteristic of a murder in the United States. According to Paz, the scene is typically Mexican because the girls are fascinated by the fighting men yet somehow indifferent to their struggle; once Rutilio has been led away and the other man left for dead, the girls still sit watching.

3. The most "fractured perception" in the story is the girls' sense that they inhabit one day and everyone else inhabits another parallel day. Being dogs for a day seems to fall within the realm of child's play, but seeing everyone else as inhabiting a different day seems more like a reaction to trauma. As people with post-traumatic stress disorder must sort among different selves they once created so as to escape the trauma, the girls

create such alternate selves ("fracture their perception") to protect themselves from the horrifying day the adults inhabit.

CARLOS FUENTES, The Two Americas (p. 100)

Explorations

1. The arrival of Mr. Nomura represents a kind of Fall for Antilia, so the two Americas might be the prelapsarian paradise with its abundant flora and fauna, its native people who lack concepts of time, work, and property; and the postlapsarian realm of highways and fast food restaurants, tourists, schedules, and security guards.

2. The narrator has created a variety of identities, depending on his audience, but he seemingly levels with the reader, claiming to be "a Sephardic Jew whose family fled Spain because of the usual persecutions" (para. 40). Fuentes's Christopher Columbus is flawed by a need for recognition that outweighs his instinct to preserve the paradise he's found. Alhough he broadcasts his discovery via a note in a bottle, he sounds more genuine when describing the beauty of the island and the rancor of European cities than when describing his hope for fame. And he almost comes to grasp his mistake: When his note brings a planeload of Japanese businessmen, he can't help but see the destruction that has resulted from his petty desire for recognition. Lest we miss the point that one explorer can launch several centuries of environmental destruction, the narrator sees in the course of his lifetime how his mission has born fruit.

3. The narrator's many allusions to oranges begin with his description of planting seeds in his newfound paradise, where they grow better than they had in Andalusia. They create a garden of perfectly "suckable, edible, renewable" (38) breasts, befitting the prelapsarian Antilia, an Eden of nakedness and unawareness (27). As a bearded white god, the narrator has an orange for a scepter, which he deems a breast that is always available, like those of the wet nurses he loved as a child. Following this allusion is a description of the idyllic landscape, forging the connection between land and nourishment. The destruction the Japanese bring culminates in flame throwers' burning his orange grove, but he takes seeds back to Spain with him, wanting "this fruit to survive the implacable exploitation of the island" (82). He also invokes Spain as a mother who once exiled him from her breast, making the connection between land and mother as he has made the connection throughout between orange and breast.

Connections

1. In "The Day We Were Dogs," Eva and Leli pretend to be dogs inhabiting a separate day so as to distance themselves from the scary world of adults, especially after the murder. Likewise, Christopher Columbus invents a new identity for himself everywhere he goes, tailoring it to the character of the local population, because his family was persecuted for being Jews. In both stories, the narrators learn that they can't really hide: the girls' separate day melds with the adults' day and Columbus fails to "act like a member of the team" (79) and returns to Spain to die.

2. Cortázar describes how Latin American writers once bemoaned their lack of a literary heritage but have recently come to see this lack as a freedom to draw from whatever traditions they choose, inventing new ones. So, if the natives believe that Christopher

Columbus is a god, he can conveniently go along with that because there are no Europeans around to impose a different story. But Fuentes is also concerned about Europeans' ignorance of other histories:

> How could Europe understand that there is a history different from the one it made or learned? A second history? How will Europeans accept that the present is not only the heir of the past but the origin of the future? What a hideous responsibility. No one could stand it. Especially me. (39)

As colonizer, the narrator must accept responsibility for the way he shapes Antilia's history, easy as it might be to accept the natives's naive version.

3. Vargas Llosa claims that two of Latin Americans' worst defects are their belief that their miseries have been imposed on them from abroad and their reluctance to see how contemporary Latin Americans have done far worse by the Indians than the original colonizers had. Fuentes's narrator mixes with the locals, remaining innocuous except for his note in a bottle. Like Vargas Llosa's contemporaries, it is the Japanese colonizers who enslave the Indians, hypocritically wondering whether to call their employees "'aborigines,' 'natives,' 'indigenous peoples,' 'Antilleans'? [because they] wouldn't want to hurt anyone's feelings" (66). Here, Fuentes mocks political correctness, the idea that those in power can absolve themselves if they simply use the right terminology.

RICHARD RODRIGUEZ, Mexico's Children (p. 118)

Explorations

1. When Rodriguez says Mexicans "commute between the past and the future" (para. 1), he means that they move back and forth between Mexico and the United States. Mexico represents the past because "things [there] are not necessarily different from when your father was your age" (32); "pulpy," "grave," "sandstone" Mexico "takes the impression of time, [whereas] the United States and its promise of the future must seem always hypothetical — occasion more than place" (30). The United States represents the future, because it is a place where all ties to the past can be erased, as when the waitress wipes away the existence of the last diner's meal and says, "you can order anything you want" (53–56).

2. Rodriguez is referring to the risk that Mexicans will forget their heritage, their families, their connections to their past; they may believe they are just heading north to get a job, but "the American job will introduce the Mexican to an industry, an optimism, a solitude nowhere described in Mexico's theology" (33). Becoming acquainted with a new value system represents a risk to the soul, especially if the value system places achieving economic success above maintaining family ties.

3. The pronoun *tú* is used as an intimate address, "the condition, not so much of knowing, as of being known; of being recognized. *Tú* belongs within the family" (50). By contrast, *usted* is used as a formal address: "spoken to the eyes of strangers. By servants to masters. *Usted* shows deference to propriety, to authority, to history" (51). According to Rodriguez, "in Mexico, one is most oneself in private" (52), and the *tú* form is for the space where one is with one's intimates. In America, one is most "at home" in

public, going out into the world as an *usted* and encountering new people, leaving the family behind.

Connections

1. Rodriguez depicts the United States and Fuentes depicts the modern world as places bent on embracing the future and forgetting the past. As the former uses the waitress at a roadside diner as a metaphor for this tendency, the latter describes the motels, pizzerias, and gas stations tourists will need in this new paradise; in both cases, the inhabitants are people on the move, treating their locale as, in Rodriguez's words, "occasion more than place" (30). The qualities of the ancient Antilia depicted by Fuentes that also appear in Rodriguez's contemporary Mexico include a reverence for Mother, whether the orange/breast of Spain in the former's case, or the country, the landscape, the Virgin of Guadalupe, or the actual mother in the latter's case. Rodriguez's Mexico seems to straddle the "two Americas" depicted by Fuentes: those who have never left live according to centuries' old traditions, but those who have been to the United States or have been exposed to too much U.S. culture through contact with television, movies, or people who have been there are likely to dream of forsaking Mexico for the supposed progress America represents.

2. Both Rodriguez and Atwood seem to believe their countries need to resist the power of the United States: Canadians feel politically as if they walk "in the footsteps of the giant" (p. 63), and Rodriguez notes how Mexican teenagers cross the border to make some dollars and end up feeling like they belong more in the United States than in their homeland. The main differences between the two writers' views are that, according to Atwood, Canadians resent Americans because they lack an international perspective, but Canada's culture is not particularly threatened by American influences, at least not in the way that Rodriguez's Mexico is by the promise of jobs that might sever her people from their past.

3. Rodriguez describes Mexican emigration as stemming from the innocent wish to earn a little money to support the folks at home, but Baldwin claims he had to leave because the United States was a hostile atmosphere for artists, especially black artists. Rodriguez does appear to regard Mexican kids who seek work in the United States to be in danger of becoming culturally lost, but not in the same sense that Baldwin describes his despairing contemporaries. Rodriguez's teenagers are losing their Mexican identities, but Baldwin's veterans and artists seem to be losing their minds. Jews who had seen concentration camps, men who had homosexual adventures in CO camps and couldn't face themselves later, women who had affairs and got pregnant while their husbands were in the service: for these people, Europe was not a place to make a living but a place to vanish.

MEXICO: INVESTIGATIONS/WEB SITES

LatinoLink (www.latinolink.com/index/html) provides news, analysis, commentary, and photo essays that explore the joys and challenges faced by those who call the United States home yet trace their roots to the Spanish-speaking Americas. It presents stories about Latinos and the political and social issues that affect them: immigration, bilingual education, affirmative action, life in the inner city, and life in the corporate boardroom.

Things Latino-Cyber-Raza (http://edb518ea.edb.utexas.edu/html/latinos.html) offers many links to Latino-related sites.

The Latino Connection (www.webspace.com/~pedro/index.html) is designed to simplify the search for information on Latino/Hispanic countries. The layout consists of individual country pages with links to country information, government, history and culture, travel and tourism, arts and entertainment, cuisine, higher education, and other related Web pages.

Mexico's Index (http://www.trace-sc.com/) provides a comprehensive list of Latino-related Web sites, with links to information about Hispanic countries.

LatinoWeb (http://www.latinoweb.com/favision/) is another listing service. The resources it lists are divided into categories such as business, government, nonprofits, art, music, education, and history.

ADDITIONAL QUESTIONS AND ASSIGNMENTS

1. In a journal entry or a collection of informal notes, discuss what it means to you to be an American citizen. How responsible are you for the decisions and actions of the U.S. government? How has reading about foreigners' perspectives on the United States in this chapter affected your view of this country? Give specific examples.

2. Interview someone who has come to the United States from another country, preferably a non-Western one. As you gather information, focus on the individual's response to our concepts of government, individual freedom, and rights and responsibilities, as well as the individual's perception of our culture as compared with his or her own. As you write an account of the interview, try to intersperse your own observations on the cultural differences with those of your subject.

3. Write a newspaper column in which you describe your reaction on finding yourself in the midst of a different culture. Even if you've never visited another country, you may recall different customs in other parts of the United States, in the city or the country, in a large university or a small college, or even in the home of a different family. Pick a specific incident and describe it, and then analyze the reasons you had trouble adjusting to the different environment.

4. Several writers in this section use memories of an earlier stage in their lives as material for an essay or a story (Baldwin, Tan, Rushdie, Atwood, Rodriguez). Take a close look at how these essays use this material and write an argumentative essay about some aspect of your cultural identity, using personal anecdotes to illustrate your points. Although your experiences will be different from the people included in this book, you may wish to include quotations from the essays you have read to illustrate the way environment shapes cultural identity.

5. Conduct further research into one of the cultures represented in this section, focusing specifically on its perception of Western culture. If the selection is an excerpt from a larger work, look first at that work. You can find more information about the culture by consulting a general encyclopedia, a journal devoted to the study of that culture, and the Internet. Narrow your topic to something manageable, such as Western influence on that culture's sex roles, educational system, or economy, or views of Western philosophy or rejection of that influence. Then write an expository essay in which you describe that culture's encounters with and reactions to Western influence.

Part Two

FAMILIES

INTRODUCTION

The selections in this section provide insight into a wide spectrum of families, varying from the Kibbutz "family" depicted by Amos Oz to Henry Louis Gates's lively multigenerational extended family in West Virginia to Kazuo Ishiguro's disintegrating family of three. None of these families fits the model of TV sitcoms, so you might start by asking the class what typifies an American family and to what extent your students' own families are representative.

Students can use their writing about family experiences as the foundation for discussion of selections within the section. If the students highlight first the differences and then the similarities among their own accounts, they will be better prepared to deal with the various images of family life awaiting them in their reading. The method might be extended to the readings themselves. Students will be confident in their ability to locate differences in family life between these cultures and their own, but they may be surprised at how quickly they compile a list of similarities. From the irritation of Amos Oz's young soldier with his mother, to Frank McCourt's finding ways to amuse himself despite his family's poverty and hard luck, students will find many points of convergence.

There are a number of possible ways to group the selections. Among the topics explored are methods of child rearing (Erdrich, Menchú, Cheever, Gates, McCourt, Filipovic, and Tanaka), the role of the family in promoting cultural values (Oz, Gates, Morley, Ishiguro, and Menchú), the concept of extended family (Oz, Gates, Menchú, and Morley), and the various relationships among family members (all selections).

Instructors may wish to consult the following familiar works in preparing related selections from *Making Contact.*

Essays

Laura Cunningham, "The Girls' Room" (*New York Times*, September 10, 1981; *Sleeping Arrangements*, Knopf, 1989).
Joan Didion, "On Going Home" (*Slouching Towards Bethlehem*, Farrar, Straus, 1968).
Jane Howard, "Families" (*Families*, Simon and Schuster, 1978).
Maxine Hong Kingston, "No Name Woman" (*The Woman Warrior*, Knopf, 1976).
Adrienne Rich, "The Anger of a Child" (*Of Woman Born*, Norton, 1976).
Richard Rodriguez, "Aria" (*American Scholar*, Winter 1981; *Hunger of Memory*, David R. Godine, 1982).
Arlene Skolnick, "The Paradox of Perfection" (*Wilson Quarterly*, Summer 1980).
Alice Walker, "In Search of Our Mothers' Gardens" (*In Search of Our Mothers' Gardens*, Harcourt, 1983).

E. B. White, "Once More to the Lake" (1941; *Essays of E. B. White*, Harpers, 1977).
John Edgar Wideman, "Our Time" (*Brothers and Keepers*, Henry Holt, 1984).

Short Stories

Rick De Marinis, "Gent" (*Best American Short Stories 1984*, ed. John Updike, Houghton
    Mifflin, 1984).
Andre Dubus, "A Father's Story" (*Selected Stories of Andre Dubus*, David R. Godine, 1988).
William Faulkner, "The Bear" (*Go Down, Moses*, Random House, 1942).
D. H. Lawrence, "A Rocking Horse Winner" (*Complete Short Stories*, Vol. 3, Penguin, 1962).
Flannery O'Connor, "Everything That Rises Must Converge" (*Complete Stories*, Farrar, Straus, 1971).
Frank O'Connor, "My Oedipus Complex" (*Collected Stories*, Knopf, 1981).
Tillie Olsen, "I Stand Here Ironing" (*Tell Me A Riddle*, Delacorte, 1961).
John Updike, "Still of Some Use" (*Trust Me*, Knopf, 1987).

BIOGRAPHICAL NOTES ON EPIGRAPH AUTHORS

1.   A contributing writer for many magazines, Francine du Plessix Gray has authored
nonfiction books on Catholic radicalism, Hawaii, and Soviet women and a novel, *Lovers
and Tyrants.*

2.   Born in South Korea, Chang-Rae Lee immigrated to the United States with his family at
age three. He received his M.F.A. degree from the University of Oregon, where he is
currently an assistant professor of creative writing. His novel *Native Speaker* won the
1996 Ernest Hemingway Foundation/PEN Award for First Fiction.

3.   Frances Rose Besmer writes for *Mount Holyoke Alumnae Quarterly* and other
publications.

4.   Patricia Schroeder, an attorney, was a member of the House of Representatives for
Colorado from 1972 to 1996, serving as the Chair of the Select Committee on Children,
Youth, and Families in her final years there.

5.   Angela Davis, a professor at San Francisco State University, has long been an activist
on behalf of the African-American community. She is the author of *If They Come in the
Morning: Voices of Resistance* (1971), *Women, Race, and Class* (1983), *Violence Against
Women and the Ongoing Challenge to Racism* (1987), *Angela Davis: An Autobiography*
(1988), and *Women, Culture, and Politics* (1989).

6.   Anwar El-Sadat (1918–1981), Egyptian military leader and president (1970–1981), is best
remembered for his work toward peace in the Middle East, in the course of which he
became the first Arab leader to recognize Israel.

7.   Philip Roth has written numerous works of fiction, including *Goodbye Columbus* (1959);
Portnoy's Complaint (1969); a series of novels featuring one character, Nathan
Zuckerman; and several postmodern (auto) biographies. He has won several awards,
including the National Book Award (twice), the National Book Critics Circle Award
(twice), and the PEN/Faulkner Award.

8.   A popular television commentator, regular columnist for the *Los Angeles Times*, and
president of the Women's Coalition, Susan C. McMillan is active in the SHE LIST (Shaping

Elections: Life Issues Support Team), a vehicle for giving a voice to pro-life, pro-family, pro-woman candidates.

9. Paula Fomby writes for *Mother Jones*, among other publications.

10. Judith Ortiz Cofer is a professor of English at the University of Georgia and the author of *The Line of the Sun* and *Silent Dancing*.

11. Robert Bly is a storyteller, translator, worldwide lecturer, and winner of a National Book Award for poetry. Two key themes in his best-selling book *Iron John* are the need to recover forms of initiation for contemporary males and the need of younger men for mentors.

12. Ved Mehta is the author of more than a dozen books of autobiography; Indian social and political history; and interviews with international historians, philosophers, and theologians. He is currently a writer for *The New Yorker* magazine and holds the Rosenkranz Chair in Writing at Yale University.

13. Norimitsu Onishi writes for the *New York Times*.

Explorations

1. In the popular media, "the breakdown of the family" usually signifies that the two-parent nuclear family is becoming less common; it may be used as a political catch phrase to hint darkly at the economic and social threat posed by fatherless families dependent on welfare. The commentators here give several reasons for the breakdown of the family. Francine du Plessix Gray cites the fact that families no longer sit down to dinner together. Pat Schroeder believes that current economic realities force women to work, if they want their children to have what they had. Susan C. McMillan sees gay marriages as "robbing a child of a two-gender upbringing," hence foiling the traditional family. And according to Norimitsu Onishi, Japanese Americans are marrying non-Japanese people because, after they were released from internment camps, Japanese Americans were encouraged by the U.S. government to disperse. Although these writers do not actually characterize the situation as "dangerous," they do use some alarming language: Plessix Gray argues that the family meal is "a set of protocols that curb our natural savagery and our animal greed" and Schroeder believes that the United States offers greater financial support for raising dogs than raising children. These writers sound so worried because they perceive the family to be the basic social glue. Without it, how can children learn their culture's rules, expectations, and benefits?

2. Several writers excerpted here suggest that the two-parent nuclear family is not necessarily the best for raising children. Frances Rose Besmer argues that a foster family provides a more nurturing atmosphere than a family where the parents are drug-addicted or incompetent. Angela Davis claims the traditional African-American system of raising children in extended families has "often been much healthier for the child and has functioned as a child care system available to working parents." Paula Fomby has nothing against the traditional nuclear family, but she wants society to acknowledge that it is becoming increasingly atypical, and she wants to broaden the definition of family to include gay families. According to Robert Bly, the main flaw of the nuclear family is that it lacks a mechanism to allow old men to help a boy break the tie with his parents without harming himself; Bly wants old men to initiate younger ones into the "ancient, mythologized, instinctive male world."

3. Unless you want to get into a heated discussion about the Middle East conflict, you should encourage students to look closely at the texts for this question. Anwar El-Sadat describes a childhood in which he derived his identity from the land; working it collectively made him feel as if he were part of it, a notion reinforced by his grandmother. Although Philip Roth's comment does not address his connection to the land directly, it's not hard to extrapolate from his view that the Jewish family is "an inviolate haven" from external hostilities to the idea that Israel, the land God chose for his chosen people, is a haven to be cherished.

4. The induction rituals described by Cofer and Bly differ primarily in regard to how the young are inducted — casually in the first case and formally in the second. In Cofer's ritual, the women gather to tell stories for the daughters to overhear, and there is no formal process by which the young are included. But in the Hopi ritual, the boy lives in an all-male area of the kiva for six weeks and does not see his mother for a year and a half; it's much more deliberate. Both rituals allow the knowledge of the older generation to be passed onto the young, helping to shape young identities.

MIRRORS:
THE UNITED STATES

LOUISE ERDRICH, Foreword (p. 137)

Explorations

1. For Louise Erdrich, the hardest part of mothering Adam seems to be the day-to-day logistical and emotional demands of caring for a child who has Fetal Alcohol Syndrome. She mentions this problem early on (paras. 5, 6), but its full impact becomes most clear when Erdrich relates her conflict with Adam over his refusal to eat dinner (10–37). Nevertheless, Erdrich appreciates the rewards of mothering Adam, including the ease with which he initially accepted her as his mother (9). But the deeper rewards have to do with gaining self-knowledge. Erdrich writes, "In the years I've spent with Adam, I have learned more about my limits than I ever wanted to know," but the pain of that knowledge is offset by the "bond of absolute simplicity, love" that has developed between her and Adam (40).

2. Most students will understand the poignancy of Erdrich's statement that a day when Adam has a seizure is "no special day" in her family. Erdrich's attitude is one of patience and resignation. Her calm, nurturing treatment of Adam after he falls shows first how much she cares, but it also shows how common this event is. The grand mal seizure would be an acute crisis in a family less accustomed to dealing with a major disability, but for Erdrich it is an unremarkable incident.

3. Some students may find the opening paragraphs of Erdrich's essay as confusing as they are intriguing. Until paragraph 5, when Erdrich defines Adam's disability, students will wonder about Adam's seizure and Erdrich's calm response. Erdrich's explanation of Fetal Alcohol Syndrome will take care of any confusion, but to help students think about the choices Erdrich has made about style and organization, it may be helpful to ask them to discuss the shift in Erdrich's tone as she begins to define Fetal Alcohol Syndrome.

In paragraph 5, Erdrich gives facts about the syndrome and states her opinion of women who drink while pregnant: "It's a lot of fate to play with for the sake of a moment's relaxation." If Erdrich had begun with this paragraph, her tone would have sounded merely judgmental, since her readers would not have understood that Fetal Alcohol Syndrome has a daily impact on her life and her adopted child's life.

Connections

1. In describing how her family came into being, Erdrich says, "it simply happened" (para. 6), but in fact it was a deliberate process. Her husband, Michael, had adopted Adam and two other children while he was single; Erdrich accepted them into her life along with their father, and she adopted the children a year after she and Michael married. Erdrich doesn't define "family" directly, but many students will understand that it is unlikely she would define it according to the nuclear model of two parents biologically related to their children. Paula Fomby asserts, "It is time for society to expand the definition of family" so that children will be able to be proud of whatever family they come from. Fomby is concerned with gay families, but her comments would apply equally well to the nontraditional family that Erdrich has helped to create. Angela Davis, in her discussion of African-American families, also refutes the idea that the nuclear family model is superior. Instead, Davis describes an extended-family model, in which grandmothers, grandfathers, aunts, and uncles are integral to the family. This model would probably appeal to Erdrich, because she recognizes that the problems that face the Native American community can best be dealt with by emphasizing tribal values (49).

2. Frances Rose Besmer talks about the challenge of meeting children's physical and emotional needs; she notes, "Intangible requirements of patience and encouragement are just as important to help a child adjust to eating meals together . . ." (p. 129). Erdrich describes her patient accommodation to Adam's complaints and demands about his food — balanced with her insistence that he must eat to avoid a seizure — before frustration overcomes her. Patricia Schroeder writes about the necessity for most working mothers to provide family income and the lack of government support for their dilemma (p. 129). Erdrich probably would agree with Schroeder's assessment of the problems of childcare, and she might also argue that the lack of government support for women's and children's needs contributes to the erosion of family and community in some Native American communities. As professional writers, Erdrich and her husband, Michael Dorris, have the advantages of being able to work at home where they can stay close to Adam and their other children; their disadvantages are that their family's demands take place in the same space and often the same time as the demands of their work.

3. A good way to engage students with this question might be to ask, Who would you rather have for a mother, Chang-Rae Lee's mother or Louise Erdrich? Lee's mother seems to live for (and perhaps through) her children — she tells her son she would die if anything happened to him, and she hates to deny him anything. She performs several roles in the household: accountant, maid, launderer, disciplinarian, driver, secretary, cook, basketball coach. Despite her many talents, she deflects attention from herself by shifting it to her husband, frequently proclaiming what a good man he is and how hard he works. She sounds overly self-effacing, the kind of mother one could not disappoint without fending off a lot of guilt. Erdrich's mothering of Adam has been a process of learning his limits and her own. She can encourage Adam to take care of himself, but she can't make him. Once she accepts that, she takes on the role of companion; she and Adam take a trip, plant trees and a garden, play tic-tac-toe. The two mothers' roles

are similar in the types of activities they perform in the house, but their attitudes differ: with healthy children, Lee's mother does a lot for them, confident they will return her goodwill. Erdrich knows Adam is only capable of cooperating, and she has to scale down her expectations and be grateful for the "bond of absolute simplicity, love" that she and Adam share (para. 40).

HENRY LOUIS GATES JR., Down to Cumberland (p. 146)

Explorations

1. Among the members of Gates's own generation are his brother Rocky, his cousin Carolyn (who died), and her husband Ernie. In the next generation after his are his daughters Maggie and Liza, and Carolyn and Ernie's three children. In his father's generation are his father, his father's sister Helen, his father's brothers Charles (who died in infancy) and Bill, and his father's white cousin Brady. In his grandfather's generation are his grandfather Pop Gates and his wife Nan; his grandfather's brother Guy; his grandfather's sisters Pansy, Maude, and Lettitia; Lettitia's husband Russell Carpenter and her suitor Rayford Logan. Two other generations are represented in photographs: in his great-grandfather's generation are Edward Gates and his wife Maude (Fortune). And in his great-great-grandfather's generation are Jane Gates (a former slave) and her white owner Brady.

2. The Colemans see one another much more often, coming together for annual family reunions and for Christmas. The Gateses gather only for funerals, so that the narrator saw them all together only twice during his childhood.

3. Gates apparently feels closest to his family when attending funerals, where the photographs in family albums and the names in his father's stories turn into "actual brown and tan and beige people" (11). Seeing his father cry at his grandfather's funeral, he feels sorry for his father for the first time. At his grandmother's funeral, Gates doesn't laugh or cry because he "wanted to be the child that day" (para. 7). And at his cousin Carolyn's funeral, he strolls about the cemetery, looking at all the Gateses, feeling "cloaked in the mantle of my family" (33).

Connections

1. In "Foreword," Adam's birth mother chose to drink alcohol during her pregnancy, causing her son to contract Fetal Alcohol Syndrome and become mentally handicapped. Among Gates's ancestors, his great-great-grandmother Jane *may* have chosen to have children with her master Brady; his great-grandmother Maude founded an episcopal church and sent her daughters to good colleges; his great-aunt Lettitia chose not to wait for Rayford Logan to return from Paris and married Russell Carpenter instead.

2. Angela Davis's observation that the African-American family has traditionally been an extended family aptly fits Gates's memoir. Davis explains that slave families were regarded by their owners as consisting of a mother and her children, with fathers sold away, so African-American families needed to create surrogate family members. The men in Gates's family tend to remain with their families, although his Uncle Bill regards his son-in-law Ernie as a poor father and wants to become a surrogate father by gaining custody of Carolyn's children after she dies.

3. Baldwin would most likely agree with Logan's own explanation in the final paragraph that he felt "free and a man" there. According to Baldwin, France was a much kinder atmosphere to blacks than was the United States, especially sensitive, gifted men like Baldwin and Logan who needed to be in a place where cultural expectations and stereotypes would not impinge on their intellectual ambitions. Baldwin might explain Logan's apparent regret for staying so long with the observation that people who were not comfortable in their own countries could never feel completely at home abroad either.

SUSAN CHEEVER, The Nanny Dilemma (p. 155)

Explorations

1. Judging from "The Nanny Dilemma," New York families who hire nannies tend to have two working parents who earn a high income, spend summer vacations in the Hamptons, eat out often (and sometimes forget to buy food for their children), are heavily dependent on their nannies ("Basically, I'm on call around the clock" [para. 13]), and let their children run the house, substituting indulgence for time and attention. Their approach to caring for their children resembles Dominique's in that she is also an absent working parent whose child is being reared by others; she hasn't seen her daughter in three years. The difference is this: Whereas the New York mothers work primarily because they gain satisfaction from their jobs, Dominique is making a sacrifice to buy her daughter an education, so that she won't have to be a nanny.

2. In her opening paragraph, Cheever informs us that Dominique has been in New York for eight years, that she believes New Yorkers are workaholics who are obsessed with money, that she has an "island accent," that she disapproves of psychotherapy, and that she believes New Yorkers are afraid of their children. We find out about Dominique's occupation when Cheever moves to Eileen Stein's comments about nannies. Readers learn where Dominique came from at the close of the second paragraph. Cheever gives her greater authority as a speaker by allowing readers to hear her views before they learn her job. If readers — presumably well-educated New Yorkers — found out right away that she's a nanny, they might take her opinions less seriously. However, not fully introducing her at the outset also implies she is not an important authority.

3. According to Cheever, New York working mothers benefit by having a "true significant other" to take care of their children (19). Fathers benefit by "sometimes get[ting] off scot-free — a lot of the time it's as if they didn't even have children" (19). Children benefit by getting a loving caretaker who even thinks about them on her day off. Nannies benefit by gaining employment that requires no green card or formal education. New York benefits by having its educated labor pool somewhat freed from child-care responsibilities: "we could close down the city," claims short-term baby nurse Myrtle Johnson (17). The city government also benefits, in that nannies compensate for the inadequate quantity of childcare it provides.

Connections

1. It's hard to imagine a nanny in the Gates family, because the relatives are so involved in one another's lives that there doesn't seem to be a need for outside support. It's hard to say about the current generation: Henry Louis Gates doesn't live in Piedmont, West Virginia, but in Cambridge, Massachusetts, where he is chair of a department at Harvard.

The women of his extended family who appear in his essay, however, have not apparently depended on nannies to make their achievements possible.

2.   Of Dominique's family in Trinidad, we learn that she has a mother, a step-father, and an eight-year-old daughter who lives with her sister. The facts that she lights a candle for her mother and that her daughter lives with her sister give the impression that Dominique is close to the women in her family, as are the women in Judith Ortiz Cofer's family, who gather in the afternoon to drink *cafe con leche* and talk about life in Puerto Rico and the United States.

3.   Susan C. McMillan insists that a child needs to grow up with parents of two different genders; in Cheever's portrait, however, the nanny and the mother generally form the child-rearing team, with the father acting as an assistant at best and an obstacle at worst. So McMillan would most likely respond that fathers — indeed, both parents together — should be more involved. (This question provides an excellent opportunity to get students to see how atypical the nuclear family is and how families can have many different configurations of care givers.) Pat Schroeder argues that many women have no choice but to work to support their families, whereas Cheever's portrait focuses on affluent women who seem to have chosen to work. Although Schroeder might take issue with Cheever's depiction of working women, she would probably agree with Cheever's observation that New York provides its citizens with insufficient child-care options.

NICHOLAS BROMELL, Family Secrets (p. 164)

Explorations

1.   According to Nicholas Bromell, a *real* American childhood affords the adult stories to tell that adhere to certain conventions, the most important being ordinariness. A real childhood is so stable and predictable that seemingly minor events become memorable dramas. It is sheltered enough from historical events that the child can believe what his textbooks tell him. But Bromell's childhood was highly unpredictable, as his parents moved about the world and his father's work filled the house with secrets he could not disclose to other children. His childhood also gave him an awareness of the world most children lack.

2.   Bromell's family seems ordinary when they're home in the United States and Dad goes to work in an unspecified office or, in a country unspecified in the essay, when they go on picnics in the desert, the men relax with cold martinis, the women look for shards among ancient ruins, and the children spy on the men. The family seemed ordinary to its members when the mother announced that the father wouldn't be home that night, or the father told them to stay out of the house until after a certain hour, or men came to debug the house. The family seems normal in the first set of situations because, in these, it resembles other families. In the second set, it seems normal to Bromell because he grew up "seeing the world double . . . not just the doubleness of adults pretending things to children but the doubleness of adults pretending things to one another" (para. 5). He adds, "Knowing no other world, this seemed normal to me" (5).

3.   Bromell uses few proper names: he mentions going to Beirut and Baghdad in 1957 and to Cairo in 1967. His parents and two brothers remain anonymous. The effect is to include readers in the sense of doubleness and danger: we are not being told all of the

details, and we know why. We get a sense of what it was like for Bromell to be a child with secrets.

Connections

1. Both the New York children described in "The Nanny Dilemma" and Nicholas Bromell and his brothers have a parent whose job limits his or her access to the children. Although Bromell's mother was consistently present in his childhood, his father might be off on an assignment for months at a time. Likewise, the children of New Yorkers who hire nannies may not see much of their parents during the week, because they are often gone from the house for twelve hours a day on the weekdays. These children are more likely to have the backdrops of a "*real* American" childhood (para. 1) — Hamptons beaches in the summer, the park year around — but the nanny's face may be more familiar than the parents'.

2. Erdrich's family is willing to center on Adam because he lacks the capacity to understand limitations: "he is at the stage of a very young child who sees the world only as an extension of his or her will" (p. 139). Once Erdrich has grasped Adam's unwillingness or inability to reason with her, she learns to accept him on his own terms, appreciating the unconditional love he is capable of giving. But along the way, Erdrich "learned more about my limits than I ever wanted to know" (p. 142), coming to admit that "it takes a certain fiber I don't truly possess to live and work with a person obstinate to the core, yet a victim" (p. 142). Bromell's family is willing to adapt to his father's restrictions because his mother has agreed to live the life of a spy's wife, and the children probably were not given a choice. But even as a child, Bromell did not seem to disapprove: "somehow we knew. . . that he did not work for money, and that his work mattered in some deeper, stronger way that could never be discussed" (2). The children benefit by gaining a much more complex understanding of history than do most of their classmates, but they lose in other ways; they have to lie about their lives to their friends, they don't have a stable social life, and they grow up with no loyalty to a particular place.

3. Anwar El-Sadat loved how working the land with people in his village made him feel attached to both, as well as to God, who made the land and decreed that these people would work it. Mit Abul-Kum's familiar landscape stimulated "an invisible bond of love and friendship with everything around [him]" (p. 131), a sense of belonging not just to his family and village, but to the land he walked on.

WINDOWS:
THE WORLD

RIGOBERTA MENCHÚ, Birth Ceremonies (p. 176)

Explorations

1. Among the Quiché Indians, the parent-child relationship serves as a model for relationships between leaders and community members. The man and woman elected as leaders bear parental responsibility for the entire community and become

grandparents to every child born (para. 1). Thinking of the community as an extended family has several advantages for the Quiché. Because they live under harsh conditions as a marginalized group in Guatemala, the Quiché need to maintain close connections with each other, offering each other material and emotional sustenance. The Quiché religion is also based on a parent-child model, in which the sun is father and the moon is mother to the people (12). The ceremonies that introduce the newborn child to family and community integrate him or her "in the universe." The emphasis on parent-child relationships in Quiché society and religion helps to remind people of their close connections with their ancestors, encouraging group solidarity and a deep commitment to traditional values and customs important for physical and psychological survival.

2. Each ceremony for the Quiché child marks an important milestone in her or his progress as a member of the community. Before the baby's birth, the mother and father together inform community leaders that a child is on the way so that leaders can prepare to accept the child into the community (1). Each child is born in the presence of carefully selected couples representing both family and community and is introduced to family and friends with ceremonies and celebrations. For eight days following the birth, the child is left alone with his mother while neighbors bring gifts (7). These gifts, and the feasting and celebration that follow, solidify the child's position as a community member. Other customs, including tying a bag of talismans around the baby's neck, binding the baby's hands and feet, and lighting candles at the four corners of his or her bed, symbolize important aspects of Quiché life that the child will eventually be expected to understand and respect (8–10). The care with which children are inducted as community members impresses on everyone the need for mutual support if the Quiché are to survive as a culturally intact group.

3. The child's education about future responsibilities begins before birth, when the mother introduces her unborn child to the natural world and to the culture by talking to her or him about Quiché life (2). When the child is eight days old, a ceremony introduces him or her to the community and the parents tell the child about the family's suffering to symbolically prepare him or her to live a hard life with dignity (9). At a large gathering forty days after a child is born, parents and community leaders promise to teach the child to follow Quiché traditions and keep the community's secrets safe from outsiders (11). They voice the expectation that the child will grow up to live as his or her ancestors did and will one day become a parent to help multiply the race. When the child reaches the age of ten, parents and village leaders again reinforce traditional values by talking to the child formally about the necessity of honoring ancestors and carrying out responsibilities toward the community (13). Throughout childhood, boys and girls are introduced to gender-specific responsibilities; girls are taught to care for the family and prepare to become mothers, and boys are prepared for their future responsibilities as heads of the family.

Connections

1. Menchú's discussion of the initiation rites of the Quiché Indians shows the importance that they place on not only the family's and community's obligation to the child, but the child's reciprocal obligation to the family and community as well. Your students may be surprised at the public and formal nature of a baby's introduction to the community and the involvement of the community in the birth and raising of the child. The leaders of the community must be present at birth if possible; the mother has a "duty" (para. 2) to tell the child about her work; the neighbors visit, bring presents, and take over the work of the household for eight days; animals are sacrificed; candles are

placed on the child's bed to show the respect the child must have for the community; the child is publicly baptized; and, at age 10, the parents and village leaders talk to the child. Gates's essay shows the importance of family ties in raising children. Gates notes that the funerals in his family served the same function as family reunions served in the Coleman family. A Bible had been in his family "for over a century, easy" (p. 148); it contained records of his family, and an old trunk contained the photographs that helped preserve memories of older generations and provide continuity to the younger members of the family.

2. The induction ceremonies described in both pieces involve rituals through which the elders pass on information to the young. In the Hopi ritual, the boys spend six weeks in the all-male area of the kiva, learning the ways of men. In the Quiché community, when a child reaches the age of ten, the parents and the village leaders tell the child he or she will become a parent and admonish him or her to never "abuse his dignity" (13). Bly argues that modern societies have no ritual to allow a boy to separate from his parents without being self-destructive. Dorris elaborates on this idea, arguing that Americans have a prolonged adolescence because we lack rituals through which to test our mettle and envision passage into adulthood (p. 273).

3. Ved Mehta's Indian parents share with Guatemalan Quiché parents the idea that parents are responsible for educating their children, whether at the "dinner-table-school" (p. 133) discussions that took place in Mehta's house or in the open air school where the Quiché child learns by observing his or her parents and asking questions about why, say, the mother blesses the wood before lighting the fire or blows on her hands before mixing the mixtamal. Moreover, in both families, children are assigned roles and are expected to follow them: In Mehta's family, the eldest daughter is expected to marry first, preferably at the age of nineteen, and in the Quiché family, the eldest son is like a second father, responsible for the upbringing of his siblings. However, Mehta's family is more like one in the United States in that it functions as a nuclear unit, whereas the Quiché family includes the community in many of its decisions.

AMOS OZ, If There Is Justice (p. 188)

Explorations

1. This question will provide students with valuable practice in making inferences from clues in the story. Fruma's comments in paragraph 29, when she recalls Rami's childhood illness, reveal that Yoash was Rami's older brother. To Rami he represents a rival who can never be conquered (100); to Fruma, her dead son was the strong one, the one who was not "delicate" as Rami was, the hero who made the ultimate sacrifice.

2. Rami's sensitivity, revealed in his anxiety over his reception by Noga, keeps interfering with his attempts to be tough. He ultimately comes to terms with an image of himself as a sensitive artist. Rami's poetry, which receives no apparent approval from his comrades in either the army or the kibbutz, has taken second place to silly jingles mocking his commander's ineptitude. His love of beauty and nature, which also has no place in a war zone, has been replaced by the love of seeing enemy planes shot down. The soldier has no time for sensitivity; likewise, his community has no need for artists. Those who are revered are the heroes, like his brother Yoash. Because of the closeness of the community, Rami's self-image reflects the values and judgments of those around him — specifically, that a war hero is infinitely more valuable than a

sensitive artist. As a result, Rami attempts to stifle his true nature, until his revelation at the end of the story.

3. Rami wants to prove his toughness, his bravery, and the gun seems to present him with the perfect chance to do so. In childish fashion he imagines what the others will say when he is dead. But what begins as a "won't they be sorry (not to mention impressed) when I'm dead" attitude is soon replaced by images of the townspeople calling him a lovesick fool. This realization is soon followed by a simpler one: He discovers that he doesn't want to die. That discovery, in turn, brings on an acceptance of self. He stops the game when he at last accepts himself for the sensitive, nonheroic type he is. Comfortable with that self-image, he no longer needs to prove himself to anyone.

Connections

1. According to Rigoberta Menchú, Quiché children learn their role in the community by working alongside their parents daily. The parents explain the meaning of each task, sometimes saying a prayer for that task. As children grow older, they begin to take on responsibilities — fetching water, tying up the dogs, for example. In "If There Is Justice," Rami apparently learned his role on the kibbutz from his mother and the people he worked with, such as his brother Yoash. He has been learning his role as an adult Israeli from his superiors and peers in the army and at home, who get excited when they spot an enemy plane (para. 36) and who are teaching him that violence solves conflicts ("People like that ought to be put down. Like Arabs. Punch him in the face . . ." [100]).

2. It is generous of Fruma to sacrifice so much for her children, but it is selfish of her to imply that they will have to pay someone back for her caretaking. If the same statements were made by the parents who employ nannies, they would be especially ironic, because the main costs they appear to pay are their nannies' salaries. If the statements were made by one of the nannies, there would be a closer parallel, because they are sacrificing their wish to live in their own countries for their children's sake.

3. Living on a kibbutz gives Fruma more parental power and responsibility than Louise Erdrich has, in that the tightness of the community makes her privy to her son's every action: she knows he has written to Noga Harish, who is having an affair with an older man. This knowledge gives her power over her son and perhaps less responsibility, because so many members of the community are involved in his life. Erdrich has less power over and greater responsibility for Adam, in that she does not have a tight community who shares in his care and she must learn that she cannot be entirely responsible for his welfare.

FRANK McCOURT, Limerick Homecoming (p. 200)

Explorations

1. When the family arrives in Ireland, the living members include the parents, Frances, Malachy, Oliver, and Eugene. We learn about Margaret, the sister who died in Brooklyn, when the father goes from shop to shop "asking for food or anything they can give to a family that has two children dead in one year" (para. 54). The information comes as a shock, because the narrator gives the impression of having thoroughly introduced the characters, and readers may still be responding to Oliver's death.

2. Readers learn that the narrator came to Limerick from the United States when one of the boys carrying their trunk hears the twins speak and asks if they're American. Angela, the mother, confirms it. Other characters in the narrative also learn where the McCourts are from when one of their children speaks, betraying a Brooklyn accent.

3. The first scene in the story, when the family arrives in Limerick, is recounted in the past tense; the next scene, at Grandma's house, is recounted in the present tense; the following section, summarizing the family's move to a furnished room and discovery of fleas in the mattress, is told in the past; the next section, describing Oliver's fever, the mother's and children's quest for coal and an onion, and Oliver's death, is told in the present tense; and the final section, about Oliver's funeral, is told in the past tense. When McCourt uses the past tense, he tends to summarize more, and when he uses the present, he tends to dramatize the scene and provide greater detail. The use of the present tense reflects the uncertainty the family experiences; the past tense highlights the family's losses. But the difference is fairly subtle. You might assign students the exercise of writing a narrative in which they switch from present to past. Students could exchange essays in class and analyze how these shifts affect the author's story.

Connections

1. Patriotism plays very different roles in the lives of the two stories' characters. In "Limerick Homecoming," the most sympathetic character is the man with advice about ridding a mattress of fleas, who makes joking reference to Ireland's "woeful history," claiming fleas were introduced by the British (para. 17). At another point, the father invokes his nationality — "I did me bit for Ireland" — when trying to talk a bartender into letting him have one more pint (62). But the locals seem as loyal to Limerick as they are to their country: when the mother asks a shopkeeper for an onion for her child, she gets it; when the father begs food from shopkeepers, they "tell him they don't need the likes of him with his Northern accent" (55). In "If There Is Justice," the protagonist's patriotism is reflected in his hatred of Arabs: When he sees enemy planes overhead, he clenches his fists and growls through his teeth, "Let them have it" (p. 192). Likewise, when he thinks of the man with whom a woman he likes has been having an affair, he thinks that people like him should be killed, "like Arabs" (p. 195).

2. As with his patriotism, the father in "Limerick Homecoming" invokes religion at his convenience; for instance, when he wants to take credit for his wife having procured coal, he claims she succeeded because he prayed to Saint Jude (she disagrees). Or when shopkeepers refuse him food, he says he's "glad to see the spirit of Christ alive in Limerick" (55). It seems that neither father nor mother make much effort to teach their children about religion, given that Frances doesn't recognize Jesus when he sees his picture in his grandmother's house. In "If There Is Justice," the protagonist's life appears to be suffused with religion. He lives on a kibbutz where people speak Yiddish and he is fighting in a war to defend land for the Jews. Yet all of this seems like a mere backdrop to the emotional center of the story, Rami's desire for Noga and his humiliation that she is with someone else.

3. Among the effects of poverty Besmer describes, only substance abuse affects the McCourts: The father's drinking both triggers and is triggered by "the stigma of failure" Besmer cites (p. 129). The McCourts' advantages over the families Besmer describes are that they live in a community that provides some support to poor people, they include two parents, who love their children and don't seem likely to abandon them, and the

35

parents are not violent toward their children (although their grandmother and aunt might be described as verbally abusive).

ZLATA FILIPOVIC, Sarajevo Diary (p. 210)

Explorations

1. When Zlata begins keeping her diary in September 1991, she has no use for politics: "I don't know what it all means. Some reservists from Montenegro have entered Herzegovina. Why? For what? Politics, it seems, but I don't understand politics" (para. 9). As the situation worsens in Dubrovnik, Zlata notices that her parents are worried, but she still claims she hasn't a clue about politics. In March 1992, however, when the Serbs start attacking Sarajevo, she becomes upset that the city is barricaded and interested in the doings of Karadzic and Izetbegovic, reporting them in her diary (17).

2. The Filipovic family tries to maintain their normal prewar life by devoting their energy to fulfilling their basic needs: they haul water for drinking and washing; they cook whatever food they can find on a wood stove in the backyard; they spend a lot of time on the phone with friends; the mother goes to work; and, during the summer, Zlata goes to school. There isn't much they can do to keep their spirits up; at one point, the electricity has just been cut off, so they cook all the food in the freezer and share it with the neighbors.

3. The early entries depict the life of a busy, happy fifth grader who is more interested in her grades and "The New Kids on the Block" than in politics; they're a little banal. But they give readers a point of reference for the later entries, heightening the impact of how much Zlata's world has changed.

Connections

1. Zlata's parents try to protect her and themselves physically by moving their beds into the living room and dashing to the cellar whenever shelling starts. Her parents also try to protect her from their worries, but not with great success: "Mommy. . . [is] constantly in tears. She tries to hide it from me, but I see everything" (para. 39). Yet, given that she watches the news all the time, lives in a bomb zone, and hears frequent accounts of violence, there is no shielding her from the war. Likewise, Frank McCourt's parents can only shield him so much from the effects of dire poverty: He sees his brother's death and funeral, his father's drinking, his mother's begging food, his grandmother's verbal abuse. Frank's mother does try to protect her children from starving by begging food and following her husband to collect the public dole so that he can't spend the money in pubs. But his father fails miserably as a provider, because he is incapable of placing his family's need for food before his own alcoholism.

2. Whereas Zlata Filipovic is alarmed and outraged to be involved in a war, Rami Rimon seems excited to be fighting an enemy. The contrast makes sense: Zlata is an eleven-year-old girl with little interest in or understanding of politics who regards the war as a confusing menace that disrupts her life and endangers the lives of her family, friends, and relatives. Rami is an older adolescent fighting in a war deemed just and necessary, and he's anxious to prove that he's as tough and brave as his peers.

3. Zlata's family fits the self-contained nuclear model depicted by Cheever, Bromell, and Erdrich in the sense that Zlata and her parents form a unit: When Zlata describes the possibility of their leaving Sarajevo, she doesn't take other relatives into consideration. The pros of the nuclear family are that they are independent, and the cons are that they are too separated from extended family members to support one another during a crisis. The Filipovics, however, don't lack for community. They seem much closer to their neighbors than is typical of the U.S. nuclear family: When the mother is late getting home on a day when there has been shelling, the neighbors all rush over to make sure she is okay when she arrives. Or, when both parents must go out, Zlata stays with the Bobars, the neighbors who share their basement with the Filipovics during the shelling and with whom the Filipovics share their freezer food.

SPOTLIGHT:
JAPAN

ADDITIONAL INFORMATION ON COUNTRY

Environment: Because 85 percent of the land on Japan's 3,400 islands consists of uninhabitable mountains, most of the population lives in the narrow Pacific coastal plains. The climate is subtropical in the south, temperate in the center, and cold in the north. Because Japan is located where cold and warm ocean currents meet, its waters provide excellent fishing, a mainstay in the country's economy.

Demographics: Over 99 percent of Japan's 125 million people are native-born Japanese. Over 40 percent of the population lives on 1 percent of the land area, making for densities of 1,800 people per square mile. This homogeneity and density may explain the Japanese group mentality evidenced in workers' and corporations' mutual loyalty and in other areas of Japanese life.

Religion: Japan has no official religion, but most of the population practices Shintoism. Known for their tolerance of religious differences, the Japanese also practice Buddhism, and some practice both religions simultaneously. About 4 percent are Christian.

Education: Ninety-five percent of the population has a high school education, and literacy is nearly 100 percent. Students must pass many qualifying examinations, and the pressure to do well is very intense. Once students enter college, however, there are no more examinations. Students accepted into the top colleges are almost guaranteed the top jobs.

Family: The family is regarded as the basic unit of society in Japan: Family responsibilities take precedence over individual desires, and family background plays a large role in determining who one marries and where one is employed. In general, employers prefer to hire people who grew up in two-parent households and who are currently married.

The traditional Japanese family had a strict gender-based division of roles, a patriarchal head, and a hierarchy by birth order. The eldest son usually remained in the household to take over the family business and care for his aging parents with the help of his wife, who had the lowest status in the household. The most important role of the family was to preserve the household resources and pass them on to the next generation while honoring the family ancestors through household-based religious practices.

The modern Japanese family evolved after World War II, when many traditional families had been fragmented and their primary concern was to secure the basics of food, shelter, and clothing. One room per family became one house per family, and the traditional extended family became less common. The "salaryman" family that became prevalent in the 1950s and 1960s had a hardworking but absent patriarch. The next generation rebelled against this pattern, seeking the love marriages they saw depicted in Western films, a wider array of opportunities for women, and childcare outside the home. The current generation seems to value individual freedom but also seems to view extreme individualism with alarm, citing American social problems, such as a high divorce rate, drugs, and homelessness, as reasons why the American model is not their ideal.

JOHN DAVID MORLEY, Acquiring a Japanese Family (p. 230)

Explorations

1. Few American students have had the experience of living with the almost complete lack of privacy Boon encounters while living with Sugama, so they will be able to sympathize with Boon's perplexity as he considers how differently he will have to live in a house without firm inside walls. To understand the "corporate" concept that defines Japanese family relationships, Morley analyzes the term *uchi*, which means both "household" and "I." The term suggests the inseparability of self, home, and family; "I" does not mean an individual, but "the representative of my house in the world outside" (para. 35).

2. Responses to this question may vary with students' ethnic backgrounds. Some may recognize the respect accorded adults in the Japanese family, as well as the patronizing attitude that accompanies that respect. (Note Sugama's amusement at his aunt's and uncle's fears.) These students may also understand the older adults' treatment of their young adult relatives: It seems that in Japan, your parents can always tell you what to do, regardless of your age or accomplishments. Those unfamiliar with this relationship will probably find vast differences between the obligations of a young adult Japanese and his or her American counterpart. Whereas the young Japanese are responsible for their parents' welfare, most Americans view themselves as responsible only to themselves and their children. (An interesting discussion may ensue if you ask students which situation they feel is better or more compassionate.)

3. The first-person narrator often causes a more limited perspective; Morley achieves a broader view of the meeting of cultures by writing through a third-person narrator. Boon's introduction to the apartment reveals him to be a foreigner: He is awed by the open spaces and especially by the concept of family indivisibility that leads to such construction. He must accustom himself to the apparent "classlessness" (36) of most Japanese homes. Perhaps more striking, however, are Boon's comic reaction to meeting Sugama's mother and his overtly Western advice to Sugama that the latter's plans for marriage are nobody else's business. In contrast, Boon's choice of living quarters, his increasing facility with the language, and his preference for Japanese food make him less foreign. By showing all this through Boon's eyes, Morley is able to remain distant. Both he and the reader can judge Boon's reactions and behavior objectively.

Connections

1. War creates "a common household unity" in "Sarajevo Diary," because the members of Zlata's family must focus on the common goal of protecting themselves from the dangers the war poses. They must all sleep on mattresses in a corner of the sitting room, must go to their own or the neighbors' basement whenever shelling starts, must stay in for days at a time when it is unsafe to go out, and must carry water from far enough away that the father develops a hernia, leaving water carrying to the mother. Whatever their individual wishes might be, the war keeps them from having much choice.

2. Menchú emphasizes the importance of keeping Indian customs secret from other communities to prevent them from learning a little and then drawing a false impression of the Indian world. According to her, Indians are annoyed when people from other cultures wear Indian clothes or try to co-opt Indian culture in other ways. Likewise, the Japanese depicted in Morley's story do not want to see outsiders adopting their culture. Boon's roommate's great-aunt and uncle are genuinely disappointed to discover that Boon ate rice and drank green tea. Whereas the Quiché try to keep their customs a secret, the Japanese try to ward off foreigners by offering them the scariest of Japanese dishes and then expressing triumph when the guest recoils from them.

3. The Indian family, as described by Mehta, and the Japanese family, as described by Morley, both hold the expectation that family members will take one another's needs into account and adjust their lives accordingly. Mehta's family expects the eldest daughter to marry the man her parents have found for her, and Sugama's family expects him to get married and to provide for his parents and live with them in the same house and to take in his great-aunt and uncle when they need a place to live. Morley spells out the difference between Boon and Sugama: Boon advises Sugama that it's entirely his own business when and if he marries, and "Sugama would clearly have liked to be able to agree with this facile advice and just as clearly he could not, entangled in a web of sentiment and duty of which Boon was wholly ignorant" (para. 44).

YUKIKO TANAKA, Mothers' Children (p. 241)

Explorations

1. Since World War II, the image of Japanese mothers has undergone several transformations. Just after the war, mothers were seen as stoic, self-sacrificing women who bravely raised their families without the financial or emotional support of a husband; given how many women were widowed by the war, this image has an element of truth in it. In the next decade, the nuclear family was exalted and mothers were depicted as doting on their homes and children, as the economy improved and a number of labor-saving appliances were introduced that freed women to spend more time with their children. The next decade ushered in the "education mom" (para. 3), popularly depicted as living vicariously through her children's academic achievement. Tanaka defends these women, arguing that the whole culture has come to place greater emphasis on educational achievement, so mothers help their children prepare for the arduous high school entrance examination. And in the 1970s, mothers were depicted as "ogres" in news stories about women who left their babies in coin lockers or who left them in "baby hotels" in the red light districts where they worked as hostesses in bars (15); Tanaka attributes the difficulty women experienced in rearing small children

39

to the sense of isolation permeating the enormous apartment complexes found in the "new towns" (4) outside urban areas.

2. Tanaka says little about fathers, other than that they leave for work earlier than the mothers, return home much later, and "are either unwilling or unable to share responsibility" (12) for childcare. Her passing remark about her friend Toda Akiko's frequent trips to Tokyo to take her son to cram school seem telling: "her husband, an unusually self-sufficient man for a Japanese husband, will not mind being left behind" (24).

3. That Tanaka is writing about urban middle-class families is first apparent when she describes "my homism" as a trend found among them (2). These families buy appliances when they become available in the fifties, move into "new towns" in the seventies, generally have two working parents or a working father and a mother who devotes a lot of attention to her children's education, and want their children to become engineers or government employees. They value financial security, and they sacrifice their time and money for the sake of their children's education, because educating the young means investing in their own future.

Connections

1. In Morley's essay, Sugama is the oldest son, so his parents expect him not only to provide for them, but to live in the same house with them. The understanding is that Sugama will eventually go home to live with his parents. In the meantime, he must be ready to host his great-aunt and uncle, who come to live with him for a few days because they fear an impending earth quake, and he lives in a quake-proof building. You might use this question to launch a discussion regarding how students perceive their responsibilities to their parents.

2. Tanaka's discussion of Japan's childcare facilities suggests that she finds them inadequate to meet women's needs: Public day care is expensive (swallowing half of Kusunose Mikiko's salary) and difficult to enroll in, and the facilities do not remain open late enough for women to pick up their children after work. Insufficient public day care has led to the growth of unregulated, often unsafe, private facilities such as "baby hotels," where children stay while mothers work in the evening, sometimes through the night. Horror stories led to government regulation, but according to Kawashima Shizuyo, author of *Children Drifting in the Darkness*, the situation hasn't improved. Tanaka criticizes the government for leaving private industry to take on a role it should be performing, subsidizing childcare, whereas Schroeder argues that the family unit is breaking down because we don't give it enough support: "We do less than any industrialized nation: In terms of tax breaks, we would do better raising thoroughbred dogs or horses than children" (p. 129).

3. Japanese families cope with insufficient government day care in a number of ways: They deal with the problem of a facility closing earlier than they can get there by hiring someone to pick up the child and stay with her until the mother gets home. Another solution is to place the child in a privately owned "baby hotel" (see answer to 2 above). There appears not to be an unskilled labor pool in Japan as in the United States from which nannies can be drawn, or a willingness among Japanese mothers to take this route; probably most significant, though, is that few working families in Japan (as in the United States) can afford the price Cheever's New Yorkers pay for their nannies.

KENZABURO OE: Japan, the Ambiguous, and Myself (p. 251)

Explorations

1. It's not exactly clear what Oe means by ambiguity: He initially uses "vague" (para. 7) to describe Kawabata's writing and Nobel speech, but he doesn't define ambiguity, other than to say it is difficult to define. Later he says Kawabata's sensibility is reflected in the poems written by medieval Zen monks, which are concerned with "the linguistic impossibility of telling the truth" (8). According to Oe, contemporary Japan is split between two sets of values: It is oriented toward the West in its drive to modernize but thoroughly Asian culturally. Its Western values have led Japan to invade Asia, isolating it politically, culturally, and socially, and leaving its people ambivalent about re-arming.

2. Much of Oe's lecture is ambiguous; it's hard to pin him down, especially when he builds multiple layers of literary allusions. Some specific points at which he sounds ambiguous are when he alludes to his success as a writer, trying to sound humble, yet obviously proud to be winning the Nobel Prize. He mentions another Nobel Prize winner, Yeats, insists that he makes "no claim to being in the same rank as that poetic genius" (11), and then draws an analogy between himself and Yeats. Oe also simultaneously praises and denigrates himself when he remarks that Ireland was "accepted into the comity of nations" (16) when Yeats won the Nobel Prize, but that Japan has been similarly accepted because of its cars and electronics, "not on account of literature or philosophy," although he has just won the Nobel Prize (16) and describes an active literary tradition.

3. Oe's comments about his family are an appropriate way to start and end his lecture because the entire piece is very personal. He moves from one association to another — most of them literary — describing how they influenced him as a writer. As he explains early on in the speech: "the fundamental method of my writing has always been to start from personal matters and then to link them with society, the state, and the world in general" (3). Also, his anecdote about fleeing the "waves of horror" (1) in the Japan of his childhood by fleeing to the woods and imagining he was Huck or Nils parallels his statement that he sees writing as a way to both escape from and reconcile himself with the problems in contemporary Japan. In regard to style, his anecdote about his son illustrates an important point in his lecture, that language is ambiguous, communicating with no more specificity than music or birdsong.

Connections

1. Tanaka describes Japanese women's primary role as supporting the achievements of their husbands and children; Oe says, "my life would have been impossible but for my wife with her abundant female strength and wisdom. She has been the very incarnation of Akka, the leader of Nils's wild geese" (para. 6).

2. According to Morley, the Japanese like to believe that Westerners cannot adapt to their way of life and that the Japanese take pride in their own cultural and racial singularity. Oe agrees that, to the West, Japan's culture has "remained inscrutable or only partially understood" (18). But he also sees Japan's singularity as somewhat compromised by its having adopted a Western economic model, leading the country to invade its Asian neighbors, and by his and others' embrace of Western literature.

3. This question is open to some interpretation, so you might encourage students to be creative, to try to imagine how it feels to be Adam or Hikari, to miss out on a number

41

of experiences the rest of us take for granted; Erdrich's own list includes receiving a high math score, reading a book, wondering at the complexity and quirks of nature, relating well to peers, and regarding his sexuality as a pleasure instead of a problem.

KAZUO ISHIGURO, A Family Supper (p. 260)

Explorations

1. Much of the drama of the story derives from the suspense created by the information about fugu and about Watanabe's having committed suicide and killed his family. If the father believes his former partner to have been "a man of principle and honor" (para. 11), does that mean he admires his partner's actions enough to imitate them? Is the delicious fish he serves his children the dreaded fugu that could kill them? Ishiguro's narrator never asks these questions, but readers can't help wondering. Without these elements, the story would have a lot less impact.

2. Ishiguro provides information about the family's relationships both by having the characters comment on them and by dramatizing them through dialogue and gesture. For instance, the narrator describes how his father struck him when he was a child for "chattering like an old woman," and goes on to observe that their conversation since his arrival had been "punctuated by long pauses" (7). The dialogue conveys this tension: the father asks directly whether the son will stay and the son gives a vague answer. The father vaguely implies that his wife's disappointment over the son's leaving caused her death, and the son says pointedly, "Surely my mother didn't expect me to live here forever" (94). The relationship between Kikuko and both men is also apparent in commentary as well as dialogue and gestures: the narrator remarks that they have always been close, and this is illustrated by the way she visibly relaxes when they are alone together. The tension in her relationship with her father is apparent in her not moving "for some moments" after her father tells her to "come here and help" him cook (81, 80). The second part of the question provides a good opportunity to discuss unreliable narrators. Can we take this narrator's words at face value? Or should we attend more to what happens between the characters than to his comments about their relationships? A good exercise might be to have students highlight all of the narrator's comments and then find evidence in the dialogue to back up his claims.

3. The story's plot would be quite different if Ishiguro had told it in the third person: Readers could more readily assume that this family supper was a farewell, with the father serving poisonous fugu to himself and his children. A first-person narrator forces us to question either that fatal outcome (since he lived to tell the tale) or the whole story's relation to reality. On the other hand, the story gains dramatic effect from being told in the first person, because we see events through the narrator's eyes, with unstated ambivalence and unresolved ambiguity.

Connections

1. Ishiguro's story is loaded with ambiguous interactions between people, starting with the fish that a friend could cook improperly and accidentally kill you with. As with fugu, it's hard to tell whether relationships are nourishment or poison, whether a son should stay near his parents in Japan or flee to California. Most issues in the story remain unresolved: Will the narrator move home or return to the United States? Was Mr.

Watanabe's killing himself and his family a sick or an honorable act? Is there a ghost in the garden or not? Did the mother die accidentally or kill herself? If she did kill herself, was it because her son left home? Is that what her husband means to imply when he says she had "disappointments" (para. 92)? Does the daughter like her boyfriend or not? Will the daughter stay near her father or flee? The imagery in the story also clothes it in ambiguity: The garden gets dim as the siblings walking in it seemingly speak candidly. The son says he can't see his mother's photo very well because "it's dark" (114). The father's face is partially shadowed as he pushes the mysterious fish dish toward his son, saying, "You must be hungry" (121). The steam that wafts up from the dish is "almost scalding" (122). It's a perfect story for showing students how literary imagery can reinforce, or even become part of, a story's plot. The first time students read it, they are likely to be so captivated by the plot that they miss the imagery. You might have them read it a second and third time, underlining ambiguous imagery or dialogue.

2.   Ishiguro doesn't dwell on the house. He mentions the tatami mat, the sliding panels that separate the rooms, the startling emptiness of the rooms, and the large sliding windows in the dining room. From reading Morley's story, one might extrapolate that the house has the three elements found in Japanese dwellings: tatami (straw mats), fusuma (sliding screens made of paper and light wood), and shoji (another type of sliding screen, with an open wood grid covered on one side with semitransparent paper).

3.   Based on Tanaka's and Morley's pieces, one can assume that the narrator's parents expected him to live with them and provide for them. Kenzaburo Oe's comments about his wife suggest that he has a fairly traditional view of marriage, but at no point does he express regret that his son is not providing for him and his wife financially. Whereas the father in Ishiguro's story is not quite sure what to do with himself, hopes that both his children will live with him, and seems angry at the independent decisions they have made, Oe sees his son as having fulfilled his own dream of understanding the language of birds, because Hikari composes music that originated in his response to birdsong.

JAPAN: INVESTIGATIONS/WEB SITES

The Japan Information Network (JIN) (http://jin.jcic.or.jp/) was set up by the Japan Center for Intercultural Communications (JCIC) to offer information about society, culture, education, and other aspects of Japanese life.

Neo-Tokyo: The Japanese Pop Culture Magazine (www.neo-tokyo.com/) covers all aspects of Japanese popular culture. Past issues have included such topics as bullying in Japanese schools, Sumo wrestlers, and the deadly fugu fish. Future issues will cover "the latest news on who is popular in Japan right now, including musicians, writers, comedians, actors, and singers," as well as "what's hot" in Japan, including the latest gadgets, popular foods, and travel destinations.

JETRO (Japan External Trade Organization) (http://www.jetro.go.jp/) is a nonprofit Japanese government-related organization dedicated to promoting mutually beneficial trade and economic relations between Japan and other nations.

The Japanese Family (http://www.askasia.org/frclasrm/readings/r000128.html) offers an article about the Japanese Family written by Anne E. Imamura in 1990 for the Asia Society's *Video Letter from Japan II: A Young Family.*

228–270 (Text Pages)

ADDITIONAL QUESTIONS AND ASSIGNMENTS

1. In a journal entry or a collection of informal notes, discuss the images of children presented in three or four of the selections. Consider such issues as the rights of children, their responsibilities to their parents, parents' responsibility to protect their children, children's need for the attention and love of a caretaker, their need for independence, and any other issues you find relevant. As you look over your notes, try to discover similarities and differences among the cultures represented. Can you come to any general conclusion about the image of children in a given culture?

2. Interview someone who grew up in a family setting different from your own. As you gather information, consider the kinds of information you're interested in eliciting. Do you want to know about sibling relationships? Responsibilities of children to parents? Influence of religious or social values on the family? Roles of males and females in the family? As you write the interview, decide what information is best summarized in your own voice and what is best delivered by your subject in his or her own words.

3. Write your own version of Henry Louis Gates Jr.'s "Down to Cumberland," in which you describe the relationships between members of your extended family and their ancestors. You might want to start by interviewing several of your relatives about their memories of their forbears, as well as their relationships with one another. As you gather material, be on the lookout for unifying themes that might help you order it in your essay. Before you start writing, reread and take notes on Gates's essay to see how he shapes his material.

4. The issue of children with two working parents is currently receiving a good deal of attention in the media. Some reports focus on the responsibility of the state to provide adequate childcare, some explore the effects of day care on the child, and some investigate the impact of working mothers on society as a whole. Research one of these topics (or choose your own related topic) by consulting magazine and newspaper articles on the subject as well as the opinions of experts found in books and interviews. Write a paper in which you present two opposing interpretations of the issue you've chosen, maintaining neutrality yourself.

5. Conduct further research on one of the cultures represented in this section (African-American, Guatemalan, Israeli, Irish, Bosnian, or Japanese), focusing specifically on the role of the family. If the selection is an excerpt from a larger work, look first at that work. You can find more information about the culture by consulting a general encyclopedia, a journal devoted to the study of that culture, and/or the Internet. Narrow your topic to something manageable, such as religious influences on the family, the role of the extended family, the place of children in the family, or the responsibility of the family to the state. Then write an essay in which you elaborate on the view of family presented in the original selection by using specific examples and quotations from the works you have consulted.

44

Part Three

TURNING POINTS

INTRODUCTION

Because many freshman college students tend to be intensely engaged in separating from their families and reinventing themselves, the unifying theme in this section should interest them. Angelou, Dubus, Ford, Liu, Heker, and Ghosh all relate the experience of making a critical discovery that pushed them toward taking responsibility for themselves, for their role in the world, or both. Other possible connections within the section include the awakening of social and political consciousness (Angelou, Dubus, Heker, Liu, Ghosh), the shattering of comforting childhood illusions (Ford, Liu, Heker), roles dictated by social class and race (Angelou, Ghosh, Heker, Liu, Gordimer, Singer), and the role of violence as a catalyst for personal growth (Dubus, Liu, Ghosh).

Students may find the section more accessible if they first discuss the various rituals associated with turning points — or lack thereof — in their own cultures. Some may identify with the scenes of alienation in selections by Angelou, Brodsky, Dubus, and Ford. They may find similarities in their own lives to the complexities and trials of growing up represented in pieces by Angelou, Ford, Heker, and Nabokov.

Some pieces look at cultures that have reached a turning point: Gordimer questions how white South Africans will adjust to their country under black rule; Dutkina tries to account for why so many of Russia's former artists and professors are selling sausages on the street; and Singer describes how elite "New Russians" are spending their money. These selections might prove a good starting point for a discussion about what students perceive to be recent, current, or oncoming turning points faced by the United States and how we can adapt to them.

Instructors may wish to consult the following familiar works in preparing related selections in *Making Contact*:

Essays

Maya Angelou, "Graduation" (*I Know Why the Caged Bird Sings*, Random House, 1970).
Nancy Mairs, "On Being Raised by a Daughter" (*Plaintext*, University of Arizona Press, 1986).
George Orwell, "Shooting an Elephant" (*Shooting an Elephant*, Harcourt, 1950).
Lillian Smith, "When I was a Child" (*Killers of the Dream*, Norton, 1949).
Alice Walker, "Beauty: When the Other Dancer Is the Self" (*In Search of Our Mothers' Gardens*, Harcourt, 1983).
Alice Walker, "Brothers and Sisters" (*In Search of Our Mothers's Gardens*, Harcourt, 1983).

Short Stories

Chinua Achebe, "Marriage is a Private Affair" (*Girls at War*, Doubleday, 1972).
Toni Cade Bambera, "The Lesson" (*Gorilla, My Love*, Random House, 1972).

272–279 (Text Pages)

Dorothy Canfield, "Sex Education" (*Four-Square*, Harcourt, 1945).
Kate Chopin, "The Story of an Hour" (published as "The Dreams of an Hour," *Vogue*, April 19, 1994); *The Awakening and Selected Stories*, Penguin, 1983.
Ralph Ellison, "Battle Royal" (*Invisible Man*, Random House, 1952).
Louise Erdrich, "The World's Greatest Fisherman" (*Love Medicine*, Holt, Rinehart, 1984).
William Faulkner, "The Bear" (*Go Down, Moses*, Random House, 1942).
Doris Lessing, "A Sunrise on the Veldt" (*African Stories*, Simon and Schuster, 1981).
Doris Lessing, "Through the Tunnel" (*The Habit of Loving*, 1955).
Jeanne Schinto, "Caddies' Day" (*Shadow Bands*, Ontario Review Press, 1988).
John Updike, "A & P" (*New Yorker*, July 22, 1961; *Pigeon Feathers*, Knopf, 1962).

BIOGRAPHICAL NOTES ON EPIGRAPH AUTHORS

1. Clive Barker is the author of a three-volume collection of science fiction short stories, *The Books of Blood* (1994), which has developed a cult following, and several best-selling fantasy novels (*Weaveworld, Cabal, The Great and Secret Show, Imajica*). His horror *films (Hellraiser, Hellbound, Nightbreed)* are equally popular.

2. Bob Seger and the Silver Bullet Band are best known for *Night Moves* (1976), whose title track reached number 8 on the charts; *Stranger in Town* (1978), whose "Still the Same" reached number 4; and *Against the Wind* (1980), whose title track reached number 5. His one number 1 hit was "Shakedown," from the *Beverly Hills Cop II* soundtrack.

3. A contributing writer for many magazines, Gail Sheehy has written a novel, *Lovesounds* (1970), and several studies of American contemporary and global life, including *Hustling* (1973), *Pathfinders* (1971), *Character: America's Search for Leadership* (1988), *The Man Who Changed the World: The Lives of Mikhail S. Gorbachev* (1991), and *Silent Passage: Menopause* (1992). The excerpt in *Making Contact* is taken from Sheehy's *Passages: Predictable Crises of Adult Life* (1974).

4. Michael Dorris, an anthropologist and writer, was the founder and chairman of the Department of Native American Studies at Dartmouth. He is the author of a memoir, *The Broken Cord: A Family's Ongoing Struggle with Fetal Alcohol Syndrome* (1989), and the novels *A Yellow Raft in Blue Water* (1987) and, with Louise Erdrich, *The Crown of Columbus* (1991).

5. Gloria Anzaldúa, a self-described "Chicana tejana patlache dyke poet and queer feminist writer" is the author of *Borderlands/La Frontera: The New Mestiza* (1987), which interprets American identity from a chicana perspective, and the editor of an anthology, *Making Face, Making Soul/Haciendo Caras: Creative and Critical Perspectives by Feminists-of-Color* (1990).

6. Günter Grass is not only Germany's most celebrated contemporary novelist but a poet, playwright, essayist, graphic artist, and sculptor. His novels include *The Tin Drum* (1959), *Dog Years* (1963), *The Flounder* (1977), *The Meeting in Telgte* (1979), *The Call of the Toad* (1992), and *Cat and Mouse and Other Writings* (1994).

7. Aleksandr Solzhenitsyn gained instant fame when he published *One Day in the Life of Ivan Denisovich* (1963), which describes a typical day in the labor camp where he was imprisoned for eight years. His next books, *Cancer Ward* (1968) and *The First Circle*

46

(1969), could only be published abroad, and the first volume of *The Gulag Archipelago* (1973–1975), an epic history and geography of the labor camps, caused the Soviet authorities to deport him to West Germany in 1974. He settled in the United States and continued working on a series of novels retelling Soviet history, which began with *August 1914* (1971). He won the Nobel Prize for Literature in 1970.

8. Malcolm X, born Malcolm Little in 1925, became a Black Muslim in jail and, after his release in 1952, advocated black separatism until a pilgrimage to Mecca caused him to moderate his views. He was assassinated in 1965. His *Autobiography of Malcolm X* (coauthored with Alex Haley) appeared the same year.

9. Sven Birkerts has published three books of essays on contemporary literature: *An Artificial Wilderness* (1987), *The Electric Life* (1989), and *American Energies* (1992). He has taught at Emerson College and Harvard University and won the National Book Critics Circle Citation for Excellence in Reviewing in 1985. He lives in Arlington, Massachusetts.

10. Alexander Theroux is the author of three novels, *Three Wogs* (1972), *Darconville's Cat* (1981), and *An Adultery* (1987); several books of poetry, including most recently *The Lollipop Trollops* (1992); plays; and two books of essays, *The Primary Colors* (1995) and *The Secondary Colors* (1996). He has taught at Harvard, MIT, Yale, and the University of Virginia; he currently lives in Barnstable, Massachusetts.

11. Kit R. Roane writes for the *New York Times* and other publications.

Explorations

1. The line from Bob Seger's "Night Moves" suggests that the speaker longs for his previous innocence, whereas the line from Alexander Theroux's *Darconville's Cat* suggests that the speaker longs to recover a previous identity, one in which he aspired to be who he is now. The lines are similar in that both express nostalgia for one's former self, but one characterizes that self in terms of knowing, the other, in terms of being. Other epigraphs in the chapter expressing these ideas include those by Clive Barker, who expresses nostalgia for a time when he didn't know the world differed from the dreamland in his children's books; Günter Grass, who longs to recover a time when the world did not know Germans were capable of administering a holocaust; and Kit Roane, whose article implies a wish to recover for the children of Sarajevo their lost innocence about death.

2. The following epigraphs show individuals dramatically changed by political changes: Günter Grass recounts spending his seventeenth year in an American prison camp and later realizing how stupid he'd been, the whole country had been, to accept the Third Reich's slogans; Aleksandr Solzhenitsyn describes whole generations "who are born and die off who do not tell each other about themselves" because their national literature has been suppressed; Kit Roane's piece portrays children in Sarajevo who have become numbed by the violence surrounding them; and the anonymous author of "Evicted" claims she feels as if she has been evicted from her country. The epigraph by Malcolm X suggests that individuals can make political changes: He describes how reading opened new vistas for him, allowing him to believe he could help black people. And the following epigraphs show individuals acting to change themselves: the adolescent Plains Indian boys described in Michael Dorris's excerpt venture into the wilderness,

inviting loneliness, stress, and, eventually, an epiphany; and Malcolm X discovers how much he'd craved to be "mentally alive."

3. This is a large and challenging question, requiring students to extrapolate from the selections what it must be like to live surrounded by death. Whereas "Sarajevo Diary" offers an innocent's account of war, Grass rails against the "overarching stupidity" that prevented him and other Germans from realizing the horror their government was perpetrating; you might ask students if they can think of any analogy from their own experience for this kind of destructive ignorance (Gangs? High school bullies? Their reading about paramilitary groups?). Solzhenitsyn's piece is probably the hardest to grasp, because students may not immediately see the link between having a national literature and being able to communicate; you might talk about freedom of the press and ask if they've ever been in a situation where they did not feel they could voice their concerns. After discussing the pieces individually, students should be able to suggest why youth in Sarajevo take death lightly, and why there were so many suicides. (Bob Seger's line may be a useful signpost.)

MIRRORS:
THE UNITED STATES

MAYA ANGELOU, Mary (p. 281)

Explorations

1. The innocent, but misplaced, sympathy of the young Angelou for her imperious employer makes readers appreciate the girl's kind and gentle nature. During her employment she grows from a naïve girl into a person of accurate moral judgment. Her final retaliation wins readers' admiration because it is motivated by principle and not a mean disposition. After her arrival, Angelou refers to her employer at least three times as "poor" Mrs. Cullinan (paras. 12, 13, 17) because she pities her lack of children. She works hard to compensate for Mrs. Cullinan's unhappiness (13). Her pity is replaced by anger when Mrs. Cullinan, acting on her friend's suggestion, decides to call Angelou "Mary" to suit her convenience. Rather than stay and compromise, Angelou decides to get fired (34). Mrs. Cullinan's final reaction to Angelou marks Angelou's moment of triumph because Mrs. Cullinan reaffirms her maid's true identity by using her given name twice (42).

2. Angelou writes that any black she knew would find being "called out of his name" an insult (30). Like other blacks, Angelou could interpret the casual arrogance of her employer as a racial slur. Her employer, fastidious about the disposition of her belongings, feels no compulsion to recognize the personal identity of her maid. After Glory recounts that she has been renamed, Angelou wonders about the former and present names of Mrs. Randall's maid. Angelou decides not to tolerate being stripped of her individuality.

3. Angelou recounts her experiences as a maid with sly humor, which shows she no longer holds her early innocent view of her employer. Many observations in the story demonstrate both the young girl's naïveté and the mature Angelou's merciless mockery.

48

The young Angelou ostensibly decides to write her poem out of pity and sympathy for her employer. However, by writing about Mrs. Cullinan in her autobiography, Angelou shows how Mrs. Cullinan deserved little sympathy. The literal description of her employer as "white, fat, old" (24) emphasizes her unappealing appearance. Students can find many examples of irony that make Mrs. Cullinan an object of ridicule, including her efforts to "embalm" herself (10) and her inability to claim the Coleman girls as daughters (11, 12). By including these incidents in her autobiography, Angelou recounts an important turning point in her life, demonstrates the false superiority of her employer, and proves that the best revenge is writing well.

Connections

1. Angelou's risky, creative act was to break Mrs. Cullinan's favorite dishes so she could be fired from her job and keep her integrity intact. There are a number of possible analogies between Anzaldúa's piece and Angelou's story: just as the brother sacrifices his sister, so the characters in the story participate in an age-old pattern in which one race exploits another. Besides being "called out of her name," Angelou is violated when Mrs. Cullinan speaks with her friends about Angelou rather than allowing Angelou to answer them directly (paras. 14–19). When Angelou can't take any more abuse, she leaves the job — an act that will allow her to reassemble herself as a stronger person. As Anzaldúa says, "The next step in the creative process is picking up the pieces and moving them around — restructuring that broken body of Coyolxhauqui" (p. 273).

2. Angelou's Southern girlhood in the 1930s resembles Gates's Southern boyhood in the 1950s in a number of ways. Both teenagers are part of an extended black community: In Gates's case we learn explicitly about his large family, whereas in Angelou's case, her interactions with Miss Glory give the impression that blacks take care of one another in a culture that is largely hostile to them. The blacks in both stories represent a mix of races — Mr. Cullinan's daughters in "Mary" and Brady's descendants in "Down to Cumberland." The differences, however, are that blacks in Angelou's story seem more financially dependent on whites. Miss Glory encourages Margaret to ignore being called Mary so she can keep her job; Gates's family, by contrast, includes doctors, lawyers, dentists, and pharmacists, and their financial independence allows them a sense of pride Angelou's family almost can't afford.

3. All three sets of girls are being groomed (in different ways) to attract desirable husbands. In "Mary," the skills the white girls learn, waltzing and balancing a teacup on their knees, reflect a leisure-class ideal of women as graceful. The black girls' skills, crocheting doilies and embroidering linens, reflect a more practical ideal of women as useful, equipped to make the home more pleasant by providing a comfortable and morally improving atmosphere. In "Quinceañera," the girls study their religion and learn waltzing, poise (how to kneel in a long dress that is too tight), and gracious conversation, suiting them for a life of social interactions in which they strengthen ties with members of their community. Of the three groups, the last receives preparation most relevant to the future they face. Angelou's black girls' embroidery and tatting is less relevant to their future lives, most of which may be spent cooking and cleaning for white families. Angelou's white girls' skills are probably irrelevant to their futures, unless they marry well and spend much of their time being ornaments.

ANNIE DILLARD, Flying (p. 288)

Explorations

1. Annie Dillard attributes her attendance at the air show to "a newcomer's willingness to try anything once," and to the way June days in Bellingham, when it stays light until 10 P.M., encourage people to stay outside (para. 2). These reasons don't lead readers to expect much from the air show. Nor do Dillard's descriptions of the stunt planes, each of which performs more or less the same "batch of tricks" (3). But Dillard starts to raise readers' expectations when she mentions that Dave Rahm has performed for King Hussein of Jordan.

2. If Dillard did not compare Dave Rahm to visual and literary artists, readers might have a harder time grasping both the sense of elation she gained from watching him and the specific visual effects of his routine (although these analogies are only accessible to those familiar with the works of Steinberg and Klee). Besides using analogy, Dillard depicts the reactions of members of the crowd (the hushed announcer and dumbstruck children). She offers precise descriptions of the plane's movements and explains how watching Rahm's performance affected her sense of time: "Like music, it split the bulging rim of the future along its seam. It pried out the present. We watchers waited for the split-second curve of beauty in the present to reveal itself" (9).

3. The main difference between Rahm's artistry as a pilot and the artistry of the earthbound creators with whom she compares him is that Rahm's work is a performance occurring in time, whereas Steinberg's writing and Klee's painting are works one can experience repeatedly and at whatever pace one chooses. And they are classified as art, whereas Rahm's performance is considered a display of skill. Dillard chooses to downplay these differences, because she wants her readers to understand that Rahm's performance exhilarated her in the way only art — her reference point for peak experiences — can.

Connections

1. Dillard foreshadows her personal turning point by describing her low expectations for the airshow; she also raises readers' suspicion that something important may occur when she describes how Dave Rahm's name is separated from the rest of the program and casually mentions that he has performed for King Hussein of Jordan. Angelou foreshadows her personal turning point in the opening of the chapter, when she quotes the white, liberal friend's remark, "Why, you were a debutante" (p. 281), leading readers to expect to learn that she was no ordinary poor, Southern black girl. These hints at what follows lead readers to engage with a story's action.

2. Clive Barker expresses frustration with the fact that children are only permitted to inhabit the places of dreams until the age of five or so; implicit in his complaint is a wish for them to visit these places at any point in their lives. In "Flying," Dillard reaches the kind of imaginative heights Barker describes. Her description of how one lives in the summer suggests that she is primed for dream travel: "Your life parted and opened in the sunlight. You tossed your dark winter routines, thought up mad projects, and improvised everything from hour to hour . . . you could wave your arms in the air all day and all night, and sleep next winter" (para. 2). Likewise, her description of Rahm's effect on the audience suggests that she believes we all crave risk on some level: "he controlled the tension of the audience's longing. You desired, unwittingly, a certain kind of roll or climb, or a return to a certain portion of the air, and he fulfilled your hope slantingly,

like a poet, or evaded it until you thought you would burst, and then fulfilled it surprisingly, so you gasped and cried out" (10).

3. For Dillard, such moments are about beauty. After seeing Rahm, she realizes that all the poetry she's memorized and art she's looked at have taught her less about beauty than has the afternoon spent watching Rahm; she seems less impressed by his performance itself than by the manner in which it expanded her sense of possibility: "Nothing on earth is more gladdening than knowing we must roll up our sleeves and move back the boundaries of the humanly possible once more" (15).

ANDRE DUBUS, Imperiled Men (p. 293)

Explorations

1. Dubus links his title to the mission of pilots who must leave the ship within thirty minutes of a Soviet nuclear attack on the United States to bomb Moscow, knowing that they will die in the mission. The essay implies that the men are imperiled in a number of other ways: They must land planes on a carrier that looks, from the air, to be the size of an aspirin tablet; the sailor who tried to rescue the pilot whose parachute pulled him into the sea must face guilt for the pilot's death, although it was not his fault; homosexuals fear the shame of being discovered to the point that they would rather die than face it; and the rest of the men's morale can suffer when Navy policies cause someone they like and admire to kill himself.

2. The effect of Dubus's not naming any of the characters but himself is to make the story seem more archetypal, as if it could have been the story of any number of ships. The information he gives about CAG and other people aboard the *Ranger* emphasizes their humanity: The sailor who failed to save the pilot wept and said he'd failed after the man died. The man who died was married to a woman whose first husband had been a pilot who'd died in a crash; the pilots and young officers get drunk when given the opportunity, possibly a way to cope with the stress of their dangerous work. CAG walks proudly and is calm and kind to the author when he embarrasses himself by pulling CAG onto the floor. Clearly the author admires him: He is happy when CAG sits next to him on the boat for Hiroshima, hoping CAG will be his guide. (This is the most obvious example; you might prod students to look at every mention of CAG in the essay and analyze how Dubus conveys his regard.)

3. This repeated question conveys the author's surprise when he realizes that the ONI *expected* CAG would kill himself rather than face the exposure from their investigation. Giving the question a paragraph to itself adds emphasis, slowing down readers so they'll absorb its meaning. The next paragraph serves to confirm what readers should have grasped.

Connections

1. This question should help students think about where and how they choose to include important information in their own writing. CAG's death would come as a complete shock if Dubus did not mention it early on. But knowing about it allows readers to look

for details relating to it, to try to understand it before reading the scene that describes it. The effect is to make us look for ways to admire the underdog as we read, so that by the time we learn the details of his death, we have already become his allies. We are also sufficiently acquainted with the fact that he'll die so that we can step back to analyze how he died and question it — which seems to be exactly Dubus's intention.

2. Dillard might add a spiritual dimension to Dubus's explanations for why pilots are attracted to flying and drinking and why women are attracted to pilots. From her perspective, flying's chief attraction is the beauty that results from the risky business of looping through the air like a gymnast, never getting lost because, if the pilot did, "the ground would swat him" (p. 290). She loves how the pilot plays with the audience's fear and expectation and desire; there's communication and a sense of artistry to David Rahm's performance. By contrast, Dubus's pilots seem to love the sense of risk and the camaraderie they share.

3. The answers to the questions are obvious; the point is to get students to consider what it must have been like to stand in CAG's shoes or in those of the girl in Sarajevo, to have death be a commonplace event. Students might be more comfortable discussing this question in small groups, where it can be easier to speak about difficult topics. Or you could have them do an in-class free write before you discuss the question to give them a chance to engage it before talking about it.

RICHARD FORD, Optimists (p. 301)

Explorations

1. From the narrator's point of view, an optimist is someone who gambles, who believes the events he wants to occur will happen because he wants them to. The narrator's parents are the optimists of the title: the narrator states this explicitly at the close of the fourth paragraph, and it's clear by the way his father talks about his job and the family's future after Boyd Mitchell's death. His mother also encourages him to "be an optimist" after that death (para. 75), and she responds to having seen her son in the supermarket — she rushes over to his car after they've parted to be reassured that he does not believe she and Boyd Mitchell were having an affair, although she isn't willing to get to know him to learn how he really feels.

2. As a child, the narrator is less of an optimist than his parents: When his father gets out of jail, he says he "wanted him to be out and for our life to resume, and even though I did not see any way it could and, in fact, already knew it never would" (53). However, his comments about his attitude when he was sixteen suggest that he was an optimist then: "when you are the age I was then, and loose on the world and alone, you can get along better than at almost any other time, because it's a novelty, and you can act directly for what you want, and you can think that being alone will not last forever" (80). He seems to have given up on optimism by the last scene: He seems lonely, he sees his mother, she says she wants to know him better but makes no effort to learn how to contact him, and, the story ends: "she turned away, finally, and left me there alone" (105).

3. When the narrator looks forward as a child, he assumes that the night his father killed Boyd Mitchell will become the defining event of his life. But when he looks back as an adult, he sees how the relative importance of events can shift over time, so that the

preoccupations of one moment tend to supersede those of another; he observes, "The most important things in your life can change so suddenly, so unrecoverably, that you can forget even the most important of them and their connections, you are so taken up by the chanciness of all that's happened and by all that could and will happen next. I now no longer remember the exact year of my father's birth, or how old he was when I last saw him, or even when that last time took place. When you're young, these things seem unforgettable and at the heart of everything. But they slide away and are gone when you are not so young" (77).

Connections

1. In "Imperiled Men," the morale of the men on the ship seems most affected by CAG's death, whereas the sailor trying to rescue the pilot was most affected by his. In "Optimists," the narrator and Penny Mitchell seem most affected by Boyd Mitchell's death and the narrator's father by the hobo's. Students are most likely to identify CAG's death as the most tragic, because he is such a heroic figure in the story; but if the extent of tragedy is determined by how death affects the living, Boyd Mitchell's death may be seen as having worse effects on the narrator's family's life.

2. An obvious (though speculative) application for Seger's line is that the narrator's mother may have been having an affair with Boyd Mitchell, unsuspected by her young son. Nor did he know enough about his mother to doubt her when she assured him they would all be fine. Being an "optimist," he simply wanted to escape and, as a teenager, thought freedom was desirable. Now he knows it's lonely.

3. Like Ishiguro's narrator, Frank has cut himself loose from his family and relishes the freedom, although the former is ambivalent about having so much and the latter is on the verge of becoming ambivalent, once he realizes that freedom means loneliness. Both young men feel as if their relations with their parents are shrouded in ambiguity — Ishiguro's narrator wonders if his father might intend suicide and murder, and Frank isn't sure why his family broke up. Neither can ask his parent directly. The differences between the two situations are that Ishiguro's narrator's father wants his son and daughter to come live with him — a mixed compliment and threat. Frank's mother is more openly affectionate, saying she wishes they knew each other better, but she makes no effort to see him again.

WINDOWS:
THE WORLD

SOPHRONIA LIU, So Tsi-fai (p. 318)

Explorations

1. In her description of So Tsi-fai in paragraph 3, Liu seems to echo the teacher's feelings: All she can see are dirty clothes, the sneering grin, the shuffling gait. But after his suicide, as she remembers him, the reasons for his behavior become clear. She intersperses her own account of his hardships with the scorn and criticism of the teacher, revealing the frustration that So Tsi-fai faced daily. The ghost that comes to claim his rightful place is the product of Liu's own mind, born of her guilt. As she ponders those events during

the next twenty years, she begins to question the fickleness of fate, wondering why she was chosen to be successful whereas he was doomed to failure.

2. Paragraphs 6, 7, and 8 make it quite clear that Liu blames fate in the larger sense but the social system in particular for So Tsi-fai's death. When we hear Sister Marie's criticisms after we've read about the responsibilities heaped on the boy, we cannot help condemning an educational system that ignores the student's life outside the classroom. Liu seems to suggest that a more compassionate approach to education is needed, one that looks into the problems students may face out of school and attempts to help students rather than simply condemn them. (It might be interesting to compare students' sympathy with So Tsi-fai with their response to "problem students" in American classrooms. Are we as willing to sympathize with the real person who's disrupting our classroom as we are with the character we know only from the printed page?)

3. This question should provide quite a jolt for those students who have been told that sentence fragments are among the great crimes against humanity. Regardless, exploring this question will prove enlightening. The musing effect that Liu achieves by using fragments in her first three paragraphs suggests the uncertainty — even the desperation — of the sixth-grader confronted with the suicide of a peer. The questioning, the incompleteness of the thoughts is reflected in the sentence structure. When she begins paragraph 4 with the standard "It was a Monday in late November," the reader sits back, ready to hear the story behind the questions.

Connections

1. Both CAG and So Tsi-fai committed suicide because they could not bear being humiliated. But their futures would have differed significantly: CAG had been an admired figure until the ONI showed up to court-martial him or insist that he resign. So Tsi-fai's life had been shameful in the eyes of his parents, teachers, and peers and would continue to be shameful unless he made some drastic changes that, as the story makes clear, he lacked the resources to make. You might ask students how their school goes about supporting students who are having difficulties, and how they might support fellow students.

2. As eldest sons, both So Tsi-fai and Sugama are expected to take on major responsibility for the welfare of the families, especially to provide for their parents and younger siblings. Sugama, a young professional in Tokyo, will be expected to live with his parents and grandfather. His dilemma is that he cannot live with and support his parents in Tokyo, because it would be too expensive for them all to live there (p. 236). Instead, if he plans to honor his familial obligation, he will have to give up his city job and go home to take a dead-end job. So Tsi-fai's family differs from Sugama's in that they are extremely poor, making it even harder for So Tsi-fai to fulfill family obligations. As the oldest son, So Tsi-fai has had no older siblings to care for him, but he "helped in the fields, cooked for the family, and washed his own clothes" (para. 6). With so many responsibilities, he has little time to give to studies. This is the dilemma So Tsi-fai faces: If he devoted himself to doing well in school, he would not be able to contribute to his family's immediate needs. But because he had so little support for his schooling from teachers and parents (4, 7) and because he gave his time to responsibilities in the home, he has failed in school — which means that he will be unable to fulfill his parents' expectation that he help them more substantially in the future.

3. Baldwin claims that his friend committed suicide because the world "despised him for his vision" (p. 18), as well as for his color, and he had too much faith in people to

despise the world back. Not long before the friend's death, he and Baldwin had a conversation in which Baldwin denied the power of love, and his friend cried; Baldwin couldn't help but wonder to what extent he was responsible for his friend's suicide. It was this death that made him decide to leave the United States, lest he too fail to survive its hostility toward idealistic young black men. Liu's response to her friend's suicide resembles Baldwin's; she feels guilty for her own better fortune and angry at the lack of support that destroyed her friend. So Tsi-fai's ghost's remarks — "I died a tragic death. I have as much right as you to be here" (14) — might have been made by Baldwin's friend (although Baldwin does not appear to have been responsible for his friend's death in the same way that So Tsi-fai's social environment was).

LILIANA HEKER, The Stolen Party (p. 323)

Explorations

1. Some students will recognize that the theft of the party happens in two ways. Ines steals the party from Rosaura at the end by demonstrating that the girl was invited not as a guest but as a servant; the thing Rosaura most values, a sense of belonging and respect, is taken from her. Rosaura, at least from Ines's point of view, steals the party by stepping outside her prescribed role and insisting on being treated as a guest. Most students will be so thoroughly in sympathy with Rosaura's perspective that the second meaning of the title will go unnoticed. A few may add that the party has been "stolen" from working-class people like Rosaura's family by the undeserving rich, like Luciana's.

2. Although Señora Ines's ignorance and class bias allow her to believe she's being generous in giving Rosaura money rather than a trinket, the child recognizes the insult for what it is and immediately presses close to her true ally, her mother. Rosaura's refusal to take the bills, as well as her stare, reveal to Ines that she has erred; however, she is paralyzed, unable to withdraw the offer but incapable of making any other gesture. Both characters realize at this point that they've been involved in a charade, and that realization makes any further pretense impossible.

3. Among the possible responses to this question are Rosaura's certainty that her mother knows nothing about friendship (para. 8), her criticism of her mother's intolerance of rich people (13), her sense of superiority to the other children in the careful handling of dishes (19), her perception of power in being chosen to distribute the cake (39) and to hold the monkey (52), and her misinterpretation of Señora Ines's comment that she is a "marvelous daughter" (68). In each case she's attempting to repress any sense of inferiority to the rich children and to reinforce her own sense of importance. And she is indeed an accomplished child — she is an achiever in school and is interesting enough to intrigue her rich friend. But regardless of the legitimacy of her pride, her naïveté blinds her to the perceptions of society. She fails to recognize the fact that to Señora Ines her accomplishments are no more meaningful than the antics of the monkey; she may be clever, but she's still the maid's daughter.

Connections

1. The similarities are numerous: Both children suffer the consequences of poverty and lower-class status in their superficial rejection by those more privileged than they. Both accept the power of authority figures either to lift them from their present state or to

condemn them to a life of insignificance. So Tsi-fai is condemned by his teacher's judgment of him as "incorrigible" (p. 319); Rosaura feels exalted by her preferential treatment at the party — until the devastating revelation that Señora Ines has been using her as a maid. Rosaura's eyes, however, reveal her strength. The cold stare she levels at Señora Ines in the end suggests that she will not only survive but also will overcome the handicaps of poverty. She does not despair as does So Tsi-fai, in part because she can rely on the strength of her mother, who stands ready to protect her. In addition, her poverty and its demands are not as harsh as his. As a result, we can expect Rosaura to prevail.

2. There are several similarities between Maya Angelou's and Rosaura's situations: Both girls are poor but are learning the ways of a higher class. Angelou learns "the finer touches around the home, like setting a table with real silver" (p. 282) while working for a white woman, and Rosaura glimpses the ease and beauty in the home of her mother's employers and longs to be rich also. But their predicaments differ: Angelou is employed by the Cullinans and has no illusions about being perceived as an equal; she needs to earn money, but she has too much pride to allow her employer to call her "out of her name," so she breaks dishes to ensure she will be fired (pp. 284–285). By contrast, Rosaura believes Luciana and her family regard her as a friend of Luciana's, and she's shocked to be offered money instead of a gift at the end of the party; her solution is to give no response other than a cold-eyed stare when Luciana's mother holds out two bills.

3. Luciana's mother gives her a fancy birthday party that will impress the parents of the children who attend and reinforce her social position. The inclusion of Rosaura, who gracefully helps to keep things running smoothly, is part of her effort to bring off a perfect party. Luciana, like Rosaura, is too young and naïve to understand how the party might be an occasion to reinforce class divisions by displaying wealth. She only wants to enjoy herself and to be sure her guests, including Rosaura, enjoy the party too. The different goals of mother and daughter are in some ways analogous to the different goals of mothers and daughters in Susan Orlean's "Quinceañera." Quinceañeras are opportunities to impress friends and relatives with an extravagant show of clothes, money, music, and food. Whereas the daughters enjoy receiving the attention and gifts, the mothers may use the occasion to be recognized for their social and organizational talents.

AMITAV GHOSH, The Ghosts of Mrs. Ghandi (p. 330)

Explorations

1. The ghosts of Mrs. Ghandi are the "very real qualities that had been taken for granted: her fortitude, her dignity, her physical courage, her endurance" (para. 11), qualities manifested in many people mentioned in the essay: a busload of people protects a Sikh man hidden on board by saying there are no Sikhs on the bus; the Sens hide the Bawas in their apartment as their cook lies to save their lives; the women in a group of people trying to dispel the violence surround the men to protect them from an angry mob.

2. Several incidents in the wake of Ghandi's assassination become turning points for Ghosh. When he is teaching the morning of the assassination, he realizes what's happened and loses his concentration: "it was a sense of something slipping loose, of a mooring coming untied somewhere within" (12). When he and Hari Sen listen to the mob interrogating the Bawas' cook, he realizes their fate depends on this frightened

man; most of the mob leaves, but a few men remain, and he remembers feeling "a strange sense of disconnection" as he walks down the driveway to shout at the men (60). This moment of expressing his outrage may have been his first step toward joining a crowd he sees the next day that is forming to confront the mob. In joining them, Ghosh relinquishes his former view of himself as an observer who, like V. S. Naipaul, might wish to join but does not. In a more general sense, the aftermath of the assassination led Ghosh to consider how he might write about it "without reducing it to mere spectacle" (81), and how difficult it is for any writer to describe violent events in an age where they tend to be aestheticized for public consumption.

3. The students at the university where Ghosh teaches seem changed by the events he describes; the morning of the assassination, they hover around transistor radios rather than flinging frisbees as they normally do. And certainly the Bawas, the elderly Sikh couple who have trouble grasping the idea that anyone might want to hurt them, are changed by the events; "with the flames visible from his windows, [Mr. Bawa] was more receptive" to the idea of going to the neighbors' house (48).

Connections

1. The Bawas' social cocoon initially prevents them from seeing the danger they face from a Sikh-hating mob, and they choose to stay home; only when they see the danger do they accept the neighbors' offer of refuge. This choice pays off, as their cook protects them, telling the angry mob that their house is owned by a Hindu. Luciana's choice to ask Rosaura to her party is naïve and unrealistic in that she doesn't realize her mother views her friend as a servant-in-training. Her mother's seeing Rosaura's willingness to help at the party as reflecting her desire to be paid is equally naïve and unrealistic. Neither Luciana's choice to invite Rosaura nor Señora Ines's decision to offer her money pays off, as Rosaura rejects the money in bewilderment.

2. The Sikhs' predicament in "The Ghosts of Mrs. Ghandi" resembles the Muslims' predicament in "Sarajevo Diary" in that both are ethnic groups that have been singled out for persecution; both groups must guard against random violence. The difference lies in the organizational apparatus of their persecutors: Whereas the Muslims are being systematically attacked by the Serbian army, the Sikhs are being pursued by haphazard, angry mobs.

3. Karahasan's point about "the decision to perceive literally everything as an aesthetic phenomenon" (para. 80) contrats sharply with the atttitude of Baldwin and his friend and their fellow artists, who, rather than "sidestepping questions about goodness and truth" (80), are eager to embrace them, to build a Socialist utopia. You might ask students to consider whether the contrast has to do with the racial or political climate in the United States after World War II versus now, or with changes in the perceived roles of artists and the arts, or with the homogenizing effect of the mass media — particularly television — on our perceptions of race, politics, and the arts (see "Future Shlock," p. 670).

NADINE GORDIMER, Where Do Whites Fit in? (p. 344)

Explorations

1. Gordimer's first answer to the question is *"Nowhere"* (para. 1), because even the gentlest African likes the idea of an Africa free of whites. Her real answer is that whites can fit

in, but they must be flexible about determining their place in the new Africa ("sideways, where-we-can, wherever-they'll-shift-up-for-us" [2]). The effect of her starting with an extreme answer is to make readers consider the question from Africans' point of view, to entertain the idea that whites don't belong there at all. Beginning this way prepares readers to accept the idea that whites will need to be sensitive to Africans' perspectives, if they wish to "fit in."

2.   For Gordimer, the critical factor in deciding whether to stay in Africa or to leave is whether it feels like *home*, with home defined as "the place you were born to, the faces you first saw around you, and the elements of the situation among your fellow men in which you found yourself and with which you have been struggling, politically, personally, or artistically, all your life" (8). That whites continue to struggle to fit in, to be sensitive to how they can help without being condescending, is critical to South Africa's future success under black rule, because it will need "the technical, scientific and cultural knowledge that white civilization has acquired many hundreds of years before black civilization, and on which, whether the Africans like it or not, their own aspirations are based" (10).

3.   When Gordimer uses "African," she means "black African." She refers to people in her own racial and national group as "the white man" (when speaking in symbolic terms) (1, 7, 9), "my fellow-whites" (when speaking of her and other whites' indignation at the idea of becoming peripheral) (10), and "white South Africans" (when suggesting black South Africans feel greater camaraderie with other Africans than with their white countrymen) (4). She also says whites will become "a minority minority instead of the majority minority we've been used to being" (11). This last usage especially helps to bolster her thesis that whites will need to adjust to their newly decreased status.

Connections

1.   Gordimer wants to prevent a violent turning point, one that might be fomented by "the stubborn mass that will continue, like a Napoleon in a madhouse, to see itself as the undisputed master and make no attempt to consider the reality of living another role" (para. 6). The potential advantage of her asking where whites fit in is that she might inspire some members of "the stubborn mass" to start facing the reality that they will need to step aside.

2.   Rosaura's mother doesn't follow Gordimer's advice; she attempts to dissuade her daughter from attending the party: "It's a rich people's party. . . . You know what you are to them? The maid's daughter, that's what" (p. 324). The result is that Rosaura goes anyway and learns that her mother was right, ends up pressing against her as she seeks a refuge from Señora Ines's insult.

3.   Both writers make the point that it is hard to live in a place where you feel people of your race are not welcome, where you can sense hostility toward you and your kind in the air. However, Baldwin's points about the negative aspects of immigrating would probably apply to Gordimer and other white ex-Africans: The new place will not feel like home, its customs will be unfamiliar, things one took for granted at home will be missed dearly, and, if one did not feel at home in the first place, one is likely to take that feeling with him or her.

(Text Pages) 352–358

SPOTLIGHT:
RUSSIA

ADDITIONAL INFORMATION ON COUNTRY

Environment: Russia's five vast regions include the European region, the Ural area, Siberia, Caucasia, and the Central Asian region. Lying between Russia's western border and the Ural mountains, the European region is the richest. It consists of a vast plain that is crossed by the Volga, Don, and Dnieper rivers. The Urals, the conventional boundary between Europe and Asia, are rich in mineral deposits. Siberia, located in the region between the Urals and the Pacific Ocean, is also rich in natural resources but, due to its harsh climate, is sparsely populated. Caucasia is an enormous steppe extending northward from the Caucasian mountains. Central Asia is an enormous depression of land that includes desert, steppes, and mountains. The plains produce grain, potatoes, and sugar beet; cotton and fruit are grown in Central Asia; and tea, grapes, and citrus fruit are grown in the subtropical Caucasian region. Heavy industry and mining of coal, iron, and other minerals have increasingly contaminated the country's main rivers, air, and soil. Deforestation and soil erosion are also widely prevalent.

Demographics: Russia's 150 million citizens are divided among 83 percent Russians, 3 percent Tartars, 3 percent Ukrainians, and over 100 other ethnic groups. Moscow has almost 9 million people, and St. Petersburg has 4.5 million.

Religion: The Soviet Union was officially an atheist country. Religion was outlawed, and 50 percent of the population regarded themselves as atheists. Religious worship is now allowed, and religious participation has increased. Russia's religions include Russian Orthodoxy, Protestantism, Islam, and Judaism, as well as native animistic religions.

Education: Literacy is almost 100 percent, and education is free and compulsory for children aged seven to seventeen. Instruction is offered in a variety of languages. To enter college, students must pass rigorous examinations.

Economy: The future of the Russian economy is still far from clear, although the forecast produced by the Russian government is optimistic. It apparently serves more political than economic purposes. Nonetheless, recent statistics have been positive: in 1995, Russia's economy contracted by the smallest amount since reforms began, whereas the country's trade surplus rose by half. Gross domestic product, a broad measure of goods and services, fell only 4 percent adjusted for inflation, down from a 13 percent drop in 1994. Unemployment was 8 percent in December 1995, although 32 percent of families lived below the official poverty level. The level of consumption was extremely low. In the beginning of 1994, meat and fish consumption was at the level of the 1960s, and milk and dairy products were at the level of the 1950s. In 1994, deaths exceeded births by 1 million people.

VLADIMIR NABOKOV, From *Speak, Memory* (p. 354)

Explorations

1. Students may respond to this question on different levels. On one level, as he rides home he realizes that he may lose his father. When he arrives home, of course, he sees

59

that this pillar of his life will not die (yet). His response in the final paragraph, "my heart welled in me like that wave . . . and I had no handkerchief," reveals that he burst into tears. On a more subtle level some students may point out that it seems to come as a surprise to Nabokov to realize on his ride home that he loves his father, that there is a "tender friendship underlying my respect for" his father (para. 7). When he arrives home, the realization that there will be no duel precipitates an equally surprising response in the boy: He appreciates, for the first time, his father's mortality. When Nabokov alludes to his father's eventual death ten years hence, he states that "no shadow was cast by that future event upon the bright stairs of our St. Petersburg house." However, he acknowledges at the same time the inevitability of death: "Several lines of play in a difficult chess composition were not blended yet on the board" (9).

2. Students will find a number of "lessons" in this essay, among them Nabokov's appreciation of the loyalty of his friend, who refuses to mention Nabokov's part in his accident, his realization of his love for his father and of his father's mortality (as discussed in Question 1), and his awakened understanding of reality (the simple way in which the duel is forestalled versus the boy's vision of the duel). In the last paragraph, the adult Nabokov adds to this list his insight into the fickleness of fate, saving the father from this threat only to kill him just as senselessly several years later.

3. Students can find combat or duel images in the discussion of the Japanese war and in the behavior of Nabokov's classmates as they pass around the magazine, in the fight with the friend who had brought the magazine to school; in the boy's musings about weapons; in the relationship between Nabokov and the cabdriver and between the driver and his horse; in his recollection of famous duels; in the "habitual exchange of homespun nonsense" with his father (7); in the slap of his uncle's gloves on the balustrade and the image of the chess game (9).

Connections

1. Both Nabokov and Liu seem to be aiming to illuminate remorse for an unnecessary death, that of a close relative in the first case and of a classmate in the second. Both stories' speakers seem genuinely saddened by their losses, but Liu's story has an extra layer of meaning: she makes clear that the responsibility for So Tsi-fai's death lies with everyone who knew him and failed to intervene in some way. Nabokov's reminiscences might have less impact if he structured his essay more like Liu's. By focusing on a near miss rather than the more dramatic death that followed it a decade later, Nabokov leads readers from preparation for the death to relief at the miss to well-informed shock at the later death.

2. The lavish party given by her mother reveals Luciana to be a spoiled child, and the behavior she exhibits toward Rosaura (particularly in sharing the secret of the monkey) reinforces that impression. In Nabokov's memoir, the evidence is more abundant: his education, his father's indulgence, the fact that he usually is transported to school by a private car. But the emphasis in the two pieces is quite different: Whereas Heker focuses on the inhumanity of the rich and the resultant restlessness of the poor, Nabokov reminisces about the leisure of the rich, which allows the family to savor such stimulating, mentally enriching activities as chess and butterfly collecting, and to become closer to one another. Heker's view reflects a disdain for the idle, insensitive rich, emphasizing the moral superiority of the poor. Heartless as she may seem to Rosaura at the beginning, her mother's primary motivation in scoffing at the party invitation is to protect her daughter from the inevitable revelation that she will never be considered

a guest at her friend's house. And the final scene reinforces that strength — Rosaura and her mother stand proud, almost haughty, as Señora Ines is frozen in a humiliating immobility. In contrast, Nabokov ascribes great dignity and sensitivity to the wealthy. Although he regrets the risks his father takes with his writing, he nevertheless respects the power of the man's money and pen. He also considers their leisurely life to be one of enrichment, both intellectual and emotional. He considers what he shares with his father on their rides and butterfly excursions to be beyond the reach of the poor; it is only in this closeness that a family can truly appreciate their dependence on one another. His dignity arises from wealth and power, Heker's from the strength of the oppressed.

3. By the last line of the essay, Nabokov means that the series of events that would lead to his father's death had not begun, either in reality or in his own consciousness. In that he is reminiscing as an adult, long after the "difficult chess composition" of that death, his point is similar to Theroux's: Both feel nostalgic for a time when they were eager to outgrow their youthful innocence.

JOSEPH BRODSKY, Less than One (p. 359)

Explorations

1. Students may see this question as more difficult than it is, so you might start by asking if anyone has studied nature versus nurture in a psychology class. They should then be able to figure out that "existence conditions consciousness" is a way of claiming that nurture takes precedence over nature, that our environment determines who we are. When Brodsky argues that consciousness can "condition and ignore existence" by acquiring "the art of estrangement" (para. 2), he is saying that one's consciousness is not subject to one's environment; once one distances oneself from one's environment, one can view it however one pleases, or ignore it altogether. Brodsky's own life shows his point in action: By age seven, he has become suspicious of all images of Lenin surrounding him and dislikes them for their very abundance. At the same age, he is sufficiently aware of people's attitudes toward Jews to lie about his nationality. And by age fifteen, he has determined that the only way for him to escape his environment is to drop out of school.

2. Students unfamiliar with this phenomenon might understand it better if you ask why students who are running for office at their college or university plaster the halls with posters picturing them and announcing their qualifications for leadership. According to Brodsky, citizens were meant to react to these "omnipresent images" of Lenin with admiration, to see "that meaningless expression on his face" as reflecting "a sense of purpose" (6). Brodsky despised these images for their abundance, although he later credited them as being his "first lesson in . . . estrangement," teaching him to regard anything he saw in plenitude as "some sort of propaganda" (8).

3. Brodsky makes it clear that he resented his schools' attempts to make him conform to the norms they defined, that he saw rejecting their values as the only way to preserve his identity. As he puts it, "the only way for a boy to fight his imminent lot would be to go off the track" (16). In his own case, "it wasn't so much a conscious choice as a gut reaction. I simply couldn't stand certain faces in my class . . . " (16). Brodsky seems to have striven for independence and spontaneity in an environment that encouraged "total surrender to the state" (13).

Connections

1.   Both writers describe the grand homes of old Russia: Brodsky imagines the "old pianos, worn-out rugs, dusty paintings in heavy bronze frames, leftovers of furniture" remaining behind the facades he passed on the way to school (para. 5). Nabokov had lived in one of those buildings, in a house with oil paintings and marble statues, alabaster bowls and crystal *objets d'arte*. The most striking contrasts are that by Brodsky's time, the facades' classical features were chipped by artillery shells, and the Soviets' equalizing decor has replaced beautiful Russian interiors with "those stuccoed walls . . . with their blue horizontal stripe at eye level" (18) and ubiquitous portraits of Lenin.

2.   Brodsky hates the name Leningrad, because the word does not resonate for Russians any more than does "construction" or "sausage" — unlike "Peter," the nickname for its former name, St. Petersburg (4).

3.   The author of "Evicted: A Russian Jew's Story (Again)" claims to be emigrating from the Soviet Union because she hears so much anti-Semitic sentiment — whether from a right-wing political group or her own neighbors. She sees food shortages and low wages as important problems but claims they are not the reasons she's leaving. Although Brodsky experienced anti-Semitism as a child, he felt more oppressed by the manner in which the Soviet system tried to make him conform and obey. The difference could stem from the different aims of the two pieces of writing: although the author of "Evicted" seeks to explain why she is emigrating, Brodsky is trying to explain how his identity formed in response to his culture.

GALINA DUTKINA, Sovs, Hacks, and Freeloaders (p. 367)

Explorations

1.   According to Dutkina, "a sov is generally a person raised in the traditions of socialist egalitarian ideology, with all the resultant personality traits (including a slavish attitude toward authority)" (para. 4). Students might also gather that a sov is someone who responds to commercials about the joys of becoming an investor by rushing out to become one, or a person who sells vodka and sausages on the street because it is the easiest — and most mindless — way to make a ruble.

2.   Dutkina's chief complaints about the old Soviet government's policies are that it encouraged "the habit of parasitism" by guaranteeing everyone a free crust of bread, health care, housing, and public education (9). When the State dissolved and issued each citizen a voucher representing his or her share of the national wealth (worth about $5), it unwittingly terrified people into becoming freeloaders, if they hadn't already. Dutkina attributes the Soviet government's failings to its having sold off its natural resources, such as timber, to offer citizens food, furniture, appliances, and cars at artificially low prices.

3.   Dutkina believes the current political and economic system is worse than the Soviet system in that people are a lot poorer than they used to be: Skilled workers, university professors, and government employees used to make a reasonable wage. Now they are either very poor or out hustling, having abandoned whatever field they trained in. The current climate is better, however, in that it is not based on false, unsustainable economic

policies (see number 2). She explains the current system's failing as the result of Anatoly Chubais' "privatization games," which did not redistribute the country's wealth equitably (10). As for remedies, she seems at a loss to recommend any.

Connections

1. Like Brodsky, Dutkina complains that Soviet Communism fostered in its citizens slavish obedience, dependence on the central government for material needs, and a taste for a safe, if monotonous existence. That Dutkina would agree with Brodsky's ideas about Marx's statement is apparent in her remarks about the boom in Russian investment resulting from commercials about the easy rewards of the stock market (para. 13). She would probably agree with Brodsky's view that the antidote to such conformity is to "go off the track," but she might also point to the financial barriers to doing so (p. 364).

2. In his excerpt from *Speak, Memory*, Nabokov depicts the West's influence on Russia when casually discussing the difference between a Parisian and a Russian duel (p. 355), mentioning the Perugino and Dutch oils in his father's study (p. 356), and the Wimbledon matches and London papers he and his father followed (p. 356); these references suggest that upper-class Russians sampled the world's art and kept abreast of world affairs. Dutkina depicts Western influence on Russia when she describes the popularity of Mexican soap operas, "where the heroes, wilting under the blows of cruel fate for the whole series, are inevitably brought fortune in the end" (9). The shows breed "new Ivan the Fool types by the millions, who dream of their own personal Firebird of Fortune" (9). Or, in commercials encouraging people to try investing, two brothers' success culminates in a trip to the world soccer championships in America (19). Although Dutkina doesn't emphasize this point, the West encouraged communism by buying up the Soviet Union's natural resources, financing the government.

3. Based on the last paragraph of her essay, as well as her statements throughout about Russians' slavish devotion to whatever ideology is current, Dutkina would probably explain the anti-Semitism cited by the epigraph's author as yet another instance of Russians' tendency to avoid responsibility and to follow the crowd, whether that crowd is working dutifully at state jobs, selling pantyhose on a street corner, or insulting Jews.

NATASHA SINGER, The New Russian Dressing (p. 378)

Explorations

1. The title has an obvious pun on Russian dressing — salad dressing. The salad is the nutritious element and the dressing is usually fatty and oversweetened; it adds flavor but does not nourish. The title suggests that Singer sees rich Russians who are obsessed with clothes as pretending to add flavor to the society, when in fact they are probably hurting it economically. This attitude is apparent when Singer quotes her subjects' earnest observations about fashion — "Cartier is for day wear" — so that any reader with a sense of irony will perceive them as somewhat ludicrous (para. 6).

2. The top status symbols for New Russian women appear to be mobile phones, filofaxes, walkie-talkies, trips to Europe and the United States, and designer clothes — preferably worn one designer at a time. For New Russian men, the top status symbols appear to be bodyguards, chauffeur-driven bomb-proof cars, and well-dressed wives or

girlfriends. These messages communicate power and sophistication to their wealthy peers, as well as to boutique salespeople and lower-class Russians. The cars and bodyguards also communicate fear of enemies.

3.   In her opening paragraph, Singer contrasts camouflage-clad troops carrying AK-47s with Jaguars and Jeeps driven by the chauffeurs of the rich. She reinforces the contrast when describing Vladimir Sloutsker's newly bombed white jeep and his subsequent purchase of a bombproof "presidential Chevrolet limousine, the kind President Clinton uses" (7) and the armed guards stationed at the entrance to the Versace boutique. The point of the initial contrast is to suggest that Russia's new wealth creates chaos (traffic jams) that the society is not equipped to deal with and resentment (bodyguards, armored cars); moreover, the rich are rightly paranoid, and even shop owners must screen their clientele with armed guards.

Connections

1.   In Galina Dutkina's statement, the "we" consists of people who could not possibly buy new furniture or appliances or cars but who "thoughtlessly spend" their money on food and clothes because they fear their money may not be worth anything in a week or a month, should they save it. The New Russians spend not because they fear their money will become worthless, but because they wish to show off their wealth with baubles and clothes: "this new nobility wants only the best" (para. 10).

2.   The characters in "The New Russian Dressing" share Brodsky's nonconformity in that they want to stand out from the crowd: According to Olga Sloutsker, "supermodels are already passé, as is Versace and perhaps even Chanel" (4). She claims she used to be "crazy about Chanel. . . . But now everybody here is wearing it, so I buy only pieces" (4). A little behind the times perhaps, Galina Grishena prefers Versace because it's "bright and attention-getting, and I don't want to be lost in the crowd" (21). Clearly, their nonconformity is superficial and sartorial, whereas Brodsky's is ideological.

3.   The Sloutskers and others seem to be emulating old Russians such as Nabokov's family in their desire to be cosmopolitan, with a key difference: The Nabokovs read London papers and buy Dutch and Italian art, but the New Russians seem primarily interested in cars and clothes. However, both groups seem concerned with protecting themselves; Nabokov's father has firearms and swords in the house and the characters in Singer's article have bodyguards and bomb-proof cars. Rather than the Russians of 1914, the New Russians seems to be copying the rich of the West, seeking to acquire all the accouterments of a fashionable life. Grishena admits in the final paragraph that they may seem "cheap" to Westerners, but adds, "we are learning, and I think maybe in ten years we will be quite sophisticated."

RUSSIA: INVESTIGATIONS/WEB SITES

Russia (http://www.west.net/~wwmr/links.html) provides a collection of links to Russian news agencies, a map of Russian Web servers, Russian online services, and many other sites.

Russia Today (http://www.ceo.cz/rtoday/), an online magazine published by the European Information Network, offers articles on a variety of topics from such agencies as the

Reuters News Service. The site also has links to other sites featuring the 1996 elections, the Constitution, political parties, parliament, the government structure, government addresses, and many other topics.

The St. Petersburg Times (http://www.spb.su/times/191-192/index.html) is the online version of St. Petersburg's primary daily newspaper.

Friends and Partners (http://www.friends-partners.org/friends/opt-tables-unix-english) was jointly developed by citizens of the United States and Russia to foster cultural exchange. It includes links to art, religion, culture, economy, politics, and many other aspects of Russian life that can be perused with its search engine.

The Russian Chronicles (http://www.f8.com/FP/Russia/index.html) is an experiment in interactive photojournalism created especially for the World Wide Web by FocalPoint f/8. Gary Matoso, a photojournalist based in Paris, and Lisa Dickey, a freelance journalist based in St. Petersburg, traveled from Vladivostok to St. Petersburg, and their photographs from their trip can be found at this site.

ADDITIONAL QUESTIONS AND ASSIGNMENTS

1. In a journal entry or a collection of informal notes, refer to two or three of the selections to discuss initiation rituals as they apply to women. Consider such issues as perceptions of women's ability to assume responsibility, rules governing their behavior, support (or lack of it) from other women, and their obligations toward men. As you look over your notes, try to discover similarities and differences among the cultures represented. Write an essay in which you discuss the image of women in a given culture.

2. Many of the selections in Part Three deal with how individuals break with the traditions and expectations of their culture as way of defining a new self or marking their entry into a new stage of maturity. In Maya Angelou's "Mary," the protagonist decides she will not let a white woman humiliate her and instead walks away from her job. As part of the process of maturing, she realizes that she cannot tolerate being called "out of her name." In a similar way, Sophronia Liu realizes she can't remain comfortable with her peers' treatment of So Tsi-fai. Using Angelou, Dubus, Ford, Liu, Heker, Ghosh, or Nabokov as a model, think of a time in your life when you either conformed or decided not to conform with what others around you had expected from you. First, describe the episode. What did you do? Why? How did your actions fit or differ from what you were supposed to do? Then, describe how you see the episode now. Were you right in what you did? Why or why not? What would you do differently?

3. One lament heard frequently today is that children are growing up too fast. Statistics reveal that problems with sexuality and substance abuse that used to be found in high schools now plague junior highs and middle schools. Parents complain that everything from rock videos to advertising encourages children to imitate adults. Using magazines and newspapers from the 1950s or the 1960s and from the present, compile information on what young people were wearing, doing, listening to, and buying during those decades. Using the information you've gathered, write a paper in which you compare the attitudes and life-styles of young people in the two periods, focusing on two or three of the categories you've set up (for example, clothing, musical tastes, recreation). Emphasize in your paper the positive and negative features of the experience of young people in each period.

4. Conduct further research into one of the cultures represented in this section (African-American, Taiwanese, Argentinian, Indian, or Russian), focusing specifically on the transition from childhood to adulthood. If the selection is an excerpt from a larger work, look first at that work. You can find more information about the culture by consulting a general encyclopedia, a journal devoted to the study of that culture, and/or the Internet. Narrow your topic to something manageable, such as a particular rite of passage, the influences of religion on that culture's rites of passage, or the differences in rites depending on class or sex, and write an expository paper in which you elaborate on the culture's treatment of initiation into adulthood.

Part Four

OPPOSITE SEXES

INTRODUCTION

Given the backlash against feminism in recent years and the discomfort some college-age students feel about discussing gender issues, teaching this section may require a bit more energy than others. But the rewards will be well worth the effort. Your students may come to find that we don't always perceive women and men in realistic terms, preferring to stereotype them. Among the epigraphs, students will find references to "the madonna" as "female prototype" (Allen), men who would rather be "guys" (Friedman), women depicted as wives and mothers first (Ugwu-Oju), and men depicted as sexual brutes (Paglia). A class discussion of various contemporary terms for men and women may prove enlightening, easing the way into more complex analyses of related images in other cultures. Among the selections themselves, Tannen's provides an excellent opportunity to discuss male-female dynamics in the classroom; such a discussion can help students to become more aware of how they participate in class and how their participation affects others. Updike's and Keen's pieces should provoke a strong response, inviting students to opine on a subject they believe they know something about (gender roles). Students should have plenty to say about Wikan's provocative piece about *xaniths* as well.

Within the section, there are several possible subthemes, including romantic visions of relationships (Silko, Moravia, and Mahfouz), European versus Islamic views of sexuality (Minai, Wikan, and Kazantzakis), and marriage (Shostak, Moravia, and Mahfouz).

Instructors may wish to consult the following familiar works in preparing related selections from *Making Contact:*

Essays

Judy Brady, "I Want a Wife" (*Ms.*, Dec. 1971).
Annie Dillard, "The Deer at Providencia" (*Teaching a Stone to Talk*, Harper, 1982).
Gretel Ehrlich, "About Men" (*The Solace of Open Spaces*, Viking, 1985).
Barbara Lawrence, "Four-Letter Words Can Hurt You" (*New York Times*, Oct. 27, 1973).
S. J. Perelman, "The Machismo Mystique" (*Vinegar Puss*, Simon and Schuster, 1975).
Katherine Anne Porter, "The Necessary Enemy" (*Collected Essays and Occasional Writings of Katherine Anne Porter*, Delacorte, 1970).
Scott Russell Sanders, "The Men We Carry in Our Minds" (*The Paradise of Bombs*, University of Georgia Press, 1987).
Susan Sontag, "Beauty: How Will It Change Next" (*Vogue*, May 1975).
Deborah Tannen, "Different Words, Different Worlds" (*You Just Don't Understand*, Morrow, 1990).
Paul Theroux, "On Being a Man" (*Sunrise With Seamonsters*, Houghton Mifflin, 1985).
James Thurber, "Courtship Through the Ages" (*My World — And Welcome to It*, Harcourt, 1942).

Short Stories

Margaret Atwood, "Rape Fantasies" (*Dancing Girls*, McClelland and Stewart, 1977).
Kay Boyle, "The Astronomer's Wife" (*Life Being the Best*, New Directions, 1988).
John Cheever, "The Country Husband" (*The Stories of John Cheever*, Knopf, 1978).
William Faulkner, "A Rose for Emily" (*Collected Stories of William Faulkner*, Random House, 1950).
James Joyce, "The Dead" (*Dubliners*, Viking, 1982).
D. H. Lawrence, "The Horse Dealer's Daughter" (*Complete Short Stories*, Penguin, 1976).
D. H. Lawrence, "Tickets, Please" (*Complete Short Stories*, Penguin, 1976).
Doris Lessing, "A Woman on a Roof" (*A Man and Two Women*, Simon and Schuster, 1963).
Alice Munro, "Meneseteung" (*Friends of My Youth*, Knopf, 1990).
Katherine Anne Porter, "Rope" (*Flowering Judas*, Harcourt, 1930).
Eudora Welty, "Petrified Man" (*The Collected Stories of Eudora Welty*, Harcourt, 1980).

BIOGRAPHICAL NOTES ON EPIGRAPH AUTHORS

1. Paula Gunn Allen, a professor of English and American Indian Literature at the University of California, Los Angeles, is of Laguna Pueblo, Sioux, and Lebanese parentage. She has written a novel, *The Woman Who Owned Shadows* (1983), five collections of poems including *Skins and Bones* (1988), and several collections of essays including *The Sacred Hoop: Recovering the Feminine in American and Contemporary Writing by Native American Women* (1989), *Grandmother of the Light: A Medicine Woman's Sourcebook* (1991), and *Voice of the Turtle: American Indian Literature 1900–1970* (1994).

2. David Friedman writes for *Newsday* and other publications.

3. Joe Kane is the author of two nonfiction accounts of Latin America, *Running the Amazon* and *Savages*, as well as numerous articles. He lives in Oakland, California.

4. A professor of sociology at Arizona State University, Rose Weitz is the author *of Labor Pains: Modern Midwives and Home Birth* (1988), *Life with AIDS* (1991), and *The Sociology of Health, Illness, and Health Care: A Critical Approach* (1995).

5. Gerald Early is professor and director of the African and Afro-American Studies Program in Arts and Sciences at Washington University. He won the National Book Critics Circle Award for *The Culture of Bruising: Essays on Prizefighting* (1994). His other books include *Tuxedo Junction: Essays on American Culture* (1992), *Lure and Loathing: Essays on Race, Identity, and the Ambivalence of Assimilation* (1993), and *One Nation Under a Groove: Motown and American Culture* (1995).

6. Population Communications International (PCI) uses the mass media to help developing countries solve their population and related environmental and health problems. Through radio and television serials, PCI works to popularize the idea of small families, enhance the status of women, and erase fears of contraceptive use.

7. Camille Paglia teaches humanities at the University of the Arts in Philadelphia. She is the author of *Sexual Personae: Art and Decadence from Nefertiti to Emily Dickinson* (1990), *Sex, Art, and American Culture* (1992), and *Vamps and Tramps: New Essays* (1994).

8. Lawrence Wright has taught at the American University of Cairo and has been a staff writer for the *Race Relations Reporter*. He is the author of *In the New World: Growing Up with America from the Sixties to the Eighties* (1987) and *Peace Report* (1991).

9. Born and raised in Nigeria, Dympna Ugwu-Oju came to the United States to attend Briarcliff College and Syracuse University, and then returned to Nigeria for a marriage her family had arranged. She is a professor of English at Kings River Community College in California and the author of *What Will My Mother Say: A Tribal African Girl Comes of Age in America* (1995).

10. President of Nicaragua from 1990 to 1996, Violeta Chamorro worked with mixed success to revitalize her country's economy by reactivating the private sector and stimulating the export of agricultural products.

11. Miriam Cooke is a professor and director of Asian and African Languages and Literature at Duke University, as well as a translator, editor, and author. Her most recent books are *War's Other Voices: Women Writers in the Lebanese Civil War* (1988); *Opening the Gates: A Century of Arab Feminist Writing* (1990), which she co-edited; *Gendering War Talk* (1993); and *Global Voices: Contemporary Literature from the Non-Western World* (1995).

Explorations

1. Among the epigraph writers who regard women as occupying an inferior position are Paula Gunn Allen, who sees women in Western culture (but not American Indian women) regarded as Madonnas or whores or as mindless, helpless, simple, or oppressed; Gerald Early, who entertains the possibility that black women who straighten their hair are reacting to feeling inferior to white women; the Population Communications International writer, who depicts women in India, Costa Rica, Brazil, Peru, and Mexico as brutalized via infanticide, rape, battering, and genital mutilation; and Dympna Ugwu-Oju, who admits that Ibos believe a woman is worthless unless she has children. No epigraph writer overtly states that men have a privileged status, but all cited above imply that through the way they depict women.

2. Among the epigraph writers who regard women as having a privileged status are Allen, who claims that in some American Indian tribes, women "wield considerable power"; and Joe Kane, who concedes that women are becoming increasingly more successful. Among those who regard men as having an inferior status are David Friedman, who describes becoming a man as "the big impossible"; Kane, who suggests that men with successful wives are regarded as wimps; and Camille Paglia, who claims that "men must struggle for identity against the overwhelming power of their mothers."

3. Friedman, Paglia, Wright, and Chamorro agree that men are more aggressive than women; the first three also agree that men are more sexually aggressive. They seem to disagree about just how difficult it is for men to control themselves. Paglia insists that boys will be boys and it is up to women to protect themselves from them. Wright makes a similar assertion, backing up his claims with biology. And Friedman claims that a loose moral code is one of the "primal characteristics" of guys.

4. Allen, Early, Ugwu-Oju, and Chamorro agree that women are more inclined than men to be cooperative, but see cooperation differently, whether seeing a woman's destiny as identical with that of her people (Allen); participating in a communal "laying on of

hands," whereby black women help themselves to endure their degradation (Early); remaining loyal to their culture's view of women instead of those in their adopted culture (Ugwu-Oju); or leading through reconciliation (Chamorro).

MIRRORS:
THE UNITED STATES

JOHN UPDIKE, The Disposable Rocket (p. 398)

Explorations

1. John Updike claims the male body "is, like a delivery rocket that falls away in space, a disposable means" (para. 1) that has lost its use once it has delivered semen to a female. Updike extends the analogy when he describes an erection as defying gravity and implies it when he contrasts a woman's body (which "curves around centers of repose") with a male one ("taut with lines of potential force") (4). In the last paragraphs of the essay, as he describes the male body's gradual decay, the analogy comes to stand for death rather than sexuality; that is, the body will be discarded once it has served its function.

2. Updike uses the analogy of a bank account to introduce the central comparison–contrast — the differences between men and women — in the first paragraph. He changes the terms of the comparison from differences in upkeep to differences in function, form, and psychology after quoting from *Don Juan*. The comparison between shaving and childbirth leads to his central point that reproduction places very different demands on male and female bodies. (This question provides an excellent opportunity to discuss transitions.)

3. Comparisons and analogies in the essay include (a) inhabiting a male body and having a bank account (1); (b) falling as a kind of flying (2); (c) male sense of space versus female sense of space (4); (d) ideal male body versus ideal female body (4); (e) Diana the huntress versus languid, overweight Venus (4); (f) Dionysus's frequency of posing for underwear ads versus Mars' (4); (g) a penis as a small brother (5); (h) a man's body betrays its tenant less rapidly than does a woman's (6). By using comparison, Updike can discuss his subject, the male body, in constant reference to its purported opposite, the female body. He gives the impression that one can only be understood according to its contrasts with the other, reinforcing his thesis that the two are eternally opposed.

Connections

1. Updike and Camille Paglia both depict male sexuality as reckless and difficult to control. Updike interprets this as resulting from the male's "superhuman frenzy to deliver his goods" (para. 1); male adventurousness is not a drive toward death but a desire to see "what the traffic will bear — a kind of mechanic's curiosity" (3). By contrast, Paglia sees men as struggling "for identity against the overwhelming power of their mothers" (p. 393).

2. Among the male traits listed in Lawrence Wright's epigraph, Updike also alludes to assertive sexual behavior, sensation seeking, and transient bonding. Updike treats these more positively than Wright does: Wright depicts assertive sexual behavior as stemming from a natural desire to perpetuate the species. Updike might explain men's sensation seeking with the argument that they "were made for combat, back in the postsimian, East-African days" (3) and that transient bonding results from men's (natural) loss of interest in a woman once he has deposited his "seed" in her.

3. About flying, Updike suggests that the male body innately wishes to hurl itself from high windows and the edges of cliffs and that the mind must fight to stop it. Yet, an airplane "turns the earth into a map so quickly the brain turns aloof and calm" (2). Andre Dubus also emphasizes the danger of flying, noting that the pilots' training runs weren't as playful as marine field exercises generally are, that from a "fighter-bomber in the sky the flight deck looked like an aspirin tablet" (p. 294). Updike also notes that men's sense of space differs from women's, in that men gravitate toward what is outer: "The fly ball high against the sky, the long pass spiraling overhead, the jet fighter like a scarcely visible pinpoint nozzle laying down its vapor trail at forty thousand feet . . . these bring portents with them and awaken a sense of relation with the invisible, with the empty" (4). These comments reflect Annie Dillard's sense of wonder (female that she is) while watching David Rahm perform: She loves how his plane climbs and dives, frustrating and then fulfilling her expectations, how the plane resembles "a brush marking thin air" (p. 290).

SAM KEEN, Man and WOMAN (p. 403)

Explorations

1. Sam Keen uses an omniscient male point of view. He is writing for men, as is clear from his use of the first person (1 ff). Keen alludes to his own experience only when he describes holding his newborn daughter and wondering whether he will ever create anything so magnificent himself. Besides reinforcing his argument that WOMAN as creatrix is a powerful figure, this personal example reinforces his authority by showing both involvement and objectivity (ability to see both sides).

2. By WOMAN, Keen means the mythic, maternal figure — attractive, confusing, and frightening — who occupies men's minds and prevents them from interacting with women as individuals like themselves. Before the "sexual-spiritual maturation . . . journey of manhood" (1), a man will interact with all women as if they were his mother, projecting her judgments and wishes, although he will believe he is interacting with individual women. After this journey, however, he will cease "establishing [his] manhood in reactionary ways" (28), and interact with ordinary women as his equals.

3. Keen's statements about WOMAN seem to be based on his own life-views, although he sometimes alludes vaguely to "expert" sources, mentioning Freud once and otherwise citing "psychologists," "feminists," and even his friend Rollo May. When discussing fathers' absence in their homes, he writes, "Someone, using what I call SWAG statistics (Scientific Wild-Ass Guess) has estimated . . ." (16) — not a source that inspires reader confidence. Keen apparently expects readers to take him at face value because his argument confirms their experience.

412–418 (Text Pages)

Connections

1. According the Keen, the three aspects of WOMAN comprising "the trinity that secretly controls man" are WOMAN as goddess and creatrix, WOMAN as mother and matrix, and WOMAN as erotic-spiritual power (para. 3). Keen would probably classify Updike's depiction of women as the last of these. Given that Updike seems comfortable with men's tendency to seek freedom from female (civilizing) constraints, he would probably respond that WOMAN presents no threat to men's equally powerful nature but serves as a point of reference for it.

2. Paula Gunn Allen claims Western images of women depict them as essentially passive virgins, like Mary, whose only contribution is birthing, or as a witch/goddess-whore (p. 390). Keen's description of WOMAN matches Allen's summary in that he also sees them as passive, affecting men through their own internalization of women rather than through any direct action. Allen might agree with Keen that men need to move beyond their attachments to their mothers so as to see women as individuals, but she might disagree with his view that men can, or need to, question the power of femininity.

3. "Man and WOMAN" sets before men the herculean task of analyzing their relationships with their mothers and learning to separate themselves from them to become whole men; it seems easier just to be a guy and not worry about this project, particularly given the enormous changes in men's and women's roles since the sexual revolution, when traditional models of behavior were cast in doubt. Keen would probably respond to Friedman by suggesting that he engage with his notion of WOMAN rather than avoid the tasks of adulthood.

DEBORAH TANNEN, How Male and Female Students Use Language Differently (p. 412)

Explorations

1. According to Deborah Tannen, the main difference between men's and women's use of language in social groups stems from the fact that, as girls, women are likely to bond with a best friend by telling secrets and building trust, whereas men start out playing in large, hierarchical groups in which they must use language to seize center stage, exhibiting their skill, displaying their knowledge, and challenging and resisting challenges. Consequently, males are better trained for classroom situations in which "ritual opposition" (para. 5) encourages students to antagonize one another than are females, whose experiences are based on a model that emphasizes bonding.

2. Tannen's sources include books (Walter Ong's *Fighting for Life*), the work of a group of research sociologists and psychologists (whom she names), the responses of various colleagues to her work, and observations about her classroom experiences. Students may find the last of these categories most convincing, because it relates most closely to their own experience. But you might underscore the difference between Sam Keen's mentioning "psychologists" and Tannen's actually naming them.

3. Besides gender, students' tendency to speak out in class is affected by their cultural backgrounds and the context in which they speak, which includes both the number of people and the conversational styles of those people. Tannen found that when she

divided her class of twenty into groups according to their conversational styles — fast talkers, quiet talkers, and Asian students — students who had previously been silent talked a lot more.

Connections

1.   According to Tannen, men tend to speak more in discussions involving the whole class, sometimes intimidating women, or simply consuming more time. Tannen found that men try to get the floor as much as possible, whereas women tend to monitor their participation so as to avoid speaking too much. Sam Keen would probably explain men's tendency to talk more than women as stemming from their need to seek validation from WOMAN, as embodied by their teacher (if female) and female classmates. Camille Paglia might explain male students' talkativeness with: "men must do or risk something to be men" as they "struggle against the overwhelming power of their mothers" (p. 393).

2.   Dympna Ugwu-Oju's description of being a woman in the United States illustrates the tension many U.S. women feel between the conversational styles they developed with best friends as girls (or in Ugwu-Oju's case, developed in her Ibo culture) and those valued in a school or work situation. Ugwu-Oju might attribute the ethnic differences in communication style that Tannen noticed to the fact that the Asian students were raised in a culture that shuns loud, assertive talk.

3.   Like Tannen, Violeta Chamorro points to studies showing that "women traditionally lead by means of reconciliation, interrelations, and persuasion . . . while men usually lead through control and intimidation" (p. 395). Given that Chamorro is the president of Nicaragua and the widow of a political activist, she has probably had ample opportunity to note the contrast between male and female styles of leadership.

LESLIE MARMON SILKO, Yellow Woman (p. 419)

Explorations

1.   At the end of the story, as she returns to the ordinary world of her home and family, the narrator has almost buried the mythic identity of "Yellow Woman." Silva is no longer present to address her by this name; her family will call her by "another name" (para. 21). She decides to tell her family the realistic story, knowing that only her grandfather would believe in the "Yellow Woman" story. However, even as she confronts the mundane aspects of the "real" world — her mother and grandmother discussing Jell-O, the smell of cooking, her husband Al — she still believes in the mythic truth of her story (92). The time she spent with Silva will remain for her a rich mix of myth and everyday reality, bringing her closer to her Laguna heritage.

2.   Silva is presented through the eyes of the narrator, whose only title here is "Yellow Woman," a reference suggesting that Silko, too, may view her as a character in a myth. The narrator sees Silva as physically strong, acquainted with the stories of his culture, and adept at the traditional skills of riding and hunting. She fears his strength yet finds him sexually attractive (56). Later on she finds him "strange" (90), a term that applies equally well to mythical figures and social misfits. The rancher sees Silva as a generic Indian and a thief whom he hopes to intimidate but also (rightly) fears (82, 85).

3. At several points the narrator directly states her feelings. In paragraph 56, she says she is afraid of Silva and also mentions a desire to kiss him. At the story's end she states she is sad to leave him (90) and wants to go back and kiss him (91). On other occasions, her actions convey her feelings. Her heavy breathing in paragraph 52 reveals her sexual excitement. In paragraph 88 she states, "I went that way. . . because I thought it was safer." Because it was not safer for the horse, she must be talking about her own safety and implying her desire to flee from Silva and the violent encounter.

Connections

1. The contrasting styles Deborah Tannen describes are apparent in the way the narrator and Silva use language: In their initial dialogue, she asks him a question ("Will I come back?") and he answers by calling her "Yellow Woman," denying her sense of reality; they repeat this dance whenever they talk about their identities. She tries to link them to her past and he tries to place them in a mythical present (para. 10). His desire for power over her is also apparent when they are making love: he laughs at her for becoming aroused ("You are breathing so hard") and she pulls away and turns her back (53). Silva's confrontation with the rancher (78–85) also exemplifies Tannen's points.

2. Yellow Woman falls into Sam Keen's categories of WOMAN as goddess and creatrix, because she thinks often of the family she has left behind, and also WOMAN as erotic-spiritual power, because her encounter with Silva is primarily sexual. Silko's depiction differs from Keen's in that she doesn't portray Yellow Woman as a stereotype but as a complex person; Silva finds her attractive, but he does not seem controlled by her, as Keen's man is by WOMAN. (You might ask students if they perceive Yellow Woman as powerful in the excerpt.) The impact of Silko's including a male as well as a female mythical character in her story is to shift the focus from stereotypes to the characters' interaction, as well as the difference between them: The woman wants to become more intimate with the man, to determine who he is and what he wants from her, even while she thinks of the family she's left, and the man seems bent on remaining mysterious, in part as a way to guard his power over her.

3. Paula Gunn Allen's piece should help to place Silko's in context, especially the former's observation that, in Indian cultures, "the individual woman is provided with a variety of images of women from the interconnected supernatural, natural, and social worlds she lives in" (p. 390). Hence, Yellow Woman goes off with Silva as a way of living the plot of a story she has known since she was a child; the familiarity of the story makes the experience less strange. Coming home is also part of the old story ("she'll come home — they usually do" [59]); it may be that, knowing Yellow Woman will come down off the mountain, she trusts that she will return to her normal life. The story — like the comfortable family life to which she returns — anchors her.

WINDOWS:
THE WORLD

MARJORIE SHOSTAK, Nisa's Marriage (p. 431)

Explorations

1. The beads and ornaments adorning her, the dancing and music, the ceremonial oil, the building of the hut, all the rituals of marriage are designed to signal the transition from child to woman. Bedecking the bride signals the change that is to come over her; the dancing signifies joy; the building of the hut symbolizes the creation of a new family unit. The anointing with oil solemnizes the union of two people. (Students may wish to continue discussion of this question by considering the symbolic significance of the wedding rituals in their own culture.)

2. That the tribe relies on hunting can be seen in the community's informing Nisa that Tashay will not let her eat the meat of the animals he kills if she keeps crying (para. 8). They are apparently a peaceful people whose main enemies are not other people but rather the animals around them. (Note that Nisa is frequently warned of the dangers of running away into the forest.) The hunting-meat metaphor appears in Nisa's mother's lament that she will stick herself with a poison arrow (29) and in Nisa's comparing herself as a sexual being to food (42).

3. Students should enjoy this question: Nisa's mother is echoing the age-old lament of mothers: "You frustrate and shame me so, I could kill myself," adding that the only thing preventing her from doing so is the weakness of the flesh. There should be quite a variety of responses to the second part of the question, including the threat of getting on a plane or a train, of jumping off a bridge, of driving over a cliff.

Connections

1. "Nisa's Marriage" and "Yellow Woman" both suggest a social model in which men initiate actions and women respond. The narrator in "Yellow Woman" is attracted to the apparent simplicity of the mythic time inhabited by the ka'tsina and Yellow Woman, without the complex demands of modern adulthood. Silva offers the freedom-within-security of childhood, along with no-fault sex. There are no daily routines to follow; she can live in the present and focus on what is around her: "When I saw the stone house I remembered that I had meant to go home. But that didn't seem important anymore, maybe because there were little blue flowers growing in the meadow behind the stone house and the gray squirrels were playing in the pines next to the house" (p. 424).

2. The men in "Nisa's Marriage" tend to speak competitively with one another and authoritatively to women. The day of the wedding, Nisa's younger brother teases Tashay that he is too old to marry her; after she has run away from her husband, Nisa's older brother threatens to hit her if she does not cooperate. When Nisa asks why she must be with Tashay, her father tells her she's crazy and that she must follow her husband. And when Nisa tells her mother she and Tashay have had sex, her mother threatens to hurt *herself* if Nisa continues to talk this way. The conversation between Nisa and Tashay about whether she will sleep with him again also fits Deborah Tannen's observations about men's and women's conversational styles: He insists that it is his right, as it is all

men's right; Nisa says she doesn't care and tells him her "insides hurt" (para. 40). Whereas he universalizes his needs, she speaks of her own experience. The practical advantages of gender-differentiated verbal styles for the Zhun/twasi are that men give orders and women follow them, fostering order, if not a spirit of cooperation, needed by a wandering tribal people.

3. John Updike's view that "to inhabit a male body . . . is to feel somewhat detached from it" (p. 400) because a man and his penis are not always of the same mind seems like a notion specific to contemporary Western culture. But both "The Disposable Rocket" and "Nisa's Marriage" express the idea that men are oriented toward external activities like hunting and are bent on depositing their seed into a woman: Updike describes how men will take great risks to accomplish this, whereas Nisa's husband asks her, "Do you know any man who has married a woman and who just lives beside her without having sex with her?" (39).

NIKOS KAZANTZAKIS, The Isle of Aphrodite (p. 438)

Explorations

1. This question will help students clarify Nikos Kazantzakis's premises, which might be difficult for some students to identify, given his lyrical style of writing. In paragraph 4, Kazantzakis describes passing "from Jehovah's camp to the bed of Aphrodite," a phrase that explicitly identifies the deities involved and suggests their differences. Jehovah, the Judean god, is in Kazantzakis's representation harsh and demanding, whereas Aphrodite, Greek goddess of love, is earthy and ready to be pleased with humanity. The journey through the Judean mountains — Jehovah's camp — was "abrasive," whereas the destination, Aphrodite's bed, is inviting. He defines the water over which he makes the final leg of this journey as giving rise to the "feminine" mystery of Aphrodite, suggesting the gender differences between the two deities and their relation to the natural world (para. 4). The "feminine" force associated with Aphrodite is natural and inevitable; he equates it with gravity and the tendency of things and people to return to the earth (5). The force he associates with Jehovah is opposed to the feminine; it is "contrary to nature" (5), urging people to overcome human nature and rise above earthly concerns.

2. Students will be able to build on their responses to the previous question as a way of discerning the meaning to Kazantzakis's dream. He associates Aphrodite with the earth and therefore with mortality; Jehovah is a god concerned only with the afterlife, but Aphrodite inhabits the earth and, as he comes closer to her temple, seems to inhabit the narrator as well. The memory of the headless male insect being eaten by the female reinforces the idea of his vulnerability and mortality; the image of the warrior's head on the ring stone (46) once again reminds him of this disturbing memory. The dream in the last paragraph contains the image of a rose, a symbol of love and therefore also a symbol of Aphrodite. It is a black rose, associated with death, an image that recalls associations Kazantzakis has made throughout the essay between the inevitable forces of the earth (gravity and mortality) and the promises and demands of love (the goddess Aphrodite).

3. There is evidence in the first three paragraphs that Kazantzakis belongs to a Christian religion. He mentions "sin" and uses biblical phrases such as "the will of God" (2) and

"glorify the Lord" (3). In paragraph 21, he asks a woman whether "religion" can identify the clay models of women found at Kouklia as either gods or devils. This question suggests that he is accustomed to seeking explanations from religious sources. However, Kazantzakis does not have complete faith in conventional religion, as his search for Aphrodite implies. When the woman he questions replies that their "poor religion" cannot explain the female gods, Kazantzakis does not refute her criticism. As he hovers between the two forces, the Judaic and the pagan, Kazantzakis continues to think in terms of the Judaic traditions. In paragraph 6, Kazantzakis wonders what his free will (a Christian concept) will lead him to do; he wants to distinguish between good and evil, and he continues to be concerned with establishing hierarchies of "virtues and passions."

Connections

1. Both Leslie Marmon Silko and Kazantzakis begin their pieces with a moment in which the narrator is overwhelmed by the sense of being in a dream. Kazantzakis writes that "drowsiness and sweetness" overtook him and so he felt ready to let go and allow his heart to break loose (para. 1). Silko begins her story with the moment of her awakening at dawn and imagining that she is leaving Silva. She stays, however, and gives in to the myth of Yellow Woman he enacts with her. She realizes that she has "no thought beyond the moment" (p. 421) and only because of this can she give in to her own desires. The dreamlike openings of both Silko's and Kazantzakis's pieces creates an atmosphere of abandonment of the self and of everyday reality, allowing the narrators to be sexually aware and open.

2. In "The Isle of Aphrodite," the image of WOMAN as erotic-spiritual power appears in the form of Cyprus itself — "an island with so much fertility or breathed air so saturated with perilous sweet persuasions" (1); in the ample-bodied woman who makes *okas*; in the star of Aphrodite "glittering, playing, and twirling in the sky" (39); and in the "full-breasted goddess [who] lifts her veil" (43). Sam Keen would probably interpret the visions in paragraphs 40–48 as those of a man who fears being subsumed by WOMAN, by "the breath of the unfathomable" (43) as represented by a seductive but predatory female insect or a statue of Aphrodite. Keen would have a field day with the stone depicting Aphrodite wearing Ares's head or the speaker's dream about holding a rose — a symbol for female genitals in Western literature — which devours his hand, just as the mantis devours her lover. Keen would see this as an expression of the narrator's fear of "the sheer power of the female sex to work effects on the male" (p. 409).

3. Both Camille Paglia and Kazantzakis subscribe to the view that the sexes are in opposition to each other. Paglia says simply that "the sexes are at war" (p. 393) and Kazantzakis describes two opposing forces, one that pulls us toward earth (the feminine) and one that pulls us upward (the masculine) (5). Furthermore, Paglia describes male psychological development as a matter of overcoming "the overwhelming power of their mothers" (p. 393), a view confirmed in Kazantzakis's piece by his fear of being eaten alive by the feminine force represented by Aphrodite. However, Paglia identifies male sexuality as aggressive, whereas Kazantzakis identifies Aphrodite, a symbol of feminine sexuality, as voracious and demanding (41–43).

445–452 (Text Pages)

SIMONE DE BEAUVOIR, Woman as Other (p. 445)

Explorations

1. Students should find it interesting to note the many changes in attitudes since Simone de Beauvoir wrote her essay. Many will be unaware of the extent to which the position of modern women differs from that of women of even twenty-five years ago, let alone those who were contemporaries of Beauvoir. Her plea for women to dispute male sovereignty was considered radical when she wrote it; now it's seen as a relatively moderate position. Similarly, her call to women "to refuse to be a party to the deal . . . to renounce all the advantages conferred upon them by their alliance with the superior caste" (para. 13) is now a standard of middle-class feminism. But students may also be surprised to see how many current issues have been the subjects of long-standing debate. Although inroads have certainly been made, the resurgence of fundamentalism in the United States, coupled with the Catholic Church's vigorous denouncement of abortion and artificial birth control, has kept alive the issue of a woman's control over her body. Recent reports also suggest that although white, middle-class women in the job market are better off than they were ten years ago, they still earn substantially less than men for similar jobs. Thus, the professional status of women has yet to be established. Furthermore, recent developments such as surrogate motherhood raise new questions about a woman's legal rights.

2. Students are sure to find many loaded expressions in the selection. A few of them are "woman represents only the negative" and "A man is in the right in being a man; it is the woman who is in the wrong" (2); the litany of antifeminists, beginning with Aristotle (2–4); the comparison between women and Jews, blacks, and the proletariat (5, 8, 9); the analogy of the master-slave relationship (12); and the use of the term *castes* (13). Beauvoir's references, as well as her language and style, suggest that she is writing for an intellectual audience that may not accept her views. That she expects men to be reluctant to relinquish their power and women their comfort is clear in her frequent references to the collaboration of women in their own oppression.

3. Beauvoir cites a number of well regarded figures as well as myths, and in the opening section, her own experiences. Audience is important here; although interviews allow us to identify with the subject more readily and are normally more entertaining, they don't carry the same weight as references to classical scholars, respected authors, and renowned philosophers. Beauvoir is stating an intellectual case here; thus, if she included interviews or eliminated references, she could be dismissed by her audience as a single voice arguing a case that may have a few current supporters but lacks broad, long-term merit.

Connections

1. Nikos Kazantzakis would probably agree with Beauvoir's model of woman as Other, a model that implies that the existence of men needs no explanation or justification (para. 2) but that the existence of women must be explained and accounted for. Beauvoir recalls that "it is often said that she [woman] thinks with her glands" (2) and that women are associated with sex (3). Kazantzakis's representation of Aphrodite strongly associates her with nature, the physical body, and sexuality, as is suggested in his description of a woman he compares with Aphrodite. He describes her as "earthy" and "full-bodied with ample buttocks" (p. 441). Throughout his essay, Kazantzakis uses images of women to help him understand his own fears and desires better, rather than considering women

as subjects in their own right. This strategy accords with Beauvoir's contention that, from the point of view of men, "woman" exists only in relation to men (3).

2. In "Yellow Woman," the narrator moves between two worlds, that of her home with her husband and family and that of the myths of the ka'tsina spirit and Yellow Woman. The narrator allows Silva to define her as "Yellow Woman," because he calls her by this name and she willingly plays the role of the woman who leaves her home and follows the orders of the ka'tsina spirit. Silva articulates her relationship to him when he tells her "You will do what I want" (p. 424). This statement and the many commands he issues make their relationship resemble the master-slave relationship defined by Beauvoir. Still, the narrator does not seem to be entirely under Silva's control. Women in this story do not appear as the completely passive beings Beauvoir describes. The narrator has no qualms about leaving either her husband or Silva when she finds it convenient, showing she is not a possession of either. She is self-sufficient enough to arrive home on her own. Furthermore, the narrator would probably reject Beauvoir's reading of her situation. By identifying her story with the archetypal one, the narrator acquires in her own eyes some of the myth's power. She does not try to define herself against a male figure but in terms of her culture, which places her in opposition to the white culture of the rancher.

3. Sam Keen's essay depicts WOMAN as a set of archetypes, whether "goddesses, bitches, angels, Madonnas, castrators, witches, Gypsy maidens, earth mothers . . . [which] must be exorcised from [men's] minds and hearts before [they] can learn to love women" (p. 403). According to Keen, WOMAN is so powerful in men's minds that the idea of her prevents them from seeing individual women as equals; Keen's "Other" is too powerful, and a man must "take leave of WOMAN and wander for a long time in the wild and sweet world of men. Finally, when he has learned to love his own manhood, he may return to the everyday world to love an ordinary woman" (p. 404). To stop defining themselves in reaction to their unconscious images of WOMAN, men need to spend time alone and with other men so as to discover "the true mystery and power of manhood" (p. 410).

ALBERTO MORAVIA, The Chase (p. 453)

Explorations

1. This selection provides an excellent example of the use of seemingly irrelevant material to establish the groundwork for the story itself. In the long opening section, Alberto Moravia introduces his narrator's love for wildness, as well as his conclusion as a child that adult males destroy the very thing they profess to love. Without this section, readers would have less of a sense of the narrator's celebration of life. His actions and even the choice he recognizes at the end of the story would seem incomprehensible.

2. As he watches his wife board the bus in paragraph 8, the narrator recalls the hunting incident, and he does so again in paragraph 17 as he realizes that he can't confront her. In his present position, he is like his father was at the hunt: He has the power to destroy the wild creature — and he is well aware of what comes of shooting a wild bird. He first thinks that he has no choice, that nature's mandate is to kill, but then he realizes what would result if he were to confront his wife and her lover. Ultimately, he chooses

the role of life giver rather than taker. In doing this, he preserves a sense of power, but he also avoids the consequences he recalls from the hunting incident.

3.   It can be dangerous to ask students to extrapolate; too often they rely on their own experience and desires rather than on the evidence in the story to create sequels. If this question is handled carefully, however, the exercise will be valuable. A close reading of the last sentence and the third paragraph make it quite clear that the narrator will never again follow his wife, nor does he plan to confront her. He's giving in to her "wildness" in much the same way she is, refusing either to tame or to be tamed. He probably believes that his knowledge will bring new vitality to his marriage.

Connections

1.   That the narrator compares his wife to a wild bird is clear evidence of his perception of woman as Other. He is enthralled by her unpredictability and laments his newfound ability to understand her and predict her behavior. He wants his wife to be Other; he finds this quality highly erotic. He sees his wife's otherness in terms of power, which he possesses. (His decision to withhold his knowledge of her affair gives him tremendous power over her.) His wife would probably share his perception; when she senses the predictability of their marriage and the resultant waning of eroticism, she seeks eroticism elsewhere. Also, the manner of the meeting between her and her lover accentuates her desire to be perceived as wild and untamed.

2.   The key to this comparison probably lies more in the attitudes of the men about their marriages, even though the women are the partners who have temporarily left their husbands. Leslie Marmon Silko's narrator is attracted to Silva, but like the original Yellow Woman will return home after her escapade. Indeed, in the myth Yellow Woman is rescued by her husband, who desires her return. Their marriage defines them as a continuing unit. The husband of the narrator in Silko's story may be upset by his wife's absence, but after hearing her explanation that she was kidnapped by a Navajo, he will not resent her departure and will welcome her back. The wife in "The Chase" is only temporarily unfaithful, but her husband cannot be satisfied with her unless she manifests wildness. Yet this quality depends on the narrator's seeing her actions as unpredictable, a situation unlikely to result in the context of a marriage that renders her behavior quite familiar. Therefore, students will probably conclude that the marriage in the Silko story shows more promise of continuing successfully.

3.   Both Moravia's and Nikos Kazantzakis's narrators are pursuing a feminine being; in both cases, the revelations they make at the end of the pursuit are disturbing and unanticipated. The narrator's revelation in "The Chase" has to do with the independence and unpredictability of his wife, who is not at all as "domesticated" as he believed her to be before he follows her to her assignation with another man. He accepts this revelation in part because it excites him to realize that his wife is still a passionate woman, and he does not have the power to deprive her of her "wildness." The goddess Aphrodite that Kazantzakis pursues in his essay is similar to Moravia's representation of the narrator's wife as a mysterious, dangerous entity who is the essence of feminine unpredictability. The wife's wildness, however, is no more personal than Aphrodite's. Moravia writes that "wildness, always and everywhere, is directed against everything and everybody" (para. 17). It is, therefore, a destructive force, although it makes her more desirable in the narrator's eyes.

SPOTLIGHT:
THE ISLAMIC MIDDLE EAST

ADDITIONAL INFORMATION ON COUNTRIES

The term "the Middle East" refers to an area of northwest Africa and Southeast Asia. It includes the following countries: Algeria, Bahrain, Egypt, Iran, Iraq, Israel, Jordan, Kuwait, Lebanon, Libya, Mauritania, Morocco, Oman, Palestine, Qatar, Saudi Arabia, Sudan, Syria, Tunisia, Turkey, the United Arab Emirates, and Yemen. Except for Israel, these countries are all predominantly Islamic. The following section offers geographical information about the four countries represented in the Spotlight section, Saudi Arabia, Egypt, Oman, and Jordan.

Saudi Arabia

Environment: Saudi Arabia is bordered by the Red Sea to the west, the Arabian Gulf to the east, Yemen and Oman to the south, and Kuwait, Iraq, and Jordan to the north. Saudi Arabia's terrain consists mostly of salt flats, gravel plains, and sand dunes with few lakes or permanent streams. In the south is the Empty Quarter, the largest continuous sand desert in the world. It is linked to another large sandy desert, the Nafud, in the north. In the southwest, there are mountains rising to over 9,000 feet, and rain is not uncommon there.

Demographics: Saudi Arabia has over 17 million people, with 77 percent living in cities and 23 percent living in rural areas.

Religion: The official religion is Islam, and Saudi Arabia does not allow the practice of any other religion within its borders.

Education: Sixty-two percent of the adult population is literate, and there are seven universities.

Jordan

Environment: Situated in southwestern Asia, Jordan is bounded on the north by Syria, on the south by Saudi Arabia and the Gulf of Aqaba, on the east by Iraq, and on the west by the occupied West Bank. Most of Jordan's population lives on a dry plateau running from north to south, rising steeply from the eastern shores of the Jordan River and the Dead Sea. In the west runs the Great Rift Valley, a deep depression that includes the Jordan Valley, the Wadi Araba, and the Dead Sea. In the extreme east, the land slopes downward from the plateau to the semiarid steppe country of the Syrian Desert.

Demographics: Jordan's 3 million people are predominantly Arabic. Other communities in Jordan are Circassian, Shishan, Armenian, and Druze.

Religion: Approximately 90 percent of the population is Muslim and 10 percent Christian. Of the Muslims, most are Sunnites, with Shiites forming a small minority.

Education: Ninety-one percent of the adult male population and 75 percent of the adult female population is literate. Arabic is the official language, although English is widely spoken; French is the most commonly used third language.

81

459–461 (Text Pages)

Egypt

Environment: Egypt's northern coastline fronts the Mediterranean Sea; its eastern coastline fronts the Red Sea and touches the State of Israel in the Sinai; its western border is shared with Libya, and its southern one with Sudan. Over 90 percent of the land area is formed by a convergence of deserts — the Libyan Desert to the west, the Sahara and Nubian Deserts to the south, and the Arabian Desert to the east. The country is bisected by the River Nile, and the land surrounding it is both habitable and arable.

Demographics: Egypt's population of 56 million is divided among three ethnic groups: Egyptian, Bedouin Arab, and Nubian.

Religion: Islam is constitutionally established as the official religion of Egypt; about 90 percent of the population are Sunni Muslim with some Bohra Muslims and other non-Sunni sects represented. Seven million Coptic Christians form the country's largest religious minority.

Education: School is compulsory for children aged six to twelve. Forty-eight percent of the adult population is literate.

Oman

Environment: The Sultanate of Oman is located in the southeastern quarter of the Arabian peninsula. It is bordered by the Gulf of Oman and the Arabian Sea, and its land borders are with the United Arab Emirates, Saudi Arabia, and Yemen. Oman's coastline is more than 1,300 miles long, and its vast coastal plain blends into an area of hills that in turn gives way to a plateau. Oman's land is mostly barren, although the plateau is arable at oases. The extreme southwestern province, Zufar, has a rainy season and is thus very fertile.

Demographics: Oman's 1.5 million people are 9 percent urban and 91 percent rural. The population is almost entirely Arabic, except for some 300,000 expatriate workers, mainly Indian and Pakistani, who comprise about half the work force.

Religion: The predominant religion is Islam, but the practice of other religions is allowed.

Education: Forty-one percent of the adult population is literate, and there is one university.

The Hijab: The question of *hijab* (covering one's face, head, and body) for Muslim women has been controversial for centuries. The Qur'an contains two main injunctions: A woman should not show her beauty or adornments except what appears by uncontrolled factors such as the wind blowing her clothes, and the head covers should be drawn so as to cover the hair, the neck, and the chest. Some Muslims do not consider the subject open to discussion and consider that covering the face is required, whereas others believe it is not required. A middle line position is taken by some who claim that the instructions are vague and open to individual discretion depending on the situation.

DIANA ABU-JABER, In Flight (p. 462)

Explorations

1. According to Diana Abu-Jaber, the pattern of Bedouin life is to move from one watering hole to another in a large group composed of extended families, "leaving just the imprint of their feet" (para. 17), relying on the elders for guidance, having "daily contact with the beauty and health of animals, an understanding of mirages and visions, of Allah's munificent voice, of the bounty of spirit and the clean warmth of goat-hair blankets" (34). The women's jobs are preparing food and taking care of the children, whereas the men's job is to protect the group from rival groups. The fact that Sitti Jasmine's word is highly respected suggests that both male and female elders lead the Huwyatat.

2. The sheets and carpets, bangles, and coins are luxurious elements in an otherwise Spartan lifestyle; they may be a form of bank account. (You might ask the class why Abu-Jaber remembers and mentions these, and what perspective she had of the Huwyatat as a child.) The tribe's essential possessions include tents where they sleep, goats that provide them with milk and goat-hair blankets, camels that provide transportation, and swords they use to protect themselves from enemies.

3. From the story, one can glean that the Huwyatat eat yogurt, pistachios, figs, pressed apricot, and thyme, and they drink coffee with cardamom. As for where they travel and where they'll go next, as Sitti Jasmine says, they are nomads who "make the earth their home" (11). The last two questions do not seem important to the Huwyatat, because they don't seem to have a predetermined pattern for their wanderings, so far as the narrator can detect.

Connections

1. In "The Chase," the narrator is drawn to wildness, feeling that he has lost the ability to perceive it in his wife because they have fallen into a predictable routine. He follows her, hoping to recapture his former perception of her, only to discover her being wild with another man; he concludes that "wildness, always and everywhere, is directed against everything and everybody" (p. 457). In "In Flight," although the mother decides to leave the Bedouins because her "daughter is getting to be savage like wild thorns" (para. 33), Sitti Jasmine, the matriarch of the tribe, appears to disapprove of the mother's "wildness," pointing out that being part of the community is stabilizing for the child (34). The daughter, considering the story years later, has a similar attitude to that of the narrator in "The Chase": She loves how, during that time, she "was lifted out of the stream of things and . . . the movement of the Bedouin was the movement of the world, intrepid, caught in the winding tails of the spirits" (48).

2. Four groups of "others" appear in the excerpt: the exiled women, the British journalists, the enemy men, and people at Beit el Sala'am camp. The Huwyatat respond to the exiled women they meet by welcoming them to come live with them — the men who find them extend an invitation. When they arrive at the camp, women greet them with arms filled with leaves and flowers, and Sitti Jasmine tells them, "Welcome . . . you are home, at last, you are home again" (9). This response seems to fit their general pattern of offering hospitality to strangers — they tell the British journalists they are "twice welcomed" and offer them coffee (17). But the enemy men are greeted with a rifle shot to announce war and the women's "ululation of war" (28); the Huwyatat respond this way because the men are members of a tribe regarded as "enemies in a nearly forgotten

blood feud" (30). The Huwyatat give people at the encampment food, keeping their eyes averted against the evil eye. They see these people as "blind to the signs of the earth," but feel obligated to help them nevertheless, because "it is better to bless than to curse" (42).

3. Both stories depict life in a new context as romantic, although in different ways: The mother in "In Flight" has her child with her, and her new love object is conveniently accompanied by an extended family who cares for her child. Although the woman in "Yellow Woman" has left her family, she trusts they are fine and would be fine even if she did not return: She calmly pictures her child being raised by her mother and grandmother, her husband replacing her with another woman. The message is that she has given her child a good home, even if she is not in it. By contrast, the mother in "In Flight" has found a good home for her daughter (at least from Sitti Jasmine's and Abu-Jaber's perspective) but wishes to leave the Huwyatat because wandering is unfamiliar to her. The progress of her relationship with the leader's son is not delineated, but, like Yellow Woman's with Silva, it may have run its course. The cultures depicted in both stories have well-defined gender roles: When Silva tells the woman where the potatoes are, she doesn't need to ask who is supposed to cook them; likewise, in "In Flight," when dangerous strangers appear on the horizon, the men know to advance with swords drawn, and the women know to ululate.

NAILA MINAI, Women in Early Islam (p. 470)

Explorations

1. Students will probably be surprised to discover the range of responsibilities shouldered by women in what is considered a backward age. Women in the tribes looked after the herds and engaged in commerce by both producing and trading items of value. They were allowed the privilege of airing their views, enjoyed the power inherent in a matriarchal society allowing polygamy for women, and in general were valued and protected. Their only real risk was of being kidnapped for ransom.

2. Khadija's wealth and position provided the support Muhammad needed to found his religion. She contributed to the social code of Islam by acquainting her husband with the needs of younger, less powerful women. When he married the young Aysha, he began to appreciate the rights of girls, and the scandal concerning her journey with the young man convinced him of a woman's need for protection against false claims of adultery, resulting in the requirement of four witnesses before the charge could be leveled.

3. Some students may encounter difficulty in distinguishing between fictitious and factual elements in an anecdote like this; they may be prone to consider everything they read as fact. This question will allow them to explore the reasons behind and the benefits of embellishment. In opening her essay this way, Naila Minai humanizes the story, allowing the reader to identify with a figure otherwise considered too lofty for human concerns. Her accounts of the family's response to the marriage, the courtship of the couple, and Khadija's infatuation with the young employee are probably fabrications. But she hasn't gone too far; these elements are plausible, none alters the known facts, and, more important, all serve the *truth* of the story.

Connections

1. According to Minai, women's material contributions earned them the right to express their political views, even if they didn't always participate in council meetings. Women also participated in battles, by cheering, nursing, or even becoming soldiers. These observations are illustrated in Diana Abu-Jaber's story: The products the women make — yogurt and goat-hair blankets, for example — are important to the group's survival; Sitti Jasmine, the matriarch of the tribe, is the one to be interviewed by the British journalists; and when the men dash off to fight their enemies, the women ululate in support of them. Nomadic life was probably similar in the two different times and places, because land-based cultures tend to retain their traditions that were created in response to their natural environment. If women have some power because they contribute to the group's survival, that is not likely to change as long as the group maintains the same relationship with its environment.

2. In the culture described in "Nisa's Marriage" and in "Women in Early Islam," in which people have settled in towns and become Muslims, girls tend to be paired with men much older than they are through an arranged marriage. After marriage, they live with the husband's family, and they are expected to fulfill his sexual needs. Minai explains that women were supposedly free to reject a mate chosen by their parents but that this freedom was illusory because they married at such a young age. She also explains that Muhammad saw sexual desire as natural; hence, husbands and wives were obligated to satisfy each other.

3. Women seem to have more freedom in Islamic culture than do Hindu women. Whereas Pom must accept the man her parents have found for her, an Islamic woman is allowed to choose her own spouse. Moreover, she is paid a dowry as a way of giving her a little financial independence. But women in both cultures are treated as "Other," in that they are regarded as creatures who must be sheltered from the rough world of men — Pom stays with her family until her parents have found a mate (with another family) for her to join, and women in Islamic culture have little freedom to move about without their husbands' permission. Because men in a patriarchal society feared having to support other men's children, they did not allow the wives out of the house; men were the ones participating in town life, whereas women remained indoors. Also, the fact that a man could have four wives and as many concubines as he could support, whereas a woman was expected to remain faithful to her husband, created a double standard that made women objects of desire.

NAGUIB MAHFOUZ, A Day for Saying Goodbye (p. 480)

Explorations

1. The narrator appears to have killed his wife. Students may begin to suspect this when he wonders if he should commit his children to his sister's care, and they might become more suspicious when his sister asks after his wife and he thinks, "What an innocent question!" (para. 13). When the narrator wonders if his children will forgive him for what he has done and proceeds to remember first meeting his wife, students should become fairly certain. And when he sees a colleague and thinks of him as "the first witness" (35), the event should be completely clear.

2. When the narrator introduces his wife in paragraph 25, it only becomes apparent that he's thinking about her when he starts addressing her in the second person: "You were crazy about inane outward appearances and would shout at me . . ." (25). Amr Bey, "the first witness," is also introduced in the midst of an emotional outpouring — just as the narrator is longing for the days of courtship and exclaiming to himself, "Oh, the masks of lies we hide behind!" (28), he runs into Bey. The effect of mixing the introduction of new characters with the narrator's emotional declarations is to make his external reality seem like a reflection of his internal one. This pattern helps us to see how his wife's death arose out of a moment when his emotions became too much for him: "Samira once said, 'How quickly and violently you become angry, Father' " (38).

3. Dawlat appears to be his lover, which students can discern from the narrator's wondering, "what is the point of pretending to a love that is nonexistent?" and recalling, "she never stopped hinting at marriage, without caring about the fate of Samira and Gamal" (67). His admission that he does not love her, that the affair is only "a whim of revenge," makes him seem that much more self-absorbed, that much less sympathetic a character (67).

Connections

1. More than anything, this question should help students to become aware of their stereotypes about Arabs. They may have an impulse to assume that anything in the story that is familiar to them — going to a restaurant and drinking white wine, for instance — is a Western element of the story. So you might emphasize the need to use Minai as a source. That the narrator's widowed sister is intimate with his family seems to reflect their Arabic and Islamic heritage, as does the fact that he meets his wife through her uncle; family connections seem more important in that culture than in a more mobile one like ours. That the narrator expected his wife to obey him — he complains at one point of her "going and coming without permission or even letting me know" — seems to fit Minai's portrait (para. 54). That the narrator straddles two cultures is apparent in his remark about his daughter: "she is a sensible girl, religious and modern at one and the same time" (56). The most Western element of the story may be the narrator's memory of how his wife asked for a divorce.

2. The narrator defines his wife as "Other" when he remarks "the angel turned into a devil" (para. 2), and his memories of her flip back and forth between that of the slim, sweet bride who made him feel so proud and the frustrated wife who tells him she hates him. Of Beauvoir's reasons why women accept the role of "Other," those that apply to Seham include the fact that she is economically dependent on her husband and that her culture encourages men to take part in the world's affairs and women to stand behind them.

3. Economic and social factors seem to have played a part in the couple's marriage. The narrator, Mustafa Ibrahim, sees his future wife bathing, but it is only after her uncle, a colleague in the narrator's firm, calls to him that he speaks with her. Rigoberta Menchú's and John David Morley's selections discuss the importance of familial relations in marriage. Mustafa Ibrahim and his wife Seham seem to lack any kind of real dialogue in their marriage. In fact, they each take for a slogan, "All or nothing." They seem to have had an unrealistic view of marriage from the start, basing their relationship on superficial judgments rather than an appreciation and knowledge of each others' character.

UNNI WIKAN, The *Xanith:* A Third Gender Role? (p. 488)

Explorations

1. According to Unni Wikan, a boy in Sohar becomes a *xanith* by singing with the women at a wedding. A *xanith* becomes a man by marrying a woman, especially by consummating the marriage. A number of valuable social tasks are performed by *xaniths:* On a practical level, they take jobs as domestic servants, "which no woman or freeman can be induced to do" (para. 15). And on a less tangible level, they define womanhood by being less beautiful and less virtuous than women. They provide a category for prostitutes, both the acknowledged male ones and unacknowledged female ones, allowing women in general to be considered both pure and sexually active.

2. Wikan means that sexuality is defined by how people behave at a given time, not by what organs they were born with. The social status of *xaniths* in Sohar is different from that of homosexuals in the United States because Omani culture is more willing to admit and live with deviations from mainstream behavior than is much of American culture. Omanis ritualize deviance rather than denying and shunning it. Moreover, being a *xanith* is perceived as a role anyone might assume temporarily; the Omani see the desire to be a *xanith* as compulsive and somewhat degrading, but they accept it.

3. Many social rules governing gender roles in Sohar would appear bizarre to us, just as the essay's author finds it bizarre when her friend talks with a man in an alley. Westerners might find it strange that no decent woman stops to talk with a man on the street, that men and women are segregated at weddings, that men and women do not eat in front of each other, that women's arms must be covered because they are considered erotic, that a woman must have her husband's permission to visit family or friends, that newlyweds' consummation of their marriage must be verified publicly. Among the reasons that might seem bizarre to us: "eating cooked food together represents a degree of intimacy second only to intercourse and physical fondling" (13) or "the *xanith* who does deflower the bride becomes, like every other successful bridegroom, a *man*" (19).

Connections

1. In "A Day for Saying Goodbye," the narrator longs for the day when he perceived his wife as a sweet, innocent girl who told him, "You've a good heart and that is something beyond price" (p. 482). Both expected the other to live up to an impossible ideal and were not prepared to deal with the "disparities of temperament" that "put an end to love" (p. 482). The Soharis' rules against close contact between the sexes protect them from disappointment by keeping them from getting to know each other well. "Differences of temperament" probably do not lead to hateful arguments in a culture where roles are highly ritualized.

2. Women probably could not be more "Other" than they are in Omani culture because they are defined in relation to what men can do and they cannot; as Beauvoir says, woman is "not regarded as an autonomous being" (p. 446). They are not allowed to speak to men in public; they are not allowed to eat with men; they must have their bodies completely covered and their faces veiled, except when they are with their immediate families; they do not have the option to change their sexual identity as men do; they must have their husband's permission to visit anyone outside the home; they can't allow any man to step into the family compound when the husband is absent; and women are considered perfectly virtuous and pure, but men aren't.

459–501 (Text Pages)

3.   *Xaniths* do not reject their privileged status as men: Women must get permission to go
     out, but *xaniths* move about freely; women are legally considered minors who must
     be represented by a guardian, but *xaniths* represent themselves. Lesbians might have
     an easier time concealing their identity in Oman than in the United States because the
     sexes are segregated. But they might have a harder time because Islam frowns upon
     men or women who choose to remain single and because there is no culturally
     sanctioned identity available to them. They would be expected to wear a burqa and
     otherwise present themselves as unassailably pure beings.

THE ISLAMIC MIDDLE EAST: INVESTIGATIONS/WEB SITES

Islam (http://www.rahul.net:80/abadi/mideast.html) offers sites with information
about Islam, including articles, pictures, and a hypertext copy of The Qur'an.

Middle East Studies Association Bulletin (http://www.cua.edu/wwwmesabul/) is the
journal of review of MESA, an international organization devoted to Middle East studies. The
on-line version of the journal contains articles on research and teaching in Middle East studies
from recent issues, notes on new on-line resources, and numerous links to other sites.

Levant Cultural Multimedia Servers (http://hiof.no/almashriq/index.html) offers links
to pages devoted to Middle Eastern archeology, architecture, books, business, cinema, clothes,
education, food, geography, history, humor, media, music, song and dance, photographs,
politics, religion, theater, and travel.

Understanding Islam (http://darkwing.uoregon.edu/~kbatarfi/islam.html) offers a
brief explanation of Islam and numerous links to Islamic Web sites, including Islamic
Resources, The Alim Online (Qur'an and Hadith in English), The Holy Qur'an, About Islam
and Muslims, Arabic Lessons and Learning Software, OnLine Islamic book store, CyberMuslim,
and Muslim Students.

The Muslim Women's Home Page (http://www.albany.edu/~ha4934/sisters.html) offers
many links to articles about women in Islam and international women's organizations.

ADDITIONAL QUESTIONS AND ASSIGNMENTS

1.   In a journal entry or a collection of informal notes, discuss the images of the opposite
     sex (male students write about female images and vice versa) presented in selections
     representing two or three different cultures. Consider such issues as rights,
     responsibilities, innate characteristics, fantasy images, and power. As you look over
     your notes, try to discover similarities and differences among the cultures represented.
     Then compare notes with students of the opposite sex. Can you come to any general
     conclusion about the way we view those considered Other? (If you have answered
     Question 1 under *Additional Questions* in Part Three, you may wish to compare your
     responses to that question and this one.)

2.   Interview someone who engaged in a courtship ritual different from your own; in other
     words, talk to someone at least a generation older or younger than you or from a foreign
     country. Compile a list of the details of the ritual, paying close attention to the
     characterization of sex roles, the outside forces that interfered with the couple, and the
     particular joys offered by the ritual. As you write up the interview, try to provide your

reader with enough detail of setting and dialogue from your subject to create a vivid impression.

3. Create your own myth to characterize your fantasy mate. Using Silko as a guide, list the characteristics you find intriguing in a potential partner. Then write a story in which those characteristics become embodied in a mythic figure. Your story should include both high and low points and should leave the reader with a definite impression of your ultimate response to the Other.

4. Reread and take notes on Deborah Tannen's "How Male and Female Students Use Language Differently" and then research the speaking habits of students in one or two of your classes to see if they corroborate Tannen's thesis. You might see if you can get permission to tape-record conversations. Write an essay presenting your analysis, using specific examples from the material you've gathered to illustrate your points.

5. Conduct further research on one of the cultures represented in this section, focusing specifically on sex roles. If the selection is an excerpt from a larger work, look first at that work. You can find more information about the culture by consulting a general encyclopedia, a journal devoted to the study of that culture, and/or the Internet. Narrow your topic to something manageable, such as the evolution of sex roles over time, the influence of religion on sex roles, the role of government in determining or perpetuating certain sex roles or courtship rituals in the culture, and write an expository essay in which you elaborate on the images of men and women presented in the original selection.

Part Five

MYTH, RITUAL, AND MAGIC

INTRODUCTION

Myth, ritual, and magic are not common subjects in pragmatic cultures such as ours, so you might want to start by asking students when and how they have encountered these concepts. A good exercise might be to have students list the five or so most mystical experiences of their lives, take a survey of the class's lists, and then have students free write about one of the items on their list. If there's a theme that appears repeatedly across the students' lists, you might have a discussion about whether there are rituals to organize that experience and, if not, what they could be. The lists could also be used to come up with a collective definition of spirituality; the epigraphs should serve as good points of reference.

Storytelling is a prominent theme in this section (Welty, Bruchac, Mphahlele, Achebe); you might ask students to analyze and critique the extent television and movies fulfill this function in contemporary U.S. culture. Another prevalent theme involves dealing with death and the afterlife (Bruchac, Morrison, Allende, Ajayi); you might have a discussion about the rituals surrounding death in these selections, comparing them with rituals in our society. Other possible subthemes include the use of magic to achieve practical results (Abram, Morrison, Márquez, Allende, and Del Guercio); spirituality versus greed (Bruchac, Welty, Allende, Ajayi); and intersections between African-American, Haitian, and Nigerian uses of myth and magic (Morrison, Del Guercio, Soyinka, Ajayi).

Most selections are quite accessible, but Morrison's may prove difficult; you might want to offer students some background regarding the characters' histories and their relations to one another *before* they read it.

Instructors may wish to consult the following familiar works in preparing related selections from *Making Contact*:

Essays

Annie Dillard, "Total Eclipse" (*Teaching a Stone to Talk*, HarperCollins, 1982).
Friedrich Nietzsche, "Apollonianism and Dionysianism" (*The Birth of Tragedy and the Genealogy of Morals*, Doubleday, 1956).
Plato, "Allegory of the Cave" (*Portable Plato*, Viking Penguin, 1977).
Mark Twain, "Letter from the Recording Angel" (*Mark Twain*, University of California Press, 1973).
E. B. White, "Once More to the Lake" (*One Man's Meat*, HarperCollins, 1941).

Short Stories

Sherwood Anderson, "Death in the Woods" (*Sherwood Anderson: Short Stories*, Hill and Wang, 1933).

Ambrose Bierce, "An Occurrence at Owl Creek Bridge" (*Complete Short Stories of Ambrose Bierce,* University of Nebraska Press, 1984).
Jorge Luis Borges, "The Garden of Forking Paths" (*Labyrinths,* 1962).
Nathaniel Hawthorne, "Young Goodman Brown" (*Great Short Works,* HarperCollins, 1967).
Shirley Jackson, "The Lottery" (*The Lottery,* Farrar, Straus, & Giroux, 1948).
James Joyce, "Araby" (*Dubliners,* Viking, 1982).
Franz Kafka, "The Metamorphosis" (*The Complete Stories,* Schocken, 1988).
Gabriel García Márquez, "A Very Old Man with Enormous Wings" (*Leaf Storm and Other Stories,* HarperCollins, 1971).
Flannery O'Conner, "Revelation" (*The Complete Stories,* Farrar, Straus & Giroux, 1964).
Edgar Allen Poe, "The Tell-Tale Heart" (*Complete Stories,* Knopf, 1992).

BIOGRAPHICAL NOTES ON EPIGRAPH AUTHORS

1. Regarded as the greatest scientist of the twentieth century, German-born Albert Einstein received the Nobel Prize in 1921, largely for his 1905 work on the photoelectric effect. He developed the Theory of General Relativity, considered his major achievement, which revolutionized physics. After leaving Nazi Germany, he came to the United States, where he worked toward establishing world peace, among other social issues.

2. John Updike (see headnote, p. 398).

3. Joyce Carol Oates, a professor of English at Princeton University, has written many books, including the novels *them* (National Book Award, 1970), *Expensive People* (1982), and *Black Water* (1992) (based on the Chappaquiddick incident); the essay collections *On Boxing* (1989) and *American Appetites* (1990); and the short story collection *Where Are You Going, Where Have You Been?: Stories of Young America* (1974). She also writes Gothic romances and horror stories. She edited the *Oxford Book of American Short Stories* (1992).

4. American Civil Rights movement leader Martin Luther King Jr. helped found the Southern Christian Leadership Conference (SCLC) in 1957 and served as its president. He delivered his famous "I Have a Dream" speech August 28, 1963, to more than 250,000 protesters in Washington, D.C.

5. Fadia Faqir was born in Amman, the capital of Jordan, in 1956. She has written a novel, *Nisanit,* about the Arab-Israeli conflict (published in the United States in 1990), and is currently working on a second while finishing a doctorate in Creative Writing at the University of East Anglia in England.

6. Celestine Bohlen writes for the *New York Times* and other publications.

7. William J. Bennett was Secretary of Education in the Bush Administration and held the post of Director ("drug czar") of the Office of National Drug Control Policy.

8. Leslie Marmon Silko (see headnote, p. 419).

9. Mara Freeman writes about Celtic history in *Parabola* and other publications.

10. The Nobel Prizewinning poet and playwright Derek Walcott draws on classical, European, and African traditions as well as the resource of his Caribbean upbringing.

His recent work includes the epic poem *Omeros* and the verse play *The Odyssey*, which was produced by the Royal Shakespeare Company.

11. Pablo Neruda traveled the world as a public servant, living in Burma, Ceylon, Java, Spain, and Mexico. A member of the Communist party, he was not welcome in Chile in the late 1940s and took refuge in France and Mexico. However, he returned to Chile in 1954 as a celebrated poet. He received the Nobel Prize for Literature in 1971.

12. Henry Louis Gates Jr. (see headnote, p. 146).

Explorations

1. John Updike argues that spirituality "retains connotations of the volatile, the impalpable, the immaterial, the dispensable" (p. 504), echoing Einstein's definition of religion; Updike also defines spirituality as "the shadow of light humanity casts as it moves through the darkness of everything that can be explained" (p. 504), paralleling Martin Luther King's observation that the conflict of opposites lies at the heart of religion. As Derek Walcott explains it, the experience of reading a poem is as mysterious as Albert Einstein's notion of religion — it may seem like eating a sandwich or, if the reader is lucky, like taking a communion wafer. There's also a tension between opposites involved, in that reading poetry is a very private experience, yet it gives us a sense of commonality with others.

2. Fadia Faqir finds good in the Islam of eleventh-century Andalucia, which respected imagination and was "committed to the pursuit of knowledge and literacy with all their consequences" (p. 506). She finds evil in contemporary Islam, which stifles Muslim societies with its "granite, heartless certainties" enforced by "appointed clerics who claim to be the sole defenders of the Islamic faith, and who use 'holier than thou' techniques to politicize Islam beyond recognition" (p. 506). William Bennett finds good in "certain fundamental traits of character [valued by Americans]: honesty, compassion, courage, and perseverance"; that he finds evil in an apathetic, amoral culture is apparent in his appeal to parents to give their children stories as moral anchors (p. 507). And Pablo Neruda finds good in the Spanish language bequeathed to his people by the conquistadors and evil in the greed that spurred them to consume or raze everything they encountered in the new land (p. 509).

3. Bennett, Mara Freeman, and Leslie Marmon Silko all depict storytellers as the guardians of culture: In Bennett's view, they provide members of the society with moral points of reference dramatizing American virtues; in Freeman's, they are "guardians of an oral-based culture and living repositories of its history and mythology" (p. 508); and in Silko's, they help to establish a people's or a clan's identity (p. 508). However, the role of the storyteller differs for these writers in the following ways: Bennett wants stories to convey abstract notions, principles, and ideals; Freeman wants stories to fling open the "magic casements" to the world of magic; and Silko wants stories to offer "the original view of creation, which sees that it is all part of a whole" (p. 507).

4. Students might respond that professional writers are more alert and receptive than others to experiences involving myth, ritual, and magic because they deal daily in the currency of the imagination. For instance, when Neruda describes the history of Latin America, he speaks in metaphor (clearly the Spanish invaders did not swallow everything in sight, leaving behind a desert) (p. 509). Likewise, Joyce Carol Oates describes the human body as "a high-rise building with numberless rooms, corridors, corners, elevator shafts,

windows" (p. 505). Writers might be more resistant to experiences involving myth, ritual, and magic because they know their own imaginations are capable of generating such experiences, and because good writing requires critical thinking.

MIRRORS:
THE UNITED STATES

DAVID ABRAM, Making Magic (p. 513)

Explorations

1. Because we live in a culture that relegates magic to the realm of entertainment, students may be unfamiliar with the great respect and fear accorded magicians in other cultures. Although this essay clearly conveys the role of the magician in other cultures, students will most likely miss the connection between the magician and an underlying ecological balance that ensures the success of the ceremony. They may also find David Abram's lack of skepticism hard to accept. Abram consistently refuses to limit the power of his magic to his knowledge of how the tricks are accomplished. Even though he characterizes his own magic as "sleight-of-hand tricks," he does not reduce it to tricks alone. Some unknown aspect of his performance mystifies him as well as his audience (para. 3). This attitude explains his ability to entertain the suggestion in the opening sentence that he may have real powers. Most important, his understanding of the magic used to change Gedé's luck, although it uses tricks, places him in contact with "the particular powers of earth to be found only there" (17). His sense of this contact and his later matter-of-fact acceptance of his magic's success (24) convince readers that Abram takes his experience seriously and does not dismiss the successful results as coincidences.

2. The goal of Abram's travels is to do research on the intertwining of magic and medicine in Asia. He is investigating "the secrets that lay hidden within my own magic . . . [trying] to discern what mysteries my magic had in common with the magic used in traditional cultures not merely for entertainment, but for healing, fortification, and transformation" (4). The purpose for which he uses his magic changes when Gedé insists that he put his magic to practical use to help him with his fishing. Abram is initially skeptical of this plan (12), but when the magic "works," he leaves Gedé's village feeling elated (25).

3. Abram uses the descriptive and expository passages about his Balinese environment to create an atmosphere that makes his use of magic ritual a natural and inevitable response. Although it might be unusual for an American to react this way, Abram comes very close to identifying with the sensibility of a Balinese, who would share Gedé's view of the way to proceed. He unconsciously adopts this role by making a self-effacing refusal of Gedé's first offer, entering a symbolic vision of the sea universe, and even dressing, Balinese fashion, in a sarong (15). The description of Abram on the boat places him in the physical world of the Balinese fishermen, ready to accept and adapt to their code of behavior (17).

Connections

1. Both writers are skeptical of the insights they had while they were ill because they know their minds and bodies were in an altered state. But evidence in each selection suggests that the writer's skepticism is not wholehearted: Abram admits that he did not want the other magicians to view him as a competitor, because "I knew the incredible power of the imagination and had no wish to be the victim of any dark spells" (para. 7). Oates can't decide what to call her "fever-dream," but she concedes, "it impressed me enormously and impresses me still" (p. 504).

2. Gedé and Abram must work by night because fishermen don't fish on the nights when the moon is bright because the fish can see their nets (16), and Gedé does not want other fishermen to become jealous (18). Mara Freeman explains that tales can only be spun in the dark because "it was dangerous for fantastic Otherworldly goings-on to invade the normalcy of day" (p. 508).

3. Abram's and Nikos Kazantzakis's investigatory approaches are similar in that they seek to have a lot of contact with people indigenous to the places they visit; they attend to the natural beauty and spiritual dimensions of those places. But they differ in that Abram seeks to discover how the activity of making magic, of interacting with the supernatural, can have a transformative effect, whereas Kazantzakis is more interested in encountering sensual images of females that might match his fantasy of Aphrodite.

JOSEPH BRUCHAC, Digging into Your Heart (p. 523)

Explorations

1. In the first two Native American stories, Joseph Bruchac suggests that greed does not serve one's self-interest: Those who wish for something to benefit themselves end up as a stone, a tree, a drowned man, and a woman too heavy to stand. The next two stories convey the message that the dead do not want their graves disturbed, and they will punish those who try to dig them up. The third more practical message in the essay is that archeologists and looters have no right to dig up Indian remains nor the gifts that were buried with the dead to accompany them on their journeys. They need to curtail their greed and respect the dead.

2. Bruchac implicitly advises Native American readers to follow the will of their people rather than acting independently (as Squanto did when he decided to help the Pilgrims of the Plymouth Colony [para. 22]); to avoid "fall[ing] into the trap of the avaricious thinking which sometimes seems to characterize European cultures" (26); and to be wary of "the dangers of corruption" from the new wealth Indian nations are gaining from casinos (27). The stories from specific Native American peoples like Wabanaki and Seneca seem geared to arouse Indian readers' pride in their own people, encouraging them to embrace the beliefs of their tribes.

3. Bruchac indirectly advises European-American readers to restrain their greed when he contrasts the story of Captain Kidd's treasure with the Mohegan tale, pointing out that the first was a matter of "intellectual puzzle-solving," whereas the second started with a dream vision (18). He advises these readers more overtly when telling how some Abenakis tried to explain to a group from the University of Vermont why everything

looted from their ancestors' graves must be returned (25). The university detail is bound to appeal to European-American readers; it conveys the idea that even those our culture condones as legitimate grave diggers (archeologists) need to listen to Native peoples.

Connections

1. When magical events take place in David Abram's selection, he causes them, for a number of reasons: to entertain a crowd (p. 514), to develop a relationship with another magician/healer (p. 515), or to placate a demanding fisherman (p. 518). When magical events take place in the Native American stories told by Bruchac, they are caused by the interactions between humans and supernatural beings, usually as a way to warn humans that they had best follow the instructions of the elders or ancestors. In the first story, for instance, the first three men's greed and impatience backfires when they look into the pouches Gluskap had given them before they reach their lodges (para. 2).

2. As per Leslie Marmon Silko's description, the stories Bruchac tells "go back to the original view of creation" (p. 507). They also include the audience and the listeners, as they reflect their community's concerns and offer a message they can learn from, generation after generation. The last two of these points apply to Bruchac's essay itself: His concerns include the whole community's need to be less greedy and more respectful of others' wishes.

3. Bruchac would probably agree with William Bennett's point that stories should provide us with specific moral reference points, because Bruchac wants stories to help us understand why European Americans should have greater respect for Native Americans' burial grounds and why Native Americans should be wary of being corrupted by casino revenues. But Bruchac would probably disagree with Bennett's point that "the vast majority of Americans share a respect for . . . honesty, compassion, courage, and perseverance" (p. 507), because the history of Americans' treatment of Native Americans is more one of greed, violence, and racism.

EUDORA WELTY, Fairy Tale of the Natchez Trace (p. 531)

Explorations

1. Other phrases in the first passage quoted from *The Robber Bridegroom* that foreshadow trouble ahead include "the wilderness was beset with dangers," "the river the color of blood," "the boats strained in the waves," and the "savage breath" of the wilderness (paras. 3 and 4). A good exercise for helping students understand how a writer creates atmosphere in fiction would be to have students rewrite this passage to make the landscape seem more welcoming.

2. Besides drawing on life in the Natchez area, Eudora Welty uses fairy tales by Germany's the Brothers Grimm as a source, and at one point she references the Greek myth of Cupid and Psyche (41). You might ask students if they believe fairy tales reflect people's lives in any time or place or if there is something about Natchez in the time Welty writes about that makes it especially appropriate for her to use these motifs.

3. Welty explains that her hero leads a double life because "life was so full, so excessively charged with energy in those days, when nothing seemed impossible . . . that leading

one life hardly provided scope enough for it all" (55). The dramatic advantages of the double character are that readers know more than some of the characters, giving us the pleasure of anticipating when the characters will be surprised to learn one another's identity.

Connections

1. Bruchac would probably agree with Clement's response to Salome's ambitions to extend their land: "To encompass so much as that is greedy. It would take too much of time and the heart's energy" (para. 20). Bruchac believes that "the heart's energy" should be devoted to improving the lot of one's people, as in the case of the fourth man granted a pouch by Gluskap (p. 524); greed only backfires.

2. Welty seems less interested in improving her readers' morals than in recreating for them the rich cultural history of the Natchez region. Among the four reasons William Bennett gives for telling stories, the third is embodied by Welty's tale: "stories help anchor our children in their culture, its history and traditions" (p. 507). Leslie Marmon Silko's view that stories "go back to the original view of creation" (p. 507) parallels Welty's interest in using fairy tales because they tell essential stories about human nature (58).

3. Rosamond washes her lover's face because she is frightened by "what she sees in the robber's house" (Welty doesn't specify) (40). Whereas she tries to determine her lover's identity against his will, Yellow Woman asks Silva, "Who are you?" (p. 420). His reply — "Last night you guessed my name, and you knew why I had come" — suggests that she had gone with him willingly (p. 420). Whereas Rosamond is afraid, Yellow Woman is curious.

TONI MORRISON, From *Beloved* (p. 544)

Explorations

1. The three characters living in the present are Sethe, Denver (the daughter with whom Sethe was pregnant when she ran away from Sweet Home), and Paul D, who knew Sethe and Halle at Sweet Home. Halle is Baby Suggs's son, the father of Sethe's children, and, while at Sweet Home, a close friend to Paul D. Halle hasn't been seen by any of them in years, but Paul D apparently saw him by the churn, a memory that seems significant (later in the novel, Paul D recalls finding Halle sobbing, drinking milk out of the churn, because Halle saw Sethe being nursed).

2. Students should have no trouble seeing the contradiction inherent in Garner's claim that he "bought" and "raised" his "niggers" to be men. The impact of that contradiction was to give the Sweet Home men a false sense of security, possibly making it easier for "schoolteacher" to "break" them (para. 63).

3. The word "haunted" implies that the house and its ghost are separate entities; saying the house was "spiteful" indicates that the ghost envelops them, that their lives are so indelibly shaped by their history that they cannot escape the ghost's machinations any more than they can escape themselves. Hence, when Paul D first walked through the house, "a wave of grief soaked him so thoroughly he wanted to cry" (65). When he

suggests that the ghost is lonely, Sethe responds, "I don't see how it could be lonely spending every minute with us like it does" (109).

Connections

1. The second sentence's "cautionary blinker" is the word "venom." It stands out as unusual, because babies are generally regarded as innocent. It warns us that the house is no ordinary house, that it can suddenly start acting out its anger, as when Paul D cups Sethe's breasts, and the floor starts to shake, the house to pitch (para. 168). In dealing with Beloved's rage, Sethe and Denver "waged a perfunctory battle against the outrageous behavior of that place; against turned-over slop jars, smacks on the behind, and gusts of sour air" (4).

2. Morrison is probably writing for a general audience, anyone interested in contemporary literature. But white and black Americans are likely to respond differently to the chapter, depending on how familiar they are with both the historical facts and the emotional truths of slavery. Baby Suggs's remark that she sees no point in moving because "not a house in the country ain't packed to its rafters with some dead Negro's grief" (18) might give some white readers pause, as might details about Sethe being whipped and nursed by the white men (160–164). Black readers may be less surprised by Baby Suggs's remark or Sethe's experiences, because they may corroborate their general sense of blacks' treatment in this country. (This question elicits risky speculations; you might want to stick to asking how reading the selection affected students' preconceptions about slavery.)

3. Leslie Marmon Silko's comment about how the Antelope people identify themselves according to their origin is reflected in Sethe's and Paul D's explanation to Denver about why they talk about Sweet Home: Paul D admits that "it wasn't sweet and it sure wasn't home," and Sethe answers, "But it's where we were. All together. Comes back whether we want it to or not" (117; 118). Sethe expresses the same thought when she's washing off the chamomile sap, remembering Sweet Home and wondering that she can still feel nostalgic for it, "although there was not a leaf on that farm that did not make her want to scream" (19).

WINDOWS:
THE WORLD

ES'KIA MPHAHLELE, African Literature: What Tradition? (p. 562)

Explorations

1. Belonging to both the Western and the African worlds forces Es'kia Mphahlele and his fellow artists to choose between the present, represented by Westernization, and the past, represented by African tradition. In attempting to reconcile the two, the artists must balance several opposing influences: Christianity versus traditional African religions; fact-oriented Western education versus the more spiritual knowledge of family and tribe; traditional tribal philosophy versus the European language used to articulate it; reverence for the artifact versus the creative process; and the local African community versus the larger, predominantly Western, surrounding world. Specifically, the artists

choose whether to adopt Western ways, gaining power in the larger world at the risk of losing African understanding, friends, and kinship ties.

2.   African writers will need education to succeed in the world beyond the community, and that education will in turn open up still newer worlds to them. But it also opens up a gulf between writers and African tradition. Writers must attempt to reconcile the education with the traditions or risk losing their moorings. Education provides new viewpoints, new subject matter, and many other sources of enrichment for writers. However, it may alienate them from the viewpoints and subject matter to which they feel closest and about which they can write most successfully. To reject education is to cut themselves off from the larger world in an attempt (not necessarily successful) to preserve the smaller one.

3.   Mphahlele's first indication of his Western heritage is found in the first paragraph, when he refers to "Hegelian historical determinism." Among other illustrations of Western influence are his ability to understand the influence of his European education (para. 2), his discussion of parent-child relationships (4), and his essay's diction throughout. His African heritage is more evident, illustrated by his understanding of the value of the creative process (6) and his acknowledgment of the spirit of his ancestors (8).

Connections

1.   The two situations are similar in that they both involve humiliation, but there's a key difference: Whereas, when they are slaves, the lives of the characters in *Beloved* are controlled by whites, in Mphahlele's South Africa, blacks' cultural identities are controlled by Western culture. Sethe recalls the humiliation of being forcibly nursed, being beaten, trading sex for the engraving on her daughter's tombstone. Mphahlele notes that it can be "humiliating to feel that one has continually to be reassessing oneself with reference to the long line of tradition he has entered — the tradition of the West" because African heroes have been discredited (para. 2). In both situations, the possible solutions are highly complex: Sethe and other former slaves must reconcile themselves personally with the cruelties that were inflicted upon them, whereas black South Africans educated in Western mores must find a way to reconcile themselves with their traditional religion and beliefs. As Mphahlele concludes, "the past is not just a segment in time to think *back* upon. . . . We need to appreciate these distances if we are to understand what the African . . . is about" (9).

2.   Joseph Bruchac's essay suggests that Native American history was "shanghaied into the history of the West" in that its stories of gold buried to help the dead on their journey were lumped together with European stories of buried treasure to be guarded or looted. Among the customs that Bruchac believes should be preserved is that of respecting the ancestors and allowing them to remain undisturbed, along with whatever was buried with them. Bruchac is willing to accept Westerners' interest in studying Native peoples but only up to a certain point. Mphahlele believes that traditional religious values that revere the ancestors should be preserved, because they help Africans to stay in touch with their indigenous culture. But he is eager to accept Western education, because it opens new worlds, "longings and desires [he] would never have known" (6); moreover, "the very educational process that wrenches him from his moorings helps him to arrange a harmonization within himself" (4).

3.   Mphahlele describes learning to read as something that both allowed him to enter new worlds and made him realize the extent to which education had alienated him from his

own (7). The conflict Pablo Neruda expresses about his language is that the conquistadors stormed across his country swallowing everything in sight — a huge price to pay for a language — yet Neruda insists, "we came up winners" (p. 509). Malcolm X found learning to read exhilarating but also felt it gave him a "sensitivity to the deafness, dumbness, and blindness that was afflicting the black race in America" (p. 276).

GABRIEL GARCÍA MÁRQUEZ, Dreams for Hire (p. 567)

Explorations

1. Gabriel García Márquez expresses skepticism of Frau Frida's dreams in the way he initially presents her in a slightly comic manner — when asked what she does, she responds, "I hire myself out to dream" (para. 4) — and he admits to her when walking along the Ramblas that he'd "always thought that her dreams were no more than a contrivance to make ends meet" (18). But he expresses his credulity in describing dreams she's had that have come true and in recounting that he was so convinced by her warning that he must leave Vienna that he left immediately and never returned (12). Pablo Neruda, however, would not hear her dreams, insisting that the only divination comes from poetry (16); it's possible that he sees her as a competitor, given that both of them enjoy the attention they attract by being mysterious and charismatic.

2. "Dreams for Hire" partakes of some elements of the short story and some elements of the essay. García Márquez offers little exposition, leaping right into the first scene of his narrative, the tidal wave that smashes into the hotel. García Márquez returns to this scene at the conclusion of the piece. Thus, the structure of "Dreams for Hire" is similar to a framed story, in which a central narrative is contained within, and contextualized by, another narrative displaced from it in time and space. In addition, García Márquez's narrative has elements of suspense ordinarily associated with fiction, especially the mystery. Is it really Frau Frida who died? What is the significance of the serpent-shaped ring? García Márquez describes his characters in detail, using their conversation to advance arguments about the association of dreams and poetry, as when Neruda expounds his opinion of dream divination in paragraphs 16 and 17. But he also pays attention to character development; his portrait of Neruda includes the poet's physical appearance (13), his eating habits, his relationship with his wife, and his propensity to dominate others, as in the "inevitable walk along the Ramblas" (18) and the "sacred siesta" (23). These are elements of character development missing in most conventional essays. The aspects of "Dreams for Hire" that remind us García Márquez is writing factually are the writer's physical presence at the real events he describes and his representation of Neruda, a famous poet.

3. The last sentence is ambiguous, because "she was a dreamer" could be taken figuratively or literally. That the dead woman's identity remains ambiguous fits the rest of the story, where one is never certain how seriously Frau Frida should be taken or even what her real name is. It seems especially fitting that she who was always predicting disasters *may* have died in one. If the story had ended on a definitive note, its light, fanciful tone would have become somber.

Connections

1. Frau Frida links people from different communities, because dreams are the ultimate common ground. Through her profession, Frau Frida comes to dominate a sophisticated

Viennese family (paras. 8 and 9), entertains students who frequent an inexpensive Viennese tavern (10), befriends García Márquez himself (10), and presumably is hired by Portugal's ambassador to Cuba. She serves as a litmus test for people's capacity to believe in dreams; the essay's characters might be placed on a spectrum, with strong believers like the Viennese family at the one end and serious doubters like Neruda at the other.

2. Both Frau Frida and David Abram are able to use their unusual talent to give other people a greater sense of control over their own lives. Through the use of illusion, Abram helps a fisherman regain his confidence and his ability to catch enough fish to feed his family. And Frau Frida builds an entire career on her ability to interpret her own dreams as a way of forecasting the future for others. Abram discovers the significance of his talent when he realizes that, in a way, he really does have "powers" he himself can't understand (p. 514). Frau Frida, although she is matter-of-fact about her extraordinary talent and not offended by García Márquez's skepticism (19), nevertheless takes her dreams seriously and is charismatic enough to persuade others to take them seriously as well.

3. García Márquez and Joyce Carol Oates both express a wish to believe in dreams, as well as skepticism of that wish. Oates seems more anxious to give a rational explanation for the seeming power of dreams, perhaps because she is writing an earnest, nonfictional essay for a Western audience. That she is self-conscious about using the phrase "mystical vision" suggests that she (and her intended audience) are not accustomed to discussing such experiences. García Márquez's essay, on the other hand, makes its argument through narrative and is deliberately as ambiguous as his subject.

ISABEL ALLENDE, Clarisa (p. 575)

Explorations

1. In Clarisa's world, oil lamps and chamber pots stand in for electric lights and toilets and people believe that saints — some of whom are their neighbors — can help them with problems ranging from blindness to a hangover (para. 1). Clarisa believes that her retarded children are divinely blessed, but she does not believe that men walked on the moon nor that anything seen on television is true (29).

2. "Clarisa" is filled with casual references to improbable events; for instance, Clarisa's husband "must be a hundred by now, unless he has already died and the coughs and curses we hear are only echoes from the past" (5). Or "her spirit was detaching itself from her body at the same pace her wings germinated" (29). The effect of these statements is to make Allende's metaphors — Clarisa's hair as "meringue" or her walls' "sweat[ing] a greenish mist" — sound like they might also be true. The overall effect is to make Clarisa's world seem like a place where anything is possible, where reality is determined by what people believe.

3. Clarisa claims to believe that her third baby will be normal, because "God maintains a certain equilibrium in the universe, and just as He creates some things twisted, He creates others straight" (25). Her unstated reason is that Congressman Diego Cienfuegos is the father. You might ask students how Allende prepares readers for this revelation — note the phrase "discreet friendship" (24), the allusion to the politician's "sleepless nights" (24), and Clarisa's conversation with Eva about her sins (48–63). It seems

appropriate that her husband sired the two retarded children, because "for more than forty years her husband had buried himself alive in a room at the back of the patio" (4), communicating with his wife only through notes and knocks (4), declining to see her even when she told him she would die (34–38).

Connections

1. Religion and superstition are nearly indistinguishable from each other in "Clarisa": Clarisa's neighbors believe she has the power to cure a hangover or handle problems with the draft or a bout of loneliness (para. 1); many claim to have "seen a circle of light around her head and to have heard celestial music in her presence" (64). Allende sometimes sounds skeptical toward religious and superstitious beliefs, giving the impression that they were invented by humans to fill their own needs, as when she mentions St. Anthony, who finds husbands for spinsters (1). However, she also tends to present reality as equally fabulous; superstitions sound less unlikely when placed against such a backdrop. For instance, Allende mentions that the Pope was "magnificent in his portable glass cage, a white porpoise in an aquarium" (29) and that "there were enough capillary relics offered for sale to stuff a couple of pillows" (31). As for Clarisa's powers, Allende presents them as the projections of her neighbors, yet she does attribute to her "the hands of a healer" (2). Márquez seems to have a similar attitude toward Frau Frida: He wonders whether her dream revelations represent a clever way to pay the bills (p. 572), yet when she advises him to leave Vienna, he takes her advice to heart (p. 571).

2. In *Beloved*, the ghost's physical disruption of the house and its inhabitants' lives provides strong evidence of its presence; so does Paul D's immediate apprehension of it upon entering the house (p. 550). Sethe also mentions that people in the area will not come near the house (p. 554). The characters in "Clarisa" are equally willing to believe in the supernatural, but they perceive it as more benevolent; there are as many forces of good that can grant them small favors as there are of evil. Whereas Sethe and Denver are isolated from others by the ghost, Clarisa and her neighbors are bound to one another by their religious beliefs/superstitions. Toni Morrison draws us into her story by plunking us into the middle of Sethe's day, offering no background information; we must construct Sethe's history from her conversations with Paul D and her thoughts. The fragments of plot we get are fascinating, making us eager to learn the whole story. Allende offers more exposition of her characters's lives, but, like Morrison, she presents the story's fantastical elements as matter-of-factly as if they were self-evidently true.

3. Both Martin Luther King and Allende in "Clarisa" suggest that the primary tension in life is the one between good and evil. Clarisa explains that her third child will be normal because "for every virtue there is a sin, for every joy an affliction, for every evil a good, and on and on, for as the wheel of life turns through the centuries, everything evens out" (25). King does not sound so confident that "the downward pull of evil" (p. 505) will not triumph.

GINO DEL GUERCIO, The Secrets of Haiti's Living Dead (p. 587)

Explorations

1. The principal source of information in the essay is Wade Davis's research. To establish Davis's credibility, Gino Del Guercio begins by describing the background of Wade's

adviser, Richard Evans Schultes, director of the Harvard Botanical Museum, which is "one of the world's foremost institutes of ethnobiology" (para. 8). Then he notes that Schultes was too busy, so he recommended "another Harvard ethnobotanist," Davis, who was working on his Ph.D.

2.   This statement means that the chemical aspects of voodoo are secondary to the social and psychological ones. Japanese people who eat fugu experience the poison physically, but Haitians are so culturally conditioned to fear zombification that they respond to tetrodotoxin and datura by remaining in a trance-like state even after they should have recovered from the effects of the chemicals. Haitians' reactions to these chemicals are charged with their fear of losing their will and becoming enslaved.

3.   The point of this question is to encourage students to think about how Westerners look at other cultures; in this case, we are much more interested in learning about what we perceive to be an exotic set of mystical rituals (and a new medical technology) than in understanding the cultural context on which voodoo depends to function as it does. Our society compartmentalizes different disciplines so much, and sensationalizes news so much, that we tend to take too narrow an approach when studying a more holistic culture.

Connections

1.   Clarisa's optimism causes events to move in directions one would not believe possible. She refuses to let a robber rob her, gives him some money, and has a long conversation over tea with him (paras. 10–22). She gets used clothes for prostitutes from the League of Catholic Dames, musical instruments for a Hebrew choir from a German Institute, and funds for alcohol rehabilitation programs from viniculturists (24). She supports four children without help from her husband or charity (28). She predicts the exact day of her death, although she appears to be in good health (33). However, religion does not appear to play as effective a role in maintaining the social order in "Clarisa" as it does in Del Guercio's Haiti: The pimps and prostitutes remain unmoved by Clarisa's harangues and even the robber she befriended shows up at her deathbed to tell her he's become a professional who targets the rich.

2.   Whereas Wade Davis travels to Haiti as a researcher bent on solving a specific puzzle, David Abram comes to Asia with a much more broadly defined goal, to see how magic and medicine are intertwined in Asian culture. Davis arrives in Haiti with several contacts and acquires a sample of zombie medicine in a few weeks but finds it to be flawed and has to try again. He comes up with a chemical answer that does not satisfactorily explain the zombie phenomenon; he then tries a different approach and proceeds to research the culture. Abram also has a false start: He begins in Sri Lanka by being far too open with his skills, anxious to get a sense of the local response. His plan backfires, as people try to get him to cure their diseases, and he leaves the country for Indonesia. There, he spends five months immersing himself in the culture, slipping into its patterns himself and slowly gaining a reputation as a sorcerer, so that Indonesian sorcerers come to *him*. Abram sees understanding the culture as essential to his research, but Davis has to learn that after taking a purely scientific approach. Davis's approach may be more efficient, but Abram's seems likelier to yield accurate results.

3.   The excerpt from *Beloved* is replete with evidence that its characters value free will and independence as highly as the Haitians do. Sethe ran away, even though she was pregnant, because she could not bear the indignity of being nursed and beaten. The

thought of Sweet Home, beautiful as it is, makes her want to scream. The Sweet Home men wanted Sethe to choose her partner independently, although they all longed for her. Halle worked Sundays for five years to buy his mother's freedom. Beloved expresses her feelings as willfully as any two year old.

SPOTLIGHT:
NIGERIA

ADDITIONAL INFORMATION ON COUNTRY

Environment: One of the largest countries in Africa, Nigeria is bounded on the west by the Republic of Benin, on the north by the Republic of Niger, and on the east by the Republic of Cameroon. The northern part of Nigeria consists of plateaus and grasslands that are dried by the *harmattan* wind from the Sahara desert. The dry, sparsely populated central plains are covered by grasslands. Most of the country's population lives in the southern lowlands, which receive more rainfall, fostering dense tropical forests. The Niger River's massive delta divides the coast into two distinct areas. Oil is produced in the east, whereas the west has more industrial development.

Demographics: Nigeria's 88 million people are divided among 250 ethnic groups. These can be divided into four main groups: the Hausa and Fulani in the north, the Yoruba in the southwest, and the Ibo in the southeast.

Religion: The north is primarily Muslim; the southeast, predominantly Christian; and the southwest a mix of Muslims, Christians, and followers of traditional African religions.

Education: Sixty-two percent of males are literate, compared with 40 percent of females. Seventy-nine percent of males and 62 percent of females attend primary school, and 24 percent of males and 17 percent of females attend secondary school. Three hundred twenty students per 100,000 inhabitants attend college (figures from 1991).

Yoruba Religion: The Yoruba do not actively worship their all-powerful god, known as Olorun ("the owner of the sky") or Olodumare (which roughly translates as "the almighty"). He plays a similar role as the Judeo-Christian and Islamic gods — he is regarded as the creator, the almighty and all-knowing, and the final judge of mankind, yet the Yoruba apparently ignore him in their daily lives. One theory is that Olorun may have developed through the influence of early Islamic or Christian missionaries, as a simulacrum of the gods of those religions.

Some Yoruba legends have a pair of gods, the male known as Obatala, Orishala, or Orisa-nla, and his wife, Odudua, as supreme creating deities. In one legend, Olorun creates the world and Obatala and Odudua finish up the details. Obatala, often a sculptor-god, has the responsibility to shape human bodies, whereas Olorun breathes these bodies to life. In some places, Obatala also rules over all of the *orisha*, or minor gods, as king.

The *orisha* traditionally number either 401 or 601. The Yoruba explained to early missionaries that these minor gods descended from the single almighty god, just as Jesus was the son of the Christian God.

Among the most important of the *orisha* are Shango, who creates thunder and lightning by casting "thunderstones" down to earth, and Ogun, the god of war, of the hunt, and of ironworking. Ogun serves as the patron deity of blacksmiths, warriors, and all who use metal in their occupations. He also presides over deals and contracts. Eshu, also known as Legba, is another important god. He is a trickster god who has mistakenly been identified by Europeans with the devil in the past, although the Yoruba pantheon has no evil gods.

The Yoruba have great respect for their ancestors, and anthropologists debate whether the rituals dealing with ancestry are religious in nature or simply respectful. Some tribes believe that after death the ancestors become demigods, but only once they have assumed the persona of a true deity. This resembles another aspect of the Yoruba faith, the phenomenon of possession, in which mediums take on the characteristics of one of the gods. Each god's traits are so well stereotyped that mediums as far off as Haiti loll back their heads and cross their legs in a manner similar to the Yoruba when possessed by the lightning god.

CHINUA ACHEBE, The Song of Ourselves (p. 599)

Explorations

1. Chinua Achebe explains "literature as celebration" as a tribute to his precolonial inheritance, the idea that any artist's work signifies "the creative potential in all of us and . . . the need to exercise this latent energy again and again in artistic expression and communal, cooperative enterprises" (para. 2). Specifically, Achebe wants to mine the colonial experience for instances where Africans managed to celebrate themselves, despite "the din of an insistent world and song of others" (4).

2. To justify their desire to plunder Africa's material wealth, Europeans had to convince themselves that Africans had no title to this wealth, because they were inferior beings; in fact, they were regarded as so inferior that they might as well be enslaved and put to use. As Achebe points out, churchmen began to doubt the existence of the black man's soul at exactly the time that "the black man's body was fetching high prices in the market place" (14). Achebe uses evidence from Western literature (Shakespeare's *The Tempest*, Conrad's *Heart of Darkness*, and John Buchan's *Prester John*) and history (Edward Gibbon and Philip Curtin) to make these points. Except for Shakespeare and Curtin, these writers depict the African as a savage that needs to be civilized by European influences. (You might ask students whether these sources suggest that Achebe is trying to appeal to European readers.)

3. As an argument against writing in English, some of Achebe's fellow African writers have created the myth that they spoke only their mother tongue during their childhood. Achebe, however, contends that because many of these writers attended British boarding schools, they were forced to use English not only because of the setting but also because that was the only language they shared with classmates from all over Nigeria (22). Clearly, this view also applies to Africa in general, where many different languages were spoken before the advent of colonialism.

Connections

1. Achebe suggests that without a British-style education, the African writer would not have come into being, but Achebe himself developed a desire to write the African's

story when he realized that the heroes with whom he had been identifying in British novels were Europeans, whereas Africans were "those strange beings . . . on the river bank, making horrid faces" (para. 20). Achebe's conclusion, that he wants to use both his Igbo language and English, depending on the context, sounds similar to Es'kia Mphahlele's conclusion that he wants Western cultural mores and African ones that revere the ancestors to be perceived as "part of the whole pattern" in the African writer's identity (p. 565). Achebe uses examples from Western literature to emblematize the way Africans were viewed by colonizers, illustrating Mphahlele's point that the African writer tries to communicate his views in a language filled with allegory and metaphor that remain inaccessible to his own people.

2.   Both writers treat their colonial history as a heritage as well as exploitation. Although Achebe does not glow over the colonizers' language itself as Pablo Neruda does, he expresses gratitude for being able to communicate with students from all over Nigeria because the British had grouped them under one administration (22). Africa's colonial experience differed greatly from Latin America's, because the former's people were enslaved and made to feel inferior. Africans learning English were forced to come to terms with the vast literature of rationalization their colonizers generated, to rewrite their history on their own terms, using the language to negate the views of those who ceded it to them.

3.   As a child, Achebe identified with the European heroes in the British books he read, until it dawned on him that he was one of the savages depicted in them (18–20); he then realized that "stories are not innocent" (21) and that Africans would need to write their own stories if they were to control their cultural identity. Likewise, Margaret Atwood learned the kings of England during her school days, until Canada switched from being an English cultural colony to an American one; then she read American comic books and listened to American records. Only at the end of high school did she read *Canada in the World Today*. As an adult, however, she seems grateful for the cultural exposure such an upbringing gave her, just as Achebe values having gone to school with children from other tribes.

WOLE SOYINKA, Nigerian Childhood (p. 606)

Explorations

1.   The integration of Anglicanism and traditional magic will probably serve as a source of amusement for students. The characters seem to find no contradiction in weaving magic throughout the fabric of the religion they have been taught. In fact, the combination seems to work wonders as far as keeping children in line is concerned: Wild Christian's story of the encounter with the wood sprites is a case in point. Her lament that faith and discipline are no longer valued follows her account of the children's failure to obey the òrós orders to stay away from his place in the woods. Reverend J. J., an Anglican minister, respects the wood sprites, and when the children are chased out of the woods after disobeying the order, he whips them (after, of course, invoking the power of the Christian God to keep off the sprites). Uncle Sanya is punished too, for his stubbornness — one of the greatest of sins. Even the children themselves respond to the twin traditions: They abandon their evening visits to the woods after the incident with the wood sprites. Students may need some guidance in recognizing the essential similarity

of the religion and the tradition, namely, that both depend on faith in a power greater than that of any human.

2.   The stories of Reverend J. J. emphasize the need for faith (his stand against the wood sprites), perseverance (his refusal to give up preaching despite the *egúngún*'s warning), and respect for tradition (his following the old woman's orders when Sanya was ill). An interesting sideline is the narrator's confusion between perseverance and stubbornness: Try as he might, he cannot keep from characterizing Reverend J. J.'s perseverance in the face of warnings as something fearfully close to the "sin" of stubbornness.

3.   Although it is sometimes difficult for students to recognize subtle changes in point of view, a close look at the selection will reveal that even though Soyinka speaks in the voice of an adult, he sees things with the eyes of a child. His grasp of history and his ability to articulate his conflicting responses to his mother's stories (the sense that the children's fright was punishment enough for their foray into the woods, the feeling that Reverend J. J.'s perseverance was really stubbornness) are indications that we're hearing this story from an adult. But Bishop Crowther's apparition is definitely the experience of a child: The fact that the author never questions its authenticity allows us to perceive the experience as the child does. His matter-of-fact accounts of his mother's stories reinforce the sense that these are the observations of a child. Even when Lawanle pulls him away for his bath, we feel the reluctance of the child. More perceptive students will also point to Soyinka's mature vocabulary and style as evidence of an adult voice recounting these experiences from the point of view of a child.

Connections

1.   "Nigerian Childhood" offers a sense of the extent to which missionaries succeeded in converting Africans to their religion, in this case the Anglican church. The essay suggests that the missionaries did not attempt to displace the Africans' animist religion: The narrator's mother tells how her brother Sanya was acknowledged to be an *òrò* (a kind of tree demon) by all, even by her great uncle, Rev. J. J. Ransome-Kuti (paras. 3–5). Rather, the two religions are blended, so the children are told a story of how Rev. J. J. continued preaching, even after an *egúngún*, a spirit of a dead ancestor, had caused the church to collapse in the middle of his sermon (33).

2.   Throughout Soyinka's memoir, stories of the elders are invoked, making them seem as influential in the mind of the narrator as are his living relatives. The narrator takes pride in his relation to his uncle Sanya, the *òrò*, and Rev. J. J., who "actually ordered back several ghommids [wood spirits] in his lifetime" (3). Also depicted positively is the elderly woman who healed Sanya by having his family prepare food for a troop of fifty visiting *òrò* (42–51).

3.   Isabel Allende, John David Morley, and Soyinka all present their characters' superstitions somewhat matter of factly, leaving it to readers to judge their beliefs. Allende is the most likely of the three to depict her characters' superstitions as wishful thinking: She recounts Clarisa's neighbors' belief that she could cure small things like a hangover or a siege of loneliness and comments, "Her wonders are humble and improbable, but as necessary as the spectacular marvels worked by cathedral saints" (p. 576). Although Allende concedes that Clarisa's ability to heal these ills is improbable, she validates the wish to have them healed, empathizing with her superstitious characters. Morley raises doubts about his Japanese characters' beliefs by simply relating facts that contradict

them: "there was no earthquake that night" (p. 239). And Soyinka presents the stories of wood spirits and tree demons as if they were real, although he occasionally relates a detail so unlikely that it suggests he regards his characters' beliefs as superstitious. For example, "Obviously bishops were not inclined to challenge the spirits. Only the vicars could" (3).

J. F. ADE AJAYI, On the Politics of Being Mortal (p. 615)

Explorations

1. Regarding the Western-style funeral he describes, J. F. Ade Ajayi is uncomfortable with the fact that the mourners seem unwilling to accept the fact of death. When the deceased's friends go to his widow's house to console her, they feel a need to "relieve the tension" by drinking alcohol. Then someone gets "the bright idea" of playing music and getting people to dance, "including the widow" (you might ask students if they believe he makes the last detail explicit for its potential shock value), all of this "on the grounds that the good-hearted professor would not have wished for gloom at his funeral" (para. 2). The phrases quoted seem in particular to express the author's annoyance.

2. According to Ajayi, the prevalent attitude toward death in the Western world is to regard it as "a challenge to science and technology, an obstacle to be conquered" (7). Moreover, Westerners are anesthetized to the reality of death by seeing it constantly on television (7). Ajayi cites Alfred G. Killilea's *The Politics of Being Mortal*, which argues that Americans need to accept the limitations death sets and find meaning in life, "not in unlimited competition and accumulation, but in touching the lives of others for good" (8).

3. According to Ajayi, Africans embrace a sense of "continuity" because their societies are structured in terms of generations rather than in terms of social class. This means there is a "community of interest" (16) among the living, the dead, and the generations yet unborn. Hence "the aged were able to contemplate death with composure and without fear, and by their example teach their offspring about the meaning of life and change, because to them death did not mean extinction" (16). This attitude has advantages over the Western one, in that ancestors and older people are valued for their wisdom, and death implies a change of status rather than the complete erasure Westerners can't bring themselves to face.

Connections

1. In Wole Soyinka's "Nigerian Childhood," the narrator describes being visited by the ghost of Bishop Ajayi Crowther and then explains that this appearance "only confirmed that the Bishops, once they were dead, joined the world of spirits and ghosts" (p. 608). Among the bases for accommodation between Christian and African beliefs offered by Ajayi, that which fits Soyinka's story best is found in material he quotes from Boubou Hama and Kizerbo: "traditional African time includes and incorporates eternity in both directions. . . . In their own way, [bygone generations] remain contemporary, and as influential as they were during their lifetime" (para. 19).

2. Chinua Achebe claims that the statement that he invented African literature is "blasphemous" because of a taboo among the Igbo against "laying a proprietary hand

on even the smallest item in that communal enterprise in creativity" (p. 600). Ajayi's ideas concerning the sense of continuity in African culture shed light on Achebe's ideas about the artist's role: According to Ajayi, a sense of interdependence and an acceptance of death in a community paradoxically reaffirm each individual's uniqueness (12). In the course of this discussion, Ajayi cites Killilea's observation that, in a communitarian culture, "the nearness of death heightens a willingness to share and thus shatters the charade of heroic individualism (12).

3.   Both writers argue that we must learn to accept death, to revere our elders and ancestors, and to recognize that greed always backfires. For Ajayi, accepting death means allowing mourners to mourn (3 and 4), whereas for Joseph Bruchac it means leaving graves undisturbed (p. 529). For Ajayi, revering elders and ancestors provides the living with a sense of continuity, whereas for Bruchac, heeding them prevents the living from making foolish mistakes, as illustrated in the story of the four wishes (p. 525). And whereas Ajayi depicts "competition and acquisition" as part of a collective cultural effort to deny death, Bruchac depicts Europeans' grave robbing as motivated by a desire to find "buried treasure."

BUCHI EMECHETA, Ona (p. 627)

Explorations

1.   Physical prowess is an important trait for the characters in "Ona" because their lifestyle entails a good deal of physical labor; specific tasks mentioned in the story include hunting animals with spears, carrying wounded hunters back to the village, raising and butchering goats, farming, and hauling water. Buchi Emecheta establishes Agbadi's physical prowess by describing how he manages to spear an elephant in its stomach, even when he's "pinned to the sugar-cane bush unable to move" (para. 8). Ona's prowess is apparent in her fitness and agility (6), and her ability to nurse Agbadi for five days and nights while he is unconscious (18–20).

2.   There are many instances in which the people or myths are cited as authorities; here are a few: "People said that Nwokocha Agbadi spent all his life on this earth courting his Ona" (4). "People used to find it strange that a chief like Obi Omunna would go about unashamedly pulling a tiny toddler with him" (5). "People said she had had him bewitched, that she had a kind of power over him" (7). "People had thought that after a while he would get fed up with her" (110). Citing public opinion so frequently would only work in a Western story set in a place with enough sense of community that public opinion was unified; "people say" more often has negative implications in the United States.

3.   Most rituals in the story that might seem unnecessary to us have to do with sickness and death. When Agbadi has been wounded and is being carried into the village, "the disclosure of his death [must] comply with certain cultural laws — there must be gun shots, and two or three goats must be slaughtered before the announcement" (9); the benefit may be that people will not panic at the loss of their leader, but will have a chance to become accustomed to the idea, which would help to maintain order. While Agbadi is ill, goats are slaughtered daily "to appease [his] chi" (18); this is supposed to help him heal. When Agunwa is buried, her slave is supposed to jump into the grave so she can continue to serve her in the afterlife (83). And, after Ona has given birth,

Agbadi is allowed to see her once but then must leave her alone for twenty-five days (116), allowing her to give all of her attention to the new baby, as well as avoid becoming pregnant immediately.

Connections

1. According to J. F. Ade Ajayi, Westerners put the needs of the individual first and Africans put the needs of the group first. That Agbadi's and Ona's romance is disruptive to the needs of the group is apparent in the discussion following their night of boisterous lovemaking: some claim it was "bad for [Angunwa's] morale to hear her husband giving pleasure to another woman in the same courtyard where she slept" (para. 65) and Idayi confirms that they kept everyone awake (76). That their relationship causes problems is also suggested when people suspect that Agbadi's young wives show "signs of sexual neglect" (7).

2. Es'kia Mphahlele describes how before indigenous African languages became literary, they "seem to have relied more and more heavily on the spoken word, so that gesture, facial expression, inflection of voice became vital equipment in communication. Language became almost a ritual in itself, and metaphor and symbol became a matter of art and device. Metaphor became a sacred thing if it had descended from usage in earlier times" (p. 565).

3. Clearly, Ona receives so much criticism because she refuses to be docile as Ibo women are expected to be. When she rushes up the procession of hunters to ask what has become of Agbadi, one of them accuses her of having tortured and teased him with her body (13). After Agunwa becomes ill, Ona is described as "a woman who was troublesome and impetuous, who had the audacity to fight with her man before letting him have her: a bad woman" (65). By contrast, as Agbadi tells his sons, Agunwa is "a good woman. So unobtrusive, so quiet. I don't know who else will help me keep an eye on those young wives of mine, and see to the smooth running of my household" (78).

NIGERIA: INVESTIGATIONS/WEB SITES

Nigeria Home Page (http://www.webperfect.com:80/afrinet/nigeria/profile.html) is designed with the business traveler in mind. It opens with a large image of the Lagos skyline and offers links to an overview, geography, history, political history, industry, hotels, state profiles, and the national anthem.

Nigeria Information Resources Online (http://pcafs2.uncc.edu/%7Eecodili/nigeria.html) offers many links organized under the following topics: Democracy Watch, NewsWires, National Profile, Sports, Business & Education, and Culture.

The Nigerian Connection (http://eng.bu.edu/~ucheo/nigeria/info.html) offers a large number of links to many other sites. Some links found here include The Nigerian Cultural Center, The Association of Nigerians Abroad, Nigerian Newsgroup, Information about Nigeria (from the CIA World Factbook 1994), WorldWide Appeals–Nigeria (Amnesty International), Nigeria Resource Listings, and Campaign for Justice for Mr. Ken Saro-Wiwa.

Yoruba Art (http://don.skidmore.edu/academics/laronson/AH_207/YorubaArt/%0 YorubaArt.html) offers a gallery of Yoruba sculptures with text describing the myths associated with the figures they depict.

Nigeria: A Bibliography (http://www.stg.brown.edu/projects/hypertext/landow/post/ nigeria/nigeriabib.html) provides a bibliography listing twenty-eight books about Nigeria.

ADDITIONAL QUESTIONS AND ASSIGNMENTS

1. In a journal entry or a collection of informal notes, list the superstitions and religious beliefs presented in selections representing two or three different cultures. After making your list, ask yourself how you distinguish between the two categories. What are the differences between them? Write them down. How do these differences relate to one another?

2. Interview someone whose religion is different from your own, possibly someone from a different generation or culture. Before you begin, make a list of questions, such as how your subject observes religion in everyday life. What rituals does your subject participate in? Have the person describe them. Before you write up the interview, decide how you will order the questions and answers to make them coherent. When you write your essay based on this interview, be sure to use some of the subject's own words as quotations. You may want to get your subject's permission to tape the interview.

3. Rewrite a section of Buchi Emecheta's "Ona," telling the story from the point of view of Agbadi's first wife, Agunwa. You might want to choose a small section of the story, such as the night she hears her husband making love with Ona, and write a monologue where she expresses her thoughts. How would she regard Ona? How would she see her husband's interest in Ona as influencing her own life? What is her view of how women should behave?

4. Conduct further research on one of the cultures represented in this section, focusing specifically on its relation to beliefs, ritual, or magic. If the selection is an excerpt from a larger work, look first at that work. You can find more information about the culture by consulting a general encyclopedia, a journal devoted to the study of that culture, and/or the Internet. Narrow your topic to something manageable, such as ghost stories, burial rites, or ancestor worship, and write an expository essay in which you elaborate on the supernatural elements in the original selection.

Part Six

INSTITUTIONS AND INDIVIDUALS

INTRODUCTION

Although students should find the selections in this section interesting and provocative, they may exhibit some discomfort with the blurring of ideological lines in many. Accustomed to defining political good and evil in terms of Western democracy versus communism, some students may resist the negative images of America's exploitation of native peoples and natural resources in other countries, of Israelis as oppressors, and of the South African government during apartheid; equally disquieting may be the theme running consistently through the Chinese selections that those who speak freely will be persecuted by their government. Precisely because of these unsettling portrayals, however, this section is one of the most important in the text. It provides a wonderful tool for encouraging students to explore political systems before judging them, to resist easy stereotypes, and to recognize similarities among seemingly disparate cultures.

To prepare students for the kind of questioning they'll need to exhibit throughout the section, you may want to begin by asking them to articulate their perceptions of how institutions act for and against people's interests. The epigraphs will be a help here: Vine Deloria Jr., Clifford M. Lytle, and Haunani-Kay Trask all call attention to shortcomings in the U.S. system. Marilynne Robinson and Thomas L. Friedman suggest that economic entities may be superseding cultures and even national governments; bell hooks critiques how the poor are viewed in the United States; Robert Reich points to the increasing defection of the rich from the rest of society. The overview provided by these short pieces should provide a relatively easy way to introduce the kind of skepticism students will find in the main selections. As they work their way through the section, students may need to be reminded occasionally that the purpose of exploring other cultures is simply to learn about them and to recognize the ways various institutions work or fail to meet people's needs to become better able to critically consider their relationship with their own.

Among possible subthemes in the section are the individual as victim of a political system (Mandela, Paley, Suu Kyi, Weldon, Min, Zha, and Schell), the role of propaganda (Postman, Zha, Min, Fang, Schell), problems resulting from changes in political conditions (Suu Kyi, Grossman, Min, Fang, Schell), and how individuals explain their relation to institutions (Paley, Boyle, Mandela, and Weldon). Instructors may wish to consult the following familiar works in preparing related selections from *Making Contact*:

Essays

Martin Luther King Jr., "Letter from Birmingham Jail" (*Why We Can't Wait*, Harper, 1963).
Walter Lippmann, "The Indispensable Opposition" (*Atlantic Monthly*, Aug. 1939).
George Orwell, "A Hanging" (*Shooting an Elephant*, Harcourt, 1950).
Jonathan Swift, "A Modest Proposal" (1729).
Henry David Thoreau, "On Resistance to Civil Disobedience" (1849).

646–653 (Text Pages)

Barbara Tuchman, "An Inquiry into the Persistence of Unwisdom in Government" (*Esquire*, May 1980; *The March of Folly*, Ch. 1, Knopf, 1984).

Short Stories

Nadine Gordimer, "Some Monday for Sure" (*Not for Publication*, Viking, 1965).
Shirley Jackson, "The Lottery" (*The Lottery*, Farrar, Straus, 1949).
Ursula K. LeGuin, "The Ones Who Walk Away from Omelas" (*The Winds's Twelve Quarters*, Harper, 1975).
Thomas Mann, "Mario and the Magician" (*Stories of Three Decades*, Knopf, 1964).
Herman Melville, "Billy Budd, Sailor" (1891).

BIOGRAPHICAL NOTES ON EPIGRAPH AUTHORS

1. Marilynne Robinson's 1982 novel *Housekeeping* was nominated for the Pulitzer Prize; her most recent book is *Puritans and Prigs* (1996).

2. Vine Deloria Jr., a Standing Rock Sioux and a professor of political science, has served as executive director of the National Congress on American Indians. His books include *Custer Died for Your Sins: American Indians, American Justice* (with Clifford M. Lytle) (1983); *American Indian Policy in the Twentieth Century* (1992), which he edited; and *God Is Red* (1993).

3. Nader Mousavizadeh is an associate editor of *The New Republic*. His *The Black Book of Bosnia* is a collection of that magazine's analysis, reportage, commentary, and editorials on the Balkan crisis.

4. Haunani-Kay Trask is a professor of Hawaiian Studies and Director of the Center for Hawaiian Studies at the University of Hawaii in Manoa. In 1986, she published *Eros and Power: Promise of Feminist Theory*. One of her more recent books, *From a Native Daughter: Colonialism and Sovereignty in Hawai'i* (1993), addresses the political and cultural struggles of native islanders.

5. Robert Reich was President Clinton's first-term U.S. Secretary of Labor and is the author of several books, including *Tales of a New America: The Anxious Liberal's Guide to the Future* (1988), *Public Management in a Democratic Society* (1990), and *The Work of Nations: Preparing Ourselves for Twenty-First Century Capitalism* (1991).

6. Born in Canada of Russian-Jewish parents, Saul Bellow grew up in Chicago, where his first novel, *Dangling Man* (1944), takes place. Among his later novels are *Henderson the Rain King* (1959), *Herzog* (1964), *Mr. Sammler's Planet* (1969), *Humboldt's Gift* (1974), and *The Dean's December* (1982). He won the Nobel Prize in 1976.

7. A 32-year veteran of ABC News, Ted Koppel was named anchor of *Nightline* when the broadcast was introduced in March 1980. He coauthored *Nightline: History in the Making and the Making of Television* (1996) with Kyle Gibson.

8. David Guterson's books include *The Country Ahead of Us, the Country Behind: Stories* and *Snow Falling on Cedars* (1993).

9. Octavio Paz (see headnote, p. 86).

112

10. A professor of English at City College in New York, bell hooks has written fourteen books in the past seventeen years, including *Ain't I A Woman: Black Women and Feminism* (1982), *Talking Back: Thinking Feminist, Thinking Black* (1989), *Black Looks: Race and Representation* (1992), *Outlaw Culture: Resisting Representations* (1994), *Art on My Mind: Visual Politics* (1996), and *Killing Rage: Ending Racism* (1996).

11. Nuala O'Faolain writes a daily column for *The Irish Times*.

12. Population Communications International (see p. 68 in this manual).

13. American essayist and novelist Susan Sontag has said her desire is to be an *écrivain*, that is, a writer without specialization. Among her books are *The Benefactor, a Novel* (1963), *Against Interpretation, and Other Essays* (1966), *Death Kit* (1967), *I, etcetera* (1978), *Illness as Metaphor* (1978), *AIDS and Its Metaphors* (1989), and *The Volcano Lover, a Novel* (1992).

14. Thomas L. Friedman is a foreign affairs columnist for *The New York Times* and the author of *From Beirut to Jerusalem* (1991).

Explorations

1. There are numerous possibilities for the first part of this question, and students' answers will depend on their interests. Some possible options: Welfare has been changed dramatically, because the government claims the middle class and the rich resent it; free speech is under fire on the Internet, because conservatives fear children will have access to pornography or other unsuitable information; and Congress has tried to undo such environmental protections as the Endangered Species Act and the Clean Air and Water Acts. According to Nuala O'Faolain, people in the little village in the west of Ireland where a bomb went off are rejecting the IRA's violent tactics (p. 651). And, according to Nader Mousavizadeh, Danes have not rejected the monarchy because its members have won over them through "dignity and charisma and exemplary behavior" (p. 647).

2. Of the "rules and regulations" under which Americans have supposedly agreed to live, the "fortunate fifth" described by Robert Reich (p. 648) have rejected the idea that the rich should share their wealth by contributing to public facilities. Reich might respond to Marilynne Robinson's comment that our "social cohesiveness and economic vitality" (p. 646) may not have failed us insofar as we won the cold war, but otherwise, they have; we can hardly claim social cohesiveness when our most privileged citizens are gradually cloistering themselves from the rest of the society. Vine Deloria and Clifford Lytle would also probably take exception to Robinson's view on the grounds that Indians have always had a much more socially cohesive culture than European Americans and our "economic vitality" has historically been one of the prime reasons for our policy of genocide against them.

3. bell hooks's comment points to the compartmentalization of our culture; just as we assume only psychologists and other professionally trained counselors know how to listen to people, so we assume that only a gifted few educated artists can create. Students might assume that if a person has the capacity to create art, she would have the capacity to support herself, and that self-support would take precedence over painting or writing. Students may agree with hooks that inhabiting a certain social class frees people from suffering, if they define suffering as material deprivation; if they define it more broadly, they might argue that anyone can suffer.

4. Haunani-Kay Trask believes that Westerners should not have imposed their ideas about social structure on Hawaiians, because they only served to alienate native peoples from the land, allowing the invaders to profit. Susan Sontag believes that Western countries should impose their beliefs about human rights on other countries; to avoid doing so because we believe only we should have such rights is "colonialist and condescending" (p. 652).

MIRRORS:
THE UNITED STATES

GRACE PALEY, Six Days: Some Rememberings (p. 655)

Explorations

1. Grace Paley is clearly frustrated by being in jail, but she is also very curious about her jailmates, and she intersperses their narratives with her own (paras. 4–11, 24–27, 32). The effect of her not describing feelings explicitly is to compel readers to construct her story from the cues that she gives, such as when she receives a note from home and bursts into tears (3) and when she admits that she had been trying not to complain because others had much longer sentences (16).

2. Paley's choices to forgo quotation marks or conventional ways of identifying speakers suits the setting of her narrative because she finds herself in a confusing world where the social rules aren't clear to her. Women approach her and ask questions without making introductions. For instance, the first person who speaks to her calls her "white girl" and asks if she's been arrested before (4). In this milieu, literary conventions seem like formalities, like so much unnecessary small talk. Other stylistic choices include using abrupt transitions, sentence fragments, and one-word sentences, as well as organizing material associatively, as if in the order the speaker remembers it. These devices are appropriate, because the narrator claims she does not fully remember the six days (even which year it was); the devices give the impression of a time spent in a partial fog.

3. The prison was most likely moved for one or a combination of several reasons: the real estate became too valuable to justify keeping it there; the prison became too small for the number of women flowing to it; and/or the neighbors objected to its presence. Paley was sorry to see it moved because prisons "ought to be in the neighborhood, near a subway — not way out in distant suburbs, where families have to take cars, buses, ferries, trains, and the population that considers itself innocent forgets, denies, chooses to never know that there is a whole huge country of the bad and the unlucky and the self-hurters" (38).

Connections

1. Marilynne Robinson's epigraph suggests that Americans lack the benefit of an oral tradition and the capacity to dissociate economic and political institutions: If we had more of a sense of history, we would not mistake capitalism for democracy. We seem to have forgotten about the Constitution. Robinson wants us to remember the spirit of the law, just as Paley wants prisons to treat people as human beings, rather than merely

enforcing rules and regulations (such a prison might allow a woman arrested in a peace protest to keep her hairpins [paras. 18–20]). A more direct connection appears toward the end of the essay, when Paley laments the lack of her "own memorizing mind" (35). The advantages of an oral tradition are that the laws are learned through rituals that are part of everyday life, so everyone knows them in spirit. The advantages of having written rules and regulations is that they are considered to be objective, so that the people enforcing them need not use their own subjective judgment.

2.   The prison's reasons for taking away Paley's paper, pen, and books may have been an idea that readers have become an elite population which isn't identified with incarcerated people (Octavio Paz); that society assumes women in jail are not creative people (bell hooks); or that literature has the power to transform people (Derek Walcott) and lead them to new worlds, empowering them (Malcolm X), in contrast with the prison's goal of control. The disadvantages of the policy are obvious: People in jail need books, pens, and paper to help them grow intellectually and emotionally, to help them devise alternate ways of conceiving the world and their place in it.

3.   Paley alerts us that her memory of her time in the Women's House of Detention is fragmented, beginning with her subtitle "Some Rememberings." The first paragraph also affirms the unreliability of her memory: "I have forgotten [in] which important year of the famous sixties" in which the episode took place (1); she is imprisoned for impeding "some military parade" (1).

CORNEL WEST, Race Matters (p. 662)

Explorations

1.   This is a good question to get students to consider why it is important to keep an audience in mind when composing an essay. When Cornel West refers to we and us, he means we who care about improving race relations in the United States. The meaning of the pronouns changes in paragraph 6 to reflect the views of two specific groups, liberals and conservatives. West's use of the first person plural to include everyone reinforces his thesis that all elements of society must work together if we are to overcome our racial problems.

2.   According to West, our common destiny is more imperiled when our racial divisions are deeper because all of us "are on a slippery slope toward economic strife, social turmoil, and cultural chaos. If we go down, we go down together" (para. 10). West proceeds to say that the riots in Los Angeles proved how alienated yet connected blacks and whites are. But he does not go so far as to say precisely what might happen if the current state of affairs does not change. You might ask students if they believe West needs to supply more evidence or if his level of generality seems appropriate to an introductory essay.

3.   Rather than blame individuals, West blames phenomena that affect all of us but which have especially harsh effects on urban dwellers. The whole culture has experienced "the collapse of meaning in life" (13), a weakening of community and family ties, but urban dwellers have seen their social and cultural networks disintegrate, leaving them "rootless [and] dangling." Likewise, postmodern market culture "engulfs all of us — yet its impact on the disadvantaged is devastating, resulting in extreme violence in everyday life" (14). Last, "American politics has been rocked by an unleashing of greed among

opportunistic public officials — who have followed the lead of their counterparts in the private sphere, where, as of 1989, 1 percent of the population owned 37 percent of the wealth and 10 percent of the population owned 86 percent of the wealth" (15). The Republicans have also been a cause, as they've tried to "realign the electorate along race, sex, and sexual-orientation lines" (16). West's solutions include "large-scale public intervention to ensure access to basic social goods" (21) and courageous new leadership grounded in grass roots organizing (23).

Connections

1. Similarities and differences of race, age, and class create fewer alliances and enmities in the Women's House of Detention than do the women's roles within the institution. Rita and Evelyn are old-timers who laugh when another woman assures Paley that she's "different," that she doesn't belong there (p. 658). Likewise, Paley's beautiful young cellmate who is in for the first time insists that she will need "protection" from the others and has the name of a veteran who might help her (p. 657). Race only comes into play when the only other white woman, Helen, corners Paley and asks her why she's so friendly with the black women (p. 658).

2. West points out that as of 1989, 1 percent of the U.S. population owned 37 percent of the wealth, and 10 percent of the population owned 86 percent of the wealth. Robert Reich notes that in 1990, the top fifth of working Americans took home more money than the other four-fifths put together. Reich also points out that wealthy Americans have been withdrawing from the rest of society, supporting social services that are only for them and not contributing to public projects. West believes that economic and social trends have had a devastating impact on the country's poor, leaving them in a state of rage at the lack of opportunities for them (paras. 12–14).

3. West's concerns about the fact that we live in a "market culture" which values "acquiring pleasure, property, and power by any means necessary" (14) accord with J. F. Ade Ajayi's suggestions that the West needs to "curb the unrestrained appetite for competition and acquisition, and promote the meaning of life by reaching out to others through love" (p. 619). Ajayi would probably advise West's audience to strive for greater "continuity of life," to give more consideration to the wisdom of our ancestors (Lincoln, Roosevelt, King, as well as the departed elders in our own families) and to the needs of the generations to come.

NEIL POSTMAN, Future Shlock (p. 670)

Explorations

1. Even students who are not well versed in European history will probably recognize that Neil Postman is referring to the rise of Nazism in Germany during the 1920s and 1930s, when art, philosophy, and science were considered worthwhile only when they promoted the interests of the party and were stamped out whenever they appeared to open the door to dissidence and tolerance of ethnic, political, and religious differences. At the end of paragraph 2, Postman proposes to "worry" the reader with the idea that what happened to culture in Nazi Germany could happen in the United States — though in a different way. Later in the essay, Postman says that although a "decline of intelligent discourse" is taking place in America, intellectuals will not be driven out as they were

in Germany (4). Instead, they will simply be ignored. At the end of his essay, Postman returns to the theme of Nazism, again differentiating culture under Nazism (culture as prison) and in contemporary America (culture as burlesque). Postman's discussion of Mel Brooks's film *The Producers* encourages the reader to believe that the film predicts that Americans will become a "trivial people . . . a people amused into stupidity" (11). Because *The Producers* is built on the theme of Nazism, with which Postman opens his essay, his discussion of the film reinforces his point that Americans will accept anything — even *Springtime for Hitler* — as long as it is entertaining. This is a point students may want to debate.

2.   Postman first addresses the reader as "you" in paragraph 2, when he says he wants to "worry you about the rapid erosion of our own intelligence." The effect of speaking directly to his readers is to suggest that his argument is important to them personally. Even before the reader becomes "you," however, Postman has established an "us" in the same paragraph. The effect of creating such a collective is to suggest that we all are affected by, and are responsible for, the death of intelligence. Readers who agree with Postman's position will accept this use of "we," whereas readers who are waiting to be persuaded may be drawn into agreement by it. Postman's frequent use of "I" suggests his personal commitment and personal sense of responsibility for making "us" aware of the problems he describes. Some students may note that Postman sometimes uses "we" when he is really writing about his own views, as in his assertion "we have also seen 'Sesame Street' and other educational shows in which the demands of entertainment take precedence . . ." (17).

3.   Although Postman uses a traditional format for his argument, his language and many of his rhetorical techniques have more in common with the entertainment-dominated media he criticizes than with academic style. His essay appeals fairly openly to readers' emotions along with their reason. Students will identify Postman's use of humor as his most obvious entertainment technique. His tone throughout is ironic; examples include the title "Future Shlock" and comments such as, "There are other ways to achieve stupidity, and it appears that, as in so many other things, there is a distinctly American way" (4). He also relies frequently on humorous exaggeration, as when he says that "the Germans banished intelligence" (2) and that the Empire of Reason has given way to the Empire of Shlock (3). Postman's informal diction is another technique more common in entertainment than in academic writing. He addresses readers directly, using first and second person as well as the third; his position is openly subjective ("I wish to call to your notice"; "I cannot imagine" [5]) rather than purely objective. His evidence, too, comes from popular sources, such as films (5, 8) and television shows (15–19), as well as from academic sources such as Aristotle (2) and Henry Steele Commager (3). This choice of sources clearly suits Postman's topic, and his argument is logically constructed rather than fragmented like the television news programs he decries; however, students may differ as to whether his efforts to enlighten his audience are weakened or strengthened by his efforts to entertain them.

Connections

1.   Cornel West blames "our truncated public discussions of race" on "the predictable pitting of liberals against conservatives, Great Society Democrats against self-help Republicans, [which] reinforces intellectual parochialism and political paralysis" (p. 663). He also blames the fact that whites view blacks as "a problem people" (p. 663) rather than seeing the presence and predicaments of blacks as one of the "constitutive elements" (p. 664) of American life. West argues that instead of regarding blacks as the problem,

we need to look at "the flaws of American society — flaws rooted in historic inequalities and longstanding cultural stereotypes" (p. 664). Here Postman's argument comes in: Because we get our news from a medium that oversimplifies and trivializes the information it purports to convey, Americans do not receive a complex, realistic version of their history from their primary source of education (para. 20–21).

2. In *The Gods Must Be Crazy*, the Coke bottle brings desire and envy to a place that never had them because there was an abundance of natural resources for all. The chief had to get rid of the Coke bottle to restore harmony. In "Making Magic," the fisherman envies his fellow fishermen because they have greater luck or skill in gathering nature's bounty, so he enlists the help of someone with power akin to that of the gods in the film to restore his luck. But from David Abram's vantage point, the Coke bottle is part of a scheme to satisfy the fisherman that Abram is trying to help him, because Abram does not believe that he actually can. Abram's trip to Asia represents a reversal of the trend towards turning our history and politics into entertainment, because he is there to do an in-depth study of the knowledge of traditional cultures.

3. Postman is condemning the fact that our culture allows television to provide both information and entertainment, leaving us with little interest and attention for what scholars might have to say; no one will censor them because no one notices them. Television, Postman claims, has atrophied the American mind. James Baldwin might disagree, because he did not feel as if the culture were indifferent toward him; he experienced it as positively hostile. Baldwin might add to Postman's argument that "a man is not a man until he is able and willing to accept his own vision of the world" (p. 25); with television filling so many otherwise vacant American minds, it's little wonder we lack for "men," that is, independent thinkers.

T. CORAGHESSAN BOYLE, Top of the Food Chain (p. 680)

Explorations

1. The speaker in "Top of the Food Chain" is an American businessman or government agency representative addressing Congress (he occasionally calls the person to whom he is speaking "Senator"), explaining events and defending decisions that occurred while he was working in Borneo.

2. This question is a good opportunity to discuss a writer's voice and how students must make stylistic choices to negotiate academic conventions without sounding overblown or too informal. Boyle's speaker uses a lot of informal, colloquial expressions that are generally not used when writing: "the thing was, we had a little problem. . . and believe me, your tamer stuff, your Malathion . . ." (para. 1); "You've got to realize this is Borneo we're talking about . . ." (3); "let me backtrack a minute here . . ." (6). The speaker is also prone to abruptly changing the subject, as when he digresses to mention how people in Borneo love wearing running shorts (6). And it is often clear that he is answering a question: "You're right there, Senator, yes . . ." (17).

3. "These people" are the natives of Borneo who have been affected by the narrator's use of DDT in their area. The narrator sounds condescending to them, as can be seen when he remarks that they "dig up roots in the jungle" (3) and "they've still got headhunters . . . for god's sake" (3), as well as when he describes how much they love their running shorts

118

(6) and their cats: "no house, no hut, no matter how primitive, is without at least a couple of them" (16). "Our people" are his American colleagues who caused and "solved" the problems for the Borneo natives; clearly, the narrator sees his people as superior because they have the technology to analyze and "solve" the problems they create (8–11). The "gentlemen" being addressed are members of Congress, and the narrator is annoyed that he has to explain himself to them; he doesn't see how they could possibly understand how reasonable his actions were. For instance, when he tries to explain the magnitude of Borneo's "fly problem" (10), his underlying message is that they can't possibly have enough information to make an informed judgment about the choices he made.

Connections

1. Of the nemeses Neil Postman describes, those found in "Top of the Food Chain" include ignorance, cowardice, and neglect. The narrator's decision to spray DDT in the first place illustrates all three: He neglected to find out what the environmental impact might be; he's grossly ignorant of how introducing such a poison into the food chain can affect everything in it; and when he's explaining his actions to Congress, he's too big of a coward to take responsibility for the mistakes he made, so he tries to rationalize them.

2. Boyle clearly regards his narrator as greedy and opportunistic: In spraying DDT abroad when it has been banned domestically, he shows no concern for the impact he'll have on the local environment. Although the story never mentions the nature of his business there, it's clear that he acts from self-interest. He emphasizes that this is "the developing world" he's talking about, a place where people live in "primitive huts" and don't wear enough clothes and are susceptible to diseases — it's like "the Dark Ages." He seems to feel justified in imposing any technologies he wants on these people, because he can't see the value of theirs (palm thatched roofs that keep out the rain, for example). The narrator wants to realize his vision of a sanitized country and is unable to grasp the interconnected nature of the ecosystem.

3. The food chain is a metaphor for the way that everything in nature is linked because bigger things eat smaller things, until the bigger ones die, decay, and eventually become food for the smaller ones. In Boyle's story, the narrator introduces an element that kills a seemingly unimportant part of the food chain, flies, but it also ends up killing cats and a moth that eats caterpillars that eat palm roofs. Chinese officials explain that a ban on dog ownership is "deeply welcomed by the masses," because dogs eat more than twice what humans eat (p. 651). However, it's possible that dogs also kill rodents, which could become a problem for the Chinese if they eradicate most of their dogs.

WINDOWS: THE WORLD

NELSON MANDELA, Black Man in a White Court (p. 688)

Explorations

1. Nelson Mandela is applying for the recusal of the white magistrate who is presiding over Mandela's case (para. 5). He wants the magistrate to excuse himself from hearing

the case because, Mandela argues, an African cannot get a fair trial in a white court (6, 8) and because, as an African, Mandela does not consider himself subject to the laws his people had no part in making (6). It is the white court's racism that is Mandela's main focus; he says that he "fears that this system of justice may enable the guilty to drag the innocent before the courts." Mandela's reasonable manner and eloquence serve another purpose, however. Mandela does not believe that there is a chance he will win his own case, but he is making a larger case for his people. In paragraph 28, he says that the atmosphere of oppression he senses in the courtroom "calls to mind the inhuman injustices caused to my people outside this courtroom by this same white domination." After Mandela's articulate and passionate speech, the judge's only response is to dismiss the application (58) — a move that essentially proves both of Mandela's arguments. If Mandela's real purpose had been to win his own case, then he was not successful. But because he had a larger purpose in mind — to speak out against systematic white racism — he was successful.

2. Building on their discussion of Explorations #1, students should realize that neither Mandela nor the court believes that Mandela's application has any chance of being approved. Mandela is elaborating on the starvation and disease his people are experiencing when the magistrate interrupts his speech to say that Mandela is "going beyond the scope" of his application (32). The magistrate goes on to say that he doesn't "want to know about starvation" (34), and he demands that Mandela stick to the "real reasons" for his application (36). The "real reasons," from the magistrate's perspective, are those that stay within the bounds of the immediate proceeding. But his attempts to define the case according to the needs and expectations of the white court are unsuccessful, and Mandela manages to make the case he is most interested in: that his people are without land, the vote, health care, or food (29).

3. From the first words he speaks, Mandela shows that he fully grasps not only the legal but also the social and political implications of the court proceedings. His style and choice of words are similar to — although more eloquent than — the white men who are about to try him. He uses the conventions of legal discourse in paragraphs 4–6, for instance, in stating the purpose of his application and giving the grounds for it. Further, he asserts his equality directly by saying that he has decided to speak for himself rather than depend on counsel. Only by speaking the language of the court can Mandela hope to speak at all. As a spokesperson for his people, Mandela uses his own educational and professional equality with the white men who accuse him to support his argument that all Africans should have the same rights and privileges as whites.

Connections

1. In the societies described by both Ralph Ellison and Mandela, whites regard blacks as the "other" that defines them, yet the fact that blacks are indisputably the fellow citizens of whites "raised doubts about the white man's value system" (Ellison, p. 662). Ellison suggests that whites feel the need to oppress blacks so as to bolster their own sense of identity, but this remark overlooks the material advantages whites have gained in both countries from oppressing blacks. As Mandela points out, so long as blacks could not vote, were "without land because the white minority has taken a lion's share," and were "ravaged by starvation and disease" (para. 29), they could not feel like they could get a fair trial in a "white man's court."

2. The effect of Mandela's using "Africans" and "whites" rather than "black South Africans" and "white South Africans" is to underscore the fact that blacks are the natives of South

Africa and whites are the real outsiders. Mandela's comments in paragraphs 2 and 7 that his trial represents "the aspirations of the African people" and in paragraph 45 that he feels like "a black man in a white man's court" illuminate his choice of words.

3.   A law court is by definition an arena for what Shelby Steele calls "a struggle for innocence." In the court where Nelson Mandela presents his case, representatives for both black and white South Africans claim innocence as Steele describes. The judge speaks for his fellow whites, who assert ownership over land and power and therefore claim to be victimized in this case by Mandela's breaking of a law made by whites for their protection. The judge's position matches Steele's statement, "White racism [is] a claim of white innocence and therefore of white entitlement to subjugate blacks." Mandela pleads innocent to the charges and claims innocence on a larger scale, using (as Steele puts it) "the innocence that grew out of . . . long subjugation to seize more power." Verbally Mandela responds to the judge as what Steele describes as a bargainer: *"I already believe you are innocent (good, fair-minded) and have faith that you will prove it."* His tacit position, however, is that of a challenger: *"If you are innocent, then prove it."*

AUNG SAN SUU KYI, Freedom from Fear (p. 698)

Explorations

1.   This question is an opportunity to discuss how persuasion and explanation must fit readers' interests and needs. Aung San Suu Kyi appears to be writing for an international audience, because she explains the meanings of the four kinds of corruption the Burmese recognize (para. 1) and alludes to the Universal Declaration of Human Rights of the United Nations (5), implying that human rights abuses in Burma should be considered an international problem. She seems to hope that her essay will spur her audience to express public disapproval of the Burmese government, although she makes no practical suggestions.

2.   Suu Kyi depicts her country's government as having "incoherent policies, inept official measures, burgeoning inflation, and falling real income [that has] turned the country into an economic shambles" (3). Moreover, the Burmese people must live with "fear of imprisonment, fear of torture, fear of death, fear of losing friends, family, property or means of livelihood, fear of poverty, fear of isolation, fear of failure" (11). She depicts the Burmese people as "a traditionally good-natured, quiescent people" whose patience has eroded (3); the students leading protests express the frustrations of the people at large, even of businessmen who had learned to prosper within the system. But the Burmese government wants the world to believe that the democracy movement is a result of the people's dissatisfaction with economic hardship alone (3).

3.   Suu Kyi depicts the current political and social conditions as "abnormal" by describing them to those of us living under "normal" conditions, for instance, "the effort necessary to remain uncorrupted in an environment where fear is an integral part of everyday existence is not immediately apparent to those fortunate enough to live in states governed by the rule of law" (4). The advantages of taking this position are that she makes the current system seem unnecessarily corrupt, an aberration that needs to be corrected, and she appeals to her audience to help restore things to "normal."

Connections

1. Suu Kyi and Nelson Mandela both argue that, in the former's words, "within a system which denies the existence of basic human rights, fear tends to be the order of the day. . . . Yet even under the most crushing state machinery courage rises up again and again, for fear is not the natural state of civilized man" (para. 11). However, there are many differences between the two pieces of writing. Suu Kyi is under house arrest, but she has a limited degree of free speech. Her audience is international, and her message is that the world needs to recognize human rights abuses in Burma. Mandela is on trial for inciting workers to strike and for leaving the country without a passport, so his audience is primarily a court of law, and his message is that it is impossible for him to receive a fair trial in a country where the party he has allegedly wronged will judge his offense.

2. Although Susan Sontag argues that certain rights should be held universally, J. F. Ade Ajayi believes that each country needs to devise laws that suit its own traditions. Suu Kyi expresses Sontag's view when she argues that "just laws do not merely prevent corruption. . . . They also help to create a society in which people can fulfill the basic requirements necessary for the preservation of human dignity without recourse to corrupt practices" (4). But when discussing the ideas of Jawaharlal Nehru, she expresses Ajayi's view: Nehru was a "political modernist, but as he assessed the needs for a twentieth-century movement for independence, he found himself looking back to the philosophy of ancient India: The greatest gift for an individual or a nation . . . was *abhaya*, fearlessness" (9).

3. In "Sovs, Hacks, and Freeloaders," Galina Dutkina gives the following examples of unjust laws, damaged human dignity, and corrupt practices: During Andropov's campaign for labor discipline in the 1980s, any policeman or auxiliary could accost someone who was not at work during the day, demanding an explanation; sometimes the person would be dismissed from his job (p. 368). Currently, people employed by state-subsidized organizations don't collect wages for months at time, and sometimes when they do get paid, they end up bringing nothing home because they spend it all on essentials on the way (p. 372). Formerly proud professors wear torn jackets and humbly beg for grants from foreign universities (p. 372). The state took away people's savings and their relative prosperity with the liberalization of prices and endless monetary reforms; people no longer save, because they don't know whether their money will be worth anything in the future (p. 373). But Dutkina does not see these phenomena as linked in the same way that Suu Kyi does: Dutkina depicts her government's economic and social reforms as haphazard, whereas Suu Kyi depicts her government as controlling and deliberately repressive.

FAY WELDON, Down the Clinical Disco (p. 705)

Explorations

1. In paragraph 2, the narrator reveals that she is a former inmate of Broadmoor, a mental institution for the criminally insane, where she was committed after setting fire to her office. Her monologue is directed at a woman named Linda she met at a pub (6), who may be identified with the reader. The story begins with the pronoun "You," suggesting that the reader and Linda are being addressed directly by the narrator.

2. Some students may see the narrator as an obviously paranoid woman who believes people are continuously monitoring her behavior, even during an evening at the pub. In paragraph 1, for instance, she says, "of course there are people watching." Others may see her as a victim of the mental health system that placed her in the position of being assessed constantly, to the point that she was forced into paranoia as a natural response to having had her smallest gesture watched and judged while she was in the institution. In paragraph 13, the narrator says that "Sister," a nurse, decided who had become "normal" enough to go up for parole and who would remain. Psychiatric professionals and judges seem to have the power to decide what constitutes normal behavior. The criteria the narrator perceives at work are narrow and maddeningly contradictory. For instance, in the first paragraph she says she doesn't drink because she has "to be careful. You never know who's watching." Later in the same paragraph, she says that "it is not absolutely A-okay not to drink alcohol." Many of the criteria she believes are applied in judging who is "normal" have to do with sexual behavior and sexual orientation. She says that women who go into Broadmoor not looking like women do look like women when they leave. Men have to pretend to want to watch heterosexual "blue movies" to prove their manhood, but women can't want to watch because it would suggest a perverted sexuality.

3. The narrator suggests that "abnormal" behavior can more easily be observed in the nurses at Broadmoor than in the inmates. She says of "Sister" that "she's not so sane herself. She's more institutionalized than the patients" (13). The point is made graphically in a scene when she arrives at Broadmoor and is sadistically treated during a bath by a group of men and women who "were sane because they were nurses and good because they could go home after work" (10). A similar madness is evident in a nurse's game in which the narrator is made to be a tea bag for an entire day. The institutional setting, the narrator implies, is itself insane; the medical personnel who run institutions and the lawyers who send people to the institution are just as mad — or more so — than those they commit.

Connections

1. Both Fay Weldon in "Down the Clinical Disco" and T. Coraghessan Boyle in "Top of the Food Chain" use character-narrators who are addressing an audience in the story. Weldon's narrator talks to Linda, a woman she's met in a bar, and Boyle's addresses Congress. Both narrators seem unreliable, but in different ways. Weldon's seems a little paranoid, but this may just be a result of having been in an institution where she was constantly being watched and assessed. Her speaking style — confiding, yet betraying fear that someone watching will judge her — suits her goal of trying to convince Linda that she is sane and happy. Boyle's narrator seems unreliable, because he is so bent on rationalizing the horrors he inflicted on a region of Borneo that he is eager to minimize the damage and show that he had good intentions.

2. Some parallels between Grace Paley's and Weldon's narrators are that both women had been institutionalized for what they regard as innocuous acts, both feel strongly that they did not belong where they were, and both question the legitimacy of the institution where they're incarcerated, implying that there must be better solutions to social problems. But there are major differences: Paley's narrator is much freer to be herself, because she isn't constantly being watched. She can "burst into tears" when she gets a note from her son (p. 656), whereas Weldon's narrator holds in her tears because "they get kind of offended if you cry" at Broadmoor (para. 14). Unlike Paley's, Weldon's narrator also feels compelled to impress upon the nurses that she is heterosexual.

3. In "Woman as Other," Beauvoir writes, "humanity is male and man defines woman not in herself but as relative to him; she is not regarded as an autonomous being" (p. 446). Likewise, in "Down the Clinical Disco," those running Broadmoor treat the inmates as so many objects. When the narrator first arrives, she is ordered to strip in front of a roomful of men and women and bathed in filthy water; she is disturbed by the experience in part because the attendants perceive her as so "other" that they don't look at her or acknowledge her. It is in the interest of the institution to define the inmates as "other" and the staff as "normal," because this reinforces the staff's perceived right to treat the inmates however they wish — to maintain complete control.

DAVID GROSSMAN, Israeli Arab, Israeli Jew (p. 713)

Explorations

1. The Israeli Palestinian Mohammed Kiwan, looking for a bridge between his country's Palestinians and Jews, believes he can build that bridge with a "common man" like Jojo Abutbul, a Jew who expressed views similar to Kiwan's on television. Both men believe that much of the conflict is fostered at the institutional level, by the government and media, and are hopeful that "if the two of us sit down and talk, we can finish off all the problems in two minutes." Both Kiwan as a Palestinian and Abutbul as a Moroccan have experienced prejudice and view themselves to some degree as outsiders in Israel. Their ability to understand each other's point of view is limited, however, because Abutbul enjoys the civil privileges of being Jewish and wants Israel to be solely a Jewish nation (para. 21).

2. Early on in the essay, David Grossman refers to Mohammed Kiwan as "Kiwan." Only after Grossman makes a joke in which Kiwan becomes Mohammed going to the mountain that refuses to come to him does Grossman refer to both men by their first names (4). Students may realize immediately that Grossman uses this strategy to emphasize that these are common men (see Explorations #1) meeting as equals. He reinforces this impression by describing them collectively: "Both are solidly built, with black hair and tough faces" (48). He writes that he could "imagine them changing roles and arguing . . . each one making the other's points . . ." (51). If Grossman had referred to each man by his last name or his profession, his effort to establish their common ground would have failed. From the outside, their differences are more obvious than their similarities. The Palestinian Kiwan, a lawyer, is better educated than the Jewish Abutbul, a restauranteur who "manages the entire beach" (49). Using last names, professions, or ethnic designations would have undermined Grossman's attempts to portray them as men with intimate connections and equally intimate conflicts, weakening readers' ability to empathize with them.

3. Students will be able to come up with many examples of Abutbul's use of metaphors and analogies. Some seem apt, others seem misdirected or confusing. In general, the technique makes abstract ideas more concrete and vivid, but it also distorts them, as the parallel between substance and symbol is never exact. Abutbul first uses "allegory" — and calls attention to it — in paragraph 6, where he compares his life when he was a sleeping child to a "box" that was "deposited" with the Arab housemaid who cared for him. This "allegory," in his estimation, describes the "trust" between Arabs and Jews, but significantly, the Arab in his "allegory" is a housemaid in an inferior social and economic position. In paragraph 15, Abutbul implies that since he didn't buy his Jewish

identity at a store — did not, in other words, choose to be Jewish — he deserves a nation. Kiwan, of course, could have made the same point about being born Palestinian, but Abutbul thinks that Palestinians would feel at home in any other Arab nation. Perhaps the most uncomfortable analogy Abutbul draws appears in paragraph 25, where he describes his relationship to Kiwan — and the relationship of Jewish Israelis and Palestinians — as a marriage: "I love you, you're my soul, everything. I don't want to live with you!" He offers a "dowry" if the Palestinian will leave. This analogy, with its implications of a gender hierarchy in which the Palestinian is the unwanted wife of the Jew, seems particularly inflammatory between two men who consider wives as private possessions who symbolize their masculine honor (61). However, the expression of intimacy that slips out ("you're my soul") suggests that Abutbul realizes that the fate of the Jews and Palestinians are closely linked.

Connections

1. Clearly, fear of losing power clouds Jojo's ability to see Mohammed's point of view: Jojo is afraid that were Arabs to have their own state in Israel (as in a canton), they would rob Jews of their sovereign status (paras. 70–78). Mohammed is corrupted by the scourge of power, in that, as he implicitly concedes in his final statement, his bitterness at the way his people have been treated leads him to seek greater autonomy for them than may be necessary for them to live freely in Israel (90). As a result of Israeli Arabs' and Jews' fears, Arabs have lost their land and been discriminated against in a variety of ways, from being given poor school facilities to being alotted a meager percentage of water for farming.

2. An obvious parallel lies in the redistribution of land: In both cases, British occupation led to one group of land claimants taking territory from another group, leaving the previous holders with relatively small and unproductive portions. Additionally, whites in South Africa and Jews in Israel denied the others' rights, providing inferior educational and other facilities for them. Nelson Mandela's point that a member of a political minority who is being tried in the majority's court cannot expect to get a fair trial applies to Mohammed's fear that Arabs can't get a fair land deal when the Israeli government is making the decisions. Mandela's recommendation that the South African government stop pursuing "policies which have outraged the conscience of mankind" (p. 695) and distribute wealth and justice more equitably applies to Israel, as does Nadine Gordimer's advice that those in power quietly accept the need to share their sovereignty with those they have regarded as opponents and inferiors.

3. Religion is barely mentioned in Jojo's and Mohammed's argument. The closest the two get is when Jojo insists on "the Jewish state" (13–15), a reference more ethnic than religious, and when he talks about contrasting concepts of honor between Jewish subgroups (61). Mohammed lists the factors that are important to him besides religion: "Our land. Our education. Our definition as a national minority here. Our national symbols" (71). Naila Minai sketches the tensions that arose when Arabs made the transition from a nomadic life to an urban one, such as "glaring socioeconomic differences" (p. 472) and the loss of women's rights and security. The war depicted in Amos Oz's "If There Is Justice" seems to be regarded by his characters as an ancient blood feud with land, not religious beliefs or practices, as its chief focus.

730–742 (Text Pages)

SPOTLIGHT:
CHINA

ADDITIONAL INFORMATION ON COUNTRY

Environment: China's terrain is divided into three large areas. The central Asian high plateaus have steppe and prairie vegetation in summer and are snow covered in winter. North China's vast plains yield wheat, barley, sorghum, soybean, and cotton, as well as coal and iron ore. South China, a hilly area with a hot, humid monsoon climate, yields most of the country's rice. The use of coal as the primary energy source causes acid rain, a serious problem because less than 13 percent of the land is forested. The Three Gorges Dam, currently under construction, is regarded as a potential environmental disaster.

Demographics: Ninety-one percent of China's 1.2 billion people are ethnic (Han) Chinese; 56 minority groups make up the other 9 percent. Under China's rigorous birth control policy, couples are allowed to have only one child.

Religion: The Chinese government encourages atheism, but religious freedom is guaranteed by the constitution. The three major formal religions practiced are Buddhism, Islam, and Christianity, but even more Chinese follow Confucianism. More a code of ethics than a religion, Confucianism emphasizes loyalty to the family and the virtues of kindness, intelligence, and faithfulness.

Education: Eighty-four percent of males and 62 percent of females are literate.

Human Rights: In recent years, human rights conditions in China have deteriorated as international pressure on the issue has collapsed. The United States, for example, has not pressed human rights issues, fearing a loss of trade with China. Most dissident human rights and labor activists in China have attempted legal challenges to police harassment, prison sentences, discrimination, even the official media's vilification of them in the courts, but with little success. Because of the Chinese Communist Party's overwhelming political control of the legal and judicial process, in no case was a dissident able to get a fair hearing.

The authorities continue to use the law as a weapon against their opponents or, when expedient, to ignore it altogether. In 1994, petty infringements of laws or regulations that would not normally merit imprisonment were used to send dissidents to labor camps. At least nine labor and human rights activists have been sentenced to two- or three-year Reeducation Through Labor terms in the second half of 1994. The Chinese government has shown no willingness to change the conditions that contribute to the systematic violation of human rights, including blanket censorship of all impartial information about rights conditions and a legal system subject to absolute political control without mechanisms for holding officials accountable.

ANCHEE MIN, The Fall of Autumn Leaves (p. 733)

Explorations

1.   The Communist Party accuses Autumn Leaves of being a spy and indoctrinating children with Western ideas. The only apparent grounds for these accusations are that her father lives in the United States, where she was born and educated (para. 9). Anchee Min's

126

description of Autumn Leaves' dedication as a teacher belies these accusations: She keeps teaching even when she has a fever or has lost her voice and she lends her students her own books and rain clothes (para. 7). She appears to live for teaching.

2. To denounce Autumn Leaves, Secretary Chain describes her as a "wolf in sheep's skin" who has tried to trick her students and claims she was "using teaching as a weapon to destroy" the minds of the proletariat youth (9, 10). Min responds to the first of these, as well as to Chain's mention that she has been described as "educable" in her teacher's diary, with wounded vanity, feeling she has been betrayed and eager to prove that she is "smart" enough to see through Autumn Leaves. She responds to the second of these with a knee-jerk response — she knows these slogans, is quick to respond to anything that violates them. Chain also acts as a living slogan, as he dramatizes his willingness to persevere, despite the fact that his liver causes him great pain.

3. The U.S. equivalent of the Confucian saying is "the golden rule": Do unto others as you would have them do unto you, which the Christian Bible credits to Jesus (Matthew 7:12). Besides making Min write the saying a thousand times, Min's mother shut her out of the house for six hours and said she was ashamed to have her for a daughter.

Connections

1. The Communist characters in the story seem to confuse their culture with their economic system, in that they see Autumn Leaves's lending out Andersen's folk tales about princes and princesses as part of her effort to inculcate in her students the worth of the "old" economic system, rather than seeing Andersen's books as literature. But their desire to affirm the values of the culture as a group at the rally seems distinctly Chinese.

2. The Communist slogans quoted by Min resemble the McThought described by Koppel in that both have a vast distribution and neither requires the listener to think. The difference is that Communist slogans are distributed through posters and rallies, whereas U.S. citizens draw their "intellectual sustenance from television" (p. 649). These forms of communication suit their respective societies, because the Chinese value community, whereas Americans value individualism and privacy. Thomas Friedman suggests that the slogans of Mao's China are becoming obsolete when he points out that companies like Microsoft control access to the modern lanes of communication and once the Chinese start buying computers en masse, they'll become part of a global system of communication.

3. Students are not likely to take great offense at the phrase "American Imperialists," because the story depicts the Communists in such a negative light, with their simplistic slogans and literalist reading of Western culture. Judging from this essay, during Mao's regime the Chinese regarded American children as starving, because Chinese children collected pennies for them (para. 1), and Americans in general as aggressive and sneaky, eager to sabotage Chairman Mao's project.

FANG LIZHI, Thoughts on Reform (p. 743)

Explorations

1. According to Fang Lizhi, for a country to be "developed," it needs to have "intelligent and civilized citizens" (para. 12). Progress must be determined not only by economic

growth but also by the presence of an educated populace who understands the use of new technologies (10). He believes China needs to recognize the important contributions of intellectuals and revolutionize the way it treats them.

2.   Fang regards Premier Zhao's gaffe in Italy as a symptom of Chinese backwardness because he's concerned about the low level of cultural literacy in his country, especially compared with other countries he has visited. He wants China to be respected outside its borders. If an American official made such a faux pas, the media might highlight it as they highlighted Dan Quayle's misspelling *potato*. The American public would probably care less, though, because most probably know little about Copernicus (you might want to take a quick poll regarding how many of your students would have caught Zhao's mistake). If Premier Zhao had made his remarks in the United States, it's questionable how many people, even among the press, would notice.

3.   Fang bases his statement that intellectuals are the vanguard of the working class on the idea that they are "the ones whose labor holds the most promise for the future" (21); as even Mao conceded, "scientific and technological personnel are the pathbreakers for new forces of production" (22). Whether students find this argument logical will depend on their awareness of the current shift from an industrial to a technological economy.

Connections

1.   Fang notes that "whenever Mao Zedong spoke about intellectuals, it was in the context of 'solidarity with the masses,' 'reform through labor,' and 'reeducation'" (para. 16). Mao's anti-intellectualism is reflected in Anchee Min's essay when Secretary Chain assumes Autumn Leaves must be a spy or when he depicts Hans Christian Andersen's books "about lives of princes, princesses, and little people" as bad influences on the young Anchee Min (p. 736). Fang's essay indicates that the Communist party's policy of treating Mao as a deity had a powerful impact on China, starting in the 1950s with "pogroms . . . bent on eradicating any kind of intellectual endeavor" (13); currently, a barber is paid more than a brain surgeon, and intellectuals tend to have a low economic and political status (16).

2.   Students' responses to this question will vary according to their biases. Some may insist that the United States is a classless society, having been established as such by its founders. More are likely to respond that the United States is divided into a hierarchy of classes according to one or more of several criteria, including economic status, job status, income, ethnicity, race, gender, age, sexual preference, and residential location. Students who believe this country recognizes a "most advanced element of society" probably will return to these criteria to identify that element. (You might stimulate a lively discussion by asking them to define "advanced" in our society.) Likely candidates include the wealthiest Americans, a professional elite (politicians, lawyers, academics, science and technology experts), and perhaps celebrities. Robert Reich's candidate for the most fortunate, if not the most advanced, element of society would be the top fifth of Americans who take home "more money than the other four-fifths put together . . . The new elite . . . linked by jet, modem, fax, satellite, and fiber-optic cable to the great commercial and recreational centers of the world" (p. 648).

3.   Fang believes that respect for learning has declined in China because Chairman Mao de-emphasized the importance of intellectuals as part of his effort to exalt the role of laborers. In his insistence that "the humblest are the wisest," Mao led people to believe that, "the more people know, the more stupid they are" (15). To Fang, intellectuals are

"a progressive force in society" (26); the danger of losing them is that the reforms Fang sees as essential may not be possible without them. Neil Postman credits television with the decline in Americans' intelligence: "serious language has been displaced by the arts of show business" (p. 672). The danger he sees in the decline in respect for learning is that television has annihilated "the line that one ought to be able to draw between politics and entertainment" (p. 675). Moreover, "when a culture becomes distracted by trivia . . . culture-death is a clear possibility" (p. 678).

ORVILLE SCHELL, Fang Lizhi (p. 755)

Explorations

1. Fang Lizhi's conviction and intellectual boldness have served him well in his roles as astrophysicist, teacher, and political leader. As an astrophysicist, he had the intellectual curiosity and the flexibility to read the only scientific book available to him, Landau's *Classical Theory of Fields,* when he was forced to work in a mine and on a railroad during the Cultural Revolution (paras. 11–12). As a teacher, Fang was so bold as to encourage intellectual exchange between the University of Science and Technology (Keda) and Western institutions, as well as foster an "'unconstrained' atmosphere . . . in which students and faculty members worked openly together" (21). And as a political leader, Fang had the conviction to keep speaking his beliefs, no matter how much he was persecuted; for instance, in 1958 he was expelled from the party because he refused to recant his alleged misdeeds (8) or, in 1989, when he had been excluded from a state dinner with President Bush, Fang appeared at a press conference that evening denouncing his exclusion and raising the larger question of human rights abuses in China (33).

2. Fang's professional progress was hindered by Mao's policies in a number of ways: In 1966 he was imprisoned for a year, including time in solitary confinement (11); he was rejected for the post of vice president of Keda several times because a colleague submitted secret reports suggesting he was politically unreliable (16); he was ousted from Keda in 1987 for allegedly inciting a student uprising (26, 27); and he and his wife were forced to seek refuge in the American embassy after the Tiananmen massacre (37). Yet many of these setbacks increased Fang's renown: When he was excluded from the dinner with Bush, he won wide media attention by speaking about it at a press conference (33). Fang's professional progress was boosted by Mao's determination, despite his anti-intellectual bias, to make China competitive with the West: "Wrong or not, as a promising young scientist he was greatly needed by China in its early efforts to industrialize" (10).

3. According to Schell, Fang was harassed, punished, and finally exiled for his beliefs that there should be open intellectual exchange between students and teachers in China, as well as with researchers working in the same fields in other countries. Hence, he was accused of having "disseminated many erroneous statements reflecting 'bourgeois liberalization'" (27). Based on what students have read in this chapter's Spotlight selections, they should understand the extent to which Fang challenged Mao's anti-intellectual principles, rooted in suspicion of any new or foreign ideas.

Connections

1. International travel "influence[d] deeply the way that Fang looked at both the Chinese socialist system and the role of intellectuals within it" (para. 17); travel also brought Fang international scientific attention and acclaim, making him an international figure when the Chinese authorities began to persecute him. In "Thoughts on Reform," Fang claims that traveling affected his notion of what is meant by "developed": Rio de Janeiro, for instance, seemed very prosperous on the surface, but the inflation rate made life very unstable. Similarly, Colombia had a high GNP, but the money seemed to come primarily from drugs; moreover, in the town Fang visited, blacks were treated like slaves.

2. According to Aung San Suu Kyi, fearlessness is an admirable trait because it is essential to resisting a totalitarian regime. She says, "within a system which denies the existence of basic human rights, fear tends to be the order of the day" (p. 702). Only by fearlessly resisting the unrelenting pressure of the state can one stick to one's principles. Fang's experience supports her statements in that no matter how he was oppressed, he continued to speak his beliefs; for instance, in January 1989 he wrote a personal letter to Deng Xiaoping entreating him to release all political prisoners (31).

3. Nader Mousavizadeh explains the Danish monarchy's success as resulting from their having "[won] over the people through dignity and charisma and exemplary behavior" (p. 647). According to Schell, China's new generation of leaders has recognized the need to "re-energize its people and win their willing participation in a new drive toward economic development" (1), making political reform and democratic development their rallying cries.

JIANYING ZHA, Yearnings (p. 769)

Explorations

1. The Chinese people say they liked *Yearnings* so much because the show "brought out the best in them and made them understand better what it meant to be Chinese and how deeply rooted they all were in the Chinese values of family and human relations" (para. 9). Jianying Zha suggests that the show was also popular because of its realistic characters, elaborate plot, and simple moral message (4–5), as well as because it had the official sanction of Li Ruihuan and other public officials (12–14).

2. Students may balk a little at this question, so you might want to start by asking them which shows they think reflect "American" values, as well as how politicians have historically intersected with television. They may respond that U.S. politicians more often attack TV shows (former Vice President Dan Quayle condemned "Murphy Brown" for the title character's decision to have a child out of wedlock) or appear on them (Nancy Reagan and Henry Kissinger have appeared on sitcoms, and President Clinton played the saxophone on David Letterman, for example) than to praise them. A U.S. official might endorse a show depicting an ordinary American family, but Li's comment that the show is "a worthy model for our literary and artistic workers" (13) seems distinctly Chinese. Whereas Americans tend to think of television sitcoms as pure entertainment, the Chinese government sees them as a means to transmit values to the masses.

3. Li Riuhuan's comments on *Yearnings* carried such weight among the intelligentsia because when they read between the lines, they could see that the implicit message

was that the government wished to pursue a more moderate approach in the wake of the Tiananmen Square crackdown (20). According to Zha, the intelligentsia are writers who had been suppressed during the Cultural Revolution and who had been trying out every available literary vehicle since then. Li's approval of the show may affect them, in that a writer such as Zheng Wanlong who was under surveillance due to his participation in the student uprising was given greater freedom because he wrote for *Yearnings* (27–35).

Connections

1. Zheng Wanlong's experience parallels Fang Lizhi's in that both men were suspect for their involvement in pro-democracy activities. Zheng's signature on a certain petition was particularly damning (p. 779), whereas Fang's tendency to promote an open atmosphere at Keda made him an easy target. Zheng was interrogated daily for a year; Fang was sent to do hard labor for a year at one point and, much later, was forced into exile. Things have gone quite differently for them, though: Zheng's involvement with *Yearnings* has made him a national celebrity, whereas Fang's consistent expression of his ideas made it dangerous for him to remain in the country after the Tiananmen crackdown.

2. The Wuhan protest at a scheduled power cut does not support Fang's advice to the students, which was to "get together and think about the root causes of the things they were unhappy about," in this case, the continually rising price of the food, not its quality (p. 752). The Wuhan protesters might have questioned the reason for the power cuts, or the type of power being generated, rather than simply protesting the interruption of their TV show.

3. Television appears to pose the same dangers to Chinese society as it does to American society because in both countries it functions as a medium for foisting propaganda onto its viewers. Neil Postman might agree with the Chinese literary avant garde that the show's "official status of 'model product' and 'campaign fruit,' its crude, derogatory portrayal of the intellectuals, its vulgar, melodramatic style, and its celebration, in the service of party politics, of old Chinese values" were an embarrassment (para. 25), as was the fact that the same people who followed the students and intellectuals to Tiananmen Square could be easily reunited with the government through a sentimental TV show.

CHINA: INVESTIGATIONS/WEB SITES

China Matrix (http://www.xindeco.com/chimat/chinew2.html) offers links to Chinese sites devoted to business, government, academics, culture, and news.

Chinese Ethics (http://www.hku.hk/philodep/courses/EWEthics/) is a philosophy class site at Hong Kong University focusing on classical Chinese ethics. It contains summaries of course lectures on Confucius, Mozi, Mencius, Laozi (Lao Tzu), Zhuangzi (Chuang Tzu), and Xunzi (Hsun Tzu).

Hakka Chinese Home Page (http://www.asiawind.com/pub/hakka/index.html) is devoted to the Hakkas, an ethnic group of "Han" Chinese originally active around the Yellow River area. It covers the following topics: Who are the Hakkas?, Origin, Hakka and Xiongnu, History of

730–781 (Text Pages)

Migrations, Hakka women, Language, Influence on Japanese culture, Hakka in China and worldwide, Notable Hakka people, Genealogy, House construction, Publications and References.

Support Democracy in China (http://www.christusrex.org/www1/sdc/sdchome.html) is a volunteer community organization based in California's Silicon Valley. Its ongoing projects include programs in community outreach, dissident relief, information technology, and education.

ADDITIONAL QUESTIONS AND ASSIGNMENTS

1. In a journal entry or a collection of informal notes, discuss the concept of a noble cause as depicted in three or four of these selections. Consider such issues as the conflict between loyalty to a cause and loyalty to human beings, the individual's understanding of the cause (or lack thereof), the history of the conflict surrounding the cause, and any other issues you find relevant. As you look over your notes, try to discover similarities and differences among the cultures represented. Is it possible for individuals to identify so strongly with a cause that they consider their goals synonymous with the goals of the cause? Is any cause worth dying for? In short, can you come to any conclusion about the role played by a people's commitment to a cause in wartime or in civil conflict?

2. Research the 1994 uprising in Tiananmen Square and then try to follow up on some of the student dissidents. How did the uprising affect their lives? Are they politically active now? Write an expository essay describing the impact of the student democracy movement on the lives of some of its participants.

3. Imagine that you are one of the "natives" depicted in T. Coraghessan Boyle's "Top of the Food Chain" and describe how your way of life changed after Westerners came to your village. How is their culture different from yours? What do you value most and least about each culture? What would be the ideal attitude for outsiders approaching your village to have? (To help you get a sense of how other land-based cultures regard Westerners, you might want to search the World Wide Web, using search terms such as "indigenous peoples" or "native peoples.")

4. Conduct further research on one of the cultures represented in this section, focusing specifically on the culture's economy. If the selection is an excerpt from a larger work, look first at that work. You can find more information about the culture by consulting a general encyclopedia, a journal devoted to the study of that culture, and/or the Internet. Narrow your topic to something manageable, such as the effect of ideology on the economic system, the culture's financial dependence on the world market, the role played by economics in internal politics, or the effect of economic forces on the individual, and write an expository essay in which you elaborate on the culture's economic system.

132

SUGGESTED SYLLABI

This is a basic course description, with options for adaptations for different teaching approaches and thematic considerations. The format of the syllabus is necessarily general, making it flexible with regard to the needs of individual instructors. Each syllabus includes four short papers and one research paper. The arrangement allows for increasing or decreasing the number of papers to satisfy the instructors' wishes or departmental requirements. (We assume, however, that each paper will be thoroughly revised at least once, ensuring a significant amount of student writing.)

BASIC COURSE DESCRIPTION

This syllabus is designed for a course focusing on reading, writing, and research. In general, the paper assignments move from personal narrative to causal analysis or persuasion involving outside sources. The thematic emphasis is on recognizing how we define ourselves, beginning with an exploration of what it means to belong to one particular culture and then moving to more specific roles within a family, to a recognition of ourselves as we come of age and go to work, and finally to an understanding of the conflicts and ideologies shaping us and our culture. The syllabus can be adapted to a collaborative approach simply by giving students the responsibility for interpreting the selections and presenting their views to the class for general discussion. Similarly, papers can be worked through a number of drafts by using peer evaluation.

Weeks 1–4

Readings: "Identifying Ourselves"

Writing: Analyses of causes for misunderstandings of our own culture and other cultures (using Atwood, Harrison, Greer) or persuasive essay arguing for increased efforts to understand other cultures (Orlean, Paz, Rodriguez).

Discussion: Emphasis in readings on obstacles to dialogue between cultures and overcoming misconceptions about other cultures.

Weeks 5–6

Readings: "Families"

Writing: Personal essay describing family traditions (using any one of the readings as a model).

Discussion: Different traditions, different types of families, family roles, and customs.

Weeks 7–9

Readings: "Families"

Writing: Personal narrative or family memory responding to one of the selections.

Suggested Syllabi

Discussion: Author's personal reminiscences; effect of subjective point of view.

Weeks 10–12

Readings: "Turning Points"

Writing: Comparison of Initiation Rites in diverse cultures (for instance, Orlean, Angelou, Menchú).

Discussion: Personal and cultural functions of coming-of-age rituals.

Weeks 13–15

Readings: "Opposite Sexes"

Writing: Comparison of Western Judeo-Christian images of males and females with those of other cultures (for example, Shostak, Minai, Wikan) or definition of male or female, based on several selections (for instance, Kazantzakis, Updike, Silko, or Beauvoir). This could be done as a parody.

Discussion: Focus on how stereotypes and inaccurate perceptions reinforce traditional sex roles; contrast with writers' attempts to represent new and different points of view on meanings of "female" and "male."

VARIATION

Instructors wishing to alter readings from semester to semester may do so by changing the general theme of the course. For example, the class might explore the relationships between the individual and institutions, both cultural and political, keeping the first, second, and third sections of the basic syllabus and substituting the following for the fourth and fifth sections:

Weeks 10–12

Readings: "Myths, Ritual, and Magic"

Writing: Comparison of ritual and beliefs in different religions (using Abram, Bruchac, Allende, Del Guercio, Soyinka) or definition of magic (using Welty, Abram, Soyinka, Allende, Del Guercio).

Discussion: Explore students' relationships to religious institutions. Compare different religions presented in the section.

Weeks 13–15

Readings: "Institutions and Individuals"

Writing: Comparison of the benefits and liabilities of a given form of government (using West, Postman, and Grossman) or definition of oppression (based on Mandela, Weldon, Boyle, Suu Kyi).

Discussion: Focus on similarities among different ideologies. With this syllabus, the focus in Sections 1, 2, and 3 would shift from personal identity to relationships between individuals and others, including the state. This syllabus presents a greater challenge to students than the first, because it involves an assessment of individuals' responsibilities to nations and their ideologies and institutions.

RHETORICAL INDEX

Analogy

Argument and Persuasion

Cause and Effect

Classification

Rhetorical Index

Comparison and Contrast

James Baldwin, "The New Lost Generation"
Margaret Atwood, "A View from Canada"
Carlos Fuentes, "The Two Americas"
John David Morley, "Acquiring a Japanese Family"
Salman Rushdie, "The Broken Mirror"
Naila Minai, "Women in Early Islam"
David Grossman, "Israeli Arab, Israeli Jew"
Henry Louis Gates Jr., "Down to Cumberland"

Definition

Louise Erdrich, "Foreword"
Susan Orlean, "Quinceañera"
Amy Tan, "Two Kinds"
Alberto Moravia, "The Chase"
Kenzaburo Oe, "Japan, the Ambiguous, and Myself"
Unni Wikan, "The *Xanith*: A Third Gender Role?"

Description

Annie Dillard, "Flying"
Octavio Paz, "The Art of the Fiesta"
Margaret Atwood, "A View from Canada"
Rigoberta Menchú, "Birth Ceremonies"
Wole Soyinka, "Nigerian Childhood"
Susan Orlean, "Quinceañera"
Salman Rushdie, "The Broken Mirror"
Jianying Zha, "Yearnings"

Example and Illustration

Rigoberta Menchú, "Birth Ceremonies"
Salman Rushdie, "The Broken Mirror"
Yukiko Tanaka, "Mothers' Children"
Natasha Singer, "The New Russian Dressing"
Deborah Tannen, "How Male and Female Students Use Language Differently"
Joseph Bruchac, "Digging into Your Heart"
Neil Postman, "Future Shlock"

Exposition

Paul Harrison, "The Westernization of the World"
Louise Erdrich, "Foreword"
Salman Rushdie, "The Broken Mirror"
Orville Schell, "Fang Lizhi"
Octavio Paz, "The Art of the Fiesta"
John Updike, "The Disposable Rocket"
Naila Minai, "Women in Early Islam"
Gino Del Guercio, "The Secrets of Haiti's Living Dead"
Cornel West, "Race Matters"

136

Process Analysis

CHART OF RHETORICAL WRITING ASSIGNMENTS

NOTE: "Elaborations" or writing assignments asking students to write an essay in a particular rhetorical form or using resources are listed below. The number following the author's name refers to the corresponding "Elaborations" question for the selection.

(For the Index of Authors and Titles, see text pp. 789–792.)

Argument and Persuasion	Cause and Effect	Classification	Comparison and Contrast
Bruchac 1	Beauvoir 1	Heker 1	Atwood 1
Dubus 1	Bruchac 2	Liu 2	Cheever 2
Ghosh 2	Dubus 2	Mandela 1	Ghosh 1
Grossman 1	Filipovic 1	Márquez 2	Gordimer 2
Harrison 2	Ford 1	Menchú 1	Grossman 1, 2
Kundera 1	Harrison 1	Mphahlele 2	Kazantzakis 1
Liu 1	Mandela 2	Shostak 2	Paley 2
Moravia 1	Mphahlele 1	Suu Kyi 2	Shostak 1
Oz 2	Tan 1		Updike 1
Postman 2			Weldon 1
Suu Kyi 1			
Tannen 1			

Definition	Description	Division/Analysis	Example and Illustration
Abram 1	Abram 2	Cheever 1	Heker 2
Allende 1	Angelou 2	Kazantzakis 2	McCourt 1
Atwood 2	Brommell 2	Márquez 1	Paley 1
Beauvoir 2	Dillard 2	Tan 2	Percy 1
Dillard 1	Erdrich 2	Welty 1	Silko 1
Gordimer 2	Gates 1		
Keen 2	Menchú 2		
Márquez 2	Rushdie 1		
Orlean 1	Tannen 2		
Oz 1	Updike 2		
Percy 2			
Suu Kyi 2			

Chart of Rhetorical Writing Assignments

Narration	Process Analysis	Summary	Using Sources
Allende 2 Angelou 1 Brommell 1 Dubus 2 Erdrich 1 Filipovic 2 Ford 2 Gates 2 Liu 1 Márquez 2 Moravia 2 Orlean 2 Silko 2 Weldon 2	Angelou 2 McCourt 2 Morrison 1 Weldon 2	Boyle 1 Postman 1	Abram 1 Boyle 2 Del Guercio 1, 2 Keen 1 Morrison 1 West 1
			Other
			Del Guercio 2 (write a fictional essay) Gordimer 1 (analogy) Welty 2 (write a fairy tale)

ADDITIONAL RESOURCES

INDEX TO HEADNOTE INFORMATION

The following index is keyed to the headnotes in *Making Contact* and locates specific geographical, historical, and political information about countries found in the headnotes.

HONG KONG: geography, population, contemporary history, British influence, reversion to China in 1997 (p. 318)

INDIA: independence from Britain (p. 53)

INDONESIA: geography, European dominance of, independence, establishment of Malaysia, artistic and religious traditions (p. 513)

IRAN: Khomeini's death threats against Salman Rushdie (p. 53)

IRELAND: geography, general history, the Act of Union, nationalist uprisings, Republic of Ireland recognized, Irish Republican Army (p. 200)

ISRAEL: geography, general history, Middle East in World War I and II, establishment of by United Nations, Arab-Israeli conflict (p. 188), Six Day War, Palestine Liberation Organization, intifada and retaliation, assassination of Yitzhak Rabin, discrimination against Arabs (p. 713)

ITALY: geography, general history, nineteenth- and twentieth-century political struggles, cultural contribution, involvement in World War II, current political stability, population demographics (p. 453)

JAPAN: geography, general history, nineteenth-century arrival of Perry, expansion policy and World War II, current form of government, recent economic boom and slowdown (p. 228)

JORDAN: geography, Bedouins, general history, current government (p. 459)

MEXICO: general history, Cortes and Spanish explorers (1500s), independence, current economy (p. 83)

NIGERIA: geography, general history, Yoruba culture, Islamic Hausa people, arrival of slave traders and Christian missionaries, nineteenth-century British control of and current influence on, Biafran secession, coup by Abacha (p. 597)

OMAN: geography, general history, nineteenth-century British influence, current government, poverty, large defense budget (p. 459)

PALESTINE: see Israel

RUSSIA: history of Soviet Union, perestroika, glasnost, independence, Yeltsin, anti-Semitism (p. 352)

SAUDI ARABIA: geography, structure of government, general history, importance of oil (p. 459)

SOUTH AFRICA: geography, racial makeup, apartheid defined, nineteenth-century founding by Dutch, Anglo-Boer War, history of apartheid, 1961 withdrawal from British Commonwealth, 1994 multiracial elections, Mandela as president (p. 344), mission of the African National Congress, worldwide economic and political pressures, current political climate (p. 688)

UNITED KINGDOM: see Great Britain

UNITED STATES: pueblo culture (p. 419)

YUGOSLAVIA (former): general history, establishment of Tito's Communist government, secession of member republics, disintegration of, civil war including Serbian policy of "ethnic cleansing," Dayton Peace Accord (p. 210)

BIBLIOGRAPHY

The following sources may be useful for further exploration of literary, biographical, and historical topics and for study of particular countries and regions.

Almanacs, Series, Yearbooks

Britannica Book of the Year. Chicago: Encyclopedia Brittanica, 1938–.

Contemporary Authors. Detroit: Gale, 1962–. An up-to-date biographical source on international authors in many subject areas.
Contemporary Literary Criticism. Detroit: Gale, 1973.
Current Biography. New York: Wilson, 1940. Biographical sketches of people in the news, published monthly (except December) and annually in a cumulative volume.
Demographic Yearbook 1990. 42nd ed. New York: United Nations, 1989.
Europa World Year Book. 2 vols. Detroit: Gale, 1993. Detailed information on every country in the world.
Facts on File Yearbook. New York: Facts on File, 1941–. Weekly summaries of news events in *Facts on File: A Weekly News Digest,* indexed every two weeks, are published cumulatively in this annual volume.
Information Please Almanac. Boston: Houghton Mifflin, 1992. Detailed information on countries of the world.
Political Handbook of the World. New York: McGraw Hill, 1975–. Formerly *Political Handbook and Atlas of the World* (1927–1974), contains information on governments, parties, terminology, and so on.
Statesman's Year-Book 1992–1993. 129th rev. and updated ed. Ed. Brian Hunter. New York: St. Martin's, 1992. Detailed economic data on all the world's countries.
Statistical Yearbook, No. 38. New York: United Nations, 1991.
The Universal Almanac and Book of Facts: New York: Newspaper Enterprise Assoc., 1868–. Factual material on current and historical topics; contains chronology of previous year's events.

Atlases

Hammond Standard World Atlas. Maplewood, NJ: Hammond, 1983.
National Geographic Atlas of the World. 6th ed. Washington, D.C.: Nat. Geographic Soc., 1990.
Economic Atlas of the World, 4th ed. Oxford: Oxford UP, 1972.
The Prentice-Hall Great International Atlas. Englewood Cliffs, N.J.: Prentice, 1981.
Rand McNally New Cosmopolitan World Atlas. New Census ed. Chicago: Rand, 1984.
Shepherd, William. *Historical Atlas.* New York: Barnes, 1964. Includes maps for world history from 1450 B.C. to the 1960s.
The Times Atlas of the World. 9th Comprehensive ed. New York: Random House, 1992.

Dictionaries and Gazetteers

Columbia Dictionary of Modern European Literature. 2nd ed. Gen. eds. Jean-Albert Bede and William B. Edgerton. New York: Columbia UP, 1980.
Dictionary of Geography. Rev. ed. Ed. W.G. Moore. New York: Penguin, 1950.
Dictionary of Islam. 2 vols. Ed. Thomas P. Hughes. New York: Gordon, 1980.
Facts on File Dictionary of Religion. Ed. John R. Hinnells. New York: Facts on File, 1984.
Lacqueur, Walter. *A Dictionary of Politics.* Rev. ed. New York: Macmillan, 1974. Defines terms, provides historical, geographical, biographical information.
The Times Index-Gazetteer of the World. London: Times, 1965. Still useful.
Webster's New Geographical Dictionary Rev. ed. Springfield, Ill. Merriam, 1984.
World Facts in Brief. New York: Rand, 1986. A handy inexpensive student reference.

Specialized Encyclopedias

Encyclopedia of Latin American History. Rev. ed. Ed. Michael R. Martin and Gabriel H. Lovett. 1968. Westport, Conn: Greenwood, 1981.

Encyclopedia of World Literature in the 20th Century. 2nd ed. 5 vols. New York: Unger, 1981–1993.

Harper Encyclopedia of the Modern World. New York: Harper, 1970. Coverage from 1760 through the 1960s.

The International Geographic Encyclopedia and Atlas. Boston: Houghton Mifflin, 1979.

McGraw-Hill Encyclopedia of World Biography. 12 vols. New York: McGraw, 1973. Contains approximately 5,000 biographical entries on world figures.

The New Illustrated Encyclopedia of World History. Ed. William L. Langer. 2 vols. New York: Abrams, 1975. Arranged chronically, comprehensively covers from prehistory to space exploration.

New Nations: A Student Handbook. Ed. David N. Rowe. New York: Shoe String, 1968.

The Penguin Companion to World Literature. 4 vols. New York: McGraw, 1969–1971. Separate volumes for American; English, classical, Oriental, and African; and European literature.

Time Line

Grun, Bernard. *The Timetables of History.* 3rd rev. ed. New York: Touchstone, Simon. 1991. This edition is based on Werner Stein's *Kulturfahrplan.* The categories are History and Politics; Literature and Theater; Religion, Philosophy, and Learning; Science, Technology, and Growth; and Daily Life.

FILM, VIDEO, AND AUDIOCASSETTE RESOURCES

After a section of general resources, the following list is organized according to the parts in *Making Contact*. Within each section, the entries are organized alphabetically by title (or by author in cases where this information provides a more helpful reference). Several entries might be useful for more than one part. For these entries, the full annotation is provided in what seems to be the most appropriate part. The entries are then listed in other appropriate parts with a cross-reference to the listing with complete information.

The Directory of Distributors at the end of the list of resources can help you locate these films, videos, and audiocassettes if you cannot find them in your school or public library or local video rental store.

General

African Wisdom: Wisdom from Tribal Africa. "Malidom Some, a Dagara man from West Africa, tells his own story about his experience of cultural trauma. After years of education in Western universities, Some faces the challenges of re-integrating himself into the ancestral lifestyle of his tribe. The author disputes the basic concepts of European values and gives the audience a glimpse into the purpose and wisdom of ancient tribal traditions." New Dimensions. 1 cassette. 60 minutes.

Americas in Transition. (1982) "Provides a concise, fast-paced introduction to the underlying causes of unrest in Latin America. Examines the roots of this unrest through a close look at Latin America's history of military dictatorships, attempts at democracy, communist influences, and the role of U.S. involvement." Icarus films. 3/4-inch video. 29 minutes.

Be It Remembered. Documentary, hosted by Eli Wallach, about immigrants past and present. 50 minutes.

Black Writer Series. "Includes 16 readings and interviews. Authors include James Baldwin, Toni Morrison, and Alice Walker." American Audio Prose Library.

The Cummington Story. (1945) "The true story of a family of immigrants settling in a small New England town. The participants re-create their own roles. Shows the difficulty of cultural assimilation." United World Films, Inc. 16 mm film. 17 minutes.

Enough Tears of Crying. (1987) "Examines the struggle of Latin American feminists in El Salvador." VHS, Beta, 3/4-inch video. Women Make Movies. 28 minutes.

Masai Women. (1989) "Provides a record of the social structure, beliefs and practices of societies threatened with extinction. Examines the women's role in this male-dominated society." Filmmakers Library. VHS, 1/2-inch video. 52 minutes.

Mother Theresa. (1987) Profile of the friend of the poor. PBS. 80 minutes.

Yesterday, Today and Tomorrow — The Women of Papua, New Guinea. (1988) "Examines some of the ancient customs and rituals of tribal women and contrasts these traditional women with those who have entered the modern world." Barr Films. 3/4-inch video, VHS, 1/2-inch video. 27 minutes.

Film, Video, and Audiocassette Resources

Identifying Ourselves

Atwood, Margaret. "Atwood discusses the writing process, poetry, and the special problems of women writers. Explains some of the reasons behind Canadian Nationalism." Vancouver Women in Focus. 3/4-inch video. 28 minutes.

Baldwin, James. *Just above My Head.* "Read by the author." American Audio Prose Library. 1 cassette. 47 minutes.

Baldwin, James. "Interview focuses on Baldwin's stand on racial issues and explores the role of the artist in Western culture." American Audio Prose Library. 1 cassette. 56 minutes.

Baldwin, James. *Meeting the Man — James Baldwin in Paris.* (1972) "A Documentary on James Baldwin's life as a black man, a writer, and a political figure." Impact. 16 mm film. 27 minutes.

Baldwin, James. *The Price of the Ticket.* (1990) "Portrays the life of the writer and includes excerpts from his major works. With commentary by authors Maya Angelou, Amira Baraka, Ishmael Reed, William Styron, and biographer David Leeming." California Newsreel. VHS, 1/2-inch video; Beta, 16 mm film. 87 minutes.

Celebrating the Day of the Dead. "Explores the annual Mexican celebration." Educational Video Network. VHS. 22 minutes.

Day of the Dead. (1957) "Deals with special objects and events surrounding the annual Mexican celebration of All Souls Day." Pyramid Film & Video. VHS, Beta, 3/4-inch video. 14 minutes.

From Here, from this Side. (1988) "Examines the Mexican-American cultural relationship. Explores the issue of cultural imperialism from a Mexican point of view. Incorporates writings by Octavio Paz." Women Make Movies. VHS, 1/2-inch video, 3/4-inch video. 24 minutes.

Fuentes, Carlos. *Crossing Borders — the Journey of Carlos Fuentes.* (1990) "Follows the travels of the Mexican novelist to Washington DC, Santiago, and Buenos Aires." Films for the Humanities and Sciences. 58 minutes.

Fuentes, Carlos. (1988) "As part of his series *World of Ideas*, Bill Moyers interviews the author about his views on Latin American economics and political independence." PBS. VHS, 1/2-inch video. 30 minutes.

The Mexican-American Heritage and Destiny. (1977) "Explores how a Mexican-American who feels culturally deprived and unsure of his identity is shown his cultural heritage." Handel. 1/2-inch or 3/4-inch video. 29 minutes.

Paz, Octavio. *Octavio Paz — an Uncommon Poet.* (1979) "Presents the Mexican poet talking about childhood, activities as a political activist, and his views on poets, poetry and language." Films for the Humanities and Sciences. 1/2-inch or 3/4-inch video. 29 minutes.

Paz, Octavio. See *From Here, from this Side* in this Part.

Reed, Ishmael. *Ishmael Reed II.* (1989) "The poet is interviewed and reads selected poems." New Letters on the Air. 1 cassette. 29 minutes.

Reed, Ishmael. *Flight into Canada.* (1984) "A recently escaped modern black slave makes his way to freedom via jumbo jet and probes the contemporary American psyche along the way." New Letters on the Air. 1 cassette. 29 minutes.

Tan, Amy. *Hundred Secret Senses.* (1995) "American-born Olivia hears the stories her older half-sister Kwan has brought from China. When the two journey to Kwan's homeland, family secrets emerge to question the connections between chance and fate, beliefs and hopes." Dove Audio. 4 cassettes. 9 hours.

A Week in the Life of a Mexican Student. (1986) "Describes the lifestyle and typical week of students in Mexico." AIMS Media. 1/2-inch or 3/4-inch video. 24 minutes.

Families

Children of the Tribe. (1980) "Contrasts Japanese and Western family life and schooling." National Film Board of Canada. 16mm film. 28 minutes.

Filipovic, Zlata. *Zlata's Diary*. (1994) "A young girl faces war in Sarajevo." Penguin-Highbridge. Abridged. 1 cassette. 1 hour 30 minutes.

Filipovic, Zlata. *Zlata's Diary*. (1994) Recorded Books. Unabridged. 3 cassettes. 4 hours 30 minutes.

Great Mother. (1983) "A look at the mother/daughter relationship in Japanese culture." Video Out Distribution. VHS, Beta, 3/4-inch video. 16 minutes.

Growing up in Japan. (1992) "A look at life in Japan, from the extreme pressures of schooling, to the country's duel between Westernization and traditional influences, to religious roots in Shintoism and Buddhism, to the Japanese values of politeness, respect, and recognition of beauty." Journal Films, Inc. VHS. 20 minutes.

Inside Japan: Tradition and Family Life. (1990) "A look at Japanese culture as the old world traditions meet with the new." Centre Communications. VHS, Beta, 3/4-inch video. 23 minutes.

Japanese-American Women: A Sense of Place. (1992) "Interviews with twelve Japanese-American women about their diverse experiences growing up in the United States, showing that the women who lived on the East Coast were more isolated from Japanese culture than the women who grew up in Japanese communities of the West Coast." Women Make Movies. VHS. 28 minutes.

Japanese Young Women. (1984) "Interviews women in their 20s and 30s from all walks of life about the cultural changes taking place in their lives and their families." Communication for Change, Inc. 3/4-inch video. 29 minutes.

Walker, Alice. *Alice Walker, Part 1*. (1988) "The author discusses family violence and the position of black women in America." Films Inc. Video. 1/2-inch video. 30 minutes.

Turning Points

Angelou, Maya. *1. Maya Angelou: The Person, 2. The Writer*. (1982) "In this two-part series, the writer discusses her relationship with her mentor James Baldwin, her work regimen, and performs two compositions, 'No Loser, No Weeper' and 'And Still I Rise.'" Nebraska Educational TV Council for Higher Education. VHS, 1/2-inch video; Beta, 3/4-inch video. 30 minutes.

Brodsky, Joseph. *Winter*. (1988) "Read by the author." Watershed Tapes. 1 cassette. 64 minutes.

Brodsky, Joseph. (1991) "Interview with the author." New Letters on the Air. 1 cassette. 29 minutes.

Ford, Richard and Grace Paley. *Selected Short VI & VII*. (1989) "Read by William Hurt and Anne Pitoniak." Listening Library. 2 cassettes. 2 hours 27 minutes.

Gordimer, Nadine. *City of the Dead & A City of the Living*. "The author reads her stories, which reveal the complexity of life in modern Africa." Spoken Arts. 1 cassette. 58 minutes.

Gordimer, Nadine. *July's People*. (1993) "During uprisings in South Africa, July, a black servant, rescues his employers by taking them to his remote home village where traditional roles are reversed and he becomes their host, savior, and keeper." Blackstone Audio Books. 4 cassettes. 1 hour 30 minutes per cassette.

Gordimer, Nadine. *None to Accompany Me*. (1994) "A strong-willed South African lawyer, mother of two and a pillar of the legal foundation that seeks to represent blacks in their struggle to reclaim the land that was once theirs, seeks to reconstruct her life as her country slowly jolts towards majority rule." Books on Cassette. 4 cassettes. 10 hours.

Nabokov, Vladimir. *Speak, Memory*. (1988) Books on Tape. 7 cassettes. 1 hour 30 minutes per cassette.

Film, Video, and Audiocassette Resources

Russia Then & Now. (1994) "Combines pre-1989 and new footage to offer a contrasting look at Russia and the other former Soviet republics before and after the communist break-up." Clay Francisco Films. VHS. 80 minutes.

Russia Today: Its Land and Its People. (1995) "Combines footage with comments from young Russians to illustrate daily life in the Soviet Union. Discusses the geography, culture, traditions, law, and government of the country." United Learning, Inc. VHS. 20 minutes.

Walker, Alice. *Giving Birth, Finding Form.* (1993) "Alice Walker, Isabel Allende, and Jean Shinoda Bolen share the sagas of their lives as inspiration for their work and explore how creativity can kindle the feminine spirit." Sounds True. 1 cassette. 90 minutes.

Opposite Sexes

Beauvoir, Simone de. *Daughters of de Beauvoir.* (1990) "Award winning documentary focuses on Beauvoir's work and her legacy as one of the leading figures of the worldwide women's movement." Filmmakers Library. VHS. 55 minutes.

Enormous Changes. (1983) "Three Stories about New York City women and their personal relationships. Based on the stories of Grace Paley." Vidmark Entertainment. VHS, Beta. 115 minutes.

Islam and Feminism. (1991) "Introduces Pakistani women's movements which are attempting to fight the unequal treatment of women under Islamic law." First Run Features. VHS. 25 minutes.

Islam, the Veil and the Future. (1979) "Explores how the Islamic world deals with marriage, adultery, and divorce, as well as voting rights for women and proper feminine dress." PBS Home Video. VHS, Beta, 3/4-inch video. 29 minutes.

Kazantzakis, Nikos. *Selected Works.* Public Television. 2-inch video. 29 minutes.

Kazantzakis, Nikos. *Kazantzakis.* (1987) "Documentary captures the essence of the Greek writer with beautiful footage of Greece and excepts from his work." Centre Communications. VHS, Beta, 3/4-inch video. 29 minutes.

The Middle East — Mosaic of Peoples (an Overview). (1979) "Surveys the diversified cultures of the Middle East, focusing on the lifestyles of ethnic minorities and the coexistence of different religious sects." Coronet. 1/2-inch, 3/4-inch video. 28 minutes.

Tannen, Deborah. *That's Not What I Meant: How Conversational Style Makes or Breaks Relationships.* (1991) S&S Audio. 90 minutes.

Tannen, Deborah. *You Just Don't Understand Women: Women and Men in Conversation.* (1991) "A guide to communicating across the very separate cultures dividing men and women." S&S Audio. 1 cassette. 90 minutes.

Updike, John. (1981) "Interview with the author." PBS. 1/2-inch video, 3/4-inch video. 60 minutes.

Updike, John. *Couples.* (1993) "Explores the psychosexual natures of a group of young middle-class married couples of Tarbox, Massachusetts in 1963." Books on Tape. 12 cassettes. 1 hour 30 minutes per cassette.

A Wedding in Galilee. (1987) "The elder of a Palestinian village is given permission to have a traditional wedding ceremony for his son if Israeli military officers can attend as the guests of honor. As the event approaches conflicts arise among the villagers, the family, and the Israelis." In Arabic and Hebrew with English subtitles. Kino on Video, Ingram International Films. VHS. 113 minutes.

Myth, Ritual, and Magic

Allende, Isabel. *Giving Birth, Finding Form.* (1993) See Alice Walker in Turning Points.

Allende, Isabel. *Stories of Eva Luna.* (1991) "Presents stories, characters, and settings based on Allende's 1991 book." Dove Audio. 2 cassettes. 3 hours.

Allende, Isabel. *The Woman's Voice in Latin American Literature*. (1993) "The author discusses the events following the 1973 Chilean coup, emphasizing her anger against militarism and discussing the subject matter of her books." Films for the Humanities and Sciences. VHS. 56 minutes.

Bruchac, Joseph. *Joseph Bruchac II.* (1993) "Native American poet and storyteller Joseph Bruchac reads from a collection that mixes historical fact with Indian myth." New Letters on the Air. 1 cassette. 29 minutes.

Festival in Kano — A Study of Northern Nigeria. "Provides a picture of the inhabitants of one of Nigeria's oldest cities." Viewtech. 16 mm film. 31 minutes.

García Márquez, Gabriel. *Tales Beyond Solitude.* "Features archival footage from the author's life and clips from films on which he has worked. Films for the Humanities and Sciences. VHS, 1/2-inch video. 59 minutes.

Mammy Water — In Search of the Water Spirits in Nigeria. "Examines the rituals and ceremonies associated with Mammy Water, a water goddess worshipped by the peoples in South Nigeria." University of California at Berkeley. 1/2-inch video, 16mm film. 59 minutes.

Morrison, Toni. (1988) "Interview with the author. Reveals the true story on which *Beloved* was based and discusses the problems of slavery and its appalling legacy." Films Inc. Video. VHS, 1/2-inch video. 52 minutes.

Morrison, Toni. *African-Americans, Pt. 3.* (1990) "The author discusses *Beloved* and the teaching of African-American literature. Trudier Harris comments on Morrison's fiction." National Humanities. 1 cassette. 30 minutes.

Natives of the Narrow Land: The Unwritten History of the First Cape Codders. (1993). Narrated by Julie Harris. Scenes and artifacts from the excavation of an ancient Wampanoag campsite and a contemporary pow-wow. Mooncusser Productions. VHS, 1/2-inch video. 35 minutes.

Neruda, Pablo. (1972) "Neruda reads and talks about his poetry, and discusses the interplay between writing and politics." Tapes for Readers. 1 cassette. 30 minutes.

Neruda, Pablo. "Presents the poet giving his views on love, hate, life and death, and intercuts the discussion with poems and commentary tracing the development of Neruda's poetic vision." Cinema Guild 1/2-inch video, 3/4-inch video. 30 minutes.

Nigeria . . . Problems of Nation Building. (1968) "Produced by Leni Riefenstahl. Surveys the country's geography, economy, and people, stressing tribalism and nationalism." Atlantis Productions. VHS, 1/2-inch video, Beta, 3/4-inch video. 21 minutes.

Soyinka, Wole. *A Voice of Africa.* "Features the work and life of the Nigerian Nobel Prize winner." Includes student notebook and teacher resource book. Sunburst Communications. VHS, 1/2-inch video. 16 minutes.

Welty, Eudora. "Welty reads selected poems." Harper Audio. 1 cassette.

Institutions and Individuals

The Chinese. (1991) "A 26 program series exploring the people, history, and heritage of Chinese civilization. Includes a look at daily Chinese life and the clash between ancient traditions and government mandated changes." 1. Reform in Crisis: The Aftermath of Tiananmen; 8. Social Control in Chinese Society; 14. Sources of Social Conflict in Chinese Society; 26. Facing the Future: China Approaches the 21st Century. Great Plains National. VHS. 30 minutes each.

The Gate of Heavenly Peace, Tiananmen Square, June 4th, 1989. "Captures the shock and horror experienced by Chinese students when government troops opened fire on them in Tiananmen Square." Filmmakers Library. VHS, 1/2-inch video, 16 mm film. 10 minutes.

Film, Video, and Audiocassette Resources

Mandela, Nelson. *Free at Last.* (1990) "Documentary about the African National Congress and the release of Marxist Nelson Mandela after twenty-five years in prison for his work to stop South African apartheid." Africa Fund. VHS, 1/2-inch video. 79 minutes.

Mandela, Nelson. *The Long Walk to Freedom.* (1990) "Documentary of the turbulent events in South Africa before and during Nelson Mandela's incarceration and the triumphs experienced after his release." Landmark Media Inc. VHS, 1/2-inch video, 3/4-inch video. 28 minutes.

NBC White paper: China. (1984) "Tom Brokaw looks at everyday life in China. Time-Life Video and Television. VHS, Beta, 3/4-inch video. 100 minutes.

Paley, Grace. See "Enormous Changes" in Opposite Sexes.

Postman, Neil. *Conscientious Objections.* (1994) "In a series of essays, one of America's sharpest social critics casts a shrewd eye over contemporary culture to reveal the worst and best of our habits of discourse, tendencies in education, and obsessions with technological novelty." Blackstone Audio. 4 cassettes. 1 hour 30 minutes per cassette.

Tragedy at Tiananmen — The Untold Story. (1989) "Part of a four-part series on revolutionary China hosted by Ted Koppel. Examines the events of June 3, 1989, when student support of China's new democratic movement was crushed." Coronet. 3/4-inch video. 48 minutes.

The Wedding Banquet. (1993) "Story about the clash of customs and secrets. A homosexual Chinese man marries to appease his parents. A comedy of errors follows the young man's deception." In Chinese with English subtitles. FoxVideo. VHS. 111 minutes.

DIRECTORY OF AUDIOVISUAL DISTRIBUTORS

Africa Fund
17 John Street, 12th Floor
New York, NY 10038
(212) 962-1210

AIMS Media
9710 DeSoto Avenue
Chatsworth, CA 91311-4409
(818) 773-4300
1-800-367-2467

American Audio Prose Library
P.O. Box 842
1015 East Broadway
Suite 284
Columbia, MO 65205
1-800-447-2275

Amnesty International
Publications
322 8th Avenue
New York, NY 10001
(212) 807-8400

Atlantis Productions
2219 Thousand Oaks Blvd.
Thousand Oaks, CA 91362
(805) 495-2790

Barr Films Media Group, Inc.
12801 Schabarum Avenue
P.O. Box 7878
Irwindale, CA 91706-7878
(818) 338-7878
1-800-234-7878

BBC Films, Inc.
Video Distribution Center
P.O. Box 644
Paramus, NJ 07652
(212) 239-0530

Benchmark Media, Inc.
569 North State Road
Braircliff Manor, NY 10510-1542
(914) 762-3838
1-800-438-5564

Blackstone Audio Books
P.O. Box 969
Ashland, OR 97520
(541) 776-5179
1-800-729-2665

Books on Cassette, a division of Brilliance
1810-B Industrial Drive
P.O. Box 887
Grand Haven, MI 49417
1-800-648-2312
1-800-222-3225 (library orders)

Books on Tape
729 Farad Street
Costa Mesa, CA 92627
(714) 548-5525
1-800-541-5525

Britannica Films
310 South Michigan Avenue
Chicago, IL 60604
(312) 347-7900
1-800-554-9862

CBS Video Library
1211 Avenue of the Americas
New York, NY 10036
(212) 975-3454

California Newsreel
149 Ninth Street
San Francisco, CA 94103
(415) 621-6196

Campus Film Distributors Corp.
42 Oak Avenue
Tuckahoe, NY 10707
(914) 961-1900

Canadian Film-Makers' Distribution Center
37 Hanna Avenue, Suite 220
Toronto, ON M6K 1W8
Canada
(416) 588-0725

Directory of Audiovisual Distributors

Catholic Relief Services
209 West Fayette Street
Baltimore, MD 21201-3403
(410) 625-2220
1-800-235-2772

The Center for Humanities
Communications Park
Box 1000
Mount Kisco, NY 10549
(914) 666-4100
1-800-431-1242

Cinema Guild
1697 Broadway, Suite 506
New York, NY 10019
(212) 246-5522
1-800-723-5522

Clay Francisco Films
P.O. Box 412
Sutter Creek, CA 95685
(209) 267-5759

Communication for Change, Inc.
147 W. 22nd Street
New York, NY 10011
(212) 255-2718

Copeland Griggs Productions, Inc.
5616 Geary Street
San Francisco, CA 94121
(415) 668-4200

Cornell University
Audio-Visual Resources Center
8 Business and Technology Park
Ithaca, NY 14850
(607) 255-2091

Coronet Film and Video
108 Wilmot Rd.
Deerfield, IL 60015
1-800-621-2131

Dove Audio
301 N. Canon Drive, Suite 203
Beverly Hills, CA 90210
(310) 273-7722

Educational Film and Video Project
5332 College Ave., Suite 101
Oakland, CA 94618
(415) 655-9050

Embassy Home Entertainment
1901 Avenue of the Stars
Los Angeles, CA 90067
(213) 460-7200

Ergo Media
P.O. Box 2037
668 American Legion Drive
Teaneck, NJ 07666-1437
(201) 692-0404

Facets Multimedia
1517 West Fullerton Avenue
Chicago, IL 60614
312-281-9075
1-800-532-2387

Filmmakers' Library
124 E. 40th Street, Suite 901
New York, NY 10016
(212) 808-4980
1-800-555-9815

Films for the Humanities & Sciences
P.O. Box 2053
Princeton, NJ 08543
(609) 275-1400
1-800-257-5126

Films, Inc. Video
5547 N. Ravenswood Ave.
Chicago, IL 60640-1199
(312) 878-2600, ext. 44
1-800-323-4222, ext. 44

Flower Films
10341 San Pablo Avenue
El Cerrito, CA 94530
(510) 525-0942
1-800-572-7618

FoxVideo
2121 Avenue of the Stars, 25th Floor
Los Angeles, CA 90067
(310) 369-3900
1-800-800-2369

Great Plains National Instructional
Television Library
University of Nebraska at Lincoln
1800 North 33rd Street
P.O. Box 80669
Lincoln, NE 68501-0669
(402) 472-2007
1-800-228-4630

HBO Home Video
1114 Avenue of the Americas
New York, NY 10036
(212) 512-7400

Handel Film Corp.
2221 Raymond Avenue
Los Angeles, CA 90007
(310) 657-8990

HarperAudio, a division of HarperCollins
Publishers, Inc.
10 East 53rd Street
New York, NY 10022
(212) 207-7000
1-800-242-7737

Hartley Film Foundation
59 Cat Rock Road
Cos Cob, CT 06807
(203) 869-1818

Icarus Films
153 Waverly Place, 6th Floor
New York, NY 10014
(212) 727-1711

Impact Media
P.O. Box 442
Lebanon, NH 03766
(603) 448-0560

International Film Bureau
332 South Michigan Avenue
Chicago, IL 60604-4382
(312) 427-4545

International Film Foundation, Inc.
155 West 72nd Street
New York, NY l0023
(212) 580-1111

Journal Films
1560 Sherman Avenue, Suite 100
Evanston, IL 60201
(708) 328-6700
1-800-323-9084

King Features Entertainment
235 East 45th Street
New York, NY 10017
(212) 455-4000

Landmark Media
3450 Slade Run Drive
Falls Church, VA 22042
(703) 241-2030
1-800-342-4336 or
1-800-352-7060

Listening Library
1 Park Avenue
Old Greenwich, CT 06870
(203) 637-3616
1-800-243-4504

Live Entertainment
15400 Sherman Way
Suite 500
Van Nuys, CA 91406
(818) 908-0303

MCA/Universal Home Video
100 Universal City Plaza
Universal City, CA 91608
(818) 777-1000

MGM/UA Home Video
Santa Monica, CA 90232-2728
(310) 828-3711

MPI Home Video
16101 South 108th Avenue
Orland Park, IL 60462
(708) 460-0555

McGraw-Hill
Continuing Education Program
4401 Connecticut NW
Lower Level
Washington, DC 20008
(202) 244-1600

Modern Education Service
381 Park Avenue South
New York, NY 10016
1-800-243-6877

Mooncusser Productions
P.O. Box 752
West Chatham, MA 02669
(508) 945-0752

National Film Board of Canada
22 D Hollywood Avenue
Hohokus, NJ 07423
1-800-542-2164

Directory of Audiovisual Distributors

National Geographic Society
c/o Educational Services
1145 17th Street, NW
Washington, DC 20036
(202) 857-7378
1-800-447-0647

National Humanities Center
P.O. Box 12256
Research Triangle Park, NC 27709-2256
(919) 549-0661

National Public Radio
Audio Services
2025 M St., NW
Washington, DC 20036
(202) 414-2000

New Day Films Library
22D Hollywood Avenue
Hohokus, NJ 07423
(201) 652-6590

New Dimensions Foundations
P.O. Box 569
Ukiah, CA 95482
(707) 468-5215

New Letters on the Air
5101 Rockhill Road
Kansas City, MO 64110
(816) 235-1159

New Yorker Video
16 West 61st Street
New York, NY 10023
(212) 247-6110
1-800-447-0196

Northern Lights Productions
1050 Commonwealth Avenue
Boston, MA 02215
(617) 267-0391

W. W. Norton Publishers
Trade Sales Department
500 Fifth Avenue
New York, NY 10110
(212) 790-4314

PBS Home Video
Catalog Fulfillment Center
P.O. Box 4030
Santa Monica, CA 90411
1-800-531-4727

Paramount Home Video
5555 Melrose Ave.
Los Angeles, CA 90038
(213) 956-5000

Penguin Highbridge Audio
1000 Westgate Drive
Saint Paul, MN 55114
(212) 366-2000

Phoenix Films/American Film Institute
2349 Chassy Drive
St. Louis, MO 63146
New York, NY 10016
1-800-221-1274

Playhouse Video
1211 Avenue of the Americas
New York, NY 10036
(212) 819-3238

Portland State University
Continuing Education Program
P.O. Box 1394
Portland, OR 97207-1491
(503) 725-4891

Public Media Home Vision
5547 N. Ravenswood Avenue
Chicago, IL 60640-1199
(312) 878-2600
1-800-826-3456

Random House Audio Books
201 East 50th St.
New York, NY 10022
(212) 751-2600

The Roland Collection
22 D Hollywood Avenue
Hohokus, NJ 07423
(847) 291-2230

S&S, a division of Simon and Schuster
1230 Avenue of the Americas
New York, NY 10020
(212) 698-7000

Spoken Books
P.O. Box 18020
Chicago, IL 60618-9998
312-769-5900

Sounds True
735 Walnut Street
Boulder, CO 80302-5032
303-449-6229

Sunburst Communications, Inc.
39 Washington Avenue
Pleasantville, NY 10570
(914) 769-5030
1-800-431-1934

Tapes for Readers
4410 Lingan Road NW
Washington, DC 20007-2513
(202) 362-4585

University of Arizona Video Campus
Harvill Bldg., No. 76
Box 4
Tucson, AZ 85721
(602) 621-1735 or -5143

University of California, Santa Barbara
Learning Center
Santa Barbara, CA 93106
(805) 893-3963

University of Iowa Audiovisual Center
C–215 Seashore Hall
University of Iowa
Iowa City, IA 52242
(319) 335-2539

University of Wisconsin
University Extension
1327 University Ave.
P.O. Box 2093
Madison, WI 53701
(608) 262-1234

Washington University
Learning Resources Video Center
George W. Brown School of Social Work
Campus Box 1196
St. Louis, MO 63130
(314) 935-5000

Watershed Foundation
6925 Willow Street, NW, Suite 201
Washington, DC 20012
(202) 722-9105

Wombat Film and Video
1560 Sherman Avenue, Suite 100
Evanston, IL 60201
(708) 328-6700
1-800-323-9084

Women Make Movies
462 Broadway, Suite 501
New York, NY 10013
(212) 925-0606

In the interest of visual clarity and simplicity, only
countries treated in the selections are labeled on
this map.